ISBN 978-0-428-86555-9
PIBN 10212420

This book is a reproduction of an important historical work. Forgotten Books uses
state-of-the-art technology to digitally reconstruct the work, preserving the original format
whilst repairing imperfections present in the aged copy. In rare cases, an imperfection in
the original, such as a blemish or missing page, may be replicated in our edition. We do,
however, repair the vast majority of imperfections successfully; any imperfections that
remain are intentionally left to preserve the state of such historical works.

HISTORICAL MANUSCRIPTS COMMISSION.

FIFTEENTH REPORT, APPENDIX, PART IV.)

THE

MANUSCRIPTS

OF HIS GRACE

THE DUKE OF PORTLAND,

PRESERVED AT

WELBECK ABBEY.

VOL. IV.

Parliament by Command of Her Majesty.

LONDON:
PRINTED FOR HER MAJESTY'S STATIONERY OFFICE,
BY EYRE AND SPOTTISWOODE,
PRINTERS TO THE QUEEN'S MOST EXCELLENT MAJESTY.

And to be purchased, either directly or through any Bookseller, from
EYRE AND SPOTTISWOODE, EAST HARDING STREET, FLEET STREET, E.C., and
32, ABINGDON STREET, WESTMINSTER, S.W.; or
JOHN MENZIES & Co., 12, HANOVER STREET, EDINBURGH, and
90, WEST NILE STREET, GLASGOW; or
HODGES, FIGGIS, & Co., LIMITED, 104, GRAFTON STREET, DUBLIN.

1897.

8497.]   *Price 2s. 11d.*

INTRODUCTION.

THE first volume of the Calendar of Harley letters and papers concluded with the year 1700, immediately after the death of Sir Edward Harley, and a month or two before the first election of his son Robert to the Speakership of the House of Commons. A few of the earlier pages in this volume contain abstracts or copies of other letters written in 1700, which were not forthcoming at the time when the first volume was completed at press, but the main portion of the manuscript material here printed ranges in date between 1701 and the end of May 1711, just after Robert Harley's elevation to the peerage as Earl of Oxford and Mortimer and his appointment to the supreme office of Lord Treasurer.

The letters, private and confidential for the most part, addressed to Robert Harley and to members of his family by persons of greater or less eminence during that interesting and eventful period of our history, cannot fail to attract attention; but it will be no surprise to those readers of historical and biographical tastes, to whom the annals of Queen Anne's reign are specially familiar, to find that the main events and the characters of the leading statesmen as conceived by them will need few modifications on account of the new contemporary evidence printed for the first time in the following pages. The attraction of such correspondence, passing during such a well-known period, is rather to be looked for in the minor details of events and in the glimpses we get from it of many interesting persons not necessarily in the front rank of eminence.

On one point, however, of some historical and of great literary and biographical importance, this volume may claim to be somewhat of the nature of a revelation by recording the very intimate relations, for public purposes, which existed for many years between Harley and De Foe. That the latter had some kind of employment as a Government agent about the time of the negotiations for the Union with Scotland has been stated by the majority of his numerous biographers, and one or two stray

letters of his which have got into print have tended to prove
the statement, but the details they have been able to furnish
of such agency are practically *nil*, and of the help and advice
given by De Foe to Harley during almost the whole of this
statesman's official career nothing has been hitherto known.
Considering the amount of research given to the elucidation of
events of De Foe's life in recent times, when original contemporary manuscripts have been much more accessible, it is a
marvel that the secret has been so well kept.

De Foe's first introduction to Harley appears to have been
brought about by William Paterson's means. Under date of
April 1703 (p. 61), about the time of De Foe's release from
prison, there is a letter from him to Paterson expressive of his
unfeigned sense of having offended the Queen, and of his hearty
desire to serve her in any capacity, even in the army for a year
or two at his own charge. The concluding part of this letter
points to Paterson's having hinted to him in conversation that
some person high in the royal favour was inclined to help him
to employment. That Harley was meant seems clear from the
letter being endorsed by him as received from Paterson, though
not until May 28 following. The next reference to the matter
is in a letter from Godolphin, at Bath, where he was in attendance
on the Queen, on September 26, 1703 (p. 68), in which he informs
Harley, " I have found it proper to read some paragraphs of
" your letter to the Queen. What you propose about De Foe
" may be done when you will and how you will." On
November 4 (p. 75) Godolphin again writes, " I have taken care
" in the matter of De Foe "; and succeeding this letter on the
same page will be found one from De Foe himself, dated
November 9, to Harley, expressing thanks for the bounty
conferred on him and his desire " to make some such sort of
" return for it as no man ever made." Following this (p. 76) is
a letter from De Foe written to a friend of his own, or an
emissary from Harley, to whom, probably, the preceding letter
was entrusted for delivery. We meet with no more letters
between Harley and De Foe until May 1704 (p. 83), though
some must have been lost or destroyed, as there are references
in the extant letters to previous communications and interviews
between them earlier in that year. The dates of the May letters
are just preceding that of the appointment of Harley to one of

the Secretaryships of State. Two other undated letters, evidently written about the same time, to be found on pp. 87–89, give details of De Foe's life and misfortunes, and urge his desire to accept some service proposed to him by Harley, if the pressure put upon him by his creditors and his enemies can in some way be relieved. In the middle of the following month, a letter (p. 93) reaches Harley from an informer to the effect that if it be desired to arrest " Dan Foe," as the supposed author of a libel then in circulation, he is to 'be found at a certain address in Canterbury. From other correspondence (pp. 98 and 106) and interviews passing between them in July, it would appear that De Foe's views on public affairs were being freely expressed to Harley, and that his *Review*, the political part of it at any rate, had to some extent the Secretary's approval.

In September 1704, we find De Foe fairly started on his first Government mission, which was apparently to travel about the country inquiring into the opinions and feelings of the inhabitants, or rather the voters, in the principal boroughs ; to spread " principles of temper, moderation, and peace," and to persuade all people that the Government was resolved to proceed by those rules. The first of his letters on this topic here printed (pp. 136–38) is dated from Bury St. Edmunds, on September 28, but there is a reference in it to one written from Cambridge on September 16, not now in the collection, and it also mentions a visit he had paid to Norwich. Nothing more can be ascertained from this correspondence about the mission to the Eastern counties. On November 2 following, probably when back in town again, is a long letter (pp. 146–149), chiefly filled with the " ridiculous stuff " he hears about the " Triumvirate," namely, Marlborough, Godolphin, and Harley, and the way they are managing State affairs. There is, however, a short undated paper in De Foe's handwriting (p. 153) describing the state of parties in Hertfordshire, which was no doubt drawn up in the autumn of the same year. That Godolphin was acquainted from time to time with De Foe's views and proceedings is evident from two or three casual references in the Lord Treasurer's undated letters, which have been assigned to the year 1704 (pp. 155, 156).

We hear nothing more of De Foe until the middle of the following year, a few weeks after the general election in May (pp. 200, 203–205), and shortly before his setting forth on a similar mission of inquiry into the Western and other counties. His first letter on this subject is from Crediton, on July 30 (p. 213), and the next from Tiverton on August 14 (p. 221), in which he encloses a warrant issued for his apprehension in Devonshire on the ninth of that month (p. 218); on September 10 (p. 244) he dates an account of his proceedings from Kidderminster. Some of his letters after this time are probably missing, but among the papers dated in November of this year will be found inserted (pp. 269–272) one in De Foe's handwriting entitled " An Abstract of my Journey with casual Observations on Public Affairs," which summarises the places he visited, with curious remarks on many of them and on the men of influence connected with them. This abstract shows that his travels, after leaving Kidderminster, extended into Cheshire, Lancashire, Yorkshire, and some of the Midland and Eastern counties.

Nothing more is found about De Foe in these papers until about six months after the date of his return to London, early in November 1705. On May 6, 1706, he writes a letter (pp. 300–302) dwelling at great length on the desperate state of his affairs, and urging his claims on the Queen's bounty. He desires to " be assisted, as far as two or three hundred pounds " will do it, to free myself from the immediate fury of five " or six unreasonable creditors "; or to be sent somewhere abroad out of the reach of their hands. In a later part of the letter, he petitions for a private apartment in Whitehall, as the shelter of such a retreat might prevent his enemies' attempts to lodge him in the Queen's Bench. His *Review* and its usefulness to the Government are also referred to. It is not until the September following that Harley appears to have decided to entrust De Foe with a very important mission to Scotland, the objects of which, as the latter understands them, are given in his letter of September 13 (pp. 326–328), written on the eve of his departure for the North. A paper, apparently a copy of some of Harley's instructions, is also printed (p. 334), but is only a fragment. De Foe does not reach Newcastle-on-Tyne until September 30 (p. 333), having visited Coventry and other places out of the direct route. At Newcastle he makes the acquaintance of John Bell, the postmaster, who figures frequently

in the following pages in connexion with the affairs of De Foe
and of others. Bell had orders to supply Harley's envoy when
at Edinburgh with money from time to time as wanted, but
was kept in ignorance at first both of his right name and of
his mission; he reports to Harley on October 1 (p. 335) the
arrival of "Mr. Alexander Goldsmith," and adds, "I drank a
" bottle with the gentleman and perceive he is not nice in
" telling his name, and will own it in Edinburgh ; he says he is
" so publicly known that it would not be prudence to go under
" another name." On October 4 (p. 336) Bell again writes that
he had the favour of "Mr. A. G.'s" conversation for two or
three days and finds him to be a very ingenious man and fit for
that business he guesses him to be going about.

De Foe's first letter to Harley from Edinburgh, printed in
this volume (p. 339), is dated October 24, but it is evident from
the opening paragraph of it that he had written one or two
letters previously, which are now missing. Between this date
and the end of November in the following year, he remained in
Edinburgh, with the exception of one or two short visits to
Glasgow, Stirling, Wemyss, and elsewhere, and his letters are
very numerous and lengthy (pp. 342–461 *passim*). The
subjects of them are chiefly the temper of the Scottish people
during the progress of the negotiations for the Union, the
intrigues of the leading promoters and opposers of the Union,
and the immediate effects of the measure on the nation generally.
It is unnecessary here to give a full analysis of his observations
and views ; many of them appear in a maturer form in the
history of that great legislative act afterwards compiled by
De Foe, and it will be an interesting work for the historical
student to compare his narrative of events, written as an eye-
witness from day to day for Harley's information, with the
work on the same subject which he published two or three
years later. The occasional reference in these letters to others
De Foe had written, which are not found in this collection,
shows that some either never reached their destination or
have since been lost; one of the missing ones, at any rate,
dated 2nd November 1706, is now in the possession of Mr.
Alfred Morrison and is printed at length in the Appendix to
the Ninth Report of this Commission, p. 469.

There is a brief letter of De Foe written a few days after
his return to England at the end of 1707 (p. 473), from

which it would appear that Harley, in anticipation of his early removal from office, was quite willing that the writer should transfer his services to Godolphin; but we hear no more of him in this correspondence until just before the time of Harley's return to office in August 1710 (pp. 550, 552). In October of that year, he was commissioned to take another journey into Scotland, for the objects set forth in his handwriting, under the title "Queries for Management" (p. 616). Previously to this he had drawn up some lengthy papers containing various proposals for the improvement of trade and navigation in Scotland (pp. 584–590).

Of William Paterson we get other glimpses in this correspondence besides that to which allusion has been made in connexion with De Foe. The latter himself refers to his benefactor, when they were in Scotland together, in terms somewhat disparaging (pp. 356, 358, 359), but Paterson's own letters (pp. 18, 26, 28, 43, &c.) show him to have been much consulted in financial and other matters by both Godolphin and Harley, and Godolphin's letters (pp. 45, 60, 64, &c.) contain occasional friendly mention of him. Though there is evidence of a genuine desire on the part of both these statesmen to provide public employment of a more permanent kind for both Paterson and De Foe, nothing came of it, the claims for office of their closer political supporters in Parliament, some of them urged with no lack of modesty in numerous letters to Harley here printed, probably always standing in the way. Some passages in De Foe's letters moreover show, in spite of his reiterated expressions of deep gratitude to Harley, that his remuneration for the temporary services rendered barely exceeded the expenses incurred.

Another historical character, William Penn, contributes a few interesting letters (pp. 19, 30, 79), chiefly about his disastrous colonial experiences. In one of later date (p. 316) he complains of an offer made by somebody to recommend his son to the Duke of Ormonde for a foot company in Ireland, "which, " to say no more, is mean. Ned Southwell secretary of that " kingdom, and my son captain of a foot company, he shall go " dig potatoes first. He is entitled to a better estate in that " kingdom than to take up with so mean an employment."

Of another person, always remembered in connexion with one episode in Harley's career, it was to be expected that some new information would be gained in these papers. William Greg

—we spell his name as he himself and his relatives did, though recent historians, probably copying from the report in the *State Trials,* have adopted " Gregg " as the proper form— seems to have come under the notice of Harley early in 1705. Nothing appears to have been hitherto published of Greg's earlier history, beyond what is reported in the *State Trials,* so it may be interesting to note that he claims, not too proudly, to be a northerner by birth; for in one of his letters (p. 183) he speculates on the risks he is about to run of falling " a victim " to the rage of a boiling nation of which I reckon it my " unhappiness to be a native." His kinsman, Hugh Greg, was English resident at Copenhagen for some years, 1693–1702, during the latter part of which time William acted as his secretary. Hugh died in January 1702, and William remained in Denmark giving like assistance to the succeeding resident James Vernon. A few letters from him, when at Copenhagen, will be found among the Stepney and Ellis correspondence in the British Museum, and there are copies of documents in his handwriting among the Denmark papers in the Public Record Office, but none of his letters. Also, among the Harley papers at Welbeck, which it was thought unnecessary to notice in detail, are to be found numerous letters addressed to him between January 1702 and October 1704 by various English agents or residents at some of the European capitals.

William Greg returned to England about November 1704, and his first appearance in the following pages is under the date of February 2, 1704-5 (p. 159), in which he refers to an offer made to him by Lord Paget, probably of a travelling tutor- ship, at twenty pounds a year salary—terms which, he writes, no man, having Harley for a patron, could embrace In May following (pp. 181, 183), are two further letters written in an inflated style ; in these is indicated the nature of a mission to Scotland with which Harley proposed to entrust him. Greg arrived in Edinburgh about June 7, on which day he writes (p. 194) his first letter; between that date and September 18 (p. 248) he writes frequently on the proceedings in the Scottish Parliament in a familiar and graphic style. How many of these letters reached Harley's hands is uncertain ; very few were preserved by him. The copies printed in this volume are mostly taken from Greg's drafts of them, which, from certain marks thereon, appear to have been seized with the rest of Greg's papers when he was charged with high treason, and so to have come into Harley's custody as Secretary of State. In October 1705, Greg was back in London, and there is an entry in some accounts kept in Harley's office of a payment to him of 25*l.* in that month and of 5*l.* to him in December. Again, in February 1706 he received 20*l.* and, in April, 5*l.* Two letters from him in the last-named month (pp. 400, 401) show his very necessitous condition at the time when he obtained the clerkship in the Secretary's office. Between April and December 1707, special payments of small sums were made to him, amounting to 38*l.* in all, the last recorded being of 11*l.* on December 31, the day before his arrest. The papers here printed, about the date of his trial and execution, throw little fresh light on his treachery.

There is a long and characteristic letter of Sir Jonathan Trelawney, then Bishop of Exeter, but afterwards translated to Winchester, dated in July 1704 (p. 101), complaining that the "bearing of this Bishop of Bath and Wells (Hooper) " is intolerable, who after being possessed of two bishoprics " without ever yet seeing one of 'em, will still pretend to be " governing in mine, where I don't need his help, nor ever yet " that I know of desired his assistance." In a short letter, written a few days (p. 105) after, he thanks Harley for ridding him of his "forward co-adjutor." In June 1707, just after Trelawney's going to Winchester, Lord Poulett writes (p. 420) about the bishop's treatment of a leading Exeter merchant, in a manner which amusingly illustrates the view of his arbitrary character which even the friends of this "positive prelate," as he is styled, are compelled to take. He fears the loss of political support to the Government which will ensue if such domineering conduct cannot be checked, for "You know," writes Poulett, " the influence of the city of Exeter in the west, and that it's too " great a city to be treated at the vile rate of a Cornish. " borough, which our friend the Bishop of Winchester through " the warmth of his temper does not distinguish." At the same time his lordship prudently hints a wish that his interference in the matter may not become known to his episcopal friend.

A more famous and equally combative churchman, Dr. Atterbury, not yet a bishop, is more frequently met with among

Harley's correspondents, but only one instance of his fiery humour need be referred to here. The occasion of it was in September 1704 (pp. 125–133), when Bishop Nicholson of Carlisle threw every obstacle that ingenuity could devise in the way of Atterbury's installation as dean of his cathedral. Of course this is no newly-discovered episode in this remarkable man's life, but fresh details of it are evolved, and the vigour of his language in his reports of the proceedings to Harley add new interest to the situation. Unfortunately we have no letters of the bishop giving his view of the case, which is the more to be regretted, as a letter from him of later date (August 14, 1710, p. 565) on election matters in Cumberland, shows him to possess a pretty wit of his own which would serve him in good stead even against so formidable an antagonist as Atterbury. That the feud between them was not soon allayed is shown by a letter from the dean, written two or three years later (p. 463), in which he takes the part of Dr. Todd, who had been suspended by the bishop. One of Atterbury's undated letters contains an interesting reference to what appears to be the "Tale of a Tub." He writes, "I cannot close this letter without expressing the " satisfaction I had last night in perusing Mr. Swift's book, " which Mr. Prior shewed us. 'Tis very well written and will " do good service, but I'm afraid by the peculiar manner of " writing he will be too easily discovered." Harley's copy of this famous book, by the bye, was not bought until September 1705, and cost him four shillings. This appears from some accounts kept in the Secretary's office, from which we have already quoted.

Of the Duke and Duchess of Marlborough hardly anything of personal interest will be found. There are a few of the Duke's letters written, not to Harley, but presumably to the Earl of Portland, at that time in Holland, during the campaign of 1705 (pp. 212, 230, 242, 247, 249), but they are of a formal character. A curious tale is told of the Duke's negotiations with the Pretender (p. 681), by Captain Ogilvie, one of Harley's spies, of whom more will be said presently; but we must take into account the character of the narrator before giving it entire belief. Of the terror inspired by the Duchess among those of her sex obliged by official circumstances to be brought into contact with her, we have an amusing instance in a letter of

Lady Mansell, wife of the Comptroller of the Household, written
at the end of May 1710 (p. 542), before Harley's return to
office, but after the Duchess was held to have lost all favour
with the Queen. Lady Mansell writes :—" I am almost fright'd
" to death with the threats of a great Lady who is now retired
" from Court . . . . In a little time she says she shall
" return with as full power as ever, and that both you and
" every friend you have shall feel the effects of her utmost
" revenge . . . . The terrible apprehensions I am under
" have took all rest from me and I was forced to send for my
" doctor, who ordered me something that I had a tolerable
" night of it; but without some good news I shan't recover
" mighty soon. I won't mention the writing this to anybody
" living, hope you will pardon the doing it, for the terrors that
" enraged Lady has put me into is (*sic*) not to be expressed."
What means Harley found to allay these fears do not appear,
but he is careful to endorse this letter as having been "answered
immediately."

Among those of Harley's correspondents who may be described
as his intimate friends, at any rate during the time over which
this volume extends, may be named Henry St. John, his school-
fellow Sir Simon Harcourt, afterwards Lord Chancellor, Robert
Price, afterwards a Baron of the Exchequer, and Sir Robert
Davers, M.P. for Suffolk. St. John's private letters (pp. 73, 176,
180, 219, 256, 257) are of no great interest, except as showing
the close relations between the two statesmen in their earlier
days in office together; some of Harcourt's and Price's letters
are entertaining and instructive, as they take us sometimes
quite behind the scenes, but it is unnecessary to deal with any
of them in detail. Of Davers, nothing is known in the political
affairs of the day, but he plays here the part of the candid
friend, often giving his plain opinion of his friend's shifty
policy, but always careful to express his warm regard for the
man. A copy of Harley's reply to one of Davers's letters has
been kept, written in October 1705 (p. 261). It is a very good
specimen of his manner, full of vague denunciations of his
enemies, and equally vague professions of his devotion to the
Church and monarchy. Erasmus Lewis, the amiable friend of
Swift and many other men of mark, should perhaps also be
classed among Harley's intimates; his letters, chiefly in the

form of London·gossip, are most numerous and readable when his old official chief had been driven from power, and had retired to Brampton between May and November 1708 (pp. 489–510 *passim*). George Granville, afterwards Lord Lansdowne, chiefly now remembered as a minor poet of the period and the "polite" friend of Pope, also claims great intimacy with Harley, and writes him many letters on public matters, few of which are without some hint of the great services rendered by him and of his consequent claims for advancement. Only one letter (p. 331) gives the least evidence of any literary tastes. Among the other friendly correspondents with Harley, known to fame, we have only left space to mention John, Duke of Argyll, and his brother, Lord Ilay; the Earl of Orrery, better remembered as Charles Boyle, who in his youthful days was engaged in the famous dispute with Dr. Bentley, whose letters in this collection give evidence of considerable ability in quite another arena; and Earl Rivers, whose letters are chiefly interesting for the account he gives of his not very successful mission to Hanover (pp. 580, 591, 594).

On the return of Harley to office, in August 1710, another voluminous correspondent of his appears on the scene, John Drummond, a Scotch merchant and banker settled in Amsterdam. Of Drummond's personal history not much is to be learned from his letters, except that he was thirty-four years old at this time, had left his native country when about fifteen, but was still sufficiently well-known and esteemed there to have been offered a seat in Parliament by the Duke of Argyll and others. His character evidently stood high with the Dutch authorities and with the leading Englishmen engaged in diplomacy and the army abroad. From his own letters here printed and from the published Bolingbroke correspondence it appears that Drummond was also in constant communication with St. John, just appointed Secretary of State, who wrote to him very openly, and told him he was of more use than any of the British envoys abroad His subsequent history will be perhaps more fully disclosed when the later papers of the Harley collection shall be published. It may suffice here to add, as additional evidence of Drummond's capacity, that in April 1713 he was commissioned by Lord Bolingbroke to act with the Commissioners appointed by the Imperial and Dutch Governments to settle and preserve the trade with the Spanish Netherlands. Among the State papers in the Public Record Office is a volume chiefly filled with his letters from this date down to May 1714.

To Drummond, Harley is much indebted for advice and help in retrieving the country's credit, and for warnings against the unscrupulous schemes of certain English and Dutch financiers for turning to their own private advantage the uneasy feeling abroad which the change of Ministry and consequent expected dismissal of the Duke of Marlborough had created. On the latter subject there is specially to be noted a long letter, written in November 1710 (p. 619–622), which depicts the almost panic-stricken state of Pensionary Buys and the Dutch generally at the prospect of the Duke's removal, and strongly urges Harley to effect a reconciliation with the great commander. Harley has preserved a copy of his reply to this letter (pp. 623–625), disclaiming the least feeling of resentment towards Marlborough or any one else, and stating his perfect readiness to act with him for the public good; he adds some instances of what he had done with regard to the Duke since his return to office, which plainly showed his friendly feeling. Shortly after receiving this letter, Drummond made skilful use of it in an interview which he obtained with Marlborough, and wrote a long account of it (pp. 634–638); thus was the way paved for the temporary reconciliation between Harley and Marlborough, which is illustrated more fully in the published correspondence of the Duke than in these pages.

In September 1710 (p. 594), Drummond notes the arrival of Governor Pitt at Amsterdam, on his way home from the East Indies, and adds, " I think I have made him yours and have drunk " your health heartily with him. He will have a powerful purse " in England, and be a thorn in the side of some great men now " at the head of the Bank and India Company if they should " thwart you. Therefore if you can get him chosen in Cornwall, " pray do."

Before passing to subjects illustrated in the Harley correspondence, which have less biographical interest than those we have indicated, it is necessary that a few remarks should be made on such of the letters and papers as may seem to throw any additional light on Robert Harley himself. Of these there are none at all likely to affect the popular estimate of his character as a statesman. Godolphin's numerous letters, mostly short, but very much to the point, written to him when Speaker, and in the early years of his holding office as Secretary of State, certainly show the great value which the writer placed upon Harley's views on public affairs and upon his capacity for managing them. Well deserving of notice is a letter written in August 1704 (p. 118), from Tunbridge Wells, by a plain-spoken friend who asks leave to acquaint Harley with his observation of people's opinions of him; and other friends at a much later period, when he returned to office in 1710, are not afraid of hurting his feelings by referring to the nickname of " Robin the trickster," which his opponents had fixed upon him. His own letters, printed from drafts or copies, are for the most part not specially interesting or instructive; the style of them is very involved, and some of them show either incapacity or unwillingness to take a plain straightforward course in any direction. One curious document of a biographical character, in his handwriting, is stated to have been drawn up in the " Crown " Inn, at Faringdon, Berkshire, on September 25, 1707 (p. 451), where, being alone on a journey, as he says, his thoughts were drawn to recollect how he came into the public service, and how he had behaved himself therein. The personal revelations in this document are not, however, very coherent, and the handwriting of it grows more and more indistinct as it approaches the somewhat sudden ending. To Harley's famed associate in some of his schemes, Mrs. Abigail, afterwards Lady, Masham, we get the first reference in a letter written in May 1707 (p. 406) from Lady Pye to Harley's sister, also named Abigail, which concludes as follows : " This makes me think of " a [matrimonial] match your's mentioned, our relation the " Dresser with Colonel Masham, whom the Queen hath lately " advanced. If the same is young [I] have heard her greatly " commended for a sober woman. I believe she is the same " Aunt Brom[field] used to talk of, lived with Sir George Rivers' " lady when first we went to Greville Street. The great Lady " Duchess in that deserves great commendations, that hath " taken such care of her relations, who when low are generally " overlooked. Is her brother Colonel Hill married, as was " reported, to one of the Queen's maids ? " This is an interesting little bit of contemporary evidence of Mrs. Masham's near relationship to both the Duchess of Marlborough and to Harley, though it hardly confirms the assertion alleged to have been made by Harley, to which reference is made in the introduction to the first volume of these papers, that he had never heard of the relationship between Mrs. Masham and himself until they met at Court. There are several letters from her to Harley, the earliest in September 1707, but the majority in 1708 and 1709, when he was out of office. The chief personages alluded to in them are slightly disguised, but, while they show plainly enough that the Queen was being influenced by Harley to some slight extent through her attendant before his return to office, they are of a very unimportant character and give little or no evidence of any deep machinations between the pair. They will, however, if of otherwise little moment, at any rate serve to rebut the statements of her enemies that she was an illiterate person, for the handwriting, style, and spelling of them are quite as good as those of any, and better than those of most, of the ladies of that period. They are certainly superior in these respects to the compositions of the great Duchess herself, specimens of which will not, however, be found in this volume, if, in judging of their style, we leave out of consideration the innate vigour of expression which often makes the latter so remarkable.

The greater political events of the period covered by this volume have been so fully illustrated by contemporary histories and, of late years, by the publication of contemporary letters and papers, that it was hardly to be expected, as has already been hinted, that even in the Harley correspondence much would be found putting at all a new aspect upon them. Of electioneering and parliamentary intrigues we get many glimpses to which it is unnecessary to draw special attention, unless we except a letter of Godolphin (p. 291) written during the first session of the Parliament elected in 1705. In this communication with Harley, the Lord Treasurer sums up the relative strength of parties in the House as consisting of one hundred and ninety Tories, one hundred and sixty Whigs, and one hundred Queen's servants, that is, persons all holding offices of more or less value under the Crown and, therefore, as a rule, disposed to maintain the existing Government in power. Of these latter, Godolphin notices that about fifteen had been voting with the Tories, and the question submitted to Harley's consideration is, " Whether it " be more likely or more easy to keep the 160 which with the " Queen's true servants will always be a majority, or to get (sic) " from the 190," together with some remarks of his own on the situation.

What may without question be termed the most important domestic event of Queen Anne's reign, the Union with Scotland, is very fully illustrated. The letters of Greg and De Foe already described, contain many graphic details of the speeches and conduct of the chief supporters and opponents of this great measure in the Scottish Parliament, and of the very peculiar temper shown by the great body of Scotchmen both before and after the ratification of the Union; they are the more noteworthy, too, as being the testimonies of eye-witnesses of the struggle between the contending parties during its most critical stages. There are also occasional letters to Harley from the leading Scottish nobles who were in favour of the Union, especially the Earls of Stair and Leven, and the Duke of Queensberry. Of the shifty part played by the Duke of Hamilton with regard to the Union there are many curious instances; the most favourable view of his policy is given in a letter of his friend, the Jacobite Col. James Graham (p. 171). The year in which this letter is written does not appear upon the face of it, and the Duke is not mentioned by name, but both these omissions are supplied by a letter of the Duke of Hamilton to Graham printed in the report on the manuscripts at Levens drawn up by Mr. Maxwell Lyte and issued in the fourth Appendix to the Tenth Report of this Commission.

In connexion with Scotland, we must not omit to notice the letters of Captain John Ogilvie, of the Airlie branch he tells us of that family, for many years a spy in Harley's employ. His own account of his earlier days was drawn up in February 1705 (p. 160), and some time in that year he prepared a memorandum (p. 276) on the discontented party in Scotland, and its intrigues with the Court of St. Germains. In the same and following years we find him, under the name of Lebrun, writing from Rotterdam and Hamburgh. Later in 1706, he arrives in Paris, and writes in the assumed name of John or Jean Gassion, and, indeed, adopts that name throughout the remainder of his correspondence with Harley. Ogilvie's reports are certainly very curious and interesting, and could not have been supplied except at great personal risk; and it must be taken that his employer considered them as trustworthy on the whole, for he remained for many years in Harley's service, and had to be maintained as an officer and a gentleman during the time, otherwise he could not have mixed with persons of position good enough to possess the private information he needed—to use his own expressions, "bricks cannot be made without "straw . . . . for if I be in any Court I must make "acquaintance and drink a bottle and eat a dish of meat with "those that I think proper for my use, and it will cost me "something to keep my wife at St. Germain" (p. 308).

For a specimen of vigorous assertion of the rights of English subjects abroad on the part of Queen Anne's Government, we may refer to the story told in a letter of Dr. White Kennett, afterwards Bishop of Peterborough, dated in May 1710 (p. 606). The doctor's brother, Basil, had been appointed chaplain to the English factory at Leghorn, but he had not been there many months before the Inquisition began to threaten him. An appeal to the Grand Duke of Florence for protection, through Dr. Newton, our resident in that country, had for answer that the Inquisition was a court superior to the civil power, and that the Duke could not hinder its proceedings. Dr. Newton having reported this to his Government, he was instructed by the Earl of Sunderland, then Secretary of State, to tell the Grand Duke and his Ministers, in Her Majesty's name, "that if any molesta- "tion were given to her chaplain at Leghorn, she should look "upon it as an affront done to herself and the nation, a breach "of peace, and a violation of the law of nations, and should, "by her fleets and armies in the Mediterranean, not only "demand but take satisfaction for any such injury offered. "And if they talked any more of the Pope and Court of Rome, "he (Dr. Newton) must cut that matter short by telling them "that her Majesty has nothing to do with that Court, but will "treat with the Great Duke as other independent Princes and "States." Dr. Kennett adds that when this "noble resolution." was communicated to the Court of Florence, the Inquisition soon desisted from further persecution of the English chaplain.

Among the more miscellaneous subjects of interest to be found in this correspondence may be mentioned, taking them chiefly in their chronological order :—The sale of votes at elections (pp. 11, 13, 175, 486); petition of William Kidd, the pirate (pp. 16, 17); the little regret shown in the country at the unexpected death of William III. (pp. 35, 36); the visit of the "King of Spain" (the Archduke Charles) to England in 1703 (p. 78), "at dinner "where he was served after the Spanish fashion he ate enough "to keep a Lazarus six months"—this is described by Charles

Goring, member for Steyning, who at a later date (p. 185) gives
an equally lively account of the interference of two peers, the
Dukes of Somerset and Richmond, in a Sussex election; proceedings of Jacobites in Norwich (pp. 92, 97); Isaac Newton's
design for a medal to commemorate the campaign of 1704
(p. 151); the search for horses and arms in Oxfordshire and
Yorkshire (pp. 162–167); Richard Duke's letters (pp. 122, 133)
on the French privateers in Torbay and other matters specially
affecting Devonshire; the French prisoners at Farnham (pp. 281,
282); some Yorkshire views of politics and Parliament men
(pp. 613, 640); Earl Poulett's "prudent letter" (p. 683); letters
of Major, afterwards Colonel, J. Craustoun (pp. 250, &c.), written
when campaigning with Marlborough in the years 1705, 1706,
and 1707; in one (p. 309) he gives a capital account of the
battle of Ramillies, in which action, he says, the British troops
had very little hand, though the English commanders, including
Marlborough, Argyll, Orkney, and General Murray, appear
prominently in his narrative:—of John Philips, the poet (p. 405):
—of John Toland, "the deist" (pp. 408–410):—of John Cham-
berlayne (pp. 411, 429, 468, &c.), about his *State of Great
Britain*, and other matters:—of Margaret, widow of George
Farquhar, the dramatist (p. 415):—of Mrs. Dela Manley, in May
1710 (p. 541), begging Harley's acceptance of her *Atalantis*, for
the publication of which she had to suffer the prosecution from
which she was freed on his advent to power three months later:
—of Alexander Cunningham, the medallist (pp. 546, 566, 670,
672), who was travelling abroad at this time, and makes some
noteworthy observations, especially on the then just discovered
remains of Herculaneum:—of Richard Steele (p. 610), and of
Abel Boyer (p. 615), desiring to succeed him as Gazetteer:—and
of the Countess of Dorchester (p. 680), formerly James II.'s
mistress, a strong-worded protest against the promotion of the
Earl of Orkney over the head of her husband, the Earl of
Portmore, noticeable, moreover, for the use of the expression
"given away," in its modern, somewhat slangy, meaning of
depreciating or exposing.

There is a touch of true humour in the story told (p. 317) by
a Sussex labourer of his being kidnapped by some armed
Frenchmen and carried to Boulogne, under the impression that
he could give some information about the position of the English
fleet and soldiers. When questioned on these points, he

"replied he could not tell, for he was a day labourer, in the "morning he went to work and in the evening came home and "went to bed." His captors put him ashore again at Lydd late at night and wished him well home; but how he got that long distance, for he lived on the western edge of the Sussex coast, is not narrated.

The many letters of Lady Pye, from which one or two quotations have been already made, to her cousin Abigail, Harley's sister, should also not pass without further notice. Selections from them have been made very sparingly, some of the letters being of great length; but they are admirable specimens of the lady letter-writer of the time, being filled with artless gossip about herself, her family, and friends, with occasional glimpses of a wider world. An account of Roman Catholic seminaries in the Netherlands, in 1707 (pp. 470-472), was drawn up, it appears from a letter of later date (p. 672), by John Macky, author of the well-known *Memoirs of Secret Services.* Swift's intimacy with Harley had not been long established at the date when this volume closes, and there is hardly a trace of him except the paper in his handwriting on the "First Fruits of Ireland" (p. 609). The intention of the Whig ministry to send Swift as secretary to the embassy to Vienna is mentioned by Erasmus Lewis in August 1708 (p. 502).

The last letter printed in this volume is a dignified and touching letter of the third Earl of Shaftesbury, written just before his departure in weak health to spend the few remaining months of his life abroad, referring to his early acquaintance with Harley, and heartily congratulating the new Earl of Oxford on the distinctions he had attained.

Mr. Richard Ward, who edited the first volume of the Harley correspondence, published in 1894, was obliged by ill-health to give up the work of preparing the material for this volume, after some progress had been made with it. The completion of it was thereupon entrusted to the Secretary to the Commission.

J. J. CARTWRIGHT.

May, 1897.

CALENDAR OF THE MANUSCRIPTS OF HIS GRACE THE DUKE OF PORTLAND.

Vol. IV.

HARLEY LETTERS AND PAPERS. VOL. II.

Sir ROBERT SOUTHWELL to [ROBERT] HARLEY.

1699-1700. January 10. Spring Garden—I enclose what I learned this day of the two persons you enquired after. And since you are never to be tired with papers, I add what I lately had from Mr. Carleton in Dublin. I had only writ to him at my Lord Clarendon's desire to know how the revenue went, about the end of my Lord Strafford's government.

I pray remember the saving I gave you wherein two of my best friends are concerned; and it were a sin to the public not to consider plantation, by which, in chimney money and excise, the revenue is increased.

Sir CHRISTOPHER MUSGRAVE to ROBERT HARLEY, in Lincoln's Inn.

1700, April 25. Edenhall—I had the favour of yours at Golds-borough, the Colonel's absence is the reason that the rarities are not so forward as his discourse renders them. Yours was sufficient to entertain my thoughts and to support me in my journey which was pleasant enough. And rest assured if the country give me any vigour, it shall be employed in your service which is the great pleasure of my life. I perceive Sir Edw. [Seymour] made the speech he told us, but no reply, silence being the new mode. The Commissioners having chosen Trenchard's brother for secretary, shows the bias. I wish the execution of that Commission may answer expectations. I suppose the examination of Kidd was not very strict. My humble service to your lady and daughters and Nathaniel and the rest of our friends.

[The SAME to the SAME.]

[1700,] May 6—I easily overcame the fatigue of the journey though I keep the cold contracted in St. Stephen's chapel. Your correspondence is the best cordial and it is a singular favour, knowing your time is precious. I wish Sir William Friend may send the cargo to your brother and my son. Your brother's goodness and your influence is that which I must entirely depend on, and should I live to hear your brother had admitted him to any share with him, I might then conclude my son were provided for. My service to Sir Edw. [Harley] and your brother whom I desire to acquaint my son Kit what he disbursed for the bedding and he will pay it. If Kidd's paper come to light I suppose

that matter will be set in a true light. I think Lord Chief Justice will scarce accept it, the public wish Mr. Attorney. I pray God such men may be Ministers that will settle the nation upon its true bottom.

Sir WILLIAM TRUMBULL to THOMAS BATEMAN, in Little Scotland Yard, over against Sir Christopher Wren's back door.

1700, May 28. Easthampstead—If any good news could come from my honoured friend Mr. Harley's hands it would be extremely welcome, otherwise I am grown very indifferent. There is one thing I cannot decipher, which is why the French have taken this time to declare the agreement about the succession of Spain. If you will be so charitable as to get me some account of this matter, you know where to have it . . . .

[P.S.] If it be not too great secret pray send me word when the King goes for Holland.

[Sir CHISTOPHER MUSGRAVE to ROBERT HARLEY.]

1700, August 1—I am truly grieved for your severe distemper; it is most happy that the impostume is broke; the frequent returns of it should prompt you to take advice for carrying off that humour, and heartily wish you would be prevailed upon, not to study so hard for your late sitting up must ruin your constitution which is not strong enough to undergo the fatigue. Consider how the public, your family. and friends are concerned in your health, therefore beseech you not to be prodigal of it.

SIMON HARCOURT to ROBERT HARLEY, at Lincoln's Inn.

1700, August 5. Hereford—The news of your illness had very imperfectly reached us. Since 'twas too true I need not tell you how sincerely I rejoice at the prospect of your recovery. The Duke of G[loucester's] death was very surprising. Every misfortune to the public make my dear friend's health more valuable, and is a fresh argument to beg you to preserve yourself. You may remember I promised my Lord R[ochester] an account of the commission of the peace in Oxfordshire. Not receiving the materials from you to enable me to do it before the commission passed, I have hitherto neglected it, but send it enclosed. If you approve it, seal and send it, otherwise make what use you please of it.

[P.S.] You are well acquainted with my Lord's temper, and can judge whether the enclosed will be agreeable to him or fit to be sent. I know you'll deal with me freely.

[Sir CHRISTOPHER MUSGRAVE to ROBERT HARLEY.]

[1700 ?] August 12—Your friend never intimated any such intention neither before or after his coming into the country. And the (Colonel ?) and his antagonist had made their applications before. I am accustomed to have malicious reflections. Within a post or two I shall endeavour to make some return to yours; but the difficulties are great. It is hardly possible to judge whether 32 or 92 is more eligible, unless it were known what 92 would produce. It will require time and great labour to calculate exactly 129. I know 111 will always be pressing 109, which ought not to be.

—— to ——.

[1700, August]—The death of the D[uke of Gloucester] has raised great hopes in the late Ministers of making advantage to themselves by it. Lord Somers and Montague have determined that a commonwealth may now be erected.

A council of five Lords and ten Commoners are to be chosen by Parliament who are to execute the regal power, wherein they doubt not of obtaining their share. That this may be effected appears by these reasons. Many of the persons in possession of the executive power are their friends. The moderate men may be alarmed with fears of the Pr[ince] of W[ales.]

Many will fall into it being a new thing from a natural inclination to change; and all who are concerned in public funds will think their effects more safe thus than any other way.

And the generality of the people have been already in part and shall be fully persuaded that all the wrong things which have been done of late years proceeded from the obstinate temper of [the King ?] and his being influenced by the foreigners about him.

This they say will the easier gain credit when it shall appear that they promote a design that looks so national.

The chief difficulties are, [the King ?] may marry or the settlement may be enlarged, for the first they will propose it to him and seem to promote it, and so have means to work on his temper, create difficulties, and make delays and so prevent it.

Enlarging the settlement depends on the House of Commons, there some will be tender in regard to the Princess [Anne] others will be satisfied with the provision already made for the meeting of a parliament on the death of the King. Many will think to keep it in hand in hopes of making advantage. And those they can trust will act in concert to promote the main design. I will tell you one pleasant thing they have made D[uke] Somer[se]t believe he has a fair pretence but at all adventures he is to have an eminent post and some other such men they say are to be wrought on by suitable application.

I have told you their scheme and leave you to judge of it but enjoin you to show this to nobody.

NEWS-LETTER.

1700, August 31. Whitehall—The *De Grave* a ship belonging to the New East India Company is arrived here from India very richly laden. She has brought letters from Sir Wm. Norris of the 11th March last, giving an account of his safe arrival at Metchelpotam and that he had given notice thereof to the Great Mogul, who had ordered that His Excellency should, suitable to his character, be safely and honourably conducted to his camp, which was 800 miles distant from Metchelpotam; and His Excellency was accordingly preparing for his march with a very numerous and splendid equipage. The *Antelope* another of the said Company's ships is shortly expected, not being far behind.

One Atkinson a priest was convicted last Thursday at the Old Bailey, upon the late Act, and sentenced to perpetual imprisonment.

. A Dutch post came in yesterday; the King was gone his Progress, and would return to Dieren this night. There's nothing new from Riga.. The Swedes had quitted Zealand and gone back to Schonen, and the King of Denmark was returned to Copenhagen. The Treaty of alliance between the Elector of Brandenburg and the States General was renewed and signed at Berlin the 31st August N. S.

Letters from Paris of 8th September N. S. say that the Thursday before the Court of St. Germain, except the late King and Queen, went into mourning for the Duke of Gloucester. My Lord Manchester was still indisposed of an ague.

The Marquis of Halifax died this day.

LORD GODOLPHIN to ROBERT HARLEY, at Brampton Castle.

1700, September 5—I am now able to tell you that it's all as well as ever it was and, perhaps better, by my being easy in that which it seems was looked upon as a greater sacrifice than really I think it.

As to the measures concerted at parting, there is not like to be the least alteration in any of the persons concerned, either on this side of the water or the other, and, I believe, you may govern your own coming to town accordingly. Your company will certainly be always useful and necessary as well as extremely acceptable to your friends.

NEWS-LETTER.

1700, Sept. 7. Whitehall—The Lords Justices ordered in Council on Thursday last that the Parliament which stands prorogued to Thursday next shall be then further prorogued to the 17th of next month.

The mail from Holland of Tuesday last is not yet arrived. His Majesty is expected here the beginning of the next month. Sir George Rooke is to command the Convoy.

The Duke of Bedford died this morning, his honour and estate descend to the Marquis of Tavistock his grandson.

Letters from Paris 15th instant N. S. tell us that all the revenues which Cardinal Bouillon possessed in France were sequestered till such time as the Parliament met to give judgment against him. In the mean time his place of Great Almoner is taken away and conferred upon Cardinal Coislin formerly first Almoner in which employ he is succeeded by his nephew the Bishop of Metz.

'Twas computed the tax laid upon the Farmers of the Revenues would produce 14,443,000 livres. The Duke of Savoy was ill of an ague.

NEWS-LETTER.

1700, September 17. Whitehall—We had yesterday two mails from Holland with advice that on Tuesday the 3rd instant about ten at night the Electress of Brandenburg with the Electress Dowager of Hanover and the Princess of Hohenzollern came to visit the King at Dieren. They lay there that night and the next day went to Loo, where they continued till Friday the 6th when they took their leave of His Majesty and proceeded on their journey towards Aix, leaving the Electoral Prince of Brandenburg at Loo.

This morning came in the Dutch mail of last Friday. The Tuesday before His Majesty attended by the Electoral Prince and several General Officers reviewed five regiments of Horse, three of Foot, and the Royal Dragoon Guards, which came and encamped the day before near Loo and as soon as the Review was over they decamped in order to return to their former quarters. The Prince of Hesse younger son to the Landgrave of Hesse-Cassel to whom His Majesty has given the command of the regiment of Dragoon Guards was presented to him at the same time.

The Electoral Prince of Brandenburg parted from Loo on Thursday in one of His Majesty's coaches for Utrecht in his way to the Hague. His Majesty designs to return to England about the middle of the next month.

The Saxons began to bombard Riga the 6th N. S., they threw in then fifteen bombs and did the like the 8th when they threw in likewise some red bullets which did a great deal of damage.

General Welling had sent some of his troops towards Nerva upon the news of the Muscovites intention to break with Sweden.

The Swedish Fleet was safe in the Haven of Carlscroon and three hundred and fifty transport ships were likewise there designed to carry forces into Livonia. The King of Sweden had resolved to go with them in person.

The Elector of Brandenburg has refused to come into the Treaty of partage.

The Earl of Portland is coming from Holland; he has lost his regiment of Dragoons and the Blue Guards."

Dr. CHARLES DAVENANT to ROBERT HARLEY at Brampton.

1700, September 19—Your man has delivered to me the records, of which about two months hence you will find I have made a plentiful use. The work goes on vigorously, but is infinitely of more labour than I expected.

The King will not be here till towards the latter end of October. The discourse of a new Parliament is not quite vanished; I wish but cannot believe it.

NEWS-LETTER.

1700, September 24. Whitehall—A mail from Holland came in yesterday with letters from Dieren 20th instant, which say that the same morning His Majesty reviewed the troops that lately served in Holstein.

Letters from before Riga 16th N. S. say that the King of Poland at the instance of the King of England and the States General whose subjects in that city might suffer great loss by a bombardment, had thought fit to put a stop to the same though all things were ready for that purpose so that it is hoped this will now facilitate things towards a Peace between him and the King of Sweden.

On Saturday last the Princess of Denmark found herself indisposed at Windsor, and her physicians were sent for from London but her indisposition went soon off again at proving only to be the vapours.

My Lord Portland arrived here from Holland on Sunday night.

Letters from Denmark 14th instant say that the King was looked upon to be past danger though his small-pox was of the worst kind and accompanied with very bad symptoms; that the Prince Royal was very well recovered of his distemper, but that the Queen had miscarried.

We have an account of the arrival of two East India ships belonging to the old Company, the *Josiah* and the *Benjamin*."

NEWS-LETTER.

1700, October 8. Whitehall—Letters from Paris 13th instant N. S. say the Pope died the 27th past and that the Cardinals were to go into the conclave ten days after. 'Twas thought the Cardinal zealots would endeavour to come to a speedy choice but if they missed their aim it would probably be many months before the College agreed.

They had advice from Spain of 2nd instant that the King was then very ill, had received the Sacrament and that 'twas the common opinion he could not live many days. Upon which advice the French seemed to be putting themselves in a readiness to enter into 'the Province of Guipuscoa. Monsieur d'Harcourt having orders to bring together on that side a body of sixty battalions and fifty squadrons.

Orders were likewise given for the adding ten men to each Company of foot which new addition would in all amount to 26,000 men. My Lord Manchester had notified the Duke of Gloucester's death to the French Court who would go into mourning for it this week.

The Court of Aldermen met again this day to see if they could find out whether any mistake was committed in taking their votes at the choosing of the Lord Mayor, and after some hours debate resolved that the clerks had acted legally and according to the ancient custom of the City, which was carried by 16 against 10, so that now there can be no further pretence but that Sir Thomas Abney is duly elected.

Two mails are wanting from Holland.

NEWS-LETTER.

1700, October 10. Whitehall—A post from Paris arrived this afternoon with the following advice.

Paris, 5-16 October. The King of Spain is still alive, the false news of his death was spread abroad by a Courier of the Elector Palatine who passed through this city on Monday last in the night and the Elector's Resident went to Court on Tuesday on purpose to assure them that though the Courier said he was dead, the letters said he was alive which was confirmed by an express that came in the 12th instant from our Envoy at Madrid. Before the King sends down his General to command the troops that are drawing together upon the frontiers of Savoy and Guipuscoa it is thought he will name some new Marshals, those that seem to stand fairest for that dignity are the Count d'Auvergne, Tallard and de Tessé, the Marquis d'Uxcells d'Harcourt and Mons. Rose who commanded the French troops in the war of Ireland.

My Lord Manchester is gone to Fontainbleau for fifteen days; it is discoursed there that the Duchess of Burgundy is with child.

Three mails will be wanting from Holland tomorrow.

NEWS-LETTER.

1700, October 12. Whitehall —We have a post this day from Paris with letters of the $\frac{9}{20}$ instant, they had no fresher news from Spain than what I told you in my last.

Marshall Boufflers was going into the French Flanders to assemble the States of that country, and at the same time to be in a readiness in case a war should arise upon the King of Spain's death.

The French King had put out an Edict for the raising of eighteen millons of livres upon the Town House at five per cent. interest, and 'twas thought that sum would be brought in, in about a month's time.

A ship arrived at Marseilles the 6th, that left Cadiz in company of the Marquis de Nesmond's Squadron, which as she reports sailed directly for Toulon.

Yesterday came in three posts from Holland. His Majesty designed to be at the Hague on Thursday last, and might embark for England about the middle of the next week.

Sir George Rooke was arrived in Holland. He had met with a storm upon that coast but received no danger.

Advices from the North say that the Czar had besieged Nerva in form with an army of 40,000 men.

The King of Poland was marched with an army against General Welling, who advanced still into the country and the Duke of Courland was gone to attack the Fort of Cokenhousen.

The Swedish transports were not yet sailed from Carlscroon.

[ROBERT HARLEY to ——— .]

1700, October 16—I have received an intimation that there has lately been a meeting of some great persons, and that the Lord Treasurer has not only promised entirely to comply with the Junto but also to sacrifice the Duke of Qu[eensberry] to them. For his going in to them I never had any doubt, he has for a long time been contriving to do it, though he at the same time exclaims against them, as they do at him. I think it fit that his grace should know of the intention regarding him though I will not have it known that the news comes from me. One way to prevent it is to let the design be publicly talked of, like giving air to a mine. You may hear of a great meeting on Thursday last week in the city where I believe your acquaintance Sir James [   ] was at dinner, and also Lord Coningsby. If the duke be true to himself, and his friends be resolute, nothing can hurt him, though I know what endeavours are used to get information and complaints out of Scotland against him.

[Sir CHRISTOPHER MUSGRAVE] to ROBERT HARLEY.

[1700?] November 4—It is impossible to foresee what may be the events, but it is generally believed that 92 will be rather better. And when I reflect what care was taken of 41, there is reason to believe they will not all change their opinions. You have seen strange dejectedness, and it was great accidents that affected 115 lately. This is certain it will not be long before there must 92; and why not now? I suppose a return will be from 44. It would have been too much labour to have sent to 63.

![Sir C. MUSGRAVE to ROBERT HARLEY.]

[1700?] November 7—I think it not worth the time consulting 63: 43: 44: 68: are best able to advise in such matters and hence opportunities of understanding things, which others of necessity be ignorant of. It is apparent that 41: was well esteemed by 32: and perfect accident got 115: and 63: and 68: often lamented the unsteadiness of 32: and how little an accident dejected 101: in 32: And if 41: 45 should get 122: in 32: questions it would influence 129: which would be of the last consequence. 63 and 68 always thought fewest trials of skill the safest. If anything can be collected from general discourse 101 hath the present advantage. And in a short time there is an nececessity of 92 why should it not then be? Not seeing what advantage can be reaped by 32: which may not more probably be gained by 92, especially since 41 : 45 : 100 : are zealous for 32. What thoughts have 48 : 39 : 42 : 111 full I suppose of fears and doubts. In the multitude of counsellors there is safety, and that I suppose Nathaniel allows. I suppose 38 is sent to I trust prudence will obviate the nauseous folly of 199. Now the measures to be taken 242 : 157 : surely 64 will not appear. If 152 : 126 were good it would much influence 129 I have no faith in the prints. And the least caution blasts their assertions.

Sir EDWARD SEYMOUR to RORERT HARLEY, at Lincoln's Inn.

1700, November 8. Bradley—Next to the pleasure of seeing you is to receive the account of your welfare which ought very much to be regarded especially by those who have a true sense of saving 12d. in the pound, which I shall always remember, and expect in due time the same performance. When the Parliament will sit I would gladly learn, I cannot believe before the middle of January, and then I suppose a new one, for partitions and successions are too great to be begun in the fag end of a Parliament. I hear my friend Sir Christopher is surrounded with contenders, which he every day gives battle to successfully, in defence of that province which justly appertains to him to be master. But I learn otherwise of you : who are calmly submitting of your pretences(?) and suffer the rich pastures to be hedged in whilst you are contented to graze on the common, and to send your pitcher a great way down the stream for water when you have the fountain in your own keeping. These windings and turnings shall never serve you, for Jack Howe will have you brought to the bason, for what is in your stomach will easily be disgorged, without offence to any, especially if I am godfather and hold your head.

I intend to be in London Wednesday the 20th instant and am desirous to receive some of your tinctures before I am tainted with the mob, and in order thereunto, you would be very kind to meet me with Tom Colston on Wednesday at Egham at the King's Head at dinner. I will write to Tom whom I have not heard from ,some time to attend you with his coach. Half a dozen bottles of good wine and your company will be very acceptable.

LORD G[ODOLPHIN] to ROBERT HARLEY.

1700, November 24—Sending him a letter from Lord R[ochester] arranging a meeting for the following Tuesday.

The SAME to the SAME.

1700, [November 24 ?], Sunday—Arranging an audience for themselves and Lord Rochester, with the King at eight that evening.

[Sir C. MUSGRAVE to ROBERT HARLEY.]

[1700 ?] November 28—I hear 41 and 45 are now wanting in their visits. What effect they have had I am ignorant of. If they are now in love with 92 possibly it is a good argument for it, 242, 159 may reasonably be expected. Who ever thinks cannot affect 116. I do not know that 63 was any way instrumental in that or any thing of moment. What will become of 95, 113 152 ?

[Sir C. MUSGRAVE to ROBERT HARLEY.]

[1700 ?] December 5—I am sorry for your father's weakness, old age is an incurable distemper. Though a sheriff possibly is of no great moment, 68 has always been baffled, notwithstanding 111 assures that 31 is very sensible, and ready to do anything. And though 42 and 43 were not there, business of moment would before 93 especially in 178, which is of consequence to 92.

If 45 character be changed, will that look well ?

LORD GODOLPHIN to ROBERT HARLEY.

1700, December 14—I cannot hear the news of your father's death without taking a great part in the affliction which I am very sensible it must occasion to so tender a son and so good natured as you are. I will add no more to your present trouble but the assurances of my being very sincerely concerned in all that is so near to you.

SIMON HARCOURT to ROBERT HARLEY, at Brampton Castle.

1700, December 14. Essex Street.—1 received your commands from Oxford and endeavoured to execute them. Dr. Ratcliff in my presence wrote, and I was his porter to deliver it at the post house; notwithstanding which I find there remains a fondness for Mr. Finch and many of your friends promise themselves success for Sir Christopher and Mr. Finch, but I cannot yet change my opinion. This day I received a letter from Oxford that Sir Christopher had a universal invitation from the gentry and clergy of his own county to permit them to elect him and that he thereupon promised if they did to serve them. I wish this may not be of ill consequence, and prejudice his interest at the University. If they choose him, which I think certainly they will, 'twill be taken most heinously if he will not serve for them. I know you have a constant correspondence with Sir Christopher; I wish you would send me an authority to say he would serve for the University if they elect him.

You may direct for me in Abingdon, Berks.

HEN. ASHBURTON to [ROBERT HARLEY].

1700, December 17. Kensington—Condoles with him the loss of that excellent man his father.

The proclamation for dissolving this Parliament will be printed on Thursday and the writs for a new Parliament will be signed on Saturday or Monday, and I hope you will allow your friends to make interest for you for Speaker. You shall have all the interest I have or can make you; I wish it were more in my power notwithstanding our former difference in opinion about public matters to assure you how much I am your affectionate cousin, &c.

SIMON HARCOURT to ROBERT HARLEY at Brampton.

1700, December 21. Oxford—Last night we received the news of the dissolution, and a letter from Mr. Finch in answer to one he received from the Warden of All Souls, wherein he pretty plainly intimates that he will serve them if elected. Upon this letter the Dean, the Warden,

&c. have declared for Sir Christopher and Mr. Finch, and think they shall prevail for both. I need not tell you I wish they may, but I am in some doubt, there being an opposition now to them both, by Sir William Glynne and Sir George Beaumont. Sir George is a Fellow of New College. If anything can hazard Sir Christopher, 'tis an insinuation made use of here, that Sir Christopher will not serve the University if they elect him. This I myself heard from Sir George Beaumont, who declares that Mr. Verney of our house reports it from Sir Christopher, and that he will procure from Sir Christopher a declaration thereof under his own hand. I am not in much pain for that; but Sir Christopher is not so well known here, though much admired and valued, as we know him, and some will be misled, who have an abundance of respect for him. I sometime since wrote to you on this subject, which I fear miscarried. I know 'twill be of great service to Sir Christopher if you will write a letter to the Dean and assure him that to your knowledge, Sir Christopher will serve them, if they choose him. I find the necessity of this, and beg you not to delay it; write such a letter as may be proper for the Dean to show.

I have not any opposition yet, nor expect any at Abingdon. I wish you all success in your parts.

Postscript.—I have promised a very good friend of mine, and a zealous servant of Sir Christopher in this place to engage your interest for him with the next Speaker to take him for his chaplain.

[ROBERT HARLEY to LORD CHANDOS.]

1700, December 23. Brampton Castle—Thanks for sympathy upon death of his father. The feeling of his great loss renders him very unfit for public affairs, but is pleased that his lordship is desirous of a meeting of the Herefordshire gentlemen, since some of them "have thought fit to spring this new game of opposition." Divers years since he had parted with an undoubted interest at Leominster, upon certain promises then made and not yet performed; and he had been plunged into great expense and trouble in other places by that means. Had promised to do what he could for Mr. Gorges. Is pleased to hear Mr. Brydges is in no danger from his opponent. *Copy.*

[ROBERT HARLEY to LORD CONINGSBY.]

1700, December 30. Brampton Castle—Concerning his brother Edward's prospects of election for Leominster. The country full of lies, and a great inclination to put gentlemen at difference. Whether the magistrates of Leominster (as they call themselves) return his brother or not, it is hoped that his lordship will see so much of their practice and the mischief of it, that he will concur in a method to hit the blots which lie open and too plain to be defended. *Copy.*

[——— to ROBERT HARLEY.]

1700-1, January 2—I do heartily condole with you for the great loss you have sustained in your family. I cannot but wonder it unfits you for other matters, which, yet I believe you'll be told from another hand this post, stand in need of your help as much as ever, and that the way to overcome one sorrow, is to take a dose of new sorrow, out of a paper you'll receive from the same hand, and if you take the advice given you, I suppose that soon after you have settled your matters there, we shall see you here, for which I shall be content to be referred till then, to have an account of them. Here, now we are got within the forty days and that there's no drinking, there's not much talking. In general, 'tis computed that there's about 2,000 stand in competition, where there's room but for 513. Eleven are said to stand candidates for Weymouth and Melcombe Regis in Dorsetshire, but 'tis supposed the four that will be elected will be the Lord We████th's son, Lord Shaftesbury's brother, Major General Churchill and Mr Mich. Harvy. For Dorchester will be Colonel Trenchard and Mr Napper, if Sir Nathaniel don't use his authority with his son and command him not to stand, but resign to him, and then neither of them will have it. At Lyme will be Mr Henley, a Commissioner of the Customs, it being a seaport town, and one Paice a merchant. In Gloucestershire Sir Ralph Dutton and Mr Howe and not Sir Richard Cox, with whom Sir Ralph, 'twas said, had joined, but has since dropped him. At Southwark the two old members again, and not Mr Arthur Moore, whom both Sir Bazell Firebrass and Sir John Parsons oppose to keep out, and this last is to come in, by consent, with Mr Harvey at Reigate. At Westminster 'tis believed that Mr Secretary Vernon and either Mr Cross the brewer or Sir Walter Clarges will be chosen, on Monday next. There are five who stand at Southampton, but 'tis believed Mr Cardonnel who belongs to Mr Blaythwayt, and Mr Momparsons will carry it and young Pappilon at Dover, instead of Ailmer: and Sergisson and Dummer instead of Colonel Perry at Shoreham. I see the business of clipped money is like to be overhauled at the Bar some where. Benj. Overton is like to be chosen at St. Ives in Cornwall. There's a third party already forming to oppose the old as well as the new Court party. Sir Thomas Powis I suppose is by this time near chosen without contradiction, in Squire Newport's place at Ludlow who will hardly get in anywhere. When the election at Leominster is over, a friend of yours would be glad to hear of it.

Robert Price to [Robert Harley].

1700[-1], January 3. Foxley—The affairs of Weobley are now, I hope, reduced to a point. Mr. Thynne "had men he moneyed about fifty-three, whereof very many were usually my stanch votesmen." Birch got upwards of forty at a dear underhand sale. I had about thirty-eight, and Colonel Cornwall about thirty at 5*l*., some 10*l*., some 20*l*.

I cannot prevail with Alban Thomas to secure two considerable voters, Will Hosier a tanner, and John Rees, who are rich, active men and of the first rank in the borough. They vote for me *gratis*, but begged of me their liberty, that since I desisted they might make their markets. Cornwall offered each fifteen guineas. I desired them to reserve themselves till Monday morning. Thomas will give them but the common pay which Hosier received, being left in his house, and would return again, no promise being made. I would desire your judgment whether it were not better to give 10*l*. each or for any less sum which they can be agreed with, than lose such men, who will be very active and will out-do A. Thomas in the game.

[Henry Guy to Robert Harley.]

[1700-1], January 4—I received yours of the 31st past, but am a little concerned to find Ludlow mistaken for Leominster twice together.

It may be oversight but I do not like it. I desire you to write to Sir Thomas Frankland about it.

I will not doubt but the writ came on the time that was mentioned.

Sir Christopher Musgrave and Mr. Finch are chosen for the University of Oxford.

I am truly glad to hear that 225 hath twenty-seven or thirty majority; because it is said here he would lose it.

The King hath been somewhat out of order, but is now much better.

Enclosed I send you a letter from 163.

CHARLES CORNWALL to ROBERT HARLEY, at Brampton.

1700[-1], January 5. Moccas—Since by a letter from Lord Coningsby I observe you cannot be prevailed with to declare for me, I have consulted with my friends and have resolved to poll it to the last man, provided you will please to give me an assurance that you will not be against me, and thereby give friends a liberty to dispose of themselves and me to engage what I can of them.

Sir H[ERBERT] CROFT to his kinsman [ROBERT HARLEY].

1700[-1], January 11—I am glad to hear you have no trouble in your election at Radnor. We shall have no contest in the county as Captain (sic) Cornwall has resolved to desist, and Lord Coningsby goes for London on Tuesday, so that I suppose the general opinion will rest upon Sir John Williams and Mr. Gorges. I should be glad to see you take your turn in this county.

[HENRY GUY to ROBERT HARLEY.]

[1700–1], January 11—I received yours of the 7th instant. I hope the adverse party will not prevail against 561 : but he hath an antagonist that will stick at nothing.

The writ I find came shorter by two or three days than was intended. I know not the reason ; however I am glad it came so that the election will be next week, for then 104 [Harley] will not be long from hence ; his return is much wished.

I am reasonable well, but not quite recovered ; for I laboured some days under a difficulty of breathing, which was very uneasy.

Here is not anything new. The elections you see in the newspapers. I do not much like 165 hitherto ; I hope it will mend.

[HENRY GUY to ROBERT HARLEY.]

[1700–1], January 14—I received yours of the 10th instant, by which is fully seen the foul play given to 225, but that will be set right no doubt by 127 [petition]. You will find more cases of that kind than ever you yet knew, of which 145 of 254 hath been the great occasion ; and somewhat must be done in it or 68 [parliament] will be hereafter utterly lost. For this cause 79 [Rochester] and 78 [Godolphin] do most earnestly desire 104 [Harley] to be at 197 [London] as soon as may be, to consider of what hath been above mentioned, and several other matters of importance. The elections for 231 and 553 being over they will now impatiently expect him every day.

They are polling still at Westminster. Secretary Vernon hath the majority by much, and next to him yesterday Sir Harry Colt had it. 499 hath lost it by one voice; but I do not at all hear how the thing was, or whether there be ground for a petition.

78 [Godolphin] will be in town to-morrow: I will then acquaint him with what you write concerning 559.

I do not at all wonder at 431, it is so habitual to him, he cannot help being false.

—— to Robert Harley, at Brampton Bryan.

1700[-1], January 14—By your letter and by what they write from other parts of the country, bribery has infected them insomuch that if a timely check be not put thereto, in a little time a remedy will be applied too late; for never was the like heard of. 50*l.* or 40*l.* for a vote. God be merciful to us; for if a speedy stop be not put to this growing evil, England is undone. You are much enquired for. I am told Lord Nottingham asked for you and many others, ladies as well as lords, and other great men. As yet, your friend tells me, he hears nothing from the Lord you mentioned in your letter, which you seemed to hint he might possibly do; but he says that place is disposed of to one fit only for a pension, which if it had been 500*l.* a year, it might have been 20,000*l.* a year in the way of the revenue if a fit man had been put there.

[Henry Guy to Robert Harley.]

[1700–1], January 18—Since my last I have spoken to 78 [Godolphin] concerning the place of Bearecroft. He bids me tell you that immediately after his death the place was given to one Sheaperd at the desire of Mr. Boyle, in whose family that man had been a servant, and they had put him some years since into some other place at the Custom House. 78 [Godolphin] says he is very well acquainted with 559, and thinks him a very good deserving man, and that he shall always be welcome to him.

147 [Guy] was yesterday with 67 [the King], who asked when 104 [Harley] would come, and desired him to hasten him. 79 [Rochester] and 78 [Godolphin] did yesterday again enjoin me to write to you this night to come with speed; for they say that what you would chiefly see over is now past, and there are several things of the greatest moment which do really want the opinion and advice of 440 [Harley]; therefore I beg of you in your next let me have from you a short day for your setting forward on your journey.

220 tells me that 99 will be here some days before this month ends, and 80 is looked for within ten days. Lake and Smithson have carried it in Middlesex against Wolstenholme and Bucknall. As I told you in my last I do not in the main like 165. I thought it would have been otherwise, though I know there are very many very foul practices which will be made appear.

—— to [Robert Harley].

1700–1, January 23—I have returned all the answer Charles could at present give to the questions, he goes up along with me next Monday, and will inform anything further he can. I could not now send an answer about the King's plate, but will look out the indentures and bring them along with me. When my father had the King's plate Charles says he used no pewter. but when he used pewter he cannot recollect what quantity; neither can he the number of candles.

I was at Gloucestershire election but could do but little service; finding them all engaged about Newent single votes for Sir R. Cocks, I persuaded about 40 to give their votes to Mr. Howe, that was all I could do. The number stood thus:—for Mr. Howe 1709 ; Sir R. Cocks 1389 ; Sir R. Dutton 1248. The far greatest number of the freeholders gave but single votes, by which means through his own folly Sir R. D. lost it, for he obliging his friends to give single votes, Mr. Masters, Mr. Chester, &c. who were for Mr. Howe and him, put those they brought in to vote for Howe only, the number who did so were I believe at least 400. Your cousin Stephens was singly for Mr. Howe. Sir R. Cocks' chief supporters were Mr. Thos. Stephens and Mr. Colchester, he promised not to stand the next election.

[HENRY GUY to ROBERT HARLEY.]

.. [1700–1], January 23—When you come hither you will find a great deal more noise of the briberies and violences in several places. Your friends do think that if 104 [Harley] were here now it would be but time enough for many important things ; but 79 [Rochester] and 78 [Godolphin] are positive, that if he is not here at least a week before the 6th, it will be of ill consequence. I believe 79 [Rochester] hath not yet written to 99 to come, till he heard when 440 [Harley] would be here, but he will write to him this post. 410 is looked for speedily.

Poor Philmer died yesterday of an apoplexy. They are polling in, London. Some think Duncombe will lose it.

I wrote thus far in the forenoon, and I have since been with 67 [the king], who most earnestly enquired when 104 [Harley] would come. And though 79 [Rochester] and 78 [Godolphin] enjoined me this morning to press 440 [Harley] to come, yet this afternoon they sent me a letter to press me to do it effectually. I have written as far as I can at this time for my late illness still hangs heavily upon me.

C. MUSGRAVE to [ROBERT HARLEY].

1700–1, January 25. Gray's Inn—My father's success at Oxford may be imputed in a great measure to your kindness. He has also been chosen with Mr. Graham for Westmorland. Sir Richard Sandford came within four votes of my father, but Mr. Graham carried it by a majority of eighty-seven. My father made no manner of application, which I suppose he will not be wanting in when he sets up a friend of yours. I take it for granted he will stand for the University, who are mightily pleased with the letter he lately sent them. I am glad to find you approve well enough of the elections notwithstanding the indirect practices and the briberies. The election for the city of London was very extraordinary and very surprising.

[LORD GODOLPHIN] to ROBERT HARLEY.

.1700–1; [January ?]—I had an opportunity this morning to discourse with Sir E. S[eymour ?] about filling the chair of the House of Commons, and finding him totally decline it himself, as soon as I named you to him, he came as entirely into that as I could wish. I had no mind to lose any time in acquainting you with this because he seemed to think of speaking to you of it this day.

W. BROMLEY to [ROBERT HARLEY].

1700[-1], February 17—Give me leave to congratulate your advancement to a dignity you so well deserve. I have never till now had any reason to regret my being out of the House, but should have been glad to have made the number of voices double to those of your competitor. We that are in the country look upon your having the chair as a very good omen in this critical juncture.

WARRANT.

1700[1], February 27—To Charles Godfrey, master of the Jewel House, for the delivery to the use of the Right Hon. Robert Harley, Speaker to the House of Commons, of the same quantity of white and gilt plate as was allowed to Sir Thomas Littleton when he held the same office. Signed by the Earl of Jersey, and counter-signed by Lord Godolphin, Sir Stephen Fox, H. Boyle, J. Smith, and Richard Hill.

DANIEL WILLIAMS to [ROBERT HARLEY].

1701, March 26—Protesting against two of the clauses contained in the bill against Dissenters then before the House.

Sir CHARLES HEDGES to Mr. SPEAKER [HARLEY].

1701, March 31—I am commanded to deliver a message from his Majesty to the House of Commons this morning relating to the succours desired by the States, and the negociations at the Hague, according to Mr. Stanhope's account thereof, which I thought fit to acquaint you withal.

[LORD GODOLPHIN to ROBERT HARLEY.]

[1701, March]—Mr. Stanhope's letter is of the 5th April new style, he writes that the French Ambassador's courier was returned, and that the Ambassador had acquainted the Pensioner that the King his master looked upon their demands to be so high and so exorbitant as not to deserve an answer ; however, that he desired peace, and would maintain the peace of Ryswick and expected the States should speedily declare their intentions.

As for England that Monsieur Tallard was at London and Lord Manchester at Paris, and in either of those places, any thing might properly be transacted which was depending betwixt the two Crowns. This was communicated to him by the Pensioner who at the same time acquainted him that according to the King's desire the States had a squadron of ships of line of battle ready to sail to the rendezvous and to join the English fleet with the first wind, desiring him to represent to the King that they stood in great need of the 10,000 men promised them by the Treaty of 1677 which therefore they hoped His Majesty would not delay to send to them.

· This account seeming necessary to be forthwith communicated to the House of Commons, some answer upon the heads following is humbly submitted.

FRANCIS LLOYD to [ROBERT HARLEY].

1701, April 15—Suggesting that all able-bodied men in the Kingdom should be ordered to furnish themselves with arms, and that they should be formed into companies and regiments, and so exercised in every parish once a week till they knew how to use them. Such a course would deter the most potent prince in the world from invading the Kingdom. It might have been of pernicious consequence in some former reigns, but now that we have a prince that rules in the hearts of his people few will be so blind as not to see their greatest interest is to preserve him.

Dr. GEORGE HICKS to ROBERT HARLEY.

· 1701, April 23—This gentleman is Mr. Wanley of whom I spoke to you. · He has the best skill in ancient hands and MSS. of any man not only of this, but, I believe, of any former age, and I wish for the sake of the public, that he might meet with the same public encouragement here, that he would have met with in France, Holland, or Sweden, had he been born in any of those countries. He brings you his book of specimens, which I believe will please you, and Dr. Smith's Catalogue of the Cottonian Library, in which he hath made some amendments and could have made very many more. I desired him to show it you only that you might see another specimen of his skill, and not to detract from the Doctor's performance, for which the world hath been very much beholden to him. I wish he might be encouraged to take a catalogue of that whole library, as he hath taken a part of it for me, and that indeed would be a catalogue truly worthy of it. He hath told me of an engraver in town, that can engrave your charter and if you will do me and my book the favour and honour to let me have a plate of it, he will do me the kindness to supervise the sculpture and see it shall be most exact. I am sensible it will be not only a great ornament to my book, but of great use to the reader and I will take care it shall be for the honour of your name. If the plate should prove a little larger than my book, I can so dispose of its prints in the binding, that they shall be altogether as convenient as if they were printed on one of the leaves of every book. In confidence you will add this to your many former favours to me and my book. I have this morning begun to write what I have to say of your charter, that I may carry it on Monday to Oxford to be printed with the rest.

GEO. FOLLET to ROBERT HARLEY.

1701, May 10—If you purpose seeing Mr. Pepys' house to-day he prays to have notice at what hour, that he may forbear a little work about his books which he is upon.

WILLIAM KIDD to [ROBERT HARLEY ?].

1701, May 12. · Newgate—The long imprisonment I have undergone, or the trial I am to undergo are not so great an affliction to me as my not being able to give your Honourable House of Commons such satisfaction as was expected from me. I hope I have not offended against the Law but if I have it was the fault of the others who knew better and made me the tool of their ambition and avarice and who now perhaps think it their interest that I should be removed out of the world. I did not seek the commission I undertook, but was partly cajoled and partly menaced into it by the Lord Bellomont and one Robert Livingston of New York who was the projector, promoter and chief manager of that design, and who only can give your House a satisfactory account of all the transactions of my owners. He was the man admitted into their closets and received their private instructions which he kept in his own hands; and who encouraged me in their names to do more than I ever did, and to act without regard to my Commission. I would not exceed my authority and took no other ships than such as had French passes, which I brought with me to New England and relied upon for my justification, but my Lord Bellomont seized upon them together with my cargo and though he promised to send them into England yet has he detained part of the effects, kept those passes wholly from me and has stripped me of all the defence I have to make which is such barbarous as well as dishonourable usage, as I hope your honourable House will not let an Englishman suffer how unfortunate soever his circumstances are, but will intercede with his Majesty to defer my trial until I can have those passes and that Livingston may be brought under your examination and confronted by me. I cannot be so unjust to myself as to plead to an indictment till the French passes are restored to me unless I would be accessary to my own destruction; for though I can make proof that the ships I took had such passes I am advised by counsel that it will little avail me without producing the passes themselves. I was in great consternation when I was before that great assembly, Your Honourable House, which with the disadvantages of a mean capacity, want of education, and a spirit cramped by long confinement, made me incapable of representing my case and I have, therefore, presumed to send your honourable a short and true statement of it which I humbly beg your Honourable's perusal and communication of to the House if you think it worthy their notice. I humbly crave leave to acquaint your Honour that I was not privy to my being sent for up to your House the second time, nor to the paper lately printed in my name, both which may justly give offence to the House, but I owe the first to a coffeeman in the Court of Wards who designed to make a show of me for his profit, and the latter was done by one Newy, a prisoner in Newgate, to get money for his support at the hazard of my safety.

Petition enclosed.

The sense of my present condition (being under condemnation) and the thoughts of having been imposed on by such as seek my destruction, thereby to fulfil their ambitious desires, make me incapable of expressing myself in those terms as I ought, therefore do most humbly pray that you will be pleased to represent to the Honourable House of Commons that in my late proceedings in the Indies I have lodged goods and treasure to the value of one hundred thousand pounds, which I desire the Government may have the benefit of. In order thereto I shall desire no manner of liberty, but to be kept prisoner on board such ship as may be appointed for that purpose and only give the necessary directions, and in case I fail therein I desire no favour but to be forthwith executed according to my sentence. If your Honourable House will please to order a committee to come to me I doubt not but to give such satisfaction as may obtain mercy, most humbly submitting to the wisdom of your great assembly.

WILLIAM PATERSON to [ROBERT HARLEY].

1701, May 19—Forwards for 'his consideration' a lengthy paper headed " Proposals for the better restoring of Public Credit and more easy payment of the National debts by settling a fund of 18 per cent. per annum for the term of nine years " &c.

Something of this nature ought to be done this session. 'Is now about making a table to this proposal by which it may be known to a day when any sum the government is indebted will be paid off by this method ; and thereby a way will be shown how there need not, for the future, be a penny given or received but as designed by the Parliament, and by which the house of Commons, as they ought to be, will be the entire and sacred repository of the public credit as well as of the public moneys of this kingdom, which he knows is and always has been Harley's wish and ought to be that of all good patriots.

WILLIAM PATERSON to [ROBERT HARLEY].

1701, May 27—Has been employed since they met in rectifying and methodizing his proposal according to the information and advice Harley had given him. Discourses at some length on his financial schemes, and begs pardon for his tedious scribble. Was unwell at the time his book was being printed, which caused it to be very incorrect; another impression, with large additions, is intended, in which it will be seen that he sets up against all sorts of: monopolies, reprisals, prohibitions, pre-emptions, and exclusions. Is glad to find Harley already against some of them.

WILLIAM FULLER to ROBERT HARLEY, Speaker.

1701, June 18—Praying that a hearing might be granted to Mr. Jones, who had long been an agent for the late King, and had managed his greatest concerns in England since the Revolution, and that he would then produce such proofs and papers as could not fail to satisfy the House of Commons how the nation had been betrayed for seven or eight years past. Mr. Jones is a gentleman of a considerable fortune and unquestionable reputation ; but there are many in England that swear he shall not live to see any other Sessions of Parliament, and on Saturday last he was assaulted, which induces the writer most earnestly to entreat Harley to present this letter and petition to the House of Commons.

The writer's petition to the house of Commons is attached. His object is chiefly " to prove the illegitimacy of the pretended Prince of Wales," by the evidence of Mr. Jones and witnesses.

[SIMON HARCOURT] to [ROBERT HARLEY,] Speaker.

1701, July 14—I must never see my Lord Duke of Ormond nor the Doctor, if you are not to be prevailed to dine with the Doctor tomorrow between two and three. "The gold bowle shall not appeare." You will meet no other company besides the Duke, the doctor, his chum and myself.

EDMUND ALURED to ROBERT HARLEY.

1701, August 14—Aboard the Bristol, riding at Spithead. Asks for a letter to Admiral "Bembo," commanding the squadron going to the West Indies, who might have it in his power to give the writer a commission before the expedition returns.

[HENRY GUY to ROBERT HARLEY.]

[1701.] August 18. Bath—I received the favour of yours of the 16th instant: and do most humbly thank you about the Northern affair: I confess it nearly concerns me, for unless some remedy can be found in that matter, I must quite give over that interest. I do not see how 78 (Godolphin) can do me any good in it, nor 148. Was the business of the two justices big enough for 79 (Rochester) to stay his journey? however if it retrieves it, it will be well enough. I have this day received a letter from 76, wherein he says that he delivered mine to 67 (the King), and in mine, yours to me was enclosed to him. 76 likewise tells me that the four warrants for the Bucks for you are sent by him this post under cover to Mr. Ellis, therefore pray look after them. I truly thank you for your resolution of letting me know how matters go: you will much oblige me by it: the cypher puts it out of all fear of danger. For a more particular direction, you may please superscribe to me at Mr. Pierce his house near the great church in Bath. I hope I shall have what I desire from the waters though as yet I cannot see much; but perseverance must obtain that. I have made your compliments to Mr Attorney, who returns them heartily to you. I cannot think these addresses will signify much.

WILLIAM PENN to [ROBERT] HARLEY.

1701, August 27. Pennsylvania—I cannot forbear thinking myself safe where I have such a friend in the chair. It is the idea we have of things that rules our determinations, and if that be wrongly taken, our conclusions will be so made.

That the notion men have at an office or two is in disfavour of proprietary governments I can't wonder at, because it is not always what is just but what is profitable to themselves that is the spring of motion.

I think it is no hard task to prove that it is easier for the crown to make colonies and improve them at other folks' cost, than at its own, and that those people have a better caution and security for their conduct than a mercenary governor or those that have not so much to lose. If it be alleged that the temptation of gain will prevail with such as have power in their hands to secure themselves in unfair ways of prosecuting it, I take leave to say, no, where the King has approved of a Deputy Governor no more than if he named him, especially if he is obliged to give security for his faithful discharge of his duty to the laws of trade and navigation—which would not be denied—besides, the King has already his Vice-Admirals, Judges of the Admiralty, Advocates, Collectors, Surveyors, and Auditors in each proprietary government. I must think that so many spies cannot but be a security, and that no wise man will hazard a country to indulge a few traders, not twenty perhaps, in a whole province. And to think that a King's governor who comes only to get money, and is perhaps indigent, should not lie under at least equal temptations with a proprietary one, were a partiality. I know not what they may do, but what they have done favours my argument.

This leads me to affirm that being King's governments, the end proposed to prevent false trade will not do it, and if so, the hardship is imposed in vain. For I convinced the Lords, before whom I had five hearings upon this very suggestion, by the confession of the same prosecutor, Ed: Randall, that notwithstanding the activity and vigilance of Governor Nicolson, and the almost ubiquity and penetration of the other single eyed gentleman, Maryland since a King's government was twenty seven times a greater sinner than we were. And more, that of the nine ships, that is, sloops and brigantines, that he with too great assurance averred were gone from our province to Scotland or Holland, I found that they all answered the laws of trade but one, and she had given bond, which is all we are obliged to expect by law.

It can never enter the head of any reasonable man, that we should labour to cut the grass under our own feet, which we must do, if to let others be rich we would ruin ourselves, by being the security of the whole to the crown.

In practice, they that improve most, are the profitablest colonies to the crown, but those are known to be proprietary ones. And again, if it be considered who they are that rise more by trade than culture, they will be found to be the King's more immediate governments as they are used to be distinguished. Upon which let the question be put, who are most likely to be vicious in trade, and I believe we shall escape the stroke of the hand now lifted up at us.

Yet again, let it but be remembered that our staple is provision to the Islands, in which regard we have not the opportunity of false trade, if we had the inclination; for those Colonies are most to be apprehended, that trade above their own produce, whereas, we have not shipping to export one half of it, but in bottoms of New York and New England.

However, I think the commission of the Customs is not changed upon every trick a merchant plays in trade. Let our faults be proved, first the facts, next the malice or intention; but not behind our backs; civil causes may, but this is of a criminal nature, and a Bill to punish us before tried is worse than one of attainder.

My worthy friend, this seems to me great trifling with honour and property, when men must be forfeited in both, unheard, and which is worse, innocent, aye, meritorious; pardon the expression, I hope it is not vain; time, if I may have it and live, will secure me.

I humbly beg that if any Bill be brought in against us next sessions, I may have time to come home, and in order to it, that the King would approve of a deputy, according to the law of the seven and eight of his reign, without which no man will serve, as without one I cannot well leave the government. Here's my dilemma, abdicate, or lose my government for not doing so, if the Parliament will proceed in my absence.

The confusion these things breed here is treating government and governors in burlesque.

I shall conclude my letter, with two things. First that the preamble of the Bill, as to me, is most untrue, for I am so far from being an independent governor that no King's governor in America has obeyed and pursued the King's directions more readily and vigorously than I have done, and in all respects to my ability, submitted to his orders. In fine, I have acted the part of the King's governor at my own charges, and pray that my letters to the Council of Trade and Commissioners of the Admiralty and Customs may be called for in my justification, for the first have not used me with candour in their representation. I might add upon this head that by my grant, appeals are reserved to the King, laws of trade to be observed, and our laws to be transmitted for the King's assent. Such a grant and government cannot with justice, I think, be reputed independent.

Next, I have sunk my fortune and family 20,000*l.* above my gain by land, to make and succeed this enterprise, which the loss of the government will make one to me, and never count upon the money owing from the Crown to my father, that was at the bottom the consideration of the grant, as my petitions, &c. show.

If therefore we must lose it let us be tried, if nevertheless the King will have it, let us have our equivalent, and time to negociate this, or a gaol instead of a government must determine my hazards, labour and expense. Let it not be said that a Parliament of England, the people's last resort for right, should ex parte, deprive whole provinces of their first and chief encouragement to planting of ▬▬▬

This is the diamond, the soil but the ring, and that we bought of the natives, and have made it English property by our blood and bones as well as treasure; and to have a proviso to save us this only is a jest rather than a security or privilege.

It is pretended the King's service, but I hope reason of State shall never be one to violate property; and I am afraid, it is the service of some body else, that would have no dissenters governors, for all the proprietary ones began upon that bottom, Carolina excepted; and then our case must be desperate, that shall not be allowed such accountable powers at t'other end of the world, to be made inhabitable by our toil, hazard and great expense. I may add an other, that some people may have more governments to excise (*sic*) and governors to go halves with.

Pardon, my worthy friend, this tedious and unpremeditated letter. Sufferers are always full, but so I am of deep respect for thee.

[HENRY GUY to ROBERT HARLEY.]

1701, August 30. Bath—I received the favour of yours of the 26th instant, which gave me hopes, that I should hear from you more at large this post; but there came no letter. I beg of you to be so charitable to let me hear from you how matters go while you are in London; I will requite you, when I return thither, and you are gone from thence. Pray let me know if there be anything in that report, that 586 is so intimate with 77; but do not let him know, that I enquire after it; and likewise what the answer was about the two justices which was satisfactory to 79 (Rochester). I shall make your compliments about the Bucks. Mr. Attorney doth not go from hence this fortnight at soonest.

[P.S.] 75 thought you were at the Bath, and hath written to me to make you all his compliments and good wishes.

Dr. GEORGE HICKES to ROBERT HARLEY, at York Buildings.

1701, August 31. I have been at Oxford where all learned men have a particular esteem and veneration for you. Mr. Potter of Lincoln College, who not long since put out *Lycophron*, which is now re-printing at the theatre, hath such a singular respect for you that he desires to dedicate to you his volume of the Greek antiquities, which among many others is now printing at Leyden in imitation of Mr. Graevius's Roman antiquities which he printed at Utrecht. Mr. Potter wrote this volume at the request of Mr. Gronovius, and it is almost finished.

VISCOUNT WEYMOUTH to [ROBERT HARLEY,] Speaker of the House of Commons.

1701, August 31. Longleat—The assizes in this and the next county have passed quietly without troubling his Majesty or the Lords

Justices with any addresses of advice, but there are some secret applications made preparatory to a new Parliament.

ROBERT HARLEY to LORD ———.

1701, September 3—I am told Sir John Cotton is dead, and thereupon the trust of that noble library comes to be put in execution, wherein I have the honour to be joined with you, and will be ready to attend any summons you shall please to give.

[LORD GODOLPHIN to ROBERT HARLEY] Speaker.

1701, September 4—Since I saw you I have met with Mr. Lowndes who tells me he has seen this morning Mr. Shepherd and Mr. Heathcote at Lord Halifax's, where he opened to them his notion of the powers of the Act, in which they all entirely agreed, and were in haste to have had a meeting this night, but Mr. Lowndes coming to acquaint me with this matter, and that he was to go out of town to-night, I went to Lord Halifax and have put off any meeting upon it till Tuesday night, at which time they seem to think this tedious and difficult matter may be brought to a conclusion.

Dr. CHARLES DAVENANT to ROBERT HARLEY.

1701, September 7—Jack Howe will be outrageous with me for thus neglecting his paper. You know how tender a part 'tis in an author. My Lord Orrery did not forgive my father to his dying day for sleeping at a scene in one of his plays.

[LORD GODOLPHIN to ROBERT HARLEY.]

[1701.] September 11—Just now, at two, Mr. Dolben has been with me ; matters sharpen apace, in the Committee of the old Company. He tells me they were so angry this morning that their Governor hardly escaped a censure for having proceeded so far in hearkening to the proposals depending, and that Sir Thos. Cook durst not own he sent him of a message to me, but that Sir Thomas seemed to wish some means might be used to moderate Mr. Moore against to morrow morning, when it seems the Committee is to meet again. I am sending to Dr. Davenant to come to me to morrow morning early, to try what he can do in the matter ; in the mean time, if by yourself or Sir B. Shower, Mr. Moore could be discoursed, and the nature of this agreement well explained to him, possibly it might help Sir T. Cook, who seems to be at a plunge, and bring the Committee a little more to their wits. The greatest difficulty seems to lie in the shortness of time, the matter coming to bear tomorrow, so that there's no room to work. But when tomorrow is over, you and I and, if you approve of it, Sir B. Shower, may appoint to meet the Committee of the old Company and reason the matter fairly with them. By what I can understand, the difficulties in this agreement arise chiefly from some among them.

[LORD GODOLPHIN to ROBERT HARLEY.]

1701. September 12—I have had a good deal of talk this morning first with Mr. Moore and then with Sir B. Shower. The former seems very averse to the agreement proposed if not to any agreement, and particularly he insisted that writing their 315,000*l.* into the Stock of the new Company was absolute destruction. Sir B. Shower seemed to be very well convinced that an union was necessary, and to be intent upon finding out expedients how to compass it. I thought it might not be amiss to trouble you with this account of the several tempers in which I found them that when you come to speak with them you may the better know how to suit your discourse.

[LORD GODOLPHIN to ROBERT HARLEY.]

[1701, September 12] Friday—Being to go out of town early in the morning I had a mind to tell you that without any partiality to my friends of the old Company, I think they are in the right to expect an answer to their paper, and if there be not still at the bottom an inclination to differ in those that govern them, why should not the new Company think it reasonable to allow the old one 350,000*l.* for their dead stock, the old Company allowing them a 100 for a 100 upon the funds and submitting to a limitation of seven years upon these terms. If I had been Chancellor at our meeting tonight, I would have pronounced they ought to have agreed, and if you are of the same mind, I should hope a word or two to Mr. Shepherd and Allen would yet bring them to a conclusion upon these three points; viz.

1st. The limitation of their existence to be for seven years;
2nd. Cent for cent to be allowed for the funds;
3rd. The dead stock of the old Company to be valued at 350,000*l.*

I reckon the old Company condescend to satisfy the new one in agreeing to a limitation of their separate existence, and also in allowing them a hundred for a hundred upon their funds; which I propose they should do, and then I can't but think the new right to comply with the old in their demand for their dead stock. I ask your pardon for troubling you with this long letter, upon so tedious a subject, I hope you will excuse it because I shall not have the happiness of seeing you again these four or five days.

LORD CUTTS to [ROBERT HARLEY].

1701, September 14. N.S. The Hague—I was several times to wait on you to receive your commands before I left England, but being always so unhappy as to miss you I was resolved to take the first good occasion to give you a sincere assurance of my very great affection and honour for you. I cannot take a better occasion than this, the King of Prussia's Envoy having just now told me, in a visit he was pleased to make me, that he came straight from Count Wratislaw's who has just received an account, that the French under the command of Marshal Villeroy have attacked Prince Eugene, that they have been vigorously repulsed, lost 4000 men upon the spot, and about 300 officers, with a very unproportionable loss on the side of the Germans. The thing is very new, for I saw Count Wratislaw at eleven last night, at which time he had heard nothing of it. Monsieur Spanheim could give me no particulars; but so far as I can guess from the first view of the thing, they must have attacked some particular post; in which if they had succeeded, they would have pushed it to a general affair; for it does not seem to me that the armies have been entirely engaged. However it may possibly be of as much advantage to the Germans as a general affair since they have gained a superiority with a little loss, which blow well followed may turn the whole scheme of affairs.

[LORD GODOLPHIN to ROBERT HARLEY.]

1701, October 3. St. Albans—I have seen Lord Carlisle this morning at Gorhambury. He is going into the north, and has promised me to carry with him a great readiness of disposition to live well with our friend, which I lose no time in letting you know since he should be prepared to be also in the same temper.

VISCOUNT WEYMOUTH to ROBERT HARLEY, at his house in York Buildings.

1701, October 7—I see the City address is echoed by Oxfordshire, and possibly it will be followed by other counties. Great wisdom is necessary in penning things of that nature.

I find by a new set of queries three Parliament men were found at supper with the French Secretary; I can decipher the name only of Dr. D. Whoever they were it was an ill-chosen conversation and had little of thought.

Last year there was not so much care as was necessary in the choice of sheriffs. I hope more will be taken now, and the clerks of the several circuits should be discoursed that six good men be in the first list to avoid the objection of pocket sheriffs. Men must not be excused because they are friends or kinsmen.

If diligence is not used one of the Colepeppers will go near to succeed Sir Joseph Williamson at Rochester. Chatham has a great stroke in that election, which the Admiralty may direct.

I wish the bishopric of Hereford may not be disposed of in haste. The diocese will not be more destitute than it has been for some years past.

[HENRY GUY to ROBERT HARLEY.]

[1701,] October 12—I wrote to you two letters since you left London, in the last of which was enclosed one from 78 [Godolphin]. I wish you would favour me with a line that you have received them. But I write this to you by the desire of La 84 who bids me tell you that a 168 of 248 [   ] is dead, and that 74 hath told 69 that it is the earnest desire of 104 [Harley] that Cox be advanced and that Banister do come in anew. If this be the desire of 440 [Harley] it shall certainly be done, or if 440 [Harley] would have any other it shall be endeavoured to obtain it. La 420 doth entreat that this may remain entirely in your breast only, and that you will not fail of returning an answer by the next post, and to keep it secret.

[The SAME to the SAME.]

[1701,] October 14—This comes only to cover the enclosed from 78 [Godolphin]. I long to have an answer to my last for the person's sake who desired me to write it. Again I entreat you to keep that matter entirely secret. I wrote likewise two letters to you from Bath, but have not yet had a line of answer to any since you went into the country. Pray forego this retentive faculty of writing, and give a line or two to me.

J. TUCKER to [ROBERT HARLEY,] Speaker.

1701, October 14. Whitehall—The Worcester and Staffordshire addresses are much talked of here. They are said to be drawn both by the same hand and sent thither from hence, as I believe many others are. The King came to the Hague on Wednesday last, but brought with him a cold which he took some days before; he will embark for England the first fair wind. The Earl of Marlborough is ordered to stay behind at the Hague.

[LORD GODOLPHIN] to ROBERT HARLEY, at Brampton.

1701, October 21. London—I came not to town till last night. I do not doubt but the addresses you speak of will have a very good effect both at home and abroad where we hear all addresses of that kind are very well liked. Your letters to our northern friend will hardly come to bear at present, since I am told Lord Carlisle is come to town again, and his journey to the north ended in going but just four miles beyond Northampton. · Mr. Lowndes tells me he has drawn the scheme of a charter in order to the union of the two companies which he seems to think will do the business, but it is so very long that I have not had time to read it. I have desired him to make an abstract of it which he promises in a day or two shall be ready, and then I suppose we must have another general assembly.

Lord Marlborough writes that the King was not willing that he should come over at the same time as his Majesty but that he should come by the first week in November. The war was looked upon at the Hague as inevitable, but with all that the Dutch do not seem so fervent for it as our addressors.

[VISCOUNT WEYMOUTH] to ROBERT HARLEY, at York Buildings.

1701, November 4. Longleat—Your absence may possibly have deprived you of the sight of a pamphlet about the dissensions of the Nobles and Commons of Athens and Rome, whose author [Swift] pretends to much reading and great sincerity, but towards the end there are pretty bold reflections.

It will be convenient that the plenipotentiary who made the new treaties should be here to justify and explain them. I can easily believe he acted prudently and cautiously but even the French Generals usually go to Paris in the winter.

I guess R. will not come without being sent for, which I hope will be the first thing done.

Our Diocesan has so eased himself upon the Convocation that we talk as much of it as of the Parliament, of which my neighbour can give you a large account who will be in town to-morrow.

Sir NATHAN WRIGHT, Lord Keeper, to [ROBERT HARLEY].

1701, November 5. Cockpit—I have been under very great difficulties about getting the Parliament prorogued to-morrow morning, the Lords Justices and myself being to attend His Majesty to-morrow by noon at Hampton Court, and we are all under apprehensions that the Lords of the Council (who are in the Commission to prorogue the Parliament) may all of them desire to wait upon the King at the same time or sooner in the morning.

That there may be nothing wanting on my part or the rest of the Lords Justices we have agreed to dispatch the prorogation before we go to Hampton Court, if we can get together a competent number of the Lords and if yourself and the Commons will be ready.

We have agreed to meet precisely at nine of the clock in the morning and desire, if possibly it may be done, that yourself and the Commons will be there at that time.

The SAME to [the SAME].

1701, November 5—Informing him that the King had taken the commission for proroguing Parliament with him to Hampton Court and that the messenger had returned without any instructions. As the King may have thought some day other than the 13th inst. was more proper for the meeting, he has sent a blank commission to be filled up as might be commanded by his Majesty.

[LORD WEYMOUTH] to ROBERT HARLEY, at Brampton.

1701, November 14—R. P[rice ?] informs me that Sir J. Williams is earnest with you to stand for Herefordshire, which I hope you will do if you can secure Radnor to a good man. He tells me he will stand for Weobley, to which he has my consent and directions to engage all my interest in the County for you, otherwise for the last Knights.

Some persons had earlier accounts of what was intended than the rest of the world, for A. on Saturday said the Parliament was to be dissolved. It is so early days that no judgment can be made how elections will go, but one side are very active, I wish the other be so too. 'Tis said Mr Ash will stand for this County, and so I believe will Mr Hyde, the latter I think the more likely to carry it. Sir H. Ashurst pretends to Wilton and Mr Phipp to oppose him. Why may not Mr Foley and Sir J. P[akington] join together for Worcester, and throw Stafford, or Wych [Droitwich] upon some other friend.

It is doubtful whether the two last Knights for Westmorland will prevail now, one of them should have a reserve in case of failure. Sir D. (*sic*) Colchester will stand for Gloucester and probably Mr Hale the Judge's heir.

WILLIAM PATERSON to ROBERT HARLEY.

1701, November 22. London—I have been twice with Mr. [John] Ward and find him entirely of the sentiments that you and other considerable men are of, with relation to the late dissolution of parliament—anything the ensuing parliament will or can do might have been justly expected from the last, and this continual altering of men and measures will make the minds of people so irritated and uncertain as to reduce the nation to the state its enemies would wish. He has been prevailed with to stand for Bletchingley, which election is on Monday. I spoke with Samuel Shephard who had before sent a compliment to the citizens met at the Crown tavern last Monday night to thank them for their good inclinations towards him, and to excuse his standing for parliament man; he is capable of being in a very good disposition, and I hope humour and resentment will not make him mad as it has done some others. I shall continue in my station to speak to men I think of any consequence, but have too little time or inclination to meddle with the giddy crowd. I go this day to Hampton Court and of what passes there you shall be advised.

—— to ——.

1701, November 26. Thetford—I cannot yet inform you who will be for the County, the candidates are Mr. Townshend, Sir John Holland,

and Sir Jacob Ashley. The two first join, but I believe will not both be chosen. The Norwich election is this day, the Mayor has made 200 freemen, on purpose to turn out the two old ones, but it is thought they will carry it, for all his endeavours to the contrary. Mr. Thacker and Mr. Clark do oppose them, for Lynn the old ones, for Castle Rising the old ones and Great Yarmouth the same. I know not who will be for this place, for if we all three stand, Stone and whom his friends please will be in. Our friends meet this night to see if they can agree which two they will have, but I believe will come to no resolution. I will prevent Stone having it, for if they cannot agree, I will give it over just before the election, for to have two of, that sort will be a much greater concern to me, so will not run the hazard, for should he get in by our division it would trouble me more than the not standing myself.

Suffolk I believe the two old ones will carry it, against any that will oppose them, it is said Sir Samuel Clark will, if he can get any one to join with him.

Sir Robert Davers I fear will lose it at Bury, but they had not proposed any one against him two days since, but Mr. Hervey will put him out if possible. I ask pardon for troubling you with this imperfect account, but as soon as the election be over I will give you a perfecter, I hope before the post goes out to know who is for Norwich.

[P.S.]—I hear since the writing of this that there is opposition at Yarmouth.

A. [Lady] Pye to her Cousin Amgail Harley, at Brampton.

1701, November 29. Bath—This town yesterday chose their old members who never appeared. What we hear now is about elections, but I will not pretend to news for this day sennight as I was writing to you I received a letter from a London lady well stuffed and for want of matter I must pen some which I have never heard confirmed. At least no sheriff named for any place. I wish His Majesty mend himself in a new parliament, all parties seemed united and unanimous.

There are four gentlemen stand for Gloucester besides the two old members, such divisions will be favourable it is thought to Mr. Howe. Pray let us hear what stir your county affords, I believe few places besides this so quiet. I do not expect Sir Charles will come in for many reasons. I shall not be sorry, I only wish quiet and safety in hurry and disorder as such times are; the gentlemen that desire it have been spending ever since I left Derby in August. Such frequent elections one would think should cure people from throwing away their money.

Robert Price to Robert Harley, at Brampton.

1701, December 2. Lincoln's Inn—Our town talk is canvassing elections, giving characters and instructions. One story goes of an associate of this house who, when two benchers attended him, said whoever advised the dissolving of the last Parliament ought to lose his head, and he would do his endeavour therein. The story comes from the Bishop of Ely and Dr. Wade, and is industriously spread; the two benchers were asked the question and deny any discourse tending that way.

I am glad our country elections succeed so well. To-morrow several of us go to Brentford to assist Lake and Smithson against the boy (?) Austen and Wostenholme; and the weaker of them is to (transfer?) to Bucknell if necessary.

Sir Chr. Musgrave is in town, and much blamed by his friends for coming on his journey when so near home; it is said he is chosen for Totnes. Sir Barth. Shower is at death's door, he fell ill on Sunday at church of a rheumatism and a high fever.

[LORD GODOLPHIN] to [ROBERT] HARLEY.

1701, December 4—I was extremely glad of the favour of your letter, and to hear the elections go so well in your parts. I hope in the West they will do so too, but the North we hear will be otherwise. I wish you may not be tempted to stay longer in the country than will be convenient for your friends here. The choice of a speaker will be a very decisive stroke in this ensuing parliament, your presence here as soon as you could afford it us would be but a necessary encouragement to the endeavours of your friends, who are all very hearty and entirely convinced they ought to lay all their stress upon that thing, in which we shall perhaps have more friends than people imagine.

I write by this post to the Bishop of Exeter to muster up his squadron so as to have them here by the 30th, and should be very glad to hear by what day you thought of being in town. Lord Rochester's leave to come into England was sent by last Saturday's post.

I hear Frank Gwyn will be chosen at Christchurch in lieu of Lord Cornbury, but I doubt our friend Sir Chr. M[usgrave] will lose it in Westmorland.

Lord Marlborough is come, and very sorry not to find you here.

STANLEY WEST to ROBERT HARLEY, at Brampton.

1701, December 6. London—Congratulating him on his return for Radnor, but informing him that the talk of the town is against his being re-elected Speaker, the wagers running four to one in his disfavour. It was moreover reported to Harley's injury that he had said he did not expect to be in the Chair again, but if he were he would make the heads of those fly who advised the dissolution of the last parliament.

WILLIAM PATERSON to ROBERT HARLEY.

1701, December 6. London—We have advice of your brother's election at Leominster, of yours for the town, and of your cousin Thomas Harley's for the county, of Radnor; for which success I congratulate not you so much as your country, which will shortly reap the happy fruits thereof.

I had an opportunity last week at Hampton Court to deliver the substance by word of mouth, and afterwards to leave the contents of the enclosed copy with the King, who was pleased to receive and hear me very graciously; and when I told him it had been impossible for me to make so considerable a progress in the scheme for retrieving the public credit without your countenance, advice, and the help of your papers, his Majesty was pleased to say "Mr. Harley is a very "honest and a very capable man."

[LORD GODOLPHIN to ROBERT HARLEY.]

1701, December 9—I am very unwilling to pursue you with my letters; what I had written to you by Saturday's post of the necessity of your coming to town proceeded only from myself, but since that I have been so pressed by the most considerable part of our chief friends to write to you again upon that subject, that though I told them all I had already done it as fully and decently as I could, yet nothing would satisfy but my promise to repeat it as from them all. The truth is as things stand they are in the right, and I hope we have a very fair expectation of making such a step in the very first day of the sessions as may be a sufficient indication of all that is like to follow. But in order to that one as well as many other things it is absolutely necessary you should be in town some days at least before Christmas.

Mr. Howe has lost his election; in the West I find two or three doubly chosen. I wish it could be so contrived as to bring him in there, but in this too we shall want your help. I suppose Mr. Guy will acquaint you himself with his going to morrow to Althorp.

A. [LADY] PYE to ABIGAIL HARLEY, at Brampton.

1701, December 10. Bath—I congratulate my cousins that are passed their elections without trouble. The loss of my master's was no more than I expected; I wonder his interest held up, being the nearest poll was ever seen in Derby. Am pleased to hear he spent not a penny, the others prodigiously. He is much pressed by the town to petition, thinking themselves wronged by imposing on them fifty beggars, who were made burgesses for that purpose, otherwise Lord James [Cavendish] and he had carried it by a great majority.

My cousin Hadley had often said that Sir George Stroude was most likely to die upon the road. He was a true hoarder of pelf. I know what the public said of his charities; Marshall his old servant told my brother Rich here, twenty shillings apiece to a few parishes. His daughter hath wealth enough if that will give satisfaction.

STANLEY WEST to ROBERT HARLEY.

1701, December 13. London—Acknowledging the receipt of his letter denying the report referred to in his previous letter, which report had been circulated on the authority of "great bishops and deans," notably the Bishops of Ely and Salisbury, and the Deans of Lincoln and Exeter, but he is apt to think those reverend persons are too boldly dealt with and equally abused with Mr. Dobbins, from whom they are said to have heard the report.

[SIMON HARCOURT] to ROBERT HARLEY.

1701, December 26—This morning I met with a report industriously circulated about town which, perhaps, may have ill consequences if care be not taken. 'Tis that we are to be prorogued for a week. Peshall and some others of that stamp proffer wagers upon it. Radcliffe I have had an hour's discourse with since I saw you. He is very earnest to speak with you, and has made me promise to send him word whether it be possible for you to drink a glass of claret at his house either this evening, tomorrow, or Sunday night. If you intend him so great a favour no person whatsoever is to be there but by appointment.

Masters of Cirencester I fortunately met this morning. He is secure.

Dr. CHARLES DAVENANT to [ROBERT HARLEY].

1701, December 26—What you gave me in charge went last night to the press, and will be public to-morrow. I beg that you will send to Mr. Winnington for his papers, for I am at a full stand without them. I would likewise borrow your printed account of the Irish forfeitures for mine is lost. If you have a brief account of the English grants it would be of use to me.

A happier Christmas come to you than can possibly be expected by me.

WILLIAM PENN to ROBERT HARLEY.

[c. 1701]—I have often blamed myself I had not left a memorial of those things that nearly affect this American empire, since we see so little of an American understanding among those whose business it is to superintend it. All places as well as people and languages have their peculiarities, and a just consideration thereof contributes much to proper methods for their respective benefit. But by what reaches these quieter parts of the world you are so full of more domestic subjects, that I know not whether this will not come too soon, and call for an apology. However, this I am well assured of, the crown of England is deeply interested in our prosperity; though I must easily grant, there may be affairs nearer home of a more immediate import, and upon which may depend the very being of these Colonies in consequence.

It were to be wished, in the first place, that there were added to those ingenious persons that superintend the Colonies some of their former governors that served well. For besides that they deserve notice, they must needs supply the rest with that knowledge their experience has given them; that they who have never been in those parts of the world, cannot, though otherwise oracles, comparably understand. Next, that both governors and inferior officers were men of estates, good morals and character at home, or they are a punishment in lieu of a benefit, and to encourage persons under those circumstances to go so far, let them have double pay, and make all gratuities and perquisites punishable; and other oppressive gains a forfeiture of their places.

The people are extremely ill used on one hand, and the King on the other. For one way the officers are officiously and unnecessarily busy for the King, taking his name in vain to serve every turn of advantage or revenge, to his dishonour and disprofit too, for instance, trade is the benefit England chiefly has by these Colonies; now where it is very young and small, the people ignorant in the exactness of the laws fall sometimes under their power, the rich find ways of coming off easily, the poor they practise their duty upon to the life, that by overacting their parts, unreasonably as well as unjustly, they may recommend their zeal as meritorious to the Commissioners of the Customs, or Lords of Trade and Plantations, whereby trade is crushed in the bud, and we only turn planters, or farmers, endeavouring a self subsistence and there's an end of a Colony to the Crown; for where trade ceases the revenue cannot increase, nor England get by the foreign labour of her inhabitants: settled places and traffic will not easily be checked: they will bear strictness that know the laws, and have often been informed, but in new Colonies all ways possible should be used to excite and encourage trade, for that is serving England and the King, since a pining one will neither enrich him nor them.

The trade of tobacco, furs, and skins for Europe, some fish and whale oil, and provisions for the West India Islands, are the produce of the northern countries or colonies. Tobacco coming from only two of them,

Virginia and Maryland, except a little made in our Bay of Delaware. Now if the Crown would encourage every climate, in those things it is proper for, we could produce silk, oranges and lemons, fruit, and wine, as well as others of us, hemp, flax, tar, masts and abundance of crooks, knees, and stately plank for shipping. The mines of England have destroyed much of the timber of England and here is enough of both. If great undertakers there would fall upon it here we might supply England and give her woods time to recover, and convert these countries to arable and pasture, into the bargain.

But there is an other unhappiness that attends us, that must undo us if not cured, and that is the power of the Admiralty in the extent practised in this province. Our settlements are upon the freshes of navigable rivers and creeks, where the river may be from two or three miles over, to a stone's cast over, and 100 miles from the ocean, and the Court of Admiralty by virtue of the seventh and eighth of the King, page 502, pretends not only to try causes that relate to the King's revenue as to unlawful trade or piracy, but whatever is done in the river or creeks other ways, as debts for victuals, beer, sails, or any thing relating to the building of any small craft; so that they have swallowed up a great part of the Government here, because our commerce, by reason of the nature of our settlements, is so much upon the river and small creeks of it; and determining these causes without a jury, gives our people the greatest discontent, looking upon themselves as less free here than at home, instead of greater privileges, which were promised. This law is weakly penned, and could not be otherwise, when only Comr. Chaddock and Ed. Randol were the framers of it, for pp. 497, 502, 505, being compared, show its obscurity, if not inconsistency, and if it means any thing, it must be this, either that in the Court of Admiralty where there is no jury, there the jury shall be natives of England, Ireland or the plantations, or that all causes to be tried in the plantations by the Court of Admiralty shall be by a jury so qualified; and truly, if that court must be so powerful here, it had need do so, or the subjects of England will, at all hazards, disobey that authority.

They expect common law here, and that the laws which limit the Admiralty powers there, should here, and not that the Admiral should be above the King, the civil above the common law, or the Doctors Commons preferred to Westminster Hall. Counsellor Mompessin, thy neighbour, at Lincolns Inn, has made himself master of this business; and I hope the Parliament will not let us fall under so despotic a power as that of the Admiralty, since the Colonies of America were begun upon the public faith by private purses; and I am sure 30,000*l*. will not pay me, though people have got—by mistake—an other notion of me, nor 500,000*l*. the people.

We have passed two laws, one against unlawful trade, wherein Ed. Randal was the greatest transgressor, who ordered the collectors to ship tobacco by content at 350 lb. and 400 lb. per hogshead, while they weighed six, seven, eight and nine hundred lbs., defrauding the King of one half of his dues of 1*d*. per lb., for several years. We have also passed an other against pirates and piracy, both as well guarded and as comprehensive as we have been able. I have angered our tobacconists, for which cause they were very barren towards me in the General Assembly, but time will wear that off, I hope.

I have had all the care, vexation, and charge of a King's Governor to do the King's business, without a farthing consideration, and I hope none has acquitted with more exactness, whatever malice or envy may insinuate against us, which leads me to a late suffering that makes us very uneasy, and might be remedied there, viz. the heat of a few churchmen, headed by a Flanders camp parson, under the protection of the Bishop of London, who having got a few together, make it their business to inveigh against us, and our government. They came hither poor, and some of them are so still, yet here get their bread, and some of them estates, and cannot be satisfied to do so, and enjoy more than their proportion to the whole of the government too; but must in the pulpit inveigh against our principles, and those that regard the State, as oaths, &c. as if they would stir up their people against those whose tenderness admits them into shares in the administration, to turn them out. This is very impertinent and provoking. They will now have no office in the government unless they swear, and have power to swear others, because they know our government is under attests only, as may be easily thought, and then complain they cannot be admitted into the government because they are churchmen ; a most abusive treatment of us. Methinks some of thy church acquaintance might moderate these follies a little. The spring of this in good measure has been from Colonel Nicolson of Virginia, a line from any body to him, and from the Bishop to Doctor Brady his suffragan in Maryland, might quench this. We cannot yet be so selfdenying as to let those that had no part of the heat of the day, not one third of the number, and not one fourth of the estate, and not one tenth of the trouble and labour should give laws to us, and make us dissenters, and worse than that in our own country. I must beg thy favour in mitigating these indiscretions, and in government in supportable treatment. This country increases in improvements above some of its neighbours, but not in people; for though we have the name of people running over hither, there came not even this year above 1500 souls, and into Maryland and Virginia, each 5000, as is generally computed, though I think our people of the better sort, theirs servants and ours for the most part free passengers.

I am careful to preserve a good understanding with the natives; many hundreds of whom I expect in three days, above one is come. I hope to settle a lasting friendship with them. The northern and western were never here before. They are in nature a brave people, but much the worse for the vices they have learnt of Europeans, that should have taught them better things. I wish we may be able to retrieve them. I have sent thee one of their otter's skins, which one of them presented me with some time since, and have ordered it to be made up into a muff, if better liked in that form.

House [of Commons].

1701-2, [January 2]—Suggested resolution for an address to the King. *In Godolphin's handwriting. Differing considerably from the resolution actually passed.*

Charles Cornewall to Robert Harley, Speaker of the House of Commons.

1701[-2], January 6. Berrington — Congratulating him on his appointment as Speaker of the House of Commons.

James St. John to Robert Harley.

1701[-2], January 10—Enclosing a report (dated Jan. 9) of a conversation which he had heard the previous day at the "Lamb" in

Abchurch Lane, reflecting on the character of Robert Harley, and his father, Sir Edward Harley. A person (not in drink) had said Robin Harley was the king's enemy and a rascal who had imposed on the nation in many ways; and his father an old knave and rogué who had 10,000*l.* for bringing in King Charles.

LORD CUTTS to [ROBERT] HARLEY, Speaker.

1701[-2], January [13-]24. New style. The Hague—Though I shall certainly embark on Saturday for England, God willing : yet, upon reading a vote in the House, viz. : that Members chosen for two places must make their choice in three weeks, I humbly beg of you, if 'tis necessary, to signify my choice to the House, that I choose to serve for the County of Cambridge. I mean, if by contrary winds or any invincible accidents I should be delayed, and be in danger of lapsing my time.

I have won some wagers publicly upon your being chosen Speaker and was yesterday paid one which was a public dinner where all the Foreign Ministers were present, your health went round.

Your proceedings do you honour here, and keep me in countenance.

WILLIAM GLANVILL to ROBERT HARLEY, at Brampton.

1701[-2], January 16—When you were in town never to come and see me in my sickness or so much as to send to know how I did, give me just cause to think you no very kind son. Yet I still live to love you and have been this month persuading all my friends to vote you into the chair at the opening of the new approaching Parliament. I have always given you honest and good counsel, which had you followed you might have sooner been that great man which I now hope to see you before I die. It will look too much like French flattery to tell you I know no man fitter than Mr. Robert Harley to be a Speaker, would he be but so faithful and honest as his ingenious parts render him able. Yet I fear the gilded mace carried before a rich gold laced brocado gown, and being the first commoner of England will make my son too proud and full of himself to look down on his old friend and father Glanvill or to do him any kindness that is in his Speakership's power. However before you take possession of the Chair, if you do not think it beneath you to meet me in Collins' shop, I may perhaps say that which will convince you no man can be more sincerely your friend.

[LORD GODOLPHIN] to [ROBERT HARLEY,] Speaker.

[1702,] January 25—If you can be at leisure tomorrow night, Lord Marlborough and I would be glad to wait upon you at your own house. Lord Rochester has been dismissed this morning.

WILLIAM PATERSON to ROBERT HARLEY, York Buildings.

1701-2, January 31. London—Not having found you at home I write to put you in mind of looking over the papers relating to the Indies if you have not done so already. I have been pestered with law affairs all the last and this week, which is a sort of work I always did and hope always shall hate. Some of it is over this week, and I hope the rest will be the next, when I shall be wholly at leisure both to think, speak, and act in the great works that shall now shortly be set on foot. I am now bound to Islington to retire and refresh myself after so much trouble as I have had for some days in town.

[LORD GODOLPHIN] to [ROBERT HARLEY,] Speaker.

1701-2, February 4—Having not seen Lord Rochester till this morning since the meeting was "disappointed" he desired, he has desired me to acquaint you he shall be ready to meet those gentlemen at your house on Saturday night.

———— to ROBERT HARLEY, Speaker.

1701-2, February 11—Thomas Jones, author of the *Secret History of Whitehall*, and likewise of the *Detection of the four last reigns* (though Cook [Coke] put his name to it), is an intimate crony of William Fuller's, and used to meet him frequently at the "Feathers" Tavern near the Prerogative Office in Doctors Commons, together with George Ridpath, Elkanah Settle, Murray, Witherington, Inglesfield, &c. All which I believe the master and drawers of the said tavern can inform the House of, and of something perhaps of their Consults. They likewise used to meet at the "St. Paul's Head" in Carter Lane. James Orme, the printer, knows Ridpath writ one of Fuller's books, and I believe that George Croom, the printer, can inform the House that Jones and Settle writ the rest.

W. FULLER to ROBERT HARLEY, Speaker, at York Buildings.

1 1701-2, February 23. The Fleet—Denying the charge that he had said that Robert Harley was one of those whom Thomas Jones had charged with having taken French money to betray the interest of the nation.

[LORD GODOLPHIN] to [ROBERT HARLEY,] Speaker.

1701-2, March 8—You were pleased to tell me to day in the House of Commons that what the Queen was to speak from the throne was to be to the same purpose with that she said at Council.

I wish you could have time to make a draught of it yourself, and appoint us to come to your house to morrow night to see it. I think her speaking can't be deferred longer than Tuesday.

She is very unwieldy and lame; must she come in person to the House of Lords, or may she send for the two houses to come to her.

[The SAME to the SAME.]

1701-2, March 9—I agree entirely the best way will be to go on to day as if no occasion of interruption had happened. I perceive the Whigs will be of that mind generally. I suppose the Queen will come to the House, but I doubt whether she has any robes.

We must desire to come to your house to night to show the draught. You may speak to whom you like to have there.

[SIMON HARCOURT] to ROBERT HARLEY, Speaker.

1701[-2], March 14. Stafford—Had I thought it possible for me to be wanted I should long ere this time have been with you; but I have persuaded myself that the greatest part of those we differed with are ready to fall down and worship. The fatal news created an universal astonishment: for about two-hours in the country, but seems now to' be forgot, at least not to stick on any persons so much as the judges who are of opinion, as I am informed, that their commissions determined on the demise of the King. You would very much oblige me with any account of what is transacting in Parliament or at St. James's. What is the received opinion concerning the Judges' commissions, and the Chief Justice of Chester, whom you know I honour ; whether Secretary Hedges be restored, a new Privy Council sworn, or when the Scene is to open ? If you can spare time on Tuesday for a line or two, direct to Shrewsbury, if on Thursday to Hereford.

ROBERT PRICE to ROBERT HARLEY, Speaker.

1701-2, March 14. Stafford—The surprising news of the king's death met us at Worcester, which startled the judges, neither knowing the duration of their commissions nor what to do; the like influence it had over us at the bar, who were unwilling to quit the profitable part and yet as averse to be actors in the pageantry of our Circuit judicature whilst twe had a dead king amongst us. However, the judges and counsel determined to proceed which we have hitherto done, though not with full crop of business. I never saw so few mourners as were at Worcester, nay, them of the godly party who said their friend had lost a friend, which I believe to be true and is too well known.

I wrote to my Lord Keeper this post to know whether it be best for Serjeant Powlett and me to keep the Sessions, our patent being determined, though I believe the Association Act and the Queen's proclamation might sufficiently justify us. As your friendship put me in the post of judicature I was in I would not be willingly dropped ; nor would I supplant the Serjeant, though I believe his age will be objected against him, but hope I shall have no other set over me.

Sir R. TRACY to his kinsman [ROBERT HARLEY].

1701-2, March 15. Dorchester—The great change that has lately happened in the government must produce several alterations in offices and employments under it ; and I hear the opinion is that the Judges' patents are determined : but I am doubtful what is proper for me to do upon this occasion because one may as well do too much as too little. But I am sure I cannot be mistaken in addressing myself to you (my great friend) for the continuance of your favour and friendship to me, and to beg your advice whether it may be fit for me to make any application before my return to London and to whom. I owed my patent from the late King to your great kindness, and I am not conscious of anything to make me doubt of your interest to procure me another from the Queen.

[P.S.]—People were a little shocked at first upon the news of the King's death, but they are now very well satisfied, which the gentlemen have expressed at this place and Salisbury by their unanimous addresses to the Queen.

A. [LADY PYE] to ABIGAIL HARLEY, at York Buildings, London.

1702, March 25. Bath—Affairs being so settled and going on in the same channel makes our loss of so great and good a King little felt at present. I never saw so short a sorrow as was here and am told it is the same in London and the High Church are elevated. hereabouts. Your thoughts of the country frighten me and should you really be at liberty by the ending the session soon and do as you hope 'twould make me change my mind and steer towards Derby instead of London. I think it fit to pay my duty there to Lady Pye otherwise I'm much off the journey. " One affair was all new rigging which this mourning hath put a stop to and we have all fitted out ourselves here, we hope as well and much more . reasonable than we hear ' things are at London. This is the country for cloth and by this means we got in mourning with the first." I am pleased my sisters were to wait on you. She of Richmond may have motive for her cheerfulness, the doctor hath been long esteemed and employed by Lady Hyde and the Rochester family, and their friends are the likeliest to rise. I heartily wish they will be his friend. He is an ingenious man and she's very notable, improves acquaintance with the great ladies of those parts. Pray have you seen our city sister, who I hear shines in jewels.

WILLIAM PENN to [ROBERT HARLEY,] Speaker.

1702, [March] 28—I am leaving town till the hurry of your affairs is over, my health being very ordinary, but I intend to wait upon you to-night if I am not forbid.

SIMON HARCOURT to ROBERT HARLEY.

1702, March 30. Gloucester—Since London is barren of news give me leave to send you what this place affords. This morning our Assizes began : there was a very full appearance of the Grand Jury of the best quality in the country. Amongst others Sir John Guise and Jack Howe were returned and appeared. The Grand Jury being called over and Sir John Guise called as foreman, they desired liberty to choose their own foreman, which the Judge permitted them in open Court to do; and seventeen voted for Mr. Howe, and four for Sir John. Whereupon Mr. Howe was sworn as their foreman.

NEWS-LETTER.

1702, April 7. London—Letters from Rome of 25th say that sentence had been pronounced against the Marquess del Vasto to lose his head, that since that a servant of the said Marquess had pursued in the street and murdered one of Cardinal Furbin's, and that things are like to grow in great disorder between the Ambassadors of the Empire, France and Spain, but the Pope has desired them to dismiss their armed men declaring that he would have the sole dominion in Rome. The guards are doubled at Naples and their forces including foreigners will be 16,000 foot and 600 horse. Sir Lambert Blackwell is arrived at Venice from England as Envoy from Her Britannic Majesty. Four French vessels are arrived at Ragusa under Spanish colours who take all the vessels from Dalmatia that carry provisions and other supplies to the German army in Italy. We are in great expectation to hear of action from Italy, the Duke de Vendome being resolved to enterprise something considerable before the coming up of the Imperial troops. Letters from the Imperial auxiliary army under Prince Nassau Sarbruck near Mulheim of 8th give account of their having attacked and defeated several bodies of French that they met with in that diocese upon which account Mauritz Governor of Ban sent a trumpeter to demand of the Governor of Seidgburgh if those hostilities were committed by his order or no, who said that the Prince of Nassau, General of the Emperor's troops ordered the same, on which the trumpeter went to the camp at Mulheim where he told that the forces that committed those hostilities were not to be looked upon as Prussian or Dutch but the Emperor's auxiliaries. Those from the Hague of 14th say the affair of the Duke of Wolfenbüttel continues as it was, those princes with the Electors of Bavaria and Cologne seem resolved to abide by the French and to stand and fall by that power : that the excessive coldness of the weather with snow hail and frost for six days had obliged the Emperor's General to canton their horses in the villages near Mulheim and to defer the siege of Keyserwart, otherwise the trenches had been opened on the 7th.

Edinburgh 31st, last Wednesday a proclamation was published requiring the taking the oath of allegiance, and signing the same with the assurance to her present Majesty by all ranks of people that were, by an Act of Parliament on the 23rd May 1693, obliged to take the same to the late King William and Queen Mary, and under the same pains and upon the recusation ; and in particular they having all their arms above a walking sword and their horses above £5 price taken from them, and the times limited for doing the same are 1st of August for electors of Members of parliament, and others by 1st July. This morning his grace Duke Hamilton and the Earl of Tullibardine and Lord Ross set forward for Court and are to be followed by the Marquis of Tweeddale and the Earls Marischal, Rothes, and Leven, Sir John Home and others all leading men of the Episcopal party, and it is said a great part of their errand is to solicit the calling a new parliament, at which the Presbyterian party are much alarmed, as dreading the consequence of parting with the Convention Parliament.

This day the Queen and her Royal Consort Prince George of Denmark went for Windsor and will return on Thursday, but I hear the interment of the King that was to be that night is put off for some days longer by reason things cannot be got in readiness.

There is said to be three candidates for the place of Master of the Horse to the Queen, viz., the Dukes of Somerset and Ormond and the Lord Marlborough, who arrived from Holland on Sunday morning, but most think the latter will have it. In the meantime Her Majesty has appointed Sir Stephen Fox and Sir Benjamin Bathurst Commissioners to manage the same, and it is believed Her Majesty will not bestow it till after the Coronation, as well as several other places.

Some talk of an alteration that will be among the Judges, their patents being determinated upon the death of the King, but this we must refer to a little time, and others there are that make a doubt whether the grants made by the late King are not become void by reason the Crown was settled on him only for life, but those are points which only the learned in the law understand.

By the death of the King the States of Holland are under some difficulties about the command of the Army. It is probable my Lord Marlborough, who is Captain General of all the forces of England and has a Commission as ample as General Monk's formerly was, will not submit to be commanded by the Dutch Velt Marshal, nor he again by the English General, upon which it is said that the States have proposed that His Royal Highness Prince George of Denmark may command both armies as generalissimo as His late Majesty did, and that the same hath been communicated to the Seven Provinces, five of which have already sent their consents. It is believed the States do this also to put off the [the remainder illegible].

St. George [Ash, Bishop of] Clogher to George Follet, York Buildings.

1702, April 24—The Archbishop of Tuam and I were to enquire for you on Wednesday to recommend the enclosed petition of his son to the Speaker. I desire you also to think of the mathematical servant for Lord Abercorn's son, who is expected here in less than a week.

The Earl of Montagu to [Robert] Harley, Speaker.

1702, April 29. Montagu House—Asking his assistance in helping on a bill then pending in the House of Commons "called Hind's Bill about the building of Albemarle Ground," if he find it just and reasonable.

Lord Godolphin to [Robert Harley,] Speaker.

[1702,] May 5—The Queen designs to be at the House tomorrow to pass the bills. I was told you had thoughts of coming to see Lord Marlborough this night who is not yet well. I hope to be with him before nine. In case you design him that favour it may be necessary to let him or me know it that orders may be given for your seeing him.

Dr. Drake.

1702, May 9—An account of the examination of Dr. Drake before the House of Lords concerning the preface to a book called *The History of the last Parliament.* See *Journals of the House of Lords,* same date.

CORONATION MEDALS.

1702, May 9—Receipt given to Isaac Newton, Master and Worker of the Mint, for 515 gold coronation medals, weighing 308 ozs., 13 dwts., 12 grains, for the use of the members of the House of Commons, signed by F. Fauquier.

Dr. John Potter [afterwards Archbishop of Canterbury], to Robert Harley.

1702, May 12. Lincoln College, Oxford—I entreat your acceptance of this second edition of *Lycophron,* which, by the help of an ancient manuscript copy lately sent from Holland by Mr. Graevius is far more complete than that published by me about five years ago. I am highly sensible of the great honour you have done me in allowing your name to be prefixed before my Greek Antiquities, of which I have already received forty sheets very finely printed, with all the cuts; and the rest will be finished within three months, if my Dutch bookseller does not misinform me.

[Lord Godolphin] to [Robert Harley,] Speaker.

1702, May 21—I take it I am to be at your house to-night about the speech, if it be not so, be pleased to let me know.

I have mentioned the chaplain of the House of Commons to the Queen several times. Her answer this very morning was that those things she has given were all pursuant to promises made by the King, and that she will be sure to take the first occasion to present him, now she is at liberty. At first when I saw your hand upon the outside of the enclosed letter it gave me a great deal of satisfaction to think you had forgiven that torrent of impertinence which dropped from me last night, but when I came to read it I concluded it was an old letter which must have been mislaid by some neglect of my servant██

[Lord Godolphin to Robert Harley.]

1702, May 28—I do easily believe the Scottish nobility are gone down angry and that some special friends of ours of the English, have contributed to make them so. However I am not without hope that things will end quietly there.

I never took so much pains in my life to satisfy any body as Sir Ch: M[usgrave] in every thing from the first moment I spoke to him, but it's pretty hard to follow humours so changeable and uncertain. He would not be in the Ordnance, and when it was too late then he would be. At first he would not be a Teller because it was a sinecure, and afterwards when he had kissed the Queen's hand for it he would not take it because it was not Mr. Palmes's.

The Queen has taken it from my Lord Villiers, and I believe will not be easily hindered from giving it to some body else if Sir Ch: M[usgrave] does not accept it.

I have said all I could think of to persuade her to leave it to my Lord Jersey, but to no purpose hitherto. However I shall not give over proposing expedients for that, as also to get Mr. Palmes's place at liberty for Sir Ch: M[usgrave] since no other will satisfy. I wish with all my heart that four or five of these gentlemen that are so sharp set upon other people's places had mine amongst them to stay their stomachs.

William Penn to [Robert Harley].

1702, May 29—Pardon this freedom, pray, and give me leave to solicit thy favour for the bearer, Capt. Fitch, in a recommendation to Sir G. Rooke or Col. Churchill for a fifth-rate to the West Indies or elsewhere. They will thank thee for it in a year's time, so brave, sober, and able a little fellow as he is in the service.

Francis Gwyn to [Robert Harley,] Speaker.

[1702, May].—My Lord Rochester will expect you about four of the clock in the afternoon to-morrow; and when you come pray take notice to his Lordship that I spoke to you from him that an address should be made from the House to the Queen that she would please to employ none in the Army but natural born subjects; Lord Marlborough desires it for there are some that had promises from the late King that Lord Marlborough cannot put off any other way, though he hath hitherto delayed their ——. Pray take notice to Lord Rochester I said this to you, for I forgot it when I saw you in the House.

[Sir SIMON HARCOURT to ROBERT HARLEY].

1702, June 3—I hope due care is taken, but am confident it is not, unless by yourself, concerning the law. · Whatever is intended must be speedily done. The circuits ought to be appointed the beginning of next week. If the alterations are deferred till the circuits are appointed and ·the term worn·out, 'twill be an argument certainly made, if it do not prevail, against any alteration whatsoever.

THE ALLIED FORCES.

1702, June [1-]11. A relation of the retreat of the Allied Army under the command of the Earl of Athlone from their Camp at Klarembeck to Nimeguen.

On Saturday the 10th the Earl of Athlone received advice, that the Duke of Burgundy having · Marshal Boufflers with him, was dis-camped with the great army, several great detachments having joined him, particularly that of the King's Household and the Regiments from Brabant, and that he took his march through the Plains of Goch, and so by Genappe, seeming to incline towards the Plains of Mocker (commonly called the Mockerheide) just by Nimeguen having begun their march yesterday morning about eight o'clock without sound of trumpet or beat of drum.

By the several accounts we had of this sudden march, their design seemed to be, to get between us and Nimeguen, by which means they would have cut off our provisions, ammunition, and forage, and being very much superior to us in numbers, as well Horse as Foot, this town with several others would have been at their mercy.

Upon this my Lord Athlone called immediately a Council of all the General Officers where it was resolved unanimously to begin our march about eight o'clock the same evening according to the following disposition :

All the baggage to march to Nimeguen leaving Cranemberg on their left, the first line to march in column between the woods at the head of our Camp, and Cranemberg by the side of the woods in which (by this time) the French had posted a great body of Foot and Dragoons, and the second line between the first line and Cranemberg leaving Cranemberg on their Right.

About break of day, my Lord Athlone made a halt, and receiving further advice of the strength of the enemy, it was resolved that the Cavalry should put themselves in battle in the Mockerheide to cover the march of the Infantry, and the Infantry at the same time to keep along the hills, making halts, and putting themselves in battle from time to time, as the Generals that lead the Infantry should think fit, keeping always in sight of the Cavalry that they might be ready to sustain them, in case of a violent shock.

About eleven in the forenoon the Infantry had gained defiles and lined the hedges, and the French Horse advancing in great numbers, with the troops of the Household at their head, began to press very hard upon my Lord Athlone, who continued to make his retreat in very good order, causing his squadrons to pass through all the overtures where the Infantry was posted in the hedges, and other proper places, and keeping at the same time as good a front as the ground would admit of whilst a considerable body of our Horse were ordered to gain the hills upon the right, where there had liked to have happened a disorder, by the troops of the French Household charging some of our squadrons just as they were wheeling to gain the hills, by which means they pushed them upon the Foot, and occasioned a little confusion to two or three Battalions, but by the good conduct and vigour of the General officers that happened to be there it had no ill consequences and the enemy was soon repulsed.

On the other side there happened a violent shock between some of the squadrons of the French Household and some of ours among which were some Danish Squadrons and my Lord Albemarle's Carabiniers, who distinguished themselves on this occasion and the French Squadrons were vigorously repulsed with a considerable loss, and not without some on our side, both parties charging sword in hand, without firing.

When our troops were got under the cannon of the town, which began now to play upon the enemy, the Queen's forces under my command who had the honour to close the whole retreat retired likewise in good order, and the troops of the French Household coming very near me towards the last and seeming to dispose themselves for an attack, the Prince of Wurtemberg was pleased to join me in person, at the head of a body of Horse and to give me his assistance until the very last. I should be unjust, if I should not take notice upon this occasion that his Highness behaved himself with that intrepidity which seems natural to his family.

Brigadier Ingoldsby supported with a great deal of gallantry the character of a brave man and good officer, executing my orders with a great deal of promptitude, and acting in every post committed to his care, with a great deal of conduct and indeed all Her Majesty's officers and soldiers and particularly the battalion of Her own Regiment of Guards expressed a great deal of gallantry and good inclination on this occasion.

My Lord Athlone who commanded the whole in chief omitted nothing that was necessary to make this retreat with a great deal of good order and gallantry, giving or sending his orders everywhere, where he thought it necessary.

All the Foreign Generals in their respective posts were very active, and carried on the retreat with a courage and unanimity that made it succeed for even our enemies own it as bold a march and as good a retreat as could be made.

Our whole Army lay under arms Saturday night as likewise did the enemy and this morning a great body of Horse and Foot advanced towards us as if they designed to undertake something, but we had intelligence before noon that it was only to cover their march, and that their whole army filed off towards Cleves by the way of Cranemberg, upon which my Lord Athlone immediately ordered the Cavalry to pass the river here, and designs to march with them himself to morrow towards Skinkenskons in order to observe the enemy, leaving the Infantry here till further orders.

When the siege of Keyserswart is over and that army can join us, and when our English Horse and Dragoons and the rest of our English Foot comes up, and when we have all the rest of the Allies' forces that have not yet joined us, I hope we shall be able to return our enemies their compliment and especially when the enterprise of Landau begins to operate.

I do not pretend in this relation to give an account of any passages but what I saw myself or what I had from the mouths of several of our Generals of what passed in their respective posts and consequently may have omitted several particulars.

I forgot to mention that the Prince of Wurtemberg was detached in the night with a great body of Horse upon the left of our march and that I detached Colonel Frederick Hamilton with three battalions of Her Majesty's Foot to secure his retreat in case of necessity as well as to take care of the highway of Norgina by which the enemy might otherwise have easily fallen in upon us in our march; and they both rejoined us afterwards at the entrance into the Mockerheide.

I have a Captain of Sir Bevil Granville's regiment mortally wounded and have lost some men upon advanced posts but we have had so much work upon our hands that it has been impossible as yet to know the certain number, only that I am assured that it is not considerable.

[Lord Godolphin] to [Robert Harley,] Speaker.

1702, June 13—I send you with this, sealed up, Lord Peterborough's notions, which I desire you to keep till I see you.

An express is come from Scotland with an account that the Duke of Hamilton and the opposing party there, finding themselves the weaker, had protested against the continuance of the parliament and were withdrawn from it.

[Simon Harcourt to Robert Harley.]

[1702, June ?]—I shall live in pain till I have some account from you of the intended law advancements. I know you will set me at ease as soon as you can. I can't doubt of Serjeant B. and am in hopes of for R. P[rice]; at least that B. will not succeed. Your kind concern for me in the case of Serjeant Birch, had I no other reason, is of itself sufficient to assure me you will interest yourself for me, especially if it may at the same time be a service to the public. There is a very eminent man to whose name or character I believe you are no stranger, Capt. Baker. He was employed by the late Commissioners of the Treasury to be Solicitor of the Treasury; but I could not believe possible that he should have been now continued. I can't think it for the public service that a scandalous, ignorant, broken informer should be continued in such a post. I'm sure, if it be not a public concern that keeps him in, 'tis my interest that he should be removed. There is a very honest man who is and for some time has been employed as a solicitor in the Queen's business, one Mr. Borrett; he is brother to the Borrett who married Lord Chief Justice Trevor's sister. The solicitorship of the Treasury is lately carved (?) out of that Office. 'Twill save a salary, be a reward to honesty, if that be a proper argument to use, and an advantage to the public, as well as to your humble servant, if Borrett might be put into the post Capt. Baker now holds. It properly belongs to him and is part of his business; however if it be possible let Baker be turned out. Should any necessity compel him to attend me in my office I would not speak with him, without witnesses.

[Sir Christopher Musgrave to Robert Harley.]

[1702, June ?] Saturday—Our friends are all under great dissatisfaction to hear from the Whigs that the Parliament will speedily be dissolved, and that it is not intimated to them, and cry out that elections shall be at the assizes and harvest. The assizes begin at York 18 July, at Carlisle 11 August, at Appleby 15 August. So that in our counties the elections must necessarily be when the Judges are there, and the same will happen in other countries. Therefore if possible prevent these apparent prejudices and a general clamour. I have heard nothing from his lordship.

[LORD GODOLPHIN] to [ROBERT] HARLEY, York Buildings.

1702, July 7—The Queen appoints half an hour after five tomorrow at her back stairs. You will please to send in your name.

I have had a letter from Lord Marlborough by this day's post, but no news. The army was to march next day.

T. B[ATEMAN] to ROBERT HARLEY, at Brampton.

1702, July 23. London—Westminster poll was shut up this morning as follows: Mr. Cross, 3195. Sir Walter Clarges, 2932. Sir H. Colt, 2605. Lord James Cavendish, 2298. Sir H. Colt has demanded a scrutiny. The City election likely to go for Mr. Heathcote, Sir R. Clayton, Sir John Fleet, and Sir Wm. Pritchard.

WILLIAM PATERSON to [ROBERT HARLEY].

1702, August 6. London—I had not access to my Lord Treasurer till yesterday. He received me very favourably and frankly, telling me he was surprised to see me look better than I did ten years ago. After this we had some general discourses of the state of the revenue, deficient funds, the Indies, and such like. He was also pleased to give me leave to write a note at any time when I should want access, and promised I should not want access to such public papers as I might want in the way of my study, or anything else he could help me to; and expressed his sense of my capacity for these kind of things far beyond my merit. However I cannot say but it helps to stir up the desire I have to come as near as his or my other friends' expectations as I can.

Some are apprehensive that you will not be speaker next parliament, and that Col. Granville or Sir John Trevor will be chosen.

I never would fainer have seen you than now and would come down the week after next but am so unsettled that it is impossible unless somewhat be done to make me more easy than at present I am; for it is now absolutely necessary to determine to make the thoughts of the public either all or no part of my future business. I have thoughts of removing to a house in St. James's Street, Westminster, near Arlington House, which seems to be very well situated for the benefit of air, as likewise for my more easy access to persons and places.

[LORD GODOLPHIN to ROBERT HARLEY.]

[1702, August] 14, Friday—Whatever is to be done upon the loan to the Emperor, if it be not done quickly it will lose its effect; and if it be 'twill do more good now than treble that sum three months hence; I beg leave therefore to suggest some thoughts which you may either speak of to Hughetan, or write to Holland, or discourse to Monsieur Vryberghen, according as you shall judge they may be of any use.

I will suppose when the Ministers of Vienna desire 400,000 they would be pleased with 300,000 crowns, from England and Holland at three several payments. The first I would propose Hughetan should give us credit for and pay at Frankfort by the 15th of October, old style; the second to be paid by Holland about the end of November at what place shall be judged proper, and the third by England upon the 1st of January, by which time we may have funds of our own applicable to it, so that Hughetan's credit need not be made use of but for the first payment of 100,000 crowns, nor for above three months' time.... :

¶ I doubt there will be also a necessity of finding credit very soon at Genoa and Leghorn, for the support of the expedition in Catalonia, if these troops either continue there, or go to the Duke of Savoy, but that I can do by Sir Theodore Jansen, or Sir Lambert Bl[ackwell].

The Scots Parliament has given the Cess without much contraction. It will be necessary by Sunday at furthest to put an end to their sitting.

ADMIRAL GEORGE CHURCHILL to [ROBERT HARLEY].

1702, August 8—Recommending the son of a friend of his, Mr. Dobyn of St. Albans, and one of his brother Marlborough's chaplains, to the Speaker.

[WILLIAM PATERSON to ROBERT HARLEY.]

1702, August 15. London—Reporting another interview with Lord Treasurer Godolphin He was very free and open, the subjects discussed being the state of the revenue, the affairs of the Indies, with some touches upon the nature and effects of trade in general. Finds that Godolphin has done very great things since he came to the head of the revenue, and that his head and his heart are entirely in it, and rightly set for this or indeed for any other principles that can concern the good of his country. In order to apply himself more effectually to these things he had taken a house in James Street, Westminster, where he had a key into the Park, and would be near his business and have good air; he was promised ready access to Godolphin as occasion required, and all manner of encouragement in his studies of financial affairs. Desires an interview with Harley.

[LORD GODOLPHIN to ROBERT HARLEY.]

1702, August 18—It is very true as you observe that three new parliaments in the three kingdoms near the same time are not very usual, but in six months after a new reign if any parliaments are necessary, there must be new ones. I hope ours is like to be a good one, but no time is yet appointed for either of the other two. The Duke of Queensberry's not being yet come to London delays all resolutions concerning Scotland. Lord Rochester's commission is renewed. Prince Eugene seems to be much pressed in Italy. All the world cries shame for his having been so much neglected, but I don't find that saddle is like to be placed anywhere but upon the right horse. The Queen having resolved to go next week to the Bath, I have thoughts of drinking the waters there for three weeks or a month. Mr. Paterson is to come to me to-morrow.

[LORD GODOLPHIN to ROBERT HARLEY.]

1702, August 20. St. James's—I thank you for the enclosed from Amsterdam. A little success this summer would go a great way to root out all those impertinences which one hears of from that side.

Our last letters from the Army were of the 13th. They had been a whole day within cannon shot of the French Army, some men and horses killed on either side, but night coming on before the defiles could be forced, it's not improbable but they may separate again without a battle, and possibly it's not the worse if they did, supposing the report proves true which we have that Prince Eugene has beaten the king of Spain's army.

Mr. Paterson has been with me full of many notions for the public, both in foreign and domestic affairs. I am apt to think the most use that can be made of him will be by his correspondence and the intelligence he may give. I have encouraged him to go down into the country to you, and if he goes before my journey to the Bath I will be sure to write more at large to you by him.

[HENRY GUY] to ROBERT HARLEY, at Brampton.

1702, August 22—I write to you in some trouble, because I wrote to you so long since as the 4th instant, and have not heard from you, which makes me fear that you are not well. I had much rather your not writing were want of kindness, than want of health, for the first will do you no hurt, the latter will. Therefore I earnestly entreat you, that you will at least let one of your servants send me a line or two how you are.

This is the chief errand of this letter, and therefore I shall not crowd it with much else.

You hear already of the victory obtained by Prince Eugene, which is as the prints have it, but the King of Spain still lies near him entrenched in an inaccessible place, and hath sent for the Prince of Vaudemont with the 10,000 men that remained with him; so that it is thought there may be a second battle if the French will.

The Queen goes to the Bath on Tuesday or Wednesday next, and the Lord Treasurer goes with her to drink the waters.

I beg of you the satisfaction of hearing from you one way or other.

The displacing Sir John Munden doth much please the City.

Mr. Dummer came to me about his proposal for sending vessels still to the West Indies, which hath hung so long. I brought him to the Lord Treasurer, who upon a full discourse of the matter, went so heartily into it, that he despatched and settled the thing that very day at the Council, and I think Mr. Dummer's first boat sails on Monday next. I find that without this method the proposal had never took effect, or at least not in a long while.

THOMAS FOLEY to his brother[-in-law] ROBERT HARLEY, at Brampton.

1702, September 1. Witley—Recommending Dr. Sacheverell for the post of Chaplain to the Speaker. Is a stranger to him farther than the enclosed letter, but if he answers the character he must needs be a very worthy person.

Enclosing

Sir J. Pakington to Tomas Foley, at Witley.

N.D.—The gentleman's name who presents this to you is Mr. Sacheverell, and his character is as great in the University of Oxford as are his relations in the House of Commons, whom I am confident you have often heard mentioned there with great respect. I understand Mr. Harley is to be our Speaker. I do not know whether his chaplain that served last Parliament is yet provided for; if he be, I desire the favour of your letter to Mr. Harley in Mr. Sacheverell's behalf, who in every respect will acquit himself like an honest, ingenious man, and I am sure the House will be so well satisfied with him as to do all they can for his promotion.

[HENRY GUY to ROBERT HARLEY:],

[1702], September 5—I received yours of the 30th past, which was no ordinary satisfaction to me, being under the last degree of trouble and concern which way I could have incurred the unkindness of so long a silence. I confess I have reason to fear that my rules and methods of friendship are troublesome, because I cannot bring myself to neglect the least circumstance belonging to it; and they are the more so, because I hope for the same from others; but the want of this carries me no farther than a secret grief, and now and then a little complaint; for I know very well the value of Mr. Harley's friendship, and no omission shall make me doubt of it, and you will have a hard task to drive me from you. I do not wonder at the underhand dealing of 95 : he thinks the day lost in which he doth not play the knave more or less. To give you a minute's diversion, I have enclosed sent you the verses which were spoken by my kinsman Mr. Pulteney to the Queen at Christchurch, when she was retired into her bedchamber to undress. We have nothing now here but what you see in the prints; we expect some from the fleet every day, and do think we cannot be long without it. There is a great court at Bath. I hear Sir Edward Seymour, Jack Granville, Jack Howe, and Sir John Leveson are there.

[LORD GODOLPHIN to ROBERT HARLEY.]

1702, September 11. Bath—I would not omit an hour to tell you I have just now received yours of the 7th which put me out of my pain for being so long without any notice you had received my letter by Mr. Paterson. I wish you would order Franco to stay on the other side, at least till the parliament has met a fortnight, to value and improve the resolutions they shall take, and to prevent any malicious impressions of them from others, for I reckon that will be a critical time, and the whole will depend abroad upon the construction of their first resolutions.

You will have heard from London that the parliament is put off to the 20th for the reason you mention, of which all the gentlemen of these parts, my Lord Poulett at their head, were so full that it would have been an unaccountable perverseness not to have indulged them twelve or fourteen days' time.

The last Thursday's Gazette will have given you the particulars of what we hear from the fleet. I have a short letter from Methuen by the same packet in which he seems full of assurance that expedition will have success.

Sir J[ohn] L[eveson] G[ower] is here, but I am not free enough with him to talk of the meeting mentioned in your letter. Here also is Colonel Gr[anville] and Mr. Howe; Sir Edw. Seymour gone to Exeter but to return next week. They had all taken an impression that the expedition of our fleet was ridiculous and impossible to succeed. How they came by it I can't tell certainly, but I doubt I can give a shrewd guess.

The letters from our English merchants at Lisbon as well as those from Methuen say that the King has publicly signified himself free from all engagements with France and resolved to live in entire friendship with England, so I reckon if we succeed at Cadiz it will be our own fault if we do not come into the alliance with the rest of our confederates. The rains we see here every day leave me no hopes at Venloo or Landau, but they abate, at the same time a great deal of my apprehensions for any insult (sic) upon Prince Eugene's still much inferior number.

[Lord Godolphin to Robert Harley.]

1702, September 16.· Bath—I had a mind to trouble you with . the enclosed rough draught (*missing*). of : what I have prepared for her Majesty's speech to the approaching Parliament being uncertain how long before the time of their meeting I may have the good fortune to see you, and being also extremely desirous of your thoughts and amendments upon it before it be exposed to any body else. I have drawn a line under such expressions where I am doubtful either of the expressions themselves, or that they are not proper in the paragraph where at present they are inserted. I am sensible that events may happen between this and the time of speaking which may necessarily require alteration in the speech, but I consider that the better any thing of this nature is digested before it comes to be seen by many persons the better one shall be able to defend it from any wild or inconvenient proposals of alteration. I hope therefore you will be so kind as to make your remarks and observations upon it with all freedom.

Just now an express arrives from the Duke of Ormond with an account that they meet with more difficulty in their enterprize at Cadiz than the last news had prepared us for. The ship that brought the letters heard great firing of bombs and mortars after she left the fleet, which she supposed to be an attack of some Castle at the entrance of the port. God send we get well off with this business. The Dutch agree to join with us next year in sending ships and land men to the West Indies. The arrival of this express calls me to Court, so I must beg your excuse for this hasty scrawl. Lord Marlborough writes hopefully of Venloo, &c.

[Henry Guy to Robert Harley.]

[1702], September 17. I received yours of the 11th instant, which is the second I have have had from you, and this the third I have written to you. I find mine of the 4th of August is miscarried, but there was nothing material in it. My friendship God knows is very useless; but such as it is, you shall have it at your service with an entire heart, and with such an integrity as nothing shall shake. 75 (Sunderland) is so dangerously ill that I much doubt his recovery. I tell you this with anxiety enough, for to part with so old and so true a friend must go near to the heart of an honest man. If he comes to any condition to receive it, I shall make the compliments of 104 (Harley) to him. There was never any doubt but the commission of 79 (Rochester) would be renewed, if he pleased : I do not hear that he thinks of leaving this place. You may safely write again to 163, for I do not think he is returning, especially if there be any hopes of bringing that Court farther than a neutrality. I pray God our friends act soberly and reasonably; I hope they will; I am sure all is lost without it; some hot men do talk very largely. 135 will take what care may be; but you know how little it is in their power very often to stop a heat and fury of that kind. I believe Mr. Dummer so very able a man that the giving assistance to any of his proposals will be a credit to him that gives it. The fort of Venloo is taken, and that by a very brave action of my Lord Cutts : the town must be taken, and we believe it is so by this time. Yesterday I saw Mr. St. John, who complained that he wrote to you three weeks since, but could get no answer. To mollify him I told him I was much longer before I had one. Pray write to him, for he seems to take it unkindly. He wished you in town, and I entreat you in your next to let me know when you will come. There is no other news but what is in the prints, which I suppose are still sent to you. Just now I have received an account that 75 (Sunderland) is so far better that they have hopes of his recovery; which doth not a little joy me.

[LORD GODOLPHIN to ROBERT HARLEY.]

1702, September 27. Bath—I will observe the hints you are so kind as to give me relating to the Queen's speech, and to everything else. The Queen will be at London about the 12th or 13th of October.

Lord Marlborough's affairs go on very prosperously. I wish I could show you some of his letters, but that must stay till I have the happiness of seeing you.

I have the Queen's leave to be a week at Newmarket, and her commands to meet her Majesty at London.

Dr. Davenant desires to be secretary to the Commissioners for the Union, and I believe would not unqualify himself to be of the House of Commons.

[HENRY GUY to ROBERT HARLEY.]

[1702] September 29. London—This comes to acquaint you that my poor Lord Sunderland died yester morning. The loss of so true a friend sits heavy upon me. My heart is so full that I cannot say more to you at present, nor is there anything of moment to tell you. Only I beg of you to let me hear from you, and when you will be here. For my friends go away so fast that I would fain still hear from you, who are one of my chiefest.

[HENRY GUY to ROBERT HARLEY.]

1702, October 6. You are entirely right in your thoughts that this of 75 (Sunderland) will take away a strange jealousy in many of 137.

The Queen comes from Bath on Thursday next; lies that night at the Duke of Somerset's at Marlborough, the next night at Windsor, and will be at Kensington on the Monday following.

This business of Cadiz, which no doubt you hear of, hath proved unlucky.

I earnestly entreat you to let me know by the next post what day you will be here, for I have many things to impart to you, some of which I would the same night that you arrive.

[LORD GODOLPHIN] to [ROBERT HARLEY], Speaker, at York Buildings.

1702, October 19. I left a book at your house this morning put into my hands by the Archbishop of Canterbury to convince me how little inclination the Convocation were like to have towards an accommodation, when at the same time he said he came with a spirit of healing so different from what appeared in them that he had actually taken out of the press some books that had been written, and hindered others designed to have been written upon the subject of contention, on purpose to avoid all occasion of increasing the flame and the divisions that had been so violently and unfortunately kindled and fomented in the church, and then he conjured me that I would use my interest and endeavours to pacify and allay these differences and to preserve the peace of the church.

I told him that I could not at all pretend to be a judge of the matters in difference, but that I thought all matters of difference at this time must needs have very ill consequences both in church and state and as a well-wisher to both he might be assured I would not neglect any thing in my power to compose and heal them.

So he desired me to take that book which he said was written by Mr. Atterbury, and judge if it were possible to be tame and quiet under such provocations, but having neither time to read it, nor knowledge enough of those matters to judge of it, I thought the best thing I could do with it was to leave it at your house and desire your directions for any steps you would have me make in this matter, not being willing indeed to meddle with it one way or other, but just as I may have the favour of being instructed and guided in it by you.

[LORD GODOLPHIN to ROBERT HARLEY.]

[1702, October 23] Friday—I have just now four posts from my Lord M[arlborough]. They have taken the citadel of Liége by storm, and with a very vigorous behaviour of the Queen's subjects he hoped to be soon master of the Charterhouse, and says the French having decamped and quitted St. Tron they might have been able to carry their conquests further if the season did not now oblige him to put the 40,000 men in the Queen's pay into winter quarters, which he is doing as fast as he can, and hopes to be here by the end of the month.

He has the honour to be named in the address of the House of Lords, which is to be presented this evening to Her Majesty.

I am afraid Prince Lewis of Baden has been worsted upon the Rhine.

[LORD GODOLPHIN] to [ROBERT HARLEY,] Speaker.

1702, November 3. I received your letter so late last night, that I could not do anything in pursuance of it, nor so much as thank you for it, till this morning, and being now at my Lord Nottingham's office, upon a particular business, which will detain me till after the House of Commons sits, so that I cannot speak to the persons necessary to move anything this morning there, upon the subject of your letter, but will take all the care I can that they shall be furnished with all the necessary papers for the information of the House; this being in my opinion a better method than either to stay till my Lord Marlborough comes, which depends upon the winds, or than to go upon ways and means, till the occasion be first settled for which the money is to be raised.

. I shall therefore desire my Lord Ranelagh, Lord Coningsby, Mr. Secretary Hedges and Mr. Blathwayt to-morrow morning at the Treasury, to adjust what shall be opened to the House before they go into the Committee, and by whom, unless you offer me some more proper method between this time and tomorrow morning.

A thousand thanks for the favour of your medal.

Yesterday by the Queen's command, I wrote to the Archbishop of Canterbury, that she would see the form of prayer for the Thanksgiving Day before it was sent to the press. I had the enclosed answer from him, in which you will see he complains of some heats in the Lower House; he would have explained them to me last night more particularly, but I would not enter upon it with him. I believe he was uneasy too about what had passed with you relating to the Bishop of Worcester, etc.

I designed to have sent you the Archbishop's letter but have mislaid it.

[LORD GODOLPHIN to ROBERT HARLEY.]

1702, November 4. I am glad to see that in Holland they have a mind to prosecute the war. I wish I could see a little more of that inclination in England, for when they see how untowardly we proceed about our land forces I shall not be very much surprised if it puts them upon other measures. I made my complaints this evening at the Treasury to Mr. Solicitor who happened to be there, he seemed to think another meeting at your house tomorrow night might rectify what is past, and adjust matters better for another day. I can submit in most things to better judgments but am at present so out of patience with Sir Edward S[eymour?] that I am sure I can meet him nowhere but to scold.

I met the two deans this morning at my Lord Nottingham's and desired them three (*sic*) to prepare what might be proper for the Queen to answer in case of a separate address from the clergy, since which I have not heard what has passed in their affairs.

My brother the provost of Eton has informed me that the Warden of All Souls is dead, and recommends Mr. Adams a chaplain of the Queen's to be prebend of Canterbury. I shall not move in anything of that kind but as you will guide me.

Thinking it might be very soon in my power to put Dr. Davenant into the Commission of Excise, I got my Lord Privy Seal to propose it to him, as you will see by the enclosed (*missing*) just received from him, as also that vanity and folly well rooted are not to be cured, even by necessity itself.

[LORD GODOLPHIN] to [ROBERT HARLEY,] Speaker.

1702, November 7. The votes of yesterday with the assurances which I have had that no angry thing shall be stirred in the House of Lords, without further provocation from the House of Commons, give a fair prospect of a speedy and quiet end of this session, of which I am extremely glad for many reasons. The Queen's answer to the clergy was altered according to the desire of the enclosed,* which I return to you. Lord Nottingham tells me the answer has the particular good fortune of pleasing both sides.

[LORD GODOLPHIN] to [ROBERT HARLEY,] Speaker.

1702 November 10 Tuesday at 2. I give you many thanks for the favour of your letter, which I happened to receive but this morning. Before I had it the Queen had signed the warrant for adding two persons to the Commission of Prizes, one Bretton, & one Gostling; the former is Customer or Collector of Dover, an experienced officer of the Customs, of good repute; the latter is wholly unknown to me but recommended by Sir E. Seymour whom I was willing to humour in it. He tells me this Gostling has lived long in Spain and is perfectly well qualified for this employment; but I suppose he must take it upon trust from somebody, as I do from him. If you had named any of those gentlemen mentioned in yours before it was too late, I should have liked better a great deal to have done just what you would have advised in it. I beg you would let me take this occasion of desiring to be informed by you if the bill about occasional conformity is to extend to any persons

---

* Missing—Atterbury's?

that are not Her Majesty's natural born subjects. My question arises from Colonel Granville's having been with the Queen last night to ask if the Prince would have any clause offered to exempt him from the force of the intended act. Now though the Prince has no scruple of receiving the sacrament in our church, yet I thought the Queen seemed almost equally unwilling either that he should be forced to do it or that he should need any clause to exempt him from doing it.

According as you hinted to me the other day, my Lord Nottingham will send to those gentlemen to meet us tomorrow morning at his office, but I doubt whether I shall be able to come, my cold being much increased since I saw you.

I hope the House of Lords will take the expedient of sitting as a House in St. Paul's church, it was the best I could think of for the easing of that difficulty.

I shall not be able to come out to-night to the meeting of the Commissioners for the Union.

LORD CUTTS to [ROBERT HARLEY].

1702 November [14–]25. N. S. The Hague—I heartily congratulate the justice done you by the Commons of England in placing you in the chair, which you have hitherto so worthily filled. I had the honour of a letter from you some time since, which I should have been proud of answering "incessantly"; but, besides that I had at that time my hands so full of business, I had not a moment's time at command : I knew nothing would be done in the Isle of Wight affair till winter. I now most earnestly desire your favour in it, when Lord Marlborough comes over, that Morgan may be removed, it having been a great injustice and hardship upon me, to have such a man forced upon me, after the good services I had done, and the bad ones he had been guilty of. I know a word from you to my Lord Marlborough will carry a great deal of weight, as well as to my Lord Nottingham, and such others as you think fit.

Lord Marlborough has thought it for Her Majesty's service, that I should stay here to command the forces in his absence; telling me (in private) that the grand Pensionary and some of the leading men here desired it; the winter quarters not being likely to pass over without some movements. He is pleased to leave me full powers, which I shall use with my utmost care and discretion.

[LORD GODOLPHIN] to [ROBERT HARLEY,] Speaker.

1702, November 16—I have employed Lord Ranelagh and another person to second the Solicitor General's endeavours with the Duke of Ormond, though if we should bring him to see his error I doubt it is too late to hinder the effects of it.

ROBERT WEST to [GEORGE FOLLET?].

1702, November 20—The day after I attended you to York Buildings, one Mr. Lane (said to be a trustee for the Earl of Clarendon) and one Mr. Blackmore appeared publicly at the Court of Aldermen, delivered papers there in the name of the New River Company, and opposed the sealing of the new lease or licence to Mr. Morris of erecting a water-engine in the fourth arch of London Bridge. To this they added a report amongst the Aldermen and some of the Common Council, that Mr. Morris or his agents had offered to come to terms with the New River Company designing thereby to create a jealousy in Mr. Morris's friends, that he would endeavour to evade his contract with the City for lowering their water rents to 20s. *per annum* for private houses. This disabled me from doing anything more towards an accommodation and made the other party so shy, that I can't ask him a question tending that way. So far as I can find amongst the Common Council men I conversed with, this opposition made by Lane and Blackmore has done Mr. Morris service, and so far exasperated the Common Council against the New River Company, that they will take upon them to seal the lease if the Court of Aldermen defers it beyond next week. Some of the Aldermen themselves, who violently opposed sealing the lease, grow cooler since those gentlemen appeared for the New River, because their opposition now will be construed an opposition to the interest of the City. I had an intimation from some friends of Mr. Morris, that a project was proposed to interest the City in some part of his works, and if that should be done, there will be no room for an accommodation, and the New River Company may suffer more prejudice than they could do by Mr. Morris singly. If that Company would desist from all further opposition, I believe I could yet be an instrument of serving them, which I would be glad to do for the sake of my Lord Clarendon, and of that truly great man your friend [Harley ?], for whom I have all the honour due to so much merit.

[Lord Godolphin] to [Robert Harley,] Speaker.

1702, November 21—I have heard nothing this morning from Dr. D[avenant], and the vacancy begins now to be so public that I am tormented out of my life. However I will not dispose of the place till after I have seen you tomorrow night, which if it be easy to you I wish may be at my house about nine because the Council will hardly rise till that hour. In case you come to my house before I can be at home I will leave out a book of curiosity to entertain you till I come ; in the meantime I had a mind you should know how little time longer I can keep this place in my hands, that no opportunity might be omitted of quickening the Doctor's resolution.

[Lord Godolphin] to [Robert Harley,] Speaker.

1702, November 24—I did not think fit to tell the Doctor nor his friend Lord Privy Seal that he should not have that place if it fell, and this is the top of what he calls a promise. I have not yet had one word from my Lord Privy Seal upon the noise of this vacancy in the Excise, by which I conclude the Doctor has yet no thoughts of it, and whatever his pretext may be, I doubt he is at the bottom vain enough to think it would be too great a loss to the public if he should exclude himself from the House of Commons. The papers relating to the expedition at Cadiz have been brought this morning by Lord Nottingham to the House of Lords. They have been so calm as to appoint Thursday for the reading of them in a full house ; and if the House of Commons suffer no new incident to interfere with the dispatch of the supplies I am not out of hopes but the session may yet end with the old year, which I think would be a better new year's gift to the whole kingdom than they have had to brag of this long time.

[LORD GODOLPHIN] to [ROBERT HARLEY,] Speaker.

1702, December 9—The Queen having granted to my Lord Marlborough and the heirs of his body the honour of a Duke as likewise a pension for the support of it during her life, his friends have encouraged him to think it will not be difficult at this time to get this latter grant confirmed by act of parliament to him and the heirs of his body.

In this he has desired me to ask your advice and assistance, and whether there should be a message from the Queen in writing or by word of mouth. Sir E. S[eymour ?] has been very gracious to him in this matter.

[The SAME to the SAME.]

1702, December 10—Lord M[arlborough] desires me to return you his thanks for your letter of last night and to tell you no pains shall be neglected in his affair. He has had some talk with Sir Christopher Musgrave yesterday and great professions from him and Sir E. S[eymour ?], but much warmer from the younger part of the House. Mr. Secretary who will have the Queen's order this morning to carry the message is to show it to you before he delivers it. If you would be at liberty this night I would come to you after Council is done to talk a little about the madness of yesterday, and to have your opinion of a thought I have had concerning that matter. Does anybody think England will be persuaded that this Queen won't take care to preserve the Church of England ? And do they forget that not only the fate of England but of all Europe depends upon the appearance of our concord in the despatch of our supplies ?

[LORD GODOLPHIN] to [ROBERT HARLEY,] Speaker.

1702, December 12—I cannot dissemble to you that I am very much concerned at the little success which I find the Queen's message is like to meet with in behalf of Lord Marlborough, especially since it comes chiefly from those of whom I thought we had deserved better. I should be extremely glad of your direction and of your help in what is fit to be done.

[LORD GODOLPHIN to ROBERT HARLEY.]

1702, December 14—I give you a thousand thanks for your patience last night when I had so little, and for the calm and sincere advice you gave me. I have had time since to reflect upon all you said, and have full power from my Lord M[arlborough] to leave this matter wholly in your hands to give it the form, tomorrow, which you think will be least disrespectful to the Queen.

I am told Sir E. Seymour has an expedient to offer, of continuing the grant for Lord Marlborough's life instead of the Queen's, but this expedient seems to me to have all the difficulties in it which complying with the message itself would have, and none of the advantage.

I am also told that Mr. Finch has an expedient to offer of desiring the Queen to grant my Lord M[arlborough] a sum of money out of the prizes, but this I take to be a most preposterous thing, for when there is a difficulty of making a grant that is only future and perhaps may never come to bear, will they give a sum of money from the public, or would any body take it when the nation is so deeply taxed and the money wanted every day in the week for the public service ?

I hear the gentlemen will meet at your house without the lords and endeavour to agree upon what shall be done tomorrow. I beg the favour that as soon as they go from you, you will send me a letter to my Lord M[arlborough]'s at St. James', with an account of what they shall conclude upon, with your own opinion of it, by which I am sure my Lord M[arlborough] will guide his directions to his friends tomorrow.

In the meantime I will only add my own opinion that the chief thing is to avoid a division in the House because the consequence of that will be, as you said yesterday, that men will look upon themselves to be listed. Now upon anything to be said in the House by Mr. Churchill which my Lord is ready for, to prevent a division or struggle in the House, I should think a rise (*sic*) might be taken to make an address to the Queen showing an uneasiness for not complying with the message from the inconvenience of the precedent and at the same time a satisfaction in Lord M[arlborough]'s services and the great justice her Majesty had done to his merits, the whole is submitted to you and those gentlemen. The Queen will be this night at the commission for the Union.

[LORD GODOLPHIN] to [ROBERT HARLEY,] Speaker.

[1702, December] 18. Friday—I am told advantage is taken from the clause added this day to the Prince's bill to blow up the House of Lords into the thought that this is a tack against which they have lately declared themselves so positively; and above sixty have signed it. If they are kept up in this thought I doubt it may prove the loss of the bill, which would be very uneasy to the Queen; and I do not see how to prevent it unless upon the report so many other saving clauses be offered as will tire the House and give them a handle to leave out all the clauses of the bill and this among the rest. You have been so tired with my letters of late that I have had good intentions to forbear troubling you a good while, but this new alarm has overthrown them all.

[LORD GODOLPHIN] to [ROBERT HARLEY,] Speaker.

1702, December 19—I am glad to find by the favour of your letter that the report of the Prince's bill is not to be till Monday, for then there's no danger of its being in our House so as to disturb our passing the bill for the Land Tax before the holidays, which I take to be of great consequence, and I hope the Queen may come Wednesday morning to pass it; and if it were possible to stave off a free conference about the bill of Conformity till after the adjournment, perhaps it were not the worse. Upon this subject and some others, if it were easy to see you, I should be very glad to see you to-morrow at five in the evening either at my house or your own as you like best.

[LORD GODOLPHIN to ROBERT HARLEY.]

[1702] December 24—It's above a month since Auditor Done gave in a petition at the Treasury to resign his place to Mr. Drake. I then discouraged that expectation very much, but did not name your brother neither then nor never but to the Queen and yourself. If I had given the least countenance to the request I am apt to believe they were ready to have made oath there was no money in the case, but I was unwilling to ask that question for fear of bringing the difficulty stronger upon me. By this and by other things I agree it looks as if he were not like to hold out long. However if any tolerable expedient arises of bringing your brother in, even in his lifetime, I shall readily go into it, for next to yourself I would sooner have him in the Queen's service than anybody I know in the world, and I think it would be of great advantage to Her Majesty. I don't wonder you found Sir C. M[usgrave] a little easier in the business of Holland. Lord Nottingham has brought his brother and Sir E. S[eymour] into it also ; but it is all upon the condition the Dutch will agree to prohibit the commerce by letters, without which condition they are all satisfied we cannot pay our army abroad another year, and our merchants concerned in the remittances make so much noise about the great fall of the *agio*, which is occasioned by great drafts of money by the French from London and Amsterdam, that unless Holland can be brought to agree with us in this point, to say the truth, I doubt both we and they shall be brought into greater difficulties than perhaps are yet foreseen.

If the Prince meets with a disagreeable opposition in the House of Lords to his bill, he is obliged to his own servants for it. The whole proceeding of that House yesterday looks to me as if they were afraid the time were too short for madness and extravagance.

[Lord Godolphin] to [Robert Harley,] Speaker.

1702, December 25, ten at night. Sir Thomas Cuddon's son was put in only to finish his father's receipt of this year, as being probably better able to adjust that account than anybody else. Of late that receipt has been in the hands of the Chamberlain of London, the frequent occasion of loans from the City in the last war made it almost necessary at that time, and though that occasion may now, I hope, be less, yet whoever is Chamberlain of London will look upon himself to be disobliged, if the receipt of the taxes should be put into any other hand. The Chamberlain is the servant of the City, and if they have a mind to take away all or part of his profit and apply it to the Orphans' stock I don't see but that they may do it, but I will desire a little of your advice in this matter if you will do me the favour to call at my house about nine Sunday night, by which time I hope we may have the Dutch letters. However I would wait upon you sooner but that I go to-morrow to St. Albans and intend to bring the Duke of Marlborough to town with me Sunday.

Account of the Earl of Stamford's reception and entertainment at Zell and Hanover.

1702—Lord Stamford, as I remember, arrived at Zell the 15 day of August new style, and came directly to the English envoy's house there, desiring him to carry his Lordship the next day to the Court which was then at Winhusen, a German mile distant from Zell, and his Lordship expressing himself as having a mind to shoot, which was then the sport of the Duke of Zell, he was offered to stay and lodge at that country house, which his Lordship accepted and passed about a fortnight in that place. All strangers are generally received in that Court with great civility, but the Duke's envoy at London having recommended his Lordship in a very particular manner, there was something more than ordinary in the kindness shewed him at Zell. His Lordship had seen the Elector before he came to Zell. The Electress was then at Berlin and the Elector at a place called Herrenhausen, about an English mile distant from Hanover. His Lordship had a coach and six horses to carry him from Hanover thither when he pleased, and—they say—he was very constant both at dinner and supper with the Elector till his Electoral Highness took his journey toward the mines, which—some people say—was at least hastened if not purely occasioned for the decent avoiding his Lordship. 'The Electress returned from Berlin eight or ten days before the Elector came from the mines. His Lordship was upon the place to expect her Electoral Highness; was very graciously received by her and had a very long and very private audience. His Lordship's visit proving something longer than was expected, orders were given at the Elector's stable to furnish no coaches nor horses to any stranger unless they were characterized persons; but this change was supplied by a pair of horses lent by the Electress to his Lordship. It has been observed that his Lordship distributed English gloves and some other toys in an unusual manner to persons about the Court. To the Electress his Lordship presented a great many Common Prayer Books of the last edition with the *Princess Sophia* printed in them. I thought at first it had been for the love and value his Lordship had of the liturgy, but I found I was mistaken because his Lordship would never appear at the English envoy's chapel, though invited thither by him, and informed that he might hear an English sermon with the prayers of the Church of England if his Lordship pleased. His Lordship has affected to speak very highly in praise of Her Majesty once or twice in public. 'Tis to be hoped he has done the same in his private audiences. One Madame Bellmont, a noted lady, who is in favour with the Electress, has been his chief confidant, and 'tis to her that all the discontented politicians address themselves, Papists and sectaries. She is of the former communion, and I may safely say she is one of the most silly creatures that ever was born and bred in it, not to say anything of the scandal which her person has so justly deserved. There is one thing observable in a Peer of England, that his Lordship gave the title of *Excellency* to all these ministers, which is never done by any gentleman. His Lordship's companion was a Dutchman, whom he brought with him from London. As to guards or armed chair or any other such distinguishing marks of honour done to his Lordship, if he has not done them to himself, they must have been invented for him by others, for nothing of that nature has been seen here.

[LORD GODOLPHIN] to [ROBERT HARLEY], Speaker.

1702-3, January 6—I can't but tell you that I am glad of your vote yesterday though I am not without my fears that the condition of it may be looked upon as too much imposing by our friends on the other side of the water. Nobody can give it so good a turn to them as yourself and I trouble you with this letter chiefly because you might know there will be an opportunity of sending to Holland this night, if you send your letters to either of the Secretaries' Offices; and, sitting so late as you did I doubt you could not have time to write much by last night's post.

'Tis high time to help Mr. G—— at Han[over]. I wish you would tell me to whom I might order Mr. Taylor to pay some moneys to be returned him.

Auditor Done languishes much as I hear, but I find besides a great occasion of making a particular Auditor for the revenue of the Customs which is now so bulky, and it is plain the two auditors of imprest have more other business than they can despatch.

[The SAME to the SAME.]

1702-3, January 8—I am much obliged to you for your letters. That from the West Indies is entertaining, but the news we have from Bembo [Benbow] grieves one's heart.

, I am glad to hear old Mr. Hill is so sanguine, I wish I could be so too upon that subject; not but that I hope the States will comply, but the consequences, if they should not, are dreadful, and too great a venture.

[The Same to the Same.]

1702-3, January 14—I find by the stopping of the money bills the Queen's servants in both Houses are vying who shall be maddest. Before I had heard of this piece of prowess I was desirous of an opportunity of speaking to you tomorrow evening, and this makes it still a little more necessary. In the meantime if the House of Commons would not go upon the bill sent down this day from the Lords till we had tried our strength once more in the House of Lords upon the Prince's bill it would be an advantage to us in that matter, but I dare not say this to anybody but you, because I am satisfied use would be presently made of it to a quite contrary effect.

[The Same to the Same.]

1702-3, January 15—Considering that probably some things may happen today and tomorrow that may much alter the state of those matters of which we are like to discourse when I see you, I am contented not to give you the trouble of coming here till Sunday.

[The Same to the Same.]

1702-3, January 21—I am sorry in this case that I can't advise the Queen to grant the office of Auditor of the imprests for life. Mr. Attorney says that matter is wholly as the Queen pleases, and the fact is that all Auditors of the revenue that have been made the twenty three years last past have been only during pleasure. But the two Auditors of the imprests are of older date, and when their patents were granted everything was given for life because more would be given for it.

The last letters from Holland give no good prospect of the matters depending there. I doubt the augmentation will come to nothing, and if so I could wish it had never been proposed. But the *Rubicon is passed* and we must endeavour to make the best on't that we can. How far or whether it be reasonable anything of this should be explained at all in the appropriating clause must be submitted to better judgments.

I am told by some that there seems an inclination in the House of Commons to take the bill of Conformity as the House of Lords have left it.

[The Same to the Same.]

1703 [January ?]—We received the Queen's pleasure upon most of the particulars spoken of at the last meeting, as I take it, the next day; but it was thought proper no part of it should be published till the Parliament was over.

The King had promised Windsor prebendary to Mr. Fleetwood; that of Christ Church to the Duke of Devonshire's chaplain, who has been satisfied with Westminster, that Christ Church might be free for Dr. Burton, at Lord Nottingham's very particular instance, while the King was alive and since: so that I believe you will agree all these were engagements. However I am apt to think the Queen would have passed over any of them at first in favour of your chaplain before she herself had confirmed these engagements, if some of the Bishops (as I casually learned from the Archbishop of York) had not led her into a notion that chaplains of the House of Commons used to be preferred once in three years: and I confess this sounds enough like a maxim of the Bishop of Salisbury.

I am extremely much obliged to you for the kindness of your expressions. I can sincerely return you the Spanish compliment

"Io lo meresco."

[The SAME to the SAME.]

[1703] February 6—Sunday ought to be a day of rest to all people, and to you particularly; and yet I find by the Duke of Marlborough as well as by myself that we should much desire to see you at my house to-morrow before five, if it will consist with your convenience.

A. [LADY PYE] to ABIGAIL HARLEY at Brampton.

1702-3, February 27—[Derby.] I wish [your brother] the Auditor much joy of his place. Both of us were heartily glad when we heard it (being for life makes it so valuable) though perhaps I am one of the last ere I expressed it. I could wish another friend at the Temple had good business, or some other advantage as his parts and merits deserve. The lawyers and their fry the attorneys in these parts complain their gains dwindle. A good sign I think unless it is want of money makes people less litigious. It is a scarce commodity. Tenants for one dead year make large complaints, and many that one would think should be wiser are alarmed at taxes, thought with King William all would, cease. I have conversed so little of late, that I know not whether people are glad or sorry that the Occasional Bill is dropped, but moderate men I should think cannot be displeased; at least the Dissenters are obliged to the Lords. It brings to my mind what was told me yesterday, indeed very pleasant, that Mr. Child poor gentleman who despatched himself was for sorrow this Bill was lost; a good Derby ale notion, though was told it was the opinion of some gentlemen. Your last told me, you writ any stuff; what then must I call mine. All, yours was new to me, that pray when next you favour me transmit again some more London chat.

[Sir SIMON HARCOURT] to ROBERT HARLEY, Speaker.

1702[-3], March 13. Stafford—Whilst you sit at helm you must forgive the importunity of your friends who desire to be informed. Whilst the parliament continued that was a reason why no alterations were made; wherever I come, I am told the campaign is altogether as good a reason, and the success of that must be expected. I endeavour to give satisfactory answers, but most of our friends are growing infidels. Though this be no news to you, yet the consequence seems so very mischievous, I cannot omit giving you this hint. I should be the easier at this distance from you, if you would give me some account, whether anything be yet done, or is to be expected before the war is ended. It is with some difficulty I contain myself on this melancholy subject, but I know how precious your minutes are. I'm sure I'm far from thinking of anything particularly myself, whilst you permit me to claim so large a share of your frendship as you have always honoured me with.

[Lord Godolphin to Robert Harley.]

1703, March 28—The Earl of Thanet has been with me several times and always easy, but not so at first in relation to the Lieutenancy. However I believe that matters will be brought to pass.

I forgot to tell you that I sent to desire Lord Galway to come to town about the affair of the Cevennes. I had a mind to speak with him upon it and to have his assistance. He has given me a sort of a scheme which I think very reasonable, if we can but get ourselves in a condition to attempt such things as are reasonable; but while we are in such uncertainty as to the event of the Bavarian war we shall scarce resolve upon anything. I doubt we have too many irons in the fire. We can't be in the Mediterranean, in Portugal, upon the coast of France, and in the West Indies all at once. The Queen had my Lord Galway's paper when I was with you, or else I should have remembered to have shown it you.

R[obert] Monckton to Robert Harley.

1703, April 3—I was with his Grace (of Newcastle), yesterday morning, and I doubt not you will find him disposed to concur with you to your satisfaction. But this is chiefly to tell you that you must of necessity appoint your time when you will be with him. He will otherwise think that you are not so sincere with him as he desires to be with you, and says positively if you do not you are content that you should be interrupted. I beseech you do not neglect this caution I presume to give you and let me be honoured with giving him the notice of it. I do not do it to impose myself upon you but that he expects your answer by me; and further as I wish my Lord Treasurer may be as much in debt to you upon the account of the one House as he is for the other.

A. Lady Pye to Abigail Harley, at Brampton.

1703, April 14. Derby—This house is not convenient as my family grows up, otherwise I've not much reason to dislike the place, for the town is much increased in gentry and good building since we have lived here. Mr. Sacheverell is just come with his family, hath left Nottingham since his lady's death, but the young and airy person of our town is Lady Evory turned of 80, that in her apartment I fancy myself in London upon a lady's visiting day.

We hear the Duchess of Marlborough bears not her affliction like her mistress, if report be true that it hath near touched her head.

Js. Stephens to Robert Harley, Speaker.

1703 April 23. The surprising news in this country is the death of Colonel Price; he died by the sword. A drunken quarrel happened between him and Mr. Thomas Baskervile of Aberedow, he gave the Colonel several wounds of which he died within twenty hours after the rencontre. Every state and community has its critical periods, death knocks at the gate of palaces as at the meanest cottages; such is the fortune of duels, to-day victorious, to-morrow vanquished.

I am pressed on by some friends to request the favour of you that you'll be pleased to put me into the Commission of peace for the county of Radnor. I am growing old and shall quit my practice; and as to my estate 'tis as considerable as most of the justices.

[LORD GODOLPHIN to ROBERT HARLEY.]

1703, April 27—After I saw you last night I received the enclosed from Mr. Paterson which I trouble you with that you may judge what is proper to be said to Franco and write accordingly. The last line of his news from Cologne about the having taken their cannon and baggage is impossible to be true.

Enclosing

[William Paterson] to Lord [Godolphin].

1703, April 27—There is herewith enclosed a translation of Franko's last letter, in which he insists that he may have leave to come over, his affairs as agent of the East and West India Company of Holland making his speedy return indispensably necessary, it being a matter of trust that cannot otherwise be discharged.

[— Franko] to [William Paterson].

1703, May 1 [new style]. Amsterdam—I am at present quite out of my element, and in much concern, lest you, and the good work which we have happily brought so far, and managed with so much sincerity and faithfulness should now after all be otherwise than could be wished. And to say my thoughts I can't imagine what should be the reason of your long silence, and to be plain, if in a short time I receive no advice from our friend in York Buildings, or from you, I am resolved to depart for England, since I find my masters the Directors of the East and West India Company are still more and more uneasy at my staying here, and the disorder of their affairs by reason of my absence from England. I therefore cannot be easy till I have my dismission, that I may with satisfaction part from hence.

By the enclosed Dutch Courants you'll see how matters stand on this side. We were in great apprehensions of the Lines being forced, and thereby a way opened for the conjunction of the French and Bavarians, and our fears were increased by the more than ordinary staying out of the Dutch Post; but we were comforted with news from the Hague, that the French after having five times attacked the lines near Stolhoven were beaten off and forced to retreat to Strasbourg, this came with an express from Lieutenant General Goor, and at nine o'clock at night I received the enclosed note from the Postmaster of the Cologne Comptoir. I would fain have sent you Prince Louis of Baden's letter to the States, but could not procure it this Post. In it he very much commends the courage and bravery of the Holland troops, and says further, that in case they had not been in the lines, he must have retired to Frankfort, and left all free to the French. I hope this success shall give new life and courage to public affairs everywhere. Bonn is now besieged, and the cannon and mortars will begin to play on Monday next. The Duke of Marlborough and General Opdam are to have a powerful army not only to cover the siege but if need be to act offensively against the French. There is to be another army by Hulst in Flanders, which is hoped shall do something considerable on that side.

We had this day French letters which had almost all been opened, and mentioned nothing of the business at Stolhoven, but the Antwerp Courant does in this matter, as in all others lie bitterly for his master. That paper is commonly a rhapsody of all sorts of deceit and lies, but I reckon the truth will at last get uppermost, and that the poor Flandrikins will begin to have their eyes open when they come to be near or quite ruined.

The Camissards in the Cevennes make a daily progress and get frequent advantages over the King's troops, and upon the whole, if the Allies do anything tolerably in their management of the following part of this war Louis le Grand is like to have work enough in his latter days. We are certainly informed that his troops under Villars and Tallard are but in a very ordinary condition, having undergone many heavy fatigues, and that not a few of them have deserted and many more are dead, and that the remainder are very sick and weak. The cavalry are also very much disabled and in a poor case.

D[ANIEL DE] F[OE] to WILLIAM PATERSON, London.

1703, April—I cannot omit that in the little information I have from my very few friends I meet with from every hand the notices of your concern for my present suffering. And as I am assured my gratitude for the kindness of my friends will be the last virtue that will forsake me, so my sense of your regard for me on whom I have laid no obligation lays a debt on me I can no otherwise pay than by my thankful acknowledgments.

Tis vain for me to complain of the misfortune of my present condition, since you can render me no services for which you shall not receive reproaches from all parties. Nay, even the Dissenters, like Casha (*sic*) to Cæsar, lift up the first dagger at me; I confess it makes me reflect on the whole body of the Dissenters with something of contempt, more than usual, and gives me the more regret that I suffer for such a people. Shall I own to you, that the greatest concern I have upon me is that the government whom I profess I did not foresee would be displeased, should resent this matter? I had it not in my thoughts that the Ministers of State would construe that as pointing at them which I levelled only at Dr. Sacheverell, Dr. Stubbs, and such people my more direct antagonists; thus like old Tyrrell, who shot at a stag and killed the King I engaged a Party, and embroiled myself with the Government.

Sir, my sense of this has led me, to the lowest submissions I was capable of in a letter I wrote to my Lord Nottingham and some other applications made since. Nor is there anything so mean (which I can honestly stoop to do) that I would not submit to, to obtain her Majesty's favour. I acquainted my Lord Nottingham that whereas persons condemned for capital offences were frequently spared upon their entering into her Majesty's service, if Her Majesty would grant me the like favour I would surrender myself at the head of her armies to any Colonel of Horse her Majesty should appoint and serve her a year, two or more at my own charge: not doubting I should die there more to her Majesty's service than in a prison; and that if by my behaviour I could expiate this folly, I should esteem it more honour to me than if I obtained her Majesty's pardon by petition. I omitted nothing to express the unfeigned sense I had upon my mind of having offended her Majesty, and I repeat this to you that you may know and be assured, and may if you please so far answer for me that I really am a hearty penitent on that account, and that I am not ashamed to be ashamed of it.

I cannot but with regret look back on the former discourses we have had concerning things done before now, and you, must remember how willingly I always offered you to make my acknowledgments to a certain gentleman whom I always honour for his character among wise men, more than the greatness of his share in the royal favour. If I have rendered the hopes you gave me of his favour desperate by this disaster, 'tis a misfortune as great as all the rest. If not, beseech him to suspend his resentments till my future behaviour may convince him that, of all the gentlemen known to me only by character, he is the last I would disoblige, and the first I would humble myself to, because of the just respect I have entertained of his wisdom and honesty. As to my present circumstances, I can only say as of him that repents without hope, I find them desperate, and that neither sense of the offences nor future amendment will atone, so I am fled, and tho' I do already find 'tis no very difficult thing for me to get my bread, yet as I expressed to my Lord N., methinks fleeing from her Majesty's justice is a sort of raising war against her, and I would fain lay down these arms. Nor had death been the punishment should I [have been] so long before I had come in and thrown myself upon her Majesty's clemency, but gaol, pillories and such like, with which I have been so much threatened, have convinced me 'I' want passive courage, and I shall never for the future think myself injured if I am called a coward.

I hope by my misfortunes I shall not lose the influence of your friendship, and, if you find it necessary to make any postulata of future loyalty and my obedient submission to, or service for, the Government, if you believe me master of any faith, or that I have any principles of honour or honesty left, you may depend upon my punctual performance. If you should find room for my name in your conversation with the gentleman I mentioned—I suppose I need not name him—if, you find him inclined to have compassion for one who offended him only because he did not know him, venture in my name in the humblest terms to ask his pardon, and whether ever I am restored to my native country or not I shall never name him but with some epithet suited to express his merit. Let him know that I solicit you with more earnestness to convince him of my sense of his resentment, and my earnest desire to be set right in his thoughts, than I do for the obtaining a recall from this banishment, forasmuch as I value the esteem of one wise man above abundance of blessings. Accept my repeated thanks for the friendship you show in concerning yourself for me. My vows for your welfare and prosperity and continue your goodness and kindness to your exiled friend.

Endorsed by Harley.

"Received from Mr Wm. Paterson Friday May 28, 1703 at one o'clock."

[LORD GODOLPHIN] to [ROBERT HARLEY,] Speaker.

1703, May 8—The matter of the Earl of Thanet would have been easy enough if he had liked it when it was first mentioned but now I doubt it much; however I will labour in it to the utmost, though I must own to you at the same time I should be very indifferent in the matter but upon the account of one person whom I shall always be very desirous to satisfy, if I can, and when I can. The letters from Lisbon gives us hopes once more that the treaty with Portugal is at the very brink of being concluded.

CAMP AT HOGTELN.

1703, May 24—Plan of the order of battle at the camp at Hogteln, under the Duke of Marlborough and Mons. D'Auverquerque, showing the positions of the general officers engaged, and of the battalions and their commanders.

[LORD GODOLPHIN] to [ROBERT HARLEY,] Speaker.

1703, May 26 — I have acquainted Lord Nottingham with the discourse I had yesterday with the Dean of Canterbury [Hooper] and the desire he showed of keeping his present preferments in the church for two years after he was made bishop of St. Asaph. His Lordship seemed well pleased to hear he would accept of it but at the same time to wish that he would not think fit to insist upon keeping them all; particularly the parsonage of Lambeth as being near, and most in every body's eye he thought he could shew him it would be for his own service and reputation to part with; and concluded with saying he would send to him to come to his office to-morrow morning. I can't say that I think my Lord in the wrong as to his reflection; however I had a mind to let you know just what we talked upon this occasion that you may have it in your power to prepare or not prepare the Dean for my Lord's message just as you think proper.

[The SAME to the SAME.]

1703, June 9—I shall always be ready to wait upon the Dean of Canterbury at any time or place, but the Queen coming to Hampton Court to-morrow morning to meet the Council it may probably be easy for him to take that opportunity and save himself the trouble of going ten miles farther.

The MARQUIS DE GUISCARD to [ROBERT] HARLEY.

1703, June [9–]20. Rotterdam—I take the liberty of sending to your excellency a copy of the history of my undertakings which I have been obliged to have printed on account of the evil proceedings of certain persons. It is absolutely necessary that your excellency should be informed of these matters in order that you may in future accord me your protection, which I earnestly ask. *French*.

[LORD GODOLPHIN to ROBERT HARLEY].

1703, June 16—Mr. Stepney's letters by last night's post mention the treaty with the Duke of Savoy as no longer a secret but the public talk of Vienna, where they expect it will soon be signed, the Comte d'Aversbergh being on his journey to Turin for the concluding of it. The rest of the letters from Germany seem to think that country almost free from their apprehensions of the junction, the storm being now going towards Tyrol, with intention to cut off the communication to Italy; but if the Duke of Savoy declares as we expect, that may give the French business enough in Italy also. Sir George Rooke is not yet at Spithead, as I thought, but expected there every hour. The intelligence he has learnt from prisoners is of no great consequence, but he seems to think the prizes he has taken very considerable. As for Mr. Paget I do not think any one more fit to be encouraged, and you need not doubt but any advances you think proper to make him will be made good.

I think we shall send Mr. Hill to Savoy. His public errand will be to negotiate for some assistance to the Cevennois, but I hope he will have some further instructions also.

[The Same to the Same.]

1703, June 30—I have perused, your letter and the inclosed from Mr. Paterson, whom I always looked upon as a useful man and find him so by the account Franco gives of him in his papers, which till this day I had scarce time to run over, but I must own to you I don't well understand what it is in which he proposes to be employed, but I shall be glad to be informed by you to-morrow if you will give me leave to come to you about noon. Formerly Mr. Paterson's schemes used to run much upon lessening the interest paid for the public money, but that seems now in good measure done to his hand. The encouragement he proposes for himself is very small in respect of any considerable service to the public, so that if his notions and ours together can form any proposal of employment for him which is reducible to practice I shall be very desirous to encourage and assist him.

[Robert Harley to his sister Abigail Harley.]

1703, July 6—I hope now I shall very quickly see my dearest sister, my wife will move the camp speedily and I shall not be long after. We have had a very uncertain summer which hath much affected all the rich meadows on the Thames, yet the farmers near the town wish for scarcity to increase the price of their grain.

In Scotland they quarrel with one another, yet not one of them will venture to cure their wound. They agree together against a protestant successor till he comes to buy it himself, but since they are for selling themselves I pray God they do it not for good and all.

This day sevennight Lord Marlborough went to persuade the States and their Generals that he might attack the French in their lines; I have not seen any body since the post came in, but it seems to me by their motions that they resolve to do it, which with God's blessing may be of great consequence and advantage, though I scarce believe the French will stay to venture the shock since they passed their time so ill with poor Mons. Opdam's army, though treble his number.

Lord Scudamore is come over and to town, though I have not seen him, not finding him at home, nor he me.

R[ussell] Robartes to [Robert Harley].

1703, July 28—Enquiring what was the reason of the delay in his being appointed groom of the Bedchamber to the Prince, and asking for an interview with the Lord Treasurer. His brother Radnor was mightily surprised that there should now be any hesitation since he, as well as the whole town, took it for granted the thing was done and determined.

[Lord] G[odolphin] to [Robert Harley].

1703, August 17—I spoke to your brother to-day to send Mr. Robert Cunningham to you, and I enclose a bank bill of 100l. with which you may please to encourage him to apply his pains either to Scotland or to

France, as you think it may be most probable for him to make any discoveries to the advantage of the Queen's service.

That matter of the Justices of the peace in Cumberland seems to be every way a sore thing. I shall meddle in it but as little as I can. I find we are running headlong into all the same stops for which we blamed others and which gave us a handle to their disadvantage; but unless one will serve particular ends and particular turns, endeavouring to serve the public will not support one. I believe all the friends Sir Christopher M[usgrave] has had there thirty years have not done him so much service altogether, as I have had the good fortune to do, though still an unprofitable servant.

I hope Sir George Rooke will be this evening called to the Cabinet Council and be satisfied in all his pretensions.

P.S.—I have a letter from Mr. Guy that brags much of the benefit of the Bath.

Dr. GEORGE HICKES to ROBERT HARLEY, York Buildings.

1703, August 21—I have been two or three times to wait upon you, to speak about some things before you go into the country. My infirmities will not bear the motion of an hackney-coach, and of a good walker I am become one of the most indifferent sort, especially upon London stones. I intreat you therefore to appoint me an hour to wait upon you. I promised to get you the enclosed paper which was worn to rags before I had it. The critic is old Dr. Biram Eaton who has read Horace over, as they tell me, many hundred times, oftener, I fear, than he has read the Gospels.

[HENRY GUY to ROBERT HARLEY.]

1703, September 2. Bath—Just now my Lord Treasurer gave me the enclosed to send to you. My son Mansell went this day from hence into Wales.

[LORD GODOLPHIN to ROBERT HARLEY.]

1703, September 2. Bath—These waters help my stomach and head but I have a violent cold which disorders me very much.

The thread of intelligence which you are following will I hope be very useful and successful for the Queen's service, and Her Majesty to whom I have communicated it is of the same opinion. She commands me to desire you would continue your endeavours to learn as many particulars as you can, and to tell you she does not think any body else is so diligent as to interfere with you in that matter. Lord Nottingham has written for leave to go to Burley about the middle of this month, but I believe the Queen will not grant it till towards the latter end of it, by which time she proposes to be at Windsor, and that the parliament should not meet to sit till about the beginning of November. Sir E. S[eymour] has been here and looks very well; his promises have been as full as usual; perhaps his performances will be so too. Mr. Mansell has passed by this place on his way to Wales. I was very well pleased to see the letter you sent me from Sir Christopher Musgrave. I should hope the proceedings in Scotland might help us a little to open people's eyes, those of the North especially. I suppose the Queen will send to the Duke of Queensberry to adjourn the Parliament for some short time and to come up hither with her other servants to advise her what measures are most proper to be taken as to that kingdom, her English counsellors by what I find being generally unwilling to meddle with it.

[Lord Godolphin to Robert Harley.]

1703, September 10. Bath—I am to acknowledge the favour of two letters from you with several papers enclosed all which are very useful and instructing. I can find times to read them without any trouble but between these waters and my own distemper I am seldom easy to write. As above ten days since the Queen sent an instruction to the Duke of Queensberry in Scotland that unless he could have strength to obtain a supply without tacking it to the Act for security of the Kingdom, he should adjourn the Parliament for six weeks and come up to London in that time with the rest of Her Majesty's servants, I have just now had news of his having received this instruction, which will be so little welcome to most there, I mean the Queen's servants, of what party soever, that I am apt to think they will use all possible endeavours to comply with her desires in it, but whether their united strength will be sufficient time only can determine.

Sir E. Seymour is returned here for the second time to make his court. He looks very well in my opinion and owns himself that he has had great benefit from a medicine given him by my Lord Guernsey.

I am very well pleased with your news from the Duke of Shrewsbury.

[Henry Guy to Robert Harley.]

1703, September 11. Bath—I received yours of the 7th and gave the enclosed with my own hand to the Lord Treasurer. I read him your just application of that piece of Horace. Sir Edward Seymour is here and Jack Howe. My Lord Treasurer is well and the Duchess of Marlborough came on Thursday.

—— to Robert Harley, at Brampton.

1703, September 23. London—In obedience to your commands I give you the following account of the affairs of Scotland from a good hand. On Wednesday the 15th instant a proposal was made to go upon the Supplies and my Lord Commissioner did promise that if they would allow a first reading of that Act, they should have three days to go upon their Liberties before a second reading were demanded. But this was rejected with some hard reflexions on the promises from the Throne which were alleged always to end in some trick prepared beforehand to obviate them. Mr. Fletcher having offered some overtures for limiting the Crown and securing the liberties of the nation, the Court proposed a vote, go upon the Supplies, or upon Saltoun's overtures. But the country party finding that they would divide upon Saltoun's overtures, and so the Supplies might be carried did persuade Saltoun to withdraw his proposal and proposed the state of the vote, go upon the Supplies or upon the Liberties of the nation, whereof the latter was carried by a great majority. The Marquis of Montrose had a speech showing that they had had nothing but a shadow of their government for many years past, that the measures of their statesmen were wholly determined by English councils, that they had an opportunity now to redress themselves, which if they did not improve, they must resolve to be slaves for ever. That they ought to remember what the asserting their Liberties and Independence had cost their forefathers, and for himself he was for all fair and peaceable means, but if these could not prevail he was ready to hazard his life and fortune in so honourable a cause. The Earl of Roxburgh and Earl of Rothes had speeches to the same purpose and a mighty ferment arising in the House my Lord Commissioner was very warmly greeted, in so much that some did not stand to affirm that he had yesternight received advice from my Lord G——n. for what he proposed that day. The Commissioner used the softest words he could to pacify them and told them that the day being then far spent, it was not time to enter on business but that the morrow they should meet and consider their liberties as they had resolved. So the next day they met being this day sevennight, and after calling some business of the day my Lord Chancellor by order of the Commissioner adjourned the Parliament to the 12th of October.

My Lord Commissioner had first given the touch of the Sceptre to all, the Acts passed, except only the Act of Security. Amongst those Acts which have received the Royal Assent is the Act for settling the power of peace and war in the monarch only with advice and consent of Parliament and the Act taking off the prohibition that was on all foreign wines or liquors which was carried by the Court interest, and protested against by Duke Hamilton and near ninety of his party as dishonourable to the Queen, inconsistent with the Grand Alliance and prejudicial to the safety, trade and interest of the kingdom. My Lord Commissioner is now upon the road and some say post for London. It is pretended that the taking off the prohibition on French and Spanish wines is to enlarge the customs, that the Queen may be thereby enabled to support the Army at least for some further time, while supplies are not granted by the Parliament, but if that be the design I'm afraid it will not answer the end. It is said that there never were such reproaches cast upon the Throne, nor more bold things said with respect to standing for liberty, than the day before the adjournment of the Parliament.

W. BROMLEY to [ROBERT HARLEY].

1703, September 25—I know it must be vain in me to give an approbation of a scheme so prepared and so transmitted to me, yet I cannot forbear saying I think it the best method could be taken to lay the load where it ought to be. But every one is not sufficient for these things, they require the ablest hand, and it is you only can raise a building suitable to this foundation.

For want of estimates and appropriations it does not so plainly appear for some years at the beginning of the Revolution as afterwards what the expenses of the army, navy, and civil list were intended to be, at least not to me, after what searches I have been able to make.

I presume you know Lord D   and Sir T. D   cannot be prevailed on to serve again in Parliament. I do not hear that the University are yet fixed; the Master of the Rolls [Trevor] and Sir W. Whitelocke are both talked of by some.

[WILLIAM PATERSON to ROBERT HARLEY.]

1703, September 25. Westminster—At parting I was in hopes by this, to have advised you of a more quiet, and happy conclusion of this long Session of the Scotch Parliament, from the hope, that twelve or fifteen at least of the madmen were grown a little more tractable and tame; but it seems the fit is returned. However, though the Queen's servants did not in the beginning seem to act with such prudence and foresight as could have been wished, yet now at last they have made no small part of amends, and thereby left their opposers so very much in the wrong, both in the matter and in the manner, as possibly will not a little contribute to the more easy accommodation.

I have now a long time been, and am still as sensible as any, of the loose foot, not only that Kingdom, but likewise all the remote territories belonging to the Crown of England are upon, and consequently of many of the real grievances; and shall be always a well wisher, and seeker of their redress, but am apprehensive, that neither the temper, nor judgment of these new Northern reformers, will be capable of contributing much thereto, therefore wish they may not have contrary effect.

It is from the Queen, that not only her own subjects, but the most valuable part of mankind, can most justly and reasonably expect protection and relief; and next to her, to the Successors of the Protestant Line, who, not by divisions and separations, but by closer unions, and better understandings, can ever hope to be enabled to do the great and good things expected from them. And it is towards the accomplishment of those glorious ends, that the thoughts, and endeavours of all good men ought to be employed.

Because I heard it had got a great name with not a few in Scotland, I have within these two or three days been forced to put myself to the grievous trouble and pain of perusing the pamphlet called, "The Right of the two British Monarchies," but cannot say I have learned, or profited anything by reading, or rather saying over this heap of words without understanding, unless in matter of caution towards spending my time better, than looking over any more of the author's works.

I have likewise finished my readings upon the works of our learned Council of Trade, and tho' I always expected to find them but little in the right, yet now I wonder, how they could possibly make shift, to be so very far in the wrong, as they are in most of all they have done. So that you may well venture to think, I have had but an uneasy week's work.

However I must say, the perusal of their performances hath given me some fresh and new views of the means of putting some of the most considerable things in the Trade and Navigation upon another and better foot; but of this I hope to be able to say further at your return.

I am glad to see the siege of Limburg so soon and happily over, since among other mischiefs, that might have attended the delay, or miscarriage of that, or anything relating thereto, the gratifying the humours of those who envy the Duke of Marlborough might have been none of the least, since they already began to pretend, he had left his post and station in the Grand Army, to head a small party in attacking so poor and mean a place, only, as they would have it, for the sake of a considerable sum in contributions.

But as I am particularly glad for this, so in general am sorry to see the matters in Germany and Italy, upon the Rhine and elsewhere at no better pass: God Almighty give the wisdom, temper, and other qualifications needful for this difficult and dangerous conjuncture. *Copy.*

[Lord Godolphin to Robert Harley.]

1703, September 26. Bath—I have found it proper to read some paragraphs of your letter to the Queen. What you propose about Defoe may be done when you will, and how you will.

As to the talk of the hot men of either party, perhaps I have not that due regard for it, which I ought to have, because I am really so extremely indifferent as to any consequences of it, relating to myself; but I am not so in what concerns the Duke of Marlborough and I must own the conduct of Holland in this summer, gives but too just a handle for clamour against our great expense of carrying on this war in their country. The Admiralty must answer for itself.

But though the hot men of both sides may agree in finding the same faults,. they wont agree in assigning the same ▬▬▬ of them, since their anger does not arise from the same grounds ; one side being moved by an inveteracy of a deep root, against anything that is uppermost but themselves, and the other only by the immoderate pride and ambition of a few men ; and we have seen something like this in Scotland where both parties unite to disturb the Government, tho' entirely opposite to each other, but that matter is for the present at an end, and 'tis time my letter should be so, for what relates to Scotland, for the future, I hope we shall have time to talk of it, at London.

[HENRY GUY to ROBERT HARLEY.]

[1703], September 27 [Bath]—Lord Godolphin goes from hence to-morrow for Newmarket. The Queen is pretty well of the gout and goes next week to Windsor. The King of Spain is believed to be now at the Hague. The Duke of Vendôme is retreated back from Trent.

LORD CONINGSBY to [ROBERT HARLEY].

1703, September 28. [Dublin]—I had not the honour of yours of the 11th till last night occasioned by four packets coming in at once, otherwise you may be sure I would not have been so long before I returned my humble thanks for it.

I wish it may be in my power to do any service here. I hope you and every body else will believe I don't want all the inclination imaginable, neither will I ever fail to remember the advice your good father gave me when I came first into this country, not to forget I was an Englishman, but it must be allowed the times are very difficult at this juncture money being beyond imagination scarce and trade low, for the people are the hardest in the world to be persuaded to do anything that is agreeable to what is truly their interest.

The Commons have opened their Session with attacking Mr. Annesley, one of the trustees who is one of their members, for a paragraph in the first report, wherein is laid an imputation on all the judges of the kingdom ;. and before they heard him in his place have condemned it as you'll see by the enclosed vote, their zeal exceeding their knowledge made them add the word Protestant in the vote which gave Mr. Annesley an opportunity when he appeared in his place yesterday to deny that ever he signed any report wherein are such words as the vote mentions, upon which they were so gravelled they were forced to adjourn the debate till this day. As there are some wise and moderate men amongst them we are not without hopes this affair may fall and that they will proceed with the public business. I shall not fail from time to time to send you accounts.

Tho: Lloyd to [Robert Harley].

1703, October 1. Tyne[mouth] Castle—The news that is stirring in
these parts is that the Scots are very high, drinking the Prince of Wales's
health in Scotland as publicly as we drink the Queen's in England; and
that they have a design upon these northern parts, but since their
parliament is prorogued are more moderate.

The Duke of Argyll died last Wednesday morning of the black
"janders". at Cberton, a house that was Captain Bickerstaff's within a
mile of this place. He is to be embalmed and lie in state until his son
Lord Lorne comes out of Flanders, and then to be carried into Scotland.

[P.S.]—Brigadier Lloyd's regiment of dragoons are ordered into the
north, two troops to do duty in this place, two at Berwick, one at
Carlisle, and the rest at Huse (?). This brigadier is a son of Sir Godfrey
Lloyd's, was page to the late King, and out of the house of Leighton in
Shropshire originally.

—— to Robert Harley, at Brampton.

1703, October 5. London—The present Scots news are, That the
Duke of Argyll who immediately upon recovery of his dangerous sickness at Edinburgh, which I suppose you heard of, came to his house
near Newcastle to visit his mistress, and died there on Thursday last.
The account hereof is written hither by his brother Lord Charles who was
present at his death. The providence of God in this end of that great
gentleman, not only for station and interest, but for eminent parts and
endowments of mind, is remarkable as following so soon after his
slighting the grave exhortations he had in his late illness to reform his
vicious and scandalous course of life, if God should bless him with
health. His son the Marquis of Lorne, who was a considerable time
under the tutelage of Mr. Alexr Cunningham, is a very hopeful person,
being sober, thoughtful, a good husband, and having to a more than
ordinary degree the promising character of being a strict observer of
his word: so that it is expected he will not be inferior to his father in
all his good qualifications. I wrote to you in my last that the
Commissioner was on the road which I did on the credit of the Scots
[torn] which did generally agree that the day for his taking journey
was fixed to [torn] that I wrote in, and though it happened otherwise,
yet I find that the [torn] was true; but that he finding some of the
most eminent of his side, as the Marquis of Atholl now Duke of Atholl,
the Lord Chancellor Seafield, and the Viscount of Tarbet now Earl of
Cromarty, so dissatisfied with some of his proceedings, as to be in
hazard of going over to the other side, did put off his journey for some
days to endeavour a reconciliation, but in vain, as I am informed. On
the contrary the breach is so widened, that the Commissioner has
refused to sign a late Act of Council in favour of the Duke of Athole
tho' passed after the ordinary course of law. His Grace came off
hitherward from Edinburgh on Tuesday this day sevennight in the
afternoon and with him the Earls of Morton, Wigton, Balcarres and
Stair. The letters bear that the Duke of Athole comes off the day
after, and the Chancellor and the Earl of Cromarty a few days after
him. None of the Country party are as yet to stir but are to wait the
event of the divided Court party there fighting it out amongst themselves, supposing they may come in time to a share in the spoil. The
Scots Wine Act makes a great noise and occasions divers reflections in
this place. I have heard some members of parliament declare that they

look upon it as the opening a back door to the enemies of England and as the putting in practice already their other Act, whereby they are empowered to observe a neutrality in the wars of England when they please. The Court party to whom only that Act is ascribable are like to be put to a hard shift now to satisfy people here about it. I hope to give you at meeting an account of some circumstances relating to that Act sufficient to "evocuate" all that can be said to excuse it. I can assure you that the Country party had an Act prepared for giving satisfaction to England concerning their friendly inclinations as intending a perpetual alliance with them on terms more favouring the interest of both nations, than (those on) which the late Treaty of Union was prosecuted, which Act was to have [*torn*] by them, if they had not been surprised with an unexpected (adjournment ?). I hope to procure a sight of the copy of that Act for you.

LORD CONINGSBY to [ROBERT HARLEY].

1703, October 9. [Dublin]—The votes of our Commons here I believe you see, and the several addresses have I presume come to your hands, you must not wonder if they contradict one another; but if you have a mind to make a judgment of the people rather do it by the votes than the addresses tho' they too but faintly express what they aim at, at this time. The remonstrance that is preparing will describe them more strongly but that will be likewise far short of the debates that framed it. Three or four heady gentlemen of the South, backed by the Northern party to a man, carry on all these heats, their reasons are different but their end is the same, which is to make my Lord Lieutenant unsuccessful; and I have too much reason to fear they will accomplish it, and when that's done it will require that very wise measures are taken to prevent more dangerous consequences. I am sure in the temper they are in they should not sit whilst we are on business, and that what they aim at above measure and the true reason of the several long adjournments of the Supplies (*sic*). I could say much more but will defer it till I have the honour to see you which I hope to do soon.

[WILLIAM PATERSON to ROBERT HARLEY.]

1703, October 9. Westminster—It is now fourteen days since I gave you the trouble of a line as I do now by reason that Lord Treasurer is not yet come to town. I have nothing to say of any great weight, only to repeat that the face of affairs both at home and abroad requires another kind of resolution and vigour than perhaps ever yet appeared in the councils, especially the public and more solemn councils of this nation, and how we are prepared for this God knows; for humanly speaking I see no hopes unless yourself and two or three choice men of the greatest reputation and interest shall show another kind of readiness and address, and another sort of courage and resolution, than you and they have done yet in this reign.

When I look upon several things and persons as I find them I wonder how things have stuck or how they do stick together. Upon the whole I am now of opinion that the world is much more capable of keeping right and of being in good order than ever I thought it, and that there are many more things of consequence that would keep right and go well as it were of themselves if people would but let them.

I expect to have a whole collection of matters at your return, but care not for committing them to writing, especially till I have seen my

Lord (Godolphin) and settled the necessary preliminaries of this new work I am about to begin...

This letter is almost as confused and involved as the public measures are at present; however I venture it to your hand.

[LORD GODOLPHIN to ROBERT HARLEY.]

1703, October 12. Newmarket—I received yours of the 2nd, with the several papers enclosed at this place, from whence I shall not think of troubling you with any more than to tell you I hope to be in London by the 16th, and that I shall not be there long without seeing you; and that you will prepare the heads of what is proper to be said to the Parliament.

GEORGE HOOPER, Dean of Canterbury, to [ROBERT HARLEY].

[1703,] October 14. Lambeth—The great trouble you have been pleased to take upon you of bringing me towards the Bishopric of St. Asaph, makes it my duty to add this other of knowing what has chanced to intervene in my proceeding to it. The last Friday, when the Confirmation had been appointed for the following Tuesday, and the Consecration for the next Sunday, I was sent for by my Lord Keeper; and found that in the Faculty come to him under the Seal of the Archbishop, that part of it which was word for word the same with that which had passed the Broad Seal for Bishop Barrow in 1670, and for Bishop Lloyd in 1680, for Bishop Jones in the late reign, had been much canvassed in two meetings for that purpose by his Lordship and Mr. Attorney and Mr. Solicitor, and many exceptions taken to it. It gives leave *Recipere in commendam Archideaconatum Asaph et Rectoriam de Landrinio*, and also *Tria quaevis alia Beneficia Curata vel non curata*, with a liberty to exchange those three at pleasure &c. My Lord Keeper's objection, and which he said he was concerned to insist on, was that leave was given to hold more benefices than two; which was against the very statute that had raised the power of licensing: and that his confirming of such a licence would be the attempting a power to dispense against an Act of Parliament. There were other questions that had been made: one in particular concerning the inconsistency of an Archdeaconry with the Bishopric: and another that related to all those *Commendams* in general: whether they being in the *Recipere*, and into which I was not to enter by institution and induction, would be good in law. That they were not good in their opinion I plainly perceived: and tho' I could remove my Lord Keeper's difficulty by changing the *Curata vel non curata* into *Quorum unum tantum sit Curatum* or by leaving the *Tria Beneficia* quite out: yet I found there was a difficulty of my own for me to consider, and I was to think whether it would be fit for me to go on with a Faculty, that was brought under such a disparagement; and would be known abroad to be held invalid by the chiefest of the profession. I understood clearly from my Lord Keeper and from another of the company that it would not be advisable to trust to such a title for the better half of the Bishopric: and besides I saw it was necessary for me however to go back for a new Warrant and Faculty. Proposing therefore my case to my Lord Nottingham and finding that I could not be secure but by Act of Parliament, I desired his Lordship to move the Queen that the other *Commendams* which were in the *Retinere*, and which only were sure

might be enlarged, and that I might keep Exeter not only for two years but thenceforth until such a security should be got for the Archdeaconry and Landrinio; and Lambeth for a year, and thenceforth in like manner: I proposing that the year certain of Lambeth should go to the making amends for the incidental charges now rising anew. This was moved on Sunday to the Queen, but demurred to, because the Archbishop who had the promise of Lambeth for Dr. Gibson might already have given away Dr. Gibson's living to another: and how this matter stood, my Lord Nottingham was to inquire. Upon inquiry his Lordship had it confessed to him on Tuesday that the Doctor had not parted with his living; but it was intended for one that had none, a worthy man, that was newly persuaded to take the oaths &c. (a cousin of his Grace's). This answer my Lord carries to Windsor next Sunday, and intends to move the Queen again upon it; hoping that my Lord Treasurer will be there then from Newmarket, and contribute to the dispatch of a business that if it lies long will be subject to various reports. It was unhappy to me that my Lord Treasurer has not been in town, and therefore I have put a paper into my Lord Nottingham's hand, that his Lordship may the better conceive the reasonableness of that which I have desired. A copy of it, I have here inserted, in the loose paper for your perusal, and am now after all this tedious account to beg your pardon for pursuing you so far, and into a retirement you seldom enjoy, with such an impertinence.

H. S[T. JOHN] to ROBERT HARLEY.

1703, October 16th—I have waited thus long before I returned you thanks for your obliging letter, because I thought it unreasonable to interrupt the pleasures of so keen a sportsman as you are, in this season. But since the time of your return to London draws near, it may not be amiss to use you a little beforehand to that which you must bear so much of when you are in town. News I pretend not to send you, because wherever you are I believe you still bear more than you care for, and the chit chat of this place will bear transcribing no more than one of Sir Chuffer's speeches. There never yet was more gravity and less thought, more noise and less mirth.

I suppose you know that the second part of a very famous History [Clarendon's] is ready to be published. Before it is a very long and politic epistle to the Queen, full of temper, and the calmest counsels. Most of those who have seen it are of opinion that it is full as well writ as the preface prefixed to the first volume.

That you may return quickly to town and bring up, the only good thing a man can go into the country for, health and fresh recruits of vigour, is what I ardently wish, who am from my soul, dear Mr. Harlay (sic) your faithful unalterable friend, &c.

[P.S.]—I cannot close my letter without renewing a petition I formerly made to you, and which I hoped you was not very averse to granting, which is that you would take my word once for a chaplain, as there is nobody I can recommend that I esteem half so much as the person I recommend him to, so you may be confident I believe you will have no reason to repent your choice if it falls upon Mr. Stratford, but you know him yourself and have heard of him from others.

[LORD GODOLPHIN to ROBERT HARLEY.]

1703, October 21. St. James's—I have received the favour of your letter and shall be very impatient till I can have the satisfaction of seeing you. I have spoken with Lord Nottingham about the vacancy of a Welsh judge. Cox is to succeed Paulet, and he tells me you spoke to him for Banastre to succeed Cox, but has promised that shall be deferred till you come to town. I hear Sir Christopher M[usgrave] will be here next Saturday, and of all hands that anger is gone out against me. I am of the Scotman's mind that was not afraid of death but disliked the "cukery."

―――― to [WILLIAM] PATERSON, in Westminster.

1703, October 23. [Hanover]—At my return here from Hamburgh I found two letters of yours. I intend to write next post to the Speaker. I hope you will deliver my letter and endeavour to learn of him whether he really desires I should write to him as often as anything occurs here which I may think worth his while. I wish you had given me your sentiments more fully about Scots affairs. Pray let me know what you think may be the consequences of the Queen's refusing her consent to the Act of Security, as also what are thought to be Her Majesty's chief reasons for so doing, since I fancy her compliance in that matter might have contributed very much to the quiet of her own reign in the ancient kingdom. And I am afraid there are but few who think that her care of those who are named to succeed her hath been a strong motive on the other side. I should be glad also of an account of what passed in relation to Lord Marchmont's overture, since however ill concerted that Act may have been; I cannot think but it was resented with more passion, more seeming contempt and scorn of the House of Hanover than one would think became the prudence of a wise assembly. As for the opinion of people here concerning the proceedings in Scotland, I can say but little, the Elector and his ministers being very reserved on that head. It is natural enough to think that some things could not be very pleasing, witness what I have said about my Lord Marchmont's overture, and another which they say was made by Lord Roxburgh for excluding from the crown of Scotland those of the Lutheran persuasion ; which appeared somewhat odd especially considering the good opinion every body here had conceived of his Lordship and the civilities he received from the Electress and some others of her family.

The Emperor's affairs seem to grow worse and worse daily. Count Stirum's loss is found to be much greater than was at first believed; the list which I have seen makes the killed and wounded mount up to very near 5000. We are in continual fears of hearing of Tallard's joining the Bavarians and other French in the Empire. If that happens the Emperor ought not to look upon himself as very safe even in his capital, especially considering the progress the rebels make in Hungary. In a word the prospect of affairs everywhere seems to be very uncomfortable, and unless the new King of Spain's expedition hath the hoped for success I see not well what can save us.

[LORD GODOLPHIN to ROBERT HARLEY.]

1703, October 25—Since I received the favour of your letter I have been at Kensington. The Queen would have the summons sent as usual and the Prince's Council ordered to attend.

If you will call upon me tomorrow in the evening and carry me to Kensington I will stay at home till you come.

Your news from Newfoundland is very good, and so is the arrival of the Lisbon fleet; but all this will not hinder the great clamours which

I hear are preparing against the management of our sea affairs, which must needs be very disagreeable to the Queen and particularly uneasy to the Prince; in short I expect to see the whole Government torn to pieces, with no friends to support it but some few in place, and it cannot but vex one the more to see them lost for so very trivial an occasion.

THO : LLOYD to [ROBERT HARLEY].

1703, November 2. Tynemouth Castle—Mr. John Campbell, brother of the Duke of Argyll is in possession of Cherton house (*see* p. 70 *ante*), and another on behalf of the Duchess. They have turned out the Duke's mistress, and are both at law about the estate and goods.

LORD CONINGSBY to [ROBERT HARLEY,] Speaker.

1703, November 3. Dublin—The committing Sir William Robison for giving into the house the estimate of the debt due to the Army in the same method it ever was in this kingdom has obliged me to stay here longer than I intended, and has prevented my being to do my duty at the first opening of the Parliament. I intend to leave this place this week and make as much haste as possible to attend the service there, and when I won't fail to give you a particular account of all our transactions.

[LORD GODOLPHIN to ROBERT HARLEY.]

1703, November 4—I have been with Mr. Secretary Hedges and left with him the paper of names and settled the method he is to take in concerting matters from time to time. I believe he will take to his part very faithfully and diligently and be desirous on all occasions to receive his instructions from you. He seemed to agree Sir Edward Seymour would thwart everything, but that he must be called to two or three meetings at least, till his opposition became open and avowed. Besides these meetings and those agreed upon last night to be at your house, it is necessary above all the rest that the Duke of Marlborough and you and I should meet regularly, at least twice a week if not oftener, to advise upon everything that shall occur; and if you will give me leave to propose let Saturday evening at the same time and place be the first meeting. In the meantime I must beg you to be careful that neither of our names be mentioned, as to our knowledge of the least tittle of the discourse betwixt Lord Nottingham and Sir Christopher Musgrave as to the conversation his Lordship had with the Queen.

I have taken care in the matter of De Foe. It would avoid a good deal of trouble and uneasiness if Mr. Mansell would recommend Banastre to be the Welsh judge. I shall speak to the Queen this night about the affair of Sir Christopher Musgrave.

DANIEL DE FOE to ROBERT HARLEY, Speaker to the House of Commons.

1703, November 9th—As there is something surprising in your bounty to a mortified stranger, so I am more than usually at a loss in what manner to express my sense of it; but at the same time that you stoop to do good you subject yourself to a necessity of bearing the impertinence of a thankful temper.

Of all the examples in sacred story none moves my indignation like that of the ten lepers who were healed by our Saviour. I, like that one grateful wretch am come back to pay the tribute of thankfulness which this so unexpected goodness commands from me.

And, though I think myself bound to own you as the principal agent of this Miracle, yet, having some encouragement from you to expect more particularly *to know my benefactors*, I cannot but wish for that discovery, that my acknowledgments may in some measure be proportioned to the quality of the persons, and the value of the favour.

It remains for me to conclude my present application with this humble petition, that if possible I may by some means or other know what I am capable of doing, that my benefactors whoever they are may not be ashamed of their bounty, as misapplied. Not that I expect to be able to merit so much goodness, but as a grateful temper is always uneasy to be loaded with benefits, so the *virtue* which I call gratitude has always so much pride in it, as makes it push at a retribution, though 'tis unable to effect it. Whoever are the principals in this favour I cannot but profess myself a debtor wholly to yourself, who till I may be otherwise instructed appears the original *as to me*. And in the kindness the manner is so obliging, and all the articles of it so generous, that as a man astonished at the particulars, I am perfectly unable to express my sense of it.

Only in the humblest manner I can most earnestly pray that I may have some opportunity put into my hands by Providence to make more explicit acknowledgments. And that as I have received such an obligation as few ever received, I might be able to make some such sort of return as no man ever made.

And as I am sure I write this from an honest heart readier by far to perform than to promise, so I take the freedom to repeat the assurance of a man ready to dedicate my life and all possible powers to the interest of so generous and so bountiful benefactors, being equally overcome with the nature as well as the value of the favour I have received.

D[aniel De] F[oe] to James Stancliffe, Ironmonger Lane, London.

1703, November—One trouble always brings on another, and as you have embarked for me in the first part of this matter, you must not refuse to be the messenger of my acknowledgments.

I can hardly promise myself that what I have wrote will express my sense of the obligation I have upon me to Mr. Harley, and I wish you would make it up by saying everything you can imagine a man overcome with kindness ought to say.

I am at some loss about the papers I told you I had prepared to publish on my enlargement. I would do nothing of that nature that should be offensive to my benefactors, but I am persuaded none of that party of men which are touched by me have any hand in an action so generous as this, and am of opinion what was in my thoughts that way would rather please than disoblige those that can entertain any thought of kindness or compassion for my case, yet I shall continue to stop the press in this case till I hear your opinion, though the substance was never so necessary to my own vindication.

The Earl of Rochester to [Robert Harley,] Speaker.

[1703,] December 17. New Park—That which occasions my troubling you now is to acquaint you I have an offer made me by a gentleman, a member of your house, to put into my hands the patent that Saracole hath had from the late King for his water engine, if it may be of use to the New River Company, which I am inclined to think it may, because Soames is pretty earnest to purchase it. I am told I may have

it on pretty reasonable terms, which I shall be willing to venture upon
if you think it may be useful to our interest in the water shares; and I
must give my answer within five or six days.

The Earl of Bradford to his cousin [Robert Harley].

1703, December 20—This is to bring you my humble thanks for your
invitation for Christmas Day, and to assure you that there is no person
whatsoever I would more willingly attend than yourself; but lying still
under a cloud in my own country, the reasons of which are not known
there; and finding no intention in you last night of removing that
worthy person we spoke of from his elevated post, though no ways
obstructing this other intended preferment, will make me appear so
awkward a guest as will render me altogether unfit for the celebrating so
great a festival and to make a part of so good company, and therefore
I do very unwillingly hope you will excuse me.

The Earl of Rochester to [Robert Harley]

1703, December 22—I give you many thanks for the favour of your
letter last night. This affair is only to know your opinion whether I
should buy the patent which Mr. Wilkins has in his power to let us
have for the New River. If we have it not Soames will have it, and
Mr. Wilkins by my son sent me word he could defer parting with it a
little time, but not long.

Your approbation or dislike of this bargain is what I would be glad
to receive, or that you would yourself discourse with Mr. Wilkins, and
one way or other finish this affair with him, or let him see the reason
why I do not determine it within the time he was willing to allow me
for it.

[Lord Godolphin to Robert Harley.]

1703, December 25—I heartily return your good wishes and with
more reason for the sake of the public which I hope you may live long
to serve. The Colonels of the army are most of them as arbitrary as so
many Pachas and none of them perhaps more so than Brigadier H.

I shall take care to give the Queen, the letter directed to Her
Majesty.

The Duke of Marlborough is gone this morning to Petworth in order
to meet the King of Spain at Portsmouth, though we have not yet any
authentic news of his being seen from the coast.

Part of Callemburgh's squadron is passed by the Downs; this makes
me but the more in pain for not hearing of Fairborne.

Matters grow worse and worse in Germany; and what Sir E.
S[eymour] told us long ago, begins now to be true, viz.: that we had
nothing to trust to, but our Portugal expedition.

I am glad to hear you talk of calming people in these holidays, and
should be glad to have your directions what part I could be able to take
towards making men a little more moderate.

I have not only thanked Mr. Solicitor [Harcourt] myself, but done him
the best offices I can to the Queen, and tomorrow I will speak to my
Lord Keeper to dispatch the matter of Banastre, for which he seemed to
be much concerned.

I believe the person who writes that long narrative is Redmond Joye,
a scandalous perjured fellow, as I have heard by Mr. Keightley and

Mr. Southwell. I fancy too that Lord Coningsby can give some account of him.

I have much to say to you about the Scotch Examinations, and an account to give you of some particulars of it, where the Duke of Marlborough's name, and mine, are mentioned. What you write of Lord Cromartie is true, and the Duke of Queensberry has complained of him for it.

CHARLES GORING [M.P. for Steyning] to ROBERT HARLEY, Speaker.

[1703,] December 28—Lest you should not have an account from any other hand of the King of Spain's character and person as we have it here, I trouble you with this. Yesterday Sir George Rooke told me his passage from Holland to Spithead was but forty eight hours : and that the King is of an extraordinary good temper, and not the least out of humour, sick or well ; his person is well both as to his looks and shape, and so much exceeds his picture that he that drew it ought to be hanged, he's a little thoughtful in his temper, and very observing in his looks. I saw him at dinner where he was served after the Spanish fashion and ate enough to keep a Lazarus six months. The Dukes of Somerset and Marlborough came on board about four o'clock and after waiting about half an hour, the Duke of Somerset was called in and delivered his letter and compliment. After a little time the Duke of Marlborough went in and the other came out ; then the private gentry and amongst the rest your humble servant, who was presented by my Lord Granville by the name of Count Goring, and next to me my Lord Scarbrough by the name of Doctor. This morning the King came on shore at eight, where the mayor made a speech and Sir George Rooke vouched for the truth of it ; he's gone to Petworth, goes to morrow for Windsor and so back. He has a great respect for all members of Parliament, and if you should go see him he'd certainly kiss you.

[LORD GODOLPHIN to ROBERT HARLEY.]

1703-4, January [24 ?]—I forgot last night to mention Mr. Paterson, since which I had the papers enclosed from him, which will not suffer me to forget him any longer ; but I must own his notions seem to me for the most part very confused, not to say impracticable, and he talks still of *retrieving public credit*, as if money were still at 8 per cent. However I have some doubts that the public necessities may in this coming year bring money to a higher interest, and I am very willing to do anything that you shall think reasonable for Mr. Paterson.

Attached to this letter are two papers in a copyist's handwriting on the state of the Revenue, and making suggestions for its improvement. The first is dated January 5, 1703-4. The second, dated Westminster January 24, 1703[-4] is apparently addressed to Harley, for it contains the following addition in Paterson's handwriting :—

" I have likewise some affairs relating to yourself to discourse you about, but you are now grown so inaccessible-and in such perpetual hurry as I do by no means understand, and, to be plain, I begin to [be] afraid there is something fatal in it, and my concern for you is so great that though I doubt I have already suffered in your opinion by free speaking, yet the friendship and regard I have for you will not suffer but that I do it once more ; and whatever be the issue, when you give me a fair opportunity I shall discharge what I think is my duty to my friend, to whom since our first friendship I am after due search and consideration I am not conscious in the least of being wanting in sincerity; and, were it not that I am afraid 'it would look too like presumption, I durst venture to say, even in prudence. I write likewise to my Lord Treasurer this morning and shall enclose a copy of this letter excepting the last paragraph."

Dr. CHARLES DAVENANT to [ROBERT HARLEY].

1703[-4], January 31—Some of the company has been so impertinent as to spread a foolish lie of what passed t'other night at your house between me and Mr. St. John, and have represented as if I had been mightily insulted and that I bore it with Christian patience. There was indeed a word dropped that might have been improved into a quarrel by any who wanted to have a quarrel upon his hands, or that desired to quarrel in such a manner as to be sure of being prevented. For my part I'm not conscious that anything was said unfit for Mr. St. John to utter or me to hear. In a tavern perhaps I had replied somewhat more angrily than I did to one expression of his but I judged it indecent in the highest degree to push a matter in the Speaker's house. When I opened myself it was in order to an éclaircissement with one for whom I had always an esteem and inclination to like and love, and into whose company I might casually light as I did then. I expressed some resentment of what he had formerly done and that I was willing an end should be put to the difference, but intimating that tho' I was fat and near fifty yet being the son of a Lieutenant-General I did not think myself hors du combat. What he replied to this in another place might have gone farther. I cannot help being a little nice in this matter, and were I fourscore I should be loath to lose the reputation I have hitherto preserved in more than two or three trials. I hope nothing of this comes from Mr. St. John. By the laws of hospitality you are bound to do us both equal justice and to say what really passed, if the story has any further progressed.

WILLIAM PENN to [ROBERT HARLEY].

1703-4, February 9. Warminghurst—If I keep no better distance to thy great post and greater qualifications thou must impute it to the easiness thou hast long indulged me in. Nor at this time do I think I ought to be in pain for an apology, since I write upon a subject agreed, and by an authority allowed of, and long after the time expected.

I need not tell so knowing a person that the colonies in America have been almost all made by private undertakers; some to enjoy their consciences more quietly, others out of necessity, and lastly some involuntarily, as being delinquents. New England, Connecticut, Rhode Island, Jersey, Pennsylvania, and Virginia and Maryland too in part, were begun on the first foot, but the two last (Virginia especially) have been frequented by the necessitous, and much stocked with criminals, which compared with New England, &c. for the time of planting, shows evidently how much better the Colonies thrive in proprietary hands than under the immediate government of the crown, so that which 'tis suggested the crown loses by trade, through the over indulgence of proprietary Governors, is, if that were true, much more than answered by the greater improvement, and trade that in proportion follows upon such improvement, in proprietary governments, to say nothing of their better regiment as to manners, and common conversation. Now this is our unhappiness, that though we in New England, Rhode Island, Plymouth, Connecticut, New Jersey, and Pennsylvania went thither to be quiet, by ample grants from the crown, to make and keep our selves easy and safe in our civil and religious privileges, yet we are made extremely uneasy by officious and turbulent persons, who to recommend themselves to the Bishops and especially of L —— here, do us all the despite they can, in the name of the church, and the revenue; though the church enjoys the same liberty they do that made those Colonies, and though the Queen's officers both in the revenue and Admiralty are in those respective Colonies, and may as freely exercise their powers as if they were in the kingdom of England. So that there is nothing more to do or desire but to have the Government, that they may be lords of our labours, have all the employments in their hands, and make us Dissenters in 'our own countries; a design barbarous as well as unjust; since it was to be free of the church's power and out of her reach we went so far, and not to make Colonies for her, but from her, for our selves.

' And as we are a people not over and above in the interest of the clergy, too many of them seem engaged to undermine us even there. I wonder what they would be at, where they think we will or can go next. Now I humbly conceive, this work is very dishonorable to the Government and extremely disserviceable, for it sours the people, disheartens them in their improvements and trade, for one is the spring of t'other, and the Colonies must, and I assure thee do, dwindle; yet I will venture to say that we have done more to make a country in twenty three years than any of the Colonies called the Crown's have done in a hundred years, for Virginia has not a town bigger, if half so big, as Knightsbridge, while we have severall bigger, and one as large, as Windsor; New England, as Reading or Shrewsbury, and twenty as big as Maidenhead; so Plymouth and Connecticut; and for New York—a Dutch proprietary improvement, the West India Company—one as big as Bath, to say nothing of several pretty little towns in the Jerseys, where converse, education and traffic are to be had, the way to make a country and civilize mankind, as well as for preservation.

Now for my own immediate affair, I have waited these two years to be off or on, about my government; to be confirmed in it after the shake given in a former Parliament, or since it was and is so great a part of my grant, and much of the reason of my undertaking and vast expence, as well as many toils and hazards, and consumption of the best share of my life, that I may have an equivalent or some suitable consideration.

I asked of the Commissioners for Trade and Pl[antations] 30,000*l.*, of which I am contented to take one moiety in things to be found there, not thinking the sum a proportionable satisfaction for what it has cost me, to settle and support the Government and Colony, and what I may reasonably expect by it to me and mine in the present and after time.

First the undertaking was chiefly encouraged by the grant of Government, which cost me 10,557*l.* in less than three years time, which was many thousands more than I received for land, which my own interest made so valuable and not the Crown's.

. 2ndly: I have paid the Deputy Governor out of my private estate, as well as supported myself in government and here also to maintain and preserve it against the attempts of our enemies from 1681 to 1703.

3rdly. I never had but 2000*l.* English sterling and that but three years ago, which did not pay my last voyage thither, living two years there, and my return, much less my attendance in town two years more, to obtain some favourable issue upon the reason of my hasty return.

4thly. My case is very singular in two respects, one that I had a debt upon the crown of about 16,000l. of money lent by my father for the victualling of the navy 1667, which was shut up in the Exchequer; the other is, that I have sown largely, as the crop upon the ground shows, but I never reaped one yet, which is not the case of the most of the other Colonies, so that instead of enjoying it for a satisfaction, it becomes a perfect mine to me and my family as well as an irreparable disappoint-ment of the people that made it a country, who were neither criminals nor necessitous, if there be not a due consideration to confirm the laws and constitution I have settled them under, and reprise me and mine, for the present and future loss that must accrue to us by the resignation of the Government. I asked indeed some honorary mark, as a founder of the Colony, viz., as the first—hereditary—Privy Councillor or Chief Justice, or the like, which I shall not insist upon, contenting myself with the rights of landlord and lord of the manor of the country. But in a letter to our great friend the Lord High Treasurer I would accept of 20,000l. [remainder missing.]

[Lord Godolphin to Robert Harley.]

1703-4, February 10—Mr. Lowndes tells me we had so good a day yesterday in the House of Commons that I think I shall scarce need to trouble you any more this session about the business depending there, though I know very well that matter must be always watched from hour to hour, and there's no such thing as safety till the Black Rod knocks at the door.

William Penn to Robert Harley, Speaker.

1704, March 3—Give my leave to put thee in mind of thy kind appointment of to-night and pray suffer me to enclose the instances that parallel the case of the New Yorkers. I know that whole affair and 'tis calamitous enough.

Ri[chard] Avenant to Robert Harley, Speaker.

1704, April 24—I perceive there is an unhappy dispute betwixt the governors of Stourbridge School (as you may please to see by the paper of the case and proceedings enclosed) about the choice of a school-master, which I am sorry for because Dr. Hallifax and my partner Mr. John Wheeler, my good friends Mr. Will. Tristram (who is some relation to me) and Mr. Richd. Baker, son of Mr. Nic. Baker late of Worcester, who are four of the governors that voted for one Mr. Woodin, and afterwards for peace sake named others as third persons for an accommodation and particularly now insist on one Mr. Wentworth as candidate for it, are very much concerned they cannot prevail with any one of the other four to vote for him, but still adhere to their first nomination, who it seems is one Mr. Underhill, son of one called Dr. Underhill, formerly of Ludlow and brother-in-law to Mr. Peter Piercehouse, trainbearer to Lord Somers when Lord Chancellor, whom he now solicits against my friend's interest, and Mr. Piercehouse saith he will petition the Queen and Council on Mr. Underhill's behalf. My friend's adversary governors are purely influenced by two or three that would govern the town and neighbourhood, for they are nothing of themselves; one is Mr. John Sparry being a stingy humorist, Humfrey Jeston and Mr. Edward Milward two old easy men, and the other one Thomas Oliver a butcher, but do as they are led by others. I am earnestly solicited by my said four friends to use my best interest with you on their behalf, that if possible this Mr. Underhill may not be imposed upon them and the town; therefore I am bold humbly to entreat your interest and favour in their behalf: who tell me that Mr. Wentworth will attend you next Thursday (if you please to admit him) that you may see him and talk with him as to his fitness, and by whom to be examined in London as to his learning, if you advise that way, and to whom you would please to advise him to solicit for him in this matter: and receive your full directions. I perceive the Bishop of Worcester is by Lord Somers procured not to be against Mr. Underhill so that I find my friends are loath to abide by his determination of the matter or examination of Mr. Underhill. Mr. Wentworth will procure you the School Charter to read if you please, and if it be thought fit Mr. Wentworth should be examined by divines and schoolmasters in Stourbridge neighbourhood, (though he is a stranger to them and many of them may be influenced by those that lead if not drive my friend's adversaries) yet I believe on your speaking to him he will submit thereto: but then my friends pray this examination in the country may be by Mr. Ashenhurst, archdeacon of Derby and rector of King's Swinford two miles from Stourbridge; Mr. Newry, minister of Kinfare two miles thence: Mr. Bowles, rector of Enville four miles thence, Mr. Howard of Kidderminster five miles; and Mr. Parkinson chief schoolmaster of Birmingham eight miles thence, or any three of them, to determine this matter for this time, in which a majority otherwise cannot be had. I beg you will excuse my boldness in giving you so many troublesome letters and have nothing to plead for myself but the liberty you gave me.

Meeting of THE PRIVY COUNCIL.

1704, April 27. St. James's—Record of Robert Harley being sworn of the Privy Council and taking his seat at the Board. *Signed by Edward Southwell. Royal Seal.* With copy of the Oath taken by him.

SAMUEL OGLE to [ROBERT HARLEY].

1704, April 29. Dublin—On behalf of the Presbyterian ministers of Ireland, whose pension of 600*l.* per annum granted by Charles II., doubled by William III. as an acknowledgment of these gentlemen's services in remaining in that country during all the time of King James's power, and keeping their people together to make a stand in defence of the protestant interest; and confirmed by Queen Anne, which was distributed in small proportions among a great number who had not congregations sufficient to maintain them, had been withdrawn by a vote of the Irish Parliament.

RICHARD AVENANT to ROBERT HARLEY, Speaker.

1704, May 6. Droitwich. I troubled you with papers and letters concerning a school [Stourbridge, *see* April 24] which I hope you received. I humbly beg you'll befriend the affair; in case you have any person to recommend the one...moiety of the electors will give their votes to whom ever you recommend.

[DANIEL DE FOE to ROBERT HARLEY.]

1704, May 12th, Friday—It is a particular misfortune to me, that I had not the honour of seeing you last night, and 'tis the more so, in that I received no orders when to give my further attendance. And yet, Sir, I had waited with all the patience became me in this particular, till your affairs had permitted, or your pleasure approved, of giving me audience; had not my uneasiness at this time prevailed on good manners from the following occasion :—

I know the duty lay on me to conceal the favour I received in your admitting a man lately made despicable to so near and so advantageous a conversation, and therefore have carefully concealed from all the world what otherwise I should have valued myself upon on all occasions, that I had the honour so much as to be known to you. But it is impossible for me to describe the confusion I was in, when I was publicly told on Wednesday last, when, where, and how often I had the honour of your conversation, and imagining their intelligence was *ab inferis*, expected to hear every morning the particulars of our discourse.

I am confident you will pardon the importunity of this letter, when you reflect how earnest I was, not only to acquaint you with this, but also to let you know the accident which brought it to pass; and the method by which any ill consequence from it may be prevented.

I am your most humble petitioner, that you will please to abate me all those ecstasies and extravagances a necessary acknowledgment of your generous concern for me would lead me to. I can no more express myself, than I can forget the obligation, and I choose to be perfectly silent from the impossibility of putting my sense of it into words, and the hopes I have that the same providence, which I humbly recognize as the first mover of your thoughts in my favour, will yet put an occasion into my hands by faithful and useful application to satisfy you that I am the gratefullest wretch alive. *Conclusion torn off.*

Postscript.—If you please to let a note be left, or any other way, with the maid servant at Mr. Auditor's Chambers, I shall call there for your orders, or directed [to me] at Jones's Coffee house in Finch Lane next the Ex[change].

[DANIEL DE FOE] to ROBERT HARLEY.

[1704, May 16,] Tuesday—It is very unhappy that I who have so seldom the advantage as well as honour of your notice should meet such united interruptions in the least occasion of its return.

I received last Friday a letter appointing me to wait on you on Thursday evening at six o'clock. I was at the coffee house after four that evening and no letter was come, and by the exactest notice I can have the messenger did not leave it till after the time I was to have been at the place. As soon as I received it I took care by a letter left at your house to signify the disappointment and to entreat your further orders. To my surprise they tell me the person who left the letter called again to know if it had been delivered. This causes me to suppose my letter has not reached your hands, though left with your porter last Friday night.

I impatiently wait to receive your orders and to inform you of the disappointment, wishing, if possible, the time may come that you may find this neglected fellow serviceable or at least make him so.

Meeting of PRIVY COUNCIL.

1704, May 18, St. James's—Certificate that Robert Harley, Speaker of the House of Commons, was that day sworn one of the Queen's Principal Secretaries of State. *Signed by John Povey.*

The COMMISSIONERS for TRADE and PLANTATION to ROBERT HARLEY, Secretary of State.

1704, May 19. Whitehall—Informing him that the principal Secretaries of State were appointed Commissioners for Trade and Plantations, in addition to those whose duty it was to give their constant attendance, and asking for his assistance on extraordinary occasions.

Signed by Lord Dartmouth, Robert Cecil, Ph. Meadowes, Wm. Blathwayt, John Pollexfex, and Mat. Prior.

SIR WILLIAM TRUMBULL to [ROBERT HARLEY].

1704, May 20. Bath—Congratulating him on his appointment as one of the Secretaries of State.

SIR J[OHN] BLAND to [ROBERT HARLEY].

1704, May 21. Hulme—Amongst the rest of your friends give me leave to congratulate you on your Secretary's place. I had letters this post to remind me of securing my election in time, for upon your appointment they apprehend there will be a new parliament, and in answer I have written that I had satisfied my curiosity enough, and had been at so much expense and trouble about elections and attending the parliament that I was resolved to decline the service this next election ; and as I am mayor I cannot return myself if there be a dissolution betwixt now and Michaelmas. I am glad to hear Mr. Coke hath got such a fat sinecure and hope he is so too.

SIR RICHARD COCKS to ROBERT HARLEY, at Whitehall.

1704, May 22. Near Evesham—I think it my duty to tell you the papists in these parts were never so armed and horsed. They and their servants to the number of ten rode through Evesham on a market day with pistols and other fire-arms. Their pretence was to go to a cock match. The country are very uneasy at it and by their repeated instances force me to write ; and I believe if you inquire you will find them better horsed and armed than any other gentlemen in England of double their fortunes. I can speak knowingly that most if not all those that were uneasy under King William do not seem to be in a good humour now ; and many of them have before given too much occasion to make the fearful uneasy and expect some ill design against the Queen and the present establishment. I know too much to be silent and hardly enough to complain of ; and am in no apprehension of danger from this often baffled, deluded, and I think contemptible party.

The DUKE OF NEWCASTLE to his cousin [ROBERT HARLEY].

1704, May 22. Haughton—I may say without compliment your being in the secretary's office is the greatest encouragement to me, and the Queen could not have done herself and her subjects more service.

If the Duke of Marlborough can recover, as you hope, this mismanagement of the Germans it will be the more glorious for him.

H. [HUMPHREYS] BISHOP OF HEREFORD to [ROBERT HARLEY].

1704, May 22. Hereford—I do with a heart full of joy most sincerely congratulate your advancement to a place of so great honour and trust.

I know it is a laborious and difficult station, having spent some time in a secretary of state's family in a very difficult time also; but I know Mr. Secretary Harley is more than *par oneri* as well as *honori*, and will make the work of it easy to himself as well as happy to the whole nation.

LORD CONINGSBY to [ROBERT HARLEY].

1704, May 22. Hampton Court [co. Hereford]—I do with as much pleasure as any body congratulate your being placed in the station I hear you are, because I am sure it will be a great satisfaction to the kingdom to have the post filled with one upon whom in our present circumstances they may depend. Her Majesty, my good Lord Treasurer, and other ministers who are most trusted by her will quickly find the difference of having one in that employment who is entirely in her and their interest, from another who it is to be doubted had strange and mistaken views.

J. GRAHAM to [ROBERT HARLEY].

1704, May 23. Levens—My respect for you as well as my obligations to you justly require all manner of acknowledgments I am capable of. Though I have been long out of the world, I do not forget that it is both practical and necessary for old courtiers not to omit their respects to new ones; indeed I am much pleased with the news of your succeeding Lord Nottingham, and as I do truly rejoice the Seals are in so good hands, I am pleased they are so soon disposed of, for we are in the Country putting out and into places much faster than at Court. I was very much satisfied with the late strokes and changes, and hope by this of Sir Roger's we may expect in time a finish, and cannot but honour Sir William and his way of proceeding, not doubting but in time he will make a thorough one. Things done severally and by degrees will be the most lasting. I cannot doubt but in due time some chops will be sent northward where in my poor opinion they are as necessary as in any place of England. I am in dirt and rubbish when at home, plagued with public business when abroad, and nothing to keep my mind in quiet, but more such news as I had last post. I will take this occasion, because correspondence when not necessary is troublesome, to pay my respects to the Auditor, not doubting but I shall soon have occasion to give him a letter of thanks hearing last week Grannondinus, at whose door my   had laid a month hath now dispatched it. Next to Sir William my thanks are due to your brother, a favour I will never forget. When Sir Roger, Sir Nicholas, the Thracian, Sir Chuffer's successor, and my worthy friend young Sir Roger, meet I desire my respects may be thrown amongst them wishing them all happiness and a good tip (?) for these parts, now the neighbouring kingdom affords not one drop of wine, but for our comfort we hope there is a prospect of good agreement there. Excuse this trouble from one that wishes you happiness and success in this new employment, and in all things you undertake, since I daresay your deeds as well as your wishes will tend to the good of this poor Nation.

John Tutchin to Robert Harley, Principal Secretary of State.

1704, May 24—I have had concerns with all the Secretaries of State for several years last past. I need not tell your Honour it was not for my private advantage, but the service of my country is my business without purchase or pay. And I desire the same favour of your Honour as I had from my Lord Nottingham who never tired me with a long attendance; I wish I could say no worse of him. Your Honour well knows that the French fleet is put to sea, and when I have discovered to your Honour that it was victualled by her Majesty's subjects from her Majesty's dominions, and have shown your Honour the names of the ships and their masters, the places whence they came, and the ports in France where they delivered the provisions, I conclude it will be worthy your notice, which, God willing, I intend to do at your office in a day or two's time.

The Same to the Same.

1704, May 26—Further on the subject of a clandestine trade with France, by which means their fleet had been victualled. The reply to his letter may be left at Mr. Peter Hall's, at South Office in Green Dragon Court in Southwark.

Sir Robert Davers to [Robert Harley].

1704, May 27. Rougham [Suffolk]—Pray give me leave to wish you joy of the honour bestowed on you. I remembered what you said to me just before I took my leave of you, that the Whigs would not come in, but when Lord Nottingham laid (sic) down it was reported here that he was turned out, and the Whigs upon it grew more insolent than they were before, and said all things were to come into their hands again; and many were named to be secretaries, but when I heard you had that place I was at ease again.

Recommends Mr. Turner, a nephew of Sir Symond D'Ewes, for the living of Transton, two miles off, worth about 20l. per annum, which is likely to become vacant.

Sir Richard Cocks to Lord Berkeley.

1704, May 27—I sent a letter of congratulation to Mr. Secretary Harley and indeed without a compliment I believe most people in the Protestant interest are pleased with his preferment. When my pen was upon my paper I could not forbear giving him an account of the fears and uneasiness of many the best affected to Her Majesty's government at the unusual grandeur of the Papists; at their appearing in arms at public places, and at the number of their good horses; as for Papists in our county they are so inconsiderable they are not worth taking notice of, and without any further inquiry; I know by the report of men of undoubted reputation many have lamented it when they have seen them appear at fairs and ride in numbers well armed through market towns on market days.· When we put the laws in execution against the Papists in order to disarm them and to take away their horses, in those places where we could find no arms nor any horses worth five pounds there are many horses for coach and saddle of much greater value, and there are visibly arms for the master and his servants. Her Majesty has no subject that wishes better to her person and government than I do, and therefore I could not but officiously give Mr. Secretary this hint to inquire if common fame spoke truth: viz., that if over all England there were the same practices. The laws oblige them not to go above five miles from their own houses, and their fears or modesty made them exactly comply with those laws: but now all those rules are broken and their whole business is to go from one public meeting to another thirty or forty miles distance under pretence of cockfighting. I have of late confined myself as if I was obliged by law so to do; and they go publicly armed abroad as if they had no law to hinder them.

I should be very glad that they had no other business but 'cockfighting and that no Papist, or those that are worse, Protestants, who are dissatisfied with Her Majesty's most gracious government, of other counties and distant parts met them there, but this is not my business nor is it in my power to inquire into it; truly my Lord who are now deputy lieutenants I do not know but I am certain that the best friends to Her Majesty have been turned out of the Commission of the peace, and for no other fault that I know of than that they had an aversion to popery, loved King William, and were most devoted to Her Majesty. This I know that the Papists and their adherents threatened to turn them out, and that they were turned out accordingly. But why should I tell your Lordship news of Gloucestershire, you know those that were turned out never had a thought in their hearts but what was for Her Majesty's service. You know that all those that have been since put in, are not reported to have used Her Majesty and her government with due and just tenderness and regard. If what I have mentioned proves true (which I wish it may not) I believe and hope there will be orders sent to the officers all over England and then you shall find nobody more zealous for Her Majesty's safety and preservation or more glad and ready to obey all your Lordship's commands.

The MAYOR AND JURATS OF RYE to ROBERT HARLEY, Secretary of State.

1704, May 30—Whereas there have been several suspicious persons lying up and down the country for these five days last past and the agent of the sick and wounded having an order from the Board for apprehending them, Mr. Francis Young, Mr. Michael Cadman, Jeremiah Grevell the agent, Morgan Warner, and Henry Barker, riding officer of the Customs for East Guildford pursued and apprehended this day four of the said persons, the other making his escape. They agree to the description in the *Gazette* given of the men who broke gaol at the Marshall's, but deny those names. The Agent has given the Commis- sioners of the sick and wounded an account of it, as likewise Mr. Stanley Gower, Marshall. If they should not be proved to be the said persons we think them to be very suspicious and thought it our duty to acquaint you of it.

[DANIEL DE FOE] to ROBERT HARLEY, Secretary of State.

[1704, May ?]—As I took the freedom to say to you so I cannot but repeat to your honour. I am at a loss how to behave myself under the goodness and bounty of the Queen, her Majesty buys my small services so much too dear, and leaves me so much in the dark. as to my own merit that I am strangely at a stand what to say. I have enclosed my humble acknowledgement to her Majesty and particularly to my Lord Treasurer. but when I am writing to you, sir, pardon me to alter my style, I am impatient to know what in my small service pleases and engages. Pardon me, sir, tis a necessary enquiry for a man in the dark that I may direct my conduct and push that little merit to a proper extent.

Give me leave as at first to say I cannot but think though her Majesty is good and my lord Treasurer kind, yet my wheel within all these wheels must be yourself, and there I fix my thankfulness as I have of a long time my hope. As God has thus moved you to relieve a distressed family, 'tis my sincere petition to him that he would once put it into my hand to render you some such signal service, as might at least express my sense of it, and encourage all men of power to oblige and espouse grateful and sincere minds.

. Your farther enquiry into the misfortunes and afflicting circumstances that attend and suppress me fills me with some surprise, what Providence has reserved for me he only knows, but sure the gulf is too large for me to get ashore again. I have stated the black case, 'tis a melancholly prospect, and my fears suggest that not less than a thousand pounds will entirely free me. 'Tis true and I am satisfied 500*l.* or 600*l.* at most joined to this I now receive will open the door to liberty and bind all the hands of creditors [so] that I may have leisure to raise the rest, [in] perhaps a year or two, but the sum is too large for me to expect.

. Indeed this debt is raised by doublings of interest on bonds, the length of time having increased the burden. I was rising fairly to clear it all when the public disaster you know of began, but, that entirely blasted all my affairs and I can easily convince you was above 2500*l.* loss to me all at once.

I forbear to say all the moving things to you I could on this head. All my prospects were built on a manufacture I had erected in Essex, all the late King's bounty to me was expended there. I employed a hundred poor families at work, and it began to pay me very well. I generally made six hundred pounds profit per annum. I began to live, took a good house, bought me coach and horses a second time, I paid large debts gradually, small ones wholly, and many a creditor after composition whom I found poor and decayed, I sent for and paid the remainder to, though actually discharged.

But I was ruined *the shortest way,* and now, had not your favour and her Majesty's bounty assisted it must have been one of the worst sorts of ruin. I do not mean as to bread; I firmly and, I thank God, comfortably depend on the Divine Goodness that I shall never want that. But a large and promising family, a virtuous and excellent mother to seven beautiful and hopeful children, a woman whose fortunes I have ruined, with whom I have had 3700*l.*, and yet who in the worst of my afflictions when my Lord N[ottingham] first insulted her, then tempted her, scorned so much as to move me to comply with him, and rather encouraged me to oppose him.

Seven children, whose education calls on me to furnish their heads if I cannot their purses, and which debt if not paid now can never be compounded hereafter; is to me a moving article and helps very often to make me sad.

But, I am, I thank God, furnished with patience, I never despaired and in the worst condition always believed I should be carried through it, but which way has been and yet remains a mystery of Providence unexpounded.

I beg heartily your pardon for this tedious espistle, the miserable are always full of their own cases, and think nothing impertinent. I write thus, for 'tis too moving for me to speak it. I shall attend the orders and hours you appointed to-morrow evening.

Postscript.—I presume to send the enclosed open for your approbation. You will please to put a seal to it.

[DANIEL DE FOE] to ROBERT HARLEY, Secretary of State.

[1704, May ?]—The hurry of your affairs is my mortification as it deprives me of the opportunity of waiting on you, and I take this way to supply it because in our short interviews I omit too much what I would say.

Before I go on to what I would now write I desire to premise to you, that your proposal of my going to H.[anover ?] is really and sincerely very acceptable to me, and particularly as you were pleased to tell me I might do you some service there, the present useless posture I am in being my particular affliction.

I entreat you to believe me without compliment that besides my being by inclination and principle heartily in the interest of the Government, so I am particularly in a great variety of obligations and more than commonly by my own affections linked to your personal interest, and shall be glad to distinguish myself in any thing and at any hazard for your service.

I confess my own pressures, which are sometimes too heavy and apt to sink the hopes I conceived from your goodness, force me to importune you, but I cannot but believe you resolve to help me without my so frequent solicitations. I, therefore, ask pardon for my impatience and go on to tell you that the voyage you propose is very acceptable to me and my very choice, unless I may render you more service else where which you will determine for me. But this need not hinder, but if you please to move my Lord Treasurer in my behalf one thing may be done for me which I humbly represent to your thoughts.

Either that one branch of the Auditor's office (for I am assured it is divided) may be bestowed on me, which I can order to be done privately and put in a person to supply for me till my return, or that his lordship will appoint me a convenient private allowance for subsistence on which I might comfortably depend and continue to be serviceable in a private capacity whether abroad or at home.

I solicit the first on two accounts, first because matters of accounts are my particular element, what I have always been master of; and secondly because it will be a certainty in which I may bring my sons up under me to be in time serviceable to their father's benefactor.

I persuade myself a word from you to my Lord Treasurer would do this for me and I humbly though earnestly press you to consider it for me. I beg leave to tell you that I will order my affairs so in this office that no one shall know me to be in it till something may happen to make it reasonable to appear in it.

If this cannot be then I refer the last to your goodness that if possible I may be delivered from the unsufferable disorders of my affairs, and that my going abroad may be as speedy as you please. Pardon my urgency in this matter and admit me I entreat to as speedy an audience as possible that I may at last enter into your interest and service, and show you whether I am qualified to merit your favour or no.

Robert Harley and Benjamin Edwards.

[1704, May to November]—A short account of Mr. Harley's proceedings upon the information given to him by one Benjamin Edwards.

On Saturday the 27th of May 1704 Mr. Harley received a letter which mentioned a great discovery that person could make of a treasonable correspondence with France and enclosed a list of ships No. 1, who carried on that trade.

Mr. Harley immediately according to the direction sent to the writer of the letter, who came to him next day being Sunday, and proved to be Mr. John Tutchin, who promised that Edwards should attend upon Tuesday May 30th at five in the afternoon, who came and Mr. Harley heard his relation and desired him to put it in writing as soon as he could.

Accordingly on Thursday June 1st Edwards brought his information in writing, a copy whereof is No. 2.

Mr. Harley gave Edwards all imaginable encouragement and immediately laid the whole matter before Her Majesty and the Lords of the Committee of Council upon which the necessary directions were given. Amongst other directions a list of the names of the ships and masters with the places said to belong to Ireland, was delivered to the Lord Lieutenant of that kingdom with orders to take all possible care to seize such ships and make further discoveries. Duplicates of the same were also, for more safety, sent to the Government in Ireland. The like, as far as concerned Scotland, was also transmitted to the Secretary of that kingdom. Divers other methods were also used to know the truth of this and to make further discoveries.

The list given in by Edwards being particular but to two places in England to which ships belonged, immediately care was taken to make inquiries in each of those viz.: Lyme and London. And upon discourse with Edwards it was thought most probable to make the discovery in London. In order to promote this, which required secrecy Mr. Harley consulted one of the Commissioners of the Customs viz. Mr. Mainwaring, who agreed that Edwards (not knowing the names of the vessels, but averring he could distinguish them upon sight) should go with the proper Officer of the Custom-House from time to time up and down the river to make his discovery, as any ships came in; and the Officer had private directions accordingly. Edwards pretended that he did do so; at least for a little while he did, and no discovery could be made. Saturday June the 24th Mr. Masters, who had carried prisoners over to Calais, came to Mr. Harley. He had left Calais the Tuesday before, June 20th, and gave an account of an English ship which had been carried in by a French privateer, and was immediately released and was come for the river.

Edwards, being informed thereof goes to see her, and affirming she was the pink he mentioned in his list and which he saw at Bordeaux, Mr. Harley sent to the Commissioners of the Customs, who, it being a holiday, did not sit, but he had word sent that this was a ship of one Thompson, whose apprentice Mr. Craven was come on board, and that long before the ship came in, the said Thompson had made applications about her, and the Commissioners of the Customs had made a report upon it. However Mr. Harley asked Edwards, if he would swear what he had related, that he saw lead delivered out of that ship at Bordeaux, which he accordingly did, and thereupon Mr. Harley issued out his warrant, a copy whereof is, No. 3, and sent one of Her Majesty's

messengers,- and ordered Edwards to show him the said ship and
Mr. Craven.

The next day being Sunday Mr. Harley laid the whole before Her
Majesty &c. at Windsor. ,

Tuesday June 27th Mr. Thompson gave in a Petition on behalf of
his ship, stating his case, as it afterwards was proved in the Court of
Admiralty. A copy thereof is No. 4.   No

Wednesday morning June the 28th Mr. Harley put the ship into the
hands of the proper Officers of the Court of Admiralty, and gave
instructions and strict charge to Mr. Glasier proctor to His Royal
Highness to prosecute the same and to give it all imaginable dispatch.

After this Mr. Harley spent upon several occasions much time in
examining witnesses relating to this ship viz : Robert Poulson, Cæsar
Deavon, Jeffery Stretch, Samuel Maron, whose examinations with
others were transmitted to the Court of Admiralty, where they may be
seen.

: July 27th Edwards made a complaint that he offered to advance
three hundred pounds for the ship's loading more than the appraise-
ment, Mr. Harley sent immediately to Mr. Glasier, and upon
examination found that, like other things, to be a fiction.

Edwards Sept. 14th complained to Mr. Harley of the delay, whereupon he ordered a letter to Mr. Crawley that day to hasten the trial;
and several other things of that nature to avoid prolixity are emitted,
which would appear by the several letters.

As to the stopping trade with France, that Mr. Harley has not been
wanting in his duty therein many instances, if it were necessary, can be
produced. And as to Edwards, his offers to hinder it, and his story of
advancing money, Mr. Harley must refer to his own proposals written   No
all with his own hand; copies whereof are No. 5, No. 6.   No

Mr. Harley's observation of him made him resolve to have him put
everything he had to say in writing.

Edwards was so far from receiving any discouragements from
Mr. Harley that it was generally talked that Mr. Harley had been too
zealous or violent in prosecuting that matter : unless Edwards thinks
this a discouragement, that upon his bringing Tutchin with him one day
to the office, Mr. Harley told him, when he had any business to speak
with him, he should come alone: and this seems to be a great crime,
for the *Observator* presently inserted the story of Trade with France
into his weekly paper.

After all Mr. Harley had done to quicken the trial of the ship,
Oct. 26th he received a letter by the Penny Post from Edwards complaining of the Admiralty Court, and desiring his assistance and advice
to apply to the Lords.

If there have been any delay in the Admiralty Court or- any other
misbehaviour towards Edwards they are answerable for it; Mr. Harley
having no concern upon that head.

It is humbly desired to make an observation or two upon the Paper
he has delivered in to the Lords.

1. That it will appear by comparing that paper with the several other
Papers, all under his own hand the copies whereof are mentioned
above, how much improved he is in his evidence.

2. His confidence as well as malice to Mr. Harley is manifest, in that he
says he got him (the ship) seized with the Master and super cargo:
without taking notice it was done by Mr. Harley's warrant; and then
he adds *who were discharged for what reason I know not*, though he
was told the Law would not detain the persons.

3. He says he had solicited to get a trial but could never yet obtain it; whereas he knew, that the trial was over, the ship and most part of the lading restored, some days before he delivered in this narrative.

Their Lordships can best judge what credit is to be given to what this man says against plain matters of fact, and things which carry uncontrollable proof with them.

If anything requires further answer or explanation relating to Mr. Harley it shall presently be done with all truth and brevity.

J. SMITH to JOHN HARE in Talbot Court, Gracious Street.

1704, June 5. Lynn—My occasions calling me to Norwich the last week I thought fit to give you with some remarks the hints of which may perhaps be useful to Mr. *Observator*, nor will I relate other than what is real, true and matter of fact.

It is first to be marvelled at that one Nash should be suffered to hold a Perkinite conventicle as he has done publicly for some time, where the little Welsh gentleman is prayed for and Her Majesty omitted. Their number about three or four hundred and what is most to be wondered at this is held under the nose of the Bishop and within the precinct of the Cathedral.

The next thing I present you with is as comical as real. About fourteen or twenty days ago three of Her Majesty's officers who lay there for recruits, one day in their cups a jollity one of the captains beat a drum while two other captains carried halberts before him as sergeants; their speech at each corner of the streets and market place, for they beat in that manner all round the city, was for all whores and rogues that were willing to serve Her Majesty were to repair to the 'Black Swan,' &c., which I cannot think any other than to be a very high affront and indignity offered to Her Majesty and her Commission; one I think they say his name was Nall. What prosperity can be expected from our armies when such profligate fellows are in command.

No less comical was that of the other day, a Perkinite brewer came to a bookseller of the same city and demanded if they had the spirit of presbytery, I suppose there may be a pamphlet so called; the man being from home she made him a goodly curtsey saying, no indeed sir we sell nothing but spirit of 'scuringrake,' clapped his tail between his legs and went away muttering, as greatly affronted though the poor woman was innocent of the matter.

The next observable I met with was of four or five of the same stamp, who in their cups at an ale house there, about five or six weeks ago, on their bare knees drank Perkin's good health and wishing that he were as well settled on the throne as Her Majesty. I think these were the words as laid in the indictment, but the honourable magistrates of that place commiserating the condition of their friends, if it should have come before a Judge at the next assizes, as every honest man did wish it would, called a private sessions by an adjournment, and like honest men and good subjects acquitted 'em all, having before committed to jail the informer. One of these was a barber, another an ale house keeper, the third a weaver, but the best jest was 'twas done at the sign of the Church.

The records of the court will confirm the truth of what I say.

WILLIAM HALLIFAX to [EDWARD HARLEY].

1704, June 3. Old Swinford—Informing him of the election of Mr. Painter of Newent to be their schoolmaster (at Stourbridge?), Mr. Wentworth having declined the office.

CAPTAIN EDWARD SHADWELL to the QUEEN.

1704, June 8—Petition for the grant of letters patent for erecting an office of insurance in the Kingdom of Ireland for the support of widows and orphans. His father John Shadwell Esq. a justice for Middlesex, Norfolk and Suffolk, had been a great sufferer in the time of the Rebellion. Referred to the Duke of Ormonde.

DR. JOHN POTTER to ROBERT HARLEY, in York Buildings.

1704, June 9. Oxford—This second volume of Justin Martyr, whereof I desire your acceptance, was printed by one who was formerly my pupil, and is not yet published, being reserved for the Dean of Christ Church's next New Year's gift. What there is in it of mine is not worthy your notice, being very little, and that put together in haste to complete the edition.

J. W. to ROBERT HARLEY, Secretary of State.

1704, June 14—If Dan Foe be the supposed author of the libel titled 'Legions Address to the Lords,' you will find him at Captain Roger's at the city of Canterbury. If a messenger be sent privately I do not doubt but he will be taken, and when he is committed of the matter, the reward promised I hope will be due to your Honour's humble servant.

LORD CONINGSBY to [ROBERT] HARLEY.

1704, June 17—I fear you will scarce have better news from Portugal till you have another General. Can there be a more proper man for that service than Lord Galway, who has capacity sufficient both for minister and commander-in-chief; and if Luttrell were recommended to the King of Portugal's service, I dare say he would be found a very useful instrument in that country.

The DUKE OF SCHOMBERG and LEINSTER to [ROBERT HARLEY].

1704, June 17-28. Estremos—I received with great satisfaction the news of your promotion to the Secretary's office. I have a great opinion of affairs in the hands of such ministers and hope much in your favour and assistance to the relief of this distressed expedition. *Signed.*

COURSEY IRELAND to [ROBERT HARLEY].

1704, June 19. Limerick—Warns him against a wicked and dangerous woman named Jane Hansard who was mixed up in a plot to murder King William, who had lately come over to England and was lodging at Mr. Mathews, near the Mews Gate, at Charing Cross. Describes her appearance, skill in opening letters, forgery, &c.

SIR S. FAIRBORNE to [ROBERT] HARLEY].

1704, June 19. Bath—Asking for employment on land until he was again required to go to sea.... The ships he had lately brought in were so very foul and ill-manned, and so unfit for service, that he was not sorry at his arrival to find the Prince's leave for his coming to Bath, it being impossible to protect trade or do service with such ships.

SIR JOHN BLAND to [ROBERT HARLEY?].

1704, June 20. Hulme—Urging his claims for a place. "I did not stay above ten days in Yorkshire and never visited my corporation but one piece of a day, and that with all the privacy imaginable, for I am not yet determined whether to stand again or no, having had enough of the trouble and expense of elections."

The ARCHBISHOP OF CANTERBURY to [ROBERT HARLEY].

1704, June 21 and 22. Lambeth—Two letters concerning the remittance of 6000l. to Lord Raby ambassador at Berlin, collected for the benefit of the protestants of Orange. Signed "Canterbury."

ABEL BOYER to [ROBERT] HARLEY, Secretary.

1704, June 26—Giving information that Sir George Maxwell, Captain Levingston, Captain Hayes and others having with them a young lord to whom they paid great respect; also three ladies, and three Frenchmen, one of them an Abbot, who all three pass for Scotchmen, though they cannot speak the language, had lately gone from the Court of St. Germains to Scotland, by way of Holland.

EARL OF LEVEN to [ROBERT HARLEY].

1704, June 20. Edinburgh—Since you were pleased to allow me the liberty of writing to you, I hope you will not take it ill that I make use of that privilege at present, although it relates mostly to my own private concerns. The information I had before I left London of a design to give me some trouble in the Parliament on pretence of correspondence with Captain Fraser, but indeed because of my endeavours to discover the plot, made me desire an exoneration or remission which Her Majesty did not then think fit to grant, therefore I insisted no further therein; but in the full confidence of Her Majesty's protection I returned home with a real design to advance Her Majesty's interest to the utmost of my power, but to my very great surprise at my arrival here I understood that there was a formed design against me and some lawyers bespoke for that purpose, nor do they make any difficulty to own in common discourse that I am to be attacked in Parliament, and are determining as I hear what my sentence shall be: some talk of prosecuting me for high treason, and the more moderate talk of declaring me incapable by a vote. I find plainly that my not being able to procure a remission has increased and encouraged the ferment against me. I see their project is either to frighten me from attending in Parliament or, if I do attend, to imprison me upon an indictment; and in either of those events to deprive me of the occasion of showing my zeal for the promoting of Her Majesty's interest and service, which is really what I am more uneasy about than for what concerns myself. Now I must intreat you to consider my circumstances, and beg your assistance, that I may yet obtain a remission before the Parliament sit. What I am accused of is correspondence with Captain Fraser last summer. I need not give you the trouble of any account of what was my part in that affair, having discoursed you fully thereon before I left London, and shall only say that it will look very strange if I be brought to any trouble for my zeal for Her Majesty's service and the peace of her dominions. I have been several times to wait on the Chancellor but he has not been pleased to let me know anything of his measures, but carries with so much reservedness that I see he neither trusts me in public matters nor befriends me in my own concerns, and if I have both the Ministry and the opposing party to struggle with innocence will hardly be able to protect me. There have been insinuations made that if I will neither by myself nor by my influence assist the Court nor go unto their measures, that then I shall not be prosecuted, but this I will by no means comply with. I beg to have the honour to hear from you before the Parliament sit that I may know what I am to expect that I may manage myself accordingly. If a remission can be obtained the late Secretary Depute if called for can give a draught thereof in the ordinary form, for it is very like the present Secretary Depute will not be very frank in that matter.

As for our affairs in general, I hear that there are not many of the opposing party that will go into the Queen's measures, and even some of those who pretend to be of that number deny it lest they lose their interest with their party, and they are still in the expectation that something or other may fall in to prevent the necessity of their declaring themselves in Parliament which our heats if not prevented are likely enough to produce ; so that whatever the present Ministry may pretend it is certain that the chief expectation they can have of success is from the hope of the concurrence of those who were formerly in the Administration and who, notwithstanding the discouragements they have met with both last year and this by the changes, are still willing to give their assistance providing those in the Administration will use them with kindness and confidence, but how prejudicial it may be and inconvenient if they find themselves neglected and their friends exposed to the fury of their enemies is easy to be imagined especially when things cannot be done without them. I beg you ten thousand pardons for this great trouble which necessity obliges me to, I entreat you may concern yourself for me. I have written to my Lord Treasurer also and I am very hopeful that by his and your means Her Majesty may be persuaded to preserve one entirely devoted to her interest and service from the rage and violence of my enemies. I have not yet had the honour to hear from you which makes me fear that letters do miscarry.

SIR H. BELASYSE to [ROBERT HARLEY].

1704, July 1. Brancepeth Castle, near Durham—After I fell under her Majesty's displeasure, which I reckoned the greatest misfortune of my life (and how far I deserved it I leave to you to judge) I then resolved the passing the remainder of my time in a retreat, but by the little experience I have had of that way of living I find it is not so agreeable to me as I expected or could have wished. Therefore if her Majesty should be graciously pleased to employ me in her army in Portugal or recommend me to the King of Portugal to serve in his (in both which I don't believe they abound with officers) I should hope in that case to have an opportunity of restoring myself to favour by my faithful services.

JACOBITES in ROTTERDAM.

1704, July 1—Statement in Harley's handwriting and signed "Ri Biron" to the effect that Captain Byron (*sic*) had recently spent a week in Rotterdam, during which time he often saw Sir George Maxwell, Mr. Hayes (who had formerly been a volunteer in the navy under Sir Thomas Hopson, and another Scotchman whom they called Sir James, about thirty years of age, a sallow complexion, who wore his own very long hair of a dark brown colour. Byron dined with them several times at the "Rose and Crown" ordinary. There were other Scots and Irish in the town at the same time. All these persons afterwards went to the Brill, where the English landlady of the "White Hart" complained of the Scotch officers' rudeness and their drinking the Prince of Wales's health. Maxwell and the others, after a visit to the Hague, went on board a Scottish ship called the *James* carrying about sixteen guns ; a few women were with them. William George Pennington, who keeps the "Rose and Crown" in Rotterdam, was a Catholic, his wife and children being Protestants, and kept correspondence with France and with disaffected persons in England. Gilbert Black, a Scotchman, now a wine merchant, was formerly a priest. No person asked Capt. Byron to seize or apprehend Sir George Maxwell and his followers but he advised with Mr. Vernon whether such seizure was justifiable, and the latter thought it was if it could be done out of the town ; but they got out of his reach.

The EMPEROR LEOPOLD to the QUEEN OF ENGLAND.

1704, July [1-]12. Vienna—It is my duty, upon receipt of the news of the successes with which God has been pleased to bless the first oper-ations of our armies, against the Elector of Bavaria, to congratulate your Majesty upon such a result, and especially for the active part which your brave troops have taken under the leadership of Lord Marlborough, who is well worthy of the high esteem which your Majesty entertains of him. I therefore perform my duty in this letter, and I hope shortly to repeat the office upon the further successes of our armies. I request also that your Majesty will allow Lord Marlborough, when he pleases, to receive from me some little token of my appreciation of his brave and prudent operations. I am anxious to anticipate this request because I have heard from one of my ministers that at one time Lord Marlborough was somewhat wounded that it had not been done. *Italian. Copy sent by Robert Harley to the Duke of Newcastle. Endorsed in Robert Harley's Hand* "Written all with his own hand, wherein he gives the title of Majesty."

J. MACKEY to [ERASMUS] LEWIS.

1704, July [2-] 13. Florence—I did myself the honour of writing to you by last post, since that I met with a gentleman just come from Toulon and going to Rome that I had sometimes paid money to by King William's order for services done in France, he was then Procureur-Gen-eral for the Duke of Bouillon and now wears the habit of an Abbot and is a Canon under the Cardinal d'Estrée at St. Germains. He told me that he was still very capable to do service to England if they employed him. I told him that I was now shuffled out of the pack and had nothing to do in the management of these affairs but that I would write to one that hath. He says whenever you want to know the sailing of any squadron of ships, their number, and how many months' provisions he can always give you notice to Genoa, or now the Post is open to Holland, thither, and that nobody can come to St. Germains or go but he can give you notice.

I write this to you because I know you understand it better having managed it so well at Paris.

He tells me that at Toulon they have fifty men-of-war now of line of battle, but that they have neither provisions nor seamen for above forty, of which seventeen three deck ships are already fitted, they have no troops there, and abundance of country people mixed with their seamen.

Count Toulouse lies every night on board his ship and they talk of putting quickly to sea.

Ri. Biron to [Robert Harley].

1704, July 2—The knight's name which he could not remember was Sir Henry Winfield. Cannot add anything to the statement about Sir George Maxwell and others given above, and explains at some length the difficulties in the way of arresting these people in Rotterdam without full authority from the States General to the governor of the town. It is a great mortification to him to have any crime laid to his charge after having served thirty-one years in the royal navy, and he hopes for a favourable construction upon what he has done in the matter.

Commissioners of Sick and Wounded to Richard Warre.

1704, July 5—Enclosing particulars of the examinations of the four persons seized by the Mayor of Rye, one of whom said he was Dr. William Davis, born in London, bred at Oxford, and had practised physic for about fourteen years past in the Canary Islands, and was detained a prisoner there four months before the declaration of the last war; he had procured his liberty by Mr. Methuen's interest. The other three persons were also connected with the Canary Islands, Samuel Swann, an English merchant there for thirty years, another the Dutch consul, and the third a Spanish gentleman.

Signed by R. Adams, Ch. Morley, and Wm. Churchill.

The Bishop of Norwich to [Robert Harley].

1704, July 5—He who promised an account of Mr. Nash's prayer last Sunday could not get an opportunity his doors being shut against all but the party. The conventicle is in his own house, which is near the Cathedral, but not within the precincts of it as the letter suggests.

I wish this sort of men were more loyal and dutiful, and behaved themselves better towards Her Majesty, who so graciously does extend her mercy and clemency to all her subjects.

I hear they offered, for twenty guineas down to pay one hundred at Michaelmas if by that time the Elector of Bavaria was not possessed of

Vienna and the Duke of Anjou of Lisbon. The last good account from Portugal; and the news of the glorious victory the Duke of Marlborough obtained over the French and Bavarians must put them out of countenance.

With all those who truly honour the Queen, and love their country I return hearty thanks to God for this great success. I also sincerely congratulate you upon the prosperous execution of counsels, in wisely laying and concerting of which, I have reason to believe, you had so great a hand.

The other reports in the letter you sent, that Captain Nall did beat up for whores and rogues, &c. and that others were indicted at a private sessions for drinking the health of the young man in France, as I am informed, are very true.

———— to ROBERT HARLEY, Principal Secretary of State.

1704, July 5—Our club met and Lord St—— and the rest of us have paid our money to oblige us for once to dine at the King's Head tavern in King Street. One has promised to bring two knights, viz. Sir James Collett and Sir B. Gracedew to our club. They say John Toland is in England and hard at work at his pen. Dan de Foe the like; both which authors will be published shortly. De Foe's book will be called the *History of Superstition*, and is already subscribed for by many. Mr. John Peirce the reputed author of the *Million Letter* is in England, but where I cannot learn. If I am kept secret, in time I shall know all these affairs, which I will make it my uttermost endeavour to do, to serve the Queen and Government.

[DANIEL DE FOE] to ROBERT HARLEY.

1704, July 7—I can easily suppose your being full of good news, this week has left you little leisure, and under that head am a little in pain for the diet.

I confess myself also something impatient to have it from yourself that I had explained the 'Review' to your satisfaction, and that in reading it you have been pleased to note the caution I mentioned that it was to be wrote not as if the objectors were of such quality as to whom the style should be unsuitable.

But I must own neither of these moved me to give you this trouble I cannot put it from my thoughts, that success of affairs, as it is the prosperity of a nation, so 'tis the felicity of a Ministry. Methinks this victory abroad might have its advantages at home.

Tho' I think it my duty to give this hint, I shall presume no farther without your command, which I shall be as glad to receive as faithful to obey.

Postscript—A new King they say is chosen in Poland.

ROBERT HARLEY to the Rev. [DR. STRATFORD].

1704, July 8—Whitehall—When Dr. Atterbury kissed her Majesty's hand for the deanery of Carlisle, she was pleased to tell him that she was glad of that opportunity to show him the respect she had for him, and that what she had given him was but a beginning of her favour. I hear he had more said to him by the Lord Treasurer upon that subject, and I need not explain to you the meaning of it.

WILLIAM CARY to [ROBERT HARLEY].

1704, July 9. Clovelly—My most hearty thanks to the Lord Treasurer for having me so much in his mind and favour as to declare to you his kind intentions to do something for me. "By sixteen or seventeen years' war my estate which 'mostly lies near the sea has felt more than the ordinary calamities of it, and hath been lessened in its income beyond most of my neighbours living in the inland country, and that a considerable jointure upon it, and four small children, and the Act of Parliament procured the last session for dismembering it, are motives which concur with my ambition " to serve her Majesty.

DR. JOHN RADCLIFFE to [ROBERT HARLEY].

1704, July 10—I give you many thanks for the good news I received and nothing could make it so acceptable as the hand it came from. I wish I could send you anything from this place besides water, here is neither love nor scandal, wit nor beauty, so that Scotland is as like to be invaded as this place lampooned.

[The EARL OF LEVEN to ROBERT HARLEY.]

1704, July 11. Edinburgh—I have the honour of yours of the 29th of June, wherein I have new proofs of your great concern for me, for which I return you my most humble thanks and entreat the continuance of your favour. I shall give you no trouble at present as to what concerns myself. But since you was desirous to have some information of what passes here with relation to public affairs, I reckon myself obliged to give you an account thereof, so far as they come to my knowledge, but I am kept so much a stranger to the politics and present management, that any account you have from me will be very lame.

The Parliament hath met twice. The first day there was nothing done save the reading of Her Majesty's Commission to the Marquis of Tweeddale to represent her royal person, and then the House adjourned to this day, when Her Majesty's letter to the Parliament was read and then my Lord Commissioner and Chancellor made their speeches as is usual. Thereafter there was a paper offered by Mr. Seton, one of the Commissioners for the county of Aberdeen, by way of Resolve, which you have here enclosed. This paper was read and ordered to lie upon the table; but there was no notice taken thereof by any of the Queen's servants, which was thought very strange. There was nothing else of moment passed in the house this day.

I cannot but take notice of the management of those who have the administration in their hands of the treatment that I and many others who are entirely upon the foot of the Revolution, meet with: for none of the Ministry have given us the least account of affairs, or how they are to be managed, nay I may say they are so far from either trusting us, or advising with us, that we are scarce treated with common civility. But notwithstanding of this I am persuaded that all of us will use our utmost endeavours to promote Her Majesty's service, and will join heartily in the settling the Succession in the Protestant line, and if things succeed not, it shall be none of our fault.

There was a meeting three or four days ago in the Duke of Atholl's lodgings in the Queen's house where were a great many of the nobility and others who are judged to be against the Succession. They had that matter, I hear, under their consideration, and what might be the proper methods to disappoint the settling thereof. It was likewise proposed by some, that if the Succession should carry, that then some of the limitations might be so adjusted, as to take place even in Her Majesty's lifetime. This meeting makes a great noise, and the more, that it has been hitherto so little noticed by those who have the management.

The procedure of the Ministry in neglecting so much those who have always owned themselves to be for the Succession, such as the Marquis of Annandale, myself, and many others, when at the same time, many of less interest and colder inclinations are courted and caressed, makes many doubt whether they be in earnest in what they propose or not; and sure I am this way of theirs is prejudicial to Her Majesty's service.

We are so jealous of English influence and letters are so ready to miscarry, that I thought it prudent to make use of a borrowed hand and to forbear signing; both which I hope you will excuse. I need not give my Lord Treasurer any trouble at present, since I hope you will let him know any part of this letter that you think necessary. I had the honour to receive his letter under your cover.

The paper enclosed runs:—

Resolved that this House will stand by and defend Her Majesty's person and government, and will not name her successor to the crown of Scotland this session of parliament; but will make such conditions of government to take effect after Her Majesty's death as may best conduce to free this kingdom of all English influence, to the end it may be in a condition to treat with England on a federal union.

ROBERT HARLEY to the DUKE OF MARLBOROUGH.

1704, July 11–23—We have very unfitting returns to make for the news we have from your Grace. You send us accounts of a glorious victory, and we can only return your Lordship an account of a series of follies committed in Portugal. Her Majesty hath done her utmost to repair and retrieve their errors. Lord Galway goes towards Portsmouth tomorrow morning, and there is to be sent immediately, besides the 1,500 recruits, a regiment of foot and a regiment of dragoons from Ireland instead of Stanhope's and Stewart's regiments of foot, which are lost, and a battalion of guards under Schrimpton. These are already ordered, and Monsieur Vryberg is acquainted with it, and also Mr. Stanhope is written to press the States to come into their proportion of the augmentation. Besides this, Lord Galway proposes a second convoy should go the beginning of September, and to raise 18 troops of dragoons and 1,000 horses to mount ours and the Dutch troopers in Portugal. This is communicated to Mr. Stanhope to lay before the States; and if your Grace could ever spare so much time from doing great things for us, one word from your Grace would be very effectual in Holland to make them comply. For I fear if they should be backward, it would have very ill effects next winter with us here, and give handle to angry men to do mischief; and I doubt not there are emissaries now in Holland who are endeavouring to sow the seeds of jealousy there. *Copy.*

STEPHEN SEIGNORES to ARTHUR MOORE, in Bloomsbury Square.

1704, July 12. London—I have written to my friend in Geneva to explain what was expected of him. I made him the offer of 200*l.* a year for his trouble in finding out able persons willing and zealous for the common cause to be sent to several places, whom he should manage and reward upon such terms as he should agree with them; but in case of some extraordinary services, viz. for engaging some clerks of the offices to serve us, they should have an augmentation of reward proportional to the benefit we should reap. As for the manner of carrying on the correspondence we shall agree among ourselves, and as it would be of an ill consequence for him if he should be discovered, I have told him that we do not expect he should give anything under his hand except the correspondence, that should be between him and me.

JONATHAN [TRELAWNEY], Bishop of Exeter, to [ROBERT HARLEY].

1704, July 15. Exeter—I beg pardon that I am forced to break in upon you again so soon, even before I can receive the favour of your answer to my last, but the bearing of this Bishop of Bath and Wells [Hooper] is intolerable, who after being possessed of two Bishoprics without ever yet seeing one of 'em, will still pretend to be governing in mine, where I don't need his help, nor ever yet that I know of desired his assistance. He pretends, as I understand from the other office, that I employed him to desire the Bishop of London to beg Bovey Tracy from the Queen for Mr. Elford fourteen months since. I know not this Mr. Elford but by a late affront which he put upon me, when, being the other day as Minister of Newton appointed to preach a sermon at my Confirmation, he took the liberty without any consent of mine to run a hunting after this new living (which the day before happened to be void) and sent me word by another raw clerk he had left his sermon to be preached for him; so that if I had not, on the spot, found another graver man to tell the people their duty on that occasion, they might have been to seek for it, as much as I was for a preacher.

But as to the Bishop of Bath and Wells and the story he tells, I must take upon me to say this with truth. I know not that I ever wrote him in my life, but in answer to a letter of his; much less that I ever went so low as to ask a favour of him or to desire his assistance in procuring one from any other. I know not, upon the utmost recollection that I ever mentioned Elford's name to him, and I am very sure that if I knew the man as well as I do now, I never should do it (in his favour) to any one. If I had made so mean an application it would seem strange to me that I should forget it so soon as within three or four months, to apply to my Lord Nottingham for another; that Her Majesty could be so forgetful as to grant me the request; or his Lordship so unmindful of a prior obligation, as notwithstanding that, to enter Her Majesty's promise to Mr. Cook in his book, and leave it minuted there for this man to play with.

But since a letter of mine to that purpose is pretended, I shall not at present dispute a matter of fact, with a Bishop who makes himself so sure of it; 'twill appear I hope, if there be any such thing, and speak for itself. Nevertheless I still beg leave to say that I insist upon Her Majesty's promise for Mr. Cook (whose character will deserve the favour) and on the proof of it, the minute in my Lord Nottingham's book to that effect; or if that be not thought sufficient to determine this matter, the letter itself which I received from my Lord Nottingham to acquaint me with Her Majesty's grant, which I shall send up from Trelawney when I return thither, and can look it out from among my papers there, as I intend in a fortnight or three weeks' time Nor shall

I think that I have justice done me, if this living be otherwise disposed of. For since the Bishop with so much heat and malice makes it 'a point of honour (on this trifle) to raise and persist in this opposition to me, it concerns me as much to defeat him now in his revenge, as I did formerly in the grounds of it, when I was forced by my Lord Treasurer's favour to wrest out of his hands the precentorship of my church here, which he would have carried over in commendam to a Bishopric that never was thought before his time to need one, and which was in my own commendam when I first came hither.

I am in all this on the defensive only, and I hope not so much out of my way as he is, when he pretends to fill people's heads with a notion that my Lord Treasurer and I are to model the elections in our county for the next (to make it a Court) parliament; which if it be so, I hope this foreigner will not be helped to set himself up on any terms in opposition to us. I do not trouble my Lord Treasurer in this matter, though I know myself sure of his protection whenever I am driven to call for it; but when I have taken the liberty to put it into your hands, I presume to conclude upon the safety of my honour and interest.

The EARL OF ABINGDON to [ROBERT HARLEY].

1704, July 15. Rycott.—Sends a letter signed "G. U." which states where the writer is to be found, as he supposes in a dark room and clean straw. Had received others from the same hand speaking of plots against the Queen, one of which had been sent to Secretary Hedges.

W[ILLIAM] BLENCOWE to [ROBERT HARLEY].

1704, July 15. Bath—This morning I received your letter, with the two enclosed in cipher. These I have explained and sent back with the deciphering interlined having written over each number the letter which it imports. Besides those numbers which are intended to signify single letters there are a few which stand for whole words. I have guessed what some of these mean, 49, 97, 54 Fleet, Ships, War; but these not being often repeated I have not that certainty which may be required. Those other figures 68, 43, 63, 66 which appear to signify names of persons and places, are left unexplained, as I can judge of them only by circumstances.

SIR W. HICKMAN to SIR CHRISTOPHER MUSGRAVE, Bart. at his house in Leicester Street in Swallow Street, near Piccadilly.

1704, July 17. Gainsborough—As there will be a great want of justices sitting at Retford in parliament time, owing to deaths, Sir Thomas Willoughby and he recommended Mr. Jonathan Acklam, of Bawtry, to be put into the Commission for Notts. Acklam had left off practising as an attorney, had a very good estate of 800l. a year, and acted as a land tax commissioner. Mr. George Wharton of Retford, who was about to marry a relation of the writer's, and had a good fortune, was also recommended to the Lord Keeper, but nothing appeared to have been done.

COURSEY IRELAND to [ROBERT HARLEY].

1704, July 18. Limerick—Mrs. Handsard was in London on some dark design but what it was I can as yet give no account; she has a working. 'ploding' head, her whole time is taken up in dark secret studies. The little advantage the French have had this campaign did so much exalt the Papists in this Kingdom, that they grew insolent and took liberty of talking more largely than ever they durst since 1691. In short they are as ripe for a new rebellion now as ever they were in the years 1641 and 1688. But thanks to our late success against the Spaniards and Bavarians their spirits are in some measure depressed. The present state of this Kingdom is very poor and miserable; little money is to be seen in it. A fat cow which would have sold for near 3*l.* within two or three years is now worth but 20*s.*; 120 lbs. of butter formerly sold for 40*s.* is now at 11*s.*; best wool 6*s.* the stone of 16 lbs. weight; wheat 2*s.* the bushel and barley 14*d.* In my opinion it would be an advantage to the public of England that some of the Queen's ships were victualled here at Cork; 3000*l.* would go as far here as 5000*l.* in England.

ROBERT HARLEY to the REV. W CARSTARES.

1704, July 20—I was extremely satisfied to see your hand on the outside of a letter, for I was afraid I had some way or other forfeited your good opinion which I would not do, because I know you to be so just you would not change your opinion without good reason, and so much a lover of your country that you would not be averse to any one who is so great a well-wisher to your nation as myself. And this principle I confess gives me much concern about Scotland for I can assure you I have no other motive. It is strange that men should run into destruction with their eyes open, that the only thing which can preserve them and unite all of the Revolution principle is the Succession; and yet because England suggests it, that is the reason against its acceptance. The world beyond sea says the succession is to be kept unsettled for a lame arm to beg by; but when the Queen offers (as I am told) to repair the Darien loss can there be a more general advantage proposed? or is it not the design for a few to make the advantage to themselves hereafter? can there be any other point to unite the honest people of Scotland but making the partition—who are for St. Germain and who are for Protestancy.

As to yourself I can assure you no ill impressions are made here of you, and I am sorry the great person you mention should distinguish himself so peevishly and weakly to your prejudice. I know your wisdom and moderation put you above such things. *Copy.*

ROBERT HARLEY to the EARL OF LEVEN.

1704. July 20—When anything doth not go as it ought in your kingdom I am heartily sorry for it, because I love your nation; and I am a servant to you as well as a well-wisher to the kingdom. I am concerned when you are *hors de jeu*, because I am so fully satisfied of your ability as well as zeal for the public, and I can never believe things will succeed well wherein your Lordship's aid is not made use of. I must own that what we hear from them is incomprehensible to me, and I cannot solve the phenomenon to see so many persons of different parties, understandings, inclinations, and interests, all join to oppose— what? Why the only thing which can secure the kingdom, or not deliver them over, as we do dead carcasses, to undertakers and projectors to practice upon, viz., the settling the Succcession. The two things from Scotland we have yet seen are proclamations of war against

England and nothing of good to Scotland. Can Scotland live by negatives? Or is England to be whipped into that which was voluntarily offered at the Union, when the greatest advances which ever were made by England were then agreed to, and have been since scorned and refused. Are those gentlemen in earnest to do good to Scotland who have endeavoured to ridicule an Union and yet now pretend to be for it? Who have pretended to believe poor Mr. Hodges' chimerical book, and yet at the same time would have us believe they are true Scotchmen and would be glad of a real Union, by which they mean somewhat either very imperfect or very impracticable. Will not the example of Poland carry some influence with it, and show how far faction and avarice can carry people to the destruction of their country, and at last find themselves deceived and make a very sorry retreat?

Will not the nation when they are cool, which will quickly happen, make reflections that they might have had everything which was reasonable, even their losses about Darien repaid, and nothing asked but for their own good. Will they not be apt to turn upon their evil leaders and give them their just doom?

You will please to forgive the overflowing of my zeal and affection to the noble Scots nation, whose ruin, if Heaven be not more merciful, will be upon their own heads. *Copy.*

ROBERT HARLEY to [LORD SEAFIELD] Lord Chancellor of Scotland.

1704, July 22. Whitehall—I have received positive information that one Col. Macdonald and one Monroe, an officer, are gone this week from London towards Scotland, having several letters and a packet, pretty large, for Sir George Maxwell the Jacobite. They seem much to depend upon what Maxwell will do there. I am going to Windsor to lay the whole discovery before the Queen, and send you this notice, hoping that the persons will be apprehended as soon as they can be found. The less noise made of this will promote the further discovery. *Copy.*

GEORGE VERNON to ROBERT HARLEY.

1704, July 23. Farnham—Congratulations and a request to forward an enclosed letter to his son at Constantinople in the packet which goes to Sir Robert Sutton.

G. GRANVILLE to [ROBERT] HARLEY.

1704, July 25—I find that Sir Christopher Musgrave has been taken ill without hope of recovery. Nobody is more heartily concerned for this accident than I or more sincerely wishes he may overcome his distemper, but in case of the worst, I take the liberty to offer myself to your friendship, upon which only I rely, and to put you in mind of one who will never forget the obligation.

THE EARL OF SEAFIELD, Lord Chancellor of Scotland, to [ROBERT HARLEY].

1704, July 26. Edinburgh—I have received the honour of yours of the 22nd and communicated it immediately to my Lord Commissioner and we have given such orders that if those you name be not

already here I am hopeful they shall be taken and their papers secured.
If we get their papers this information may be of consequence, but if
not the Habeas Corpus law will bring them out of prison though we
had them. I am indeed afraid there is too great a disposition in this
country for disorder and confusion, and I am sorry that we have not
had better success in Parliament; if we can now get supplies for the
forces it is all we can expect, but that would give Her Majesty time to
determine and take measures for the settling of this nation. I entreat
you may continue to inform me of what may concern Her Majesty's
service here, and I shall omit nothing that is in my power.

[Sir Simon Harcourt to Robert Harley.]

1704, July 29. Gloucester—I assure myself you are a most sincere
mourner for our dear friend Sir Christopher. Every good man is
undoubtedly much affected with it. I wish you find it capable of being
repaired. I saw the vice-chancellor at Oxford, I wish he was as well
known to you as to me. I am sure his good conduct in everything you
command will make you think he deserves your favour. You will very
speedily receive from the University an address for the Queen's goodness to the Clergy, in granting the first fruits. Mr. Stratford will
inform you as to my affair for the University ; I am fully informed by
his silence. From others I am surprised with an account that the Dean
is engaged solemnly for George Clark, by which means I believe Sir
Humphrey will be chosen, but this is not worth your thinking on.

Jonathan [Trelawny], Bishop of Exeter to [Robert Harley].

1704, July 29—An indisposition and the course of medicines which
I was forced to use have hindered me from acknowledging sooner the
favour of your letter and your just and friendly sense of the attempt
upon me. I am now also to thank you for the firmness and despatch
which you have been pleased to use in rescuing me from it. I am
obliged to Her Majesty for ridding me of my forward co-adjutor, and
to my good patron the Lord Treasurer for the part which I doubt not
he took with you in making known to Her Majesty that indignity.

Robert Rochford, Attorney-General [for Ireland] to the Lords Justices of Ireland.

1704, July 29—Report in favour of Captain Edmund Shadwell's
petition for letters patent for erecting an office of insurance in Ireland
for the support of widows and orphans. *Signed.*

The Battle of Blenheim.

1704, August 2—A description of the standards and ensigns taken
from the French at the battle of Blenheim and deposited at the Tower
of London in the following December. In all Colours 83; Staffs and
Pieces 47. Total 130.

The Same.

Same date—A list of the chief prisoners taken at the same battle.
Marshal de Tallard and 33 others.

[DANIEL DE FOE to ROBERT HARLEY.]

[1704, July]—I am convinced you are thronged with business of so much more weight than the particular before me, that I ought not to expect you can think this way; but, 'tis the debt I owe to your orders as well as my willingness to embark in your service which obliges me to acquaint you that pursuant to your directions of getting ready for this very day I have been preparing and fitting out in order to have been on horseback this morning.

I confess it afflicts me to see the day appear and myself unfurnished with the main thing, the very substance of all the rest, *your instructions*. Methinks I look like the Muscovite ambassador at Constantinople, who appeared as Envoy and had everything ready but his orders. Indeed I cannot jest with myself heartily on this head, because I reckon it my great misfortune, and though I shall never attempt to dictate to you, yet from the leave you have given me to use more freedom than otherwise I should, I crave a liberty with all possible respect both to your judgment, and to your design, humbly to represent:—That if this journey be for your service, as I hope it is, or I should be very sorry to be employed, it cannot be for the advantage of that service, to have me straitened in time, and the latter part of the season come on, before I shall have room to answer either your charge or expectation. I would not be an unprofitable servant, the unfortunate as I have noted elsewhere are criminals in politics, and ought to be laid by; if I have the season for acting I dare answer for it I won't miscarry but the night comes, winter will be upon me, in which of this affair I may say no man can work.

I acknowledge when you first did me the bonour to converse with me, and began the discourse of these things in particular, that very part so hit what I have had on my thoughts some years that I adjourned all my hopes, and all the thoughts I had, some of which were of much greater appearance, believing this a thing so absolutely useful, so exceedingly profitable in its event, and so suitable to my genius, that though I had some things of a more capital nature before me. I closed with this as *the thing* which I thought the Ministry most wanted and myself most capable of.

I had before now tendered you a Scheme of General Intelligence, but I thought this would much better go before it.

I had a design to propose your settling a private office for the conducting matters of this nature, so directed as neither in general to be suspected of what it should act, and yet be as publicly known as any other. That in this office openly and without the help of Mr. St. John's back stairs, a correspondence may be effectually settled with every part of England, and all the world beside, and yet the very clerks employed not know what they are a doing.

But all this I thought would be better subsequent to this journey and I firmly believe this journey may be the foundation of such an intelligence as never was in England; if I did not think so, I would be your humble petitioner not to let me go, and earnestly remonstrate against it.

I cannot close this long letter without observing something from your last discourse with me.

You were pleased to note that the Queen held the hands of the Dutch, and the Dane, from falling on the Swede, and the reason was just because in case of a rupture the Danish, the Prussian, and the Lunenberg troops must be recalled, &c.

I entreat you to consider whether a squadron of English and Dutch men-of-war may not effectually bring the Swede to reason without concerning the Dane or the Prussian in the matter, and if he will break with the rest, he will be ill handled at last, but I am persuaded our fleet may, if well directed, do all the work, and the Empire would soon have another face. I need not tell you the advantage of a Saxon Army on the Danube and a grateful King in your interest who will certainly acknowledge his being saved by our hands.

I have said too much, I ask pardon for the freedom I use.

NEWS LETTER.

1704, August 10. London—Yesterday we received the four Holland mails that were due, the freshest being of Friday last. The accounts they give of the affairs of Europe are that the Muscovites have again beaten General Schlipenbach near Narva, which place they expect soon to be masters of, as it is said they are already of Dorpet. In Poland things are much as they were, King Augustus and the King of Sweden with the new king are preparing to fight it out.

The French in Italy since the taking of Verceil have enterprised nothing, but refreshed their men; but the Duke of Vendosme is preparing for another siege. He has also detached 10,000 men to go and join the Grand Prior to enable him to oppose the Germans re-entering Lombardy as they design with a bigger force.

The principal malcontents in Hungary, according to letters from Vienna of the 2nd, have rejected the ample terms of accommodation offered them by the Emperor, and have begun their hostilities with greater rage than ever, burning and destroying all before them, but it is said 15,000 men will be drawn from the Empire to enable General Heister to chastise them.

They write from Augsburg of the 8th that the army of the Allies was decamped, as was that of the enemy after they had levelled their entrenchments near that place and left 4,000 men in garrison, but the same evening they perceived the Imperialists drawing towards that city and at the same time the advanced troops of the Bavarians arrived with the baggage, and a postscript to a letter says there has been action, that the Bavarians were beaten back, but the truth of this we must refer to our next. The Confederates lay all waste in Bavaria leaving nothing for man and horse to subsist on. The Marshal de Villeroy has possessed himself of all the passes in the Black Forest from Offenburg to Homburg and it is said designs to attack the lines.

The Dutch army is in the neighbourhood of St. Trond. On the 9th the detachment under the Marquis d'Allegre joined the Marquis de Bedmar; General Salish has taken [Fort] Isabella and draws in great contributions. The States are sending a vast quantity of ammunition for the Danube.

Paris letters of the 11th say that the Count de Toulouse returning with his fleet to the Isles of Hyéres the 25th received an express from the Viceroy of Catalonia with an account that Admiral Rooke having left the principal part of his fleet about the Straits mouth lay himself with 25 ships of war near Malaga, upon which Toulouse sailed and arrived at Barcelona on the 1st instant, where a conspiracy was discovered in favour of the House of Austria, in which above 300 persons, many of consideration, were found concerned.

Edinburgh, the 3rd. The Parliament met to-day according to their last adjournment and went upon the consideration of a Petition given in by the Marquis of Montrose for confirmation of his claim to the duty of sheriffdom of Bute and others belonging of the Duke of Lennox, the Lord Advocate pretending the Queen's right, and under her claimed the Earl of Bute ; but the Parliament gave it for the first and then the House adjourned till to-morrow when they are to go upon the petition for the payment of arrears and misapplication of funds during the last reign to the value of upwards of 100,000*l.*, being found to be sunk. in some great men's pockets that were then the premier ministers.

It comes now confirmed from Paris that their privateers meeting with a fleet of twenty four Barbadoes ships took nine of them and carried them into Brest and Nantes, and Count St. Paul bid fair for our Virginia fleet which are now safe arrived in the Downs, and since the loss of the *Falmouth*, the *Gloucester* and *Moderate* have had a sharp engagement with two French men-of-war of 60 guns each, about the chops of the Channel, but the French at last bore away, the *Gloucester* lost about 70 men by the bursting of a gun and some powder blowing up. The Lord Paston has completed the levy of his new raised regiment. The Marquis of Miremont has listed several hundred French refugees to go to the assistance of the Camisars, their body is to be made up here and abroad to 6,000. An express arrived just now of the total defeat of the Bavarian army.

Messengers.

1704, August 9—The names of the forty messengers and the places where they live. Signed by Thomas Atterbury, clerk of the cheque.

News Letter.

1704, August 10. Whitehall—This afternoon arrived an express from his Grace the Duke of Marlborough to my Lady Duchess written on horseback with a lead pen, a copy whereof follows.

August 13 N.S. 1704. I have not time to say any more than to beg of you to present my humble duty to the Queen and to let Her Majesty know that her army has had a glorious victory. Monsieur Tallard and two other generals are in my coach, and I am following the rest. The bearer, my aide de camp Colonel Parks, will give Her Majesty an account of what has passed. I shall do it in a day or two by another more at large.

The gentleman who brought this express is gone to Windsor to give Her Majesty an account of the particulars, which will be published at his return.

Thomas Foley to his brother[-in-law Robert Harley].

1704, August 12. Earl Stoke—I hear Sir Edward Seymour is recovered, and have this day sent my man to Bradley of a "how d'ye." 'Tis repeated Sir E. Seymour did not shave his beard from the time he lost his place till last Warminster sessions where he appeared very gay, new shaved, with a fine long periwig, and was a very great beau ; and having had the misfortune to lose his staff ordered it to be cried in open Court at Warminster. Lord Rochester is expected next week at Lavington within a mile of this place. I desire you will let me know whether there is any other Thomas Harley besides the Knight of Radnorshire, for there is one who calls himself by that name, says he is a younger brother, lives in your family, hath a place of 60*l.* per annum under you, is very much in your favour, and expects a greater place being a near relation to you. I, having never known-such a person should be glad to know if there be any such.

The ARCHBISHOP OF CANTERBURY to SECRETARY HARLEY.

1704, August 12. Lambeth—Asking him to present an address to the Queen from the Bishop of Oxford and his clergy, not being able himself to go to Windsor for the purpose, and to cause it to be printed in the Gazette.

SIR RICHARD COX, Chancellor of Ireland, and the EARL OF MOUNT ALEXANDER to the DUKE OF ORMOND.

1704, August 12. Dublin Castle—Sending him Attorney General Rochfort's report upon Captain Shadwell's petition with which they express their agreement. [*See* July 29, *ante.*] *Signed.*

VISCOUNT WEYMOUTH to [ROBERT] HARLEY, at Whitehall.

1704, August 15. L[ong]leat—I beg that you will please in my name humbly to congratulate the Queen on the glorious victory obtained by her armies under the command of the Duke of Marlborough.

MARIUS D'ASSIGNY to ROBERT HARLEY.

1704, August 16. Kentish Town near Highgate—Urging upon him the importance of fortifying Gibraltar, the writer having lived near there three years and knew its weakness; and offering several new inventions in gunnery of his own.

JOHN CHAMBERLAYNE, Secretary of the Society for Promoting the Gospel in Foreign Parts, to [ROBERT HARLEY].

1704, August 18. Petty France, Westminster—On behalf of Mr. Hales, a brother of Sir Thomas Hales, member for Kent, who has spent seven years in travelling through Germany, Italy, &c., and is more master of High Dutch, French and Italian, than of his mother tongue. *Signed.*

MEMORANDA by ERASMUS LEWIS.

1704, August 18 — Giving particulars of Mrs. Middleton, *alias* Brown who was concerned in the Assassination plot and who had owned herself to be the person that hid the Duke of Berwick.

NEWS LETTER.

1704, August 19. London—They write from Turin that the Duke of Savoy had caused to be signified to the Ministers of the Emperor, England and Holland, that he had occasion for a further supply of 10,000 men, and it would be necessary he should have them before the end of the campaign, upon which those ministers despatched expresses to their sovereigns. His Royal Highness since the loss of Verceil has sent orders to his ministers in the Courts of the Allies to declare his firm resolutions to continue firm in the Grand Alliance notwithstanding his present ill circumstances. And the last letters from Turin say that Mr. Hill is upon concluding a fresh treaty between that Court and England, and it is said considerable sums must be supplied by England and Holland for the support of the Prince.

According to letters from Paris of the 15th, on the 13th a courier arrived from the Duke de Vendosme which left his camp on the 7th and brought advice that the general designed to march with his army on the 11th or 12th to pass the Doria and make the siege of D'yre and that the Duke of Savoy was preparing to pass the same river to oppose him, and it was said that Count Albergotti would join the Duke de Feuillade to make the siege of Cony, though letters say the latter is to march with his troops for the Rhine.

They write from Vienna that the rebels continue to make a horrible ravage in Styria, Moravia, &c., and have burnt above 100 villages. The Elector Palatine before he left Vienna recommended to the Envoy of Holland to write to his masters and acquaint them with his immutable friendship for them and his zeal for the common cause, adding that he was troubled that the pains he had taken to accommodate matters with the Hungarians had had no success, it having been found that the heads of the rebels rejected all the tenders made them by the Emperor upon the promises made by the French and Bavarians of an utter destroying the House of Austria, for which it is said the King of the Romans has declared he will never forgive the Elector.

We have two Holland mails due and we long for their arrival to hear what measures the Elector of Bavaria takes since the overthrow of his army, whether or no he is drawing his scattered troops together (his left wing having not suffered so much as his right which was composed of the French troops and were totally cut in pieces or made prisoners), or is making his accommodation with the Emperor. Of this we are assured from the last letters that the Duke of Marlborough was resolved to give him no breathing time, but to pursue his blow and follow him wherever he should hear he was.

It is remarked as ill conduct in Count Tallard in permitting our army to pass the morass and the two rivulets which covered the camp without opposition, where they might have made a very great one, and on the contrary cried out, Let him come, make him a bridge of gold; nor did another action of this great general savour less of folly, for whilst he was a prisoner in his Grace's coach he sent a message to his Grace to spare his dear infantry who were in flight, and he would give orders they should not fire on the English.

Our letters from Scotland of the 12th bring nothing considerable from the proceedings of the parliament. They are going upon the consideration of the plot, but since neither the papers relating to it nor the witnesses are sent down to them nor are like to be, they cannot do much in it, but their sessions would soon terminate.

Last night Colonel Parks was sent back again express to the Duke of Marlborough with directions to his Grace about the Marshal de Tallard and the other General officers which are prisoners, and we hear are by order of Council to be brought for England, and no doubt will make a pleasing spectacle to the generality of people, being more for their 4s. in a pound than ever yet they saw. The Queen and Prince returned this evening to Windsor. The noise of a plot is a sham, the persons in custody of messengers are about other illegal practices.

Postscript.—We have just received two Holland mails which give an account that the Elector of Bavaria with the Marshal de Marsin is retired with his broken forces under the cannon of Ulm, having drawn out the garrison of Augsburg and others to join him, and expects to be joined by the Marshal de Villeroy, and that the Duke of Marlborough with the whole Confederate army (Prince Lewis to that end having quitted the siege of Ingolstadt) is marched in pursuit of the enemy. The Marshal de Tallard with the other French General officers are sent to Frankfort. The Paris Gazette takes no notice of this battle.

A[BEL] BOYER to [ROBERT HARLEY].

1704, August 21—Enclosing a translation of a manifesto to be issued by the Marquis de Miremont, Commander in Chief of the forces of the Queen of Great Britain in Piedmont. Gives description and particulars of a Franciscan friar named Soulier, formerly one of Count Tallard's chaplains, now in town and in constant communication with France. He is of a middle stature, his face ruddy and full of pimples, has crisped hair (unless he has lately put on a wig), wears a sword and dark brown clothes ; and generally to be found at a coffee house in St. Albans Street, three doors on this side the house that was lately burnt down. If Mr. Fitzgerald is found serviceable it will be necessary to provide for his subsistence, he having nothing to depend upon. It is advisable not to let him have any money but in very small sums, he being a very ill husband of his purse and given to gaming. Has been obliged to keep him from starving these four or five days ; but he (Boyer) has much ado to get his own livelihood. *Translation enclosed.*

NEWS LETTER.

1704, August 22. London—They write from Riga that the city of Dorpet surrendered upon Articles to the Czar of Muscovy who was there in person and entered the place sword in hand, and caused the garrison to march out in three bodies. The Governor with the other officers were conducted to Narva, and the rest to Pernau and Riga. The Swedish General Lewenhaudts has gained a victory over some Muscovites and the troops of Oginsky and took 22 pieces of cannon, 40 standards and 300 carriages laden with ammunition, killed 309 Poles on the spot besides others in the pursuit.

From Warsaw of the 9th, that the new king would take the field with his forces in a few days, that Prince Alexander Sobieski was arrived there and was going after the King of Sweden who has passed the river Wynele, and is marching for Russia to meet King Augustus, who on the other hand is moving to meet him, so that we daily expect to hear of a bloody battle from the north. The Swedes have plundered and burnt 60 villages in the Province of Sendomir belonging to the nobility which adhere to the King.

From Turin of the 12th, that nothing considerable has passed in the armies. The French make continual motions with a design to surprise the army of his Royal Highness, but as yet have attempted nothing. 25 soldiers are brought prisoners to Turin, and several are in irons in the camp for carrying on a conspiracy in favour of the enemy.

From Switzerland, that the Republic of Venice is upon the point of declaring against the two Crowns, and in order to it are arming apace. The Emperor will not receive the Pope's letters in justification of what passed in the Ferrarese and the Imperialists talk high at Rome that that court must expect in a little time to pay dear for that comedy. Cardinal Delfino is dead which makes 16 vacuities in the Sacred College.

Paris letters of the 23rd say that Count Toulouse is sailed from Barcelona towards the Levant to meet a fleet of English merchantmen that are on their return from Smyrna, that his fleet is composed of 52 men-of-war and 20 galleys, besides a great number of other vessels, carrying in all 2,582 pieces of cannon and 23,933 men. An express from the Marshal de Villeroy has put the Court in a consternation, and though the particulars it brought are kept private yet it is said the army in the Danube is routed and the Marshal Tallard with a great number of officers are taken prisoners.

The accounts given in already of the battle of Blenheim are so ample that there is little to add. Never did any age produce a more glorious victory. Our great expectations are now to hear of further action if the Elector of Bavaria continues about Ulm. The Duke of Marlborough and the other generals are resolved to attack him there if it be practicable, or else by straitening him oblige him to march for the Rhine and pass that river into the territories of France, having already quitted his own country to the Confederates; and it is wrote that a deputation is coming from Munich in the name of all the States of Bavaria to desire the Duke of Marlborough's protection like as Augsburg has done.

Edinburgh, 15th. The Parliament are upon the consideration of the public accounts and have discovered a cheat of 40,000*l.* sterling by Sir William Menzies in his farm of the duty of excise on Beer and Ale which was sunk between him and the Lords of the Treasury, and they have resolved that he shall make the same good. Our African and India Companies having on Saturday last given orders to Mr. McKensey the secretary to arrest and seize an English ship from East India then in Leith Road, which he effected by gratiating himself with the captain and the crew by first accepting a treat on board, and then inviting the captain &c. on shore, at which time they sent boats off and seized the said ship by way of reprisal for the *Annandale* seized some months past in the river Thames, which was there as forfeited. The next day the Company sent to notify the matter to the Commissioner, who appeared extremely surprised and offended at the action, as were the Chancellor and other Court officers. The *Medway* of 60 guns has taken and brought into Plymouth two French Privateers, one of 32 guns and 150 men, the other of 28 guns and 130 men. There be letters from Holland by the last post which say Sir George Rooke has beaten the French fleet, but the report deserves no credit. Yesterday a proclamation was published for a general Day of Thanksgiving to be observed on the 7th of September next for the late glorious victory. There were killed of the Queen's subjects in the late battle 51 officers, and 133 wounded.

The DUKE OF ORMONDE to SECRETARY [ROBERT] HARLEY.

1704, August 23. Whitehall — Approving of Captain Shadwell's petition for a grant for erecting an office of assurance for the support of widows and orphans by the voluntary contribution of subscribers in the kingdom of Ireland. *Signed.*

A. [LADY] PYE to ABIGAIL HARLEY, at Brampton.

1704, August 23. Derby—My mother's health was much increased while she stayed here; she was able to walk up the Peak hills to see

Chatsworth, the greatest wonder of the place, which is much beautified since I saw it this time four years. Lady Crewe's marriage with Lord Torrington caused much chat in these parts. They were married upon the road, and two days after lay here in this town on the way to Buxton the daughter Lady Harpur and her sister Miss Crewe knew nothing of it till the public post brought the news. Having both a good spirit and purse she is more likely to deal with his lordship better than the last poor lady. Our public good news of late has caused a general rejoicing and raised our English General above all detracting tongues; the country people say there is something for their money, which I fear will rise heavy this next year. The farmers complain much, all sadly burnt up; I never remember more heat to continue so long as this summer. I suppose you heard of Sir Cholmley Dering's marriage to a great fortune and pretty young lady.

Dr. H. ALDRICH, Dean of Christ Church, to [ROBERT] HARLEY.

1704, August 24. Christ Church—Sending him a letter which he had received from Cambridge, where he never had a correspondent. The writer spells his words like a no-scholar; but perhaps he had only a mind to send a specimen of his Cambridge talent in bantering.

NEWS LETTER.

1704, August 24. London—By letters from Madrid of the 5th of this instant we have an account that the King had fixed the 1st of September for returning to his army, that in the meantime a new regulation was made for the Spanish troops by which the officers are obliged to have their companies always full, which considering at the same time how ill they are paid many have resigned their commands, being not able to live on the service, besides they complain of the fatigues of the last campaign and how ill the army was supplied with necessaries. The Viceroy of Catalonia has demanded a reinforcement of troops to keep the Barcelonians and others in order whom he finds wholly inclined to the interest of Charles the 3rd.

Those from Vienna of the 13th say, that the departure of the King of the Romans for the army on the Danube was fixed for the 20th of the same; that General Heister was returned for Hungary to put himself at the head of his troops, and advances to attack a great body of the rebels that were posted near Oedemberg and it is said that the said General is to be joined again by the Croats, as also to be reinforced with some troops from the Danube. In the meantime the rebels have absolutely rejected the Emperor's last concessions, are very rampant, committing great disorders on all sides, having been buoyed up with promises of great assistance from France and Bavaria, which finding themselves frustrated of by the defeat of the enemy it is probable they will now show a better temper and accept what before they rejected.

They write from Augsburg of the 16th that since the defeat of the French and Bavarian army the Elector hath drawn what troops he could together out of his garrisons in Bavaria and Suabia, and particularly four squadrons and eight battalions that were in that city had quitted the citadel and were marched for Ulm, also the Electress of Bavaria and her children have quitted Munich, and are gone post for Ulm. The consternation is inexpressible.

They write from the camp of the Allies of the 17th that they are extremely embarrassed with the prisoners which they took in the late battle, which amount to upwards of 11,000, besides 1,200 officers, and 120 standards and colours. The Marshal, Tallard, had the honour the day before the date to dine with his Grace the Duke of Marlborough, as did his son, and several other General officers that are prisoners; and a company was given the Marshal to mount the guard before his lodgement. It is said his Grace complimented the Marshal at the first view, and said, that he was sorry that this misfortune should fall on him having had the honour of his personal acquaintance, to which the Marshal replied, that since it was so he thought it his happiness to have fallen into his Grace's power.

Edinburgh, 17th. An action brought in for allowing the exportation of wool, seeing there is not a consumption in the kingdom for half that is grown, and the scarcity of money here is attributed in good part to the want of coin which that commodity brought in. The Duke of [*torn off*] the Marquis of Annandale, the Earls of Marchmont, Crawford, and the rest of that party keep their cabals together, and are tooth and nail for the court of Hanover and abjuration, and it is believed will make an attempt to bring in the latter before the Parliament rises. One Chartres, an officer in the Horse Guards, is suspended by the Duke of Argyll, captain of the said troop, for having had the impudence to place himself at the commanders' table, and when he was turned out to draw upon the gentleman that was commanded to do it.

The Lord Portmore is arrived from Lisbon, and gone to Windsor to wait on the Queen. The Lord Chief Justice Trevor is lately married to the Lady Barnard, widow of the late Sir Robert Barnard of Brampton in Huntingdonshire. The East India ship that was seized in Scotland belongs to neither of the two companies, but is a separate trader, and they now pretend their reason for it was that she broke bulk there, which was contrary to their Act of Parliament.

JOHN TAYLOR to ——.

1704, August 24. The Secretary's Office at Whitehall—I enclose you the Observator wherein you will find a complaint of a conventicle kept in your city by Non-jurors and Jacobites, and desire you to shew it to your Magistrates in order that they may take care to suppress it, whereby they may testify their zeal for her Majesty's person and government; otherwise they may be taken for such like disaffected persons themselves.

JOHN DALLEY to ROBERT HARLEY, Secretary of State.

1704, August 25. Barnet—We are just now going in all haste to the borders of Scotland the bishop having finished his message here and having received letters from the two Colonels to meet them at Newcastle upon Tyne. Please write to me there by the name of Miles Crowly and let me have directions to some Justice of the Peace that may secure us all there. I will give it to him or compass some way how to do it. If you do not do this all I can do is to get us all secured in Holland by your envoy there; it will be easy to do it there. I never saw any man so fearful and so wary as the bishop is since the taking of those people. There is no coming at him till we come to Newcastle where we will have a stay. You know I cannot get them taken without exposing myself in public view to them to be the person that betrayed them, so that I must take private measures to do it. I want a bill of twenty guineas enclosed in your letter to Newcastle. I expect you shall have the Colonels as well as us taken there.

R. HALES to [JOHN CHAMBERLAYNE].

1704, August 26. Copenhagen—Giving details of his travels in Germany and Sweden and the means he had taken for disseminating the *Soldier's Monitor* and other treatises.

NEWS LETTER.

1704, August 26. London—Letters from Turin say that now they believe the design of the enemy is not to besiege Yvre or Verue, but to endeavour to attack His Royal Highness in his entrenchment. They have taken away all the palisades about Verceil and have undermined the works in order to blow them up, and leave the place, it being too big to keep, and the air of it will not agree with strange bodies. A detachment from the Duke de Feuillade's army has been beaten near Coni. His Royal Highness has frequent conferences with the English envoy, and they talk of a negociation on foot, which is at present kept very secret, that will produce a great change in the affairs of Europe.

According to what they write from Venice, the French ravage all the country about Verona, and have so posted their troops that they have in a manner blocked it up on two sides, upon which the Regency have given orders for their troops to march that way to cover their territories and repel force by force, and have at the same time resolved to arm considerably, and it is believed the late victory obtained by the Confederates will be a means to induce the Republic to declare against France, the vote before in the Senate upon debating the point having been in a manner upon an equilibrium.

The Emperor's forces which retired into the Trentin have since received several reinforcements, and still possess divers passes in the Adige, so that they can enter Italy again when they please, which however it is believed they will not do till the war in Bavaria is over.

Our letters from Switzerland speak no further of the neutrality for Savoy, the Cantons having a mind to sit still and see the fate of the liberties of Europe disputed. The Protestant Cantons are inclined to the common cause, but the Catholic Cantons appear wholly in the interest of the two Crowns, and there are considerable feuds at present amongst themselves about the affair of religion which is heightened by the Pope's Nuncio, and the Minister of France.

Edinburgh the 15th. The affairs of the public accounts take up great debates in the House, and few understand them, and it is believed will turn to little account. This day a Bill was brought in for excluding all Commissioners from shires and boroughs that have any public post or pension from being members of Parliament, as also for additional number of Barons or Commissioners of shires to balance the number of peers made in the last reign and present, and the same was read the first time.

We hear some persons come from Holland in the *Soardyke* yacht report that the French and Bavarians, upon the advance of the Duke of Marlborough towards Ulm, retired towards the Black Forest, to avoid coming to further action, and that afterwards Ulm surrendered to the Confederates; but this report is not to be relied upon, but we must await the arrival of the next post. The Antwerp Gazetteer takes notice of the late battle on the Danube, but says upon the whole that we had more men killed in it than the enemy, which is certainly, untrue, though to be sure we lost a great many men in a fight of five or six hours with troops that are esteemed the best in Europe; and the general account is that in that part of the army belonging to the Queen and States about 6,000 were killed or wounded, and it fell rather heavier on the right wing, however it be so a glorious a victory was not too dear bought. On Wednesday night last Mr. Arthur, Mr. Mallone and Mr. Coleman, lately taken into custody of messengers, were admitted to bail, and are bound to appear the first day of the next term in the Court of Queen's Bench. It is thought one Hurly an Irishman is the informer against the aforesaid three gentlemen, who are of the same country.

Dr. F. GASTRELL to [ROBERT HARLEY].

1704, August 27. Christ Church [Oxford]—I shall make it my business to deserve the confidence you are pleased to put in me by the most faithful accounts I can give you. The university is very sensible of the kindness intended them by her Majesty, and when the Charter comes out all jealousies will be removed concerning the disposition of that royal charity. The Dean of Christ Church is most heartily and entirely your humble servant in all companies and upon all occasions. Had heard that one Mr. Griffith was designed for the Archdeaconry of Brecknock; he is a person very worthy upon all accounts to be taken care of, it will be of service to the church to prefer him.

LORD CUTTS to [ROBERT HARLEY].

1704, [August 28—] September 7 new style. The Duke of Marlborough's camp at Spire—I thank you for your letter and presume to accept your generous offer of being my friend, and when a favourable occasion offers shall ask your protection. I am glad you think I have done my duty.

P.S.—I don't pretend to write you news, knowing you have it from Cardonnel.

NEWS LETTER.

1704, August 29. London—The Cardinal de Fourbin, according to letters from Rome, has lately had a long conference with the Pope upon the affairs of Italy, in which he assured him, that the King his master had so ordered matters as to put a speedy end to the war in that country, at which the Pope showed great satisfaction, and replied that he would contribute his prayers towards it, and, as it is believed, something more underhand, or else the Imperialists had not been turned out of the Ferrarese. Cardinal Pignatelli has had an audience upon the subject of the affairs of Poland, and it was observed that the Pope appeared cold in the cause of King Augustus, and talked of misgovernment and a mistrust he had of his Catholicism, which confirmed the opinion that many had of him before, that with France he has underhand supported the party against that Prince.

The news of the taking of Donauwerth by the Allies and their entering Bavaria, has mightily disturbed the Queen Dowager of Poland, and induced her to send her son-in-law the Elector a supply of 40,000 crowns, which however is a sum so trivial that it will scarce answer with that prince one night's play, much less enable him to carry on a war with the Emperor and his Allies.

The Pope has lately refused to fill the vacant bishoprics in Spain, upon the nomination of Philip the 5th, as well not to add fresh fuel to the Emperor's present resentment against the Court of Rome for its partial proceedings during the course of this war in favour of France, as not to disoblige Charles the 3rd, who has anew declared his sole right to the said nomination, as the veritable successor to Charles the 2nd, and not knowing yet which way the success of the war will turn.

The Elector Palatine before he left the Court of Vienna left a commission with his Privy Councillor Ruckley to go to Prince Ragotzy, and it is believed that Prince will at last think fit to send him the necessary passports demanded in order to it; in the meantime they write from Buda that that Prince had given an assault to Segedin, but was beaten off with a great loss, and that they had no account since which way he was turned. We long to hear how the late victory upon the Danube operates with these people, but we must have patience till the arrival of the three Holland mails that are now due.

Edinburgh, 22nd. I lately told you that an Act was brought in Parliament for allowing the transportation of wool, and that the same was read then a first time. This day the same was debated in the House, and upon the votes whether export or not, it was carried in the affirmative. After that another vote was put whether it should be with an additional duty, which was also carried in the affirmative. The Privy Council hath at last declared prize a Dutch ship laden from the Canaries with wine, taken by Captain Gordon, for having a French pass, which was discovered to him by the cook of the said ship in revenge to the captain who had the day before beaten him, and she is ordered this day to be brought into Leith Harbour, in order to the selling both bottom and cargo, but the Dutch seamen are kindly used, and are to have their pay.

Our port letters have nothing in them worth remark. It is said the Dutch had recalled six of their capital ships from the fleet in the Straits before the taking of Gibraltar by Sir George Rooke. The French fleet under the Count de Toulouse is said to have orders sent him to return to Toulon, so that their pretended orders to seek and fight Sir George Rooke was nothing but bounce. I hear his Grace the Duke of Ormond, Lord Lieutenant and General Governor of Ireland, designs to set out hence for that kingdom, the 10th of the next month. Last night Irby Montagu Esquire, a Colonel of the Guards, brother to my Lord Halifax, fell from his horse near Newington, and immediately died, being a corpulent man. We hear the King of Denmark and the States General use endeavours to engage England in a war against Sweden, in favour of his Polish Majesty, but some considerations for the House of Hanover prevent our Court from engaging into such an alliance, there being a prospect of a match between his Swedish Majesty and a Princess of that House. The Queen has appointed Doctor Sherlock, Dean of St. Paul's, to preach before her on the 7th proximo, the day appointed for a Public Thanksgiving for the late glorious victory.

—— Dusouley to [Robert] Harley.

1704, August 29—Warning him against the great number of French priests and monks undoubtedly living in London and ever plotting against the government. Two of them were mixed up in the plots against the late king and were put under arrest, but were released at the solicitation of the Portuguese envoy and sent abroad; nevertheless they returned some time afterwards to London where they still are. One, is named Michel Lebreton, the other Pierre Maudin, the latter passing as a teacher of languages, thereby gaining introduction into many houses. A third priest is named Soulié. The writer can supply sufficient evidence to justify their arrest. Charges Louis Delafaye with carrying on a correspondence with the Abbé Renaudot in Paris, and submits that a person so badly disposed to the government should not be continued in employment.

THE EARL OF ABERCORN to [ROBERT HARLEY].

1704, August 29. Dublin—When I waited upon you in your office you did me the favour to offer me letters of recommendation in my son Paisley's behalf, as to such foreign Courts I designed he should travel to. I only delayed accepting thereof, till my son had in some measure fitted himself to appear in the world by learning his exercises at the Academy of Lewarden; but it seems that Academy is broken up, upon the death of the chief person who managed it, and I am now sending orders to Monsieur De Choutens: my son's governor, to remove ihim from thence to Wolfenbüttcl. The Court of Hanover being in my son's way thither, it might seem want of due respect in him to Their Highnesses, and in me of due deference to the Protestant Succession' as by law established, if he should pass through Hanover, or reside in the territory of Princes of that family, without behaving himself as becomes him upon that occasion. I should be glad therefore to have my son Paisley introduced at the Court of Hanover by Her Majesty's Minister, there, and that you would please to honour my son with two or three lines to his Excellency.

STANLEY WEST to [ROBERT HARLEY].

1704, August 29. Tunbridge Wells—The company here seem wholly employed in the amusements of the place and nothing passes of concern to the public. The news of the late glorious victory was received with universal joy; few seemed displeased at that surprising success. The Lord George Howard promoted and encouraged the public rejoicing and told me, that though he was a Catholic yet he was very glad of the news as considering the interest of his estate in it. Here are few persons of quality, several have been here but not together. The Lords Leinster, Burgavenny, Howard of Effingham, Howard of Escrick, Villiers, and Barnard are gone; the Lords George Howard, Petre, and Fanshaw are still remaining and also the Duchess of Cleveland who is a constant player with the gentlemen only, and hath had bad success.

For want of other information, be pleased to give me leave to acquaint you with my observation of people's opinion of your Honour. You have a happier fate attending you, than any in the present Ministry, or in former either. You are entirely master of two opposite parties, both think you to be theirs and confide in you as such, to promote their several different interests: whatever distinguishing favour you show to either side, doth not lessen your esteem in the other party, 'tis all ascribed to a depth of policy which they cannot comprehend and which they say is peculiar to yourself, but is not a leaving the party; and in such an unprecedented manner do you manage the heads of both parties, that both sides believe, at a proper time and occasion you will show yourself entirely in their distinct interests. I am very glad to see so eminent a post free from the reproach that usually hath attended it, and to observe your Honour stand so right in the people's opinion; being very confident you will so manage the weaknesses and follies of both sides as will in the issue redound to the true interest and advantage of the Kingdom. The Duke, the Treasurer and yourself are called the Triumvirate, and reckoned the spring of all public affairs; and that your interests and counsels are so united and linked together that they cannot be broken, nor in any danger of it during this reign. Particular notice was taken here of the Duke's letter, as addressed to yourself and not to the elder Secretary: remarks on that were plain and obvious: your concerting that march with the Duke justly entitled you to the first notice of its success. I have heard of people's talk, that you fall in with this Ministry, not for any particular value or esteem for the persons but as what the Court had resolved upon to be the Ministry; if the Court had appointed my Lord Rochester, or any other person to be the Prime Minister, it would have been the same thing to you, and that your aim is in time to be the Prime Minister yourself. Some others say that no gentleman's interest in England could have been equal to yours, had you accepted of no place at all, but only the Speaker's, which they say would have been constantly entailed upon you, nobody could have stood in competition with you; that then the Court would always have courted and feared you, and the Country been managed by you, and that the profits of that place under such considerations were preferable to the Secretary's office, for that being under the command of the Court, there must be an absolute compliance with every direction, or a quitting it, and in that case you can never afterwards be so popular, nor stand so right in the people's esteem as you did before. Thus people take the liberty to express their sentiments of great men, and differently to judge of their actions. I humbly beg your pardon for this great freedom, which I hope you will impute to my very great zeal, for your interest and service, and apprehension that it might not be altogether impertinent to let you know the people's talk. When I lately waited on you you were pleased to express a desire of creating a good correspondence abroad and at home. There is a gentleman now in Flanders who I think very capable of serving you in this matter, at his return I will sound him and acquaint you if he is willing to undertake it. As for affairs in the City and rise of reports there, I cannot think of a person proper to inform you; as for myself, I am more retired from company and more in the country than I used to be, and am not so conversant with persons and reports, as would be of any use to you, but if anything should come to my knowledge, of service to the public, or to yourself, my zeal for both would oblige me to give you the earliest information.

INSTRUCTIONS to RALPH YOUNG, messenger.

1704, August 29—You are to make all diligence to go to   for the apprehending of the several persons in your warrant specified.

You are to go first to the Post Office, where you are to keep your residence until you have effected your business, or received orders from me to come back.

Deliver the letter to the Mayor as soon as you conceive that your have need of his assistance, as well in searching in the Town as also on board all vessels, which shall be outward bound.

If you want directions or further assistance deliver a letter to Mr. John Ord, an attorney who is recommended as a person very capable of being useful to you.

You are before the post comes in to deliver the letter directed to the Postmaster giving him the highest cautions of secrecy.

You are carefully to watch the coming in of the post and endeavour to be in the house near at hand when a letter directed to Mr. Miles Crowly is called for, whom you are to apprehend with as little noise and clamour as may be! He is a very tall lean man, has some hollowness about his eyes, very long fingers with freckles upon them and his hands. In case any person different from him now described should call for the letter oblige him to tell you where the party himself is, and secure him till he conducts you to his lodgings, or wherever else he ordered that person to bring the letter to him.

If the person above described comes himself for the letter, you are to seize him and use your utmost endeavours to make him discover where the other two persons may be found. It is possible there may be but two, one person besides him that comes for the letter.

You are to be diligent in your search that none of the said persons get on shipboard or into Scotland, and you must be particularly careful in searching any ship you suspect may be bound for Holland. And if you seize the persons be careful to secure all their papers, mark them and seal them up distinctly, that you may be able to swear from where you received each paper; be sure you search their clothes, also the heels of their shoes which are made hollow on purpose to carry letters.

You are to give this letter to the Postmaster directed according as a letter is expected that is directed, and observe whether the person opens it or no. If he opens this letter or by other circumstances you judge him to be the person meant you are to seize him immediately, but with as little noise and disorder as may be, that you may not give the alarm to his companions whom you are to endeavour to prevail with him to discover to you, one or both of them being of more consequence than this person himself.

It is expected you should use your utmost application to seize this person, it being impossible to give particular rules that may suit every accident which may happen.

You are every post, by letter, to give me an account of your proceedings.

News Letters.

1704, August 31. London—The difference between the Imperial Court and that of Rome increases insomuch that the Emperor has refused to receive the Pope's letters in justification of himself of what happened to the Germans in the Ferrarese, he laying the whole contrivance and conduct of that matter upon his officers, but this sort of varnish being too common in that Court the asseveration of his infallibility in this case goes for little.

Several conferences have been held with the Ottoman envoy at which Count Rappach and Count Maximillian Brunes with some others of the Eldest councillors of the Council of war assisted, in which the said envoy gave the most solemn assurances possible that the Porte would inviolably observe every article of the Peace of Carlovitz, but at the same time he was told that some Turks were joined with Ragotzy, to which he replied that they were only deserters from the garrison of Temisware, and if the Emperor's forces should happen to take any of them, and would send them to the aforesaid place, the Porte would be glad of the occasion to convince the Emperor by the severity of their punishment, that it is far from the inclination of the Grand Seignior, that any of his subjects should join with Ragotzy in his rebellion to disturb the Emperor.

Postscript. By three Holland mails just arrived we have these particulars, that the French have undertaken nothing yet in Italy, that the Protestant Cantons showed an extreme joy at the victory obtained by the Allies, that the Court of Vienna appeared ravished at the same, and that Prince Ragotzi had sent to demand of the Emperor the conditions he had before offered him; that his Imperial Majesty, as an acknowledgment of the great and signal service done him by the Duke of Marlborough, had made him a Prince of the Empire and Marshal de camp of his armies.

The Elector of Bavaria and the Marshal de Marsin after the battle of Hochstedt retired with their battered troops, not making above 17 or 20,000 men, towards Ulm, of which the Elector made Monsieur Bottendorf Governor, leaving a garrison of two regiments of French and six of Bavarians, and then retired through the Black Forest to meet and join the Marshal de Villeroy, which it is said he has already done by the valley of Kintzig, but that together they make not above 30,000 men.

The Duke of Marlborough with the Confederate Army pursued the Elector and arrived before and summoned and invested Ulm on the 21st, and, after the exchange of some prisoners, together with Prince Eugene pursued his march with the army of England and the States towards the Rhine, and was to be at Bruschall near Phillipsburg on the 5th proximo. Prince Lewis and General Thungen with 20,000 are left to carry on the siege of Ulm, which place, some advices say, has already surrendered, and the Electress of Bavaria, who could not join her husband, is with her children returned to Munich, and has sent to demand the Emperor's protection, as the Estates of that country have done, their Prince having deserted his country, and to the Duke of Marlborough to desire an accommodation, offering to surrender Verne and Ingolstadt upon condition the Duke will let her enjoy her country and the said towns, to which the Duke answered that the last of the said places must be demolished, and the troops of all the garrisons come into the service of the Allies, and that she should have 500 men allowed her for her guard &c. In the meantime his Grace makes long marches to besiege Landau, so that the Elector of Bavaria is now in the same condition as his brother the Elector of Cologne.

Paris letters of the 1st of September mention the great consternation they were in at the news of the defeat of the Danube, that upon it orders were sent to the Duke de Vendome to make a detachment of 10,000 men for the Rhine, and the Duke de Feuillade of 3,000. They own their loss to be 6,500 killed, 3,000 wounded, and 8,000 prisoners. That on 26th the Marshal Villeroy joined the Elector of Bavaria, and that their army makes 60,000 men.

Edinburgh, 24th. Yesterday our parliament passed the Act for transportation of wool, so that they may now draw it from the north of England and Ireland and send it to France. The Commander of the English East India ship that is seized here petitioned the Parliament to be released, but the House would not meddle in that affair, but left it to the decision of the law. That Duke Hamilton and the Laird of Saltoun had hard words and were near coming to blows. It is said the Parliament will be adjourned to-morrow and an end put to the Sessions.

LORD GRANVILLE to ROBERT HARLEY, Secretary.

[1704, August 31.]—Desires to know how Her Majesty would have the general thanksgiving observed at the Tower and other garrisons.

The last time the Queen went to St. Paul's the Tower made a triple
discharge of cannon ; a single discharge in more remote places would
probably be sufficient.

. . .

RICHARD DUKE to ROBERT HARLEY, Secretary.

1704, September. Otterton, ten miles from Exeter—This year I
am within two of eighty years, and whatever defects I may be loaded
with I cannot accuse myself of much flattery. You know that nothing is
more common than to wind and warp to a man in high place; but I
seek our common good.

A great man, a traveller on this road last week, left behind this
universal pleasing report, that you, in conjunction with my Lord
Treasurer or without him, should be the medium of recalling my
unlucky neighbour [Sir E. Seymour]'s white staff. Sir William
Courtenay and his numerous accomplices have been brought to throw
out, and over awe, my son's election at Ashburton, a borough I bought
by old Sir William Courtenay's commanding persuasion, and in which
my son still hath the true interest.

Sir Edward Seymour, when he had the white staff, prevailed with the
Lord Keeper to throw out several of our most valuable justices, five round
me worth about 100,000l., and put in one of 100l. per annum; threw
out Sir Jo. Elwill worth 50,000l., the most necessary justice in the
county, living but two miles from Exeter, who stands so fair with the
judges that the last assizes they invited him and many of the outed
justices to eat with them. I desire you may have the honour to rout
Sir Edward by inducing the Queen to restore the justices of this great
kingdom county, as has been done in lesser counties.

It is necessary to take off all murmuring from the merchants and trading
little ships, which employ no less than 20,000 men and horse in our
division of the county; for there are now four French privateers sailing to
and fro all Torbay over, which have hindered the fishing and trading all
this summer. If I had not lent some muskets to beat them off, they had
carried away a bark of 50,000 healing stones of Sir William Yonge's and
my son's; they however only set her sails on fire, which our men quenched.
The privateers then ran four leagues to Lyme, and came but a quarter of
an hour too late to take a Lyme ship worth 6 or 8,000l.; we suppose we
killed two or three of their men for which I deserve a medal. Exeter
and Dartmouth merchants are not a little vexed that the greatest bay the
Queen of England hath should be thus and so long tormented with
such pirates, which may be avoided by one swift sailor of 30 or rather
of 40 guns. I would not have my name mentioned at the Admiralty,
though I study to serve all, and gave notice of these pirates to Sir
William Drake some weeks since, to acquaint the Admiralty hereof,
but nothing has been ordered for our better protection.

Postscript.—Since writing of this my neighbour seaman saith those
French rogues have taken two colliers.

GENERAL H. LUMLEY to [ROBERT HARLEY].

1704, September [1–]11. New style. Langenkandell—Assuring him
of the satisfaction with which he received the news of the Queen having
made so good a choice.

JOHN BELL to ROBERT HARLEY, at Whitehall.

1704, Semptember 2. Newcastle [on-Tyne]—Promises to carry out his instructions concerning Miles Crowly. Is just going to Sunderland where are seven doggers or vessels going to Holland, in order to secure any persons going over sea without a pass ; and his friend Colonel Villiers at Shields will be instructed to take the same precautions. *Signed.*

FRANCISCO DE LA TORRE to [ROBERT HARLEY].

1704, September 2—Giving information against John Corso, an Italian, who pretended to have been robbed of 30,000*l.* by Captain Kidd, and who was intending to substantiate his claim by means of false witnesses, having been directed to appear before the High Court of Admiralty.

WILLIAM PENN to ROBERT HARLEY.

1704, September 2—I send a case very extraordinary and an offer as commendable. He is a gentleman, the son of an old Parliament Colonel and a brave man, I recommend it to thy favour, if thy good judgment approves of it ; and when the Queen gives it the Duke of Ormond—who is apprised, and his Secretary, of it, with liking, as I hear—pray encourage the Duke to answer the gentleman's request. The petition will be drawn to-night for the Cabinet to-morrow, if the enclosed case receives thy approbation. I hope to wait upon thee at Windsor and therefore waive my privilege to-night.

Enclosure.

PIERCE ARNOP.

The case of Pierce Arnop, of Crookhaven in the Kingdom of Ireland, Esquire.

The town of Crookhaven lying at a considerable distance from any other English settlement and a fort, that had been maintained there for the defence of the harbour, being demolished by the late King James, the French privateers in the late war gave such frequent disturbances to the few English inhabitants who remained there that they deserted the place, and upon the peace, the said Arnop came to settle there with a few English families his tenants.

Upon the breaking out of this present war, the enemies' privateers appearing frequently upon that coast, the said Arnop left his house and betook himself to an old ruined castle which he repaired, provided with small arms, and made defensible against a sudden surprise, at his own charge, so that his small force became an awe upon the privateers, that they durst not land thereabouts as formerly, and gave protection to divers English ships that put in there.

In the month of July 1703 two large privateers came to the harbour, and made show of attempting to land, but finding him provided to oppose them, they suddenly stood off again, and soon after the said Arnop descried from the top of a hill a considerable number of ships in the offing, which afterwards appeared to be the Jamaica fleet, and considering the danger they might be in from the said privateers, and others which then were cruising upon that coast, he adventured though in sight of the privateers, to go off in a small boat, and went on board them at six or seven leagues distance, advising them of the danger and persuaded them to come into the harbour, which they accordingly did, the wind being contrary to their proceeding for England; of which service they were so sensible that the commanders of the ships collected a considerable sum among themselves, offering to make him a present thereof, which he refused, his circumstances being then such as to stand in no need thereof; all which appears by certificate under the hands' of the commanders of her Majesty's ships and the merchant men of that fleet, and for which he had the honour to receive a letter of thanks from Mr. Secretary Southwell by order of his grace the Duke of Ormond.

The said Aruop continuing to do all the services to the English that lay in his power, such of the malicious Irish who held correspondence with the enemy incited them against him, and gave them an account of his small strength, whereupon in the month of April last, a French privateer came near the harbour shewing Dutch colours, and seeming to be in distress, the said Aruop sent off a boat, with his son and five men to their assistance, who with much difficulty escaped being taken, by landing on the other side, but could not return to the Castle, so that the French landing sixty or seventy men and the said Aruop having but two or three people with him, after resisting them for above two hours, found himself necessitated to surrender upon their promise to use him well; but as soon as they came in they fell on plundering his house and abusing his person, till his wife brought them all her rings, jewels, gold, and silver, so that they carried away all that was valuable, even to their very clothes; and when they returned on board their ship, the captain was very angry because they had not brought the said Arnop with them, and sent them ashore again to fetch him, but he being escaped they lay two or three days in the harbour, came divers times on shore, offered rewards for his person, burnt all his houses, with a considerable quantity of corn, and other things of value, and killed all his cattle that they could meet with without injuring any other person, so that he is not only deprived of his stock and his being, but dares not settle again upon his lands during the war, unless the government shall be inclined to maintain some small fortification there for the security of the place.

The said Arnop desires that as his sufferings have befallen him only for his services to his country, he may receive a competent reparation for the same from the public, and upon his being paid what may be thought reasonable he is willing to be obliged to repair the old fort at his own charge, if the Government will furnish it with ten guns, sufficient ammunition, a gunner, and a detachment of twenty men out of the nearest garrison, giving him the government thereof, at such pay as shall be thought fit, on condition to repay his charge whenever the said pay shall cease.

JOHN BELL to [ROBERT HARLEY].

1704, September 4. Newcas[tle-on-Tyne]—Since I wrote last I have been to Sunderland and Shields to secure both ports that no passengers should go beyond seas that had no passes. Upon my journey I was reflecting upon Col. Macdonell's name and recollected that he married a sister of the present governor of Tynemouth Castle, Col. Villiers; and I believe it may be the same man enquired after, if I see him I shall know him. Lest he and others of them should go off at Chester in the Street, six miles south of this place, and so cross the country for Tynemouth Castle I have laid a trusty friend to keep a watch. I received a letter last post for Mr. M. Crowly, which I keep with that sent by the messenger till called for. .

[Dr. Francis Atterbury] to the Bishop of Carlisle.

1704, September 4. Bishopthorpe—I came hither on Saturday evening and intended to have set out this morning in order to pay my duty to your Lordship at Rose Castle, but am stopped by a letter of your Lordship's to his Grace, part of which his Grace hath been pleased to communicate to me. And therein I find that your Lordship is firmly determined not to give me institution your self, should I wait upon you for it, unless I do openly and freely revoke and renounce three propositions relating to her Majesty's Supremacy there specified, and which seem to your Lordship desirable from something that I have heretofore asserted and published. My Lord, there are many reasons for which I can by no means comply with this, or with any such proposal, and with which there is no need that I should at present trouble your Lordship; especially since your Lordship hath in the same letter desired his Grace, that, in case I consented not to your proposal, he would please to admit me and send his Metropolitical Mandate for my installation. His Grace, I find, is very ready to fulfill your Lordship's desire in that respect—as I am also to take that method of being instituted—as soon as your Lordship shall have made such a remission of your right and authority in this case, under your episcopal seal, as may be a legal and effectual warrant for his Grace's giving me institution, and my receiving it. To this end I may, I hope, be permitted thus to offer myself to your Lordship by letter for institution, since your Lordship hath expressed a concern [for] the unnecessary expenses of my coming to Rose Castle in order only—as your Lordship is pleased to speak—to be sent back by you. And therefore without waiting in person on your Lordship—as I was ready to have done—I will expect your Lordship's pleasure here at Bishopthorpe. Hoping for such dispatch from your Lordship as may enable me safely to proceed to my instalment without further delay. *Copy in Atterbury's hand, headed* " My own letter to the Bp of Carlisle," *to which is added,* " Extract from the Bp of Carlisle's letter of Aug. ult., to the Ap of York."

Sir C. Musgrave to [Robert Harley].

1704, September 6. Edenhall—I should be guilty of the greatest ingratitude imaginable if I omitted any opportunity of paying my utmost acknowledgements to you for the many favours you have conferred upon me and the family. The friendship and regard you had for my father have induced you, a very unusual thing now a days, to continue your acts of kindness to the family, when none of them can pretend to have the least prospect of making any other return than a poor acknowledgment. You have been pleased in a very obliging manner to take notice of my brother Thomas, who of late years has reaped great advantages from the favour of you and yours.

On Monday Colonel Graham came hither, and yesterday most of the persons of the greatest interest in Westmorland dined here and after some debate it was resolved to let this election go uncontested, and the rather since Mr. Fleming has had the advantage of a month's time to solicit the country, nobody else offering their service, and this Parliament not being long lived. But it is likewise resolved that my brother shall forthwith make his application and offer his service to the country in conjunction with Mr. Graham upon the calling of a new Parliament. This morning the Colonel went for Levens. We frequently drank your health. Tomorrow I go to Carlisle to entertain my Corporation, and to keep the jubilee.

Our victory by the prints appears every day greater. I hope by the assistance of Cousin Lyster (who is so kind as to act as my Commissioner of Accounts here) to give a present dispatch to my affairs so that in three weeks time I may have the honour to kiss your hand.

[*Postscript.*]—The weather is very bad and the country very poor. I am glad to hear Sir John Bland succeeds Mr. Roberts in Ireland.

"ANONYMUS" to [ROBERT HARLEY].

1704, September 6—Warns him that Mistress Anne Webb, but twelve years of age, grand-daughter of the late Lord Bellasis, was about to be sent by her father out of England to a nunnery in Flanders or France greatly against her will, and begging that a writ of *ne exeat regno* might be issued in order to prevent her going. Thinks that some law should be passed which should prevent papists' children from being forced to abandon their country, to convey their estates abroad; and become slaves to the Romish priests. Has read Mr. Sacheverel's arguments against the Dissenters' private education; but it cannot be denied that the Dissenters have the same holy religion, the same loyal affection, to our Queen, and the same love to our country, as ourselves.

QUEEN ANNE'S BOUNTY.

1704, September 6. St. James's—Order in Council approving draft of Charter for incorporating such persons as her Majesty shall direct to be inserted therein by the name of the Governors of the Bounty of Queen Anne for augmentation of the maintenance of the poor Clergy. *Signed by* John Povey.

H. ST. JOHN to SECRETARY HARLEY.

1704, September 7. Whitehall—Informing him that Lieutenant Lesly formerly belonging to the Earl of Donegal's regiment had been "broke" under the Queen's order, and was still out of employment. *Signed.*

"THOMAS from FLORENCE" to———.

1704, September 8. L[ondon]—I could not immediately forward the enclosed letter by reason of several here in town being committed to prison on suspicion of keeping correspondence with France and Spain, and of whom Mr. Peter Kearny is still in custody. Wherefore I desire that you may let all those that are any way in the dominions of France or Spain not to be writing to any here, it being severely forbidden by the laws and very dangerous and pernicious to the Government. I suppose you have heard how all means are used that possibly can be, to extinguish the superstitious idolatry of popery in the Kingdom of Ireland. I hear one Anthony Martin, a popish friar, is to be executed in Dublin. Yesterday the Queen, Prince George and all the nobility went in great pomp to the church of St. Paul to assist at the singing of the *Te Deum* in thanksgiving for the blessing bestowed on the army in gaining such glorious victories abroad. *Copy.*

N.[STRATFORD] Bishop of Chester to [ROBERT HARLEY].

1704, September 9. Chester—Thanking him for having appointed his son his chaplain; and also for the relief which the poor clergy of his diocese would, as he hoped, in due time receive from the Queen's Bounty.

Dr. Francis Atterbury to Robert Harley.

1704, September 9. Bishopthorpe—When I came hither on my way to Carlisle this day sevenight, I found a full stop put to my journey onward by the Bishop of Carlisle, which I thought myself obliged to give you an immediate account of. But the Archbishop—who invited me hither, and hath received me with all manner of kindness—pressed me to delay writing till he could receive another letter from the Bishop, in answer to one which he would then send him, and which, his Grace was persuaded, would have its effect. In expectation of that answer I have stayed at Bishopthorpe all this week. 'Tis this day come, and I find by it that the Archbishop's judgment and persuasions in the point have not prevailed, and have therefore obtained at length his Grace's free leave to lay the whole matter before you. In which if I shall seem too particular and tedious I beg you will please to impute it to the earnest desire I have to approve every part of my character and conduct to you. Besides that you will be the better able to judge of what is fit to be done in this matter above, when you are fully acquainted with all the steps taken in it below.

Before my coming hither letters had passed between my Lord of York and the Bishop of Carlisle in reference to my institution, which the Bishop told his Grace—in a letter received by his Grace the day I came to Bishopthorpe—he would never give me unless I revoked some propositions which he thought deducible from some passages in my book about Convocations, and derogatory to the Royal Supremacy. He referred the Archbishop to the 213th, 214th and 215th pages of the second edition of my book for these passages; which the Archbishop consulted, and so, by his Grace's desire, did several other eminent clergymen, members of the Church of York; and they all entirely agreed with his Grace that there was nothing contained in my book, on the head of the Supremacy, which there was the least occasion for me to retract or explain myself upon. The Archbishop wrote to the Bishop several times his sense of this matter very fully and freely, and pressed him now once again either to let me wait upon him for institution, or to appoint commissioners—as is usual—for that purpose, or to remit the matter to him, as Metropolitan, in due form, by an Act of Requisition, under the Episcopal seal of Carlisle. This last proposal the Archbishop made with relation to the Bishop's desire—expressed in his last letter to the Archbishop—that the Archbishop would himself institute me, which the Archbishop would have gladly done, but did not think a request made by letter only a sufficient warrant for him to interpose by his Metropolitic authority. I have enclosed a transcript of that part of the Bishop of Carlisle's letter which relates these particulars, and I have sent also a copy of the letter which I wrote to the Bishop of Carlisle on this occasion, though I had never received from him any return to my former. [See under Sept. 4, ante, p. 125.]

This morning the Bishop's answer to my Lord of York's letter came, and in it he declines both the methods proposed by his Grace, and insists now that I should come to him and make a personal tender of my patent, which he had before forbid me to do. Accordingly I shall set out for Cumberland early on Monday morning, where I expect to find all manner of delays and affronts; though indeed the affronts are not so much to myself as to the Queen's Mandate, which was never before, I dare say, so disobeyed and trifled with in any one instance since the Reformation.

He hath twenty-eight days allowed him by the 28th Canon, before which, in presentations of a common nature—though that, I presume, is far from being the case at present—the Bishop is not bound to institute, nor can the presentee regularly lodge his appeal with the Archbishop of the province. It is probable he may make use of his privilege in this respect, and keep me in attendance at Carlisle for some part of this time—as he hath already done at York—to be the discourse of the country and province.

Nor is it unlikely that he may except against the form and tenor of my patent, which includes no express presentation to him, nor is he mentioned in the mandatory part of it, which is directed to the Chapter and includes the Bishop in general words only. However thus, I believe, all the patents for Deans of the New Foundation run, and entitle the respective deans to institution wherever it is necessary ; and thus, I am sure, in particular ran Dr. Graham's, my predecessor's patent, and he had institution upon it, which would not in my case be necessary to be had from the Bishop, but that the statutes which Henry VIII. presented to the Church—upon refounding it 37 *regni*—say : *Volumus ut ille pro Decano habeatur, et acceptetur, Decanique officio in omnibus fungatur, quem nos aut successores nostri nominandum eligendum et præficiendum perque literas patentes magno Sigillo nostro aut successorum nostrorum sigillatas episcopo* Carliolensi *præsentandum esse duximus. Quem quidem decanum sic nominatum electum et præsentatum post episcopi institutionem præsentes canonici assument et admittent in decanum &c.* This statute, I think, till it shall be altered, entitles the bishop to the right of institution ; and altered it may be by the same authority which framed it, whenever the bishop by an arbitrary, unbecoming use of his power shall deserve to lose it, for another statute says : *Reservamus tamen nobis et successoribus nostris plenam potestatem et authoritatem statuta haec mutandi, alterandi ; ac cum illis dispensandi et—si vidibitur—nova condindi.*

Upon the whole, I submit to your wisdom what steps may properly be taken, in order to assert the validity of the Queen's grant, and oblige the Bishop, without farther delay, to comply with it. To your favour—and my Lord Treasurer's goodness—I owe the grant itself ; and hope by your favour not only to have it made effectual to me—which is now as much her Majesty's concern as mine—but to be supported also against the injuries and indignities which are thus heaped upon me.

I hope to be able to tender my patent to the Bishop at Rose-Castle on Thursday morning next, and will then trouble you with an account of the event. If he refuses the institution, or delays it, I think of going to Carlisle, and there waiting the Queen's pleasure. In the meantime, I beseech you to look into the mentioned pages of my book, and see whether there be any word there relating to the Queen's supremacy, justly liable to exception, and which Mr. Attorney General himself—as much his business it is, to support the Prerogative—would not allow to be true.

And should you farther please by a line to the Archbishop of York to desire to know his sense of my notions and expressions in this matter, it would give his Grace a proper occasion of justifying me to you ; which he neither will nor can decline, though a bishop of his own province be concerned in the dispute.

Postscript.—Next to the favour of removing the obstacle at present laid in my way, what I should heartily intreat of you is that you would please to think of some way of having this charge—brought against me by the Bishop—examined and heard ; that either he or I may publicly clear ourselves of it, or bear the blame, if we do not. For the stroke is not levelled only at the Deanery of Carlisle, but at all my future hopes ;

and permit me to say that you yourself—to whom I am well known to owe this station—are struck at also in it.

"Thomas from Florence" to Father John Mac-Gauly, at St. Ambrose, Prague.

1704, September 11. London—I protest writing is very dangerous in this government. Several have been taken up here on suspicion of keeping correspondence with France or Spain. I suppose you have heard of the late Acts of Parliament which were done and sealed by the Queen and Council for the succession, against popish heirs, as also of the banishing all priests who actually have no parish, and they are to be listed in the sessions of the several counties, their name, age, country, and where they received orders; so that in a short time, that superstitious and idolatrous popery will be extinguished in Ireland, for better means are taken since the Duke of Ormond went there than ever were taken before, all doors being shut against such people. I hear Oliver F. G. with all his Oliverians are very poor and true. The Queen and Prince went to St. Paul's on the 7th to return thanks for the victory of the allies and for the taking of Gibraltar, but the misusage and disorders which the soldiers committed after capitulating and giving their word of honour has mightily lessened the honour of the enterprise, for they were used far worse than those of Vigo were.

The Parliament of Scotland is very troublesome for they cannot well agree concerning the succession of the Crown; moreover they insist mightily to have free trade with England and elsewhere. 'Tis thought the Queen will prorogue the Parliament for some time.

Dr. Francis Atterbury to Robert Harley.

1704, September 16. Carlisle—The matter between me and the Bishop is now perfectly ripe for such a determination as Her Majesty shall be pleased to give in it. I waited on the Bishop yesterday at Rose and tendered my Letters Patent to him; upon which he observed—as I apprehended he would—that they were not directed to him, nor was he at all named in them, and he did not know therefore how far they might concern him. However—he said—he received them *de bene esse*, with a reservation to advise and consult upon the matter of them as he might see occasion; and ordered a public notary, who was ready there for the purpose, to put down this his reservation in writing. After this he produced a paper, wherein, in order to my institution, he demanded a new sort of revocation from me—not that of the three propositions, which I before transmitted to you; and which he now said he no longer insisted upon, but a retraction of a particular passage in my book. I desired leave to retire and immediately drew up my answer to it; a copy of which and of the demand made by his Lordship I here presume to inclose. After this, his Lordship, in some disorder, said he would proceed to my institution step by step, and in the first place demanded my orders, and a testimonial of my learning and manners. I told him I had not brought them, apprehending that since I had been before collated to two dignities in the Church, I should not have had now such a demand made of me; besides that I was in my Letters Patent styled the Queen's Chaplain in Ordinary. However, he insisted upon it, and then said he would proceed to examine me, as to my learning, but after he had said it, paused awhile, and added, 'Perhaps

'that would be too great an affront to me?' To which, I took the
liberty of replying, 'As many affronts as his Lordship pleased, I was
'prepared to bear them.' He then abruptly, and with some heat,
broke off, and produced a paper—which a notary had written fair before
I came—deferring his answer to my request for institution till October
12, that is for the whole twenty-eight days allowed the Ordinary in
common institutions by the 95th Canon. I represented to him the
hardship of this delay upon two accounts, because I was on the 16th of
October to be at London, in waiting, and was also to prepare a sermon
for the Queen on November 5th, my Lord Almoner having desired me to
preach his turn on that day. The Bishop, however, insisted upon the
twenty-eight days allowed him by the Canon. At last he told me that,
though he appointed that distant day, yet, if he was ready for me, I
should hear of him sooner. But this is as his Lordship shall think fit; for
his positive orders are for me to attend on the 12th of October; which I
was the more surprised at, because the Bishop had himself kept me back
seven days from tendering my Letters Patent by intimating his
unwillingness that I should come to him from Bishopthorpe for
institution, and ought not therefore to have taken the advantage of a
delay which he himself had directly occasioned. My Lord Archbishop
of York was so sure of the Bishop's dispatch in this case—after his
Grace's hearty and repeated applications to him on my behalf—that he
uses these words in a letter to me, which I received this morning: 'I
'have had time this morning to write a new letter to the Bishop,
'wherein I have spoke my mind freely. I hope, if he will not institute
'you, he will at least suffer you to proceed to your appeal without any
'delay, by giving you his peremptory denial at the first, and waiving
'the twenty-eight days the Canon allows him to give his answer in.'
   After all the Bishop's intentions, I find, are to write an account of
what he hath done, this post, either to you, or to Mr. Secretary Hedges;
and if he find it is not approved above, and receives a letter in answer
to it that the Queen expects his immediate compliance, he hath
publickly professed that he will proceed to institute me without a
minute's delay. And so I doubt not but he will, when such an
intimation of her Majesty's pleasure arrives. In order to my obtaining
which, I beg leave to observe:—
   In relation to the Bishop's first objection against the form of my
Patent, that it is exactly, almost to a word, the same with the Patents of
all my several predecessors in the Deanery, since the foundation of it.
And if his Lordship therefore have a right to institution—which I have
good reason to doubt, it having been omitted as often as it hath been
practised—by virtue of the statute of the Church, a transcript of which
I formerly sent you; then I also have a right to demand institution in
virtue of a like Patent with those upon which some of my predecessors
demanded and obtained theirs.
   As to his second objection, relating to my opinion about the
Supremacy, my Lord Archbishop—before whom the Appeal must at
length lie—hath often told him, and you, I daresay, are satisfied, that it
is wholly groundless. Besides that, it is of dangerous consequence for a
Bishop to impose such unprecedented and illegal tests upon persons
coming to them for institution, and proffering to qualify themselves
according to all the obligations laid on them by the canons and laws now
in being. And for my part, rather than make any such retractation of
any one thing I have said concerning the Supremacy, I would choose
to undergo any difficulty, and even to lose the benefit of those Letters
Patent, which her Majesty hath so graciously granted me.

Postscript.—I have made a discovery here which if upon further search it holds good will be of advantage to Her Majesty in her right of patronage, and help forward those noble ends which she is pursuing. I reserve an account of it for the time when I shall wait upon you in London.

JOHN, ARCHBISHOP OF YORK to [ROBERT HARLEY].

1704, September 18. Bishopthorpe—I can truly say I have done all that was possible for me to do, both towards removing the objections which the Bishop of Carlisle had started against Dr. Atterbury's being admitted to the Deanery, and if that could not be done, then towards the persuading his Lordship to grant me his authority to admit the Doctor myself, which I would readily have done; and in hopes of that I kept the Doctor here a week before I would let him go to Carlisle. And when that had not effect, by endeavouring in the last place to prevail with his Lordship, that in case he did not think fit to institute the Doctor upon the tendering to him in his own person the Queen's Letters Patent, that he would at least give him a peremptory denial at the first, that so he might bring his Appeal to me immediately without waiting twenty-eight days for the Bishop's answer—as the canon allows him so much time for the giving his answer. I hoped this last thing would have been done, but I find by letters from the Bishop and from the Doctor, which I received just now, that it is not:

I presume the Doctor has by this post given you an account how the matter now stands. I find the Bishop has done it to Secretary Hedges, to whom he has sent up the form of recantation, which he proposed to Dr. Atterbury to be subscribed by him in order to his admission, with the Doctor's reasons why he could not, as also his own reasons why he insists upon such a recantation. So that now the whole matter lies before you, and I suppose it will be laid before her Majesty, who, I doubt not, in her great wisdom will find out ways for the putting an easy end to this unfortunate squabble.

DR. FRANCIS ATTERBURY to ROBERT HARLEY.

1704, September 18. Carlisle—I write this chiefly to acquaint you that I had the honour of your letter this morning at Carlisle; where the Bishop hath endeavoured underhand to put all manner of affronts upon me, by keeping all here from paying the respects usual on this occasion. But he hath not succeeded entirely to his wish. The Mayor and Aldermen have been with me; and I hope in a little time to be able to traverse all his measures. I went to the Cathedral yesterday, and made use of the Chancellor's seat, and preached there as a stranger. I was very particular in the trouble I gave you last post, but I had good reason to apprehend that all circumstances would be told above by another hand; for which reason I thought it proper to lay them nakedly and truly before you. I have only to add an earnest repetition of the request, made in my last, that her Majesty's pleasure may be intimated to the Bishop as soon as conveniently it can, and in such a manner as may not encourage this, or any other Bishop thus presumptuously to disobey her Broad Seal for the future. Permit me to say to you, that if this attempt of the Bishop be passed over unresented, you are likely to have frequent troubles of the same kind given you; for it will pave the way towards laying an unbecoming restraint on her Majesty in the disposition of her preferments—especially the remote ones—and will make the several Chapters depend more upon the Bishops and less upon the Crown than they do already.

The Bishop's complaint of me in relation to my notion of the supremacy is frivolous and groundless, and his demand of retractation—in order to institution—uncanonical and illegal; and therefore he will not, I trust, in any degree be countenanced in it.

Institution is indeed, by the Statutes of Henry VIII.—given to this Church—made necessary to instalment, but there is, as I before acquainted you, another statute which gives the Crown a liberty of dispensing with any of them. Accordingly, upon searching the registers since I came hither, I find that of the ten Deans which preceded me four at least—and I believe I shall find more—have had *nonobstantes* in their patents, which have superseded this and other statutes. The only two Deans in Queen Elizabeth's time, Sir Thomas Smyth, and Wolley, the Queen's Latin Secretary, were mere laymen, and consequently could have no institution. Sir Christopher Musgrave's brother,—who was made Dean in 1684—had a *nonobstante* in his patent for being a Master of Arts only, the Statutes of the Church obliging the Dean to be at least a Bachelor of Divinity. And then *nonobstantes* from the Crown to its own statutes, as Founder, and Supreme Visitor, are doubtless at this time safe and legal. Our Statutes were never under the Great Seal, but were injunctions only given us by two bishops, commissioned by Henry the Eighth, who indeed had their powers for this purpose under the Great Seal of England.

What I aim at from hence is to let you see that the Bishop may, by a dispensation with the Local Statute, be passed over, and the Chapter immediately applied to for installation, if that method shall be found requisite. But for my part, I presume, it will be more for the Queen's honour at this time, that the Bishop should be made to do his duty. And her Majesty may then be pleased to consider how far it may be fit to lodge the same power in his hand afterwards.

The sly pretence of zeal for the supremacy will not, I daresay, make any impressions to my disadvantage, especially if some way be found out of having that matter solemnly examined and sifted to the bottom, which is what I above all things desire. When he is forced out of his demand of retractation, he will, I doubt not, endeavour to find little faults in my Letters Patent, and rest upon them—which indeed are not drawn, or amended, with all the exactness that might be wished—and still, by that means, delay and affront me here in the face of a country, where I am utterly unacquainted; unless he be made speedily sensible that every indignity of that kind which he throws upon me will return upon himself, upon the event.

And indeed his nature and character are such—as I have learned from good hands since I came hither—that he is not to be managed after a milder manner; and will be found to be so much more obsequious in all his future conduct, as he shall, on the present occasion, be more roughly dealt with. I speak not this at random, but will be answerable, at any rate, for the event. Notwithstanding his being born and bred and Bishop here, there is scarce anybody in the country who thoroughly approves what he hath done in my case; though they stand aloof a little to see what interest he hath above, and how far her Majesty will interpose in it. Both Mr. Musgrave and Colonel Graham have in private laboured the point with him; and both my Lords Carlisle and Thanet have presented me with venison, since I came, with what other views I know not, but to be sure not with that of countenancing the Bishop in his measures.

I thank God that as yet I have been able to keep my temper entirely, and have neither said nor done anything, which the Bishop can justly lay hold of. I presumed to send you the very worst words I uttered in my last, and even those were not spoken in an offensive manner. The Chapter of the Church, summoned by the Bishop to be present at that time, will be my witnesses in this case, though they are his creatures.

Postscript.—The Archbishop, I suppose, writes to you this morning and will, I doubt not, do me justice on this occasion. But his influence or the few bishops of his province being what he hath reason to secure (*sic*), I cannot expect otherwise than that he represents things somewhat tenderly and warily.

K. Hastings to [Robert Harley].

1704, September 19. [London]—To be an informer hardly suits a gentlewoman, but the great concern she has for the Queen's safety compels her to inform him that a set of gentlemen had lately come out of France, most of them Irish Roman Catholics and in the service of the French King, with designs against the Queen. Begs that her name may not be made use of; his commands may be sent to Bolton Street, Piccadilly, where she lives.

The Archbishop of Canterbury to [Robert] Harley.

1704, September 20. Lambeth—Promising to recommend a treasurer for the Corporation of the Bounty of Queen Anne. *Signed.*

The Same to the Same.

Same date and place—Is obliged for extracts sent, and glad to see such marks of application and judgment in Lord Raby. Recommending his kinsman Edward Tenison for the post of treasurer; he has been bred to the civil law, and knows business well, has in land and money an estate worth above 4,000*l.*, and was concerned in the Old East India Company.

Richard Duke to Robert Harley.

1704, September 20. Otterton near Exeter—You have much honoured yourself, by your most kind letter of the 9th instant, which I had not given you occasion for, if I had heard that any other would, being really affected with my own defects; but living in the daily full sight of Torbay, and hearing the complaints, and observing the necessity, that some or other ought to inform some person of your station of our circumstances, and you being best known to me, and most willing to assist us, having but little to do more in this world, I thought without presumption I might give you an opportunity to serve our most gracious Queen and this kingdom and county. Insomuch that I can now tell my neighbours, that there is good hopes, at last, that by your means a man-of-war of 40 guns may be sent to cruise on this coast, for the welfare of Plymouth, Exeter, Dartmouth and Lyme, in which towns are so many merchants who bring more benefit to Her Majesty than the cost of a fifth rate ship will amount unto, besides the calming of the thoughts say of 20,000. And for our outed justices, I have some confidence, my Lord Poulett and my constant friend hath not occasioned the laying aside any of them, nor so much as knows one half of them, nor ever advised with Sir Edward[1] Seymour thereabouts, who is a man of so many passions and perturbations, and swears and swaggers amongst the seamen in his late progress here within five miles of 'me,' that I would rather whisper in your ears than write what I hear. A church canon being with him did reprove him 'and his unsound opinion about the Resurrection,' that some suppose he is not sound in his head, as he hath been. I shall trouble your busy hand no further about him; only his great informer whom he hath preferred and by whom he might be excited to regulate our commission is an attorney that all know. And I know it will be for Her Majesty's service and your honour to accommodate those two great matters, which concludes these, without expecting one line from your posting hand.

Enclosure.

Seeing you intimate for particular outed Justices, they were in all twenty nine of which some are dead; those that occur, are—

*Sir Hugh Acland, Bart.; omitted on the last commission of 2,000*l.* per annum.
*Sir John Elwill 1,000*l.* per annum and valued in Bank etc., 20,000*l.* in money.
Moses Gold Esqr. 1,200*l.* per annum, besides money.
*Christopher Savery 1,200*l.* per annum.
*Richard Duke Esqr. 1,000*l.* per annum.
*Richard Lee Esqr. 600*l.* per annum, 5,000*l.* in money.
John Cholwich Esqr. 600*l.* per annum, 5,000*l.* in money.
Peter Beavis Esqr. 400*l.* per annum, near a great town.
William Ball Esqr., a lawyer that had the chair, 500*l.* per annum.
Richard Burthogge, a doctor as learned as any in this county, 500*l.* per annum two miles from Sir Edward Seymour's in the great town of Totnes.
John Coplestone Esqr. 600*l.* per annum, near Plymouth.
Mr. Shepherd Esqr. 600*l.* per annum.
Dr. Pyne 400*l.* per annum, near Sir Francis Drake.
Southcott Lutterell Esqr. 600*l.* per annum.
Mr. Ilbert worth 20,000*l.* per annum (*sic*).
Mr. Downe Esqr. 400*l.* per annum.
Mr. Fountaine 400*l.* per annum.
Philip Shapcot a lawyer 500*l.* per annum.
*Martyn Ryder Esq. a lawyer 500*l.* per annum.
*Jasper Ratcliffe Esqr.; valued at 40,000*l.*, 600*l.* per annum.
*Sampson Hele Esqr. 2,000*l.* per annum.
Those that have asterisks (*), have either been Sheriffs or Parliament men.
Two others have been restored Mr. Davys and Mr. Northmore*, whom you know and was an attorney.
You are pleased to say, Her Majesty is willing to dispense her favours impartially, whence I conclude she knows not of the outing of so many, without any cause assigned, who might do her and the country most convenient service.
This is true in fact and may occasion many prejudices: not two of all these but receive the sacrament in the Church of England, and I

am sure, you do not want wisdom to make a right use of this account for her great Majesty's service, our country's good and quiet, and your own satisfaction to serve all.

JOHN MAYER to ROBERT HARLEY.

1704, September 22—A long letter giving his reasons why he thought the siege of Landau would not succeed.

SIEGE OF LANDAU.

No date—Plan of the arrangements for attacking the fortress.

ADAM CARDONNEL to ROBERT HARLEY.

1704, September 22. Camp at Weissembourg—By the copy of an intercepted letter from the Elector of Bavaria to the Electress which my Lord Duke transmitted to you the last post you will have seen that mention is made of another letter sewed up in the trumpeter's livery. By good fortune we had kept the same trumpeter ever since he came to us before Ulm. On Friday I had his coat taken from him while he slept, wherein I found that other letter, which having been since unciphered I now send you a copy. The Duke is gone this morning to wait on the King of the Romans at the camp before Landau where his Majesty did not arrive till last night.

It is reported that M. de Coigny is marched with a detachment of ten or twelve battalions towards Brabant.

Note by Harley. The copy he mentions of Duke of Bavaria's letter he forgot to send.

SIR STAFFORD FAIRBORNE to [ROBERT HARLEY].

1704, September 26. On board the *Exeter* in Torbay—Notwithstanding all his endeavours since he had his orders the weather had made it impossible for him to get out of the Channel; two ships had been disabled and two more damaged. Was driven into this bay with the *Revenge, Medway, Mary, Rochester,* and *Deptford.* In his opinion it was too late in the year to cruise in squadrons in the channel, and that his ships were all foul the cleanest of them being six weeks "from the ground." No ship to sail well should be longer from the dock. Desires the Prince's leave to come ashore, having very urgent business of his own, and any private captain being fit for his command.

NEWS LETTER.

1704, [September 26—] October 6 new style. Camp at Weissembourg. On Friday the third in the afternoon seven hundred men of the garrison of Landau made a sally out of the town, and Prince Louis of Baden being at the same time in the trenches gave such orders for their reception, that they were immediately beat back with the loss of above twenty men without doing us the least damage.

On Saturday the Prussians began a redoubt for the security of their attack on the left, and part of the second parallel from the right was finished, the King of the Romans being in the trenches gave orders for the battery of mortars to fire about eleven at night.

Yesterday a lieutenant and eighteen men came over to us from their town, who confirm the great fatigue the garrison undergoes which occasions great desertion, and that we have already dismounted several of their cannon.

Last night the redoubts and parallels between them were finished, and our men have now begun the sap in search of the enemy's mines in order to make a lodgment upon the counterscarp.

The Prussian battery of thirty pieces of cannon is flanked, and will be ready to fire to-morrow notwithstanding the badness of the weather.

His Grace the Duke of Marlborough intends to go to morrow to wait on the King of the Romans before Landau.

[DANIEL DE FOE to ROBERT HARLEY.]

1704, September 28. Bury [St. Edmunds]—I did myself the honour to write to you from Cambridge on Saturday the 16th instant, and was in hopes to have received your orders as hinted there by Friday. How I have spent the time the last week; how I received an odd alarm from London occasioned by Mr. Stephens the messenger of the press, who really treats me ill, how this occasioned me making a trip to town, how staying but two days there, I happened of a smart encounter with Mr. Toke of East Grinstead. These are things I purposed not to have troubled you with, till I had the honour to finish the affair I am upon.

As my last signified my desire to come to this place, and that not receiving your countermand I should pursue that design, I have accordingly spent a few days here. Sir R. Davers who rules this town, carries matters very high. Sir [Thomas] Felton the other member, we hear today is dead or dying and I doubt they will make but an ill choice. If it be possible to bring that gentleman off, it would do great service, his interest in this county being very strong; but, of this I crave leave to be particular hereafter.

I cannot but beg leave to lay before you that I am surprised to find my name in the written news letters of this day as taken into custody and committed by her Majesty's order for ill-treating Sir George Rooke, &c. I hope if there be any suggestion against me on that or any case, you will please to reserve me to answer to yourself; it cannot be, that I can be guilty of anything to displease you, nor of anything willingly to give you cause of dislike. If Sir George is scandalized at me for anything, at the same time professing I have not designed him any affront, I beseech you to take me into your protection, upon that head, and I am ready to make such acknowledgment as you shall think reasonable.

I have been exceedingly concerned at this case, and was coming up post to throw myself at your feet, and put myself into your hands, but being very unwilling to leave what I am upon, till it is finished, I have ventured to stay, depending on your goodness to me in this case.

I write this from Bury where I hope I have not been useless; Norwich I have perfectly dissected, and was directing my course to Lynn, but this unhappy Newspaper I confess discomposed me, and I spend the time in visiting the sea-coast towns here, till I may have a line from you at this town, where your farther orders will both comfort and direct me. If I do not receive some signification from yourself by certificate or otherwise, I shall hardly know how to govern myself; for my stirring about may be dangerous, and I am in danger of being taken up as a person fled from the Queen's justices, and in such a case may have my papers taken from me, and at least seen, which would be 'as bad. For this reason I am very shy of myself till I have the honour of your protection, which I entreat by first post.

I am informed here, this Newspaper is written by one Mr. Fox, who, they say, belongs to the Secretary's office. If anything could have been in it, I flatter myself, I should have it from yourself, from whom, if I were guilty of high treason, a letter or a verbal command should cause me to come and put myself into your power.

I cannot conceive what I can have offended in, and shall desire but this favour, that Sir George Rooke may be referred to the Law. If I have offended him, I am willing to be left to the Law ; and ask him no favour, but if the Government will espouse the quarrel of a single person against another, any man may be crushed.

I have not taken the freedom my inclination guided me to, and which I really thought the case of Sir G. Rooke required, because I saw you disliked another man on that head, and as I hope I act from different principles with those people, so I always remembered my obligation to you and believe and hope to satisfy you I shall never do anything to make you think I forget it.

'Tis something hard that while I am spreading principles of temper, moderation, and peace, through countries where I go, and persuading all people that the Government is resolved to proceed by those rules, I should be chosen out to be made the object of a private, high-flying revenge under colour of the Government resentments; for be it that you find Sir G. Rooke faithful and that this fight or victory at sea be the first proof of it, I can at this distance acquaint you that the improvement made of this victory abroad by the mad men of his party at home is such that, speaking of the peace at home which is the design I am upon, and which I suppose her Majesty, yourself and all good men embarked in, perhaps we may see good cause to wish that victory had been a defeat— and though I were to suppose Sir George himself under the management of your hand, yet I am free to tell you, that the High Church party look on him as their own.

The victory at sea they look upon as their victory over the Moderate party, and his health is now drunk by those here, who won't drink the Queen's, nor yours. I am obliged with patience to hear you damned, and he (sic) praised, he exalted, and Her Majesty slighted, and the sea victory set up against the land victory; Sir George exalted above the Duke of Marlborough, and what can the reason of this be, but that they conceive some hopes from this, that their High Church party will revive under his patronage.

Now, sir, I leave this to your judgment whether be Sir George Rooke concerned or no, whether the unreasonable acclamation be not made from other principles than joy at a victory.

If he is to be the patron of that party, whether he see it, or not, if he is to be a head for them to value themselves upon, whether purposely or not, he is a fatal instrument to ruin the Peace we speak of. Indeed, 'tis my regard to your orders and that only, restrains me on that head, for the case requires to be spoken to, and if the Government espouse the case against me in this, the broil will be removed from High Church and Low Church to Rookites and . . . . (sic) the consequences this has already in the country, and the check it has put to the advances peace had made, are visible, and I shall give you particulars as soon as I come up, and conclude with this presumption—at least Sir George Rooke must be won over to disown the proceedings of this party, and to check those which affront the Government on his behalf, or the civil feuds of parties will increase rather than diminish, my commission will be in vain, and you will find the temper of the gentlemen, who are to come up the 24th of next month less governable than you expect. I am running out into the usual freedom, with which I hope you will not be offended. I can not but think it my duty to let you see there, what you would be displeased to see, if you were here. Sir, I have another grievance to lay before you, with an earnestness particular to my usual solicitations. Mr. Chris. Hurt, of the Custom House, the same whose name you have in your pocket book has been with me all this journey, and a very useful person I have found him in the work I am upon. He is under concern at my staying longer than I expected, and having asked no leave at the Custom House, where he is not a little marked out as a Dissenter, expects to be ill treated for this absence. The least notice from you will remove the possibility of it, and though I conceal the bottom of the business, yet he serves it faithfully, and I know not how to want him. I therefore entreat that you will please to get a note of leave from my Lord Treasurer directed to the Commissioners of the Customs for *Christopher Hurt, Quay-man,* to be absent on his private occasions.

I would have hinted that the magazine runs low, and is recruited by private stock, which is but indifferent. I acknowledge myself not a good husband, but as my ill husbandry is only where I find it absolutely needful, I venture not to be sparing, and hope you will find cause to approve it, and trust my choice of instruments and methods. I again entreat your care of my assistant, it would heartily concern me, and I believe yourself, if he should be divested of his livelihood for the absence here, while the bottom of it is your and the nation's service. I cease to importune you farther and waiting to hear further from yourself ask your pardon for the length of this.

Postscript.—The extraordinary goodness of the season, there having been no rain these three weeks, makes me offer it, if for the service, to stay out as long as you please. If I should be straitened and you please to order me to draw for a supply and on whom, I hope the success of the affair will answer it beyond your expectation. Please to direct to Alexander Goldsmith, at Mr. John Morley's in Bury.

Sir C. Hedges to [Robert] Harley.

1704, September 28. Whitehall—Here has been nothing considerable since you went, only I have taken up the disperser of the Address, one Sammen a weaver, a tool of De Foe's. I can get nothing out of him against others, but I have sufficient evidence against him. I cannot find that Cowdall is in England, but am in a fair way for discovering the undertakers for a licence.

Sir George Rooke came to St. Helens on Sunday, having suffered no damage on his voyage home. I believe I shall meet him at Windsor tomorrow.

Dr. Francis Atterbury to [Robert Harley].

1704, September 28. Carlisle—The bishop received yesterday his orders from Mr. Secretary Hedges, who deferred writing a post, after you were pleased to write to me, in order, I suppose, to convey the harsh message in as soft words as he could find out, and to have time to answer the Bishop's arguments point by point, which he did, I find, very carefully and respectfully, and without any the least intimation that the Queen was offended at the former delay. His letter, however hath prevailed so far that the 'Doubts and Difficulties in matters of Law and Conscience,' which the Bishop laboured under are quite dispelled, and he hath sent to me to receive institution tomorrow, which, had you been in town, I would humbly have begged leave to decline, till I had laid before you my Doubts and Difficulties also about his Lordship's right of conferring it upon me. But in your absence, whose favour is my only support in this matter, I must be content to pass through the usual forms, without making any immediate exception to them.

I am to the utmost sensible of your kindness to me in freeing me so speedily and so effectually from the rude and barbarous treatment I have here met with. However, give me leave with all humility to say, that the favour you have designed and done me will not be complete till you shall be pleased to put this dispute between the Bishop and me some way upon a foot of being heard and considered by our superiors, that I may be freed as publicly from the imputation of opposing the Queen's supremacy, as I have been loaded with it—and loaded without the least hopes of gaining the point pretended—as I have learnt from sure hands; but in order only to blast me if possible, and leave a mark upon me for the future. Pardon me therefore, for saying that till the impressions, which this opposition was designed to make, are by proper methods utterly effaced, I cannot truly enjoy the honourable post her Majesty hath given me, nor be perfectly easy even under all that favour which you have been pleased to show me, and which shall to the last moment of my life be acknowledged, and, whenever it is in my power, by God's blessing, returned.

If you shall judge that by what hath been done in this matter already a full stop is put to any further consideration of it above, I must submit. However even then I hope you will allow me to right myself, as I am able, in my private capacity ; under the assurance that I will take no methods of doing it, which may misbecome me, or be any reflection on those who have interposed on my behalf.

E[rasmus] Lewis to [Robert Harley].

[1704, September]—Since you left this place I have been informed that one of the young ladies mentioned in the warrant you sent down to Harwich last Friday is daughter to Lady Webb, and the young woman said to be her servant is her companion that is to be put into the same monastery with her. They are both conducted by a priest who calls himself George Wharton, merchant ; but are not yet come to Harwich. Perhaps you may have heard of one Guardi whose uncommon familiarity with his master Lord Jersey has made him more known than a man of his rank would otherwise have been ; but he will be still more famous if it be true, what is now generally reported, that he is married to a young lady with whom he was ordered to treat for Lord Villiers.

The enclosed verses (*missing*) were sent me from Hinchinbrook and 1 believe were made there. Sir George Rooke writes that he has not lost the least boat in this expedition. I am told Mr. Graham sets up lame Fleming against Mr. Musgrave.

E[rasmus] Lewis to [Robert] Harley.

1704, September 28. Whitehall—Mr. Wharton and his ladies went down to Harwich on Tuesday. By next post I hope to report that they are brought back. His true name is Briars. The several expressions that the Bishop of Carlisle condemns in his Dean's books were collected and shown about in Lambeth before he had this preferment. The Court of St. Germain has retrenched some pensions since the battle of Hochstett. My Lord Chief Justice has taken up Bishop Gifford and other Romish priests. Mr. Secretary Hedges has been taken up with examining printers and publishers of pamphlets.

Sir Charles Hedges to [Robert] Harley.

1704, October 3. Windsor—We have three mails from Holland which brought you as many letters from the Duke of Marlborough, which have been read to the Queen but have nothing in them very material beyond what is known of the progress of the campaigns in the Netherlands and Spain.

Viscount Weymouth to [Robert Harley].

1704, October 3. Longleat—The death of my younger son sits so close to me that I have not philosophy enough to overcome it, which added to my former ill health renders me unfit for any business. I have therefore this day begged the Lord Treasurer to lay my small office at Her Majesty's feet, with all imaginable thanks for her grace and goodness to me.

R. Warre to [Robert] Harley.

1704, October 5. Whitehall—The warrant to Young the messenger enclosed in a letter to the Mayor of Newcastle was sent away on Saturday September 23, but I have yet heard nothing of him.

My Lord Portland came to town yesterday; he left the Hague on Sunday. Mr. Montagu, Lord Halifax's nephew, came with him, and his tutor Monsieur Guagin brought me this afternoon a box which Mr. Secretary Hedges having opened found it was the instrument of the Duke of Mecklenburg for entering into the Grand Alliance.

E. Lewis to [Robert] Harley.

1704, October 5. Whitehall—The three prisoners brought up from Harwich complain very much of their confinement and I believe they will soon be released for want of evidence. The priest says now his name is Brears (sic), not Molyneux. I can find nothing new among the Hawkers but Sir Humphrey's praises of his own bill.

Adam Cardonnel to [R.] Warre.

1704, October 6—The Electress of Bavaria has not yet sent any return to the offers made her by the King of the Romans, though the time allowed her be elapsed; however it is not doubted she will be obliged to comply at last.

Anne Maria Webb.

1704, October 6. Whitehall—Undertaking by John Webb, of Red Lion Square, esquire, and John Molins of Dover Street, gentleman, for the appearance before either of the Secretaries of State of Anne Webb, daughter of Sir John Webb, who was taken going beyond sea with a pass under a feigned name. *Draft.*

1704, October 10—Our last letters from England have put us out of our fears though not answered our hopes from our fleet. We cannot reproach the Tars with doing anything that may eclipse our glory. Posterity must decide who has the best title to the victory, for I believe neither of the parties concerned will depart from their pretensions as long as they live. Bad sermons I see fly as fast as bad news. We have that from St. Paul's already, and I am surprised to see a performance of that learned Dean with less life and elegancy than most of the country addresses. No comfort yet from our damned siege. It is almost vexatious to see so much done for a stupid people that can do nothing for themselves. The work there in most perfection is a stage for the King of the Romans to mount and view anything that may be performed worth his royal contemplation. It is thought the Electress of Bavaria must yield to the terms the Imperialists are willing to give her.

John, Archbishop of York to [Robert Harley].

1704, October 16. Bishopthorpe — Hearing that Dr. Plume the minister of Greenwich is in a dying condition, and that some are making applications to the Queen for that living, desires that it may be given to Mr. Turner who had been petitioned for by some of the nobility and chief persons about Greenwich. The Dean of Carlisle [Atterbury] set out this morning from York on his London journey; he intends giving her Majesty a sermon on the 5th of November.

A[bel] Boyer to [Robert Harley].

1704, October 18—Asking him to countenance his design of publishing a journal of the Duke of Marlborough's campaigns in Germany. Somebody had been beforehand with him in this scheme; however only as to the title, for upon perusal this journal is no more than a lame abstract of public papers.

News Letter.

1704, October 21. London.—The letters from Paris of the 24th by the Holland mail—of Tuesday last which came yesterday—bring a confirmation of the retreat of the Portuguese from the river Agueda near Ciudad Rodrigo, which they were not able to pass by reason of the works made at the fordable places on the banks of that river by the Duke of Berwick, and the opposition he gave them; and the Paris Gazette says that their cavalry advanced into the plains on the other side of the river, but could not draw the enemy to a battle, and that one hundred of their horse rencountered five squadrons of English dragoons which covered the march of the Portuguese army, and made them retire with precipitation; but says that on the 8th the whole Portuguese army appeared again, but made no attempt. But this account being loose and romantic we may expect a different one by our next Lisbon mail.

On the 20th an express arrived at Court from the Duke of Vendome with advice that he had driven the enemy from their posts about Verrua, that his great artillery was arrived, and that he had disposed all things for the siege of that place, and would open the trenches incessantly : this place is looked upon as a bulwark to Turin.

The Duke of Savoy continues encamped at Cressentino, and has caused process to be made against the officers that so ill defended the posts and the retrenchments de la Faille. His Royal Highness complains highly of the irregular proceedings of the Swissers.

The French write that they have taken of the Duke of Savoy's troops twenty-six battalions, besides some cavalry, but that he has still, including the German auxiliaries, twenty-four battalions and a good body of horse. The Marshal de Villeroy is gone to Flanders, where he is to confer with the Elector of Bavaria about means to prevent the siege of Trarbach, or else to make a diversion by the attack of some other place.

The accommodation with the Hungarians is not like to be so soon effected as was imagined. The Ministers of France and Bavaria with Prince Ragotzi labour to prevent the same, and the rebels demand as preliminaries two points which it is believed the Emperor will never comply with, vizt., That all the fortresses in Hungary shall be garrisoned only with natives, and that the Jesuits shall immediately quit the kingdom and never return more, and be dispossessed of their estates there.

By letters from the camp before Landau of the 20th it is remarked that on the 18th we attacked some part of the counterscarp but the enemy's works being not enough destroyed we were several times repulsed, but at last we made a lodgment eight paces from the palisadoes. On the 20th the enemy in a vigorous sally drove us from our lodgment, but letters of the 22nd assure that on the 21st in the evening we retook the counterscarp, on which we are raising batteries to make a breach in the town, so that the same cannot hold out many days. It is said the King of the Romans is resolved to grant the garrison no other terms than to make them prisoners of war.

Letters from the Duke of Marlborough's camp of the 20th say that Colonel Blood marched from the army that morning with eighteen pieces of cannon, under the convoy of three regiments of infantry, that he was to be followed the next day by twenty-two battalions and forty-eight squadrons, and that they were to join the Friday following at Homburg where the Duke of Marlborough designs also to be in person, and to march for Treves and Trarbach. A detachment of six regiments of foot and four of horse from the Dutch army is also on their full march for the Moselle. The French have also made a detachment of 6,000 men to march the same way and join the Marquis de Regro. The King of Sweden is marching towards Cracow to crown King Stanislaus, which is to be performed on the 28th instant by the Archbishop of Lemberg ; the Cardinal primate is still at Dantzic. The greatest part of the Russia fleet is now arrived, two men-of-war are ordered to carry Admiral Mitchell to Holland, who is to adjust with the several Admiralties there their quotas of ships of war for the next summer's expedition according to the treaty of alliance, which they never sent yet, and those which they sent the year past were sorry ships, that which Admiral Calenberg was on board carried but sixty-four guns, and was presently disabled.

Our seamen grumble that they have not a month's pay given them as bounty money for their service in the late engagement, as they had for that at La Hogue, which was not half so long nor near so smart.

A convoy is ordered to be got ready to bring over the Duke of Marlborough. It is believed that the Bill to prevent occasional conformity will be brought in again this session.

HENRY GUY to [ROBERT HARLEY].

[1704, October 22.] Sunday—I cannot express to you my affliction for the sickness of my worthy friend your son. I thank you for the good news you sent me that they came out so well, the kindly season, by which the accidents of cold will be prevented, will I hope contribute much to his recovery.

NEWS LETTER.

1704, October 24. London—Letters from Poland say that General Brand with a body of Poles, Muscovites and Saxons has laid siege to Posnia, and that they hope to be masters of that city in seven or eight days. A party of Saxons has recovered a great part of the treasure which the King of Sweden extorted from the inhabitants of Lemberg: they have also plundered and laid waste the Archbishopric of Guesna belonging to the Cardinal Primate, and another party of them surprised and took the Sieur Towianski, Palatine of Lowizie, a creature of the Cardinal Primate, within five leagues of Dantzic, and with him 180 fine horses and 15,000 crowns in money. This man has been a terrible incendiary against the King; but he is now sent for Saxony in order to atone for his revolution principles. The Cardinal Primate who continues to shelter himself at Dantzie labours with the Foreign Ministers there, to intercede for this person, knowing the just punishment he deserves, but they have declined to intermeddle in the matter.

The King of Sweden has quitted Russia, and his army is marching in three columns towards the Vistula; one of which is commanded by His Majesty, the other by General Reinschild, which marched towards Lublin, and the third under King Stanislaus towards Cracow in order to be crowned there.

The King of Poland continues at Pultawa and his army is cantoned thereabouts, and it is not yet known which way he will move upon the approach of the King of Sweden, but it is generally believed he will avoid a battle. It appears now by letters from Berlin that the Prussian forces that are on their march are only to guard their own territories and not to join the King of Poland as auxiliaries.

The letters from Vienna give little hopes of a sudden accommodation with the rebels of Hungary, who have not on their parts observed the cessation of arms during the treaty, but possessed themselves of Cassovia, Eperies, and Sentre in Upper Hungary where they found a very fine train of artillery and great quantity of ammunitions of war: they seem also to be preparing for an irruption into Moravia.

We expect in a post or two to hear of the taking of Landau, the Governor of which place, Monsieur de Laubaine, has made a better defence than did Monsieur Melach in the former siege two years ago; but the reason the Germans have been so long about it is their sparing of their men, though the French have cut off a great many in their frequent sallies.

The consternation is great in Bavaria upon notice they have given them that after the above siege is over, the troops of the Emperor, the King of Prussia, the Danes and Franconians shall come and quarter upon them to chastise them for their obstinacy; in the meantime the Imperial Commissaries exact vast contributions in that country.

Yesterday about noon an express came to the Admiralty from Sir John Leake, who commands the squadron that is left at Lisbon, giving an account that the Marquis de Villadarias has actually besieged

Gibraltar by land, while at the same time Monsieur Pointy has by sea with ten men-of-war, and that he was going to its relief with fourteen men-of-war; but the garrison being well provided with all necessaries is looked upon to be in no great danger.' '"

Yesterday being the first of the term Mr. Robert Ferguson appeared upon his recognizance in the Court of Queen's Bench, as did Tutchin the Observator, whose trial is appointed to be on the 4th proximo: also Abraham Gill, the conventicle preacher at Wisbeach, appeared in the same Court, where the Justices of the Peace that caused him to be impressed into the Queen's Service, to prevent an Information being brought against them, made it appear that he had two wives at the same time, and children by them both, that he had forged orders in the Church of England, that he was a common disturber, debauchee, &c. : which he is ordered to answer on Saturday next. An information was brought against Rawlins the printer for a libel called *Legion's Address to the House of Lords*. This day the Parliament met according to their last adjournment, and the Queen came to the House of Lords and, the Commons being sent for up, made a most gracious speech. in substance vizt., reminds them of the present and remarkable success of her arms this summer; hopes that they are disposed to an improvement of the present advantage, and accordingly desires such supplies as are necessary for the carrying on the next year's service, and for our performing our treaties with our allies, and the rather for that some of their just pretensions are depending ever since the last war; believes that they will find some changes necessary for the next year which were not mentioned the last session, and some extraordinary expenses incurred which were then unprovided for; and lastly recommends union at home. The Commons resolved on a congratulatory address, to go on the Queen's speech on Tuesday, and the call of the House on Thursday sevennight; and adjourned till tomorrow.

VISCOUNT WEYMOUTH to [ROBERT HARLEY].

1704, October 24. Longleat.—Asking his advice whether to resign his place at the Office of Plantations or to apply to the Queen for leave of absence. His desire to lay down his office proceeded not from being uneasy or weary of the Queen's service, but the loss of his son had quite unfitted him for business and he was unwilling to receive the profits of a place, the duties of which he was not in a condition to execute.

J. BISHOP OF NORWICH to ROBERT HARLEY.

1704, October 26.—Has received the enclosed statement from his receiver of the Tenths, to the effect that Jacob Hudson of Ipswich with 700l. of that revenue in his hands had gone to Holland. Desires a Secretary of State's letter to authorise his capture.

NEWS LETTER.

1704, October 31. London—The ensuing occurrences we have by the Holland mail of Friday last which arrived yesterday, vizt.—
From Warsaw of the 23rd that on the 18th King Augustus passed the Vistula with his army and came himself and took his lodging in the castle of that city. The next day the King of Sweden with his army arrived near Prague and sent some of his troops to the bank of the river opposite to Warsaw to learn if the King of Poland had put a garrison into the place, upon whom the King caused the cannon to play, and has

disposed his forces so as to oppose the Swedes passing the Vistula. The King of Sweden is retired to Pultowa but his troops continue in sight of Warsaw.

The Duke of Vendome opened the trenches before Verrua on the 22nd instant, though it is thought impossible for him to carry on the same considering the rigour of the season. Letters from Venice say that Count Leinengen having received his reinforcement only attends the return of the officers which he sent to Piedmont and Vienna to march; the Grand Prior, having also received the reinforcement sent him by the Duke of Vendome, so that he is now twenty-two battalions and forty squadrons strong, observes very narrowly the Imperialists.

Prince Ragotzki according to letters from Vienna of the 25th continues to insist upon extravagant demands, and amongst the rest to be Prince of Transylvania, which the Emperor will never grant, but rather endeavour to divide the heads of the malecontents till the siege of Landau is over, and then pour in more troops upon them and force them to a submission on easier terms.

The Electress of Bavaria and the King of the Romans are come to an agreement by which that Princess is immediately to deliver to the Emperor the city of Passau and Straubingen and all the other places along the Danube from Passau to Ratisbon, with the artillery and munitions in them, and accordingly the places named are already put into the hands of the Imperialists, and there is a suspension of arms and great hopes that the Electress and States of Bavaria will entirely submit to the Emperor.

The siege of Landau according to our accounts of the 1st instant proceeds as well that they hoped to be masters of the place in ten or twelve days more. Prince Lewis in visiting the trenches was in danger of being killed by a cannon ball, his horse was wounded and fell to the ground, and the prince bruised in the left leg.

The Duke of Marlborough has taken possession of the city of Treves and the fort of St. Martin, the French having quitted it upon his approach. It is said they have also abandoned Saarbrück. Trarbach was invested on the 3rd by the cavalry and the next day by the infantry.

The Elector of Bavaria having on the 28th drawn together all the forces of the enemy with a design to march and attack the Dutch army under Monsieur de Overkirk, but having communicated his design to the Marshal de Villeroy, who arrived at Tirlemont at the same time, he not only disapproved the same as hazardous, but also when that would not do, produced a written order of the French king's not to attempt anything, upon which the Elector mounted his horse and returned to Brussels full of discontent, and the troops were ordered to return to their garrisons. M. Tallard with the other French General Officers are arrived at Rotterdam, in order to their transport to England.

According to the account from Spain the siege of Gibraltar was to commence in form the 20th instant, the Marquis de Villadarius having with him an army of 14,000 men including the 3,000 French landed by Monsieur Pointy.

On Sunday in the afternoon some pickpockets at Covent Garden Church, giving it out that one of the galleries cracked and was falling, put the people into such a consternation that they pressed out with that violence that two women were trampled to death and several sorely bruised. In the meantime the pickpockets played their game so well that they got a power of gold watches and other

E 82470.

K

good booty. On Saturday last died the famous and learned physician Mr. John Locke being upwards of seventy years old.

Yesterday Sir Owen Buckingham, the new Lord Mayor, according to custom and _{usu}al ceremony went to Westminster and was sworn, and afterwards returning dined at Drapers Hall. All that was observable was that very few aldermen accompanied his Lordship, which was inter-preted as disrespect, but then this was sufficiently made up by the honour the Duke of Somerset, Lords Somers, Halifax, and some others did his Lordship in dining with him.

LORD CUTTS to [ROBERT HARLEY].

1704, November [1-] 11 new style.   The Hague—The Duke of Marlborough, forseeing it would be late before he could come for England, having given me leave to pass this winter there, after having stayed three winters successively in these parts, gave me leave to come forthwith, Mr. Lumley and Ingolsby—two younger Lieutenant-Generals —being still with Her Majesty's forces in Germany. I left the Camp at Weissenburg on Monday was a fortnight, and arrived here on Friday last late at night ; and wait only for the arrival of the convoy from England, to come over with Mr. Churchill, who sent me word yesterday from Rotterdam, that he expected it every hour. All which you'll please to lay before the Queen and the Prince, that, if Her Majesty or His Royal Highness hear of my being here, they may know the meaning of it.

[DANIEL DE FOE to ROBERT HARLEY.]

1704, November 2—I am very shy of burthening you with trifles, while the Nation's burthens load you, but *pardon me* that I am extremely solicitous on your account. If it be so, that my low station renders my concern very useless to you, yet I shall not less show my sincere endeavour and at worst incur your censure as impertinent, not as unfaithful. The freedom you always gave me, and which I think it was never more my duty to take, obliges me to talk to you in terms too coarse for the distances between your character, your person, your merit, *and me.* I beseech you place my want of decency to the account of my passion if possible to render you service.

I wish for an occasion to show you by anything. besides this cheap empty way of word service, what I would do, suffer, or risk, for your advantage ; that the sincerity with which my soul is swelled for your service might by some demonstration challenge your belief ; and I might if possible discharge myself of the weighty debt of gratitude, and please myself with having done something worthy of you obliging, and of. me obliged beyond the common rate of service and obligation.

Among the crowd of things which press my thoughts, and the various ways my impotence of thought offers both to discharge my exceeding obligation, and if possible be useful to so bountiful a benefactor, admit, sir, as the best I can offer, a genuine candid observation on the public affairs as under your conduct—and yet who am I that I should pretend to advise you, qualified to advise a nation.

It wounds me to the soul to hear the very Whigs themselves, and who, for saying so I fancy in the Confederacy which you hinted you had some notice of, tell me, and speak it openly *you are lost;* that your interest in the House won't keep you in the Chair, that the party suppressing you there will consequently ruin your interest in the Queen's favour, and give a new turn to your management at Court. I confess it fills me with indignation to hear this spoken with an air of satisfaction by a Party who ought to know, if blindness from Heaven had not seized their understandings, that in your fall, *pardon my calling it so*, from the management, the ruin of their interest is as effectually contained as 'tis possible for consequences to be in their original cause.

But the children of light were always darker in temporals, than the rest of their neighbours, and we are willing to be fools to please our fancies, though to the destruction of our judgments, but above all they are the most implacable in censure—and they cannot believe Mr. H—— honest and true to the Moderate interest, because they once thought him otherwise. But the principal reason I find, because they saw themselves in the case of the disciples who were disappointed when they found our Lord did not restore the temporal kingdom to Israel; or like the Mother of Zebedee's children who looked to have them all to be Lord Chancellors, and Lord Treasurers, and one to sit on the right hand, and the other on the left, and was angry our Lord did not grant it, though he declared it was *none of his to give*.

I rejoice that I have had the honour of doing your character justice, and have some converts to boast of; but as my little merit shall be the last thing I'll plead, so I only hint it now, to let you know the blemish, as they would have it be called, on you, as a person not in the right interest, has had a vast extent and requires some conduct to raze out. Pardon me, had your enemies nothing to boast of but the 'voice of our foolish friends, I grant this not worth your notice but as it is apt to fall in with other capital mischiefs, it merits your consideration, and some method to suppress it.

If you'll allow the vanity of the expression, *if I were a public Minister*, I would if possible know what everybody said of me, and I have formerly instanced Cardinal Richelieu to you on that head; please to give me leave though the words shock my soul as I write them, and I believe them to be impotent forgeries, yet I repeat them, that you may make use of them as you see cause.

"Mr. Harley is *out*, he has *lost* his interest, the House will certainly *lay him by* and if there be nothing else in it, 'tis a trial of the strength of the House, and a proof he *has lost ground;* besides both sides are against him, he has trimmed so long on both sides, and caressed both Parties, till both begin to see themselves illtreated, and now as he loves neither side, neither side will stand by him. All the Whigs of King William's reign expected to have come in play again, and had fair words given them, but they see it was but wording them into a Fools' Paradise, and now the two ends will be reconciled to overturn the middle way. If he is out of the Chair, they will soon work him out of the seals, and Lord Godolphin out of the Treasury."

They call the Duke of Marlborough, the Lord Treasurer, and yourself, *the Triumvirate* who manage the State and that if this knot be broken in the House first, they will prevail with the Queen to continue the Duke of Marlborough abroad, all this winter, under pretence of going to concert measures with the Princes of the Empire, and so they will easily put by all this scheme of management.

This ridiculous stuff had never reached your ears, if I had not observed some coherence between it, and what you were pleased to mention to me as designed, and by which it seems either to be publicly concerted or at least concluded and talked on as a thing finished.

As our friends were always fools, it amazes me to hear them promise themselves a general ease on a capitulation with the High Church, Liberty, Occasional Licence, and God knows what.

I shall give you no comments on this ungrateful text, I leave it to your sedate thought; I struggle with my utmost to expose the folly of it, and with encouraging success.

Nor is it the danger to you from these people. I hear discourse that would have moved me thus far to assume a post that so ill becomes me. But as these little capillary veins of malice receive the little venom they contain from some fountain of larger dimension, so I recommend that fountain to your discovery and prevention.

I remember when having had the honour to serve the late King William in a kind like this and which his Majesty had the goodness to accept, and over value by far, expressing some concern at the clamour and power of the party, at his express command I had the heart or face or, what else you will please to call it to give my opinion in terms like these:

" Your Majesty must face about, oblige your friends to be content to be laid by and put in your enemies, put them into those posts in which they may seem to be employed, and thereby take off the edge and divide the party."

It would be an unsufferable vanity to offer you the detail of that affair, but the end of thus arrogantly quoting myself is as follows :

Sir, the Whigs are weak they may be managed and always have been so. Whatever you do, if possible divide them, and they are easy to be divided. Caress the fools of them most, there are enough among them. Buy them with here and there a place; it may be well bestowed.

If you have him not already, as all I can talk with that are friends *wish* you had, my Lord Somers, whom all allow to be a great man, must if from them, weaken and distract the Party. Such a man cannot be bought too dear, and if gained entirely would secure your interest. 'Tis pity two such men should not understand one another—if it be so. *United*, what may you not do! *Divided*, what mischief must ensue to both, and the nation in general !

I humbly entreat your accepting these hints. 'Tis my fear of a conjunction of extremes, which are doubled from the connection of what I hear abroad, and what you observed. They talk of this conjunction as of a thing done, and you would wonder at the follies and hopes some weak people discover at this novelty.

I have had some thoughts, though it be but a project, that the bringing an Occasional Bill upon the anvil in such a juncture would be of the last service in this case. 'Twould break the Confederacy, 'twould blacken and expose the party, yours are sure of giving it a toss at last, and there are a crowd of present advantages to be made of it. To bring it in by trusty hands, and blast it at last would confound the thing itself, ruin all the confederacy, brand the Party with the scandal of opposing the Queen, and breaking their promise in the Address ; 'twould sink their character, and they would go home with such a fame, as would cause fewer of the same men to come back again next Session than may otherwise he expected.

These two things have lain so strongly on my thoughts, always employed, and solicitous to serve your interest, that I could not satisfy myself without giving you the trouble of perusing them ; and pardon me, if I say I think I write of them with more earnestness, and concern, than I should if I were petitioning you for a reprieve from the gallows.

I beseech you place it all to the account of my zeal to serve you, and to prevent if possible a public disaster to the nation, which I think must be the consequence of a blow to your present greatness and conduct to whom we all owe much, if not all, of the present prosperity of England. I have some subsequent thoughts on this subject, which, if this pleases you, you may command at a word, as you always may.

JOHN DUBOURDIER, Minister of the Savoy, to ROBERT HARLEY.

1704, November 4—Petition on behalf of certain French protestant ministers imprisoned in the castle of Vincennes, that they might be exchanged for an equal number of French priests taken at sea.

SIR JOHN BLAND to [ROBERT HARLEY].

1704, November 6. Doncaster—Regretting that a fit of the gout prevented him from coming to town. Designs to go thirty-three miles to-day in his chariot and so troop on till he meets with a place in the coach. Has ventured very hard in coming up now, but hopes the air and travelling will recover him.

—— to the EARL OF GALWAY.

1704, November 10. Gibraltar—Our garrison is about 1,300 men, whereof 200 are sick and wounded, and half the remainder on duty every second night so that a man cannot be spared to work, which occasioned the Prince to get 500 sailors and artificers from the fleet, who work night and day. The enemy has twenty-five cannon battering continually against the face of the bastion on the waterside and the curtain, they are from twenty-four pound ball to forty-eight, except two of twelve pounds and five mortars of a small diameter and do no great harm. Their cannons have dismounted all our guns on the two bastions and curtain of the land gate where their only attack is made, and fire furiously against the works, but cannot bring their artillery to bear so low on the foot of the curtain to make a breach only upon about fortypaces that wants the *chemin couvert* and glacis, but the breach is not practicable to mount having still ten foot clear from the ground of good wall, and every night we carry off the rubbish; as for the rest of the curtain it is firm and good. They are now upon some old walls running from the castle to the bridges, and have made a small breach through, but of the greatest difficulty to mount both by reason of its situation and several lines of defence, on the back of which breach I am making now a second work within the Castle to oppose them, if they can mount the breach, and from whence we are sure to drive them; as for the curtain below that is battered. I have pulled down several houses and [am] making another rampart parallel to the first, from whence we can make good all our fire that is taken away by their battering the parapet of the first rampart. I have run a double range of palisadoes of the fosse seven foot high of good oak and made two flanking works to scour the same, and am also carrying a mine from the ditch under the *chemin couvert* and so under the glacis the whole length of the curtain which I hope to have ready in three days, and ready to spring, if they should attempt to lodge themselves on the glacis; but as our garrison is small we have got 500 sailors and artificers to work with us night and day, and in case the enemy makes any attempt, all the boats of the men of war will be manned to flank the enemy on their march, which will be a 1,000 paces all the way exposed to ours and their fire, and the only thing we want is more men, and if the place is lost that will be the cause. Wherefore we hope your Excellency will send about 2,000 immediately to us, and in my opinion there is nothing but the men or great rains can save it. As for tools and necessaries we had none but what the fleet furnishes. This is the true state of our condition, and we hope a speedy succour may be sent. *Copy.*

HUGH CHAMBERLEN, Senior, to the SPEAKER.

1704, November 11. Dalkeith Castle—A long letter dealing with the questions of national credit and the currency.
Accompanying the letter is a very long paper headed "Overtures for a current credit humbly offered to the Honorable House of Commons by Hugh Chamberlen, senior, formerly physician-in-ordinary to King Charles the Second."

The SAME to the QUEEN.

1704, November 11, Edinburgh—A humble address on the same subject as the preceding letter.

The DUKE OF NEWCASTLE to [ROBERT HARLEY].

1704, November 15. Welbeck—Part of my servants are already gone and others must come after me ; and I continue fixed for Monday sevennight and hope in a few days after to have the honour of your company, the satisfaction of your conversation is one of the chiefest I promise myself in town. The ill will of some people is not to be questioned, envy and ill nature furnishing them with malice. But I think it is your own fault if ever you let them add to that power.

[LORD GODOLPHIN to ROBERT HARLEY.]

[1704,] November 16—Mr. Warre brought me your letters which I herewith return, having had the honour to read them to the Queen and to give Her Majesty the letter from the Queen of Denmark. There seems nothing to be answered upon any of them but to Lord Marlborough about Dantzic, who I believe will know well enough without it what he has to do there. And I hope besides that he will have left Berlin before a letter can reach it from hence.
I don't see but that in Holland they ought to renew the conferences for the protection of Dautzie, though they don't see the King of Prussia's treaty, provided they will admit Palmquist, and then Sweden and Norway might both join with the rest to be guarantees against each other.

ADAM CARDONNEL to [R. WARRE ?].

1704, November 17. Cassel—We came yesterday from Frankfort to Marburg where we found the Landgravine of Hesse with one of the young Princesses. The Landgrave did not expect we should have left the Army so soon, but hearing at Rheinfels we were come forward, he sent Monsieur Borirebourg, a Colonel of his troops, post to my Lord Duke to pray he would stay one day and His Highness would be with him intending to entertain his Grace with hunting the wild boar. My Lord Duke has returned his compliments and prayed his excuse, intending to pursue his journey to-morrow morning towards Berlin. We travel fifteen hours in the four and twenty, night and day, and hope to be at Berlin on Sunday ; you will please to take care of the enclosed.

My Lord Duke would be glad if Mr. Secretary could contrive a passage for Count Gallas before his Grace comes to the Hague which you will please to acquaint him with. He was received last night at Marburg and here to-night with all the marks of honour and respect possible.

The EARL OF GALWAY to [ROBERT HARLEY,] Speaker.

1704, [November 20–] December 1 [new style]. Lisbon—I've received the honour of your letter by Colonel Dobbins, but since I came here, you may be assured I shall lay hold of all occasions to serve any person who has the honour of your recommendation, and particularly Colonel Dobbins.

I'm mightily obliged to you for the good opinion you have of me, I will endeavour to do all the good I can but fear I shall not do all the good I would. Solicitations are very dilatory in Holland ; this service requires a speedy resolution and quick execution. If England would exert itself on this occasion by timely and necessary succour, it would both save great sums and do the business effectually, for of all things time is most precious.

I flatter myself much with the honour of your favour and protection in the House of Commons for the Portugal establishment that we may have our share in the augmentation of forces I hear the House intends to give the Queen.

You'll find by the enclosed account the state of Gibraltar, I hope the succours I send thither will arrive in time to save so important a place.

BENJAMIN EDWARDS.

1704, November 23—Information delivered at the bar of the House of Lords by Benjamin Edwards and produced by Lord Haversham on this date.

Is[AAC] NEWTON to [LORD GODOLPHIN,] Lord Treasurer.

1704, November 24. Mint Office—Sending him a design for a medal to commemorate the campaign of 1704.

A memorandum at foot in the Bishop [Lloyd] of Worcester's hand that he agrees in all things to the medal as corrected by Mr. Newton, with some slight exceptions.

DANIEL WILLIAMS to [ROBERT HARLEY].

1704, November 29. The hint you gave me about my Lord Treasurer, lest my not asking might be misinterpreted when I found him there, emboldened me to ask the favour of his presenting us ; which he was pleased to declare his willingness to have done, but that his affairs required his going thence before the time appointed. This I informed the ministers of, and we all meeting him on our way to the castle,I stepped aside to his Lordship, not for any matters I had to speak, but that their observation of his civility might introduce a momentous and kind proposal of yours, which I find will be highly esteemed and thankfully embraced.

I sent you word by Mrs. M. that I was well assured Mr. Johnson is very frequently with Lord H———on, and not knowing when your leisure will allow me a little time, I must beg leave to inform you that I have an account from New England representing Colonel Dudley as one unagreeable and very dangerous to the present government if any trying exigency should occur. I thank God for restoring health to you and family and must congratulate you on their defeat who attempted tacking the Bill. The world will still more see the unkindness its hot promoters have for the protestant succession or kingdom, though I almost equally fear it from a zeal for the little charity yet remaining, for I foresee how disposed and advantaged our folk will be to preach and talk for a total separation from the Church of England ; to say nothing of their utter incapacity to preserve the government who are as yet as zealous for it as any. Nor will there always be want of a trial when so many potent pretenders are excluded, especially in a nation so selfish and hurried by disgusts. God hath honoured you above any in procuring the settlement of the protestant succession. Pardon my folly if I mistake in saying, the Bill against occasional conformity is apt as well as intended to undermine it; you and the best part of our present ministry in the state as well as church. Nay had you seen the tottering state of our stocks last night you would [realise] the crisis the apprehended success of our violent men would cast us into.

INFORMATION of BENJAMIN EDWARDS.

[1704, November.]—Draft of a long statement, in Harley's handwriting, of his proceedings upon the information of Benjamin Edwards regarding the discovery of a treasonable correspondence with France ; with observations on the paper delivered to the House of Lords by Edwards.

LEOPOLD, DUKE OF LORRAINE to [ROBERT HARLEY].

1704, December 9. Luneville—Having learnt that the Emperor has had the goodness to recommend my interests to the Queen, I have thought it my duty to beg Her Majesty to order her generals to give all the assistance in their power towards the preservation of a State which his Imperial Majesty wishes to protect; and as I know the opinion which the Queen holds of your merit, I flatter myself that on this occasion you would accord me your good offices with Her Majesty. *Signed.* *French.*

PAUL BRETON, Merchant of Amsterdam.

1704, December 18—A Petition for his release from prison where he was confined on a false charge of high treason.

JEAN EICHER to MR. BROWNE, to be left at Mr. Low's a mercer's at the Hen and Chickens in Bedford Street Covent Garden.

1704, December 20—Has not received four or five of the letters said to have been addressed to him in October and November. Suggests some methods for securing greater secrecy, asks for information concerning the English navy, and for London newspapers. *Written partly in cypher.* Attached is a copy of the letter with key to the cypher. *French.*

MEMORANDUM.

'1704, December 29—Bassett a French priest returned into France about five years ago. Doctor Bassett a Roman Catholic physician is now in England and further enquiry will be made concerning him. *In Erasmus Lewis's handwriting.*

The EARL OF CARLISLE to [ROBERT HARLEY].

[1704,] December 29. Hind[erskelf]—By this day's post I have received two letters from you both bearing date the 26th with Her Majesty's commands, the one directing me to make enquiry what horses have been bought up within my Lieutenancies, and sent it into Scotland, the other directing me as Governor of Carlisle to stop all serviceable horses going for Scotland, and to take an account of their numbers, owners and to whom and what places they are designed. Both which directions I shall carefully observe and give you an account from time to time of what happens. I have not heard of any horses bought up within my Lieutenancies in order to be sent into Scotland. I am apt to believe that part of her Majesty's information may be a mistake, the country not affording horses any way useful or proper for military service. If such a thing had been, I should have been very sorry her Majesty had received the information of it from any other hand sooner than from mine.

The BAILIFF and BURGESSES of Leominster to the QUEEN.

1704, December 30—Petition for a confirmation of the charter of incorporation originally granted to them by Queen Mary and confirmed by Charles II. With a reference of it to the attorney general and solicitor general for a report thereon. *Seal of the Corporation.*

[The COUNTESS OF ORKNEY?] to [ROBERT HARLEY].

[1704?]—I am very glad of any mistake which has given me the satisfaction to receive the favour of your enquiring after me in so obliging a manner, all that I will say upon it is that you shall ever find I shall deserve so to be esteemed your faithful friend. I must give myself the pleasure to tell you, that I have heard so much to your advantage of late that I must pray for the continuance of your humility, and for mine, in having so deserving a friend. As soon as my Lord Orkney can venture abroad he will wait of you to give his thanks for your thoughts of him, you are the only person that he thinks he ought to depend upon, and therefore we hope you will finish his affair since you know in point of time 'tis so necessary and find some way to let him know he may have leave to kiss the Queen's hand, and when.

STATE of PARTIES in HERTFORDSHIRE.

[1704.]—This county is under several characters.

That part of it adjoining to Bedfordshire and Buckinghamshire is Whiggish and full of Dissenters. That part adjoining to Huntingdon, Cambridge, and Essex entirely Church and all of the High sort.

The Gentlemen of the Royston Club settle all the affairs of the country and carry all before them, though they behave with something more modesty, or at least carry it closer than in former days.

There is a monthly meeting of the gentlemen of all the neighbourhood the first Thursday in every month. They used to drink excessively and do a thousand extravagant things, but .they behave much better now. They have built a large handsome square room well wainscotted and painted; 'tis hung with the pictures of King Charles I., Charles II., King James, and King William at their full length, well painted in good frames, 10 or 12 foot high.

They have a monteth of silver of about four gallons which cost them 50*l.* They raise some fines and forfeitures, which formerly were improved to the increase of drunkeness, but now they do some charities and are much reformed.

Here Justice ———— and the then club resolved the pulling down the Quakers' meeting [house] at Hertford in 1683, for which the proprietor afterwards sued him and recovered sufficient damages to rebuild the house.

Mr. Freeman is master of all this part of the county as to parties. *In De Foe's handwriting.*

[LORD GODOLPHIN to ROBERT HARLEY.]

[1704.]—I thank you for the favour of your letters but I shall not trouble the Queen to read them to her to-night, because if I saw her I could not avoid troubling her with another thing which I am sure would be so uneasy to her, as to hinder her from sleeping.

All yesterday the generality of the Whigs, and this morning too some of them, treated the intention of sending for the old Electress as a ridicule, but Mr. Boyle has been with me just now to tell me, he finds the Whigs of the House of Commons very much changed in that matter, and they now talk that they should not have moved anything so disagreeable to the Queen, but if it be moved there is so much security for England in it, that 'tis impossible for any of their party to oppose it ; and if they did, the thing is so popular, they should lose themselves with the country, and with one another.

'Tis not imaginable how uneasy this will be to the Queen, and I don't know which way to prevent it, unless we can be strong enough to quash it in the House of Commons, which can scarce be hoped for, if all the Tackers and the Whigs join in it. I am sorry I did not know this before you made your visit to his Grace this evening, who perhaps might have been of use. I intend to-morrow morning to see if I can get any of the Whig Lords to make their friends in the House of Commons a little more passive. I give you the trouble of this letter to-night, not expecting any answer, for I am just going to bed, but because you might be forming your thoughts, against I see you to-morrow, to find some expedient to keep the Queen from so great a mortification as I know this will be to her.

[LORD GODOLPHIN to ROBERT HARLEY.]

[1704.] Windsor—Mr. Secretary Hedges sends me word he has summoned the Lords to attend the Queen here to-morrow upon the Lisbon letters, but thinking rather by yours that you will not be of the number of those that come, I send you back your Dunkirk papers, without any remarks, as well because I have not time, all the Scots Lords being to dine with me to-day, as for that I am very sure you will judge full as well of that matter without my assistance.

I cannot but take notice of Dr. Atterbury's particular good fortune in having expressions made him at the same time by Lord Thanet and

Lord Carlisle, and am willing to hope it is a good omen of what may follow.

The letters from Lisbon dated 23 days after the battle at sea, take no notice that they had heard the least word of it. I must own I don't see much occasion of summoning the Lords upon these letters, for till the Fleet returns it will scarce be possible to give any pertinent directions in the matters they contain.

I beg to hear from you again by this night's post if you have made any change in your intentions for Monday.

DR. FRANCIS ATTERBURY to [ROBERT HARLEY].

[1704.] Bridewell—Since I waited on you yesterday, a book has come to my hands entitled *Presbyters, not always an authoritative part of Provincial Synods* &c. written by Dr. Gibson, or one of his friends on that side, in order, at this juncture to revive the dispute between the two Houses, which has so long lain quiet.

'Tis written in answer to a few passages in a book of Dr. Brett's, which came out near a twelvemonth ago, and was by this time almost forgotten, so that the real design of this answerer must be, not to obviate any impressions that book may have made, but to stir up the ferment anew against the meeting of the Convocation; which is a convincing instance in what sort of temper those gentlemen are, and how little is to be expected from them towards the composure of our heats, if proper and pressing methods be not taken with them and that instantly. The book is undoubtedly written with the Archbishop's privity, if not by his direction, and therefore I thought it my duty to give you some account of it, before you discourse him. And whenever you think fit to let me wait upon you for a quarter of an hour, I shall be ready to offer what I have further to add on the same subject on which I spoke last night to you.

I cannot close this letter, without expressing the satisfaction I had last night in perusing Mr. Swift's book, which Mr. Prior showed us. 'Tis very well written and will do good service, but I'm afraid by the peculiar manner of writing he will too easily be discovered.

[LORD GODOLPHIN] to ROBERT HARLEY.

[1704.]—I return your draft of the Queen's letter to the King of Prussia, which I think is very right.

I had not heard a word of Benjamin Edwards, till by your letter; whoever be his patron, I think he is not like to do him much honour. So many disagreeable things as one meets with every day make me quite weary of my life; I have often envied your happier temper in these matters.

The Duke of Marlborough desires the gentlemen of the House of Commons may be summoned to meet at Mr. Boyle's to-morrow night at eight. We are just going to battle in the House of Lords.

LORD GODOLPHIN to ROBERT HARLEY.

[1704.]—Not knowing where or how to send to De Foe, I trouble you with his letter, desiring the favour of you to let him know that I think it might do service, if he could let us know the names of the persons concerned in carrying on these designs here in London, and the place of their abode.

I hear there are letters come from Sir Cloudesley Shovel, and that the troops landed in good condition, but that he must return to Lisbon to take in more provisions.

LORD GODOLPHIN to ROBERT HARLEY.

[1704.]—I am very glad to see you are eased in the Welsh affair. I am sure you should never be troubled if I could help it, in anything, though I find I must submit to be so while I am alive; the impertinen. cies I meet with are innumerable.

As to De F[oe] I should think he might be made use of where he is without further charge to you, but I shall be glad to talk with you to. morrow, if you will call upon me as you go to Kensington; about him and some other things.

WILLIAM HARLEY to [ROBERT HARLEY].

1704-5 January 3. Landau—Being under great obligations to you when I was under hard circumstances in England some few years ago, I think it my duty to acquaint you that when I parted from England, when you would have put me into some employment, I came to Germany with a nobleman of this Empire who knew me in my prosperity, and knew my services and sufferings during the wars in Ireland. I served but one campaign when I was preferred to the command of a troop of horse and am every day in hopes of being advanced higher. Recommends the bearer of the letter to his favour.

[SIR SIMON HARCOURT to ROBERT HARLEY]

1704-5, January 6—The Dean of Carlisle acknowledges what he has to be entirely owing to you. He is under great uneasiness for fear of being thought too pressing. I have undertaken to let you know the Dean of Wells is now in waiting and will be very proud of receiving your commands to wait on you. If you consider on what terms the Bishop and Dean of Carlisle stand, you will not blame the Dean's impatience to be out of his power.

I received the Secretary's orders for tomorrow night. I'm in great pain least some false step should be taken in the matter we discoursed of last night. You remember what H. S[t. John] said to us in the chamber sometime since after the rising of the House. I shall herein as in every thing submit myself to your conduct and hope you'll set me right.

The DEPUTY LIEUTENANTS of Westmorland to the EARL OF CARLISLE, at Hinderskelf, in Yorkshire.

1704-5, January 11—We have made enquiry concerning horses bought in our country by Scotchmen or carried into Scotland by any, and we do not know that any horses of value, or more than usual, have been carried into Scotland. Signed by Wm. Pennington, R. Musgrave, Edw. Stanley, Hen. Blencow, and Tho. Brougham.

WILLIAM GRAHAM to DR. FRANCIS ATTERBURY, Dean of Carlisle.

1704-5, January 11. St. James's—You need not give yourself and friends the trouble to meet tomorrow at the place that was appointed, because I am now resolved never to comply with the proposal made to me yesterday. I am glad the business, as the Solicitor General told me, may otherwise be done, which I hope may be to your content.

ADAM CARDONNEL to [ROBERT] HARLEY.

1704–5, January 12. Whitehall—My Lord Duke desires you will mention the enclosed papers to him at the Cabinet Council in order to receive the Queen's directions to signify Her Majesty's pleasure to Mr. Davenant at Frankfort to employ his good offices in conjunction with the Dutch Minister to induce the Princes of Rotenburg to accept of an equivalent from the Landgrave of Hesse Cassel for the Baillage of Rheinfels.

TER. MAGRATH to [ROBERT HARLEY].

1704–5, January 18. Berwick—In pursuance of orders he had seized on the 15th inst. a horse belonging to Patrick Butter a Scotchman going to Edinburgh with a pass from Lord Seafield for himself and servant without naming horses. This was the only serviceable horse that came that way ; as many as do come through will be seized.

The EARL OF CARLISLE to [ROBERT HARLEY].

1704–5, January 22. Hinderskelf — By the enclosed, which is a letter from my Deputy Lieutenants you will see that we know nothing of any horses bought up in our counties by Scotchmen, or by others for their use. I dare say the information given to her Majesty of this affair is false. We do not seem to be so very apprehensive of our neighbours as you are at London ; howsoever I have given directions to put the militia under my care into the best condition I can. If there be reason to apprehend any trouble from Scotland, the likeliest way to prevent any attempts or designs of theirs is undoubtedly to have a competent number of forces quartered upon the border, if they can be spared ; and indeed that seems necessary, for the weakness of our frontier garrisons will be an encouragement to them to make incursions upon us, if they are so inclined.

I desire the Queen will give me leave to make one Mr. Aglionby a deputy lieutenant.

J[OHN]. E[RNEST] GRABE to Dr. FRANCIS ATTERBURY, Dean of Carlisle, at Chelsea.

1704–5, January 22. London—I have told you that His Majesty the King of Prussia hath some time ago not only given to two of the chiefest clergymen in his dominions the title of Bishop, but also commanded the English Liturgy to be translated into the German tongue, in order to be introduced (although perhaps with some alterations) first into his chapel, and afterwards with the consent of the people into other congregations ; of which translation one of the nominated Bishops hath sent last August a copy to His Grace the Archbishop of Canterbury, to be presented to Her Majesty the Queen of England. I have likewise intimated to you, that it would mightily confirm the King of Prussia in his design of introducing the said Liturgy and also direct him to let the Bishops be duly ordained (which otherwise will give occasion to the Papist to ridicule the Protestant Episcopacy), if Her Majesty from the foresaid present of the Liturgy would take an occasion to declare in a letter to the King how much she was pleased with it, and give him at the same time a .hint of the consecration of . the titular Bishops according to the custom not only of the English but of all Christian Churches through the whole world ever since the foundation of them. This is not only my hearty wish, but also the great desire of the Chaplains and the nominated Bishop in the King's Court at Berlin ; as you know from the letters, which partly you have seen, partly been told of. And therefore I beg of you, that you would propose this matter in the best manner you can, to one of Her Majesty's Privy Council whom you think most inclined to speak to the Queen about it effectually.

Postscript.—Any of your letters will find me, if directed to Mr. Coligne's, an apothecary's, in Leicester Fields, where I lodge at present.

ROBERT HARLEY to [JOHN VERDUN].

1704-5, January 25—I understand from Sir Stephen Evans that you are desirous to speak with me. I would have you recollect yourself and resolve to be open and candid, and then you will find the advantage of it. Saturday in the evening I will send for you and it will be then in your power to make me your most humble servant. *Copy.*

SIR O[WEN] BUCKINGHAM, Lord Mayor of London, to ROBERT HARLEY.

1704-5, January 30. Goldsmiths Hall—Asking him to obtain leave for him from the Queen to go into the country in order to get rid of a very great cough which Dr. How acquaints him is turning to an asthma.

[JOHN] VERDUN to SIR STEPHEN EVANS.

1704-5, January 31—As I have promised you I have opened my heart to Mr. Harley without reserve. He promised me that he would see me again, but he has so much business that he has forgotten me. I desire that you would ask him to have so much charity as to admit me to bail. Nothing will come to my knowledge but I will let him know it.

NEWS LETTER.

1704-5, February 1. London—Letters from the camp at Gibraltar of the 11th relate that the garrison have since the 2nd made several vigorous sallies but have been repulsed with equal loss and that the besiegers have carried on their works to the covered way, and the other fortifications, but have deferred to give a general assault till the succours were arrived from the frontiers of Portugal, which would consist of 3,000 Spaniards and 5,000 French ; and that the Baron de Pointy was sent for the Court of Madrid to consider about blocking up Gibraltar by sea, the confederate fleet being returned to Lisbon.

Nor does the siege of Verrue prove a less knotty piece of work to the French than the above to the Spaniards, for according to letters from the Duke of Vendome's camp of the 19th the snows and rains have fallen in such abundance that their whole time for several days had been spent in clearing the trenches of water and preventing them being overflown by the Po.

This siege proves a terrible mortification to the Duke of Vendome who dares not assault the place by reason of the strength of the garrison and the multitude of mines they have made under all their works besides retrenchments within retrenchments nor is attacking the Duke of Savoy's camp at Crescentin less impracticable, the waters of the Po being excessively swelled, and that Prince has strengthened the same with 5,000 fresh men drawn from his garrisons, so that upon the whole it is believed the French will be obliged to turn the siege of Verrue into a blockade, after having lain before it about four months and lost above 12,000 men.

The sheriffs of London and Middlesex allowed the common panel of juries, so that Rawlins for libelling the House of Commons, and others of the same faction that are under prosecution, may expect tender usage from their brethren, but the Queen little justice.

The Bill for qualifying justices of the peace that is now carrying on in Parliament exacts that none shall be qualified for that commission unless he has an estate of 300l. per annum, excepting in the several counties of Wales and some of the northern counties 200l. per annum, and in Butland 100l. per annum, be reckoned as a qualification, but in corporations it shall remain as at present, where the mayors are usually justices by charter ; this will prevent a great many sorry and mean persons getting in the commission. Yesterday the Lords ordered their thanks to the Bishop of Peterborough for his sermon and that he be desired to print the same. The commons ordered the same to Doctor Stanhope. Yesterday the Lord Lucas departed this life, by whose death that honour is now extinct as the estate was long before. Yesterday an express arrived from Gibraltar which left that place on the 12th of January O. S. which gives an account that the garrison was in so good a condition that they feared nothing from the enemy, and that Admiral Leake was daily expected back from Lisbon.

JAMES MUNDY to ROBERT HARLEY.

1704–5, February 2. Sergeants Inn—My friend Mr. Warre informed me of the honour you did me in speaking to the Queen on my behalf, but withal he told me that Her Majesty seemed unwilling to add to the number of her Sergeants at this time. In King William's time they were eight or nine in number and I believe seldom less than six in any reign ; and now since the death of my Brother Birch there are but five, three of whom attend always in the Chancery and one in the Queen's Bench, so that Mr. Recorder alone is left for our Court, and the affairs in the City do take up most of his time, so that in truth the Queen has never a Sergeant at the Common Pleas Bar, where they are all supposed to attend, for the Queen has other Counsel in the other Courts. My Lord Keeper intended the number should never be less than six, and therefore, on the death of Sergeant Birch, designed me to fill up the vacancy, and for that purpose spoke to the Queen, and has since recommended me to your favour.

WILLIAM GREG to ROBERT HARLEY.

1704–5, February 2—Lord Paget upon hearing that I was out of business and willing to go abroad, having sent for me, offered such terms, as no man, who had your Honour for a patron, could embrace. Twenty pounds a year did surprise me, and yet when the meanness of my cir. cumstances would have tempted me to close with his Lordship's conditions, prudence bade me stay and try whether your Honour could not better my fortune, which I should look upon as desperate, were it not in so good hands.

The Earl of Carlisle to [Robert Harley].

1704–5, February 2. Hinderskelf—By the enclosed letter from the officer commanding at Carlisle you will see that no serviceable horses have passed our way into Scotland.

I beg to know the Queen's pleasure in relation to Mr. Aglionby, whom I would make a deputy lieutenant.

News Letter.

1704–5, February 3. London—At Falmouth 28th ult. at night the Alliance packet boat arrived from Lisbon in ten days with a mail, and brought over about thirty passengers most soldiers who report that about three weeks since the squadron under Admiral Leake except Dutch men of war returned into that port from Gibraltar, which place they left in so good a posture as to fear nothing from the besiegers, having a garrison of 3,000 men and a sufficiency of provisions and ammunition for four months.

Plymouth 30th, her Majesty's ship the *Medway* commanded by Captain Littletone has taken and brought in here the *Philip*, a privateer of St. Malo of 32 guns and 330 men which he took after an engagement of two hours in which the privateer had killed and wounded between forty and fifty men, but the *Medway* lost but one. Thirty other prizes are brought into the same port by her Majesty's cruisers. On Wednesday last Admiral Dilks sailed from Spithead with the fleet under his command.

The House of Lords read a second and third time a bill for treating a union with Scotland and passed the same ; and agreed to the report of the address relating to some mismanagement in the Admiralty which it is said has been much softened since the first draft, which we long to see in print.

Dr. Francis Atterbury to the Queen.

1704–5, February 4—Petition for the rectification of the date of his patent for the deanery of Carlisle, vacated by the preferment of Dr. Grahame to the deanery of Wells. With report of Sir Simon Harcourt thereon, dated February 14, in favour of such rectification.

John Verdun.

1704–5, February 5—A list of persons in custody under Secretary Harley's warrants, including John Verdun who had been confined thirty-four days, with the messengers' charges for keeping them.

Captain John Ogilvie.

1704–5, February 5—A statement drawn up and signed by Ogilvie for the information of Harley, by whom it is endorsed as received on this date, to the effect that he was in the army of King James and went abroad with him, as having taken the military oath he thought himself obliged to follow that prince's fortunes. Ogilvie was sent to Savoy and then to Catalonia, served through the wars there, and had a pension of 800 livres given him. On the death of James he left his court and went to the coast of Normandy with his wife and four children. When Queen Anne granted an indemnity to the Scots he went back to St. Germain to ask for a pass and some money to carry him over, but it was refused him, though the rest of his countrymen were allowed to go. In the month of December [1702 ?] however he hired a fishing boat, embarked with his family and landed on the Sussex coast. Ogilvie went at once to Sir Edward Selby, a justice of the peace, and told him who he was and where he came from; but some custom house officers came the next day to tell him he would not be allowed to depart without an order from the Secretary of State. An express was thereupon sent to Lord Nottingham, who despatched a messenger to bring up Ogilvie and his family to London at his own expense. Arrived there he, his wife, and daughter were kept prisoners for six months at extravagant charges for diet and lodging, so that he has run into debt to the extent of 130*l*., for which he is liable to arrest at any moment.

Ogilvie adds that he has given the lords of the council, without being forced or threatened, information about the treasonable correspondence carried on between France and England; and offers his services in intercepting such communications if he be sent to the Sussex coast, which and the measures adopted by these correspondents he knows well. But upon the whole he is willing to be disposed of as the Queen to whom he owes his life may think fit; he having no way to live but by his sword, being bred a soldier from his infancy.

News Letter.

1704–5, February 6. London—From the camp before Verrue of the 24th that they had received some fresh artillery and expected more, of which they are in great need, what they already have being for the most part rendered unserviceable. Several detachments of horse and foot are sent to Quieras near Turin to besiege that or some other place, in order to oblige the Duke of Savoy to quit his camp at Crescentin, to succour that place. The cavalry with some battalions are gone to the plains of Turin, to make a diversion and waste the country, so that the Duke of Savoy seems to be hard set.

From France the letters from before Verrue, speak of little else but the misery their troops are reduced to, in fighting against the elements, their trenches for eight days having been filled with snow and water, and the batteries covered above two foot deep, so that they could not play. Yet notwithstanding these difficulties, the Duke of Vendome will not quit his design.

The army under Count Lynengen consists but of 6,500 men, destitute of all manner of necessaries, so that a great many of them desert, and are become almost desperate, but Prince Eugene is preparing in a few days to go to Piedmont. The affairs of Hungary appear every day in worse state.

The Spaniards carry on the siege of Gibraltar as though they designed it the work of an age. The Baron de Pointy is returned again to Cadiz. The French labour to put a strong squadron to sea. The Marshal de Villars is gone to command on the Moselle, where he will have the flower of the troops of France and Villeroy in Flanders; and in all probability the approaching campaign may be decisive to the war.

The port letters I'll omit nothing material being in them, only it is worth remark, that the joint East India Company have sent out seventeen ships which makes fifty that they have abroad, so that the trade will be drove more extensive than ever.

It is said that on Thursday next the Lord Monthermer is to be married to the youngest daughter of the Duke of Marlborough.

This being her Majesty's birthday, the Court appeared very gay, but on Sunday her Majesty will go into mourning for the Queen of Prussia, to the great mortification of the shopkeepers by reason it will spoil their spring trade.

Sir Richard Cocks to Lord Berkeley, Lord Lieutenant of Leland.

1704–5, February 6—I am satisfied it is the principle of the Papists to place their preservation in the ruin of their Queen and country, and they have prepared horses and arms for that purpose. They have too many adherents. They have great friends in power who give them notice of everything that is designed against them. I gave you last summer an account of the number of their horses, and of their insolence in riding in armed bodies through our market towns [co. Gloucester] on market days to the dislike and terror of the people; but all that came of it was that in a few days the papists knew what I had written, and I was left as a mark for them to vent their malice on.

I could not procure two more deputy lieutenants to assist us in carrying out your orders of the 18th January, the justices being unwilling for the above reasons to act against the papists or Jacobites. Mr. De la Bere and I therefore resolved we would no longer delay and ordered Major Carter to search Mr. Wakeman's house, who is the only papist or non-juror in this division; he found no arms or powder, or any horse worth five pounds. He heard however that ten good horses had been sent away about ten days ago, and this account we had also from others.

Horses and Arms in Oxfordshire.

1704–5, February 9. Com. Oxon. North Division—According to orders directed to us dated the one and thirtieth day of January 1704–5, we went to Brize Norton, made diligent search in the house of Mr. Greenwood, found neither horses or arms.

From thence we went to Tusmore and diligently searched the house of Mrs. Farmer, and there found one birding gun and one large fowling gun, and in the stables three black geldings fifteen hands and a half high with blazes in their faces and bobtails, owned by Captain Lile.

From thence we went to Souldern and searched the house of Mr. Weeden and there found one birding gun and in the stables one slight chestnut mare.

From thence we went to Somerton and diligently searched the house of Farmer Collindridge, and there found one birding gun but no horse of five pounds value.

From thence we went to Farmer East's of the same town, made diligent search, found one birding gun but no horse of five pounds value.

From thence we went to North Aston and diligently searched the house of Farmer Goodman, found one birding gun but no horse of five pounds value.

From thence we went to Kiddenton and diligently searched the house of Sir Charles Brown, found two birding guns of his own and one of his butler's, but no horses at all.

From thence we went to Woodstock Park and diligently searched the lodge of Mr. Colvert, found two birding guns but no horses.

From thence we went to Cassenton and diligently searched the house of Mr. Reynolds, found one birding gun but no horses.

In searching of which houses we were seven days with three men each.

Thos. Napier.
John Connopp.

1704–5, February 9. Com. Oxon. South Division—According to orders directed to us dated the one and thirtieth day of January.

1704–5, we went to Sherborne on the third of this instant February and made diligent search in Mr. Gage's house where we found one birding gun and no horses or other arms.

From thence we went to Watlington and searched the house of Shepheard and found neither horse nor arms.

From thence we went to Watlington Park and searched the house of Mr. Stoner and found neither horses nor arms.

From thence we went to Stoner House and searched there and found one slight grey mare which Mr. Stoner used a hunting for his health and promised her forthcoming when desired, and found no arms.

From thence we went to Greys and searched the house of Mrs. Kennedy and found a little black mare in the stable under five pounds value and no arms.

From thence we went to Maple Durham and made diligent search in the house of Mr. Blunt, where we found four birding pieces, one of which we seized, and in the stable eight geldings and mares above five pounds value.

From thence we went to little Stoke and made a diligent search in the house of Captain Grimsditch, where we found no arms, nor horses in the stable.

From thence we went to Dorchester and searched the house of Farmer Day, and found no horse above the value of five pounds, and no arms.

From thence we went to Sandford and made diligent search in the house of Mr. Powell, and found no arms and in the stable one little horse not worth forty shillings.

From thence we went to Waterperry and made diligent search in the house of Sir John Curson and found neither arms nor horses.

From thence we went to Great Milton and made diligent search in the house of Mr. Francis Curson, and found neither arms nor horses.

From thence we went to Oxford and searched the Roman Catholics residing there and found no arms, but one horse of Mr. Kimber's not worth three pounds.

In searching of which houses we were seven days with three men each.

> JOHN CLERKE.
> RICH. CLERKE.

1704–5, February 9. Oxford—May it please your Lordship. In obedience to an order of Council dated the eighteenth day of January 1704, and transmitted by your Lordship to us whose names are hereunto subscribed Deputy Lieutenants of the County of Oxon, we did immediately issue out our precepts to proper Officers of the Militia effectually to search the houses of all papists and reputed papists, and all other persons within this County of Oxon refusing or neglecting to take the oaths to Her Majesty, by seizing all arms, ammunition or horses according to the Acts of Parliament. These are to certify that according to our precepts the Officers employed in this affair did on the ninth day of this instant February make their return to us of what they had done and delivered the same to us to be transmitted to your Lordship which we have here enclosed sent to you.

> FRAN. CLERK.   EDW. COBB.
> RL LYBBE.   SEB. SMYTHE.

NEWS LETTER.

1704–5, February 10. London—At Edinburgh the anniversary of King Charles's martyrdom was pretty decently observed. The court of judicature did not sit and the public offices were shut, and the best lot of people appeared in black; but a person who is fled thither from England for being author of Legion's Address and goes by the borrowed name of Allen (though his true name is Pierce) with some others of his kidney kept the calves head feast at the house of one Fowler in the Cowgate, by which we may see what sort of people they are that libel the present House of Commons.

The people are very busy in arming themselves throughout Scotland, and there is a great talk there of an alteration to be made in the ministry and the Duke of Queensberry and his party are again coming into place.

A party of the Marquis of Lothian's dragoons did last week by order of the Earl of Marchmont, Sheriff Principal of Berwickshire, apprehend a party of seventeen English dragoons including their officers and carried and secured them in Greenlaw Prison. The reason of this was this party made a practice of coming over the borders and kidnapping and pressing away men, and had nine with them when taken which they were carrying off; it is said they will be detained till they send home eight more which they have carried off before.

Sir Thomas Dilkes continues detained at Spithead by contrary winds so that he cannot prosecute his voyage for Lisbon, which is to be lamented there being some fear that the garrison of Gibraltar may be in want of the necessaries which he carries before his arrival, especially if the Duke of Anjou comes before the place and the French and Spaniards press the siege to that degree as it is pretended they will.

The Earl of Albemarle, the grand favourite in the late reign, with Sir David Mitchell, Count Gallas the new imperial minister, and Colonel Baynenbourg who took the Marshal de Tallard prisoner, are arrived from Holland. Sir George Rooke being recovered from his long indisposition went yesterday to Court to wait on the Queen and Prince. The information brought by William Colepeper Esquire against Sir Jacob Banks for striking him two years ago in Windsor Castle is to be tried the next assizes in Bucks.

LORD CUTTS to the DUKE OF MARLBOROUGH.

1704–5, February 11—Memorial praying for the payment of his debts in consideration of his services at the battle of Blenheim and elsewhere. *Copy.*

LORD CUTTS to LORD GODOLPHIN.

1704–5, February 13—To the same effect as the preceding memorial to the Duke of Marlborough. *Copy.*

YORKSHIRE HORSES.

1704–5, February 15—Two certificates signed by Sir George Cooke and Samuel Mellish, justices for the West Riding, of the number of horses sold in the several towns and fairs in the wapentake of Strafford and Tickhill, and in the wapentake of Staincross and Osgoldcross, since Michaelmas, 1704, showing the sum paid for each horse, which varied usually between 3l. and 10l.—none fetched more than 15l., except one from South Kirkby sold to Lord Granby for 100l. The majority of them are said to have been sold " to a neighbour."

YORKSHIRE RECRUITS.

1704-5, February 15—Return by Sir George Cooke, Samuel Mellish, and Thom. Vincent, that the constables of the wapentakes of Strafford and Tickhill, and Osgoldcross and Staincross have not brought in more than sixteen recruits to be enlisted by virtue of the late Act of Parliament. Most of them had been shipped to Holland to serve in Lord Orkney's regiment.

A similar return from magistrates of the West Riding within the Morley division (R. Musgrave, W. Calverley, and Fran. Lindley) gives the names of fourteen recruits who had been drafted into three different regiments serving abroad. Other persons whose names they had not ascertained, had gone and "listed themselves voluntarily."

NEWS LETTER.

1704-5, February 17. London—The siege of Verrue moves heavy and the French contend not more with the enemy than the elements, the snow having fallen again in abundance on the 1st and 2nd inst. at night which retarded their works; however at times they batter the Donjon with twenty pieces of cannon, and a work that covers the bridge of communication with seven, and Monsieur Lepara the famous engineer, who arrived in the camp before Verrue on the 10th and has now the directions of the siege, hath by a courier given the King an account that he hoped in a few days to have breaches wide enough to give an assault to the place as also to the fort which covers the bridge.

Paris letters of the 20th say that the Spaniards are in great hopes to be masters of Gibraltar before the garrison has received a fresh supply of munition &c., which they believe they are in need of from the sparingness of their fire. They write from Metz that the Marshal de Villars was preparing to open the campaign with some enterprise.

Dublin the 10th. This day our Parliament met and his Grace the Duke of Ormond our Lord Lieutenant went in great state to the Parliament House, his coach was drawn with eight horses, his livery very fine &c. His Grace made a speech of which it is hoped will have a very good effect and that the Parliament will soon dispatch the public business.

A Dutch privateer called the *Neptune* has taken and brought into Falmouth a French ship of good value from Martinico bound for Nantes and the *Golden Moon*, another privateer of the same nation, has brought into the aforesaid port a Spanish ship of 500 tons from St. Domingo which had on board the late Governor of the place with his lady, family and effects. This ship is said to be very rich. On the other hand the Paris letters this post confirm that the *Brittania* galley from Smyrna is carried into Morlaix, which though the French value her too high yet her owners say that she is really worth 40,000 r. but these are accidents that cannot be helped and must be reckoned among the calamities of war.

The Earl of Dysart (a Scottish honour), a principal member of the House of Commons of the church interest, is removed from being Lord Lieutenant of the county of Suffolk and the same is conferred on his Grace the young Duke of Grafton. A villainous letter has been sent to the magistrates of Oxford from some calves man, exhorting them to shoot through the head any of those gentlemen that were for tacking the Occasional Bill, should they stand at the next election for members of Parliament, but the country knows how to prize their true patriots.

This morning Mr. Mountague and the other counsel for the Aylesbury prisoners with Mr. Harcourt, the Clerk of the Crown, met at the Lord

Chief Justice's Chambers to make up the records in order no doubt to bring that affair before the House of Lords by writ of Error.

W. Bishop of Llandaff to [Lord Godolphin ?].

1704-5, February 19—Hearing that Dr. Bull, his Archdeacon, is to be preferred to the bishopric of St. David's, asks that he might have the archdeacoury in addition to the bishopric of Llandaff, which is so "scandalously poor," that the meanest bishopric in England is twice as good, "I have struggled in it with poverty now twenty-six years and "have even undone myself in endeavouring to live up to the dignity "thereof."

Richard Warre to [Robert] Harley.

1704-5, February 20. Whitehall—In the enclosed letter to the King of Prussia, the titles of the deceased Queen are inserted. It seems not very proper, at least not necessary, but since the King has mentioned them all in his letter, he may perhaps expect them in the Queen's. If you do not approve it, the letter may be transcribed with such other alterations in it, as you shall be pleased to direct.

I beg leave to observe that the King of Prussia gives himself in his letter the title of Prince of Orange, with the addition of such others as depend on it. The succession to this Principality is not I think yet decided, and I find upon inquiry and search the Queen has not in her former letters given him that title, for which reason it is omitted in this letter.

News Letter.

1704-5, February 20. London—Portsmouth the 18th, this day Sir Thomas Dilkes sailed again with ten men of war and a fleet of merchant ships for Lisbon, and will be speedily followed by Sir [John] Jennings with thirteen or fourteen men of war more, the Government being as resolute to preserve Gibraltar as the Spanish Court is to retake it.

Last night a farce was acted at Court to end the carnival where was all the fine singers and a mighty concourse of nobility and gentry. The validity of the marriage between Mr. Fenwick and the Lady Grosvenor having been for several days hearing before the delegates at Sergeants Inn in Fleet Street last night the same ended and the court gave it in favour of the Lady against Mr. Fenwick, it appearing that she was not according to the proof made *compos mentis* at the time of the pretended marriage in France, so that the same is null and void and Mr. Fenwick has lost his expectation of a rich bride.

On Saturday last the Earl of Bellomont of the kingdom of Ireland was married to Madam de Overkirke, daughter to Monsieur de Overkirke the Dutch velt marshal.

Sir Geo. Cooke and Samuell Mellish to Henry Boyle.

[1704-5, February 21]—The copy of the Order of the Privy Council was but very lately sent to us by Mr. Hewit the clerk of the Militia, with a copy of your letter to your Deputy-Lieutenants of the West Riding. There being no more at present than ourselves, residing within the wapentakes of Strafford and Tickhill, and Staincross, the rest being in London, or attending the Parliament, or remote from us; we certify, that we have carefully perused the said order and letter, and for want of Militia Officers we have prevailed with Mr. Thomas

Waterhouse the late Muster Master to take our warrant to search for such horses in papists' hands, as are above the value of five pounds (there being but five papists in these wapentakes able to keep such horses), he being very capable and always on such occasions ready to serve the Government. He hath brought this day to us the account as follows:—

Mr. More of Barnburgh hath four horses which have been viewed by one of us, and neither of them worth five pounds. Mr. Perkins a lodger with him owns he hath two geldings of the value of twenty pounds each sent to a fair to sell four days since, if unsold promised to bring them to us. Mr. Anne of Frickley hath seven but all used in husbandry none of them of the value of five pounds, two of the best have been seen. Mr. Hansby of Tickhill hath five, three mill horses, a mare, one foal, none of the value of five pounds, but he sold three good horses a mouth since to the Honourable Mr. James Sanderson, son to the Lord Castleton. Mr. Ratcliffe near Rotherham hath three galloways, none worth five pounds.

Sir Edward Northey to the Queen.

1704-5, February 21—Report in favour of the petition of the Bailiff and Burgesses of Leominster. *Signed.*

News Letter.

1704-5, February 22. London—The States General (as letters from the Hague of the 27th assure) make the utmost efforts to be as early in the field as the enemy and all the hired and best troops are to serve on the Moselle. The Pensionary has received advice that the Duke of Marlborough will return for Holland by the middle of March, with ample instructions from the Queen his mistress to confer with the Deputies of the States General about secret affairs touching the management of the war. His Excellency is also expected with great impatience to regulate the operations of the next campaign.

Weymouth the 19th, yesterday passed by Portland Admiral Dilks with the convoy for Lisbon, with a brisk gale at east, and it is believed he has got clear of the channel.

Our merchants had yesterday the bad news of the loss of a homeward bound Guinea ship off the Lands End named *Dalby Thomas*, taken by a French privateer. She had on board 4,000 ounces of gold besides a very valuable cargoe. The company has also an account of the loss of another of their ships in Guinea which was drove on shore by a French privateer.

The delegates were almost unanimous in the case of my Lady Grosvenor mentioned in my last, only four civilians of the six dissented; the four bishops and five judges were unanimous in their opinions that it was no marriage, and that the Lady was not *compos mentis* at the time of the consummation.

A great many merchants and eminent traders in this city daily break, but none hath made more noise than the failure of Mr. Pitkin, a whole-sale linen draper, whose debts are about 70,000l. but that which has raised the clamour against him is that before he went off he grasped all sorts of commodities which he could into his hands with a design to cheat, upon which his creditors have made application to the House of Commons for relief. This morning the Earl of Huntingdon departed this life after two or three days sickness. I hear the Duke of Argyll is to be her Majesty's High Commissioner in the next session of Parliament for Scotland. The Commons have passed to day and sent up to the Lords, the last money bill. The Lords have been upon the list of Justices of the Peace, and have resolved to address her Majesty about the same.

VISCOUNT SCUDAMORE to ROBERT HARLEY, in York Buildings.

1704-5, February 23—Asking for an interview to speak about his standing for Parliament at the next election.

E. LEWIS to [ROBERT HARLEY].

1704-5, February 24. Whitehall—The petition of Captain Francis Sterry is in a particular manner recommended to you by the Duke of Marlborough. The trial comes on next Tuesday. In case the gentleman be brought in guilty of murder Mr. Cardonnel tells me his Grace desires you to procure his pardon that he may be despatched to his post.

NEWS LETTERS.

1704-5, February 24. London—The Paris letters of the 28th confirm that their grenadiers had taken the eminence on this side the place, but the besieged returning posted themselves on the top of that hill, so that the assailants finding themselves between two fires were obliged to retire no doubt faster than they came up. It is said the Marshal de Tesse has orders sent him to raise the siege if he finds he cannot carry the place in a very little time. The Court expects to hear that a general assault was given on the 18th or 20th.

Prince Eugene with the forces designed for Italy have received orders to begin their march with all expedition upon the pressing instances of the Duke of Savoy. The enemy is at present quite upon the Moselle.

Edinburgh the 17th, this day the officers of this city begun to make a list of all persons here from 16 to 60 years of age to be armed and disciplined, to conform to the Act of Security. The Privy Council have remitted Captain Green and his crew to be tried for piracy in the Court of Admiralty and his indictment is preparing to be given him this night or on Monday. They have also ordered the Lord Advocate and Solicitor Advocate with four others of the most eminent lawyers in the Parliament house to assist the Fiscal in the prosecution and will appoint some to be assessors to the judges.

Our Barbados merchants have an account of the loss of a ship of theirs which had on board 700 hogsheads of sugar, which came from that plantation in company of four or five more. The merchants are also in pain for their fleet from Viana and Lisbon laden with wine and fruits which however it is hoped they may be safe, though it is certain they are blamable to run without convoy and their losses generally proceed from thence.

It is said the Duke of Norfolk is in England, will take the oaths, and will in a little time appear in public and to that end his Grace's coaches and equipage are getting ready. I hear the Earl of Huntingdon who died in the 29th year of his age of a malignant fever, has left 1,200l. per annum to his sister, a moiety of which is to go off upon her marriage, 400l. per annum to his bosom friend Colonel Stanhope, and 100l. per annum to a young gentleman reputed to be a natural son of the late Earl, his father, who was no ways provided for before, besides other legacies, but the honour with the gross of the estate is descended to his half brother.

1704-5, February 27. London—Dublin the 20th. This day a Bill is ordered to be brought in, to have accounted as regulars all such of the Romish clergy as shall refuse or neglect to register themselves as appointed by a former Act of Parliament. On Tuesday next the House of Commons is to go upon the consideration of a supply and there is a great appearance that the Parliament will dispatch the public business with all cheerfulness. A letter has been dropped at Cork pretending that a general massacre was designed to be of the Protestants on the 24th inst., but the thing is so improbable, the Romanists being all disarmed and the power in the Protestants' hands, that the same is little minded, however the officers are all ordered to their posts.

Our port letters have nothing in them worth remark. The Lords have addressed her Majesty in relation to some alterations which they desired might be made amongst the present list ■ the justices of the peace. Her Majesty was pleased to answer to this effect viz. that she had given directions as desired by a former address which she was in hopes would have prevented any further application, however she should find the matter of fact.

LUDLOW CASTLE.

1704–5, March 7—An inventory of all the goods in Ludlow Castle, delivered by William Gower to Captain Thomas Jones. The different rooms, closets, &c. are named and the furniture in each described, the President's rooms, Prince Arthur's room, and the Chief Justice's room being apparently the chief apartments.

SIR C. HEDGES to [ROBERT] HARLEY.

1704–5, March 10—I send you what my Lord Duke of Marlborough thinks may be the heads and substance of the answer to Count Lescherain's memorial as near as I can remember. You will please to put it in what terms you think proper and oblige the envoy with as many good words as you can. His Grace is of opinion that is necessary to be done, and it can't be in a better hand than yours. The Earl of Seafield desires that the horses of the Scots nobility and gentlemen now going to Scotland should not be stopped, and they refuse to take any passes. I have spoken of it to the Lord Treasurer who thinks some order should be sent to the governor of Berwick or such other officers as have directions for stopping horses going to Scotland, that the Scots nobility and gentlemen should be unmolested in their passage. If they are stopped going to the Parliament it may make a great clamour, and the officers may not have discretion enough to distinguish without some directions.

SIR M[ICHAEL] WARTON to [ROBERT HARLEY].

1704–5, March 11—Having in all places of late met a report of my being made a lord, though I hope there is nothing in it yet I thought fit to have recourse to your favour to put an entire stop to it if there should be any such intentions. I ambition nothing but my ease and quiet which I find so absolutely necessary to support my ill health. I have seen enough of business and bustle, and am much better pleased when my friends tread the stage than to be there myself. I hope you'll pardon this trouble in giving my positive opinion in this matter.

SIR J. BLAND to [ROBERT HARLEY].

1704–5, March 14. Hulme—I was retreated into Lancashire for a little ease and for the recovery of my health, but Mr. Lowther and

Mr. Ward are so busy treating at Pontefract that I must be forced to go over the next week to secure my point, for I do not doubt but they will be disappointed in their design, for my friends are very staunch for me. The Low Church party, as they call themselves, and the Dissenters of all kinds, join together in all places and have the assurance to say that they are the persons that the Government approves of and will countenance, and positively assert that when the house rises the tackers will all be displaced. What grounds they have for being so confident I know not, but if any such thing be, I should be desirous of a fair exchange betwixt an Irish and English place.

CAPTAIN JOHN OGILVIE to [ROBERT HARLEY].

1704–5, March 18—Has considered the three proposals made to him and would rather serve the Queen on the coast of Sussex than in Scotland or abroad.

The EARL OF MONTAGU to [ROBERT HARLEY].

1704–5, March 20—Asking that on his elevation to a dukedom there might be a warrant for his son to be Marquis Monthermer instead of Viscount, as before.

VISCOUNT SCUDAMORE to [ROBERT HARLEY].

1705, March 25. Holm Lacy—Had declared his intention of "standing for Parliament man" at the last Hereford assizes, and many of the gentlemen of the county had promised him their support at the next election, and doubted not to carry it if honoured with Harley's support.

GERVASE ROOKE to ROBERT HARLEY.

1705, March 25—Enclosing a petition from certain prisoners in the Fleet prison protesting against the ill-behaviour of John Bradshaw one of the late turnkeys of the prison, who, with other persons, stood armed outside the prison in order to prevent any food or other necessaries being brought to them. *Petition enclosed bearing 22 signatures.*

JOHN CHAMBERLAYNE to [ROBERT HARLEY].

1705, March 27. Petty France, Westminster—Recommending Mr. Hales, who had come as far as Hanover on his homeward way. He has been named to her Majesty more than once for employment, so that his brother Sir Thomas and the rest of his friends think that nothing but a proper application from Secretary Harley is wanting. By sending him to Berlin a most acceptable service will be done to Sir Thomas Hales, Sir George Rooke, and all the Kentish gentlemen of that side.

G. GRANVILLE to [ROBERT HARLEY].

1705, March 28 — The Lords Commissioners for Trades and Plantations deliver their report to-morrow upon the complaints against my brother [Sir Bevil Granville, Governor of Barbados], and the complainants have made powerful interest to obtain a re-hearing in case the report is against them. These men have not gone about so much to deny or extenuate their own crimes as to recriminate upon the Governor, and are at the same time the accusers and the only evidence to prove their own allegations. But upon the whole this mighty cry ends only in this one single point—that the Assembly of the Island when they had prepared a house for the Governor's reception ordered their treasurer to furnish his cellars with the accustomed provision of liquors, and this is alleged against him as a breach of the Queen's instructions against receiving presents. By the Queen's order profitable presents were meant and not those which cost more to the receiver than the giver, since we very well know that those liquors were chiefly for their own drinking, and that in the great concourse of so many people at his house they have eaten and drunk him out of least threefold. I therefore earnestly entreat your attendance at the Council to-morrow.

[COL. JAMES GRAHAM] to ROBERT HARLEY.

[1705,] March 30. Preston—In my way home I have stayed here two nights with a very good friend [the Duke of Hamilton]. And much to my satisfaction according to your promise, and to obey your commands, I trouble you with what follows: the chief thing recommended to me from Lord Treasurer was that my friend should make the matter of the treaty easy, which he presumed would not be disagreeable to him since it is what he was for last year. My Lord and you may both depend upon it, that he desires it as much as any man in either kingdom and will to his power promote it, but saith plainly he fears it will not be possible to make either that or anything so easy as formerly, since the nation is generally disgusted by our last Act of Parliament; and by all the accounts he hath from Scotland the people seem averse to any correspondence with us, till that is repealed. What his own thoughts are upon the present circumstances in that kingdom, you sufficiently know, so I shall not repeat, yet taking all things as they now stand be they as bad as some, as well as others represent them, it is his opinion all the help that can be had, will be requisite and necessary to keep temper amongst them. He protests and I do believe him he hath nothing in view, but to keep things in peace, to contribute to that with all his power, to demonstrate his service and inclinations for the Queen's Service and to give undeniable proofs of it, an opportunity he hath been seeking and wishing for since she came to the Crown; and appeals to Lord Treasurer to whom he hath made these professions, and whom he loves, desiring nothing more than that everything may flourish under his administration. Now, he and I both are very sensible that professions of this kind are too general, and many persons in both kingdoms make them, when many at the same time act contrary or at least are mistaken in what is the true interest, wherefore he doth desire that from my Lord or you he may be fully instructed to what points his skill and service may be required, and may be plainly informed without reserve how he may be most useful, which will be a certain rule for him to walk by and secure him from all misrepresentations, which every one may be liable to, by which means his own actions and conduct will plainly appear, and he himself have the merit or reproach of them.

If I durst presume to give my opinion, it is that by no means this occasion be lost that some way may be thought upon before he leave this country to have a more plain and close correspondence with him, that he may be fixed to points and see his way clear before him. I wish you and he were together a few hours, or send anything to him by an express messenger, he will in a few days take a journey into Staffordshire to see an estate fallen to him there, which will be very convenient to impart anything to him. If you desire it I shall let you know when he moves.

As to all that passed between you and me in relation to my friend, we have fully and largely discoursed it over; he is extremely well satisfied with what you say and doth not at all doubt anything you are pleased to answer for, and desires you will give his service to Lord Treasurer and receive the same yourself. It will be unnecessary to say more on this subject now, so I will take my leave of you, as I am this moment doing of my friend and going for Levens where I shall be glad upon any occasion to receive your commands.

Postscript.—This is writ in haste and I have no copy of it, so I desire you will keep it should any occasion be hereafter to have recourse to it, for I am jealous of mistakes happening when things of this nature are transacted by such ways of corresponding. I am to my good friend the Auditor, the worthy Thracian, young Sir Roger, an humble servant. I would gladly give my service to one knight more but dare not, yet hope you will for me. Through all the countries as I came as great preparation for war in order to elections as now upon the Moselle for real campaign.

Since I writ this letter reflecting upon all the discourse between my friend and me I think it very necessary to add to what I have already writ, that nothing may be left doubtful or anything that is said lead you into mistakes whereby we may be reproached afterwards, that he insists upon knowing plainly to what point and in what manner his service and assistance are expected, to which he saith he will give a very full and positive answer, and which way soever he acts it shall be done above board and is well to be considered before he comes there. His task will be difficult enough having all his enemies in power, yet all resentments will be laid aside when it appears to him that the Queen and Britain's interest is what is aimed at.

PETITION of SIR JOHN CREWE of Utkinton, Cheshire.

1705, April 7—For leave to establish three annual fairs and a weekly market at Tarporley in Cheshire. Referred by Robert Harley to Sir Simon Harcourt, who on April 10, 1705 reported in favour of the petition.

ANNE PUGH'S PETITION.

1705, April 7. Admiralty Office—A recommendation to the Queen of the petition, which had been referred to Prince George of Denmark, of Anne Pugh, widow of Captain Richard Pugh who had been drowned when the *Norwich* was lost in the West Indies. Signed by Prince George.

GEORGE VERNON to [ROBERT HARLEY].

1705, April 8. Farnham in Surrey—The other day the officers of this parish took up a stranger in this town being a Frenchman and brought him before me. Upon examination he calls himself Mr. Jean De Camau, he is about twenty-one years of age and a native of the Province of Languedoc being born in Toulouse. He owns himself a Roman Catholic and pretends he came into England about three months ago to see some Protestant relations at London, but names only one, and that is Mr. Dugua, a gentleman who lives in Soho. From whence he came to this place purely as he says to make a visit to the French Bishop who is a prisoner here, and to keep the solemn time of Easter with him He confesses he never had any passport but says he has been a traveller, that he left France some years ago, and came through Holland to the Brill where he embarked for England. He seems to be a gentleman of a liberal education and says his relations are Counsellors of the Parliament of Toulouse, but he is not altogether consistent with himself upon his examination. I find no letters about him either to the French Bishop or any of the ecclesiastics here prisoners. He says his curiosity led him to pay his duty to the aforesaid Bishop, whom he had seen at Paris about three years ago. I have taken his parole to appear whenever I shall call for him and entreat the favour of your direction what I shall do with him, whether you will please to order his release or command him to attend you at Whitehall.

Postscript.—I presume you will hear from the gentleman himself or some of his friends who perhaps may give you some further account of him.

Appended are a report of the examination of De Gamau, and two letters in French and one in Latin, from him to Harley, as Secretary of State.

N. BOOTHE to ROBERT HARLEY.

1705, April 9—I desire you to be my friend with the Lord Treasurer in a matter I will communicate to you when I wait upon you. At present I shall be employed in the Cheshire election and am going to assist Mr. Offley and Mr. Boothe with my interest, which is considerable, having a great many of my own tenants that have voices and wholly at my own disposal.

LORD RABY to [ROBERT HARLEY?].

1705, April 11. [Berlin]—Before the Marquis de Prié fell ill he had put this Court upon a project in favour of his master, which would be much for their advantage too if it succeeded, and they give in to it very willingly and only fear the consent of the Swiss, which is the chief thing and I look upon as the most difficult. The project is in short—though they desire here mightily it may be kept as a secret, and I hope you will manage it as such—that this king shall give eight thousand men more out of Prussia, that the allies shall let four thousand more of this king's troops now in the service of the Empire join them, and that the Protestant Cantons shall declare against France, and shall also join four thousand more to them, and that England and Holland shall send their "religionaires" which they reckon shall be about five or six thousand, in all about twenty-one or two thousand men; that when the Protestant Cantons shall agree to come into this project, they shall underhand erect magazines in Switzerland, for the march of these troops who shall at first join Prince Lewis on the Rhine, who shall make a movement to amuse the French, whilst those troops shall march through the forest towns to the Canton of Berne, and through that into France, having the town of Geneva behind them, and Switzerland, to furnish them with provisions; and that they shall disperse declarations in France that they come only to establish the Protestant religion and liberty of the French, by which means all that are left of the Cevennois and those inclined to the reformed religion will flock to them; and the French having no troops in these parts, they make make what progress they please, and perhaps by such an unexpected stroke, they may do more mischief to France than any other way; and should they fail they have always the Swiss to retire to. The Protestant Cantons are to take

Savoy under their protection, and the Duke of Savoy is to give them some advantages from thence to make them give into this project, and there is to be a strict league, defensive and offensive, between the king, Duke of Savoy, and the Protestant Cantons, who the Marquis will have to be mightly inclined to break with France. *Endorsed in Robert Harley's handwriting* "Secret." Extract out of Lord Raby's letter."

A. KINEIR to [ROBERT HARLEY].

1705, April 14. Whitehall—In answer to yours, concerning Mr. Houstoun this is to acquaint you that he obtained in June last 50*l.* for himself and some of his fraternity for services done at the Revolution. I believe the reasons inducing our secretaries to procure him that favour were that they, being preachers of that bigoted set of Presbyterians whom we called Cameronians, so troublesome in former reigns, upon the Revolution influenced their followers with a zeal for that interest, and engaged them to list themselves in the regiment then raised under the Earl of Angus, and now commanded by Brigadier Ferguson.

LE MOYNE [DE BRIE] to [ROBERT HARLEY].

1705, April 17—Offering to acquaint him with what he was entrusted to Scotland, in hopes of having his liberty and the return of the money he had spent.

The SAME to [the SAME].

Same date—Protesting his innocency in a long letter of the charges brought against him.

ROBERT HARLEY to LE MOYNE DE BRIE.

1705, April 17—Acknowledging the receipt of the two preceding letters the first of which he concluded was intended to be private, and the other to be public; and promising him an interview, if he be resolved to be candid and ingenuous. *Copy.*

LE MOYNE [DE BRIE] to [ROBERT HARLEY].

1705, April 20—An insolent letter apparently intended as a denial of having written one or both of the previous letters.

LE MOYNE DE BRIE.

1705, April 26. Whitehall—Warrant for the arrest of Le Moyne de Brie, as being an alien enemy and spy. *Approved by Lord Chief Justice Holt and the Attorney General. Draft.*

The SAME.

Same date—Declaration delivered by Le Moyne de Brie to the Lords at the Cabinet Council of his journey to Scotland as an emissary of the King of France.

JOHN CHARLTON to ROBERT HARLEY.

1705, April 26. Jewel Office—Requiring him to return the "parcells of gilt and white plate," with which he stood charged as Speaker of the House of Commons, to the Queen's Jewel House, under penalty of a process being issued against him. *Signed.*

WILLIAM FLEMING [of Rydal]. to [ROBERT HARLEY].

1705, April 28. Manchester Court, Westminster—If Lord Treasurer and you are in earnest about my standing for the next Parliament, I shall be glad to discourse with you as soon as possible, for I doubt not I could yet make a very great change in the present prospect of affairs in Westmorland, being by yesternight's post solicited to stand there.

Though may be no man in the kingdom' hath been worse used since King William's death that hath so much affection for her Majesty's service, and that hath so good interest in the counties as I have in Westmorland, Cumberland, and Lancashire, and though I can as little bear ill-usage as any man in England, yet I designed not to concern myself much in two of those counties this next election, but continue in town till that bustle was over, and look after some private business.

E. LEWIS to [ROBERT HARLEY].

1705, April 29. Whitehall—Williams was taken this morning. It appears he was going with two young men into France. One of the young men is seized with him, but must be released immediately unless a warrant is issued to keep him.

[LORD GODOLPHIN to ROBERT HARLEY.]

[1705, April]—This is only to return you my Lord Raby's letter [see April 11] to which I am apt to give credit. That's a strange humoursome Court, and like enough to give trouble to all its neighbours, we must manage them as well as we can, but there's no patience except the Duke of Marlborough's that is of proof against all manner of impertinence.

I shall be very unquiet till we have the next letters from Flanders, I don't think it unlikely the French may be of opinion their present circumstances will require the hazarding of a battle; in which if they succeed, they may spare troops for the support of the Duke of Anjou, and if not, they will take the resolution of letting the States be masters of the peace.

[SIR JAMES LONG to   .]

[1705, April ?]—You could not have sent to any man that knows the affairs belonging to the borough of the Devizes so well as I do.

The Low Churchmen are so firmly united that I believe no money will prevail on them to do anything in prejudice of their party and Mr. Diston spares no pains or cost to support their interest, and on all occasions they are countenanced by my Lord Sunderland, my Lord Wharton and a great number of Justices of the Peace in the neighbourhood; and I am sure if you give five hundred pounds for a Common Councilman, Diston will give a thousand and out bribe you on all occasions. Mr. Child wants five votes who must vote singly for you, or for you and Mr. Webb, or else you can't prevail, for they are now nine votes before Mr. Child; but if five men give both votes from Mr. Diston and Mr. Methuen it will answer, but can you think that whilst your party are bribing those five men Diston will not bribe off some of Mr. Child's.

To be short in this matter, Sir Fra. Child and Mr. Diston have spent I verily believe three thousand pounds a year in law and bribes since the last election and Diston has still been too hard for Sir Fra., and now

Sir Francis is away C. finds he labours in vain. He would give out or rest a little and let you try if your purse can outdo Mr. Diston's, but I hope you'll do nothing unless Sir Francis joins in the expense which will be endless. Sir Simon Harcourt, Serjeant Hooper, Pratt, King, Eyres, or any of the great counsel can inform you what suits in law are now depending and that all the charge is borne by the members of Parliament. Burn this and take notice that it comes from me, no man wishes Mr. Child's party better than I do, but I would have some other person spend his estate and not you.

, The only place in our county for any man to be elected a member of Parliament is my Lord Abingdon's borough of Westbury where his Lordship recommends both members and always succeeds. I am informed Mr. Robert Bertie is willing to desist; if so, it is easy to gain an election there with my Lord's recommendation, encouraged by Lord Weymouth and Mr. Lewis, who have both good interest and are respected in that borough. Mr. Lewis's father served many years and was much esteemed by all the electors. If you try at this place it will be best for Mr. Robert Bertie to stand until the election day, and then there being no person to oppose you a little gold will serve to half a dozen dissatisfied electors, and gain you an election in a quarter of an hour without any manner of opposition; and you need not appear in the borough until the election day, but may lodge privately at my brother's four miles from Westbury, and he will be able to do you some service.

WILLIAM PENN to [ROBERT HARLEY].

1705, May 1—This gentleman [Aruop] has received the thanks of the East India Company and the Turkey, as well as of the Virginians and Jamaicans, in a very sensible manner, and they are ready to recommend his allowed services to the Queen's bounty and further favour. Sir Ch. Hedges promises to do his part towards the Queen's favour, and I persuade myself thou wilt please to co-operate and, after so long an attendance, not think his importunities impertinent. The merchants allow him to have saved 200,000*l*. to the kingdom, certainly it entitles him to her bounty, as his interest and voluntary courageous endeavours recommend him to the command of that place of Crookhaven; which he would be glad to owe to thy English heart and good sense.

"HARRY" [ST. JOHN] to his "master" [ROBERT HARLEY].

[1705,] May 1—I am just going out of town and shall not be able to return till my election is over. You will, I am sure, take the trouble of getting the Queen's hand to some orders, which I left directions with Mr. Lynn to prepare. My departure being sudden, and not having an opportunity to see my Lord Treasurer, though I have been twice to wait on him, I desire you to excuse my absence if you think it necessary. I have received a letter from Lord Duke [Marlborough] wherein he writes that he hopes the Solicitor General will appear for him; that is the expression at Woodstock. I did not fail to shew it to Harcourt.

LORD POULETT to [ROBERT HARLEY].

1705' May 2. Hinton—In the country little matters appear very great and I am sensible everybody is represented to be very officious who concern themselves about them, but my duty to my country and my unfeigned respect for Secretary Harley engage me to submit it to him whether Frank Gwyn's being chosen Recorder at Exeter be of any moment or consequence. He has been the fire brand of all this side the kingdom in the elections, and many gentlemen of Dorset, Somerset and. Devonshire court him as Lord Rochester's representative and Sir Edward Seymour's successor in his Western Empire, so that he is now respected as the person who can support men in the keeping or obtaining places in the "Publique of their Utopia." There almost wants nothing but Sir Chuffer [Seymour]'s death for this management of Mr. Gwyn's to take effect at Exeter. The spirit of that city does not only in a great degree influence Devonshire, but Cornwall also. Even now it appears in spite of the Bishop, whose clergy preach nothing but the Church being now in the greatest danger, and the Bishop himself is often named in their pulpits as an enemy to the Church. The gentlemen are so much inflamed by these firebrands that it won't be easy to check this temper even in this particular at Exeter, which is not yet public to any degree, but pray don't let me ever hear by another that I writ this. Extravagances here are very great, but I presume they are not unknown to you, so that I will not trouble you further.

[E. Lewis to Robert Harley.]

1705, May 5—The inferior part of the family at St. Germain believe they are shortly to remove from thence, but they do not know where. Some say they are to retire to a remote place in case of a peace ; others that they are to live at Brussels in order to a nearer communication with England and Scotland.

A. [Lady] Pye to her cousin Abigail Harley, at Eywood.

1705, May 5. Derby—My sister Severne left us this day sevennight after three weeks stay ; she came from Lady Pye's in Charterhouse. I had not seen her in eight years, she is grown very fat and unwieldy and is thought very like her majesty. I doubt she hath an idle husband whose chief care is to spend. It seems most of the Salop gentry are great drinkers. She seems easy, having a clear jointure he cannot touch. Sir Charles [Pye] cares not how little time he spends in London, which he hath taken effectual care to avoid in declining being a member of the new House; indeed it cost him some pains to persuade his friends to believe what they would fain have had otherwise, knowing his the best interest.

Within an hour or two are expected Lord James Cavendish and Mr. Parker our recorder. The county perfectly quiet none opposing the old members, and for the town never was known the like, all being agreed I think to get it or lose it at a cheap expense. There hath been little or no public drinking since Christmas, nor once heard a shout, that formerly was used to be deafened; but Mr. Harpur and Stanhope labour under-hand very hard, the others by their absence giving them fair play. Shall be glad when it is over, that the young squire Dick's thirsty acquaintance may be at an end, who, it seems, fancy my ale. You say I've a tolerable hand at it.

R. Hales to ——.

1705, May 5. Hamburg—Giving a long account of the Protestant churches in Silesia, some translations he had undertaken, and of his visits to some European cities.

STANLEY WEST to ROBERT HARLEY.

1705, May 7—Enclosed is the short compliment Doctor Gower made the Queen. It was first intended in Latin according to some precedents of the University but by advice from Newmarket it was translated into English, in which it runs not so smooth as in the Latin. My uncle commands me to express his thanks to you for the concern you have expressed for this designed affront put upon him, and that you have undertaken to convince yourself of the injustice done him by asking Her Majesty's opinion of her reception at St. John's College. If you can recover the original papers delivered to Mr. Lewis, it will there appear the order and multitude of scholars, the loud and uninterrupted acclamations of *Vivat Regina* on their knees through all the Courts in thickset numbers as the Queen passed forward and backward, which the Gazette says nothing of.

E[DMUND] POLEY to SECRETARY HARLEY.

1705, May [8–]19 N.S. Hanover—I have received your letter informing me that her Majesty has thoughts of removing me from this employment, and am sensible of your friendship in giving me early notice of it.

The QUEEN'S MESSENGERS.

[1705, May 8]—Rates for Messengers' services allowed in the Queen's Establishment :—

For keeping prisoners close with diet 6s. 8d. per day.

For keeping a prisoner close that finds his own diet 5s.

For Post journeys to be allowed 6d. every Post mile and 2s. each stage, and though two or more go together, no more to be allowed than 2s. a stage.

Journeys to fetch prisoners and the like when they do not ride post to be allowed but by computed miles of the country 6d. per mile and 2s. a stage.

A messenger's allowance when abroad on journeys 10s. per day and 5s. for an assistant when an extraordinary case requires one.

When prisoners through poverty cannot find themselves an horse, the messenger to be allowed 3d. per mile for bringing them up.

The allowances whilst attending us abroad and not travelling 5s. a day.

Nothing to be allowed for searching ; and expenses on guards and constables in taking prisoners to be allowed with caution, in respect to time and difficulty of the service, by the respective officers which pass the bills.

No allowance for delivering summonses ; nor anything to be charged for carrying messages or letters within the Liberties of London and Westminster.

Some journeys to be ascertained at the old allowances.

	£	s.	d.		£	s.	d.
To Windsor	1	18	0	To the Hague	25	0	0
To Hampton Court	1	0	0	To Dublin	30	0	0
To Richmond	0	15	0	To Kensington	0	3	4
To Greenwich	0	10	0				

And the like allowances for the like distances.

The contents above (title only excepted) are faithfully transcribed from the establishment of the Household, compared and examined by us—Thos. Atterbury, Wm. Sharpe, Clerks of the Cheque.

THOMAS BLISS to ROBERT HARLEY.

1705, May 9. Maidstone—This day our election for burgesses came on. Sir Thomas Colepeper and myself are elected. Lord Guernsey's son Heneage Finch, the other candidate, lost it.

H. [COMPTON] BISHOP OF LONDON to [ROBERT HARLEY].

1705, May 9—Her Majesty is informed that "Bail's [Bayle's] French Dictionary" is translating into English, in which, it is said, are contained many lewd, obscene, and "prophane" stories not fit to be mentioned; and therefore she would have you mind her of it the first time you wait upon her, that she may have your advice which way to stop the impression before it comes out.

DR. HUMPHREY GOWER to [ROBERT HARLEY].

1705, May 10. Thriplow near Cambridge—I hope my nephew West has given your Honour such an account of my engagements to Mr. Annesly that will satisfy; he is a scholar and has been long of my acquaintance as such and has acquitted himself in all University business intrusted to him with great approbation. These considerations easily inclined me to promise him my assistance at the approaching election. To him it was positive and peremptory, not so to any other; though much application was made to me for Mr. Windsor, before we heard of Mr. Godolphin, but I kept myself in such liberty, as to my second vote, that I can dispose of it to the Lord Treasurer's son as I intend it.

You were misinformed in the matter concerning me about the Queen's late gracious visit at Cambridge. I do not use to prate so greatly about such grand matters. It is an extravagance to suppose that so great a thing could be done on so little an occasion. I never could believe it and therefore could not say it. I do remember, indeed, that something like that was said in my hearing not by way of assertion but supposition; which if I ever repeated (though I neither remember nor believe I did) it was only by way of repetition from others, and not with approbation. I speak it positively because such a suggestion seemed to me little less than ridiculous. I cannot think anyone here believes anything of it. One thing more and I relieve your Honour. Mr. West represents Mr. Annesly as turbulent, &c. his interest here is not gained that way. I am sure, not with me. The public is engaged in matters of grand consequence and fundamental concerns. They are enemies to England that would disturb the counsels of peace at home, or slacken or obstruct the proceeding in the war abroad. May they not prosper that attempt anything that way!

[LORD GODOLPHIN to ROBERT HARLEY.]

[1705, May 10.]—Thursday night at 11—I hope you won't trouble to write to-night, but I shall have some small curiosity when I wake in the morning to know if you got anything out of that woman. After I left you I heard them cry in the street "The news of the French King's sickness and death." Is there any foundation for that report ? I took it to be a mockery only. Colt has out-polled Cross above 600. I doubt that can't be recovered ; but I am not in pain about that so much as for Woodstock. I fear it does not go well.

[LORD GODOLPHIN to ROBERT HARLEY.]

[1705, May 11] Friday—The woman that could tell you so much must needs know more, but whether she will tell it or no, God knows; it is most probable St. Paul may land arms and perhaps some money in Scotland, but I don't think he will stay upon that coast, but rather return again, or go north about into the soundings.

It may be worth considering whether the Irish Transport might not be strengthened from hence, but if the Privy Council be left to themselves, they will scarce do anything either right, or quick enough. I could wish therefore that the Lords might meet at the Office to-day at noon, or if you have taken other measures, so as that is not convenient, to-morrow. I am going to Kensington, and at my return shall be glad to know, which of the two you like best.

This battle at Woodstock vexes me very much, what good will it do us to have Lord Marlborough beat the French abroad if the French at home must beat him.

I believe the stopping of the ports in France might be to prevent any notice of St. Paul going out.

"HARRY" [ST. JOHN] to [ROBERT] HARLEY.

1705, May 15. Bucklebury—I came back yesterday from Wiltshire to this place, where I found the letter my good natured Robin writ me. Part of it, translated into English, I take to signify 'that the Queen thinks well of my services, which is a very great pleasure to me, for upon my word I have nothing more at heart than doing all I am able to promote her measures, of the goodness of which one cannot have a better proof than this, that all the knaves and fools in England are confessedly or secretly in opposition to 'em. You are mistaken in thinking that I have been busy in elections, I did all I was able to serve Lord Duke in that of Woodstock; my own gave me no trouble. Harcourt's I could not influence, and there is so much merit in being against the tack, whatever some wise men may think, that Nevil was not to be opposed.

I am extremely obliged to you for the trouble you have taken on my account; you have wound up the bottom for me, and from this time till winter I have as little to do as a Teller. If the death of the Emperor should give occasion to the Queen to send any one to Vienna, it would be a journey but of four or five months, you can best tell whether upon this change there would be any credit to be got by such an expedition; I know you will use me like a friend and I refer myself to you, for I have no opinion in the matter myself. Adieu dear Master no man loves you more entirely than Harry.

SIR ROWLAND GWYNNE to [ROBERT HARLEY].

1705, May 15. Hanover—I am sorry that those gentlemen of the House of Commons who professed themselves so zealous for the Church of England, which Her Majesty hath always protected with great care and tenderness, should push the Bill against occasional conformity so far, as to endauger (the credit at least of) the Government, in so dangerous a war, and I am glad to see that Her Majesty is so sensible of the consequences that might follow such a design.

I must attribute the good measures since taken by Her Majesty to proceed from her great wisdom and virtue, being assisted by the wise counsel of my Lord Duke of Marlborough, my Lord Treasurer and yourself, and I doubt not but you will be supported by the next Parliament, if you will employ only moderate men and pursue moderate counsels, which I cannot doubt, and take such men to assist you as you can depend upon. We have sufficient experience that no violent party in England could ever stand long.

There is a lady here who calls herself Countess of Bellamont, her father was an Earl of Ireland with that title; she is a most violent Papist and Jacobite. She came to this Court long since, pretending to be married to Prince Robert [Rupert] and was kindly received here thereupon; but she does all the ill offices she can to the English here, and amongst the rest, did raise a report that I was an enemy to the Duke of Marlborough. As soon as I knew this, I writ to his Grace upon it who knows me too well to believe it and hath done me the honour to write me a letter to justify me.

I have offered my service to the County of Brecon for the next Parliament. If I am not chosen there, perhaps I may be elsewhere, and if I am I will heartily join with my Lord Duke, my Lord Treasurer and you, in whatever measures you take to serve Her Majesty, to the utmost of my power. But if I am not chosen, I should be much obliged to you and them if you will obtain for me some employment abroad, wherein I may serve Her Majesty and live with reputation.

There are many letters come to this Court, that Mr. Poley is to be recalled. If I had the honour to serve Her Majesty in this Court, I believe I should be as capable of it, as any other that could be named, and of serving their Lordships and you and your friends, both at present and in futurity. I have writ to my Lord Duke upon this point, therefore I pray at least that you will put a stop to the declaration of anybody till you hear from his Grace.

Their Electoral Highnesses are all well and I sent you a part of a letter of the Electress's to me in my last to you. I can further assure you that they have a very great and just esteem of you.

W[illiam] Greg to [Robert Harley].

1705, May 16—Mr. Warre happening to come in just as I was going to make my most humble and dutiful acknowledgments to your Honour for your unexampled goodness and generosity to me, I should certainly have dreamt of being damned to ingratitude, had I upon my coming home suffered sleep to have seized my eyelids, before I had committed to paper the deep sense I shall ever retain of the infinite obligations your honour has laid upon your Creature, who humbly craves leave to assure your Honour, that he would sooner forfeit his head than the favourable opinion you have been pleased to conceive of him, and hopes to be believed when he presumes to add, that had the overture been made him by any other, even in the like eminent post, the difficulties in the management of so delicate an affair, and the danger necessarily attending a miscarriage would have made him take twice four and twenty hours, instead of once, to consider of it; and if my circumstances should at last have tempted me to have closed with it, yet means might have been found to disengage myself from so ticklish a task, for one that requires no such trial of skill.

The late Earl of Dalkeith was not dead many days when a gentleman of my acquaintance proposed my being governor to the young Earl; which I excused myself from, by telling him, I had no talent for a pupil-monger. But I must confess, I was much more puzzled for a handsome excuse, which Mr. Paizant of Sir Charles Hedges's Office told me, that he had recommended me to Mr. Stanyan, who thereupon wanted to speak with me.

I should be very sorry to be so understood as if I meant to value myself upon the refusal of either of these offers. If I may be vain on any account, it shall be in the satisfaction I have to think with myself, that I am once more brought upon the stage, though in a vizor mask; and that ere long it will be pulled off, if I chance to play my part well in that disguise; which no piece of money can encourage me to do so much, as the hopes of your Honour's future favour and protection upon my return. The scene being laid in Scotland, I shall begin with Scotland Yard here by addressing my letters for your Honour, to Mr. Batéman, till such time as I hear that you are come up to town again, as fearing your Honour may not have had leisure before your going down, to give your orders to the Post Office, about the other address which I humbly beg may not be forgot.

I shall only add that I will take all possible precaution to prevent a discovery, and likewise not to pretend to be too great a discoverer myself, but where I am well informed; so that your Honour may expect to be entertained with nothing but what I have very good vouchers for. I wish the business may not have taken air at your Honour's Office by reason of my frequent attendance there. For my part, I never gave the least inkling of the matter to any mortal, nor ever shall.

I conclude with my best wishes for your Honour's good journey into the country, and safe return to Court, where may the Queen never want such a Servant, the Commons such a Speaker, nor I, such a Patron.

E. LEWIS to SECRETARY HARLEY.

1705, May 17. Whitehall—Shadwell's man is come up from Romney, but Mr. Secretary Hedges has directed him to return again thither till the proposals he has made in writing are fully considered. He offers to discover all clandestine trade and secret correspondence provided he is allowed to go to and from France with all sorts of merchandise freely. This is a great trust, and I believe Shadwell and he think to make a fortune by a monopoly of French trade, but on the other side if a right use can be made of this man he seems to be a very cunning knave and capable of anything he really undertakes.

Mr. Ellis's room in the other Office is shut up.

Mr. Churchill desires he may not be hindered from printing Bayle's *Dictionary* provided it be castrated to the Archbishop's satisfaction.

EDWARD HARLEY to his father [ROBERT HARLEY].

1705, May 19. Westminster—I spoke to Mr. Bateman according as you ordered, I gave the Dr. his guineas, he presents his humble service to you. And the next morning I went to Mr. Friend's chamber to give him his (because I thought the Dr. would take it amiss if he saw me give him); he refused to take them, and told me that he was ashamed to take them, and that he had taken enough. I could not persuade him.

by any means to take them; he desired me to present his humble service to you. I do desire to know what I shall do with them. I have sent as many of the verses that were spoke at the Election as I could get. Mr. Philips honoured me yesterday with a visit, he desired me to present his humble service to you, he went this morning to Oxford. The writing master as I was speaking to you of send me word that for half a guinea entrance he would teach [me] to write; I desire to know what I shall do.

Sir John Bland to [Robert Harley].

1705, May 20. Hulme—We have had a great bustle in this county for knights of the shire occasioned by Mr. Stanley's ungentlemanlike proceedings. The first notice was that the election was to be as last Tuesday and then notice sent to all places that it was not to be till Tuesday following; and to delude Mr. Shuttleworth Sir Roger Bradshaw was with Mr. Shuttleworth on Monday at Liverpool election and on Monday in the night Mr. Stanley marched towards Lancaster with about fifty, and the next day went privately into the Castle and demanded of the Sheriff to return him and Sir Roger Bradshaw, which had been done if Mr. Heysham had not by chance heard of it and demanded a Poll for Shuttleworth which run thus the first day, Stanley 19: Shuttleworth 17: Bradshaw 9: and the next day the Manchester single voters got in and set Mr. Shuttleworth 50, the majority, and if the Poll had not been yielded on Saturday morning Mr. Stanley would have been 6 or 700 short of Shuttleworth, for he had then 400 single votes in town to poll and we would have sent him in twice that number. So my Lord Derby hath not that interest in this county as is represented above and his haughty treatment of all the gentlemen will never be forgot. Cheshire election comes on next Wednesday and I believe the old ones will carry it, and 'tis two to one my Lord Hartington loses it in Yorkshire.

Now that I have done with election news, give me leave to ask your advice as to my own affairs. I have the misfortune to have three stewards that have cheated me and must lose abundance of money by them, and must put my concerns now into new hands which will require some time, and I have had the gout so long in my stomach that all my physicians say I must troop to the Bath or march off. These two matters render a trip to Ireland very difficult this summer so if my Lord Treasurer thinks fit to excuse me this year I will make a summer's campaign there next year with my family. I beg the favour of you to present my humble duty and respect to my Lord Treasurer, and to honour me with a line that I may know how to steer my course.

W. Greg to [Robert Harley].

1705, May 23—Being just going to my horse (which I have bought with a design to bring back again) I esteemed it my duty to leave for your honour the repeated assurances of an inviolable fidelity and indefatigable industry in the discharge of the great trust and confidence you have been pleased to repose in me; and I most humbly crave that if at any time your Honour shall think fit to mention the name of a volunteer to the Queen, that you would assure Her Majesty that I shall think I have ended my days gloriously should I, upon a discovery, fall a victim to the rage of a boiling nation, of which I reckon it my unhappiness to be a native.

I beg pardon for putting your Honour again in mind of giving your orders to the Post Office, concerning the direction'.you were pleased to approve of. as soon as you come to town, because I humbly conceive the secrecy of the affair will chiefly depend upon it.

After hinting to your Honour that I have bought a horse though of no high price, you will easily be induced to believe that what with accoutrements and other necessaries for so long a journey, my stock is considerably diminished before I set out, so that I foresee plainly an unavoidable miscarriage for want of money unless timely supplied by your Honour's order. Should I draw a small bill upon Mr. Bateman, which yet I will not do till the very last extremity, nor then neither, if I can raise credit at Edinburgh. Indeed the two payments your Honour was pleased to order me, if free from all encumbrance at my setting out, had been sufficient to have enabled me to have gone through with the undertaking. But as your Honour may remember, I signified in a letter a month ago that my circumstances were such then, that had I been to go the next minute I could not get out of London under 20*l.*, so that your Honour may easily judge to what a *modicum* the whole is reduced by this time.

E. Lewis to [Robert] Harley.

1705, May 24. Whitehall—Mr. Howe has let his house to Mr. Walpole, and complains among his friends that you delay the necessary despatches for his going to Hanover. Some say Mr. Montagu does no longer desire to be sent to Vienna, but I have not seen him to discourse with him upon that subject. Mr. Warre is at Chelsea, where he seems to decay very fast. "The Colt " has routed a squadron of Sir Humphrey Mackworth's miners; I wish he may not have exceeded the law.

Dr. Francis Atterbury to [Robert Harley].

1705, May 25. Chelsea—I received yesterday the following account from Dr. Todd: "I have done what I can to trace the man and am informed that he crossed the road from Kendal and went to Wakefield, and that there a horse he had borrowed was taken from him, he having given a false account where he would inn. I suppose he will scarce return to these parts, but stay about Yorkshire, and perhaps after a while endeavour to return to Scotland. If he be a man of consequence a messenger might be sent and command given to the soldiers who are upon the line of the kingdom to surround him that he could not well escape. I shall write to a relation who is a justice of peace in the bishopric to do what service and as privately as he can in this affair. He had three guineas of Lady Lonsdale out of her opinion of him and good affection to the government."

I take this opportunity to make my acknowledgments to you for the late favour of your assistance towards fixing my patent beyond exception. I beg you to believe that I had not given you any farther trouble on that head had I not found, upon search, that a resignation was necessary to make the Deanery vacant, and consequently that it was necessary to make my patent subsequent in its date to the resignation. I had carefully inquired into the Records at the Rolls, where there are many grants of deaneries made vacant upon a promotion of the former deans • greater deaneries; but there is not one where the deanery is not aid, in the grant, to have been made *per resignationem;* though there ath been an omission of enrolling those resignations.

I shall probably begin my journey northward before I have the honour of waiting upon you here, at your return. The Bishop, I find, hath been trying all ways to create opposition to me in the Chapter when I come down, and to hinder me in the exercise of those rights and powers which do most evidently belong to me. I will do—as hitherto I have done—all I can towards avoiding a contest with him; and will be sure to enter into none, but where I have the clearest evidence on my side, and where the point is worth contesting, and I should be injurious to the post—into which by your favour I am put—█ I did not assert it.

WILLIAM BORRETT to [ERASMUS] LEWIS.

1705, May 25. Inner Temple—I acquainted you yesterday with what haughty insolence Hannan behaved himself towards me, for which and for want of new security he was last night again taken into custody and is now in Newgate.

Le Moyne de Brie moved to be discharged or bailed for want of prosecution, but I acquainted the Count that he was an alien enemy and a spy, and a very dangerous person; and the reason why he was sent to Newgate was for his safe custody, and because we have had several such criminals escape from the Gatehouse and the Marshal's Prison.

I shall go to Epsom to-morrow, but shall attend you upon the first summons.

CHARLES GORING to [ROBERT HARLEY].

1705, May 25—Knowing your inclinations for a jest I cannot omit giving you the following account of our proceedings in relation to our election for knights of the shire which began yesterday at Lewes. The candidates Mr. Lumley, Sir George Parker, Sir Har. Peachy, Mr. Trevor. But what added, if not to the interest of the two latter, yet to the splendour of their party was that the Dukes of Somerset and Richmond appeared at their head and such a sight having been seldom seen at Lewes, it was thought by all the inhabitants it must of necessity carry the election, but *multa cadunt* &c., for before they began to poll the high sheriff [Turner] produced the resolves of the House of Commons against Lords of Parliament appearing at elections, and told their Graces they should go off the bench before one man should be polled; the Duke of Richmond swore he would not go off; the other began to debate and told the sheriff the resolve of the House was no law, &c. The sheriff replied whatever was done by the Commons in Parliament he would always abide by as his representatives, even to the last drop of his blood, "and if you do not go immediately off the bench, I'll adjourn the court." "Mr. Sheriff," quoth the Duke of Somerset, "you had acted more like a gentleman had you told us of this before we came here." "My Lords till I came here I had nothing to do to tell you, neither could I believe you would come where you knew you had nothing to do, and I would have you to know I am as good a gentleman as yourself and know as well how to behave myself," &c. He ordered the under sheriff to make way and he himself went off with them, and our Dukes immediately with their stars disappeared, which brought all their party under a cloud.

Postscript.—The two Dukes employed the rest of their time in seeing a puppet show. I can give you no account of the success of the election.

A. [LADY] PYE to ABIGAIL HARLEY at Eywood.

1705, May 28. Derby—At present I believe the discourse in all parts turns on the same subject, I mean elections, which now will soon be over.

Was glad when ours was past, finding little less trouble than if Sir
Charles had stood. We hope we have sent up two good members, the
Recorder Parker is generally esteemed and looked on as a rising man.
Notwithstanding a fair poll, Mr. Harpur's friends say he will petition
provided the parliament prove to his mind. The county election over
on Thursday, no contest, though it is generally thought had my Lord
Hartington stood one had been outed. It is reported to-day he hath
gained it by poll in Yorkshire, but first rumours seldom are to be
depended on. Leominster poll I found recorded a vast interest, the
gentleman with fifty votes. I fancy him like the Kentish warm
spark who hath lost it by many hundreds to Sir Cholmley Dering.

It is said this week will be married our cousin. Pye of Faringdon and
Mistress Curzon, said to be made by the Bishop of Durham and the
young gentleman's own inclinations last year at the Bath when he was
younger brother.

I hope the Secretary's family are all in health. Doubtless Radnor is
not a little proud he keeps to them.

I would gladly scribble on but the post hour is come, and besides I
am at the end of my 'latten' having scrawled all the chat I know.

[MAJOR JAMES CRANSTOUN] to ROBERT CUNNINGHAM.

1705, May 29. Camp at Elft near Sierck on the Moselle—You will
expect news from me in which I can give you but little satisfaction.
We expected to have made a glorious campaign and certainly the Duke
of Marlborough had laid his measures so that if his friends and the allies
had kept touch with him in what they promised the enemy could not have
hindered our designs; which it seems were to have opened the campaign
here with the siege either of Thionville or Saarlouis, and from thence to
have besieged and taken Metz, which, if we had done no more, secured
us of winter quarters in Lorraine, from whence we should raise contributions even to the gates of Paris, and it cut entirely off the French
communication with Strasburg, Brisach, &c., whereby these must have
next spring fallen into our hands. For this design the States had it
seems engaged to have a magazine both of meal for bread to the army,
and of hay and oats, at Treves sufficient to supply our whole army when
joined for five or six weeks, because it was foreseen that the army assembling only here and this being a mountainous bare country there could
not be forage so early in the fields as to supply us. It is said the States
really gave their orders for furnishing the magazines at Treves, but the
commissary employed there in chief to do it has either been in correspondence with France and treacherously neglected it, or else has spent
the money and could not do it, so the magazines fall mightily short of
what is necessary, and the Commissary for fear of punishment is
deserted into the enemy. The Electors on the Rhine hath also
promised to the Duke to furnish a sufficient number of horses for drawing
our great train of artillery, now when they are wanting they say it was
impossible for them to find so many horses. The Duke went up the
Rhine before us and went as far as Rastadt to speak with Prince Louis
of Baden at his own house. It is said they concerted that the Prince
should either have come himself or at least sent a general with 12,000
or 14,000 men of his army to march to Saarlouis on the one side while
the Duke should march up on the other and so invest it. Their troops
were to have been here as soon as we, and now we are here a week and
they are not yet come. We expect also 10,000 Prussian troops which are
on their march to join us sent by the King, and to be paid also by him.

The want of all these hinders us yet from acting anything. We came here on the 22nd by a prodigious great march from near Treves and found Marshal Villars encamped in a prodigious strong ground just before us, his left wing extending near the little town of Sierck on the Moselle, and his right running out towards Thionville. He was entrenched before we came and has fortified his camp every day since, and though we lie and look at each other yet we cannot possibly come at him though we were six times his force. Some talk that the Prince of Baden refuses now to march till he know what terms he has from the new Emperor. What truth is in this I know not but though it is certain the Duke designed the siege of Saarlouis, and I fancy does yet design it, it seems uncertain if we shall be able to execute it because of all these disappointments, and that the enemy have such a superiority now in Flanders that they are besieging Huy, and that taken may proceed to somewhat else of so great consequence as will oblige the States to call back their troops, for which view it is said they are now already hiring boats at Coblentz to carry them down with more expedition in case it be necessary. If those leave us we can probably attempt nothing here this summer. We have at present here with us now since the Palatine troops joined us eighty-three battalions of foot and ninety-four squadrons of horse and dragoons and reckon if the Prussians and Imperialists were joined us we should be near 25,000 men stronger than anything the enemy can make on their side even though they had received 10,000 men from Flanders. Thus much for news. My very hearty affectionate respects to your lady, humble duty to Monsieur Du Berry and service to our other friends. Pray write to me soon and at great length. Let me know if you have got occasion to send down the Poole's *Annotations* to my sister which I left with Mr. Taylor. Write me what hopes you have of our Scots affairs and whether the Duke of Queensberry goes down.

[LORD GODOLPHIN] to ROBERT HARLEY.

[1705, May.]—I received the enclosed to-day from Mr. Ellis, one does not know how to reconcile the air of sincerity he takes, with the little assistance he gives towards finding the clear truth of this whole matter; nor do I see, if there were nothing more than folly or stupidity to be imputed to him, how he can continue in the office with any sort of satisfaction either to himself or to Mr. Secretary Hedges.

He is my old acquaintance, and I have always had a good opinion of him, but I wish he would let us know the naked truth of this matter; there seems still to be something in what he has said and in what he has done very unaccountable if there be nothing more than yet appears to us.

MAYOR AND ALDERMEN OF COVENTRY to SECRETARY HARLEY.

[1705, end of May.]—We thankfully acknowledge Her Majesty's concern for the peace of this city expressed in your letter, on receipt of which we drew up an order forbidding strangers from meddling in the election and the voters from carrying clubs, sticks, or weapons. Three of the aldermen refused to join us in this, and one of them, Mr. Thomas Palmer, gave countenance to the riots. Mr. Thomas Smith and Mr. Thomas Chiswell, the present sheriffs, and some of the constables, showed a backwardness in doing their respective duties.

Your letter was also communicated to the candidates and endeavours used to bring them to agree to some proposals for preserving the peace;

but neither Sir Christopher Hales nor Mr. Grey consented to them or offered any other.

On the day of the election, Tuesday the 22nd inst., these candidates' party seemed resolved on their former course of riot and violence, but the other candidates forbid their men rallying or bringing sticks. The mayor and some of the aldermen sat up all Monday night with the constables and watch, who were charged not to strike with their staves or halberds, but to apprehend such as they should find breaking the peace. About two o'clock in the morning the disturbance began. Mr. Grey appeared rallying his men about three o'clock, and we saw him with above a hundred men without sticks between four and five, but when the numbers increased and they understood that our attendants were not to strike they got sticks and clubs, and gathered stones and brickbats to throw at us.

A terrible riot ensued about five, some of the watch were knocked down and their halberds taken from them and broken. The mayor was wounded in the face by a stone thrown at him and was also struck with a stick by Mr. Humphry Burton the younger, a country gentleman that come to town on this occasion. One of the watch apprehended Burton, but William Haywood, a constable, rescued him. Further attempts to disperse the rioters proved impracticable, and appeared likely if continued to be attended with slaughter and blood.

The rioters then marched the streets and at nine o'clock possessed themselves of the town hall with 600 or 700 men, and continued there during the three days of the election, being Tuesday, Wednesday, and Thursday; and most things were done as this rabble pleased. Many voters were beaten, knocked down, dragged along the ground by the hair and inhumanly abused.

Signed by Samuel Billing, Mayor; and Edward Owen, William and John Snell, Fra. Cater, Thos. Diston, and Jonah Cryne, Aldermen.

Copy.

"Passages of Dyer's News Letters."

1705, May to July—

1705, May 5. London—We hear that seventeen strangers are like to be chosen in Wiltshire, not one of them having a foot of ground in that county, to the reproach of the electors for not having a value for the honest loyal neighbouring gentry.

1705, May 10—We have an account of pretty many elections since my last, but fortune has favoured the wrong side in them, for Mr. Nevil has carried it at Abingdon against Sir Simon Harcourt by thirty odd voices, &c. On the other hand Mr. Gape has carried it at St. Albans notwithstanding a great Lady went thither to oppose him, whose endeavours it is hoped will succeed no better at Woodstock in favour of Brigadier Cadogan an Irishman.

1705, May 17—We have an account of a great many more elections made since my last, and upon the whole a sort of an equilibrium seems to be between the parties, near seventy of the Tackers are already chosen. In Essex Sir Charles Bar[ringto]n and Sir Richard Ch[il]d have lost it by a great majority, though they polled more freeholders than in the former elections. But the Whigs have found a way of granting quit rents of forty shillings per annum resignable upon the tender of sixpence; besides the Quakers in general throughout the kingdom in this election vote against the Church.

1705, May 19—For Warwickshire their old representatives Sir Charles Shuckburgh and Sir John Mordaunt, the last a Tacker, have carried it, being set up by the general consent of the gentry of that county. One Captain Lucy, supported by the interest of three or four gentlemen, and the assistance of all the Dissenters, attempted to have come in, but was very much distanced, as you will see by their number on the poll, viz., Sir Charles Shuckburgh, 1984; Sir John, 1884; Mr. Lucy, 1116. The Bishop of Worcester refused the latter his interest upon application to his Lordship by reason a fanatic preacher is kept in his family.

On Thursday last came on the much contested election for the University of Cambridge. The candidates were the Honourable Arthur Annesley Esquire late Fellow of Magdalen College, who had 183 voices, and the Honourable Dixey Windsor Esquire, Fellow of Trinity College, who had 170, opposed by Francis Godolphin Esquire, my Lord Treasurer's son, who had 162 voices, and Sir Isaac Newton, a late made knight, who had 117, and notwithstanding there was all the management and delays possible, and the Heads of the Houses against the two first, it was carried for them to the unspeakable joy of the hopeful and promising part of that University, by which we see that the sense of both Universities was for the Occasional Bill, and that they approved of the Tacking of it by choosing the same members that joined in it. I hear the poll of Woodstock will be printed, that it may be seen who they were that polled for the Brigadier, whose grandfather was governor of Trim in Ireland for the Parliament, and his grandmother was daughter to the famous Hardress Waller, on his father's side. His pedigree was proved at the election by an epitaph that was made last summer by one of the Heralds' Office, and was never yet on a tomb.

1705, May 29—Sir John Packington had a banner carried before him whereon was painted a church falling with this inscription, For the Queen and the Church Fackington. It was observable that as they were marching through the Foregate Street in Worcester they met the Bishop's coach in which was a nonconformist teacher going to poll for the Captain, but the horses at the sight of the church (as it was believed) turned tail, overturned and broke the same and very much bruised the holder-forth's outer man, and this raised no small admiration that the Bishop's horses should be afraid of a church.

The cry of the Whiggish rabble at the election for the county of Chester during this election was "Down with the Church and the Bishops"; and when about 60 of the clergy headed by the Dean came to poll they said Hell was broke loose, and these were the Devil's black guard; they abused the Bishop, though according to his peaceable temper he did not intermeddle in the elections, and to complete their outrage broke the windows of the Cathedral and another church.

1705, May 30—The report of my Lord Keeper's sudden removal begins to wear off, most believe there is nothing in it, but given out by the Whigs to encourage their party, and dispirit the other, or else to shake his Lordship out of that post, as they have done before by my Lord Nottingham and Sir George Rooke cut of theirs.

I hear some great men that are in post of honour, have lately applied themselves to my Lord Keeper to remove from the commissions of the peace several considerable gentlemen in the country where they live, by reason, and for that cause only, that they were Tackers, nay there was no other reason given against one gentleman in Cambridgeshire, but he had given his vote at the last election for one that was a Tacker, but this was thought not a sufficient reason by his Lordship to comply with their humour, though it may be a sufficient one with some people for his Lordship's removal.

The Honourable Charles Bertie, Treasurer and Paymaster of the Ordnance above 20 years, is removed from that place, and succeeded by Colonel Harry Mordaunt. The reason of the remove of this good old royalist is not said nor nobody knows but the Queen, and one or two more, unless it be that for which the Justices of the Peace should have been removed.

I hear the Earls of Rochester and Nottingham have been lately with the Queen. God send Her Majesty no worse counsellors!

1705, May 31—At that for Sussex— Turner Esquire refused to take the poll, unless the Duke of Somerset removed out of Court, which he obliged him to do, after some high words had passed, the High Sheriff producing a vote of the House of Commons against the Peers intermeddling with elections, which however they have done more in the electing this parliament than ever.

The Quakers in Buckinghamshire voted all of them against my Lord Cheney, though he was the person that brought in and procured a bill in their favour about signing a declaration instead of an oath. At Brentford several hundreds of them polled against Smithson and Lake as they have done against the Church interest all England over, which no doubt will be remembered, and placed to their account in bar of future favours.

1705, June 2—We have an account of six Tackers more that are chosen since my last, of which number are Sir Ed. Seymour and Mr Snell, who carried it without opposition for Exeter; though endeavours were used to have brought in a gentleman that lately lost it at Cambridge, but the loyal city would not be put upon by the University's refuse.

1705, July 3—The Court and Country party are very busy in caballing, and the last set of Ministers club by themselves. Upon the whole it is feared this sessions will scarce answer the expectations of the Court, so perverse are the minds of some men.

1705, July 17—London. Mr Wesley, a beneficed minister in Lincolnshire, who formerly wrote the Life of Christ, which he dedicated to Queen Mary, but lately unhappily writing against the Dissenters, and since that giving his vote for the Tacking interest at the election in the county, and his reasons in writing for his so doing; he was in the first place removed from being chaplain to a regiment, which is worth about 100l. per annum, &c. In the next place after a thousand insults in his house and streets of Jacobite, Perkinite, &c., was arrested and carried to Lincoln gaol in a violent manner for some debts contracted by the smallness of his income, the numerousness of his family, and other accidents of Providence; but it seems he was pertinacious, and would not retract his book (being fact), otherwise he might fare better.

1705, July 21. London—The manifesto of the Church of England that was endeavoured to be suppressed, is now again sold publicly about the streets, the bookseller being resolved to take the benefit of his copy, and stand the test of the law, and the pretended remarks that are printed in it strengthen and not confute the assertions of the author.

[Endorsed by Harley. Passages of Dyer's News letters.—[Received], September 11th, 1705.]

SIR CHARLES HEDGES to MR. WHITWORTH.

1705, June 1. Whitehall — I send you enclosed a copy of the report from the Board of Trade, in relation to the manufacture of tobacco, which some people now endeavour to establish in Moscovy, together with the original Order of Council upon the same subject. You will use your best endeavours and exert your utmost power, with your usual prudence and discretion, to destroy those materials that are brought from hence to Moscow, for the carrying on of the manufacture already mentioned ; and order the persons concerned therein forthwith to return home, Her Majesty having ordered a Privy Seal to be issued out for recalling them. When you shall have destroyed the utensils of their trade, you are to acquaint the Czar how much Her Majesty resents her subjects taking upon them to enter into contracts of this nature, without Her Royal permission, and their monopolising the trade of tobacco, and thereby imposing extravagant prices on the Czar's subjects. As on the one side you are to discourage all monoplies, so on the other side you are to give all the countenance and assistance you can, equally to all Her Majesty's subjects, who endeavour in a fair and open manner to carry on the tobacco trade, which is so much to the advantage of both nations.

P.S.—When you have your audience of the Czar, you'll let him know that Her Majesty having forbid her subjects under the highest penalties to enter into treaties of this kind without the sanction of Her Royal Authority, it will be impossible for them to make good the contract they have made with him, and Her Majesty hopes from the Czar's friendship that he will not expect it from them.

Next post you shall have the Privy Seal for calling home Mr. Martin and his wife. *Copy.*

Enclosures (*Copies*).

At the Court at St. James's, the 31st of May 1705.

Present :

The Queen's most Excellent Majesty in Council.

Upon reading this day at the Board a Report from the Lords Commissioners for Trade and Plantations in the words following, viz. :—

May it please your Majesty

In obedience to your Majesty's commands signified to us by the Right Honourable Mr. Secretary Harley, we have examined a Petition of several merchants of Virginia and Maryland complaining of undue practices in Muscovy by some of your Majesty's subjects in relation to the vending and manufacturing of tobacco there, we have heard the Petitioners and likewise Nathaniel Gold, William Dawson, Edward Haistwell, Samuel Heathcote and others, as also Joseph Martin in the behalf of his partners, who are alleged to be concerned in the said practices, and upon the whole matter do find that the said Nathaniel Gold and others had made a contract with the Czar of Muscovy, here in England in the year 1698, for importing certain quantities of tobacco into his dominions, which they accordingly did perform, and wanting a vent for the same, whereby great part of the said tobacco became dry and like to be unfit for sale, unless the same methods as in England were used for the preservation thereof. They had thereupon sent over Peter Marshall and his wife versed in the cutting and rolling of tobacco, together with instruments and materials necessary thereunto, with a design as they allege to recall the said persons immediately after their having performed this particular service, without allowing them the liberty to employ their skill in the rolling or cutting any tobacco of the growth of the dominions of the Czar. And we do likewise find that the said Mr. Joseph Martin, merchant of London, by his son Samuel Martin and James Spillman, his correspondents at Moscow, has very lately made a contract with some officers of the Czar, for the importation of other quantities of tobacco into those dominions from England, as likewise for the sending thither as many persons skilled in the spinning and rolling of tobacco as the Czar should require, together with the instruments, engines, materials, and liquors commonly used in that work, to be employed not only for the manufacturing of English tobacco thus imported, but even for the tobacco of the growth of Circassia, a large province appertaining to that Prince, by which means his subjects would become equally skilled in that mystery with any of your Majesty's subjects dealers in tobacco, which proceedings being of most pernicious consequence to the trade of your Majesty's subjects and the welfare of your plantations, we are humbly of opinion that the persons mentioned to have been already sent to Moscow by the first contracts may be immediately recalled by Letters of Privy Seal to be sent to your Majesty's Envoy for that purpose, and that the engines and materials already there be ordered by your Majesty to be broken and destroyed in the presence of your Majesty's said Envoy, as likewise that the said Martin and correspondents and all other persons whatsoever be directed by your Majesty's Declaration, in such manner as your Majesty shall think proper, not to send any persons versed in this mystery or any instruments and materials for the same, or employing any persons therein, notwithstanding any clause in His said Contract, obliging them to a matter so injurious to other your Majesty's subjects. And whereas the Petitioners, merchants and planters of Virginia and Maryland, do suggest that several persons are soliciting for themselves at Moscow the sole trade and entire importation of tobacco, exclusive of all others into those parts, we further humbly offer that your Majesty would be pleased to direct your Envoy at that Court that he be equally and impartially assisting to all your Majesty's subjects in the Free Trade of such tobacco of the growth of your Majesty's plantations as shall be imported into the dominions of the Czar. All which nevertheless is most humbly submitted.

DARTMOUTH   WM. BLATHWAIT
ROB. CECIL   JOHN POLLEXFEN
PH. MEADOWS   MAT. PRIOR

1705, May 26.   Whitehall.

Her Majesty in Council is pleased to approve thereof and to order, That the Right Honourable Mr. Secretary Harley do forthwith prepare a warrant for Her Majesty's Royal signature to pass the Privy Seal for recalling the said Peter Marshall and his wife out of the Czar's dominions, and that he cause the same to be sent to Her Majesty's Envoy there for that purpose, with directions to him to take care for the safe conveyance of the said persons into this

Kingdom, and also to cause the said engines and materials already there to be broken and destroyed in his presence, in the most private and effectual manner that may be. And as to the proceedings of the said Mr. Martin's correspondents in making a contract with a foreign Prince without Her Majesty's knowledge and allowance in a matter so injurious to other Her Majesty's Subjects, Her Majesty is pleased to declare her utmost dislike of so much thereof as relates to the manufacturing in Muscovy the native product of Her Majesty's dominions and furnishing the persons and materials necessary thereunto, which is contrary to the interest and usage of Her Majesty's Kingdoms, and to order that the same be signified to the said Martin and his correspondents, and that they, and also the Russia Company and all other persons whatsoever, forbear to send any persons into Muscovy versed in the mystery of spinning and rolling of tobacco, or any instruments or materials for the same, or to employ any persons therein, as they tender Her Majesty's displeasure and will answer the contrary at their perils; and the Lords Commissioners taking notice in the said report that several persons are soliciting for themselves at Moscow the sole trade and entire importation of tobacco exclusive of all others into those parts, it is further ordered by Her Majesty in Council that Mr. Secretary Harley do also prepare for Her Majesty's Royal signature the necessary letters and orders to Her Majesty's Envoy relating to the said trade, and otherwise as shall be most proper according to the tenor of the said Report.

Sir C. Hedges to Secretary Harley.

1705, June 3. St. James's—Upon reading Mr. Stepney's letters which go herewith, Her Majesty thinks it for her service that you lay before her on Sunday next at Windsor the instructions which I understand you have already prepared, for a minister to the Emperor, that being a matter that requires despatch.

R[obert] Monckton to [Robert Harley].

1705, June 5. Hodroyd—You were pleased to say to me you would be in town again as soon as your election was over. Let me implore your protection and friendship in a matter about which the Duke of Newcastle is interesting himself with the Lord Treasurer on my behalf.

Richard Duke to Robert Harley.

1705, June 7. Otterton—Since my last six French rogues carried away our boat where it lay in our harbour two miles from my house and but four from that of Exeter; and my dying daughter Duke riding on the sea cliff to take the air heard a French privateer halloo at her coach. All which affrightens us daily until you send us your cruiser of 40 guns. Neither trading, nor coal, nor stone, barks which employ ten thousand and pay her Majesty great customs, can adventure one-half league to sea; and but two days since Lieut. Butson, who lives on the sea shore but two miles from my house, borrowed some of my muskets to defend his neighbours, and had a warrant from my son the justice to set a watch of six men till we have a sight of the cruiser. If you want a captain for it, my neighbour Captain Manston who three or four years since commanded the *Foresight* and took six prizes worth about 40,000*l.*, may procure a good number of seamen, which is difficult now to do.

Our present necessity pleads aloud for us all, that we may have lime
and sand to manure our lands for wheat this next season ; and how
shall our labouring men be employed without building stones ?

W[ILLIAM] GREG to [ROBERT HARLEY].

1705, June 7. Edinburgh—I write your Honour this first letter
upon my return to my native country in worse health than ever. I
enjoyed in ten years I was out of it : so that nothing but a deep sense
of the great obligations I lie under could have prompted me to take pen
in hand this post, which I was unwilling to let slip without acquainting
your Honour with the little I have been able to learn under my present
indisposition, since my arrival.

This day the Parliament was prorogued to the 28th instant notwithstanding the ship having on board the Commissioner's equipage came
safe yesterday into Leith Road, under convoy of Her Majesty's ship
the *Nightingale.* I am not particularly informed of the true reason of
this prorogation, but it would seem as if matters were not duly prepared,
as yet, for opening the Session.

The poverty this country labours under at present is so great, that
any project for remedying such an epidemical distemper, must needs
find an easy ingression here. And accordingly, they are willing to
forget the fatal Isthmus for an Island they fancy may prove more fortunate. The scene of this imaginary wealth is laid in Madagascar,
from whence two Deputies arrived here about six weeks ago, who offer
no less than five millions of money and fifty sail of ships, to have themselves and their worthy fraternity enfranchised here. They have been
lately with B. in the country, by whom I hear they were very well
received. Should such proposals ever be hearkened unto, 'twould puzzle
C. himself to reconcile hanging of pirates one day with harbouring them
the next.

The merchant whose name I left with your Honour, being gone
abroad, I humbly crave your commands (if at any time you shall think
fit to lay them upon your creature) may be directed for me at Mr.
Thomas Crombie's, a merchant here. The least intimation of your
Honour's orders being given about the direction I have been, I doubt,
indiscreetly fond of, would put me beyond all fear of a discovery ; the
better to prevent which, I shall for the future forbear setting my name
to my letters, humbly begging pardon for this empty one.

E. LEWIS to SECRETARY HARLEY.

1705, June 8. Whitehall — I have long since drawn drafts of
letters, for the Queen's own hand to the Emperor and the King of
Prussia, which were accordingly sent away from the other office without
my knowledge. Her Majesty sealed them herself and we have no
copies, nothing being ever entered till signed.

Some people are very angry the Exeter election is not in the Gazette,
and say it was left out by order, though the fault is really in the Postmaster of Exeter, who has not yet transmitted an account of it to the
Postmasters-General from whom we have our lists.

Some great men have given out that Mr. Ellis bears the blame of
others and suffers in his own reputation and fortune because he will not
discover——. You'll easily guess who are capable of so malicious a turn.
My Lady Power is in custody.

The Queen has given Lady Betty Bruce, Lord Ailesbury's daughter,
leave to come home.

[WILLIAM GREG to ROBERT HARLEY.]

1705, June 9. Edinburgh—Since my first of the 7th from this place, I have been in company with the senior of the two gentlemen Deputies from Madagascar. His name is Captain Bryholt by whose discourse I found that he not only had been with B. but likewise with several other of our Grandees and particularly the Earl of Wemyss in the country. He first intended, as he said, to have come down by land, and accordingly had bought a horse, which he afterwards sold and took the opportunity of the ship that brought the corpse of the late Countess of Cromartie hither. He seems to be a notable talking man, and that is talent enough to impose upon those that nibble greedily at every bait.

But lest a project so far fetched should not succeed so speedily as they could wish, a homespun one is set afoot here by a gentleman who of all men living once was thought to have the worst turned head that way. Mr. Law who killed Beau Wilson in England is the man, and so fond is the Commissioner of this project for a Land Bank (since money fails) that the day before yesterday his Grace sent for the *quondam* Rake in order to discourse him fully upon this important point, so very necessary at this time. He proposes the striking tallies for 50,000*l.* sterling at first and then proceeding according as issues are made.

This day about noon, Sir James Falconer of Phesdo, one of the lords of the Session, and a member of parliament for the shire of Kincardine, died suddenly of an asthma. He was a gentleman of good parts and extraordinary probity and reckoned one of the best Judges on the Bench.

I humbly beg pardon for this blurred paper and bad tools, &c.

(Draft in Greg's handwriting.)

CHR. PRICE to [ROBERT HARLEY].

1705, June 11—I had waited on you at Brampton had not our county election happened at the time of your being in the country, where I was deeply engaged in endeavouring to get the two Morgans chosen for our representatives against the two new candidates Sir Hopton Williams and Sir Thomas Powell. One of the former lost it by a small majority and very irregular proceedings of which you'll hear in the house of commons. I happened to nick the point and laid Sir Thomas aside by bringing the much better part of the hundred he lives in (of which I am too) to give their voices for the Morgans. This has nettled the two baronets to that degree that they do publicly vow revenge, and declare they'll do me all the prejudice they can; they are now making all the interest they can to get me out of the commission of the peace.

[WILLIAM GREG to ROBERT HARLEY.]

1705, June 12. Edinburgh—The day before yesterday being the Anniversary of the St. Germain gentleman's birth, it was observed here in corners with a great deal [of] devout drinking, as happening on a Sunday; insomuch that Captain Bryholt, who pretends already to a more than ordinary acquaintance with the best sort of people here, assures me, that when he went yesterday morning to wait on some of them, he found thirty still half fuddled. This is hint enough, whereby to judge of the pulse of this boiling nation, which all their extraordinary pretences to sanctity and reformation above their neighbours could not hinder from hugging an airy phantom, which if ever realized must needs prove their ruin. I was in no less than three several taverns with a design to have observed their various humours of that obscure birth-night, but happened to fall in with such a discreet set of men, as carefully forbore all healths, but those of the company. Captain Bryholt having been no inconsiderable part of the subject matter of two former letters, what passed between him and a merchant yesterday in my hearing, may perhaps deserve a place in this as giving further light into this project, which meets with encouragement here from the Indian and African Company. He was indeed for mincing the matter as much as possible, by telling the merchant that there were not above 10 sail of ships belonging to Madagascar, nor more than 1,000 Europeans upon the Island. This may come nearer the truth than 50 sail, which yet I am told he has promised to B., of whom he owned to myself that he has had an audience of two hours' length. In consequence whereof, he is now about buying two ships to go for Madagascar, of which B. with him is already king, since the Captain happening to be in company on Sunday did instead of pledging the health of the day drank that of B., which I take notice of as serving to show if not the emptiness of the project at least the vanity of the projector.

That your Honour might see we have our Tutchin too, I presume to send you a bad imitation of no good original. If I may hope for your pardon for this once I shall take care to trouble your Honour for the future with no more impertinencies of this kind unless everything may be possibly reckoned such that comes from me.

(Draft in Greg's handwriting.)

JOHN CHAMBERLAYNE to [ROBERT HARLEY].

1705, June 15. Petty France, Westminster—Recommending Robert Hales for public service in Switzerland among the Grisons, or in those parts.

[WILLIAM GREG to ROBERT HARLEY.]

1705, June 16. Edinburgh—There's nothing talked of here at present save the changes newly made in the Ministry, which few, I find, are much displeased at. I shall not trouble your Honour with our conjectures about the candidate for the Privy Council and Privy Seal, that being best known to your Honour only say our politics, if A. should be made President of the former, as 'tis talked, then he may come to be as much influenced as F. whom they stick not to compare already to R[ehoboa]m, who followed too much the advice of young men.

The 12th instant, I acquainted your Honour that Captain Bryholt met with encouragement from the African and Indian Company here; and now I am to inform you, that upon his giving out (how truly I know not), that before he came from England he had obtained Her Majesty's pardon for all Scotch pirates in Madagascar, they are inclined, to grant him their pass and protection, for trading with negroes between the said Island and Brazil, for which purpose he has shown them an agreement made between the Portuguese and him, by virtue whereof he is to have 40l. sterling for every negro he shall bring from thither and the Company here so much per cent for their pass; which they hope may turn to good account; and the more, in that he undertakes to send for Scotland, not only all pirates, natives of this kingdom, but promises to extend the Queen's Pardon to all those that are willing to pass for such. By which means, they look for a shoal of seamen and a squadron of ships, laden with the treasure of the Indies, to enrich the country in the world that stands the most in need of it, and that is the least solicitous how they come by it in their present exigencies. In the meanwhile they are not a little beholden to England (though loth to own it) for a supply of 16,000 guineas newly brought into this country by such as are willing to store themselves with Scotch linen before the 25th of December next. There are also 5,000 great cattle sent into England, as foreseeing the time is but short for driving that beneficial trade. Yesterday Captain Green's frigate came first out here.

* *(Draft in Greg's handwriting.)*

DR. ARTHUR CHARLETT to [ROBERT HARLEY].

1705, June 19. University College, Oxford—I was very sorry my absence on Wednesday hindered me, from paying those respects due to you, which the Vice Chancellor would, had he been present. I did not hear till late, on Tuesday that you were at the 'Angel' and then was assured by Dr. Edwards, that you were very early to be at Windsor next morning, so that I took boat to a country house on the river for two days' rest.

With this excuse, our Theatre Catalogue presumes to wait upon you, as also a noble invention of our excellent Professor, Mr. Halley, to fix and determine the motion of Comets.

Dr. Wallis's house being given by his son to the University, for the use of the two Savilian Professors of Astronomy and Geometry, we are going to erect a very convenient Observatory thereupon, on which the University will expend a considerable sum of money, enabled there-unto by the late kindness of Her Majesty's Exchequer in giving us the arrears of Hen. VII.'s. pension so long due.

[WILLIAM GREG to ROBERT HARLEY.]

1705, June 21. Edinburgh—They are so much taken up here with a succession of trifling projects for increasing the coin of a moneyless nation, that go where one will he meets with nothing else. But I who am very void of all design either to enrich them or myself ought not to heed these their amusements nor would I have mentioned them to your Honour but that they must serve to plead my excuse for the emptiness of this and my preceding letters of which for what they contain your Honour might have been spared the trouble, but that I was ambitious at any rate to approve my diligence to you.

Her Majesty's High Commissioner is not a little uneasy at the D[uke] of Q[ueensberry's] long stay in England his presence being thought more necessary here, in order to second with his interest the measures of the Court, insomuch that though the Parliament be to meet this day seven-night, yet 'tis thought it will be adjourned for eight or ten days to wait the Duke's coming before they enter upon business. This is what is talked at the Abbey of Holyrood House and I may say the all that is fit to impart to your Honour.

The great scarcity of money appears in nothing more than in their recent inability to furnish provisions for a small cruising frigate appointed to guard the coast, so that the captain rather than be out of business is willing to take that in a manner upon himself. They begin to be sensible of the great loss they will be at after the 25th of December when they shall see their small incomes curtailed of 80,000l. which their black cattle and linen cloth brought them in yearly from England.

1705, June 26. Edinburgh—Though the Parliament be to meet the day after to-morrow yet the members scared by frequent prorogations come but slowly up to town, which however a general joy overspread last night upon the public entry (as I may call it) of Duke Hamilton, whom several coaches and six together with a good body of the inhabitants on horseback met some miles off and accompanied him to his lodgings in the Abbey; whereof he is Bailie or Keeper, though indeed a stranger would have rather believed him to have been Lord and Master of the same by the great mirth and revellings in the houses and streets, till break of day, upon this occasion. Some days before he came to town, the Marquess of Tweeddale and the Earls of Roxburgh and Selkirk having been to give him a visit at his country house, he received them with this compliment that *he had a fatted calf for returning prodigals*, looking upon himself it seems to be the Father of his Country: and now that he is come to the capital of it, he is I hear hugely pleased to see himself furnished with an unexpected topic for hindering the imposition of a Cess or Tax for the subsistence of the Forces, and it is this: the Earl of Dalhousie who is lieutenant colonel of the Foot Guards being indebted 150*l*. sterling to some tradesmen here and proving deaf to all their dunning, they laid their heads together how they could best come by any part of that sum, rather than lose the whole, and accordingly, hearing that he had some rich liveries a-making, they sent to his tailor's house and arrested the same, and because the man suffered them to be taken away, the Earl enraged at this affront came with a file of musketeers and taking the poor tailor out of his bed on Sunday morning caned him to some purpose. I am sensible how unpardonable it were in me to entertain you with such a silly story at any other time but this when B. with his followers (which are not few) are glad of any handle for baffling the designs of the Court by representing how well such lawless gentlemen deserve bread who think nothing of sporting on the liberties and even the lives of their fellow subjects; and at the last also they told of a late instance from the country where some soldiers of Colonel [Grant's?] independent company repaired to the house of one of the Earl of Mar's tenants, and because the country fellow would not go along he unhappily lost his life in his own defence, for which the Earl swears he'll have them hanged.

1705, June 28. Edinburgh—This day the Parliament met for the first time but was adjourned to Tuesday next being the 3rd of July because a great many of the Members are not come up, so that neither Her Majesty's letter was read, nor consequently any speech delivered from the throne, which I, as an eye witness, can assure you was very well filled by a young Commissioner [Argyle], whose graceful mien and becoming carriage, accompanied with an air awful beyond what was expected from one of his years, did at once both charm and challenge respect from the beholders, and I believe, let the censorious world say what they will, Her Majesty could not in the present juncture of affairs have made choice of a fitter person for bearding the Hector of Hamilton, who was not long silent after the Commissioner's and Chancellor's Commissions were read: for the House being ordered to be called over and as is usual the first Officers of State taking place in the list immediately after the Commissioner, no sooner was the President of the Privy Council called according to the old list but up stands the Hero and in a huff told the Chancellor, that this was calling a nonentity, there being no President of the Privy Council for the time, and that therefore, though he had all the respect imaginable for the Queen and her Officers of State, yet he could not sit still and hear such an encroachment upon

·his right and privilege. The Chancellor answered with his wonted calmness, but all he said could not satisfy his Grace who still insisted upon his right. However orders being given to go on with the call of House, and Mr. Baillie of Jerviswood the late Treasurer Depute coming in course to be named, as knight of the shire for Clydesdale, Mr. Fletcher rose up, and protested against calling Jerviswood, who he said was no more a member of parliament, as having once accepted Her Majesty's Commission for being Treasurer Depute, which office he positively affirmed was altogether incompatible with his being a knight of the shire for Clydesdale and that therefore from the minute he accepted of the said commission, the former representing character ceased. Mr. Baillie answered for himself with general applause that 'twas true Her Majesty was once pleased to confer upon him the office of Treasurer Depute which he did accept with a design to serve both the Queen and Country, and that Her Majesty having been lately pleased to resume the same, he had as readily resigned it, not doubting but that Her Majesty would be much better served. But that as 'twas during the interval of the Session of Parliament, he had accepted Her Majesty's Commission, so he never had the honour to sit there by virtue of the same, so that his title to the honour of representing the shire of Clydesdale was not thereby forfeited. 'Tis remarkable that Fletcher was not seconded by any one member, yet he would not desist for all that, and not being able to answer what the Chancellor said for Mr. Baillie, the madman, as I remember your Honour once rightly called him, was so impertinent as to tell his Lordship, that he kept up a controversy after the whole House had let it fall. The true ground of the ill-nature and spleen which Fletcher has vented against Mr. Baillie arises from the latter's apostasy from the Country to the Court Party.

The next thing which came upon the file was a controverted election for the shire of Clackmannan, which seemed now to be at an end by the death of Mr. Burnside, one of the persons elected, and accordingly Sir Tho. Burnet of Layes, a mighty stickler for the rights of the Barons, desired that Mr. Abercrombie of Tullibody, the surviving competitor, might be forthwith admitted, and in this was seconded by the Dukes of Hamilton and Athol. But the Chancellor and all the rest of the Officers of State were of opinion that the matter should be delayed and a competent time allowed for acquainting the electors therewith, in order to have their determination: but it being urged by Fletcher that it was only cognizable by the Parliament, and there appearing no visible issue of this debate otherwise than by a vote, it was readily agreed to by the House, and the Motion being made and the Question being put by the Chancellor, admit or delay? 'twas carried, *admit*, by a very great majority, and accordingly Mr. Abercrombie was admitted. Whereupon the Country party began to shrug triumphantly, and from this small advantage at the opening of the Session, presage no less than a complete victory over the Court party before it ends.

(Drafts in Greg's handwriting.)

Viscount Townshend to [the Duke of Newcastle].

1705, June 29. Rainham—I trouble you on account of a petition of several of the freemen of Norwich against the Mayor, who has behaved himself in a very arbitrary and illegal manor. The ill practices he has been guilty of would certainly have put the whole town into the utmost confusion, had not the freemen been pacified by the assurance they should have right done them. I can assure your grace his behaviour in relation to the election for the town was no less scandalous, for there was nothing omitted that could be thought of by him and several others in the town to deter the freemen from voting for those honest gentlemen who, after all their indirect practices, had the majority by a very great number; and yet the sheriffs would make a double return. All the Mayor's actions have been attended with so much partiality and so much violence in order to support his party that there will be an end of government in Norwich, if he escape without punishment.

LORD POULETT to [EDWARD HARLEY].

1705, June 30. Hinton.—I will write you nothing of the confounded practices of our opposers at the election since you have seen Mr. Palmer who can tell you a great deal of his part; but since their defeat they flame more fiercely as if only a little water was thrown on them, and they rage with the overcoming hopes this next session to destroy our friends and their moderate interests as they phrase it; but here their loudness proved but a sign of weakness in reason and numbers, and I believe they are made of the same stuff all their party.

Though I have time in abundance to do myself the honour to write to your brother I consider he has none to spare; so I choose rather to take the advantage of applying to him by you in behalf of Edward Parker *alias* Southcote, of Buckland Toutsend [Tout Saints], near Kingsbridge in Devonshire. He is a very honest gentleman of two thousand pounds a year, but a Roman Catholic, so desires a protection from the Council for four coach horses and some hunters, he being a sportsman. It is a common courtesy to grant it, if Secretary Harley will do him the honour to move it in Council.

MEMORANDA [by DE FOE.]

[1705, June ?]—To be furnished with something new to inform the people I converse with, at least when anything extraordinary happens which may be had more authentic than ordinary.

To have a certificate as from the Office that being travelling on my lawful occasions I may not be stopped by any malicious person on the road—or, which may be worse, searched.

To settle a method how to write, &c.

Charges to be directed as shall receive orders.

To get leave for the same person [Hurt, *See* p. 138 *ante*] who went with me before to be absent at the Custom House.

To be going as soon as possible. The Assizes will else not overtake me only, but be before me

If may suit with convenience—be gone Friday next.

Some special instructions.

[DANIEL DE FOE] to ROBERT HARLEY.

[1705, July 2,] Monday.—I am sincerely thankful to your solicitous thoughts for me, though I avoid ecstasies on that subject.

I have the Pass, and doubt not its being effectual, and assure you of my making no use of it, but at the last extremity.

I give you joy of the good news which I received with one hand the same moment I received yours with the other, and which I take as a good omen, and both contribute to send me out cheerful and easy.

I send you herewith six of the "High Church Legion;" the bearer, who is my brother in law, and who may be depended on, is the same person [who] carried the Coventry affair, yet knows nothing of the principal affair. He is charged with the like number for my Lord Treasurer, but if you demand them, will deliver them, since if you would please to concern yourself so far as to let my Lord Treasurer know they come by your hand, it would be a double favour. I persuade myself now, you are convinced Lesly has not been the author of the "Memorial." I am fully possessed with a belief that not him (*sic*), no, nor Dr. D[ra]ke, but the latter as a tool, an amanuensis to his Grace. *Lætantur Lares &c.* There are his marks, his strokes, there is his spirit, his gall, and in short his picture. I am concerned to see your orders betrayed and buffooned. That wretch, Stephens, makes the Government perfectly impotent in these matters and the booksellers and he together make sport at your orders.

Indeed I write this without private design or ill will to the man; his being a rogue was useful to me, and I bribed him always to my advantage. But in this case they act under his patronage. An instance of this you will have to-morrow when the "Memorial" is to be published answered paragraph by paragraph.

As this is done purely to sell the book which the town is eager for, and which I think the Government is highly concerned to prevent, so the answers are always trifles, and the design, which is dispersing the original, is fully answered.

If you send for that fellow, and, severely reprimanding him, arge him in it, you may effectually damn this project in its embryo, for he knows the hand it comes by and may go and seize it in the press, and will be frighted by your threats. For villains are always cowards.

The licence you give me to use this freedom, joined to my concern for the case, is my excuse for this, and I hope shall be accepted so. This minute I go away, and shall do myself the honour to write at large on all occasions.

The DUKE OF NEWCASTLE to SECRETARY HARLEY.

1705, July 4. Welbeck—There are reports of a great many changes but I always fancy the town make more than there really will be. Both for his civility to you and my being sooner in a condition to fit up Powis House for myself makes me not sorry for that about the Lord Keeper [Wright]. I cannot say so of all the other rumours.

I enclose you a letter from one of the knights of Lincolnshire, believing you are not very sorry for the defeat of lofty Sir John [Thorold ?].

[WILLIAM GREG to ROBERT HARLEY.]

1705, July 5. Edinburgh—The 28th past being the first day of the meeting of the Parliament, I had the honour to acquaint you, that the Session began with *Banter*. I was in hopes to have been able to have informed you, by the last and this ordinary, that, banter apart, they had entered upon business. But the Commissioner contenting himself with the reading of Her Majesty's letter, and enforcing by a short (but handsome) speech what Her Majesty was pleased to recommend, did determine me to defer the giving you an unnecessary trouble, seeing I could not possibly procure copies of the Commissioner's and Chancellor's speeches, nor a list of the members of parliament. Such an excuse from a diving Dane (*sic*) in matters so seemingly discoverable without any great difficulty, may perhaps create but an indifferent opinion of my diligence. But I beg you to believe, that no pains have been spared for obtaining the said copies, which I hope to be able to send you by the next post. You have here enclosed the first day's minutes of Parliament which came not out till to-day.

. 1705, July 7. Edinburgh—Yesterday about one o'clock in the afternoon, the Parliament met again for the third time, and continued sitting till half an hour after eight; during which they decided a controverted election for the Shire of Ross, in favour of the Laird of Inchculter against Balnagowne. Then the House took into consideration Her Majesty's Letter, and accordingly, the Marquess of Annandale proposed, that before all other business, they should go upon such limitations and restrictions of the same successor with England, after Her Majesty's decease, as should be for the honour and interest and advantage of the Kingdom of Scotland.

. The Earl Marischal rose up next, as the mouth of the Country party, with this Resolve: That the state of the trade and coin of the Nation shall be entered upon, previously to all other business.

After him, the Earl of Mar gave in a Resolve: That preferably to all other business, the circumstances of this Nation with relation to England should fall under the consideration of the House, and in order thereunto, that a Treaty of Union betwixt the two kingdoms should be set on foot.

. This Resolve how important soever was not thought worthy to enter into competition with the other, and therefore was ordered to lie upon the table, so that the rest of the time was spent in determining which of the two: Annandale's Proposal, or Marischal's Resolve should remain Master of the Field; and after a great deal of dust raised on both sides, it was at last put to the vote and carried by the Country party, by thirty-seven votes.

But matters did not stop here; for the Court party finding, that such a positive and peremptory Resolve would fetter them too much by tying up their hands from bringing in any other business, whilst it was in agitation bethought themselves of a softer sword in its stead, and this was, *Overture*, accordingly the question was stated—To consider of the Trade of the Nation, by way of Overture or Resolve; and it carried—Overture by a considerable majority. 'Twas remarkable that many of the Country party came readily into this moderate measure; as foreseeing also how much they must needs have been hampered, should the Resolve have passed. Nor were the Gentlemen of the flying Squadron less forward as finding it a fit opportunity for re-admission into grace and favour; among this set, one may modestly reckon N., who has the honour of this nice distinction; which being approved by the Chancellor, who said, That Resolves at the opening of a Session were of dangerous consequence, the Hero of Hamilton rose up and bawled out, My Lord Chancellor, dangerous or not dangerous, Resolves have been the things that have saved us hitherto. Nor was Fletcher long silent, upon this occasion, who told the Chancellor, that his Lordship *put the plough before the oxen* in the management of this debate: For, says he, the Question is not so much concerning the method as the matter and this he thought was the miserable circumstances of the nation or nothing, and that these required such a Resolve to save from sinking was to him beyond all exception. This the best account I can give of what passed yesterday in Parliament which stands adjourned to Tuesday next at 10 o'clock, being the 10th instant, when you shall have a true list of its members. In the meanwhile I beg leave to send enclosed a printed copy of Her Majesty's Letter, accompanied with the Commissioners and Chancellor's Speeches which came not out here, before yesterday at noon, though you cannot be supposed to be unacquainted with the substance of either at this time of day.

(Drafts in Greg's handwriting.)

WILLIAM BROMLEY to [ROBERT HARLEY].

1705, July 7—Your chaplain Mr. Stratford having acquainted me that the Queen has been pleased to give him a canonry of Christ Church in Oxford, and how instrumental you have ███n in the procuring it I return you my humble thanks for this and all other your favours to him. I have a very good opinion of his ingenuity and virtue.

COURSEY IRELAND to ROBERT HARLEY, at Whitehall.

1705, July 7. Dublin—Mr. Secretary Southwell had informed several of my friends that I had disobliged the Duke of Ormond by a letter I wrote to you, wherein I complained that young gentlemen and noblemen's valets were posted in the army when some men of experience, merit and integrity were forgot. I had no design of complaining of his Grace or the Government, to hope thereby to be advanced to some valuable post or employment as some men do, &c.

DR. HENRY ALDRICH to [ROBERT] HARLEY, in Whitehall.

1705, July 7. Christ Church—On Friday last we installed Mr. Stratford canon, gave him possession of his lodgings, and chose him Treasurer. He is sensible he owes his preferment entirely to your favour. Should I add my own thanks and the College's for so good and useful a brother, I am afraid it would look a little impudent, in me at least who am too much indebted to you upon my own account.

SIR JOHN BLAND to [ROBERT HARLEY].

1705, July 8. Hulme—Enquiring whether he could be excused from going to Ireland this summer on account of bad health. Things are very quiet and easy in these parts and in Yorkshire, but in Cheshire 'tis otherwise.

[DANIEL DE FOE] to ROBERT HARLEY.

1705, July 9—When with your usual goodness, you were pleased the last time I was with you to order me to put down in writing anything I had to propose on my private account, it put me on considering whether the same secret hand that first put it into your thoughts to do me good might not perhaps yet farther move you on my behalf.

I am not insensible to the tenderness you treat me with, and though I am not ever crowding you with my empty acknowledgments as things I know you are above the ceremony of, yet you have bound a grateful fellow so close to you that nothing can be too great for me to attempt for your service. I only want the occasion which must come from yourself.

When I come to talk of myself, the story is melancholy enough, and yet I am loth to give you the trouble of it.

What I write of peace it seems raises war to me, and those people who were easy before grow troublesome now, though they must needs know me less able than before the last trouble to discharge them, and as those who offer this are most of them of the contrary party, I see the design is, if possible, to put a stop to my writing. But why do I trouble you with this, to ask you anything that can relieve this capital defect, is what I have no merit to pretend to.

But I remember when you were pleased, the last bill I received from you for which I ought to repeat my thanks, to say something of bringing it to a certainty—pardon me for restraining my requests, though you give me too much freedom. I know not whether what I have from you be from the public, or your own private. Though the bounty to me is equally yours, yet this difference it will have : that though I hate to be craving, yet, as I hinted once, I was fitter for a pension than an office, by which I meant respecting the service I may do among the Party.

So might the service I may do merit a private allowance by which the necessary cravings of a large family of seven children might be answered. What else I can raise in the world would soon set me at ease as to creditors, whereas the eager prosecution of enemies will at last disable me either to support the first, or discharge the last.

I know not how to build this proposal, but on this foundation, that I hope 'tis in your power to make me deserve it.

I hope you have more confidence in me than to think, what you supply me with for the expense of the services I go on, shall be in the least misapplied, and though I cannot persuade myself that good husbandry should straiten the work, and was something too expensive in the last, yet really the many particulars obtained, and the short time performed in, obliged me to expenses, and I thought it well bestowed. Nor, unless you prescribe me, shall I spare, where the service I am upon requires, since I am satisfied this thing will be of various uses to the public.

All this is to signify to you, that the money you are pleased to furnish for this affair, which I hope is out of the public stock, as the use is for the public, relates to its proper expense, subsistence or allowance being hitherto unconcerned in it.

Nor should I take this freedom, but wait your leisure, to reward me as your own judgment shall persuade you I merit, having always reason to acknowledge you forward to assist me. But—sir, the man is demolished, and the wound is too deep [for] common industry to heal, and he that made you the first physician has entailed the rent charge on you, and makes my Lord Rochester's verses on women true of me

> " That authors beggar-like will haunt the door,
> " Where they received a charity before."

Make me merit all you do for me, if I can do nothing, why assist me at all? If anything, then the public bounty will not be lost. :

'Tis the hopes of the party to see me fly, and I believe they would bribe me to be gone. If my pay is a harm to them, 'tis a use to the contrary. My petition to you, sir, is to make me serviceable, and the Queen's bounty will follow, for no man serves Her Majesty for nothing.

I have answered this " High Church Legion," I have dedicated it to my Lord Treasurer, from your hand, sir, my Lord cannot but accept it, and perhaps to my advantage, if not, I am sure 'tis for the public good ; and if I lose by it, I'll publish it, and flatter myself you will not be ashamed of the performance.

I forbear to trouble you any more with my case, I lay this at your feet, and, throwing myself wholly on your goodness, humbly ask your pardon for the freedom.

Postscript.—The messenger Stevens has brought or will bring some people up for the ' Dyer.' I pray that a seeming reprimand &c. may suffice, else the charge will lie.

[DANIEL DE FOE] to ROBERT HARLEY.

[1705, July 10,] Tuesday morning—I wrote the enclosed [i.e. the preceding letter] last night, though had I ▮▮▮ you I believe my heart had failed me in delivering it, for I could never yet speak for myself.

I wait with impatience your last order and shall attend at four this afternoon according to your direction.

I long to acquaint you that I am told Dr. Atterbury is author of the "Memorial," and that George Sawbridge and Abel Roper are the publishers, but your messenger Stevens, too much a friend to that party, took such care of the orders given him to discover the printers, that some hours before his search a person was sent privately to all the booksellers and gathered them in again.

Mr. Pooley in some company yesterday gave a great encomium of the book very publicly. I have sent you herewith the rough of the answer. I hope it will please you, and any hint you please to give shall be added. If you please to give me leave, I would address it to my Lord Treasurer, or to yourself, it should be in the press today if possible. I beg the favour of your perusal of it—the printing shall not stop my journey an hour.

[WILLIAM GREG to ROBERT HARLEY.]

1705, July 10. Edinburgh---When I sent the 7th instant a printed copy of Her Majesty's Letter to the Parliament 'twas natural to have expected at the same time, a dutiful Address by way of answer accompanying it. But the *Ante omnia* (for so they call here the settling of the Succession) has thrown our Patriots so off the hooks that they are in too waspish a humour to be mannerly. However you will have perceived by my last that they did not carry all before them, but rather that matters went as favourably for the Court, as could well have been expected for that Sederunt, in which the Ministry did prudently divert a dangerous Resolve, as I then informed you.

This day the Parliament met again about the usual afternoon hour and continued sitting till five. The most part of the time was employed in bandying about a controverted election for the Stewartry of Kirkcudbright, which after all was not discussed. So that the general overture carried last Sederunt concerning the Trade and Coin of the Nation was only minuted into four particular ones ; viz.

Mr. Baillie of Jerviswood, the late Treasurer Depute, moved that Mr. Law's Project (mentioned in my letter of the 9th past), for establishing a Land-Bank and Paper-money, might be taken into consideration.

The Duke of Athol made an overture against the importation of Indian muslins, and calicoes.

Mr. Cochran of Kilmarnock presented a third against the importation of English and Irish victual ; and

The Earl of Eglinton gave in a fourth against the importation of Irish butter and cheese.

All which were ordered to lie upon the table, and then the House adjourned till Thursday 10 o'clock.

Though I have a written list of the Members of Parliament ready by me, yet by reason of the above mentioned controverted election, I cannot send it till next post, being loth to send what is not exact.

The enclosed minutes of the 3rd came not out till yesterday : and as for written ones, we have no such thing. (*Draft.*)

1705, July 12. Edinburgh.—This afternoon the Parliament met between one and two, and took into their consideration the proposal and overtures mentioned in my last. But a proposal from Dr. Chamberlen, brother to the Professor well known to your Honour and physician to the Duchess of Hamilton, having been recommended to the House but omitted in the minutes of the last Sederunt, it had the preference due to its seniority, and being read, was marked a first reading and ordered to be printed, of which I hope to send you a copy by the next post, together with one of Mr. Law's proposal, which was also read and marked a first reading.

After these proposals, they proceeded to the overtures, and first of all, to that given in by the Duke of Athol against muslins, calicoes, holland &c. which with all the particulars (sail-cloth excepted) offered in the draft, was approved of, and marked a first reading.

It were endless to entertain you with all the speeches made on this occasion. The Hero whom in justice I always single out from the Herd, though forward enough for the Act, yet considering well his Duchess's interest in England, even in these moveable womanish commodities was loth to give up tamely her pretensions and therefore pleaded strongly in her absence, that what stock of table and bed linen his wife was already furnished with might not be prejudiced by the Act, whensoever she had a mind to bring it to Scotland, hoping the prohibition was only to be extended to personal wear and tear and not to table and bed linen, with which he supposed most of the members present to be so well provided that they could not reasonably flatter themselves to outlast them.

They went next upon the overture against the importation of butter and cheese which in the draft was only restricted to Ireland, yet before they could lick it into a right shape, England also in this particular must run the same hard fate and fall accordingly under the lash of this prohibitory law. Whilst these melting matters were in agitation the Commissioner's brother, who votes as High Treasurer, rose up and maintained, That if the tenor of the Act did not run thus: *Irish and Foreign butter, English* must also be understood. Whereupon Duke Hamilton, to do him still right, stood up and said, *That matters were not come to that as yet nor hoped ever should.* But Fletcher nettled at the reserve, rose up and said, *He wondered why anybody scrupled to mention England, since England used no ceremony with them.*

The Victual overture fell last under their consideration, but happening as it was couched to run counter to the genius of the House, it was put off till next Sederunt, and only ordered to lie upon the table, without being marked a first reading.

The only Vote that passed this day in the House was concerning the adjournment of the Session (as they call it) or Supreme Court of Justice, and which at last carried in the negative by a vast majority. The Earl of Marchmont had given in a draft of an Act, last Sederunt, for adjourning the same; but the lawyers foreseeing how prejudicial such an adjournment would prove to their trade found means, it seems, to deal so effectually with the Register's clerks, that when the draft was called for nobody knew what had become of it; upon which the Chancellor as Speaker of the House and the Marquis of

Annandale as Marchmont's second, in my hearing expresssed their just resentment of the bad treatment of the House in general and the 'slight offered to Marchmont in particular.

List of Parliament men sent. (*Draft.*)

JOHN GELLIBRAND to [ROBERT HARLEY].

1705, July 13—My advice is that Mrs. Croom be forthwith taken up and committed to Newgate. She has confessed upon oath before Mr. Lewis that she has sold many copies of a book declared to be criminal, and she will not bring forth the person from whom she had them. If however at any time after the author, printer, or original publisher be discovered you may drop your prosecution of her. The book has made a mighty noise and Mrs. Croom having been taken from her stall at the Exchange a prosecution will be expected ; besides this woman has an ill character, and her husband is a printer and a non-juror, a viler fellow does not live. The sending her to Newgate will make her believe you more in earnest. I am morally assured if this course be taken that she produces the party from whom she had the books.

'[ROBERT HARLEY] to the ATTORNEY-GENERAL [NORTHEY].

1705, July 13. Whitehall—Sends report on the Fleet Prison received from the Lord Keeper, in which three things are proposed for preventing future abuses. Asks his opinion, and that he will hear what Col. Leighton has to offer on the subject. (*Copy.*)

[WILLIAM GREG to ROBERT HARLEY.]

1705, July 14. Edinburgh—The day before yesterday I had the honour to send you an account of the proceedings of Parliament that afternoon, together with a list of the members that compose it. Upon a review of what I then wrote, I find myself engaged by promise to send you by this post copies of Dr. Chamberlen's and Mr. Law's proposals both which are here inclosed, with the minutes of the 10th and 12th which are not printed the next day as in England, but only the day after the next Sederunt when they are read again.

Yesterday the Parliament met again between one and two. A draft of an Act was presented to the House for prohibiting the importation of molasses; which was read and ordered to lie upon the table.

Then the question was started whether the House should go first upon the state of the Coin or Trade of the Nation. With respect to the former Mr. Baillie of Jerviswood moved, That Mr. Law's proposal might be considered as containing, in his opinion, a more rational and practicable scheme than that of Dr. Chamberlen. Whereupon Fletcher rose up and run it down with his usual ill-nature, calling it a *Contrivance to enslave the nation ;* which heavy charge the Earl of Roxburgh took up, and said, that a gentleman, who had employed his time and thoughts purely to serve his Country, if he should meet with no suitable encouragement from the public, ought at least to be treated with good manners. This went not without its answer from Fletcher, who fell into such a passion, as thinking himself taxed of ill manners, that I verily think (for I was present) had he been near Roxburgh they would have gone together by the ears: insomuch that the Commissioner, willing to prevent any bad consequences that might arise from what had passed in his presence, thought fit to confine Roxburgh and Fletcher to their chambers, as soon as the House was up. The Earl was too *mannerly* and respectful to dispute the authority which put him under arrest : but the Laird, who boasts that he never made his court to any King or Commissioner, made no bones of breaking it, pretending 'twas not the Commissioner's but the Marischal's business to keep the peace of the .House. However after a little fluttering, he was advised. by his friends to return to his cage, where he still continues under confinement.

After this heat was over, the House launched out into a *mare magnum;* I mean the further consideration of the Duke of Athol's overture against the importation of muslins, calicoes, holland, dorneck damask &c. where they did so traverse one another, that after two long hours' debate they made little or no progress therein, but were fain to defer it till next Sederunt. Among the many speeches made about the precautions necessary in a matter of that moment, what was insinuated by the Lord Belhaven deserves to be taken notice of. His Lordship recommended it earnestly to the wisdom of the House, to consider how far the African and Indian trade might come in time to be affected by such a prohibitory law, in case it should take place; though in the same breath he allowed that at present they were not in possession of a foot of ground in the new world, nor of any island or port leading thither. This instance does cross the common proverb of *Scotchmen being wise behind the hand,* whereas this though too late would make it out, that we either are, or ought to be so, *before.*

The draft of the Act against the importation of victual from England and Ireland lies still dormant ; the House looking back with a wise affright upon the scarcity they laboured under some years ago. So that they proceeded to (*sic*)

That discharging all English, Irish and Foreign butter and cheese, except what should be imported in order to be exported again; which though awkwardly enough churned by our Lairds, yet the honest gentlemen fearing that they would never be welcome to their country wives, unless they carried an Act which so highly imported their dairy got it, after some amendments, marked a second reading and approved by a great majority; a copy of which Act, you may expect as soon as I can possibly procure it. The House stands adjourned to Tuesday next.10 o'clock being the 17th instant.

This evening a fleet of Dutch Herring Busses under convoy of a man-of-war came up the Frith. (*Draft.*)

LE MOYNE to ROBERT HARLEY.

1705, July 17—I most humbly beseech your lordship to take in consideration the miserable condition to which I am reduced being destitute of all help, without friends or money and now obliged to send for my "closes" rather to prolong my misery than to help it. I beseech your lordship to have mercy upon me, &c.

[WILLIAM GREG to ROBERT HARLEY.]

1705, July 17. Edinburgh—The 14th instant I acquainted you with a strange proceeding in Parliament, the day before, occasioned by a proposal of one Mr. Law, whom Fletcher was for confronting with

Dr. Chamberlen in full Parliament there to reason and debate the matter, so as the House might be the better satisfied, which of their proposals was the most practicable and advantageous. This the Earl of Roxburgh thought very unfair, to oblige a gentleman to come to the Bar, without first knowing whether he himself was willing to appear in so public a manner, especially since he had not dedicated his book to the Estates of Parliament, nor put his name to it; and therefore, his Lordship said, That Mr. Law or any gentleman, that had employed his time and thought for the good of his Country ought to be treated with good manners. The answer Fletcher made was, *That if anybody taxed him of ill manners, they were unmannerly and not he.* To which the Earl replied, *That what he had spoken was not pointed at any particular member, with a design to accuse him of want of manners, but was rather an appeal to the justice of the whole House, how hard it would be to stage a gentleman for his generous endeavours without his consent; but since that member fancied himself struck at, he might if he pleased, take it so.* Upon which Fletcher rose up and said, *I take it as I ought.* The Commissioner, as I said in my last, foreseeing that a challenge would ensue upon this unmannerly proceeding in his presence, gave orders, as soon as the House was up, to put them under arrest, to which Roxburgh readily submitted, and continued in his chamber where it was laid on. But Fletcher, whom the officer found at the tavern, alleged very artificially in order to make his escape, that he had certainly mistaken his man; he for his part having given no occasion for any such arrest, and therefore desired he would give himself to wait again upon the Commissioner and understand his pleasure aright, promising verily to stay till he returned. Whilst the wheedled officer was gone, Fletcher, who had sent the challenge, took coach immediately with his second Lord Charles Ker, went down to Leith, where he continued all the next day, expecting his adversary, who being very uneasy under his confinement whilst Fletcher was free, got friends to speak for him to the Commissioner, who at their request was prevailed with to order the arrest to be taken off. Upon which the Earl went also with his second, Mr. Baillie of Jerviswood, down to Leith about six o'clock in the evening when he found Fletcher at the place appointed. The seconds were for making up the business, but Fletcher insisting upon satisfaction for the affront offered him in Parliament, the Earl was willing to give it him in the usual way, had not Mr. Baillie stepped between them, and said that his Lordship having a great weakness in his right leg so that he could hardly stand, 'twas not to be expected that this quarrel could be decided by the sword and therefore desired some other way might be agreed on. Fletcher having foreseen that this objection would be started had provided a pair of pistols and desired very *cavalièrement* his Lordship to take his choice. But whilst Mr. Baillie was raising new difficulties as that his Lordship's weakness did equally disable him from firing on foot, as from pushing, they perceived at some distance a party of the Horse Guards that had been sent out in quest of them; the seconds glad of this handle to save the honour of their principals, fired the pistols in the air and returned hither.

I am heartily sorry that I am now to acquaint your Honour with a proceeding in Parliament to-day, which, though not so strange as the above mentioned, is of infinitely greater consequence to this Island.

The Country party having certain intelligence of the Duke of Queensberry being upon the road and fancying themselves not altogether unacquainted with the nature of the errand he came upon, were so alarmed at the news of his approach, that they were prevailed with by D[uke] H[amilton] to postpone the further consideration of proposals and prohibitory laws for one Sederunt, and endeavour what in them lay to baffle the measures of the Court, by rendering ineffectual and fruitless a journey so long wished for by those who wish well to the Succession and which now I am afraid is like to prove too late. For no sooner was the House called over this afternoon, but Duke Hamilton rose up and spoke to this purpose :—

This day twelvemonth, I had the honour to present to the House a noble Resolve, which being absolutely necessary then, I am of opinion another of the like nature will be no less so now : and it is this :—

That this House will not go to the nomination of the same Successor with England, till such time as we have a previous Treaty about our Commerce and other concerns with that nation; and that we will proceed to such limitations and conditions of Government as may best secure the independence and sovereignty of the Crown and Kingdom of Scotland.

A Resolve so directly opposite to what Her Majesty had recommended in her letter was briskly attacked by the Marquis of Annandale who said, He was sorry that in the front it began with the exclusion of a Protestant Successor. The Duke who thought himself obliged to vindicate his Resolve from so black an imputation said, That he wondered how anybody could pervert and wrest the natural sense of words as plain and obvious in themselves as that one and two make three : that it was not meant by them, to exclude a Protestant Successor simply, but only the same with England till we had a previous Treaty, and then and not till then was the time for going into their Succession : and that 'twas strange if 100 years' experience could not teach us wisdom, during which we had felt the fatal effects of English Councils and influence ; that this was the only opportunity left not only for bettering our condition and of saving us from slavery for ever.

There were several pretty warm speeches made upon this head, but the Duke and Marquis having engrossed most of the discourse for four hours together which were spent in the agitation of this important point, it was at last put to vote—Approve the Resolve, or not, and carried, Approve, by a majority of 43 votes. (*Draft.*)

JOHN CLARKE and ALEXANDER VALIERE.

1705, July 18. Whitehall—Protection to the above-named persons, who have occasion to travel into the country for their private affairs. Signed by Robert Harley.

[WILLIAM GREG to ROBERT HARLEY.]

1705, July 19. Edinburgh—In my last of the 17th I gave you an account of what passed in Parliament that day, which, I am now to acquaint you, was pitched upon by D[uke] H[amilton], both last year and this, as being his wedding-day, which he said before he went to the House he had observed to have always been lucky. This was modest to what his party said of him, when he opened the House, *That he was certainly inspired :* and so indeed he was if a torrent of talk had been an extraordinary gift. He treated Marquesses that day as disdainfully as if they had been his menial servants ; for besides the bantering expressions mentioned in my last, which he let fly at the Marquis of Annandale when he opposed his Resolve, by a long and handsome speech, I now remember further, this was a provoking *one, That he wondered to hear a long and strong speech end at last in a great empty nothing*; and after the Marquess of Montrose had made a short speech before he voted to this purpose, That he doubted not but he should be censured by a party in the House, for giving his vote against what he had voted for last year; but that as then he had good reasons for so doing, he had now more powerful ones to the contrary:—the Duke said, *I am not at all surprised at that noble Peer's unsteady principles, he has changed so often that we have a fair chance for his coming about right again next year.*

Thus far I flatter myself, I shall be believed; but if I should say, that, 'b' [*sic*, "the Duke himself" *crossed out in draft*] has been shrewdly suspected by his own party, since the Parliament met, I dare hardly expect to be equally credited though there be nothing more true.

There's a considerable party in *green* that are not only Q., but R. at whose head 'e' puts himself, who being lately in close cabal with 'b' the whole gang were extremely offended, that the latter was so much D. and taking 'e' by the hand, said, they would stand by him, though 'b,' who was but one man, should leave them. Whereupon he went out of the room in a huff, in hopes that some of those high flying gentlemen would have followed him but seeing they did not in haste, he went down to the Abbey whither half a dozen came, and after reasoning the matter more calmly together 'b' brought them over to his opinion, and still insisted, that theirs was too rigid, barefaced and declared.

To-morrow the Parliament meets again, when 'tis thought, they will resume the consideration of their Resolve concerning the Trade and Coin of the Nation, which they had postponed out of complaisance to the Duke, who had it been still to be given in, I believe the news we had yesterday from Flanders, would have marred it. (*Draft.*)

Sir C. Hedges to [Robert] Harley.

1705, July 23. Compton—I am glad Sir B. Granville stands so well with the Queen and Council, being of opinion, upon all that I heard of his business, that he was most unreasonably prosecuted. Mr. Tucker tells me the Lords want to know the reason for putting a stop to the exchange of prisoners till further order. You may please to acquaint them that the Commissioners for Sick and Wounded having proposed to carry over eight hundred French prisoners for five hundred English, and the Lords taking notice that the French fleet wanted seamen, and understanding also that the French did commonly stop the exchange boats when they thought our seamen were wanted here, though they had their own men delivered, and did frequently take that advantage, since by the method of exchange the French prisoners are first sent over, it was thought fit to stop the exchange for the present.

I am told that Mr. White member for Chippenham is dead.

The Duke of Newcastle to [Robert] Harley, in London.

1705, July 23. Haughton—The Duke of Marlborough has done enough to silence even envy and malice itself, if some men were not destined into the hospital of the incurables. I never saw a pamphlet stuffed with more gull, more falsehoods, and indeed more trivial stuff, the greatest part of it. Indeed the style of this scandalous libel is as imperious as King John himself, full of groundless assertions, but sure he was as short-sighted as when he sent the fair one to be imprisoned by you, for there is a general detestation against the book.

Henry Guy to [Robert Harley].

1705, July 24. Earl's Court—I find that Mr. Poley is coming presently from Hanover and leaves no one there but a Dutch secretary whom you know. I did last week trouble you with a letter to him to Mr. William Pulteney, in which was a bill of exchange. I have sent another letter to him for Mr. Pulteney this post. I entreat you to recommend to Mr. Poley that those letters be delivered to Mr. Pulteney when he comes thither, because mine are to hasten him over to the Parliament here.

A. [Lady] Pye to Abigail Harley, at Auditor Harley's at Eywood.

1705, July 25. Derby—All counties have suffered by this long drought, yours must yet more by fruit and hops; this is no time for tenants and landlords together. It is well we have victory abroad for the charge [we] are at. Money is a scarce commodity, excepting where good places help out. Our countryman Mr. Cook [Coke?] since his [election] is not so revered by the High Church, because he had so much declared against it. It is thought they will endeavour to oppose him against next choice, but that is a great way off if Her Majesty lets them sit their full time as the last did. Yesterday heard Mr. Cook was talked to marry Mrs. Winchcomb, Mrs. Packer's sister.

The Duke of Marlborough to Lord [Portland?].

1705, July 27. Vlierbeek—I do not doubt but that Lieutenant General Hompesch has given you an account of all the particularities of our good success in entering the lines, and beating those troops that came to oppose us.

As you know that I have no thought, but of what may be good for the common cause, so I should be glad to hear from you, what the States General wishes to have done, and how far they can enable me to do it; by which knowledge, I should be the better able to press it forward here. Pray let me hear from you some times, and let me have your own thoughts, which I promise you shall be known to nobody but myself.

Our Army is in great heart but you know this country is such, that it is very hard to force an enemy to fight when he has no mind to it. My thoughts at present are very much employed to be master of Louvain, it being a very proper place to have our magazine for bread, for as yet we are forced to have it from Liége, which is very hazardous, the enemy having a great garrison at Namur, and Jean another troublesome place behind us.

Henry St. John to Robert Harley.

July 27. Whitehall—I have received a letter from Captain Wentworth, and have given directions for his being supplied with the necessaries demanded &c. *Signed.*

Henry St. John to

1705, July 28. Whitehall—Reverend Sir

Δημόδοκ' ἔξοχα δὴ σε βροτῶν αἰνίζομ' ἀπάντων
Ἤ σε γε Μοῦσ' ἐδίδαξε Διὸς Παῖς, ἤ σε γ' Ἀπόλλων.

The compliment Ulysses made Demodocus, you will give me leave to begin my letter with. He sang the Grecian heroes, and was equal to the task, but our age has the advantage of them in having produced a greater Captain and a better Poet.

You have done me an honour I did not deserve in dedicating your Ἀνακρεων Χριστιανὸς to me, I shall be very happy if it lies in my power to be useful to you, I am sure I shall be so to the world in encouraging your muse, to which end I desire you to accept of some wine which I have just received from Portugal.

Οἴνου δε μηκέτ' ὄντος οὐκ ἔστιν Κύπρις
Οὐδ' ἄλλο τέρπνὸν οὐδὲν ἀνθρώπους ἔτι.

Eu
Ba
Vi
y.

[*Note by recipient.*]

Ἔξοχα δὴ σε βροτῶν, ὦ " Ὅμηρ, αἰνίζομ " κ. τ. λ.
Te longe supra reliquos laudamus, Homere!
Seu te Calliope docuit, seu major Apollo.

[Daniel De Foe] to Robert Harley.

1705, July 30. Crediton—I do myself the honour to acquaint you that I reached this town yesterday, though extremely fatigued with the violent heat, but this country has been cooled with plentiful rain, and is now very refreshing.

I have nothing to complain of in the success of my design, except in Dorsetshire, where the exceeding harmony between the Dissenters and the Low Church, the disposition of the former to peace one with another, and of the latter to moderation make my remarks something useless The only two warm people, Colonel Strangeways and Sir N. Napier, have acted with more caution and less success than ever, and had Lieutenant General Earle and T. Freak put in for the county they had carried it beyond all possibility of miscarriage.

The Dissenters are indeed too easy, and do not struggle, having met with no ill-treatment to move them, and particularly the inferior Clergy are the most temperate here of any place I know, a certain proof that the different temper of other counties is owing (at least much of it) to their inflaming the gentry. At Salisbury 'tis quite another thing, the Bishop's candidate for the town, Mr. Harris, lost it, and the Bishop's friends were very ill treated by the Clergy at the County election. The Bishop's gentlemen, the Dukes of Somerset and Bolton, received strange insults, and his Grace of Somerset was insulted in the streets of Salisbury by the mob.

Here also things are in terrible disorder. The election of Honiton is an abridgement of Coventry and F. Gwyn has particularly distinguished himself. In Exeter, the conquest the Bishop made over his clergy, and the further improvement his lordship makes of his victory renders him formidable, and exceedingly chagrins the party; but his lordship, as they say, still declaring himself for the Occasional Bill, comforts them

Fisher, the former representative of the clergy, was expelled by the Bishop last week for want of institution and induction, and had a severe admonition given him to be resident at a small cure he has in the country, on pain of suspension. Several others of the High Church Clergy feel the effect of his lordship's displeasure, and are under like prosecution.

All agree here, had my Lord Treasurer given his letter to the Bishop to have set up his son, Sir Edward Seymour had lost it here. If that had happened the party had received such a blow they would never have recovered.

I go this day to Exeter again to furnish my informations at that place, and thence to Plymouth; shall come round by the north coast of this country, and be at Tiverton in about ten days, where the honour of a letter from you would be a satisfaction and encouragement, directed to Alex. G[oldsmi]th, in a cover to the Reverend Mr. Josiah Eveleigh, at Mr. Francis Bere, Merchant in Tiverton. I met an express, and two Lisbon mails on the road Friday last, some little particular of that affair other than the prints inform would furnish me with means to let them know I shall be useful; for all our party here are politicians especially the Parsons (God bless us) who once a week settle the conscience, twice a week the State, and it could not but afford me some speculation to see at this place, where the Dissenting parson is my friend, the post coming in on Sunday morning, the people devoutly resort to the newshouse, as they call it, first, and then to Church.

I am almost ashamed to tell you how expensive I am, and yet not extravagant, but I am resolved not to balk the design, leaving all things of the sort to your kindness, and to judge by the effect, wherefore having a little supply of my own at Plymouth, I forbear to press you on that head, if you please to convey to Kingsland what you think convenient for the support of this affair, against I may reach Bristol. I shall then be obliged to draw, and my wife, who is my faithful steward, will not diminish it one penny. I have nothing more worth your notice.

[WILLIAM GREG to ROBERT HARLEY.]

1705, July 31. Edinburgh—When the necessity of a grand-aunt's affairs, left desolate and helpless by the death of her husband, obliged me indispensably to make an excursion for some days, which terminate in this, I remember to have undertaken to send though late, an account of what should pass in my absence; but the gentleman whom I had bespoken for that end having been obliged to go out of town the next day and not yet returned, I should be hard put to it what apology to make, had I a less favourable judge to deal with.

Being just come back, as the post was going off, I can only acquaint you, that this day there was a Resolve given in by the same hand with that of the 17th namely: That this House will not enter upon a Treaty with England before they have settled the necessary limitations and conditions of Government. Which Resolve was only carried by 3 votes. Fletcher made a speech in favour of the Prince of Prussia. (*Draft.*)

The DUKE OF NEWCASTLE to [ROBERT HARLEY].

1705, August 1. Welbeck—I am sure the new Speaker will need
more assistance than the new Secretary though loaded with both
provinces. I question not our Condé de Peterborough will not be out
rhodomontado'd by any Don of 'em all.

The same letters which told me ten days ago of Mr. Smith's being
fixed upon for Speaker said the Parliament would sit the beginning of
November. If the business of the Session be dispatched early I hope to
get the Queen's leave to come down to my usual exercises, the want of
taking which earlier has been the reason my indisposition has been so
long troublesome to me; and I think I may say the Privy Seals have met
with a quicker dispatch after they came hither than they did for many
years when the seal was in town.

[WILLIAM GREG to ROBERT HARLEY.]

1705, August 2. Edinburgh—When I acquainted you the 31st past
with Fletcher's having made a speech in favour of the Prince of Prussia,
it ought naturally to have been ushered in with the Resolve that was
calculated to make way for it. But the hurry I was in upon my return
to my post hindered me from narrating matters in their order and extent;
which I hope your wonted goodness and indulgence will easily pardon.
The Resolve was couched in these or the like terms, viz. :—

That this House will not treat with England before they rescind the
prohibitory laws lately passed in the Parliament of that Kingdom, against
the subjects of the Kingdom of Scotland.

The dire Decree (as they call it here) against the Scots was the said
gentleman's darling theme of declamation, which he opened with all the
rhetorical display he was master of; and after he had taken asunder the
Act and railed plentifully at each paragraph thereof, he concluded, That
there was no way left to make the Scots a happy people, but by sepa-
rating from England and setting up a King of their own : *not* K. J[ames]
the 8th (or rather the St. Germain gentleman), because he would never
content himself with Scotland alone, unless endeavours were used to
bring England also under his obedience, nor could we be secure from
those threatening inconveniences which we so happily escaped under his
father's reign : *not* one of the House of Hanover, because they maintain
Consubstantiation which to him was as absurd as Transubstantiation :
and therefore we ought to choose the Prince of Prussia, who was of our
religion, and able besides, by his powerful interest abroad, to secure us
from any uneasiness from a jealous neighbour.

As the M. of A[nnandale] has all along appeared a champion for the
Court, and consequently lost ground with a set of gentlemen who would
pass for the only Patriots, he seemed ambitious of regaining it, when he said
last Sederunt, that if England could not be brought to reasonable terms,
he would go sword in hand into the field and force them to it. This
expression savoured too much of the Hero, to be let pass easily by the
heroic Duke, who took him up roundly, saying, That he believed he
might go sooner into the Union than his Lordship would do into the
field.

George Tollet to Robert Harley.

1705, August 4—Is informed the Bishop of Meath is at the point of death. Craves leave to put two names before him, namely Dr. St. George Ash, Bishop of Clogher, and Dr. Edward Smith, Bishop of Down and Connor, as fit to succeed to the bishopric.

The Earl of Westmeath to the Duke of Ormond.

[1705, August 4, received]—I make bold to mind you to speak to Mr. Secretary Harley for a pass to Holland for myself and my son and two servants, having no other business but to settle my son there for his education.

Sir Nathan Wright, Lord Keeper, to Robert Harley.

1705, August 4. Powys House.—I desire your favour to excuse me from attending the Queen to morrow in Council. My dear wife is buried but three days since, and myself indisposed and not fit for business.

My son, the clerk of the Crown in Chancery, is desirous to retire from business with the Queen's permission in favour of Mr. Francis Hayes, of the Inner Temple, well qualified and older than my son; so that what in effect is desired is no more than to exchange one life for another that is older.

I sent you the warrant for Mr. Samuel Birch to be Attorney General for Wales in the room of his brother Serjeant Birch, which you will please to lay before the Queen, when you shall think proper.

G. Granville to [Robert Harley].

1705, August 4—I have had the honour to wait upon my Lord Treasurer several times since you was pleased to acquaint me that his Lordship had something to offer to me. He has however continued silent and I remain under the same suspense in which he has thought fit to keep me for almost three years.

I am now informed that a certain undertaker in our county, who pretends to direct the frowns and smiles of the ministers as he pleases, has engaged to remove me from my small government there, and has promised it to one of his creatures. And in the very instant of time when I have been made to expect the favour of the Court, I am threatened with its displeasure. It will be a very great surprise to me if I should find your friendship less powerful than his enmity, and therefore from the assurances you have been pleased to give me, I find myself more inclined to hope, than to apprehend. But which way soever it is to happen, I wish it were once determined, for to be out of doubt, is in a great measure to be out of pains.

It is so well known to everybody how much I have devoted myself personally to your service, that I flatter myself you will confound my interest a little with your own, since the injuries that are offered to our friends are so many affronts to ourselves; and I should be sorry, especially at this time, that the world should have any occasion to reflect that you want power to protect a man who has so publicly and upon all occasions avowed himself with the greatest zeal and respect your &c.

The Duke of Newcastle to Robert Harley.

1705, August 6. Welbeck—As to Mr. William Cooke's intention to contest Harley's nomination of a clerk of the signet. Is glad the Duke of Marlborough will send for the Prussian and Palatine troops, for nothing of consequence is to be expected from General Lewis, and the Duke's army should be made as strong as possible.

[William Greg to Robert Harley.]

1705, August 4. Edinburgh—Yesterday the Parliament went upon Trade, in pursuance of the proposal contained in the minutes of the 2nd here enclosed, and after some time spent in debating which branch of it should fall first under their consideration, 'twas at length agreed to enter upon that of the Fishery as what might be made the most beneficial to the nation, if rightly managed; in order whereunto 'twas proposed, whether it would be best to rouse the Herring with Scotch or Foreign salt. But the House being mightily divided in their sentiments about it, to end all further debate, a Vote was stated—Rouse the Herring with Scotch or Foreign salt, and it carried,—Foreign salt.

Then the House for encouraging the Export, took into their consideration, what drawback should be allowed upon white Fish and how much upon Herrings and 'twas only proposed, that 10*l.* Scots should be allowed upon the barrel of the former and 4*l.* Scots upon the barrel of red Herring and 3*l.* upon buss Herring. (*Draft.*)

Henry Gibbs, Alderman of Canterbury, to Robert Harley.

1705, August 6. Canterbury—Forwards affidavits sworn before George Hall, the mayor, and himself, of Andrew Gentil of Holy Cross, Westgate in Canterbury, leather dresser, and Jean Misaubin, schoolmaster there, concerning boastful words spoken by one M. Chevalier and other French prisoners there and at Dover.

Henry St. John to Robert Harley.

1705, August 8. Whitehall—Had received the petition of three persons pressed at Derby who had gone over to the regiment in Ireland; and had written to the mayor of Derby on the subject, from whose answer it appeared that these men did not come within the terms of the Act relating to enlistments. As to the alleged absences from duty of some of the regimental chaplains at Gibraltar, had received from there a return of those with their regiments and of those absent. Comments on the petitions of Mary Westcoat, Ann her daughter, and others. *Signed.*

G. Granville to Robert Harley.

1705, August 8—Expressing in elaborate terms his gratitude for some favour received.

William Greg to Robert Harley.

1705, August 9. Edinburgh—I omitted to write last post, though the Parliament sat that day, in regard what passed then in the House would not afford material enough for a letter, the whole Sederunt having been taken up in adjusting the several drawbacks to be allowed upon Herrings and white Fish, which after a long debate, were agreed to, thus : 24*l.* Scots upon the last of Red-herrings to be exported ; 18*l.* upon Buss-herrings, and 9*l.* upon Boat-herrings and all white Fish, in general out of Her Majesty's Customs, which 'tis feared will be thereby impaired unless an equivalent be granted, which the Court laboured hard for, but without success.

Yesterday the House was upon the same Act, which, after adding several clauses, they finished and then proceeded to consider the Draft of an Act presented by the Duke of Hamilton for erecting a Council of Trade, which was only marked a first reading, the further consideration thereof being put off till to-day when the Parliament met again with a design to have finished the same ; but little or no progress was made therein except what passed with respect to the nomination of the Commissioners who appear to compose the said Council of Trade. The Court were for giving the Queen the nomination of them, and the Country party stood up for the Parliament, so that after a great deal of reasoning about that matter, it was at last put to the Vote, and the Country carried it against the Court by 11 votes.

To-morrow the Parliament meets again in order to determine the number of the Commissioners and their several salaries.

I beg leave to send with the minutes of the 3rd instant a printed list of the members of Parliament, which came out only to-day, as appears by the date, and yet I hope the written one, I had the honour to send you the 12th past, will be found to agree pretty well with it, the most material difference being in the addition of two members for the shire of Ross, which were not in mine, and I still much question whether they ought to be there at all, a representative for a Northern county of my acquaintance having cancelled them with his own hand, when I borrowed of him the Rolls as they stood last Session. (*Draft.*)

Hugh Stafford to All Constables and other officers in the County of Devon and also to Charles Sugg.

1705, August 9—Whereas, I have received information against Daniel De Foe for spreading and publishing divers seditious and scandalous Libels and false news to the great disturbance of the peace of this Kingdom, and that he is a person of ill fame and behaviour, and is now lurking within some or one of your parishes, tythings, or precincts :—

These are in her Majesty's name to will and require you and every of you, on sight hereof, to make diligent privy search within your said parishes, tythings and precincts, in all suspicious houses and places within the same, and to be assistant to the said Charles Sugg in searching for and apprehending the said Daniel De Foe, and when found and apprehended forthwith to bring him before me to be examined concerning the premises, and to be dealt with as the Law directs, hereof you and every of you may not fail at your utmost peril. (*Signed.*)

"Pray, Sir, Do not lose this paper," is written by De Foe at foot of the above. [*See* Aug. 14 *post.*]

The Earl of Galway to [Robert] Harley.

1705, August 9–20. Montemor—I am going to Elvas to hasten the preparations for the siege of Badajos, which is absolutely necessary for the conquest of the province of Andalusia, which I always esteemed the only way to attain the ends of this expedition; by that we become at once masters of the wealth of Spain and of the key of trade. I am sensible I shall meet with great difficulties, but if I cannot bring the Portuguese to take the field this autumn, I expect to do no good with them. The greatest opposition I meet with in everything is always from Mr. Fagel, who is supported and encouraged in it by the adverse party to the alliance, so you may judge how the service is likely to go on here. Lord Peterborough sailed from Gibraltar the 24th with a fair wind. All things seem very well disposed for him in Catalonia.

Henry St. John to [Robert] Harley.

1705, August 10—An official letter concerning the memorials of Major-General Cunningham and Major Jones; and the supply of horses to the armies abroad and the charges incident thereto.

Robert Harley to the Earl of Sunderland.

1705, August 10—Some private suggestions and advice on Sunderland's mission to Vienna. Count Wratislaw is a growing favourite and like to have much credit with the Emperor; also Baron Szeitern (?). Whatever causes for dissatisfaction these men may have given us, his lordship may be trusted to treat them with that urbanity of which he is so much master, and so render them less hurtful.

Henry St. John to Robert Harley].

1705, August 11. Whitehall—I was a little concerned yesterday at what you told me just as I went away. I would not be guilty of any irregularity even in the most trivial matter of form, and whilst you are Secretary I should not forgive myself if I committed any indecency. I find several notifications of the Queen's pleasure about commissions, signed by me, when it was the Queen that gave the directions herself, and in the books I see the same method was observed before I came in. I look on the bit of paper I sign to be nothing more than a voucher to the officer that goes to desire his commission may be prepared, that he tells truth when he says the Queen or Prince has granted it to him, which makes it not so ridiculous as to deserve laughter.

Should I pretend to signify the Queen's pleasure to a Secretary of State, I should be a coxcomb. However, I will take care to have the form altered for the future. Forgive, dear Master, this trouble and believe you have not in the world a more faithful sincere friend and humble servant than &c.

Robert Price, Baron of the Exchequer, to [Robert] Harley, at Whitehall.

1705, August 11. Exeter—We have a comical high sheriff here, Mr. David Long, who was bred a farmer, but worth thirty or forty thousand pounds. He is very honest and generous, and drinks to the Queen by the name of " the good old gentlewoman, two times with all my heart." He does not drink out of bottles, but pulchers, as he terms them, that is great jars of claret, and that is his usual way of living.

I hear Justice Nevill is dead. I have no friend but yourself and if I might have a remove to the Common Pleas it would be to my advantage. All the Judges but the Chiefs and Justice Gold have passed first through the Exchequer before they came to other Courts. I have by your favour more than I merit and am ashamed to make this application.

Last night we had such a hurricane here that it was next to the great wind and lasted 5 or 6 hours. · God send good news from sea !

[WILLIAM GREG to ROBERT HARLEY.*]

1705, August 11. Edinburgh—When I had the honour to send you, the day before yesterday, a printed list of the members of Parliament, I began to blame myself for over hastily anticipating it by the written one I sent the 12th past, as fearing mine had been less exact.

But yesterday I was confirmed in my conjecture concerning the two supernumerary representatives for the shire of Ross, when being in the Parliament House, I heard the Rolls called over twice but neither of the gentlemen left out in my list once named.

All the progress made yesterday in the Act for a Council of Trade was only the fixing the number of Commissioners to twenty one, whereof seven are to be chosen out of the Lords, and the like number out of the Barons and Boroughs, and of these three Estates seven make a Quorum. This is to be done the 14th instant, to which day the House stands adjourned. But lest they should not meet again in the same giving humour they happened to be in yesterday, a couple of authors came to be considered for good services to their native country: and these were, Mr. Hodges who, besides the 400l. sterling ordered him, might also have expected, had he been here, the thanks of the House, which Mr. Anderson, the other champion, had, together with a promise of the like reward, which, in the present low ebb of the Treasury, cannot be so readily paid as was the tribute of thanks. Mr. Atwood's book, which gave occasion to the latter of these gentlemen to draw his pen, is ordered to be burnt by the hand of the hangman.

Though I be very sensible how little my letters deserve to be acknowledged, yet for one to be in doubt for two months, (in which time I have written eighteen from this place) your Honour will allow to be no small pain. I covered every one of them according to your direction, which I will continue to do, as often as anything passes here worth your knowing.

[WILLIAM GREG to ROBERT HARLEY.]

1705, August 14. Edinburgh—In my last of the 11th instant, I had the honour to acquaint you that this day the Parliament was to proceed to the nomination of the Commissioners of the Council of Trade, for whose names I beg leave to refer your Honour to the other leaf.

* This is copied from the original letter received by Harley. A draft of it in Greg's handwriting, slightly differing in forms of expression, is among the other drafts of his letters from Edinburgh which are here printed. The other original letters from Edinburgh do not appear to have been preserved. The drafts were probably seized with the rest of Greg's papers in January 1708, when he was tried for high treason.

Whilst they were going upon the said nomination, 'twas pretty remarkable that the Barons stayed in the House, whilst the Lords and Boroughs withdrew, the former into the Session House, and the latter into the outer House, where the Advocates plead.

In nothing has the Duke of Queensberry bestirred himself more since he came down, than in this affair, he having gone about both yesterday and this forenoon soliciting in favour of the Court, which has carried the day, notwithstanding Duke Hamilton's endeavours to the contrary, at which he seems to be so nettled, that I find some are of opinion, he may be attempted to lay hold on this handle for trumping up the plot again. Be it as it will this day's method of proceeding promises a like success to the Court, when a Treaty of Union shall be considered.

I humbly beg leave to send your Honour the enclosed mock Acts, which some say were sent down from London, though others are of opinion that they have been framed here. They are so very satirical and severe that I was some time in suspense, whether I should presume or not to trouble you with such impertinences, and nothing certainly could have determined me but an ambition to approve my diligence, were [it] only in blotting paper, and what I have written hitherto will, I fear, be thought little better. (*Draft.*)

[DANIEL DE FOE] to ROBERT HARLEY.

1705, August 14th. Tiverton—I received but this day the honour of yours at Tiverton. Your concern for me fills me with grateful thoughts how to render myself a yet more suitable subject for so much goodness, and encourages me to bear up under the desperate resolutions taken to ruin me.

Providence, and some dexterity of conduct (pardon my vanity), have hitherto rendered all the measures of the party impotent and unsuccessful, and yet I have not omitted one part of my work, nor balked one town I purposed to call at, Barnstaple excepted. I cannot, however, but divert you with the short history of this matter.

The miscarriage at Weymouth happened by such a casualty as no man could foresee. My letters directed for the friend now with me called Capt. Turner, to be left at Weymouth, were taken up by one Capt. Turner, Commander of a Guernsey privateer, then in that port. The ignorant tar, when he found things written dark and unintelligible, shows them to all the town ; at our coming however, he restores the letters, drank a pint of wine with us, and calls for one himself, which it seems afterwards he went away and never paid for. The people of the house demanding money for it next day put him in a fret and that vented itself in his railing at this letter all about town, till the Mayor sent for him ; the imperfect account he gave filled the Mayor's as (*sic*) foolish head with jealousies; and the Assizes being at Dorchester away he runs to the Judges, and gets a summons for Mr. Fenner, the Dissenting Minister, and two or three more whom I had visited, and carries them to Dorchester, where the Judge, whose name I think is Price, examined them and dismissed them.

But this blunder has had a worse effect since,—when I came to Exeter and having appeared publicly among my friends, and being after at Crediton a day or two, the party thought I was gone. One of the Aldermen blustered that he was sorry he did not take me up and list me for a soldier, Colonel Britton's regiment being there.

At my return I appeared publicly, walked several times on the walks of the church, called the Parade of the party, went to the church, the bowling green, the coffee house &c. with some of the principal of the citizens, and Mr. Alderman and his brethren took no notice of it.

I went from thence to Totnes, Dartmouth, and Plymouth, and the day before I went the Judges came to town.

The party then took heart, and as I understand applied to Mr. Justice Price who, in his charge to the Grand Jury, tells them there are several seditious persons come down into the country spreading libels, &c., and embroiling the people, and advises the justices to apprehend them. The first effect of this was that at Crediton a country justice grants the enclosed warrant [see Aug. 9, ante] against me, and searches the town with constables, and particularly the Dissenting minister's house. But I was then at Liskeard in Cornwall.

The first account of this I met with at Bideford, where some gentlemen coming into town from the Assizes, told the people the Judge had named me to the Grand Jury and given directions to apprehend me, wherever I might be found.

By this report I had been insulted in Bideford the next morning. But the mayor being out of town, the next principal magistrate whom they call a justice, as having been mayor the year before, was my particular friend, and here was the first and only time I showed your Pass, taking the hint from your letter of using it with caution. This so encouraged the magistrate and all my friends, that I might have assured myself here of protection, and the measures of the other party in the town seemed entirely broke. But I was privately informed that they had sent away a messenger express to have me stopped at Barnstaple as I came along. Had not the danger of my own private affairs and the warrant from London, being roused by this noise, lain a little upon my thoughts I had more publicly ventured the worst effects of their malice; but not knowing what of that sort might be in it I avoided Barnstaple and having a particular friend a S. T. P. Dissenter, whom I carried with me all this circuit from Exeter, I have visited every town so securely by being lodged among friends, that I am now under the nose of the justices concerned in the enclosed warrant, and yet out of their danger.

To-morrow I leave this town and county, and presuming your directions for my return proceed from your apprehensions of my personal hazards and are the effect of that concern for me which I can never enough acknowledge, and not from an alteration in your opinion or design of having this work done, I proceed with resolution, through more difficulties than these, to pursue all the orders I shall at any time receive from you. The success I have had in this part I persuade myself will fully satisfy you as it has encouraged me to say that "Seymskeyes Western Empire" may with much ease be overthrown and his successor defeated, and had I come here sooner by half a year it had felt a great blow ere now. As to apprehensions of my friend who is with me betraying me I assure you of the contrary. Nor are you betrayed to him, nor does he suspect I correspond with you, or have the honour to converse with you. I am not serving a master I have so little value for, you may depend upon me, that neither by fraud or folly the confidence you are pleased to place in me shall ever be disappointed.

I wrote you from Exeter, which I hope is come safe; in that I took the freedom to mention a supply; indeed I have been more expensive here than I expected, but it has been purely to perfect the work, and I think I may say I have a perfect skeleton of this part of England, and a settled correspondence in every town and corner of it.

I go directly to the Bath, where my companion leaves me, and Mr. Davis, my brother in law, who has the honour to wait on you, comes to me with another friend, who will travel into the North with me.

By my brother, anything you please to convey to my wife will come safe, but rather by bill than in specie and sealed, because I have learnt in all these things to make agents without acquainting them with particulars.

I humbly entreat your letter which Mr. Davis will bring me to the Bath, and so no danger of a miscarriage, and till then forbear troubling you any further.

[Captain JOHN OGILVIE] to ROBERT BRYAN [HARLEY], merchant in London.

1705, August 14 [New Style ?]. Hamburg—Since my last I have got a great deal of insight in the thread you are desirous to be informed of. In short it is of the deepest consequence and regards your country and not the ancient city. You will admire how I should come to know a thing that regards another place than the ancient city but it is matter of fact and I am sure of it. I will write nothing of it till I come to Holland. I hope to part from this in ten days; I could wish to be but one even with you. Depend upon it there will be strange negotiations this winter with some in your country, I am afraid to mention to you what I know. I beg of you let nobody see this letter, not your best friend, nor must you communicate it to your mistress as yet for if it take vent all is spoilt. Only keep your mind to yourself for the space of two months, but I must tell you that you may thank God you did gain the battle of Blenheim. Be not impatient for I will not write my mind till I come to Holland.

H. ST. JOHN to [ROBERT HARLEY].

1705, August 14. Bucklebury—Dear Master, I send you a draught of a report on the mine adventurers' petition; I have delayed it as long as possible, and when you have corrected what you think fit, it will be time to send it in form to you.

[P.S.]—I will be at Windsor on Saturday and have given directions to Mr. Lynn if the orders and other papers cannot otherwise be dispatched in time to send for me, and I'll be in half a day in London.

ROBERT HARLEY to the Hon. BARON PRICE.

1705, Aug. 14—As to the Speaker those gentlemen who like not Mr. Smith have nobody to thank but themselves; they might have had another, the Solicitor [Harcourt], but they would not come in to him, nor to any one else. As to your humble servant, I beg you to bear that down all you can, for I ran the hazard of my life last time, and having once escaped with a few scratches I don't desire to go again into the bear garden. (Copy.)

[WILLIAM GREG to ROBERT HARLEY.]

1705, August 16. Edinburgh—Yesterday the Parliament met about the usual hour, and after some amendments in the minutes of the preceding Sederunt, the Earl of Rothes moved, that the draft of an Act he had given in the first instant, for choosing all officers of State, &c. Privy Councillors, and Lords of the Session &c. by Parliament, after her Majesty's decease, might be taken into the consideration of the house, before all other business. It was read accordingly, but no further progress made therein; Mr. Fletcher having stood up, and with my Lord Rothes's allowance, obtained a reading to his overture for limitations upon the successor, which are much the same with those he gave in about two years ago, but a little more methodically digested, being now divided into twelve articles, and therefore not unfitly called by some twelve *Tabulæ*; and every whit as sacred and inviolable too, if the gentleman's word had been taken for it. But it proved no small mortification to him to find, after he had harangued the house above half an hour and spoken particularly to each of his twelve limitations, that even though the whole house was for limitations, yet few or none did approve his overture (a copy whereof you have here enclosed) which made him say, that he was sorry to find such a profound silence in the house at the proposing of limitations, when to his knowledge, out of it, many had shewn that it was their earnest wish and desire, they should be brought in. He, however, endeavoured all he could to carry them by way of *claim of right*, and not by an Act of Parliament, which he said was leaning upon a shadow and cheating the nation; whereas were they turned into a *claim of right*, no subsequent Parliament could annul or repeal it. No arguments used by the Court party to shew a claim of right impracticable in the present circumstances of the kingdom, whilst her Majesty was alive, could prevail with him to drop what he had once advanced, but on the contrary, he showed himself the more stiff and tenacious; alleging in favour of his limitations, by way of claim of right, the Magna Charta, which being the basis and foundation of English liberties, the people he said forced a king then actually upon the throne to grant.

This debate, whether the house should go upon the limitations by way of an Act of Parliament, or by way of claim of right, lasted four full hours, and after all, was let fall, the latter way being found altogether unfeasible, which Fletcher perceiving was resolved to turn the mouth of the cannon upon his own party, and since he could not carry his limitations in his own way, in my hearing, he said : *well is it so ; I'll serve them a trick for it*. And therefore out of malice and spite dropped his limitations, and went into the draft of an Act presented by the Lord Belhaven for regulating the present constitution, which Act, together with that given in by the Earl of Rothes, was marked a first reading, and a controversy arising which of the two should be preferred next Sederunt, that was put to the vote, and my Lord Rothes's carried it. Accordingly it was brought in this day before all other business, but Mr. Fletcher thought to have diverted it by renewing the controversy about his overture, whereupon the Earl of Stair, who is allowed to be the best spokesman in the house, took him roundly up, saying, that Mr. Fletcher was resolved to do by his limitations as the ape did by her young ones, that grasped them so fast, till at last she stifled them ; which comparison did so throw him off the hooks, that he rose up and recriminated upon the Earl thus, that his Lordship stretched the prerogative till it had well nigh cracked, when he opened the declaration for arbitrary power. These unhandsome reflections were quickly put an end to by the Chancellor, who moved, that the house might proceed to consider my Lord Rothes's Act, paragraph by paragraph, which they went through and after several amendments and reasoning thereupon it was put to the vote, whether after the decease of her Majesty without heirs of her body her successor to the crown of Scotland [England *in draft.* *See Aug.* 21], being at the same time King of England, the officers of State, Privy Councillors, the Lords of the Session and Justiciary should be named by the King with advice and consent of the Estates in Parliament, or by the Estates in Parliament assembled, and it carried, *By the Estates in Parliament,* by a majority of twenty three votes.

This is a short account of what passed in Parliament both yesterday and today, where I was present both Sederunts.

The Parliament is adjourned to Tuesday next, by reason of the Commissioner's indisposition, which the Chancellor signified to the house.

SAMUEL LYNN to SECRETARY HARLEY.

1705, August 17—Concerning the wreck of the transport *Mary* bound for Jamaica, wherein forty eight soldiers had been drowned, whose places are to be supplied from the Portsmouth garrison. Encloses copy of a letter from Capt. Samuel Atkinson, of the Transport Office, about the refitting of the ship.

The ARCHBISHOP OF CANTERBURY to ROBERT HARLEY, at Whitehall.

1705, August 17—Enclosing a paper from the Commissioners for redemption of captives at Machane, from which it would appear that the Moors claimed for thirty two English captives sent home twenty six barrels of powder and sixteen slaves; and that for thirty four French Protestants to be redeemed there were due to the Moors thirty two barrels of powder, seventeen slaves, and three thousand four hundred gunlocks.

M. CROWE to the DUKE OF NEWCASTLE.

1705, August 19-30. Genoa—Nothing will make better blood than a hearty bottle of Hermitage, so sends him a present of wine, and reports the movements of the British fleet off the coast of Spain.

The DUKE OF NEWCASTLE to [ROBERT HARLEY].

1705, August 20. Haughton—I return you my most sincere thanks for both yours. 'Tis very melancholy to see any prospect of there not being so good a harmony between all the Confederates as has been, but all the world must do Her Majesty this right, that she has done her share or more in all parts of Europe, and some of the Confederates have done theirs so ill, not to give it a harder name. A French gentleman, one M. Rosigad, who was some time governor to the Duke of Somerset and the late Lord Anglesey, was with me on the 9th instant and wrote me a letter a day or two after, that the Deputies of the States had frustrated my Lord Marlborough's designs and opposed fighting the French, upon which his Grace was very angry, or to this effect. I was then a little surprised when there were no foreign packets, that there should be such a surmise. I did once design to have sent you the letter, but that I thought you would laugh at me for a country fool that believed all I was told; and if I find it, when I come to Welbeck I will send it to you. If you have any occasion to mention this to anybody I desire you will keep M. Rosigad's name private though he did not write it to me as a secret, and I only mention it now to show that some people had an expectation of this some time before.

I came to this place to stag hunt, and was twelve hours on horseback which has given me such a bile, that I am easy in no posture but in bed. I beg your pardon for troubling you with it, but 'tis to show you the reason why this is not in my own hand.

I hear my Lord Keeper [Wright] is whitening the sashes of his windows and sprucing up his house, I question he does not do it to repair my house, but to be a sparkish widower to bring some lady thither. *Signed.*

[WILLIAM GREG to ROBERT HARLEY.]

1705, August 21. Edinburgh—Before I presume [to] trouble your honour with an account of this day's proceedings in Parliament, I am to beg pardon for a false transposition in my last of the 16th towards the latter end; when in stating the vote about the choosing the officers of State &c., after her Majesty's decease without heirs of her body, instead of saying, *her successor to the crown of Scotland, being at the same time King or Queen of England,* I find upon review to have said, *her successor to the crown of England,* &c. which I humbly conceive alters the reason of the thing, and therefore hope the escape will be imputed to the haste I was in towards the close of my letter, which was not in the post house before I perceived my mistake, but I was fain to let it pass as it was or else lose the post, the house having sat late that day.

Mr. Fletcher having failed in his attempts against the crown (as I acquainted you the 16th instant) turned them to-day against the church: which gave occasion to the Chancellor to say very justly of him, that he was *Athanasius contra totum mundum.* This assuming gentleman, as he was never yet pleased with any model of civil government, so neither the church must in her turn escape his censure. And accordingly he attacked her in one of her most sensible parts, called a synod, and particularly that of Merst and Teviotdale, which he charged with gross encroachments upon the legislative power of her Majesty and Parliament, in imposing lately new oaths and bonds as terms of communion upon all ministers and probationers, and this without any allowance from her Majesty's Parliament or General Assembly, yea without their privity or knowledge. In this heavy charge he was seconded by the Earl Marischal, a man of the same kidney; but they both missed of their aim, in that they very fairly outshot themselves by their over-hasty zeal to wound the Kirk through the sides of a synod, for want of exhibiting a formal libel, which they not having then in readiness the Marquis of A[nnanda]le, her Majesty's late Commissioner to the General Assembly, thought himself in honour obliged to stop the mouths of these gainsayers, which he did so effectually that Fletcher being gravelled, had nothing else to say, but that he would make it appear that his Lordship whilst he presided in the Assembly had done such illegal things as he could not answer for; and therefore desired the

Chancellor might appoint a day not only for making good his charge against some high-flying churchmen but their Commissioner too.

This controversy being let fall, another soon arose upon a second reading of the Earl of Rothes's Act concerning the choosing of officers of State, Privy Councillors, Lords of Session, &c. which latter were no sooner mentioned, but the Duke of H. attacked also the College of Justice in the most sensible part, the head, and for presenting a clause to be inserted in the said Act, which clause runs thus :—

That after her Majesty's decease, instead of one President of the Session, three be chosen out of the fifteen which compose the said college, to preside by turns every two months.

This clause met with a great deal of opposition but more particularly from the Earl of Stair, who alleged that in England, neither the courts of the Queen's Bench, nor Common Pleas, which latter, he said, answered to the College of Justice here, had any more than one President. To which Duke of Hamilton answered, that he desired the house would reflect a little, from whence the model of this court of judicature first came, which, he said, was from Paris in the reign of King James the Fifth, where they had still three Presidents. At length, after a great deal of debate, it was put to the vote—Add the clause or no—and it was carried in the negative by a considerable majority. After which, the house proceeded to consider the rest of this merry Act, for such your honour will allow it to be, when I shall have entertained you with what the Earls of Balcarres and Stair said upon the next paragraph, which bore that the officers of State and Privy Councillors could not continue longer than six years, and that at the end of three years, the one half should go off, and the other half in three years more, and that the same officers of State and Privy Councillors could not possess the same posts till full six years were expired after their removal. As to the term of years, the officers of State are hereby insured of their posts, the Earl of Stair said, that whatever privilege the sovereign was like to lose, by the choice of his officers of State being lodged in the estates of Parliament, he was sure the officers themselves were like to be no losers by such a reasonable time. And as to the one half quitting the stage after they had played their parts three years, the Earl of Balcarres stood up and said, that by what he could remember of Roman story, these masters of the world, when they were about modelling their commonwealth, sent to Greece to consult with their wise lawgivers ; and that as to his knowledge, this model the Parliament was upon was borrowed from the canton of Berne ; so he was of opinion the house would do well to send deputies thither and wait their return, before they concluded anything in a matter of so great moment. At which pleasant fancy the whole house burst into a loud laughter.

HENRY ST. JOHN to [ROBERT] HARLEY.

1705, Aug. 22. Whitehall—I have received from the Earl of Arran a state of the matter relating to Mrs. Allen's petition transmitted to me with your letter of the 7th instant, a copy whereof I send you here inclosed.

And in answer to your letter of the 9th relating to the officers of the company at Newfoundland, I have received an account of that matter from Major Lloyd who commands that company. He pretends that Lieutenant Moody who was first Lieutenant thereof having been found in a particular manner to encourage the late mutiny at Newfoundland

—which endangered the whole garrison—as has been since, he says, proved by the oath of a very creditable person, taken before a master in Chancery, he conceived him unfit to continue an officer, and therefore prayed a commission for one Mr. Phillips, who I find has a commission to supersede the others, for which the Prince's directions were not signified by me.

As to the other Lieutenant, Mr. Gully, the said Major Lloyd alleges he was taken a prisoner in France, whereupon he proposed one Mr. Latham an Engineer upon the place, to be Lieutenant in his room, for whom I find there is likewise a commission passed, though without any notification from me. But since Mr. Gully, I am informed, is returned to England, I conceive he ought not to suffer for the misfortune of being taken prisoner in going to his post; and I must observe in the other case, that should it become a practice to break subalterns upon a bare suggestion from their superior officer, the consequences would be very mischievous. *Signed*.

[William Greg to Robert Harley.]

1705, August 23. Edinburgh—Having been obliged to break off somewhat abruptly last ordinary, I humbly beg leave to continue the account of the proceedings in Parliament that day before I presume to entertain your honour with what passed yesterday.

I then had the honour to acquaint you, in what a burlesque and bantering manner, the Earls of Stair and Balcarres treated poor Scotland's fate after her Majesty's decease, in being like to be molten down to that golden calf state, where, in my humble opinion, the Sovereign will have little more to say than the Doge of Venice has in that Republic. For in this Caledonian Commonwealth, not only the power of choosing the Sovereign's servants is lodged in the Estates of Parliament, and their periods of duration fixed and determined, but even the priority of withdrawing is prescribed ; which is to be in the same manner as they ride the Parliament here, where the Boroughs go before the Barons and the Barons, the Peers, who close the cavalcade ; just so must the youngest Burgess, Baron, or Peer, go off first according as they are called in the rolls of Parliament. This retrograde way of removing seemed so very preposterous to the Earl of Stair, that he said, he should have rather been for the fattest goose going off first, intimating thereby, that some of the officers of State might make a better hand of it in three years, than others, whose places were less profitable, could do in the whole six. The Lords of the Session and Justiciary are to enjoy their places during life, and when any of their own number, or of the Officers of State, comes to die, during the interval of Parliament, they are to be supplied by the Privy Council, and this choice to be approved or disapproved in the next session, as the Estates of Parliament shall think fit.

Yesterday the house took into consideration the Lord Belhaven's overture for a triennial Parliament. His Lordship was seconded in his proposal by the Dukes of Hamilton and Athol as judging it one of the most necessary rectifications of the present constitution. They not only pleaded in behalf of a triennial Parliament the claim of right, wherein *frequency of Parliaments* is asserted, but they likewise alleged the example of a neighbour nation as a precedent, which latter these two noble Lords never allow of, but when it makes for them.

The servants of the prerogative (to do them justice) were not silent here. As to the claim of right, they said, no more could be meant by frequent Parliaments, therein asserted, but frequent sessions of Parliament, of the want of which the subjects had no cause to complain ; and as to the example of the English nation the Chancellor, in my hearing, said, that for ought he could ever learn, England did not brag much of it. Besides, that any such innovation in her Majesty's time would be an encroachment upon the prerogative, the power of calling, adjourning and dissolving Parliament when the Sovereign pleases, being a right inherent in the crown, and plainly asserted as such, in an Act of Parliament anno 1661.

To elude the force of so express an Act in favour of the prerogative, some were for tracing the constitution up to its original, others, not to go so far back, fancied to have found some footsteps of what they were contending for in the year 1691 before which, they said, no adjournments had been heard of.

The Chancellor conceiving it to be his proper province to set this matter in a true light rose up and made a very handsome speech, desiring those who were so very fond of a triennial Parliament, as a part of their ancient constitution, to be convinced that they laboured under a great mistake, if they thought any such thing ; for as much as he could make it appear, that the representing the collective body of the people, by frequent elections from among the Barons and Boroughs, was but modern, when compared with their other rights and privileges, the whole body of the Barons having had formerly a hereditable right to sit in the house, as well as the Lords : and that as for the Boroughs, they were seldom changed, and when any new members happened to be elected, they never exceeded four or five. So that in effect, it was still the self same Parliament.

All this did [not] satisfy the two Dukes, who were not otherwise to be determined, but by a vote of the house, which being stated thus, whether the Act for a triennial Parliament should take place as a limitation upon the Queen, or upon the successor? It carried, upon the Queen, by a majority only of five votes.

Flushed with this success the Duke of Hamilton fancied nothing too hard for him, how unreasonable soever it might be, and therefore very briskly moved, that this Act should commence the first of November next. The Marquis of Annandale opposed him as stoutly, declaring that this would be a retrospect, and therefore of bad consequence. The Duke being seconded in his motion by few or none, the court moved that since this Act was to be a limitation upon her Majesty, it might not take place before the 23rd of August 1708. Others proposed as a medium, the 23rd of the said month 1706. To decide it between these two last motions, it was put to the vote, whether the the Triennial Act should take place one year's hence or three years, and it carried three. So that according to the tenor of this Act though her Majesty may dissolve this present Parliament, and call a new one before the said 23rd of August 1708, yet the Parliament now sitting cannot continue longer than three years reckoning from this day.

The continuance of this Parliament and the commencement of the triennial being determined, the house went next upon the capacities and qualifications of those who were to compose it, and excluded all farmers, collectors, surveyors and managers of her Majesty's Customs and Excise from being members. The Duke of Hamilton was for turning them out of doors immediately, but being soon ashamed of his motion he dropped it.

The Act thus gone through was put to the vote—whether approve it or no? and it carried, in the affirmative, by twenty eight votes.

The Duke of Marlborough to Lord [Portland ?].

1705, August 24. Corbais—After all the pains and care that was taken for the getting of ten days' bread to enable us to make the march by Genap, and the finding the enemy behind the little river Ische, I thought the victory so secure that I cannot as yet forgive those, that were the occasion of our not attacking the Elector, and Monsieur Villeroy. When I have the honour to see you I shall tell you my mind very freely of this matter, and I think show you very plainly that if there be not other measures taken for the next campaign the French must by degrees get the better. Orders are given for the attacking of Leuwe, and the levelling the lines, and if I see after that the Generals are resolved to attempt nothing else, I shall then have a mind to get into England early. I should be glad as a friend you would let me have your thoughts on this, for I would not willingly do anything that might give occasion to people to think that I were dissatisfied, though I must own to you I am very much, for as it is ordered by Monsieur Slangenberg I have not the tenth part of the authority I had last year. I am sure I serve with all my heart, I wish I could be as sure of others.

William Penn to [Robert Harley].

1705, [August] 24—I send the enclosed (*Cf.* Aug. 28) by the author. If you will not help him to help you what can he hope for? Do something I beg, after kind words and fair looks. He has hung too long upon expectations, and that is the plague of Courts. Pray look kindly upon it to Lord Treasurer to-morrow, whom Sir Charles Hedges hindered me just now from speaking to by letters he brought him. Let my son have thy good opinion. He knows it must go to the Admiralty, but is satisfied if it has not some recommendation it must be abortive.

[William Greg to Robert Harley.]

1705, August 25. Edinburgh—When I acquainted you the 19th inst. that the Court party had carried that day the nomination of the Commissioners for a Council of Trade I remember to have then foretold what came yesterday to pass: namely the revival of the Plot, which was indeed designed to have been trumped up immediately after the reading of the minutes of the preceding Sederunt, had not the Treasurer Depute rose up before the Duke of Athol, who was fain to have patience till my Lord Glasgow had represented to the house the absolute necessity of granting her Majesty a supply for the support of the Government, or else of disbanding the forces, which had now neither money nor credit whereby to subsist, the funds applied to that use having been exhausted last month.

This seasonable overture was no sooner made but my Lord Duke moved to know if there was any answer given to the address of the house sent up to her Majesty last session of Parliament, in relation to the Plot, and whether or no the papers relating thereunto had been transmitted according to the humble request of the house. And withal moved, that a day might be appointed for enquiring into that affair. He was seconded by the Duke of Hamilton who produced a copy of the Duke of Queensberry's letter to the Queen the 11th of August 1703, which he read and thereafter made such a comment upon it as obliged the Duke of Queensberry to rise up and speak for himself, which he did very handsomely to this purpose, *That he did never transmit to her Majesty any account of the Plot but upon informations which he could always make good;* that he did not disown there might be truth mingled with some falsehoods in so intricate affair, and that he was very willing that every man's part in it might be enquired into. Whereupon the Dukes of Hamilton and Athol desired, that a day might be appointed for examining that affair, which they did in such pressing instances, that the Commissioner saw himself in a manner obliged to satisfy the house so far as to let them know, that he had received a letter from her Majesty in answer to the address of the house, which letter he said he would look out, and then signify her Majesty's pleasure to them. This promise from the throne did not satisfy the two Dukes, who still insisting to have a certain time prefixed for enquiring into what, they said, was called in England the Scotch plot, the third Sederunt next week was named for that purpose, when the papers also relating thereunto are to be laid before the house.

Then the house returned to the consideration of the Act presented by the Earl of Glasgow for granting her Majesty a supply for the maintaining of the forces, garrisons and frigates within the kingdom. This overture was seconded by the Marquis of Annandale and a great deal was said by him and the other servants of the crown, to shew the indispensable necessity there was of doing something very speedily in this matter. And yet notwithstanding the reasonableness of this motion, a member made another, as if he intended not only thereby to delay the granting any such supply, but even entirely to defeat it; which was, that no supply should be granted till such time as the Acts already passed in the house had got the royal assent. The Duke of Hamilton is too much leader to content himself simply with seconding, and therefore though he did not dislike the motion made by the said member, yet he started one of his own which aimed at baffling whatever should be offered by the ministry in favour of a present supply. He alleged that the circumstances of the nation were so very low, that it was in vain to talk of granting what the nation had not to give; unless effectual measures were first taken for bringing in money into the kingdom, for which end, he was of opinion that since our black cattle could not be sent into England after the 25th of December next, a drawback should be allowed upon beef to be exported, which being a good commodity not only in Holland, but Spain, he said he saw no reason why the Parliament of Scotland might not open a trade with that kingdom as well as England had done, and not only with Spain, but even France too, whereby considerable sums would be saved, which are paid to the Hollanders for insurance.

The Court nevertheless, still urging the necessity of a supply, the Country party, the better to avoid giving any, did industriously improve the jealousy first started by the member who proposed a delay, till the Acts already passed were touched; and even the good old Earl of Marchmont came at length to believe there might be some ground of jealousy, as if the Commissioner might have instructions to adjourn the Parliament, as soon as the supply should be granted. To remove which suspicion the Commissioner assured the house, that he was not stinted, nor doubted but her Majesty would allow the time for finishing what Acts might be judged necessary for the good and advantage of the nation. By which assurance the house seemed to be cured in a great measure of their jealousies and were clear for giving the Act of supply a first reading, provided it had not a second, before the house came to a conclusion in the matter of a treaty of union with England, and had considered the several branches of trade in relation to the prohibitory clauses contained in the English Act. To which overture, given in by the Earl of Rothes, Mr. Fletcher offered an additional clause in these terms—That the house will pass such laws as shall regulate the balance of trade to the advantage of this nation, before the Act of supply have a second reading—which clause being put to the vote—add the clause or no; it carried in the negative, by a majority of 31 votes. In mentioning the exact plurality of votes, by which Fletcher's clause was thrown out, I beg leave to correct here an error in my last concerning the majority, by which the country party carried the triennial Act; and that was only five votes instead of eighteen, which had indeed been the odds in some other vote, set down in my table book, upon which I inadvertently stumbled, and though perhaps that mistake might never have been enquired into, yet I thought it too material to conceal it, because thereby a judgment is to be made of the strength of the Court party.

This afternoon, the house was to have gone upon the consideration of a treaty with England; but instead of making any progress therein, our topping declaimers contented themselves with trying their talents in railing plentifully at the prohibitory clauses contained in the English Act. So that the further consideration of the treaty itself is deferred till Tuesday next.

[WILLIAM GREG to ROBERT HARLEY.]

1705, August 28. Edinburgh—When I acquainted you the 25th how a day, designed for business of the last importance to this kingdom, had been wholly spent in making angry speeches against the Parliament of England, I was indeed unwilling to enter into the detail of what was spoken in the house when I was present all the while, as fearing my memory would not serve me to give any tolerable account of such a vast variety of things; besides that I must confess, my spirits were almost exhausted in hearing only, had time allowed me to have made an essay for your entertainment. But upon second thoughts yesterday, I took pen in hand in order to try the utmost stretch of a bad memory, which, with all the powers and faculties the writer possesses, is never so cheerfully employed, as when he is in the way of his duty, however he may come to fail in the discharge and performance of it.

Mr. Fletcher was the first that vented his spleen in his usual fierce and violent manner against the usage done this nation, as injurious, insolent and unneighbourly; and advanced that the English Act of Parliament, in the terms it was conceived, struck at the sovereignty and independency of the kingdom of Scotland. To fortify which assertion he cited the preface to the Border Laws by the Bishop of Carlisle [Nicolson], where in an advertisement at the end, his Lordship thinks fit to amend. "Be it enacted thus" to "Both houses unanimously desire, that it may be enacted." From whence, Fletcher inferred that this kingdom must needs be looked upon by the English to be in a state of vassalage and dependency. Notwithstanding the great indignities he complains of, he said, he was for an honourable treaty with England, with this proviso, that the prohibitory laws be repealed before the treaty should commence. For which purpose he gave in a resolve, which was read and ordered to lie upon the table.

Another member stood up and gave a quite different turn to the hardships pretended to be put upon this nation, and more particularly, with relation to what our proud Scotch stomachs cannot digest, and that is the word, alien; to declare us such, he said, was not in the power [of] an English Parliament; his reason was, that what was our undoubted right by the law of nations could not be taken from us by any municipal law, since we were under the same sovereign and paid allegiance to her; and that it was so, he alleged the authority of Coke in the case of Calvin. And therefore he looked upon that part of the Act, whereby we are declared aliens from and after the 25th December next, unless we settle the succession in the same manner as it has been settled in England, to be an error, which he hoped the new Parliament would be soon convinced of. But upon a supposition that even they too should continue in the same error, then said he we will gain a point, for which many of their kings have so earnestly contended, an entire renunciation to all claim and pretension of superiority or dominion over the kingdom of Scotland. And upon that supposition, he was of opinion that part of the English Act of Parliament by which we are declared aliens ought to be engraven on brass. This gentleman (who is my particular friend and no enemy I can assure you to the interest of the Court, to which he is newly brought over) aiming more in what he said to show his parts, than any thing else, sat down without being seconded; whereas Saltoun wanted not his followers, as well as adversaries. Among the latter, one may always reckon the Earl of Stair, who however on this occasion so far joined with him, as to own, he thought this nation had been unkindly dealt with by England, in declaring us aliens; but as to the prohibitory laws, he did not think that so strange, since we ourselves began first some time after the restoration of King Charles the Second. Now said he there being no remedying our grievances but by a treaty, since the two Parliaments understood one another as little as two distinct worlds, he was much for having it an honourable one as any man in the house; but then he did not see how that would be brought about if we should insist to have the minatory and prohibition clauses in the English Act first repealed. Therefore, he was for a plain Act or a treaty without any such clause. The Earl Marischal [Kintore] thought this proposal so very dishonourable, that he rose up and said in a huff, that whoever proposed any such thing, in his opinion should be treated as they deserved, and what he meant by that he believed the house understood pretty well; and upon the Chancellor's asking what he meant, he answered plainly, hanging. The unwarrantable freedom of this peer, who next to Hamilton is the Hector of the house, was not heeded by the Chancellor, who, notwithstanding Marischal's severe sentence, made a speech, wherein he agreed in most things with the Earl of Stair; but withal added, that the prohibitory laws lately passed in England were not perhaps so great a grievance as their Act of Navigation, which had proved of far worse consequence to this nation than the prohibitory laws could be. And therefore wished for nothing more than to see an honourable treaty set on foot, in which both one and the other might be taken off.

The 19th past, I find to have acquainted you that "e." was not only Q. but R. and this he put beyond all doubt when he declared, that though formerly he had been for a treaty with England, as much as any man, yet ever since the Act lately passed in the Parliament of that kingdom, he had changed his mind, and therefore was now of opinion, that considering the indignities done us, the first step we ought to make, before we commenced a treaty was to address her Majesty, that she would be pleased to interpose her authority with the Parliament of England for redressing the grievances complained of, before any treaty should be set on foot. In this, he was seconded by the Duke of Hamilton, who delivered himself on this occasion in the most moving and pathetical manner I ever heard him speak, and the courage of our ancestors being his common place, he enlarged upon it with all the rhetoric he was master of. I am, said he, for an honourable treaty, but to be thus cudgelled into one, was below the courage of our ancestors, and he hoped it should never be said that their descendants had grown so degenerate as to lie down grovelling in the dust, and patiently receive the stripes and lashes that should be laid upon their backs, without repining. No! we had a gracious Queen, whose protection as a common parent we, as dutiful and humble children, ought first to implore against the bad usage done us by our fellow subjects, who strive not only to make us a dependent people, but her a dependent Queen, as he said she must necessarily be, if their Act of Parliament should take place the 25th of December next, that fatal period, when to think of a total separation from his gracious sovereign made his heart almost to bleed. He, good man, could not bear the thoughts of it. This harangue, being more popular than to the point, had the less weight with the house, which seemed to be more taken with what the Earl of Aberdeen (who as I formerly hinted, was Chancellor in King Charles the Second's time, and for whose judgment, though he be now somewhat broken in his parts, the house still retains a great deference) advanced. He said, that since after the 25th of December, Scotchmen were to be looked upon in England as aliens and strangers, the first thing the Parliament ought to do was, in his opinion, to put the English upon the same foot in Scotland. And as for their prohibitory laws, we might make the like with respect to the commodities we had of them; and that then both nations would be even, and equally free to begin a treaty; but then, said he, it must be rather a treaty of alliance and commerce on our part, and not of union, to conclude which, he did not think this present Parliament sufficiently impowered and instructed from their constituents; and that therefore a new one ought [to] be called on purpose to consider of a matter of such great importance, as was that of an union between the two kingdoms.

As Fletcher had the first word, as soon as the Marquis of Lothian's draft of an Act for a treaty was read, so he was resolved to have the last also by throwing in a bone of contention about a safe conduct for the Scots Commissioners, in case of a treaty, who being aliens, he did not know he said but the English might come to send them all to the Tower, whenever they pleased. He was seconded in this by the Duke of Hamilton, whom the Chancellor took up roundly taxing him of want of knowledge in the law of nations, whereby, he said, the persons of Ambassadors and Plenipotentiaries were held as sacred, and that ours would still be looked up to be the more so, even upon a supposition of their being aliens, than if they were really fellow subjects.

This day has produced as little progress in the business of a treaty, as did Saturday last, save only, that the draft of an Act presented for that purpose by the Earl of Mar has had a first reading, which it got just as the house was rising, the whole afternoon having been trifled away in idle repetitions of such like speeches, as that whereof you have a copy enclosed, with which Mr. Fletcher entertained the house for half an hour at their sitting down to-day, and after that in pursuance of his

,theme, gave in a draft of an address to be sent to her Majesty which had no better fate than the rest of his overtures have had this session, that is to say, was fairly let fall to his great mortification.

—— to [ROBERT HARLEY].

1705, August 28—About ten days ago Mr. Penn told me that you would send for me when you next came to Town, for without your leave and appointment I would not presume to go ■yself. I know as well as anybody what construction both the violent Whigs and Tories would put on such a meeting, and I grant it becomes your prudence on such an occasion to be cautious, as it is both my interest and duty to be secret. I have learnt by experience and observation on whom to depend, and how to behave myself in such a complication of parties, principles and designs. But, for declining to be a mercenary tool I have been basely sacrificed and abandoned by those who you know have as little kindness for you in particular, as they have generosity for the Public, and when they thought it likely I would not be always patient of ill usage (though since the King's death I have not writ a word in the common disputes) they loosed all their little curs of Booksellers and others upon me at once, knowing I could not be able to satisfy my creditors (though my debts were very small) if they came upon me all together. This was the utmost they could do, and shows what they would do, but with no fair or thinking person has it done me any dis-credit; though I doubt not they would ruin me with all others as well as themselves. 'Tis but a moderate sum on the obtaining of which I would stipulate (under forfeiture both of that and the protection of the giver) to owe no man living at any time a farthing. This I declare not to you, to whom I have the honour to be so well known, by way of excuse; but as the only thing their malice can object, however they may aggravate or represent it. When you please to admit me nearer, I doubt not but to give full satisfaction as to all points, and if I have any learning or ability, I desire to be entirely directed by your orders in all I may do for the future: wherein it shall be my continual endeavour to recommend myself to your care by my diligence and fidelity. A method may be easily found to make me useful to yourself and the public, without incurring the censure of any faction or letting it be known to your best friends, till I have time and opportunity to wear off those prejudices which my own want of experience and the treachery of others have raised against me. I look not therefore at present for any public employment but to be provided for either in the way I have mentioned in my letter to Mr. Penn, or as in your judgment shall be thought more convenient. I hope the Lord Treasurer, if I be not extremely out in his character, interest and inclination, will not be averse to my request. I know what sort of folks he has to manage, nor need it ever be told that he gives me any countenance. But I'll give you no further trouble till I have the favour to discourse with you which I humbly and earnestly beg may be with the soonest, I being ready to wait on you when and where, and how you please to appoint. I desire you would not impute it to ignorance or disrespect that in this hasty note, 1 have not observed the usual style and form. I have by degrees broke off a great part of my tattling and mean acquaintance, frequenting no coffee houses, as I never hereafter design to do; being convinced that they are few that can improve, and fewer still that can deserve our trust. In short, Sir, I am sure 'tis in your power, and I hope 'tis in your will, to make me a new man without changing my old principles : for this has been my chief misfortune, to be left at large to my own caprice and humours, without any certain patrons or settled business, and having neither estate nor relations to support me. But it ought to be considered likewise that I was young, and that now seeing my faults and mistakes, as well as discerning my true friends and interest, I may correct whatever was amiss, and become another person in the prime of my age.

I lodge at present at one Mr. Norcon's near the Sugar-houses in Battersea, where or at Mr. Penn's lodging in Spring Garden any message will find me.

WILLIAM BORRETT to [ERASMUS] LEWIS.

1705, August 30—Has Mrs. Bankes' and Mr. Addison's informations against Hannan, also Hannan's account of charge for fitting the *James* brigantine out for sea. Mr. Attorney-General could not prefer a bill upon that evidence.

Afterwards Mr. Attorney had one Capt. Ridley and Mr. Shales before him and made a report to Mr. Secretary [Harley] of their evidence; then directed the writer to attend at the Old Bailey to get Hannan continued until next sessions, on the ground that the most material witness was a prisoner in France.

[WILLIAM GREG to ROBERT HARLEY.]

1705, August 30. Edinburgh—Yesterday the Parliament sat upon private business, and this day they were upon the Plot, of which nothing could be made by all the papers sent down as yet, which occasioned the Duke of Hamilton's calling them *Glenderule's knapsack*, as having been for the most part those which were found about him when he was secured. Besides these the Commissioner acquainted the house, that the rest might be expected with her Majesty's convenience, as also such persons as the laws of England would allow to be sent hither; and that her Majesty in the mean while desired they might proceed in that affair with such calmness and sedateness as to prevent all heats and animosities amongst them; for which reasonable advice, his Grace said he thought he had observed some ground the other day, which reprimand the Duke of Hamilton taking immediately to himself, showed such a regard for Her Majesty's commands from the mouth of her Commissioner, that he did not bawl the whole day, but contented himself with a modest vindication of his own innocence without attacking any person. The Duke of Athol was not so much upon the reserve, but complained of all offices done here by a fellow servant, meaning the Duke of Queensberry.

I must not forget to acquaint you, how mightily the House of Commons were commended by the Duke of Hamilton for disagreeing with the Lords about christening the plot which their Lordships, he said, thought fit to call the Scotch conspiracy, whereas the Commons, as much the more friendly and neighbourly god-fathers, would not give it so hard a name. Of this encomium, squire Stought or Stoughter (I cannot just tell which) one of the representatives last Parliament for Northumberland, together with two other English gentlemen, were ear witnesses.

The QUEEN to [the EARL OF PEMBROKE].

[1705, c August 30]—You are immediately upon the receipt of these our instructions and your other despatches, to repair to the Hague, and at your arrival there you shall acquaint the Pensionary and such other of the principal members of the States as you shall think proper, of our constant resolution to maintain and improve the strict friendship and alliance between us and the States General, and of our readiness to concur in such measures as may best conduce to attain the ends of it. If you find it necessary you shall demand an audience of the States General, at which, having delivered to them our credential letters, you shall assure them of our great value for their friendship, and our constant affection for the good and welfare of their State, with such other expressions of our good will to them as you shall judge proper. And particularly you are to set forth to them the kindness we have upon all occasions shewed to their State, whose amity we do so highly prize, and for whose welfare we have so tender a regard, and have given so many instances of our endeavour to gratify and make their subjects easy.

And as a further testimony of our great value for their friendship, we have sent you, in whom we place an entire confidence, not so much to expostulate upon the misfortunes which have lately happened, as to prevent the evil consequences which may hereafter follow such proceedings.

We are very unwilling to remember what is passed, nor do we take notice that the same hath happened twice very lately, for any other end but that the serious consideration of it may show the necessity of a speedy cure.

You are therefore to represent to them that we have no views but what regard the welfare of all our allies, and how much it is for their interest and that of the common cause that they take such speedy and effectual resolutions as may render our joint armies more useful, for we cannot but impute the disappointments which have lately happened to their placing less confidence in the Duke of Marlborough this year than the last—though they have had experience of his happy conduct more than once—and that the opinions of inferior officers in the army have taken place preferably to that of both the Generals. You will plainly represent to them that it will be very uneasy to our subjects to give supplies another year, for a war which is to be carried on after this manner. Therefore we persuade ourselves that our good allies the States will find an effectual remedy in this case.

You are also to assist our Envoy extraordinary during your stay, in pressing such things wherein you judge you can promote our service, and particularly in obtaining a convention for one year at least to prohibit the carrying naval stores to France.

You shall constantly correspond with the Duke of Marlborough, our Captain General and Ambassador extraordinary to the States General, and with such other of our ministers in foreign courts as you judge to be necessary for promoting the service you are employed in.

You shall observe from time to time such further instructions and directions as you shall receive from us or one of our principal Secretaries of State, with whom you shall constantly correspond, and transmit unto him an account of all matters which shall happen in the course of your ministry. *Sign Manual. The body of the paper is in Harley's handwriting. There are also several drafts of the same, with alterations.*

The SAME to [the SAME].

[Same date.]—Whereas we have ground to believe there are emissaries from the French king who have made attempts to persuade some persons in the Seven Provinces to accept of a peace, and having made a sort of proposal to that end.

You are therefore to use your utmost diligence to find out how far this hath gone and the particulars, as far as you are able, of what hath been done in it. You are to discourse the Pensionary and such other particular persons as you shall judge proper, and show them our opinion that we cannot consent to a peace with France until Spain and the Indies be restored to the House of Austria, and without reasonable satisfaction and security to all our allies. You are therefore at large to explain to them that a peace upon any other terms will be both insecure and dishonourable; and that the state of the affairs of France, both as to their armies and especially their treasure, is such, that there is very good ground to hope in one year for such a peace as may answer the ends for which we and our allies entered into this war.

This affair by reason of the divisions and factions which are in the Seven Provinces is of a delicate nature, and therefore we recommend it to your prudence so to treat it that it may show them our opinion and resolution, and yet not precipitate them into any hasty measures with France, but to unite them nearer to us, if possible, in a more vigorous and hearty prosecution of the war. *Sign Manual. The body of the paper is in Harley's handwriting. There is also a draft of the same written by Harley; endorsed, "Additional instructions. Read to the Queen, August 26th, 1705."*

[WILLIAM GREG to ROBERT HARLEY.]

1705, September 1. Edinburgh—Yesterday the Parliament met again with a design to have resumed immediately the further consideration of the Act for a treaty of union with England, had not Mr. Fletcher moved immediately after the reading of the minutes, that the Address of the house to her Majesty last Session might be printed, to let the world see, that they had been in the way of their duty, how much so ever traversed in it by a Parliament to which the cognisance of what they called a Scotch plot did not at all belong. This motion was greatly opposed, but at length agreed to, together with an overture of his hindering any more than the two Secretaries and six of the nobility to go up to London without leave of the Privy Council, that the house might not be hindered by the person that made it, to proceed to the Act for a treaty; to which, the Duke of Hamilton offered the following clause to be added:—

That it shall not be in the power of the Commissioners to alter or derogate from the fundamental laws, ancient customs, privileges, rights, dignities, or offices of this realm.

This clause being calculated for preventing an incorporating union, or rather any union at all, was so laid open by the Court party, who represented the inconveniences that would attend it, with a great deal of good reasoning, that it being put to the vote—Add the clause or no? It carried in the negative.

This in short was the whole business of yesterday. What has passed in Parliament this afternoon has been a very good day's work, the house having gone through the whole Act for a treaty and finished the same, in such a plain and simple manner as not only leaves out all clogging clauses in the body of it, such as that offered by the Duke of Athol for not entering upon a treaty, till the clause of alienation contained in the English Act should be repealed; but likewise gives the nomination of the Commissioners to her Majesty. It is true indeed the house agreed, that the clause, declaring Scotsmen *Aliens* after the 25th of December next, should be first rescinded, before the treaty commenced. But then the debate having run for three hours, whether the Duke of Athol's clause should be inserted into the body of the Act for a treaty, or done in a separate Act, Address, or the instructions to be given to the Commissioners? the question was stated at last:— Add the clause to the Act, or in a separate way? And it carried, separately, by two votes only. Nevertheless the Duke of Athol entered a protestation of adherence to his clause, as did several others whose names were accordingly marked at their desire.

The day was already far spent, when the Court gained so much of the Country, which the latter perceiving, would fain have put off the nomination of the Commissioners till the next Sederunt; but the ministry finding that they had got the ball at their foot, were resolved to push matters briskly. And accordingly it was put to the vote:—Proceed or delay? And carried Proceed. Whereupon the Duke of Hamilton rose up and declared, that he was for giving her Majesty the nomination of the Commissioners, which sudden turning of the tables made his whole party stare and look aghast. His reason for so doing, though very plausible, did not satisfy his country friends. It was in vain for him to allege the duty he owed her Majesty which (to do him justice) he expressed on this occasion in a most respectful manner, as also the confidence he had of her Majesty's making a good choice. And admitting, says he, that she make a bad one; where's the danger? Seeing what ever shall be treated of by the Commissioners of Scotland must come before a Scotch Parliament, there to be approved, or rejected, as they shall think fit.

Several gentlemen of the flying squadron and particularly the Marquis of T[weeddale] and Earl of Roxburgh finding that this matter was ripe for a vote, rose up and made their excuses to the Chancellor, why they were not at freedom to compliment the Queen with theirs, which, they said, would signify nothing if given, seeing they could not go along with the Act itself, when it should come to be approved; which it was at length, by a majority of four votes only; as was also the nomination of the Commissioners given to the Queen, by much the same number.

It will be easily believed, that Fletcher fell into one of his fits, when he saw the nomination was like to go as it went, and so impudent was he, as to say, that the giving the nomination to the Queen was in effect complimenting the English ministers (and particularly, my Lord Godolphin) with it. This went not and without a reprimand from the Chancellor, who snubbed the madman roundly.

ERASMUS LEWIS to the SECRETARY [HARLEY].

1705, September 1—Is desired by Mr. Borrett to acquaint him that a true bill was that morning found against Hannan, who was thereupon sent to Newgate. Hannan showed so much disorder and timorousness that he will probably discover all he knows.

ROBERT HARLEY to the LORD MAYOR [of London].

1705, September 3—Thanking him for the great zeal he had shown to the Queen and her government in suppressing those pernicious libels so industriously spread by ill-intentioned persons. *Copy.*

DOCTOR P. ALLIX to [ROBERT] HARLEY.

1705, September 3—Asking him to procure for his son John Peter Allix, Fellow of Jesus College Cambridge, the office of lecturer at St. Antholin and St. John the Baptist in London, in case of Mr. Laizamby's death, he having got the approbation of the best people of the two united parishes by preaching three times amongst them.

MEMORANDA on VALIERE.

[1705, September ?] :—
[*In Godolphin's hand*]—I can't but much approve of this service. The proposal seems to be in a hand very like the man's writing who came to me from Hughetan.
[*In Harley's hand*]—No, it is one Valiere a very active man. Mr. Schutz hath another letter that Doctor D. being turned Whig, Pousin will return the ring to Monsieur Tovey.
[*In Godolphin's hand*]—This I suppose is the man that gave the Secretary Hedges a hint to stop Hannan's letters.
[*In Harley's hand*]—I found out that he was going to France, and upon discourse with him and several conferences this paper was the result, and we expect an answer from La Touche in a few days, but the first charge will be two or three hundred pounds.
[*In Godolphin's hand*]—It will be very well worth it.

WILLIAM ALDERSEY to [ROBERT] HARLEY, Secretary.

1705, September [4–]15 new style. Hamburg—Mr. Warre has probably acquainted you with what I wrote to him since the arrival of Captain Ogilvie. The latter is well satisfied with his coming hither and designs to stay about fourteen days. I have paid him 50*l.* and send his receipts.

[WILLIAM GREG to ROBERT HARLEY.]

1705, September 4. Edinburgh—The first instant I acquainted your honour with a surprising step made by the Duke of Hamilton in favour of the Court, when he declared he was for giving her Majesty the nomination of the Commissioners for treating of an union with England. And if this must be owned to be pretty odd, and indeed unaccountable (unless he thereby aimed to be chosen one of the number) I am afraid, what this day has produced, will be taken for a prodigy, which is, that Fletcher is turned courtier too. I should be loath to advance any such paradox, had not I been present in Parliament, when he gave in a draft of an Address to her Majesty, for using her royal endeavours with the Parliament of England to get the clause in their Act, whereby the subjects of this kingdom are to be adjudged aliens after the 25th of December next, repealed. The manner of doing this was so much to the liking of the Court and so little to be expected from a professed enemy, that the draft did not take, as being too humble, or rather too mean. For he pleads the present poverty of the nation, as a reason for the paucity of Commissioners, whom he would have go no farther than the Border to treat; which was found impracticable. And therefore the draft of an Address presented by the Earl of Sutherland, being free from those exceptions, was preferred to be the ground work of the intended Address. Which way of getting the Alien clause taken off being not judged effectual by the Earl of Marchmont, he gave in the draft of a separate Act for that purpose, which coming a day after the fair, I mean, after the Act for a treaty was passed, it only furnished matter of debate for three hours during which many members, grudging the Court the ground they gained the other day, stood up for; but the ministry did strenuously oppose it, as thinking, it would weaken and shake the Act which had cost them so much pains to build up. And therefore, they were willing to try their strength by a vote; to understand the state whereof aright, I beg leave to put you in mind of what was agreed in the house the first instant, with relation to the Alien clause, namely, that the Commissioners to be nominated by her Majesty on the part of Scotland should not commence the treaty, till such time as the said clause in the English Act should be repealed. Now, to-day upon second thoughts, the house to give the more weight to what they had unanimously agreed on last Saturday, added the word ordered, so that their resolve runs thus:—Agreed and ordered *nemine contradicente*, that the Commissioners &c. The Earl of Marchmont being of opinion that an Address to her Majesty would be very proper, whatever might be the fate of his separate Act when put to the vote, the state of the question was proposed thus: whether an Act and an Address, or the order of the house and an Address, would be the most effectual way for hindering their Commissioners to treat, before the Alien clause should be removed out of the way; and it carried, Order and Address by a majority of almost two thirds of the house. The Duke of Athol, before stating of the vote, had proposed that instructions to the Commissioners might in his opinion be as effectual a method as any of the other two, but in this his Grace had the misfortune to be seconded by few or none; and so his motion was let fall.

After this, the house went through the Earl of Sutherland's draft, paragraph by paragraph, and with much ado, licked it into some tolerable shape; for to me it was surprising to find so few masters of style, even about the throne itself; where the Chancellor and other officers of State were reduced to a yawning indifference, by that time they were got half way through the Address. This censure may perhaps, seem too free and bold; but I wish there [may] not be found some ground for it, when the loyal Address comes to Court.

I must not forget to tell that the Duke of Hamilton had almost marred the merit of Saturday's motion, by a very unseasonable one he started to day; which was this, that seeing he was at a loss in what capacity to look upon his countrymen, with respect to the Queen after the 25th of December, did therefore propose to the wisdom of Parliament, whether or no an assertory Act for recognising her Majesty's title to this crown would not be preper to be enacted at this time. Such a scruple did so startle the ministry that the Lord Justice Clerk rose up and said, that there was no other assertory Act necessary now, for recognising her Majesty's right and title, than what was presented by his Grace himself the first session of this Parliament; after which, if any body durst call in question, to whom their allegiance was due when Christmas should be over, he ought to be tried for his life and fortune. This was so home that the Duke is not like to trouble the house with any such cases of conscience this session ; which he finding is now drawing near a close, presented an overture for encouraging the exportation of beef ; which had a first reading, after which the House adjourned till to-morrow, 10 o'clock.

WILLIAM COURTENAY to [ROBERT] HARLEY.

1705, September 5—Informing him that he had been to see Hannah and had entreated him to confess all that he knew.

[WILLIAM GREG to ROBERT HARLEY.]

1705, September 6. Edinburgh—Amongst the several overtures of Acts given in yesterday, such as, for discharging all sorts of merchandise in general to be imported from England, and tanned and best leather in particular, by Mr. Fletcher ; the taking the duties off linen and woollen cloth to be exported out of this kingdom, by the Duke of Athol, and for the exportation of wool, by the Lord Justice Clerk (all which had a first reading marked on them), none were so very much foreign to the business of trade, as one presented by the Earl Marischal, for having one or two Scotch ambassadors to represent her Majesty's person, as Queen of Scotland, at the first general treaty of peace that shall be concluded, and these to be accountable to the Parliament, though his lordship was so complaisant as to let her Majesty have the naming of them. This novelty was opposed by the ministry, as a limitation upon her Majesty, besides the unseasonableness of such a motion, till such time as people saw the issue of the treaty of union, which should it prove incorporating, there would be no need of distinct ambassadors. However the generality of the house were so taken with a thing so much (as they fancied) for the honour and interest of this nation, to which no manner of regard was shown by the English in any treaty, that after an hour's debate, it got a first reading. Fletcher finding the house so favourable to the Earl Marischal's maggot, thought his for hindering the nobility from going to London, with[out] leave from the Privy Council, did bid as fair for a first reading, which he urged for ; but being put to the vote, it was thrown out, and that by one single vote. However, he had the satisfaction of railing at the courtiers, in a long winded harangue made for that purpose.

Today the house was upon private business, the enumeration of the evidences mentioned in the minutes of the 30th past being put off to another diet.

The DUKE OF MARLBOROUGH to Lord [PORTLAND ?].

1705, September 7. Tirlemont—I have this night received the honour of yours of the 3rd and I think myself very much obliged to you for it. However uneasy some things may be to me, you may be sure I shall not leave the Army nor do anything else that I can think can do any disservice to the Queen or common cause ; but that which I thought and do still think is that when every body is convinced that nothing more can be done this campaign, that then it might not be thought unreasonable for me to desire to be in England, but I do assure you that if you and the Pensioner do seriously think that my staying at the Army can do us any good, I shall continue there though against my own opinion ; but I know not what excuse to make to my Lord Treasurer who presses me to be in England at least a fortnight before the Parliament meets. You may depend of it that what you write to me shall never be seen by anybody but myself, and if you would write to Lord Treasurer so that he might consent to my stay, it would make it easier to me, and I daresay he would not let your letter be seen if you desired it. If I had been at the Hague you may be sure I should have hindered the letter being printed before the States had had it.

I must say so much for myself, that I do serve the common cause with all my heart, and wish as much prosperity to the States as any subject they have, so that I can't think I deserve the slight of not having my letter answered, but I will not complain since you think it is what enemies may make use of.

[WILLIAM GREG to ROBERT HARLEY.]

· 1705, September 8. Edinburgh—Yesterday the house took into farther consideration the draft of an Act presented by the Duke of Hamilton, for encouraging the exportation of beef and pork, and went through the same, allowing a drawback of twenty pence per barrel on each. They also approved the Duke of Athol's overture, for taking off the duties upon all linen cloth and woollen manufactures that should be exported. After which, Fletcher's overture for discharging the importation of all sorts of merchandise from England, after the 25th of December, came to be considered. A prohibition so very general as this was by no means to the liking of the Court, who therefore opposed it with all their might, and were seconded by such members among the royal boroughs as foresaw the many mischiefs that would thereby accrue to this nation, without doing any great hurt to their neighbours.

Fletcher being well aware, that this project was like to run the fate of all the rest, insisted to have a vote of the house, whether to proceed to a general prohibition, or to particulars only ; which being thus stated, it carried, particulars, wherein a considerable progress was made, when a motion by the Marquis of M[ontrose ?] for a delay, seconded by the Marquis of T[weeddale] and others, put a stop to the farther consideration of these matters till this day ; and then the house instead of resuming, thought it more advisable to refer them to the Council of Trade.

The ministry having thus got fairly rid of an overture, which of all others would have hampered them most, renewed their instances for granting her Majesty a supply, without which the forces must, they said, be disbanded. And such was their credit with the house and the cogency of the arguments they made use of, that after some struggle they obtained a supply of six months, amounting to 36 [000 ?]l. sterling for maintaining the land forces ; and of one month, for fitting out three frigates, the grand fleet of this kingdom, against spring.

The DUKE OF NEWCASTLE to [ROBERT HARLEY].

1705, September 10. Haughton—I return you a thousand thanks for diverting from me a troublesome Embassy, in which you have showed your kindness, for it would have been very uneasy for me to have declined anything Her Majesty and that Lord did require of me, who am so entirely both by duty and inclination bound up in their interest ; such a sudden journey would always be very troublesome to me.

I am very sorry for the death of Sir Charles [Shuckburgh, master of the buckhounds], if I may offer my poor thoughts it may be very convenient to be under no promise for the disposal of that place for I know several gentlemen of very good interest that are sportsmen who would be more obliged by such a place than another of double the value.

The Grand Jury have done themselves and the Government right; his G——— has yet given greater marks of his good nature and veracity in the secret history, but he should not have given a more favourable character of himself than ever any other writer did, unless he would have fixed his name.

A[LEXANDER] G[OLDSMITH *alias* DANIEL DE FOE] to
ROBERT HARLEY.

1705, September 10. Kidderminster—My absence from the Bath, where I had appointed my brother to meet me and where having waited two days I could not satisfy myself to spend my time, occasioned me to miss him longer than I intended and consequently to defer my giving you an account, that by him I received as well the supply as the repeated expressions of your concern for my safety, for both which I owe more acknowledgments than I can express this way. I spent about eight days, the interval I mention above, in going back into Somersetshire and that great vale of trade extending from Warminster on the south border of Wilts to Cirencester in Gloucestershire, which lying so out of the road I could not otherwise take either going or coming without omitting places of equal moment.

Here I shall give you an account, and I hope to satisfaction, of strange and unaccountable people, as well as practices in the late election, with a survey something particular of the towns of Warminster, Westbury, Bradford, Trowbridge, Chippenham, Calne, Devizes, Malmesbury, Bedwin, Ludgershall, Marlborough, Cirencester, &c.

Here I am to note to you, that Watt White, member for Chippenham, is dead, and that all the gentry of the high party, who here act like devils more than men (*pardon the expression*), are embarked to get in, if possible, that scandal of the county, Col. Chivers, and the design is not so much to have the man in the house, as to shelter him from the prosecution of my Lord Bishop of Salisbury, who prosecutes him for most impudent language, of all which I have the particulars.

Sir, there cannot be a greater piece of service to the public, nor can anything tend more to carrying future elections in this county, which now run higher and worse than in most places in England, than to prevent this project, and one step above would do it effectually, viz.: putting Chivers out of the Commission of Peace, to which he is really a horrible scandal—for by being in that power he influences the town, sits diligently at every Petty Sessions, and awes the people. He was at this work when I was at Chippenham. This may be done obliquely, no man need know who hurt (?) them, his character will most clearly justify it, and no man can object. If he is out of the Peace, he certainly loses the election.

Lord Mordaunt stands against Mr. Chivers, but his interest is but weak yet. Bristol, Gloucester and Bath are entirely reformed cities, and the moderate interest prevails amain.

Devizes and the whole county of Wilts are corrupted and abused by the *Iron-chest* a modern proverb now known in this country as universally as the alphabet ; the meaning is the receiver general of the county is Sir Fra. Child's brother, whose influence so rules by lending money, that whoever is needy is sure to be bought off. The remove of that one article would make twenty members more, of which I reserve till I have the honour to see you. I am now moving North ; shall be at Shrewsbury to-morrow and at Manchester Thursday, from whence I'll do myself the honour to write again, and where I may receive any orders from you, if you please to direct to Robert Davis, to be left at the Posthouse at Manchester till called for, for I shall go to Liverpool and come back thither.

I am, I bless God, got clear of all the enemies I apprehended, and am everywhere received with unusual respect.

It a little surprised me at Gloucester, when Mr. Forbes, the dissenting minister, bid me at parting give his humble services to you, for he knew [not] I had the honour to be known to you. I can no way divine his intelligence, unless Mr. Auditor might mention it to him.

[WILLIAM GREG to ROBERT HARLEY.]

1705, September 11. Edinburgh — This day the Chancellor acquainted the Parliament, that the Commissioner had received the rest of the papers concerning the Plot, that had been laid before the House of Lords in the Parliament of England. But the house did not think fit to make any farther enquiry into these matters by reason of the Duke of Queensberry's absence, occasioned by the sudden death of his brother the Earl of March who died the day before yesterday of a drinking bout the 5th instant at General Ramsay's house, where the poor General also fell within an hour of the other, though but ingloriously in such a field, after the laurels he had gathered before Namur, last war.

The house has been amused the whole afternoon with the Earl Marischal's overture, mentioned in my letter of the 6th for reviving a piece of State that has been long in desuetude. Nothing now will serve us, but we must have Ambassadors and Plenipotentiaries of [our] own, forsooth, distinct from those of England at all public treaties wherein the honour and interest of this kingdom (for so runs the tenor of the Act) may be any ways concerned. We are so new-fangle of every thing that would make us stout and look big abroad, that there was no attempting directly to dislodge the fancy. So that the ministers were fain to go another way to work, by raising a thousand difficulties how these representing gentlemen should be maintained. To remove which difficulties some proposed the laying on a month's cess, (as they call it here) or supply, to be raised and applied only to that use, whenever the exigence of affairs shall call for the presence of our Ambassadors. Others were for a "Fond" of credit, by which the public faith of the nation represented in Parliament, should stand engaged to her Majesty to make good what expenses she should be at in rigging out and maintaining her Scotch Plenipotentiaries. Mr. Fletcher, envying the Earl Marischal the honour of his fantastical project very naturally thought of supporting it with as imaginary a Fond. And to refine upon the Earl's plain draft, he was for lodging only the representing character in Scotsmen who should have estates in Scotland, so that nothing would satisfy him unless the English were excluded. Such an unreasonable clause from him was not at all to be wondered at. But I must do the house the justice to say that every member almost opposed it, as what was both unreasonable in itself, and would bar all Scotsmen's preferment in England. So that after an hour's struggle Fletcher was forced to let his favourite clause fall. But still the difficulty recurred about the Fond, without which the ministers said the Act would be ineffectual, and therefore pressed, that since the house thought it so much for the honour of her Majesty to be represented at public treaties by Scotch Ambassadors, and with all so advantageous to her ancient kingdom, these gentlemen might not be a rent charge upon her, which they said, they must be, if not otherwise provided for. And accordingly, they proposed that a clause of provision might be added to the Act. This met with abundance of opposition from several, who, though clear for establishing a Fond in a separate Act yet urged, that it would not be tacked to the Act itself, which was to be perpetual, whereas the clause contended for by the ministry was only temporary. In fine, after a long debate, which the Court party managed with all their art, a vote was to decide it, whether the house should proceed to approve the Act or delay it till such time as they had found out a Fond to answer the design of the Act—and it carried approved. After which the draft of an Act for settling the Fond desired had a first reading, and then the house adjourned till after tomorrow.

Sir John Buckworth to [Robert] Harley.

1705, September 11. London—Thanks for favour and encouragement lately shown to the body of the City in approving their just resentment of all scandalous reflections on our good Queen and her faithful ministry. We have some hopes that Mr. Recorder [Lovell] may be made a judge as a reward for his good services to the public, and as it highly concerns the public to have that place filled with a deserving person the City seems unanimously to desire he may be succeeded by Sir James Montague, as most acceptable to it. This lord mayor's time is short and he will be succeeded by at least five gentlemen of another stamp, and I wish I could say, as good magistrates as the present ; and if the office of Recorder become vacant in either of their years, it is odds but we may have an ill man put in. At present we are sure to have one we like.

[Robert Harley] to Mr. Valliere, peruque maker, Throckmorton Street.

1705, September 11—I received the news prints from your lady, by which it is plain they can if they please give dispatch to this conveyance. I desire you will exert yourself to establish it. I received your letter yesterday of a new way you propose ; I must leave that entirely to your judgment, for I cannot pretend to know that matter ; but in this time of action the quicker the intelligence the better the trade. I desire again you will be careful and diligent.

[Robert Harley] to the Count de Lionne.

1705, September 11–22. Whitehall—Signifying that leave is given to the Count to go to France by way of Holland for four months on his parole to return again. He is indebted to the Duke of Marlborough's lively representations of the circumstance of his affairs to her Majesty for this concession. *Draft.*

[WILLIAM GREG to ROBERT HARLEY.]

1705, September 13. Edinburgh—In my last of the 11th inst. I acquainted you with the untimely death of Lieutenant General Ramsay, who died so poor, that his only daughter has this day petitioned the Parliament for the payment of what debt he had contracted for clothing the regiment of foot guards, whereof he was Colonel. This debt, amounting to 4,000l. sterling was deemed so much the more just in that the deceased General so far consulted the honour of his post, that rather than see his men go naked he choosed in a manner to pawn his own private fortune, which is so much affected on that account, that the young lady can never touch a sixpence of it, unless relieved by the Parliament, who therefore went very cheerfully into a proposal for granting a month's cess. And accordingly the draft of an Act for that end had a first reading.

After this, the house went upon the business of the day, which when I heard proved to be only a continuation of the former day's amusement about the Ambassadors who, when they shall appear upon the stage, must by all means be handsomely provided for at the cost of the country, how little soever it may be able to bear the charges of one who is to have allowed him a month's cess, or 6,000l. sterling, payable within a month after her Majesty shall have signified her royal pleasure to the Privy Council.

Before the Act for such a fund came to be voted and approved, the Earl of Cromartie excused himself from voting, in regard he could not see, how any foreign prince or state would ever treat with Ambassadors, who though under one and the same sovereign with those of England, yet the crowns being distinct and independent, their interests must be different also, and consequently clash with one another.

What passed in the house after this was over is not worth troubling your honour with, being an Act for easing the town of Glasgow of debt.

The DUKE OF MARLBOROUGH to LORD [PORTLAND?].

1705, September 17. Tirlemont—I have had the favour of yours of the 12th and am obliged to you for your kind and if I may say just thought of me that I would not leave the Army whilst there is any likelihood of service ; though it be late in the year, I am not in despair but that something may be done, since Monsieur Slangenberg is gone as he says sick to Maestricht. Since you think I may leave the Army about the beginning of October there is no occasion of writing to Lord Treasurer, for he does not desire I should do it sooner, believing I might then be in England a fortnight before the sitting of the Parliament.

We shall march tomorrow to Diest and the next day to Aerschott where we shall employ three or four days in levelling the rest of the lines which we are masters of. I shall then use my utmost endeavours to inform myself of their line from Werckteren to Antwerp; for we may depend upon it that they will not come out of their lines. I hope there is no need of my giving you assurances that my utmost endeavours shall always be used for the continuation of the good correspondence between the two nations, I being fully persuaded that if ever we should be so unhappy as to disagree, France would make such use of it, as might prove very fatal to both England and Holland. I hope your occasions will not call you so soon for England, but that I may have the advantage of finding you at the Hague.

C[RAVEN] PEYTON, M.P. for Boroughbridge, to [the DUKE OF NEWCASTLE].

1705, September 18. Stratton Street—I am much concerned at those pains you mention to be troublesome to you. If you'll be pleased to give me a description of the nature of them, I can by discoursing with our best physicians (whom I see every day) perhaps learn by that means their sentiments more sincerely than by any other. The Whigs and Court are unanimous about the Speaker, and we shall certainly have a considerable majority. We cannot reckon the others to be above a hundred and seventy, though they depend upon being near the number I formerly mentioned. We think here Mr. Harley might have had it, but your Grace undoubtedly knows his reasons for declining, better than I do. Some Whigs indeed declared against him, and it is plain from whence the hint came, but the generality being determined to gratify the Court, if he had stuck to his point those gentlemen would have come in to him. My Lord Carlisle has been in town and the reconciliation with his lady is not effected, though much desired by him; so he is gone again into the north.

Private letters from Holland all agree that there is a project of a treaty of peace on foot at Aix-la-Chapelle.

[WILLIAM GREG to ROBERT HARLEY.]

1705, September 18th. Edinburgh—I did not presume to trouble you with any of mine last post, by reason the proceedings of Friday were hardly worth while as relating mostly to private business. This day the house was to have gone previously to all other business upon the consideration of the report of the Commissioners for stating and examining the public accounts, but that Fletcher found means to usher in the Sederunt with a new draft of a petition to the Commissioner and Estates of Parliament in consequence of one presented on Friday last by the Marquis of T[weeddale] on behalf of the merchants trading to France and Spain, for obtaining her Majesty's passes and protection against her ships of war, privateers, and those of her allies. The ministers were altogether against a thing which they thought her Majesty was not at liberty to grant. But others that were for it took occasion to argue in its favour from the tenor of her Majesty's letter to the Lords of the Treasury for releasing the Dutch Canary ship brought up some months ago. So that the whole house addressed the Commissioners, for representing to her Majesty the reasonableness of their humble request, to which they hoped for a favourable return, by his Grace's good offices.

After this, the house went upon the foresaid report which consumed the whole afternoon. Then the Parliament was adjourned till Friday, when everybody expected it would have risen; but it would seem, the Commissioner waits his orders touching the several Acts passed this session, though others say he has received them, but such as cut off the Council of Trade, Triennial Act, and that about choosing officers of State after her Majesty's death; and that therefore his Grace had taken upon him to remonstrate to her Majesty the uneasiness the nation would be under at so great a disappointment.

WILLIAM BORRETT to [RICHARD] WARRE.

1705, September 19. Inner Temple—Dyer the news writer was tried and convicted for writing libels and false news in the time of Mr. Baker, my predecessor, and still lies under that conviction.

The Same to the Same.

1705, September 21. Inner Temple—Forwards particulars of five libels published by Dyer in August 1699, for which Dyer was tried at Guildhall on June 15, 1700. In three of the cases he was found guilty, but exceptions being taken by Dyer's counsel against the information, Lord Chief Justice Holt took the Postea into his custody to consider it, and to keep it as a security for Dyer's good behaviour. Since which time the matter had not been stirred.

William Courtenay to [Robert] Harley.

1705, September 22—I showed Hannan your letter. He has sent you his answer to it, which comes short of what I expected. I know not what to make of him, he "snakes in and from the subject"; but however he commissioned me to tell that he knows of wicked practices carried on by merchants and that he has two things which he will never discover to any soul alive but you. He is a trifling fellow but I am sure will buckle at last; I'll be always at him till he does.

le Moyne to Robert Harley.

1705, September 30. [Newgate, *endorsed*]—Beseeches the Government to take pity on his miserable state, and to put him on his trial or discharge him. His clothes are all in pieces and he dreads the rigour of the coming winter. Begs to know the crime he has committed to deserve such unheard of hardness. Is very much obliged for the two guineas Harley had sent him.

The Duke of Marlborough to Lord [Portland?].

1705, October 1. Herenthals—I have had the honour of yours of the twenty-six of last month; and as to your calculation of the time for my journey to Vienna, I believe it is very just, which makes me of the opinion the Queen will not willingly consent to my going; and I am sure if she thinks I can be of any use to her in England, I shall have no other thoughts, but being obedient to whatever she commands; though at the same time I must own to you that if some care be not taken for the fixing of the Court at Vienna, as to the operations of the next campaign, and that so solemnly as that it may not be in the power of Prince Louis to alter it, all will go wrong, for if he governs it, their campaign will not begin sooner than the month of July, by which France will be able to make use of all their troops in this country till that time, which will disappoint the advantages which otherwise we might have by opening the campaign, but of this I shall be able to explain more particularly when I have the honour of seeing you, which was the reason of my desiring to find you at the Hague. As it is reasonable this army should continue in the field as long as is necessary to hinder the French from sending a detachment to the Marshal de Villars, I have accordingly written to Prince Louis to know how long he intends to keep the field; for as there must be at least three weeks' time for the march of a detachment to go from hence for Strasburg, so we may reasonably leave the field a fortnight before Prince Louis, which makes me think that if I do not go to Vienna, I may be at the Hague about the end of this month, so that ten days after I may be going for England. If this be not too late for you the same convoy may serve us.

[Major J. Cranstoun to Robert Cunningham.]

1705, October 1. Camp at Herenthals—I have received your letter, which by the date of Mr. Harley's that came with it I take to have been written in the beginning of August, but being addressed to Mr. Carstairs who is often very negligent it had lain there till about ten days ago when an officer of ours coming to his home and finding it on his table sent it to me. I thank you heartily for your news, you give me a fuller and more particular account of what passed in our Parliament than any we had here, though many of our officers had letters by every post. Everybody writes that after the Duke of Queensberry came into the Parliament the opposing party begun daily to lose ground, and but for him the ministry had succeeded as little in this as they did in former sessions. All seem pleased here that they have passed the Treaty Act, plain as they call it and unclogged, and though few expect much success from it or hope for any equal union with England, yet this will let the world see more plainly where the stop lies, will justify our nation and may be a means if we cannot obtain a reasonable union with England, at least to unite us amongst ourselves, which will be still a great blessing. I think there is a unanimous address from our Parliament to the Queen to have that clause in the English act making us aliens rescinded, and a resolve that our commissioners though named shall not treat till this is done. I should wish to know whether you think this will be complied with or not ; most here continue to think the English ministry as little sincere in their designs of a union as ever, and some who pretend to be Whigs and know that party in England very well tell us that the managing Whigs such as Lord Wharton, Lords Somers and Halifax, and even Mr. Harley, whatever they may pretend, are really the greatest enemies to the Union, and will though indirectly yet effectually obstruct it, because it is by the present confusions and difference that they make themselves necessary to a Court that in their heart hates them. I pray you as far as you judge proper write me your opinion of this which I am very loth to believe true, and write to me in general what hopes thinking, honest and impartial men with you have of any success from a treaty this winter. Most of our army here are Whigs and staunch ones, and so are very glad to hear that the Court have now for the first time declared themselves so much above-board as that of the Lord Treasurer's recommending Mr. Smith for Speaker seems to be. If this is sincere things must go well in the ensuing Session.

We have not here made any progress in the war this campaign answerable to our own and our friends' expectations of us. Faults there have been and miscarriages, and those great too, but where to lodge them is hard to tell, and we hope you will not look too narrowly into them since it cannot probably do any good. It is certain that when our army was on the Moselle Prince Louis and the Germans disappointed us much ; they neither came to join us at the appointed time, and the magazines at Treves were not provided as was undertaken, nor were there horses to draw our great train of artillery as the Electors and Princes on the Rhine had undertaken to have. In all this the Duke of Marlborough was innocent and ill used by others, but people who are ill-natured pretend to censure in him the project of going there with an army of 80 or 90,000 men to lie seven or eight weeks—which he must have done to have taken Saarlouis and Metz—in a country where the French who have been long masters of it say they could never subsist 25 or 30,000 men six weeks, and then it was the worst season of the year for forage, the corn being then but in the beard and not fit to cut. They say that when the Duke found the French did not detach after him as expected, he should have made his army halt at Duiren or mid-way, whereby he must have kept the French in awe and respect here and hindered them to attempt anything while our army was à porteé to come back, and have saved the forage about Treves and Sierck till all was ready for the siege and then it might have served us; or if· he could. not stop his army at Duiren he might at least have kept them about Trierwyler on this side Treves, for he then knew that neither the magazines were provided ·as promised, nor Prince Louis and the Germans and the Prussians ready, or that they could keep there. Yet notwithstanding of this we marched to Sierck and lay uselessly consuming forage for a fortnight in that very country which should have supplied the army during the siege of Saarlouis; so that they say if our allies had joined us at last we should have been obliged either not to have undertaken, ·or to have abandoned the siege for want of provisions and forage, and so the French besieging Huy and Liege, they say, was a favour to us and saved our credit in giving us a handsome pretence to abandon a design we should have been forced however to quit with greater disgrace.

This is what the ill-natured people amongst us and such as envy the Duke of Marlborough's glory say of the first part of our campaign; nobody denies but the Duke came in season to relieve the States who were trembling for their towns, but they say they neither sought nor expected that he should have brought back his whole army to them or abandoned absolutely the designs laid on the Moselle; they expected only such a detachment to strengthen Monsieur d'Overkerque as might have enabled him to keep the enemy in a little respect, and hinder their greater progress, though not to put him in a condition to fight them. However our returning here had once a great success, and the passing and forcing the French lines was a great action and wholly the Duke's own. The States opposed the very attempting it as a rash and impracticable thing, and indeed so did all their Generals and perhaps most if not all ours also; so that the Duke both laid the project himself and by his authority and interest at the Hague with great importunity did but at last obtain their consent to make trial, and orders to their Deputies and Generals only to second and follow him if he succeeded, or help to make his retreat if he miscarried, but not to share the danger with him. So that none dispute him the sole glory of this action, which if it had been followed out as begun, gave us all Brabant except the town of Dendermonde, and consequently both Antwerp and as much of Flanders as we had last war.

The not pursuing the advantage we had got here has been the beginning of misunderstandings and quarrels among us which have come since to a greater height. Few blame the Duke for not pushing Monsieur Caraman and that body of foot with which he retired, though it is certain and soon afterwards appeared he and they might have been all either taken, or cut in pieces with very little loss. for we had more than troops enough then come over to have destroyed him, and our horse and dragoons were already getting before and surrounding him when the Duke made them halt and let him go off; but as there was a rising ground behind him whither he was retreating, and the Duke really neither did nor indeed could at that time know how near the Elector and Marshal Villeroy were with their whole army, and Mousier d'Overkerque's army were but marching up at a distance and were not yet entered the lines, the Duke very prudently thought it better to let that body escape than perhaps by pursuing them bring himself rashly into a general action with the enemy's whole army before the half of his own were come within distance enough to join and second him. But Caraman being gone off and all the French squadrons who had offered any opposition entirely routed, our army marched on to Tirlemont, where a single battalion which was in garrison did upon the very first summons lay down their arms and yield themselves prisoners of war without retarding us one quarter of an hour. Yet unhappily the Duke halted here, and encamped so unluckily that it was the only spot after coming so far he could have encamped in so as to lose all the fruits of his victory, for had he marched forward to Louvain or but to Parc, which is but two hours farther, he was master of Louvain and all the enemy's great magazines there, and of Mechlin also, and so they could not hinder him to besiege both Liere and Antwerp. Or in place of marching to Louvain had he turned to the left and marched towards Jodoigne he necessarily forced the Elector and Villeroy either to fight him which they would not have done, or to retire towards Massy and Namur, and so abandon Brussels and all Brabant and Flanders. It was so plain a thing that we should not have halted, at least not encamped at Tirlemont, that not only all the inferior officer but even most of the common soldiers who had served in the last war and knew that country cried out at the time to their officers that we ought to march on to Louvain or at least to Parc for it was but ten o'clock in the morning when our army came to Tirlemont. Some general officers spoke and gave their advice publicly, of whom it is said the Earl of Orkney was one. Monsieur de Slangenberg, as he has taken great occasion to talk of since and to throw odium on the Duke about it, did come up to the Duke and congratulate him on the glorious success of the day, but also told him that we had done nothing if we lay still there and that we should march on to Louvain or Parc. The Duke himself owns this to be true and says he made this very answer to Slangenberg. "I am very glad, sir, to find you are of my opinion for this is my judgment of it too; I think we should march on, and I entreat you go back and dispose your Generals to it." Monsieur d'Overkerque, who had the day before made a feint and crossed the Mehaigne with his army and had all that way to march back again in the night farther than our troops had, was indeed pretty far behind with his army, and his troops having marched that night and morning considerably farther than the Duke's were certainly more wearied, and I believe it is agreed that he had sent to tell the Duke that his troops were wearied and could not march much farther; yet this being yet but ten in the morning the whole army might have rested four, nay five or six, hours to refresh and yet marched time enough that night to Parc to do the business and prevent the enemy. But it is said that when Monsieur Slangenberg went back from the Duke he neither returned to give the Duke an account what the Dutch Generals would agree to in this, and some say that before he got back to the States troops they had actually pitched their tents or were pitching them, which if true one would presume he as being one of the generals of the foot must have known it or given orders for it before he came up to the Duke. However it be, it is certain even the Dutch foot might have marched that day to Parc, and those who know an army and what soldiers are, know very well that upon occasions like this where even the common soldier is sensible of the reason of what he is to do, and especially in the joy of success and victory, soldiers with little entreaty will even outdo themselves and march and fatigue double with cheerfulness what their officers would at another time compel them to. There we encamped and lay all that night and those who take pleasure to satirise say that the pleasure of writing letters with an account of that day's great success to the Emperor, the Queen, the States, and others, and that of signing warrants for safeguards, of which above two hundred were writ and signed that afternoon, took people up so much that they forgot to pursue the advantages which were certainly in their hands. The orders were given out at night for the army to march at three next morning, but they did not actually march till seven.

The Elector it is said when our army first halted at Tirlemont stood upon an eminence observing us, and upon our halting long he waited there betwixt hope and despair, having given all over for lost, but when he observed the first tents pitching he cried out three or four times in a rapture *Grace au Dieu, Grace au ciel*, and then ordered his own troops to march, and without obliging them to keep any order bid every man make the best of his way to Louvain. They marched and marched all the night long, and yet though our army did not budge till next morning, our advanced squadrons and even some of our infantry came time enough to interrupt the rear of their army in crossing the river and to take some hundreds prisoners, by which it appears if we had but marched even at three in the morning as ordered, and sent our horse and dragoons before we might still have hindered the better half of their army from crossing the river, and have cut them off. Next it is said again that since we did nothing of all this yet at least when we did at length come up and see they had got over the river Dyle we ought then immediately that same day to have thrown bridges and forced our passage over while our troops were fresh, bold and flushed with victory, and theirs outwearied, dispirited, in confusion, many of them scattered and behind in the woods, and all under a panic terror of us, and the avenues and passes of the river yet unfortified, and that this was much liker to have succeeded than our attempt afterwards when they had recovered themselves and been fortifying all the accesses for sixteen days together and considered and posted their men in the best manner for their defence. As to the attempt we made thereafter to pass the Dyle whether it could have succeeded with us if it had been pushed, and what were the real reasons it was not, is more than I can inform you of, because even our great men differ and vary in their accounts of it. I think it is allowed this project was also of the Duke of Marlborough's own laying, and was well enough concerted supposing the thing practicable in the main, but Count Oxenstiern who, as Lieutenant-General in the army under the Duke's command, had the command of the troops detached from us in that attempt, though he had a far shorter way to march and more hands to work with, yet had got but one bridge laid over the river and half of another, while Lieut.-General Hucloem who commanded the six battalions and some squadrons detached from Overkerque's army, though he had much farther to march, had yet laid all his bridges and passed all his foot, chased the enemy from hedge to hedge, and had at last posted himself so well that he was able to have maintained himself there even for days together. Our people loitered and were in suspense as it were in laying the bridges, and indeed they say that where they did lay them the ground on the other side was impracticable for cavalry being *marécageux* whereas they might have found firm ground a very little farther below that. However they were but laying the second bridge about break of day when the Duke came there himself and being as it is said asked by Brigadier Ferguson who commanded in that detachment as Brigadier under Oxenstiern why we halted, and if we should not march on, the Duke made him answer grasping his hand " Hold your tongue, you know nothing, I have given my word to do nothing without consent." From that it is said his Grace rode and called the Dutch Generals together to Council, and asked if they thought it proper to go on and push the thing. It is talked that Monsieur Slangenberg should have said he doubted if we could sustain our head, meaning the front that should go over. Monsieur Salis it is said refused to give his opinion before his Velt Marshal who was there gave his first, and Monsieur d'Overkerque seeming to doubt if the thing could be carried, the Duke said there was then no time to reason on it but either to resolve to go on or immediately call back the troops that were over, and the Generals hesitating and seeming to show by their mien they did not think it advisable to push it, the Duke immediately ordered some aides de camp to go to Hucloem and Oxenstiern and order them to retire their men and take off their bridges. Hueloem raged and refused at first to retire being well posted, but having peremptory orders sent him again, obeyed with great regret. Some, and I think most, blame Count Oxenstiern for not having laid more bridges and passed more of his men, and this has given many people some ground to think Oxenstiern deserves a little the character some have of a long time given him as a man not too forward to expose his person to danger.

Upon the miscarriage in this attempt there begun I think first to appear some dryness and misunderstanding betwixt the Duke and some of the Dutch Generals. The Duke's friends justified his projects as good and well laid and practicable, and complained that he should be liable to be controlled and his good designs prove abortive, and the common good and his glory be obstructed by the Dutch generals slowness or over-wariness. The Dutch and their friends again sought to justify their own conduct by censuring the Duke's projects as rash. However these things were discoursed in private yet they did not break out publicly till the last attempt we made to force the enemy at the Ische, where the Duke was positively for attacking and all the Hollands Generals were of opinion it was a desperate thing, and perhaps sought to make it appear yet more difficult than it really was, though it must be owned that not only they but I think most or all of our own generals did think that affair so difficult that it was not to be attempted without hazard of ruining our army. Monsieur Slangenberg carried [himself] haughtily and roughly on that matter, and is accused of stopping the cannon on the march that day and forcing his own baggage to go before it, and it is said he spoke frowardly and harshly to the Duke. It is sure that both he and all the Hollands Generals took it ill that they were not put upon the secret of that design and complained this was treating them ill. You must have seen the letter the Duke wrote to the States on that attempt's miscarrying. Mr. Stanhope published it, which it is thought was not agreeable to the States and was the occasion why they allowed the letters written to them by their Deputies here and Generals to be published also. Many wished the Duke had not allowed his letter to be published because that rankled men the more and put the Dutch who were accused in it to justify themselves by canvassing and censuring the

Duke's conduct, and the dryness grew on this to so great a height that it was like an open breach. Generals Salis and Slangenberg seemed to take it hottest, and Slangenberg who by all is known to be a man of so uneasy and intractable a temper that he never yet could agree with anybody equal to or above him, spoke very free language everywhere, and writ two long letters in Dutch by way of narrative and vindication of himself and the States Generals, wherein he is satirical enough. General Churchill hearing that he spoke too freely and disrespectfully of his brother, and being informed these letters were detracting of the Duke's reputation sent Brigadier Palmes to him to tell him that if these things were as he was informed he expected to meet him and have satisfaction, and if it was otherwise he expected he should show his letters to Mr. Palmes. Slangenberg denied to have ever spoke unbecomingly of the Duke, and did show Brigadier Palmes his letters and so there was no more on it. It is believed the States have in their prudence taken care to prevent the ill consequences these jarrings must have had in obstructing the service, for Slangenberg soon after left the army on pretence of going to the Spa, and it is thought he will not be employed again, at least not in an army with the Duke; and we have it that the States have given the Duke a more ample power and authority over their troops than he had before. However the Dutch still censure us for many things particularly for keeping no discipline in our army, for which there is indeed but too much ground. They say our people have been, if not allowed yet connived at, in marauding and plundering of purpose to force the country wherever we came to come all in and ask safeguards, which bring in incredible sums of money. They and others also complain a little that the Duke does not advise so much either with the officers of experience and in the highest characters of his own and the States army as with two or three favourites whom he himself has raised, such as Brigadier Cadogan, Brigadier Palmes, and Brigadier Meredith, who are men of little service and experience. It is certain our army is now very weak and we have lost this summer in the British troops almost as many men by marauding and desertion, though we have not fought at all, as we lost last summer though we had two bloody battles. You will hear that the Duke is now at the Hague, and it is said is to stay only a day or two here when he returns and goes to Vienna. It is hoped the Queen and the States will increase their army here next summer, and it is believed that if the Duke do not agree to some other German progress for us, we shall endeavour to open the next campaign with the siege of Namur.

Dear Sir, I have wearied myself with writing this long scribble to satisfy your desire of knowing what has passed, and what is talked amongst us, and have writ on some things I know with greater freedom than prudence will allow, but I hope my letter will go right, and know it is safe with you. I desire earnestly to hear from you for I am still in pain about your condition. I shall be in garrison at the Bosch and you may address for me directly there, and in general I may now tell you at any time hereafter that there needs no other address for me in summer but to me in such a regiment in the army under the Duke of Marlborough's command, and in winter to me at the Bosch putting still Holland at the bottom; the letters will hardly ever miscarry. I have just now a letter from my wife with the agreeable news of her safe arrival at Rotterdam. I will write you to from the Bosch and will always mind both you and your family with as great tenderness and exactness as I shall myself and my own.   H

[*Two copies of this letter are attached to the original.*]

SIR ROBERT DAVERS, M.P. for Suffolk, to ROBERT HARLEY.

1705, October 2. Rougham—I hope your interest will not come into choosing Jack Smith Speaker for I very well remember what you said to me about him, and desire you may not have Cassandra's fate, for I take her to be a (gilt?) and was ravished at last. Do you not remember that you told me my Lord Treasurer bid you tell me and all your friends he would not suffer a Whig to come into place nor a "leagh torry." I will not launch out but will say we have been most barbarously used by one that we have not deserved it from. I have often told you that those vile wretches the Whigs only watch for an opportunity to tear you and that Lord to pieces, and you have always agreed with me in that matter; and we that have stood by that noble Lord and you to be called factious and sent home with a paper on our backs to be torn to pieces by the mob! I do hope nothing of that matter lies at your door. I beg pardon for this egression (*sic*).

"HARRY" [ST. JOHN] to [ROBERT] HARLEY.

1705, October 2—Dear Master I am just going by Dr. Garth's directions into the country for a few days. I have taken the best care I can that nothing may suffer during my absence in which I am concerned, and I depend on you for making my excuses. If I can recover my health perfectly against the meeting of Parliament, I promise you to make amends for this absence.

ROBERT HARLEY to [WILLIAM] DISTON.

1705, October 3. Whitehall—The malice of ill willers to the government and the licence of the scribblers is come to that height as to leave nothing without the marks of their rage and fury; amongst other things they have libelled the grand jury of which you were the worthy foreman. However it is not fit that these men should go on thus without correction, so you may be assured order is taken for prosecuting this libel. *Copy.*

[The SAME] to the ATTORNEY-GENERAL.

1705, October 4—Mr. Hannan, now in Newgate, having made offers of doing very considerable service to the Queen if he may be admitted to bail until the Session after next, you may admit him to bail, unless you have any objection.

Several persons now under bail for printers' libels have repeated them, and I am to ask you what ought to be done with them.

SIR JOHN GIBSON to [ROBERT HARLEY].

1705, October 6. Portsmouth—With the assistance of Capt. Henry Player and the Constables had searched every hole and corner of the house of Mr. Pugh, tobacconist, but had not found the person expected. Had heard that he had been seen since at Gosport, and on the way to Southampton.

[HENRY ST. JOHN] to [ROBERT] HARLEY.

1705, October 7. Bucklebury—Dear Master, I am sure you will not think me impertinent if I trouble you with a letter, to tell you that I recover strength apace, and hope in a week's time, or ten days at furthest, to return to my friends and my duty, since you cannot have a more faithful nor more zealous servant than myself, and therefore you are in some measure concerned in my recovery; at least I would fain find a reason to make you so.

I received a letter from Shrimpton with papers enclosed from the Alcaide; they contain some matter of complaint which I thought much more proper to make your brother busy than to trouble you with.

I hear you remove this week to the Cockpit, I hope they will think it as reasonable that I should at last have some place to be in while I am in this employment, as that Mr. Blathwayt should still enjoy a very good house for having been in it.   Your faithful Harry.

The DUKE OF MARLBOROUGH to LORD [PORTLAND ?].

1705, October 8. Herenthals—You will have seen by a copy of the Emperor's second letter, which I sent to the Pensioner by the last post, how extremely I am pressed to make the journey to Vienna; I did at the same time acquaint him that I would be at the Hague next Monday, but that I did not intend to stay above two or three days at most, for I must return again to the army, and if you are not otherwise engaged I shall be glad to dine with you on Tuesday, till when I shall give you no farther trouble.

A. [LADY] PYE to her cousin, ABIGAIL HARLEY, at Auditor Harley's at Eywood.

1705, October 8. Derby—I was just three weeks and two days in town so I tell Sir Charles he must not reckon it a London journey. I could not get to see many of my own relations but nothing so much troubled me as to miss your sister Hutchins. I am heartily glad your sister is so well disposed; she looks brave and jolly. I had a sight of the fine earrings and necklace. I never saw any youth so grown as your nephew Ned Harley. His countenance shews him a sweet nature, not injured in the least by the small-pox. When you see him I guess you'll be told what a visit I made in his absence to his chambers and how I came acquainted with his good old landlady. In good manners I should have mentioned your brother the Secretary in the first place, whose greatness doth not make him forget his old acquaintance and relations, being still the same cousin Robin Harley; he was so kind soon to find me out and invited me to dinner.

I saw Cousin Hadley twice in town, and one day at Barnet. The eldest son much improved, looks cheerful like other young men of his time, that I suppose he has laid aside his high mathematics.

NEWS LETTER.

1705, October 9. London—Paris letters of the 12th say that Barcelona is surrendered to King Charles and that his Majesty entered that place on the 23rd. That all Catalonia had declared for him as had part of Arragon and divers fortified places.

Those from Lisbon on the 4th say that the confederate army is passed Badajoz and marched into Castile in hopes that the Castilians will declare for King Charles.

Edinburgh, 2nd. This day the Council met and gave commissions to several persons to seize and "forefault," all provisions that shall be brought from Ireland, allowing them twenty-five soldiers four sergeants and ten dragoons to attend them. The Commissioners grace declared that it was her Majesty's royal pleasure that a pardon should be granted to the remainder of Captain Green's crew which was agreed to, and the Lord Advocate was to take care of its passing the seals. Our magistrates were chosen also, but I shall not trouble you with their names.

Portsmouth, the 6th. On Thursday happened here a great storm which did much damage to the shipping in which the *Scarboro* man of war was forced to cut her main and mizzen masts by the board to secure her from driving on shore, but afterwards she rid it out and we fear a great deal more damage was done to the shipping in other ports.

Yesterday the Quarter Sessions began at Guildhall when the Recorder in his charge to the grand jury directed them to present the public houses that take in seditious libels.

[ROBERT HARLEY] to MR. VALIERE at the sign of the Peruque in Throckmorton Street.

1705, October 10—I am very well assured you are discovered by several persons where you are : the particulars you shall know as soon as I see you, which is very necessary I should do very speedily, that we may think of some other place. Therefore hasten up unless you expect an immediate return from ———— this day or to-morrow.

[JOHN OGILVIE *alias* LEBRUN] to [ROBERT] HARLEY.

1705; October [12-]23 [new style]. Rotterdam—I arrived here on Wednesday last, and my friends parted some time ago for Hanover. Not that I believe they will wait on the Court, only divert themselves at Lamspringe. When they come for Amsterdam you shall know more. What I had to say to you, I have sent it under cover to my wife, but I could not tell if my addressing of your letter to Mr. Robert Bryan would come to your hands unless it were put under cover to somebody, and there is none that I will trust on that head. So when this comes to your hand when it is a little dark you may send your porter for my wife and she will give you my letters ; but depend upon it she will not send them. You must cause your porter put off his livery coat when he brings her. She lodges in Drury Lane at the sign of the Boot and Slipper nigh the Horse Shoe tavern. I send you here a letter from Mr. Aldersey. I wish you could render him any service for he is the honestest man among all the English merchants. Stratford is not what you believe him. I thank God I had nothing to do with him.

[The SAME] to ROBERT BRYAN [HARLEY].

1705, October [12-]23. Rotterdam—I had the honour to acquaint you from Hamburg that I would not fail to give you a full account of what I did learn there; so I now perform my promise and it is as follows. If you remember I told you that there was one gone to Scotland to sound the Duke of Hamilton; that person is returned and his Grace's answer is that he is most willing to enter into measures for the Prince of Wales, but it must be upon sure footing, that is, in the first place he must know what party he hath in England, and what they can do for his service there; in that he must be entirely satisfied of. In the next place there must be a body of troops landed and money sent for to carry on the war with a good train of artillery and when he is satisfied of all this he will declare himself but not before, but in the meantime they will put the nation in the best posture of defence they can. This is all I can learn as to them.

Now as to what else I learnt is as follows—The King of France is designed to try another method and that is, to propose a peace with the Queen that she shall reign peaceable all her life, but that Her Majesty shall take such measures as that the Prince of Wales shall succeed to her; that is to be proposed immediately. There is a person in London for that effect, who returns his answer by way of Hamburg to a person that stays there for that end that he may acquaint Monsieur de Torcy with what passes, and if that fail then there will be measures taken to gain Scotland and send in men there. As for the men there is one hath undertaken· to find 12,000 men and shipping to land them in Scotland or in the north of England for a sum not much exceeding six hundred thousand crowns.

If the battle of Hogstat [Hochstet or Blenheim] had not been lost to them this had been put in execution, but the loss of that battle put them by all their measures that they were obliged to look to their own preservation. Now you'll wonder how I came to find out all this, so I will be frank with you. When I came to Hamburg I was received very well by my Lord D[rummond] and he carried me to a company where he did use to eat with, so amongst these men who does I see but an old acquaintance though in disguise; he is a Major General just now in the French Service, his name is Count Belke, he is a Swede born but hath passed all his time in France he is also Colonel of the Royal Almonry (?). I being known to him, for I have served where he commanded, and then my Lord D. telling him of all my sufferings, I did ingratiate myself so in his esteem that he was never without me; so he gave me a full account of all this. There is also one there, he is a Swede, his name is General Tisenhangen, he was formerly a Brigadier in the French Service but is now Lieutenant-General to King Augustus of Poland, but he would not serve against his own Prince; but King Augustus allows him all his appointments and he is entirely in the French interest and assists Count Belke; this Count Belke is nephew to the famous Marshal Belke that was in Sweden. There is another Monsieur Lebate, he is a Frenchman born and Colonel of a thousand horse in the King of Denmark's service. He was forced to quit France above twenty years ago for fighting a duel; this man assists Count Belke in all his private negociations. You must know that the Court of St. Germain knows nothing of all this, neither will they have them to know anything of the matter till it be just ready to be done. I was desired by Count Belke to go to France and to assure Monsieur de Torcy that in case the Treaty with England did not take effect he would answer upon the pain of his head for the 12,000 men I have told you of; and he did give me Monsieur de Torcy's cipher to take a copy of that I might writ to him. He is to see to find some body to speak to the Duchess of Tyrconnel to see if she would persuade the Duke of Marlborough to be a good instrument in the Treaty of Peace. Count Belke told me that his friend at London told, that is, wrote him word he had proposed it to

R 2.

the Queen but as to that I did not believe, neither will I touch on that point; but when I am in France and see how Monsieur de Torcy relishes the thing then you shall know more at large. I think I have performed my duty since I have been at Hamburg, for your Resident, nor none else could ever have dived into this, for these men are above the keeping of company with any thing of merchants except it be for their own ends. You may judge it must cost me money to keep their company, but I have still twenty pounds left; now if I go to France I cannot hear from you till I return, but there is one thing I must acquaint you of, that I am almost ruined by the indiscretion of some whom you trust, for Mrs. Richeson could tell that I had a bundred pounds given me and that Mr. D[rummond] in Amsterdam was to give me more. Now your Honour must know to whom you did communicate this, for from myself it never came. You know my life and couse-quently the lives of my poor family depended on it. There is not such another prating lying bitch as she is in England. It hath gone to Mrs. Fox's ears and Floyd's, and they have writ against me to St. Germain, as you will see from my wife; so I pray you when you come to see Mrs. Richeson inquire of her when she heard of me, and you must tell her that I am no man of honour to you, for I did promise to go to the army and on that consideration you had ordered some money for me; but as I had broke my word I should have none, but if you did catch me I should be punished. This you must take care to do forth-with, for she hath told up and down that I can do the Government more service where I am than at London. My wife will let you see the letters I received from France. I have sent them on that account that your Honour may see the danger I lie under. However if you take right measures with that bitch then all may go well again, for my party is pretty strong at that Court and then the authority that I am backed with from Hamburg will go a great way to support me. But be as it will the Queen did give me my life when last in prison, and with the grace of God I shall never be ungrateful but venture always and on all occasions that life she did give me to serve her. But we may suppose the worst and that they take me and throw me into the Bastille, then I hope your Honour will still persuade the Queen to settle a maintenance on my poor wife and four small children.

WILLIAM COURTENAY to [ROBERT HARLEY].

1705, October 13—Harman would fain know when you would have him wait on you, and I long to see him do something to please you that we may see whether or no he deserves all the great favour you have shewn him. He ought to make a solemn declaration of what he knows, otherwise I'll deliver him up again. I live on the Stone Terrace next the Iron Gate near Mayfair.

GUSTAVUS ERIKUS NERIBAN to ROBERT HARLEY.

1705, October 15. Gosport—Informing him that the Portuguese spy arrested with letters about him directed to many eminent gentlemen in England had been handed over to Sir John Gibson, deputy governor of Portsmouth, who had sent him to London. Being very conversant with most languages the writer could be very useful in apprehending foreign disaffected persons who might come over, and desired employ-ment. He had made a declaration before Sir John Gibson that Dutch merchant ships frequently supplied the French nation with ammunition and stores of all kinds.

William Courtenay to Robert Harley.

1705, October 15—Hannan was with me last night. I desired him to double his despatch towards an accommodation with you by making out those matters you required at his hands. His answer was that Mrs. Banks bespattered him to such purpose by giving out that he was an informer and discoverer, that none of the illegal traders among the merchants would keep him company, and consequently impossible for him to do anything at present. Thus the little shuffler prevaricates and abuses your mercy and I refer to your own wisdom what is proper to be done to this little dog.

Robert Harley to Sir Robert Davers.

1705, October 16—I do assure you I have the same principles I came into the House of Commons with; I never have willingly nor never will change them. It hath been my misfortune for twelve years past almost every session to get the ill word upon one occasion or other of both parties; for the good word of one side I did not court it, and that of the other I lost it only upon such occasions by which they ran into those extraordinary things which gratified none but their enemies, as appeared by many instances. At length I was thrust into the forlorn hope, in the affair of Speaker; I was very sensible of the risk I then ran. I am glad that I was in the least capable to serve my friends, though I must tell you I suffer to this day for that affair; but that is no matter. Since then I have laboured with the utmost application to prevent our friends doing anything unreasonable, anything to give a handle to the enemy to do them hurt, or to lose their interest in the nation. I have honestly warned them, I have publicly and privately foretold them the consequences of what they were doing; but tares have been sown in the wheat, and impracticable measures suggested by those, who whatever else they meant, did not intend the public good— but this is more proper for discourse than a letter. I will therefore add no more of myself but that I defy the world to say I have directly or indirectly done anything against the common interest of the Church or Monarchy of England, but this is too much to any one but so good a friend. As to what I mean by reasonable—it is this, the Queen hath nothing to ask for herself, she will protect nobody in doing ill; therefore it is easy to agree what is reasonable to defend ourselves—and as to the Lord hinted at in your former letter, to my knowledge he never left those that complain, they went away from him, and then are angry. As to the load laid upon me, it is unjust, and I can not only bear such a load with patience but despise it.

I never have got by the Public, and I can retire with ease every hour in the day to the same plenty and more peace than I now enjoy, and I shall think myself as great a man in my own bowling green at home, as now in a toilsome office at Whitehall. (*Copy.*)

Sir John Gibson to [Robert Harley].

1705, October 16. Portsmouth—The other day an Italian was brought before me with the enclosed pass and letters. The pass is of a pretty old date, besides I did not think it usual for a foreign minister to give passes of this sort. This made me secure this person, and send the pass and letters to you to learn your pleasure.

Enclosed is a document dated 28th August, 1705, with a fine seal, purporting to be signed by Giraldi, envoy to the Duke of Tuscany and Vincent Tucci, his secretary, certifying that two Italian seamen belonging to the ship *Stella* anchored at Plymouth are come to London on some business; and it is desired that they may have liberty to return on board, without any manner of hindrance.

News Letter.

1705, October 16. London—We have nothing from the Upper Rhine, the new levies that are making for the Emperor in Bavaria are carried on with great difficulties, the youths that are fit to bear arms choose rather to fly the country than take service, but there is orders to prevent that and force them; 16,000 men will be quartered in that country this winter to make them suffer for their disaffection they having a great inclination to rebel again.

Edinburgh the 9th. Yesterday morning his Grace the Duke of Argyle her Majesty's High Commissioner set out from Newbattle the seat of the Marquis of Lothian for Court accompanied in the coach only by his brother the Lord Archibald Campbell, and this morning set out hence for Court, the Marquis of Annandale Lord President of her Majesty's Council; as will my Lord Chancellor the Earl of Seafield and the two Secretaries of State on Monday next.

Shields the 12th. Yesterday came in here two ships from the east country who report that they came from Russia &c. with a great fleet of merchant men with their convoy but meeting with contrary winds, they suppose they are put into some port in Norway..

There is advice from Dover that Count St. Paul is put to sea with a squadron of men of war from Dunkirk but care is taken to bring home our East India ships that are put into Kinsale with a sufficient force not to fear him whatever his designs may be of putting to sea now.

Roger Mompesson Esquire, some time since a member of Parliament for Southampton and of the society of Lincolns Inn but withdrawing to America upon the account of some incumbrances, is made Chief Justice of New York and other Colonies under the Government of the Lord Cornbury, which is worth about 500*l.* per annum; he is an honest gentleman and a learned lawyer and succeeds in it Mr. Attwood. My Lord Keeper designs to keep his first Seal on Thursday next in the Middle Temple Hall of which house his Lordship is a member; the Masters in Chancery and the other officers that are dependants on that high court have been to compliment his Lordship upon his accession to that high court and had as complaisant a reception.

It is talked that the Earl of Bridgewater will be made Lord Chamberlain to the Queen by the resignation of the Earl of Kent and that his Lordship will be succeeded in his place of Master of the Horse to the Prince by the Marquis of Monthermer.

News Letter.

1705, October 18. London—Letters from Switzerland give an account that the cantons are solicited on all sides for their troops, the ministers of France and Spain press them to renew their ancient treaties by virtue of which they are bound to supply them with a body of troops in case they are engaged in a war as now in this juncture they are.

The Pope also by his Nuncio has demanded of the catholic cantons several thousand men by virtue of their ancient alliance with the Court of Rome but for what end the Pope demands these troops is not known, but the same causes divers reflections. However the general opinion is that he will not do any thing that shall widen the present difference with the Emperor especially in this conjuncture when Charles the Third has so fair a prospect to get the crown of Spain.

The cantons of Zurick and Berne have not yet ratified the treaty which the Republic of Venice has renewed with them which was so much opposed by the ministers of France and Spain, by virtue of which they are to furnish that Republic with 4,000 men.·

From the confederate camp before Badajoz October the 11th N. S. our forces having drawn together in the neighbourhood of Elvas the Marquis das Minas who commands in chief having held several councils of war about the operation of the campaign in which after divers and various sentiments it was resolved to besiege Badajoz, according to which and all the commands being adjusted the army marched and on the 2d. passed the river Guadiana without any opposition from the Marshal de Tessé which we expected and on the 3rd came and encamped before this place.

On the 4th we opened our trenches before the gate of Merida within 100 paces of the covered way during which the enemy made a great fire but killed and wounded very few. On the 6th the heavy cannon arrived in the camp and last night we began to throw our bombs into the town and this day we play upon it from three batteries of heavy cannon and our engineers doubt not but to be masters of the place in ten or twelve days, the Marshal de Tessé who is posted with 7 or 8,000 men three leagues from our camp being in no condition to give us disturbance much less to relieve it.

Lisbon 13th. We are in great hopes soon to be masters of Badajoz and the garrison it is said is not above 2,000 strong and this evening the Marquis Das Minas's son arrived with good news from the camp, upon which a rumour is spread that the place is surrendered.

Falmouth 13th. This day the *Alliance* packet boat, Captain Green commander, arrived here in ten days from Lisbon with a mail and brings the report as above that Badajoz had surrendered but on this we dare not depend by reason the letters from the camp speak as though it would be a work of ten or twelve days.

Yesterday the Lord Mayor, Court of Aldermen, and Recorder presented the Lord Mayor elect to the Lord Keeper for his approbation of the city's election, it being an ancient compliment, and were treated according to custom with cake and burnt wine, at the same time they complimented his Lordship's accession to that high dignity. This morning his Lordship sat the first time in the Middle Temple Hall where was a great concourse of persons of note to usher his Lordship to the bench. On Tuesday the Joint East India Company held a court and having resolved to borrow 100,000*l.* to be employed in trade, the same was subscribed immediately before the court rose. The yachts are in Holland to bring over the officers of the army that are members of Parliament to be here at the choice of a Speaker. Cardigan house in Lincolns Inn Fields is taken up for the Duke of Shrewsbury who is suddently expected over with his new Duchess.

News Letter.

1705, October 20. London—Cardinal Radziowsky, primate of Poland, died at Dantzick on the 13th inst. about noon in the sixty third year of his age, and the twenty second of his Cardinalate, and has left behind an incredible wealth, most of which he has given to the new Queen who was his relation.

This monster raised all the troubles in Poland but could not live to see them ended, and died of mere grief at the treatment of the Pope, who deprived him of all his offices and benefices for his disobedience to the holy see, which brief of the Pope's was affixed to the gate of his palace at Dantzick, and at three Romish churches in that city by the Castelan Posaniecky, which struck the Cardinal to the heart.

The Pope's nuncio has declared that his master will not bestow this vacant cap on any bishop that is in the interest of the pretended King.

King Augustus's faithful friend Monsieur Sinigielsky invested Marlembourg in Prussia on the 29th past with 3,000 Poles and some Saxons, and on the 1st instant took the place sword in hand, and cut all the Swedes in pieces that he found in arms, and gave the city to the plunder of his soldiers as their punishment for taking in a Swedish garrison.

Paris letters of the 23rd say that the faithful Catalans have put a great supply of cattle into Barcelona, and that the place defends itself so well that in all appearance the enemy will be forced to quit the enterprise, and the rather for that Prince Circlas de Tilly is marching into Catalonia to command the troops that are marching thither from divers parts of Spain. These letters add that the Viceroy was slightly wounded in a sally, but that the trenches were not opened before the place on the 9th instant.

Shields 14th. This day arrived here one of the Russia fleet who made her passage from Archangel in five weeks, but was separated from the fleet and three men of war their convoy twelve leagues west of the Cape, and believes they are 100 leagues behind ; upon which four men of war more are sailed to meet them and secure them from Count St. Paul.

A great many officers are come from Holland in the last packet boat, but the yachts are still in the Brill which are to bring over the Polish and Venetian Ambassadors and some other great men.

This morning died William Elson Esquire member of Parliament for Chichester, who came to town but last night, by whose death Mr. Bromley has lost a vote, as have the Whigs by the death of Colonel Dore.

Sir Richard Temple and some other officers that are members of Parliament are arrived from Holland, as are others from Ireland.

Major J. Cranstoun to [Robert Cunningham].

1705, October 20. Camp at Calemthout—I wrote to you at great length about five or six weeks ago enclosed under cover to Thomas Harley, and that under cover to Edward Harley, the Auditor, as you directed. I wish my letters have gone safe to your hand, because I wrote upon some things with greater freedom than perhaps prudence would have well allowed. I have nothing of news to write now since you will know of the Duke's journey to Vienna more than probably any of us here do, and that we have taken the little place of Santoliet, but by besieging it have given the enemy opportunity to *enlever* from us four battalions of foot and the best part of a regiment of dragoons which we had put into the town of Diest, having determined to keep that place Santoliet and some others within the enemy's lines as frontier garrisons for this winter. Diest had only a slight thin old Roman wall and dry fosse about it, and that broken down too in some places, and the breaches only made up with palisades which we had lately put there, and built a little redoubt or two in haste upon the eminences that commanded the town. However all this did not make it a place of defence, but having so many garrisons near it we reckoned that if the French had attempted against it in winter we could have drawn force enough to oppose them ; but our troops now not being gone yet into garrison, and the army come all together at this distance from it to cover this unlucky siege, the enemy took the occasion, and we foresaw and feared it, so that in that view partly not only the Duke of Marlborough but even all the Dutch generals opposed the design of besieging this place, as a little hole of no use to us when taken ; and indeed now that we have it we are razing the works, but as it lies on the borders of Zeeland and several partisans used to nestle there and infest the province, the States of Zeeland were so obstinate to have it taken that the Duke was forced to yield, and we paid dearly for it. The subject of this is to acquaint you that Brigadier Ferguson died at the Bosch on the 12th instant of a high malignant fever. The Duke being lately at the Hague had wrote to him to meet him there, and acquainted him that he was going now to declare him Major General, and would send him the Queen's commission so soon as he got to London, but left him here this winter to command in chief all the British troops as well horse as foot on this side during the winter. The Brigadier had had a fit or two of an ague at the Bosch, but it seemed gone off, and he had been well for above a week, but his ague recurred at the Hague and he was ill, yet his lady being brought to bed of a daughter but a week before he would not stay but hastened home, and by travelling in the cold was seized so ill that he was carried speechless from the waggon to his house and without knowledge : those fits recurred every day from Sunday till Thursday that he died. All the English themselves and even his greatest enemies while he was yet alive allowed he was by much the best officer we had in all the British troops. He was brave, knew the service ; had great and long experience in thirty years constant service ; and the Duke was so sensible of this that when he had anything difficult or of importance to do he constantly employed him even out of his turn. Our regiment has a great loss, and I in particular more than they all, for he allowed me all his confidence and all his friendship. Many have already put in for our regiment as Lord Mark Kerr, Lord Edward Murray, but principally Colonel Macartney, who having but a new raised regiment which must probably be broke at the peace, he seeks to obtain ours, and has found the way to get Brigadiers Cadogan, Meredith, and Palmes to recommend him, and they you know are looked on with us as the three great favourites with the Duke. Lieutenant Colonel Borthwick, who is our Lieutenant Colonel, is allowed by all indifferent people to have the only just right to it. He is an honest plain brave man, and a good officer, has served several years with reputation in Sweden before the Revolution, was invited to be captain in our regiment at its first raising, was severely wounded at Steenkirk and made then major to us by the King, and has continued now near fourteen years Major and Lieutenant Colonel to the regiment, and so, by his rank and the course of his service as well as by his merit and bravery, ought to have the regiment in justice. If he gets it my preferment to be Lieutenant Colonel ought and I hope will follow in the same course, but if any other Colonel is brought over his head it stops of consequence both my advancement and all the officers in course below me. Both he and I have found more friends in the army on this occasion than we durst have hoped for, for he has the good wishes of all who have not a particular interest in some of his competitors. My Lord Orkney who, both by his quality of oldest Lieutenant General of the foot and his being at the head of the Scots troops here, has a right both to advise and to be bold with the Duke in what relates to Scots regiments. My Lord, I say, professes to be our friend and we have all ground to believe he is sincere, but he is modest and is shy to meddle, so that if his Lordship does us the honour and justice to recommend us yet we have reason to fear he will not be importunate or urge it unless he finds his Grace inclined. Mr. Cardonnel and Colonel Durell, who are both gone to Vienna with the Duke, have promised us all their interest, and we believe they are sincere, and have taken such measures as Mr. Cardonnel will find his interest in our preferment. The Duke seems at least as favourable to Colonel Borthwick as to any of his rivals, for when he first spoke to him he bid him make a memorial of his pretensions and give it him, and when he gave it to his Grace the night before he went for Vienna the Duke took it very favourably, and told him that he knew the particular circumstances and constitution of our regiment very well, would have a tender regard to it, and assured him the regiment should not be disposed of till he were satisfied. But this we fear may be a design to give Colonel Macartney our regiment and give Borthwick his, which is what I know the favourites all solicit, but the Lieutenant Colonel will not accept of Macartney's regiment, both as it is new and must be broke, and as he by his ill conduct has already run it over head and ears in debt; and our whole officers and soldiers have such a terror of Colonel Macartney's coming upon our head, that they are all in despair about it, looking upon the regiment as inevitably ruined, for he who has already squandered all his own and lady's fortune, and I fear her children's also, and has in one year by his gaming and rioting run his own regiment in debt, and is so much himself in debt that he can now neither go to England or Scotland, must by these measures not only oppress but soon utterly ruin any regiment he gets. So in these circumstances we reckon we have no measures to keep, and though it is an unusual thing in the army yet we have made a joint petition, signed by all the officers of the regiment present in camp, except the Lieutenant Colonel who as interested could not handsomely appear in it, mentioning to be in their own names and at the desire of all the serjeants, corporals, and soldiers of the regiment, wherein we narrate the manner of our regiment's first levying, their serving out of principle of religion, the King's constant encouragement to us to continue on that foot and giving us frequent instances that he would put no officer amongst us, but such as were of our persuasion and acceptable to the regiment and that party in Scotland; so we beg his Grace to give us our Lieutenant Colonel for Colonel, or if he will not do that at least to give us some man of merit who may be less unacceptable to us all and to our friends in Scotland than Colonel Macartney is conceived to be. This petition I delivered myself to the Duke as he took coach for Vienna, and as it is by some termed a bold action, and by others a vigorous address, but by most indifferent people here approven of, so however it may perhaps be taken ill out at my hands, as being a field officer I must be reckoned the chief in it, yet most think it will effectually exclude Colonel Macartney, who was not very favourably stated with the Duke before, and I know when he spoke for our regiment, the Duke gave him no answer at all, and to Lord Mark Kerr he said only that he might speak to him when he came back to the Hague; to Lord Edward Murray he answered "My Lord, your service is not so great, you are but a captain yet, and I cannot give you a regiment when so many field officers are to provide for." Colonel Preston, of Lord John Hay's dragoons, certainly puts in for it too, but he is sick at present, so I know not how or by whom he applies, but it is believed the Duke will not dispose of the regiment till he goes to London, and there we fear that the Duke of Argyle and Duke of Queensberry with the rest of our ministry will strike in and recommend some man of quality in Scotland for it, which will create us new and more powerful rivals if the ministry join to interest themselves. If Borthwick must lose it and we have another Colonel put upon us, we all agree to wish the regiment may be given to the little Duke of Douglas, for his education preferable to all the world except our Lieutenant Colonel. But since Borthwick has the justest pretensions, and by his preferment we hope all to rise in our course, it is natural to insist for him as far as we can. He will go to London I believe with the Duke to solicit his own right, and will wait upon you and beg your assistance, and I would too, since my interest and his are the same here, but we cannot be both absent from the regiment, and my wife being here a stranger I cannot think to leave her whatever come of it. I have writ to Lord Philip-haugh by last post but I find since by our gazettes that our Commissioner, Duke of Queensberry, and Secretaries are come off from Edinburgh, so I must earnestly entreat you, my dearest friend, to interest yourself a little in this, where not only my fortune, but my honour and reputation are so much concerned. My friend's, the Lieutenant Colonel's, interest and mine are the same or almost so, for though it is true they may give him the regiment and yet put another Lieutenant Colonel over my head, yet to be sure if he gets not the regiment I cannot be Lieutenant Colonel. I entreat that how soon our great men arrive you will sound them and learn how the Duke of Argyle, Duke of Queensberry and the Chancellor and Secretaries are disposed in favour of Borthwick, and whether they design to recommend any other and who it is, and that you would without losing time inform me of it so as I may know it before the Duke of Marlborough returns to the Hague, where he is determined to be back by the last of November at latest, because we may take our measures here upon your information, and if it is found that different persons shall be recommended at Court, or children and others who will not serve in the war, perhaps that may incline the Duke to dispose of the regiment here before he goes over to prevent his being solicited for different persons or people he may not incline to have. And in case our great men are not yet arrived I wish you would sound Sir David Nairne who probably may know their mind. I know you will speak both to the Duke of Queensberry and the Duke of Argyle, that if Colonel Borthwick get the regiment nobody may be put over my head as Lieutenant Colonel, since it would reduce me to despair; and if they should do that I know not but I should be inclined rather to quit my commission and throw myself upon Providence than bear it. At least I am sure if I were a single man I should not balance to it. If Ormeston, the Justice Clerk, come to Court, he is the Lieutenant Colonel's neighbour and his good friend, and I hope will be useful to him. I shall write to you when the Duke returns how he seems disposed. In the meantime I depend upon your giving me information of what part our great folk will act in it, and that as soon as possibly you can. Address your letter directly for me, of the late Brigadier Ferguson's regiment in garrison at Bois le Duc, Holland, and it cannot miss me. I desire to be affectionately remembered to good Mrs. Cunningham.

Postscript.—I have by this same post wrote myself to the Duke of Queensberry and sent him a double of our petition, begging his favour · for the Lieutenant Colonel and at least against Colonel Macartney. If the Earl of Leven come to Court I hope he will favour the regiment and the Lieutenant Colonel's and my pretensions; so pray apply to him.

JOHN SHOWER to [ROBERT HARLEY].

1705, October 27. Clerkenwell—Acknowledges the present of *The Memorial of the State of England.* It appears to him the most judicious and seasonable of anything lately printed, sets the real state of our case in a true light, with excellent judgment and eloquence. Desires twenty five copies to be sent to him that he may promote the spreading of it.

S[ALWEY] WINNINGTON to [ROBERT HARLEY].

1705, October 27—The kind concern you are pleased to express for my affair in the House gives me great assurance of success in it, for a just cause supported by your interest cannot fail. I have troubled you with the case which is faithfully represented and, unless there be perjury on the other side, will appear to be as I have stated it. The only difficulty is the mistake of the town clerk in not entering upon the poll the two persons who voted for Mr. Foley; but as the fact is certainly true and will be proved by twenty witnesses I hope the negligence of the officer will not turn to my prejudice.

NEWS LETTER.

1705, October 27. London—Our port letters say that on the 23rd our Russia fleet safely arrived in Tynemouth road, but we have worse news from Hull concerning our East Country fleet from Hamburg Dantzick &c. which is that three of her Majesty's frigates with twelve sail of merchant-men (most Dutch) had fallen in with Count St. Paul's squadron consisting of seven frigates and five privateers, with whom her Majesty's frigates maintained a fight for several hours, but it was feared most of them were taken and carried to Dunkirk; the rest of the fleet (they having been separated in a storm) have with them twelve Dutch men of war.

There was a great contest on Thursday and a great many warm speeches in the House of Commons before the choice of a Speaker was made each side endeavouring to lessen the abilities of the contrary candidate. Against the honourable gentleman that fills the chair they objected a speech he made in the house in the late reign for keeping on foot a considerable body of regular troops as necessary in that conjuncture, of being at a late meeting in which a peer was present about agreeing upon a person to be Speaker, &c. all which was easily answered. Against the other they printed his juvenile travels with a ridiculous index made to the book argued from Mr. Tilly's sermon, the want of judgment that body might have where such principles were taught in the choice of their members; but this signified little on either side, the numbers carried the election. It was observable that there were 457 members sworn and but 455 gave their votes and two great men of the long robe are suspected to have withdrawn. Of those who have places or dependencies at Court about fifteen or sixteen gave their votes for Mr. Bromley, of which number George Clarke Esquire was one, who yesterday, or as some say the morning before, had his dismission sent him, he was Secretary to the Prince, and one of the Secretaries of the Admiralty.

NEWS LETTER.

1705, October 30. London—Monsieur Balmquest the Swedish minister at the Hague (according to letters from thence of the 6th) communicated that day to the States a letter which he had received from Paris bearing date the 2nd, giving an account that Barcelona capitulated on the 14th, and that the next day the cavalry marched out through the gate of St. Anthony and the infantry through the breach with three pieces of cannon, but as the garrison was marching out a disorder happened upon the account that the ■ice Roy would take with him the prisoners, so that the capitulation being broken, the Vice Roy with the garrison were made prisoners of war and most of the latter had taken service with the allies, and the Vice Roy was conducted to the tent of King Charles, and the Marquis de Aytona with another general officer to that of the brother of the late Prince d'Armstadt.

Letters from Ostend and Dunkirk of the 3rd confirm the unhappy news we had from Hull of the loss of three English men of war, two of good force and the other of thirty or forty guns, and twelve or thirteen ships of the East Land fleet which were brought into the latter place on the morning of the date by Count St. Paul's squadron, but the said Count was killed in the action. His fleet consisted of thirty-one sail and came from the Baltic, but we are told that not above three or four of them had naval stores on board.

Shields the 26th. Fifty five sail of the Russia fleet are come in here and their convoy are riding at the bar. There is advice that part of the East Country fleet are put into Owsley Bay.

This morning the five yachts arrived from Holland with my Lord Portland and several foreign ministers and other persons of quality and officers on board.

Yesterday being the anniversary for swearing the Lord Mayor elect at Westminster, his Lordship went thither in his barge by water attended by the several liveries in their barges as usual, and having performed that ceremony went to the several courts in Westminster Hall and invited the Lord Keeper and judges to dine with him at Vintner's Hall. He returned in like manner and the Lord Keeper and Judges honoured his Lordship with their company, but there were no other of the court officers there, as did his Grace the Duke of Beaufort, the Earl of Winchelsea, the Lord Granville and the Lord Bishop of London. Sir James Montague is made one of the Queen's Counsel. .

[DANIEL DE FOE] to ROBERT HARLEY.

An Abstract of my Journey with casual Observations on Public Affairs.

1705, July 16 to November 6—I set out from London July 16. Having concluded to make no observations within twenty miles of London I proceed to the several stages.

> July 16.—Brentford. Lodged at Justice Merriwether's—he was a justice, but turned out of commission in the general displacing moderate men.
>
> > Note.—Justice Lamb of Acton, who was a goldsmith in Lombard Street, is now the high flying and ruling justice of that side of Middlesex, the same who swore to the flash of his pistol in the case of Ni. Charleton.
>
> Reading—They are all well there, and there is no doubt of a good member in the room of Mr. Vachell. I have

the exact list of the magistracy of all the chief towns in Berks.

17. Newbury a large trading town but choose no member, but they influence the elections at Ludgershall and Great Bedwin, and a very good story about the Bruces, who now petition, is to be told here.

18. Salisbury.—Here I have the whole account of the County elections and the parsons rustling my Lord of Salisbury, and Mr. Westfield, his steward, and the mob insulting the Duke of Somerset and stopping his coach in the street.

19, 20. At Blandford. No corporation, the county too much governed and the town entirely by Seymour Portman and Colonel Strangeways. Had Major General Earle plied his interest well they all say the other had lost it.

21. At Dorchester. A good for nothing town; one member is [Awnsham] Churchill the bookseller; the other —— [Napier] chosen by the interest of Colonel Strangeways. People here very moderate.

22. Weymouth—here the disorders of my letters hindered me staying to do what I proposed.

23. Lyme, a town entirely united, and all the Churchmen very moderate and well affected.

24. Honiton, a terrible mob election here, but Sir Jno. Elvill, of Exeter, is so cowed by Sir William Drake and Francis Gwyn that he dares not petition.

25. Exeter. Here I have the list of all the parties exactly, and a model how Sir Edward Seymour may be thrown out against another election without any difficulty at all.

Here I learnt the history of the family of Col. Rolles, and how the young gentleman, knight of the shire for Devon, will be brought off from high church.

August 1. I left Exeter and went to Totnes, Sir E. S[eymour's] town as we call it, though he has not one foot of land nor a house in the town.

2. Dartmouth, a bubbled town engrossed by the Herns, but the story of a ship called the Constant Tacker is a mistake.

3. To Plympton, a little town, all low church and very well united, but a poor place. Lord Chief Justice Treby's town.

4. To Plymouth. I have the skeleton of this town.

5. To Saltash.

6, 7. To Liskeard and Bodmin.

8. To Launceston. There is nothing to be done in these towns, they are wholly guided by the gentlemen and the townsmen, know little, but act just as they are bid. My Lord Granville governs several of them, my Lord Treasurer, more. I thought it was throwing away time to stay among them.

9, 10. Bideford.

11. Barnstaple.

12. Tiverton. Here the alarm of the Devonshire justices hurried me too fast, but I have established correspondence at all these towns.

14. Taunton—have an exact account here.

15. Bridgewater, and here also.

16. To Bristol.

19. Bath. A contest here, between the people and the magistracy, will come before the house.

20. To Chippenham. Here Watt White being dead, that scandal to all good manners Colonel Chivers puts up, he is the profoundest rake and bully in the county, and is put up here by the gentry on purpose to screen him from the Bishop of Salisbury, who sues him for most impudent scandalous lies raised of him. Of this I have the particulars as also of his scandalous history, and 'tis the humble request of all the county on that side, at least, that he may be out of the commission of the peace, for he is a scandal to the country.

22. To Devizes. Here is the same petition against the Iron Chest, the history of which is worth relating.

23. To Bradford, Trowbridge, and Westbury, the skeletons of all those towns are complete, with all the vale here for fifty miles.

24. To Devizes again, and from thence to visit young Duckett chosen for Calne, the same Sir Charles Hedges petitions against ; of him the story how the Atheist Club at Oxford used him—his character.

25. To the Bath.

26. Back to Bristol, the history of the revolution of this city is large and edifying, and I have an exact scale of the people, their trade, and magistracy. Stayed here four days.

30. To the Bath again, Chippenham and Calne, thence to Malmesbury and Cirencester, here I had the story of the election, which it seems Mr. Cox has given over, or else the briberies on both sides would have made strange work.

September 1. To Gloucester, a perfect change here, the history of which I had from Mr. Wade, brother to Major Wade of Bristol, and from Mrs. Forbes. This city and Bristol are perfectly reformed and new modelled.

2. Tewkesbury, a quiet trading drunken town, a whig baily and all well.

3. Pershore and Evesham, great contest at the last for Sir Richard Cox (Cocks), and a great deal of foul play.

4. Worcester. Here I forebore to examine as to the magistracy, you having full knowledge of persons and things.

5. To Leominster. I went on a particular obligation to visit a Quaker, one Bowen that I had been engaged to by his brother here, but as being Mr. Harley's town I did nothing here.

7. Bewdley. Of this town I have a long and useful history, and of the election there.

8. Bridgnorth. Of this town I have a full account, and of the throwing out Sir Edward Acton.

10. Shrewsbury. Of this town I have an exact list.

11. Wrexham.

12. Chester, and of this also.

13. Liverpool, and here also.

16. Warrington ⎫
17. Manchester ⎪ No magistrates in any of these towns.
20. Bolton ⎬ Choose no members nor have any officer
21. Rochdale ⎪ but a constable.
22. Halifax ⎭

23, 26. Leeds, Wakefield and Sheffield—No members chosen
here neither. Here I have made useful remarks on
trade, and observe that, frequent elections having no
influence here to divide the people, they live here in
much more peace with one another than in other parts.

29. Derby. The parties were exceedingly inveterate here,
but begin to unite very much.

October 2. Nottingham. This is a violently divided town. I have
the exact schedule of their leaders.

6. Leicester. A monstrous story here about the elections,
and the contending parties here daily together by the
ears.

8. Lutterworth. Here Justice Bradgate rode a horseback
into the meeting house, and told the parson, as he
was preaching, he lied. A highflying town, but no
corporation.

9. Coventry. Of this town you will see the history at large
in print.

15. Daventry. Famous for an infamous parson who among
other things swore himself a freeholder, whereas he is
not the incumbent, but curate only.

16. Northampton. Of this town I have a draft.

18. Wellingboro'.

19. Huntingdon.

21. Cambridge, done before, but the story of the colleges dis-
commoning Mr. Love, the late Mayor, and his indiscretions, are very remarkable.

25. Bury. Here the case of my Lord Hervey and Sir
Dudley Cullum, and the measures taken on both sides of
the approaching election, are observable.

28. Cambridge again, to move some friends that came thither
from London on private business of my own.

November 1. To Sudbury, and have the particulars of their management
of the last election.

3. To Colchester.

5. To Chelmsford.

6. To London.

In all parts the greatest hindrances to the forming the people into
moderation and union among themselves, next to the Clergy, are the
Justices.

Wherever there happen to be moderate justices the people live easy,
and the parsons have the less influence, but the conduct of the justices
in most parts is intolerably scandalous, especially in Wilts, in Lancashire,
in Nottingham, Leicester, Warwick, Northampton, Suffolk, Essex and
Middlesex.

DAN: WEAVER to [ROBERT HARLEY].

1705, November 8. Berwick—Now his Excellency Major General
Maine, governor of this garrison, is in London serving Her Majesty
and the nation in Parliament, and Captain Bladen whom his Excellency

left Captain Commandant being out of town. I have the honour of being Commander here in Chief for the time being. I therefore think it my duty to inform your Honour that about three weeks ago one Mr. Colin Campbell rode post to London through this garrison, and returning back this day towards Scotland, and I hearing that there are a great many discontented gentlemen in that kingdom and that he had been an officer in the Highlands but had been broke as a person concerned in the late Scotch plot, and by his sudden return suspecting he was about business that might be prejudicial to Her Majesty and her Government, according to the custom of examining all gentlemen that come into this garrison with arms, I sent for him and after asking him a few questions he did confess that he was accused of being concerned in the Scotch plot, and that he lay nineteen months in prison upon that accusation, and was out upon bail and that his hasty business to London was to discharge his bail, the first day of last term, which he has done and has other business of law affairs in Edinburgh which calls him back so suddenly. Which story seems to me to be very suspicious because I was concerned in things of this nature myself, only it was in a better cause with his Grace the Duke of Devonshire, the Earl of Stamford, the present Lord Halifax, and a great many other noblemen; for after lying so long in prison without making any confession he seems the fitter to be trusted by the party, and therefore I thought it proper to give your Honour this account because if your Honour thinks fit to have his business inquired into in England or Scotland, or to have him stopped and searched and examined if he comes this way again post for London, whatever your Honour in your great wisdom thinks most proper to be done for the service of Her Majesty I shall most readily obey your Honour's commands, because I believe you well design them as much for Her Majesty's honour and interest as I am sure I am her most dutiful subject.

[Lord Godolphin to Robert Harley.]

[1705, November] 10. Saturday — I have not had time this morning to thank you for the favour of your letter last night. I shall be sure to let the Duchess of Marlborough know your concern for *her* election, which is a great one to her, and Monday I will endeavour to send Mr. Killegrew's solicitor to wait upon you for your orders.

By the way I have been told this day that our Solicitor-General is wavering again, but I don't know how to believe him so weak to say no more. I have a letter from my Lord Sunderland which refers to your letter but shows little hope of the business of Hungary.

I have nothing from the Duke of Marlborough.

The affair of Barcelona is not clear in Mr. Secretary's letters but they tell their doubts in a manner that leaves me none; but I wish we could hear from the fleet or even from Lisbon. The French say the King of Portugal is dead.

A. Harley to her Aunt [Abigail Harley?].

1705, November 13. London—At Lady Glasford's we met the lady of Shere Lane. She was wonderfully set out with her jewels that don't see the sun above once a year. They say she is breeding. There will certainly be heirs enough to that great estate. She will save by wearing a stiff gown, buying candles in the city, selling broken glass bottles for basons and such utensils. There is daily expectation of another court mourning, Queen Mary being given over by the physicians and not like to recover, a sister of Prince George's is like to die, and the King of Portugal very ill. There is no question now made of the taking of Barcelona, it is certain it was surrendered the fourth of last month; my Lord Galway has lost his arm but is in a way of recovery. My Lady Abingdon has surrendered her place of lady of the bedchamber by my Lord's persuation though sore against her will; he would not let her continue in her place because he had lost his.

DR. FRANCIS ATTERBURY to [ROBERT] HARLEY.

[1705, November 14 ?]. Wednesday — My Lord Treasurer still speaks to Mr. Brydges in such a manner as if he designed that our address should be proposed by us in the Lower House, on Friday. That cannot be—since the imparting of it to the bishops—without a discovery of what hath been doing; and therefore I humbly beg that my Lord may speak to him on that head in such a manner as will leave no doubt. Mr. Brydges invited me yesterday on purpose, as I found, to propose the insertion of a new clause, complimenting my Lord Treasurer upon the management of the Revenue. But though I should be glad to have such a clause sent down to us, yet I think it too late for us now to propose it, and besides I was resolved to determine upon nothing farther in the matter without your direction.

I intend, if you please to give me leave, to wait upon you at your office, either late this evening, or, at farthest, to-morrow at noon; when you will please to let me see the draft of what is intended to be sent us. The expressions concerning my Lord Treasurer's wise administration of the Revenue will be too high to go down with us.

SIR R. COTTON and SIR THO. FRANKLAND to SECRETARY HARLEY.

1705, November 23. General Post Offiee—Forward extract from a letter of M. Vanderpoel at the Brill complaining of the inconvenience and danger caused to the postal service from Holland by the crowding of officers and soldiers, with their baggage, into the packet boats which were not built for such purpose; and urge that proper transport ships should be provided for the service of the army.

[ROBERT HARLEY] to — HANNAN.

1705, November 26—You having been admitted to bail upon your own desire and having had so long time to refresh your memory I do not doubt you are now prepared according to your promise to do that service to the public which you professed you could and would perform. You know that there remain but two days for you to determine one way or the other. (*Draft.*)

MEMORIAL of WILLIAM HEWER, of Clapham, co. Surrey.

1705, November. Being returned the last year as High Sheriff of the county, her Majesty, on consideration of his long service in the Navy from 1660 to 1689, his many infirmities from old age, being upwards of sixty-five years, was pleased to excuse him from serving. Understanding however that endeavours are being made to put him on the list for the ensuing year, he prays Harley to intercede with Chief Justice Holt in the matter.

HENRY ST. JOHN to [ROBERT HARLEY].

1705, December 3. Whitehall—The Queen was pleased to tell me she stopped Colonel Dobyn's commission, because she remembered my Lord Marlborough had spoken to her about the disposal of it. I am informed my Lord Marlborough had promised it to Colonel Rodney, who was killed in a duel in Catalonia. I thought it proper to acquaint you with this.

VISCOUNT LISBURNE to [ROBERT HARLEY].

1705, December 20. Crosswood—Complaining of certain non-Jurors who had been put into the commission of the peace soon after the death of the late King, and asking that there might be a new commission for the county. He had already troubled the Lord Keeper with this subject, who had promised his assistance.

The STATES GENERAL of the NETHERLANDS to ROBERT HARLEY.

1705, December 30. The Hague—Asking him to give his advice and support to Monsieur Buys who was going over to England as envoy extra-ordinary. *Signed. Seal of Arms.*

The EARL OF SUNDERLAND to [ROBERT HANLEY].

[1705, December 31 ?] Monday—Will you do me the favour to let me know whether I am to give the Emperor's *lettres de cachette,* and his letters of recreance, to the Queen when I shall kiss her hand [on my return from Vienna], or whether I should give them to you when I wait on you. I asked Lord Treasurer who told me he could not tell which was customary.

[LORD GODOLPHIN to ROBERT HARLEY.]

[1705, December] Wednesday—I have not been well yesterday nor to-day or I should sooner have thanked you for your letter which I received last night.

I am entirely of your mind that it is better the Commons should adjourn, rather than be put to find business for themselves; and besides, it will lay the delay of the Parliament's rising at the Lords' door.

I doubt there will be a necessity of the Queen's coming to the House before the end of the Session, to pass the Annuity Bill, which cannot stay much longer.

I will see Mr. Paterson as soon as I can.

The enclosed from Sir Roger Mostyn I received this morning. I have often had alarms of the same kind, of the same person's illness, so that I don't lay much weight upon this notice, only I take this occasion to know your thoughts as to that place, or whom you would recommend in case it were vacant.

I desire you to consider the enclosed draft of a speech, and send me your amendments, at your leisure.

I should be very glad if I might see you to-morrow or Friday night.

s 2

DANIEL DE FOE.

[1705?]—A list of towns in England with the names of the agents residing there to which "remarks, &c." were sent. *In De Foe's handwriting.*

MEMORANDA on Scotch affairs, by Capt. JOHN OGILVIE.

[1705?]—There came a sort of a scheme from Scotland to the Court of St. Germain telling them that on the conclusion of the Union was a proper time for the King of France to send in some troops with some money and ammunition and some arms and some officers; and if the Prince of Wales would come himself the most of the kingdom would join him withal. They said it would redound much to the King of France's service in Flanders for the most of the English army must come home to quench that fire which would in fact make the French masters in Flanders, and if they were beaten they did not doubt but they would retire into the Highlands where they could always defend themselves, or make a good capitulation for themselves. It was not signed but I perfectly did know the hand.

After this Caron, who commands a ship of 36 guns, went to the north of Scotland. Then Mr. Huck [Hooke?] was sent and after that Robert Murray came to St. Germain and immediately his brother John who was sent there in the time of Lovat's affair returned with him, he is there as yet; and after that Charles Rina was sent whose father is an Italian but himself born in England; he is not returned as yet. When I came away there was a Scotch gentleman there privately, but for my life I could not have a sight of him nor could I learn his name, but I was certainly informed that there was a person from St. Germain to the Court of Sweden to represent the deplorable condition of the Prince of Wales, and it was once whispered that the Prince of Wales should go and make some campaigns with the King of Sweden on purpose to ingratiate himself in that prince's favour, but the certainty of this I cannot affirm but he is very pressing to go to the army in Flanders.

The chief heads of the discontented party in Scotland are—
Duke Hamilton.
The Earl of Nithsdale, papist.
The Earl of Traquair, papist.
The Earl of Home.
The Earl Marischal.
The Earl of Errol, Constable.
The Earl of Breadalbane, Highland following.
The Earl of Strathmore.
The Earl of Aberdeen.
The Viscount of Stormont.
The Viscount of Strathallan, he is but young.
Lord Fraser, in the North.
Lord Drummond, and his brother called Lord John.
Logie Almond, a cousin of the Earl of Perth, he is a bold man and hath a following.
The Duke of Gordon, but they are afraid he will not risk but on sure grounds; however his following will rise for they are most part papists.
The Duke of Athole supposed to be but lately joined.
As to the Highlands there is Lochiel a good following, the Macdonalds, Glengarrie and Copick Macdonalds, the Stuart of Apren. the Captain of the Clanronald, the whole Macgregors headed by one

Rob Roy commonly called by that name. All the Frasers of Lovat's family.

Clona Ogilvie, a brother's son of the old Earl of Airlie, he can make a good party in Angus. This is besides a vast number that comes not in my mind as yet: to mind Mr. David Floyd who keeps a correspondence with the late Queen, his letter I did see. Mr. Fox keeps the same with my Lady Middleton: Fox is a canny jade and very capable. Mrs. Capeman and Mrs. Oldrich was at St. Germain, there came from that place just now the wife of Larne who was father to that Larne that was the evidence in the time of the ███████ion plot; she is here now but I believe it is only her own private business hath brought her. The frigate from Dieppe keeps still a correspondence with the Coast of Sussex.

Mr. Lindsay keeps still correspondence with my Lord Middleton, for I did see one of the couriers deliver a great packet to my Lord Middleton's secretary and I did perfectly know Lindsay's hand but I know he does it every week. Doctor Taylor, also Sir William Elwes who is one of the Board of Green Cloth at St. Germain, he hath a considerable salary for the expense of his intelligence he furnishes from England; now who is his correspondent, here is the question. I do know some but suspect others, for I will not affirm what I am not certain of.

Bishop Nicholson, he lives in the north of Scotland, and Bishop Gordon, popish bishops.

Alexander Drummond, priest, who was bred in the Scotch College of Paris receives all letters from the Principal of that College and he distributes them according to the private directions. There is some letters goes by John Drummond in Amsterdam directed for Père Cupignie, that is the Principal Mr. Jennens; some others are directed for Jean Cupignie, that's my Lord Perth, but they have other ways. There's just now a young man one John Drummond gone home, he did belong to the Scotch College, there's also another John Wallace he was formerly governor to my Lord Drummond and it was he who bred him papist, he once was a minister.

Now if you have a mind to send me to Scotland you had best do it soon, for I may be there before those sparks part that was sent from France. Certainly I shall do you better service if I come there before they part than I can do you otherwise, but as to that what you please, only I wish with all my heart I could render you service and not be as a cipher, for I declare if I had twenty lives they should always be at the Queen's service by reason she did give me mine.

——— to LORD GODOLPHIN.

1705-6, January 3. Dublin—Taking notice of a reward offered in the "London Gazette," of 200*l.* for the discovery of the author of the "Church of England Memorial," and of 50*l.* for the apprehension of Edwards, the printer of it, I write to inform that there has lately come to this city a printer who says he worked three years with Edwards, and many things were during that time printed against the interest of the Government; and a certain Lord and another person, whom he named, used to come to read and correct some of the matter printed, and were looked upon as having had a hand in penning the Memorial. This printer, finding work scarce, designs to come to the west of England, and if you should think the examination of him might be for the public service, I will make some excuse to come over with him, and endeavour to get further information, if my expenses are paid.

[LORD GODOLPHIN to ROBERT] HARLEY.

[1706, January] 9. Wednesday—This letter will be given you by Thomas Edwards, brother to the printer, who brings me a man that comes from his brother to tell me it will be necessary to seize some persons before the noise of his brother's coming in or being taken, or else they will run away. I would not speak with the man myself, and therefore I lose no time in sending the printer's brother and the man to you, that upon your speaking with them you may give such orders as you think proper.

The EARL OF PERTH to CAPTAIN JOHN OGILVIE.

1706, January 10. St. Germain—I know your coming will not be acceptable to the Queen; the reason I cannot tell; only I believe it is somewhat from England. Until I speak to Her Majesty I can give you no answer, and so soon as I have spoken I shall write to the Scotch College to Mr. Wallace, and you may send there to enquire for my letter on Tuesday at night.

The SAME to the SAME.

Same date—On Wednesday at ten in the morning I will meet you at the Scotch College on the Fossé St. Victor. Pray fail not to meet me there.

DAVID EDWARDS to ROBERT HARLEY.

1705–6, January 10 — Promising to discover everything that he knew and informing him that he had sent an account of persons and papers to his wife, who can tell more if Harley thought fit to see her.

[LORD GODOLPHIN to ROBERT HARLEY].

[1706, January 11 ?] Friday—I take the thing you mentioned in yours last night of Sir W. Ashurst to be wild enough, but that does not make it impossible to be attempted, and therefore I would be glad to know if you would have me write to the Speaker about it, or speak to any one else.

I hope there will be no great difficulty to-day in fixing Mr. Conyers in his throne though at the same time his behaviour shows we ought not to have taken such pains in the matter but for [our] own sakes.

The business of Lubeck grows a dangerous thing, but I don't see how any remedy can be so properly applied to it as at the Hague, where the Ministers of all the 'Guarands' are present and may concert and agree in such resolutions as upon consideration of the Treaty of Travendahl they shall find most suitable to the present case.

When Monsieur Schultz presses so much for the exchange of Vaudencourt and shows so much jealousy of Plessens being here, and of Prussia's intrigues, might not you ask him, how these things cohere since Vaudencourt's liberty can be desired for no other use but to carry on Prussia's affair. Have you no sort of curiosity to ask him also what is the occasion of the gentleman's coming over who had Mr. Stanhope's pass for himself and three servants. I have not heard anything more of that matter.

. Since I began this letter I have received the enclosed from your friend Mr. John Colt, who is an exceeding worthy person.

JAMES CRESSETT to [ROBERT HARLEY].

1705-6, January 11—I should not have given you the trouble of this letter had not Baron Schutz, who is much indisposed, obliged me to insinuate to you some way or other what follows relating to the Lubeck affair. 'Tis so much the Elector his master's interest · to calm those troubles which are beginning in his neighbourhood that his intentions can be no way suspected, and though his Electoral Highness is not to be named or to appear in the front of expedients upon this occasion, the sense of his Court is, that if the Powers concerned in the guarantee of the Treaty of Travendahl will propose the withdrawing of all armed forces on both sides out of the Bishopric, giving their declaration at the same time, that neither Danes nor Holsteiners (till the thing is juridically decided) shall return into that country and that the administration may still remain in what they term *possession civile;* 'tis the opinion of Hanover that a proposition to this effect may be relished and prevent the great disorders which threaten those parts, the point of honour being now saved on the Danes side if the resentment can be as well stopped on the other, since these last violent proceedings. I hope I am not mistaken in this matter, which I promised Monsieur Schutz either to tell you by word of mouth or to acquaint you with it in writing.

RIOT IN NEWBURY.

1705-6, January 12—Deposition of William Littler, sergeant to Capt. Vicaridge in Col. Godfrey's regiment, before Fr. Negus, to the effect that on January 10 the justices at Newbury, finding that four men brought before them were fit to serve as soldiers, had delivered them over to Capt. Foxon and other officers by whom they were put in the care of the deponent, and other sergeants; but on their passage through the town several of the townsmen came out with pistols and other arms and rescued the recruits, the sergeants being knocked down, shot at, and sorely beaten. The rioters also declared that if they could find the officers they would "knock 'em o' th' head." Further attacks were made upon them late at night, and upon the officers, and Sergeant Sharp had received a blow, of which, deponent believed, he was since dead.

MARY EDWARDS.

1705-6, January 12—The examination of Mary Edwards, wife of David Edwards, the printer of the *Memorial of the Church of England. Signed, and sworn before Robert Harley.*

DAVID EDWARDS to ROBERT HARLEY.

1705-6, January 12—A long letter of explanation and exculpation, and accusing Sir Humphrey Mackworth of having something to do with the circulation of the *Memorial.*

Baron Schutz to Robert Harley.

1705–6, January 14—Asks if the instructions had been sent to Lord Raby touching the introduction of the Elector [of Hanover ?] into the Electoral College, about which he had recently written to Harley. *French. Signed.*

David Edwards.

1705–6, January 15—A list of persons to be arrested, implicated by Edwards and his wife in their statements about the publication of the *Memorial of the Church of England.*

Messengers.

1705–6, January 16—List of the messengers employed, with brief notes in Harley's handwriting, such as " capable," " superannuated," " seems honest," " honest," " drunken, good rider," " Irish," &c.

Baron Schutz to [Robert Harley].

1705–6, January 17. London—As my indisposition continues and 1 am unable to call upon you, I do not wish to omit informing you of the latest orders which I have received from his Electoral Highness concerning the affair of Lubeck.

His Highness thinks that the only way to prevent war on that account is (1) That neither side should put any troops into Eutin or anywhere in the Bishopric. (2) That the civil possession should remain in its entirety with the Prince Administrator, that is to say the enjoyment of the episcopal revenue and the administration of the government. (3) That Her Majesty and Holland and the other guarantors of the treaty of Travendahl, should guarantee this civil possession, and should bind themselves to prevent the Administrator from being disturbed. (4) That the King of Denmark should withdraw to the islands the troops which he has brought thence which are in excess of the numbers he is entitled to have in Holstein by the treaty of Travendahl. That is the only expedient which can prevent Sweden from coming to extremities and his Electoral Highness from assisting the Administrator, as his quality of guarantee of the peace of Travendahl and his engagements with Sweden and the House of Gottorp oblige him. *Signed. French.*

A. B. to Robert Harley.

1705–6, January 21—Though I am deterred by the character usually fixed on informers to come before you in person to accuse Dr. Charlett, Master of University College in Oxford, who last summer received by the carrier and dispersed through the University great numbers of the *Memorial of the Church of England,* &c., yet in duty to the Queen and Government I think myself obliged to assure you of the fact, the notoriety whereof in Oxford and particularly in his own College will clear me from the charge of forging this story to his prejudice. A little art used would no doubt make the Priest squeak (if he knows the author or authors), whose fears for his person and hopes of preferment by serving *any one* will work more steadily upon him to make him discover, than his zeal for the Church will make him hold his tongue.

Riot at Newbury.

1705-6, January 21. Westminster—Examination before Erasmus Lewis of William Littler, sergeant in Captain Vicaridge's company in Col. Godfrey's regiment; and of John Kay lieutenant in the same regiment. *See* Jan. 12, *ante.*

Two papers giving slight additional details of the Newbury riot. The three justices concerned in the matter were Mr. Head, Mr. Wightwick, and Mr. Kingsmill.

[Lord Godolphin] to [Robert] Harley.

[1706,] January 22. Tuesday—I found Mr. Buys today as full of two memorials he was preparing as his head was last night with entertaining his guests.

The Attorney spoke to me today about prosecuting of Stephens in the Duke of Marlborough's name. I told him I thought the Duke of Marlborough's mind would be to have him prosecuted in both your names or in neither, and so indeed I understood him before he went out of town.

I don't hear when they intend to proceed upon the Place bill, but my thought is that the sooner it comes the better. While yesterday is fresh in their minds, I am apt to think gentlemen will be more easy than if you give them time to harden one another.

David Edwards to Robert Harley.

1705-6, January 22—Thinks he has not fair play. The messengers ought to have gone to Waltham Abbey. They had taken up the wrong woman, though one whom he had seen in company with the right one at Mrs. Mackworth's house in Shere Lane. Desires he may be heard before Mrs. Mackworth is called in.

John, Bishop of Quebec, to [the Commissioners for the Sick and Wounded].

1706, January 23. Farnham—A report has been spread in Farnham that you intend to take away the prisoners here and transfer us to other towns in England. As I see no one here and enjoy perfect tranquillity in a solitude which I have often desired without daring to hope for, I cannot help calling your attention to the pain which it would cause me to be removed and to find myself again in the discomfort which was my lot at Rochester, where you placed us at first. I understand that the report has proceeded from a request which some of the inhabitants of this place have presented to the Queen, perhaps as much out of jealousy for Mr. Clement our commissary as for any good reason. Without entering into this matter I beg that if you close the prisons of Farnham you will leave me here with my ecclesiastics. The Queen and Council having been willing up to now to allow us this little town as our prison on our word of honour not to leave it, I am persuaded that you will have no difficulty in obtaining permission for us to stay here on the same conditions. To allow us to remain in a spot which I believe to be one of the most lonely in England will do much to mitigate the hardness of a captivity which may yet last a long time. *French.*

P. Mews to Doctor Adams, in Little Rider Street near St. James's, Westminster.

·1705-6, January 23.. Farnham. Castle—The petition.;of the inhabitants of Farnham lately presented to Her Majesty is grounded upon very good reasons. The small pox has raged in this place with great fury for several months,,and the infection daily increases by the fresh supply of soldiers for the guard of the prisoners. This has struck so great a terror upon the country people round us that the trade in general is incredibly diminished, and the corn market, the chief support of the place, is in a manner deserted. This misfortune does already sensibly affect this little town, and if it continues may be of fatal consequence to it.

The Commissioners for the Sick and Wounded to [Robert] Harley.

1705-6, January 25. Sick and Wounded Office—Enclosing the preceding and other letters from Farnham, and informing him that the only prisoners of war there were the Bishop of Quebec and his ecclesiastics who were on parole, and one Roach David, and that if David were moved to Southampton there would be no necessity for a guard there.·

It is certified by Bartbo. Clements and Peter Proy that the small pox was brought into the town by a baker and not by the soldiers.

Adam Cardonnel to [Richard] Warre.

1705-6, January 25. Whitehall—I have laid the letter from the Justices of the Peace for the county of Worcester before my Lord Duke, whereupon his Grace has given orders that the officers who were appointed for that county be tried at a court martial for the neglect of their duty in not attending the justices, and that others be immediately hastened down thither. His Grace has likewise given orders that the officers shall accept of any men that are tendered to them provided they be hale and well set, without insisting on their being five foot eight inches high as the letter mentions. This the Duke prays the Secretary will intimate to the justices and give them the Queen's thanks for their care, to encourage them to go on.

J. Cranstoun to ———

1705-6, January 27. Edinburgh—I have seen most of our great men here and have talked in freedom with E. of L[eve]n and the President, but from all that, can give you no distinct and satisfactory account of things here. There have been no meetings at Pett Steels (sic) of late, principally, I believe, because the heads of that party are all absent, so it is not easy to guess what they will be for when they meet; but few here seem to hope much good from the advances made in the English Parliament towards an Union, and either will not believe them sincere or think it will be offered on hard terms, and without any real advantages to us. Many seem rather inclined to wish we may secure our own Government by restrictions upon the power of the Sovereign as to the disposal of places of trust in the Government, sinking the office of Secretaries of State, regulating the representation in Parliament and the elections to it, and to have all things done hereafter here, either by the Sovereign in Parliament or in a well-regulated Council. I find some of our present Ministry even what you have given their opinion to some of their friends here, that this is like to be what we have safest to trust to, and several of their friends here seem of the same opinion. By anything I can learn whatever changes the Queen shall think fit to make it will be hard if not impossible for any set of a Ministry at present here to obtain anything in our next session of Parliament. We have changed so often of late, that things are spoilt indeed and our Government has lost all credit and authority, and is losing every day more and more. The Duke of Q[ueensberry] desired I should write to him, but hitherto I can learn nothing whereby I could hope to inform of anything that could give him any light or real knowledge of things here. We wait with impatience to see what will become of the Commons' Bill with relation to us.

LE MOYNE to [ROBERT] HARLEY.

1706, January 28. Newgate—Imploring his aid and protesting his innocence in the pretended Scotch affairs, which were only pretexts for other more particular matters; notwithstanding that he had tried to appear mixed up in them in order to obtain the confidence of Marshal Tallard and to get help from him. Also that he knew nothing about Lord Nottingham, in whose family he always behaved like a child; that he had been told that Lord Nottingham passed for a Jacobite, but that he neither heard nor saw anything all the time he was with him to which he could attach any importance. Begs Harley to present the petition to the Queen which he enclosed, praying to be allowed to appear " au tribunal du Bailly " after his ten months imprisonment in Newgate. *French*.

The ARCHBISHOP OF CANTERBURY to ROBERT HARLEY.

1705–6, January 30. I send another letter from Redmond Joy. What he would now have I cannot tell unless it be money, which seems to be the main scope of this sort of men.

PRISONERS.

1705–6, January 31—List of persons in custody under Secretary Harley's warrants, shewing the names, twelve in all, the messenger in whose custody each was, the length of confinement, and the cost of their maintenance.

VISCOUNT LISBURNE to ROBERT HARLEY.

1705–6, January 31. Crosswood—Complains of attacks made upon him by enemies, and sends copies of two letters giving great insight into the principles of a certain person and his party.

DOCTOR JOSEPH BROWNE, of St. Paul's, Covent Garden.

1705–6, February 1—Confession that he had caused Hugh Meers to print a copy of verses entitled *The country parson's honest advice to that judicious lawyer, &c.*
Examination of the said Hugh Meers, of Blackfriars, attached.

—— to THOMAS, LORD FAIRFAX, at Leeds Castle, near Maidstone.

1705–6, February 2—Giving brief account of a meeting of Papists at the post house in Tadcaster. They included Middleton of Stockhill; Plumton of Plumton ; Vavasour, Talbot and Moor, all of Bramham; Michael Anne of Bramham Biggen, Hammond of Scarthingwell, Gascoigne of Parlington, Rider of Scarcroft, and Littleton, Sir William Vavasour's priest. Sir W. Vavasour himself was not there, not being yet returned from London.

RIOT at NEWBURY.

1705–6, February 2. Whitehall—Examinations of Lieut. John Sotheby and Sergeant Thomas Sharp, both of Brigadier Meredith's regiment, before E. Lewis, about the attack made upon them and other officers at Newbury.

JOHN BELL to [ROBERT HARLEY].

1705–6, February 8. Newcastle [on Tyne]—In obedience to commands had waited upon Mrs. Shaftoe, who lived at Killingworth about four miles off and was told that her daughter had been taken to France five years ago by two daughters of Sir Theoph. Oglethorpe, one of whom returned on the outbreak of the war, the other removed from Paris elsewhere. Mrs. Shaftoe's daughter went to wait on the Duchess of Perth, fell ill, and on her recovery turned papist and went into a nunnery as was supposed. The mother said that if she could but see her in England she would be satisfied without troubling herself about her religion, but was quite out of hopes of ever seeing her again. He had known Mrs. Shaftoe many years, and she and her family were always reckoned good church people; she had brought herself low in the world by engaging in law suits with some great people.

SIR EDWARD NORTHEY, attorney general, to ROBERT HARLEY.

1705–6, February 9—I have perused the several informations touching the riot of Newbury, but as the name of only one rioter is given I cannot frame a prosecution thereon, but advise that copies of these examinations may be sent to the justices there with commands to make further enquiry into the matter.

SIR EDWARD NORTHEY, attorney general, to ROBERY HARLEY.

1705–6, February 9—Has perused the Act of James II., cap. 8, and finds that the importing of gunpowder, arms, &c. by way of merchandize for the Queen's service is legal, and any merchant may be licensed to import such goods.

[Lieut.-Col. J. CRANSTOUN] to ROBERT CUNNINGHAM.

1706, February 11. Bosch—I wrote to you from The Hague after my commission as Lieutenant Colonel was out and since by Lieutenant Alexander Gordon, of the Earl of Orkney's regiment, by whom I sent you the holland you wrote for made up in three pairs of sheets. I addressed him to William Elliot the laceman to find you out. It is now long since he went from this and I hope the linen has gone safe to your hands. I sent you the account enclosed in my letter, and as Major Peter Gordon of Earl Orkney's regiment was to have raised recruits for my company in place of his son who though a child is my ensign. I wrote to you to have given him the money at your convenience in order to raise me men, but I find by letters of his to our paymaster since, that as he acts as agent for our regiment he has taken up 200*l.* at the Treasury to give those of our people [who] are making recruits in England and so I have since written to him to take money of that in his own hand for any men he raises to me.

I consider that if you get my tweezer case from Collma you will have money to pay for it, and my wife complains sadly that she has no pewter in her family and the people here where we take rooms grudge to furnish anything. I have a family now of six persons that eat within doors and I have yet neither dish nor diblet as we say nor any sort of household furniture and I never was less in condition to provide or more under difficulties for money ; however I must get now and then as I can what is absolutely necessary, for Officers now here especially those of any character live much higher than they did last war and have every thing in good order. I must therefore dear friend give you the trouble and my wife desires it as a favour that you will buy for her, two dozen of fine pewter plates of what they call your hard metal, one dozen of good ordinary plates not so fine though not coarse either, and one dozen of soup plates for broth that is in all four dozen of plates and with these one entire service of pewter dishes of good pewter. Mrs. Cunningham or at least the pewterers will tell you what a service is and how many and what sort of dishes ; for my part I do not know but I think it is nine in all of larger dishes and what they call your assietts together. My wife desires that the whole may be of the very newest and best fashion now used and with them she would have a pewter ring to set a dish in on the table. I suppose the whole commission may come to 9*l.* or 10*l.* sterling and I have written to Major Gordon that he may give you what money it stands above what you shall have in your hand and that I desire if the pewter is bought he will send it over to me with the mounting of our regiment because it will come safest so and free of all expense to me so I entreat when this comes to your hands you will take the trouble to call for Major Gordon who is every day at Man's Coffee House and he will tell you when the last of our mounting is to come over and if you with good Mrs. Cunningham's assistance will get the pewter ready and put it up in a box and deliver to Major Gordon he will send it over and give you what money you want ; or if he should not give you the money I shall upon your very first letter take care to remit it to you from this. I would hope that Charles Collma has given you my field standish snuff-box and little square lined box together with my tweezer before this and if he have you may easy pack these up in the same box with the pewter. I wish all may come over with the clothing because I shall not find another occasion so convenient again before next winter and my wife is indeed in great want of the pewter.

If Collma has not yet given you those things he is very indiscreet to me and I entreat you'll tell him so and press him a little and that when you find a convenient opportunity you will also remind Sir David Nairne about Madam Fullerton's money in his hand and to get up my note of 30*l.* I am brought very unluckily just now into a snare that is fallen hard upon me and has reduced me to great difficulties at this time when I have my equipage to make up for the campaign. There is a young man Mr. Ker son to Gilbert Ker, Sir William Ker of

Greenhead's brother who being bred a surgeon came over last year to the army in hopes to have got in either to the hospital or some regiment. He followed the camp all summer without getting into business and at the end of the campaign being straitened of money he applied to me to carry him down to Holland. I recommended him to Captain Lawson of our regiment and bid him give him what little money he needed and take his Bills for it; not dreaming he would take above 8*l.* or 10*l.* at most and not doubting but his bills for that on his father or his master James Pringle at Edinburgh would be answered but he took up 200 guilders from Captain Lawson and gave him bills for I suppose 260 pounds Scots or thereabout upon Mr. Pringle the surgeon. These bills have been protested upon which I wrote home and though both Mr. Brisbane, Mr. Pringle and my brother at Crelline have spoken earnestly to his father Gilbert Ker, he refuses peremptorily to pay one farthing of it and now Captain Lawson has actually stopped both the sum of the ill and expenses of protesting, &c. off of me and I have been forced to pay him 200 and odd guilders. The youth went over to London to seek employment so soon as he got the money from Lawson and indeed before I saw him. I cannot say but he is a very modest virtuous youth though he has been indiscreet and much in the wrong to me to take up above twenty pounds when he spoke to me only of six or eight; but I neither know where he now is or how to address to him so I must entreat you'll inquire at Mr. Wilson surgeon to our Hospital, who is married to Mr. Inglis's daughter, or at Dr. Oliphant's or Dr. Inglis's brother who is surgeon to the Hospital and also to Lieutenant-General Lumley's regiment; and if any of them can inform you of him you would call for him and tell him how ungratefully he and his father requite me for my kindness, and see what course he can propose to get me paid, and ask him at least to write earnestly to his father to pay the money to my brother-in-law Mr. Brisbane who will give him up the bills. This loss could never have fallen upon me at a worse time and I know not really how to overcome it.

I hear the D. of Q——— is come and that he is again at the head of Scotch affairs. I hope you have not forgot to entreat his Grace will be pleased to honour me so far as to give the Duke of Marlborough thanks for advancing me which may do me service here. We are informed that Earl Leven is certainly to be Commander-in chief in Scotland but I still hope the D. of Q——— will procure to Major General Murray the regiment of Guards, with the character and pay of Lieutenant General.

I entreat you write to me what measures are really taking towards our Union and what hope you have of it, or what sort of an Union they are like to endeavour, all write that there seems greater dispositions on both sides to it than ever and as it is certain the Whigs do now carry all before them so if they are serious I hope somewhat may be done. The Gazettes say Duke H[amilton] is written for, I would gladly know in what view. I entreat when you get this you'll write me a long letter for indeed nothing delights me so much as your letters do and I long to hear from you. Oh, if it was but once in my power to serve you as I have been now this twenty years constantly receiving pleasures and material favours from you. Alas, I can only return them in wishes, and those I have a pleasure to make for you. I never forget either you or your little family and my wife has a great concern in you, she gives her affectionate duty to you and to your Lady as does my sister Tibbie. My wife has had a most severe time in child breeding and continues yet very downish though not altogether so ill as she used to be, I reckon if it please God to preserve her from miscarrying again she will fall to lie in about August. My service to honest Thomas Harley, I wonder I do not hear from the Isle of Man. I give my blessing from my heart to good Mrs. Cunningham and the little family, may our good God in mercy preserve them long to you and you to them for a great comfort to each other. I shall be impatient till I hear from you and will ever love you as I ought.

Baron Schutz to [Robert Harley].

1705–6, February 14–25. London—Announcing that a treaty had been made between the Elector [of Hanover] and the Duke of Wolfen-buttel, whereby the Duke recognised the Electorate and gave up his part of the Duchy of Lauenburg to the Elector, who on his part would give an equivalent to the Duke. *Signed. French.*

Count D'Hompesch to the Duke of Marlborough.

1705–6, February 17—Applying on behalf of the Elector of Bavaria for a pass for a gentleman of his horse to come over and buy six horses in England. *Signed.*

T. B. to Robert Harley.

1705–6, February 18. [Lichfield post mark]—Mr. Dyer the news-writer says in his letter to Mrs. Newton at the Bull in Lichfield that on the 30th of January last at Bristol was made the effigies of King Charles I., which they there set upon a mastiff dog which carried him about the city, and afterwards was brought to a block, and there they cut off the head of this effigies. Some persons in our neighbourhood pretend that they are assured from good hands that this will be a bloody summer in England, and that we shall certainly be invaded by the French.

C[harlwood] Lawton to [Robert Harley].

1705–6, February 28—Since you did not mislike my beer, I beg you will accept of all I have left, which is but poor eighteen quart and eighteen pint bottles. Having small cellarage I seldom have much at the end of a session ; but I shall soon broach another vessel, and then some more shall be at your service. I know whatever I said last night I spoke to the gentleman. But as my late Lord Sunderland, to whom I sent an account what was expected (both by the Duke of Hamilton and Mr. Penn) long before peevishness showed itself in relation *then* to a general pardon, which he said publicly over his tea, he was for, but did nothing in it, and from thence received wounds he could never recover, so I honestly tell you that I fear that those I love and honour will hurt themselves by being wanting in this matter. Once I knew men, whose names I shall ever forget, who perhaps might tamper enough to make them apprehensive of God knows what future mischiefs. What one reason can there be against putting them, since they are of all parties, at ease ? I protest, upon all the recollection I can make, I know not one man of my acquaintance, of the party you mentioned, who would mislike a general pardon. But if it should be resolved to send down one, be pleased to let me know so, and I dare undertake an act of grace shall be accepted with an avowed cheerfulness.

[DR. FRANCIS ATTERBURY to ROBERT HARLEY.]

[1706, February?] Thursday. St. James's—I have been thinking of what you mentioned last night and take leave further to suggest to you that perhaps the proper time for the Queen's saying what will put an end to this dispute may be, when the Address comes to her from the Convocation, which will be about ten days hence, and may be deferred a day or two longer, if that be found requisite; by which time the House of Commons may probably have some way or other shewed itself in such a manner as will give room to have a word or two dropped in favour of that part of the Clergy which is in her and their true interests, especially if an address comes to her from the Lower House separately, which may, I believe, be compassed, if such a method be thought expedient to open the way for what she will be pleased to say. Words may be inserted in the Address which will naturally give her the occasion. And the like may be done, if both Houses should join in the same application, which is the more usual way; for when the Bishops' form comes down to us, we may add a clause, which will effectually bring on that matter, and which they will not think it convenient to refuse joining in. You may be pleased, Sir, to consider of this method, and— if you approve it—to intimate it to some other of our members most able to make it the sense of the House, though in that I apprehend no difficulty. Such a public step will prevent jealousies, and yet leave room to have matters concerted by more private applications, and place the management of this affair in the hands of a certain member of our Body, who, unless he hath the direction of it, and such assurances given him, as may put him beyond suspicion of being carried further than he intends to go, will scarce fall in heartily with it. In order to it, it will be convenient that I should not appear much in it, and therefore that I should wait upon you at such times, when it may be least observed. When you think fit to command my attendance, Dr. G. may let me know it, and by him, if you please, I shall send any letter I take the boldness to trouble you with on this head. By this means I shall be able to give you the best lights, as matter arises, especially if I can learn what is intended and where it sticks.

But I must take the liberty to add, that this, or any other proposal of the same kind will go near to be dashed, if the present scheme, for confirming the whole set of old Chaplains at once, take place; and that therefore cannot, I should think, be too soon prevented. Especially since my Lord Chamberlain intends, as I hear, this very day to send orders to as many of them as are in town—two-thirds of the number— to come at a certain time together in a body to be sworn.

[LORD GODOLPHIN] to ROBERT HARLEY.

[1706, February?] Tuesday—I am glad to hear you are better and so submissive to the doctor's care. The bill is brought in with very good intentions and chiefly to hinder the House of Commons from beginning with that matter. I am to see it tomorrow night. I think the shorter and plainer it is the better; but something of that nature seems unavoidable, the Scots having done it.

I desire the favour of you to send Mr. Lewis to St. James's to speak one word to the Duke of Marlbororgh and me about something that is to be written by this night's post to Mr. Robinson at Monsieur Vryberghen's request. They begin to be uneasy in Holland about the King of Sweden, and I hope they will join in despatching that guarantee. After to-morrow I will try to go to St. Albans for two or three days in hopes to get rid of my cough and hoarseness which continue very uneasy upon me.

GEORGE SMITH to [ROBERT HARLEY].

1705–6, March 4. North Nibley, Gloucestershire—My chief employment this whole winter has been from time to time to hold petty sessions among my brethren in commission for impressing soldiers, and we have so well succeeded that out of the two hundreds Berkeley and Long Tree we have raised above sixty men. One man, however, Joseph Webbe, of Wotton Underedge, rather than serve his queen and country, got a sharp knife and cut the great sinews of his legs above the heels, whereby he is become a cripple and hopes to be maintained by the parish. If neither common nor statute law will make it felony, I wish he may be brought before a court martial and, for example's sake, shot at the head of some regiment.

[LORD GODOLPHIN to BOBERT HARLEY.]

[1706, March 6] Ash Wednesday—The merchants we met with yesterday came to a resolution, that the properest way of effecting the loan for Prince Eugene will be for the Queen, instead of a letter to my Lord Mayor, to sign a warrant for a Commission under the Great Seal appointing   to be trustees for taking subscriptions for the loan of this 250,000*l.* sterling, and for the managing the returns of it to Prince Eugene and taking the security for repayment of the principal and interest. To-morrow they will bring me the names of the Commissioners they propose to be inserted in the warrant; if you please to order one to be prepared against the time of the Council meeting, with a blank for those names. I take it for granted the ground of the warrant for this Commission must be the same that is mentioned in the enclosed draft of the letter which I return you herewith.

What Franco writes must I suppose have come from our Coffee House politicians here in London; 'tis unimaginable what ridiculous accounts of all kinds they send over to Holland every week.

[LORD GODOLPHIN to ROBERT HARLEY.]

[1706, March 10] Sunday—This reason why I went to your house so unseasonably this morning was because I go to Newmarket tomorrow for four or five days and I had a mind to have shewn you a draught of a speech for the Queen to make at the close of the session, which I shall now leave in the Duke of Marlborough's hands for your correction. I had also a mind to tell you that when the Queen has recceived the Address of both Houses about Sir R. Gwyn's letter it will be right for her Majesty to give you her commands to acquaint Monsieur Schultz with what has been done by the Parliament upon that matter, and desire him to communicate it to the Court of Hanover. Of this too I hope the Duke of Marlborough will speak to you when you are well enough to give him leave. Mr. Secretary Hedges has told me that Mr. Heysham the Barbados merchant dropped some words to him the other day as if to-morrow the House of Commons would desire to have some account of the Queen's Message to them about the members that might be concerned in writing the Memorial. I wish they would do this because I don't think they would gain any very great advantage by having a plain narrative of the matter of fact sent to them, which if they stir that business I should humbly advise. I shall not trouble you with anything in answer to your letter about the pamphlets you have directed, only, that relating to the Duke of Marlborough being a little nice I hope you will make him read it before it be printed.

If there be any occasion I shall beg the favour of hearing from you in my absence.

D. EDWARDS to ROBERT HARLEY.

1705-6, March 11.—I humbly entreat you to consider my circum-stances, being three-quarters of a year from my house has driven my wife into an indigent condition, having little or no business. They make a heavy hurricane about my coming in, and curse my popish wife, bell, book, and candle. No sooner they touch the printer or publisher but they are blown up as if there was wild fire to their tails. They won't meet with a fool that will keep out of the way almost eight months upon his own expenses to save their bacon. I would have burnt the book before I had concerned myself in it had I understood their drift.

[LORD GODOLPHIN] to ROBERT HARLEY.

[1706,] March 14. Newmarket—Your amendments in the draft of the speech are very just; I am only sorry to observe you have not amended the conclusion, which I doubt wants it.

I wish your presence in the House of Commons may be able to make them take some effectual resolution about manning the fleet, since that matter does but too plainly want their immediate care.

W[ILLIAM] BLENCOWE to [ROBERT HARLEY].

1705-6, March 15. Launceston—On the difficulties he had met with in decyphering a letter sent to him. After discovering as he thought what most of the characters signified he was surprised to find the matter concealed under the cypher to be a gibberish language of which he did not understand a word. Should be inclined to believe himself mistaken in the key, if any cypher could be thought capable of being reduced into a sounding language by two keys differing in many letters. The first words of the letter as the key explains it are *Precloss quannupila sa monne*, and it goes on in that kind of canting language. Will keep the cypher, and use more pains to make an intelligible interpretation of it unless Harley, who knows from whose hand it comes, believes that it is incapable of a better explication.

—— to ROBERT HARLEY.

1705-6, March 20—There is one John Paston Esquire, who lives at Great Appleton near Lynn Regis in Norfolk, a professed, bigoted papist that has for several years and does still keep a priest in his family openly and publicly, by name one Hall, who in defiance of the laws travels and employs his daily arts and devices to pervert and reduce several of the commonalty of the neighbouring towns, who resort there every Sunday morning to hear mass. They marry, &c., without licence, and have perverted abundance to the Romish creed. If speedy care be not taken with them there will be more mischief done than can be thought of.

[LORD GODOLPHIN to ROBERT HARLEY.]

[1705-6, March 22] Good Friday night—I think as you do in your letter t'other day that the Tories are more numerous in this Parliament than the Whigs, and the Queen's servants much the least part of the three. My computation runs thus: of the 450 that chose the Speaker Tories 190, Whigs 160, Queen's servants 100, of the last about 15 perhaps joined with Tories in that vote of the Speaker, by which they mounted to 205, and so afterwards more or less, in almost every vote. Except in the Place Bill, that is the *clause*, the 160 voted always with the body of the Queen's servants. Now the question in my opinion is, whether it be more likely or more easy to keep the 160 which with the Queen's true servants will always be a majority, or to get (*sic*) from the 190. I think their behaviour in this Session has shown as much inveteracy and as little sense as was possible, however I should be always of opinion to receive such of them as would come off, but I see very little reason to depend upon that or upon them afterwards, and further it ought to be considered that for every one we are like to get from the 190 we shall lose 2 or 3 from the 160, and is it not more reasonable and more easy to preserve those who have served and helped us than to seek those who have basely and ungratefully done all that was in their poor power to ruin us : and when they find themselves disappointed, they would willingly make a little fair weather again, in hopes only as I think of a better opportunity next winter, if we have ill success, and if we have good, of making a merit. As for the Clergy, they always say themselves it is easy for the Queen to get them into her interests. I think so too, if they be once thoroughly satisfied which is the right way to preferment. As for idle stories they make not the least impression upon me, I mind only what men do, and not what others say they do, so that as far as my friendship is of any value, you need not apprehend that 'tis in the power of another to take it from you.

As to the *narrow measures* of any in the House of Lords, be they who they will, I may presume to say such measures are wrong; I take it our business is, to get as many we can from the 190, without doing anything to lose one of the 160.

CHRISTIAN AUGUSTUS, DUKE OF HOLSTEIN to [JAMES CRESSETT].

1706, March 22. Gottorp—I am greatly indebted to you for the favourable reception you have given to Major General Count von der Natt, and for the good offices you have rendered me to the Queen, in order to decide her in favour of my re-institution into the Bishopric of Lubeck. It seems as if the King of Denmark were willing to relax his pretensions, but as there is nothing yet fixed in the matter, and as possession alone would not any more than before guarantee me from fresh insults, unless I were protected by a renunciation by Denmark on the model of their pretended rights, and unless the infraction of the treaty of Travendahl were at the same time completely redressed, I shall be obliged to insist all the more on the offering of guarantees because the re-institution is nothing but a way to facilitate the rest.

I beg you will reflect thereon and represent to the Queen the necessity to which I am reduced of not being able to stop at possession only. I am sure that you will see that in order not to have to solicit the guaranteeing powers again, I cannot act otherwise. I recommend also to your protection the liberty of commerce for my subjects and the payment of arrears, as also to assist Monsieur de Leyencrona minister from Sweden, who is entrusted with that matter _by me. *Signed.* *French.*

MONSIEUR SALADIN to [ROBERT HARLEY].

1706, March 22. London—Asking that his servant, who had been in the hands of a messenger nearly two months, may be released and his horses returned to him, as those taken from others had been. *French.*

D. EDWARDS to ROBERT HARLEY.

1706, March 29—I was very cautious what I delivered for fear of being wrong but, by all the transactions maturely connected together, 'twas Mr. Bromley's lady brought me the copies [of the Memorial of the Church of England], and I wish she might be viewed. They make such hectoring and bouncing that they'll lay me in a jail for my life, and that I can't find the woman. What induces me to believe 'twas Madam Bromley that brought it is, that she told me 'twas recommended by both Universities, and I know he's the darling of one if not of both; and you'll find in their letters to me large promises of being my friends in a more public manner, and it was whispered to me in the time of my absence that the votes of Parliament were designed for me if Mr. Bromley should come in for Speaker.

W[ILLIAM] BLENCOWE to [ROBERT HARLEY].

1706, March 31. Marston—Acknowledges receipt of papers in cypher. The work will require a pretty deal of time and application for the cyphers used in the several letters are different and none of them easy. Sees no word through them all written in plain characters, by which might be judged in what language they are written; in this his honour [Harley] might have given him some assistance. Is sorry he has not been able to give a better account of the last letter in cypher received, which he new returns enclosed.

M. SALADIN to the EARL OF RANELAGH.

1706, April 2. London—Asking that his servant and his papers might be handed over to him. And that five or six hunters which he had bought for himself and friends to be sent to Geneva might be either given up or sold. *Signed. French.*

M. DE ROBETHON to [ROBERT HARLEY].

1706, April 2. [Hanover]—I shall follow your orders concerning the letter you are writing to the Electress.

663, 1356 did not fail to write to 715 three weeks ago to put off the embassy, but I think none of that will be any good, no more than the rescript which was sent you on Tuesday about that matter.

Craggs is still here and does not speak of going away. That is very mortifying for 1356. 319 talks loudly for 867, 52, 94, 536, 837, 589, but 399 wishes him to go away at all events for a time, and made him a compliment yesterday by 1252, who assures me that when the 52 is once gone they will find means to prevent his returning. Do not speak of this yet for I shall not believe he is gone until he actually goes, as 319 leaves nothing undone to make him remain. 1252 will make him carry 692, 431, without which he could not leave here as he owes money on all sides. Scott thinks that Hutton will go soon. I will make Mr. Howe understand that you have done all that was possible in his difference with Mr. Craggs. *French. Copy in Harley's handwriting.* "Brûlez, Monsieur" *is written at top of the letter.*

A. LADY PYE to her cousin, ABIGAIL HARLEY, at Eywood.

1706, April 3. Derby—I wish your sister a son, the family not being overstocked. I should be pleased to renew my acquaintance with her; 'tis many years since I saw her when a very young lady. I am glad your niece Popham has brought an heir to her husband's family, but pray let not a great aunt make you look grave. I don't intend to be so till I'm a grandmother and that's not likely to be in haste, though I wish hereafter I may have as good a hand at marrying my children as servants. Yesterday we had a wedding, my own maid; and by this day sennight my girl's French woman and the chaplain have agreed to conclude; with many more since I lived here, that I begin to be weary to fit servants and then part, though these two last I must not complain of, have been both eleven years with me.

JAMES CRESSETT to [ROBERT HARLEY].

1706, April 5. Deptford—Being obliged to return some answer to the letter I lately showed you I think it my duty to trouble you with the sight of what I write. I write likewise to General Bavieres, who is an old friend whom I esteem and value, having known him long before I was plagued with any of the northern broils. I hope there may be an end of this honourable correspondence which, as I do not think it becomes a private man, so am I sure it was not of my seeking. *Copy of his letter to the Duke of Holstein enclosed.*

H. [HUMPHREYS] BISHOP OF HEREFORD to [ROBERT HARLEY].

1706, April 6. Whithorn—Promising to obey the Queen's instructions that he should enquire into the irregular proceedings of which Mr. Dobbins had given information.

BARON SCHUTZ to [ROBERT HARLEY].

1706, April 12. London—Having called twice at your office to communicate to you the reply of the Electress to the question you made me when you sent me the address of the Parliament concerning the letter of Sir Rowland Gwyn and the Queen's reply, and my health not allowing me to go out much, I thought I ought not to put off any longer sending you the said answer which is to be found in the enclosed extract. I expect also to receive by the next post the orders of the Elector on the subject. *French.*

H BISHOP OF HEREFORD to [ROBERT HARLEY].

1706, April 13. Whithorn—Informing him that he had been to Hereford and made all enquiry into the wicked and infamous action reported to him ; and that he had examined the man who rode upon the ass, and his master; that they protested they meant no ill, but there was sufficient moral evidence to shew that it was done with a profane and blasphemous intent. He had also ordered a private enquiry to be made of the behaviour of these madmen in churches at any time ; and exhorted the town clerk of Hereford to stir up the mayor and justices to prosecute this matter to the utmost, and have also obliged Canon Watts the present residentiary to assist.

ROBERT HARLEY to ROBERT YATE, at Bristol.

1706, April 13. Whitehall—Some weeks since a letter came pretended from Dublin, which said that one of David Edwards the printer's servants would make discoveries relating to the libel, " *The Memorial*," &c. Since then Edwards has surrendered himself and done what he can to promote the discovery ; and I believe he is a real penitent for the mischief he has done the nation. Now I understand one Baily, who was Edwards's servant at the time the libel was printed, is in your city with one Bonny, a printer. I desire therefore you will examine Baily upon oath with great privacy as to his knowledge about the printing of " *The Memorial*," &c., who brought the copy, who corrected it, where the books were sent, &c. I hear there are some people in Bristol intimate with Baily whom you should also examine, more particularly one Mr. Arthur Bedford, whom I believe a very honest man and a well-wisher to the Government. (*Copy.*)

ST. JOHN BRODRICK to [ROBERT HARLEY].

1706, April 18—There is another person of the name of Thomas Brodrick besides my brother. He is a relation, but one with whom I have no manner of conversation nor can tell where he may be found, but I will make it my business to enquire. His father is in Jamaica in an office there, and has sent for this young man to come over to him. The father is a very honest man and of a good character ; I hope the son has not been guilty of anything that may subject him to your displeasure.

JOHN GELLIBRAND to [ROBERT HARLEY].

1706, April 19—I herewith send you Dyer's letters. They are four hundred and eleven, and with what you have, which are a hundred and ninety-seven, makes in all six hundred and eight. They commence from the November before King William died and come down to last November. I think his foreign news is what you have no where else, and his home news is very scandalous, especially since it passes with impunity. However I believe in a short time there may be found a way to prevent it as well as punish him.

I hope you do not forget me in relation to my being admitted into my former office of Clerk of the Cheque to the Messengers.

Postscript. These letters cost me 20*l.*, at which price they are yours.

JOHN TUTCHIN to ROBERT HARLEY.

1706, April 20. London—It lying in my way to be informed of many grievances dangerous to the public, I think it my duty to inform the ministry in order to a redress of such evils and never make them public till out of hopes of remedy.

I heard great complaint in the Savoy Precinct concerning the usage of the men brought out of the country for land service, fresh lusty young fellows are kept there stifling for want of room in the prison where they soon die or become unserviceable; some of the parish have told me that a much greater number die in a year in that prison. than in the whole parish besides. This put me upon inquiry and I find that the Keeper or Marshal of that Prison is one MacMahone, an Irish papist who came over from St. Germain with the ███ughter of Mrs. Cellier, midwife to the pretended Prince of Wales. His Deputy one Murphy, another Irish papist, was tried and condemned for a pirate.

I leave it to your honour's consideration whether these persons are fit for such a trust and how likely our army is to be recruited with healthful able-bodied men when such persons have the management.

DR. W. S[TRATFORD] to his "brother" ———.

1706, April 22. Christchurch [Oxford]—We had a sermon yesterday which I am afraid will be reported to our disadvantage. It will be to no purpose to urge, that it was by the most silly and most worthless person of the whole society. He will be supposed to be the mouth of the College; and I only give you this account that you may be able to contradict the aggravations of it. Read preached in Dr. South's turn. His text was, 'As then, he who was born of the flesh persecuted him who was born of the spirit, even so it is now.' Had there been any particular expressions that would have borne a censure, I would, though the Dean was absent, have done what I could to have had the Chapter taken notice of them. But there were only general hints, that are capable by enemies of an ill construction: that the Church, ever since the Reformation, had been persecuted, by Papists in Queen Mary's time, by fanatics, instigated by Papists, in the late times of rebellion etc.: that the same was now endeavoured at: that they shewed what they designed by the persecution of the clergy in Scotland: that they would do the same there, if ever they had power again etc.: that many who were nursed up among us, who were partakers of our sacraments, betrayed us etc.: that we were not to be dismayed whenever the clouds gathered, that God would find some way to disappoint them. I attended diligently, and I profess to thee this is the best account I can give thee. It is said at the close he bid them arm themselves against the fiery trial that was now approaching. I did not hear any of those words, but so many [credit] them, that I believe there might be [some] such. 'Fiery trial' is the word, and it is said that Sacheverell has been outdone by one of Christ Church, and no doubt it is at Lambeth before you will receive this. Pray communicate this with my respects to the Dean. I wish he would be pleased to go with you to the Secretary, to give an account of this, and to contradict any worse representation that without doubt will be made of it. I pray go to Dr. South and let him know there are some who are so silly as to think to do him credit by it, others who are so malicious as to design him mischief and say this preacher was put up on purpose by him and instructed what to say. It would be of service to the College, and to Dr. South too, if he would take some notice to him of this folly. This useless [man, not] to say worse of him, may do the society more prejudice than all honest men with their utmost endeavours can do service.

Jo. Forster to Robert Harley.

1706, April 26. Newgarthside.--I thought good to acquaint you that I am afraid that the Jacobites have some designs in their heads this summer, for they have been very busy in caballing and plotting all this spring, and have had many meetings under the pretence of visits; and their emissaries are going like bees to and fro. They laugh at anything of an Union and to divert that business they have had a story amongst them that still the King of France will give Scotland far better terms than ever they can expect from England, that Scotland may have the freedom and liberty of trade to all the French and Spanish plantations abroad, provided that Scotland will furnish France with forty thousand men, which men the French King will pay and maintain at his own charges. They say that there are great sums of money remitted to the malcontents in Hungary on purpose to keep the war on foot on that side, and that matters will be so managed this summer that a final stroke will be given to the war; for they say that the French King will have one hundred thousand men more in arms than ever he had in all his life. Now upon all these considerations, why may not some men be sent into Scotland and money remitted thither on purpose to breed a broil in those kingdoms, for since I can remember I never saw the Jacobites in such a heart and look as if they did expect some mighty matters. I hope that you will forgive this boldness in me, for it is my hearty and sincere love to my Queen and country that induces me and I wish that I could in any manner be serviceable to them.

Postscript.—I have not been well all this spring so have not stirred abroad so much as I used to do, otherwise I fancy that I might have known more of their designs.

The French Refugee Ministers in England to the Queen.

1706, April 26—Asking for her usual grant of 15,000*l.*, of which 12,000*l.* would be for the refugees, and 3,000*l.* for the petitioners. *Seven signatures. French.*

Robert Harley to — Price, Clerk of the Peace for Radnorshire.

1706, April 27. Whitehall—Enclosing a copy of a letter from the Privy Council calling for a return of all the Papists in Radnorshire. *Copy.*

Dr. R[obert] South to Robert Fbeind, Second Master of Westminster School.

1706, April 27.--Though as I told you, and that with great truth, I have neither expectation nor desire of anything from the Court, yet since every man of sense ought to be so just to himself, as to endeavour the best he can to be dealt with only according to the merits of his own behaviour, I am I confess by no means willing to have my name traduced and tossed about by the tongues of a malicious party, only for the folly and indiscretions of another.

And therefore let me beg this favour of you, that when you have occasion next to visit my Lord of Exeter, you would with my humblest duty and service to his Lordship plainly and impartially lay this matter before him.

And I doubt not but his Lordship's known generosity and love to justice, as well as his goodwill to me, are such that he will be ready to set this business (howsoever it may have been represented) in its true light, and to give that just account of me and my utter unconcernment in this whole affair (which by all that is sacred I avow); yet in case he should meet with any great persons prepossessed with any spiteful stories of this nature against me, he would so far inform and rectify them that I may find so much fair and equal dealing from the men in power as to suffer as little by them as I look for from them.

This I shall account no small kindness to me and the sooner you do it the more effectual is it like to prove for my vindication.

Dr. William Stratford to [Robert] Harley.

1706, April 27. Christchurch—It is with great satisfaction that I can let you know that the sport here is over, and that nothing that I can hear of was either said or done that could give the least offence, either to any private person, or to the public. It was ended on Friday before our *Comitia* began. All concerned in it came to the Theatre. There were the Duke of Beaufort, Earls of Plymouth and Denbigh, Lords Craven and Granville, Sir J. Conway, Sir William Glynne, Mr. Leake, Mr. Bertie, Mr. Wenman, Sir J. Walters, Sir R. Dashwood, Sir R. Jenkinson, Mr. Morley, Mr. Goring. There were some others whom I knew not, but they seemed to be cockers of a lesser denomination than the others. The compliment that is usual to persons of their quality was offered to them and accepted by them. And the Lords and the Commons who were members of Parliament were presented with the foreigners who were there to their degrees. This was the only conversation that they had with any scholars whilst they staid there. And I must beg leave to say it for our credit, that I believe it was never known upon any other public meeting that has been that ever the scholars so readily and so generally abstained from it, as they did from this. The Duke with some of his company went to-day to Sir Robert Dashwood's. I suppose by Monday we shall be clear of all the company.

The exercise will be printed, but I beg leave to trouble you beforehand with the little share we had in it. We must desire some allowances may be made for it, it being done upon very short notice. The Dean set the music before he left us, and it gave great satisfaction. The ode had been most of it used upon a former occasion, but we had not time to prepare one on purpose. We were afraid the exercise would have been too short, and therefore Dr. Smalridge was desired to present Dr. Grabe with all the ceremonies that are performed in a solemn act. Dr. Grabe was one whose character would bear such a respect, and the novelty of it was an entertainment to the strangers. It having been a new thing there, I have presumed to trouble you with all the little speeches Dr. Smalridge made upon every part of the ceremony, and I beg leave to add that it happened to be that part of the exercise which was most taken notice of by the Resident of the King of Prussia, and the foreigners, as well as by our own university.

Dr. Gastrell tells me he has troubled you with an account of what passed in our church on Sunday last. I had last night a letter from my brother, Dr. South, in whose turn the sermon was preached, to desire me with great earnestness to clear him of it in as public a manner as I can. We have no other way to vindicate ourselves, for whatever the preacher might mean, his expressions were so general that no censure could be fixed on him.

J[OHN] LEBRUN [*alias* OGILVIE] to [ROBERT HARLEY].

1706, [April 29-]May 9 [new style]. Rotterdam—I was afraid
that you should begin to have a bad opinion of me by reason of my not
writing to you as you ordered me, but when I shall give you the reasons
why I did not I hope you will be convinced of my fidelity to you. In the
first place, I will never write by Mr. D[rummond] for my hand is known
to all these people and also my Lord Drummond was all this winter in
Holland and his brother with him, where they stayed often at Mr. D's in
Amsterdam so that was a dangerous consequence for me ; and in the
next place I had but little to say but what the newspapers did acquaint
you of, and to trouble you with stories that is nothing to the purpose is
what I cannot be capable of. But the truth is I was obliged to wait the
Court's pleasure to see what answer they would return to the message
that I brought from Hamburgh. I suppose you have my last letter by
you that my wife did give you, so that I need not enlarge on that
subject ; so that now I am ordered back with the Court's orders to those
ministers *incognito* I could wish to be with you before I went ; but I
am afraid that would spoil all for it would be found out that I went for
England,' and also the time that it would take up, but you may depend
upon it that I shall write to you every post from Hamburg by Mr.
Alderson, and if you think it proper that I stay any time with those
ministers and go along with them I shall, for in doing so it will be easy
for me to drain into the bottom of what they negociate there or elsewhere in those Countries, for you may judge that I can never be
suspected by them since the Court hath sent me back.

All the affairs of Scotland depend upon what shall be negotiated in
those northern parts, however there was a frigate sent from Dunkirk to
Scotland with some orders, it was a frigate of thirty six guns commanded by a Scotchman whose name is Caron and I believe he declared
his message at a house of the Earl of Errol's the Constable of that
kingdom : it stands upon a rock in the sea almost. The Lord's mother
is a very intriguing wily lady as is any in Britain, she is sister to the Lord
Perth and Melfort. What the message was I cannot tell but when I
come back from Hamburg if you think it fitting I can take a turn down
to Scotland where I am certain to find it out ; but before I go down I
shall have the honour to see you. I am much obliged to you for your
goodness to my poor wife, she is there still for I durst not venture to
bring her away for fear of giving of them suspicion of me, and at the
same time I am afraid that the Queen at St. Germain can take
them and put them into a monastery ; and to bring them away I know
not what to do with them unless you could persuade the Queen to
do something for me that I may make them live and not starve.

I made some remarks when I was at Wolfenbüttell but that I shall
leave till my next, only I shall tell you he is in the French interest
entirely. I must also tell you that my poverty is a great hindrance to
any intelligence, for I had but fifty pounds at Hamburgh and my staying
there, coming back and my going into France did eat it all up which if
I had been master of a little money I had stayed at Court ; for to find
out matters of that nature one must have money to eat and drink with
several sorts of men. Since the business of Fraser our Court of
St. Germain will suffer nobody that belongs to them to take any money
from Versailles as you will see by what I send you here enclosed and
you may judge what I can do on such small allowance. Therefore I wish
you would order me a little money and your orders what you will have
me to do. I must also tell you that my ingoing to France I was
afraid of myself, as you'll see by the first letter I had from my Lord Perth

bearing date the 20th of January that I had reason; but when they found that I was trusted by the French Ministers then you'll see how they changed their note by my Lord's letter dated the 20th or so and his next dated the 29th of March and also the 6th of April. I have sent these letters to you that you may see that I deal frankly and uprightly with you. I was afraid by my reading of the Gazettes that you were to quit the Ministry before I could get this length, for I only arrived here last night having parted the 28th of April from France, which if you had quitted it had been a great misfortune to me, for truly I reckon on no friend but yourself for I have not the honour to be known to my Lord Treasurer, so I must have perished. So I beg of you if you be to quit that you will acquaint me, at least if you can get nothing done for me, for I will have to do with none else, come in your place who will, for I am satisfied that you are a man of honour and generosity and will never fail in what you have promised me.

I shall say no more at this time till I hear from you, only recommend my miserable fortune and family to you and I wish that God prosper them no better than I shall ever be faithful to you. Direct for me à Monsieur Lebrun, chez Monsieur Andrea Brun merchant in Rotterdam; but since it is from England let it be backed in English. Let me hear speedily from you and send me back those letters of my Lord Perth's, for they may be of use to me and if you can order me a little money, it will come in good time to me at present although God is my witness it is not for the lucre of a little money that I risk my life in this nature to serve the Queen and you, for you must be sensible that were I found out my life would pay for it. But it is my gratitude to Her Majesty that did give me my life when it was in her power to have taken it away, and in the next place to see if I can merit to oblige Her Majesty to provide for me which I do not doubt but you will be mindful of me, I pray you to pardon this way of writing to one of your character, I know it does not become me and were it on any other occasion, I would not presume to take the liberty, God reward you for all your favours.

W. [Talbot] Bishop of Oxford to [Robert Harley].

1706, April 29. Caynton near Newport in Shropshire—I cannot say anything upon my knowledge of Mr. Pocock's title to Chinner. His being presented to a living of that value to which he could not have the greatest pretensions has occasioned some jealousies, how well founded I cannot say, but this 1 am sure of that if he came in upon simony, that pest and bane of the church, I heartily wish he may be displaced. But those making the charge against the present incumbent should be well satisfied with the proofs they have to support it.

W. [Talbot] Bishop of Oxford to his "brother," the Rev. Samuel Dunster at Lord Maynard's house in Pall Mall.

1706, April 29. Caynton—I can give you no other answer than what I have returned to Mr. Secretary Harley, viz that if Mr. Pocock came into Chinner upon simony I heartily wish you success in turning out a wretch that could be guilty of so vile a practice; but I would advise you before you proceed further to have not only Mr. Thornicroft's allegations against Mr. Pocock laid before some judicious and honest lawyers, but likewise the proofs by which he supports them, that they may judge whether they will bear the stress he may lay upon them.

Dr. Hugh Chamberlen to [Robert Harley].

1706, April 30—Concerning his proposals for the establishment of a "current credit."

le Moyne de Brie to Robert Harley.

1706, May 4—Another letter pleading for his liberty and depicting his "dismal condition" and "disorder of body and mind" in the strongest terms.

G. Granville to [Robert Harley].

1706, May 4—The honour you do me in sending me such assurances of your friendship is a sufficient reparation for the disappointment for which your letter seems to prepare me. I had heard what was designed from public report but could no way be induced to give credit to it after so solemn a promise and such repeated assurances as I had received, especially not having given the least colour of pretence for so unusual a treatment. But however I am contented to suffer provided the Queen's service may be the better for it. As for my future expectation I look upon-all that to be at an end; but as long as you shall please to honour me with your friendship I must always look upon myself as a gainer.

A. Lady Pye to her cousin, Abigail Harley, at Eywood.

1706, May 4. Derby—When I was in London I heard Col. Hill admired Mrs. Collier. It was his company that was long quartered here and are newly gone, which most are glad of. Our celebrated beauty Mrs. Warren is also at London; I gave Sir Charles an account of a duel betwixt Capt. Cremar and her brother and he told me he would relate it to you. I begin now to think Sir Charles's absence very tedious but hope he is on the road having no letter this post; he hath met with many lets and delays in his business and at last I doubt can't sell his house at Twickenham. I think we had best live at it, and have the advantage of seeing my friends which this distance deprives us of. But I can proceed no further till I've returned my dear cousin abundance of thanks for the fine flowers which I received this day se'nnight. They are by far the best I ever saw and the Indian mighty beautiful. Am sorry you would be at the charge, enough to stock a garden instead of bosoms; must own a more welcome present could ne'er have been thought, for my girls are wonderfully delighted. Our milliners have brought down flowers this year, but very ordinary things. We have lately had a fine modish lady, Mrs. Key. One would not guess she so lately had three children at a birth, is yet pretty but on the wane. She told me a great deal of Lady Shrewsbury and such stories as made me very sick of her Grace. But with all that the ladies now begin to admire her and even the graver sort such as Lady Falconbridge &c. She also saw Lady Scudamore after her wedding; said she looked well in her fine clothes. We have now Mrs. Munday in our neighbourhood that is thought as pretty a black woman as most is.

[Daniel De Foe to Robert Harley.]

1706, May 6th—As the last time I had the favour of audience with you, you were pleased to tell me you desired to speak with me on account of " The Review " &c. I have often endeavoured to have the like honour and begun to hope something might offer in which I might be useful to you.

But I am not only unhappy in frequent disappointments, but my unhappy circumstances making those disappointments more severe to me than I believe you would have them be, forces me to give you this too tedious narrative, humbly to state to you my present case and earnest request, and entreat your pardon for the importunate plainness, a liberty you were pleased frankly to give me, and which I have been too apt to accept of.

My case really admits no ceremony, being come to that crisis, that without some powerful aid, or some miracle which I ought not to expect, I shall soon be rendered entirely useless both to the public and myself.

But why do I look to you, or move you in this matter is a question offers some shock in my writing this.

Pardon my positive way of speaking, I don't say I merit, at least anything but pity—but you have had the goodness to put me in hopes that something was reserved in my favour. If I have mistaken you, I am wrong indeed, and would be glad to be set right, that I might not expect and make you uneasy with my importunities.

This reserve you were pleased to say with your usual tenderness for me you would have to be useful to me, and therefore kept till I was free.

But the prospect of the freedom looks every day more dull upon me, and I foresee I shall never master it, unless I can take off some of the most furious people, who resolutely oppose me, and which is worse, I find it will be, if contested, a very doubtful point, whether I am within the meaning of this Act or no, and am therefore advised not to attempt it.

Now, as the risk of disputing is too great, since I must surrender myself first into the hands of the unmerciful, and that to take them off by treaty is absolutely necessary, no man that is my friend advises me to attempt it by law, since when they in particular are shaken off, I shall be as effectually free as by the act, all the rest being under obligation to a composition, which they have received part of and cannot go from.

Thus, sir, my freedom depends on a private treaty, which treaty without assistance I cannot carry on, and meantime have been so close pursued since I saw you, that I am but by miracle yet out their hands, and am obliged to quit all conversation and make a retreat altogether disconsolate and such as renders me useless and incapable.

This urges me to say if there is such a thing, if her Majesty's bounty has anything in reserve for me I entreat of you one of the two following particulars, and 'tis fit I should leave it to you to choose.

1st, that I may be assisted, as far as two or three hundred pounds will do it, to free myself from the immediate fury of five or six unreasonable creditors, after which I shall by my own strength work through the rest in time. Or, that according to your kind promise, which I cannot but claim, you will please to send me somewhere abroad out of the reach of their hands, and that her Majesty's bounty may be someway applied to the support of my family.

I really know not whether this thing I call her Majesty's bounty be what I ought to speak of in this manner or no, I pretend to no merit I have done but my duty.—But indeed, I have been unjustly ruined, and that in her Majesty's name, and I am now implacably pursued purely on account of my endeavours for her Majesty's service.

If these are merits I have some claim and I flatter myself your intercession, sir, will improve it.

I cease to go on with this sad story, and though my case renders me now next to desperate, yet-I can not enlarge on my complaint. I am not weary attending at your door, nor do I repine at staying your leisure—But the risk I run so much as to pass and repass, is of the last consequence to me, and though I resolve if possible not to be taken by them, yet there's no defending against a surprise.

The loss I sustain also, in the want of conversing with you, appears to me destructive of all the designs laid by me, for your service. The correspondence I had settled by your order in most parts of England, and from which on all occasions I could have rendered you service, dies and declines for want of that assistance which you were pleased to allow was necessary to me, viz. of a servant to assist. and of frequent communication of things to keep intelligence alive.

The very charge is too great for my reduced condition, and the number of letters too many for the few undisturbed hours which I have left me.

Thus I am rendered useless to you, in that which I hoped once to have brought to a perfection beyond even your own expectation, and in which I have been at no inconsiderable charge over and above what you have been pleased to allot for that work.

I hope you will think all this proceeds from a mind grieved that I cannot be made that useful instrument to the public I would be, and whatever may look self interested you will pardon, for though it is true I importune you in the first I above all covet to show you that I would not be thought to enjoy your favour not to your advantage.

I have several things to move you in, that I cannot comprise here. Mr. Ducket has been in town, that affair being delayed not only sinks my interest and correspondence in that country, but puffs up the high interest in the country to a vast disadvantage, and I have much to say on that head worth notice.

I would be your humble petitioner for a private apartment in Whitehall, where I am told it is in your power, to admit me, and having an opportunity now to clear myself of the Queen's Bench by an accident, which I want to inform you of, I might, by the shelter of such a retreat, prevent any new attempts upon me there.

I have also something to inform you of, of a design forming against yourself, which I should be glad to be instrumental to disappoint, but all these things receive their interruption, as I, a continued mortification in the want of that access to yourself which formerly I enjoyed.

I am impatient to mention also the subject of the three last Reviews, which, if you have not seen, is my loss, since without doubt I might be enabled by you to have carried on that subject exceedingly to the Government's advantage.

I humbly refer all these things to your consideration, and wait to dispose of myself by your direction.

JOHN LEBRUN [OGILVIE] to ROBERT BRYAN [HARLEY] merchant in London.

1706, May [7-]18 [new style]. Rotterdam—I did take the liberty to write to you about twelve days ago in hopes that you would have sent me your orders by this time. If I had come over to you in the time that I have waited here it would certainly have been better than to have stayed here to no purpose where I can render you no service, but bring myself to be suspected by those that sent me, and also render me incapable of either serving the Queen or you, and make myself miserable. For I leave it to you to judge what they will imagine of me to stay here and not go about my affairs that I was sent for, they are no fools that I have to deal with. Besides I shall spend the little money that was given me to bear my charges, so I earnestly beg of you that you'll not suffer me to be ruined for my good will to you; but if you think I can serve you let me have your orders, and you may depend upon it they shall ever be obeyed if it were even to the hazard of my life. If you could give me some person in London to address your letters to it would do well, for you see I have found out one here, therefore mind it for Mr. Lebrun at Mr. Andrew Brun's there must be no more for he is Jacobite but our letters will be safe. You must give me somebody in London that is not in the Government, for I do suppose if I should put in a letter into the post house directed for Mr. Robert Bryan it would not come to your hands unless it were under a cover to somebody, this you may clear me in and you shall hear from me every post be where I will. Had I received your orders just when mine came to your hands, I might have been with you and almost back here again by this time. I am uneasy to know if my letter came to your hands safe. I had almost forgot to tell you that there was two Scotchmen at St. Germain just come over and was to return back immediately, they were not men of any character but they have been both of them trusted with letters formerly to my knowledge; but as to that I shall say no more until I shall have the honour either to see you or at least hear from you, but whatever you please to order me I am content of, but what you resolve do quickly, otherwise I must be gone for I dare not answer it to stay here.

D. Edwards to Robert Harley.

1706, May 7—Forwards proof sheet of a pamphlet entitled *Slavery in Disguise*, which he found in his warehouse on returning home after eleven months' absence, with remarks on the handwriting of the corrections made.

Lord Chief Justice Holt to [Robert Harley].

1706, May 8—I received your letter wherein you signified the Queen's pleasure concerning Mr. Stephens standing in the pillory. I shall be always ready to obey Her Majesty's commands on the least intimation of her pleasure, but it so happens in this case that the times of his standing in the pillory are part of the judgment and are confined to tomorrow and Friday. Therefore I cannot suspend that execution unless I have Her Majesty's command under her sign manual counter-signed by the Secretary of State and under the seal of the office.

The Same to [the Same].

1706, May 9—I received your second letter this morning and am afraid I have given you a great trouble which I could not avoid. Since it is Her Majesty's pleasure to extend her mercy to Mr. Stephens I have taken care to prevent his being put in the pillory.

Yorkshire Papists.

1706, May 13—A list of all the Papists and reputed Papists within the three bailiwicks of Holderness in the East Riding of Yorkshire, showing their "qualities," occupations, abodes, and the value of their estates, if any. Among them are Ralph and John Brigham, Robert, Viscount Dunbar, Marmaduke Langdale, Robert Dolman, George Meltham, William Constable and Thomas Crathorne. The majority are farmers, their families, servants and labourers. The return was taken at Hornsea and is signed by five justices, viz. Robt. Hildyard, Hugh Bethell, Rich. More, Wm. Thompson, and Wm. Lister.

The Same.

1706, May 14—Similar list of all Papists and reputed Papists within the Wapentake of Ouse and Derwent in the East Riding of Yorkshire. Among them are George Palmes of Naburn, and his four infant children, Marmaduke Palmes, William Palmes, and Peter Middleton of Stockeld in the West Riding. The justices signing the return are Tho. Hesketh, Tho. Stillington, and W. Headlam.

The Same.

Same date—A similar list for the divisions of Buckrose and Dickering in the East Riding of Yorkshire. Among them are John Constable of Caythorpe his wife, and Frances Partridge, his grandchild. The justices signing the return are Will. Strickland, W. Osbaldeston, J. Legard, Tho. Sowtheby, and Rich. Osbaldeston. Another copy of this list has the additional signature " M. Peirson v.c. Ebor."

Adam Cardonnel to Lord William Paulet.

1706, May 14. Maestricht—My Lord Duke commands me to make his compliments to your Lordship and to let you know he would have been very glad on your account as well as for Mr. Irvine's merit to have preferred him in the new levies, though he really thinks he is better where he is; and as to his present request for a brevet of Lieutenant Colonel, his Grace does not now concern himself with the troops in England, therefore advises your Lordship to make immediate application to the Prince, where I hope you will succeed, for I do assure your Lordship I was heartily concerned at this gentleman's disappointment. I concluded he was sure of his pretensions, but it is the case of abundance more who had the like favourable promise.

Isaac Bernard to the Queen.

1706, May 15. London—Describing himself as a German Jew, and a jeweller in Duke's Place, asking to be sent into the enemy's camp as a spy. *French.*

Yorkshire Papists.

1706, May 18—A list of all the Papists and reputed Papists within the divisions of Hunsley Beacon and Bainton Beacon in the East Riding of Yorkshire. *Includes* George Meltham of North Cave, wife and four children; Philip Langdale of South Cliffe; Alexander Mont-gomerie and Marmaduke Langdale of Sancton-*cum*-Houghton. The justices signing the return are Cha. Hotham, Ing. Daniell, Edw. Barnard, Jo. Moyser, and Tho. Alured.

LORD CONINGSBY to [ROBERT HARLEY].

1706, May 20—Asking for an order that one Coleby, deputy-chamberlain to Mr. Gascoigne, accused of robbing the Irish Exchequer of 1200*l*., who had been seized at Chester, might be sent over to Dublin. *Enclosed is a letter from William Robinson from Dublin on the same subject.*

R[OBERT] MONCKTON to [ROBERT HARLEY].

1706, May 20. Holroyd [co. York]—I congratulate you upon this glorious success when things seem coming to a crisis. All the rest have been striking at the branches but this gives a blow to the root, when the trunks all shake. And now that all is put under his feet I beg your interest and intercession to my Lord on my behalf. He knows how much he has said to make me expect the marks of his favour without importunity. If you are pleased to be as earnest as the Duke of Newcastle my Lord will not cast me off with the reprobates.

[DANIEL DE FOE] to ROBERT HARLEY.

1706, May 21—I am loth to break in upon your joy, and no man more sincerely congratulates it than I; though my clouds darken my own expression of it and make me reflect that it is hard all the Queen's friends rejoice but I.

My melancholy story, however, is not the design of this. I cannot expect but you are in hurries too great to think of my trifling affair, but I could not but send you the enclosed. Perhaps you may make use of them to my advantage, if not, it is fit, I should recommend them to you, to use at your pleasure. It is always a cordial to me to see you, but now, when so much more suppressed than ever, it would be par-ticularly so. Will a short essay on those mighty affairs be accepted from me in this juncture? is a question, which if answered by you, sir, would help inspire the performance.

JO. MOYSER to [ROBERT HARLEY].

1706, May 22. Beverley—The Queen having been pleased to grant her letters patent for a brief towards assisting this Corporation to repair a part of a noble old minster in this town that is fallen to decay, the trustees appointed agreed with undertakers for laying the briefs, collecting the money, and paying it in at certain times. They also took security of them for performance of the covenants, but one of the under-takers had since absconded and the others for their protection desired an advertisement (draft of which was inclosed) to be inserted in the *Gazette* or *Postman*. The Gazetteer had however declined to publish it, being prevailed with, it was suspected, by the absconding person; Harley is therefore begged to order him to make the announcement.

JOSEPH BROWNE to [ROBERT HARLEY].

1706, May 24—The Lord Keeper is quite willing to pardon me about the paper called *The Country Parson's Advice,* &c. I hope you will give me leave to wait on you and offer such testimonies of my submission as may satisfy you that I am thoroughly convinced of my error.

LORD GODOLPHIN] to ROBERT HARLEY.

[1706, May 25 ?], Saturday—Finding by the letter I had this morning from the Duke of Marlborough that our news of the quitting of Antwerp is not true, and that he thinks first of attacking that place, and Ostend not till after he has taken Antwerp, I incline to think it may be necessary to be tomorrow at Windsor to change that method and send back Captain Pitts to desire him to begin with Ostend while he may have the assistance of our ships lying before it, but this with submission both to his judgment and yours.

H. BISHOP OF HEREFORD to [ROBERT HARLEY].

[1706], May 27. Whitborn—I was at Hereford and did all I could to find out the bottom of the wickedness there but it is perfectly stifled. Though Mr. Dobbins was zealous at first to find out the matter, yet a considerable man in the city told me that the rakes having fee'd his son Hill, he was cooler. It is a wonder that since these rakes still continue to break windows, frighten people, and commit frolics, the justices take no notice of it. As for what was said to be done at Kinnersley it was not so bad as reported. Neither the dogs nor the rakes touched the bread or wine, nor the communion table. It is true the dogs came into the church and some of them into the chancel and towards the steps leading to the altar, but were called back and the rakes talked and tittered, or muttered as the minister says, in the seat and then went out. I am told of two that were in the seat and have employed one or two privately to pump them, for the minister and wardens if they know will own nothing to the purpose.

ROBERT HARLEY to [SIR EDW. NORTHEY,] Attorney General.

1706, May 30. Whitehall—Yesterday Dr. Browne brought one Mrs. [Anne] Watkins to be examined relative to the affair [*of the Country Parson's advice to the Lord Keeper*], for which he is to receive judgment. *Signed. Examination enclosed.*

S. WHITEHALL to ROBERT HARLEY.

1706, May 31. Dover—Excusing himself for some alleged neglect in observing the travellers to or from the continent. Clerke and Bara have been frequently together at Deal of late.

J. K. SCHUTZ to [ERASMUS] LEWIS.

1706, May 31. London—I have received a letter from the City of Augsburg repeating their former petition, desiring an answer for which they have waited ever since Secretary Harley told me that something will be sent over to them. You may direct for me in Princes Street near Stocksmarket over against the Golden Ball.

MADAME DE SALTY to LORD [GODOLPHIN ?].

1706, May 31. Paris—Begging for the release of her husband Monsieur Nanquelin de Salty who had been detained a prisoner in the Island of Jersey for five months, he being accused of nothing except of having passed to that island to avoid the menaces of his enemies. *French.*

BARON SCHUTZ to [ROBERT HARLEY].

1706, June 3. London—Enquiring whether the queen was willing that his master the Elector should use his good offices with the King of Sweden to deter him from invading Saxony and to sound him on the subject of making peace with King Augustus. *Signed. French.*

REDMOND JOY to ROBERT HARLEY.

1706, June 3—Informing Harley that a man who was confined with him had confided to him that he was negotiating with one Squire Howard and his son for the sale to them of certain carbuncles or jewels which had been taken from the Great Mogul's daughter.

The ELECTRESS SOPHIA to the QUEEN.

1706, June [7–] 18 [new style]. Hanover—Credentials for Louis Justus Sinold, Baron Schutz, in pursuance of the Act of Parliament for securing the Protestant succession. *Copy. Latin.*

JOHN OGILVIE to ROBERT BRYAN [HARLEY].

1706, June 9. London—Since I had not the opportunity to tell you my mind last night I have here set down what I think most material, however it must not be as I think, for you are judge what is most proper to be done for the Queen's service and yours. I shall here let you see what may be done when I have delivered my message to Count Belke. I may desire to stay by him till he sees what success his negociation hath, that I may carry the laurel branch to the Court of St. Germain. If I obtain this from him then it exonerates me at the Court and puts me in a condition to serve you, for you shall be advertised of every step that is taken and if he, Count Belke I mean, finds any encouragement of the negociation then Scotland is to be advertised that they may put themselves in a readiness. I truly do believe it will be myself that will be sent to them, there will be also all sorts of ammunition sent and money, and I am apt to believe that the Duke of Berwick will go and command if the Duke of Hamilton thinks it fit; but I found the Court of St. Germain was afraid of the Duke of Hamilton's being colder than he was in their business, but some thought that scruple was only raised by my Lord Middleton's agents, for my Lord Duke of Hamilton will have nothing to do with my Lord Middleton, they never were friends but all business that relates to Scotland is entirely kept up from my Lord Middleton for the Scots abhor him. If I go to Scotland that I am persuaded, I shall know the bottom of these last affairs which you shall be advertised of from time to time. When I return to France, if you think it proper I shall stay as long as I can at Versailles, I may still learn something and I shall send my wife to the Court of St. Germain that she may learn still something among the ladies there that may be of service to you, for my wife is cunning abundantly and very close minded and hates the Queen for you see she hath little other reason. I can let you see a letter that the Queen refused to recommend me to Monsieur Chamaliar for a post in the army, but that is some time ago, however we have not forgot it for to refresh my memory I still keep that letter about me, so you see my obligations to the Queen. The reason of her refusing me that small favour I shall tell you when I wait on you, it will make you laugh heartily, I shall bring you all their addresses that is of consequence when I come to you next. Now on your part you must give me somebody here at London to address your letters to for in Holland Mr. Andrew Brun will serve for there is no fear of him for he hath no business with them, he is only a friend I have made myself for my own ends. I pray you to set down in writing all the heads of what you would have me to do. and also mind that bricks cannot be made without straw for if the heart of me were never so willing to render you any service it is impossible whilst I am in poverty, for if I be at any Court I must make acquaintance and drink a bottle and eat a dish of meat with those that I think proper for my use, and it will cost me something to keep my wife. at St. Germain, now none of these things can be performed without money as I found by experience when I was last at Versailles. I am loath to speak to you of money for fear that you shall think it is for money that I serve you but you are judge yourself that it is impossible to do any business to the purpose without money. If I had it of my own I should not matter it, for it is not a little money that I mind it is your generosity that I am persuaded of to provide for me and my poor unhappy family when you think it convenient; and I declare that my whole trust is in you because you have been so good as to promise me as much. If you think that my wife can be of little use at St. Germain then I could wish her here for you see how it is with her and if ever they find any reason to be jealous of me they will put her up and my children also in a monastery to keep me to my good behaviour, but if she should come here unless your Honour can get something done for her she shall perish here and my children also; but as to all that I have said I refer myself to your orders for that shall be my law. This will be tedious for you to answer me all this but there is a necessity for it for without that I can never be easy and when I have an audience of you they are so short that I cannot mind what I have to say. Now I shall say no more but beg that you will dispatch me, for it is an affair of great consequence to me, it is just the life of me and my poor family, for if they suspect me in the least they will dissemble till they catch me in France and then I shall be made an unfortunate example; for you may judge that they have their agents in Holland to take notice of things. It is come Monday a twenty days since I left Rotterdam, whereof I have been a fortnight here, so when their letters come to Rotterdam they will expect that I must answer them the next post to let them know that they are come to my hand and also to advertise them that I part for to go to Count Belke, and since I am not there to do this it may give them a jealousy of me and upon this there may be spies set to work to see if I have not been in England and I am but too well acquainted with the Queen's Italian temper. So I beg of you to take it to your consideration and dispatch me for it would vex a body to lose their life unworthily in doing no service, for I protest—if the venturing of my life could serve you I should never make a scruple of it. You must provide me a pass and in it for a servant wench that did live formerly with my wife that I have a mind to send to her, for a French servant does not so well with a English woman; and if she should be obliged to come away she can never bring her three children here, for a French servant will not come, neither will I trust any of them. I did think it convenient to give you the trouble of this before that you go to Windsor that you may have nothing to do but dispatch me when you return.

[Lieut.-Col. J. CRANSTOUN] to [ROBERT CUNNINGHAM].

1706, June 10 old style. The Camp at Rousslaer—I received the pewter, field standish and wainscot box all right and now have the account. The pewter is excellent good and perfectly well chosen. It could not have been better. I had the honour the very day before we marched out of the Bosch to have the Duke of Argyle, Lord Dalrymple, and some other officers of note eat out of it for the first time at my house.

I am persuaded nothing would contribute so much to my wife's health as her going to the Baths in Egland, which all physicians agree are sovereign for that, but she neither inclines to go till I can go with her, and indeed if she did I am not in a condition at present to send her. The expenses of the coming over to me, my getting my commission as Lieutenant Colonel, and making up a new equipage and then taking up house, have all dipped me so deep that I shall not recover in two years.

I am ashamed to trouble you with Charles Collima, he is so slow; but now when all company are in the country he might find time to finish my tweezer. If he makes my tweezer really fine and good I do not value for a guinea or two what he take for it, because some of the instruments having belonged to Lord Angus I would keep it as a relic while I live. It must have in it a knife, pen knife and fork, scissors, pair of good pincers, compass, foot of measure, bottle screw, pen and crayon and bodkin, with a leaf of ivory if possible and what else is used.

I proposed to have writ to you soon after our glorious action at Ramillies, but was constantly either marching with the army or on particular command for a fortnight after it, so that I can write no particulars now but what you must have already heard from many hands. The British troops had very little hand in the action, only the Scots brigade of foot in the States service with Major General Murray and the Duke of Argyle had an honourable share in it. The Duke led the Scots brigade with a battalion of the Dutch guards, and was himself the second or third man who with his sword in his hand broke over the enemy's trenches, and chased them out of the village of Ramillies pushing on into their very lines of foot. He received three shot upon him but happily all blunt. Major General Murray, who was posted on the left of the second line, was so happy visibly to save the Duke of Marlborough, who fulfilled that day all the parts of a great captain, except in that he exposed his person as the meanest soldier. The attack being to be made by the Dutch on our left against the enemy's right where all the King's household and their best troops were, the Duke put himself at the head of the Dutch horse, and the guards du corps, mousquetaires, and gens d'armes happening to encounter them, ten of the Dutch squadrons were repulsed, renversed and put in great disorder. The Duke seeing this, and seeing that things went pretty well elsewhere, stuck by the weak part to make it up by his presence, and led still up new squadrons there to the charge, till at last the victory was obtained. It was here where those squadrons being renversed and in absolute *déroute* and the French mixed with them in the pursuit, the Duke flying with the crowd in leaping a ditch fell off of his horse and some rode over him. Major General Murray, who had his eye there and was so near he could distinguish the Duke in the flight, seeing him fall, marched up in all haste with two Swiss battalions to save him and stop the enemy who were hewing all down in their way. The Duke when he got to his feet again saw Major General Murray coming up and run directly to get in to his battalions. In the meantime Mr. Molesworth quitted his horse and got the Duke mounted again, and the French were so hot in the pursuit that some of them before they could stop their horses run in upon the Swiss bayonets and were killed, but the body of them seeing the two battalions, shore off to the right and retired. The Major General thereafter observing the Scots brigade and Dutch guards likely to be oppressed with numbers, though contrary to the opinion of Count Oxenstiern who commanded there as Lieutenant General, did yet march up some battalions to their relief, which made the enemy's brigades turn, and contributed a great deal to the victory. Of the British foot only Churchill's and Lord Mordaunt's battalions were engaged in the attack, as being detached and joined to ten other foreign battalions they suffered a little but not much, and acquitted themselves with great bravery. The Earl of Orkney who commanded the British infantry upon the right had marched them over the *ruisseau* and bog and was himself on the head of the English guards and first battalion marching in to attack the village of Offuz, and was already come under the enemy's fire when Brigadier Cadogan came with orders as he pretended from the Duke, and obliged him to retire.

It is certain if we had been allowed to attack there and possess that village, we took the enemy's lines on their flank, and we had cut off or taken prisoners their whole body of infantry entirely so that not a battalion had got off, for we were betwixt them and the way they were to retreat, and, as it was their infantry which saved their horse in the retreat, stopping at times and obliging our horse in the pursuit to halt and pay respect to them. So that their body of horse got freely off, and if we had cut off their infantry, our horse having no body of f_{oot} to oppose them would in the pursuit have got in with their horse already shattered and broke them quite, and had also gained a league of ground by going over on our right with the foot. My Lord Orkney had led over there, whereas when Brigadier Cadogan obliged my Lord to return over that brook and bog with the foot and dragoons who with a squadron of Lumley's had already, though with some difficulty, got over, the generals then on the right fell a disputing what to do, and at last agreed to march to our left up to second the Dutch, and while we marched that way, the enemy's horse being routed by the Dutch, their foot plied at last and gave way and fled; but we were so far behind that it was long before our horse got up, and our foot could not overtake the enemy, having defiles to pass. It is suspected much the Duke really gave no orders to call Earl Orkney off, but that Cadogan having viewed the ground where we were to attack before at a distance, or perhaps rather relied too much on what is marked in his charts believed there was another *ruisseau* and morass betwixt us and the village of Offuz which would be impracticable, and upon that took it on him in my Lord Duke's name to call the troops back. But we had not only passed all the morass already with all our infantry, but both Lord John Hay's and Ross's dragoons with one squadron of Lumley's were got over, and the rest could have followed. The Earl of Orkney with the company of grenadiers of the guards were actually got into the village, so that all the difficulty was got over, and the victory had been yet infinitely more complete if we had been allowed to push on there. Some heats and words have been since among some of our Generals about this matter, but I hope it will be let fall; since though an unhappy mistake it was no doubt well designed, and since God has given us however a victory both signal and glorious beyond all expectation, and of which the success is so much even beyond what we durst wish for that we may justly say of it with the poet

Quod, optanti, Divum promittere nemo audebat, volrenda dies, en attulit ultro.

Since things have gone so very well it would look ill to search too narrowly into little mistakes. Lord John Hay did great service in the pursuit and deserves great honour, for with his own regiment alone he broke in *à la hussarde* sword in hand and at a gallop upon two battalions *du Roi* and killed or took them all prisoners, but lost several men in it, receiving not only their fire but a fire from three other battalions from behind hedges both on his flanks and rear. We are now blocking up Dendermonde and besieging Ostend and Nieuport, but I hear this day that by cutting the *digues* and letting in the sea the country is so overflowed that Monsieur d' Overkerque cannot approach near enough to Nieuport to raise batteries and is obliged to go to Ostend. We hoped if those two towns had fallen our next attempt should have been on Dunkirk, but we cannot get there unless we have Nieuport; so it is like we shall turn either to Ypres or Menin but more probably to Menin first. The enemy cannot with all that comes to them from the Rhine bring any body of foot together this summer to face us anywhere, and all that seems to be feared is that, whilst we have one body besieging and another covering here in Flanders, they attempt an irruption into Brabant to give a check to the few troops we have to spare there. Three battalions of our English foot and three troops of Lord John's with three of Major General Ross's dragoons are to embark with the descent fleet. It is said the three battalions will be *La Lo* (*sic*) Farrington and Macartney's. Pray write me all the particulars of our happy Union and if possible send me the scheme or propositions. Seek not to frank my letters but put them in the common post which is always the surest and speediest.

James Cressett to Robert Harley.

1706, June 13. Deptford—Having not long since desired your favour in what related to my disbursements in the late King's reign, I beg leave to put you in mind of the same that you would at your own time move my Lord Treasurer in it, of whose justice and generosity I can never doubt. This debt though not great lies heavy upon me, who am charged with no small family, but under whatever uneasy circumstances I may be no complaints shall be heard from me. Though I was forced to leave the service being ruined both in health and fortune with ten years service, yet I presume so much on your equity that you will upon occasion testify for a man who lives in obscurity, my retirement having in no way diminished that zeal which becomes a good subject.

The Same to [the Same].

Same date and place—Enclosing the preceding letter which was intended to be shewn to the Lord Treasurer, and offering to give all the information in his power concerning the Northern affairs.

Sir T[homas] M[ansell,] Comptroller of the Household, to [Robert Harley].

1706, June 13. Britton-ferry—Your letter reached me yesterday at Margam where I went to see my father who every day visibly decays. I told him I felt obliged to be down in London at which he seemed to be much concerned but said nothing. If he does not enjoin my stay with him I will be in town the latter end of next week. I own that by what yet appears to me there is very little reason to move, knowing that my personal appearance in anything is of little use. But if you think it 'tis enough and I submit my opinion to your judgment. I should be sorry to see anything miscarry that is under your care, but since you were pleased to touch upon a scheme, give me leave to say I am very sorry for two or three things that are done; and even they that roar most at them are in my conscience very well pleased at them, for their notion is that things must be worse before they will be better; the English of that need not be explained.

Robert Harley to the Rev. W. Lancaster.

1706, June 14. Whitehall—I shall give you a short account of a very long insult and piece of impudent treatment I received this day in my own house. I came home very late to dinner; while I was at table with my family and other friends I received a solicitation in writing to contribute something to the erecting a new chapel somewhere about Russell Street. To this I immediately ordered my porter to return answer, I would do something for that charity, but I should take my own time and my own way to do it. This I thought to be a very full answer, but about an hour after my daughter going away from dinner was insulted by a man in the habit of a clergyman, but in the spirit of a dragoon or rather a hussar. I understand his name is Yates, who it seems had not pleasure enough in exercising his ribald language upon several of my servants for an hour together in my own house, but after he had frightened my child he thought he might with a good title insult me. His gown protected him from the correction he deserved; the great regard I have for you obliges me to give you this account before I take those measures the law appoints for such an insufferable insult. If this pretended clergyman be a person you have no concern for I beg your pardon most heartily for the trouble given you upon this account. *Copy.*

Baron Schutz to [Robert Harley].

1706, June 15–26. London—Assuring him of the satisfaction which the Elector will receive at the announcement that the marriage of the Princess of Hanover with the Prince Royal of Prussia was pleasing to the Queen; also begging to be informed what were the Queen's intentions concerning the propositions made by the Elector for an accommodation between the King of Sweden and King Augustus. *French.*

The Same to [the Same].

1706, June 17–28. London—A formal request for the Queen's approval of the proposed marriage between the Princess of Hanover and the Prince Royal of Prussia. *Signed. French.*

[The DUKE OF NEWCASTLE to ROBERT HARLEY.]

1706, June 17. Houghton—I thank you for the account you give me of the Union, and find what we said to be true, that when they had got their land tax lowered as much as they could, they would not abate us one member for it. Nay I find artifice has had a very ill effect with them, though many of them said when they came first to town, they should ask a greater number to exonerate themselves (as they called it); yet did seem as if they would have been content with thirty-six of the Lower House. But I suppose our pilots, by ▮▮ hand they have in the present negociation, hope afterwards to steer those northern vessels. But I would not have them trust too much to a trading people who always seek the advantage of their own commerce, let it come from what part of the Indies it will.

The REV. W. LANCASTER to [ROBERT HARLEY].

1706, June 17. Queen's College [Oxford]—This is humbly to acknowledge the honour, and I cannot but add, the very great kindness of yours when after such unheard of provocations from one belonging to me, you would vouchsafe to let me know it from your own hand.

I confess myself to be in great confusion to find a person, whose countenance I and my friends in this place do above all things in the world desire, affronted by the insults of one bred up (if I might say so of a man that has no breeding) and enriched by me. He has always been a tool to churchwardens and other officers in collecting briefs and charities; and because they are commonly men of trades who are skilled in dunning, they have imposed their arts upon him, and put him upon taking no answer from servants, frightening children; taught him that he must speak with the lord or master himself, to thrust his head into all companies, to tease and try every body with importunity, and in short have made him an ecclesiastical dun. I hope you will cure him of this, which I by my advice could never do, and because he has many very good qualities for a curate in that parish.

LORD CONINGSBY to [ROBERT HARLEY].

1706, June 19—Our two Knights are, I am told, now upon the road with our address. The day it was agreed on my poor little boy was dying with convulsions which prevented my being there, and as the clerk of the peace informed me, Mr. Stratford prepared it. By whom they design to be introduced I know not; but it was my intention to send it to you had I been present.

J[OHN] AISLABIE, M.P. to ROBERT HARLEY.

1706, June 19. Ripon—Forwards some informations received from the mayor of Ripon and other justices in a matter about which he had himself made enquiry, viz. words alleged to have been spoken by a lawyer to the effect that all who frequented any public worship where the queen was prayed for were rebels and traitors. *Copy.*

REDMOND JOY to [ROBERT HARLEY].

1706, June 21. Newgate—A long letter giving incidents in his life, his services to King William after the surrender of Limerick, the circumstances under which he became acquainted with certain emissaries from the French Court, his relations with father Andrew Hurly, &c.; and begging a favourable consideration of his case.

D. EDWARDS to [ROBERT HARLEY].

1706, June 22—His coming in to serve the Goverment has provoked a restless party that make it their business to study his ruin, and all the people he dealt with are set against him. His landlord has threatened to seize what he has if payment is not made to him on Tuesday next. Begs to be put into some post.

The WEST INDIES.

1706, June 25—A tabular statement shewing the working of a scheme which was started in 1702 for sending out a monthly packet boat to the West Indies, endorsed " The West India Correspondence how propounded and how performed by E. Dummer." *Printed.*

REDMOND JOY to ROBERT HARLEY.

1706, June 26—Encloses a petition to the Queen, and offers to " set and take " Col. Morgan O'Brien, Major David Barry, Col. John Stephenson, father Hurly and other popish emissaries who are now in town.

R[OBERT] MONCKTON to ROBERT HARLEY, at his Office in the Cockpit.

1706, July 1—I am now with your great and good friend at Welbeck. It is reported they have allowed the " bonny blewcaps " forty five, to complete the measure of our House, and those to be chosen out of theirs. This will make them refined Scots that are to be twice chosen. Pray let him know what the number and how the method is, and let me desire you not to shew the least neglect towards so solid an interest and sure friendship. All that I value myself for is to think you cannot forget how much I contributed to fix it for you.

SIR WILLIAM ELLIS to [ROBERT HARLEY].

1706, July 1—I thank you for the description of Japan. 'Twas too small for me that knew so little of that country. I have not seen the numbers of the dead weight that are to be transported hither at our charge. I am extremely obliged for the great favour you offer me, and if I knew any persons worthy such a recommendation I would present them. I think the pot boils over everywhere, and if 'twas in my power I would empty it before I put more in.

The DUKE OF NEWCASTLE to [ROBERT HARLEY].

1706, July 3—I am sorry the winds are so strong in the contrary corner. I should be glad to know if the young Admiral is as well pleased with his sister's preferment as with his own, and whether it will not make a breach between old friends.

˝. I think the Lord Thanet's protestation was much more ridiculous than Sir George Rooke's refusal, I suppose his Lordship was not pleased with that part of the Address relating to the Ministry.

As to the Union I believe it is pursuant to what I told you before I came out of town that they still continue their intentions to send it to all the members to sign that they might stand by what they have done. I am disposed to give it all the assistance I can in Parliament because I hear some former Treasurers are resolved to oppose it in opposition to the present, which will make me more warm in the defence of it, yet 1 cannot but think if some of the Commissioners had not been so artificial, we might have had better terms in a plainer way. If it be sent into the country to be signed I suppose you and others will insist that it rest a little time with each member to consider it before they sign it, or that a copy of it be sent down before the instrument itself be brought to be signed, for though nobody can be more cordial for the Union than I am yet I will peruse it first if it be desired I should sign it.

I wish I had thought of it before, I could have saved you the trouble of so much argument with his Grace [of Canterbury], whom I believe to be a very honest man and may be a very deep divine for ought that I know, yet I take him to be one that can go as little out of his track as a Spanish Don. (*Original and copy.*)

DE LA MARCK, DUCHESSE DE DURAS, to the EARL OF FEVERSHAM.

1706, July 7. Paris—Although distance prevents our having frequent intercourse yet it does not hinder me from feeling assured that if you can give me the pleasure of obtaining leave of absence from the Duke of Marlborough for Monsieur de Montenay [a prisoner at Lichfield], who is an old friend of mine and for whom I should be very glad to obtain this favour, you will exert yourself for that purpose. I shall be greatly obliged to you and I assure you that none of your nieces honours you more particularly, or is more entirely. your humble and obedient servant. *French.*

LORD POULETT to [ROBERT HARLEY].

1706, July 8—The continued glorious success every where abroad can never fail of making a perfect union at home with any you are pleased to give your hand. My heart is so much with you that I shall make no scruple of signing as you do, though I am not prepared with an exact copy of the articles, which are no great secret. I do not doubt you will always have so many real friends as to shew your enemies in anger and disappointment, which I earnestly pray for as the happiness of England.

SIR SIMON HARCOURT to [ROBERT] HARLEY.

1706, July 10. Abingdon—I consult you as my Oracle, on all difficulties. I received a summons, this instant, from Mr. Dorrington to attend at the signing the Articles of Union, on Monday next. His letter was in a very pressing style, and that the Lords Commissioners for England take it for granted that all the Commissioners, who are not against it, will come up on purpose to sign it. I need not tell you how very inconvenient 'tis for me to come up, but be the prejudice to my affairs never so great, I am determined to come, if you say I must, or advise me to it. I beg you, if this comes time enough to you this night, to write me two words, by this night's post to Oxford; if you can't write this night, if you write by to-morrow's post, I will stay in Oxford till I receive your commands.

The SAME to the SAME.

₁ Same date and place—To the same effect as the above, for being forced to send that letter by a chance-coach, for fear of miscarriage he repeats his request for advice.

L. S. to SIR CHARLES HEDGES, Secretary of State.

1706, July 10. Conway—Complains of the judges of that circuit, Peasely and Gwynn, having acted contrary to her Majesty's commission, and brought fear upon many honest gentlemen, by declaring publicly in court that they had the Queen's commands to assure the Non-jurors that as she looked upon them as her father's best friends so she doubted not that she should find them so to her, and that she was resolved to screen them from exorbitant taxes and other hardships they lay under. Their conduct had encouraged some Jacobite justices in Merionethshire to prevent the new levies and to discharge several soldiers in the officers' absence who had enlisted. They had favoured papists and the malignant high party, and magnified that nasty pamphlet called the *Memorial of the Church of England*, both of the judges in the writer's hearing having said that it could not be answered and of any book it ought to be next esteemed to the Bible ; and they had moreover presented many copies to the gentlemen of the several counties in their circuit.

WILLIAM PENN to [ROBERT HARLEY].

1706, July 14—My son has sent me so melancholy a story upon our friend's answer to him I must break out into complaints upon him after many promises of providing for my son here, and Rooth in Ireland, and speaking of nothing less than 600*l. per annum* for reasons he knows and thou mayst guess, he talks now of speaking of my son to the Duke of Ormond for a foot company in Ireland, which to say no more, is mean. Ned Southwell secret[ary] of that kingdom, and my son captain of a foot company, he shall go dig potatoes first. He is entitled to a better estate in that kingdom than to take up with so mean an employment. Besides, it was a civil employment he chose for him and promised him, showing his aversion to a military employment as well as myself. I beg of thee to urge for a civil employment though in Ireland, of 5 or 600*l. per annum* or give him 1000*l.* to pay his two years expenses in fruitless waiting, and let him go live of his own. If my steady—and secret and public—regards for the Queen's service, divers ways—that every body had not the power or talent to do beside myself—have so mean a conclusion—to say nothing of the worry the Lords Commissioners for Trade &c. have brought upon me, by a long and fruitless attendance and expense—from my country, to keep it—it is high time to retire, and lament our unhappiness. But my poor son may have this just reflection, and I the satisfaction, of his seeing his conformity to the world to be his ruin, instead of his advancement, and I can forgive our great friend, if that could be his reason for slighting him. I have opened myself very freely, to thee, bear it, perhaps it will be the last time, and thy easy methods, so much thy honour and wisdom, have given me the presumption to believe thou wilt both help and forgive. Thy most faithful and unhappy friend.

J[OHN] AISLABIE, M.P., to [ROBERT HARLEY].

1706, July 15. Ripon—Has received the informations he had sent up, with the Attorney-General's opinion and 'directions thereon, and has delivered them to the mayor of Ripon in order to the prosecution [*see* June 19 *ante*]. Sends an address from the Corporation and desires the honour of having it presented to the Queen by Harley's hands.

DOCTOR SAMUEL PRATT to [ROBERT HARLEY].

1706, July 18. Windsor—The Queen has bestowed upon me the Deanery of Rochester, vacant by the death of Henry Ullock, D.D. and I humbly beg when next you come to Windsor to bring a proper warrant for Her Majesty to sign because the giving me a good despatch will be for her service.

ROBERT HARLEY to MR. STANIAN [Abraham Stanyan, envoy to Switzerland?].

1706, July 19. Whitehall—I trouble you with this on account of one Mistress Shaftoe who has made her escape from a convent in France and is now in Switzerland. Though she and her family are wholly unknown to me I have remitted one hundred crowns to a person in France who undertook to get her out of the convent as others had been delivered before. She has written to her mother at Newcastle for money to bring her over but her mother is grown so very poor it is not in her power to send her any supply, but I am willing to furnish her with money to bring her back to her native country since I have gone so far already. Therefore if you please to pay her any sum you think fit not exceeding twenty pounds I will pay it to your use immediately to any person you shall signify to me here to receive it. You need not tell her who the money comes from, for she knows neither my name nor my person. *Draft.*

EDWARD ABRAHAM.

1706, July 19—Information of Edward Abraham of Kingston, co. Sussex, labourer, before Carew Weekes, Esq., a justice of the county, that he had been taken out of his bed on the 9th inst., his house being about two hundred yards from the sea, by eight armed Frenchmen, and carried to Boulogne. There he was put before the mayor and afterwards before the governor who asked him where the English fleet and soldiers were. He replied he could not tell for he was a day labourer, in the morning he went to work and in the evening came home and went to bed. After keeping him at a public house until the following Friday he was carried back to England in the same vessel and put on shore near Lydd between ten and eleven on Saturday night; the master of the ship on leaving told him he wished him well home.

BARON SCHUTZ to [ROBERT HARLEY].

1706, July 20. London—Asking him to fix a time at which he could call at Harley's house or office in order to present to him M. de Bosire (?). *French.*

CHIEF JUSTICE HOLT to [ROBERT HARLEY].

1706, July 20.—Craves leave to represent to her Majesty that the companion of one Taylor, who had killed a man and had received the benefit of the Queen's mercy, should also be treated with the same leniency.

ROBERT HARLEY to WILLIAM BRENAND.

1706, July 23—I heartily wish it were in my power to serve you with the Earl of Derby, but my want of the least acquaintance with his Lordship renders me incapable of doing it.

As to the message you brought me from my Lord Duke [of Queensberry] you may assure him that it has long been my opinion that he is capable of doing the best service of any person in that nation, and I therefore was for his being employed. I believe now he has an opportunity of serving himself and at the same time doing the greatest thing for the advantage and settlement of his own country such as no man ever had before in so easy a way. What I mean is as to the Union, which I might plainly shew it is his Grace's interest to promote. *Copy.*

JOHN LEBRUN [*alias* OGILVIE] to ROBERT BRYAN [HARLEY]; in London.

1706, July 23 [old style]. Hamburgh—I wrote to you from Holland, directed it for Mr. Robert Bryan merchant in London without any other cover. If it be not come to your hand send to the post house and enquire for it. I told you in my last that I did see Dr. Taylor and Mr. Cotton, Mr. Redman his governor, all just come from France. They are all at Rotterdam. It is true they were frequently at St. Germain but I believe there is no danger of either of them. As to your giving a licence to the Doctor, you] are wise and know what is proper. It is true if you give him a licence it will make you greatly esteemed amongst the High Church party for he is mightily considered amongst them although on my conscience I think him no conjuror. I have seen several other people who were come from France. Among them was one Watt or Watts, who was once servant to old Father Galio, the late Queen's confessor, an Italian Jesuit. I do believe he is sent, for he is a fellow they can trust, having served a cunning master.

I desire you'll think of finding some person in Holland that I may send your letters to. I beg of you for the future to keep touch with me, for disappointments of this nature render me unable to go through with any design although never so willing, for as I often tell you there is no making of brick without straw.

JOHN LEBRUN [*alias* OGILVIE] to [ROBERT HARLEY].

1706, [July 26-] August 6 [new style]. Hamburg—I received the honour of yours this day, it was very welcome you may judge. Had I had money sufficient when I came here I had gone to Silesia and met Count Belke where I might have learned several things from him, but without money I durst not venture into so barbarous a country, however I will let you see what measures I have taken. In the first place I have sent him his orders and I have written at large upon every subject that I may draw an answer from him to the purpose. I have told him that his master must see his answer so that I believe it will be full enough, which if it be I design to send it straight to you, but you must not keep it above a post but only take a copy and send it to me to Rotterdam, for you are sensible I must not go on without it, neither must I stay any time in Holland after I come there. It is true I could send you a copy of it but I am willing to convince both the Queen and my Lord Treasurer of my sincerity to her service, and also that you may have no reproach for your kindness to me; but it must be sent me immediately or you must acquaint me that I may send and bring away my family out of France. However I am resolved to venture it being fully convinced of your honour and generosity, the sooner I go for France the better, for you may be assured that there will be great preparations for the next year to retrieve their losses, so that if I were there I would be serviceable to you, at least I think so, but whether I can or not I promise you that I shall use my endeavour. What I told you of the King of Prussia is true for it was Count Belke that was sent to him; Count Belke's trustee is here and told me how the Count was received and the promises that passed; but the raising of the siege of Barcelona spoilt all and then the battle, but in a little time you shall know more. I hope to be instructed in the whole matter before I part.

Sir EDWARD NORTHEY, Attorney-General, to ROBERT HARLEY.

1706, July 27—You having by your letter of the 20th instant mentioned that a Countess Dowager [of Huntingdon] of this kingdom had been married to a French prisoner of war, who sometime since had leave to go to France upon his parole and is now returned three months before the expiration of the term that was allowed, and asked my opinion what Her Majesty may legally do for the benefit of the lady's children by her former husband and show her just resentment of so great an affront done to her authority; I do humbly certify you, that by her intermarriage all the Countess's ready moneys and personal goods and chattels in her possession, by the law became her husband's, and he is also entitled to her jointure for their joint lives. And an inquisition being found Her Majesty will thereby be entitled to the moneys, goods and chattels, and also to the jointure during the coverture, unless the Countess before that marriage, with the consent of her now husband, assigned her interests therein to trustees to be at her disposal, which it is probable (if she took any advice before this marriage) was done. The French prisoner being here, I do not know how the woman marrying him can be punished. Without doubt she will find her punishment by the consequences of such a marriage.

CAPTAIN ROBERT READING.

1706, July 27. Lewes—Henry Pelham, T. Pelham, and William Nelson, justices of Sussex, report the result of an examination of one Robert Reading, alleged to be a captain in Brigadier Brudenell's regiment, who had been taken in custody by the Custom officers at Bourne on his landing from France in a small boat with three Frenchmen. Reading stated that he had embarked at Lisbon, having leave from Lord Galway to come to England about business concerning that regiment, but had been taken prisoner in company with Col. Lundy and Ensign Foliott, off Plymouth by a French privateer, sent to Caen, and afterwards set at liberty on his parole to return in three months.

G. GRANVILLE to [ROBERT HARLEY].

1706, July 29. North-end—The last letter I put into your hands was dated the 8th of this month, and no answer being yet sent, may not so long a silence be subject to mis-interpretation ? I am still of opinion the greatest difficulty in this affair is that of creating a mutual confidence between you. When once you come to believe one another, I take it for granted a good agreement will soon follow.

[The DUKE OF MARLBOROUGH to ROBERT HARLEY.]

1706, July 29—I am not a very good judge of manifestoes or declarations, but I think the success of this will depend upon the diligence and vigour of the Generals that command, for if they do not at their first landing carry all things before them, and at the same time take all the care possible that the soldiers are not permitted to plunder, but that every man that does not take arms against them should be treated with all humanity and friendship.

I have been informed that the Dean of Carlisle, and Dr. Smalridge, make compliments to Her Majesty, but at the same time are as violent as if they were governed by Lord Rochester; as I know you esteem them, I would not fail of letting you know what is written to me concerning them.

————— to ————.

1706, July 29, new style. The camp before Menin—A long account of the preparations for the siege of Menin. *Copy.*

LORD CUTTS to ————.

1706, July 30. Dublin—Contradicting a report of his death and stating that he hoped to be in England soon after the Duke of Ormond's arrival in Ireland. *Copy.*

BARON SCHUTZ to [ROBERT HARLEY].

1706, July 31. London—Asking leave to procure a recommendation from the minister of the Grand Duke of Florence. *French.*

PRINCE GEORGE OF DENMARK.

1706, August 1. Admiralty Office—Reporting that Captain Thomas Smith late of the sloop *Bonetta* had been dismissed the service for great irregularities of conduct, by sentence of court-martial, the particulars of which are enclosed. *Signed.*

ROBERT PRICE, Baron of the Exchequer, to [ROBERT] HARLEY.

1706, August 2. Coventry—This day I finished the campaign at Coventry where there nearly 150 indicted for riots at the last election of members. Sir Chr. Hales and Mr. Hopkins the candidates appeared with their friends on both sides, the mob so numerous and violent that I despaired of doing justice there, but I have brought both sides to so much temper that there is a prospect of fair weather. The Union affair

I doubt not but will take amongst the generality ; I have laboured in it heartily, publicly and privately. The gaols have been very empty, and there has been but one criminal executed in the whole circuit, and that was a fellow that murdered his wife in Lincolnshire, tearing out her bowels with his hands, a matchless barbarity.

I do not see but the fire of parties is pretty well over save in Northamptonshire, which shows most heat. Mr. Sacheverell preached the assize sermon at Leicester and could not forbear giving the dissenters and occasionalists a "flurt as most of them do." Otherwise the discourse was good and ingenious, and with all zeal and duty to the Queen.

B[RIDGET], COUNTESS OF PLYMOUTH to [ROBERT HARLEY].

1706, August 7—Not having met with success in the only thing I had in view to incline me to keep my marriage to Dr. Bisse any longer concealed, we now resolve to settle in the country, but before we go, I hope you will excuse my troubling you with my thankful acknowledgments for the honour you do Mr. Bisse in owning him related to you, and also for your obliging endeavours for his promotion, which shall ever be as gratefully remembered, as if they had succeeded to our wishes. Had he obtained what was desired it would have made me entirely easy, by the reasonable hopes it would have given me of a reconciliation with my family in a little time. What you have done already encourages me to beg the continuation of your favourable assistance as you shall have opportunity ; and I hope you will not refuse me the favour you had the goodness once to offer, which was to own Dr. Bisse as your relation to the Queen, and to acquaint her with our marriage. If you please now to take this charitable part upon you, I would beg it might be done when you are at Windsor on Sunday next, we designing to own it in the country the Monday after, and I hope you will also intercede with her Majesty on our behalf, as you shall think it proper on this occasion. I am sensible I ought to ask a thousand pardons for the freedom I have taken with you in writing this letter, not having the honour to be known to you ; but to go about making any excuse, would but add to the trouble given you.

J. [MOORE] BISHOP OF NORWICH to [ROBERT] HARLEY.

1706, August 7—Acknowledging the receipt of the catalogue of the books of Triglandius, late Hebrew professor at Leyden.

G. GRANVILLE to [ROBERT HARLEY].

1706, August 8—After I was forced to leave you last night I received the enclosed packet from Sir Humphrey [Mackworth] with a copy of one from his neighbour by which you will find, as we imagined, he is of his counsel. I had written him a general letter upon other heads before you told me Sir William's mind, in which I dropped a hint concerning his friend, wishing him to give him good advice : the consequence of it you will see in his letter, and since it was not to be imagined but they would consult together, I hope it was a right step to prepare and soften the counsellor before hand, lest he should have brought some obstruction which now he promises not to do. He has always professed a great deal of kindness to me upon old accounts, and I believe him so far as to

think he will not be a hindrance to an affair in which he finds me
personally concerned, and besides I know he would be glad of any
occasion to continue himself in your good graces. You will find by this
letter that we are to expect the utmost diffidence, what ground there is
for it I can't tell, being wholly a stranger to former transactions. But I
hope whatever is agreed in the present case will be religiously observed
on both sides, nor can I doubt it since you are concerned in it. Sir
William's aversion to Sir Humphrey may perhaps make it best to
conceal this letter from him, though I believe you will approve it, both
as a prudent and necessary step, as you at first seemed to think it.

ROBERT HARLEY to SIR THOMAS TRAVAIL [or TRAVELL, M.P. for Milborne Port].

1706, August 10—I am very sorry to hear of your misfortune and
heartily wish it were in my power to assist you out of this difficulty. I
have consulted with Mr. Joddrell who is very zealous to serve you. All
the ways I can think of which have been ever practised are—to send
notice to the officers and sheriff to see whether they will run the venture
of detaining you; to make application to the Speaker; or to apply to
the courts of justice for a writ of privileges. *Copy.*

S. WHITEHALL to [ROBERT HARLEY].

1706, August 13. Dover—Reporting further suspicious proceedings
of Barra and Clerke, who employ boatmen and fishermen to carry
letters to France and declare they have Harley's authority for so
doing.
[Attached to this letter are copies of correspondence between
Secretary Hedges and the Mayor of Deal, 15–22 August, on the same
subject.]

B[RIDGET], COUNTESS OF PLYMOUTH to [ROBERT HARLEY].

1706, August 17—I received the honour of yours of the 13th with
great satisfaction and am highly sensible of the obligations you have
laid on me, by your undertaking the charitable part of interceding
with the Queen on my behalf, and for the honour you have done Dr.
Bisse in owning him as your relation to Her Majesty, whose great
goodness (I find by yours) moved her to express a compassionate regard
for me on this occasion. I am encouraged to hope, Sir, by the favours
I have already received from you that you will endeavour to improve it
if any opportunity offers. Could I give myself leave to put you to any
further trouble, I should beg you would present my most humble and
dutiful acknowledgments to Her Majesty, if you find it would not be
thought too great a presumption in me at this time.

B[RIDGET], COUNTESS OF PLYMOUTH to [ROBERT] HARLEY.

[1706, August 25 ?]. Monday—The obligations I have already
received from Mr. Secretary Harley, and the assurance he gives Dr.
Bisse of the continuance of his favour makes me hope he will forgive
me troubling him with a letter to acquaint him that the Duchess of
Marlborough did me the honour yesterday to introduce me to the
Queen in a very obliging manner, and that Her Majesty had the goodness to receive me very graciously. I hope, Sir, you will approve of

my making this step, which I imagined necessary since the declaring of our marriage, before any application could well be made to her Majesty in favour of Dr. Bisse; and I please myself with the hopes that when any opportunity offers you will have the goodness to use your interest for him. This, Sir, as I am sure it will be more effectual than any addresses I could make by my own friends, so is it what I could much rather wish.

[DANIEL DE FOE] to ROBERT HARLEY.

1706, August 23—Though I had not the honour to wait on you last night, your letter forbidding, I cannot but give you the trouble of letting you know God Almightly has heard the cries of a distressed family and has given me at last a complete victory over the most furious, subtile, and malicious opposition that has been seen in all the instances of the Bankrupts Act.

I earnestly wish and long to give you the particulars, in which something very unusual will divert you. I cannot but communicate to you one thing, nor can I stay till the time I am to wait on you for it. There is a letter or manuscript, for 'tis as big as a book, brought I suppose by a messenger express from Scotland, to be printed here. 'Tis unhappily written, and full of mischief against the Union, but particularly addressed to the dissenters and insinuating that their destruction is intended and will be compassed in it. It seems to imply that the presbyterians in Scotland are alarmed at it, that the ministers and assistants keep days of prayer and fasting against it, that they foresee it will be fatal to their establishment and would invite the dissenters into the same notions.

It is something particularly wonderful that has brought this to me but I suppose I shall be applied to to get it printed. I encourage them to it as far as I can without appearing too forward. If I can lay my hand upon the manuscript you will be sure to see it, and if I cannot prevent its publication then, I shall but ill recommend my capacity to you as fit to be employed abroad.

I shall more largely explain this when I have the honour to see you on Saturday night. I am exceedingly fatigued with this afternoon's struggle.

LE MOYNE to " MR. ADDISSON, Whitehall."

1706, August 23 and 24—A letter of thanks for the kindness shown him during his close imprisonment; and begging that Addison will continue to use his good offices with Harley in order to obtain his (Le Moyne's) complete discharge. *French*.

JOHN WILLIAMS to ROBERT HARLEY.

1706, August 25. Treworgey near Loo—Touching the capture of some seamen by a Sally rover, some of whom had sailed in a merchant ship from Fowey, which the writer had represented in Parliament when Harley was Speaker. The men would no doubt be released if, by Harley's influence with the Queen, she would demand them.

JOHN LEBRUN [*alias* OGILVIE] to [ROBERT HARLEY].

1706, August 23. Hamburg—This is the second letter I have written since I came to this place, and once before I parted from

Holland, but I have never heard from you since I parted from London, which makes me afraid that some of mine may have miscarried.

The remainder of the letter repeats much that was written in his letter of the 6th August.

ROBERT HARLEY to WILLIAM BRENAND.

1706, August 24—I received the favour of both your letters and by the first I understand that I had been too forward, but I protest I had no other aim in it than serving the Duke [of Queensberry] and the public at the same time. The world sufficiently knows how backward I have been to meddle with Northern affairs so as nothing could draw me into them, but this was so plain a case that upon your invitation I came in to give my helping hand to his grace ; for to tell you plainly the Duke may make himself the greatest man in Scotland by complying with the promoting of the Union, in which no man has more interest than himself, or may let himself be —— (sic). At present he may have what he desires, his enemies are in the meantime endeavouring to do it without him, or fling the odium of the miscarriage upon him, which no man is great enough to withstand, or even the delaying of it. In short I find little whisperers have great credit and a farthing candle is fancied to be clearer than the sun. I have no interest in this affair, only to serve the Duke, but I will learn hereafter not to be over officious to do people good against their wills. *Copy.*

SIR CHARLES HOTHAM to [ROBERT HARLEY].

1706, August 31. The *Eagle* riding in Torbay—Concerning the serious illness on shipboard of Col. Soames, who would have died had he not been conveyed under General Earle's orders to Sir William Courtney's house about five miles from Torbay. Lord Rivers had been applied to for permission to leave Soames behind as he was quite unfit for service, but Lord Rivers said he had no power to give any officer leave to stay. Harley is therefore desired to procure an order to that effect, as on shipboard Soames must certainly perish. Col. Dashwood died on Saturday after three or four days illness.

Fate having now altered the design of our first expedition I heartily wish we may succeed in the enterprise we are now upon ; but I fear if the wind continues as it is one fortnight longer, the same time will be requisite to take in a supply of provisions, especially for the horses.

I have now no expectation of waiting on you and the rest of my friends the ensuing session of parliament. Give me leave therefore to wish that everything may proceed to your desire and satisfaction, which I'm sure the public will reap the benefit of. I have no novelty from our element to acquaint you with, only Sir Cloudsley Shovell outdoes Mons. d'Ruell. J. Earl tells me he gave you account of that day's diversion.

JEAN GASSION [*alias* OGILVIE] to ROBERT BRYAN [HARLEY] in London.

1706 [August 28–]September 7, new style. Rotterdam—I have been at sea and put back again so that I am fully resolved to go by land. I have lingered here on purpose thinking I might hear from you but I have no so good luck. However I find Mr. Brown goes for Bruges so you may try one letter that way, but let it be mystically that no body can understand it but myself; but let me know if the things be matter of fact that I did desire to know and send me the papers I desire, for they can be of no use to you, and if ever they have any suspicion of me they may be serviceable. You may direct as I have told to Madame Gassion at St. Valery sur Somme, and you may put it under cover to M. Andrew Brun in Bruges. This will do for one or two times, but I do not venture to write by him anything that is of consequence. I shall be very uneasy till I hear from you. There ▬ no letters come from Count Belke, but he is at present with the King of Sweden, negotiating some affair or another, but when he writes I shall learn something of it.

John Netterville to [Robert Harley].

1706, August 31—I will not trespass on your precious time therefore shall be short. I have, since the honour I had of seeing you, been at several places in order to serve those ends we proposed. I find most of those I would have discoursed are out of town. I intend to adjust and order matters so that you shall have often what occurs to me worth your notice. As to affairs in Scotland, I have I think settled matters, so that I shall hear what may be of use. I will not be wanting to serve Her Majesty and I will venture to say that I will serve my Lord Treasurer, and you will find you will not repent any favour you are pleased to show me. You must expect from me no compliments or ceremony, I will write as I speak. I find by some that at St. Germain they are exceedingly melancholy, at their wits' end, I will not write to any till I first advise with you. I am persuaded by your advice we may profit somewhat by what we may pick out of Monsieur Premolie the Emperor's Envoy's secretary, as we may by what I may learn from Mr. Henningham that writes the Portugal Envoy's letters, who tells me without reserve what the Envoy knows. There is a Cardinal called Sacrapanti, the name of a family as I am told. You may easily learn the Cardinal's names. The post (?) thickens and parts. This cardinal amongst others is this M. Premolie's correspondent. I find till the nights are somewhat longer boats will not be ordered to carry letters to and fro between England and France, and that when it is settled it will be on Sussex coasts as formerly. If you think fit there is a burgess for Preston in Lancashire dead, Sir Alexander Rigby has complimented the Earl of Derby with his interest in that place which with my Lord's being Chancellor of the Duchy of Lancaster, my Lord may recommend whom he pleases to serve for that place, which I thought fit to let you know, that the Queen or the Lord Treasurer may speak to my Lord Derby to choose a person of estate as well as figure that may be for your interest. My Lord will obey, and perhaps will be glad to show his interest to the Court. I have been at the Grecian coffee house, and have met with some one angry with my Lord Treasurer, who talks big and tells me he knows many members both of the High Church, Low Church, and Whigs, that care not for you nor my Lord Treasurer, and in parliament great matters will be done. I am told that Ferguson says Paterson is a blockhead, has neither head nor interest, a superficial fellow, though countenanced by my Lord Treasurer. I could wish you would advise me, give me directions how to proceed more effectually to serve you. The Lord Treasurer you will see to-morrow, as you will the Duke of Ormond. I hope then you will settle matters as you were pleased to promise me. You may find difficulty to read my hand, but when you are used to it, that difficulty may be over. The members of parliament, I mean the leading members, out of town. I will be with some of them as soon as they come to town. Sir John Pakington very angry, resolves in Parliament to speak his mind freely. Tho. Cæsar was sent to the Tower. I purpose to see you within four or five days, and intend to call at your house about seven or eight of the clock at night, the rest only to beg of you to throw a veil over my infirmities and forgive them for they are great and many. I must rely on your goodness so great that I humbly hope for as much of it as will amount to a pardon.

G. GRANVILLE to [ROBERT HARLEY].

1706, September 3. Northend—The enclosed letter was brought me this morning. Our other friends keep a profound silence. You may judge I believe by this of their intentions, for this elaborate piece of nonsense I suppose was concerted among them, they being at the time of writing all together. Since they can refuse so fair an opportunity of making such considerable and apparent advantages, they have no doubt some greater thing in view, and it must be something very great indeed that can outweigh your offers of service here. When they find themselves disappointed, they will then repent too late. Since you have acted by a third person, perhaps that great gentleman thinks to do so too, and has therefore made Sir Humphrey his secretary. The hand he writes is as puzzling as his mysterious sayings. I shall not enter the lists with him in so particular matter without further instruction. I am here within reach of your commands which I shall fly to receive whenever you please to appoint.

Postscript—I must not forget to let you know I have done you justice to Berenice, she is at the Bath and I have not yet received any better instructions, when I do you must expect again to be troubled.

WILLIAM PENN to [ROBERT HARLEY].

1706, September 8—Lest I should not see thee at Windsor, I send the enclosed petition. I know whose province it belongs to, but he has promised to give it in Cabinet, and I only beg he may have it (Sir C. H[edges]) time enough, for I fear he has lost the other, though so necessary a service to the Queen and public. I also enclose a letter just come to hand, that I could not refuse to send, because I would do to others as I would be done, though an uncourtly way of arguing; thinking I am not mistaken in my hero. I wish thee all true happiness.

The QUEEN to the Ranger of Waltham Forest.

1706, September 8. Windsor—Requiring him to kill one fat stag of this season and to deliver the same to Secretary Harley. *Signed.*

[DANIEL DE FOE to ROBERT HARLEY.]

1706, September 13—I was coming to wait upon you and take your last instructions, when I met with your order to despatch without any further conferences. 'Tis the more afflicting to me because you are pleased to signify that something unhappy relating to yourself is the occasion, in which I condole though I know not directly the occasion. But on my own account this is a particular disaster, because I had a great many enquiries to make, in order to my conduct in the affair I go upon. Not but that as Abraham went cheerfully out not knowing whither he went, depending on Him that sent him, so I willingly go on, entirely depending that I shall have such instructions as shall not disable me from effectually answering your expectation.

I only entreat your leave to remind you, that as you have acquainted Her Majesty and my Lord Treasurer with my going, the success of my journey is the more my concern, lest want of information rendering me useless, the want of capacity or diligence be judged the reason of my miscarriage.

Under these anxious thoughts I beg you to consider, that I am without the heads of the Treaty, without the characters of the gentlemen who were here, and without the knowledge of what has been transacted in the councils here, in order to dictate to me what I am to observe. Hence I shall seem ignorant of the sense of England, and of what is expected here, or intended from hence, and thus I shall be so far from knowing the people I go to, that I shall appear not to know those I come from.

However, that if my notions are wrong I may be set right by your instructions, I beg leave, though it be beginning at the wrong end, to set down how I understand my present business as follows:—

1. To inform myself of the measures taking, or parties forming, against the Union, and apply myself to prevent them.

2. In conversation and by all reasonable methods to dispose people's minds to the Union.

3. By writing or discourse, to answer any objections, libels, or reflections on the Union, the English, or the Court, relating to the Union.

4. To remove the jealousies and uneasiness of people about secret designs here against the Kirk, &c.

I beg the orders you please to give me may mention if I am right in my thoughts of these things, and that you will give me as much light as possible in your further pleasure concerning my conduct.

I cannot quit this without mentioning the matter of expense. I confess when you told me it is out of your private, and that the government should be at no charge, it straitened my thoughts and I am the more limited in my designs—Indeed I'll put you to no expense for extravagances, but in the affair if I am a good husband I shall ill serve you. If it be proper to print anything there, some charge will attend it, and for intelligence of things I would not be sparing.

I entreat you to give me the proper limits of expenses, that I may not make you uneasy on that score, for though I hope I need not assure you, that what I shall take shall not be misapplied and that I shall bring nothing back, leaving any consideration for me or mine to your usual goodness; yet I beg you will please to hint to me for my government what you think fit on the head of charges.

I have received your bill of 25*l.*, and with the utmost expedition have equipped myself as the sum and the time will permit.

I mention the first not by way of complaint of anything, but my own misfortune—who having, as I acquainted you before, parted with so much as horse, saddle, bridle, pistols and everything, I am forced to buy all new—yet refurnished with two horses and all necessaries, I assure you I have no fear of highway men—and *cantabit vacuus* is my motto, and if I reach Newcastle I shall be in condition very fit to wait upon Mr. Bell. As to family, seven children, &c. *Hei Mihi.* No man that ever served you shall trouble you less than I with complaints of this nature. But if I have been honest, I must be naked, and am less ashamed to tell you so than I should be to tell you I am foresworn and have made reserves. I need say no more. You were pleased once to make me hope her Majesty would have some concern for me when free. I have now naked liberty—and cannot but recommend the circumstance to that bounty which I trust you will move on my account. Thus, sir, you have a widow and seven children on your hands, but a word I presume from you will ease you of the burthen.

I ask your pardon for this representation to which my present circumstances compel. I shall be no more unfortunate in that affair. I have been considering about treating of the Union in the "Review" and unless your judgment and orders differ, believe as I shall manage it must be useful, but beg hints from you if you find it otherwise.

I entreat letters from you directed to Alexander Goldsmith, to be left at Mr. Joseph Cater's in Coventry, where I shall be God willing on Thursday or Friday at farthest.

If anything supplemental offer the next post, for ditto, to be left at Mr. John Drury, bookseller in Nottingham, and the next at Mr. John Coningham's at Manchester.

Postscript.—Pray please to give me the positive day the Parliament are to sit down. Just taking horse.

Dr. W. Lancaster to [Robert Harley].

1706, September 13. St. Martin's—I beg leave to send to you the enclosed printed paper that's now gone round the kingdom wherein is a scandalous story, told in as scandalous a manner of the ridiculous behaviour of the parish priest of S. Martin's, upon a message sent to him by a Minister of State upon the news of that glorious victory at Ramilies; of his open discontent and uneasiness upon the good news; his foolish slight and contempt of the minister's servant, and of his drinking &c.

I assure you, I was that very day upon my visitation at Halsted in Essex above forty miles from London, that I lodged that night when the rejoicing was here, at Chelmsford 25 miles from S. Martin's, as Mr. Fitch, Serjeant Comines and many other gentlemen who were there with me can witness, and Dr. Bramston my official, and my own servants now in town are ready to attest upon oath; as that the next day after that rejoicing I dined in Essex and returned not home till night when all was over.

I know there needs no more be said to undo the credit of any man of my profession, than to charge him with drinking, disrespect to the Ministry, and being dissatisfied at our successes; and I think so well of myself, as to believe those writers might as well charge any man in England as myself with any of those odious things, and in confidence that you (who are supposed to be that Minister of State) do believe well of me, and will be ready to do me right I do humbly apply myself to you, and request of you to use your authority to call this noted libeller before you, at least to know of him who was the Minister of State, and how he came to report so scandalous untruths and publish them to the world.

This parish has enjoyed great peace and quiet ever since I came here till now, but I do not know how long it may continue, since we know it is written, "Smite the shepherd and the sheep will be scattered abroad." The story seems published on purpose to make divisions, and it has its effect beyond what I could have expected, but I know under whose protection I am, and I cannot without the greatest pleasure in the world acknowledge what advantages and favours I daily enjoy.

BARON ROBERT PRICE to ROBERT HARLEY.

1706, September 13. Bath—Since I wrote to you from Coventry giving you an account of the proceedings in the riots, I have been in North Wales and thence am come here for my health, my old foe the cholic still afflicting me. Study and serious thought being forbidden I must comply with the humour of this place, and gratify myself in letting you know how the world goes here. The Bath has not been known at any time to be fuller than now it is, the Duke of Norfolk, the Duke of Beaufort, the Duchess of Shrews▬ (the Duke being gone hence and left her behind), the Lord Hyde, who is just gone, Lord Grantham, Lord Gore, Lord Granville, are the principal quality with abundance of Ladies. The Duke of Norfolk is said to have a design upon Sir Nich. Sherborne's, of the North, daughter and heir, who is here also, who has upwards of 3,000l. per annum and red lettered. The Duke lives great both in table and equipage.

Sir John Germaine has been very ill and went hence two days since to Lord Berkeley's, to marry his fair daughter. He carried off 700l. he won at play, which is to make his lady a present and equipage; she is twenty-two and he fifty-six years of age, she has 6,000l. and he settles 500l. per annum pin money and 1,200l. per annum jointure, but it is his late Lady's estate in Northamptonshire, which the Earl of Peterborough designs to push for, and by this politic settlement hopes to ensure it. There are about fifty known gamesters and sharpers come here from London; they want cullies and are forced to devour each other.

I am sorry to hear the Controller Mansell's affairs go on so bad in Glamorganshire; the gentlemen of the country proposed to him some terms of election, that they would agree him to be knight of the shire next parliament, but would have Sir Edw. Stradling for the borough, which he refusing, Capt. Jenkins has declared he will oppose him for the county, and Sir Edw. Stradling will stand for the borough; and they are now as busy on all sides making of interest and spending of money as if the election was next month. Messengers have been here to the Duke of Beaufort for his interest, who told me he had promised them. Lord Leicester and Lord Windsor have done the same. I fear in my heart Mansell will be hard put to it.

ROBERT HARLEY to Dr. [WILLIAM] LANCASTER.

1706, September 14—I received the favour of your letter while I was in the midst of dispatches for Windsor, and other places upon this great occasion of joy; otherwise I would have waited upon you, which as soon as I return from Windsor I will endeavour to do, but not being easy to let you remain under any disquiet, upon occasion of that most impudent and groundless reflection which seems to be aimed at you, as far as it is in my power to relieve you. And therefore I give you liberty to use my name, that I did not send any message to you or to your house upon the news of the battle of Ramilies, because having been at church the Sunday before I knew you were not at home; and in the next place I never heard from any person whatsoever anything relating to your conduct that savoured of any disrespect to the Government; but I have from the pulpit heard you make very zealous discourses for the present Government. I have not leisure now to say more upon this subject but as soon as I come to town again you may be sure I will omit nothing that is in my power to justify you. *Copy.*

Sir David Nairne to [Robert Harley].

1706, September 17. Whitehall—Having received her Majesty's commands to send an account to Scotland of the great victory obtained over the French in Italy, that I may be the more enabled to do the same exactly I beg you will do me the favour to send me an abstract of the particulars.

Lord Poulett to [Robert] Harley.

1706, September 18. Hinton—I most humbly thank Mr. Secretary Harley for the sensible obligation and great honour of your letter with the good news, which was the more welcome to me, because these repeated great successes must lay all the enemies of the Government flat at your feet. Sir Chuffer apprehends himself very near dying, but I fear friends not being well prepared at Exeter for that time will be their own disappointment by the Bishop there having put his foot in it ; reckoning that city is to be managed like an obsequious Cornish borough. If it be suffered the cheerful joy of this county of Somerset for the wonderful successes of this summer will be very much disturbed by an unnecessary militia muster, which is only to insult your friends in elections. The Shire Knights and several other considerable gentlemen too many to name make it their humble petition it may be prevented. Colonel Berkeley's regiment is ordered to muster the beginning of next month, if you think fit by speaking to Lord Ormond to prevent it, you will very much support your interest here. It is absolutely necessary to inform you that one Henerie Brett of Wick-Taunton in Somerset is so much the officious drudge of the tacking party that he very insolently and impertinently thwarts your friends here in everything so as to give them a great deal of trouble. I had sooner proposed the leaving him out of the commission of the peace for the county of Somerset for want of a sufficient estate, for he is desperately contemptible in his family and fortune ; but his differing the last election I thought at that time would appear like personal resentment in me.

I beg pardon for troubling you so long with such little matters, but it being somewhat necessary to the service here.

The Archbishop of Canterbury to [Robert Harley].

1706, September 19—Has taken care that her Majesty's pleasure be known to all the ministers within the bills of mortality.

The Duke of Newcastle to [Harley ?].

1706, September 21. Welbeck—States the miserable condition of the troops garrisoned at Hull, who are lodged in the citadel without fire, and half-starved by the bad weather, and urges the necessity for some speedy redress. *Signed.*

William Paterson to [Robert Harley].

1706, September 21. Edinburgh—I have now been fourteen days in this place, and find at least as much want of temper and more ignorance in the changes relating to the Union than I expected. However I cannot but hope when the treaty comes to be opened in

Parliament it will meet with better acceptance than some who are in
doubt about it at present apprehend. People have been and are yet
pretty much out of town, but in a week or two they will be here, and
the meeting of the Parliament on Thursday come sevennight will open
the scene.

The Duke of Queensberry and the rest of those in the administration
are now in town and appear very hearty and unanimous, which gives
those who are for the Union great encouragement. When anything of
moment happens I shall communicate it to my Lord Treasurer.

George Granville to [Robert] Harley.

1706, September 21—Enclosed I send you the verses, which I have
endeavoured to improve pursuant to your remarks. I have only
differed from your advice, in omitting the imitation of the Latin
Epigram, which appears to me not to be exactly of a piece with the
design of a prophesy, which is too grave to admit of any epigrammatic
mixture. I therefore send it you by itself with the Latin, and if there
is anything good in it, 'tis in the niceness of the turn line for line. Nor
would I indeed be thought to make anything my own, that is not really
so. The Thracian had an objection to the allusion to Juno, but that
image referring to nothing but the difficulty of the commands, you
seemed to lay no great stress upon it yourself, and therefore it remains
unaltered. If that criticism were just, it would be impossible to use
any allusion at all. For instance, if I should say my Lord Marlborough
fought like a lion, it might be told me I say he fought like a beast. If
I should compare him to Cæsar, I might be told that likewise is a
reflection, for Cæsar fought to enslave his country. If I should think
of Alexander, there I should be out again, for Alexander fought to
tyrannize over mankind. If I compare my mistress to Venus, will
any body think I mean to call her a strumpet. Where the meaning is
obvious, and there is no room to suppose you refer to any thing but the
conduct, the bravery, and the execution of a design, one must be very
much a hypercritic indeed to enter into the causes of it. This being
the only correction I have waived, I thought it might be necessary to give
my reasons for it, for I am very apt to follow any judgment rather than
my own, especially in a case that seems the least doubtful; and I have
ventured to be the more positive in this because you yourself appeared
to lay no great weight upon it. Such as the performance is, you are
are entirely master of it, to publish or conceal as you think fit, for I
intend nothing but with absolute submission to your judgment. It was
intended only as an addition to the British Enchanters whenever it
came to be again represented, and with the ornament of a proper scene
would have been a kind of theatrical monument to the honour of the
Queen. But in this division of the playhouses 'tis possible that opportunity will be lost, and therefore I was willing my design should be
known, though it should never come to be executed.

Postscript.—I have heard nothing since from our Polish agent, &c.
or I had waited upon you.

[Daniel de Foe to Robert Harley.]

1706, September 22. Leicester—The short journal of my travel hither
is not worth your note, only to tell you I was locked up by a rain of
forty-eight hours without ceasing, and that we have not had one dry
day since I set out. This though I stayed but one day at Stourbridge

fair, made me march very slow, the country here being very deep and wet. I hope to make more haste when I get over the Trent, the ground being harder.

I am disappointed in not meeting your instructions at Coventry, as by my last in obedience to your order I directed. If they meet me not at Nottingham, I shall hope for them at Newcastle, to be left at the Posthouse, or with Mr. Bell.

I have put off my design of going to Manchester because I doubt it being late and yet know not the day the Houses will meet at Edinburgh, and the badness of the ways makes it long enough getting thither. I entreat your favour that I may not fail of your letters at Newcastle without which I shall be extremely at a loss how to proceed; till then I go on cheerfully.

Postscript.—I think it my duty to acquaint you that there is a book published in town whose title I do not remember—nor, unless I could see the "Courant," I cannot describe it other than that 'tis said to be written by one that calls himself a High Churchman, in which besides a great deal of virulence and High Church poison I am told the whole memorial is couched, and as it were reprinted. 'Tis boasted of in this country as a defiance to the Court and indeed the impudence of the party is intolerable in these parts, and such as I never met with the like in England. They say here that 'tis wrote by the Coventry parson Kinderly, others that Mr. Bromley and a club are the authors, others that the "Memorial" authors have done it, and particularly I am told it was printed by — Taylor in Paul's Church-yard; I mean the young man not old Taylor, who I suppose has more wit. This I thought my duty to acquaint you, and ask your pardon if it be officious.

WILLIAM COWPER, Lord Keeper, to ROBERT HARLEY.

1706, September 24—I am glad the Queen commands me to bestow the living on so good a man as Dr. Trimnel. I thank you for your kind encouragement of me to give you trouble. Having not heard you mention in so long a time the concern you so kindly undertook to manage for me, made me fear you meant by your silence in that particular to signify to me I had somehow forfeited that favour. But my being sure I was not conscious I had so done, gave me still some hopes my apprehensions were not true. If I have in anything through inadvertency given you the least offence I beg you to deal plainly with a plain man and let me know it. I daresay the truth when laid open will set all right.

JOHN SPECIAL to [ROBERT HARLEY].

1706, September 25—Informing him that he had some acquaintance with the French prisoners at Nottingham and that he knew they had communication with France by way of Scotland.

WILLIAM COURTENAY.

1706, September 26—Certificate by Catherine Lady Fermoy that she knew William Courtenay in Ireland, and had been often at his father's house; he was the son of Thomas Courtenay and was one of the Courtenays of Newcastle [co. Down ?]. Witnessed by Canton Haly.

WILLIAM COURTENAY to [ROBERT HARLEY].

1706, September 27 — Forwards the above certificate which he describes as Lady Roche's, the widow of John Lord Roche and Viscount Fermoy. She lodges at a poulterer's house next to an oil shop facing St. James's Market. Mr. Haly the witness was her son by her first marriage. The writer will leave nothing undone to prove himself an honest gentleman and a faithful subject, and those that abused him to Harley not so.

LORD POULETT to [BONERT HARLEY].

1706, September 28. Hinton—Reading last post that Lord Hatton was dead if you think it not improper I should be glad, to be better able to serve, to snoceed to his government of Guernsey. If you are free and think it advisable I would beg your interest in it.

J. PULTENEY to LORD GODOLPHIN.

1706, September 28. St. James's—I am informed my Lord Raby is soon to be recalled from the Court of Berlin and that the Queen has not yet made choice of any person for that character. If so I shall think myself very happy to have my son [Daniel] sent to that Court rather than to Denmark, the air being much better and the way of living much better at Berlin than at Copenhagen, especially for one who has no very strong constitution. Besides he has already spent some time at the King of Prussia's Court and, I'm persuaded, will be very well received there. I do not think it reasonable that this change, if Her Majesty consent, should be any extraordinary charge to the Crown, and I am well content to bear the expense.

My son is now at the Hague, and I believe a letter by next post from Mr. Secretary may stop him there if this change be approved of.

[DANIEL DE FOE] to ROBERT HARLEY.

1706, September 30. Newcastle[-on-Tyne]—I have everything here according to my expectation and yours, as to Mr. Bell, and am unhappy only in wanting your letter of instructions, &c.

Your letter to Mr. Bell put me to some difficulty, mentioning to him that you should draw a bill on him, whereas I had no bill but your letter without your name, and with some other circumstances in it, which were inconvenient to show him. But Mr. Bell was pleased to believe me, and has supplied me twenty five pounds, and given me his letter of credit to Edinburgh for a supply in case of farther occasion, in which I shall be as sparing as may consist with the duty I owe to your service, and the more so, because you have not been pleased to limit me in particulars.

I have had a severe journey hither but it begins to mend now, and the two last have been the only days without rain since I left London, which has made me longer getting hither than I expected. I shall lose no time, I came hither last night and I shall go away to-morrow for Edinburgh. If you will please to favour me with yours directed to Mr. Bell till I can write from Edinburgh he will forward it to me.

Methinks I look very simply when to myself I reflect how I am your messenger without an errand, your ambassador without instructions, your servant without orders. I beseech your honour to let me not be to seek of anything which may furnish me to answer your expectations to do her Majesty and the Union the service which you design, and for justifying your choice in the honour you do me in singling me out for this work.

I need say no more, you know without a strict correspondence it will be impossible for me to act by your measures, or to know what course to steer. I entreat your pardon for my importunity on this head.

CHIEF JUSTICE HOLT to [ROBERT HARLEY].

1706, September 30—The last night I waited on the Queen to give Her Majesty an account of my circuit, and particularly of the several prisoners whose cases were referred to me by the Queen's order signified under your hand. As for the first Thomas Lyford, condemned in Surrey, the Queen in consideration of his youth and hoping that if he be put into some laborious employment he may be reformed hath been pleased to extend her mercy to him: the like to William Hayes, condemned in Kent, because by his means the rest of the highwaymen were apprehended, and the parties robbed regained a considerable quantity of the money and goods taken from them.

But upon my representation of the case of Evan Evans and his brother William Evans, the Queen, hath been pleased to leave them to execution, for they are very notorious highwaymen and so have been for many years, and are a common danger to the Queen's people by whose spoil they have acquired much. This I thought to acquaint you with, because their friends may presume to give you trouble in their behalf.

THE DUKE OF CAMBRIDGE.

[1706, September ?]—A list of titles suggested for the son of the Elector of Hanover. Duke of Cambridge, Marquis Pontefract or Canterbury, Earl of Milford or Norwich, Viscount Teignmouth or Merioneth or Wallingford, Baron Northallerton or Taunton or Henley or Tewkesbury or Agmondesham. *In Harley's hand.*

Note by Lord Godolphin.—I have nothing to say to this matter but I should be glad to speak a word to you tonight or tomorrow morning.

INSTRUCTIONS to [DE FOE].

[1706, September ?]—1. You are to use the utmost caution that it may not be supposed you are employed by any person in England, but that you came there on your own business and out of love to the country.

2. You are to write constantly the true state how you find things, at least once a week, and you need not subscribe any name but direct for me under under cover to Mrs. Collins at the Posthouse, Middle Temple Gate, London. For variety you may direct under cover to Michael Read, in York Buildings.

3. You may confidently assure those you converse with that the Queen and all those who have credit with her are sincere and hearty for the Union.

3. You must shew them this is such an opportunity that being once lost or neglected is not again to be recovered. England never was before in so good a disposition to make such large concessions, or so heartily to unite with Scotland, and should their kindness now be slighted——

Copy. Incomplete.

CHR. PRICE to [ROBERT HARLEY ?].

1706, October 1—I am addressing you now for protection from a mob. We have had the greatest affront offered to the Queen's authority in enlisting a man this day se'nnight by virtue of an act of Parliament in the town of Abergavenny that ever I knew. We are actually in danger of our lives in taking informations for the punishment of the rioters. We must have a countenance from our superiors otherwise we shall never be able to bring the mob to justice, and the Queen's officers must never pretend to beat up for soldiers in Abergavenny. I have communicated with Lord Chief Justice Holt who will heartily engage in the matter. The other justices have represented the case to your acquaintance. I desire an answer by next post, wherein you may please to signify your countenance, for 'tis absolutely necessary for the service of the Government. They gain strength and encouragement by their victory, and we know not where it will end, if we have not encouragement from above.

JOHN BELL to [ROBERT HARLEY].

1706, October 1. Newcastle[-on-Tyne]—Yester night came to town Mr. Alexander Goldsmith (De Foe) in his journey to Scotland and sent for me and inquired if I had an order to pay him some money, I told him I had a letter from a gentleman that mentioned him and would supply him with what he had occasion for. He told me about twenty five guineas would serve him at present and desired a letter of credit to my friend at Edinburgh for what he shall want there. I shall give him a letter to the General Postmaster at Edinburgh to furnish him with what he has occasion for, with some restrictions. I drank a bottle with the gentleman and perceive he is not nice in telling his name, and will own it at Edinburgh, he says he is so publicly known that it would not be prudence to go under another name. I have read part of a book under his name; it may be his own but be pleased to let that pass, what I write is wholly to yourself. He is to dine with me today and then shall be further acquainted with him. I shall say nothing of what I formerly writ to your Honour about only beg the favour of a small room in your thoughts when business of greater consequence will permit.

JOHN BELL to ROBERT HARLEY.

1706, October 1. Newcastle—Enclosed I send you a letter from Mr. Goldsmith (De Foe) and shall wait your honour's commands for what I have next to do, having supplied him with what money he has occasion for at present.

G. GRANVILLE to [ROBERT HARLEY].

1706, October 2. Northend—Being informed yesterday at your office that you begin your journey to Herefordshire tomorrow, I take it this must be a day of business and will not therefore interrupt you.

I troubled you with a request by Mr. St. John on behalf of my brother upon the vacancy of the Government of Guernsey. I wrote to the Lord Treasurer to the same purpose and by yesterday's post to Lord Marlborough. I hoped this opportunity might come seasonably, to work everything easy about declaring Mr. Crowe. I have no diffidence upon me in relation to your good offices, but if you have made any step in it by which we may guess what is to be expected from others your information would much oblige me.

Postscript.—It would be a favour to let me know how I may direct to you in the country in case any thing should happen in your absence that might be necessary to communicate to you. What may I say to Berenice in answer to the last case I sent you.

The guns have informed us we are to wish you joy of some new success.

[DANIEL DE FOE] to ROBERT HARLEY.

1706, October 2. [Newcastle-on-Tyne]—My last of the 30th past from hence informed your honour of my arrival here. I had parted from hence this morning, but have had the misfortune of one of my horses failing, worn out with the fatigue of the journey.

Mr. Bell has, however, cured this breach by furnishing me with a horse, which though it has increased the expenses of the journey twelve pounds, yet the necessity I presume will excuse me to you, and the horse shall be at your honoured service at demand. This, as now ordered, will retard me not above half this day and I shall, God willing, reach Morpeth tonight.

JOHN BELL to ROBERT HARLEY.

1706, October 4. Newcastle—I have had the favour of Mr. A. G[oldsmith *alias* De Foe]'s conversation for two or three days and find him to be a very ingenious man' and fit for that business I guess he is going about. I wish him good success. He had occasion for more money than I mentioned to your Honour in my last, having occasion to buy a horse at this place, he had of me forty pounds 17s. 6d. and I have given him a letter of credit to the Postmaster General for twenty pounds more, and if his stay be long there he is to write to me to give him fresh credit, which I shall do if your Honour approve of it. Enclosed I send your Honour his letter he left with me; he went for Scotland on Wednesday last.

I had a letter from a friend of mine to my Lord Sunderland in my favour, which letter I enclosed to Mr. Carr, who writes me it came time enough to strengthen my interest, there being as yet no presentation from the Commissioners of the Customs to my Lord Treasurer for a Collector, so that it seems necessary to make application to my Lord before the Commissioners present one. However I leave it to your Honour to do as you think fit.

J. D'ALAIS to [ERASMUS] LEWIS.

1706, October [4-]15, new style. Hanover—The cessation of arms, agreed upon between the King of Sweden and the Regency of Dresden for ten weeks, has had hitherto no other good effect, but to put a stop to hostilities on both sides. Deputies from several parts of Saxony have made proposals to his Swedish Majesty, but could not work upon him, nor bring him to any terms for the good and tranquillity of their country. Some have proposed to maintain at their own charges a sufficient number of his troops to secure him that country, provided he would send back the rest, and be contented with the contributions he had already raised. Others have desired of him to assign equally quarters to his troops throughout the whole Electorate, to prevent the speedy and utter ruin of those who are oppressed by quartering too great a number of them. But these and several other proposals offered to his Majesty instead of working any good for the ease of the Saxons, have created such jealousies and divisions amongst them, that that Electorate must be entirely ruined, or King Augustus must abdicate the crown of Poland, as his Swedish Majesty insists upon.

[The DUKE OF NEWCASTLE to ROBERT HARLEY.]

[1706,] October 5. Welbeck—I shall acq████t Mr. Monckton with what you write about him. I am very glad my Lord Treasurer will remember his early and fast friends and humble servants. I wish you had had as certain advice of this victory which report makes Colonel Moor to bring, as you had of that out of Italy, let any ill natured faction never so much dislike it; and I continue my wishes that the next post may confirm to us that the Duke of Marlborough has surprised us with a victory when we thought the campaign had been ended on that side.

If I asked too many questions in my last to you, blame yourself, you led me to it.

JOHN GASSION [*alias* OGILVIE] to [ROBERT] HARLEY.

1706, October [9–]20 [new style]. Paris—As to our news here I can send you nothing that is comfortable, for we are all in a confusion since the unhappy affair of Italy, for we begin now to see where the faults lay when it is out of time to help it. We had a minister, Monsieur Chamillard, for the war and the finances. As to the first he knows nothing of the matter. He is to be laid aside and Monsieur de Senlis is to come into his place. He is a man was bred with Monsieur de Louvoy. Monsieur de Ponchartrain managed all the affairs of the marine, and understands them as little as the other does the affairs of the war, but who will have his place is not certain as yet, for Monsieur de Villeroy he will never command any more; but notwithstanding he is still a favourite with the King and is now in waiting. To inform you a little of the mistakes that fell out, the first was that Monsieur Ponchartrain having an interest in the West India Company, he ordered twenty two men of war for their convoy which should have joined Count de Toulouse, and if they had Admiral Leake durst not have attacked him, so from that we date the affront at Barcelona. Monsieur Chamillard contributed a great deal for that his son-in-law Monsieur de la Feuillade might have the glory of reducing Turin. He kept back 10,000 men which were designed to have joined the King of Spain. The next fault was to advise the King to send for the Duke of Vendôme to come to do nothing and to lose Italy. In the meantime however we do not fear to re-establish our affairs before the next campaign, that is if the galleons come safe home with money, we shall have at least 100,000 men. Monsieur Catinat will go to Italy with the Duke of Orleans. Monsieur de Harcourt will attend Monsieur de Vendome with a *camp volant* the next campaign. I have given you here what is material and I send you a lampoon which will show you the humour of the people.

Your descent that was designed for this country put us to a great deal of trouble and expense. But to have landed betwixt La Rochelle and Dunkirk they would have been cut in pieces for there was a vast army on the coast. Also it was no conduct in the enemy to name so little a mean fellow as Cassalie for one of the chief commanders. For let the French be never so discontented they will never rise but with someone who is noble. They have that vain glory that they misprise anything that is not noble; and you may easily judge what harm such a man would not have done who had formerly been a baker's boy and esteemed a murderer. Monsieur l'Abbé Guiscard hath no reputation here. Had they sent my Lord Galway or Schomberg that would have made a greater noise; but since their conduct was bad the better for us. *French verses enclosed.*

H[ENRY] S[T. JOHN] to [ROBERT] HARLEY.

1706, October 10. Bucklebury—I thank you dear master for the notice you give me, which I shall keep with the strictest secrecy to myself, and make the proper use of it. I suspected him to be a rogue, but did not know whether he might not be of use if he could discover the practices of the person in whose secret he pretended to be.

I hope to be in town this day sevennight at furthest, and suppose before the end of the month we shall see you there. I enclose to you an *Observator* which I received last post enclosed from the Duke of Marlborough, and had his directions to show it you. I believe Mr. T[utchin?] will be soundly drubbed; I hope every honest Englishman would approve of it—says my letter. If I had some friend that would concern himself to get the author and printer both well beaten, for I cannot nor will not bear any longer this barbarous usage from this rogue, nor his patron Lord Haversham. Adieu.

NICHOLAS REILLY, Mayor of Newcastle on Tyne, to [ROBERT HARLEY].

1706, October 11. Newcastle—The person who called herself Countess de Maille, whereof we gave you as particular information as we could get, hath been kept in our gaol ever since her first commitment (being now above two years) to the great charge of the town. At the last assizes she applied herself to the Lord Chief Baron, who let her out on bail to appear in the Queen's Bench on the first day of next term. *Signed.*

E. LEWIS to [ROBERT HARLEY].

1706, October 19. Whitehall—The substance of the Elector's letter to the Duke of Marlborough was that the King of France had hitherto made proposals of peace only in a private manner, but now did it publicly by him, and was ready to treat in any place between Mons and Brussels. His Grace's answer was that it was a matter of great importance in which he could make no step without the Queen's commands.

[The DUKE OF HAMILTON to ROBERT HARLEY.]

1706, October 22. Holyrood House—You'll see by the Minutes what we are doing; we go on in reading the Articles and Minutes upon them, for information. Many of our merchants that were very fond of the Union, upon examination, alter their inclinations, and say, as it is calculated at present, it will be far from being advantageous to the trade of this nation. But this must be farther illustrated before we can come to true light in that matter. We had a long debate in the House the other day about the calculations, so they contended strenuously that there should be no new calculations made, but that we are to rely upon what had been made above. But there being several errors made appear in this day's proceeding, they agreed to name a Committee to inspect that matter anew, for the shyness in the preceding day's debate had created great jealousy in that matter, which made them yield this day to a new inspection into that matter, but the hurrying and averseness to come into this matter with deliberation, are far from being agreeable arguments to come into what has been treated. The generality of the people don't seem fond of it, since it has been exposed. I don't know what we within doors may be but there is a great ferment amongst all ranks of people in this nation at present.

I long to hear from Aberc[orn ?] how my brother Orkney does, for I hear he has been ill at Ghent.

I have nothing more to add at present, but that I desire you may make inquiry of the occasion of your letters being called for by the Comptroller of the Post House. So honest Mason, adieu. *Copy.*

SIR C. HEDGES to [ROBERT HARLEY].

1706, October [22]. Tuesday—I can't omit acquainting you the Parliament is to meet and sit the 21st of next month and the friends to the Union in Scotland have got so much ground that private letters say the difficult part is over. The foreign letters to-day say King Charles's affairs are in an ill posture in Spain. Cuenza is taken by the Duke of Berwick, and the garrison which is considerable are prisoners of war. We have no letters from the fleet since the 10th and hear of but three transports driven back, so there is good hope they are gone forward to the rendezvous which upon this misfortune was appointed at Lisbon. On the other side all succeeds to our wishes in Italy, in case they will give the investiture of the Duchy of Milan to the King of Spain. I believe Mr. Lewis has acquainted you with an extraordinary credential Monsieur Spanheim has for resuming his character if Her Majesty will declare Lord Raby shall continue the same he has with His Prussian Majesty. The old gentleman, who was with me to-day, seemed much out of countenance when I appealed to him as an experienced minister touching the method of making this proposal, but I write to the Duke of Marlborough for his opinion, whether he thinks it advisable to gratify the King in this particular, and Lord Raby is to stay at Berlin till further order. Mr. Lewis tells me he has given you an account of the Elector of Bavaria's proposals. Lord Treasurer has framed an admirable answer to them, which I hope will defeat the proposed conference and keep the Dutch, if possible, from secret negociations.

D[ANIEL DE] F[OE] to BOBERT HARLEY.

1706, October 24. Edinburgh—According to your commands in the only paper of your orders viz. of writing constantly to you, I continue to give you the general state of things here.

I am sorry to tell you here is a most confused scene of affairs, and the Ministry have a very difficult course to steer. You allow me freedom of speaking allegories in such a case, it seems to me the Presbyterians are hard at work to restore Episcopacy, and the rabble to bring to pass the Union.

We have had two mobs since my last, and expect a third, and of these the following is a short account. The first was in the Assembly or Commission of Assembly, where very strange things were talked of and in a strange manner, and I confess such as has put me much out of love with ecclesiastic Parliaments. The power, *Anglicé* tyranny, of the Church was here described to the life, and *jure Divino* insisted upon, in prejudice civil authority ; but this was by some tumultuous spirits who are overuled by men of more moderation, and, as an Assembly they act with more wisdom and honesty than they do in their private capacities, in which I confess they contribute too much to the general aversion which here is to the Union; at the same time they acknowledge they are unsafe and uneasy in their present establishment. I work incessantly with them, they go from me seemingly satisfied and pretend to be informed, but are the same men when they come among their parties—I hope what I say to you shall not prejudice them. In general they are the wisest weak men, the falsest honest men, and the steadiest unsettled people ever I met with. They mean well, but are blinded in their politics, and obstinate in opinion.

But we had the last two nights a worse mob than this, and that was in the street, and certainly a Scots rabble is the worst of its kind.

The first night they only threatened hard and followed their patron Duke Hamilton's chair with huzzas from the Parliament House quite through the city—they came up again hallooing in the dark, threw some stones at the guard, broke a few windows and the like, and so it ended. I was warned that night that I should take care of myself, and not appear in the street, which indeed for the last five days I have done very little, having been confined by a violent cold. However, I went up the street in a friend's coach in the evening, and some of the mob not then got together were heard to say when I went into a house, " There was one of the English dogs, &c." I casually stayed at the house I went then to, till dark, and thinking to return to my lodging found the whole city in a most dreadful uproar and the High Street full of rabble.

Duke Hamilton came from the House in his chair as usual, and instead of going down the city to his lodgings went up the High Street, *as was said* to visit the Duke of Athol. *This*, whether designed by the Duke as most think, or no, but if not was exactly calculated to begin the tumult, for the mob in a vast crowd attending him thither waited at the door—and as these people did not come there to be idle, the Duke could have done nothing more directly to point out their business, the late Lord Provost, Sir Patrick Johnstone, living just upon the spot.

The mob had threatened him before, and I had been told he had such notice of it that he removed himself. Others say he was in his lodgings with eleven or twelve gentlemen besides servants resolved to defend himself, but be that as it will, the mob came upstairs to his door and fell to work with sledges to break it open, but it seems could not. His Lady in the fright with two candles in her hand that she might be known, opens the windows, and cries out for God's sake to call the guard. An honest townsman and apothecary that saw the distress the family was in, went to the guard which is kept in the middle of the street, and found the officers very indifferent in the matter, whether as to the cause or, as is rather judged, through real fear of the rabble; but applying himself to one Capt. Richardson, a brave resolute officer, he told him he could not go from the guard without the Lord Provost's order, but if he would obtain that order, he would go up.—In short, the order was obtained and the Captain went with a party of the guard and made his way through the rabble to Sir Patrick Johnstone's staircase. The generality of them fled, some were knocked down and the staircase cleared, and three or four taken in the very assaulting the door.

Yet they fled not far, but hallooing and throwing stones and sticks at the soldiers. Several of them are very much bruised and the brave Captain I am told keeps his bed. However he brought down his prisoners, and the Tolbooth being at hand, hurried them in, and made his retreat to the guard. In this posture things stood about eight to nine o'clock, and the street seeming passable I sallied out and got to my lodgings.

I had not been long there, but I heard a great noise and looking out saw a terrible multitude come up the High Street, with a drum at the head of them, shouting and swearing and crying out all Scotland would stand together. "No union." "No union." "English dogs," and the like.

I cannot say to you I had no apprehensions, nor was Mons. de Witt quite out of my thoughts, and particularly when a part of this mob fell upon a gentleman who had discretion little enough to say something that displeased them just under my window. He defended himself bravely and called out lustily also for help to the guard, who being within hearing and ready drawn up in close order in the street advanced, rescued the gentleman and took the person he was grappled with, prisoner.

The City was by this time in a terrible fright, the guards were insulted and stoned as they stood, the mob put out all lights, nobody could stir in the streets, and not a light be seen in a window for fear of stones. There was a design to have shut the gate at the *Nether Bow*, as they call it, which is a gate in the middle of the great street, as Temple bar may be, and the design was to hinder the guard in the city and the guard in the *Canongate*, as they call it, from assisting one another, and cut off their communication.

But my Lord Commissioner prevented that by sending a detachment of his guards up the Canongate Street—as from Whitehall to Temple bar—who seized upon the Nether Bow and took post there with every soldier a link in his hand being in his arms.

During this hurry, whether they omitted shutting the North Port, as they call it, which goes to Leith, or that it was not yet ten o'clock I know not, but a second rabble of five hundred, some say a thousand, stout fellows came up from Leith and disporting themselves in the street continued the hurry in a terrible manner.

About eleven o'clock my Lord Commissioner sent for the Lord Provost and desired him to let him send a body of the guards into the city—which they say is what never was admitted before, and some say the Lord Provost hesitated at it for a long time.

I cannot send you the particulars of that part—but about midnight a body of the guards besides those posted at the Canongate entered the city, drums beating, marched up the High Street to the Parliament Close, and his Grace the Duke of Argyle mounted at the head of the Horse Guards to have seconded them. After the foot came my Lord Provost, the Bailiffs and Magistrates with their officers and links, and these clearing the streets the mob was dispersed. They have six I think or thereabouts in prison, and the Council is now sitting to take some further orders for preserving the peace.

Two regiments of foot are sent for to quarter in the City, and I hope as before, this mob will, like our Tackers, be a mere plot to hasten what they designed to prevent.

What further happens in this matter I shall as it occurs not fail to acquaint your honour with.

—— to [ROBERT] HARLEY, at Brampton.

[1706,] October 24—Though I know it is only to tautologize to your knowledge, as the English orator phraseth it, to give you any account of the proceedings of the Scots parliament, yet I shall venture to give such as I have had.

On Saturday they considered the first eight articles. The Justice Clerk and Sir David Dalrymple read what was in the minutes relating to them, and the Commissioners of the Treaty explained them and answered all the doubts and objections made about them. There was nothing considerable said and little opposition made. Some moved for reading the Act of Settlement and Succession in England with the limitations, which was done; others moved not only to read the Act of Coronation in England but to have it printed. Kincardine Bruce moved it and urged it much, and Sir Thomas Burnet of Lee desired a vote about it, but his party was not for it. It was said that as the Queen had sworn to maintain Episcopacy in England so also to maintain Presbytery in Scotland, and that she and her successors would swear to maintain those governments within their respective limits, as other did, Lutherans, Calvinists, and Papists. The party could not so much as carry it to have the motion marked in the minutes.

· There are several other members arrived in Edinburgh. Some think that the opposers of the Union will endeavour to muster all their numbers after the consideration of the articles to reject it.

It is not known whether after the consideration of the Articles is ended the question will be in general, approve or not the whole, or whether there will be a question on each article. The Commission of the General Assembly's address is come to Court. It is modest, desiring only care may be taken to secure their Church government in that part of Britain. The merchants are in pain about the Lisbon fleet in the news of its being dispersed by the stormy weather, and five or six ships taken by the French privateers. They are also in fear for the East India and Virginia fleet, they being both very great ones and the last of two crops and about a hundred and fifty sail, besides ships from other places which are with them.

Some say that the Electoral Princess of Hanover was not with child as was believed at that Court; but as none but Halifax says that, some thought she miscarried by the fright on the fire which happened in or near her apartment, but all say that she is now with child.

Mr. Southwell has another lusty boy.

There are exceeding many horse robbers here and in great troops which makes many uneasy.

Radziowski, nephew and heir to the Cardinal Primate, designs to return shortly to France where his family is. His pass from Marlborough was of August. There is an order as is said to release the vessel he came over from Calais in. Prince George took physic yesterday.

· The Lord Poulett writes that he will come as late as he can to town, having no great encouragement to come soon.

D[ANIEL DE] F[OE] to ROBERT HARLEY.

1706, October 29. Edinburgh—In my last you had an account of two mobs, in particular Church and Street, but as you were put in expectation of a third mob there I purposely referred it to this post to let you know that this particular sort is expected within the House itself.

There is an entire harmony in this country, consisting in universal discords, the Churchmen in particular are going mad, the parsons are out of their wits, and those who, at first, were brought over, and, pardon me, were some of them my converts, their country brethren being now come in, are all gone back and to be brought over by no persuasion.

The mob you have heard of are affrighted with the loss of the Scots Crown, and the parsons maliciously humour it, and a country parson who preached yesterday at the High Kirk before the Commissioners took this text:—" *Behold I come quickly ; hold fast that which thou hast, that no man take thy crown.*" He pretended not to mean an earthly crown, but made his whole sermon a bald allegory against the Union. I confess I had patience to hear him, but to an exceeding mortification.

The House is now going on, they have confirmed the Act of the Council for suppressing the rabble and bringing in soldiers, and thereby suppressed a new clamour which was raising against the bringing the soldiers into the city, at which it was begun to say this was not a free parliament, but that is over. Now 'tis said this was a mob raised by my Lord Commissioner, and that his Grace did it on purpose to have an opportunity to suppress them. The third mob is expected in the House where 'tis said when the party see the articles put to the vote, if they cannot carry their part, they will protest, take Instruments as they call it here, and leave the House, and then they pretend to say the nation will take arms, and the Highlands are to be brought in—and indeed if this should run so far I fear the Church will join the worst of their enemies against this Union.

They are now a going to fast all over the Kingdom and therein to give the ministers occasion to pray and preach against it, and as soon as that is done tumultuous addresses are preparing in several parts of the country.

And thus you see what a nation you have to do with here. I am as diligent with caution not to be suspected as possible. I have not the success I hoped for, but I continue to push on and think I do no harm.

I have printed one essay, which I transmitted the last post. I have the second in the press, which, if it does equal service with the first, I shall not so much grudge the expense.

I wrote you last post how I hear I am treated in England, as to my Lord Chief Justice Holt. I beseech you to concern yourself in the case, that I may not be ruined while I am at this distance. My secret enemy is being very vigilant and furious. I am told they will bring the publisher to a trial while I am absent and he cannot procure me, for which I shall be eternally reproached.

Sir, you may depend upon it I shall be pursued to the utmost, if your power be not my screen. I earnestly, therefore, entreat you will not forget me in this condition.

E. LEWIS to ROBERT HARLEY.

1706, October 31. Whitehall—By direction of Mr. Secretary Hedges I had begun to make enquiry privately, who the persons were that printed Lord Peterborough's memoirs, but I have since received orders to let that matter take its course, for my Lord Treasurer and Mr. Secretary Hedges are both of opinion, that the book when published can never do so much mischief now, as it would if endeavours were used to suppress it. Your letter that came to me yesterday under cover from Mr. Thomas was safely delivered to Lord Treasurer.

Sir Lambard Blackwell desired me to acquaint you that he had been here to offer his services if you think fit to employ him at Vienna.

Mr. Dartiquenave who was one of the Agents of the Revenues in the late reign is made Paymaster of the works in the room of Mr. Lloyd who died last week.

Captain Cartwright is gone to Flanders to pay the English forces there, he is succeeded in Mr. Bridges's office by Mr. Sloper who quits Mr. Howe's service.

I send you enclosed two letters from Scotland, which mention nothing of what I hear from others, that the morning after the tumult had happened Duke Hamilton sent to the High Commissioner to assure him he had no hand in it, and that he believed 'twas an artifice of his enemies to blacken him, and terrify people from opposing the Union.

We have no mail from Holland though the wind has constantly been very fair. Sir Thomas Frankland says two packet-boats put to sea from Harwich last Sunday, and as soon as they were out of the port were chased by several French privateers, one took to the north and the other to the south. The latter is come back safe into Ousley Bay, the other has not been heard of, so that he believes she is either taken or put into Norway, and that the reason why we have no letters from Holland is because there is no boat there.

It is given out here that Baron Price's son shot himself at Genoa, but I am very well informed that he was not his own executioner, there was jealousy in the case occasioned by his own ill conduct, which was the most imprudent in the world.

NEWS LETTER.

[1706,] November 2—The Parliament of Scotland, on Friday the 25th of October, did only approve the Privy Council's method of securing the safety of the Parliament and tranquillity of Edinburgh by the regular troops being brought into that city. Some were against the continuing of them, Duke Hamilton opposed the voting thanks unto the Council for what they had done and the ordering it to continue the same care in the same way for the future; the debate continued about four hours, and the joint vote was carried in favour of the Council's acting by a majority of above 66. It is still more probable that the Treaty will be approved by a very great majority; but the common people, many Presbyterians, and most of the Jacobites are against it.

Some write that Duke Hamilton and his friends say that the mob was encouraged to get a pretext for those new guards to the Parliament. The Lord Chancellor moving to the House to know their mind concerning the prisoners, Duke Hamilton said that though they had taken a part of Errol's privilege from him by introducing and authorizing those new guards yet they ought not to take from him the rest of his right, which is to judge and try all riots during the sitting of Parliament, and it was not disallowed. The Parliament adjourned from Friday till Monday.

Guiscard is gone to Holland.

The Polish Count Radziowiski is gone to Holland. Halifax when he invited him to dine told him and the foreigners to dine with him and to come *Mercredi* and to the English he named Tuesday, so the English came on Tuesday and he waited long for the others but they came not till Wednesday and then he had no dinner for them but desired their company on Thursday; he mistook *Mercredi* for *Mardi*. Judge Price's son was found shot dead in his chamber in Genoa, a pistol lying by him, and money, watch and other things about him, those of Genoa say he shot himself. It is said that Cron, governor of Barbados, is to go first to Spain as Envoy to King Charles.

The *Nassau* a third rate stranded at St. Helens, one man only lost.

The packet-boat near Chester was lost but the passengers saved, many vessels and one of 24 guns lie in that sea between Dublin and the other coast.

The French letters speak much of their progress and advantages in Spain, and that Galway is retired towards Denia and has possessed himself of an advantageous post there, and **has** sent some forces to Alicant to secure it.

They say that Albergotti was come to Susa on the 28th ultimo with 18,000 men and artillery and expected Orleans with more artillery and troops. Orleans had had a fall from his horse but had no great hurt thereby.

It is reported that King Augustus has defeated the Swedes, but some think this needs confirmation.

There is great pains taken for promoting Auditor Mainwaring's interest at Preston in Lancashire.

They say that some prisoners have made their escape from Dover Castle.

It is said that the Duke of Orleans declared Mistress Sire is gone from Paris to Grenoble to be with him.

The Thursday's post brought a letter from Annandale, under cover to a gentlewoman, to a friend of his ten miles westward from London as some say.

Mrs. Cleverin is like to be favoured by a great man's inclination.

Some say that there is a great misunderstanding, if not rupture, betwixt a person of great consequence and his lady.

It is said that the Venetian lady is to return hither to Cardigan.

The Duchess of Cleveland was introduced by Grafton, Northumberland, and Quarendon the first day of the term, when for continuing of the bail she swore that she feared personal hurt, and for a proof of her not having malice she said she had married him who had nothing. Fielding answered that she had no malice when she married him, but his having now 50*l.* per week etc. However his bail was continued.

D[ANIEL DE] F[OE] to ROBERT HARLEY.

1706, November 5. Edinburgh—Since my last the face of affairs I hope is a little mended, and after a very long and warm debate on Friday whether they should proceed on the Union, or go first on the securities of the Church it was passed—proceed.

On Saturday they sat till near eight at night and the speeches on both sides were long and warm. Duke Hamilton raved, Fletcher of Saltoun, and the Earl of Belhaven made long speeches, the latter of which will be printed—the clamour without was so great that a rabble was feared, though the guards are numerous, and were drawn out in readiness.

Addresses are delivered in from several places and more preparing, but 'tis observed the addresses discover a fraud which shows the party here at their shifts. The addresses are found in the cant of the old times, deploring the misery of Scotland for want of a further reformation and the security of the church and the Lord's covenanted people, but when the names come to be examined they are all signed by known Jacobites and Episcopal men.

There has been a further expectation of a mob and some practices have been used to infect the soldiers, but the Earl of Leven called the

-guards together today and made a speech to them. They had been possessed with a notion that they should be sent to the West Indies as soon as the Union was over. My Lord Leven, I hope, has re-established them and the proceeding since is more favourable.

Last night the grand question was put whether the first article, or in short the Union itself, should be approved or not—and carried in the affirmative, which being on King William's birthday is to me very remarkable and encouraging.

I had today the honour to be sent for by the Lords Committee for examining the equivalents, and to assist them in the calculating the drawback on the sale, the proportion of the excise, and some *addenda* about Trade.

They profess themselves obliged to me more than I merit, and at their next Committee I am desired to dine with them. I am looked on as an Englishman that designs to settle here, and I think am perfectly unsuspected and hope on that foot I do some service. Only I spend you a great deal of money at which I am concerned and see no remedy if I will go through with the work. I have now great hopes of it though today the Assembly men make a great stir; in short the Kirk are *au wood*, pardon the Scotticism.

The Earl of Leven to [Robert Harley].

1706, November 7. [Edinburgh]—Nothing material has occurred since my last. Only this, on Monday the 4th the Parliament had the first article of the Treaty under their consideration, and at last we brought it to a question, approve or not, which we carried in the affirmative by a considerable majority, although there were even some of our friends that had some difficulty as to the voting of that article until all the rest should be first agreed to. All is quiet here, although I cannot say it would be had we not guards within this city, for there is a very great confluence of people here in town, and the ferment is great amongst the mob. When anything falls out worth your notice you shall be informed thereof.

D[aniel De] F[oe] to Robert Harley.

1706, November 9th—In my last I hinted to you what the Church was doing as to their Address or Protest against the Church of England constitution. I herewith send you the thing itself—and as to the general opinion it gains, here I must own it does some harm—but not what it was expected, for while it was in debate, like the English fleet while it lay at Torbay, it kept all France in suspense, so the country expected the Kirk would have protested as the Burghs have done against the Union in general as destructive to the civil interest and the interest of the Church in general; but instead of that it contains six heads, as you will see, all which suppose the Union as real and certain.

I had this day the honour to be in the Committee of Parliament appointed to examine the drawbacks and equivalents and they have desired me to assist them. Their debates will end in making explications on the heads of excise and drawbacks, and I believe I shall have the honour to form them.

I shall in my next I hope be able to give you a scheme of their demands, and as I believe I shall have the honour to draw them out for them. I would be glad that after I send you a draft of this subject I might be instructed what will or will not be conceded in England, since it is so ordered that I am in their Cabinet by some management and can influence them more than I expected.

Now to lead them to anything which England will not comply with, or to put them off of anything which makes a difficulty here and may be complied with, is equally acting against the Union.

Their lordships have resolved to commit the drawing up the explanations to me, and if directed I might do more service to both kingdoms than I could have expected. If therefore my service here be of any moment I shall beg to be instructed, or if I take wrong aims, to be excused.

Next post I shall transmit a draft of the things in debate.

Postscript.—All the gentlemen lay elders protested in the Assembly against the address.

J. Herbert to Robert Harley, in York Buildings.

1706, November 10. Oakley Park—Asking that he would endeavour to prevent his being Sheriff of Montgomeryshire, as he had not received a farthing from the late Lord Herbert's estate in that county since he died, and he had been at a heavy charge to secure the reversion to himself and his posterity.

[D. Fearns to Robert Harley.]

1706, November 12. Edinburgh—I have not written since the 4th because I would not multiply when there's nothing certain or more material, or worth your perusal. The first article of the Union was voted and passed after much struggling for several days; on the sixth, some frivolous address read to please parties, and the Chancellor hath too much inclination to please parties. One instance is that a certain poor Lord who was brought up and bred a Roman (*sic*) is introduced into the parliament without taking the formula prescribed by act of parliament, 1700, for preventing the growth of popery, alleging that he was never popish, though known to hundreds as a professed papist and bred so; and yet the said Lord votes against the Union and all good things. On the eighth several addresses were presented and read from several villages, that are no royal boroughs or corporations, such as Hamilton which is but Duke Hamilton's seat, Falkland a village joining the palace of Falkland, one of her Majesty's country palaces, of which the Duke of Athole is but keeper or tenant at will, as other noblemen are of other parts, forests, and palaces since 1602. An act for a supply of eight months cess extending to 40 and 50,000 pounds English, to maintain the forces, guards and garrisons, and some frigates for next year, which would maintain many more forces than are here ; besides the customs, excise, crown rents, &c. if rightly applied, but managers make large chips out of other people's timber to keep their fires always burning, so *quicquid delirunt reges plectuntur Achivi*, and the poor Achivi feel the smart of all, which frets and galls them under such oppression.

Duke Hamilton was four hours with the Lord High Commissioner last week in his apartments and went out as well as came *incognito*; and he is with the Chancellor very frequently.

This day, the twelfth, the parliament met at eleven and sat till six at night, and had the act for the security of the Presbyterian government of the Church as by law established here befor them. The protestators gave in their protest that the Act was no security to the church; one of the protestators was the Earl of Kincardine now, formerly Sir Alexander Bruce.

I lodge in one Mr. John Monro's house, her Majesty's armourer, a very honest man and faithfull, at the sign of the Half Moon near the Netherbow.

The EARL OF STAIR to [ROBERT HARLEY].

1706, November 12. Edinburgh—I had the honour and satisfaction of yours from Brampton Castle; the irregular appearance of the' mob and the addresses procured from all corners against an entire Union were as you rightly consider the opposers' last shift, and indeed the engaging so many persons by their subscriptions is a malicious step against the Union, but by patience we have prevented the ill effects of these commotions and are entirely master of this city to secure the Parliament, where we are near two to one.

This day we have finished our Act for the security of our church, without making any alterations for the Address from the Commission of the Kirk to which they were ill advised, though that doth give them full assurance of the continuance of their government after the Union, yet there is no insinuation of Divine right to check the Church of England, nor is there direct exemption from the power of the Parliament of Britain in which we found you very nice? and likewise we have not insisted upon the exemption from the Sacramental test, for which in our private communings we had one pretty fair encouragement.

I was for having this done at London as a part of our Treaty and I did foresee that the want of that article might lose us the populace; but I reckon from this day forwards, the ferment will abate and when the Ministers find themselves safe, they will soon make the people easy and quiet. We shall be obliged to proceed slowly but I hope we shall have all the material articles of the Treaty approved before the Parliament meets, and for some small explanations, not at all inconsistent but upon the foot of the Treaty, I hope they shall not stick with you, such as to give premiums or drawbacks to the exportation of oats and meal as you give to wheat and barley, and to white herrings as you give to your pilchards or the like. It may be our people might be in a better disposition towards the Union upon some small delay, but then it's impossible ever to seek a disposition in our Parliament, especially in our noblemen who are indeed the greatest losers, therefore I beg that no ear be given to any delay, for our stage is narrow that it cannot hold all that at present are hearty for the Union, and we will soon come to differ amongst ourselves if we continue upon our present establishment.

[DANIEL DE FOE] to ROBERT HARLEY.

1706, Nov. 13. Edinburgh—In my last I acquainted you with the present posture of the affair before the Committee of Parliament. The difficulties before them are the drawbacks and the equivalents, the taxes, and the trade.

The first head is —viz. speaking as themselves :—

We have some difficulties, how can we remedy them, we cannot add any article or take off any, that will require a new Treaty and consequently a new delay and the Lord have mercy on us if we have another Session here !

Will England admit of explanations ?

My answer—pardon me, uninstructed in the case—Without doubt England will admit the Parliament of Scotland to declare their construction of any article of the Treaty, provided it be agreeable to the true intent and meaning of the Treaty, and to reason and justice.

Upon this foot you will have an explanation offered on the following heads, and were I better informed from England, I could perhaps lessen, encourage, or discourage those explanations.

1. That their two-penny ale which is sold but for 2s. 4d. per gallon more than our small beer should pay as small beer only, or, as I offer, be advanced to a middle rate of excise between strong and small, in proportion to its advance of price, which seems just.

2. That their own Acts of Parliament obliging them to cure fish with foreign salt, and those Acts being by the Union to be continued; they are to understand English salt as foreign salt in the sense of those Acts, it being so now. Or else after the Union they shall be prohibited using the rock salt of England, which will be to the loss of England, as well as a hardship on Scotland.

3. That whereas they are obliged to salt all flesh for exportation, or for victualling their ships, with foreign salt; they may use their own or English salt, paying the duty for it, else they are not on equality in trade with England who salt most of their ships beef with English salt.

4. That the tax upon coals payable by the chalder in England be explained on the weight of Scots coal in proportion, they not selling by measure.

5. And the bounties on corn be explained to include a grain called bear, which is much the same as barley, but differs a little.

These are what are at present before them and as the rest offer, for there will be more, I shall acquaint your honour.

Meantime it would be very serviceable if I might know, whether those explanations are agreeable to England or no; since it will be in my power to shorten them very much, though if allowed, it will give some ease here to a nation that really are in a terrible ferment, and it is unaccountable how it increases.

At Dumfries they have burnt the Articles in the market place—at Glasgow, they were about it, but the magistrates prevailed with them to forbear on promise to sign an address against it.

It would amaze you, if I should give you the trouble of repeating the ridiculous notions people here have entertained against their own happiness, the libels, the absurdities, and the insults on that head are intolerable.

The High Commissioner has had letters sent to threaten him with pistol, dagger, and variety of assassination, and the unusual numbers of Highlanders makes some people very uneasy here; there being more of them here now, than has been known. Indeed they are formidable fellows, and I only wish her Majesty had 25,000 of them in Spain, a nation equally proud and barbarous like themselves. They are all gentlemen—will take affront from no man, and insolent to the last degree. But certainly the absurdity is ridiculous to see a man in his mountain habit armed with a broadsword, target, pistol or perhaps two, at his girdle a dagger, and staff walking down the street as upright and haughty as if he were a lord—and withal driving a cow, bless us—are these the gentlemen? said I——

As to the Union, though I hope well and the Government stick close to it, yet I must own 'tis yet a dark prospect.

The difficulties are many and the people obstinately adverse, and if any insurrection happen—which I must acknowledge is not unlikely—I crave leave to say the few troops they have here are not to be depended upon; I have this confessed by men of the best judgment.

The officers are good, but even the officers own they dare not answer for their men, and some of the wisest and most discerning men here wish two or three regiments of horse or dragoons were sent but near the borders, as silently as might be. All the forces this Government has to make a stand are not 2000 effective men, and of them I question whether 1500 could be drawn together.

I have more objections of trade to make, but they are not ripe. I wish I might know what steps to take in this affair. Mr. Bell has sent me a farther supply.

Postscript—I am written to—to offer my service to my Lord Halifax to acquaint him with matters here. My respect and indeed obligation to my Lord make it very agreeable to me, and I have this post wrote to his Lordship. But as I am yours in duty abstracted from, and exclusive of, all the world I thought myself obliged to acquaint you of it, and on your orders shall at any time desist.

D[ANIEL DE] F[OE] to ROBERT HARLEY.

1706, November 14. Edinburgh—I sent you a post or two since my Lord Belhaven's speech, which I presume has diverted you. I enclose you a short comment upon it, which has made some sport here, and perhaps done more service than a more solid discourse.

Since my last the Parliament voted the Act for the security of the Church, and refused the Articles the Church recommended; at which the Church are very angry, and the rabble at Glasgow has been very tumultuous upon that end.

The Church has today voted an address to cure the suggestion too justly cast on them against the succession, viz—that the growth of popery may be prevented, the open profession of it suppressed; that the succession being undeclared gives the greatest hopes to the party of the Prince of Wales, &c.

This is a healer, but does not fully recompense the folly of their last.

Today the house has debated whether they shall go upon the second article with a proviso, or begin at the 4th article, and have agreed to go upon the second; but the majority is not above twenty five, whereas they carried it against the Church affair by a majority of seventy and a good jest at the end of it, that all the protesters and adherers, which were twenty five, were of such as were the known enemies of the Church. 'Twas very odd and diverting to find these gentlemen vote that the Act was not a security sufficient for the Church, and especially Sir Alexander Bruce now Earl of Kincardine, formerly expelled the House for saying the Presbyterian Church was inconsistent with monarchy.

Postscript—The floods here are so great I question even the post being able to travel.

SIR RICHARD MYDDELTON to [ROBERT HARLEY].

1706, November 15. Chirk Castle—Asking that Mr. Ambrose Thelwall might be excused for the third time from being Sheriff for Denbighshire. *Signed.*

[The DUKE OF NEWCASTLE to ROBERT HARLEY.]

1706, November 16—Enclosed is a copy of a letter I received from Mr. Special on Thursday last and of the answer that Wenman told me he returned him to it, and though I find his chief business seems to aim at getting of money to support his extravagance, and although I had a different account of his debt from what he writes and have often observed him not to be consistent with himself in his discourse, yet the sum he asks being but small, I leave it to you, whether you think it proper to remit it him, and enjoin him to come up in two or three days after he is at liberty, to give you an account of his negociation, that you may thereby judge whether he will be able to make any discovery or no.

As you were kept prisoner by the floods, I fear I shall be so much longer, though I wrote my Lord Treasurer word, I hoped to have dispatched my affairs to be there the first week in December, and I find his Lordship desires I would not make it longer, yet I am certain he would not have me and my family hazard drowning, for the like has never been known here within the memory of man. There is no getting within a mile or two of any bridge upon the Trent, and all that pass go over in little boats. Your friend Mr. Monckton with his lady have been stopped two or three days and are at last gone to Nottingham, but I question whether he can be able to ferry over there. I am confident a great many members cannot possibly get up, and whether that may make the Parliament adjourn for eight or ten days, you are the best judges that are upon the spot. Pray satisfy my Lord Treasurer that as soon as the waters abate I will come up.

I wish the huddled up and mysterious peace between the two Kings have no ill consequences, and that France be as much surprised in it as we are. I shall be very glad to have your thoughts, as soon as the next foreign post comes in, upon this point.

I always wish that they you mention would make use of their own good understanding, I am sure they would find it better than that of those who importune them, and I am in that particular of the memorialist's opinion that friendship founded in ambition is not of long duration. I am certain their apprehension will let them see the difference of a true friendship on the same interest with them, from a dissembled one that is only designed for a step to their own dominion.

I am very glad of what you write to me about my Lord Keeper [Cowper], I wish you two always friends, for I own I have a great inclination and respect for him.

D[ANIEL DE] F[OE] to ROBERT HARLEY.

1706, November 16. [Edinburgh]—Since my last the Parliament have voted the second article of the Treaty—viz. yesternight after long struggle and several attempts to put it off, as first—a motion to make a recess, to acquaint her Majesty what a ferment the nation was in and how the matter was vigorously opposed by the whole country, and to lay it before her Majesty in an humble address. This was put to the question and passed in the negative or rather according to the method here, Delay or Proceed, and carried—Proceed.

Then the main question was put:—

Approve the second article or not approve, and carried "approve" by a majority of fifty eight. Thus in Parliament things go right enough, but really everywhere else the nation is in strange confusion, and the threatenings of the Church party are very high and plain.

The rabble at Glasgow has driven the Provost out of the town, and he is fled hither; the reason was he would not address. They have sent up their Address and a great many whose hands are to it have sent up letters to the Lord Chancellor, that they were forced to sign it against their minds; yet the address was received and read, the Provost flying for his life. They have broken up his house and plundered or defaced his goods.

The lenity of the Government is taken as fear, and the Kirk is stark mad that they have, as they say, no security and that their Articles are rejected.

The Cameronian address, though of no great moment, I send because you should see some of the spirit, for though Hepburn that sends it is a mad man, that is mad in zeal, and has been deposed and disowned by the Kirk, yet they talk his very language now every day in their common discourse, and I dined to-day with a minister who told me were the weather permitting they would have been at Edinburgh before now with 15,000 men. They exercise their men and appear with arms and drums in Glasgow, and indeed those things tend to a strange conclusion. The next sitting of Parliament will enter on the main question, I mean the third article, and if it pass we shall see whether they dare make any disturbance or no.

I wish her Majesty would be pleased to have some forces on the border, for if there is the least violence here all will be in blood; an appearance of some regiments on the border would at least encourage the troops here, who are not otherwise to be depended on. You will excuse my presumption in offering anything that looks like direction; no doubt her Majesty will let nothing be wanting here to succour that interest which appears so hearty, and which if they are not supported will, if an accident happens, be sacrificed to all manner of the most barbarous insults.

D[ANIEL DE] F[OE] to ROBERT HARLEY.

1706, November 19. Edinburgh—I have the satisfaction to write your honour that the Parliament has now voted the third article by a majority of thirty.

I am not willing to fill you with the apprehensions of people here, nor am I very phlegmatic on that head myself, and therefore when I shall tell you that the Commissioner has been threatened with daggers, pistols &c. and now that the last two sittings being within dark he was insulted by the rabble in the street at his return—great stones thrown at his coach and one of the guards wounded—I yet shall add that I am of opinion his Grace will go through with the matter. I confess I thought it an ill concerted measure that last night the Commissioner drove through the town so hastily, the foot guards running, and the horse galloping, at which the mob hallooed and the enemy insults them, "the Commissioner was run away" &c. Indeed it betrayed too much concern, but that is not my business.

The Church has not yet done, and though in the "Review" I am defending her proceedings, which you will easily perceive I do, not that I like them, but to check the ill use will be made of it in England; yet I doubt she will go on till no honest man can defend her.

Addresses are now coming in from the respective Presbyteries in order to justify the Commission's first address, and as by the enclosed which is the first of them you will see the nature of them, so I doubt others will be worse yet. All the West is full of tumult. Glasgow is mad.

I was going to see what I could do there but met several of the honest people flying, and all advised me not to venture. So I have much against my will played the coward and made my retreat, but I think to go the next week *incognito*, if it be practicable, only to observe and be able to give you exact particulars. The Commissioner is come down from the House to-day by daylight, when they have debated but not yet voted the fourth article. They came down without any disturbance as I yet hear of.

The ministers are quieter here now than before, but in the enclosed petition or address you have two in particular who were here in the Commission, and have been in the country to procure it viz. John Bannatyne and Linning, two firebrands and who merit to be marked as incendiaries, of whose actions I doubt I shall have occasion to give you further account, and I wish they don't bring themselves to want her Majesty's mercy.

I do myself the honour to congratulate your safe arrival from the country, and especially if the waters have been equally violent as here, where it exceeds all that has been known in this age.

JOHN BELL to [ROBERT HARLEY].

1706, November 19. Newcastle—I stopped the Scotch mail till I wrote a letter to D. Fea[rns] and ordered him ten pounds which he will be very glad of, having spun out his small credit there, and the business has suffered as he tells me for want of supplies. I presume this recruit will make him easy for some time.

I also wrote to Mr. D[e] F[oe] and told him your hurry of business since you came to town would not give you time to write to him, but you would do it by next.

Mr. D[e] F[oe] knows nothing in the least from me of D. Fea[rns'] concerns in that country, and the like Mr. D. F[earns] knows as little of Mr. D[e] F[oe]'s, and this your honour may depend upon, and nobody could have kept matters more private than I have done.

A letter from each of them enclosed, which came to hand yesterday.

LORD CUTTS to [ROBERT HARLEY].

1706, November 19. Dublin—Upon application from your friend Colonel Jones—Lieutenant Colonel to Lillingston—I give you this trouble to inform you that Colonel Lillingston the last winter got my leave to go to England for a reasonable time; when he was there he found ways to make an interest to stay longer from time to time. He has never made up any one account either with his Lieutenant-Colonel or any officer of the regiment, since the first money issued out for the levying of the regiment not even for subsistence; and by his getting leave to stay in England he has been out of my power, so that I could not oblige him to accounts, or any thing else, which has made that regiment in so bad a condition. I wish you would speak with the Duke of Ormond, and my cousin Harry St. John, upon this matter, because I am informed, that Lillingston is now soliciting to get his English accounts postponed, which would be a rigorous piece of injustice to the officers of his regiment. I farther find, upon examining his clothier here, that in his halfmounting, he has not bespoke half his due complement (which we supply by interposing the orders of the Government), and that he has obliged his clothier to give him a note under his hand not to pay the off-reckonings of the officers' servants to the officers, but to him, which we have likewise overruled besides many other severe, irregular, and arbitrary steps too long to trouble you with.

I have wrote to the Duke of Ormond by this post upon this matter, and proposed Jones to have the regiment, and to pay Lillingston 200*l.* or 250*l.* a year : which would be just, since Lillingston don't go, and much for the Service.

JEAN GASSION [*alias* OGILVIE] to [ROBERT HARLEY].

1706, November [19-]30 N.S. Paris—Since I had the honour of yours from our friend at Hamburg I have written to you wherein I desire you to let me know if my letter came safely to your hands. I also did give you the best information I could for the encouragement of your wagers but of late there is nothing to be relied on for the measures of the Court is so changeable that they alter every week, for to be plain with you who is our friend they are in a confusion. We have no money, our troops unclothed and ill paid are in a very bad condition, so what measures will be taken God knows for paper notes will not go for the merchants at Paris lock up their shops, no credit ; for when a Colonel comes and demands cloth for his regiment the merchant tells him plainly paper notes will not pay his creditors so he had rather shut up shop. Therefore I am afraid our army will not be clothed this year, there is vast multiutdes of militia to be raised this year, but they are not clothed. They talk we are in a treaty with the Swiss for 50,000 men, and some think we will reduce Barcelona with the Duke of Orleans' army before we go into Italy, but as to the truth of this I cannot be positive, Were I in a condition to live at Court I could better judge of things but that is expensive and I am but poor for I have stayed there as long as I am able but it was not the right time of the year ; but now is the time and if you have any intention to venture on wagers you must advertise me in time that I may go and live at a place that I may learn what is matter of fact to acquaint you early how to venture your money, I believe you know how to direct to me and if you have any difficulty in it you may but give your orders to our friend in Hamburgh who will send them safely to me, be of what nature they will. I have sent you here enclosed the letter I wrote you word of 'some time ago, a copy of it I mean, and whatever measures is taken in that affair you shall be acquainted from time to time, but there is nothing to be done at this time unless there were a breach betwixt England and Scotland. I could be sent there if I had a mind but I did decline it believing I may render you more service here. I pray you let me have your advice and let me know if this hath come safely to your hand for you may judge I will be uneasy till I know that your correspondence is sure.

D[ANIEL DE] FOE to ROBERT HARLEY.

[1706, November 21 ? Edinburgh]—Since the other part I have attended the Committee ; the first false step I discovered was that the vote yesterday upon the fourth article was designed as an alteration of the article.

I took the freedom to say if they broke in upon the articles to alter the terms of them, they unravelled the Treaty and would come to the necessity of a new Commission. But that I conceived all their amendments or regulations might be brought into an Act explanatory of the articles and founded upon them, and while these explanations consisted with equality, proportions and reasonable constructions they might expect the Parliament of England would hear reason, whereas if they went on to direct alterations they would fall into inextricable difficulties and indeed dissolve the Treaty, or at least endanger it. This they all adhered to and resolved to call the vote of yesterday an explanation in the Minutes if they can, though perhaps that may be too late.

Then they desired my opinion of their demand of a drawback on peas, oats, and oatmeal, which the Northern members pressed for and the people are very clamorous about. I put them off from a bounty on oats or peas by assuring them, England will always buy them, and there could be no pretence for a drawback or bounty for exporting that which was always wanted at home. The justice of this prevailed with the Committee and so they have agreed to waive that. But on oats ground, or oatmeal, they are positive and really the reason of it. convinces me. They drive a great trade to Norway for deal and timber and they purchase them and sometimes bring silver to boot with their oatmeal.

On the other hand from Ireland they do the like and undersell Scotland, and the bounty will enable the Scots to send larger quantities— and I cannot but add (to you sir) this may help England who now trades to Norway wholly for ready money, and perhaps in time may come to save a great deal of it by supplying them with oatmeal. So their explanation on this article is to have 2s. 6d. drawback on oatmeal only per quarter. Then we had a long debate what price the oatmeal must bear, when the bounty should be due, and the price of oatmeal being an uncertain thing especially in England and hard to determine, I offered an expedient (viz.) that the prices should be stated on the whole corn. I proposed 12s. per quarter. My Lord President demanded it at 20s., Mr. Paterson offered it at 13s. 4d. and there it passed, and so the amendment will be thus : —

That a bounty of 2s. 6d. per quarter on oatmeal shall be allowed when the price of oats in the port where the said oatmeal shall be exported does not exceed 13s. 4d. per quarter. This I presume will be the work of the next meeting of the parliament, and if they get it passed as proposed and the amendments offered by way of explanation, I hope all will be agreeable to England and to the common interest.

The Committee then proceeded to the matter of the excise and very great difficulties appeared then.

They all insisted that by true proportion and the rules of equality their two penny ale here ought to pay but as small beer—but the people are uneasy and afraid to be left to the mercy of the excise office to construe the law upon them. And indeed the clamour of the people would be intolerable should the strong beer duty be demanded on their ale, which though called ale is little better than small beer, and really sells under 10s. per barrel.

However to come to a certainty they are content that the excise come up to a proportion and this they calculate at 2s. per barrel and so the people pay 9s. per barrel only to be sure, and to bring this to be offered in the terms of an explanation their Lordships put it upon me to draw it up for them against the next meeting of Parliament, which will I suppose be Wednesday. The rough of the said draft I herewith enclose your honour and wish I had time to have your opinion of it —I have done it with as much indifference and impartiality to both sides as I can, and as I see no shadow of any other medium I believe it will be approved here, and I hope in England too. The drawback on salt will be the next difficulty, and there is a strong demand for a draw-back on their pork exported for sale. I mentioned it and Mr. P[aterso]n thought I had started it for them and hinted as much after we came out, which only served to convince me he conversed with but few, since the merchants concerned are many and make a great cry about it, and I think it every man's business that wishes well to this work to allay the spirits of this agitated people, at the expense of everything that can be easily parted with.

'Tis true drawbacks and bounties will put back the equivalents, but they are but few and the consequences of denying them very great. When paid they are paid by themselves and I daresay the reasons will sway England to do any reasonable thing to make the people easy.

I wish my Lord Treasurer informed that a report was spread here when my Lord Annandale proposed the Succession with limitations instead of the Union, that there was a letter in town from his lordship to direct the accepting it—and that his lordship wondered they should not close with it at the first offer.

[Daniel De Foe] to Robert Harley.

1706, November 23. Edinburgh—In my last I gave you the Address of the Presbytery of —— and it was feared that all the presbyteries would do the like, nor do I question but endeavours have been and are still used to procure them, though I hear of no more yet come in.

The eyes of the people begin a little to open, and I had the honour to hear an Assembly man tell me yesterday he was afraid some were gone too far, and that they were to be only the cats-foot ! and he would have no more to do in it. I do not claim the honour of converting him, though he compliments me on that head. But my last Essay, which I transmitted to your honour by post, has had some effect, for Hodge's book which indeed has done more mischief than a thousand men is so much exposed now that it is grown into contempt, and a gentleman did me the honour to tell me to-day that it has stopped three Addresses which were coming out of the North, and that a gentleman reading it among about twenty that had resolved to address, they all laid it aside. I am not pleading my merit, sir, but to let you see how easily this people have been imposed upon, that a little plain arguing would bring them to reason again. I hope things begin to look a little better here. They have given some vent in the parties to the first fury and now the three first Articles are over they seem to be calmer.

At Glasgow we hear of no more tumults though here was a flying report of 15,000 men got together.

Col. Areskin is highly blamed even by his own friends for his imprudences, who being Provost of Stirling drew out the militia to sign an Address, and with his sword drawn in one hand, and his pen in the other signed it, and made the rest do so also, with some very indecent expressions which in any Government but one so mild and forbearing as this would have been otherwise resented ; but he is a malcontent and declining in his fortunes, though otherwise a very honest man.

However, these things do them no service nor has it been any help to them that Fletcher of Saltoun made a speech to tell the Parliament the trade to England was no advantage to them; or to see twenty members vote against a communication of trade with England, in which even Duke Hamilton himself abandoned them, and a very pretty proposal was offered as follows, which none of them could answer :—

Why gentlemen are you against the clause if the communication of trade be no advantage, is it not a passive article?

Cannot we let it alone, and make no use of it—the English by this article don't bind us to trade, they only lay open their trade to us, to enter into or let it alone, why should we refuse the liberty?

They go tomorrow on the fifth article, they have been debating it last sitting, and here is a mighty popular objection against [it] on account of their shipping.

· The enclosed will explain it more particularly which I wrote at the desire of the Earls of Abercorn and Sutherland and some members of the Commons, to prepare them against tomorrow's debate.

And thus I believe I must do, on every article as they come to be debated, the objections in some cases are so dull and so gross, and yet so 'puslie' on one side, and the honest gentlemen so ill informed of things here on the other, that really I blush for them sometimes, and am ashamed to instruct men, whom I thought I had not been able to inform of anything.

They have reprinted the book of rates here though it is not yet published—but I foresee they will want an exposition upon it, for many that have seen it are not one jot the wiser, and honestly protest not to understand it.

They go on calmly now, but some foresee that there will be the greatest struggle about the general, when after all the particulars are run through they shall be in danger at last in passing the general question.

On this some of the Lords that are sincere friends to it, and under some concern on that particular account, sent to me yesterday to desire I would write one Essay more, on the generals of the Union, the common interest of trade, government and religion.

· This as within my sphere and the substance of my silent commission hither (pardon me that freedom) I have accepted, with some seeming reluctance, as having raised me enemies here already &c.

If this be finished time enough, I hope it may be of service, and I shall not be sparing to disperse them, though I venture putting you to some charge, and indeed I am a chargeable messenger to you, but, if I had been to spend my own money, I profess I could not have forborne these things, and for the sake of the public service should have ruined myself.

If I am too forward, I beseech you, sir, restrain me by your orders, for I have no other uneasiness. I seek the service by the directest methods I am master of. If I err the misfortune will be mine, but indeed, indeed (*sic*) sir, want of instructions is a melancholy reflection, and makes me frequently think myself an unworthy instrument.

· *Postscript*—I cannot but hint my own misfortunes to your remembrance, and by you to her Majesty's goodness, as you were pleased to give room to expect.

JOHN BELL to [ROBERT HARLEY].

1706, November 23. Newcastle—Has received letter of 19th inst., with one enclosed to Mr. D[e] F[oe], which had been forwarded to him under cover to a friend. Incloses a letter received this day from Mr. D. ff[Fearns], to whom the same friend had paid ten pounds. Hears his matter about the post office is over and settled by the Lord Treasurer's order.

D[ANIEL DE] F[OE] to [ROBERT HARLEY].

1706, Nov. 26. Edinburgh—I cannot express to your honour what a cordial the favour of your letter was to me. After such a strange and surprising silence I thank God, my faith in your regard to me was too firmly fixed to suffer me to neglect my duty, but I own I have been under perplexity and discouragements innumerable. I shall trouble you no more with them.

My success here I am in hopes will answer your expectation, though the difficulties have been infinite. If no Kirk devils more than we yet meet with appear, I hope all will be well, and I begin to see through it.

If I understand the cautions you are pleased to give me in your letter, they respect England as much as Scotland, and indeed I am afraid of erring most that way, and am therefore very wary.

Though I will not answer for success, yet I trust in management you shall not be uneasy at your trusting me here.

I have compassed my first and main step happily enough, in that I am perfectly unsuspected as corresponding with anybody in England.

I converse with Presbyterian, Episcopal - Dissenter, Papist, and Non Juror, and I hope with equal circumspection. I flatter myself you will have no complaint of my conduct. I have faithful emissaries in every company, and I talk to everybody in their own way, to the merchants I am about to settle here in trade, building ships &c.; with the lawyers I want to purchase a house and land to bring my family and live upon it. God knows where the money is to pay for it !

Today I am going into partnership with a member of Parliament in a glass house ; tomorrow with another in a salt work, with the Glasgow mutineers I am to be a fish merchant, with the Aberdeen men a woollen, and with the Perth and Western men a linen manufacturer, and still at the end of all discourse the Union is the essential, and I am all to everyone that I may gain some.

Again I am in the morning at the Committee, in the afternoon in the Assembly. I am privy to all their folly, I wish I could not call it knavery, and am entirely confided in.

You'll pardon me this excursion on myself ard bear with this allay to it, that I really have spent a great deal of your money and am like to do more. Yet perhaps not so much as by Mr. Bell's account, since he sent me in his last more and sooner than I expected, of which however I am not the worse husband and have about 20l. yet in hand, though the press drains me and I am something behind to it.

I assure you, and entreat you to believe me I am not in anything extravagant in this sharping dear place, but where the design I am in presses me then indeed I am not sparing. My own affairs I have recommended to you but too often, and had not mentioned them now though severely pressed there, only to assure you I cannot relieve them from hence ; though my wife wrote me last week she had been ten days without money. I submit it all to that Providence which when he sees good will smile, and till then I must wait.

I shall strictly observe your directions and act with the utmost caution in every thing.

The regulation of the clause about foreign ships has passed against the scheme I offered, but I shall take the first occasion with my Lord President to set them to rights in method.

While I wrote the above I am sent for by my Lord Cessnock to the Committee, where I understand Mr. Paterson is to be also. Though I never saw him there yet the result I shall add to this, that gentleman is full of calculates (*sic*), figures, and unperforming numbers, but I see nothing he has done here, nor does anybody else speak of him but in terms I care not to repeat.

WILLIAM COWPEN, Lord Keeper, to [ROBERT HARLEY].

1706, November 26—As he cannot attend the Council on Thursday has sent the lists of Welsh sheriffs to Mr. Blathwayt. Mr. Townsend should not be nominated Sheriff for Denbigh, ■ case the three on the list are excused; he has, Lady Russell states, but 100*l.* a year to keep a wife and five children.

The COUNT DE BRIANÇON to [ROBERT HARLEY].

1706, November 26—Asking that the term within which William Carrell had been ordered to leave England, might be extended for two months and that he would give security for his good behaviour during that time. *French.*

The EARL OF STAIR to [ROBERT HARLEY].

1706, November 26. Edinburgh—It is neither to the honour of the treaters nor so safe for the treaty to have alterations, but indeed it is absolutely necessary to carry along our friends who are not disinclined to the Union, and I hope they shall be so managed as not to break squares. 'We have made good progress of late, but it will be impossible to get all finished before January. I believe your Parliament cannot now be forced or delayed, nor can you take the Union much under your consideration till it is finished here, but the material articles being ratified, the occasion for the Queen's laying it before the Parliament and the necessary supplies for the next year will keep you in work till the recess at Christmas. What I pointed out in my last against delay was the inclination I found among the opposers and some fearful friends to have some recess until the ferment amongst us might cool. I am persuaded a recess would but increase it and break us amongst ourselves. There can never be a better disposition expected in our Parliament; for if there be no violent or open rebellion to chase us from this place, though we proceed slowly yet I am confident we shall conclude the Union in such terms as need not stick with you.

I acknowledge there's great ground to believe the opposers are so bold and resolute that they will spare no means to obstruct the ratification of the treaty, and will take off foully some persons that may be most forward, or else raise the country in arms, towards which there are too many open steps made already.

We have all the encouragement we can wish from Her Majesty and her ministers there by their firmness to the measure, but I could wish to hear of your troops in the north of England and Ireland, for it encourages our enemies to think you have none near. And though the officers of our few forces are gentlemen of honour, yet the continets (*sic*) may be tainted with popular apprehensions, and the belief that after the Union they shall either be disbanded or sent to the plantations; and if the country should rise, they are few, exposed without help or hopes of relief. It is easier to stifle ill inclinations than to reduce open rebellion upon popular sentiments, therefore I long to hear of the troops; and upon the arrival of the Duke of Marlborough I doubt not they are ordered to march. For the first effect of the country's rising would be to chase us home, and the balking of the Union at this time may be an irreparable loss to this nation, and to the liberty of Europe and our religion.

[Daniel De Foe to Robert Harley].

1706, Nov. 28. [Edinburgh]—I have the honour of your second letter with the enclosed paper of observations, which I have transcribed and here returned according to your directions, and shall not fail to observe the cautions you were pleased to give me.

The gentlemen kept me so late the last post night that I closed your letter in some confusion, the post being just going, else I had sent this paper back that night.

I observe by these papers it is expected the Parliament here should pass the Articles entire.—I fear they will never be able to do that, but as I wrote you in my last they will only make their demands and explanations in an Act of Parliament which they will annex to the Union. It is my daily business to convince them and remove new started difficulties in this case, and if it had not been my good fortune to be there that night they had blindly gone into direct modelling the Articles.

The Parliament has been two days upon the sixth article, and have at last referred it back to the Committee, where I shall have some more opportunity to debate it with them. I gave you an account what I had done in the several cases of the oatmeal, which I hope the Parliament will confirm, but they have altered the rate of oats from 13s. 4d. to 15s. per quarter in the standard of price.

I have also proposed a modicum by which I put them off from laying any duty or prohibition on oats from Ireland—not that it signified much but that I avoid loading the case with amendments. I had a great tug about this trifle, for they would have 16s. per quarter on their groats or oatmeal, and 8s. per quarter on the oats, which must then have been altered in England.

Looking in the book of rates it appears that in England there is 5s. per quarter on oats now as imported from Ireland.—This I showed them was sufficient still and might stand for the whole island only with this addition—that every quarter of groats or oatmeal shall be deemed as three quarters of oats, within the said Act.

This, I believe, will pass; the house today has been warm upon the drawbacks on oats and peas, but the gentlemen of the Committee stood their ground on my notion of there being always a market in England.

I omitted enclosing the draft of my proposal for the excise, for they kept me so long I had not a minute for the post. I ask your pardon for the omission and have sent it herewith.

This terrible people the Churchmen have not yet done, they have now in debate a protestation against the Act of Security as insufficient.

God Almighty open their eyes !

Also here is a protestation today from the West, where they burnt the Articles. I shall get a copy of it to send per next post. I am sorry to see in the paper you enclosed me that all the amendments seem to be desired here to be referred to the Parliament of Britain. I daresay the gentlemen here would come in to it, but should they attempt it the whole Treaty will be lost. The very word, Parliament of Britain, is grown terrible here and the people are so foolishly possessed with their having no justice there that 'tis to say nothing to attempt it. On the other hand the entering into those few amendments or explanations mightily quiets and eases the minds of the people especially of the wiser sort.

I take this liberty on two accounts :—First, that I may have your orders that if I must not go on to lessen their demands, or put them off from some by granting others, and the like, but insist plainly that they must pass the Articles and refer the rest &c. I may know how to obey you punctually—but then I beseech you to bear with me in saying all the interest here would never carry the Union without blood.

Secondly I offer this, that if you incline as I hope you will in England to grant the heads, I daresay they shall be trifles, and I hope to put them off from a great deal that they now insist upon.

Postscript—I could not refrain sending you a piece of my Lord Belhaven's poetry in answer to the Ballad.

I daresay you will believe it a mere original, and I believe he may challenge all the world to match it or to answer it.

You will also see by it, I have managed so in the Ballad that he does not suspect it, but believes it my Lord Haddington. The Doctor he means is your next neighbour, Dr. W——d. This morning I put abroad privately the enclosed lines upon it also. The Ballad is printed.

[SIR THOMAS MANSELL to ROBERT HARLEY.]

1706, November 28. Margam—I can never believe you would put me upon anything that was not right, and though I had no intention nor inclination to mention my father's death yet I have done it to both, because I intend to kiss your hands in three weeks, which I suppose none can think a long time considering what affairs I have here.

JOHN BELL to [ROBERT HARLEY].

1707, November 29. Newcastle[-on-Tyne]—I wrote you by last post that I would pay Mr. De Foe one hundred pounds which will be done without fail.

Your honour is pleased to take notice of my affair in the Post Office, and hopes I am easy in it—for answer my masters the governors of the Post Office have taken away part of my farm and given it to the post-master of Durham to oblige Sir H. Liddell; though I believe Sir T. Frankland will put things as they were before if your honour be free in the matter.

G. GRANVILLE to [ROBERT HARLEY].

1706, November 29—I would be particular only in one request, which is that I may be permitted to keep my little government in Cornwall, notwithstanding anything else that may happen. It gives me some interest in that county which I shall know how to turn to her Majesty's service, for which reason only I am desirous not to part with it. This hint I thought necessary because I take it for granted, as inconsiderable as it is, there will be soliciting for it as soon as 'tis known there is any intention of providing otherways for me.

PROMOTIONS IN THE PEERAGE.

1706, November 29—

Earl of Kent	- a Marquis.
Earl of Lindsey	- a Marquis.
Earl of Kingston	- Marquis of Dorchester.

To be made Earls -
{
Lord Wharton.
Lord Poulett.
Lord Treasurer [inserted by Harley].
Lord Cholmondeley.
Lord Walden [inserted by Harley].
}

To be made Barons -
{
Lord Keeper [Cowper].
Sir T. Pelham.
}

The above memoranda are in Godolphin's handwriting, with the two exceptions noticed. The paper is endorsed by Harley. "Dignities, Lord Treasurer."

D[ANIEL DE] F[OE] to ROBERT HARLEY.

1706, November 30. [Edinburgh]—The Parliament has sat three times, since I wrote to you—they have passed the seventh article not in the exact terms, but on the foot of the paper I sent in my last.

I am sorry to say it, but 'tis really true the Union may be carried on and I hope perfected on reasonable explanations, never, with leaving it to the parliament of Britain; 'tis my sphere to lessen them as much as possible and in this I think I do my country good service, and this country no injury.

I am sorry to tell you the war here is begun, the Glasgow men, a hundred only very well armed, are marched, and two hundred are to follow ; the Stirling men, Hamilton men and Galloway men are to meet them.

Expresses coming in today of this the Privy Council, who had yesterday ordered a proclamation against them, have despatched a body of dragoons to meet them, and I must own the well affected people here attend the issue with great uneasiness. I had heard of the West countrymen's resolutions and purposed to have gone among them myself, but the Committee calling every day for me; I thought myself able to do more service here—and Mr. Pierce whom you know of offering himself, I sent him with my servant and horses, with some heads of reasons if possible to open their eyes. He is very well known among them and very acceptable to their ministers who are the firebrands, and I hope may be serviceable to cool the people, if he escapes the first fury, but I confess myself in pain for him. He is sincerely zealous for the public, and will merit a pardon for what has passed, if he performs this service, whether he has success or no.

The Parliament has this day passed an Act to repeal the Act of security and discharge the musters and the appearing in arms that were made lawful before. I shall not fail to give you an account of every step on both sides.

[LORD GODOLPHIN] to ROBERT HARLEY.

[1706, November]—The Queen having given me the enclosed draft of a letter you had prepared for her to sign to the Elector of Hanover, and the Duke of Marlborough having in his letter to me desired there might be some expression in her Majesty's letter which might give rise to his desiring some troops of him, so I have presumed to offer to your thoughts the amendments in the margin which are humbly submitted.

[The SAME to the SAME.]

[Same date]—The Queen expects you will bring her the letter again
for the Elector of Hanover; but since it is to be sent to Berlin it may
be time enough perhaps to send it next post.

I am glad you are so sanguine as to think the madness loses ground.
I must own to you it frights me the more to see they can have a
strength in a matter which is not really supportable by one argument.
I am of opinion that Lord N[ottingham]'s having a Roman Catholic so
long in his family and to teach his children French, will appear a pretty
sufficient indiscretion if Le Moyne comes to be opened (*sic*) which I
doubt, if t'were but for your sake, he must be; and as for Sk[   ]r,
he must forthwith make you master of what he knows, or be treated
with all the severity the law will admit of.

SIR WILLIAM COWPER, Lord Keeper, to [ROBERT HARLEY].

1706, December 1—I did not know but your reason, of delaying the
business you write about, might continue longer, for which cause, as
well as that it was fit it should not be made public till necessary, I
forbore to make any inquiry about it, lest it should take air, before it
was agreeable to Her Majesty's service it should do so; and I would
forego anything rather than in the least endanger her service.

I would choose a town in Kent called Wingham, the land whereof hath
been for the much greatest part, and an adjacent manor, in my family since
the time of my great grandfather: but I am not so sure that 'tis not in
any other's titles, as I desire to be. I will do myself the honour to write
further to you as soon as I am sure of that matter, and give you the
instructions you command me.

WILLIAM STONOR to his nephew [   ].

1706, December 3. Brussels—It being natural for every body to
desire to spend the latter end of their days in quiet at home in their
own native country among their friends and relations, asks him to find
some friend who would recommend him to the Queen's mercy and would
procure him a licence to come and live quietly under her government.
Had not served since the beginning of the last peace, and the reason of
his first going abroad was that being a younger brother, his father dead,
and his elder brother (father of the person addressed) also, he was obliged
to try what fortune he could find abroad, but was now wearied of roving.
Endorsed " Received from the Duke of Marlborough."

JOHN BELL to ROBERT HARLEY.

1706, December 3. Newcastle[-on-Tyne]—I beg your favour and
assistance in a matter which I think is my right. I have been Postmaster of Newcastle, South and North Shields ever since the Revolution,
and in the infancy of it was very serviceable to that interest at my own
hazard, as Mr. William Carr who was then in this town can give you
an account.

I farm the by-letters of the Postmaster-General for which I paid
twenty-four pounds a year for several years; then they raised me to
thirty pounds. Several attempts have been made by Sir Henry Liddell
and Mr. Robert Ellison, his son in law, to wrest part of the benefit of

my farm out of my hands, not with design for the public good or for the benefit of the people of South Shields in general, but for a private end of their own—the obtaining it for the Postmaster of Durham who had married Sir H. Liddell's maid. They had made two former efforts to effect this, and now ventured on a third by a representation to the grand jury of Durham, copy of which is enclosed, and of my answer thereto. Sir Henry Liddell being now in town will push the matter with all imaginable expedition.

WILLIAM BORRETT to [E. LEWIS].

1706, December 7. Inner Temple—The Sessions at the Old Bailey are over. Susanna Gough is continued till the next, but Thomas Joy is discharged, as also Le Moine de Brie notwithstanding the Common Serjeant was told he was a spy and an alien enemy. I have however continued them in Newgate till Monday next, that Mr. Secretary may consider what he will please to have done with either of them. I gave you a caution long ago not to commit spies or such persons to a prison of gaol delivery.

D[ANIEL DE] F[OE] to [ROBERT HARLEY].

1706, December 7. Edinburgh—In my last I gave a particular of the increasing rabble at Glasgow, which grew to that height that the Magistrates and honest townsmen pressed for some soldiers to be sent with all speed, and Finly, one of the leaders of the mob, boasted he would be at Edinburgh in two days. You will please to observe this Finly is a mean, scandalous, scoundrel fellow, carried arms in Dumbarton's regiment, and a professed Jacobite, and I believe that is one reason the Cameronian people, though equally disaffected would not join him, at least not so as to march from Glasgow or from their other towns.

I think I noted in my last how the prudence of the Duchess Dowager of Hamilton prevented their assembling at Hamilton, and I am sorry to tell your honour that thirteen ministers of parishes in their several pulpits read the paper handed about for their assembling.

They excuse it here by saying it was only a legal summons for the people to muster and exercise, as by the Act of Security they might do, and by custom used to do. But I say no more, their best friends here are ashamed of it—they did not meet it seems, for the Duchess of Hamilton having received the proclamation and Act of Parliament sent orders to all the places in her country and particularly to her own tenants not to meet upon any terms, and particularly threatened her own tenants with dispossessing them, if they presumed to appear in arms ; had his Grace, the Duke, behaved like this, matters had not come thus far.

Wednesday night, the detachment of dragoons which went from hence with the horse grenadiers of the guards and a second detachment who marched out of Fife by way of Stirling bridge were ordered to march all night with the utmost expedition to Glasgow. We had several reports of action happening between them, and that the mob having taken possession of the Castle at Glasgow had killed several of the dragoons. But this is contradicted.

'Tis true they have kept a court of guard in the Bishop's house, which is the remains of an old Castle, but I cannot think they will defend themselves there. We expect the event here with great impatience.

The Parliament have been today on the article of the malt tax, and have made a determination, which I like the worst of anything they have done. Not that I think it material in its nature, but that 'tis an absolute breaking in upon the Articles and to me a breach of the equality which is the foundation of the Union.

They put it first, whether Scotland should be exempt from it for a certain time, or for ever, and carried it only for a certain time by a majority of thirty; then after a long debate it was put whether the time should be for seven years as in the Salt, or *during the War*, and with great difficulty it was carried for the latter; and this was so nice a turn that the House was equally divided, and my Lord Chancellor's vote carried it.

I need not tell you the long argument to prove that Scotland cannot bear this tax, the only argument I saw of any force was this, that the malt here is very ordinary and does not produce equal with the English—but when I alleged two things to the gentlemen here—

(1) Why then do you demand equal bounty on exportation, and
(2) that the malt in England used only for distilling is worse than theirs, and pays the full—

they knew not what to say.

I cannot help saying that these tumults and terrors have brought all this mischief on, and 'tis impossible to avoid the amendments.

I hope some expedient will be found in England to bear with them, for the yet greater benefit of the whole, and that her Majesty will be the great intercessor between the Nations that these things shall not break a Treaty of so much consequence.

Postscript—The Dutch fleet is just arrived, and with them near two hundred men, officers and servants for recruits, which is some help to us here.

The above was written, but by a mistake kept too late for the last post, for which I ask your pardon, but make amends in part for it by adding that this short war is, God be praised, at an end. The detachment of dragoons are come back from Glasgow, and while I am writing this they are marching by the door with Finly and Montgomery, the two leaders of the Glasgow rabble, whom they seized in Glasgow without any resistance, and all things are restored there, and by this stroke I hope all is at an end.

The Church also begin to face about again, I wish they had been wise enough to have done it sooner. Last night they concluded upon a letter in the Commission of the Assembly to be written to the several Presbyteries, to exhort them to use their endeavours in their several districts to persuade the people to peace, and to prevent all tumult and disorders.

The draft is not finished but I hope to have a copy of it against next post.

D[ANIEL DE] F[OE] to ROBERT HARLEY.

1706, December 7. [Edinburgh]—The enclosed [*i.e.* the preceding letter of same date] was wrote at three essays, and yet I am obliged to add a fourth.

Since all the proceeding of the forces at Glasgow of which you see the issue in the enclosed, the mob has been up there again as furious as ever. I confess I thought it a wrong step to let the dragoons quit the town again so soon. As soon as they were come away the rabble rose again and took all the magistrates prisoners and declared that if their two men were not restored and sent home again, they would treat the magistrates just in the same manner as they should be treated.

They took the parole of some of them, and let them go to Edinburgh to solicit, and they were here as soon as the prisoners. What the issue of their solicitation will be I know not, but I suppose they will force the Government to hang these two men and to send the dragoons back again. Of everything that occurs you will depend upon an exact account.

My Lord H[alifa]x has not given the return his Lordship promised my brother to the letter I sent, so I have not wrote since, but whoever I write [to] you may depend entirely on my absolutely concealing that anything but my own affairs drove me hither.

Postscript.—If you please to convey to me in a letter the draft of your coat of arms, I will only use it to make you a small present of the manufacture of this country.

D[ANIEL DE] F[OE] to [ROBERT HARLEY].

1706, December 9. Edinburgh—I sent you an account last post of the taking of Finly and Montgomery, the two ringleaders of the Glasgow rabble, and their bringing into the Castle here.

They had no sooner brought them away but the rabble rose again there, took the magistrates prisoners and sent some of them hither, assuring them if they did not procure their two men again they would burn their houses &c. The foolish men frightened with the rabble were here as soon as the prisoners. They have been, I hear, today before the Council, who as they very well deserve, bid them go home, and take better care of the peace of the city; for that must be owned, had they timely done their duty, these rabbles had been suppressed before they came to a head. I suppose these foolish people will force the Government to hang those two miserables.

Finly behaves very haughty and positive, declares himself a Jacobite, talks of dying and I believe expects no other. The other, I hear, has a pen and ink allowed him, and perhaps may tell some tales. The Committee of Council have been three times (or the Lord Register from them) to examine them; what has passed there, I presume you will not expect I should be able to acquaint you of.

The Committee of whom I have often hinted have been to-day on the Salt.—The other party insists on having 10s. per barrel instead of 8s. 4d. drawback on white herring.

I was sent for and took upon me to oppose it, first I convinced them even by their own account that 8s. 4d. which is allowed in England was 1s. 8d. more than the salt came to which cured the fish, and was clear gain to the importer. Then I undertook to prove that, on a new demand, the same drawback being allowed in England would increase our fishing so much as to make us rival them, and perhaps supplant them in all the Straits trade, and so lessen the encouragement of their fishery, which was much of it exported from England.

They are come to no conclusion yet, but I am to attend again to-morrow and to give in my reasons in writing and my calculation of the duty and the drawback.

I obtained copy of their resolution or report rather on the Customs, which is pretty enough, and I believe will please you; they are all very honest hearty gentlemen, and zealously for the Union.

I am your humble and earnest petitioner not to let it be known that you have this copy from me. It would so lessen my esteem among them, that I should be very ill-used by them, and no more consulted with on any occasion.

I have also estimates of the respective customs on goods here, to which I am to draw farther replies, and to present them at the next sitting.

These things take me up some time, and indeed made me lose the post for my last letter for which I again humbly ask your pardon.

If you will please to give me any hints in the things now before them, and whether you approve my endeavouring to lessen their amendments, it will be very useful and encouraging in this matter to me particularly.

I am printing a single sheet entitled a Letter to the Glasgow men, but which I presume may be useful to all the rest to open their eyes a little; it is not out of the press tonight, so I shall not be able to enclose it till next post.

Mr. Bell writes me I must write to you for farther orders, if I make any more demand on him. I have not yet made any demand nor shall not as long as I have any thing left; but then if you do not permit me to do it, I shall pass my time very ill here, and be worse as to return.

I hope you will please to approve both of my work and of the expense when I render you my account, and that in the meantime you will please to recall me in time, when you do not think fit to subsist me any longer. I have, I confess, spent you a great deal of money here, and it is the most expensive place I was ever in.

But indeed that has not been my expense, I have laid out myself and your money in the true service I came here for, and I flatter myself, I have been useful.—I earnestly wrote to you, to be limited in my expenses, and I would not have exceeded, and I have not been the larger for the liberty you have given me.

I have had 75l. and a horse of Mr. Bell and I have just thirteen guineas left, about six of which I propose to lay out, for the effectual spreading this letter at Glasgow, and over all the West, and therefore purpose to print about 2500 of them and send them to Glasgow, Lanark, Hamilton, Stirling and Dumfries. I beg you will please to signify your mind about expenses, and if you think me too forward you need but a word to restrain me. I'll stop immediately, otherwise I am every day saying something in print that exposes these people here, and encourages the thing.

I earnestly entreat your thoughts about the salt, the drawbacks I mean, and about the Committee's report.

LORD WALDEN to [ROBERT HARLEY].

1706, December 9—Enclosing a list of the titles he had made choice of, by a gentleman who would satisfy Harley that none of them were in any family whatever. *Enclosure wanting.*

The BOROUGH OF LEOMINSTER to ROBERT HARLEY.

1706, December 12—Understanding that boroughs and market towns are to have a preference in the Queen's Bounty to the clergy and that a distribution thereof will shortly be made we presume to address you on behalf of this place, where the maintenance for a minister is by much too slender an encouragement for a man of parts and industry, and such a one the largeness of our town and parish requires. *Seal.*

D[aniel De] F[oe] to Robert Harley.

1706, December 12.   Edinburgh—Since my last nothing material has happened, the house sits diligently on the report which I sent you last post.   The Glasgow magistrates received a check from the Government, as they deserved (for really they have been too accessory to all this mischief) and are sent home, and there is no more done with the prisoners yet.   The paper I mentioned in my last about the Glasgow men I send you enclosed, 'tis a plain but course (*sic*) expostulation, and they flatter me it has done a great deal of service here.

I foresee a great debate will arise here about settling a Court of Appeals, and I enclose you a paper on that head.   I wish I could have your opinion on the subject, because I fear something to be offered here that may be erroneous in fundamentals viz.

· A Court of Appeal in Scotland will be insisted upon to be established here.   If it be composed of Peers, they will object for they dare not trust their own Lords.   If of Commons how will it consist with the Lords being the sovereign judicature ; if there is no Court of Appeal at all they will either be forced up to England with their causes, which will be intolerable, or they will have the Lords of the Session be a Sovereign Judicature, which seems still worse.

I may do much in stating this case having some notions of the matter which I digested before I thought of coming hither—but I entreat your directions in this case as far as you think convenient.

Postscript—The post is miscarried to-day, the weather is so bad, and snow so great ; there is no travelling.

The Parliament have granted to-day an equivalent to the breeders or keepers of sheep for their not exporting wool to France and other parts. I suppose they are to pay it themselves.

· D[aniel De] F[oe] to Robert Harley.

1706, December 14.   Edinburgh—This post affords me very little matter worth a letter, the Parliament has not sat since Thursday, and the Commissioner being each day on the Committee in person I have not been sent for.

The present close debates are about the drawbacks on salt, and an encouragement of 20s. per last on exporting fish, which they will allow to the merchant out of the money from England.

The hopes of tumult and noise being over, the designs are now if possible to argue them into something that they think may shock England.   I am as watchful on this as I can on all occasions.

The rabble at Glasgow are not yet quiet, though not so dangerously uneasy as before.   However, the Government has thought fit to order a detachment of foot and dragoons to march thither to protect the magistrates.

Postscript—By the enclosed you will see a little more of the temper of the West.

D[aniel De] F[oe] to Robert Harley.

1706, December 16.   Edinburgh—I have not the honour of any from you lately, the Treaty goes on here in Parliament pretty well, my fear is the clogging it with amendments.   As I hinted in my last the rabbles and noise of the party have pushed them upon amendments and there was no possibility to avoid it.   Now the diligence of the party is employed if possible to bring them to agree to such amendments as they know the English cannot comply with. Thus the party would fain have drawn them into an allowance for exporting wool. I told them it was declaring against the Union, and they had as good do nothing; even the Committee, some of them too much interested, seemed to stagger in it, but at last came to resolve against it and to have a satisfaction to the sheep masters in the room of it.

The sixth article is passed today with an addition to the drawback on fish 20s. per last, and a licence to salt the provisions for ships on inland trade with their own salt paying English duty.

I confess the alterations are numerous and confused but I take them hitherto to be not very considerable and none of them fatal to the Union in general.

Here is a Church dispute started in private by some ministers to me, for they take me for their friend, and I am so, more to their interest than their management; but it is serious and considerable, and I entreat your private judgment for my government, for a Committee of the Assembly are to meet me privately upon it.

Their request is honest, and if I can have a favourable answer, they will depend much on it, and it will reconcile a great many to the Union, and they believe I have interest enough in England to lay it before the Queen, and before such great people (they do not guess who) as may be of service to them.

If the Union goes on, say they, the Queen is declared Queen of Great Britain, the Coronation Oath must be altered and the subjects must renew their oath.

If the oath be imposed upon us the Ministers half of us will be turned out of our livings, if we cannot swear to a Queen of Britain as on the foot of the Union, for that is swearing to episcopal magistracy and swearing to the Union. Now though we can acquiesce and be passive in a Union with Prelacy yet to swear to it is an active subjection, and we cannot do it, our national oath is direct upon us and we must be undone rather than submit to it.—We have sworn to the Queen, and we will keep it inviolably to the last drop, but the other is against our consciences and we cannot do it. Nay, if as Queen of Scotland, her Majesty should require us to take the same individual oath of allegiance over again, we could not do it, for having sworn already, to do it again would be multiplying oaths, which we hold sinful and could no more do it, than marry or baptize twice over.

The next thing is the abjuration oath, if this be imposed upon them in the terms as now worded in England, there are not ten ministers of the Kirk will hold their places, and the confusion will be incredible.

The case is this—The oath expressly says, or the Act, for I have them not here, that the successor must conform to the Church of England, now for them to abjure any successor but such as shall be of the Church of England, is to join in excluding their own Church from the succession —which they say is not reasonable, nor can they in conscience comply, but they are content no person shall succeed that is not a protestant, and they desire the general term protestant may be allowed, or else they can never abjure.

Thus I have stated their questions, I assure you the persons proposing them are sober wise and judicious friends to the Union, and solicitous for the general quiet, hearty zealous promoters of her Majesty's interest, and the succession ; but scrupulous to a nicety about oaths, episcopacy and such things as those.

I give you their own words, and as near as I can do not alter—I beseech you assist me with your thoughts. I know nothing in this country in which I may be able to render her Majesty equal service as in this, and the turn it will give to the opinion of the priests will be unexpected—and indeed their management has done incredible injury to the case.

Some medium I hope will be found out, and I beg your thoughts whether it may not be in England rather than here, because to do it here would start such a cloud of scruples as will alarm all the clergy here and especially in the West, and may endanger a real commotion. The people who have broke this to me are few and have promised to keep it private if possible to have it remedied, and if it be you gain the whole body of ministers at a blow. You will pardon my warm way of expressing it. I confess I am concerned in my thoughts that some way may be found out to make them easy.

D[ANIEL DE] F[OE] to ROBERT HARLEY.

1706, December 17. Edinburgh—Since the enclosed [*i.e.* the preceding letter] we are informed the dragoons who we thought went to lie in Glasgow to keep the peace there have been to apprehend some persons who, upon the confessions of the two prisoners they have here, are accused of being principals in the tumult here.

We are told they have taken seven, who they are I cannot yet learn, but a party of dragoons being detached this day we suppose it is to receive the prisoners and bring them hither.

My messenger is not yet returned from the West, we hear the people have been gathering a little in Galloway and the West but nothing considerable. I again recommend the case enclosed to your thoughts.

D[ANIEL DE] F[OE] to ROBERT HARLEY.

1706, December 19. Edinburgh—I wrote you a long letter last post, relating to the Kirk and the uneasiness of the ministers. I doubt my account was something confused.

I have since conversed more closely with them on that head, and not to run out in particulars, the sum of the matter is as follows :—

(1.) The Union *as such* they are not against and some of them profess to be very willing to come into it, but they complain they are treated haughtily and at first something rudely.

The overture or act of security for the Church was hurried up only among a few. Large amendments and long considerations are in hand on account of trade, taxes &c. but matters of religion are hurried on too fast, the Commission thin and the members not come up, and all their motions or demands, public or private, received with haughtiness and contempt. As to the Bishops, they are not inclined to any opposition on that account ; other than by the formality of a Protest or Declaration to satisfy their consciences as to submitting to episcopal legislation.

From this short abridgment, I crave your pardon for the freedom of giving my opinion :—

These are a refractory, scrupulous and positive people.

It is in the power of the Government to inflame them to the last degree, and were the design their destruction, they might easily be driven into the agency of their own ruin.

On the other hand if they are managed with a little lenity and tenderness, if used kindly, you may yet have them heart and hand for the Union—and I cannot but say it is yet worth while and not too late.

I know the moderation of your honour's principles, and as it is agreeable not only to the interest but inclination of her Majesty with all her people, so I cannot but repeat it, that a little of that gentleness exercised here, instead of what has been a little too warm, would quench all this fire.

If it be needful for me to descend to some particulars perhaps nice enough for the government of this matter your orders shall be observed on the first notice by your humble servant.

I had this day again the honour to dine with the Committee at the Lord Cessnock's. The occasion was the debate to come on this day in Parliament about the salt tax. The motion they expect is either a total exemption from the duty as insupportable to the poor, or a lengthening out the term of seven years to a longer time (*sic*).

The case I doubt will go hard. I see no argument has any room on the other side, the people being so possessed of the burden that the word insupportable is in every mouth, and they run away with it without any consideration.

However, I proposed to examine what quantity of salt per head the people could expend, and so to consider whether it was really insupportable or no. It happened to be a new thought to them and I was amazed to hear even the gentlemen themselves guess that the people consumed two bushels English measure per head per annum, and it was an equal surprise to them, when on a stricter examination they came all to be convinced that less than two pecks Scots measure, which is not quite $1\frac{1}{2}$ pecks English, was the utmost they expended—and my Lord Cessnock by calling his servants found his family of twenty four did not use two pecks each per annum, not reckoning children nor strangers. On this foot they think themselves furnished for the debate at least better than they were before.

But just as they were preparing to go into the House they are all in a surprise at an unhappy accident which happening this morning, kept the Commissioner back till near one o'clock, a duel fought in the Park this morning between the Duke of Argyll and the Earl of Crawford. The quarrel it seems was trifling, from a bottle. I have not yet the particulars, but am told the Duke of Queensberry having some notice of their resolution took their paroles not to fight—how they have thought fit to break through that engagement I know not yet. They have neither much harm, so the hurry of it is the most. Will. Kerr, brother to the Earl of Roxburgh, was with the Earl of Crawford, and Lord Deloraine with the Duke.

The dragoons have brought several prisoners in this afternoon from Glasgow and Hamilton, among which are some of the Duke of Hamilton's servants, their names and particulars shall be in my next.

Postscript.—The House have not gone through the clause of the salt to-day.

D[ANIEL DE] F[OE] to ROBERT HARLEY.

1706, December 21. Edinburgh—I doubt I throng you with letters, the variety here affording every day fresh matter. The debate about the salt I wrote you in my last is not yet come on, the House having been embroiled on another head viz. the drawback on pork and beef.

This is an article long plotted to hamper the cause if possible.

The Committee had unwarily reported the beef and pork in one article—I must acknowledge there seemed some reason in their demand on pork of which they have a large and increasing trade from Aberdeen, only to Italy, Leghorn and Genoa; and they say shipped off 1,000 barrels there this last year, and as the pork being fed with corn is a great article of the consumption of corn, I the sooner came into it, which Mr. Paterson pretended to give me a caution for afterwards, as if I had put it into their heads. But 'tis a sign to me how little he conversed with the gentlemen concerned since it was always in their mouths every time I was with them, from the first discourse of the salt tax.

But this bringing the beef in is a most ridiculous thing, since though they have the same thing now and a bounty paid to boot, they do not nor can export ten barrels of beef a year for sale, one year with another.

If Mr. P[aterso]n represents any branch of this thing as above in my prejudice, he does me wrong, and I beg leave to be favourably construed and heard to it. I must confess I am sometimes shocked in my thoughts at the multitude of amendments here, though this is a most insignificant thing in itself, neither kingdom exporting any quantity of beef for sale.

However, the party boast of a victory and say they have secured the Union from being ever finished, and yet they carried this but by one voice, and that was Seaton of Pitmedden, an honest Whig too, and for the Union, but biassed in this case. This discovers what I wrote you before, that the present design was to load the Treaty with such amendments as they think will ruin it in its consequences, and this is the only card left to play.

The affair of Crawford and Argyll made more noise than mischief, and is all over, but the Duke has not got any reputation by it. I earnestly crave your thoughts on my last.

D[ANIEL DE] F[OE] to ROBERT HARLEY.

1706, December 24. Edinburgh—This unhappy debate about the drawback on beef and pork has held them here all this week. The case was thus. The Committee had unhappily voted it together :—No drawback on pork or beef exported for sale.

When it came to the House, the drawback on pork appeared so reasonable, there was no withstanding it, and the Vote being whole, the beef went with it. Everybody laughs at the demand for a drawback for beef when Scotland exports none for sale to any part of the world, but this trifle being carried made the party very cheerful thinking they had gained some ground, but all this proved their loss, for the very folly of the Vote brought this addition to it this day viz. That this should be subject to the Parliament of Britain—which was carried to the infinite mortification of the party.

I hear nothing more about the prisoners. There are three now in the Castle, and two belonging to the Duchess of Hamilton in the town.

Since my last I have had a long account from Mr. J. P[ierce] whom I hinted to what purpose and when I sent into the West, he has been at Dumfries and in the Highlands, has been with John Hepburn the Cameronian minister, and with some of the most resolute of that party, and I hope has been very serviceable to cooling and calming the minds of an ignorant and deluded people, and I must do him that justice I believe has been very useful.

· I have a large account from him, which I had sent you this night—But I confess myself in some disorder tonight, the account of the death of my father coming just as I was writing this.

Postscript.—Tis very long since I had any account from you whether mine come to hand.—Enclosed is the vote passed today about the salt.

John Foley, to his kinsman, Robert Harley.

1706, Christmas Day. Lisbon—The Prince of Brazil was proclaimed on their New Year's Day in very great splendour. We are making all things ready for a march through this kingdom, but our poor regiment continues still unfortunate and the Colonel was yesterday given over by his physicians.

John Philips to Robert Harley.

1706, December 26. Christchurch, Oxford—I received your present from Dr. Stratford yesterday. I suppose the Doctor deferred the payment till now that it might seem to make a Christmas box.

D[aniel De] F[oe] to Robert Harley.

1706, December 26. Edinburgh—I am unhappy in all this nego-ciation that your more important affairs permit you not sometimes to cast an eye this way and spare me the consolation of a line or two.

I acquainted you in my last I had a letter from our itinerant [Pierce], which I had not then time to abstract; I must acknowledge he has suc-ceeded there beyond expectation, and has done such service there as no man in Scotland but himself could have done, nay he has gone where no man but himself durst go at this time.

He has been at Dumfries, in the Mountains of Galloway, in the Dales and almost everywhere, he has been with Mr. John Hepburn, the Cameronian bishop, spent three days with him, and with his disciples, heard him preach and pray without intermission near seven hours to a vast congregation several of which came twenty four miles on foot to hear him. He has opened his [Hepburn's] eyes in several things, and he shows us he has been misrepresented in several others, and he authorizes me to assure you there is no danger from him unless some new artifices succeed to influence them.

Some persons of quality here and sincere for the Union, having the knowledge of his being there, have been with me for this two or three days pressing me to write to persuade him to stay there longer, being all convinced of the suitableness of the person, and the serviceableness of the design, for 'tis public here that he is in Galloway and 'tis the only place from whence any real danger is apprehended.

Indeed nothing restrains me in this case but the article of expense and having said the needful on that head I cannot add, for it is not for me to dictate to you.

If I had of my own to carry me through this affair, I would not say a word, and I fear I am too plain.

'Tis hard if the endeavour we use here (and shall I say it, the hazard of our lives, for in both cases that has been evident) in pushing on faithfully and sincerely a cause of this concern should not be supported by the Government.—And nothing has more prescribed me than when you were pleased to say it comes from yourself.

I earnestly entreat your approbation of what I am doing, and a word or two about supply, for without it, 'tis impossible for me to render you the service I strive for. I am, and shall be, as sparing as is possible.

D[ANIEL DE] F[OE] to [ROBERT HARLEY].

1706, December 27. [Edinburgh]—My last was the 26th; what the Parliament has done in the salt tax I enclosed you and that clause is since passed.

I am very sorry to see things run so heavy here. But I am sometimes afraid the worst is not passed here yet. The Court here is very uneasy and I doubt not but there is some cause for it.

I have acquainted you of the appearance of mobs and tumults and I hope they are over—but it has been observed that unusual concourse of strangers and Highlanders are resorted to town in these few weeks. At the ferries of Leith and Queen's Ferry unusual numbers of men armed and horses have been seen to come over, and some circular letters have been discovered sent privately about. This makes honest people here very uneasy, and I must own I am not without just apprehensions.

Yesterday there was a great Council at the Abbey, and to-day the Parliament met—there was no business done, but to form the enclosed proclamation, which passed not without great opposition and a protest with a number of adherers. 'Tis certain there are some secret designs on foot, what they are time and Providence alone can discover.

In this critical juncture J. P[ierce] is returned. I cannot attempt to give you the history of his journey in particular, but 'tis a most unaccountable thing to think how the Jacobite subtlety had imposed upon the ignorant people there and brought them to be ready to join with almost anybody to raise a disturbance.

Hepburn, the minister, though mad man enough, declares against tumult and arms, and J. P. says there is no fear there; the worst people are about Hamilton and that side of the country and principally because they have the worst engines about them, and are daily deluded by the party of that fancy. Finly, though a prisoner in the Castle, openly drinks King James the 8th's health—and 'tis as good a thing as he can do. I have made Mr. J. P. write word of it into Galloway.

And to let you know that I leave no stone unturned in this work, I have procured letters from some dissenting ministers in England to Mr. John Hepburn, and to some of his principal neighbours, to qualify and persuade him, not to peace only, but to persuade his people to the like. After all, I assure you 'tis a very critical juncture, and things are ripening apace; it will be either a Union or all confusion in a few weeks more.

Nothing afflicts me so much as not to hear from you, or have the least hint what measures to take. I resolve not to stir, while I can with any tolerable safety be here, either in public or private—but if any disturbance happens I shall have an ill post.

My Lord Leven has appeared to-day by a friend plainly to me to desire the return of Mr. J. P. and they are sensible he has done service there, nor is there a man in town dare go there but him—and they are very jealous of those people. Upon these repeated solicitations we have agreed he shall go immediately.—Indeed I expected they would have considered that he could not be out a month with himself and two horses, for my servant goes with him, and spend for aught they know his own money.—However there was not the least mention of it—so I have furnished him for the journey out of my little stock left. I have said.

enough of that affair, and beg your pardon for it. I am satisfied you will do what you think needful.

Postscript.—The above was wrote yesterday, the consternation here increases and I see every honest man loaded with concern even in their countenances, they say there are above a hundred strangers come into town to-day. The Sheriff depute of Lanark, that is Deputy Lieutenant, issued out circular letters for assembling, they say he sent sixty nine letters. I have removed my lodging, for I have been openly threatened to be the first sacrifice.

JEAN LEBRUN [*alias* OGILVIE] to [ROBERT HARLEY].

1706 [   ]—I forget to tell you last night that there was a man ordered to go and sound the Duke of Hamilton to know what might be expected from him and also to make him great offers-in case he would be hearty in the affair, one of them was to make him Duke of Chatellerault in France as his predecessors was before him ; but his answer was that he was for having of the young man restored, but before that he would come to any resolution he would be satisfied of what he had to trust to, in the first place what force the King of France would send them and what money, what artillery, in short everything. In the next place he would know who in England was in their party and what might be trusted too from them. The messenger that was sent could not satisfy him in either, therefore he and the rest fell upon this expedient, that my Lord D[rummond] should be spoken with to see if he would undertake to go in and represent all this to the King of France, being he was a man of quality and well known to them and also the Duke of Hamilton's cousin german and the Duke of Perth's son, having been educated at the Court of France and a Roman Catholic, so they did not doubt but the King of France would be entirely confident in him, and likewise they on the other hand was persuaded of his sincerity towards them and that he would persuade them of nothing but what was matter of fact ; but after all he was not very fond of the employment or thought it would expose him too much to go in, therefore the Court was consulted to see if they thought it proper, but what their opinion was you saw by the letter to me last night. There is several gone and come since to them but it is impossible for me to know anything of their affairs unless I go to Scotland, but that I cannot do until I return from Pomerania, then I make no difficulty but to dive to the bottom of the whole affair. You'll see by the Countess of Erroll's letter that I did give you last night that she hath a good opinion of me, she calls me the bearer, if you took notice what I did tell you last night I believe it is not needful to repeat it over again since you put down the heads of all ; so I pray you to consider what you would have me to do that I may be gone, for if I stay long here all will be spoiled, and besides I may lose my life at my return and do neither the Queen nor you any service. You promised me to send me some money to send to my poor unfortunate family, I wish you would do it soon for their misery presses me to the very soul. You see their conduct at St. Germain to promise me great things when there, and after they had sent me upon their business to suffer my poor wife and children to starve ; it is a wonder to me what they think I am made of, if they think that I have a heart or soul in me, but this is the way they treat everybody and manage their affairs. They did suffer poor Canon to starve for want of bread who was one of the best officers that they had ; however I owe them no obligation never did I take any oath to them, for when the King died my heart went with him. Since I have taken the oath to Queen

Anne, I am her subject and obliged to serve her and if they will be such fools as to trust me let them take it for their pains, for I am doing my duty when I serve her Majesty; besides I have a tie of gratitude, she gave me my life when she might have taken it away, so that in my conscience I am persuaded that I do nothing derogating from a man of honour. I hope God Almighty will assist me to both serve her Majesty and you, for if you did know the will of my heart to serve you in any thing that I thought could oblige you I am certain you would be content with me. I can say no more but that I shall never disobey your commands let the risk be what it will. God bless and preserve you.

FOREIGN MINISTERS.

1706.—

The Baron de Spanheim, Ambassador Extraordinary from the King of Prussia.

Signor Mocenigo, Ambassador in ordinary from Venice.

Count Gallas, Envoy Extra-ordinary from the Emperor.

Monsieur Hoffmann, Resident from the Emperor and King of Spain.

Monsieur de Vrybergen, Envoy Extra-ordinary from the States General.

Monsieur Ronsencrantz, Envoy Extra-ordinary from Denmark.

Monsieur Leyencrona, Envoy Extra-ordinary from Sweden.

Monsieur Acunba, Envoy Extra-ordinary from Portugal.

Monsieur Giraldi, Envoy Extra ordinary from Florence.

Count Zefferini, Envoy Extra-ordinary from Florence.

Count Briançon, Envoy Extra-ordinary from Savoy.

Baron Schultz, Envoy Extra-ordinary from Lunenberg.

Monsieur Stingens, Resident from the Elector Palatine.

Monsieur Berry, Resident for the Duke of Zell.

Signor Imberti, Secretary to the Venetian Embassy.

Monsieur Vecelli, Commissioner of Trade for the Emperor.

DR. GEORGE HICKES to ROBERT HARLEY.

1706-7, January 1—Sir Andrew Fountaine hath twice asked me to let him come with me some time before he went out of town to wait upon you, when I next dined with you. He is in all respects a very worthy gentleman. I pray you let me know by Mr. Wanley when I may bring him to wait upon you. The day obliges me to wish you a most happy new year.

D[ANIEL DE] F[OE] to ROBERT HARLEY.

1706[-7], January 2. [Edinburgh]—I wrote you at large last post. The fears we were there in vanish apace. I have, *incognito*, got into the company of some of the people who came here on the design I mentioned. They own the design was to have gone in a body to the Commissioner and then to the Parliament and demanded an answer to their petitions. They do not deny that if the people had taken that occasion to have risen they would not have been ill-pleased, nor, I suppose, backward to encourge them all they could. But I do not find they were very forward to venture their own heads in the fray; and this balks all their designs, for I observe they are like the Pharisees in the gospel, that bound heavy burdens on other men's shoulders but would not touch them.

Some of them I understand are gone away again; and indeed the dearness of this place, where people pay from 2*s*. to 5*s*. a night for nasty lodgings, would soon make them weary of their attendance; and their private discourse is of addressing the Queen. I was glad when I heard that, but cannot imagine what they can ask of Her Majesty or what they can have the face to say for their cause.

The Union meantime proceeds apace, and this day they past the 16th, 17th and 18th articles about coin, weights, and measures.

I wrote you at large about the Kirk. I hope, though you do not think fit to reply to me, you will take that case in thought. They are now on an act to be proposed to the House to put a test upon all Englishmen engaging places in Scotland equivalent to that in England.

If nothing better can be found out for me, I could wish you will please to settle me here after the Union. Perhaps I might do her Majesty a service of one sort while I was in an office of a different face, but of that hereafter.

H. [COMPTON], BISHOP OF LONDON, to [ROBERT HARLEY].

1706-7, January 3—Your last has so amazed me that I know not well what to say to you. I am ready to lay down my life for her Majesty's case, but what can I do? Justice and honour constrain me still to implore the Queen's consideration. If it had been upon my own account I had obtained this promise from her, my own unworthiness might be a reasonable motive to have sunk quietly under the disappointment; but when the promise was obtained upon the just account of a retribution of a public service without the least regard to any private interest of my own, it is a bond too heavy for me to discharge. And therefore whatever her Majesty is pleased to lay upon me I must lie down and be crushed; though whilst I have health I shall ever pray for her long life and prosperity, and bewail my own undeserved misfortune.

Postscript.—Can any in common honesty, or just regard to her Majesty, press her for that for which she has already passed her royal word?

Endorsed by Harley.—" Mr. Ayloffe."

PHILIP STUBS to [ROBERT HARLEY].

1706-7, January 4. Sion College—On behalf of Mr. Tyler who had assisted the writer for a year in his care of St. Alphage, London, and the Greenwich Hospital, and who had been recommended for preferment by Mr. Westfaling.

JOHN BELL to [ROBERT HARLEY].

1706-7, January 4. Newcastle[-on-Tyne]—Enclosed is a letter just now received from Mr. D[e] F[oe], he tells me the affairs in that place are in a fair way to have another turn than what we had an account of last post.

I perceive his stay in that place may be longer than he expected, so consequently he will have occasion for more money, and so will Mr D. F[earnes] by what I perceive. I therefore beg the favour of you to give me your commands and they shall be obeyed having so much credit at Edinburgh as will supply their occasions there.

For your satisfaction I have sent you a note of what I have paid. Mr. D[e] F[oe] has had 89*l*. 8*s*. and a horse 14*l*. The last ten pounds was but lately paid him and perhaps he has not taken notice of it to you. Mr. D. F[earnes] has had 15*l.* according to the enclosed note. In all £118 8 0 which if you please to order to be paid into the Salt office or post office they will me credit on my account for the same.

Mrs. Shaftoe has had a letter from her daughter that she is got safe to London with an old woman, but what she has writ they conceal from me and are much of the opinion with the lady that the Government has sent for her. I humbly beg your pardon for troubling you with what these trifling women imagine. I wish you a good New Year.

Newcastle 1706.

The Right Honourable [Robert] H[arley] is Dr. to J. B.

October 2, paid Mr. D[e] F[oe]	-	-	-	£40 17 6
November, paid ditto in Edinburgh -	-	-	-	£52 10 6
December, paid do. in Edinburgh	-	-	-	£10 0 0
				£103 8 0
October 11, paid Mr. F[earnes]	-	-	-	£5 0 0
November, paid ditto in Edinburgh	-	-	-	£10 0 0
				£118 8 0

D[ANIEL DE] F[OE] to ROBERT HARLEY.

1706[-7], January 4. Edinburgh--I wrote you last post, that the apprehension we were under here began to vanish, the day begins to shine after all the nights of cloud and darkness we have had here. The crowd of strangers lessens amain. They had, as I am informed by some of their own friends, three private meetings and one general meeting to consult what to do.

Duke Hamilton proposed to his people to wait on the Commissioner and beg him to give them time to address the Queen, but the difficulty was how to get to him. No single man would do it, and to go in a body as they designed they knew they would not be admitted.

I am told that in one of their meetings some force was proposed, but they found themselves too weak for the attempt. At their general meeting it was offered to draw up a petition or address to the Queen, to offer the Succession and an expedient for the Union, or at least for a delay; but the Duke of Athol told them his men would not come into the succession, so that vanished. Then a protest was proposed in which was to be expressed their detestation of the Union in terms bitter enough, their being imposed upon in the Parliament, the guards and power of the Court and the bribes of English money having frightened or debauched the Parliament from their duty; that they are betrayed, bought and sold, and are to be enslaved to the English.

. I am promised a sight of the draft proposed; if I can get it, I shall not fail to transmit it per next.

In this little scheme of their affairs, I have acted a *true spy* to you, for by an unexpected success I have obtained a converse with some gentlemen belonging to the Duke of Gordon who are very frank, and I daresay the particulars above are unknown to the Commissioner himself. Their Assembly broke up without any conclusion.

. I cannot help giving you the satisfaction of letting you know that I believe the business as good as over here, and if I may yet beg a line from you, it should be for your orders, when to leave this place or how to govern myself.

I confess I have had an uneasy post here, under so many frequent fears of murder, tumult, rabble, &c.; but I resolve not to be uneasy in any of your commands. My chief uneasiness [comes from the] want of now and then a line from you, without which I am in so many doubts whether my letters reach your hand, whether my measures here please you, and the like; that indeed is very discouraging at this distance.

I shall very impatiently wait your direction about my stay here or coming away. If you please to order me away my former solicitation for a supply ends with a small order for travelling charge; and I say this to convince you that I have never solicited for any thing but the absolutely necessary disburses, and am very forward to put a stop to them. I think you will expect me to attend your orders for staying or going, and I shall do so, as a duty to the service, but when I see myself incapable of more service, I shall think very much of the charge.

The nineteenth article was passed yesterday with some amendments, relating to their own Courts, &c., which England will not be much concerned in. Today they sit on private business and I believe about fourteen days more will end the Session, and I may give you joy of the Union.

D[ANIEL DE] F[OE] to ROBERT HARLEY.

1706[-7], January 6. Edinburgh—I have little to say today but to confirm what my last hinted, that all the fears of the matter are now over on this side, and the Angus men, &c. are most of them dropped away as silently as they came. I wrote you earnestly last post for your orders about my going or staying when the Union is over here, and I repeat my request on that head, but am to acquaint you they press me here to stay a few weeks after to quiet people's minds about it.

I am to leave that wholly to you, by whose breath I would direct all my measures on this head and therefore again most earnestly entreat your thoughts on that subject. They have begun today on the twenty-second article.

The EARL OF STAIR to [ROBERT HARLEY].

1707, January 7. Edinburgh—I have not for some time offered you any trouble in our affairs, but now we have this day got over the twentieth and second article of the Treaty, and I doubt not next week we shall transmit it to you ratified by our Parliament.

The alterations were more to please some members here than considerable in themselves; they are all either consequential to what is done in England, as bounty money for exporting of oats or oatmeal when you allow the like to your grains, and to our herrings as you do to your fishes; and generally all are alterable by the Parliament of Britain or subject to its regulations, so these can create no difficulty with you. However it may well be mentioned that our Parliament continues two or three weeks, lest some of these alterations may be mistaken in your House and because the rendezvousing in arms is only suspended during this Session.

The temper of our people begins to soften, but the aversion continues unaccountably; the discoveries we make every day do inform us of dangers that I hope are prevented, but too general to be prosecuted at present.

I wish you many happy new years.

D[ANIEL DE] F[OE] to ROBERT HARLEY.

1707, January 9 (for so they write here from New Year's day). [Edinburgh]—I hope I may now give you joy of the Union, the twenty second article having passed last Tuesday night by a majority of forty voices.

Yesterday the house sat, but did no business but quarrel. The Duke of Athol had made a formal protest against the vote of the day before, so had several others, as you will, I presume, see by the minutes. The Duke of Argyll said it was indecent, illegal and irregular, the Duke of Athol defended it and reflected on the Duke of Argyll, and words rise at last to a loss of all decency on both sides, giving and returning the lie in the open Assembly. The house took it up and made them both give their words to stand by the decision of the Earl Marischal, Earl of Leven, General and Lord Errol, Constable, or to be committed, so I hope 'tis at an end. There is some expectation of another illnatured paper from the Church about an oath to be imposed upon Englishmen here, and having the honour to wait on the Commissioner last night, I find his grace is something apprehensive of it; I have since been with some of the ministers and am not out of hopes of getting it stopped.

Yesterday was a day of disaster and Scotland has lost one of the best men in the nation, I mean as to public matters. My Lord Stair was in the house and made an extraordinary speech on the debate on the twenty second article, and was found dead in his bed in the morning; he was alive at four o'clock and spoke to his lady, went to sleep and waked no more in this State. He is generally lamented, and had he died a little sooner would have been very much wanted in the house, where he was one of the most useful members in the grand affair.

D[ANIEL DE] F[OE] to ROBERT HARLEY.

1707, January 11. Edinburgh—I wrote you last post the account of the broil in the Parliament on the protests, and of the sudden death of the Earl of Stair.

The house have since been taken up upon the proposal I hinted of an oath &c.; which is thrown out. It was hatched in a private cabal of parsons and proposed to the Commission, but the ministers were prevailed on to refuse it, and I hope I may say without vanity I have been useful in that part. The rejecting it there stabbed it to the heart and though it was offered in Parliament it the sooner sunk there.

The ministers pressed hard for an explanation of the clause in the Abjuration Oath binding the successor to be in the Communion of the Church of England, and indeed it seems to me so rational that I cannot but think they ought to have it, not that ever a Presbyterian King is likely to come, but it would be hard to make the ministers abjure a Prince for being of their own persuasion, and England that dispenses with the Quakers taking it at all, and accepts their affirmation for an oath, will never scruple this; and if not done half the ministers in Scotland, and some sincere friends to the Union, and who have been very serviceable in it, will be turned out of their places, which will make here intolerable confusions.

One line from you to the Commissioner here would soften all this, and I persuade myself you will be sensible of the necessity. The Council are sitting to-day on that Article of the Kirk's representation respecting the encouraging papists, the number of popish priests, &c.

The Earl of Leven to [Robert Harley].

1706–7, January 14—My want of health has hindered me from doing myself the honour to write to you for a considerable time. I shall not now trouble you with the detail of our procedure in relation to the Treaty of Union. No doubt you have had them from time to time. I shall now acquaint you that this day we have voted and approved the last two articles of the Treaty, so that nothing now remains to be done but to pass a vote upon the whole, which I hope may be done in a few days. There's somewhat yet to be done concerning the equivalent, and relating to the proportion of the forty five Commoners betwixt the Shires and Boroughs, and also concerning the method of choosing both the Peers and Commons, but these things being what only concerns us and not England, we incline to finish the Treaty before we take those things under consideration and the rather because there may be particular concerns many of us may have in them that may occasion some difference amongst us, and for this very reason I believe those who have opposed us all along in the Union will do their utmost to prefer the consideration of the representation to everything else, but I hope they shall not be able to carry it.

I have always twice a week accounts from the country and have people there to observe what's adoing, and by all the accounts I have all is quiet and the ferment amongst them is much abated. I have been at some pains in this matter and not without success.

——— to ———

1706–7, January 15. York—'Tis the public report here that one of your most intimate friends newly created a P—r, is about marrying his son to a prodigious rich heiress of our persuasion; and that he designs to effect it by measures, though lawful, yet unprecedented in these parts; at which his and your avowed enemies (for I have heard of it from no one else) begin to raise great clamours. Perchance there is nothing in it, and I have given you an unnecessary trouble; but if it be so that he wishes it, and finds the methods of compassing it to his mind difficult, I believe I may be serviceable to him, and possibly contrive to give a fair beginning to it with her own (at least seeming) consent, to all the world; which once done the rest would admit of no difficulty. And you may be satisfied beforehand, that matters can very easily be so managed, that if they should not succeed, 'twill be absolutely impossible for anybody living ever to have the least suspicion of such a design; and you may depend upon my entire secrecy as I do on yours of what I write; which known, would do me irreparable prejudice.

I have the utmost intimacy with those that have the keeping and disposing of her. I can have all free access imaginable to her for as many weeks or months together as I please. I can place one of her own sex with her, on whom I can securely depend, and be present myself to instruct her daily how to work the young lady, without this gentlewoman's being entrusted with, or ever suspecting my real design, which I can make her believe is in favour of another person of her own persuasion, by whom she is already employed to try to procure my interest for him. I am the person in the world that will be the least suspected for such a design as this upon her. And though I know her so far prejudiced by education, that 'twill be impossible to persuade her (whilst under the eye of her guardian) to consent to this match, yet I have a thought, which improved by your friend's and your further advice, may not improbably put her into your power, by her own request; without her suspecting why, or what is designed by it. If he aims at this match, and my assistance is necessary to compass it, upon your answer I'll come up to town (if you so order me) to discourse him and you more fully about it, and receive your instructions. Though possibly you may remember me, yet should you desire a character of me, to judge how far I am fit to be trusted or employed here, inquire of either of those to whom I present my service in the enclosed. As my proffer to serve your friends here proceeds from that esteem and affection for you which your obliging behaviour wrought in me from our first acquaintance, I am satisfied you'll never suffer it to prejudice me, but will burn this, my hand being very much known.

'Twould be a satisfaction to me to know this has not miscarried. Trust no one; frank not, nor enclose yours to any here. I know your hand, and 'twill suffice that yours bears the same date and from the same place mine does.

A. LADY PYE to ABIGAIL HARLEY, at Aywood.

1706-7, January 15. Derby—I obeyed your orders about the young ladies' muffs which the gentlewoman sent up above a fortnight since. I could not get her to allow but a small matter for the feathers, she thought most of them too ordinary to use and altogether not enough for half a muff; but I suppose she wrote to them herself to satisfy and where the money might be paid. I can't say she hath all such feathers as those I sent you, but for amends makes them up much better, for we were but young at the trade when yours was sent; that if dear Cousin hath not worn it out pray bring to London (for I presume you come at spring), and I will have it made wider and wadded with a finer wool that the hairs may not come out. To make the figure exact, I fear the feathers were laid too thin. I am very glad the Auditor's lady gathers strength. My Cousin Hadley tells me poor Cousin Yates is dead, most women at her years have a release from the dangers of childbed. Sir David Hambleton had better success with my neighbour Mrs. Wilmote, who went to lie in with her Mother La Marrow, lay near three days but both mother and child like to do well.

Sir Charles and Dick returned from the Bath last week. That place is half full of company, mostly quality; it becomes a fashion to winter there. Dick was very weary of it, and won't own much benefit, but hath better looks and more flesh on his back than I've seen him have a great while.

[LORD GODOLPHIN to ROBERT HARLEY.]

[1707, January 16]—I suppose you intend to produce these papers to-morrow night. There does not seem anything very material in them, more than that the Governor of Maryland should be upon his guard.

De Foe's letter is serious and deserves reflection. I believe it is true and it ought to guide us very much in what we are doing here, and to take care in the first place to preserve the peace of that country.

D[ANIEL DE] F[OE] to ROBERT HARLEY.

1707, January 16. Edinburgh—I am now with joy to acquaint you that the Treaty of Union received the touch of the sceptre this day, and an universal joy of the friends of both nations runs through the city. The Church has made some struggles, but they are faint and opposed by the most worthy, learned, and to be valued, of their number, who deserve regard and Mr. Carstares in particular merits great consideration on that account. It is not my business to recommend persons. I wait now your instructions whether to stay or come away.

D[ANIEL DE] F[OE] to ROBERT HARLEY.

1707, January 17. Edinburgh—Since the papers I lately sent you, I have printed here two essays, one I enclose you here, the other shall be sent the next post. The business seems now to be over, but the dissatisfactions of the Kirk begin to revive, on the two following occasions, which I think 'tis very needful to acquaint you with. The Kirk especially the ministers moved for an explanation of the Abjuration Oath the thing I formerly hinted; but no notice was taken of it, nor of the following.

Just at the breaking up of the Parliament on Thursday, they supplicated again against the clause which leaves the Church of England to make any Act they shall see fit for their own settlement, and that it shall implicitly be passed without being reconsidered here. 'Tis true, as they allege, the Church may bring in some things inconsistent with, or invasive of, the Church here, or the Dissenters in England, and 'tis passed of course, and thus they make the people very uneasy about here. 'Tis true also that if the Church of England should make an Act the most reasonable in the world, and it should be brought hither to be confirmed, the whole nation would cry out murder, and the clergy roar out prelacy and the Covenant.

You will pardon my freedom of expression; they are a restless uneasy people but tender usage and cool counsels may manage them; and you are too much master of such measures to need that I add anything on that head.

I enclose you also a (piece ?) like a posthume birth brought to light just after the work was over. What possessed the man is hard to guess since he has ever since I have been here, and before, professed himself for the Union and often in my hearing declared the Church could not be safe without it. But this is an instance of the change in temper I mentioned above; the man is a worthy good man, popular in character, a great preacher, and, which you will think strange by his poetry, a man of wit, a good judge, and of a clear head; in short, he is in himself the very reverse of the pamphlets. What dark interval has possessed him at such a juncture is every man's surprise to know. But 'tis most surprising to see with what greediness the town runs with him. I shall take him to task in the best manner I can, but 'tis a tender point, and as I have studiously preserved an esteem with all his friends and which I have found very much to the purpose in what I have been doing here, so I must use him wondrous gently and shall only take him to task for his falling on the English dissenters, which indeed everybody blames him for. I shall by next post transmit you the copy of what I say to him and anything else that occurs. There was a hard pull in the Commission of the Assembly on the 14th and 15th to obtain a remonstrance to the Parliament against the things above noted, but it was carried in the negative.

DR. W. LANCASTER to [ROBERT HARLEY].

1706-7, January 21. Queen's College, Oxford — Dr. Hody the Greek professor of this University died here this morning and the nomination of one to succeed him is in Her Majesty. The salary is 40*l*. a year, and though so small would be a great assistance to a fellow of a College. If the Vice Chancellor might have leave to recommend a person eminent for knowledge in the Greek tongue, and one who would be useful to us in publishing some things in that language which would do honour to the University, both at home and abroad, I would beg you to recommend Mr. Thwaites to Her Majesty, who by the unhappy loss of his leg must all his life be confined to his studies in the University.

THOMAS ADDISON to [ROBERT HARLEY].

1706–7, January 22. Delahay Street—Recounts his past services as Collector at Whitehaven, King's searcher at the port of Carlisle, Commissioner for the hearth money and collector of excise in the four northern counties, of which he was deprived in King James's reign. With Sir John Lowther since Lord Lonsdale he had seized the arms at Workington which, with the stores and munition procured from Chester and Carlisle, had saved Londonderry. Was first Commissioner for sick and wounded seamen and for exchanging prisoners of war from July 1689 to July 1698, but had only received eighteen months' salary and was 1,800*l*. out of pocket. The considerable business which he had at Whitehaven being lost by his long absence, his small fortune much exhausted, his old friends dead, and his health impaired, he begs to be put into some useful post in England.

BARON SCHUTZ to [ROBERT HARLEY].

1706–7, January 23 — Concerning the amendments to Prince Charles's renunciation. *French.*

DR. JOHN POTTER to [ROBERT HARLEY].

1706–7, January 25—These wait on you to return my most humble thanks for the great favour offered in your last, which I should thankfully accept, but that for several years last past I have almost wholly applied myself to theological studies, which I have propounded as the end of all my other studies from my very first admission in the University, nor have aimed at any farther progress in the Greek, or any other human learning, than might be subservient to the profession of Divinity. So that I am wholly unfit to compose constant lectures upon classical authors, which the Greek Professor is obliged to read at least once every week of the University term; but I shall always be ready to serve my church and country to the best of my power in the way of my profession. I am, Sir, highly sensible of my great obligations for your many undeserved favours, particularly for this last, and that other of my being her Majesty's chaplain; for which all I can return are my most hearty wishes and prayers for your prosperity.

[EDWARD HARLEY] to [his sister] ABIGAIL HARLEY, at Aywood.

1706[7], January 25—Excuse me to my wife that I do not write by this post. My brother was taken very ill this evening when I was with him at his office and so continued till he was let bleed. He is now much better.

D[aniel De] F[oe] to Robert Harley.

1707, January 27.   Edinburgh—I cannot but return my humble acknowledgments for the honour of your letter of the 21st.   It is my singular joy that the constant accounts I have sent have been to your satisfaction.   Indeed I have been very sad on the account of my having had no line for now eight weeks, and feared myself forgotten.

I confess there seems equal occasion of somebody here now as before, and indeed if a person were constantly here, provided he had no public mission, it would be very useful   The implacable parsons are unsufferably insolent and now they fly in the face of everybody, friend and foe, and the coals are blowed on all occasions by the others.   I sent you [in] the last letter the attempt of one Webster, a minister, against the Dissenters; I here send my answer to him.   They are now laying their heads to defame the Dissenters to render them suspected to the people.

It is in vain to go about to excuse these people, they are proud, passionate, ignorant, and jealous.   I have hitherto kept myself unsuspected, have whispered and caused it to be spread that I am fled hither for debt and cannot return, and this particularly that they may not suspect me.   Under this reproach, though I get some scandal, yet I effectually secure myself against suspicion.   Now I give out, I am going to write the history of the Union in folio, and have got warrants to search the Registers and Parliament books, and have begun a subscription for it.   I tell them it will cost me a year's time to write it.   Then I treat with the Commission to make them a new version of the Psalms, and that I'll lock myself in the College two years for the performance.   By these things I effectually amuse them and I am perfectly unsuspected.

Then I am setting weavers to work to make linen, and I talk of manufactures and employing the poor, and if that thrives I am to settle here and bring my family down and the like, by which trifles I serve the great end, viz. a concealment.

I would be glad you would please to consider the case I wrote about the Abjuration Oath, which is very hard upon them.

I humbly thank you for representing favourably my poor endeavours for the service here.   If her Majesty was informed of the circumstances of my family from whom I have been so long absent, and whom I effectually stripped just before by my surrender, I persuade myself it would move her royal goodness to some compassion.   I need but represent it to you.   I leave the rest to yourself, but must own to you I am distressed in my mind on their account.   I ask your pardon for running out on that here.

The present affair is about settling the representation here, which they have in part agreed, as you will see by the minutes—'tis now strongly contended to keep out the eldest sons of noblemen from the house, and the house are now sitting upon it, the barons struggle hard for it, and the nobility to get them in.

I am to thank you for your hint of a supply.   Indeed I have been expensive, but I daresay the money I have laid out is expended to the very directest end you desire it.   But I am now attended with a new disaster.   Mr. B[ell], who is my only resource, is gone to London, and I suppose will kiss your hand ere this reaches you; he is a capable faithful and judicious gentleman.   I suppose if you direct him he may supply as well in London as here, and hope he will wait on your orders for that affair.

Postscript.—They have carried it in the house for the admitting the sons of the nobility, but it was by dexterous management, they had a majority of fourteen only, and the people rail at it abominably, but that wi[ll be] over.

The ARCHBISHOP OF CANTERBURY to [ROBERT] HARLEY.

1706-7, January 28—I thank you for your civility to that excellent man Dr. Potter. He cannot accept of the Greek Professor's place if offered ; having of late turned his study wholly to divinity.

I believe Dr. Hody was inclined to resign that place, and in that case, he would have recommended Mr. Mills who assisted him in fitting his last book for the press. I know that my Lord President, whose godson Mr. Mills is, would hold himself obliged to you if you moved for him. I think Mr. Mills would fill the place very well, judging of him by his books. I hope this will find your honour in better health than, I hear, you had the other day.

[The EARL OF GODOLPHIN] to [ROBERT] HARLEY.

[1707 ? January.] Wednesday—I have no skill in forms but I cannot see any objection why the Bishop might not have either of the titles you sent me that will most oblige him, for he is certainly duly elected Bishop of Munster, and 'tis nothing but injustice and chicane that keeps him out of that see.

I have nobody to propose to be a Welsh judge, nor no objection to him you propose. Should not you speak of it to my Lord Keeper ?

JEAN GASSION [*alias* OGILVIE] to ROBERT BRYAN [HARLEY].

1707, February 2. Paris—I write this upon hazard not being sure it will come to your hands, therefore I shall say very little only to acquaint you that I received a letter from our friend in Hamburg. He tells me not to write any more by the correspondent that he did give me in Holland, for they are gone out of the way ; this he told me he had advertised you of, but what makes me in pain is 1 had just written to you about 20 days before I received this advice from Hamburg, and in your letter there was one of consequence signed C. B. and I am troubled to know if it came safe to your hands or not. If it did not I would have you advertise me, for I have still a copy of it which I shall send as soon as our friend gives me a correspondent in Holland. I have much to say to you but must not venture till I have a correspondent in Holland settled by our friend in Hamburg. You may believe me it is a great trouble to me not to be in a condition to send you the goods you designed me to send. I pray you do not think it my fault for I protest I had rather lose my life than you should have a bad opinion of me, but I must tell you at the same time that I can work no impossibilities, for if you will have me to send you merchandise that is proper for your market you must remit me wherewith to purchase them. Our friend in Hamburg can tell you my strength when I parted, so that it is long since I was run out, and you know what I did complain of the last year ; let not that be the fault this year. I need not explain myself for a word is enough to the wise. You may give your orders to our friend in Hamburg who will send them to me, and I promise you they shall be obeyed for nothing shall fail on my side, only I cannot make brick without straw ; but it is in your power to remove that obstacle and the sooner the better, for after the market a commodity is never so good.

D[ANIEL DE] F[OE] to ROBERT HARLEY.

1707, February 2. Edinburgh—I omitted writing the last post perfectly for want of subject, being at present entirely taken up in mere cavil and continual dispute with the clamorous clergy. If I have done any service since I came hither I think it is now, for these men are really the *boutefeus* of the nation, and if they talk against the Union everybody will do so also. However I have picked out some who are for it, a very very few I have brought over, and I have so set those against the other, that like Satan's kingdom divided against itself, the furious temper cannot stand. These reconciled parsons begin to call the other mad men and they call these apostates, and the people divide just as their leaders, but peace will prevail and I hope gets ground. I hope the affair shall not come down again for amendments; if it does the latter part will be worse than the beginning and I shall be sincerely afraid of it, several of the best men being gone or going, some into the country, some to England ; nothing ought therefore to be more avoided than its coming back hither for amendments. I thought it meet to hint this because I see the party seem to promise themselves something of hopes in difficulties to be raised in England that shall occasion its being brought hither again clogged with something proper to be disliked here.

There is also one critical day here yet, which I apprehend will put them into some confusion but as it is wisely deferred to the last, so if the Treaty does not come down again, the breach it will make cannot be fatal, and this is when they come to name the persons for the first representative. The parties here, the temper of the persons, the circumstances and the forms render it impossible to avoid a brush when this comes on the stage. But if this should be first entered on and amendments from England come after, pardon my freedom, it will endanger breaking the whole affair.

On these and several other accounts I thought it my duty to give this hint, though I question not but your own judgment will agree that it is very necessary to keep it if possible from a return hither, and indeed so necessary that the sum of the affair will seem to depend upon it. If this can be avoided, the heat of the ministers will abate, and one kind thing done for them, *I mean that of the oath*, which I hinted before, and which you were pleased to tell me in your last you would consider of, all would be easy and a little management would reconcile them all, or at least take off the edge of their discontent.

Indeed, would her Majesty afford the charge or grant me a very moderate request I know no way in the world I could serve her interest more in than making only a trip to London, and then come down and spend a year at least among a people unacquainted with peace, moderation or temper, but of that hereafter.

Postscript.—Since the above I am surprised with the accounts we have here of your sudden illness—God Almighty in mercy to these yet unsettled nations preserve a life so necessary to their immediate felicity ! Indeed, I have often thought to use the liberty you are pleased to grant me on that head. Though the vigour of your mind qualifies you for uncommon burdens yet we have *all these treasures in earthen vessels*, 'tis a new turn to the text but I presume it will hold. The body is not made for wonders and when I hint that denying yourself needful and regular hours of rest will disorder the best constitution in the world, I speak my own immediate experiences, who having despised sleep, hours, and rules, have broken in upon a perfectly established health, which no distresses, disasters, jails, or melancholy could ever hurt before. I beseech you, pity your country in the sparing yourself for a work so few but you are able to go through.

DR. GEORGE SMALRIDGE to [ROBERT HARLEY].

[1707], February 12—My Lord Archbishop of York told me this morning that upon the notice he had of Dr. Jane's life being despaired of he applied himself to the Queen in my behalf; that her Majesty was pleased graciously to remember the promises she had made to you and to his Lordship, but that she had been informed that I was one of those who flew in the face of the Government by representing the Church to be in danger, or to that effect. His Grace could not learn from her Majesty whence she had received this information, that he might put me in a way of proving it to be false. His Grace gave me both his leave, and his advice to communicate this to you. I am sure my own conscience acquits me from having done anything to forfeit the Queen's favour. It will be no great prejudice to me to lose this preferment, which would not add to my present income, but lessen it. But I shall reckon it a great unhappiness to lie under her Majesty's displeasure. I humbly submit my case to your consideration and favour and know that I cannot leave it in better hands.

D[ANIEL] DE F[OE] to ROBERT HARLEY.

1707, February 13. Edinburgh—I had closed the other letter before the Parliament was over—and gave you an account of names [of representatives in the first parliament of Great Britain] but by guess from the common opinion. Since that the whole is finished and very happily without any broil and the true list of the names is on the other side to which I refer.

List of sixteen Peers and thirty 'Barons' annexed.

[DANIEL] DE FOE to the [EARL OF GODOLPHIN] Lord Treasurer.

1707, February 22. Edinburgh—I most humbly crave your Lordship's pardon for presuming to write to you at this distance, but hearing of the very unhappy illness of Mr. Secretary Harley and the subject of my writing concerning more particular your part in the government, I mean the revenue, I thought it my duty to lay the following case before you. Your Lordship knows well that in this place there is an open trade with France. And as this trade is very considerable, so on the prospect of an Union I perceive there are several wheels at work to lay schemes of private trade from hence for England; some of which I may get insight enough into to acquaint you both of time, place and person if you command to search farther into it.

But the main particular I give you this trouble upon is this, here are great commissions from London already for the buying up wines and brandies on the supposition that they shall be freely conveyed to England after the Union, and that England will not so far disoblige Scotland at first as to obstruct it. 'Tis true an obstruction of that kind would do some harm here at first, as it will be improved; but if they are assured of a liberty, as I find the merchants of London encourage them in it, your Lordship will find the inconvenience very great and the quantity before the first of May incredible. Here were three ships entered last week and all the wines are bought up, and I am informed there are eight more at the Orcades waiting to come in—and this place is unusually and prodigiously full of English money at this time. I need not trouble you with any notes of the consequences of this and how easily twenty or thirty thousand pounds duty shall be avoided by the merchants in this case, the best wines being now sold here for 11*s.* per hogshead, brandies at about 13*s.* and so of other things.

Nor shall I presume to offer my thoughts of expedients in this case without your immediate commands, only presume to lay it before you as what I thought for her Majesty's service for which I humbly ask your pardon.

Postscript.—If your commands direct me to note the quantities of wines bought and by whom in London, I suppose it may not be difficult, and perhaps where lodged.

D[ANIEL DE] F[OE] to ROBERT HARLEY.

1707, February 23. Edinburgh—If I have omitted my constant advices to you, it has been under the very uneasy reports spread here both of your first illness and after of a relapse, and several flying reports have alarmed me with the account of your being dead. I will not trouble you with my concern on that score ; the loss to the whole Island is what I hope God in his mercy to them will not afflict them with in many years.

My close concealing my acquaintance with, much less employment from, you, rendered it impossible to know anything from other than common intelligence, but having a letter from Mr. Bell this day that he had the honour to wait on you the 8th and no mention of your indisposition, revives my hopes of your health and renews my very pleasant labour of thus conversing with you.

I wrote you a large letter last week, but cautious of the case of your health sent it to Mr. Bell, who I hope will do me the honour to put it safe into your own hands. The town rings here with a report that the Test Act is repealed, as far as concerns the Dissenters, but the various manner of its being told here makes me doubtful.

I should improve it to the utmost advantage here against Presbyterian jealousies, if I had the certainty of fact. However as it is, I begin to make some of them blush at their suspicions of English sincerity.

We are surprised here with an account that the whole treaty has passed the Committee of the House of Commons ; it is so good news that I cannot but suspend my expectations till a confirmation arrives of so valuable a thing.

I troubled you with an invective by Mr. Webster here against the English dissenters. I have had another railing bitter pamphlet on the same head from him, but so taken up with ill language, scurrilous personal raillery, and little sense, that I cannot think it worth giving you the trouble of it. Raillery and ill manners have just the same effect here as in other places, viz. to sink the character and reputation of the author.

The Parliament have now before them the several requests of the commission for plantation of kirks, and valuation of teinds as they call them here, or tithes as with us. This very day they are upon naming the members for the first Parliament, the quarrelsome work I hinted in my last : The Peers, as expected, are as follows, but I do not yet hear they are determined in the house :—

Duke of Queensberry, Lord Chancellor.

Two Secretaries of State.
Marquis of Tweeddale.
Marquis of Montrose, Lord President of the Council.
Marquis of Lothian.
Earl of Sutherland; Earl of Roxburgh.
Earl of Rothes; Earl of Glasgow.
Earl of Stair ; Viscount Dupplin.
Lord Ross—the others not named.

The people are strangely irritated here, and there is a spirit of bitterness and slander gone out among them. The mob are a machine; the Jacobites have wound them up to a pitch and nothing but time, management, temper and success can reduce them to the proper medium. They must be let run down gradually or they precipitate at once into all manner of confusion.

I have had several letters and some hints I guess from the other newly altered part of an office near you, which I long to give you the history of, if you please to command it. I presume you will suffer nothing of that to be to my prejudice, and permit me the freedom of taking your honour for the concealment from all eyes or ears but your own.

I am not to be pumped or sounded, and yet would be glad to have a hint from you where I should be wary, and where not. Perhaps here may be no need of caution. I believe you are all in the true interest and if I may be open I would be glad to know.

I have little in this world to boast of but my fidelity, and as that is to you before all the world, so I entreat a hint from you, whether I may be free in case of such suggestions as ——. We hope he is not dropped. —'Tis hard if the persons who say they employ him do not stand by him. Pray let me know if you are in anything uneasy and the like.

These if right are kind things and to one circumstanced like me should be improved, but if wrong can have no influence on me who as before have neither hands to act, mouth to speak, nor purse to receive favours but as you direct. I humbly entreat your hints for my conduct and as frequent orders as your affairs will permit.

The Archbishop of Canterbury to [Robert Harley].

1706-7, February 23—I hope Mr. Mills will answer expectation. In one thing I committed a mistake in my letter, in which I said he was my Lord President's godson, instead of his being his son's tutor ; which I think is not material. The confinement which my tedious fit of the gout occasioned has made me so tender that I have not been a long while at the Council at Kensington, though I ventured last Thursday to wait on the good Queen there. I hope I shall be more hardy in a little time. If in my absence anything should be moved about making Croydon a Corporation, I would entreat you to say that I desire to be heard before anything passeth; my rights as Archbishop being much concerned in it. I believe Mr. Solicitor will say so too as also Mr. Attorney.

Dr. William Stratford to [Robert Harley].

1706-7, February 24. Chester—My father died, as I expected he would, without any other money than that which he had with him for daily expense. I am afraid all his brethren will not approve the example he has given them in one point. After having been in the dignities of the Church for forty years he has left a less estate behind him than he was possessed of before he had any preferment.

I suppose you have heard that Sir. John Bridgman has sent to Mr. Edward Finch a presentation to Wigan. If the presentation is good the Bishop's revenue will be considerably diminished and there would not be many competitors for the see if they knew the true value of it, and had no hopes of being removed from it. Though whoever succeeds will find himself obliged to my father, he having refused to renew several leases because the tenants presuming upon his age would not agree to any reasonable terms.

JOHN BAKER to ROBERT HARLEY.

1706-7, February 25—Asking leave to be allowed to wait upon him with a petition to be presented to the Council, Lord Sunderland having told him how very kindly Harley had espoused his interest there.

DR. HUGH CHAMBERLEN to ROBERT HARLEY.

1706-7, March 1—Laying claim to the initiation of the system of " current credit" then employed, and recently approved by parliament, and asking for a suitable reward from the Queen, as it is below any government to make use of the labours of private persons without more ample gratification than usually passes between common chapmen.

D[ANIEL DE] F[OE] to ROBERT HARLEY.

1707, March 4. Edinburgh—My last represented my fears of the returning the Treaty hither on account of the Oxford clause. 'Tis very mysterious to us why that affair was not included in the Act of Security for the Church, and I fear it was kept *in petto* as an ambuscade against the bill. I will not despair of anything but it is a new danger here, and some good friends to the affair seem under great apprehensions. Indeed here are disgusts and dissatisfactions among the great ones which give room to apprehend an ill effect of any thing to be brought before them again. Some are disgusted, as I wrote before, that they are not in the British List, others at want of places. But I cannot but observe though by the bye the equivalent is the main disgust, many had swallowed large morsels of it in expectation, and I daresay little enough of it should go as designed, if it were in the management of some people.

As it is everybody says that the nobility will . . . . . . it, and that the only hope is they will fall out about sharing it, which is likely enough.

The persons who they say are uneasy begin to complain loudly and if the temper and moderation of the Commissioner, who indeed is the soul of this whole affair, does not help it, I doubt lest they may come to calling one another some names, which the bystanders may be apt to say are true on both sides. Though I write my apprehensions of things, yet I shall not be discouraged from my small endeavours and wait your further instructions.

BARON SCHUTZ to [ROBERT HARLEY].

1707, March 8. London—I have just received your letter of the 7th inst., and I have seen in it with much satisfaction that her Majesty has given orders for the recognition of King Stanislaus and for the guarantee of the peace of Poland, without any restriction or condition.

With regard to the renunciation of Prince Charles by Denmark nothing is suggested but that the States general shall assist in it, and as to the publication of the decision of the Lubeck affair by the Council at Vienna, my paper notes that the Imperial court in order to avoid such publication gives out that England and Holland are not in favour of it, which the Elector is very far from believing, but he wishes the queen should know this, in order that she may prevent such an impression reaching the king of Sweden, and also may let them know at Vienna that she does not find it well, after England and the States have done everything to prevent the Lubeck affair from disturbing the North and have always shown how much they desired to see the matter settled at Vienna, that the fault of the delay should be imputed to them. It will be necessary however that the Imperial court shall not know of this news having come to her Majesty from the Elector, who has no object but the common cause, in communicating to her whatever will assist in it. *French.*

D[ANIEL DE] F[OE] to ROBERT HARLEY.

1707, March 10. [Edinburgh]—I have now I hope the satisfaction of seeing the fruit of all this mischief, the effect of all the labouring, fighting, mobbings, &c. viz.: Union, and while I write this the guns are firing from the Castle and my man brings me up the Queen's Speech. Methinks *Nunc Dimittis* comes now in my head, and in writing to you I should say:—Now let me depart from hence for my eyes have seen the conclusion. I confess I believe I might be serviceable here a long time yet. But everybody is gone up to solicit their own fortunes, and some to be rewarded for what I have done—while I depending on your concern for me and her Majesty's goodness am wholly unsolicitous in that affair. I wrote earnestly to you and to my Lord Treasurer about the import of wine and brandy; three ships more came in yesterday and ten more are at hand, and two hundred tun of brandy is sent for from Holland. If it shall pass into England why shall your honour not permit me to buy you a tun of rich claret here, which I may do as cheap as you buy a hogshead, and I'll take my hazard that it shall be extraordinary on my own risk.

J. P[ierce] is this day gone for England, he has been at first useful to me, but since some who were fond of having an agent here employed him out of my way, of which more hereafter. I have not recommended him to you. I am now on the old doctrine of peace, and her Majesty's Speech is my happy text, and I please myself in telling your honour it gains ground. I have been invited to Glasgow where I must have been torn to pieces, if I had gone before, but I think to venture a round thither and to St. Andrews and spend every minute to the best issue I can that the charge I have put you to may not be ill laid out; and now I am impatient for your orders which way to steer my course, which I entreat I may have the honour of as soon as possible.

BARON SCHUTZ to [ROBERT HARLEY].

1707, March 10. London—The Duke of Marlborough tells me that in Holland they have struck two lines out of the draught renunciation, and that it will be well I should speak to you on the matter before the post goes out. Not having found you at your office to-day I shall not fail to return there to-morrow. The Duke has not told me what it is they have struck out. *French.*

[—— to BARON SCHUTZ.]

1707, March 11. Hanover—I send you the reply which the Elector made to the memorial of Monsieur Friesendorf and to the letter of the Administrator, to which we think her Majesty and the States could conform, and that the affair of Eutin should be promptly finished as much by the renunciation as at Vienna; and that we should send ministers to Hamburg for the conferences, about which matter I wrote last Tuesday and therefore have nothing to regret. There is no question that Monsieur de Goertz is likely to settle anything with Monsieur Tessin ; about that we hear nothing more. The former of these gentlemen has transported himself to the quarters of the King of Sweden, the other is at Leipsic, and they have little communication with each other. A new incident has happened which will show us how anxious are the people of Gottorp to profit by the stay of the King of Sweden in Germany. The canons of Lubeck of the faction of Gottorp, taking advantage of the time during which those of the other faction are suspended, have proceeded to the election on the fourth of this month of a coadjutor, and have elected the son of the administrator who is an infant of seven or eight months, relying on the treaty of 1647 between the Chapter and the House of Gottorp, which assures the election of this House for six generations and which is confirmed by the treaty of Travendahl. According to us this election of a coadjutor is a new and strong reason for pressing on the affair of the renunciation, as it shows how much the King of Sweden takes the affair of Eutin to heart and how much the Gottorp party are inclined to anything which will stir up incidents capable of producing disturbances. We must labour therefore to deprive them of all pretexts, and Mr. Stepney must induce the States to behave quite differently in all these affairs and to follow the same line as the Court of England. The States which are now so favourable to Denmark(?) could not render this Crown more signal service than to dispose her to give satisfaction to the House of Gottorp in relation to her pretentions which are so well founded, and to put matters into such a state that if the King of Sweden attacks them, he should be obviously the infractor of the peace of Travendahl and should bring on himself the guarantors of that treaty. I agreed upon this with Monsieur d'Almesch this morning. He arrived here yesterday and leaves thus tomorrow. He had an official audience this morning with the Elector.

French. Copy in Schutz's handwriting.

BARON SCHUTZ to [ROBERT HARLEY].

1707, March 12. London—As it appears that Holland has struck out the most essential part of the draft renunciation I do not doubt that her Majesty will insist on it being left as it stood before. Seeing that it is she who pays the four thousand pounds sterling and who ought to control the matter, I am persuaded that her Majesty will dispose the States not to cause further delay. *French.*

CHIEF BARON SIR EDWARD WARD and BARON SIR THOMAS BURY to [ROBERT] HARLEY.

1706[-7], March 14. Dorchester—We received your letter last night relating to the weavers, combers and other labourers in the woollen manufacture at Taunton, Tiverton, and Bristol, and her Majesty's commands to enquire into that matter, and to take care the offenders be prosecuted effectually. We have no commission that extends to Bristol. No judges go there nor are any assizes held at Bristol oftener than once a year, which is the long vacation. As to what relates to the Counties of Somerset and Devon, we are obliged by our commissions to go next Monday to Taunton for the first, and stay there four days, thence to Cornwall, and thence to Exeter for the County of Devon, where Commission day is Friday the 28th inst. We have communicated with Serjeant Hooper, whose part as the Queen's Serjeant it is to advise and assist in the proceedings.

D[ANIEL] DE F[OE] to JOHN BELL, at William Carr's Chambers in Lincoln's Inn.

1707, March 18 : Edinburgh—Your ordering me to write no more to you at London left me at some loss for a post or two, and I wrote to Mrs. Bell to direct as formerly by Sir Thomas T——. I am glad your stay in London is somewhat longer and particularly for the conveyance of the enclosed. When you wait on Mr. Secretary again giving my humble duty to him be pleased to move him in the following cases.

I have been extremely desirous to choose out one tun of rare claret here for his own table, and as we are all assured that it will come free into England, and all the world are buying it up, the goodness and the cheapness make me earnest to have his commission, considering I may buy him a tun as cheap as his honour informed me he gave for one hogshead in London, and this trade being my old business I persuade myself my palate cannot be deceived in what will please him.

My other request is that he would be pleased to let me have a short quartering of his arms, in order to make him a small present of this country's manufacture. Perhaps it may be to the honour of Scotland and to his own very good liking. In this you will particularly oblige me, and I shall at large inform you of particulars as to the manufacture when I see you.

As to my coming up, I have neither feet to travel nor tongue to say when, but as I receive orders from him whom you have the honour to converse with, and if you will make it your particular request to obtain me the favour of a letter, I shall place it to the account of the many favours received of you.

D[ANIEL] DE F[OE] to ROBERT HARLEY.

1707, March 18. Edinburgh—I have not wrote so constantly as usual having nothing material to communicate, but private Bills in Parliament, horse races at Leith, fire in the city and such things, which are not worth disturbing your thoughts with. To tell you that my Lord Hopetoun's horse won the Plate, that a fire burnt three or four houses and five people, that the parliament have been busy about a quarrel between the Doctors and Surgeons (knaves all!) to determine which shall have the greatest privilege to kill people and be paid for it. These things will be so far from informing you that they will not so much as divert you. Indeed should I tell you the story of ecclesiastic frenzy in these parts and draw a scheme of north country bigotry, I could make you merry in spite of your most serious concern for the public peace.

I find there is bigotry without popery, and God's priests ride upon God's people as well as the inferior Clergy of less pure Churches. Certainly the Clergy here have more to account for than in other places, where the customary slavery of other nations is inverted but is every jot as fatal as there. The priests lead aside silly women, these silly women more silly men; the women are the instructors, and the men are mere machines wound up just as the spring goes at home. Thus, as the velocity of motion doubles and increases as 'tis remote from its centre, so if the priest be chagrined at the Union, the good wife rails at it, and the husband grows mad. This has put a notion into my head which if ever I were to write a book should take up a good part of it.

I have heard of the circulation of the blood, and great discoveries have been made of late on that head. I think it wo██ be very instructing to write an essay upon the circulation of the brain, in which case more wonders would be found out in this clear air here, than could be hoped for even in a journey to the Moon. You'll pardon me this excursion; indeed the moral of it all is instructing, the ministry here strangely influence the people, and the conflict between Mr. Webster and me here has discovered more of it than I could have imagined was possible. His attempt has had two very fatal designs in it, though I thank God I can without vanity say I have defeated him in both:

1. To argue the sinfulness of the Union as a breach of the National Covenant, and inflame the people on that account.
2. To represent the Dissenters as no friends to the Kirk, and not fit to be depended upon, and so break the general friendship of the Nations.

Thus one design was to inflame, the other to divide.

To his first, I printed a short piece to prove the National Covenant was so far from being broken that it was not at all concerned in the Treaty. He cried fire at this, said I had blasphemed the Covenant, that everybody ought to shun my company; that if I came into his Church while he was preaching or praying he would stop and proceed no farther till I was removed. But when he saw the best ministers in the City my constant friends and visitants, it put him distracted, and he goes about railing at my morals, calls me drunkard, swearer, blasphemer, and I know not what, for which he has the pleasure of seeing himself laughed at. To his second piece I published three tracts. I. A sheet called, "The Dissenters vindicated," &c. which I sent your honour long since, to this he replied with little ▉ut ill language which made his own friends blush for him. I had printed a reply to him bitter enough, but when I considered my business here was peace, reconciliation and temper, I thought it was better to use him gently, and as to his railing it did me no harm, that wise men would see the beauty of moderation, and bearing reproach was better than returning it; especially having my eye to the work before me. So I suppressed the book and wrote another which I call " *A Short View of the State of the Protestant religion in Britain, as it is professed by the Episcopal Church in England, the Presbyterian Church in Scotland, and the Dissenters in both.*" Here omitting to mention the man, I have as clearly as I can stated the case, and the differences among us all, how far we ought to agree and how behave where we cannot.

This has gotten me a complete victory and the moderate men of the clergy come every day to thank me for it. I have sent it you, enclosed by this post, though 'tis rather too bulky for a letter, and I recommend it to your reading, and its author to your concern when at this distance too likely to be forgotten. As I told your honour in my last my design, if you approve it, to stay till I see the issue of the General Assembly, so I entreat your orders about it. I must own 'tis too much in the power of the ministers here to ruin the peace of this Nation, and this makes me think the meeting of the General Assembly here a thing of more consequence than otherwise it would be at this time, and I repeat my humble motion that their Session may be as short as may be.

I am in nothing more unhappy in this affair than that your extraordinary affairs permit you to favour me but very seldom with your directions, and methinks I look too much a volunteer in the Service.

However, I resolve to omit nothing I can do. And I doubt you find I spare no charge to carry on the work I am upon in the best manner I can, and to push the great work of reconciling the minds of the people to one another and to the Union.

To this purpose I have in the "Review," which I humbly beg you will please to cast your eye on, begun a long series of discourses on the reciprocal duties of the two nations one to another after the Union.

In my management here I am a perfect emissary. I act the old part of Cardinal Richelieu. I have my spies and my pensioners in every place, and I confess 'tis the easiest thing in the world to hire people here to betray their friends. I have spies in the Commission in the Parliament and in the Assembly, and under pretence of writing my history I have everything told me.

I am in daily conferences with the ministers who are members of the Assembly and hope they will come more moderately inclined than was expected. They now solicit me to write to my friends in England among the Dissenters to assure them that they are not concerned in the scandal raised on them by Webster, which I shall do. In all things I labour to reduce them to temper and union of affection both with England and with one another, and indeed I think my work is harder and more perplexing now than it was at first. In all which I study to approve myself to your judgment, that having put you to a very great expense that expense is faithfully applied, and not entrusted with an unprofitable servant.

I entreat your directions about a tun of wine.

G. GRANVILLE to [ROBERT HARLEY].

1706-7, March 19—Lord Marlborough having to depart tomorrow, I have written to him to recommend myself to his favour that in some kind or other the frequent promises I have had may have some effect with the Lord Treasurer that I may be no longer left at large as I have been. Last year no particular application was made to him, and 'twas attributed to that that I met with so unexpected a disappointment.

The DUKE OF QUEENSBERRY to [ROBERT HARLEY].

1707, March 20. Holyrood house—On Monday in the afternoon I received from the Queen's messenger the exemplication of the Act of the English parliament ratifying the treaty of Union. It has been read in parliament here, and ordered to be recorded as her Majesty directs.

I am very glad that great affair passed so cheerfully with you. I wish this nation had been as wise and embraced it as readily; but I hope the advantages of it will soon convince many of their mistakes.

D[ANIEL DE] FOE to ROBERT HARLEY.

1707, March 25. Edinburgh—I have now seen the finishing of this happy work. The Union has been confirmed, as they call it here, that is proclaimed at the Cross, and this day the Parliament is at an end and all is over. I have wrote your honour my thoughts of staying to see the Assembly meet and act my part among them, then to make a tour to Glasgow, Aberdeen, and St. Andrews to preach peace and good manners to the preachers of truth and sedition, for such some of them are.

When I signify my design 'tis always subjected to your opinion and in hopes of your direction, in want of which I am obliged to satisfy myself with a negative allowance and take your not forbidding me for an order. I entreat you to favour me with your approbation of my measures, or your orders, and withal to signify to me what course I shall steer next.

Postscript.—I hear the bill for securing the right of printed copies is stopped. I beg of you, in respect of your encouragement of letters and diligence in learning to give it your help.

At the closing the Parliament the Commissioner made a short speech which I presume you will have a copy of. And I cannot but observe that a motion was made to recommend Mr. Paterson to her Majesty, and if my labour had not been always to conceal myself I might have had the same honour—but I have nobody to recommend me, but yourself to whom I leave it. I am sure he has the credit of a good stock in the face and is applauded for some things I actually did in the Committee. I beg I may not, however, be forgotten.

[The Earl of Godolphin] to [Robert Harley].

[1707, March]—If you have prepared any answer for D[e] F[oe] pursuant to the papers I sent you last night, when you send it to me I will speak to Sir David Nairne to dispatch a flying packet with it because I think it is of haste.

On the same page is an answer from Harley.—I wrote to your Lordship this morning that I understood it to be your mind that I should send the observations to F[oe], and I did intend to send it to the postmaster of Newcastle who sends it privately to him, for I suppose it is not proper he should be thought to correspond with any here; but I will do as your Lordship please.

[D. Fearns] to Robert Harley.

1707, April 1. Edinburgh—Occurrences are now become very barren here, so have nothing interesting to write, only to keep within your orders, and to make some remarks and take observations.

The Marquis of Montrose and the two Secretaries of State went to Court yesterday, as the Earl of Marchmont and some others went latter end of last week, and the Lord High Commissioner &c. say they go on Thursday and several others soon thereafter, which make the facile people say that that concourse of goers shall spend the equivalent at Court.

There is mighty talk amongst the people in general about the new settlement of one Secretary for North Britain, and that the same runs between Q[ueensberry] and Chancellor, indeed they say though Q. hath done so and so, yet he was in the Revolution, and went over to King William, when the other acted for a long time (like Doctor Charlock) against both till interest brought him to; true it doth not belong to me to comment too high, *sed caveat emptor*, and the first would be more grateful if he had but two lawyers and honest men his deputies &c.

The shares of the African Company here sell apace and already much English money comes into our bank daily. I am afraid that you cannot have time to think of many things I write to you, especially of late about D[uke] H[amilton's] Cameronians and the proposal of raising 1,000,000*l.* yearly and to sink in 13 years, &c.

Have received your orders by J. B[ell] for which a thousand thanks and though you think I may be extravagant, but upon account you shall find that I have not spent a farthing in vain. If you order me soon up very little matter more may serve, if any further orders pray to let me know as soon as your convenience can allow, either by yourself or Mr. Bell, and whatever comes to me to the care of our Postmaster-General, Mr. George Mann, or by Mr. B. comes safe; we need not be shy about matters and things now.

The Hon. H[ENRY] PAGET to [ROBERT HARLEY].

1707, April 2—Promising to write to Captain Wager on behalf of Sir Hugh Middleton, a volunteer on board the *Grafton.* This ship would not however join Captain Wager till she came to the West Indies, being one of those ordered to convoy transports and trade first to Lisbon.

D[ANIEL DE] F[OE] to ROBERT HARLEY.

1707, April 3. Edinburgh—Mr. Bell being come from London has I doubt stopped the delivery of my last. I have at present nothing material to write. We are preparing for the General Assembly, and though I hope well, yet I am now busier than ever, but it is a nice point to act, and the parsons here are unaccountable people, humourous, jealous, partial, censorious, haughty, insolent, and above all monstrously ignorant. I shall omit nothing I can to influence those of them that are *come-at-able* and hope for a good issue and a short sitting.

The great men are posting to London for places and honours, every man full of his own merit, and afraid of everyone near him: I never saw so much trick, sham, pride, jealousy, and cutting of friends' throats as there is among the noble men. I presume you will soon see the effects of it at London, I wish some of our friends had not so much hand in it. Last night I waited on the Commissioner to wish him a good journey, and take my leave. He received me very obligingly. He is pleased to say more of my small services here than I have a face to repeat, and has promised to recommend me to the Queen and to my Lord Treasurer. If his Grace be sincere, I cannot miss to meet with some help when 'tis joined with your prevailing assistance.

I shall no more afflict you with solicitations for your orders. I proceed by my own undirected judgment, giving you a constant account and am forced to take your long silence for a tacit professing your satisfaction. If I flatter myself in a mistake I am doubly unhappy. I am spending your money a little freer than ordinary on this occasion of the Assembly, but 'tis from my sense of the danger if it miscarries, and I have some engines at work among the ministers. In short money will do anything here.

Some angry men are chosen but the rancour of the temper is abated exceedingly, and I hope shall more abate. After the Assembly I entreat your orders what to do. The Commissioner sets out for London this day.

JEAN GASSION [*alias* OGILVIE] to [ROBERT HARLEY].

1707, April 5. Paris—This is the fifth letter I have written to you without so much as the least information to let me know if any of them came safe to your hands. I have a great deal to say to you that I will not trust to paper on such uncertainties; therefore I beg of you let me hear from you as soon as ever this comes to your hands that I may know how to take my measures both for your satisfaction and the behoof of the company. If I had heard from you I certainly would have returned your several commodities that would have been of value in your parts. It is not my fault you have not had them for I am willing to serve you at all hazards.

If I had wherewith I would send my wife and children to your parts, but I have not money to bear their charges, and at the same time it is only to you I must send them, for under heaven I have no other support or refuge.

WILLIAM BORRETT to ERASMUS LEWIS.

1707, April 5—William Dawson was tried and convicted at the last Derby Assizes for speaking treasonable words. He was sentenced to stand in the pillory the two succeeding market days, and also fined five pounds, and to find security for good behaviour. The judge would have set the fine much higher had the man been worth a groat, but says he may continue long enough in prison before he can pay that fine, or find sureties for his conduct.

[D. FEARNS] to [ROBERT] HARLEY.

1707, April 8. Edinburgh—Had nothing worth your consideration since my last, except that the bank had instructions not to leave guineas at the currencies here of 23s. 8d.

Today the General Assembly—to which the Earl of Glasgow, a modest good man, is Commissioner—met, read his commission, her Majesty's letter; the last moderator Mr. Wishart preached a pathetic sermon upon Elijah's being taken up triumphantly into heaven for his zeal for the service of God and suppression of grievous evils and immorality, and his injunctions to Elisha. Then the rolls were called, a list of three candidates to be next moderators were given in according to custom by the late moderator Mr. Wishart; three others by the General Assembly. The choice fell upon Mr. Starling, of the late moderator's list, Principal of the University of Glasgow—who was lately in company of Mr. Carstares and judges him to be a modest good man. Appointed their Committee to draw up an answer to Her Majesty's letter and some other small matters; adjourned to Thursday next when intend to have their meeting; for matters seem to run in a safe channel unless some supervenient unlucky accident occurs. I need not give [you] relation of the Duke of Queensberry's, Lord High Commissioner, taking journey on Thursday last, the Chancellor on Friday, their retinues, and receptions at Berwick &c. because you must needs have all before this comes to hand, yet all were great. As to them I sent enough before; if your Honour doth not mind them it is certainly for want of time; and if we should slip good opportunities accidents may prove first to good meaning men in the end (*sic*).

DR. F. A[TTERBURY] to [ROBERT] HARLEY.

[1707, April 9.] Wednesday. Chelsea—The Archbishop told us today that they had considered our application and schedule of prerogatives, and were prepared to shew us that several things therein contained were not true. However the Queen's supremacy being concerned in it, they had resolved to lay it before her Majesty. We went down, and immediately agreed to desire the Archbishop if he laid the case before her Majesty, to lay also our previous vote before her, wherein we declared that we had no intention to debate the validity of the late prerogative, to which we had humbly submitted. But the Archbishop avoided receiving that message, by keeping the prolocutor five or six minutes without doors till the Bishops had adjourned themselves to Saturday. We have deputed the prolocutor and two more to wait upon his Grace with that vote at Lambeth.

H. BISHOP OF LONDON to [ROBERT] HARLEY.

1707, April 10—The bearer Robert Stephens desired me to give you his character. He is the most useful man in the place of messenger of the press that can be found, for nobody understands so well where and when to find out prohibited books. Indeed since whiggish and Commonwealth books have been so much in fashion, that malicious sort of people have so run him down that he has been able to do little service ; but if you please to give him encouragement and get him his salary I am sure you will find him very serviceable.

W. GREG to [ROBERT HARLEY].

1707, April 10—I beg leave to put up a petition now in my own behalf, which this day's post from Edinburgh has determined me to do. I was in hopes to have spared your Honour the trouble by having such an account of my business there as might enable me to satisfy my creditors and consequently to continue quiet in your service. But though matters are adjusted the best they could be in my absence yet the payment being put off till the end of the year you will imagine how impossible it will be for me to subsist in your service until then, unless the method you proposed be put in practice which your illness and other incidents have hindered you from doing, though now about ten weeks ago. But my uneasiness increasing daily I crave your Honour to order me ten pounds to stop the mouths of two troublesome creditors.

The EARL OF SUNDERLAND to [ROBERT HARLEY].

1707, April 11—What Count Briançon desires is that you would write to Lord Raby to press the King of Prussia in the Queen's name to give his consent to the publishing the ban against the Duke of Mantua ; the Duke of Savoy not thinking himself secure in the posses. sion of the Montferrat till that be done. He desires also that you would write to Lord Marlborough at the Hague to speak to Mr. Gerstoff at the Hague to engage King Augustus to do the same.

D[ANIEL DE] F[OE] to ROBERT HARLEY.

1707, April 12. Edinburgh—I have the satisfaction of writing you that the Assembly goes on here with all manner of calmness and quietness contrary to the hopes of some, and I must own contrary to my apprehensions. I have not failed in plying them hard with arguments and persuasions in print, in discourse, and by other instruments which I have employed. I will not presume to say I have been anything in the success, but I have done my duty.

The hottest of the clergy are extremely cooled by this surprising alteration, and some of them are very much ashamed of their former behaviour. I converse not much with them that are for it, for they need not the physician, but I single out the opposers, and am daily and almost hourly in their little clubs and cabals. They begin to solicit me now not to represent them to their disadvantage in England, and value themselves upon their negative behaviour—what they did not do to excuse themselves from the blame of what they did.

And now I entreat your directions how to steer my course. I have been long here without a word or hint how to govern myself, but now it seems absolutely necessary to have some orders, and I humbly recommend it to you to determine for me, what course I shall take. I did propose a small circle here among the clergy to cultivate the good temper that appears among them, and then to leave this country; but I have no satisfaction in undertaking anything without your orders. I entreat one line for my government whether to go or stay here, or come for England. For without your directions I am a mere image without life, soul, or action.

WILLIAM GREG to [ROBERT HARLEY].

[1707], April 15—My uneasy circumstances put me upon thus importuning you sore against my will, for without paying the ten pounds to-night I must expect to be affronted before I get to the office to-morrow morning; and in that case I shall be forced to take my leave of it, since I know not how to continue in it.

[D. FEARNS] to [ROBERT] HARLEY.

1707, April 15. Edinburgh—Nothing worth your perusal since my last, but what your Honour must needs have at the Court seeing all suspicion of English influence is now out of doors, for as I said frequently before, the people that were most against the incorporated Union (except the too strict Presbyterians) do say that whatever may be wrong in the Union, they enter into the same to their own people, and not to your ministry and do hope and expect to have all their grievances redressed, after a just and fair representation, by her Majesty and a British Parliament, and there are many schemes in forming.

The General Assembly at first were like to have had some infractions and divisions, the strict sort of them pretending, that the true Protestant religion and their government established by law had not full security by the Union, and designed to make remonstrances but the majority of the Assembly (the Commissioner and the Moderator being calm sedate men and well affected to the present settlement) being moderate, and pains being taken upon the former in making it apparent to them that the Presbyterian government was never secured till now, some of the former were convinced of their mistakes and the remaining part of them (which was very few) finding that they could not mend their matters have acquiesced and made no further stir, but went on the plantation of some vacant kirks, and transplanting of ministers; so judge that they will not sit long but part good friends.

Yesterday I went to wait upon the Duke of Gordon at his country house about two miles from hence being he was to go to Castlegordon to day or tomorrow, walked abroad with his Grace an hour before dinner alone and he obliged me to dine with him alone also, so that we had about three hours private converse; he has no exception against the Union but one. He expects his son the Marquis of Huntly and his Lady (the Earl of Peterborough's daughter) here the latter end of this or beginning of next month, and if your Honour do not order me hence sooner I shall wait upon him some way out of town, as his father ordered me; we expect good things from this marriage.

I beg your Honour, as you have plentifully provided for me hitherto as I have been more chargeable than I expected which was impossible for me to prevent for reasons which shall be made clear to you, that you would give immediate directions by what hand you think fit, whether there be any further use for me here, or whether I should return, or be useful elsewhere to her Majesty or your Honour, for under God my dependence for earthly matters is upon yourself, for it should grieve me that suffered formerly so much in the service to the of myself and family), I should be thought chargeable without doing service to the public.

If Stair had lived he had seen me provided for after the Union in the government, but your Honour is now my plight anchor, wishes might be provided under your own wings, corrections as well as whole directions, were it never so mean being proper for a gentleman of my education. God bless and reward you. And I must take the liberty to add one word more, viz. that Mr. Bell hath been very punctual to observe your Honour's commands in relation to me, and I believe so to everything else.

John Bell to Robert Harley.

1707, April 18. Newcastle[-on-Tyne]—I send a letter from Mr. Fearns as also one from Mr. D. F[oe] which was returned me from London, which your Honour may please peruse and either give him or me directions about the contents. I have paid Mr. D. F[oe] 40*l.*, and D. F[earns] 20*l.* I perceive they will want more money so shall supply them till I have your order to the contrary. I have spoken to Mrs. Shafto about her daughter. She told me she had been ill used and exclaimed mightily against Madam Oglethorpe. She said she would have her daughter's case put in print, so you may see what is got by mistaken charity.

The Archbishop of York to Robert Harley.

1707, April 18—Desiring him to take some speedy opportunity of putting the queen in mind of Mrs. Mitchell's case, her Majesty having promised to grant her a pension, after talking with the Prince about it.

D[aniel De] F[oe] to Robert Harley.

1707, April 22. Edinburgh—I presume you will now have notice that the Assembly is up and all things grow better that way every day. The Address will come away tonight and the Earl of Glasgow in the morning.

I am much at a loss how to manage myself about the affair of trade here, what the Court in England seemed to desire was as I thought to allow some latitude, and now by her Majesty's Speech it looks quite another way. But as to the thing itself I crave leave to note, if no exception be made for the Scots, it will make ill-blood here and they talk loudly here that the Union is broke before it is begun. If an exception be made, the end will be defeated and all manner of doors are opened to perjury by transferring of property and innumerable frauds. And after all, the quantity brought in is but small compared to what is talked of—I could do some service in this if I knew what the measures are—the whole Fleet is but forty two sail at most.

The foundation laid here for clandestine trade is, beyond all this, fatal to both the revenue and to trade; and as I am let into some of it, I am the more moved, nor do I see any possibility of wholly preventing it, without an army of officers.

I am too far to offer schemes for this here. I have said enough to solicit you to think of me and shall not press you on that head only thus far, his Grace the Duke of Queensberry gave me his word and his hand to recommend me to her Majesty, and I persuade myself will second any motion you will please to make for me. I am informed, I know not how true, that my Lord S . . . [underland ?] is no friend to me on an occasion which concerns yourself; the particulars I refer till I have the honour to see you.

D[ANIEL DE] FOE to ROBERT HARLEY.

1707, April 24. [Edinburgh]—I cannot write to you now without concern, and I fear heartily the unravelling of all we have been doing. The new votes of the House of Commons make the most unaccountable fermentation here, that if the next news does not cool it I shall need no new orders from England about staying or returning, for really there will be no staying here for me nor hardly any English man.

The importation of all their goods to England free of duties is they say expressly capitulated in the article of free communication and the English ought to have known the consequences of the interval as well as they. The vote of the house they say is directly against the Union, and they talk of meeting and declaring the Union broke. I dare not write to you the murmurs of the people, and my worst misfortune is that I can make no answer to it, and though I thought my reputation established here, yet I must confess this shocks it; they come crowding about me reproaching me every hour with what I have said of the honour and justice of the English Parliament. "Aye, aye" says one of them, "Now you see how we are to be served! and what we are to " expect from a British Parliament! How early they begin with us, and " what usage we are to have whenever our advantage clashes with their " interest." I am exceedingly harassed and fatigued with them, and I know not what to answer, because I do not know what the measures are. I tell them (though I know nothing of it yet) that there will be an exception for Scotsmen, and have printed the clause of the last Act, with some remarks, shown the necessity of the preventing the abuses about tobacco and the drawbacks, and I endeavour to buoy them up with hopes. But 'tis a strange hurry they are in, and if something is not done to cool and satisfy them I acknowledge I apprehend the consequences. Here's one gentleman that shows a letter from London as he says by a Parliament man, which says that even those Scots who shall be excepted shall be obliged to come to London to prove the property of their goods, and the difficulties at the Custom house will be chargeable and vexatious, so that the exception to the Scots will signify little.

I entreat you to consider these things and give me a hint what I must say to defend the case and make the people easy. This early ferment is very unseasonable.

Sir Edward Northey to [Robert] Harley.

1707, April 25—Having received her Majesty's commands to prepare, and having prepared a declaration for continuing the members of the present Parliament, I think it my duty to send it to you. I have also returned the commission for constituting a Council in Scotland which you received from Sir David Nairne. The commission for the new Council for the purposes mentioned in the Act of Union will be the same as this, leaving out those powers that do not concern the preserving public peace and order.

D[aniel De] F[oe] to Robert Harley.

1707, April 26. [Edinburgh]—I write to you now upon a very odd and unhappy occasion, I shall say little to the fact, but refer to the enclosed. But my apologies are to you for giving you the trouble of it.

By the manner of the letter you will see I have obtained upon the Clergy here every whit as much as I have represented to you, for this was a great opposer of the Union. I would have gladly razed out his compliment upon me as what no way becomes me to be the messenger of, but I could not send you the letter blotted. You see what a charge I have laid upon me, which I know not how to dispense with, and as I am directed to send it to you and the Archbishop, I enclose a short letter to his Grace, that you may at your pleasure deliver it yourself, or send it to his Grace without acquainting him that it came through your hands.

The case is indeed horrid and becomes her Majesty's justice. But the secret history of it is this—

1. The murderer is grandson to the Earl of Melville and a near relation to the Earl of Leven, and 'tis very much feared my Lord Leven should intercede for him.
2. Her Majesty's exemplar justice will be very grateful to the country here, who have an exceeding resentment of the fact, and the Burgh of Inverkeithing is preparing an address to her Majesty for a proclamation and reward for apprehending him.
3. He has behaved himself so notoriously impudently since the murder as gives a general abhorrence of him, and to pardon him will form a sad prejudice among the people here.

I shall not presume to give my opinion here but have laid it before you, as the minister has been pleased to command me.

As to other matters I refer to my last and wait your commands.

Postscript.—I am sorry to tell you my friends write me word I shall stay here till I am forgot.

If you think fit to deliver the enclosed, you will be pleased to cause copy the letter and seal the outer one.

[Erasmus] Lewis to [Robert] Harley.

1707, April 28—I have a letter from Mr. Cardonnel dated at Berlin the 30th inst new style. The Duke left Leipsic the day before, and, having received an express from the King of Prussia that he would take it extremely ill if his Grace did not make him a visit, set out accordingly for that Court.

JOHN PHILIPS to EDWARD HARLEY, at Mrs. Beresford's house in Little Dean's Yard.

1707, April 28. Christchurch, Oxford—As soon as I received your letter I enquired about the nature of the Westminster gratulatory verses, but could not meet with a satisfactory account, nor so much as one copy that might be of use as an example. However I have procured at last some verses which (as far as I am able to guess who am a stranger to the Westminster method) may pass tolerably for a King's scholar. You may expect them on Wednesday night.

The SAME to the SAME.

1707, April 29. Christchurch, Oxford—According to my promise I send the enclosed verses. I wish they were better for your and your friend's sake. However I hope you will accept them as they are, since I could procure no better. I don't know what inscription should be put to them; I suppose the gentleman they are designed for knows what is proper in such a case.

SIR SIMON HARCOURT to [ROBERT HARLEY].

1707, April 30—I beg leave to inform you that I have prepared a draft of the proclamation for holding the first parliament of Great Britain, and laid it before the Lord Keeper and two Chief Justices, who have approved it. I am now commanded by the Lord Keeper to draw the form of a writ according to the articles of Union directed to the Privy Council of Scotland, which is to issue the same day the Proclamation passes. The Privy Council of Scotland ought to be settled and in being at that time; you will forgive me for putting you in mind of it. That commission certainly is to be settled by the Scotch lords, or at least with their privity; I hope it is done, I have heard nothing from any of them concerning it.

BARON SCHUTZ to ROBERT HARLEY.

1707, April 30. London—Enclosing an extract from a letter from the Electress recommending Monsieur Winde to the Queen for some post in England. *French. Extract enclosed.*

The EARL OF SUNDERLAND to [ROBERT HARLEY].

1707, May 2. Whitehall—Asking him to meet the Lord Treasurer, Lord Keeper, Lord President, and some of the Scotch Lords to consider the constitution of the Privy Council.

BARON SCHUTZ to [ROBERT HARLEY].

1707, May 3—As the Duke of Marlborough could not write to you before leaving Hanover, he wished me to inform you that he agreed with Mr. Robinson that he should go to the conference at Hamburg as soon as the King of Sweden had quitted Saxony. *French.*

A. LADY PYE to ABIGAIL HARLEY, at Eywood.

1707, May 12. Derby—Indeed our neighbourhood is much improved of late, makes me less care for country visiting, which good manners notwithstanding compels me to. Last Thursday dined at Sir Edward Coke's at Langford. He hath long had fine gardens, now the house is as neat within, nothing wanting but a lady which he hath been so long considering, doubt will be difficult to fix, though here they have already given his cousin, widow to great Coke of Norfolk. It is said she is worth 40,000*l.*, kept all her estate in her own power, besides large settlements at marriage. The good natured man hath greatly added to the prejudice of his eldest son, upon whom it will be hard, notwithstanding the great estate, whilst his mother and Lady Anne Walpole live. Last summer they made Sir Edward a visit of ten days, cost him 200*l.* to entertain them, which amongst country gentry was thought high doings ; had enough of her irregular hours ever to think of for a wife, could he hope to obtain. To-day's letters mention Lady Anne Popham married to General Harvey, but know not who it is, nor what he hath besides the officer. This makes me think of a match yours mentioned, our relation the Dresser with Colonel Masham, whom the Queen hath lately advanced. If the same is young have heard her greatly commended for a sober woman. I believe she is the same Aunt Brom[field] used to talk of, lived with Sir George Rivers' lady when first we went to Greville Street. The great Lady Duchess in that deserves great commendations, that hath taken such care of her relations, who when low are generally overlooked. Is her brother Colonel Hill married, as was reported, to one of the Queen's maids?

SIR C. HEDGES to [ROBERT HARLEY].

1707, May 13—I here send you the best account I can get of the Muscovite ship which the Envoy of Sweden desires may be stopped in the River of Thames and not suffered to go out of port, upon pretence that the said ship is fitting out in warlike manner with intent to disturb the commerce in the Channel and North Seas ; and according to the Report of the Marshal of the Admiralty, by whom I have made inquiry and to whom I crave leave to refer, I do not find that the Envoy of Sweden has any just grounds for his demands, the fact not appearing to me to be as is represented by his letters. But if it were authentically proved, which is necessary in this case, with humble submission it is a point that may very well deserve to be further considered before any arrest be made, since the taking in of guns and arms, or goods contraband in their own nature, by her Majesty's subjects and friends in the port of London and entered for a country in amity, is not prohibited by any law that I know of, unless her Majesty had published a prohibition thereof, and I take the Envoy's construction of the treaty in this case to be more than can be clearly deduced from the words and plain intention of the articles he mentions, and I humbly conceive there may be more ill consequences attend the stopping of this ship in the river than can be, by a fair turning it off, in regard of the great trade her Majesty's subjects have in the Czar's dominions, who is a Prince too easily induced to resent it. But if there are any English seamen on board this ship they may be taken into service without giving any occasion for complaint.

The EARL OF GODOLPHIN to [ROBERT] HARLEY.

[1707], May 14. Wednesday—I have been this morning endeavouring to fix the Custom house officers for Scotland. Mr. Honley is named for one, and there is a blank left for the Secretary. I have not yet ventured to propose De Foe for fear I should never get him to go down with Mr. Lowndes unless it be recommended from you.

[The SAME] to the SAME.

[1707, May 15]. Thursday—Monsieur Schultz has shewed me this morning the despatches he received from his Court by the last post. I desired him to communicate them to you which he said he was just going to do. I think it seems reasonable that the Queen should write such a letter tomorrow to the King of Sweden as the Elector proposes; but I wonder why the Emperor, who is alarmed sufficiently as appears by my Lord Manchester's letters, should neglect to desire the Queen's interposition. I am afraid the reason of it must be for fear she should require him to stop his troops from going to Naples.

D[ANIEL] DE F[OE] to ROBERT HARLEY.

1707, May 15. Glasgow—I hope your charity will determine for me that something extraordinary has restrained my writing thus long. I found by a sudden stop of my letters that some were opened, some intercepted, and three letters current to my wife came not to hand till a long time after the course. This, and this only, interrupted my conversing with you in the usual manner which was my pleasure as well as my duty till I saw the course of letters clear and found the stop of letters was only delay, though I knew not, nor yet know where.

I stayed in Edinburgh till the Assembly broke up and after that the Commission, and after that the Synod of Lothian, in all which I have perhaps been more jealous than needed, but I always thought the cautious part the safest in these cases, though it were too much, since over caution may do harm, but too little can do no good. After I saw all clear of the priests I thought to have travelled a little as I hinted to you formerly, but I am posted here to bully a clamorous people, and as I mentioned I think in my last if the Parliament had not dropped the Drawback Bill, I must have fled this country and come away without your commission, which I should have been very loth to have done. It is scarce possible to describe to you the disgust that affair gave here and what use was made of it, and as I am posted here on the frontiers, I could not breathe hardly for the importunate queries of the friends to the Union, what would become of them, and what the Parliament would do with them, and the like. I won't perplex you with these country impertinences on that head, I write this only to satisfy you how I have been employed here for some time.

Now the main affair is over they are frighted afresh with the accounts they say come from London that notwithstanding this the Custom House officers will stop their goods. I have not had the honour of a line from you a long while. I humbly entreat a hint or two in this affair what to say and what to do, for I am at a great loss how to answer and indeed in the general how to behave myself. Nor do I yet know whether my negociating pleases you or not, being to act wholly on my own judgment in every case. I am now to offer another thing. I am at the City of Glasgow and unless I receive your contrary directions

I design to take a short tour and come back hither and stay a week or ten days here. You will be sure matters are changed that I dare to show my face here where it had been death to have been known but a few months ago. I am acting my part with the magistrates and the ministers, for the rest I do not concern myself. I am arguing the great concern England has shown for them in letting fall the Drawback Bill and pressing them to suitable returns of duty and moderation; and I am pleased to tell your honour I am heard in it, and that I think I am doing more service now than ever since I came into this country. And here I beg your leave to give one hint. There are officers sent down to the Customs and Excise; I make no complaints, nor do I say there is yet any cause, but I humbly move that who ever are sent may be commanded to use all the courtesy, civility and calmness possible here. Nothing else can oblige this surly, haughty, vain humour of the poorest and meanest people. I have been often moved on the head, though the gentlemen should be in the right and it consists with their duty, yet, if they have any regard to the nature and temper of things and folks, they must wink, abate, and bear with circumstances. In short, this people may be drawn, the contrary I need not mention.

I have now another thing to mention. Mr. Bell is gone again to London, and he will acquaint you I have been no good husband for you. Indeed, I hinted the measures I took about the Assembly of which I was really heartily afraid, put me to no small expense. But I have been forced since to supply in part family demands, my long absence making it absolutely necessary and indeed impossible to avoid. I shall be sorry to have your censure in this as invading your bounty, but I hope your honour will prevail to have an honest and I hope faithful engine supported while abroad. However I thought it my duty to inform you of it. For I will not have (no not bread) without your knowledge, and will desist whenever you summons me away.

I am to dine on Wednesday with the Presbytery of Dunfermline and the next week at that of St. Andrew's and shall then come back hither. I cannot help expressing my joy at the visible success of my negociating here—and though I am alone too little for it, yet I think nothing more needful than this work, for this is a fermented and implacable nation.

JOHN TOLAND to [ROBERT HARLEY].

1707, May 16—I may take it as my text that *I own myself disappointed;* for this time two years I made sure of some preferment before now, not only because my Lord Treasurer was pleased to promise I should be taken care of when he received so favourably my letter to Mr. Penn, and by reason of the particular service I was generally acknowledged to have done him in writing *The Memorial of the State,* with the further pains I was at in making *My Lord Marlborough's Defence*, it being none of my fault that it was not published, though without receiving as much as copy-money for either: but likewise because I think I may, without fearing the least imputation of vanity, look on myself as much more deserving on many other accounts not fit to be named at present, and a great deal more capable in all respects, than several in the long list of such as have been employed in that space of time. I am as glad not to have the recommendations, as I should be sorry to have the merits of some of these: and should I ever have it in my power to show my resentment, as none can be sure that I shan't, and all will own that I ought, the worst thing I could do will be justified by the bare history of their preferment, whereof nobody is better acquainted.

from all hands with the principal circumstances, though 'tis impossible for any man to unravel the whole mystery. I except all that ought to be excepted : and as for the rest, I have neither bought with some, nor sold with others, being an absolute stranger to all bargaining; I have neither betrayed nor been betrayed; I am neither akin to this family, an enemy to that, nor a retainer to any ; I have never a favourite brother or sister, nor am myself for such gentle services in the good graces of any Lord or Lady whatsover; I have neither flattered nor lampooned with my prostitute rhymes; and, to omit all other considerations, I have threatened no discoveries of past or present transactions, nor have I bullied any great men by myself or others. I have, on the contrary, forgiven all the faults of the Government to the virtues of it. I have silently endured the greatest hardships imaginable, I have been extremely modest in my demands, and though my circumstances would not permit me to be as backwards to ask as others were to give, yet I am conscious to myself, that I never asked or expected any thing that was unreasonable, and that would not be a greater credit for them to give than for me to receive. I know it is an ordinary maxim with certain ministers to consider men no further than as they may be useful or hurtful to their own designs, these extremes equally meeting in the centre of preferment. But I begin at last to suspect the truth of what I have been often told, and as often disbelieved, that the supposed want of such qualifications is not the sole cause of exclusion to me, though the churches of all kinds were never so much in my interest; as neither the Bishops nor the Dissenters are any longer my enemies, whatever some hotbrained pert fellows from Christ-church or anywhere else may pretend, and of which they'll soon receive a demonstration.

I heartily beg your pardon, sir, for discharging my mind with this freedom to the best friend I have upon earth. I have all the assurance conceivable, that if it had depended upon you, I should have been made easy long ago. You have supplied me now for two whole years out of your own pocket, in diet, clothes, lodging, and all other expenses; for whatever some might imagine, I had no other resource in the world but your protection and friendship. Indeed at the beginning I thought, and so did our friend Mr. Penn who led me into the notion, that my Lord Treasurer had ordered me this provisional support, till something became vacant proper for me to accept or execute : but at last I began to gather the contrary from diverse infallible circumstances, and that I became a real charge to you alone, without being on my part any way useful or necessary, at least not made so. This has given me more uneasiness than is possible to express, it overwhelmed me every time with shame, and yet I always found myself under the unhappy necessity of being troublesome. Though all sorts of people took it for granted, as they still do, that I had a good pension in order to a better employment, and that several congratulated me on this account, whether they wished me well or otherwise ; yet I left them all in the dark except some particular friends, to whom I privately discovered the true state of the matter, and who it was in reality I ought to thank for my life and well being. I had the satisfaction to hear many of them expressing themselves on this occasion very obligingly; some of them affirmed, that though they had been deceived in you before, they would ever think well of you hereafter : and truly all the world are persuaded you are my patron, and look on me as your creature ; though few of them are aware how much I ought to regard myself as such. But you may firmly depend upon it, sir, and I give it you here under my hand, that setting aside all considerations of your politic capacity, wherein I ever admired and approved your impartial measures, I have inviolably resolved to run your good or bad fortune, for the future, and to have no other interest but yours. I have no doubt concerning it, but that this is the most certain method of being always for the good of my country; and this is the true reason why I have made no further court to some great persons to whom I was lately recommended, but only to show myself friendly and forgetful of old quarrels or injuries, that I might blunt the edge of their malice, and remove such obstacles out of my way.

Now, as to my going for about six weeks out of the kingdom, I do assure you, sir, by all the professions I have already made, that I am not going nor shall go either to Berlin or Hanover, nor upon any account or errand whatsoever relating to those Courts, as some foolish people might insinuate to you after my departure: for I am not ignorant that pains enough have been taken, and from very different or rather opposite quarters, to ruin me in your opinion, which still increases my debt of adherence and gratitude. But I am really going over on the pressing invitation of some particular friends in the seven provinces, that love my person and favour my studies. There are *arcana literaria* among us, which I hope may divert your leisure hours; and besides its being indifferent whether I passed so much of the summer there or in the country here, I have great reason to believe that I shall be no loser by the journey. 'Tis high time for me to have new clothes, linen I shall buy cheaper there, and I design to retire for the rest of the summer into the country as soon as I come back. Now for these purposes, as well as for my subsistence till November next, and for the discharging of my small debts which can never be possibly prevented till I have something fixed, that I may know how to bring both ends together fifty pounds will be sufficient. I have kept an account of all I have received from you hitherto, and I make no question but if I live I shall be able to repay you, as you have enabled me to pay others; for I never can nor ever will discharge the obligation.

JOHN GASSION [*alias* OGILVIE] to [ROBERT HARLEY].

1707, May 16—It is a long time since I had anything that was comfortable to acquaint you of, and as to the glorious victory we have obtained in Spain over my Lord Galway, I know you have a full account of it from the public gazettes so that I shall not trouble you with the particulars, only I shall tell you what the consequence may be after the battle. You know the Duke of Orleans joined the army where they did continue their march towards Valencia; but when they came within four leagues of the place the town sent out their deputies with the keys. They fell on their knees to make their harangue but the Duke of Orleans suffered them to sit on their knees until they had finished and afterwards told them he would speak to the King about them, but in the meantime ordered them to stay; and that kingdom is taxed to the value of eight million of "cobes" for their rebellion, so that whole kingdom is reduced. The Duke of Orleans is gone to Madrid to speak with the King of Spain and after that to return where he is, to march with a part of the Army through the kingdom of Aragon to reduce it, and with the rest the Duke of Berwick is to march to Barcelona and Monsieur de Noailles is to enter Catalonia by the way of Roussillon where the whole three armies are to join and besiege Barcelona. I do believe they will amount to very nigh 50,000 men, and if the King of France send them from France what is necessary for the carrying on the siege they will certainly take it, and I believe raze it afterwards; but if the King should fail to send those things then it can never be attempted for the Spanish army hath neither ammunition nor money, but I am hopeful the King of France will not fail. We are all over-joyed that it was the Duke of Berwick that gained the battle for it will make him famous, and also pass for a great captain when he shall be sent to assist the restoration of our King. Now as to Flanders our army is about 100,000 men, so we are in great hopes that we shall not be beat, for the whole general officers are men that are chosen by the Duke de Vendome, so we hope the best. I shall trouble you no further at this time only in a little time I hope to be nearer to you. I have written a great many times but cannot tell if you have received them, however when it shall please God to send us anything that is good you shall have it.

Sir Simon Harcourt to [Robert Harley].

1707, May 18—I send you enclosed the warrants you delivered to me yesterday at the Cockpit. There must be a clause in your warrant for determining the letters patent of Generalissimo of England and Ireland, which I have added. The drafts are fairly transcribed and ready for her Majesty to sign if you approve of them. The warrant for High Admiral and all other warrants relating to the Navy are to be directed to the Attorney General only.

John Chamberlayne to [Robert Harley].

1707, May 19. Petty France, Westminster—My good old father had the luck to see about twenty editions of his State of England published before he died. Since his death I have put out two or three, but as England is happily swallowed up in the name of Great Britain, to the everlasting honour of the present Ministry, I am encouraged by my friends to prepare a new Account of England and Scotland under the aforesaid name. I have accordingly settled a correspondence with divers learned and ingenious Scotchmen at Edinburgh and here in town, who have kindly promised me their best assistance, and so have the Bishops of Sarum, Norwich, and Carlisle for books, &c.; but I am still at a loss for several valuable books especially those marked thus + in the enclosed list, which I can find nowhere unless in the noble library of Mr. Secretary Harley, and if your Honour would permit my friend Mr. Wanley to look for them, they should as soon as possible and very punctually be returned with a very deep sense of the obligation.

Postscript.—Since I have been ill, I amused myself with drawing up these Rules, some of my friends tell me they are indifferently good, if they have the fortune to please you I shall be hardy enough to give a copy to a Foreign Minister, for whom they were chiefly intended.

D[aniel De] F[oe] to Robert Harley.

1707, May 21. Stirling—My last was from Glasgow of the 15th. I am now at Stirling, in the circuit which I hinted to you before; I gave you an account of myself at large in my last to which I refer. I cannot but think myself obliged to lay the state of things before you as clearly as possible, and if for want of your commands explicitly guiding me I err in my conduct I hope for your pardon—since it is impossible for me to judge at a distance what is your pleasure being so absolutely destitute of your directions in this affair. The country here was very easy on account of the Union, and I began to boast myself of the happy success. But two things have given so much disgust here that I am amazed to see how soon these people are to be turned about to extremes. Dyer in in his letter says, the lawyers have found out a method to stop the French goods without breaking the Union ; and this is spread over the whole kingdom, being printed again in the Edinburgh Gazette. Now as to this affair, I remember I formerly hinted to you my thoughts, and had some public notice been then concerted, and the Court here taken some measures to have corresponding with it and discouraged the import I believe, much of the mischief might have been prevented, but that is passed.

My humble conclusions formed from serious observation here are that (1) if a general stop be made you put the whole nation here distracted; (2) with a partial stop, they will be very well pleased.

I explain myself thus :

To stop or seize our goods who are Scotsmen is highly injurious to us, as our market here is destroyed by the flux of goods brought in by the English on a prospect of trade to England, who when they shall be obliged to sell here will glut the market and lower the price, and so you ruin us for what is your own fault, which is not fair.

In this part indeed they seem to have reason, for if the stop be general, the case will be very miserable here with a great many, and the clamour intolerable.

They say if their goods are stopped, the Union is directly broken and the article of a free intercourse of trade destroyed.

And indeed this to me seems evident too, and the exception in the House of Commons implies as much, and this is what I am so earnest for direction about.

I am clear, however, that the importations of foreigners and English ought to be stopped, and though concealing and transposing properties may be practised yet you will find it something easier to discover properties here than in England, especially considering the entries are already made without any caution, and the proprietors in most cases discovered, and I have made some observations that in their season will be useful that way. I am also to assure you, that if this medium be agreed on, it will give an universal satisfaction here, for 1st, they cannot pretend any breach of the Union and 2ndly, their pride is fully gratified as well as their purse, and they all cry out it is just to stop the encroachments of strangers.

I ask your pardon for thus freely giving my thoughts, and as I know you put the stress upon the giving just satisfaction to the subject I presume it my duty to give you the sense of the country.

This is the scheme I have also followed in speaking to Dyer's newspaper, and I endeavour as 1st, to allow what they claim as to their own goods, so to show the reasonableness of stopping others. In which I hope I am right, and entreat a hint if I am not, but I am sure, I am right as to the people here in preparing them to acquiesce in all the proceedings, but just as far as touches their separate properties.

I am informed the Custom house is settled for this country, is there no room for an absent servant to be admitted ? I formerly hinted that a general survey, such as Dr. Davenant has in England, would be of great service here, and I am persuaded if I had the honour to acquaint my Lord Treasurer of the steps I formerly hinted about clandestine trade, which some have taken and are making large provision for, his Lordship would find such an employment absolutely necessary, considering the infinite creeks and coves here in which frauds will be carried on, and where 'tis impossible without an army of officers to prevent it. My brother writes me, he has had the honour to see you, and you were pleased to say my Lord Treasurer had mentioned me in the matter of the settlement here. I have nobody to recommend me but yourself, save that the Duke of Queensberry promised me to recommend me to my Lord Treasurer and to the Queen also.

I repeat my humble entreaty to you to be thoughtful of me, that I may no longer be thus chargeable to you.

DR. GEORGE SMALRIDGE to [ROBERT HARLEY].

[1707,] **May 23**—Asking his advice whether he should accept the well-endowed lecturership at St. Dunstan's if it became vacant by the promotion of Dr. Blackall to the bishopric of Exeter. If the professorship [of Divinity at Oxford] should be granted him the lecturership could be thrown up; but if he should miss the chair, this preferment would make the loss of it sit easier.

DR. WILLIAM GRAHME to [ROBERT HARLEY].

1707, May 24. St. James's Place—I would have waited on you this morning by Her Majesty's order with the enclosed address which I had lately the honour to present to the Queen at the request of those gentlemen whose names are to it, but that just now I am commanded to be at Kensington before ten o'clock. It is Her Majesty's pleasure that it should be in the next Gazette and that it should be signified by whom it was presented, namely by Dr. William Grahme, Dean of Wilts, Clerk of the Closet in Ordinary to Her Majesty. You will be pleased to excuse my giving you this intimation by letter, because though it was my inclination I could not possibly pay my service to you in person.

D[ANIEL DE] F[OE] to ROBERT HARLEY.

1707, May 23. Wemyss—My last to you from Stirling gave you my scheme of the national discontents here about the wine and brandy. I mentioned two things, but spoke to one only. The next is the affair of the equivalent—and why is not the equivalent come down, says the country man, you were to pay it by the 1st of May, and you have broke the Union in that, and where is it all this while? Now the Treaty is finished you do what you please with us, and thus we shall be used in everything; this in them is very serious language.

Great advantage is made indeed of this, not so much pretending it shall not be paid, but that time is not kept with them and agreements not performed, and we have a story whispered here that the Duke of Hamilton came the first of May in the night and protested at the Cross of Edinburgh, that the Union was broke. I do not I confess believe the thing, but these reports joined with the want of the money makes a great deal of ill blood here, and does unspeakable harm. The government knows how to apply suitable remedies to these mischief and I doubt not will do so, but I thought it my duty to hint my observations.

The apprehensions of the people here at the stop of their goods are very great, and I confess if that matter is not cleared up and the property of Scotsmen set free, together with some settled method, how the property of Scotsmen may be ascertained and determined, the discontents will run too high and I apprehend new tumults very much. I have spoke my mind freely in print in the "Review" and printed one here to show the justice of preventing frauds, but I must with it own, and indeed my own judgment joins in it, and I believe yours also, that the true property of Scotsmen should be admitted free. I wish I had but two lines from you to direct me in this affair, 'tis really a difficult time here, and I think more so than when the Union was in agitation, for the whole nation is in a ferment, about the French goods and the equivalent.

I might do you much more service, if I had but now and then a letter of proper hints from yourself. I know you are in a hurry and I lament the occasion, but indeed, things here are of consequence, and a little disorder here would give things a bad aspect, and have too great an influence on credit, trade, funds, and all those things.

The matter, therefore, mourns to be settled. I beg your excuses for the liberty I take, which I think my duty.

[Sir Simon Harcourt] to [Robert] Harley.

[1707, May 25 ?]—The patents for High Admiral and Generalissimo, and the Lord Treasurer's, will be brought to you before eleven this morning. I thought proper to revoke the former patents by a distinct instrument for that purpose. 'Twould have looked odd to have revoked the office, and in the same patent granted the same office to the same personage. You will be pleased to let my warrant bear date before the revocation. I was not able to send you a certain answer last night. *Enclosing drafts of patents with alterations.*

Lord Coningsby to Robert Harley.

1707, May 26—I spoke yesterday to my Lord Chancellor and my Lord Treasurer in behalf of Sergeant Birch, and found the first named his friend and the latter so inclinable that I cannot but conclude it done, and so I told Mr. Sergeant this morning.

George Tollet to Robert Harley.

1707 May 26. Navy Office—Forwarding two letters dated 17th and 24th May respectively from Charles Sergison, complaining of some trouble he has met with from a new justice of the peace [for Sussex] and a commissioner of the taxes started up amongst them, who out of pure zeal is raising Sergison's taxes to lower his own, and is like to be a troublesome fellow in the neighbourhood. As this man cannot be removed, he would be glad to get an honest gentleman and a neighbour of his, of fair estate and character, also put into the Commission, if his old friend [Harley ?] would please to do it for him. In the second letter, after an assurance that his honoured friend will comply with his request, he states that the gentleman's name is Leonard Gale, Esq., of Crabbetts in Sussex, bred at the inns of court and holding an estate of 700l. or 800l. a year.

Baron Schutz to [Robert Harley].

1707, May 28—Asking him to fix a day for receiving the gentleman named Winde sent over by the Electress. *French.*

[The Earl of Godolphin] to [Robert] Harley.

[1707, May ?] Wednesday—I have received the favour of your letter and must needs say I thought it an odd question that Mr. Attorney asked me, as if he did not know how he was to prosecute, better than I could tell him.

I have seen the clause you mention and think it in some particulars impracticable and in others unreasonable, and so I believe it will be thought in the House of Lords, but how you will be able to deal with it in your House I cannot judge.

The Duke of Marlborough desires Mr. Stepney may have leave from the Queen whenever he sees he may best be spared to make a step to Mildenheim for one week, to settle his Grace's affairs there, and that you would please to take the Queen's pleasure, so as to let Mr. Stepney know it by Friday's post.

I believe Mr. Buys would be glad that the Queen's pleasure upon his two memorials were also signified to me at the Treasury upon Friday morning.

[The Earl of Godolphin] to [Robert] Harley.

[1707, May] Thursday—I hope you are not the worse for your kind visit yesterday. I shall continue uneasy, till I can get your brother to say something to my Lord Poulett from me, for till I am well enough to go to the House of Lords, it will hardly fall in my way to see him myself.

Holland seems to be a good deal frightened with the noise of the French preparations for the Upper Rhine. I mean the party there for a peace, which is a strong one, make that use of it and blow them up at the same time to be uneasy, without any ground, about their Barrier, and make them jealous of the power of England, but I should think it might be no hard matter for Mr. Stepney to set those people right as to this last point by showing them, as is true :—

That England has a great power when the Sovereign and the nation are of a mind to exert it for the protection and security of their neighbours, because it is indeed their own, but it never will nor never can have the same power to disturb or oppress their neighbours as France does, which is an arbitrary Government.

The letters from Turin speak very hopefully : in short, if Holland can be kept right six months longer, all will go well.

Marg[aret, widow of George] Farquhar to [Robert Harley].

[1707, May ?]—I most humbly beg your honour's powerful inter. cession to the Queen for her gracious charity to a distressed widow and fatherless children, who without some immediate redress must inevitably perish ; the late experience of your honour's great and generous nature encourages me to beg your assistance to the Queen for my future sub. sistence. I never yet received a farthing from her Majesty except ten guineas by the hands of the Duchess of Devonshire upon the presenta. tion of my husband's poem. I hope your honour has perused my petition and certificates to the Queen.

[*Another undated letter of the same writer to the like purport is attached to this.*]

RICHARD KING to [GEORGE ?] TOLLET.

1707, June [1–]12 new style. Camp at Meldert—The 21st and 22nd May N.S. our army assembled at Lambeck near Hall. The 25th my Lord Duke having intelligence that the enemy were marched out of their lines thought fit to march the 26th to Soignies in hopes to find some occasion to engage with them. The 27th my Lord was informed that the enemy marched towards Villeer Perwys with design the day following to take the Camp of Nivelle in order to cut off our communication with Brussels. To prevent which his Grace returned with the Army the 28th to Lambeck, where understanding that the enemy had marched to Sombref with intention to send a detachment either to take Louvain or Huy, he was obliged, to hinder their making any such attempts, to march with the army the 29th to Dieghem, the 31st to Terbanck near Louvain, and the first instant to this place. The enemy made several movements two or three days after we arrived here, and at last fixed on the Camp of Giblon encamping with their right at that town and their left towards Hevileer, having by that means the Ruisseau of Noirmont and Gefuage before the greatest part of their line, which renders their camp so strong that there's no possibility of attacking them in it, without running a great risk of being repulsed. So that I believe we shall not move from hence before the French decamp, which I hope want of forage in a short time will oblige them to do. By the enclosed Order of Battle you'll find that we have 96 battalions and 164 squadrons which at a moderate computation will amount to 85,000 men. The enemy has certainly more battalions and squadrons than we have, yet I am assured we are considerably stronger by reason their battalions and squadrons according to the report of all their deserters are mighty weak.

We understand that Prince Eugene was to march yesterday towards Dauphiny. If this obliges the French to detach part of their army from hence to oppose him we shall make a much better campaign on this side than a great many imagine. It is strongly reported here that the Emperor has actually entered into a Treaty of Peace with France, if so it will be happy for us if we can make peace on the same conditions the French offered us the last winter.

I'm much obliged to my friends for the Engineer's post in the Ordnance they obtained for me last winter, and to you in particular who contributed so much to it.

[*A plan of the order of battle at the Camp of Soignies on 26 May, 1707, is enclosed.*]

SIR JONAT[HAN TRELAWNY], BISHOP OF EXETER to [ROBERT HARLEY].

1707, June 2—I had done myself the honour of waiting on you this morning had I not feared my interest in your porter is no better now than it was in the two late attempts I made with the same design. I know I need not trouble you with any earnest request for the hastening the warrant for the *congé d'élire*, for I am vain enough to believe I am so far in your favour that any affair of mine will never find any stop with you; but my present business is to ask you whether the Queen has been already pleased to sign the first warrant, or only given you orders to bring it to her to be signed, because being commanded yesterday by my most noble patron the Lord Treasurer to pay my dutiful acknowledgments to Her Majesty this morning I must be directed by your answer in what method and how far I am to make them.

J. AISLABIE to [ROBERT HARLEY].

1707, June 4. Ripon—Asking for preferment for his kinsman, Edward, son of Sir Edward, Blackett who had passed his examination and was entered upon the list of lieutenants in the Admiralty. He had served several years under Captain Fairfax, and was now on board the *Albemarle*. If no commission could be obtained for him at home, he would go with Sir Cloudesley Shovel's squadron then ready to sail.

JEAN JUSTIN DE GREIFFENBERG to [WILLIAM] GREG.

1707, June 8. Amsterdam — Excusing himself for having left London without seeing him again. *French*.

LE MOYNE DE BRIE to [ROBERT HARLEY].

1707, June 8. The common side of Newgate—I have found myself so many times engaged above this two years to show you my submission, but always with so little success that I don't know how to move your mercy or justice, &c.

SIR SIMON HARCOURT to [ROBERT HARLEY].

1707, June 10—I send you herewith my report on Mrs. Oglethorpe's petition, if there be anything in it you do not like, I will alter it. I have been beset this afternoon about it, first the prosecutor Frances Shaftoe was with me, who is not to be satisfied without fire and fagot. An agent from the Lady Oglethorpe afterwards came and waited for the report, whilst 'twas transcribing an agent from Mrs. Oglethorpe came also for it, and a dispute grew between them which should have it. The gentleman who came from my Lady was very pressing for it, and that the young gentlewoman might not have it sent her. I thought it most proper to send it to you, and could not help sending you an account of this passage. I have had no summons to a Council to-morrow.

BARON SCHUTZ to [ROBERT HARLEY].

1707, June 10. London—I enclose you the extract of which I spoke, and I take this opportunity to express to you that the Elector has again pointed out to me in his letters which I received today that he thought it would be most useful that the affair of the renunciation should be settled, since that would tend to prevent the house of Gottorp from angering the King of Sweden, and would strengthen the impressions which the Ministers of France and Bavaria wish to give him that the maritime powers were only trying to amuse him and to gain time until he had quitted the Empire. *French. Extract of letter from the Czar enclosed*.

D[ANIEL DE] F[OE] to ROBERT HARLEY.

1707, May 10 [June 10]—I wrote you last post. I have nothing to add worth your note. The weather having been favourable I am travelling through the towns and disputing with the rigid and refractory clergy who are the worst enemies of the Union. I act all this of my own head, for having no direction from you I am loth to be idle and live upon your expense, without forwarding the work I came hither about, and I hope you will believe that I do my utmost not to be so expensive as I am sensible I am without pursuing the true end of the charge.

I am not able to say anything more to what I have formerly hinted about myself; I know absent and forgotten are frequently synonymous, I have no dependences but on yourself but while I see such men as Rigby, Isaacson, &c. in commission I cannot but hope you will cause me to be remembered.

I formerly hinted my proposal of a survey of the outposts and still wish for it; but if not, the accounts or complements of the accounts, things I pretend to be master of, would be suitable for me. I throw myself wholly on your concern for me, and persuade myself, while you are my intercessor I cannot be denied.

Endorsed by Harley.—"D. F., dated May 10 1707, by mistake for June 10. R[eceived] June 17."

ROBERT HARLEY to D[ANIEL DE] F[OE].

1707, June 12—I have received your letters very constantly, and I cannot think that anyone has miscarried. I am sure I have taken care to represent your services in the best light from time to time where it may do you service, and I hope I have not been an unprofitable servant. I am very sorry that you, or your humble servant, should bear reproach for doing what others could not or would not do, but it has been often so, I have set up my rest, and therefore it is not in their power to disappoint me. I count upon all that impotent malice, inveterate spleen can do by misrepresentation, and notorious forgeries to do me hurt. I am prepared for all; and the wrath is greater against me because their weakness as well as villanous arts happen to be detected. And if God spares me life, I think I shall be able to pull off the mask from the real atheists and pretended patriots—but too much of this now.

You are in the right to put the Duke of Queensberry in mind of you, repeat it again. It will serve to cover your friends in doing you justice. I need give you only a hint. As to more particulars I desire you will write a letter to Lord Treasurer (enclose it to me), proposing your own service and where you can be most useful. He thinks Surveyor of one of the Ports, if that meets with your approbation propose that, or any other alternative, the sooner the better.

I cannot let this letter pass without a few words upon the point of trade. The true state of the matter is this—upon the view of the Union, Dutch, Jews, Swedes, Danes &c. struck into the notion of bringing in goods before May 1st, which arose from one certain gentleman's giving great commissions, thinking to have swallowed all the profit; this set everybody agog to get the pence; the malicious world reports, and names the men and sums of money ventured by those in both Houses, but be sure you do not believe that, for it is impossible that persons of all sorts, colours and pretences can be such knaves—and what has passed since is only accidental, which the men of the world interpret to very wrong ends. However, the House of Commons would have rescued us from the scandal and obliged Scotland; they had contrived to make the cheats do justice and at the same time indulged the Scots with an opportunity of getting clear and honestly 150,000*l.*, to speak with the least—but Satan hindered—the Scots—but I should more truly say one person only—solicited against their own nation, under pretence of the Union, whereas there is nothing plainer can be said in words (for any case which is contingent and is to happen) than the words of the Union against the practice. What is more, no one lawyer of credit would ever pretend to stand by the contrary opinion, but it was hoped that power, faction, and noise, which are the same, together with fear of offending Scotland whom they hoped to enrage, would bear the cheats out in this barefaced fraud. When they found that a middle way was discovered, to indulge the Scots and make the others pay, then they were surprised and to hinder it, all the tools were to be used—*Acheronta movebo*—What was the present end you know, what is to come God knows, but this is certain; if our Scots frien■ knew what a sweet morsel these people have taken out of their mouths they would turn their rage the right way. I will add but two things more, those goods (though they should come in quickly) will come to no market, and the next thing is that the wines, brandies and other goods of the growth and manufacture of the kingdom of France are entirely forbidden here, and can no way be brought in, either before or since the Union, but as prize goods, and then the duty is fixed high and this is as plain as A. B. C.

You will excuse me for being so large upon a head, which is so copious, and as extensive as the vast volumes of cheat and knavery, but you will quickly guess at the true state of affairs relating to this matter by these short hints. I think it will be for your own service as well as the public, that you consider what method is the best to prevent future frauds in the Customs, and to allay the heats of our new friends, and send it as soon as you can in writing.

I desire you will send me an account of what money you have received from Mr. Bell, and the times when; he being now in town, I am clearing with him, and L[ord] T[reasurer] says it is not fit you should be longer at my charge, which I hope is for your good.

Copy endorsed by Harley :—" Enclosed to Mr. Bell.*"*

R. MONCKTON to [ROBERT HARLEY].

1707, June 16—Though you so oft denied me audience I made myself sure of my *congé*, but was this morn compelled for Yorkshire without that satisfaction. I excused you for your reservedness because I fancied you now suspected I came to tease you about our pretentions to your principality. I had other things which more concerned yourself and myself to have consulted you upon, as you voluntarily promised me the privilege of in my new province more proper for a Grahame than an epistolary correspondence, but as to the other I ought to tell you how highly your friend resents it though I beg of you be sure to take no notice to him of this information as you desire I should keep his friendship; but when they have not only waived their own pretentions but in the way to engage him more have added also their solicitations for Jessop, you may be sure they won't fail to fire him at your opposition from whom he had much more reason to expect assistance. And you are the more to blame because this is a thing that Jessop—who is more particular to him then anybody—may pretend to very reasonably, which is not always happening, when nothing can fall within the extent of the supreme Courts—as he says—too good or too great for such a full figure as your man makes.

There is the other great man, on whom you have spent so much powder, told my Lord Hartington that he was extremely sorry that he did not think of Jessop the other day when he, expostulating with you for being always on the banter and you made him such sincere professions, that he did not propose Jessop as a test to you and a satisfactory performance of all you promised.

D D 2

I gave you these hints that you may if you please act upon them. both. And as a friend tell you I think it for other reasons the best advice I can give you. I am sure 'tis sincerely meant.

The DUKE OF MARLBOROUGH to [ROBERT HARLEY].

1707, June [16-]27—I have had the favour of yours of the 10-21 with the enclosed copy of Monsieur Chamillart's letter, he is mistaken as to Monsieur Blanzac, and I shall take care to inform him. We are here under great uncertainties, for our friends in Holland are desirous of good success, but will not consent to the venturing a battle for it, they would be glad of action, so that it did not engage us so far as to venture the whole, which is what can't be promised, for if we are once engaged, that matter will depend on the resolution of the enemy. We are in great expectations of hearing that the Duke of Savoy and Prince Eugene have forced their passage, which is generally thought must oblige the Duke of Vendome to make a detachment; this is one of the reasons that makes our friends not willing to venture a battle till they hear of their success.

EARL POULETT to [ROBERT HARLEY].

1707, June 16. Hinton—My unfeigned respects for Mr. Secretary Harley are too strong for my apprehensions of being thought an officious body here in the country, in recommending Mr. Nicholas Wood, merchant in Exeter, to you, which I am the more free to do because I have neither private interest nor pleasure in so doing, but a perfect duty to the Queen's service engages me in it. He has an absolute interest in the Chamber of Exeter and by his great trade and generous living has a mighty sway in that city; but because he won't give this up tamely to the late Bishop of Exeter, there is a personal difference between them; and his being opposite heretofore to him has raised such prejudices in that positive prelate that I know my Lord is incapable of having any tolerable opinion of him, so that he turned him out from being one of the receivers in the county of Devon, which in respect to the public though I was Lord Lieutenant of that county I did not concern myself to meddle in it.

Now Sir Jonathan is translated to the top of preferment, Mr. Wood can't see his great favour, without justly apprehending his power will persecute him in all the vexatious disturbances of his trade by partial directions to the little officers of the Customs there who are all his creatures. You know the influence of the city of Exeter in the west and that it's too great a city to be treated at the vile rate of a Cornish borough, which our friend the Bishop of Winchester through his warmth of temper does not distinguish. I am sure I live in that respect with him that it's not out of the least prejudice to my Lord I write this, for I profess I am his friend and servant, but none of his friends can be ignorant this is his temper, nor do I write this out of any personal favour for Mr. Wood, for I can take the Government to witness that I never presumed to give any trouble for the least preferment to any one friend of mine, but Mr. Wood has been here with me and has satisfied me so much of his good disposition that I dare answer for him in acting what is right as to the choice of a Recorder in Exeter whenever Sir Ed. Seymour dies, who stood singly upon his interest in that city; and in the next elections of Parliament you may there experience this truth, for as Mr. Wood has an interest to be chosen himself, so he will be entirely at my Lord Treasurer's devotion; but his city pride won't submit through the Bishop, and all that Mr. Wood desires is only to have that regard and protection from the Government that of common right is due to every subject, for though the law will maintain his right he thinks 'tis a great unhappiness to be forced so often to contend for it, as he has been through these occasions I take the liberty to acquaint you with. I durst not trouble my Lord Treasurer with so very long a letter, and thought I should be faulty if I did not by you make it known to him, the circumstances of a man who can be most useful to the Government, in this city. I expect so much regard to myself as that the Bishop of Winchester shall never hear anything of this, and beg the favour to know whether this came to your hand; and if it be agreeable I should give any encouragement to Mr. Wood in his disposition towards the public.

SIR JONATHAN [TRELAWNEY], BISHOP OF WINCHESTER, to [ROBERT HARLEY].

1707, June 18—Thanking him for his congratulations on his appointment and asking for the restitution of his temporalities from the day of his predecessor's death, which he has the more reason to hope for, because the rents of the bishopric are so unequally divided that the Lady day payments do not exceed 600*l*.

[ROBERT HARLEY] to the [EARL OF GODOLPHIN] Lord Treasurer.

1707, June 19—-Though as the wind is now changed I am very like to trouble your Lordship again tomorrow, yet I think it my duty not to omit sending to you a letter I received this day from my Lord Poulett's servant. I find his caution would not permit him to send it by the post, and I believe your Lordship is well informed of the interest in Exeter. I am sure he has taken pains and been at charge to fix a right interest there, and to show it upon the death of Sir Edward Seymour. Your Lordship will please to observe the freedom wherewith he writes to me, which is not fit for any view but your Lordship's from whom I ought to conceal nothing. I will write such answer upon this subject to my Lord Poulett as you shall please to direct me. I take the liberty also to enclose to your Lordship a letter I received from Fearns an agent of mine in Scotland, because De Foe is now gone into the country, and I cannot tell what account your Lordship may have had of what he represents: he is a formal fellow, but very faithful and in credit with the Kirk.

This puts me in mind to tell your Lordship a matter which I have touched before, and is really so unaccountable that I can scarce satisfy myself it is possible: and yet I have positive assertion of particulars more than is fit to trouble your Lordship with in a letter. It is about ——Scot —— I have it from one who converses with his relation and gives an account of all his proceedings from Hanover hither. He says that he left his servant behind him and ordered him to meet him at The Hague as he did, that he wrote to his own Court that he was taken sick upon the road, which was the occasion of his stay and that he wrote letters to this purpose from Paris, that he saw the Prince of Wales upon whose birthday this man met him here in London to rejoice on Tuesday was seven-night. This is so very extravagant that I cannot reconcile it to common sense unless he is a refiner like his countryman Johnson, and thinks to make discoveries (of nothing) by acting a nonsensical part.

But I must now begin a matter which is to my weak judgment of greater consequence, and that is to give your Lordship a short account of what passed at the meeting of the three Chiefs, with the Attorney and Solicitor at the Lord Chancellor's about the Lord Treasurer's Patent ; I hope you will be pleased to oblige the Attorney to give your Lordship a particular account of some circumstances which in my poor judgment will give more light than anything else which will be suffered to appear, and will particularly show that there was scarce so much labour used about the ship money as has been about this, most certainly not in so little time, and I must humbly beg as your Lordship's faithful servant and one that will be so to the utmost, that I may not be joined in it. I cannot with open eyes be partaker in these dark projects; and my soul shall never enter into their secret. I cannot see how any one who is of the House of Commons can foreclose himself from that debate, that the *present* Parliament is not dissolved. I am confident no Judge will dare give an opinion in a point where he has neither law nor precedent to direct him, and especially in what principally affects the the House of Commons, and of a matter they know no more than the Bishop of Salisbury does of the countries he has described in his second volume of Travels, where to my knowledge he never once set his foot. But this is the Original Sin, *hinc prima mali labes*--the notion of the Parliament being whimsically and consequently metaphysically dissolved and reviving again is the fountain of mischief; one absurd thing allowed has drawn too many pernicious consequences after it, and will produce too many hereafter more than at present can be foreseen; though too much way has already been given to this tinsel fancy, it is not too late to stop it; and I cannot see any way of preventing endless mischief and creating new divisions in the House of Commons more formidable than any have been yet of late, but by beating down this opinion of the Parliament being transubstantiated; the elements and accidents the same but the substance altered. I think this is so gross and substantial nonsense, that the power of the Queen will scarce find believers enough to give it credit, and I hope the doctrine will meet with no support from that quarter. It is fit now I should beg your Lordship's pardon for being thus tedious, it is possible that it is my fault and proceeds from weakness that I apprehend this matter so much. Your Lordship will bear me witness that I have opposed the monster from the first of its appearance, and I am sure that I have no other consideration in it, or any motive whatsover but what springs from a sincere zeal for the Queen's service, and a heart firmly devoted to your Lordship.

Thus far I had wrote and going to take a little fresh air, I met a chairman in the Park who gave me the honour of your Lordship's letter. I sent the enclosed immediately to my Lord Chancellor. After your Lordship has received my Lord Chancellor's letter and had the patience to read mine hitherto, it is fit I should contrive to be very short, though I hope your Lordship will before you determine anything have a sincere state of this matter and all that passed at the meeting which I will only touch very briefly. The Judges were told it was necessary and thought to be so; each of them spoke to the point and then it was summed up that they were of opinion it was necessary; upon this it was objected that it was not apprehended that the Judges were of that opinion, upon much discourse it came to be settled that they thought it expedient only. Then it was started what Commission the Lord Treasurer must have, it was agreed that it must be verbatim with the present one; then it was started that his Lordship must have a Pardon for what is passed (but that is to be kept in reserve), it was also said that the Chancellor of the Exchequer by consequence must have a new Commission, and how much exception that was liable to. By these short hints your Lordship will judge the truth, and what will more plainly appear when your Lordship has the full detail of this matter, and how little foundation there is for this project which is designed to be the corner stone of more mischief. I hope if they are permitted to be worried into this opinion that we may have leave to show by parity of reason that all the Judges' Commissions, but more particularly those of the Exchequer, are also vo█.

I most heartily beg your Lordship's pardon for this most tedious letter.

RICHARD LONG to ROBERT HARLEY.

1707, June 24. Stockton—I left Edinburgh on Friday last and thought it fit to acquaint you of the dissatisfaction I saw in Scotland about the Union, not knowing whether you had heard of it, because the Scots gentlemen that are for it do apply themselves to you, and not the dissatisfied party. In Edinburgh and to northward especially they cry so bitterly against the Union, cursing those great men of theirs that gave consent to it, frequently talking about him whom we believe to be the pretended Prince of Wales as the true heir, and desiring the bad success of the Duke of Marlborough. They do not this in private, but in taverns and along the road when they meet anyone. The people that live in the south part and who use English markets are more moderate, yet one may see fifty men before one that is for the Union in South or North.

JEAN GASSION [*alias* OGILVIE] to [ROBERT HARLEY].

1707, [June 28–]July 8. Rotterdam—I arrived here on the sixth with my wife and children. I thank God I have got them out of the danger I was most afraid of.

It's true that you will perhaps blame me that I have not answered your expectation, but I am persuaded that you will not when you consider that it's not in my power to perform impossibilities. You know I have not money of my own to maintain me at a Court such as the French is, and there is not a man on earth can render you any service at that Court unless he have money to spend ; for such an affair will require it.

You may depend on it the King of France designs to restore the Duke of Bavaria and raise Barcelona ; and for the Duke of Savoy's entering Dauphiny it's what they are not afraid of, and I positively tell you that I do not think it possible for him, all passes are so well guarded, and when he comes he'll find an army as strong as his own. It's believed that Monsieur de Vendome will besiege Menin about the end of the year.

DR. J. E. GRABE to [ROBERT HARLEY].

1707, June 28. Oxford—Thanking him for obtaining the Queen's favour and bounty in relation to the publication of the first volume of his edition of the *Septuagint*.

John Forster to Robert Harley.

1707, June 30. Stonegarthside—I humbly presume to give your Honour the trouble of a line. I did give Colonel Stanwix some hint, ere his Grace the Duke of Marlborough went abroad, that there was a design this summer to disturb the peace of these nations viz. : that the Jacobites in Scotland and England had thoughts of setting up the Prince of Wales, and that there were emissaries sent from one to another to carry on the thing; there was one went there out of this country this spring, that went by the way of Scotland into Ireland, and came back to Scotland and went into the north of Scotland, and is there still, he goes by the name of Peter Stranger, and those that did converse with him do say he came upon that design, he is sent by some Londoners or some in the south parts. There was in the beginning of this month a gentleman of the name of Mr. Donnald at Sir Patrick Maxwell's and other gentlemen's houses, who are professed Jacobites. This Mr. Donnald as I hear is lately come from France.

This last week I met a gentleman that lives in Annandale, he told me that the Marquis of Annandale, the Earls of Nithsdale and Wigton, Lord Stormont and several gentlemen had a meeting and that those noblemen and gentlemen that incline that way had dispersed and resigned their authority to the Marquis of Annandale, and had given him the chief jurisdiction or superiority over most part of Nithsdale and Galloway viz.: that at his call or summons all the sensible men should rise in arms, and that these noblemen had been speaking to some of their tenants to provide themselves with horses and arms. Duke Hamilton should have been at this meeting but did not come; the Marquis of Annandale is now at Edinburgh.

I hear that Colonel John Johnston, the Marquis of Annandale's brother, is now in London, he was a Captain in my Lord Dumbarton's regiment, he went to France soon after he got out of Newgate, for he and others were committed to Newgate just at the Revolution; he stayed all King William's reign in France and about three years ago came into Scotland. It is supposed that letters or other intelligence may come to him from France, as I am told that he turned papist when he was abroad.

It is said that they have frequent accounts of what happens abroad, having so many relations and acquaintance in all parts, possibly their letters may come in other men's names and not in their own names.

Some time ago I was told that the ringleaders of this party in Holland had made settlements and conveyances of their estates to prevent forfeiture, and that there were commissions from the Prince of Wales amongst them. They have been very busy all this spring but carried matters very quiet and close.

I humbly beg pardon for this trouble and freedom, hoping that your generous character will freely excuse me, for I do heartily wish that I could be serviceable to my Queen and country, humbly desiring that my name may not be made use of, for I live among those that generally are inclined to the Prince of Wales.

If you are pleased to vouchsafe me the favour of a line, direct for me at Newgarthside to be left at the Post house in Carlisle, and it will come safe; and if anything hereafter happen that I think may be of use, I shall acquaint your Honour.

The Privy Council.

1707, July 1—Certificate of the Privy Council that Robert Harley one of the Principal Secretaries of State having delivered up the old signet of that office which was thereupon broke before Her Majesty, and having received a new signet, did again take the usual oath of one of Her Majesty's Principal Secretaries of State. *Signed by John Povey. Seal of the Privy Council.*

D[ANIEL DE] F[OE] to ROBERT HARLEY.

1707, July 8—I gave you some of my thoughts last post and some instances of Jacobite insolence. I cannot but acquaint you of what I think, not without ground, gives a great many sober people a great uneasiness and I must acknowledge has some appearance of mischief in it. The intolerable boldness of the Jacobite party in the Northern Highlands is such now, and in some of the Lowland provinces, also in the North, that unless some speedy care is taken to prevent their disorders, the consequences cannot but be fatal. About fourteen days since they rabbled the whole Synod of Ross and maltreated the ministers, and this by a made rabble of men disguised in women's clothes, of which complaint having been made to the Council I presume you have a particular.

But the thing I particularly instance now, is that the Duke of Athol who now makes himself the head of the discontented party has appointed his great hunting. I have not learnt the precise day, but the Lord Sinclair and several other of the popish and Jacobite gentlemen on Fife side, where I now am, are already gone to it, who are known to be no sportsmen, nor ever used to go. The Jacobites report their King James VIII. will be on show quickly, some report he is arrived *incog.*, but all agree there is some mischief in hand; and the forces here are so contemptible that if any commotion happen they can do nothing. After all, the secret talk among some of their privadoes is that they have 30,000 men ready at a word, and good people are very uneasy. But the particular reason why I write this is the easiness of the attempt supposing a party of these desperate people should offer to surprise the equivalent, and it is but this day that I strangely had an occasion to hear something like it whispered, as it comes directly from some that know more than everybody imagines. I thought it my duty to hint this, 'tis a doubtful time here, and such a bait would flush the whole party and push them headlong into general confusion. If you think it may conduce to the public service I shall willingly hazard myself to go north, and make myself master of as much of those mysteries of iniquity as can be obtained in order to give you seasonable intelligence. If you approve it your orders should come by the very next post.

JEAN GASSION [*alias* OGILVIE] to [ROBERT HARLEY].

1707, July 12. Rotterdam—I must advertise you that there are emissaries in Scotland and that the Court will be tampering with that nation more than ever. Lord Melfort is come to St. Germain to live on purpose for that end, for believe me there is a numerous discontented party in Scotland and the Prince of Wales is become very vigorous. They have also some people from them with the King of Sweden to represent their deplorable condition to him and to beg his assistance; and I doubt not I may render you service at the Court of Sweden by the means of Count Belke who is there for the French affairs, and he can never mistrust me since I had letters of credit to him once. If you think that my going down to Scotland to see if I can find out their intrigues be of any service to you I am content to do my endeavour, but there is one thing you must take care of, and that is there is a priest that stays with Lord Drummond who is correspondent to the Scotch College, and he receives their letters and distributes them. This priest has no kindness for me and will keep all things as close from me as he can, but if he were removed I am sure I should know of every letter that came. So I would have you send him away. You need but speak to some of the Scotch ministers to advertise him to leave the kingdom or he would be taken and sent away.

DAVID EDWARDS to ROBERT HARLEY.

1707, July 12—Asking for assistance and agreeing to accept the post of messenger of the peers if the salary might be 100l. a year, the same as it was when Sir Roger Lestrange officiated.

HENRY GUY to ROBERT HARLEY.

[1707,] July 12. Earl's Court—I have been several days successively to wait upon you but could not have the good fortune to see you. I go away very early on Monday and I cannot easily depart in peace without bidding you farewell, for such a valuable friend is not to be found every day. Therefore I will again come this afternoon and hope to find you not gone to Windsor. I the more desire it because so long a journey joined to my age and infirmities may give me a reasonable doubt whether I shall ever see you more.

PRIVY COUNCIL.

1707, July 14—Heads of the business to be brought before the Privy Council upon appeals from the Plantations and other matters.

EARL POULETT to [ROBERT HARLEY].

1707, July 16—I think myself under an indispensable duty to make my humble acknowledgments for your letters. I wrote in general in Mr. Wood's favour that you might know his character to be very well disposed and capable of being very useful to the public service in this part of the kingdom, and in that respect only I desired he should not be discouraged, which he has some reason to apprehend, being turned out of half the receiver's place in the County and all the little officers of the Customs in that city recommended by his utter enemy. I desire particularly to know if I might encourage him to stand for Parliament man at Exeter where he has an interest to be chosen on his own credit, and I dare answer I could prevail with him as shall be judged most fit. How his character of a Churchman may agree with the present dispositions is a mystery to me, and I shall with patience wait at home till the unriddling of the Juntissimo. I will not presume to add more but that enemies' actions have made in general all of the character of Churchmen more reasonable than any words of friends could do, and it has so effectually wrought that I find them earnest to give any proofs of the convictions of their folly that can be derived from men of their principle. Sir Chuffer went to London to receive Lord Stourton's moneys; he has abandoned all thoughts of the public.

The Duke of Bolton to [Robert] Harley.

1707, July 16. Epsom—Enclosing a letter written from Lulworth on the 11th inst. by Robert Corbin and Richard Davis but posted at Blandford, twenty miles from there, stating that many small arms had been landed at Lulworth Castle, that several French were there, and that the writers were afraid to live in their houses. Has sent the information to Mr. Serjeant Bond, who is deputy custos, and has directed him to send an account of his proceedings in this matter; and if any necessity requires will call some of the deputy lieutenants to his assistance.

Lulworth Castle is now a Roman Catholic's, I think his name is one Wild (Weld).

Guernsey.

1707, July 18 (received)—Depositions taken in Guernsey concerning arms being put on board in France for Scotland. Attested by Eleazar Le Marchant, Charles Andros, and James Careye. *French and English*.

D[aniel De] F[oe] to Robert Harley.

1707, July 19. Edinburgh—I am sorry to say that I look now as one entirely forgot. That having the honour to be sent hither and not thinking it my duty to abandon my post without your orders, have now neither capacity to stay nor orders to come away. The Commissioners of the Customs are sitting every day and filling up the places with persons as usual supplied with more friends than merit. I have been in hopes from what you were pleased to hint to me that I should be thought of. I entreat you will please to interpose your interest on that account, which I doubt not would be effectual. If nothing be to be expected, it is a favour I persuade myself you will not deny me, to let me have a hint from you, and a help to return me to serve you some other way.

I gave you an item of a design to surprise the equivalent, were it real or not, I thought it my duty to communicate it to you. I believe their heart will fail them. However, I took this method, in which I believe I did not amiss, that I effectually spread a report that there was such a design, which I believe will make half the country go out to meet it, and quite make the attempt impracticable. Ignorance and prejudice have raised a clamour against the Exchequer bills that they say are coming. I had wrote half a sheet to explain the advantage of them and their answering money in their effect on trade, but I am run too low to print for there is no printing here but at an expense. I shall disperse some written copies that I may continue to do what service I can when straitened from doing what I might.

I fear, sometimes, you have thought me too chargeable here, but if you will permit me to give you a scheme of my way of living and what I have been doing, I persuade myself you will be convinced I have not misapplied neither the time, nor the money. I am, I confess, impatient to have some directions what to do, and how to govern myself, and entreat your pardon for my importunity. It has been reported they are discontent here at the many English who come hither for places; but that I think is groundless report. But one thing I ought to note. It gives a very great distaste here that the officers of the excise are obliged to gauge on the sabbath day. It would be also a caution needful to be given that the English officers should not frequent the Jacobite conventicles, which will soon render not them only odious, but so encourage them, that they will think themselves supported, or at least approved by the English Government. These hints I thought needful to give you the trouble of.

[The EARL OF GODOLPHIN] to [ROBERT] HARLEY.

[1707, July 22] Tuesday. Windsor—Since I saw you I have seen letters by the way of Ostend which say the Emperor was possessed of Naples without opposition. I offer to you whether Sir Philip Medows should not be directed by this post to press the Court at Vienna to send a detachment of those troops to Spain without loss of time and while the fleet continues in those parts.

Perhaps this has been done more than once, but upon this news there can be no harm in repeating it.

SIR ROBERT PRICE, Baron of the Exchequer, to ROBERT HARLEY.

1707, July 23. Abingdon—Concerning the trial before him that day of one James Murray for highway robbery on August 15. Patrick Graham, the only witness against the prisoner, had deposed that he and Murray, with others named, had stopped two ladies in a coach in Maidenhead Thicket, from one of whom they had taken a guinea and a half, and a purse of silver from the other, but the latter telling them that she was the wife of an officer in the army the money was returned to her. The party were said to have gone afterwards to Staines, and Murray had four or five shillings for his share. The jury had acquitted Murray as two persons of quality had given him a good character.

JOHN CHAMBERLAYNE to [ROBERT HARLEY].

1707, July 24. Petty France, Westminster—After my humblest thanks for your great favour to me, I am bold to trouble your Honour again in behalf of the good old Archbishop of Armenia, who according to the Oriental custom, ushers in his petition with a small present of some of those books printed by him in Holland, for the use of his countrymen. What he desires, Sir, you will be pleased to see by the enclosed from the Archbishop's agent Mr. Cockburn ; he was put upon that request by the Czar's Ambassador, who has promised him his master's protection as far as his vast territories extend themselves, and through which the old man desires to return home ; but he, the said Ambassador, tells him also that the renowned Queen of Great Britain's pass will convey him much further.

JEAN GASSION [*alias* OGILVIE] to [ROBERT HARLEY].

1707, July 25. Aldgate—Announcing his arrival in England.

The EARL OF SUNDERLAND to [ROBERT HARLEY].

[1707] July 26. Windsor—Congratulating him on the good news just arrived from Provence, and hoping to see him at Windsor on Monday.

PRIVY COUNCIL.

1707, July 28—Heads of business to be brought before the Privy Council.

The Mayor, Recorder, and Justices of Chester to Robert Harley.

1707, August 2. Chester—Regarding the charges made by one Bourne against Richard Taylor, of robbing the Exchequer. Taylor had been allowed to escape, the evidence not being sufficient. Signed by Puleston Partington, mayor, R. Comberbach, recorder, Hugh Starkey, Peter and William Bennett, and D. (?) Puleston.

John Chamberlayne to [Robert Harley].

1707, August 4. Windsor Castle—I am but too sensible how troublesome I am to your Honour in an affair, small indeed in itself but very great to me, not only because I shall find my account (as everybody does) in the Queen's grace and favour, but chiefly because my credit and reputation lie at stake, having been so foolishly sanguine as to promise my bookseller, and some of my friends, that I could easily obtain Her Majesty's privilege &c. This is the first time I ever sold a bearskin before I had caught him, and I am sure it shall be the last. Sir, you were pleased to tell me that the Queen found a great many faults in my book, they shall all be mended, if it be possible in the next impression, especially if Her Majesty would direct her officers neither to deny me lists nor give me false ones when I apply to them, for there I believe are the greatest of my faults, I am sure 'tis there I meet with the greatest difficulties. Sir, if Her Majesty will vouchsafe to grant my humble request, I beseech you let it be for this my first edition, which will be ready against the opening the first Session of Parliament of Great Britain ; 'twill encourage me to spare neither pains nor cost in making my book as useful as possible (in order to which I have settled a noble correspondence at Edinburgh), and moreover it will protect me from such pirates and plagiarists as Miege, &c. who rifled and transcribed almost half my father's book to compile his *New State* &c. I heartily beg your Honour's pardon for being thus tedious and troublesome, but perhaps I shall owe a little of your favour to this importunity ; I am sure I shall, a great deal of it, to your known goodness and patronage of such as do but aim at learning and exerting their poor talents in the best manner they can.

Postscript.—My honoured friend, Dr. Arbuthnot, intends to attack my royal Master again upon this affair.

A. Lady Pye to Abigail Harley, at Eywood.

1707, August 4. Derby—I returned from Buxton last week, where I spent ten days to oblige my eldest girl, who prefers that Bath and the waters to all other medicines ; and it agrees with her as the Somerset waters do with your sister. This town daily increases. When we came first but one coach besides ours, now thirteen kept, and more talked of. Naming a coach reminds me of the misfortune of mine, lent it from Buxton to carry some ladies home, who so well loaded it that it quite unjointed and fell to pieces, past mending, that I dare not venture to visit out of this town, and spoils me for Nottingham horse race where will be abundance of company. The French [prisoners] contribute much to the plates. Though [I have] lived so near never was at it, which few besides myself can say. Mrs. Gray that seldom stirs out appears then always in great splendour. She hath lately built a fine school and endows it well for poor children to learn to read English, write and account, likely to be more useful than many grammar schools. She credits the single life to refuse so many great offers. I think they now let her alone, but I have not seen her a great while.

Our two eldest now both want a little polishing, and Dick is grown so strong will bear the town air better than formerly, which has been one occasion of our staying in the country; swimming and shooting have done more for him than all the doctors. Sir Francis Mulinax' daughter, Lord Howe's niece, is just upon marriage with Mr. Plumbtree, burgess for Nottingham, a good clear estate, and a mighty good character he hath for well-bred, ingenious and sober; her fortune in this age esteemed small being 2,000*l*. The scribbling humour is upon me, but don't be frighted it comes very rarely, and I may not of a long time be so troublesome; but to be serious, dear cousin as soon as read burn this most trifling paper if you love me.

[DANIEL] DE FOE to ROBERT HARLEY.

1707, August 5. Edinburgh—My last long letter prevented the enclosed and without supposing it had been sent you in a public manner. We are told here that my Lord Mar has suppressed the Address, and they are very angry with him here for it.

Notice has been sent from some merchant in London to their principals here that all their ships will be confiscate and their goods spoiled, and that their seamen are all pressed or, as I tell them is more likely, run away for fear of pressing. The merchants here have they say sent orders to their friends in England to give no security, but to demand their goods and if not delivered to give bills of parcels to the officers who detain them and to sue them for the money. If this be so, it must be by procurement from London, that method being unknown here, and the persons I believe are W. A. Stuart, Thos. Coots, &c. who are the principal merchants in London concerned in this affair, with Mr. Elliot in Round Court, laceman; if these could be made easy, this whole affair might be closed.

Now they begin to be convinced here that if the first bill had passed in Parliament Scotland had been safe and also gainers, and they blame the Scots merchants for opposing it; a short hint how to behave in this affair would give me a great help. Indeed the Jacobite party make great use of it, and it does an unspeakable injury as to the tempers of the people, which began very much to abate in their ill influences but now increase again. The brewers are now going mad, in their turns. I hinted the case in my last, several of them gave over work, and the servants finding others did not, went yesterday in a tumult to those houses that were at work and put out their fires and let their liquor run about house; and the like disorder today also. Where it will end I cannot yet foresee.

I entreat the hand of the enclosed may not be seen because I obtained it by a private correspondence, which it will be necessary to keep up, and being a known hand it would be both unfaithful to him and entirely close the door of my intelligence on that side if I should not conceal him.

Postscript.—The equivalent is safely lodged in the Castle this night.

D[ANIEL DE] F[OE] to [ROBERT HARLEY].

1707, August 7. Edinburgh—I wrote you in my last that the equivalent was arrived in the Castle—I think it my duty to give you a distinct account of the circumstances of that affair here, I mean with respect to the humours of the people. I must confess the ill blood occasioned by this is such, and so much has it revived the old heats that were the Union now to be transacted it would be impossible.

I am never, you know, for searching an evil to be amazed at it, but to apply the remedies. The capital quarrel is at the bills come down; were the people here that are to receive it men of trade, or were there any such thing as paper credit here, or were the Bank here in hands that were not secret enemies to the public good, or had the bills had a running interest upon them—this matter had been better. But as it is, pardon me to foul my paper with some of their language; 'tis necessary you should know it, though you have the happiness to be remote from it and out of its reach.

First at England in general—Did we not say they would do what they pleased with us when they had us in their power ? Did not Mr. Hodges tell us they were a tricking, faithbreaking nation, and now we have given ourselves up now they unmask, now they begin with us—others—aye, and they begin early too, one would have thought that in policy they might have dealt smoothly with us at first, but now we see how we are to be treated they contemn us so much that they do not think it worth while to wheedle us of the Bills—Here's the English money that was to circulate among us and encourage our trade and now 'tis come in bits of paper. What are their banks and exchequers to us, our gentlemen carry them down to pay their heritable debts with, and who do they think will discharge their lands for bits of paper that if they will be paid must be sent 400 miles or more to get the money where those people have neither friend nor correspondent.

I confess I am tired with filling your ears with these things. But really the gentlemen of the Bank have been much in the wrong. If they had expected their bills should have been made current, they should have brought sealed notes with interest and set up a small cash here to answer them, something like the subscription for circulating exchequer notes. Credit you know well is what cannot be forced. It is a mere consequence of wanting no credit. He that can have his money when he will, will refuse it and let it lie, or take paper for it. But he that is asked to stay for his money will certainly demand it. If the Bank therefore has done this, they have put their reputation on the tenters, and stretched it farther than it will go. The prudence of which is at their own door. I write this on taking it for granted what I suppose is true, that the Bank has thus sent their bills to offer in payment, and I am glad to hear the people lay it on the Bank, rather than on the Government.

I am to have a meeting in a day or two with the four gentlemen who come from England, Sir John Cope, &c., who it seems desire a private conference with me on this head. I am not sensible I can do them much service but I shall tell them heartily and frankly what they have before them. It is most certain if they offer any man a bill till some other step is taken to make the people easy, it will be refused, and if one be refused all the rest are waste paper. In the last letter I hinted the arrival of the carriages. It is not to be described the fury and indignation of the people on the sight of it, cursing their own guards that brought it, in stoning the poor fellows that drove the waggons, nay, the very horses. I saw one of the waggon drivers wounded with a stone on the face, which if it had not glanced on his shoulder, first I believe had certainly killed him. They call it the price of their country and the poor people are incensed by the subtile Jacobites and too much by some of the Presbyterian ministers, that they go along the streets cursing the very English nation. This is a melancholy story but I thought it was necessary you should be informed how it stands. Till the matter of the bills, and the wine and brandy, is adjusted there can be no temper expected here. I hope something may be done afterward.

It must be time and management which must bring them to themselves again. Meantime I omit no occasion of throwing water upon this flame but cannot honestly boast of any success; I mean just now. I hope better.

JEAN GASSION [*alias* OGILVIE] to [ROBERT HARLEY].

1707, August 8—Offering again to go to Scotland or anywhere else so as not to be idle, and gives some information about Robert Murray, a brother of John Murray, who was proclaimed at the time of Fraser's plot. Robert had gone from Scotland to St. Germain and had also been at Versailles.

D[ANIEL] DE F[OE] to [ROBERT HARLEY].

1707, August 9. [Edinburgh]—I am in hopes mine come constantly to your hand, and therefore I repeat nothing of what I have wrote. My own case I leave wholly with you, and doubt not, but my Lord Treasurer will be pleased with the choice I have made of being serviceable rather than profiting of his Lordship's goodness. I refer that wholly to his Lordship's direction, only pray the return with his farther orders as soon as may consist with convenience. I am not to be discouraged, either with danger or difficulties by this work. I know that the more disordered they are here the more need of what I am upon ; and therefore when I give his Lordship a very melancholy account of things it is neither to enhance his opinion of my services nor to suggest that I am either weary or afraid of the undertaking ; and I speak this now because I really am going to give you a very melancholy account of things.

The ferment runs every day higher here, and the ill-blood of this people is so much increased that there is no speaking among them, but with the utmost caution. Not but that I am apt freely enough to speak, but if I should give way to talking in cases which would move the patientest man on earth to lose his temper I should deprive myself of the opportunity of doing good another time. I, therefore, hear all their ill language, and only desire them to have patience, till they see the end of things ; and to moderate as well as I can, but 'tis a fit of lunacy just now, and when the spirits are evaporated it will cool again. I hinted to you a sermon preached at a communion by Mr. John Anderson, of St. Andrews ; last Sabbath he preached again at the Grey Friars Kirk in this city, his text Hosea 7 v. 8, " Ephraim is a cake not turned. Strangers have devoured her strength, and she knows it not," here he railed at and abused the English nation, denounced God's judgments against the people for uniting with a perjured and a godless people as he called them, and in short flew in the face of the Union and the Government in such a manner as really is unsufferable. He has in conversation the same style and goes up and down enflaming and enraging the people—he is a bold popular man, and thereby the more mischievous. I have taken no notice of it other than gently in discourse, for really it is not the time to do it just now. But if the Government here had a hint given them, that her Majesty has an account of and is displeased &c. at such dealing, and they directed my Lord Advocate to send for and reprove him gently, perhaps it might give a check to his raillery; and as that is the common method here of treating their ministers it will make no new motion. This man is really a fatal instrument at this time because he is esteemed a good man.

I shall not trouble you with the artifices of the Jacobites to inflame those things. How men were employed to go about the streets and cry out upon Scotland, and call the brewers' men Scotch rogues, and Scotch dogs, just as passing in the streets, and so make the people believe it was the English excise men, and such like methods to exasperate the people against them, which makes the poor fellows afraid to go about their business.

In this ferment we are now and till the affair of the ships is over it will be no otherwise. My fear of it is, its increasing and refounding a national aversion, which is the great thing we hoped the Union would have worn off, and which the ministers in particular do now especially strive to spread in the minds of the people, and which if it goes on will be past cure.

I must confess I never saw a nation so universally wild and so readily embracing everything that may exasperate them. They are ripe for every mischief and if some general step to their satisfaction is not taken I do not yet foresee how they will certainly precipitate themselves into some violent thing or other on the first occasion that offers (*sic*). It seems a perfect gangrene on the tempers, and like the general method of such exasperations it reconciles smaller things to promote this greater. Different interests, differing parties, all join in a universal clamour, and the very Whigs declare openly they will join with France or King James, or anybody rather than be insulted as they call it by the English. 'Tis the happiest thing in the world that the Union is finished. Were it to act now it would be all confusion and distraction. I have nothing to say in this relation but that it is much short of the fact. I wish heartily some medium may be found out in the case of the wines, stop of the ships, and particularly the impressing their men; for though I hope things will cool then, yet really such heats as these are dangerous in taking too deep root. I thought myself obliged to give you this account. I ask your pardon for its length.

The DUKE OF NEWCASTLE to [ROBERT HARLEY].

1707, August 11. Haughton—I make my humble acknowledgments for the draft of the Privy Seal. I think if the person who drew it could make the Thistle a little more conspicuous it would not be amiss, and you may be assured if Her Majesty approves of it, I do: and now all other offices make use of the Seals of Great Britain. I wish this was dispatched that I might do so too; I have not enclosed the draft, supposing the person has another by him.

I wish the good news that is postponed may answer our hopes about Toulon. I not having the good fortune to see you before I came out of town, made me believe I had committed some unknown sin, that I had the punishment not to take my leave of you.

JAMES BOURNE and RICHARD TAYLOR.

1707, August 12. Sandford, co. Salop—Affidavit of James Bourne, of Talk upon the Hill, before Thomas Sandford, regarding the escape of Richard Taylor, charged with robbing the Exchequer, from his custody.

BARON SCHUTZ to [ROBERT HARLEY].

1707, August 13—Having informed the Marquis de Lassay that until a reply shall be received from the Duke of Marlborough, he cannot have permission to return to France, he has strongly urged me to write to you to beg that he may not be obliged to go to Nottingham before the reply comes, but may remain in London. Hopes that in consideration of the great interest taken in the Marquis by the Electress this favour may be granted to him. *French.*

SIR ROBERT DAVERS to [ROBERT HARLEY].

1707, August 18. Rougham [co. Suffolk]—The 'sizes are now over for our county, and I expected that upon the new commission for the peace the gentlemen I gave you a list of would have been in. I had your promise as well as my Lord Chancellor's that the gentlemen should be in; I wish those that oppose their being in were to answer it at the bar of the house of Commons, for I think it is a barbarous usage to keep out of the commission gentlemen of the best estates in a county.

Now, dear namesake, forgive me for being plain with you and thinking you have not been sincere with me. If it be in your power to put those gentlemen in, who is to blame? If it be not in your power, say so, and I will never ask you to do it.

I do wish my good friend Mr. Harley had never left the Speaker's place of the house of Commons. I will reserve the rest for our meeting.

[The DUKE OF NEWCASTLE] to [ROBERT HARLEY].

1707, August 18. Welbeck—The Justice in Eyre of the north side Trent has never been out of this family since the Restoration, but when I made it my request to the late King that he would bestow it upon William Lord Kingston, and when the King gave it to the Duke of Devonshire, I never came at Court was the only reason, as the King said, that he thought I did not then care for it, or else I should have had it as well as my grandfather and father-in-law had. There being none but this Forest and a small jurisdiction in Needwood on this side Trent, everybody knows there is no manner of profit, it is only the honour of the command. The Duke of Devonshire has not only no estate in the Forest nor no house, nor in the county except some few tithes, so that I believe Lord Hartington could not think much that it should be restored into the old channel. So I beg you'll be pleased to make my humble request to the Queen from me, for this command. I know you will not lose a moment's time, and that you will do it in the best manner. No mortal knows my mind in this matter but you, and I leave it to you to speak to Lord Treasurer in this affair in my name or not as you think best. Pray you send me word by the next post if you would have me write to Lord Treasurer upon this matter.

JOHN BELL to [ROBERT HARLEY].

1707, August 19. Newcastle[-on-Tyne]—Has received a letter from Sir Thomas Frankland and Sir Robert Cotton, from which it appears that he is likely to be ill-used by the taking away of part of his farm of the posts, it being proposed to send the South Shields letters by the Durham bag, in order to gratify Sir Henry Liddell and his son, without doing any service to the public. Desires Harley will speak to Frankland, so that the letters may come in the same way as they have done since the Revolution, for so long has he been postmaster. Mr. Carr knows this very well and will also write about it.

Copy of letter from the General Post Office enclosed.

D[ANIEL DE] F[OE] to [ROBERT HARLEY].

1707, August 19. Edinburgh—I am glad to tell you the affair of the wines &c. which we are told are delivered, seems to abate here, and this clamorous party are now turning their tongues to other subjects. I cannot say they rail less but I have the comfort to be able better to defend any case and better to understand any other case than that. Two cases now occupy their gall which I thought it my duty to signify to you.

The great quantities of goods run here as well openly and insolently as secretly I hinted at before. In order to make themselves amends upon the merchants and come at a complete discovery the Commissioners have summoned in general all the merchants, as well those suspected as not, to come in and swear whether they have not defrauded the Queen of her Customs and to tell upon oath, how much since the 1st of May. Now I am not saying this is against their law, for really they have such a barbarous law being a remnant of the old suppressed tyranny, nor am I debating whether the Queen shall get money by this prosecution, yea or no, for certainly if prosecuted the Queen must get 20,000l. or multitudes must be perjured, or be undone, and unable to pay. But I humbly represent to my Lord Treasurer that a rigorous prosecution of this case will be attended with infinite murmurs and discontents and serve more to that fatal design of alienating this people from the Government and the Union than all that money can countervail.

1. The Kirk exclaim and say this is practising that old abhorred custom of multiplying oaths, which tends to perjury &c. That it is leading people to destruction by forcing them to perjure themselves or be ruined, which multitudes cannot resist. That however such a law is in force it is against the law of nations, in which it is everywhere a maxim *nemo tenetur scipsum accusare*. That this law has rarely if ever been practised and is not now in any Christian country and the like.

2. The people say this is the first test of the moderation of the British Government, in which 'tis apparent the subjects of Scotland are to meet with nothing but severity : that 'tis against the Union, in which all the subjects are to enjoy equalities in trade, mutual restrictions &c.; that the subjects of England cannot be thus purged, and all laws to produce an inequality are to be repealed ; that this has been a time of as it were an *inter-regnum* in trade and unusual liberties may have been taken ; that this is a design to punish the conscientious offender, and let the hardened sinner escape ; that this will be of no use any farther, for it will put them upon measures in which the nicest and most scrupulous will be able to swear for the future ; &c. I act in this I hope the part my Lord means I should act, viz. to acquaint his Lordship what measures here may work ill, and what not, and have no other prospect in it. I am sensible this proceeding makes great additions to the ill-temper here, which really is too great already not to merit a great deal of caution.

If this matter were pushed now to extremity I cannot express the confusion it would make here ; for really, half the nation are in the crime. But measures to prevent it may better be used to all extremities than retrospects especially on the foot of this exploded law. The debate by Council in the Exchequer Court here was very long, and yesterday the Lords adjourned it to the third Wednesday in November, and this makes me lay it before you that my Lord may be judge whether it will not rather be held as a rod to awe them, than otherwise.

The next thing I note is the Council here settling justices, or Commissions of the Peace, in which I doubt they distinguish too much such as were not for the Union. Though some of them being men of temper and honour are at the same time well affected to the Government, and being gentlemen of absolute superiority in their several countries it will be a little too much dishonour to them and perfectly alienate them to see their vassals in the Commission and themselves subjected and left out. This matter the constitution of things here makes to differ from England and in such case the law and course of justice will be obstructed, since those vassals dare not, and will not, act without the authority of their chiefs, though they were of greater estates than their chief.

These things I humbly offer as my own observations, if it be your pleasure I may lay before you some names wherein this is particularly mischievous. I should be glad to know if my answer to my Lord T——r's letter reached your hands and if possible see myself delivered from the present circumstances I am in here, which I need not explain to you.

JOHN OGILVIE to [ROBERT HARLEY].

1707, August 20—You ordered me to give you in writing what I had to say concerning my family. In the first place your honour should procure them some money to buy them a bed or two and some other little furniture, that I may take them a little house at a small rent, that they may be settled before I part; and that something may be settled on them for their subsistence. In the next place that your honour will give me your word that in case of death or other misfortune befalling me you will see them taken care of that they may not be miserable in the world.

I pray your honour will be so good as to order me some little money for the present to subsist upon, for I declare on the word of a Christian I have not twenty shillings in my power at this minute, and yet I am seven in family, so it will not last long, and to hear my poor children cry for bread, and I have none to give them, is very melancholy.

JOHN OGILVIE to [ROBERT HARLEY].

1707, August 21—I have sent this day to take Mr. Hill's house. It is in Strutton's ground, but after his having consulted his wife he has raised the price of it, for instead of 20l. he demands 22l., besides the taxes which will amount to fifty shillings more; I think that is over much for me. There is also another house in Marcham street, and the rent of it is 28l. besides the taxes which may amount to forty shillings. Now I am afraid that house may be too much out of the way by reason you were pleased to tell me you would honour me so far as to go sometimes into it. There is another little house on the other side of the Park below Stafford house, but it is very little indeed; I may have a pass key to go through the Park from it. The rent of it is 19l., besides the taxes. My wife tells me she would engage to furnish it prettily for 40l. I pray your honour to be pleased to send me word what you would have me do. You told me if I would go to Scotland for a month's time, if you think I may render you service in so doing I am content, if not I am for whatever your wish is.

THOMAS FOLEY to his brother[-in-law ? ROBERT HARLEY].

1707, August 23. Witley—Though the affairs of this county are not worth your minding, yet perhaps it may not be unacceptable to you to have a short account of the proceedings here since Mr. Bromley's death.

As soon as Mr. Bromley's death was known here Sir T. C. Winford declared he would stand and Mr. Pitt sent to offer his service to the country, but said if the generality of the gentlemen thought of setting up anybody else, he would desist and give them his interest. On Thursday last at the Assizes at Worcester there were a great number of gentlemen, who were all for Mr. Pitt. Mr. Lechmere who had not declared of either side, came to them with a proposal of accommodation for the quiet of the country, that one of the gentlemen that stood should come in now, and that if Mr. Walsh and Sir John Pakington would not stand the next time that the gentlemen there should give their interest to Sir Thomas Winford and Mr. Pitt for the next Parliament. Several gentlemen were very shy of saying any thing to this because formerly Mr. Walsh had made an ill use of it, and they said they would not trust him unless he would give it under his hand, but at last they agreed on this, that they could engage for none but themselves, but if Sir T. Winford and Mr. Walsh and Mr. Cox would give their interest to Mr. Pitt this time, and if Mr. Walsh would desist the next Parliament, they would endeavour to persuade Sir John Pakington to desist and give their interest to Sir Thomas Winford and Mr. Pitt. With this proposal Mr. Lechmere went to Sir Thomas Winford, who said Mr. Walsh was on the Grand Jury but he would send an answer by nine o'clock the next morning. I went home that evening. The next morning Sir T. Winford sent a paper to this purpose that he could not give up the rights of the freeholders. This answer exasperated the gentlemen very much, who said this was a trick, that the proposal came first from Sir T. Winford's friends, that they were not fond of it, but complied with it for the peace of the country, and pressed Mr. Lechmere to tell who sent him, who at last named the Bishop of Worcester. By this you see our country is like to be in as great a flame as formerly, and though the generality of the gentlemen seemed inclined to live neighbourly and to have the country quiet, yet the heats &c. of one or two persons who pretend to moderation have prevented that which would certainly have been for the advantage of both the gentlemen who stand now, for the ease of the country, and consequently for the credit of her Majesty's government; for it would have given a great check to party, and faction on both sides.

PAMPHLET.

1707, August 23—A printed pamphlet of seven quarto pages, so dated in Harley's handwriting, headed "Some Queries which deserve no consideration, answered paragraph by paragraph, only to satisfy the ridiculous inquiries of the trifling P——r that made 'em public."

DR. FRANCIS ATTERBURY to [ROBERT HARLEY].

1707, August 29. Chelsea—I have enclosed a just state of the matter of fact for the truth of which I will be answerable in every particular. The only thing that I doubt of—and I have therefore expressed that doubt—is, whether ever there was any attempt to frame articles of inquiry upon the pretended Statutes of our Church, before the Restoration; in which point—though I presume, it is not of any great consequence—I shall take care to have speedy and $_{sure}$ information. In the meantime, I humbly beg that you will please to let this matter be laid before the Queen, so early as that I may have her answer to my petition before you leave the town: otherwise, I shall be either forced to submit to the Bishop's right of visiting on the 25th of September, or lay myself open to the ill consequences of declining it.

I shall have a book ready to present to the Queen about the end of next week, and would humbly hope that I may be allowed to wait upon her at Windsor about the same time, if not sooner, with my petition.

CONYERS FILBRIDGE to the EARL OF SUNDERLAND and ROBERT HARLEY,
Secretaries of State.

1707, August 29 (endorsed)—Had served as a volunteer in Lord Mohun's regiment, but upon his arrival from France yesterday, where he had been for nine months past, was confined in the Savoy. Gives some information about the proceedings of several Scotch and Irish ships at Havre, Rochelle, and Nantes, and desires an early hearing in a matter which concerns her Majesty's and the nation's interests, the masters of these ships being well known to him. Esquire Ogle, parliament man for Berwick-upon-Tweed, knows the writer's family and himself.

JOHN BELL to [ROBERT HARLEY].

1707, September 2. Newcastle[-on-Tyne]—I herewith send a letter from Mr. D[e] F[oe]; which came to my hand last night.

Some posts ago I made bold to put you in mind to speak to Sir Tho. Frankland in my favour that he would be pleased to let the South Shields letters come to Newcastle in my bag, as they always have done till the time Sir H. Liddell made interest with Sir Thomas in favour of the postmaster of Durham. Mr. Carr wrote to your honour about this before.

JOHN OGILVIE to ROBERT BRYAN [HARLEY].

1707, September 4—This Dennis Connell is the young man that did belong to me. I did carry him to Hamburg with me and placed him with Lord Drummond, and so he went to Scotland with him and continued till the priest caused him to be turned away. After that he came to me again, but I ordered it so that Lord Perth ordered him back again, and it is he that is gone down to my Lord; so that it's I that am the occasion of placing him there, for I shall know everything that shall pass while he is there.

THO[MAS] CHIFFINCH to [ROBERT HARLEY].

1707, September 5. Gravesend—Informing him that in accordance with his instructions he had searched the Flanders fleet for Dennis Connell but had not been able to find any one answering his description. Mrs. Taylor at the "Red Lion" had stated that Connell left London on Wednesday or Thursday last, that he was a young, well-shaped, middle sized man in a fair natural wig, had two or three scars on his forehead, was clothed in a red, blue, or dark-coloured coat, and had the King of France's head cut in steel tied to his watch.

Sir Robert Davers to [Robert Harley].

1707, September 6—Acknowledges reply to his letter about the justices for Suffolk, and continues his remonstrances. The gentleman that was said to be an attorney was never so; he has been called to the bar several years, and has at least 1,200*l.* a year, a brother to Folkes that was of Gray's Inn. The other objection he did not expect from the Lord Chancellor, for young men may be fitter than old men, and his lordship has already put in several young ones. Would do anything in the world to serve Harley, having the same high opinion of him that he always had; and if——(*sic*) should spoil him it would grieve the writer heartily.

Henry St. John to [Robert] Harley.

1707, September 6. Whitehall—I have received your letter wherein you have by Her Majesty's command referred to me the petitions of Baron Le Duc, Katherine Fletcher, Margaret Strother and Isabella Mercer, and am to acquaint you in answer thereto, that as to Baron Le Duc I can only say that I believe the man is very poor and an object of compassion, and as to the others I find them to be widows of officers of the army who have lost their lives in the service. Upon which matter I take this opportunity again to report my humble opinion to her Majesty that though there are a great many objects of this kind yet there is no settled fund or provision made for the relief of the widows whose husbands lose their lives in her Majesty's service, but what the officers themselves of the army under the command of my Lord Duke of Marlborough, and of the marines, do allow out of their own pay to the widows of officers of those corps only who happen to be killed in service ; and for want of some provision of this kind, there are a great number of poor widows and fatherless children of officers who have been slain and lost their lives of other corps in the service this war, who are in a very miserable condition and stand in great need of relief.

Edward Harley to his aunt, Abigail Harley, at Bywood.

1707, September 7—We went to St. Pauls. Poor sister could not go, her face was so swelled. The Queen and Prince looked very well. Dr. Sherlock preached. His text was in the psalms, "Verily there is a reward for the righteous." He made a very good sermon. My Lady Mayoress and my Lady Ashurst sat under me and scolded all the time. The Lord Mayor and Court of Aldermen said they would not come to Paul's if they had not their own seats, but there came an express order from the Council that they should come and take the seats that my Lord Chamberlain [gave them]. Pray pardon this scrawl being very much tired.

Lieut.-Colonel J. Cranstoun to ——.

1707, September 10. Ghent—The enclosed packet for our good friend Mr. Cunningham, containing an instrument in parchment from the Duke of Argyll in favour of a friend of Mr. Cunningham's, qualifying him to be his Grace's chaplain, I have taken the advantage to send over by the bearer Sergeant Parke of our regiment who with some thirty more who are become infirm and unfit for further service are now discharged, and such of them as have a right to it are recommended to be taken into Her Majesty's Hospital at Chelsea, as the Sergeant himself is. I neither could give him so particular a direction to our friend's house as might be necessary, though I know it is in Russell Street.

We have now got near the end of a campaign that has been the most inactive here, and the most unprosperous and unfortunate for the Allies everywhere of any we have yet had in the war. Thus Providence is pleased to defeat and laugh at all the projects and proposals of us poor mortal creatures, and to teach us that the race is not to the swift nor the battle to the strong, but that when we hug and exalt ourselves most in our own strength and in our thoughts anticipate victory to ourselves and destroy our enemies God can make our strength weakness and our hopes vain, as he can at other times give us victory and success against appearances, that we may see and be brought to acknowledge that it is not unto us but to God the glory belongs and that He raises and casts down when and as He pleases. It is impossible not to make this reflection in observing the course of this whole war, where we have ever been least successful when we reckoned most upon ourselves, as the first year while we were yet but weak and our Army and Generals that were strangers to each other, after we had been beaten within the ramparts of Nimeguen God enabled us in that one campaign to clear all the great country of the Maese and with a rapidity and torrent of success to take the towns of Venloo, Ruremonde, Stevenswaert and Liége. Next year when flushed at this success and thinking to do yet greater things we were reduced to consume the whole summer in marching and counter-marching before the enemy's lines, and with difficulty in the close took the two poor small places of Huy and Limbourg. The third year when we despaired of doing anything here and the Empire was at the very brink of being swallowed up, by our going up into Germany, a dangerous project and perhaps the result of despair, God blessed us in it and gave us all those glorious and unprecedented triumphs of Schellenberg, Hochstadt, Landau, and Traerback, which elated us so much that in the fourth year we had already in our thoughts overrun Lorraine and ended the war at once by going to the gates of Paris; but God was pleased to defeat all our projects there and to humble us by making all we attempted miscarry and we were forced to come back with shame to stop the current of the enemy's victories, and though we stole in over their lines thereafter by their negligence yet we let slip out of our hands the opportunity of profiting of it and of gaining all this country, and were thereafter twice forced to desist and lay aside the further attempts of forcing them again at the Dyle and the Ische, and end that campaign ingloriously enough with taking the two small places of Leuwe and Sanfleet.

So that observing the difficulty or impossibility of forcing the enemy any more in their lines, which being then become shorter were more easy to be defended, we began the last campaign without the least hope or prospect of success in this country, to that degree that on the fixed belief that nothing could be done here measures were laid down and already resolved upon of only looking first to the enemy's countenance here, and approaching their lines to consume the forage a little; and that then my Lord Duke should have left the British foot in conjunction with the States troops to defend only our own towns, and gone himself, with all the British cavalry and with the Hanover and

Hesse troops he had expressly in that view made stop upon the Moselle, into Italy to have joined Prince Eugene and endeavoured to save the Duke of Savoy then given over for lost, whilst we had nothing before us but these melancholy ideas and this uncomfortable prospect of things; but God who orders all things as He pleases moved the French in confidence of their strength to forsake their true interest and all the wise and prudent rules by which they usually walk to come out without their lines and force us to fight them at Ramilies, where we gained a victory which though bloodless (for on both sides there were not above 1900 killed) yet wholly discomfited and broke their army, gave us all this country, and allowed us before they could recruit to take Ostend, Menin, Dendermond and Ath, all strong and well fortified towns, from them, while they neither durst or indeed could bring so much as the face of an army into the field against us. At the same time in Spain Lord Galway came to Madrid and drove King Philip to Burgos and, if seconded as he might have been had drove him quite out of all Spain and probably if once out he had never returned again.

In Italy Prince Eugene, after forcing a thousand difficulties impossible and unsurmountable to any but himself, joined at last the Duke of Savoy, forced the lines of Turin, and beat a much greater army than his own. These successes with a knowledge of our own strength and the increase we made this year to it, and an opinion that the enemy could not recover the prodigious losses of last campaign, made us lay no less designs for this year than of either forcing the enemy to fight and beating them here at our first entry to the field or, if they durst not face us, of taking Mons. Tournay and their strongest towns before their face and forcing our way into the very heart of their country here, and by that glorious noble and well concerted design on Toulon on the other side, to have in this one year ended the war so advantageously as that France should have been for ever ruined at sea and reduced to accept such conditions at land as we pleased to impose.

These were our confident hopes in May last when we took the field and God has so far blasted them that our designs in Toulon have cost infinite expense and much blood and proven wholly abortive, the enemy have beaten and ruined us in Spain, and hardly left us footing enough for our King to retain the title we gave him. They have overrun the lazy and sleepy Empire and not only maintained and paid a great army in it all the year, but by vast contributions sent money into France to help the King's other affairs; and here they equalled our numbers and though they did not find it meet to fight us yet, by taking up in time a strong and advantageous camp they have kept us at bay upon our part of the country the whole campaign and put it out of our power now to undertake anything for the rest of this year. What may be the success of the war next year God only knows, but hitherto I think by this it appears visible we have ever been disappointed when we reckoned most upon our own strength, and have succeeded to a wonder when we desponded and trusted least to ourselves.

Address to me in Col. Preston's regiment either to the Army or to Bridges (Bruges ?).

The Same to [Bonert Cunningham].

1707, September 10. Ghent—We are all very melancholy and my Lord Duke is of late for the most part much out of humour and peevish with the bad success of the war and the most unprosperous campaign we have made everywhere this summer, which in all probability if we

still desire to obtain a good and solid peace will make the war last a
campaign or two more yet before we shall be able to bring the French
to submit to such a peace, this having been the happiest and most successful campaign to them everywhere of all they have yet made this war;
and no doubt may encourage them yet, however low in their treasury and
affairs, to hazard and struggle a campaign or two more if possibly they
can find funds for the war. Especially since it is plain that in the worst
events can befal them, and though our success hereafter shall enable us
to take all from them, we should probably require no more than the
peace of the Pyrenees which we now insist on.

It seems but too clear we can never hope to obtain any success on this
side and in this country that can force France to yield to so great demands
as we make, unless we could bring an army of at least 25 or 30000 men to
the field superior to what they have, for as their frontiers are all covered by
very strong towns and well fortified, and ours are all open, so we cannot
make any siege with hopes of success unless we have troops to spare
from our army sufficient to carry on the siege and yet leave
our army equal to fight them and cover our convoys, which
cannot well be done without such a superiority at least ; and as this whole
country has everywhere such natural strengths of rivers, woods or
morasses, as it is easy for a weaker army so to post themselves either in
Brabant, Flanders, or Hainault as that they cannot be attacked even by a
better and stronger army without the greatest disadvantage and a manifest hazard of losing a battle, so while it shall be the enemy's interest
not to fight, we can never hope to bring them to a battle.

Indeed we lost a fair opportunity once this summer when they lay at
Pieton and Seneff, and we came to Nivelle in view of their camp, and
with our right wing encamped within less than a league of their left, where
though it is I believe most certain that no general in the world ever
desired more sincerely and anxiously to fight, and to push the war in
earnest than my Lord Duke does yet, by not taking all the right
measures at that critical time that might have been taken, the enemy
escaped out of our hands. We came to our camp in the evening and
seeing the enemy lie still in theirs, and being persuaded they would march
that night in the night or early in the morning to escape us, my Lord
Duke was persuaded to command a detachment of forty squadrons of
horse and all the grenadiers of the army out to advance near to their
camp in the night, and either by their presence deter them from marching
till next day that we could move and attack them, or if they did march
to fall upon their rear and so by engaging them to retard their march
till our army could come up to engage them in a general action. This
was well and had taken but that Count Tilly who was to command this
whole detachment in chief is an old man, and though a notable officer yet
by his age become perhaps too cautious and slow for such an enterprise,
as Lieutenant General Schultz of the Danes who commanded the foot
next under him; and then Count Tilly being both a man of quality and
high character as General of the Horse to the States was it is said
piqued and perhaps not without ground that the Duke in laying the
design when he resolved to send him and Lieutenant General Schultz
upon it should not at first have sent for them and himself have acquainted
them with and concerted with them upon what he designed they should
do; but on the contrary there were orders sent to Tilly only that he
should come to such a place where he should find the detachment and his
orders. It was eleven at night before he came to where the detachment
was lying on their arms. He found his orders there writ on a piece of
paper as they would have been done to any officer of the most inferior

quality; it rained heavily, was pitch dark, and no house near, so that it was an hour before a light could be got for him to read and know his orders, and no guides being there who knew the country and many defiles before him. It was another hour before guides were found and it still continuing dark and raining the whole night he was shy to venture to march the detachment so near the enemy in the dark, so that in reasoning upon this the night was spent, and Major General Ross who was also upon the command did with difficulty obtain his leave to advance with two squadrons to reconnoitre, which he at last did and by that time day broke, perceived the enemy were already in full march, and had only left a strong rearguard to make their retreat. He instantly sent back to Count Tilly to inform him of it, and beg he would advance, but the grenadiers who were far behind could not get up in time and so the enemy got off, though we understood afterwards that the Duke of Vendôme, from this manœuvre believing he could not get off without losing one wing of his army, had marched a little and then halted and drawn up and formed his whole army in the plain of Rouelx to expect us as we should have come out of the defiles. Finding we did not pursue him he continued his march with great diligence all that day and night and next day till he got into the plains of Cambron, sending all his baggage and cannon and even his army's tents off to Mons for expedition; whereas if the Duke of Marlborough had at our first coming to the ground at Nivelle made that detachment, and sent for Count Tilly and concerted with him, which he perhaps had a right to expect in good manners to his quality and post, they might have had daylight enough not only to have sent some squadrons before to have reconnoitred the defiles and way that led to the enemy's camp, and seen how far the detachment might with safety have advanced in the night. But indeed the whole detachment might have got through some of the defiles before it became quite dark, and they could have marched the more boldly in the dark if by reconnoitring they had known the ground better whereby the detachment might have been up with the enemy time enough early in the morning to have engaged their rear so soon as daylight came, and thus brought their whole army to a stand till ours could have come up and made it a general action, or as it was had we known that morning that the Duke of Vendôme formed and halted his army without the defiles, we might have been with him, or yet if my Lord Duke in place of resting all next day at Nivelle, which believing the enemy gone it is probable he did, because the detachment horse and the grenadiers had been under arms for a whole day and a long rainy night, and had that morning after they had notice the enemy was marching run like horses for two leagues in hopes to fall in with them, which two leagues they had again to march back to their camp, whereby they were indeed terribly fatigued and harassed, and so probably my Lord Duke thought fit to halt that day to give them rest; but had he marched the army on that morning towards Soignies and let the grenadiers and the forty squadrons have reposed themselves only a few hours, they might have followed the army on the rear and made the rearguard with the baggage, and by the army's marching and having a nearer and more direct way than the French, we should that day either have fallen in with them on the march or have forced them to quit their design of going to Cambron, and retired within their lines by Mons, whereby we should have got betwixt them and Flanders and might have continued our march over the Scheldt and invested either Tournay, Lille, or Ypres as we pleased, before they could have got up to hinder us or throw themselves behind their lines as they did since, for they had marched more than we, were yet more fatigued, wanted their bread and everything, so that they could not then have continued their march to dispute the passing the Scheldt with us, for they brought but two or four pieces of cannon with them to Cambron and no bread waggons, which being on their march from Mons and Charleroi to Gembloux when by our sudden march from Meldert they were obliged to march in all haste too, their bread waggons could not come up to them in some days thereafter so that for two days after their wearied troops came in to the camp at Cambron, one ammunition loaf gave half a pistole in their army and one day's march more had made almost all their infantry desert them. This, is the only advantage I have ever heard my Lord Duke has had in his power to have got over the enemy all this summer, and it is most certain it is not for want of zeal and good inclinations that it was not taken, but it must and undoubtedly may justly be imputed to the frailty of human nature, by which the greatest and wisest men cannot at all times see all they might do but make unwilling escapes and neglects by which advantages offered are lost, and he is the greatest man, and in war the greatest captain, that makes fewest of those. I wish the bad success everywhere this summer may not discourage our parliament from continuing to push on the war with their usual vigour which if we can do but a little longer we certainly must bring France to reason and secure Europe by a lasting, firm, and solid peace upon equal and sure grounds by putting France out of a capacity of breaking it. I think it is and will be reckoned with you a great advantage of the most importance that the Queen has it in her power by law to continue this present parliament yet three sessions more, which I hope shall be more than sufficient to end the war and settle the nation in peace. I shall long to hear from you after your return from the country, and shall write to you again when I know where our regiment is to be in garrison, which I presume will either be as last year at Bruges or here in this town.

D[ANIEL DE] F[OE] to ROBERT HARLEY.

1707, September 11. [Edinburgh]—You have always allowed me the freedom of a plain and direct stating things to you ; if I should not do it now I should not be just to you, much less faithful to myself, and I entreat your pardon for this from the true and necessary part of it.

If I were where I have had the honour to be, in your parlour, telling you my own case, and what a posture my affairs are in here, it would be too moving a story, you could not, I am persuaded, pardon my vanity, you have too much concern for me, and too much generosity in your nature, you could not bear it.—I have always been bred like a man, I would say a gentleman, if circumstances did not of late alter that denomination, and though my misfortunes and enemies have reduced me, yet I always struggled with the world, so as never to want till now. Again, I had the honour to come hither in a figure suitable to your design whom I have the honour to serve. While you supplied me, I can appeal to Him that knows all things; I faithfully served, I baulked no cases, I appeared in print when others dared not to open their mouths, and without boasting I ran as much risk of my life as a grenadier in storming a counter scarp. It is now five months since you were pleased to withdraw your supply, and yet I had never your orders to return ; I knew my duty better than to quit my post without your command. But really, if you supposed I had laid up a bank out of your former, it is my great misfortune that such a mistake happens. I depended too much on your goodness to withhold any reasonable expense to form a magazine for my last resort. 'Tis true I spent you a large sum, but you will remember how often I entreated your restraint in that case and particular directions, but as left to my liberty I acted as I concluded I ought to do, pushing every work as thoroughly as I could; and instead of forming a magazine for myself, if you were to see me now entertained of courtesy without subsistence, almost grown shabby in clothes, dejected &c., what I care not to mention; you would be moved to hasten my relief in a manner suitable to that regard you were always pleased to show for me.

I was just on the brink of returning, and that of mere necessity, when, like life from the dead, I received your last, with my Lord Treasurer's letter. But hitherto his Lordship's goodness to me seems like messages from an army to a town besieged, that relief is coming, which heartens and encourages the famished garrison, but does not feed them; and at last they are obliged to surrender for want, when perhaps one week would have delivered them.

What shall I farther liken my case to? 'Tis like a man hanged upon an appeal, with the Queen's pardon in his pocket; 'tis really the most discouraging circumstance that ever I was in; I need not tell you that this is not a place to get money in. Pen and ink and printing will do nothing here, men do not live here by their wits. When I look on my present condition, and reflect that I am thus, with my Lord T——'s letter promising me an allowance for subsistence in my pocket, and offering me comfortable things, 'tis a very mortifying thought that I have not one friend in the world to support me till his Lordship shall think fit to begin that allowance.

The prayer of this petition is very brief, that I may be helped to wait, or that you will please to move my Lord Treasurer that since he has thought fit to encourage me to expect assistance in order to serve the Government in this place; he will be pleased to make such steps towards it as may prevent my being obliged to abandon an employ of such consequence, to my own ruin and the loss of the capacity I am now in of doing his lordship service. I need say no more to move you to this, I entreat a speedy reply and supply.

DR. FRANCIS ATTERBURY to [ROBERT HARLEY].

1707, September 11. Chelsea—I have enclosed the petition so worded as you were pleased to direct. I am extremely concerned to find that there should be any difficulty in procuring the Queen's interposition towards doing herself right in so plain, and so important a case, and wherein, I am sure, the Bishop so far distrusts his own power, that, upon the least word from the Crown, he would desist from his attempt. How it can be thought worth while to pleasure him, not only by sacrificing me, but even at the expense of the prerogative, I presume not to guess. But if that be determined, and the honour I have hitherto had of being known to depend entirely on you cannot prevent it, 'tis to no purpose to complain. I must make myself as easy as I can under the mortification intended me; the use of which in some other respects I easily see, and shall endeavour to make such an use of it, with regard to myself, as becomes me.

However, if you please to look back on what passed at the beginning of last winter, you will permit me to say that I have not deserved such usage. My Lord Treasurer himself knows I have not. And as little and useless as I may be for the future, there have been occasions wherein my services may be compared with any the Bishop either hath done, can, or will do for those who now think fit to encourage him.

May they find his gratitude equal to the obligation they are now going to lay upon him.

As to what you were pleased to say to me at parting about other matters, I will venture to promise for our body that they shall lie by this winter without doing anything, if that will please. I dare undertake for this and humbly beg therefore that no point may be strained to the prejudice of the constitution when—it will certainly appear—there is no manner of occasion for it.

Copy of petition and statement enclosed.

The EARL OF PEMBROKE, lord lieutenant of Ireland, to [ROBERT HARLEY].

1707, September 11. Dublin—Though I have this day answered your letter concerning the troops, yet I cannot but in particular write this other to you to shew the obligation I have for your favour and kind expressions in that letter. But in thanking you for the care you have taken in the business of the Council you must excuse me if I express it just contrary to the words by which you are pleased modestly to mention it, for I am sure her Majesty's business there has had an advantage by my being here, where I can only say my endeavours shall be sincere.

[The EARL OF GODOLPHIN] to SECRETARY HARLEY.

[1707,] September 14. Windsor—I return you many thanks for your letter with enclosed papers, which I shall keep for you till to-morrow not having had any opportunity of acquainting the Queen with them who is abroad performing the ceremonies of Holyrood Day.

I am glad to see Lord Rivers turns his thoughts so much to his business, but he seems to desire more positive instructions in some particulars than perhaps can well be given him at so great a distance.

I doubt we shall not have many Lords here tomorrow to give the Queen their opinion upon the particulars he mentions. The wind seems more obstinate than ever.

CAPTAIN RICHARD BIRON to ROBERT HARLEY.

1707, Sept. 16—*Fubbs* yacht at Sheerness. Among the passengers which came on board this yacht bound for Rotterdam, with Mr. Vernon, envoy to Denmark, was one Francois Armand, a Roman Catholic, come from France since the war without a pass. By advice of Mr. Vernon had secured him and sent him in custody to the commissioners at Chatham, for further examination.

JEAN GASSION [*alias* OGILVIE] to [ROBERT HARLEY].

1707, September 16—I have been several times with Charles Dunster since I had the honour to wait on you. I have made it my business to inform myself of all I could from him both as to the inclinations of the nobility and people in general and of their intentions, for there is no man can give me a better account than Charles for he was born in the Highlands himself and he speaks their language. He told me that they want but an opportunity to rise, for if the Prince of Wales should go to them, or the Duke of Berwick in his name with some good officers, arms, ammunition, and money they will join him unanimously, and that they long for the occasion. He further adds that there is not a man in that kingdom more dangerous than is the Duke of Athol, he says my Lord some time ago made a review of all his men in arms, and that they did amount to 4000 men; but he says there was few or none stayed at home and there was some other loose men that did not belong truly to him joined him at that review, but Charles says my Lord did not act prudently, for it made an éclat. Lord Breadalbane did more wisely for he hath several markets or country fairs and it is the custom there that all the country people go under arms to those fairs, so my Lord went and did take the occasion of this and reviewed his men, which did amount to 3000 resolute men that will follow him without asking of questions. There is one thing that is to be observed of my Lord and that is there never was any of those ministers that is Presbyterian and did comply, that is did pray as the Government did ordain, for Our King William or Her present Majesty that durst possess any benefice or preach in his jurisdiction. Since the Revolution, there was once one did go, he was sent by the Senate who was sitting at that time in Inverary, a place that belongs to my Lord Argyll, but when the minister came there and was waiting for his auditors behold there comes a party of thirty men armed and carries him away with them dragging him over heels and through water to the neck and still threatening to shoot him at a post. When he was upon his knees and a napkin on his face just ready to be shot, then it was ordered that a party of my Lord Breadalbane's men should come for to rescue the minister, so both parties presents their arms and threatens to fight; but at last it was agreed that the minister's life should be saved and my Lord's men should have the honour to have rescued him, but that the minister should swear never to set his foot in that country again, which the poor minister performed. But the general assembly did well believe it was all a contrivance of my Lord Breadalbane, but the minister would not let it be said for he was so affrighted that he did believe it was all in earnest. My Lord's name is Campbell but he is no friend of my Lord Argyll, on the contrary all my Lord Argyll's own men that is good for anything will follow my Lord Breadalbane whenever he pleases to call them even in spite of my Lord Argyll, for let my Lord Argyll pretend what he pleases this is the truth. There is one thing that I presume to advertise you of, that is you will never get a perfect and true account of things relating to that kingdom from any of their nobility, for they are all ambitious as the devil and every one of them would be esteemed great and powerful in his own country and would gladly have you to believe that they are capable to suppress everything that may arise there of themselves, and this they would have you believe till the disease be past remedy and all this is to ingratiate themselves to the Court and keep their places, and in the event you'll find that if any mischief fall out they will only run away and fly to you for shelter. I need not give you a character of them, for I know you are too wise not to have found them out before this time and to have seen clearly through them. They are as I have said ambitious envying one another and not a bit of trust is there to be put in the greatest part of them, for you may believe me a man of honour is rare to be found amongst them; they have a subtle cunning and some of them is men of letters and some may be men of honour, but it is those that hath travelled and seen a great deal of the world, and I wish you may never trust more of them than you are sure of. I pray you to pardon me for this freedom I take to write to you in this nature for I am sensible you are too wise to need advice from so poor a despicable creature as I am but it is the love I have for your person and I should be very sorry if anything should fall out while you are at the helm that might give you any uneasiness or that any of them might impose on you. It is the nature of many of them to love to fish in troubled waters and I must be so frank to tell you that it were my interest also to fish with the crowd, but I must confess I were a most ungrateful rascal and void of honour if I did, for in the first place I owe my life to Her Majesty and which is more I owe the preservation of my poor infants and family to you.

I remember you inquired of me who was the correspondent here from St. Germain I forgot to name you my Lord Molyneux was, and my Lord Weymouth, but he is timorous. You must know they believe a great many that is Protestants to be for them, if an occasion were offered I could name some; for Roman Catholics I need not name any for that's granted. I am sorry I forgot to speak to you about the removing of Mr. Alex Drummond the priest that there might be some way fallen on to remove him. I did see a letter from him this night and in the tail of it was there how to address to him, which is for Mr. John Johnston, to the care of John Mitchall, periwigmaker at the Netherbow, Edinburgh. Now if you will but give orders to arrest all such letters I will engage you shall find some that is worth the pains. I do expect a letter from Scotland, how soon it comes you shall know, but let no consideration. whatsoever on my account hinder you from making use of me if you think I can be serviceable to you. I have taken a house for three years and I have bought some furniture but cannot pay for it as yet. Mrs. Richeson found me in Westminster Church, she fell down on her knees and begged me to pardon her, but I told her I did not know that ever she did disoblige me ; however she roared and cried and since she hath been going to hang herself, but I have all her love letters to this boy, I never did see anything so droll unless it were Don Quixote's letter. I am sure they would make you laugh heartily, the first time I come I will bring them on purpose to make you laugh.

C[HARLWOOD] LAWTON to [ROBERT HARLEY].

1707, September 17—I beg you will forgive me saying that I believe it would not be a false step if the promises which I am sure have been made to Sir John Pakington were now upon the death of Mr. Stepney made good. Ministers who remember promises, and who take not too much notice of what passes in a House of Commons, may be as safe as if they do otherwise.

When the Parliament meets I know how little time you will have to spare, and if your affairs will not allow me an audience I beg I may have a copy of the number of Roman Catholics, of which list I am pretty positive I can make a good and seasonable use, as you shall be judge when I have done.

[The DUKE OF NEWCASTLE] to [ROBERT HARLEY].

1707, September 17. Haughton—What accident has made the scales fall from the eyes of my Lord the Sovereign [Godolphin], for when I came out of town he was in love with almost all that society [the Junto] if not with every individual person of them. I am very impatient to hear what effect your wholesome advice has had. I am confident you do remember I have observed for above a year past that these measures would of necessity drive them into extremes, and I am every day more confirmed in that opinion. Pray God direct them for that which is best for our good Queen, the best of Princes.

D[ANIEL DE] F[OE] to ROBERT HARLEY.

1707, September 18 [Edinburgh]—My impatience urged me to write a long and importunate letter two posts ago. I would not be construed that I doubt your concern for me, but fear you are not sensible of my incapacity of waiting, as I am circumstanced in this remote place. I do not in the least doubt but you will so far carry on what in your meet goodness to me you have begun, as to move my Lord T——r to remember me and I will be easy in depending on it, that I shall not be obliged to make a dishonourable retreat from a place where I have worked myself into a capacity of serving both countries. I, therefore, give you no more trouble of that sort, though hard pressed &c.

It would be of service if I could know particularly how the affair of the wines stands, that I might manage the clamour of the people here as much to advantage as possible; you will depend safely on its being cautiously used.

We are taken up with a discourse of several people landed in the West of Scotland from France and Capt. Murray is apprehended. The Council are sitting on it today and I doubt not you will be rightly acquainted with the particulars. I hope there is nothing dangerous in agitation yet, but I must own and have often thought to hint it; the humours of that party are at present under such fermentation, so encouraged by the successes of the French, and so unhappily backed by the common disgust that should the King of France but support them, not with men for they need them not, but should he send about 200 officers, arms, and ammunition, artillery &c., to furnish them, and about 100,000 crowns in money, he might soon get together 12 or 15,000 stout fellows and do a great deal of mischief. Nor is it so much the inclination of the men as the money dispersed among the landlords, the lairds, and Jacobite gentry that would bring them in, and the men follow of course. I confess this would be a very fatal diversion as things stand here now, and I hint it because 'tis a juncture in which it would be of worse consequence than ever with respect to other parts of the world.

JO: FORSTER to [ROBERT HARLEY].

1707, September 18. Newgarthside—I humbly presume to give you the trouble of a line once more. Since I wrote my other which was about the beginning of July last I had a different account than what I wrote to you, viz. that that party in England which does favour the Prince of Wales was against attempting anything by violence, but they hoped that this winter might produce a peace and that the Parliament would disband the army and that all interest imaginable should be used in the country to get men of that kidney into the House of Commons; and the better to effect this the Prince of Wales was to take upon him the profession of the Protestant religion, and they report that he has not gone to mass for several years past, and that the French King would be at liberty to send them what forces they desired in case they could not accomplish their designs in a parliamentary way. Now, I am much afraid that some violent attempt is suddenly intended, for I do lately understand that Duke Hamilton has his messengers going with letters very throng to and fro to England, and I do observe that the Jacobites of both kingdoms have very frequent meetings under pretence of visits or some slight occasions.

It is said that at the Duke of Athol's hunting, those that met there entered into a band of association and sent some of their number over to

France. It is reported that Duke Hamilton has been picking up large horses all this summer and has put them into parks. The truth of this I will not assert but one thing I do know, that there were men employed this spring to find out sizeable horses and buy them. Here are some Irishmen come over that inform me that the natives of that kingdom have had an expectation of the Prince of Wales's landing in Scotland ever since the beginning of summer.

I hope that the Prince of Wales's motions might be observed at no great expense.

ROBERT DAVIS to ROBERT HARLEY.

1707, September 20—I crave leave to remind your honour of your promise that you would not only take care that my brother [in-law] D[e] F[oe] should be supplied, but also spur my Lord T——r to settle that affair on him before your honour goes in the country.

I hope that neither your honour, nor my Lord T——r, will not now neglect him while all the world sayeth he hath been very serviceable, and will so continue both in private and public (if he be not too much neglected), which with submission my Lord T——r he may stand in need of before he is aware. I beg your honour's pardon for this trouble, and hope his condition with his sickly, large and needy family here may be sufficient motives to move you and my Lord T——r to a speedy resolution; not only to fix that affair on him, but order him a supply; that he may not be put to such straits as I am informed he is in a strange place. I shall be very glad to receive your honour's commands in order to relieve him a little.

JON. DAVIDSON to JON. JOHNSON, at Edinburgh.

1707, September 23. London—The 22nd of this instant Mr. Moor set out in the stage coach with Plutarch's volumes. I give you this account to prepare you for a visit in his way to the north. Our news is that the Duke of Orleans has invested Lerida in Spain, where there is a garrison of four thousand men and an English commanding officer in it; it was invested the 13th, and the trenches opened with forty pieces of cannon playing against it. The D[uke] of B[erwick] was to be up with him the 14th with his army returned from before Toulon. The Duke is made a Grandee of Spain *du premier classe pour lui et ses descendants* and Philip has parted with Crown lands lying about Valentia to maintain the dignity. The Elector of H[anover] is come to the army on the Rhine and M. Villars has sent an officer to compliment him upon his arrival and sent him four pieces of Burgundy wine. The campaign in Flanders is at an end, the French retiring into their lines. The Duke of M[arlborough] is expected in Holland the 14th of October: the King of France has sent the Prince of Asturias a diamond for his cap valued at 800,000 crowns. Our Scotch Secretaries are at the Bath with the Duke of Queensberry and the Earl of Morton. I have sent you Mr. Strahan's bill.

1 set of Plutarch's lives in 5 vols., 1*l.* 3*s.* 0*d.*

E. LEWIS to SECRETARY [HARLEY].

1707, September 25. Whitehall—Revell the messenger brought hither yesterday a young woman, whose name is Molloy, by mistake for the Countess de Maillé, who I hear is gone to make a visit to the French prisoners at Nottingham, but is expected back from thence this week. I have received from my Lord Manchester's secretary a large packet sent to him from Milan to be conveyed to Lord Peterborough, I thought it might not be proper to let any letter of his Lordship's pass through my hands without knowing the contents, and therefore I got it opened and have sent it to Mr. Addison to lay it before my Lord Sunderland, though there is nothing very remarkable but that the Marquis de Visconti has desired him to convey a letter from him to the Queen, and that his Lordship's correspondent at Milan tells him he hopes his Lordship will be made Viceroy of Sicily for the good services he has rendered King Charles the Third. When my Lord Sunderland returns me the packet I will make it up and send it as directed. My Lord Treasurer I suppose will let you know whether my Lord Peterborough sends the Marquis de Visconti's letter to the Queen or sinks it.

ROBERT HARLEY.

1707, September 25, Thursday. Crown Inn, Faringdon in Berkshire—Being alone upon a journey I have had occasion to reflect upon the present situation of public affairs in England, which has drawn my thoughts insensibly to recollect how I came to be drawn into the public service, and how I have behaved myself therein.

I will not here mention what was done by my father, my brother, my cousin, and myself at the Revolution, that may be proper hereafter for the instruction of my son, as also that he may know what brought those very great expenses we were after at in elections, and trials in the House of Commons, all which sprung from one cause, and were the consequences of our acting upon principles of honour and integrity, and of the envy and malice of other people. I must also pass by Duke Schomberg's pressing my father's being Lieutenant of the Ordnance upon his going to Ireland, and that he would have extorted a promise from him to accept it. This was chiefly managed by Lord Montagu, at present Duke of Montagu. Many other things I pass by, and will but only touch those matters which necessarily lead me to the point I proposed. I will very briefly pass over everything until I come to the beginning of this reign, and shall mention no more particulars at present, than are necessary to show how I came concerned with several great persons as well as with public affairs. In the second session of the second parliament of King William and Queen Mary, and called in the end of the year 1690, I came into the House upon my petition for Radnor. The bill for taking accounts having miscarried the session before was revived again in this, and I was chosen a commissioner, the youngest and last of nine, and was in all the commissions which after were passed during that reign, of which a particular account is more proper than to insert it here; only in general after the first years and little more every session there were new ballotings, and many arts used to destroy it or render it useless, but though all others were changed one time or other, Mr. Foley and I continued the whole time, being chosen by a majority.

During that time I had many overtures made to me, sometimes to be Secretary of State and very earnestly to accept Sir Robert Howard's place of Auditor of the Exchequer, who then lay ill. I was offered to *have it made easy to me and that the commission might determine* and I be left out. Several other things were offered to make it sure to me and easy, and the aforesaid Duke Montagu was sent to press me in it divers times, and once particularly his Lordship came to me in King Street and met Lord Ashley now Earl of Shaftesbury, which I mention only to put myself in mind of some particulars which then happened worth noting. During my being in the Commission of Accounts, I was generally twice every year to wait upon the King, viz. at his first coming over, and the night before he went away from Kensington, were the usual times. The first conversation I had with His Majesty was very long, free, and very particular, and it began in the year 1691 upon a very extraordinary proposal about Toulon. The whole of that affair is very well worth putting in writing. Ever after that the King grew more and more free in his discourse both of persons and things, and as I never came to him but when I was sent for, so I thought it my duty to attend upon my Prince's summons. That year of the second disbanding the army he did not send for me to take leave of him when he went; but he told me before and after, that I had treated him like a gentleman, and foretold what would happen. But this is an affair to be treated by itself, as also those conversations I had with His Majesty—which are proper to be set down—for I will never mention anything he was pleased to say to me, but what have been told by other persons; as for purpose the Earl of Sunderland, while the King was alive, told me before others that I knew the King would have turned out Lord Somers to have had the sum of 200,000*l.* out of the Irish forfeitures. This was offered and pressed very [much], but I would never enter into that negotiation, or give any encouragement to it; but perhaps more of that in another place it not being proper here. *In Robert Harley's handwriting.*

The EARL OF SEAFIELD to ROBERT HARLEY.

1707, September 25. Edinburgh—I have received the honour of yours concerning Mr. Robert Murray now prisoner in the Castle of Edinburgh, it gives no further light in that matter. You say there is one can charge him but that you cannot discover his name without Her Majesty's allowance. He would certainly have obliged us to have set him at liberty on bail, had it not been for those papers were found in his custody when he was taken. I have sent a particular account of them to my Lord Treasurer who I doubt not will acquaint you with it. We are doing what is in our power to apprehend John Murray, if he is in this country I believe he will have difficulty to escape. I caused search the two last packets, but there was no letter found with the direction you mention but any letter of consequence may better be opened at London as here, if Sir Thomas Frankland or any of the Post Office be advertised. However I shall continue to cause search the packets so long as I continue here, which will be all the next week, and if you have any commands for me in answer to this I shall be glad to receive them though I be on the road; for your letters will come to my hands and I shall give such orders as in any case arise.

E. LEWIS to [ROBERT HARLEY].

1707, September 27. Whitehall—Sir Stephen Evans tells me Mr. Greg will not close with his offer, as looking upon the encouragement not to be sufficient. There were great contests in the Council on Wednesday night about a clause in the bill against popery which made void all settlements made by Papists within these last twelve months, though upon valuable consideration. Lords S[underlan]d and Con[ings]by were for it, and the Lord Chancellor leaned that way but was brought over to the other side by the steadiness of the Attorney General and Lord Chief Justice Holt, and an amendment was made.

Yesterday morning I was informed that one of the queen's waiters in the port of London died the night before. This morning I hear it is given to one Mr. Cornwallis an ancient inhabitant of Alsatia; I speak in the language of Shadwell's " Libertine."

[DANIEL] DE FOE to ROBERT HARLEY.

1707, September 29. Wemyss—When I read over sometimes my Lord Treasurer's letter, which I carry in my pocket, I think 'tis impossible I should be in the case I am. Since therein his Lordship mentions that he knows my necessities.

I cannot but think it hard to be left so in a strange place, and where, I speak without vanity, I had made myself capable of doing ten times more service than I, or any ten can do by new measures; why the service as well as the man is so forgotten is not for me to enquire. I bless God I have never been driven to importunities with my friends, and were I in England though I have misfortuncs that crush me, yet I shall never be so reduced as to solicit bread and sue for subsistence.

I know it is your supposition that they will supply me, for you never would have left me to this, I have too much experience of your concern for me. I humbly entreat but this last favour as the *coup de grace* to send me out of this torture. Give me your orders to come away. I'll ever be your faithful and sincere servant, whether subsisted or not, I'll be the constant friend of your family and interest in mere remembrance of your past care of me. It is my aversion to quit a post I am placed in by your order and which without your order I ought not to abandon, but the bravest garrison may be starved out, and it is my duty to tell you when I am not able to hold out any longer. I had a letter from my brother, who tells me you ordered him to write to me I should be supplied, and I had resolved to come away the last week but for that letter ; I will make hard shift till if you please I may have a line in answer to this. I, know my Lord T——r will be at Newmarket, and if I am left to his return 'tis impossible for me to wait.

If I do not come away this month, the roads will be impassable, and to subsist here of myself the winter is not for me to pretend to.

Besides if my Lord had answered his own letter and I had gone on here I would have proposed my making a trip up, though I had come post back again, and have convinced you of what use it had been for me to have been among our Scots members at the meeting of the Parliament.

I beseech you, sir, to believe me that nothing but necessity can oblige me to this, had I been in a condition I would have conquered all delays with a patience should have forced my Lord to remember—but it is not with me as it has been, and I can hold out no longer, and 'tis a double affliction to me to tell you so.

Postscript.—Tomorrow the Synod of Fi[fe me]ets. I have been very busy among the ministers there for fourteen days passed ; for this I have found to be a maxim for managing here, if you will form anything here it must be by the ministers. I am invited to dine with the Presbytery of Kirkcaldy today, being the day before the Synod, and shall have the honour to sit in the Synod the next day and hear all their proceedings ; and, which is more than ever was allowed to a stranger, have liberty to give my opinion in any case—though not to vote, that cannot be. But you may judge by this whether I am not come a length to render me capable to serve the interest, and 'tis great pity it should be all blasted at once.

[ABIGAIL MASHAM to ROBERT HARLEY.]

1707, September 29. London—All that has happened new since you left us relates to myself, which is :—the 22nd day I waited : and in the evening about eight o'clock a great lady came and made a visit till almost ten. I was in the drawing room by good luck, and as she passed by me I had a very low curtsey, which I returned in the same manner, but not one word passed between us, and as for her looks, indeed they are not to be described by any mortal but her own self. Nothing but my innocence could have supported me under such behaviour as this. When she had ended her conversation with the Queen, I was gone to my lodging to avoid seeing her again that night, but she was so full, she could not help sending a page of the back stairs to speak with me : when I came to her she told me, she had something to say to me and desired it might be the next day either at her lodgings or mine which was easiest to me, and then she would trouble me no more. I desired I might wait upon her where and when she pleased, then says she, I will send for you tomorrow. I waited all day expecting to be sent for, but no message came ; at last, between eleven and twelve o'clock, this letter was sent by her footman, which I have taken the liberty to inclose with a copy of my answer, the next morning, before she went her journey to Woodstock, if you care to give yourself the trouble of reading them ; and I beg you will let me have her letter back again when we meet. I hope in God it will not be very long before you return : I have paid the 200l. to Mr. Bateman according to your order. The Queen wants me, and I must conclude.

Her Majesty approved of your letter to the Bishop.

EARL RIVERS to [ROBERT] HARLEY.

1707, September 30. [Warndon *postmark*]—I thought till I had the honour of yours that all my friends had forgotten me. I have not heard from anybody what you mention. If I do you shall know what is proposed and I shall desire your advice. I design to stay here till the beginning of November, having much business and being well provided with all sorts of conveniences. Pray tell my friend St. John that since I cannot hear from him I am glad to hear of him and that " he is so well scrambled off." When either of you has an idle hour I desire you'll let me hear how matters stand.

E. LEWIS to SECRETARY [HARLEY].

1707, October 2—The enclosed from Mr. Drummond came to my hands last night. I acquaint the Lord Treasurer by this post that Mrs. Stepney desires him to accept of a beautiful Arabian horse their brother (*sic*) left at the Hague. Lord Peterborough is in great grief for that true Englishman *the Observator*.

SAMUEL MILWARD to EDWARD HARLEY, at Eywood.

1707, October 6. Knighton—Mr. Woleston intends to wait on you next week. He pressed Mr. Mason to join with you in elections, not as if you desired it but as proper for his own security. He did not give a ready or certain answer. It is thought if he refuse it will shatter his interest. There is a motion made for five or six leading aldermen to wait upon Mr. Secretary. I shall know the resolution as I return. Mr. Harnage has absolutely desisted. Lord Newport, as I hear, will be for the town of Shrewsbury or the county, and Mr. Brett's interest will fall if your purchase stands. We think it not proper to move much among the small ones, they are such a rude sort of people, until we see whether there will be any present occasion, for it is said this Parliament will continue.

J. D'ALAIS to [ERASMUS] LEWIS.

1707, October 7. Hanover—Since Mrs. Burnet has been here she has always dined at the Electress's table. She returns into Holland next Monday. I am very sensible at the loss we have sustained both publicly and privately by the the death of Mr. Stepney. I shall always preserve a very profound respect for his memory, and I can assure you that he is much regretted here. *French.*

E. LEWIS to SECRETARY [HARLEY].

1707, October 7. Whitehall—It is generally believed here that Brigadier Cadogan will succeed Mr. Stepney in his foreign employments. Mr. Walsh, Stanhope, Lord Raby, and Sir Philip Medows' merits were considered, but my intelligence says Cadogan carries the point. Mr. Walsh is uneasy under the yoke of his superior and now puts in for the Board of Trade.

Lord Treasurer has won two races.

LE MOYNE to SECRETARY HARLEY.

1707, October 8. The Common Side of Newgate—Give me leave to entreat you this once more to grant me my liberty, that I may be the quicker free from the long and hard oppression I have been under this two years and a half in Newgate.

E. LEWIS to SECRETARY [HARLEY].

1707, October 9. Whitehall—I believe you will be much surprised to hear that Captain Baker by his informations to Lord Sunderland has found means to get Clarke confined, two of his men put into the custody of a messenger, and prevailed at the same time with that messenger to deliver to him all the letters that came from France and were found about those men, without any regard to Lord Sunderland into whose hands those papers ought to have been immediately delivered. Captain Baker knew very well that Clarke was employed by you. He told me so several times, and my silence could not but confirm him in that opinion. I have taken no other notice of the two other letters I received from Clarke than barely to acquaint Lord Sunderland that I knew this man was once employed by you and I believed was so still. The *Observator* for the benefit of Tutchin's widow, printed last Saturday, makes much noise here.

SIR ALEXANDER RIGBY to SECRETARY HARLEY.

1707, October 10. Edinburgh—Introducing Mr. Moriston of Preston Grange who was one of the Commissioners for the Union, considerable both in fortune and alliances, having one daughter married to the Earl of Sutherland's eldest son, and another to Lord Boyle, the Earl of Glasgow's son.

E. Lewis to Secretary [Harley].

1707, October 11. Whitehall—I know you are apprized that Mr. T[oland] has given out that he was employed by you, and therefore I thought it needless to tell you what I had heard upon that subject, however I send you Mr. D'Alais' account of it.

All the letters from Newmarket as well as Israel Fielding's make a mystery of the Queen's illness.

Mr. Lawes sends me word Mr. Cadogan has told him he is to succeed Mr. Stepney, but I have no orders to prepare the instruments.

J. D'Alais to [Erasmus] Lewis.

1707, October 11 [new style]. Hanover—Mrs. Burnet left here yesterday for Holland. She saw the Electress two hours before her departure, and carries with her the esteem of the Electress and all the Court. Mr. Scott and his wife arrived three days ago. She appears at Court today for the first time. Toland has come here from the Court at Dusseldorf, where the Elector made him considerable presents. He went yesterday to Herrenhausen and Mrs. Burnet was there when he paid his respects to the Electress. I should have liked to have been there but I cannot pay the expenses of the journey as often I should wish. There are two young English gentlemen here who came with him from London to Holland. He told them on the journey that he was accredited by the government to the Elector for affairs of importance. *French. Enclosed with preceding letter.*

E. Howe to [Robert Harley].

1707, October 11. London—I have not neglected the first moment my health allowed me to come to this place in order to embark for Holland, nor am I able yet to stir without being carried. There is no convoy from hence for a fortnight or three weeks, but if the Queen's service requires my being sooner at Hanover, I will leave my family here and go over in the packet boat. I have received letters from my secretary wherein he gives me an account of Mrs. Burnet's having been at Hanover and very graciously received by the Electress. He also gives me an account of Toland's arrival there and that the Electress receives him three or four hours every afternoon in private, and that this scandalous fellow pretends to come from several people of quality in England. He was gone to Wollfenbüttel when the last letters came away but was to return in few days to Hanover.

Jean Gassion to [Robert Harley].

1707, October 18. Perth—I told you in my last that I was to see a person who I did believe would give me some intelligence. I find there was a design on foot to have surprised the Castle of Edinburgh but there was a fellow at the bottom of it whose name is Caer of Carsland (Ker of Kersland), but he went for London and when he came down there would nobody converse with him, for they believed he did go up to make a clean breast, and so came down to trepan them; but that design is put off till they have encouragement from France. I must tell you that the taking of Robert Murray does not signify a rush, for he was apprehended in Glasgow

a great many miles from his own house, the better way had been to have
surprised him in his own house and have seized all his papers and made
him a close prisoner; but on the contrary he hath liberty to see and be
visited by everybody, so that measures are consulted. His brother is gone
positively, but I must tell you the whole kingdom is disaffected and if
France were but able to send them 10,000 men with other necessaries
they would rise infallibly, for they are all armed already; that was done
two or three years ago. If you could fall on ▇▇me way to have them
disarmed it would be a good thing. I pray you keep the letter (See Sept.
23) that I enclosed in yours for the person he calls Mr. Moor that is to call
at Drummond's with the Plutarch's Lives; he is a priest and just come
from France. The young man that I sent down, Mr. Drummond, the
priest, would not let him be received telling it was not safe for my Lord
to receive a man come from France, but this was only a pretence for he
well did know that the young man had no letters of consequence.
Therefore he would do this to cloak his receiving of that Moor and of
the Colonel John Drummond that is lately come home a papist also. I
wish you had caused take up this priest before I came down, but I must
tell you that family is favoured by the advocate Sir James Stuart, for
every time when they hunt the deer there is a good fat one sent to him
and I know he will not disoblige that family. There hath been a
meeting of some lords in the country and they talk my Lord Duke
Hamilton hath been this fourteen days absent and nobody knows where
he was, but at my return from the north I hope to be capable to give
you a better account.

I beg of you not to forget to remit me a little money against I come
back from the north to Edinburgh for by that time I shall not have a
farthing to bring me up, and also must beg of you to take care of my
poor wife for she is lying in and I am afraid she may want, so for God's
sake be mindful of her and let me know if mine hath come to your hands.
It will be a good thing if you could make an Act for to banish all the
priests in Scotland, but I shall tell you more of that when I come up.

JOHN CHAMBERLAYNE to [ROBERT HARLEY].

1707, October 24. Petty France—Mrs. Hamilton has almost forced
me to promise that I would lay before you the enclosed letter which she
writ me some time since. You know how zealous she has been to inform
you of the ill practices of the pretended Countess de Maillé, for a
description of whom Mr. Lewis was pleased to send to me a messenger
on purpose, though if I had been half so often *at her coach side in Paris*
I should not have given him that trouble.

The last time I wrote to you I made bold to beg your perusal of that
part of my book that gives an account of our Parliaments.

T. FOLEY to his kinsman [ROBERT] HARLEY.

1707, October 28. Stoke—Mr. Lechmere joins with me in a request
in relation to his standing next Parliament at Tewkesbury. He is there
opposed by Mr. Ireton. It would be of great use to him could a letter
be procured on his behalf from the Earl of Essex, who is their Lord
High Steward. I suppose that passed between the Earl's grandfather
and Mr. Ireton's father which lays my Lord under no great obligation
to him.

Sir William Fleming to [Robert Harley].

1707, October 31—Asking him to help to prevent his being made sheriff for Cumberland, as he fears that some of his enemies may endeavour to get him on to inconvenience him, living out of the county and not having been in it for some years.

D[aniel, De] F[oe] to Robert Harley.

1707, October 31—According to your order and directions I wrote to my Lord Treasurer, and this day I had the honour of a letter from him in which his Lordship, not thinking proper to order any person on whom I may draw, proposes my brother whom I sent with my letter. Still, my Lord neither directs me when to draw or how much. I had solicited his Lordship that in consideration of my circumstances, family &c. and that I had no subsistence the last half year, that he would give me leave to draw something, leaving the sum and time to him.

Now his Lordship orders me to draw by my brother, but gives me no order, either as to sum or time, trying my modesty in a manner I dare not venture on.

I am your humble petitioner that you will please to move in my favour for the advances of that half year. I have not dissembled when I have wrote you of the difficulties I have been in, and have gotten into some debt, both here and on family account, and if my Lord please to give his allowance that retrospect he shall never find me craving. I have been all the while upon the spot, and sincerely diligent in the grand work. I leave it to your goodness and hope you will prevail by your powerful intercession.

What my Lord is pleased to give my brother, I have ordered him to bring forthwith to you, entreating you will please to give him your letter to Mr. Bell, to answer it to me; for the Exchequer bills have so supplied all exchanges from London hither that it is impossible to remit hither, by which you will observe how the project of bringing those bills hither has answered no end here, not one of them passing in payment but being immediately sent for England, and even for that are now sold at two and three per cent. discount. But of this hereafter.

It is my humble opinion that the best way to make me truly useful in the affair I am upon is to have me be eight months here and three months in London each year, and the one month travelling between, going various roads, I shall perhaps do more service in than in all the rest. I have hinted the same thing to his Lordship and if your opinion concurs I could wish to be coming forward ere the ways are too deep, and that I may be here again before the Assembly sits, which is in March.

Postscript.—I formerly gave you the trouble of a letter about the Master of Burleigh, who barbarously murdered an innocent poor man without any——(*sic*); 'tis a surprising thing to see that madman come home again and go unmolested about the country insulting and threatening the people, and boast he has the Queen's remission or pardon in his pocket.

Sir Robert Price to Secretary Harley.

1707, November 2—Your company was very much coveted at Lincolns Inn. The Scotch lords were transcendently satisfied, and the little .. hose(?)lord was stiff, but little minded, though introduced by a great duchess's present of four does.

You are much in the good opinion of our Superintendent here, J. H., and if you would but visit him sometimes he would be established; the junto have him too often.

Dr. R. Freind to [Edward] Harley, at Christchurch, Oxford.

1707, November 8—By your last from Brampton I found that an answer would not meet with you there, but I intended to have congratulated you upon your coming to Oxford. You have reproached my tardiness very kindly in writing to me again, and giving me an account of your settlement in your new lodgings, I wish you abundance of enjoyment and improvement in them. I am glad to see you begin with so much vigour and cheerfulness, the further you go the more desirous you'll be of going on, as you have in some measure already experienced. You cannot be in better books than you are now in, and I don't doubt but I shall hear you proceed in 'em. As for Logic though it be dry there's an absolute necessity for it and it must be digested, it cannot sure seem duller to you than Grammar and yet I believe you are satisfied how necessary that was. Logic is indeed the grammar of Philosophy, and you must conquer it, 'tis a rough uncouth pass but it leads to a pleasant country. I suppose you begin Arithmetic with I. Kiel, pray let me know how you go on with him. Pray will you give my kind services to Mr. Finch I will write to him in a short time. I have paid an old debt to my Lord Carteret to-night. Your cousin does pretty well, and begins to sit still now having tipped down in his dancing upon the high form and broke his head. I'm sorry to hear of Dr. Stratford's misfortune, but since 'tis only a contusion I hope 'tis well by this time. Pray use yourself to write a little larger hand. You make too free with the Secretary's name from Oxford when 'tis so notorious that he is in town. I shall always think your letters worth the postage.

W. Lord Cheyne to Robert Harley.

1707, November 8—Asking that his cousin John Fleetwood might be excused from being sheriff of Bucks. His father served not long before he died, he is not twenty-two years of age, has a younger brother and sisters to provide for, and his mother keeps in jointure half the 1,000l. per annum the estate is worth.

Thomas Addison to Robert Harley.

1707, November 11. Delahay Street—Desires that William Delle-more, or Delamar, farmer of part of the late Duke of Richmond's estate in Lincolnshire (of which the writer is a trustee) may be excused from serving as sheriff of the county, as he has but a small estate and eight small children to maintain by his farming.

Letter of Delamar, from Sutton, November 7, to William Welbye, Esq., at Devonshire House, enclosed.

J. Herbert to [Robert Harley].

1707, November 14. Oakley Park—Asking to be excused from being sheriff of Montgomeryshire or Merioneth, as he is told there is a very great man resolved to fix him for the former county, if it lie in his power.

JEAN GASSION [*alias* OGILVIE] to [ROBERT HARLEY].

1707, November 17. Edinburgh—I came to this place on Saturday night last but so wearied and ill that I was not able to write that night, for my journey hath been a little extraordinary. I went from this door through the one side of the kingdom and I came up the other side which is called the Lowlands, and I will assure you of one thing and that is if you had got a sight of the transactions of this nation from an Italian necromancer, you should not have had it more justly than I can give it you, for in the first place I wrote you no idle talk or stories but what you may entirely depend on to be truth, this you know is my way. Now to begin be assured that the most of this kingdom is entered in an association with the King of France, the troops that is to come is 10,000 men, most of them is promised to be of the Irish Corps that is in France; they are to bring money, for the troops is to be punctually paid, the officers is to have half pay, the Duke of Berwick is to command them but the Prince of Wales is to be in person, they are to bring a train of artillery and arms and clothes for 30,000 men. The Highlanders need neither clothes nor arms, in short, they engaged to join the 10,000 with 40,000 so they shall be at least 50,000 strong. The way that this great affair was carried on was as follows: when the Parliament sat Colonel Huck (Hooke), for the King of France calls him so in his letters to them, came and stayed all the time in Edinburgh the Parliament sat. After that he returned with the sentiments of some of the nobility, upon which the King of France sent him to them back with a full power to treat; the nature of the negociation was as I have mentioned, the troops was to have landed this very month, but they have received a letter from France wherein they are advertised that it's only the affair of (Toulon ?) hath retarded the expedition but nothing shall hinder it the first occasion. There's a gentleman gone from this kingdom to France to represent the danger of a delay, he pretended to go elsewhere but positively his errand is there. When Colonel Huck came last he brought a Captain John Murray in his company, but the nobility and gentry that was concerned, knowing the danger that John Murray lay under, if he was apprehended for his being here on Fraser's business, would not suffer him to stir his foot but he lay privately some times at the Earl of Erroll's, and some times at the Earl Marshal's, and at one Sir William Keith's; but Colonel Huck went boldly up and down the whole country and passed for a borderer of the English side come to buy cattle. The Countess of Errol was so complaisant that she sent to the Countess of Dunfermline for her priest to say mass to him, although her Ladyship be a Protestant. As for the negociating with the Highland clans there were other measures taken, for Doctor Gordon, who is a doctor of the Sorbonne and a bishop here over the Roman Catholics, was sent up to them to advise them to be in a readiness and to provide themselves of what arms they could. This is a short but true account and I dare venture to say without vanity that I have answered the trust that you are pleased to put in me, and I firmly believe none else could have dived into the bottom of this affair but myself and I do assure you I had great difficulty, for when I came amongst them at first they did believe I had some letters for them, but when they found I had none then they did not know what to make of me but they did believe I was entirely honest in the main. Some of them would not see me but in private, others would not let me come into their houses but met me at the hunting, and all their fear was that the country should talk that I was seen at their houses and they should be taken up on it, for they swear that if one of them be taken up, they will all fly to arms at once, and I declare I think I never ran a greater risk of my life since I was born, for had they but in the least suspected me I had been murdered and never heard more tell of, but all is safe that God will have safe. I could have performed this journey in less time and much less expense but then I should have brought you an Irishman's answer, which is a nothing, but that would have never answered the trust you have in me. I have received a line from my wife, she is gone into her house, and you were so good as to give her 20*l.* She hath sent me 10*l.* of it and I declare to you on the word of a Christian there is not one guinea of it remaining but what is spent on horse hiring and servants and guides for carrying of me through the Highland countries, therefore I must beg of you to remit me a small bill this very post.

W. JESSOP to [the DUKE OF NEWCASTLE].

1707, November 19. Sheffield—Regarding a meeting to be held about Fullwood common which could not take place owing to the absence in London of Mr. Gravener, the Duke of Devonshire's agent. If Mr. Baukos should set up at Retford he would be openly opposed by Mr. Thornhagh and his son; the latter would take it well to be offered the seat. Parson Calton knows nothing more of this matter, but has been desired to pump old Jervis, the oldest man in the town, and such others as he apprehends can inform him.

D[ANIEL] DE F[OE] to ROBERT HARLEY.

1707, November 28. Edinburgh—I have not the honour of any from you since my last; but I have an account from Mr. Bell that he has your order to furnish me with one hundred pounds and this post has accordingly remitted it hither; and as this gives new life to my affairs so in three or four days I purpose to set out for London and hope to kiss your hand, and acknowledge my engagements to your constant goodness in a few days, though the shortness of the days and badness of the way will make me longer on the road than I would be. I have little to advise of here, the vote of taking of the *noli prosequi* from the Scots merchants pleases very well, and my Lord Haversham's speech is laughed at by everybody. I am sorry my being so far off will make me late in giving my Lord his due praise, but I shall be out of his debt this post.

 I am your most humble petitioner to give my sincerest acknowledgement and the fullest expressions of duty and gratitude that a mind deeply sensible of his bounty can imagine to my Lord Treasurer.

As I come forward I shall continue to acquaint myself of the circumstances of every place and the state of things, and shall do myself the honour to write on all occasions.

ANT[HONY] LECHMERE to [ROBERT HARLEY].

1707, November 20. Tewkesbury—Has been there three days endeavouring to secure an interest, which he has some reason to believe is not despicable. Mr. Yerrow is much inclined to dispose of his vote and interest speedily unless very soon influenced by Mr. Popham through Harley. Also desires a recommendation to the Quakers, who are a considerable number in Tewkesbury and as yet unresolved for whom to vote, by a letter from William Penn.

WILLIAM MACE to [EDWARD] HARLEY, at Oxford.

1707 [November]—The town grows dull and does increase my spleen. 'Tis dismal news to tell of our misfortunes. You know Sir Cloudesley is, lost, we have had no information since the fatal wreck for not one soul, was left to tell the mournful tale. This calamity has made a visible impression upon the whole town who are something too alarmed at the sudden adjournment of both Houses on Thursday. The Queen made no speech but approved of the Speaker after he had represented himself as insufficient for so great a trust ; my Lord Chancellor replied Her Majesty was very well pleased with the choice, and would always put the most favourable construction on his words and actions, and said she didn't think fit to acquaint them with the reasons of their being called together, but that it was her pleasure both Houses should adjourn themselves to Thursday next. This has occasioned several speculations. The most probable conjecture to me is that the Court want some dispatches they expect from the Duke of Marlborough, who has negotiated the treaties with foreign Powers, which perhaps they judge worthy a place in Her Majesty's Speech. But time will soon unriddle the secret. , However this has postponed an affair that likely may make a noise, Sir H——y M——th designed to have presented his printed case to the Commons complaining of a clandestine attempt upon his life by ruffians hired for that end. I am sorry in a charge of such a high nature to hear the name of our Mr. M——l's father mentioned, but I hope my intelligence is not true. I should be glad if you would undeceive me for I suppose if this be fact you are better acquainted with the story. The Prophets continue to furnish out the talk of the town, they multiply against all opposition, about a hundred having the gift or the preparatory symptoms. The pamphlets writ against them have really advanced their interest. For excepting "Clavis Prophetica" which abounds with more wit than judgment or justice the rest are nothing but calumnies and inconsistent invectives. The Virtuosi are divided in their opinions about the puzzling phenomenon, some accounting for it by the supposition of enthusiastic delusion or imposture or a composition of both. However it be the world is like to reap some advantage by these transactions, for the pens of the learned will be provoked to set the subject of prophecy in a clearer light. Mr. Misson famous for his travels, is writing a parallel between the Ancient and Modern Prophets, wherein he attempts to prove the former had fits, tremblings, convulsions, howlings &c. as these now have. He promises something curious, for his work is the product of a whole year's collection and observation. Sir R—— B——ley, a diminutive deformed gentleman, is big with the expectation of being made straight as an arrow by Mr. Lacy, or rather I should think by Mr. Fatio [Faccio?] who is so well known for his skill in rectifying of curves. Mr. L—y is publishing his third and last part wherein he declares that unless he is able to prove his mission by miracles incontestable within six months' time he will acknowledge himself under a delusion. Though they have been prosecuted with no ordinary zeal, they have not yet received any sentence or fine, and I am very well informed my L—d C—— Just—e does not approve of the process which he thinks was entered with more vehemence than discretion. I have enlarged too far on this article and fear you begin to yawn but you'll soon recover your gaiety by reading but one page in the "Tale of a Tub," concerning mechanical inspiration. I have dwelt the longer on the subject through the barrenness of news occasioned by the want of four mails.

[DR. FRANCIS ATTERBURY] to ROBERT HARLEY.

[1707, November,] Saturday—The paper enclosed contains the last pages of a large preface to a volume of sermons; at the end of which I have been forced to consider a rude passage in a late Assize sermon, preached by Mr. West, at Winchester, of which church he is prebendary, and a creature of the Bishop of Sarum. After I have said something to his objections, what I have enclosed is to follow, and is designed to give such a turn to the thoughts of those who read it, as you desire should be given. And if there should be a little more warmth than ordinary in it, perhaps the occasion will justify it, and coming from me, it may not be amiss; and, I am sure, is the more likely on that account to rouse the clergy, with whom it is necessary to establish a confidence, in order to the promoting any public service. Nevertheless I am not willing to send it to the press till I have your direction, and for that reason give you this repeated trouble.

LONDON HOSPITALS.

1707, December 1—Petition of the Lord Mayor and citizens of London and the governors, &c. of the Hospitals of St. Bartholomew, Bethlehem, Christ's, and Bridewell in London, and of St. Thomas the Apostle in Southwark, for a royal licence to enable these Hospitals to hold and enjoy such lands and tenements as are, or shall hereafter be, given or purchased for their use, with especial reference to a legacy of 2300l. left by Sir Robert Clayton, to be invested in land for the use of St. Thomas's Hospital, which legacy was however to be void unless a licence in mortmain should be obtained within a year after his death, which occurred in July 1707. Signed by W. Withers, Mayor; Peter Joye, Treasurer, and John Fleet, President, of St. Bartholomews'; Thos. Lockington, Treasurer, and Francis Child, President, of Christ's ; Thos. Gardiner, Treasurer, and Thos. Rawlinson, President, of Bridewell and Bethlehem ; Thos. Eyre, Treasurer, and Thos. Abney, President, of St. Thomas's.

Attached is an opinion of the Attorney General, Sir Simon Harcourt, that such petition may reasonably be granted.

[DR. FRANCIS ATTERBURY to ROBERT HARLEY.]

[1707, December 2,] Tuesday—On Monday the 24th when the Bishop of Carlisle met the Chapter again in his visitation, and Dr. Todd's suspension was determined, the Bishop commanded him to subscribe a form, which in general acknowledged the Bishop's power of visiting the Church, and Dr. Todd's contempts &c., in resisting that power. Had Dr. Todd subscribed such a form, he would have been understood to allow the Bishop's power—as local visitor—of visiting upon the statutes of the Church, and therefore he would not do it. The Bishop upon that declared him contumax, and continued his suspension till Thursday the 27th, when he again commanded him to submit in that form ; and upon his refusal excommunicated him, and then, I think, put an end to his visitation the day before the rule for stay of proceedings issued here above. How these violences, and the necessity of continuing excommunicate for two months, will work on Dr. Todd, and induce him to compromise the matter with the Bishop, I cannot say ; but I hope he may have courage enough to persist in what he has done, especially if some way were taken of heartening him, by a few lines written to me, which I might in confidence transmit to him, if you thought fit, Sir, and whereby it might appear that I had laid the account of all before you, and what sense you had of it. I know not how far this may be proper but if it be, apprehend it may be of great service to keep up his spirits against the outrageous violences which the Bishop hath practised towards him. What notions they had of his being excommunicate in that country and how early it was known what the Bishop intended to do with him, the following certificate will inform you. I shall wait upon you for it again in two or three days. In the meantime I shall not be idle in the matter Dr. Gastrell last mentioned to me.

The Bishop of Winton came to Chelsea last night.

WILLIAM GREG to —— ROBINEAU.

1707, December 2. Whitehall—I have to congratulate you that you are at last delivered from a most disagreeable person as you will see by the Marshal's letter, unless indeed the last letter which I wrote to Monseigneur de Chamillart should have made him change his mind. *French. Copy. Endorsed :—"Original letter from William Greg to Mr. Robineau, under whose cover Greg's letters were sent to Mr. Chamillart, and he takes notice in his letter of his writing to M. Chamillart."*

JOHN BELL to ROBERT HARLEY.

1707, December 2. Newcastle[-on-Tyne]—In my last I acquainted you that I had given orders to pay Mr. De Foe a hundred pounds, which my friend gives me an account is paid. I also desired you to pay the value into the Salt Office, which I hope is done ere this.

[The EARL OF GODOLPHIN] to [ROBERT HARLEY].

[1707, December 5,] Friday—A great cry is made to-night at the loss of the Leicester election and that all the Court Tories were for a Tacker.

I must needs say I think it is a great *contre-temps*, to fall out among ourselves, when all our strength united is not sufficient to defeat the *whimsical* clause. What vexes me most is to see the malicious insinuations that are made upon every such occasion, and I cannot but own it is a very weak and foolish behaviour of those who are in office, to say no more.

I enclose to you an advice from Oxford, which I should have given you this morning but I forgot it, you will judge much better than I, what use can be made of it.

JEAN GASSION [*alias* OGILVIE] to [ROBERT HARLEY].

1707, December 25—After I arrived at Edinburgh the beginning of October, I found it was not worth the time to stay there as I found I could learn nothing but stuff that is not to be credited so l went to Perthshire to the house of Tho. Drummond of Foyers Almond, he is a cousin of the Earl of Perth and also of the Duke of Roxburgh his estate borders with the Highlands and he has a good following ; so from that I went to my Lord Drummond, his Lordship returned me an answer wherein he told me he had reasons for not seeing of the young man that I sent down, and that he would never see him nor me nor nobody else publicly, but if I could order it so as to come to his house unseen by anybody, he would be glad to see me for he said he had much to say to me, you have seen his letter to me. I returned his Lordship answer that it was impossible for me to come to his house and not be seen, for I did know his priest to be my enemy. His Lordship was pleased to answer me that since I would not come, he would meet me at the wood of Congosk and ordered me to bring Logie's huntsman and dogs with me and that would be the sign I was come, this letter you saw also. My Lord came he was there before me, I had conversation for about three hours with him and indeed received all the information I could desire as to their negociation with the King of France which was as follows that Colonel Huck (Hooke) came over in the time of the parliament, being sent to see what he could do to hinder the Union, but the Jacobite party finding that there was no possibility of hindering of it they designed him to acquaint the King of France that if he would send them troops they did not doubt but to find many more friends than they had formerly ; with this commission Huck returned to France and came back this last spring accompanied with Captain John Murray with credentials from the King of France to treat with the nobility and gentry. His instructions were to this effect that there should come this very winter, ten thousand men, thirty or at least twenty five thousand stand of arms, money to pay the soldiers full pay and subsistence for the officers, ammunition and a train of artillery ; with a declaration promising to maintain the religion as it is established and that no papist shall bear any public office whatso- ever, and that all vassals that will take arms and join if their lords or superiors be in the other party then all such shall be freeholders and hold only of the King. So when I received this intelligence there I was not content with what I had got but went back to Drummond of Logie Almond where I found the Earl of Breadalbane by chance, he was going to my Lord Drummond's. I told his Lordship I was just come from there, his Lordship having known me formerly had no manner of mistrust of me, so after dinner when the cloth was taken away we fell to the same track that I had travelled with my Lord Drummond, where I heard the same confirmed to me by his Lordship and Logic, only he added that the affected all ever had hindered it for this winter but he hoped it in next spring but his Lordship is very forward in the cause.

From thence I parted the next day and went by my Lord Stormont's and my Lord Paumure's and through the shire of Angus and Mearns where I found them all very ill inclined and want but a occasion to take arms and rise. From thence I went to the shire of Bacff and to my Lord Boyne's, old Ogilvie, two nights. I met with himself but he told me his son was gone to Sweden to serve under General Ogilvie, but I found his Lordship had not that clear, for General Ogilvie serves King Augustus. At Banff I did visit the old Lady Marchioness of Huntly the Duke of Gordon's mother, and there I found a nest of priests and their bishop, Nicholson, who goes by the name of Dr. Bruce. They were going to Aberdeen to an assembly, whereupon I dispatched my brother Joseph to go to them to see what he could learn amongst them for my further information, and I went my way to the Coast of Buchan to the Earl Marshals where I was confirmed without any reserve by his Lordship.

From thence I went to the Earl of Erroll's but before I came there I called at a change house about a mile from the house of the Bowers as they call the Earl of . . . (*torn off*) house, and there I sent a line for a old fellow-soldier of mine Colonel Graham, he came to me immediately, he was a particular friend of mine, he and I had served formerly in France together and we were long bedfellows. I was confident he would hide nothing from me and truly I am persuaded he did not, for he did give me a full account of everything for he was in the house all the time that Huck was there; and he is John Murray's uncle so he is perfectly well acquainted with their most secret transactions. But how soon the old Countess heard that there was a man that had sent for him she was surprised and sent for him in all haste and enquired who it was that had sent for him. He told her it was I, she desired him to be on the reserve but he told her it was too late for he found I was acquainted with the affair before so he had been frank with me. This he told me afterwards, upon which my Lord met me and told me he would have invited me to his house but that it was dangerous at this time, since that I was so well known in the country to have been seen so long in France, it might cause them to be apprehended which would be of bad consequence to the King's affairs, as they termed him. There I was confirmed of all that the Colonel had told me and more that young Boyne was gone to France to pray that King to hasten his supplies and to see to have them near *by Whitsuntide*, and that they were to be advertised before the troops embarked in France by a light frigate from Dunkirk. She was to touch on the coast of Buchan either at my Lady Erroll's or Sir William Keith's at]Bothom a place stands in the sea also.

From thence I parted and came to Aberdeen, there I found my brother Joseph and that he had learned that Doctor Gordon, who was a doctor of the Sorbonne in France, and who is a Bishop here of the popish church, was sent to the Highlands to advertise the Highland clans to provide themselves in arms and to be in readiness when called. He speaks their language and is a bishop and what little religion he has is Roman Catholic. So I thought it was my best to send my brother Joseph there amongst that set, withal praying of him to write me word from time to time what happened, particularly of what word came from France that I might take my measures, but I kept entirely from him the use that I intend to make of his intelligence. So I left that country and came for Edinburgh and there I found that Mr. Defoe was in town but nobody would suffer him in their company except the anti-monarchial men, for they believe he is sent down to be a spy over them and that his flight is only a pretence; he hath tried to insinuate himself in several companies but none will admit him. I found also that there had been a project on foot proposed by one Craford of Carsland (*sic*) but they believe he is a rogue to them, so they will have nothing to do with him.

There is one thing more I must advertise you of and it's positively true for I had it from good hands and that is, the most *of the subaltern officers of the army in Scotland is debauched and the whole generality of the soldiers*, that is if the Prince of Wales comes they'll join him, but the horse guards is entirely debauched; there is one of their brigadiers called John Maeder who hath a great hand in debauching of them. This is the substance of what I learned for my down going. I wish I could have done more for her Majesty's service and your satisfaction.

You remember I told you my Lady Erroll was very complaisant to Huck when at her house, she sent to my Lady Dunfermline for a priest and had mass said to him in her house, although she be a strict Protestant. I told you that Huck did travel up and down boldly as an English drover from place to place. The Duke of Hamilton knows of this affair . . . (*torn off*) he did not like *winter campaigns*, to lie on the ground without a bed in the winter, especially in Scotland where they could not have the conveniences that is in other armies, they have asked however of him, that is, if the Prince of Wales as they call him comes, but he is resolved to walk on sure grounds having an estate in England. There is no man more forward for the cause than the Duke of Athol and I do assure you at his last review he mustered four thousand men, but a gentleman of good sense told me he could have drawn out nine batallions of as good men as ever he saw and as well armed. They are all a little angry with the Duke of Hamilton for it was he only hindered them from rising of the Parliament, for all the gentry was on their march and came as far as the river but was stopped by a order from him. There had been a difference between my Lord Duke of Athol and the Earl of Breadalbane, but they are entirely reconciled now, you may easily judge the reason.

It is a wonder to me to see the Roman Catholic service public in every place, just as public as it was in King James's time both at Edinburgh, Aberdeen, Banff and on the Duke of Gordon's land whole nests of priests, and for those that are Roman Catholics they have their priests and chapels avowedly. The advocate for James Stuart says he will persecute nobody for fear of a change that if it should fall out then they may call this the mild government, as for example my Lord Leven is put into office as Steward of Strathearn, my Lord Perth is Constable Steward of it, but my Lord Drummond not taking of the oaths he was put in and notwithstanding he sees my Lord Drummond's priest instructing and converting of the country people and preaching to them, and yet his Lordship is so loth to disoblige that family that there is no notice taken of it. There was order given to a officer, one Campbell, to apprehend Colonel Graham, this officer kept the order above four months and never did it, at last it was given to another officer and he had it three months, at last the Colonel came to a house by chance where this officer was, but alone, the master of the house did know of the thing and advertised the Colonel not to come in, but the Colonel being a . . . (*torn off*) bold brave man said since he is alone he shall catch a Tartar if he offers anything to me; and the Colonel actually went up and drank all the night with this officer, so you may judge how you are and will be served. I find that there is few or none will take the oath of abjuration, even the Presbyterians themselves pretend they will not take it.

JEAN GASSION [*alias* OGILVIE] to [ROBERT HARLEY].

1707, December 26—I forgot to tell you that the west country was all armed in the time that they did pass the Act of Security, and for the Highlands they make their own arms themselves and if you should give an order to disarm them it's what can never be done by the army that is at present in Scotland, for they will connive together and besides it's what they fear, for they have caves made in the rocks for preserving of their arms so search who will they can never find them. But I must tell you if you do not call away the Scots army it's what you'll repent when it is too late, that is if anything fall out which they expect, and the sooner you remove them the better, but you must have others to send down in their places immediately. Your surest way is to send the Scots troops abroad that is either to Spain or Italy, as good they perish as better men. You know I did propose for you to give me an independent troop of dragoons of Englishmen, and I told you that I would do you more service than all the troops you have there can do you or will do you at this time; for let me tell you there is nothing like to set a thief to catch a thief. In the first place there shall hardly any come from France but I shall do my endeavour to snap them for I am no stranger to their haunts, and in the next place I promise you to give you account of every priest and bishop that is in the Kingdom; but I would gladly have it so that I might receive my orders from yourself and I promise you that I shall put them in execution without being afraid of any lord or laird in the kingdom. I may say it without vanity that whoever shall command the English troops in that country will not be the worse to have me by him, for it's natural to believe that a stranger must need information how to behave in many cases. Also the heads of their faction, if it was thought proper, I durst engage to apprehend the most of them in a night and that is more nor any stranger can do, for if he apprehend one the rest will make their escape and so the rebellion will begin. But what I do propose will be perhaps difficult to be obtained for me, that is an independent troop, but as to that I shall be content of what you think fit, but I only propose the most effectual way to render me capable to execute your orders who I know can break me as well as make me, if I do not answer your expectation. Therefore I pray you, if you can venture to believe any of my countrymen, answer for me and with the help of God you shall never be ashamed of the making of me. There was one thing that I would have gladly begged of you last night but I was dashed, it is that you would honour me so far as to be godfather to my little boy that was born last, he is not baptized as yet nor shall be till your convenience can allow you to do me that honour, it is what I am very ambitious to have for several reasons and one of them is, it will be a great satisfaction for me to think that one of my children shall have so good a friend when I am dead as yourself. I must put you in mind that you did promise me to help to some furniture for my house, for although it be a satisfaction to be within one's self yet it's miserable not to have a bed to lie on; so I beg you'll be pleased to think on it for what you give me to subsist on I dare not venture to lay it out for fear of the children wanting bread. I have two of them lie out of the house at present for want of a bed to lay them in and that is expensive; however I do not doubt but you'll help when your convenience will allow you. I beg you'll honour me with an answer as to the christening of my boy.

JOHN CHAMBERLAYNE to [ROBERT HARLEY].

1707, December 28. Petty France, Westminster—I beg leave to return my humblest thanks for the great honour of yesterday's letter, particularly for the wise advice about the methodising my *State of Great Britain*, the account of both parts of which you have abundantly convinced me ought by no means to be confounded; for it is most certain that although the two Kingdoms are made one by the happy Union, in many circumstances, yet they are disjoined in more; and therefore till the wisdom of the nation shall think fit to blend their laws and customs together 'twill be impossible for me to treat of them as one nation.

I can't tell whether I was more sorry or surprised to find my book returned without opening, the bulk of which, I doubt, frightened you, though the chapter of the Parliament was so short that it would not have cost you more than an hour. However since your Honour has been pleased to refuse me this happiness, I will, I must be contented, and I am the more readily so, because like truly great men, you have the art of softening your denials almost into favours.

Postscript.—If your Honour could spare me Mr. Hales's letter either to-morrow night, or Tuesday morning I should be thankful, because that letter is so long that it is impossible for me to answer it without book.

WILLIAM PATERSON.

1707, December 29. London—A document in Paterson's hand-writing, and signed by him, promising to pay Robert Harley "fifteen pounds at demand."

— HORNBECK to [ROBERT HARLEY].

1707, December 30. Hague—Among the letters of Marshal Tallard sent to Rotterdam to the merchant whom your Honour thought fit to authorize for that purpose, there were letters, copies of which having been communicated to the Burgomasters with a letter to shew them the handwriting of the person who wrote the two letters signed W. Greg, the Burgomasters have charged me to send these copies to your Highness. *French.*

W. GREG to MONSEIGNEUR DE CHAMILLART.

1707, December 30. Whitehall—You will agree that the Irish are more fortunate than the Scotch notwithstanding the Union when you learn that Mr. Palmes, one of the favourites of my Lord Marlborough, has just been named envoy-extraordinary to the Duke of Savoy, to whom, as you know, he was sent during the last campaign. Before going there however he is to make a round in the spring to Hanover, Berlin, Dusseldorf and Vienna to try and hurry the slowness of the Germans. We shall then see that the Germans have not changed their nature although they should try and do so out of pure complaisance for a lady.

I am afraid I did not explain sufficiently distinctly in the letter I wrote you a week ago on the subject of what the Parliament gave the Duke of Savoy, who, before his expedition into Provence had received the 100,000*l.* which it pleased these gentlemen to repay to their mistress. *French. Copy. Endorsed :—" This paper was found in Mr. Greg's closet in the middle of a quire of fair paper. January 3, 1707–8."*

WILLIAM GREG.

1707, December 31—William Greg, examined before the Lord Chancellor, Lord Treasurer, Lord Steward, Duke of Marlborough, Earl of Sunderland, and R. Harley, said that the first beginning of his correspondence with Mr. Chamillart was either October 24 or 28 last, that he sent his letter to Mr. Robineau in Marshal Tallard's cover; it was to desire a pass for a ship for Mr. Crookshanks; that he pressed that several times; but had never any answer to that nor any other letter; that then he wrote weekly or oftener an account of proceedings in Parliament always under Mr. Robineau's cover; that he wrote other matters, that he gave an account of the Queen's writing to the Emperor and sent a copy of the Queen's letter, and remarked that where the lines were drawn were corrections of my Lord Treasurer. He sent also a copy of a memorial from Mr. Dayrolles to Secretary Harley about the Dutch quota; he took the paper out of the book where it was to be entered, by which means he got the sight of it. The last letter he wrote was Tuesday sevennight wherein he sent the Parliament votes and remarks upon the Duke of Savoy's proceedings. He was to have had a hundred guineas if he could have obtained the pass for Mr. Crookshank's ship. That he has written to Marshal Tallard, had never any answer. He owns the letter of December 2, 1707, to be all of his own handwriting. He says that Crookshank's christian name is Robert, he told Crookshanks that he had written for him to Mr. Chamillart; the ship's name was the *Mary* of London, to go first to Guinea and then to the West Indies. *Minutes in Harley's handwriting.*

JEAN GASSION [*alias* OGILVIE] to [ROBERT HARLEY].

1707, December 31—I remember your Honour was desirous to know the name of my Lord Breadalbane's house, the strong house that is in the lake is a damned Highland name such as Collawa but his ordinary dwelling house is called Taymouth, it was formerly called Balock. You asked also my Lord Panmure's name it is Maule. I sent my Lord   letter to him by a man who is a servant to a relation of mine; at first he did believe it to be one of my brothers that had brought it and said all my father's sons should be welcome to him ; but when he opened the letter he swore a great oath that I was no more in the King of Sweden's service than he was, and if I had been in Scotland it behoved me to be about the business of France, and he could not see me for I was concerned in Queensberry's plot, but yet he wished me very well.

But his Lordship little knows that I had no mind to see him, for I never received any good nor any expectations from him nor none of his country. I trust in God he will provide for me without ever letting of me owe any obligation to them. I pray your Honour to remember some things that I presumed to write in my last letter : I shall be uneasy until I hear from your Honour.

ROMAN CATHOLIC SEMINARIES.

1707—An exact calculation of all the English Popish Seminaries in the Low Countries, with the Revenues they draw from England, and the shoals of priests and other papists that they return yearly thither, as they were exactly surveyed by ocular inspection in the years 1706 and 1707.

In Newport.—There is an English Carthusian Monastery ever since that order was expelled the Charterhouse of London by King Henry the 8th. Each father that comes thither brings with him at least three hundred pounds and some of them five hundred. They were in number this year 1707, besides their Superior Father Hunter and Father Hall the famous preacher to King James the 2nd, twenty two Fathers.

In Bruges.—There are two Monasteries of women ; the one of the Augustine order all women of quality, who bring at least four hundred pounds each of them for their portions, and many of them much more. They were this year 1707 sixty dames, amongst whom is an aunt of this Duke of Norfolk, a sister of my Lord Powis, and some of the best families in Lancashire, Yorkshire, Suffolk, and Sussex; who have small yearly pensions besides their portions. There were also near a hundred young children pensionnaires at fifteen pounds a year each.

The other Monastery is of the order of St. Clare and are now in number fifty women who bring at least three hundred pounds each, and several young pensionnaires.

In Ghent.—There is a Monastery of Benedictine ladies who bring at least four hundred pounds each of them for their portion, they were, this year 1707, thirty Dames and above forty young pensionnaires at fifteen pounds per annum each.

There is also here a College of Jesuits who have purchased five hundred pounds per annum in rents on the Town House of Courtray, and are generally as they were this year 1707, thirty Fathers and abundance of Novices.

In Brussels.—There are two Monasteries, the one of Dominican ladies founded by Cardinal Howard for forty Ladies, which bring at least three hundred and fifty pounds each, there are several ladies of quality, a sister of my Lord Stafford, three daughters of Bernard Howard and other relations of the Norfolk family.

The other of Benedictine ladies who bring at least four hundred pounds to their portion each of them ; and are this year 1707, fifty Dames, besides abundance of pensionnaires in each.

In Mechlin.—Is a convent of the Teresian order who bring three hundred pounds portion each of them ; and are in number twenty. Their ancient abode was at Hogstract in the Compein, but since the war they purchased this house and retired hither.

In Liere.—There is a convent of Teresian women who bring three hundred pounds portion each of them and are in number twenty, besides abundance of young pensionnaires.

In Antwerp.—There is also a convent of Teresian women who bring three hundred pounds each of them to their portion and are in number twenty besides young pensionnaires.

In Burrum pais de Waes.—There is a convent of Dominican friars founded by Cardinal Howard which bring three hundred pounds to their portion each of them and were this year 1707, twenty Fathers.

In Louvain.—There is a most noble Monastery of Augustine Ladies who bring at least four hundred pounds each, besides their yearly pensions from England, they were this year sixty Dames, and a vast crowd of young girls pensionnaires at school, this is esteemed to be one of the richest and finest houses in Flanders, of the English nation.

Here is also a college of Dominican friars founded by Cardinal Howard and endowed with a revenue of three hundred pounds a year. There are as yet but ten Fathers and few or no scholars being but of eight years standing.

In Liége.—There is a College of English Jesuits founded by the family of Bavaria with a revenue of two thousand pounds a year. There were this year 1707, one hundred Fathers and abundance of scholars each of which bring twenty five pounds per annum for their entertainment and learning.

Here is also a Convent of Nuns of the order of the Sepulchre each of which bring at least three hundred and fifty pounds to their portions, and were in number fifty.

In Douay.—There is a Seminary of English secular oratorians consisting of thirty Fathers, who had this year 1707, one hundred scholars at twenty five pounds per annum each.

Here is also a Convent of Benedictine monks consisting this year of forty who bring three hundred pounds each of them to their portion.

Here is also a poor College of Scots Jesuits of about twenty Fathers, and a few scholars.

In St. Omer.—There is a Noble College of Jesuits where are constantly at least eighty Fathers and some years three hundred scholars who pay twenty five pounds per annum each. This year 1707, there were not above one hundred and fifty scholars. The Noviceship of this College is at Watten some miles distance from the town where are also constantly twenty Fathers besides novices, and where also they have purchased fifteen hundred pounds a year in land. Many Roman

Catholic gentlemen come from England and St. Germain to board here. Here is also a Nunnery of thirty women who bring three hundred and fifty pounds each.

In Aire.—There is a Monastery of St. Clare now consisting of fifty women who bring three hundred and fifty pounds each. But by reason of the war are now miserably poor.

In Graveling.—Is another Nunnery of St. Clare of sixty women most of quality who bring three hundred and fifty pounds each to their portion.

In Dunkirk.—Is a Convent of English ladies of the Augustine Order. They are now sixty Dames in number consisting mostly of women of distinction and bring with them each four hundred pounds to their portions.

This account being limited to the Low Countries does not comprehend the several English Seminaries at Paris, nor the famous Benedictine Convent of English gentlemen at Lamspringe nor these in Germany.

ANT[HONY] LECHMERE to [ROBERT HARLEY].

1707-8, January 2. Stoke—Mr. Popham's agent at Tewkesbury refuses to show the letter written by Mr. Popham in my favour, therefore I beg that another may be written to him a little more pressing.

JA[MES] ANDERSON to HUMFREY WANLEY, Duke Street, York Buildings in the Strand.

1707-8, January 3. Edinburgh—I am favoured with yours of the 27th last, and give you my hearty thanks for the acceptable account you are pleased to give me, of the valuable store of Manuscripts, Charters, and Rolls in the library of Mr. Secretary Harley. May it still increase for the good of the public, and honour of the possessor. He has given sensible proofs of his goodwill to this Nation : and I can assure you he is in very great esteem here: for I never heard his name mentioned but with very much honour and respect. His noble and generous design of publishing Fordun and his Continuator, and with such embellishments, is a real and engaging mark of his affection to this Nation, and of a sincere inclination to confirm the mutual friendship betwixt the happily united Kingdoms. I am fully persuaded, that such an obliging work will meet with a very honourable and grateful reception from all good men here. It is what has been wanted and desired by many, and I'm confident it cannot come from a hand more acceptable to Britain. I must beg of you, Sir, to give my most humble duty and service to Mr. Secretary, with my very thankful acknowledgments for his favours, and in particular, for doing me the honour of acquainting me with this good design. I shall seriously consider the hints you have given me of manuscript, with his judicious remarks, and your queries. I resolve to consult a curious copy of Fordun and his Continuator, fairly written upon vellum, in the Library of the University of this place ; (whose principal Mr. Carstares and the masters, I have heard express a very grateful sense of Mr. Secretary's favours). By the glances I have taken of this book I am apt to think it is much the same with his. I am also to look upon some other copies of Fordun, some with the continuation, and others without it, and on some abridgments of them, and shall likewise discourse some knowing persons here about this matter, so as I may discover if the copies here be a transcript of Mr. Secretary's Manuscript, which I presume will contribute to make it authentic.

I shall endeavour to satisfy you in these things with all the expedition and exactness I am capable of. I am glad you did not lay your commands sooner upon me, for I have been indisposed these six or seven months by-gone, but am now by the blessing of God pretty well recovered. You have been pleased to get yours to me marked *Frank*. I wish to know of you of any cover, by which for hereafter I may address mine to you so. I have had by me for some time a copy of the Bible printed here with Cann's notes, which I designed for you; my indisposition has hindered the forwarding of it, which I shall now do by the first fit opportunity.

Sir Simon Harcourt to [Robert Harley].

[1707-8, January 5]—I trouble you with this on Greg's account. I know not what resolutions are taken concerning his prosecution; if it be determined I beg leave to acquaint you that the sessions begin next week, and a bill of indictment may be then found on which you may try him after term. Or if you have any inclination to have him tried at bar in the next term you may, but then directions must be given to have the grand jury of Middlesex summoned to meet at the beginning of the term.

Le Moyne [de Brie] to [Robert Harley].

1708, January 5. Ramsgate—It is not without regret that I leave "l'aimable Angleterre," and although the hardships and miseries endured by me there were extreme, my return to my own country will deliver me from these, and will be even capable of awaking my old affection for you. I take this occasion to inform you of the true reasons of my conduct with regard to Lord Nottingham, &c.

Concludes with an urgent offer of his services to Harley in France, whether in Paris at the Court, or at a sea-port, dwelling on the probability that the ill treatment which his country men know him to have undergone in England will make him less likely to be suspected of conveying information. *French.*

[Daniel] De Foe to [Robert Harley].

1707-8, January 5. Kingsland—I have been in town five days, but have kept myself *incognito*, being willing to have my Lord Treasurer's commands how to dispose myself before I took any step of my own. In order to this I sent by my brother as I thought it my duty to acquaint his Lordship that I attended his pleasure but have not yet had the honour of his answer.

I give you this trouble to entreat your intercession with his Lordship for an audience since I shall not be able to continue long concealed, and I have no hand to act or tongue to speak now but by his directions, to whom I resolve to be not only a faithful but a punctual servant.

Dr. George Smalridge to [Robert Harley].

1707-8, January 8—I was yesterday informed, that instruments were passing in my Lord Sunderland's office for giving the Professorship to Dr. Potter; which after the intimation I had before by Dr. Stratford was no manner of surprise, and after the uneasy state of suspense I have been so long kept in, was no great mortification to me. I am satisfied with the honour of having been so heartily recommended by you to Her Majesty, and shall take the first opportunity that is given me of making my humble acknowledgments to you in person for your many and great favours to me, which are no more capable of being forgotten than they are of being returned by me.

W[ILLIAM] GREG to [ROBERT HARLEY].

1707-8, January 8—If there be any room for an after-thought with their Lordships and your honour I humbly crave leave to add one particular to the rest, which I never called to mind before this morning. I acquainted M. Chamillart that the Muscovite ambassador had proposed his master's being admitted into the Grand Alliance; as to the success of which proposition I remember now to have said—"*mais il n'y profitera rien, n'étant nullement l'intention de cette cour de rompre avec la Suède à ce prix-là*," which how true soever in itself ought not to have been said, and therefore it can only serve to aggravate my guilt, which is alas! but too great already.

ROBERT SEDGWICK, Clerk of the Jewel Office, to ROBERT HARLEY.

1707-8, January 10. Whitehall—Pursuant to warrant dated 19 May, 1703, whereof you have had former notice, and by repeated orders to the Jewel Office, I am now to acquaint you that you are required forthwith to return into this Office the several parcels of plate you stand charged with in our books, otherwise process will be issued out against you—viz.

The two parcels as Speaker to the House of Commons:

	Ozs.	dwts.
First Warrant - - - -	3,998	1
Second Warrant . - - -	4,019	10
	8,017	11

SIR SIMON HARCOURT to [ROBERT HARLEY].

1707-8, January 14—'Tis very probable Greg may plead guilty, but yet I think it my duty to inform myself of every particular as fully, and have everything in the same readiness, as if I expected the best defence counsel could make. I must therefore entreat the favour of you to consult with Lord Sunderland at what time between this and Monday next Mr. Solicitor [Montagu] and I may be least troublesome to him and yourself.

W[ILLIAM] GREG to ROBERT HARLEY.

[1707-8,] January 15—Before my trial comes on I have one discovery more to make, which were it not of that moment to deserve a hearing as well as anything I have yet said I should not have dared to propose it. Therefore I most humbly beg that in order to my dying with as clear a conscience as I can I may be admitted once more, and but once, to discharge it of all that remains to be disclosed to their Lordships and yourself.

MEMORANDUM on FRENCH PRISONERS' LETTERS.

1707–8, January 18. Whitehall—The letters that come from France to the prisoners of war in England are some of them superscribed to the persons themselves at Nottingham and Lichfield, some are put under cover to their bankers and friends in London, others are recommended to the Secretary's office.

The Comptroller of the Foreign posts gathers all the letters he can discover to be for any French prisoner under what cover soever they come and sends them to one of the Secretary's offices.

Such part of the letters as come to the Northern Office (they being sent to both offices) Mr. Lewis either reads himself or directs one of the clerks to do it. Marshal Tallard has formerly complained to Mr. Lewis that due care was not taken of his letters, and therefore desired he would always peruse them himself and see them sent to the post, but Mr. Lewis desired to be excused for he had reasons why he must deliver them to the clerks indifferently.

Mr. Lewis has observed of late that though he laid these letters on Mr. Mann's table, yet he afterwards found them on Mr. Greg's, upon which he then made no other reflection but that Mr. Mann might possibly have a great deal of other business and desire Mr. Greg's assistance in reading over these letters; but Mr. Lewis has been lately informed by Mr. Mann that Mr. Greg used to come to him and desire him to let have the perusal of these letters, which he said were very entertaining.

BARON SCHUTZ to ROBERT HARLEY.

1707–8, January 28. London—Having received the Elector's reply to the resolution communicated to him regarding the loan I send it to you for the information of her Majesty.

The Elector is greatly obliged by the guarantee offered him, whether the money is to be borrowed in her kingdom or out of it; but he could not pay a higher interest than five per cent, which would make the loan impossible in England, and money being too scarce in Germany for the sum to be raised there within the time needed, he is unable to profit by the Queen's offer. *French.*

W[ILLIAM] GREG to [ROBERT] HARLEY.

[1707–8,] January 31—It becomes me to rest satisfied and not think of asking any further favour, were not the fetters I have deservedly dragged along for a month become so very painful that my body is not the only sufferer, considering the close concatenation between the soul and it, especially since a person in my circumstances can never be too often on his knees, to which duty my irons prove a great uneasiness and interruption. Therefore I most humbly beg your honour would be pleased to cause them to be knocked off, as what would be a piece of great (though undeserved) charity to one who must write himself no otherwise now than a condemned capital offender but sincere penitent.

THE LORDS OF THE COUNCIL to ROBERT HARLEY, Custos Rotulorum of co. Radnor.

1707–8, February 1—As there are wanting great numbers of men for the fleet designed for this year's expedition all possible endeavours are to be used to procure them. You are therefore required to call upon the justices of the county for vigorous, speedy, and effectual execution of the following matters :—

1. To cause diligent search to be 'made for all straggling seamen, watermen, lightermen, bargemen, and fishermen, to impress such of them as are able-bodied, and to put them in custody of fitting persons to be conducted to the nearest sea-port where any of her Majesty's ships may be, not marching them further than shall be absolutely necessary, the which did formerly give them opportunity of deserting and so occasion unnecessary and extraordinary expense to the public.

2. To appoint a secure place to keep the men in until a fitting number shall be got together, to give each of them a shilling for imprest money, and to allow each of them sixpence a day for maintenance money, and eight pence a day when they travel. The cost of this will be paid by the Navy Commissioners on production of proper vouchers, &c.

3. To take particular care that no old, decrepit, crazy, or unhealthy men are impressed; and to issue warrants for the apprehension of deserters.

4. To give frequent accounts to the Council of the steps that have been taken, and what progress has been made herein. *Copy.*

THOMAS, ARCHBISHOP OF CANTERBURY, to the BISHOP OF ——.

1707-8, February 2. Lambeth—I doubt not but all my Suffragans are apprized of what is doing in the case of the Bishop of Carlisle.

Though he is not of our Province, I take it to be a common cause, and of great concern to this Church ; which will never be quiet so long as that evil generation of men who make it their business to search into little flaws in ancient charters and statutes, and to unfix what laudable usage hath well fixed, meet with any success.

I write not this, as if I suspected your zeal in such a case, but to assure you of my ready concurrence with in any proper and legal means, whether by Bill or otherwise, to make this excellent Church safe in this point, both now, and to late posterity.

Such revisions are to be endeavoured in a good Reign, lest in an evil one we feel the want of them. *Copy or Draft in Atterbury's hand-writing.*

SIR SIMON HARCOURT, Attorney General, to ROBERT HARLEY.

1707-8, February 2—Hannan's trial comes on upon Wednesday. I give you this notice, that if you would have the trial stopped, you may immediately send me your commands. If we do not proceed now 'twill raise too great a clamour if we continue him longer bound over. There will be some difficulty, though I hope to get over it, at the trial. You will consider, supposing he should be acquitted, whether that had not better happen, than not try him.

FRANCIS POPHAM to his uncle [ROBERT HARLEY].

1707-8, February 7. Littlecote—My father-in-law died last Monday. What trouble my ensue I cannot tell, my father having a notion (and indeed there always was such a one in our family) that neither my father-in-law nor his father had ever any right in law to the estate. As for me in my present circumstances 'twould be easier to me if young Mr. Popham has the estate, for he'll be obliged to pay my wife's fortune and yield an estate to me long since given my wife by my father-in-law. As I shall always humbly beg your advice, so it shall be my care to deserve it by obeying your commands. What these or any other pretences may induce my father to, if I know anything of his humour, he'll lay the whole case before you.

Dr. Geo. Hickes to [Robert Harley].

1707-8, February 10—This little book is sent to wait upon you to beg your acceptance. You'll find your two Saxon wills, and your King Eadgar's Charter in it, and I think it a great honour to have had the publication of them, especially of the two Princesses' wills, which are printed with as good types as I could get, with translations, notes, and descriptions of the places mentioned in them; and if in the equipage, and appearance, in which I have sent them abroad, they are but so fortunate as to be liked by you, that will be great satisfaction to me.

[Daniel De Foe] to Robert Harley.

1707-8, February 10—The report which fills the mouths of your enemies of your being no longer Secretary of State alarmed me a little I confess, and particularly brought me to wait upon you this night. Others compliment you on the accession of your good fortune. I desire to be the servant of your worst days, and yet upon my word I know not whether to congratulate or condole. I think verily you are delivered from a fatigue which never answered the harassing you in such a manner and the wasting your hours in the service of those that understand not how to value or reward in proportion to merit. Particularly you are delivered from envy, and I persuade myself you are removed from a tottering party that you may not share in their fall.

My business was only in duty and gratitude to offer myself to you against all your enemies. My sphere is low, but I distinguish nobody when I am speaking of the ill treatment of one I am engaged to, as to you in the bonds of an inviolable duty. I entreat you to use me in anything in which I may serve you, and that more freely than when I might be supposed following your rising fortunes. 'Tis also my opinion you are still rising—I wish you as successful as I believe you unshaken by this storm.

Postscript.—I shall wait on you tomorrow evening as by your order.

H[enry] Boyle to [Robert Harley].

1707-8, February 13—I return you a great many thanks for the honour of your kind and obliging letter. I have not yet been at the office but intend to look in some time tomorrow, and when I have seen the furniture will take the liberty of sending to you about it.

Tobias Bowles.

1707-8, February 17—By virtue of a power given by the House of Lords to those whose names are underwritten, Tobias Bowles, of Deal, Esq., is required to attend at Northumberland House on the 20th inst. to give an account of what he knows of Alexander Valiere *alias* John Clarke. Signed by the Dukes of Devonshire and Somerset, and Lords Wharton, Townshend, Somers, and Halifax.

D[aniel] De F[oe] to Robert Harley.

1707-8, February 20. [Edinburgh]—In obedience to your commands I send you enclosed the state of the case in Scotland between the Bank and the people in the payment of the equivalent.

I shall always be glad of an opportunity to render you service in this or anything in my power, sincerely wishing you deliverance from all your enemies.

R. GRIFFITH to [ROBERT HARLEY].

[1708.] February 21. Radnor—I am glad that you have resigned in so honourable a manner as you have done. When about the beginning of January I had an account how the Regius Professorship at Oxford was disposed of, I was confirmed in the opinion I had when I was last at London of the designs of your good friends on the other side of the river.

CHARL[WOOD] LAWTON to [ROBERT HARLEY].

1707-8, February 27—I am very glad to find that the Church party so generally and so heartily take you by the hand, and believe me, it is in your power, by making them wise in relation to the enclosed case, to do them service. Several of them will have the good sense to give ease, but if they would generally be for it, I can answer that they will receive the reward of their good nature at the next elections. If I could speak a minute with you, as you go into the House, I would tell you some who have promised to be for giving ease, and others who I wish you would speak to. I wish you would, upon this occasion, be earlier than ordinary at the House, and I wish too that you would speak. You having heretofore spoke against harsh oaths may naturally speak in this case. The Petition will be brought in this morning, by Sir David Dalrymple, and I believe will not in relation to Scotland be at all opposed.

W[ILLIAM] THOMAS to EDWARD HARLEY [at Oxford].

1707-8, March 2—I have spoke to my Master about your note of books to be bought, but he has not as yet given me any directions about them; if they are in haste you would do well to put him in mind of them. This day the Lords of the Secret Committee made their Report which I am told was three hours and a half in reading, they have only appointed a Committee to make an Extract of the most material passages and ordered one Hind into the custody of the Black Rod for offering a sum of money to one Carter to procure an account of what information had been given the Committee relating to the affair of Valiere. I hear there is nothing in it of moment except some malicious inuendos and invidious reflections. I was in hopes I should have been able to procure a more particular account of what passed but they sat so late that I am afraid I shall not till the post is gone. I desire you will please to excuse it to the Doctor who I hope is safely arrived with you.

["K. O.," so endorsed, to EDWARD HARLEY.]

1707-8, March 4—Yesterday the Committee of the Lords made their report to their House and one that heard it but not from the beginning told me that considering the matter it was extremely maliciously contrived; it insinuated that Valiere under pretence of being a spy for us and having the protection of the Secretary's warrant was in reality one for the French, that one Barra who was of the same employment going with him to Cadiz once should say he would give 5*l.* they could bring back the news of the taking of Toulon, and that Valiere should reply he would rather give 100*l.* to bring the news of raising the siege; that he was used to be well received at Calais and brought Frenchmen on board his boat to spy out our ships, that he gave orders to have his packet thrown over when any English vessel approached him; that when he was in drink he used to talk very freely of the great liberty that was given him and how easily he could impose upon the Secretary; and that upon the coasts he was generally reputed a French spy. Afterwards there was an affidavit of one Carter read importing that one Hind had been tampering with him and offered him 200*l.* upon the Secretary's account if he would tell him what the Lords examined him about, and get him all the information he could what they were doing; but that it took wind that he had revealed the matter to the Lords and therefore never had a meeting with the Secretary as was designed; and thereupon Hind was ordered to be taken into custody of the Black Rod. But I forgot at the end of Valiere's business that notwithstanding all the informations that was sent the Secretary from several places of the suspicions they had of this man he still employed him, to which they attribute much of our miscarriages at sea. When the Duke of Somerset had done reading the Report which lasted above three hours, some Lord I know not who spoke to this effect, that they were very much be-holden to that noble Lord for giving himself the trouble to read so long a report, he thought there was several things of very great importance in it, and therefore moved that a Committee might be appointed to make an extract of the report to lay before the House that they might come to some judgment upon it; and accordingly all that were present were ordered to be of the Committee, and they sat the same night as soon as the House was up—*Parturiunt montes* &c. After these noble Lords had given themselves the trouble for three weeks with a great deal of application and examining a vast number of witnesses, using both promises and threatenings to get something to serve their turn, they have found out nothing at last but perhaps that Valiere played Jack on both sides, whereas there was nothing less expected than to have heard of the Secretary betraying our counsels to the French, informing them of all our measures, underhand employing these fellows to that end, in short to have known the cause of all our disappointments by sea and land last year. They have learnt as I somewhere read which is the top of learning, to know that they know nothing; well since they cannot lay it upon his back I hope they will share it among themselves.

JOHN GASSION [*alias* OGILVIE] to [ROBERT HARLEY].

1707–8, March 6—I have received no letter as yet from Scotland, but the reason is, I am certain, that the messenger they expected to come to them before the fleet, with advertisement to be in readiness and to take arms is not yet arrived. He will be sent by a small frigate just when the fleet is ready to set sail. If you had been in your place at this minute I should have either lost my life or you should have known all the particulars both of their ships and numbers of their troops; and I fancy I could have been very useful to you after they had landed, for I could have advertised you of every step they had taken. But since your honour is no more concerned I have done, and I promise you that it shall never be in the power of another minister to cause me ever venture my life or my honour for all the kings or princes on earth further than a soldier is obliged to do.

There is a young gentleman of the name of Ogilvie with my Lord Seafield at present, and he was made an ensign in the foot guards some time ago by Lord Seafield's means. This Ogilvie is not of my Lord Seafield's family, but of the Earl of Airlie's, as I am, therefore he was thought a very fit instrument to pump me; so he after a great deal of pains found my lodging and brought another gentleman with him who is a captain in the army also and a neighbour of my elder brother's in Scotland. These two "coy ducks" came with all the protestations of friendship imaginable and at last were desirous to have my opinion of the invasion that was threatened from Dunkirk. I told them briskly that I was astonished that they who did belong to my Lord Seafield should ask me for they might have better intelligence near him, for, said I, my lord, who is so well with the Duke and Duchess of Marlborough, needs but desire his grace or her grace to demand of her sister the Duchess of Tyrconnel, who is lady of the bed-chamber to the Queen at St. Germain and consequently knows every step that is taken at that court; and I said, I wonder my Lord Duke does know nothing, since he sees my lady Duchess of Tyrconnel always when he passes and re-passes to the Hague, for she lives at present at Delft, and not ask those questions of me for it is above three years since I left France and that interest, and had been ever since in places very remote from that, seeking for my bread. When I had said that, they looked as if they had been struck with a thunderbolt and in a minute took leave of me.

I do not know if you remember a letter I wrote to you above two years ago wherein I told you that Count Belke did propose to a certain person to go and desire the Duchess of Tyrconnel to speak to the Duke of Marlborough to persuade him to be an instrument to oblige the Queen to make a peace, and to get her brother the Prince of Wales to succeed her; but the person it was proposed to would not undertake it. I also told you that I saw my Lord Duke's name often on the cipher that passed betwixt M. de Torci and Count Belke. The reflecting on this made me answer them as I did.

W[ILLIAM] THOMAS to EDWARD HARLEY, at Oxford.

1707-8, March 9—I hear nothing new relating to my M[aster]. I doubt not but as the matters of fact are set in a true light all the trifling insinuations will be found as ridiculous as what you mention. The noise made about the dissent has not been effectual to raise the apprehensions of people high enough to justify a motion for the con- tinning of this Parliament; nay, I find that the more the endeavours are to that end, the more people suspect a design, even to that degree that I believe most people do not think there is as much in it as really there may be. When I acquainted the Doctor that the Address was moved by Mr. Annesley I did not know it was seconded by your father; when he had done I am told one Eyres (not the lawyer) stood up and said, he thought it very proper to present an Address of thanks to the Queen for having removed dangerous persons from her person, &c. Some say he was drunk, perhaps wanted to make his court.

I hear the suspending the Triennial Act has been proposed in some of their private cabals but I hope they will not find even among the Whigs a majority so desperate as to come into a motion of that consequence to the nation.

["K. O." to EDWARD HARLEY.]

1707-8, March 13—I hear the Abstract has been read to the House but they have come to no resolution upon it, having leisure to attend nothing but stopping the French invasion. It was my Lord Orford made the motion for an Extract and the Lord Sunderland seconded it. I remember I mentioned the conference between Carter and Hind as a notorious falsehood, and I was not as far as appears out in my conjecture, for Hind, being taken into custody of the Black Rod and examined, affirms that Carter met him and asked him first if he would go and drink a pot of ale, and he told him he had no money, then Carter said he would treat him, as he did and lent him a shilling besides. When they were in the alehouse Carter told him he was examined before the Committee of Lords and that he thought they designed to do Mr. Secretary a mischief, and if he would acquaint him with it and procure a sum of money he would get him what intelligence he could. Hind replied he would acquaint Mr. S—— with the proposal and accordingly did, but instead of any encouragement or thanks for his pains he was extremely angry with him and forbid him coming near him again till this business is over. The Lords asked Hind what the Secretary employed him in and he said he never was employed by him in any thing and that he came to his house only to solicit his interest with my Lord Treasurer for a place being in very bad circumstances. By this one may see one story is good till another is told and I hope a time will be found to put all the other matters in a true light. The Lords heard of a cypher between the Secretary and Greg which they wanted mightily to see, and Mr. Lewis with the Secretary's consent carried it to them, which was only one page with one letter for a name as H. for Hamilton &c., which Greg before he was in the office was sent with to Scotland, that Parliament that the Duke of Argyll was Commissioner to give what account of the affairs there that he could learn. This happened to be of a contrary nature to what they desired and was returned, being of no service to their design. All that they found by Greg's examination as I hear was that he [Harley] came late to the office and things were done in haste and letters taken down in short hand and obliged to go to his house to have them signed (whereby the clerk's shoes were worn out, a great prejudice to the Government) and such other enormous crimes. As all they have found is such frivolous stuff and most part of that only suspected, I think on the other hand it is as fair a suspicion to any impartial person that there's a great deal of malice in it, since it is managed by his avowed enemies. Though this Revolution had wholly taken up the discourse and speculations of the town and no wonder being so extraordinary, yet you hear no more of it than if it had happened in Queen Elizabeth's day and now one had as good hold one's tongue or tell a story of Tom Thumb as say anything except it be about the invasion. What may be the event God only knows but it seems to have something of Knight Errantry in it, certainly it is the most bold and daring attempt the French have undertaken this war, they used not to be very forward in engaging upon equal terms much less when there was such a superiority as we now have. It was thought they might have been blocked up in their harbour, and some do not scruple to say it was for want of good management that they were not; but since they are out the Government prepare with great application to oppose them if they should land. I think there's nothing to be feared since I have heard that Secretary Boyle is so intent upon the affairs of the nation that he hardly takes time to eat, and my Lord Sunderland sits up whole nights, and what may we not expect from such great men and of such assiduity.

Postscript.—Pray please to burn this and the other.

Jo. CHARLTON, Master of the Jewel Office, to ROBERT HARLEY.

1707-8, March 16. Whitehall — You are required forthwith to return into the Jewel Office the several parcels of plate you are charged

with in the books of the said Office, and by indenture in order to be
discharged, otherwise process will be issued against you.

	Ozs.	dwts.
The first warrant as Speaker in the late reign · -	3,998	1
Second warrant as Speaker in the present reign -	4,019	10
Third warrant as Secretary of State -	997	12
	9,015	3

[W. Thomas to Edward Harley.]

1707-8, March 16—Yesterday the Lords went upon the Extract of
the long Report of the seven Lords, and resolved upon an Address to
Her Majesty. I am told the heads of it are:—That Greg may be
made an example, that Valiere was more in the enemy's interest than
ours, that it is dangerous to connive at persons going over from the
coast to France, that there have been some neglects in the Secretary's
office by suffering papers of great consequence to lie open to the clerks;
and to desire her Majesty that these things may be remedied for the
future. I shall make no other reflection upon it than Parliament
merits.

W. T[homas to Edward Harley].

1707-8, March 18—We expect every moment to know whether we
beat or are beaten, for we seem to be a little in pain since we understand the Brest squadron has been seen off Berwick steering northward.

'Tis said the Duke of Somerset before he read the long report told
some lords in the House that he thought it was not worth anybody's
hearing, and for his own part if he was not obliged to read it he should
not stay to hear it.

W. Thomas to [Edward Harley.]

1708, March 27th—We were in great apprehension here all this week
of the French landing in the north of Scotland; but the account we had
this morning from Deal, that they were all returned to Dunkirk, has put
an end to all our fears of this chimerical expedition. Six of our men of
war had a running fight with them on the Flemish coast, whereof one is
missing, but 'tis hoped she has put into Ostend. Commander Walker's
conduct on this occasion is much blamed, he was ordered to cruise off
Dunkirk, but pretends he wanted pilots to carry him to the Dutch coast.
We had an account yeterday, that the two frigates of Fourbin's
Squadron that were come into Dunkirk reported that when they were
chased by the English Squadron under Sir G. Byng, their Admiral gave
them a signal that they should all shift for themselves. We have an
account from Lisbon, that Sir John Leake is safely arrived there.

Major General Meredith succeeds Mr. Walsh of Worcestershire, who
is lately dead, as Gentleman of the horse.

I shall not trouble you with any account of the answer to the Lords'
Address about Greg &c. it being expected to be published next Monday.
It was general to all the heads, but the accounts I have of it are so
uncertain that I shall not repeat them, lest I should not do her Majesty
justice.

[WILLIAM THOMAS to EDWARD HARLEY.]

1708, March 30—I have very little to trouble you with by this post, besides what you have in the Prints. It is expected, the Parliament will be up this week, some day, Thursday, but 'tis not yet known whether they will be prorogued or adjourned for nine days or a fortnight.

We are told here that the Tories will set up Mr. Bromley for Speaker in another Parliament. I should be glad to know the Tr——is thoughts upon that point. I hear Mr. Auditor is like to meet with very considerable opposition at Leicester from Mr. Osborn who has already made about 100 votes and treats very liberally. Mr. H. goes down with his family this day sevenight. I do not know whether they will take Oxford in their way, they have talked of it, but you will hear the certainty of it in time.

The Lords famous address is at last published. It was not to have been published till this day, but I am told the Printer was sent to on Saturday night to make all dispatch possible to have it out yesterday, so that they were forced to work upon it all day on Sunday.

That part that relates to Greg is very frivolous, and a great part of it downright falsehoods, but they are such as if true, would not generally affect either my Master's diligence or integrity. The other part concerning Valiere &c. is scraps confusedly put together, and invidious turns and insinuations through the whole. You will be better able to judge of it when you see it. It is pretty big for a packet, however rather than keep it till the carrier goes I will bring it as near as I can within the compass of a letter and direct it to the Dr. —— I am told their Lordships are not satisfied with her Majesty's answer. I suppose they expected fire and faggot.

Greg was yesterday at his own desire brought before the Lords of the Council at my Lord Sunderland's, where he delivered them a paper which was immediately sealed up and carried to the Queen. I hear it purported only a kind of petition to recommend him to her Majesty's mercy. I am assured, it is nothing that concerns my Master. 'Tis said the Queen has upon some occasion expressed a great deal of compassion for him, and has said that the usage he had was hanging him over and over.

Our News Papers from the other side are full of the rejoycings made in Holland and Flanders upon a foolish letter writ by Cadogan, that the British fleet had defeated the French upon the coast of Scotland. There has been something of a misunderstanding between the Admiralty and Secretary's Office about their putting it in the Gazettes and other prints by authority that there were but two clean ships in Sir G. Byng's squadron, whereas the former say, they were all clean but two. The very extraordinary flourishes in the late advices from the fleet and the incoherences of it together with the new style of late proclamation for apprehending Ogiley and others, gives a great deal of diversion to the town. The former shews how effectual the Lords Reports have been to stop all intelligence, and the latter proves here for the present Sollicitor is to be made Attorney. It is pitty but they should be all of a piece.

I hope you will pardon all this impertinence of a (really) domestick clerk, and put it to the account of his desire to give you some divertion with the wise things that the town is so much imployed about. Ten a clock puts one in mind of having too long transgressed upon your patience.

WILLIAM GREG'S EXAMINATION.

1708, March 31. Memorandum—Being in company with Mr. Hoskins, domestic steward to the Duke of Somerset, and who was employed by the Lords of the Committee appointed for the examination of Greg ; he acquainted me with the following particulars :—

That the Lords asked Greg a great many very hard questions about Mr. Secretary Harley, insomuch that had Greg been a thorough-paced rogue (as he said) he might have saved his life by giving pertinent answers to them. For afterwards they sent him a message by Mr. Hoskins that they were very well assured they could intercede with Her Majesty for his pardon if he would confess to those questions which they had reason to believe were all matter of fact, but Greg sent him back without any answers at all to them, for he said he knew no more than what he had already confessed. And that the queries which Greg answered were several times transcribed and several alterations made in them by the Lords to turn them as near as they could to their own advantage, and afterwards the originals were burnt, when the amendments had received an unanimous approbation (though Greg was not privy to this correction).

Valiere was very obstinate, and would not confess anything material, only it appeared by one Whitehall's report, that the Secretary had ordered him to dispatch a boat to France with Valiere if he could do it with privacy, which he the said Hoskins confessed, in all the proceedings, was the only ill thing in his opinion could be with any colour urged against the Secretary.

Mr. Hoskins says, he had fresh queries drawn up every day for three weeks together to examine Greg by, but that a quarter of them received no answers, so that then they were committed to the flames.

W[ILLIAM] THOMAS to [EDWARD HARLEY].

1708, April 1—The Queen came this evening to the House of Peers, and having given the Royal assent to the Bills that were ready, and made a speech, the Parliament was prorogued to the 13th instant. I do not know whether the speech will come out time enough for this post, it being pretty long and delivered near six o'clock.

There was one Mr. Keith, a Scotch gentleman, taken up here on Monday last soon after Greg had been before the Lords of the Council ; I do not hear his crime, but the account his wife gives is this. It seems that he had been taken into custody at the time of the Scotch Plot, and was discharged upon his entering into a recognizance not to go into Scotland. He had sometime since made application for the discharging of his recognizance, and particularly to my Master, whose answer was that he should get his own countrymen to move in his behalf and then he would do him all the service in his power. She says, the reason of her husband's moving for this was that that he designed to go for Scotland upon an invitation from his friends there who intended to set him up for member of Parliament at the next election. The gentleman that opposes his interest there has found this means to break Keith's measures, and she says Greg has been prevailed with to acquaint the Lords of the Councill that he is a dangerous man ; and some insinuations have been made to his prejudice which have occasioned his being now taken into custody. This is her story, it is very plausible, but I do not know how far it is true.

There was a little box sent you to day by the carrier, you will receive the three books I bought in it. It is said the elections will be in May, if so we shall be soon going out of town, at least some of the family.

Postscript.—To be sure you have by this time read the Lords representation. I beg leave to take notice of one thing upon which they lay so much stress, that of the Queen's letter to the Emperor about Prince Eugene's commanding in Spain, which their Lordships insinuate to be a secret of the highest consequence. My observation is this, that it was so far from being a secret, that all our prints mentioned it near three months before the date of the Queen's letter, which was November 28th, that King Charles desired it and that the Queen and the States concurred with him in it, and that the Prince was not adverse to it, if he had a sufficient force.

This is in the Postboy of September 11, in the article from the Hague of September 16. N.S.

Postboy, September 20, from the Hague September 20.

Flying Post, September 25, from the Hague September 30.

Daily Courier, September 24. Hague, September 30.

Postman, October 2, in the article from the Hague.

The Queen's letter was not the first proposal of it to the Emperor, but the last effort used to prevail with him to comply with the Queen's and the States' desire in that point.

T[HOMAS] FOLEY, Auditor of the Exchequer, to [ROBERT HARLEY].

1708, April 12—I will not be wanting to endeavour to keep up my interest at Hereford, though it will be a near struggle. Mr. Brydges' agents aim much more to put me out than Mr. Morgan, though I am satisfied at present I have more promises than either of them. If Mr. Brydges could have had, as your brother told me, your interest for the count , 'tis amazing to me he did not embrace it, since the best he can hope for is sitting upon a disputed election, the practices of his agents being the most notorious I ever knew in any case whatsoever. His extravagant expenses may gain him numbers, which at present I know he wants. I take myself to have 650 absolute promises. Notwithstanding the new freemen there cannot possibly be brought to poll more than 900, if so many, and we have all three a great many single votes. I have the Jacobites very much against me, but the Church party is very zealous for me. It would do me a kindness if Lord Scudamore would appear for me at Hereford I have promised him all the service I can do him in the county, and yet can gain no answer when I applied for his interest at Hereford.

DR. WILLIAM STRATFORD to [ROBERT HARLEY].

1708, April 14—I ordered a set of Almanacks to be left the last week at your house. I think these were all that have been put out by the Dean. The best Almanack, which was much larger than any of these, and designed by Streater (*sic*) and reprinted for two or three years together, is wanting. I hope you will receive from God one part of your recompense for the injuries you have received on account of the public, in blessing on your children. Mr. Harley is in all respects what you would desire he should be. There is but one thing I could wish otherwise. The servant who waited on him at Westminster corresponds with him, I believe often. His letters I perceive are very long. He is not very free to show them, and I never let him know that I understood from whom they came. But he has been once or twice much dejected and dispirited, and not capable of any attention, when I or his tutors have been reading with him. It has gone off in two or three days and he has been as easy again as ever. I cannot say this has proceeded from any idle stories that may have been sent to him, but I believe it would not be to his prejudice if that correspondence were broken.

The gentlemen of this county are so much divided that there will. be no opposition to Lord Rialton. Had the Duke of Marlborough come hither before he went to Holland, as he had once designed, he was to have dined at Queen's, and most of the Heads were to have been invited to meet him there.

[Mrs. Abigail Masham ?] to [Robert] Harley.

1708, April 18—I was at Court this day and if I have any skill in physiognomy, my old mistress is not pleased with me. I told you 'twas my thought on Thursday night. If I guess right am to seek why 'tis so. My Lady Giggster was there very gay and seemed extremely at ease. Ailligo's mother was also there. I was asked by a very sensible man and one that knows Courts, whether any or all of us four were not with my old mistress when she last was in town. The reason of the question I had not, and the answer I made you may guess. I shan't go till Thursday, therefore you may be sure I shall wait of you first.

Sir James Long, M.P. for Chippenham, to——.

1708, April 21—I met the Duke of Beaufort's gentleman yesterday at the place appointed and considered of the most effectual way to gain an interest in that borough [Devizes]; and I find five votes wanting which your friends think may be purchased for about four hundred pounds. They also say there are twenty-four Common Councilmen, whereof twelve are in Mr. Child's interest and twelve in Mr. Diston's, and that five hundred pounds will buy one of Mr. Diston's, friends and make a majority for Mr. Child, who can with such a majority elect a Mayor and as many Burgesses, living in or out of the borough, as they please; and by that means secure the election of members to serve in Parliament for ever. If you'll be at this charge and the matter succeed you shall ever afterwards be elected without any expense. Now as to the bribing of the five votes, you know what will be the issue of that if discovered, and Child thinks they'll make a discovery ; and as to the five hundred pounds that will not be bribery within the power of the House of Commons, it being only to elect a Mayor which must be done Friday in the next Whitsun week. This is the true state of the borough and you are the best judge of what is proper for you to do. There have been and still are great. differences between both parties and great sums of money spent by their representatives in law-suits and otherwise. If you proceed let Sir Francis Child join with you in all expense.

T[homas] Foley to Robert Harley, in York Buildings.

1708, April 24. Hereford—Mr. Prise of Westerston has declared his standing for the county, and I cannot avoid being for him without losing my election here, for I never saw any place so set upon outing another, as this is upon outing Mr. Gorges. I take Lord Scudamore to be at the bottom of it; I know his steward has ridden all about the country along with Mr. Prise under the pretence of buying timber, which I can't see what occasion he has for, especially twelve miles from home. Besides Mr. Westphaling, Mr. Trist, and all my Lord's dependents, some openly and the rest underhand, are for him. As to the town I take myself to be as secure as 'tis possible where the most open bribery is practised.

There is a report that Lord Scudamore's sister is to be married to Mr. Prise.

HENRY POWELL to ROBERT HARLEY.

1708, April 26—Mr. Rowe the turnkey told me that Mr. Greg had sent a letter yesterday to the Earl of Sunderland, and that he himself was to carry another this morning to his lordship, and he believed the purport of the letters was an account of some discovery or impeachment. What I hear further I will despatch to your honour. I do not however hear of any reprieve for Greg. In consideration of some previous services rendered, you were pleased to say that you would assist me to recover my liberty. This I leave to your honour's consideration, and that at your own time.

[Lieut.-Colonel J. CRANSTOUN] to ROBERT CUNNINGHAM.

1708, April 27 O.S. Ghent—We have been a little alarmed here at the struggles of your parties at Court. I pray God give us a good British parliament the next we have, for all depends on that. I shall never be persuaded that, if it be true that there was a design to lay the Duke of Marlborough and the Lord Treasurer aside, those who designed that could mean well or be real friends to the present government and the bottom it is settled on. There are no men free of faults, but I do not believe any man living at this time could be put in the Duke of Marlborough's place, but it would prove fatal to Britain and to the interest of the Protestant religion. Nor do I think any man can come in his place where there were either more sincere or zealous to bring the war to a speedy and a happy conclusion than his Grace is. We are now about to open a campaign which all here expect will be a warm one and full of action, and we hope may by God's blessing be so successful as soon to procure us a good peace, and upon better terms than have even yet been offered. I shall expect and I do entreat earnestly to hear sometimes from you. It will be a great pleasure to me if you will write sometimes to me, and write with freedom and at large, and let me know what alterations are made or like to be amongst great men, especially those of our country, and what progress and success the government makes in finding out those very ill and desperate men that have encouraged France to this late invasion upon us. You need only address your letters to Colonel Cranstoun of Colonel Preston's regiment in the army under the Duke of Marlborough and they will come right to hand.

[WILLIAM THOMAS to EDWARD HARLEY.]

1708, April 29—I send you enclosed amongst other papers, the Ordinary of Newgate's account of the criminals executed yesterday. I do not send it because it contains any thing extraordinary about Greg, but because it does not, which looks very odd after what happened at the execution, of which I have the following account from persons that were present. When Greg was in the cart, Sir Charles Peers one of the Sheriffs called the executioner to him and whispered him, he returned to Greg and spoke to him something that the standers by could not hear. Greg turns to the Sheriff and said to this effect:—" Mr. Harley is perfectly innocent as to any knowledge of the correspondence I was engaged in, neither he nor anybody had any hand in it, and I call God to witness that I die with a conscience clear from having concealed any thing I knew relating to the Queen and the Government." This he spoke with a very strong voice so that though the crowd and the noise were very great Mr. Harley's name was heard a pretty distance from the gallows, but what he said was not distinctly heard but by such as were in and about the cart. He seemed to be extraordinary devout, and it was observed that several questions were sent to him from the Sheriff between the offices, and he made answers to the effect I mentioned and once said, " what would they have me say ; I have told all I knew," and that he had wrote all his mind in the two papers which he gave to the Sheriff and the Ordinary sealed up, and desired they might not be opened till he was dead. Those papers were delivered soon after the first message sent to him by the Sheriff. It was expected there would have been some notice taken of this in the Ordinary's account but there being a profound silence, it is supposed those papers will be stifled. However people which guess at the nature of them make just reflections upon it. Here is nothing else that I am willing to trouble you about at this time. I hope to have the honour of seeing you in a few days : so shall not trouble you with any anecdotes.

I should be glad to receive your directions about your news while I am out of town.

EDWARD HARLEY to his Aunt, ABIGAIL HARLEY, at Eywood.

1708, May 2. [Oxford]—Your letters have met with very bad luck, the last which came from Leominster was kept there five days by mistake, Mr. Spencer being out of town. He wrote me word that he thought my uncle would carry it, I hope he may. I hear there is great opposition at Hereford, and that it is like to go hard with my cousin Foley : I should be glad to hear of that matter. There is nothing in that you mentioned of this University ; they choose their old members, the election is to-morrow. Greg is hanged at last. I hear that when he was at the gallows, Sir Charles Peers one of the Sheriffs called the executioner to him and whispered him. He returned to Gregg and spoke to him something the standers by could not hear. Gregg turned about and with a loud voice said, What would you have me say, Mr. Harley is perfectly innocent and knew nothing of it. Though the crowd and the noise was very great Mr. Harley's name was heard a pretty distance from the gallows.

WILLIAM LOWNDES to ROBERT HARLEY.

1708, May 11. Westminster—My Lord Treasurer has commanded me to present his service to you and to acquaint you that his lordship has received the Queen's pleasure for your having the plate, and will present the warrant to be signed by her Majesty when there is a certificate from the Jewel Office in due form ; but for that and passing the privy seal you will please to appoint some person to solicit for you.

RETFORD ELECTION.

1708, May 10—A List of the Voters for Robert Molesworth and William Levinz at Retford Election. The state of the Poll was :—

Thomas White	-	- -	100
William Levinz	-	- - -	57
Robt. Molesworth	-	- -	50

The names of those who voted for Molesworth and Levinz respectively are given, nearly all of them presumably having recorded their second vote in White's favour.

[E. LEWIS to ROBERT HARLEY.]

1708, May 18—I hope that nothing will interrupt your quiet enjoyment at Brampton, since your elections are over, and our rulers seem to have cast away all their thunderbolts. Sir William has declared that the young Duke of Cambridge is to make his campaign under our great general, and that in the interview of Hanover when this point was settled the Elector told the Duke his only son should be a hostage for the good will of the father to the two kings of Brentford. Thus you see we follow the French fashion, and as the princes of their blood are to serve under a great captain ours are to do so too.

Duke Hamilton is gone to the North in order to be of the number of the Elect. After he had made his submissions to Sir William and thought that alone would have procured his liberty, it was insinuated to him that to save appearances he must apply to the juncto and the Duke of Queensberry for their favourable interposition. The last was a hard morsel, but he was forced to digest it.

Her Grace is grown the gayest, wanton young thing in the world, but whether it proceeds from her being restored to favour, or from her finding herself in a state above the favour of —— I cannot tell. She is highly delighted with the verses Welsh made upon you, and fancies them the finest that ever were written, I will get a copy for you in a post or two.

Mr. Meyrick sets up in Cardiganshire upon the interest of Price and Pugh. There is a strange jumble in Glamorganshire, old friends turned foes, and old foes made friends, Sir Thomas being entirely reconciled to his brother Stradling. I hear from my own country that there will be a petition against the Auditor [Foley].

[G. GRANVILLE to ROBERT HARLEY.]

1708, May 20. Treblethick—I had not the honour of your commands till yesterday when all our elections were over. When I parted with our friend Harry [St. John], he seemed pretty confident of succeeding in some place or other, and I own I took it for granted he knew himself secure. I join with you in being under the greatest concern for this disappointment. If I could have recovered Tintagel as I have done Camelford, I intended to have nominated him, but there was a bargain struck up above these two years in Mr. Hooker's name which I could not break through upon any terms, which interest was transferred the morning of the election to Mr. Travers. Addison has likewise been brought in at Lostwithiel by an interest carried on in another name and transferred by surprise in the same manner. Upon the whole these two last elections have made us rather worse than better in this county. No endeavours of mine have been wanting nor have I spared for anything that might contribute to the public service, in which I have so far succeeded where it has been possible for me to appear, that, without your protection defends me, there is no revenge but will be taken.

Postscript.—Is there no way of bringing in our friend in North Britain ? I hear the prisoner is released and hope it is done by your means for a good purpose.

[E. Lewis to Robert] Harley, at Brampton.

1708, May 20—I have not yet had an opportunity of making your compliments to ——[Lord Halifax, written over by Harley], however I believe I may tell you for a certainty that his brother (Sir James Montague) will have the employment your friend quitted, and that this agreeable news was brought him by the company that dined with him ten miles off the day that you went out of town.

There are letters from Dunkirk which contain very surprising things, for, to justify the wisdom of their idol monarch and to satisfy the world his measures were well concerted, they declare that the Triumvirate was in their plot. I own I cannot conceive how they can be guilty of self murder, and consent to overthrow the power they themselves enjoy; but there is no arguing against facts, and some men- are so used to treachery that they love it.

Sir Edward Stradling and his brother are again at the utmost variance, and Sir John Aubrey carried his election by the favour of the latter. All Sir Edward's party forsook him because he would not agree to cast lots.

Lord Mohun has sold his regiment to one of the Dormers for 3,000*l.* ; and Dormer has sold his company in the guards to a younger brother of Mr. Cholmondeley, the new member, for 2,700*l.*

[E. Lewis to Robert Harley.]

1708, May 22—The notion of extinguishing the names of Whig and Tory and assuming the distinctions of Court and Country party, which the great men were once themselves fond of, seems now to be taken up by their adversaries, for I have heard several persons mention it since you went out of town, and perhaps you may infer the probability of it from the Buckinghamshire advice to their representatives, wherein Lord —— appears *in puris naturalibus.* By the last motion of the French to Soignies it looks as if they intended to present us battle, and not wait till we attack them. This I am sure of, that if that be the place of action we can have at best but a *cruenta* victory, by which I conceive Tacitus means in the style of our hawkers a most cruel and bloody fight, but which cannot be attended with any consequences of solid advantage. All the letters from Hanover say positively the Electoral Prince is to make the campaign under the Duke of Marlborough though our prints do not mention it, and I think it may be observed that our news writers are more cautious what they say in relation to that family, than to any other subject. I am further told that the Duke will next winter bring him or his grandmother over hither, in such a manner that they shall. have the obligation ,neither to Whigs or Tories, but entirely to himself and Lord Treasurer; whether they will think fit to communicate it to the Queen I cannot tell.

Lord Chief Justice Holt has been solicited to quit ; if they prevail, he will be succeeded by Sir J. Jekyll, and he by Sir James. The town says Lovell will succeed Baron Smith, and King be made Recorder of London.

By the liberty Lord K[ent] and his lady take in talking of the great men, one may conclude he does not expect long to hold his White Staff.

There is another copy of verses upon you which I have not seen but am told they are scurrilous.

[Sir Simon Harcourt to Robert Harley.]

1708, May 28—By the enclosed letter from Valiere's wife, who has been with me, you will see under what uneasiness they are. I advised her to be patient a little longer, since there was no step taken in order to his prosecution. If anything of that kind should be attempted she was to give me notice instantly. I think 'twould be in vain to struggle at present, since by the Act he may be detained without bail as long as that Act endures.

I must trouble you with a word about Harry [St. John]. Lord Weymouth's son being chosen in two places, sure his lordship may bring him in in one of them. Collier was yesterday with one and tells me Bromley wrote to Lord Weymouth to chose Cæsar to succeed his son, but that Lord Weymouth has modestly refused, and declared for Harry. I take it for granted that you have written to Lord Weymouth on this subject or speedily will.

Our news of the law advancements is that Holt is to surrender and Jekyll succeed, the Solicitor succeed Jekyll, Parker and Eyres Attorney and Solicitor, Lovell a Baron and King Recorder. 'Twill be as bad if it be not so.

[E. Lewis to Robert Harley.]

1708, May 29—There are several letters in town from the old lady of Hanover, full of the praises of the Duke of Marlborough for the proposal he made of bringing over one of that family into England. She says he owns he was not empowered by the Queen or either of the parties, to speak upon that subject, and that she could not therefore but think the Holy Ghost inspired him. This is now no longer a secret, some say this bold step without the Queen's privity is the cause of her illness, but whatever the cause be it is certain she is so very ill that those about her are in great concern for her. The W[higs] are much alarmed and swear the Duke shall not run away with the credit of so popular a thing as bringing over the ———. The last letters from thence say the old lady was very ill.

I hope been to wait upon my Lord Raby, who desired me to give his services to you and acquaint you with the great injustice done you by Mr. Toland, who has given out that you sent him an extract of my Lord's letter wherein he complained to you of his conduct.

Sir Philip Medows is recalled, but Lord Berkeley says he won't go unless they allow him 10l. a day, as they did Lord Sunderland.

Five thousand men are to be sent upon some secret expedition under the command of Erle. The French look upon our Moselle army to be so much a chimera that they have named no general to command on that side.

Mr. St. J[ohn] not being in Parliament has occasioned some jealousies that he has no mind to appear.

Lord Raby hopes you will take some notice of what relates to Toland.

Dr. R. Freind to Edward Harley, at Christ Church, Oxford.

1708, June 5—Your Professor by your account is not very polite, I hope he will make amends for it by being very profound. You I see are aiming at both talents now you are engaged in the study of Homer and Euclid together. I am glad you proceed so vigorously in your Greek, I was afraid you would have laid it quite aside, &c.

The Dean will not be with you till the week after next. He was showing me last night his Euclid, I remember he began it in my time, and he says he is resolved to finish it, but before that I hope you will have finished Euclid done by some worse hand. You have put a cypher too much to Dr. Hannes's legacy, but he has really left 1,000l. to Peckwater, and 6,000l. more if his daughter dies before she is married, which you have a good chance for.

My very kind services to Lord Carteret, Mr. Trelawny, and Mr. Finch.

K. O. (so endorsed) to Edward Harley, at Christ Church, Oxford.

1708, June 10th—Mr. Harley came home to Mrs. Beresford the Tuesday after the holidays very well and brisker if possible then when he went. He says all Mr. Hadley's family are well and that Mr. George is called to the Bar. I have sent you this figure of a monster that is shewed here in town, for in my opinion it is very extraordinary and worthy anybody's curiosity, they are Hungarian girls between six and seven years of age shewed about by their father's brother. He brought over a great deal of money from Holland he got by showing them there, and it is thought he receives a 100l. a week upon the same account here, for he has a shilling for every one that sees them, and more of those that are more nice and desire a private inspection.

The Bishop of Oxford's son married a great fortune whose name was Mathews, it is reported she is worth 3,000l. and 3 or 400l. per annum; she was extremely willing, for under pretence of going to the Abbey to morning prayers she went and took him up in a coach, and when they came to the place appointed the minister asked him for the licence, he said he had none, she answered but she had, and so likewise by the ring, and when the ceremony was finished desired the few spectators that were there to be witnesses of what passed that he might come to no trouble.

I hear Mr. Auditor will be in town this week or the next at furthest. Mr. John Beresford is in deacon's orders and Chaplain to the College at Dulwich. Mr. Robert is come from sea this six weeks and is resolved to go no more. There is not any news stirring otherwise I should send it; my troubling you with such mean matters I hope you will excuse, being in obedience to your commands.

Postscript.—The Queen goes to Windsor about the middle of next week there is another copy of verses, of the same subject and the same side as those I sent you, come out, I would have sent them if I thought they had not been disagreeable; Boileau's *Lutrin* is very well liked, if I knew you were not timely supplied with such books I would take care to do it.

[E. Lewis to Robert Harley.]

1708, June 17—My Lord —— and Sir William C—— are in a matrimonial state, one day very dear to each other, and the next in most violent transports of fury; for an instance of his animosity he refused to dine where Sir William was to be, and thus it is like to continue till the place you know of is given to his ———, or otherwise disposed of. The Ladies her Gr——— makes so much court to for the sake of the place from whence they came, were there at no higher a price than half a crown. The Queen's health suffers by these follies as well as the deeper designs of ——— and I am told she has a touch of the jaundice.

The poor gentleman that married Mrs. T——— **the** m. of H. ——— has made a hue and cry after the 2,000*l*. left her by her family, and it is found that 1,200*l*. of it was given to the Duchess of Or[mon]d for her being made a m——— of H———. This was a seasonable supply for her Grace's playing cash, and she had the cunning to make the bargain with her Grace of Mar[lborough] for 500*l*.; this is public and certainly true. There are snares of this kind laid for one of your allies, and I fear she will not be able to keep herself out. The *Observator* of yesterday gives you a touch of what I formerly told you of the Duke of Queensberry, whose title to sit in parliament the juncto say they will dispute.

Pray direct Mr. Thomas to acknowledge the receipt of my letters, that I may have the satisfaction of knowing whether they pass. Tom Hopk——— was one of the first whose name was struck out upon the scrutiny for having voted for Colt without a right to vote. The last Kitcat has afforded much diversion. Jacob Tonson in his cups, sitting between Dormer and Walpole, told them he sat between the honestest man in the world and the greatest villain; and explained himself that by the honest man he meant Dormer, the other was a villain for forsaking his patrons and benefactors the juncto, for which poor Jacob was severely bastinadoed. But as to order of time I should first have told you that Tom Hop——— having been admitted into that society upon a vacancy by an unanimous election, Jacob, who always hated him, bantered him by telling him this election was a banter, for the company then there was but a committee, and that all elections were to be in a full meeting. Upon this the new elect made a speech and told them he hoped his election would be confirmed by the whole society, for which calling to question the power of that company then present he was turned out of doors.

[E. Lewis to Robert Harley.]

1708, June 19. Whitehall—I hear there is a very scurrilous pamphlet in the press, wherein I have the honour to be introduced holding a familiar conversation with you, who are distinguished by the name of Harlequin le Grand as your servant is by that of Louis le Petit. Mr. Man is I am told the author, or at least has contributed the materials to it, but as I never in my life ate or drunk in his company, much less have you ever been free with him, I cannot conceive how he should pretend to be able to draw your picture or mine. As for his baseness I do not wonder at it, because I know he inveighed against you in all public places the minute that you were out, though I never told you so before, because I knew you as little cared to hear such stories as I cared to relate them.

I cannot imagine what can be intended by the embarkation in the Isle of Wight, unless it be to send them to Portugal that the Parliament may be told that service was not neglected; but in reality that is but an amusement, for the troops cannot arrive there soon enough to serve even the Autumn Campaign, for I know very well that they cannot be in readiness to sail till the 10th of August O.S., and who knows how long they may be detained by contrary winds.

By some words that fell to me from a person whom you will easily guess I gather that either they intend to attack you next year upon the business of Valiere &c. or would have you kept upon your good behaviour by an apprehension of what they would do upon that matter if you provoke them.

I beg of you that Mr. Thomas may acknowledge the date of my letters.

Sir Miles (*sic*) Wharton sends you his service, and bids me tell you he wishes you here.

[E. Lewis] to [Robert] Harley.

1708, June 24—Mr. Evelyn who married Mrs. Boscawen is to be one of the Governors of the Post, as it is said in the room of Sir Thomas Frankland, but I suppose it is a mistake and that he will come in the place of Sir Robert Cotton, who will be laid aside and rewarded with a pension. By the disappointment Sir John H. —— meets with upon this remove, and by the promotion lately made in the Admiralty, it is plain the juncto have not so much power as both their friends and foes think they have. Sir Humphrey [Mackworth] who is now ill at the Bath writes to his friends here that he is to serve for the town of Cardigan, and that Meyrick has disengaged Mr. Price of the promise he made him.

Dee, the Common Sergeant, opposes Mr. King in his pretensions to the Recordership with a good probability of success. Mr. King is likely talked of for Speaker. Radcliffe has received a letter from Oxford wherein he is told that Sir Edward Hannes will give them the sum that Dr. Radcliffe promised, but did not pay; and that it will be declared in an inscription, which has so much perplexed the Doctor that it is believed this stratagem may prevail with him to perform what he once engaged for.

E. Lewis to [Robert] Harley, at Brampton.

1708, June 26—In one of my former letters I had the honour to acquaint you that there was a notion received here as if Colonel Jones had been prefered in consideration of you; as you were no doubt surprised to hear such a groundless story should ever be raised, you will be much more so to hear that it has since made a great noise and occasioned much hurly burly. Complaints have been made to the Queen of the discouragements some people lay still under by such a mark of favour being shown to one of your friends. The Queen justifies her self and desires to know the authors of the report. Admiral Ch[urchil]l is named. He says William Ch[   ]l is his author, and he pretends to have it from Taylor, who belongs to Mr. W[alpo]le, the Secretary of War. Taylor, to vindicate himself, has made an affidavit before a Master in Chancery that he never said so, and this affidavit has been laid before the Queen. This is the manner in which some tell the story. Others say W[alpole] took a bribe for making J[one]s a Colonel, and when Lord T[reasure]r and Junto enquired how a Colonel could be made without their privity, W[alpo]le, to justify himself said the Queen did it because the man was allied to you. Whatever the foundation is I can assure you this matter has occasioned great heat.

ERSKINE WALKER to ROBERT HARLEY, at Brampton.

1708, June 29. London—Gives information of an alleged plot against Harley's life, one John Edwards living at Deal and Dover being a principal manager, and at least eight or nine more concerned in it who are supported by the Earl of Sunderland and some others till the parliament meets. Will make a further scrutiny into the matter if his story should be thought worthy of notice. Believes there is fact in it, but Harley can best judge of things of such a nature.

[GEORGE GRANVILLE to ROBERT HARLEY.]

1708, July 17. Menabilly—Having read in the news this morning that we have a vacancy in this county by the death of Colonel Kendal, I am this moment going to try my interest with Mr. Canon Kendal, who has the disposing of that burgesship, on the behalf of our friend Harry. I take the freedom to give you this notice that, in case you have not already settled some other way of serving him, you might, without any delay, second the efforts I shall make with other recommendations. The Dean of Carlisle has a good interest in him, and 'tis possible likewise the new Bishop of Exeter may have some power over him. My Lord Radnor's interest is what will contend against us, and Mr. Francis Roberts will no doubt be a competitor again. My Lord Treasurer and the Bishop of Winchester will likewise have somebody in their eye, and therefore what is done must be done with the utmost dispatch. Nothing shall be wanting here on my part, of which I will take the freedom to give you some account by the next. My stay in these parts has been much longer than I expected, but I found it necessary to answer the extraordinary civilities and respect that I have found, which has furnished me with daily opportunities of giving gentleman a right notion of things in regard to the Queen's personal service, in which cause I had the honour to embark with you from the beginning, and will stand and fall by it. I am told, and am well assured of the truth of it, that our new Lord Warden [Boscawen] has declared he will have me turned out of my Government of Pendennis for professing myself your friend. He has had the indiscretion to declare this publicly at his table. I hope you have still credit enough to support me against any such attempt, which without presumption, I may say, will contribute as much as anything to the keeping the gentlemen of this county in temper, for as inconsiderable as I may seem at London, I find myself not without consequence here.

I beg your pardon for this long 'scrole,' which was begun upon our friend's account without any thought of mentioning myself.

[ABIGAIL MASHAM to ROBERT HARLEY.]

.1708, July 21—My brother delivered yours safe into my hands this day, and tells me he goes back early tomorrow morning, by whom I send this. I repent heartily my telling my aunt (the Queen) the reason why I desired to go to Walton (London), but did not question having leave as I told you in my last. I thank you for your kind advice and I hope God Almighty will give me more grace then to be taken in any of their snares, I am very ready to believe they will try all ways to ruin me, but they shall never do it by any indirect action of my own. If theirs will take effect against me God's will be done, I must submit to what He permits. Oh my poor aunt Stephens is to be pitied very much for they press her harder than ever, since what happened lately she is altered more than is to be imagined, no ready money (courage) at all to supply her with common necessaries, really I see it so bad and they come so fast upon her I have no hopes of her deliverance, for she will put it quite out of her friends' power to save her. I have heard of the court they make to Mrs. Packer (Hanover family) from several people and told her all, while she is hearing it she is very melancholy but says little to the matter.

My Lady Pye (Duchess of Marlborough) is here still. I have not seen my aunt since my duty called me which was Saturday and Sunday in the morning, tomorrow I go again to do my duty. I don't think it any unkindness in my aunt but because my Lady Pye is here. My friend that is gone the journey you need not fear will be led into any inconvenience by the person you mentioned to my brother, for my friend is as cautious as any body can be, he knows them very well.

I shall be glad to have a line from you Saturday. God bless you and give you health. The papers are safe which you left with me but if you want them let me know when you write.

[DR. FRANCIS ATTERBURY to ROBERT HARLEY.]

[1708, July 22] Thursday—I will write immediately to Canon Kendall, and I will go to Hampstead to morrow, to Mrs. Kendall, and, if I can, will prevail with her to write also, which will be of greater moment. But I fear that way is barred up by the two great men mentioned in Mr. G[ranville]'s letter. For though the Bishop of Winchester hath lately expressed great anger towards Canon Kendall, yet I doubt not but he hath given him an opportunity to reconcile himself by this vacancy. And if he hath, some expectations that the Canon hath from my Lord at Winchester, and New College, in relation to two of his children will certainly determine him. The Bishop of Exeter will hereafter have great influence with the Canon, and at present hath some, but it centres in matters that relate to the Church and City of Exeter. I do not think it practicable to make the Bishop interpose with him for a Parliament man, and for such an one to whom the Bishop is a stranger. However, if upon farther reflection, I have any hopes of stirring the Bishop in that matter, I will not fail to attempt it, and by this very post.

[LIEUT.-COLONEL J. CRANSTOUN] to ROBERT CUNNINGHAM.

[1708], July 25, O.S. Camp before Tournay at Willemeau—We march tomorrow towards Orchies on the way to Douay to be nearer forage.

My last to you was from Ghent some days before we took the field as the last I had from you was by Mr. Twyman, Lord Finch's governor. You will be juster to me than to judge of my friendship from my letters, I dare assure you there is no day passes over my head in which you are not often on my tenderest thoughts, and wherein I do not oftener than once remember you and yours with the same concern I do my own family. Lord Finch came up to Ghent from Holland with my Lord Stair, came out to the camp with him and has stayed with him ever since till this morning that he is returned from Holland, and probably will stay at and about the Hague till he see whether this campaign is like to produce a peace. He is I think a youth of much modesty, virtue and sweetness of temper, and seems to have a good understanding and a good stock of sense. Mr. Twyman and I have been often together and always minded you with pleasure. He speaks of you with great respect and esteem, and indeed I think him worthy your friendship, and that my Lord Nottingham has made no bad choice in sending him with his son. He seems to have a good tincture of the *belles lettres* and the more polite learning joined to good manners, a staid gravity, and a good stock of prudence and discretion, with a great attachment to his patron's family, and a personal friendship for his pupil. Lord Finch could not have been so well with us anywhere as with my Lord Stair, who has indeed been very kind to him and been the best governor he could have got in the army. My little family are blessed be God in ordinary health, the two children and my sister Dickson have been ill but are better. The uncertainty we were in for some time before we took the field betwixt the hopes of peace and the thoughts of another campaign kept me then from writing. Most people thought Monsieur de Rouillé was left only to try to make the best of a weak game, but that, whenever he found the Allies were positive not to abate anything they had demanded he might have had private instructions at last to yield and agree ; because France had really come such a length in condescensions beyond what I believe any of the Allies durst have hoped for, that people wrought themselves from this into a persuasion they would stop at nothing but that as they seemed to have given us up their shirt they would give us their skin too.

However, we see the treaty broke off at last in good earnest, though I am credibly informed that Monsieur Rouillé before he parted offered formally in the King's name to yield to all except that of the 37th article limiting the cessation of arms to two months. Who were the occasion of breaking upon that article or what were their views I know not, but I fancy most of the wisest men on both sides who sincerely wish a reasonable peace have since repented it and wish rather that either of the sides had yielded that point, and perhaps the longer the campaign goes on we may see greater reason to wish it. It is certain the Imperial Ministers and Prince Eugene were not for breaking upon that point, and however the Duke of Marlborough went into the opinion of the Pensionary and those who were for standing to all we demanded, yet it is not believed to have been his real judgment, but on the contrary that he was for passing from that article, but in prudence would not take it upon him knowing what advantage his enemies at home would have made of it if any cross accident had fallen out thereafter.

All those amongst us here who are reckoned high Whigs or in with the Junto as you call them seem pleased at continuing the war and reason on all occasions to persuade the world that all the offers and advances made by France were a trick to impose upon us, though indeed I could never yet hear a good argument given to prove this, and I doubt that if we do more than take Tournay this campaign there will be many in St. Stephen's Chapel next winter of opinion we were in the wrong to push things so far and refuse offers that appeared both so reasonable and sincere. It has cost us twenty-two days open trenches to take the city of Tournay and about 3,000 men killed or wounded, officers and all though I believe there are not above 1,500 men can be said truly to be killed or so wounded as to be *hors de combat*. We are now begun to the siege of the citadel since Thursday last and our approaches advance as much as can be expected considering the nature of the place, their many mines, and the reason we have not to sacrifice men's lives for a few days more or less, and yet if the garrison makes the defence they probably will do unless some other treaty than a military capitulation gives us the place, it is not probable we shall get it before the first week of September even in your style. But I am told that Monsieur de Marigneu, major general in the citadel, after liberty obtained by a drum came out late on Saturday night or yesterday morning with some overtures of yielding the citadel upon conditions yet a secret to us here, and that after having been with the Prince and Duke and States Deputies he took post yesterday at 12 o'clock for Versailles, and is expected again in three or four days. There is certainly somewhat true in this and some kind of overtures *sur le tapis*, which if they take I believe are only made to give a decent handle and introduction to ministers coming back to take up the negotiations for peace again.

If this is [so] peace seems certain and all preliminary articles must be agreed to positively at first meeting, but if nothing follows upon this, and it proves the middle of September before we get from this place we are not sure of opening one entry into France yet for this campaign, and it were hard to tell what we shall do next that will satisfy the world who wants peace so much. Valenciennes or Douay are what we would wish to take, or next to them Bethune and Arras, but Villars keeps yet a body of 25 or 30 battalions in his lines at Lens and Bethune and is come with his main body near Valenciennes where he has made new lines and those very strong betwixt the Scheldt at Valenciennes and the Scarpe, which is a tract of ground only of two leagues over, and impracticable for most of the way; so that it will be easy with a small body to defend these and while he lies with the gross of his army betwixt the Scarpe and Scheldt with his right near their lines and extending [torn] and has bridges enough laid. I believe he imagines he will be able to cover both Valenciennes and Douay, and to be still before us in case we march towards La Bassee to force his lines of Lens, and I doubt our greatest generals think he may do it if he be much on his guard, and that unless we can overreach him and steal a march upon him with some considerable part of our army, so as to force some of his posts before he gets up to sustain it, we shall be able to do little that way and if we should get in somewhere upon him, as it is not impossible but that in so great a length of ground as betwixt Valenciennes and the Lys or St. Venant an advantage may be found. The forage is all consumed there already in the fields and there is nothing in barns this year as usual, so that it may prove difficult enough to carry on a siege there at any of those places though we could invest it. If these difficulties prove insuperable, as they may be, we seem to have nothing left that appears to us here but to sit down before either Condé, Mons or Ypres. Condé seems not worth while at this juncture, and even neither Mons nor Ypres opens France to us, and either will be hard to take in so advanced a season, both being in great part defended by morass around them, especially Ypres which seems most worth our while to take because it makes us a complete head and cover to our country and opens the way at least towards Dunkerque and the sea coast, but all of them at best leave sufficient work for another campaign before we can end the war even with the same superiority of troops we have now, provided only the French king can find bread for his army and people, and funds to maintain the same troops another year; but we hope he cannot do this, and perhaps his funds being exhausted and his people starving is what we shall owe a good peace to, more than to any conquests we can make this campaign, unless our generals have some scheme in their head we cannot yet guess at. Adieu my dearest friend. Write to me I entreat you and reckon upon my daily prayers and concerned good wishes for you and yours. Let me know what they are doing with the Duke of Douglas and what hopes there is of him. Adieu.

[Abigail Masham to Robert Harley.]

1708, July 27—My brother delivered yours very safe into my hands, I am sorry he has not business to oblige him to go back this week that I might send him to a place where I have locked up the papers you desire to have returned. I dont care to trust a servant to go to the place, but if there is a real necessity for it I must do it, for I cannot get leave to go myself. When you do me the favour to write to me say what you will have me do in that matter. I have nothing new since to acquaint you with but I am very much afraid of my aunt's (the Queen's) conduct in her affairs, and all will come from her want of a little ready money (courage) for hitherto you know the want of that has made her make a most sad figure in the world. I shall be very glad to have your opinion upon things that I may lay it before her, for that is all can be done. I trust in God and beg of him to supply her, that she may not be so blinded but save herself while it is in her power. She will give me your book and I will keep it till I shall have the comfort of seeing you which I heartily wish for, my brother tells me he never saw you look better in his life.

[E. Lewis to Robert Harley.]

1708, July 31—I hope you had a safe journey to Brampton. All your friends wish you here, where there still seems some probability that things may take another turn than they have lately done. The Muscovite ambassador set out this morning in a Dutch vessel without accepting presents or recreditives. He insists that the bailiff be executed where he did the affront. Lord Chief Justice will come up so far as to punish it for a riot.

Dr. Garth says he knows not where Crull (Curll ?) is to be found.

Coatsworth, the apothecary who affronted Radcliffe, is dubbed a doctor in Holland, and sets up here for a physician.

News Letter.

[1708, July]—I send you here inclosed an account of the great news we have received to-day, to which I shall only add a few particulars. We have not yet any account of the numbers of killed, wounded, or taken, but we are assured that this victory is yet more complete than either Hochstet or Ramillies. Our horse they say could not do much service in the battle because of the ground, but they are so much better and more entire for the pursuit. The French are quite scattered, cne part of them retired towards Ghent, where is also all their great baggage, and some say the Princes of the Blood Royal, and we hope in a few days to hear that all that is at Ghent will be prisoners of war, for we hope they cannot escape ; another part of the French are run away towards Lille, and we expect that our horse will overtake them, and not let one whole regiment get off any way. They have not saved one wagon nor baggage nor cannon. They had no cannon with them at the battle it seems, for they could not get them brought over the

Scheldt soon enough. My Lord Duke though very sick and in a fit of the fever, yet would needs be on horseback, and commanded and directed all the whole business with his ordinary prudence and courage, and has added new laurels to his crown by this action. Prince Eugene was everywhere, sometimes on the right, sometimes on the left, as if he had been Aid de Camp to some or all the generals, giving his directions everywhere, and you may be sure he did good service. None of his troops were yet joined to our army, but they are now all or most part about Brussels, so that is a new fresh army ready to push on after this victory. I do not believe the Allies have lost in all 2,000 men, though the action was very sharp and lasted the whole night. Our English troops have been in the hottest of it, and done wonders. Our joy here is very great, and so much the more that it comes on the back of the bad news you had in my last of the enemies having got into Ghent and Bruges, &c., which has in effect been the occasion of their ruin. There is nothing but rejoicing, ringing of bells, and firing of guns great and small in this town, and we have had public Thanksgivings in all our churches this evening for this great and signal victory. I doubt not our Generals will push it as far as ever victory was pushed, and that it will procure us peace very soon on whatsoever conditions the Allies please to propose. I wish you as perfect joy and contentment in it as we have.

[E. LEWIS to ROBERT HARLEY.]

1708, August 5. Whitehall—The town has been all day in a great alarm occasioned by reports of an intended assassination of her Majesty, and several papers have been printed about it, but I can meet with no person of credit who can give me any account of it.

The Great Park at Windsor is to be granted to Lady M[arlborough] for as long a term as the Crown can give. I am told that the Earl of Roc[heste]r would be Lord Chamberlain. Whether there is any truth in it, or that it is given out to raise jealousies I know not, but as far as I can trace the story it comes from Sir William's emissaries. M. de Guiscard sells his regiment.

DR. FRANCIS ATTERBURY to ROBERT HARLEY.

1708, August 14. Chelsea—Mrs. Kendall and I have both received answers to our letters from the Canon, by which I find that he is in some suspense, on the account of an idle report that hath reached him about an understanding between Mr. Roberts and Mr. Addison. I have had some opportunity of searching into that matter, and Mr. Granville hath had more, and we are both entirely satisfied that there is no foundation for such a report, and so I tell the Canon in a letter by this night's post. Mr. Kendall was chosen exactly upon the same foot with Mr. Addison: and therefore Mr. Roberts, if he petitions against one, must petition against the other also. And so, I hear from good hands, that he certainly will, having a petition ready for that purpose, which will be lodged perhaps ere this reaches your hands. I believe, there can be no danger of its being thrown out, when Mr. Addison will be able to engage one sort of men against it, and Mr. St. John, another. And therefore if Mr. St. John hath no nearer and better news than Lostwithiel, he will give me leave to give as punctual and quick an answer as can be to the Canon's enquiry, how far he may may depend upon being supported. Upon turning this matter over in my head, I see but one way wherein it is possible for Mr. Addison and Mr. Roberts to join; and that is, if Mr. Roberts should whisper to him, that if he will quit his pretensions to a choice, upon the foot he now stands, and give in to Mr. Roberts's petition, he shall be brought in upon a new foot, by Mr. Roberts's interest; and that his election shall be secured to him, not only in this, but in future Parliaments. It is possible there may be persons that for the good of the common cause may set such an accommodation on foot, ere the matter is ripened for a decision in Parliament. But it is certain that there is no tendency this way at present; and Mr. Granville—to whom I opened my suspicions—thinks it impracticable that there ever should be. However, I thought it proper to lay this thought before you, who can best judge how far it is likely to take place. Mr. Granville will write to Mr. St. John this post.

[E. Lewis to Robert Harley.]

1708, August 19. Whitehall—The solemnity of the day has been performed with a great deal of decency, but I cannot say with any visible marks of real joy and satisfaction. There were very few people in the windows and balconies, and it was to be read in everybody's countenance that they looked upon the giving of thanks for a victory at Oudenarde to be a mocking of God. However the men in office acted their parts, and put on their wedding garments. Lord T[reasurer] and Mr. L[own]des have been several times with Sir Edward Northey at his chambers in the Temple. This mighty condescension makes people imagine he will be A[ttorney] Gen[eral]; in the mean time it is a great disgrace to Sir J. [Jekyll?] that he should be passed by, and that Sir Edward should be consulted in all their affairs, and particularly the great one now depending, which Lord T[reasure]r and Lady M[arlborough] lay so much to heart, viz.: whether the Queen is entitled to any part of the galleon taken by Wager, which is said to be worth a million sterling and to have been made prize before the new act took place.

Lord Herbert has ordered two large silver maces to be bought for the Corporation of Bewdley, and my cousin has them in hand.

Father Gilbert has at last got a diabetes by drinking tea.

Mr. Reynardson, one of the directors of the Bank, is to be Collector at Bristol; and Sir Thomas Frankland's second son, now Inland Comptroller, to be cashier of the Stamps in trust for his elder brother, a member of parliament.

T. Pauncefort to Robert Harley.

1708, August 20[-31, new style]. The Hague—I gave you the trouble of a letter some time ago, since which I have made the tour of the greatest part of these Provinces. I am now going for Flanders and the army where I think to be for two or three months, and if in any place I could afford you any diversion or service, I should be mighty glad, if you'll pardon my presumption. I should desire you would let me know whether my correspondence when I am in those parts may be admitted as agreeable to you.

Lord Raby is here and preparing to go to Berlin, though 'tis said the King of Prussia will go to the army in Flanders. Colonel Godfrey and Admiral Baker have been to wait upon the Queen of Portugal here,

they are to be ready to receive her Majesty on board the yachts
at Rotterdam, on Monday next if the wind permit. Young Craggs
arrived here from Spain the day before yesterday, he came from
Barcelona the 5th of this month, he is dispatched to Lord Marlborough
from Mr. Stanhope; he came this way to get a French pass. I don't
find that 'tis any particular news of action that brings him, but I believe
to represent the state of affairs there which is but indifferent. He is to
proceed for England.

The siege of Lille goes on very well, there is a vast artillery playing
against the city, which we expect to be masters of by the 3rd of next
month at furthest; but the citadel is very strong.

We have an account of the Duke of Berwick having joined the French
army, which has passed the Scheldt and is encamped at Grammont.
Lord Marlborough lay with his army within less than two leagues
of them and was joined by Prince Eugene and all the horse, so that we
expect to hear of another battle. 'Tis said there are letters that mention
the decamping of my Lord Duke towards the French army, who give out
they will fight. There is an account here of a very odd attempt to
poison Prince Eugene, 'tis very unaccountable, but the story I have
from very good hands. There was a letter sent him directed, *à son
Eminence*, which is a character only given to the Episcopal; he flung
the letter upon the table at the reading the superscription, but afterwards
took it up, and in opening of it was struck up the nostrils. They
immediately gave him something that prevented any ill effect. In the
letter was only a piece of paper or skin very oily and nothing else to be
perceived. I presume the invention was to have the sudden smell at
the opening effectual. To make the experiment they afterwards put it
into a dog's mouth, which it immediately killed. King Augustus was
at Prince Eugene's quarters at Lille and I believe is still there, 'tis said
he is solicitous to get his horse taken into the service of the Allies, of
which he has sixty squadrons. There is an account here that our forces
from the Isle of Wight are landed near Havre de Grace on the Coast of
Normandy.

[E. LEWIS to ROBERT HARLEY.]

1708, August 21—The author of the *Tale of a Tub* goes Queen's
Secretary to Vienna. Lord Berkeley will follow in the spring with the
character of Envoy Extraordinary.

Marquis de Guiscard goes third Envoy to Turin and sets out next
Tuesday.

Lord Treasurer has cleared the arrears of all the foreign ministers by
"Tallies of Pro" upon the tin, bearing no interest. Lord Pembroke is
to be married to Lady Arundel. Mrs. Pearshal succeeds her in her
former station under the guardianship of the Knight of the Peak.

NEWS LETTER.

[1708], August 26—Yesterday there came in two Holland mails all
there is due. By it we understand that the Duke of Berwick has at
last joined the Duke of Burgundy. They joined the 18th our style.
Upon which Duke of Marlborough advanced near to them within three
leagues, so that it is next to impossible to avoid a battle. The letters
from our camp import we are to expect a bloody battle in few days.
Some are of opinion it is over two or three days ago, some four or five

. days ago. This letter is writ in the morning, some fancy even by night we may have an account of it by an express especially if we have their letter on it which is little doubted. Our last letters from Holland spoke as if Duke Marlborough posted himself so as that it was not possible for him to retire, but it seems they are and there must be [torn] decisive too. 7,000 horse from Lille has joined Duke Marlborough, some say Prince Eugene will be there in person. We talk of nothing but of battles and victories. The siege of Lille goes on, they hope to be masters of the town the 28th instant, our style, but the citadel will hold longer time, but the success of the battle will take or soon relieve the place. The accounts from Dauphiné and Provence are various, the French say they get an advantage, others say the Duke of Savoy gains ground. We have little from Catalonia, the Duke of Orleans presses the enemy there but no action of moment. On the Rhine little done; some letters from thence still mention the Duke of Bavaria's coming to the Netherlands. I refer you for a more distinct account to the prints, which I presume you will have. We have little home news. Mr. Goodsire of the Signet office tells me no grants are in their office. Our parliament to sit about the 21st of October, and the Convocation the 25th of October. Who will be Lord Mayor uncertain, Sir Charles Duncombe thinks he ought to be being his turn to be next the chair; I find some great men do oppose his being chosen. No changes or alterations at Court. General Earle with the forces at St. Heliers, the stormy weather forced them for the French coasts, and it is believed they will go [torn] thither this season. The foreign ministers go to Portsmouth to wait there for the arrival of the Queen of Portugal, who (that I hear) has not sailed from Rotterdam, but she is expected when the wind presents fair. Peterborough some say cannot get such conditions and such powers in the West Indies as he thinks necessary. He is kindly and is angry very soon; now he has access to the Queen, he has quality, courage, and wit enough to speak his mind freely to the Queen, of which I will say no more. If Duke Marlborough beats the French his enemies must become his footstool. I write this letter because you might prepare for the joyful news of victory so near at hand, Veni, Vidi, Vici. Observe that there are but very few English or Scotch at the siege of Lille; Duke Marlborough has them in a manner all with him, relying and depending mostly on them as the . best troops. This is all I can get, except some merchants on the Exchange fancy Monsieur Ducasse may be very near Spain or France with what plate or money he has got.

Some say Prince Eugene was to be poisoned but little credited though some prints have it. Burgundy's army between us and Brussels, and our army between them and Lille. Some blame Duke Marlborough's conduct for letting Berwick join Burgundy but success covers all faults. The King of France has sent Count Tessé to Rome his ambassador, to be in the league making in Italy. Monsieur Premola assures the league will be great and surely made, but we say all depends on the success in Flanders.

[E. Lewis to Robert Harley.]

1708, August 28—After a thousand difficulties raised by Lord S[underland] and Mr. H[   ], the former refusing absolutely to discharge V[aliere] by his warrant, it has been resolved to send him a message, that if he will enter his prayer next sessions he shall be admitted to bail, and lest he should not be able to procure any, intimation has been given to some persons that they may offer themselves. Notwithstanding all this Mr. Baker, as I suppose by instigation of a certain Lord, is moving heaven and earth to suborn witnesses against you, and some people tell me they hope to make this appear by legal proofs.

[E. Lewis] to [Robert] Harley, at Brampton.

1708, September 2—Admiral Wager has written to several persons that the whole value of the bullion in the ship he took does not amount to ten thousand pounds. The Queen is better and walked last Saturday for half an hour in Bulstrode Gardens. There has been a great squabble between —— [Duchess of Marlborough] and the Commissioners of taxes at Windsor. The two Parks were rated at 170*l.* No payment being made they said they would lay it before Parliament, but at last Topham with great importunity and by laying the inconveniences before her prevailed upon her to pay it.

A. Lady Pye to Abigail Harley, at Auditor Harley's at Eywood.

1708, September 11. Derby—We had an unkindly spring and now an uncomfortable wet autumn, but worst for harvest, all grain much risen. I know no news from this place worth sending. The other day making a visit in this town I met Congreve the poet, Estcourt the player, and Moreland the painter; the latter is yet here drawing some fair ladies. Twenty five years since my mother sat to him for me, which picture I have. He is much improved that I would be glad to have a head of Beck, but our little house is so filled, have not a spare place to hang it, which you will scarce credit till you see it. But when will that time come? long hath it been promised that I even despair. Chatsworth hath been well filled this summer; last week the Marquis Dorchester, Lord Rialton &c. Lord James Cavendish was going into Wales to his father in law Mr. Yale.

W. Bromley to [Robert Harley.]

1708, September 18—Since I have had the honour of your acquaintance I have endeavoured on all occasions where I could, to make appear my particular regard for you; and I can now assure you of my own very sincere disposition to enter into measures with you and the gentlemen you mention, for serving our common interest, and that I verily believe you will find the like in others.

You impute our present difficulties to the advantages that have been taken of the mistakes of others; I will not enter into a nice discussion of that point, but you will forgive me telling you what immediately occurred to my thoughts upon the reading it, an expression that I have met with of a blasphemous fellow in his prayer on one of their fasts in the late times. "O God, many are the hands that are lift up against us, but there is one God, it is Thou thyself O Father, who hath done us more mischief than they all." I beg I may be rightly understood, I intend not by this to reproach, and prevent a good agreement for the future, and therefore I will carry this no farther than to add, that I am determined, notwithstanding anything past, to join with you, not as you observe they do on the other side, though they hate one another, but in affection as well as zeal to preserve the whole, and for the service of the public.

I entirely agree, and have been a good while convinced, that the gentlemen and clergy have everything to fear from some in power, and since there is in your opinion an easy cure, I should have been glad to have known it, depending that no lines of circumvallation and contravallation can long secure any enemy against resolute and obstinate attacks and a good cause. I shall rejoice to see points brought on of such consequence in themselves, that will appear so to the nation, and that will comprehend the opinions and consequently the assistance of most people to support them. These are certainly the right points, but you must allow me to say this description is very general, and that I wish you had pleased to have been something more particular, for we must expect them from you, who have had opportunities by being conversant in business to know them, and are best able to direct. You refer to discourse when we meet, and in the mean time promise I shall hear again from you ; I shall probably be in town about a week, as I use to be, before the meeting of the parliament, and then I hope you will be more free and open, which will be necessary to unite us, and to create that confidence that I desire may be among us.

Our friends only want countenance, for even under the present cloud I think it is very evident they are the majority, and with favour and countenance we should in all places appear as considerable as ever.

I cannot conclude without asking your pardon if I have delivered myself in anything not to your satisfaction and beg you to believe I readily and thankfully embrace the offers of your friendship, which I so much value.

[E. Lewis to Robert Harley.]

1708, September 21—Lord S[underlan]d gives out that he has a letter under Greg's hand, by which he declares that the speech he left behind him was written by a clergyman. If you think fit to trace this matter I believe I may have leave to name the person who told it me.

Lord Grantham and Mr. Dunch have each a pension of 1000l. a year out of the Post House during the Queen's and their lives. Lady Fitzharding had a warrant for the same, but she died before it passed the seals.

[E. Lewis to Robert Harley.]

1708, September 28—The business of our little world stands still in expectation of the great event in Flanders, and till that be decided all things are in suspense, nor is the least payment made excepting only to those who are to attend at Newmarket, and to defray the Queen of Portugal. In the mean time nothing can be more ridiculous than to see the emissaries go about and declare the Siege of Lille was projected by ——, or was entirely against his judgment, according as the news from thence varies. The Queen comes to-night to Kensington, goes this day senight to Newmarket. From thence it is supposed she will return ten days after. A Council of the Junto will be held there, and then and not till then shall we know who will be Speaker. For several Parliament men assure me it is not yet agreed upon, though the vogue runs for Sir Richard [Onslow], whose son will in all probability carry the West India fortune.

If the judges should do that act of justice to the country, as to represent the true state of it to our governors, I am humbly of opinion it would still incline them to follow the same methods by which they have hitherto succeeded so well, I mean to empoverish us still more; for according to Richelieu's maxim, the poor the country is, the more easily is it kept in subjection; and without looking for further marks or proofs of the miseries of the nation, their tame suffering of so absolute a power in the hands of one family is convincing enough that all spirit is lost. History furnishes many examples of men who from the command of less force have aspired to sovereignty, but I believe there is no instance that ever any man who had tasted of absolute power could ever after retire to a private life, and become a good subject.

[E. LEWIS] to [ROBERT] HARLEY.

1708, September 30—The Duchess of M[arlborough's] grant of the Priory is passed; it consists of 3,600 foot and she is to enjoy it for fifty years at 10s. a year rent, with a power to dispose of it at her death though under coverture. Palmes's 1,000l. is lately settled for life. Do not the settlements for life look as if they suspected a change? Some are very angry with Colonel Davenant for sending an express to Windsor with the news of Mrs. Masham's being brought to bed, though it was by the Queen's positive order and only fell to him because he lived at Kensington.

Mr. Hopkins is gone down to Arundel, where he is likely to be opposed by Lord Lumley and Dummer.

[E. LEWIS] to [ROBERT] HARLEY.

1708, October 2—The Lords have pitched upon Sir Richard Onslow to be Speaker, and Sir Peter King is to be otherwise considered. The Queen has put off her journey to Newmarket, some say to avoid the solicitations that would be made her there when she was to be entirely surrounded by the party, others think it was purely by the advice of her physicians.

[E. LEWIS] to [ROBERT] HARLEY.

1708, October 5—The Lord T[reasurer] had a meeting with the Lords of the Junto last Thursday when they agreed upon Sir R. Onslow for Speaker, and the former declared he would stand and fall by the party he had espoused. This declaration may be owing to the ill posture of affairs abroad, our communication is now cut off every way, we want everything, part of our cannon (of which we never had a number sufficient) is rendered useless, and the flower of our army destroyed. Lady Frechville stood godmother for the Queen, Lady Thanet for herself, and somebody for the Prince, at Mrs. Masham's child's christening.

—— to ROBERT HARLEY.

[1708], October 5—The Queen was resolved to have returned this day to Windsor, but the Prince's illness occasions her staying at least till Thursday. He was out of order and feverish but is better.

The Lord Treasurer went this morning about four o'clock with flambeaux from hence to Newmarket; the Duke of Somerset and Lord Rialton were in coach with him. The Queen and Lady Thanet were godmothers and the Prince godfather to Colonel Masham's daughter.

It was generally believed that the Lord Treasurer would fix measures and capitulate with the Junto at Newmarket, but it's said now that that work will be delayed some time and it's probable that none of these Lords will go thither except those who are concerned in the diversions of that place. Some say that the Lord Treasurer finds great difficulties with the Whig Lords, that the Queen is very stiff and inflexible and will not consent to any treaty, believing that no terms which she can grant will be accepted by them. The Lord T██████r is of opinion that terms should be offered, and it's said that upon the Queen's refusing the Lord Treasurer offered his white staff to her Majesty, which she refused. The Duke of Somerset was employed to speak to the Queen but did not prevail, and the Lord Treasurer was to speak again with her about it. The Queen as some say seems very firm, and some wish that those who are her friends (as they phrase it) would assist her. Some say that the Lord Treasurer is out of humour and that if the Queen does not accommodate matters with these Lords, he will be very uneasy and will offer to lay down. Others say that the Lord Treasurer makes use of the Queen's disinclination to these Lords to bring them to the terms which he thinks reasonable or, as some call it, his own terms ; and these believe that the Lord Treasurer will accommodate with the Whig Lords, and that the Queen will comply. Some think that you should be here.

[E. LEWIS to ROBERT HARLEY.]

1708, October 7—There are great discontents at Hanover. That Court is exceedingly dissatisfied with our two Kings, who now again for what reasons I know not are grown very cold towards them, and say nothing more of the invitation upon which they were so hot last spring.

Though I conceive our affairs to be in so miserable a posture that it cannot but affect anyone who has a subsistence, though never so small, in his country, I see however that this ill blast blows this good, that I dare go, without fear of being insulted, into public places, which I could not have done some months since, and that misfortunes which usually obscure people's reason make men now more clear sighted and you would be surprised to hear men say publicly, we have spent so many millions to find out this great secret, that our General does not understand the *métier de la guerre*, that he has indeed twice or thrice thrown a lucky main, but never knew how to play his game, and that he is but a little genius, of a size adapted to getting money by all sordid and dishonourable ways, which I think never was the vice of a warlike, nor indeed of a great spirit of any sort.

One of the reasons of sending Webb over was to prevent a quarrel between him and Cadogan, and that the latter may no longer be deprived of the second place of honour.

In the Dean of Carlisle [Atterbury]'s sermon at the election of Lord Mayor some passages relating to the obedience to be paid to the governors gave offence to the Whigs who pretended his doctrine came up to passive obedience. The question being put whether the Court of Aldermen should give him thanks and desire him to print his sermon it was carried in the negative. Sir Richard Hoare was of opinion 'twas best to drop the matter and not put the question at all.

Fletcher of Saltoun has kissed the Queen's hand.

[E. Lewis to Robert Harley.]

1708, October 8—Lord Sunderland, Lord Coningsby and Sir James Forbes dined yesterday at Pontacks with their City friends, where they took Lille and raised six millions in a trice without the assistance of any but their own party, as the two gentlemen last named declared last night in all the public placés, adding that Lord Treasurer had promised to drop the Duke of Queensberry, and to surrender himself up entirely to the sage advices of the Junto. Lord Treasurer avows this himself upon all occasions, and there seems to me no room to entertain the least doubt of the truth of it.

[E. Lewis to Robert Harley.]

1708, October 9—It is now generally known that Major General Webb came over to solicit a supply of money in specie which was sent away by a clerk of Mr. Bridges, for in the present situation of our army no remittance can be made by bills.

T. P[auncefort] to —— Jones, at Secretary Boyle's Office at the Cockpit.

1708, October 14–25. Ostend—Mr. Lynn brings you the surrender of Lille, which the Duke sent in two or three lines to General Eule by a woman, and recommended to him the maintaining the port of Leffingen, which we have done for ten or twelve days very bravely. But this morning the French attacked it with ten thousand men and carried it, and took our men prisoners which were about 1200. There were a few Dutch that behaved themselves well but they blame a little our raw troops that were there. I was at our little camp when the French came up to alarm us, but it proved only to cover their attack on Leffingen. We doubt not but the Duke will soon open our passage and retrieve this, and in a day or two I hope to send you some account. If the French come nearer to attack us I believe our little army must shelter in this town till his Grace makes his motion.

Postscript.—Boufflers is retired with the garrison into the citadel to defend that.

[E. Lewis to Robert Harley.]

1708, October 15. Whitehall—The siege of Lille is so entirely the subject of all conversation that even the choice of a Speaker is not talked of, though the opening of the session is so near. I have seen a letter from Mr. Drummond wherein he says he has seen a letter from Prince Eugene to a Member of the States General giving an account that the siege proceeded so well that he did not doubt but he should dine in Lille on Sunday last. Had the event answered expectation, we should have known it ere this. On the other hand I am to acquaint you that the Duke of Somerset told a friend of mine that by the direction of the Duke of Marlborough, it was proposed at the Cabinet to raise sixteen new regiments, besides the four already ordered: and that as soon as any tolerable number was listed every one of the regiments now standing, either in Britain or Ireland, should be forthwith transported to Ostend to rescue our distressed General and his army, who are so encompassed on every side that they do not know but they may be forced to embark themselves at

Ostend in order to be carried round by Zealand into winter quarters. It is owned our battalions in Flanders, one with another, are not above 200 strong, and that if we "opiniatre" the siege as obstinately and unsuccessfully as we have done we shall have no army at all. The Court was in so profound a silence upon this subject last Sunday, that whoever had named Lille there would have been looked upon as malignant. What we are to do if we should take the city no man that I meet with can divine, for taking the citadel or blockading it are thought equally impracticable.

The death of Mr. Auverquerque is looked upon as a great loss, because it is hardly to be imagined that a successor can be found of as much credit in his country, and as obsequious to our Prince, as he was.

Lord Wharton has received the submissive protestations of Lord Treasurer with all possible scorn and contempt. He says he knows very well it was his last stake, and that he could subsist no longer without them, and he will at last not go in so far with Sir William as he endanger the credit he and his party are possessed of with the people. It is said my Lord T— cannot prevail to have Lord Somers President, though he has endeavoured it heartily.

[DR. W. STRATFORD to ROBERT HARLEY.]

1708, October 15—After much ado all the interest of the clergy on our side is engaged to put up the Dean of Carlisle for their Prolocutor. Willis will be recommended by the Archbishop. The odds on the Dean of Carlisle's side, if all members were present, would not have been, if those first chosen had all lived, above seven. But by the death of the Archdeacon of Canterbury they will now only be five. I know not whether Mr. Archdeacon Griffith, after having declared himself, without occasion, against our side the last election, will think it proper for him to appear for it at this time, but it would be of moment in the election if he could be prevailed with to stay in the country.

[E. LEWIS to ROBERT HARLEY.]

1708, October 22. Whitehall—Sir Edward Northey has observed very well that though they have at last given Sir James [Montagu] the title of Attorney General they can never give him a reputation to support it, which he might have done by the assistance of Chief Justice Holt without committing very gross mistakes, if they had not by this great delay brought his ability to be so nicely scanned.

[The SAME] to the SAME.

Same date and place.—Some thing has lately happened that may put all things into a flame again, which is that the last Holland mail brought advice that the Whig Lords had written several letters to their friends on the other side to advise them to enter seriously upon thoughts of peace, not without very plain insinuations that Lord Mar[lborough] and Lord T[reasurer] would obstruct it. You may very well believe these two princes ill brook other people's interfering with their ministry, but much less to find themselves personally struck at.

Lady M[arlborough] says she would not have condescended to ask the last grant from the Queen, but that it was promised her long before the quarrel with Mrs. Masham.

[The SAME to the SAME.]

1708, October. 28—I must send this to acquaint you that the Prince is dead and the Queen come to St. James's. This morning Dr. Sloane, and the rest of the physicians were of opinion things would have happened otherwise. Thus has the Queen lost her companion. Whoever succeeds in that quality, be it man or woman, will have a greater share in affairs than the last had. The run of the town is already Lord Pemb[roke], Admiral, Somers, President, Ireland for Lord Wharton.

The GLOVERS of LEOMINSTER to ROBERT HARLEY at Brampton Castle.

1708, November 1—We, the Society of Glovers of Leominster having met this day, according to our usual custom to elect a head warden for the next year, and finding that you were admitted freeman of our Society the 24th of September, 1688, have unanimously elected you for the ensuing year, and hope you will be pleased to condescend to do us the honour to accept of it.

Signed by Roger Edwards, head warden, and sixteen others.

[E. LEWIS to ROBERT HARLEY.]

1708, November 2. Whitehall—All acts relating to the marine run, in the Queen's name, are signed by her Majesty, and countersigned by Mr. Burchett.

Mr. Churchill continues in town till the funeral is over, and then retires to Windsor, with an intention not to appear this winter in Parliament.

It was thought at first that the Privy Council would have been named Commissioners, both because an alteration would look like discarding the Prince's servants before he was buried, and that several people might be upon their good behaviour in the winter in hopes of attaining that preferment at the end of the Session, but notwithstanding these reasonings I believe it is otherwise determined, and that the fleet will be entirely in the hands of Lord Or[ford] or his creatures. His Lordship is come to town. The cue is given out to speak contemptibly of Leake, and none but staunched men are to be employed.

The Queen is pretty well and in her own apartment. It is not to be imagined how joyful some men are at the death of the Prince.

H. BOYLE to [ROBERT HARLEY].

1708, November 4. London—The Prince's death will not hinder the Parliament from being opened on the 16th. As well as you and I love the country I can hardly pity any one for coming to town in the middle of November, and therefore cannot be sorry that your journey is like to hold especially since it will sooner give me an opportunity of waiting upon you.

[ABIGAIL MASHAM to ROBERT HARLEY.]

1708, November 6—I thank you for your last, dated the 31st of October, and find by it you have heard of my aunt(the Queen)'s great loss, indeed she is to be pitied upon several accounts, but particularly for the last misfortune of losing all that is dear to her, the only comfort of her life. You know my uncle's life has been very precarious a long time, but

I don't find (though in reason it should) that the expectation of an evil makes it be borne with much more patience when it comes; my good aunt has as much as most people. I hope in God this affliction will have no ill effect upon her health, there is care taken she shall not be alone, for since the misfortune the Lady Pye (Duchess of Marlborough) has hardly left her so long as to let her say her private prayers but stays constantly with her. My Lady's friends say it is fit she should (and they hope she always will), to keep that jade my cousin Kate (Mrs. Masham) from her. Oh my poor aunt is in a very deplorable condition, for now her ready money (courage) is all gone, because I will not trouble you with a melancholy story (give me leave to repeat your own words) she has shut and bolted the door upon herself. Oh what can one say to all these things, when I know what wise and good advice you have given her, and yet she rejects it to satisfy those monsters who she knows will ruin her. When you to come to town I desire you will give me leave to wait upon you and the rest of my good friends, whom I shall have the greatest value for, to the last moment of my life.

[EDWARD HARLEY to his Aunt ABIGAIL HARLEY.]

1708, December 3. Christchurch [Oxford]—I find by the votes that Osborne persists, and that Sir S—— H——t is petitioned against. I hear last night that the Court give out that the House of Commons is to be purged in a little time. No quarter for H———rt, H——ley, and what more of that kidney falls in their way. This has been made use of within these five days to frighten Valiere from petitioning the Parliament or making any noise about the usage he lately met with in Newgate, and lest that should not be of force enough to stop his clack it was intimated that the moment that anything of that kind was done he should be clapt up by an Exchequer writ for owling [i.e. smuggling]. This is all Jehu: too violent to hold, very clever proceedings. They may be called to an account for these matters. O most implacable Hell-hounds!

I hope God, who has so wonderfully preserved our dear friend from their hellish malice and (to use his own words) so miraculously touched the conscience of that unhappy man, that instead of being the chief instrument of his ruin proved the greatest argument of his unspotted reputation, will still continue his mercy to us.

William Paterson I hear was Tuesday voted not duly elected. A great mortification to himself, and an unknown loss to that body to be deprived of so able a projector at this pinch for money, and especially now there is talk of removing Lowndes. If you have not heard the compliment Lord Wharton received upon his Lieutenancy I believe it will please you. The next morning after he had kissed the Queen's hands a Bum comes to the door, asks the porter if my Lord was within, and to tell him, that he came from Lord Sunderland to let his Lordship know that the citadel of Lille was taken. The porter being a man very much of General Read's character, very fond of hearing news and as forward to tell it, as soon as he had received the good news, steps to the next door to inform his acquaintance of it. In the meantime the bailiff, knowing the porter's humour, calls his fellows, and finding the doors ajar, surprised the citadel and seized all within doors, an accident of much the same nature as I am informed is befallen a late Lord Lieutenant of that country, I mean the Duke of O————, the Rapparees having broken in upon him, and continue in possession. I think it is very merry. I should have been concerned if it had happened to anyone except his Lordship; for the latter I am very sorry for, though he does deserve to be used in that manner.

I am very sorry to find that so little of the great news that we rejoiced so much about proves true. People began to suspect a second Oudenarde business. They must have a care, for the people will not now be so easily caught with their shams, the trick has been too often put upon them this campaign. My Lord Mayor served Sir W——— Ashurst very comically about this news. He read him part of an old letter from my Lord Sunderland that he was desired to make the usual rejoicings upon those occasions. He immediately went down- to the Parliament House and buzzed it about that the news was confirmed. They immediately broke up in a great hurry of joy, and when they came out it proved nothing but a bite. I think he served that fellow well enough.

Pray did you take notice in the "Postboy" of Tuesday the twenty-third of November of an address from the clergy of Rapho in Ireland ? I think I never read such fine stuff in my life. It is so seraphic that it is beyond our comprehensions here. If you have it not I will send it you.

I have not heard anything of Mr. H——'s being come to town. I know the ladies are not to stir till he is there. I suppose it will soon be finished. The tongues of the Russilians are very busy in trumpeting it about at all the public places they go to. I wish it was over. I expect every post to hear of your setting forth that I may have the pleasure of seeing you. I am sorry that Mr. Thomas is-likely to be so great a loser, I hear seventy pounds, which is a great deal to lose. I am indeed amazed that any one would trust him, especially one that knew him so well.

The Baronet is of age tomorrow. I expect him here this next week on his way to London. I have told him myself often the same that you write. He has promised me to give himself up to learn French and Latin all this winter. He seems to me very sensible of his misfortune, and is resolved to improve himself what he can. I shall not fail to put him in mind of it when he is here, and I hope he will be so kind to himself as to put that good resolution in execution.

I have long ago transgressed the ordinary limits of a letter, but there is an old saying "over shoes over boots" so I think I shall go on trusting to your good nature for a pardon, and considering you are in the country where you are not either troubled with too much company or diversion, I may hope that my impertinence may be acceptable to you which is the utmost of my ambition. I wish you do not think me a very idle fellow that can find time to scribble my nonsense in such a tedious manner, but I assure you it is the time I generally use for my diversions, and I can never spend it in a more agreeable manner than in conversing with you.

Do you hear who is like to be chosen at Weobly in the room of Mr. Thynne?

I hear now for certain that Mr. Thomas Onslow is married. If I had understood dressing and algebra as well as he says he does, it might perhaps have been his lot to have worn the willow garland, but I am glad it is as it is, and I am where I be; that is what few people can truly say. But I must now put an end to my scrawl. I have gone beyond the rules of modesty. Pray send me your pardon as soon as you can, I shall be uneasy till I have it. I shall send this by London, being I think the safest way.

Postscript.—Pray let me know how you like the enclosed verses. I suppose there will be good store of lampoons this winter in town. I do not doubt but scandal is very rife already. I have one piece of news that

I forgot to acquaint you with before. I was this day told by a gentleman, who had it from a Turkey merchant, that he heard last week that my uncle Natt was very well, and that he was of late fell into such great business that he could scarce be able to get away this four or five years, which I am very sorry for. I hear that coffee will be very cheap, there are two ships laden with coffee just coming in, and several more that are come as far as Lisbon. I take this to be a piece of very good news.

Pray when did you hear of Pantalonians? I have not heard a long time. I hear Neddy is very well. I should ■ glad to know in your next who Mr. Wilkins was to marry. I must now, though against my will, bid you adieu. Pray excuse all errors.

[ABIGAIL HARLEY] to her nephew [EDWARD] HARLEY, at Christ-Church, Oxford.

1708, December 9. [Eywood]—It is trouble enough to me at any time to be forced to take medicines, but it gave me more than ordinary uneasiness Tuesday last that I durst not hold down my head so long as to own the favour received that day from you, which deserves a better pen than mine to make a suitable return. I were unjust not to allow all my acquaintance the advantage in that, but never can any have a more grateful sense of the kindness of my friends. You have in many instances been obliging and beyond expression in that kind epistle, so full of pleasing variety that nothing could be more entertaining. You are in the right, I am neither burdened with company nor news, have hardly seen a strange face since the Governor went, nor heard from any one how the world goes, have not had one letter from London this six weeks, not so much as Lady Glasford think it worth their while to converse in this dull corner, which I can easily forgive, considering most letters are made up either of mere trifles, or, what is worse, foolish reflection and scandal. For my own part have not the least regret for a retired life, so far from that, that I ever thought those most unhappy that could never know how to entertain themselves alone; though no one values the conversation of a friend more, but that must not be in a crowd. By this you will be convinced how fond I am of visiting days or those that have nothing else to do but to make up their scoundrel train, where I will leave them telling as many lies as stories.

It is a difficult thing and what I won't pretend to say, who will be chose at Weobly. To the great joy of that noble corporation there are three candidates. Friday last Mr. Cæsar came there, as it is said with my Lord Weymouth's interest; Saturday Mr. Gorges who has Sergeant Birch's, and Sir John Germain has only sent an agent, who with the help of Captain Charles Cornwall hopes to do wonders. It is certain the best bidder will carry the point. Most think and hope Gorges will be the man, his being the superior interest in the town, and all the gentlemen of the country by letters or otherwise declare themselves his friends. All ours do so, which I do not wonder at, being a likely way to quiet matters in the country and Leominster, which will be a great happiness at present to some you know, as well as a mortification to others. If it be resolved to purge the House of all friends, it must certainly be done by violence, as once it was by scoundrel upstarts, and what may not the sword and purse when united do? When one considers the vile principles as well as practices of our noble Patriots, it gives just cause to fear heaven is provoked to give us up to be ruined by this generation. I must own the affair we were so nearly concerned in last winter, gave me many an uneasy hour, could not help often reflecting upon Sir Walter Raleigh's case; if you do not remember it, at your leisure may find it in any history of King James the first. I hope the mercy of God to our friend will never be forgotten by any of the family, who so wonderfully preserved him from the most inveterate rage that has for many ages been expressed. I trust the same goodness will follow him all the days of his life, and cannot but hope that yet the time will come when his innocence will be as apparent as their malice. Have you seen the papers I undertook to convey to you? It is what I long to do and am resolved to solicit the Governor for. I have not heard a word of Mr. H—— since what I mentioned to you, am a little vexed about that affair, lest it prove any prejudice to one we all love so entirely, and all owing to womanish spite that could find no other way of being revenged for the disappointment of her own silly chimera, but by making her the subject of her chat. Though others that are wiser do, I cannot entertain a thought that persons can have any dishonourable design who acted so generously in the matter from the first: who is in the right time will show. I very seldom, of late, hear from the Pantalonians, am afraid their circumstances are very bad, which often troubles me; she would take it very kindly if you did write a letter to enquire after her. The most ungrateful news I have heard a long time is what you tell me of your uncle N—— (the fall of coffee is no equivalent). He must renounce his name if grown covetous, that crime has not yet been charged upon them. It is a melancholy thing always to be in expectation of seeing one so much beloved, and the longer one lives to find the time still at a greater distance. I have never been so ill satisfied with my fate as to wish myself of the better sex but in this case, that I might make him a visit, which I certainly would have done long ere this. I heartily wish the gentleman much joy that wanted foppery and skill in algebra to carry the fortune, do not doubt but some better is reserved for him. I cannot help mentioning last night was completed eight years since your good grandfather went to heaven. May all that bear his name, yourself most particularly, inherit his accomplishments both as a gentleman and christian. I am glad my thoughts agree with yours as to the Baronet. It is in your power to influence him more than any one else, who I am sure will improve that advantage to his good. The lady I heard Mr. Wilkins was to marry is my Lord Ferrers' fifth daughter. Since you thought fit to make excuses for the most diverting letter I have seen a long time, what must I say for blotting so much paper, and what is worse taking up so much of your precious time? I own and blush for my faults, but dare not promise amendment, which is a lamentable case, being conscious to myself that I shall certainly be scribbling again; when you are weary tell me so. I did not see the address from Bogland, am pleased with the verses and thank you for them. Adieu.

[EDWARD HARLEY to his Aunt ABIGAIL HARLEY.]

1708, December 15. Christchurch [Oxford]—I hear that the Court lost the Reading election contrary to all expectation, by a majority of about forty. Saturday the committee voted six per cent. interest for money to be advanced upon the land tax, which was used to be but five, and it was observed that Mr. Lechmere, my Lord W[harto]n's creature, opposed, so I perceive that he is not yet satisfied. He will make them submit to him yet. He swore some time since that he would unmask them quite, as I do not doubt he will. I hear a white staff will not do

Lord Manchester's business, he must have a post that will reimburse the extraordinary expenses he has been at in his embassies, it is therefore talked that he will have the places of Mr. Howe and Mr. Bridges in as large and ample a manner as Lord R——gh enjoyed them, and I do not doubt will tell the money as carefully over his grate as the other did over his. I fancy Mr. Br—— will scarcely be outed, because he has been at the bottom of all the cheating of a certain great man.

The Weobly people will have a rare time of it, I hear Mr. Cæsar was sent down by my Lord Weymouth. He refused to send down Mr. St. John: he was very much solicited to do it. I hope he will lose his interest by it, and that Mr. Gorges will carry it. I think his Lordship has shewn himself very weak in this affair. I should scarcely have acted as he has done in this case.

[Sir Simon Harcourt to Robert Harley.]

1708, December 20—I have this day fully discoursed Mr. Medlicot. He had been pressed for Cæsar [Weobly election], but could never engage his brother for a professed enemy of the Chancellor [Cowper]. He seems not to doubt his brother's consent for Harry St. John, but Sir Thomas Travaile declares he will set up his son, and much pressed Medlicot for his consent, which he was told would never be given. Mr. Medlicot hopes he may succeed if St. John appear in it; he hinted to me somewhat of a gratuity to Travell (*sic*), or to be otherwise disposed of to secure the election. I told him that was so dangerous I could not enter into it; he said he would take it upon himself whatever happened.

Has Harry no one in the army who can govern Travaile, and make this whole matter out of dispute?

[Henry St. John to Sir S. Harcourt.]

1708, December 20—Sir Godfrey Copley sent to me this morning; his business was to let me know that he had reason to believe that there would be little difficulty in bringing me into Parliament for Milborne Port. He says he has spoken with Medlicot, and that in short 200*l.* given to Travell would unite the whole interest and put the matter out of dispute.

I will make no reflexions upon this intelligence, but leave the fact with you. It is in my opinion of very small importance whether I am in parliament or not, but I would leave nothing undone which my friends seem to expect from me.

[Sir Simon Harcourt] to Robert Harley.

No date—I send you the enclosed [*see* last letter and that of January 20, *post*] that you may take what care you think proper of our friend Harry. I am unalterably fixed to come no more into the House of Commons unless I am brought thither in custody. I am not wise enough to advise Harry what to do. Perhaps the triumph over me might make them easier to him, but I should be grieved to think he sat a minute at their pleasure. There will be a controversy with out doubt about this election, and I must suspect there will be at least as much ground for a petition as there was at Abingdon. You will discourse with Medlicot. I have written to Harry and told him I refer him to your advice on this occasion.

[Sir Thomas Mansell] to Robert Harley.

1708, December 23—My Lady Giggster was pleased to send her page yesterday to my house with a good morrow. I am just now told that my Lord Queensbury is to be sole secretary for Scotland, and that he used this expression " God damn my wife and children if I will not go into the Junto." If he swears like John of Gaunt then this may not be true, though it comes from Lord Wharton's privy Councillor.

Edward Harley to his father [Robert Harley].

1708, December 20, Christchurch—I was not willing to trouble you while you were sick, am very glad to hear that you have got rid of your indisposition.

The Doctor has sent you an account of my expenses here for the last half year. I am extremely ashamed of the two articles that have so great a share in it; I mean what's paid to the bookseller and bookbinder, I have nothing to say in excuse for my fault, but only that as it is the first of this sort that ever I was guilty of, so I assure you it shall be the last.

I gave Mr. Broxholme two guineas for the Ode that is printed in the Oxford verses with my name.

You was pleased once to promise me a set of razors ; if you please to order Mr. Thomas to send them down the expense of a barber will be needless.

[Thomas Harley] to [Edward] Harley.

[1708], December 30. [London ?]—I sent you a little snuff in a bottle, and now I send you a taste of another sort to see which you like best. I do not pretend to write you news because what is material you have from a better hand. Everybody here talks of peace, but the reasoners differ exceedingly, some say all circumstances are so fair that it is impossible to fail of making peace, others say the public will be able one way or other to furnish supplies for one campaign more, and therefore it is foolish to expect an end of the war till that is over, beside the party that is founded upon war, and a senseless jargon of France Jesuits and an invisible army of 100,000 pilgrims mounted upon elephants, have not yet acquired power enough to support themselves in that most difficult and slippery state of peace. Madam Mindelheim is going over to take care of her husband, lest he should be drawn in to consent to what is so contrary to the interest and temper of the sober people of the nation.

Pray tell his Eminence I once designed to call on him to draw his pen in defence of his order, but the designs are so open that I hope he will not have much trouble, for even the moderate divines begin to start. They whilst they had to do with the polite part of the clergy one common saying served their turn (those men are too learned to have much grace), but now finding so much favour shown to their brethren of the city, who pretend to no more learning than themselves but to a great deal more grace, these moderate divines begin to think their case somewhat desperate, and their preferment doubtful ; and reason good for if an Independent or a pale-faced Baptist will do the work for which they were designed more effectually, there is an end of my moderate divine at once.

I pray God give his Eminence patience to bear this cold weather, and may it be the greatest affliction he ever meets with.

J. G[assion, *alias* Ogilvie] to Robert Bryan (Harley).

1708–9, January 1—My old friend Fargison (Ferguson or Farquharson) we have had him twice at Mr. Dunster's, but said but little to him at first, for we must take care that he have no suspicions, for he is as subtle as a fox; therefore we will draw him on by degrees.

But I have a notion in my head and if you approve of it, it shall be as pleasant as a comedy to you. The thing is Charles Dunster shall invite Fargison any night, and if you'll take your chair without a footman I shall come for you where you may be in the next room; there shall be a good fire and the room is warm, so that I hope you shall not catch cold, and there you shall hear Charles fall on the politics with him and you shall hear every word he says, and he know nothing of the matter. Charles will take care to make him as drunk as a beggar, and then you may hear him give his sentiments of everybody and everything. I should be glad to speak to you to have your opinion of something my Lady Mackan (*sic*) told me.

[Henry St. John to Sir Simon Harcourt.]

1708–9, January 20—This is the first moment, dearest Sym, in which I have grieved that I am not in parliament. I know too well the characters of men, and the circumstances of time, to imagine that any solicitation or any argument could have prevented the resolution which has been taken, but methinks it is no small misfortune to be quiet here whilst my friend is under persecution. At least I might have had some share in exposing what I could not help, and if you are to be thrown out I might have provoked them to expel me in so good company. Before this letter comes to your hands, you will know your doom. I expect it from your friendship that if you are to go out, care may be taken that I may not come in; for God's sake consent to be chosen at the place now intended for me, and let me take my chance in another. Besides the advantage to the public, there would be this private pleasure in making such a turn, that perhaps no greater mortification can be given to some people who deserve the greatest. I have written to others upon this subject, and I conjure you once more by all our friendship to give way to it. I declare to you that if you refuse me no consideration shall prevail on me to stand.

Edward Harley to his aunt Abigail Harley at Eywood.

1708–9, January 30—The determination of the Abingdon election has made a great noise in town, both parties are liberal of ill names to them. Sir S. H[arcourt] they say called a great man rogue and rascal as they construe his words, which were to this effect, " A person that has long since abandoned all truth, justice, honour, honesty, gratitude &c." I think this is pretty plain. I hear that the Dream was made use of as an argument for the motion of giving thanks to his Grace. Lord William P[aule]t said that he was sure *somebody* was the author of it, a discovery worthy of his Lordship's penetration. Though the taking notice of that libel was said to be contrary to the direction of the persons thought to be most concerned in it yet

Mr. Lechmere's zeal could not forbear it on that occasion. He, I hear, explained it all, and said that it ought to be censured, but the House burst out in a loud laugh and nothing was determined that way. They have had the impudence to move an address to the Queen to marry. Sir David Dalrymple said he thought it was time enough, but they carried it, and the Lords have joined with them. I hear my cousin Thomas Foley exerted himself very much at the Abingdon election, but nobody so much as a *friend of ours* who, I hear, had very high words with Lord Coningsby and, they say, the Lady Scudamore has not forgot. I believe the expressions he used there are the occasion of Mr. Montague's moving an address to the Queen that she will be pleased to order the production of the papers relating to Greg, from his first apprehension to his death. This was seconded by the great Lord William Paulet. This will give him [Harley] an opportunity to clear himself of several impertinent objections, and, by what I hear, I believe he designs it, having put a petition to the Queen into Mr. Secretary Boyle's hands to pray her Majesty's leave to make use of such papers that may be necessary for his justification, in case anything be objected to him on that occasion. I hope he will not only make his innocence appear in that House but publish it to the whole world. This is all the news that I have except that coffee grows cheaper every day. I cannot meet with any tolerable Spanish snuff here, and the little I had is quite gone. If I should send you any Oxford snuff you would not be able to take it. I beg your pardon for being so long and impertinent.

— VALIERE to ROBERT HARLEY.

1708–9, January 31—Begs advice about the papers taken from him by Mr. Hopkins, Lord Sunderland's secretary, viz. a little bag of acquittances and receipts, a note of three pounds, the copy of the patent of his " fridenization " and two little blank books. Had written to Mr. Hopkins but had had no answer notwithstanding his promise to return them safe.

[ABIGAIL HARLEY] to her Aunt ABIGAIL HARLEY, at Eywood.

1708–9, February 1—My aunt told me your great concern and has promised to convey this safe to you. My father writ word that Lord W. Paulet moved it in the House, and was seconded by one James Morgan of Wiltshire; he did not apprehend they could fix anything on him, but for fear of the worst was busy preparing papers, and hoped that business would now appear in a true light. I heard this day from Oxon that our dear friend has put a petition in Secretary Boyle's hand, to pray Her Majesty to give him leave to use of such papers as shall be necessary to his vindication, in case anything should be objected against him. There was no letter from him to-day, but Mynat with the news writ that it was then almost 12 o'clock, the House still sitting on Sir Edward Turner's election who (it was thought) would have the same fate as Sir S[imon] H[arcourt]. I cannot but have many fears and uneasy thoughts when I consider the implacable rage and malice of our enemies, but then our comfort is that that God who governs the world and has all hearts in His hand, has wonderfully protected and appeared for us, and it is to His mercy and goodness that we must trust, humbly imploring His protection, and that He will give us hearts to submit to what He sees best. The remembrance of former mercies is a great encouragement.

[W. Thomas to Edward Harley at Oxford.]

1708–9, February 3—I mentioned in one of my former letters a petition, the answer was read this day from the same hand, with free leave to make use of what was desired. It is talked pretty publicly that the design of bringing on that affair at this time is if possible to get a handle for clearing the house of so troublesome a person. But I believe that will be hardly attempted. Some of their people have been squeamish in the late extravagant determinations. All the cases since in dispute they say were more scandalous if possible than that of Abingdon. A certain Gatt that was not thought likely to boggle at such practices has absented himself from the question at the late elections and expressed great dissatisfaction at such violent proceedings, and ordered an acquaintance of his to assure a certain gentleman that if any such thing should be attempted as is above mentioned, he should never come into it. I am told Mr. Thornhagh, member for Nottinghamshire, thought to be a thorough man, does not like what has been lately done; which I take the more notice of because some years ago, it was thought there was a great hardship put upon him in the election of East Retford, when he and Mr. White were turned out by another set of men. Sir John G[ui]se has expressed a dissatisfaction and divided against his friends. An honourable person that serves for a city not 20 miles from B——n is a thorough stitch voter. Lord Man——r has declared within this week that he does not know of anything intended for him. The Whigs swear Lord Halifax shall be Treasurer. I shall trouble you with no more, I am afraid I have writ already more than you can read.

H[enry] Boyle, Secretary of State, to Robert Harley.

1708[-9], February 3. Whitehall—I have laid before the Queen the petition you sent me in your letter of January 26, and am to acquaint you that her Majesty does allow you to give such accounts and produce such papers to the House of Commons relating to the examinations of William Greg and the proceedings thereupon, as you shall think necessary for your justification, in case anything should be objected to you.

[Abigail Harley] to her nephew Edward Harley, at Christ Church, Oxford.

1708-9, February 7—I hope some have made a scourge for themselves and that our friend has now an opportunity of making his own innocence and their malice appear, though I am confident that was least designed by the wise managers.

To use the old stag's phrase for once, 'twould make a dog die with laughing, to think of the Matrimonial Address, which looks like the result of a consultation of superannuated women rather than senators, since they won't allow her Majesty the decent retirement that all the sex may justly claim upon such occasions; will never give her the liberty of choice. How glad would some of their wives be to have it in their power thus to revenge themselves when they were hardly cold in their graves. Methinks the next step shall be to make it penal for anyone to live a month a widow, which I hope would not want the R[oyal] assent.

I hear Mr. Ambler is dead, so great place fallen which is in Mr. Walcot's gift. Mr. Davies of Bucknell is said to stand fair for it. There is great writing and scouring about among the clergy upon these vacancies.

Maunt was here yesterday ; if your ears burned now know the occasion. I could not persuade her to stay one night.

[W. THOMAS to EDWARD HARLEY at Oxford.]

1708-9, February 15—The Ministry were extremely alarmed yesterday morning upon a sham letter writ to Lord W. Paulet Saturday night, that the Tories were to assemble all their forces in order to move an address to the Queen to invite over the next Protestant heir. This was communicated to Mr. Secretary B. who returned the noble Lord formal thanks for his information and imparted it to the Treasurer. And yesterday they drew up in order of battle in expectation of a violent attack, and now the report goes very current that there was a design to have surprised the Whigs with that motion, and but few know the true grounds of it. I could not inform myself last post what passed in the house at the delivering of the papers concerning Greg. When the titles of them were read my master stood up and said he believed there was a paper among them which he thought none in the house had seen except the honourable person that presented them and himself, viz. Greg's confession, which he therefore desired might be read, and it was accordingly. Then he stood up and gave an account of the discovery, apprehension, and conviction of Greg and said that if any member desired any further information he was ready to answer any questions for their satisfaction having obtained her Majesty's leave for that purpose. But not one person spoke a word and so they were of course ordered to lie on the table. And now they are mad that ever they were ordered to be brought in and they have reason. I forgot whether I acquainted you last post with what Lord Halifax said to a certain person that morning. However you will forgive me rather if I repeat it than if I should omit it. He ordered him to assure [Harley] that there was no design in it, that it was resolved at a drunken bout between Lord William and Sir W. St—k—d. This appears now to have been no design and indeed I thought so from the beginning. I am told there are very great heats between the Treasurer and his new friends.

EDWARD HARLEY to his Aunt ABIGAIL HARLEY.

[1709,] February 18. [Oxford]—When I wrote to you last I had no account how the papers relating to G[reg] were received in the House. I suppose by this time you have heard, but I hope you will pardon me if I send you the advices I had of it. They came in early on Saturday morning, our friend was there, and when the titles of them were read, our friend stood up and said he believed there was a paper among them which none of the House had seen, except the honourable person that presented them and himself, viz., Greg's confession, which he therefore desired might be read, and was accordingly. Then he stood up and gave an account of the discovery, apprehension, and conviction of Greg, and said that if any member desired any further information, he was ready to answer any questions for their satisfaction, having obtained Her Majesty's leave for that purpose. But not one person spoke a word, and so they were of course ordered to lie upon the table. And

now they are mad they were ordered to be brought in, and I think they have reason : what great cause have we to adore the great and wonderful mercy that God has showed to a poor family !

I hear that the morning the papers were brought in Lord Halifax said to a certain person and ordered him to tell Mr. Harley and assure him that there was no design in it, that it was resolved at a drunken bout between Lord William and Sir William S[trickland]. I have very little faith in his lordship, and I believe it was only to keep him from coming soon to the House, and that he might not be prepared, and though it is thought by our friend and some more to have been without any design, yet I cannot think it, Sir William S[trickland] being in it, for I know there passed very high words between our friend and the knight at Sir Simon Harcourt's election, whose speech by the bye I have sent you, shall be glad to have your opinion of it in your next; it is so sadly wrote am afraid you won't be able to read it. I have forgot whether I told you in my last who I meant by the squeamish gentleman I mentioned in one of my former letters; it was Sir Harry Peachy. The ministry was extremely alarmed on Monday upon a sham letter wrote to Lord William Paulet Saturday night that the Tories were to assemble all their forces in order to move an Address to the Queen to invite over the next Protestant heir. This was communicated to Mr. Secretary B[oyle] who returned the noble Lord formal thanks for his information and imparted it to the Treasurer; and on Monday drew up in order of battle in expectation of a violent attack. And now the report goes that there was a design to have surprised the Whigs with that motion, and few know the true grounds of it. I am told there are great heats between the Treasurer and his new friends ; I fancy we shall see great changes soon. I hear the Bishop of Salisbury has married Mrs. Mohun. They may cry about the hasty widower as well as the hasty widow : I think it is a little scandalous for a Bishop to be in such haste.

[William Thomas to Edward Harley.]

1708-9, March 8—You will see by Saturday's votes that Greg's papers were dropped, none of the gentlemen that were so noisy for bringing them in having thought fit to open their mouths about them, though there was a design to have put them off to another day and so to have kept them in the votes. But Mr. Bromley desired that since those papers were brought in as reflecting upon an honourable member of the House, they might then go into the consideration of them. At which Mr. Boscawen was very angry, and said he knew nobody they reflected upon. Then Mr. Secretary Boyle said, there was nothing in them, and he was of opinion that the House should not be troubled with them another day. My master said he hoped he had satisfied gentlemen when these papers were first brought in, and he was now ready to give the House any further satisfaction, and therefore desired they might be then proceeded upon; that he could not carry these gentlemen's attestation about to persuade people that there was nothing in them as long as they appeared in their votes. And so the House seeming entirely satisfied that there was nothing in them, they were unanimously dropped. I hope this will have a good effect and that —— [Harley] will make use of the Queen's leave to make these papers public.

I send you some mere scandal. You will easily find out the key of the poetry I send you, unless it be the two facts hinted in p. 7. The one pointing at a letter deciphered at the time of the Scotch plot, the other Madame Le Croy's answer when consulted by the cat about her fortune, which I suppose you and the Doctor have heard of.

ABIGAIL HARLEY to her Aunt ABIGAIL HARLEY, at Eywood.

1709, March 29. London—I hear her Grace designs building a house in Mr. Boyle's garden, to-day they were measuring the ground, and sent to all of that side the Pall Mall to pull down the mounts in their gardens that look over into it. The person that told me says they wonder she will build there, because it is so near her, she may hear everybody curse her as they go by. It is reported about that the Duke said to Lord Stair he did not know whether he should send for him to make this campaign. They talk mightily of peace, sure there is something in it, this he said. Methinks this is a blind way of talking for one that knows it is in his power to make peace or continue the war. My mother it seems sent the paper to you that I mentioned in my last. I think it is too severe upon one that is reduced to the misfortune of not being able to remedy those evils that they are sharers of as well as others, and can only be grieved for them. Our dear friend has a very bad cold and cough, finds good by the oil, has lived on gruel these two days, I am sorry is gone out to-day. I must now conclude, will thank the Governess for hers next post ; duty and service as due.

When I ended I was called down to dinner, and now have time to write a little more and send you some snush (sic). Sir Thomas Mansell has sent me a strong recruit, I will send you more another time if you like it. Dr. Gastrell was here to-day, he goes to Oxford to-morrow; I suppose will make no long stay there. I believe you will be glad the mourning will be left off. We can laugh now at those that were in such haste to buy. I wonder at two ladies to clothe themselves in white that can look clean in nothing, if that money were laid out in soap were it not better. I forgot to write you word that before I left Brampton I took occasion to tell a certain person about having no prayers in their family ; they utterly denied it, and said they had them constantly. Mr. Nevill who made a speech this session against my father and reflected on him about Greg's business, and when that was brought in spoke for him ; you know he is a great Whig. I think we can never enough admire the goodness of God in that affair. This session there was a letter sent to Lord William that on such a day the Tories intended to mention in the House of Commons the bringing the Princess Sophia and her son, and his Lordship being a great defender of the liberties of the nation, they could not address themselves to any one more able and proper to prevent so great a mischief. Immediately this epistle was sent to Volpone he sends thanks to him, a meeting was appointed, all their forces came into the House, and after some time one came to our friend and asked when the great gun was to go off. He said he knew nothing of it, thought it was only the fears of their own guilty consciences. I think this a very good banter as ever I heard. My cousin Popham presents his duty. Adieu.

THE SAME to ABIGAIL HARLEY, at Eywood.

1709, April 19. London—I hear there is a new paper comes out three times a week called the Tatler. I have seen none yet. If they are worth anything will send them you. He resolves to put in all the stories of the town, warns the gentlemen and ladies to behave themselves well. He has given an earnest that he will perform his promise, for he put in the story of Lord Hinchinbrooke coming Thursday night drunk to the playhouse, in a sad pickle, and there railed against marriage in a strange manner. His title was not put in but there were spectators enow to tell everybody who it was.

I cannot help giving you an account of the Treason Bill though it will be an imperfect one: the Governor must inform you better. It is that which in the Votes is called making the Union more complete. It is to alter the manner of trying them in the North; it overturns all their laws. The Lords passed it, sent it down to the Commons. There it passed two readings, and to make the best of a bad matter they added this clause, that in England as it was in Scotland estates should not be forfeited in cases of treason. The amendment was debated by the Lords and they added that that clause should not take place till after the Pretender's death, and so it passed yesterday in the Commons, which will make it of no effect at all. Our friend took a great deal of pains about it, they did not imagine his interest in the House so good as to bring in the clause, it vexed them dreadfully, and yesterday they assembled all their forces, the lame and blind and all, and yet it was carried but by six. It will make a great confusion in Scotland; every man of them was against the Bill; they may see how well the Court has rewarded them for acting all this session contrary to justice, honour, and honesty to serve it. I hope their eyes will be open now and they may be sensible who are friends to their country, for they have all along opposed those gentlemen that now would have served them. One says they have been like a pack of hounds following a huntsman; all are very angry now. The prevailing party had not one word of sense to say, but made long speeches. Mr. Ireton said those that were guilty of treason were men that had estates or that wanted estates, men of principles or no principles. I could say a great deal for I have heard abundance on it from everybody, but I won't tire you, for I find I have given but a blind account, being not capable of stating the matter as I should do.

They say the parliament will be up on Thursday.

DR. HUMFREY GOWER to ROBERT HARLEY.

1709, May 20. St. John's College, Cambridge—A very deserving person, Mr. Newcome, master of arts and fellow of this college, is a candidate for the school lately erected at Rochester for grammar and mathematics according to a provision made by the will of Sir Joseph Williamson. The salary will be about 100l. per annum. Mr. Newcome is at present in that city, and finds good encouragement among the electors. He is of note and eminence among us as a general scholar, likewise a very good man, well tempered, grave and serious much above his years, with very good faculties and genius for an instructor, apt to teach, communicative, and easily to be understood, a qualification very desirable but not always to be met with in those who undertake such employments. I am told one Captain Boys, one of Sir Joseph's executors, will have the greatest sway in this election, and that he will easily be determined by yourself, Lord Nottingham, or Lord Jersey; I have the honour to be known to all those excellent persons, but apply only to yourself.

A young man, but bachelor of arts, is set up by Trinity College for this place, and had the start of Mr. Newcome by about a week; but sure that will not give him precedence in a case of this nature against such a one as Mr. Newcome.

[ABIGAIL MASHAM to ROBERT HARLEY.]

1709, August 9th—I received yours by Mr. Davenant and also that by Mrs. Banks very safe, and desire I may not burn the first, till I have read it to my friend (the Queen), who wants such good instructions, and though she has had the same advice last year yet I think it cannot be too often repeated to one that shows so little courage and resolution as she has hitherto done. I have a great mind to go to London to see you before you leave that place, but shall not be able to compass that design till about the 24th of this month. Since you intend to have your wedding very private it will not be proper to give any favours to anybody, for that does not agree with a private wedding. As for your writing a letter for me to show my friend you had better not do it, for I fear she will be afraid of being examined about it, so I dare answer she would much rather know nothing of the matter, I have often spoken to her concerning Lord T's office, but never could obtain a satisfactory answer. If I cannot be so happy to secure it for you I won't attempt doing it myself. I thank God my girl is well.

JAMES CRESSETT to [ROBERT HARLEY].

1709, August 27. Cheam—I hope you are persuaded that I sincerely rejoice in all things that happen to the advantage of your person and family. The merit of your daughter was too well known for her to fail of an honourable establishment, but according to the reputation of both Lords, the father and son, you could not dispose of her better than you have done.

I am not surprised at the base and unworthy treatment which you have met with from such persons who can never forgive your having obliged them in too high a degree, however I think you ought not to despair of being forgiven by God and all honest men for having served them too well, provided you repent of it sincerely and make a steady resolution never to do so any more; party malice in a factious country supplies all defects, and whoever is well stocked with that and impudence needs no other qualification. I am trying how long and how well I can live upon this air, which is mightily celebrated for health. I have not yet waited upon the parson of Banstead though my next neighbour, but I intend to go take a lesson of contentment from him, who is remarkable for being the only clergyman in England that is satisfied, except his Grace at Lambeth. There is so much iniquity both in the foreign and domestic mysteries, that I'm afraid your time will hardly permit you to see the unravelling of it before your return to London.

LORD HAVERSHAM to [ROBERT HARLEY].

1709, September 5—I am as sensible as any man can be, of the present temper this nation is in, and could give many instances how much you are in the right, some too very personal, were it necessary; and as to our poverty, how low so ever we are sure there are some who think we are not yet poor enough, or else they would never have brought a new charge upon us. I cannot say we are hated and abhorred, but I may perhaps think some persons, however courted or b-——d (sic) and made use of, are at the same time contemned and despised at bottom abroad, and not valued at home. As for pride it must be a great judgment to any nation to have those in it who are too great for subjects, and can never be sovereigns, I mean *de jure* not *de facto*, without the subversion of a Constitution and in such cases, (I do not say it is our own) what is gained is lost, and whatever the subject has more than he ought the Sovereign has less than he should, which very often makes the one insult, and the other comply, more than otherwise they would, a state of things very threatening, and sometimes fatal, if not timely prevented. Our preliminary Articles not consented to by the Emperor show how conscientious we are in not making a separate Peace, and whatever may be now hatching I can't but fear Spain is lost. There is a worse circumstance to me than all this, a spirit of distrust, separation and distance among those who remain untainted, which if removed it were easy in a very short time, to see things all set upon a safer foot than in my opinion you seem to be at present both for Prince and People. I may be mistaken in all and am contented after so long being in Parliament to come there very little.

[ABIGAIL MASHAM to ROBERT HARLEY.]

1709, September 4—My friend (the Queen)will not consent to my going from hence till I go to lie in, which will not be till the middle of this month, the soonest, for she says I am so near my time the journey may disorder me so much that I may not be able to come hither again, and for that reason she won't let me go. I did not write you this before because I have been in hopes every day of bringing her to give me leave, and what made me the more desirous was that I might have had an opportunity of waiting upon my Lady Dupplin to wish her an uninterrupted life of happiness and contentment. I know you are so just as to believe you have not a friend in the world more heartily rejoices at her being so well disposed of than myself, and all people are satisfied of it, my enemies are so very angry at it. I can't tell you what use my friend has made of the advice was given her in your letter, but she heard it over and over. She keeps me in ignorance and is very reserved, does not care to tell me any thing. I asked her if she had gratified my Lord R[ochester] in what he desired; she answered, yes, he was very well satisfied but told me no more. I shall tell her what you said to Mr. Masham when I have an opportunity. You may venture to write anything and direct for him, perhaps they will not have the curiosity to open his letters; but make use of the names you sent me. I am very uneasy not to see you before you leave London but it is impossible for me to do it. Mr. M[asham] presents his most humble [service] to you and we both wish you a good journey, and safe back again.

WILLIAM PATERSON to [ROBERT HARLEY].

1709, September 7. Windsor—I take this opportunity by my good friend Mr. John Kemp to tell you that after a long and dangerous fit of sickness I am now here in good health. Very few knew I was so ill as I was, but among those I find I have been better beloved and much more regarded than I durst have presumed to think without experience. They carried me to a place down in Kent during my illness, and after my recovery I took a lodging here, as well for benefit of the air and riding and walking out as for business I have at present depending.

I congratulate you upon the new alliance betwixt your family and one of very good substance and repute in North Britain.

I hope to be favoured with an opportunity to wait on you once, in fourteen days or as soon after as you shall come to town.

[ABIGAIL MASHAM to ROBERT HARLEY.]

1709, September 14—I am very glad to find mine came safe to your hands for I was in some pain about it hearing nothing from you till yesterday. My aunt (the Queen) will not let me go from hence yet, for the reason I acquainted you of in my last, besides, now she is afflicted with very sore eyes which makes her mighty melancholy, together with the thoughts of Lady Pye[the Duchess of Marlborough]'s being to be near her this night and is to stay as long as my aunt does, this is what my Lady's eldest daughter gives out. I have heard the same thing of the second child which you write of, and have mentioned it to my aunt, who says she will never consent to it, but her saying that does not put me out of fears; for you and I know my aunt has made resolutions often and they have prevailed with her to break them, and they have too much reason to depend upon that weakness in my poor aunt. Mr. Safe would have seen you instead of this messenger, but I being out of order, he did not care to leave me; and you may write freely your mind and send it by the bearer who is an honest servant of ours, and we send him because he is very trusty and careful. I have ordered him to deliver the letter as soon as he gets to town and call for an answer when you shall command him. I wish you a good journey.

LORD HAVERSHAM to [ROBERT HARLEY].

1709 September 15., Richmond—I can make no other return to your letter of the 12th inst. than a firm and sincere resolution never to abuse or forfeit the confidence you have honoured me with. I would give you an immediate instance how much I rely upon it, by an openness becoming the sense I have of so valuable an obligation, were I certain this letter would not lose its way. I shall therefore reserve that till I wait upon you, at a time when the contingencies of the campaign will be over and one may be able to take a better view of schemes, operations and actions, and how far men are changed from a privative nonchalance to a positive concern for the public, a spirit I fear too noble and generous for our northern clime, especially too in so unhappy a situation where we want the blessing of a warm and ripening sun.

DR. STRATFORD to [EDWARD HARLEY].

1709, September 21—Soon after you left Oxford I had a visit from a very sensible, accomplished young gentleman, Mr. St. Coef. I am sure you must have heard of his father, who is Burgomaster of Rotterdam. The young gentleman is newly come to England. He bewailed the loss of their troops in the late carnage, but said the States were more concerned at the spirit the French had gained by the late battle, than at their own loss. When he left Holland all were of opinion that the apprehension of troubles in the North would determine the States to make a peace. A friend who came from London the same day told me that he had met last week in different places with Mr. Fletcher of Saltoun and Colonel Hunter, both lately come from Holland. Both happened to speak how much the Duke of Marlborough's interest was sunk in Holland and to give the very same reasons for it. They said the first thing that had lessened his interest there was his attempt to be Vicar General. But that which had given the great blow to his interest was his quarrel with Mr. Harley.

G. GRANVILLE to [ROBERT HARLEY].

1709, September 22—I will not fail to observe your directions in regard to the Duke of Beaufort, and am much mistaken if this alteration in his condition should make any alteration in him. But you must give me leave to say I must have some assistance to confirm him in such notions as I may have opportunities to advance, by introducing him as occasion may happen to proper acquaintance. There must be a confidence created among some persons, and a knowledge of one another's intentions, or everything will lie loose. You may depend upon it that I will omit nothing in my power that may contribute to the ends you desire, for whose service I shall ever have an inseparable attache (*sic*).

I am much mistaken if I cannot likewise answer in the same manner for the friend with whom I am, notwithstanding any suggestions that may have been, &c. We constantly remember you, I can't say in our prayers, for I fear we don't all pray, but in our cups, for we all drink, and when our hearts are most open, your image is most conspicuous.

Postscript.—I beg leave to present my most humble service to your whole family. I can't say (Collier ?) is entirely in the land of the living, for it is his hour of being very drunk, but as much of him as lives is entirely devoted to you.

[SIR THOMAS MANSELL to ROBERT HARLEY.]

1709, September 26. Margam—This comes to welcome you home, I fear after the worst roads and weather that have been known this time of the year; and 'tis well you came as you did, for we have had such storms and floods all last week and especially Sunday that I am a very great sufferer both by the sea and rivers, which I must endeavour to patch up immediately, else shall lose considerably. I intended to have waited on you this year at Brampton, but the season is so far spent, and I have so much to do here that 'will be impossible for me to be happy in your company till I come to town, which at present I don't design till towards the end of November.

When I first heard that we lay upon the field of battle, concluded our victory could not be great, when we contented ourselves with that single honour; and could a great man have found in his heart to have parted with intelligence money, they would either have fought two days before or two days after they did. Peace is what I long to see, and so we have it 'tis no matter what they have done; but I'll never believe we shall have one, till the war can no longer be carried on.

Our harvest is not near in, and the crops especially wheat but indifferent, so that our country without the assistance of Palatines will go near to be starved before the year comes about.

ABEL BOYER to ROBERT HARLEY.

1709, October 18—Be pleased to give me leave to congratulate your safe return, and to acquaint you that some body has been before hand with me in publishing a journal of the Duke of Marlborough's campaign in Germany: I mean however only as to the title; for upon perusal of this journal, I find it to be no more than a lame abstract of public papers. Therefore if your honour will be pleased to countenance my design, I despair not of performing something less unworthy of my Lord Marlborough's great actions, and more acceptable to the public. I hope you will not be displeased with the reading of the enclosed letter, which I have caused to be printed, not only because it gives a clearer account of some passages in the battle of Blenheim than any we have hitherto seen, but also because some expressions in it are as good as a large panegyric upon the English conduct and valour. *Quod si ab hoste doceri fas sit, quin et laudari?*

Sir Simon Harcourt to [Robert Harley].

1709, October 22. Norfolk Street—I lately received a letter from Peer Rivers, by which I see you have made him believe I am much more considerable than I am. He desires to hear from you. I have catched at this twig, being determined, on some occasion or other, to break in upon your retirement, and give you the best handle I can to let me know you are alive.

Samuel (afterwards Lord) Masham to [Robert Harley].

1709, October 22. Kensington—In obedience to your commands I acquaint you of Mrs. Masham's being brought to bed last Wednesday of a girl.

[Sir Thomas Mansell to Robert Harley.]

1709, November 10—I was happy with yours last night which the fish man brought the Captain, and he to me. I can't yet tell when I shall be in town, but believe it will be the first week in December, and shall call of H. St. John who if I can seduce will bring him along. I reckon the Land Tax will be ready to pass by the middle of next month with which I am content, but if the wisdom of the House gives the Malt for more than one year I should be glad to give my negative, as also to any extraordinary methods of raising men, which perhaps can't be dispensed with till after the holidays, but they may go for what I know hand in hand with money matters, which will prevent idle people from asking questions, and prolonging the Session. I shall be glad to find that there are more Lord H's, and that they would print for the good of the public, who don't yet see their state. I wish well to all good men that have no other view than the welfare of their country and to the others what they deserve.

Ker of Kersland to [Robert Harley].

[1709, November]—I send you enclosed a double of a letter of the Cameronian Officers to me; and although the sum due to them be but small yet in regard I know the government hath at present many pressing occasions for money, there is nothing that can be thought upon to be sufficient to give satisfaction to these headstrong people but what I shall readily go into, being fully sensible how much at this critical juncture it is the interest of the government to have those people in a good temper, which will be no small disappointment to the hopes and endeavours of a set of men who ought to be better employed. As for the money I received if the weighty affairs that lay upon me, and the many hands I behoved (*sic*) necessary to employ for so long a time be considered it may be thought a miracle that matters were managed with so little charge to the public. I believe I shall have something of moment to tell you on Wednesday evening; for yesternight one who was sent to me to desire me to a meeting to-morrow dropped to me some things further.

I am hopeful if right methods be taken I sh▮ keep the Cameronians from going to methods of ill-designing men ; and shall open the eyes of the presbyterian party in Scotland and the protestants in Ireland who are just now settling a correspondence among themselves in both kingdoms, some of the commissioners from Ireland having lately been with myself.

Enclosed with the above is paper endorsed "The Cameronian Officers to Mr. Ker." [October 26, 1709.]

You may remember that at the time of the late invasion you gave all imaginable assurance of justice to be done us by England in satisfying our bygone arrears while we served in the Earl of Angus' regiment of foot levied by the late worthy laird of Kersland, your predecessor, upon his and our expenses. And we being fully convinced of your honour and honesty assured ourselves you had sufficient warrant for what you said at that time; and indeed we shall never impute the non-performance to any neglect in you but allenderly (*sic*) to those concerned in the government, although we deserved better treatment. But it seems to deserve either well or ill at a government's hand must receive the same reward; otherwise our service at Dunkeld—where we had the honour to defeat the enemy's whole army after they had routed General McKay and the whole regular troops then under his command at Killiecrankie, where we put effectual stop to the enemies' progress at that time—had not been forgotten. And although this and sundry other pieces of eminent service are well known to the whole kingdom, yet we find all promises made to us are broken. You can bear witness of our readiness to have opposed the French last year had they landed ; and what if that attempt should be renewed, as there do not want abundance of presumptions that way from several corners of this country.

But it is probable we may have the misfortune to be looked upon by the English (who are strangers to us) as not deserving their while to take notice of us, but it is well known that we under the conduct of your worthy predecessor durst look our enemies in the face and defend ourselves against all their fury ; and seeing you are now in London we write entreating you would let us know whether we may expect the performance of these promises made unto us anent the payment of our arrears, yea or not. We trouble you no further at present, but we still retain a due value for you and an esteem for the family you are honoured to represent.

DR. STRATFORD to ROBERT HARLEY, at Brampton.

1709, December 5—The Archbishop has exerted his visitatorial power in a very extraordinary manner at All Souls. Mr. Blencowe, who was once your servant, received an admonition to go into orders within the time limited by the statutes, or his place would be declared void. He applies to my Lord Sunderland, who writes a letter to the Archbishop to let him know that whereas the Warden of All Souls was very troublesome to one who was of use to her Majesty's service, in deciphering letters, by requiring him to take a new profession, which would hinder him from attending her Majesty's service. Her Majesty required his Grace to interpose and to restrain the Warden from giving Mr. Blencow any further trouble. This, I believe, is the first letter of this nature that ever came from the Crown to a Visitor. His Grace immediately sends the letter to the Warden enclosed in one of his own. In his own letter the Archbishop requires the Warden immediately to obey my Lord Sunderland's letter, and to publish both his own and my [Lord] Sunderland's letter to the society within so many days, and to register both. He is the first Visitor that ever sent orders to the Governor of a Society entrusted to his protection, to break the Statutes of the founder. Upon what he grounds his pretence of a power to dispense with the statutes I know not. I cannot hear that he has the least colour from the statutes for any such pretence. I take the case to be altogether as arbitrary as anything done by the late Lord Sunderland at Magdalen College; only there they make the Visitor the tool to do that for them, which they then did in the King's name. The question is what remedy a Society can have against their Visitor, when he acts not only without any authority from the statutes, but contrary to those ends for which the power was lodged. The Warden is now at London upon an appeal from two other Fellows. I wish he may be well advised there, and have courage to oppose it. This extraordinary proceeding has alarmed the whole University. The reason is very remarkable: a new profession would hinder him from attending the Queen's service. As though he would not have as much leisure to decipher letters if he was in orders, and lived in the College, as he has now that he attends terms and circuits. I suppose my Lord Sunderland does not know that Dr. Wallis was in orders.

If the orders to read out new prayers with the other prayers were sent into Scotland, there would be no occasion to imprison the minister to prevent the people from coming to hear the common prayers.

Dr. Stratford to [Robert Harley].

1709, December 21—200l. will be a very ample allowance for all expenses whatever for my Lord Strathallan and his servant. My Lord Stawel had no more, and my Lord Carteret has no more. Both of them lived very handsomely and within their allowance. I have given my Lord Dupplin an account of this to-day. My Lord Dupplin is pleased to tell me that the gentleman who is with him has orders to leave here as soon as he has seen him settled there. I must beg you would be pleased too to take care of that. His stay with my Lord Strathallan could be of no service, but might be very inconvenient.

I have had an opportunity this week of writing with great freedom by a very safe conveyance to a gentleman at Rotterdam.

So solemn a prosecution for such a scribble will make the Doctor [Sacheverell] and his performance much more considerable than either of them could have been on any other account. It works more than I could have expected. He is visited and presented by clergy and laity. Those whom he has used brutally, forget their past resentments on this occasion and visit him. I hear Sir Simon Harcourt has promised to be one of his counsel.

When the motion was for addressing for Hoadly's Mr. Bromley said it was very extraordinary, and he was afraid it might be looked upon as an affront to the Queen, to desire her to prefer him for writing against a sermon which she had ordered to be printed. It is said the Queen, when the address was delivered to her, turned off without giving any answer.

The Vicechancellor has the mortification to see another of his creatures humbled. The Warden of All Souls has been at Lambeth upon an appeal of his Fellows against him. He is obnoxious, and several blots have been hit already, and more I am afraid will appear in a little time. The Archbishop rebuked him severely in Court. He will hear more when the Archbishop's determination comes, for which he has taken a month's time.

The Bishop of Winton [Trelawney] storms at Jack Dolben. He sent for him and desired him not to engage in this [Sacheverell?] affair. Dolben excused himself upon a promise he made to great men, I suppose Somers and H[alifax]. His Lordship swears he shall not come into the House again by his means. But his Lordship swore so once before.

BANK and INDIA STOCK.

1709—A table shewing the prices day by day for the months in August, September, and October of Bank and India stock. Signed by John Castaing, and addressed to Arthur More [Moore?].

ABIGAIL HARLEY to her nephew [EDWARD] HARLEY, at Oxford.

1709-10, January 26. [London].—The D[uke] and D[uchess] returned from their retirement this week. It is said he has made great submissions where they are due. She being desired to send to him to return, said, No, they were gone upon their own affairs and might stay their own time; her Grace cannot submit. The address I told you of is sunk, though an impeachment was threatened. Sa[cheverel]l put in a long plea yesterday, I have not seen it. Great heats yesterday in the House of Commons upon the Self Denying Bill, sharp speeches on both sides, begun by W[ortley] Mon[tag]u; Dol[ben] said the quondam S[ecretar]y was like a fox that had lost his tail, had got two monkeys to his assistance, Sir J. Jekyll, the other I have forgot, a very witty and as mannerly comparison. What pleases me is, they affirm a person came in October last from Shrewsbury, and has been here incognito ever since, raising up an evil spirit that never appeared till within these two days; this you know the truth of. It is said in one of the men of war lately taken by our enemies was £50,000 in fine pictures and furniture for your neighbouring castle [Blenheim?]. The lottery will be full to-night, if not so already; all the old hoards are broke up.

LADY DUPPLIN to her aunt ABIGAIL HARLEY.

1709-10, February 5. Dupplin House—I wonder Sir Godfrey [Kneller] has not finished the pictures, my Lord Kinnoull thinks they are done and talks often of writing to have the money paid and the pictures sent down. I find the Parliament won't be so dull all their session as they were at the beginning, though there is nothing affects the people here so much as Dr. Sacheverell, one party adores him and the other would hang him. They think me very stupid that have so little concern about the matter and show so much indifference that I have not read the sermons yet; they were promised me but I have not got them yet.

[ABIGAIL HARLEY to her nephew EDWARD HARLEY.]

1709–10, February 28. [London]—The Governor (R. Harley) is much out of order, got a terrible cold at the (Sacheverell) trial yesterday and increased it to-day, yet if not worse resolves to go to-morrow. I hope you have some friend that gives you an account of what passes there each day. I wonder you should imagine I would be there, never had a thought of it, ha'n't so much as read the sermon, and have had as little concern about it on either hand as any mortal. As I detest unjust prosecutions from any side, so. I may be partial to him but shall never add a grain to his vanity.

[ABIGAIL MASHAM to ROBERT. HARLEY.]

[1710, February]—I was with my aunt (the Queen) last night on purpose to speak to her about Dr. S[achevere]ll and asked her if she did not let people know her mind in the matter. She said, no, she did not meddle one way or other, and that it was her friends' advice not to meddle. I desired to know who she called her friends, she said Mr. Anthony it was his opinion. I fear there is some truth in what you have heard of the D. Bradford for bishop. I heard the same thing and told my aunt of it; she made me this answer, that he was a very good man, but would not say whether he was to be a bishop or no, nor who recommended him for one. I shall be very glad to know why Mr. Anthony does not think it proper to make our friend one.

ABIGAIL HARLEY to EDWARD HARLEY, at Oxford.

1709–10, March 2 [London]—Last post I told you the Governor was indisposed with a great cold, indeed came that night very ill from Westminster Hall, was so ill all day yesterday was forced to keep his bed till near eight at night; had sweat a good deal and found relief by it. About that time Sacheverell's mob pulled down Mr. Burgess's meetinghouse, and burnt it in these [Lincoln's Inn] fields, did not so much as spare the poor woman's clothes that lived in the house, but burnt all she had but a feather bed. From thence they went to four more, and showed the same rage. As they were gutting that in Drury Lane some horse and foot guards came and dispersed them, seized several who were committed, and several were killed in their zeal for this good cause. They attempted the same in the City, but the weavers rose, and then the train-bands so secured all there; now we hear nothing but drums. The Fields have now several companies of the train-bands to secure the houses from the insolence of the mob. This is methinks an odd way of defending passive obedience and non-resistance. It was told me that in Oxford the same is done, till you tell me so I shall suspend my crediting that. The mob insulted my Lord Chancellor and Lord Wharton last night, and caught Dolben and were going to hang him upon a tree till he swore he was not Dolben nor a parliament man. They threatened Gil[bert Burnet] of Sarum, had they proceeded there even to Vol[pone] would have had some pretence. I pray God it stop here. This is apparent that had the least care been taken yesterday when our ministry had notice of it, all this tumult had been prevented, but I believe that was not their desire. To-day Lechmere summed up the evidence, if it may be called so, against the Doctor, then they adjourned till to-morrow when his counsel are to be heard. All peoples expectations are fixed on Sir Simon Harcourt, and everybody desires to hear him. I hear the Dean of Carlisle [Atterbury] was present to hear himself severely reflected on the other day by General Stanhope. In my opinion those clergymen were most prudent that kept out of the way of it. What is mankind that a nonsensical harangue from a pragmatical insignificant man should make such a terrible work ? It is confidently said this will be made a handle to obstruct a peace. Sir Simon Harcourt is chosen at Cardigan by a great majority not yet returned. Numps [Sir Humphry Mackworth ?] will have but an ill time of it, if he petition as it is said he will, though a High Churchman his honesty in his mine adventure will hardly maintain his character. I forgot to tell you the Queen was at the trial yesterday, not to-day. She appeared very pensive ; the mob huzzaed her, joining the Church and Sacheverell. We could not go to bed last night till near morning, and since up some or other have been here to see how we did, so that I have writ this in strange haste which forgive : so farewell.

Mrs. Beresford sent to desire Neddy might be fetched hither, they threatened to tear her house [at Westminster School] down and broke the windows, one is gone for him.

Postscript.—Neddy is just come home well.

ABIGAIL HARLEY to EDWARD HARLEY, at Oxford.

1709-10, March 4. [London]—Very glad I ever am to have a letter from you to thank for and do it heartily for that received last night. I wish I could give you a better account how things pass here, but really hearing so many, and some very confused accounts, can hardly give any tolerable one. The managers finished upon Thursday ; among these the best judges say Parker spoke the best, all of them with great heat and bitterness, severe reflections which you know are sorry arguments at best. Walpole asked a Lord if he did not think Parker spoke best of the managers ; he answered he could not say so because he was one of them. Lord William Paulet had his part who never fails doing it well. Yesterday the counsel for the Doctor began his defence. Sir Simon Harcourt spoke for near two hours to the first article, and so well that had there been no watches none had thought the third part of the time spent ; no heat or indecent language, gave everything a noble turn with mighty force of reason, quoted the sermons of twenty Bishops ; several Archbishops have abridged the Homilies, and he desired to know whether the Lords would receive that or the Homilies themselves which were ready in court. They allowed him what method he thought properest for his client. When the governor comes back I will give the best account I can what is done to-day, am sorry you have it not constantly from a better hand, am sensible mine is very defective. You know Lord Coningsby is one of the managers ; he is always talking and the other day with great passion saying to a gentleman, I always was against the father and will be against the son (meaning the Pretender), was answered, aye, my Lord, and against the Holy Ghost too. It is pleasing to me I can tell you the mob are all dispersed, and so they might have been at first had the government desired it. Mr. Burgess sent to several Lords and Secretary Boyle to acquaint them that he was

threatened and insulted Tuesday night, with a promise they would be
with him next night; and had this return, that they would send a
guard at seven Wednesday night, which had they done had prevented
all the mischief that followed. A man being killed when they first
began pulling down his meetinghouse, all the mob ran away saying they
should be found accessories to his death; nobody coming to disturb
them a second detachment fell on, and proceeded as my last told you.
The train-bands are still upon duty, I suppose will continue till the trial
is over, which is like to last some days yet. My Lord Chancellor complained to the House how he was insulted. I believe had they not
apprehended themselves in danger little regard had been had for others;
somebody talking to Lord Wharton about the Dissenters, he said he did
not care if they were all damned.

It is current about that the peace cannot be obstructed, the Dutch
will not be wheedled out of it; that he may be sure to have a share in
all they dislike, they say now that Harley persuaded the States to send
those men Plenipotentiaries, and pretend they have letters of his to
that purpose. The Governor is not come home that I can tell nothing
what is done to-day, it is late. Adieu.

The Governor is just come home; little passed at the trial to-day
more than reading those parts of the Homilies proper for the cause and
several sermons, among the rest one of the Bishop of Sarum's; his
Lordship stood up and produced another of his own to contradict that,
a noble vindication. There has been hot work in the Parliament house,
were going to send Lechmere to the Tower for giving ill language; the
occasion he proposed a bill to be brought in for securing the Queen's
person and government; was told that was too great to be entrusted
with any person.

Sir Michael Warton, M.P. for Beverley, to [Robert] Harley, York Buildings.

1709-10, March 6—This morning Sir John Thorold sent me word
that Sir Simon Harcourt would come into the House and that if he
did Lechmere would move to send him to the Tower. Let me know if
he comes to-day, for I am but an occasional member, but would not be
wanting to serve him. I hope he will be Chief Justice in order to the
Great Seal hereafter. I hope the Queen will think it high time to be
Queen.

[Abigail Harley] to [Edward] Harley, at Oxford.

1709-10, March 7 [London]—You can hardly imagine the pleasure
yours last night gave me, you have certainly a right notion of the
darling doctrine, it is fresh in most people's memories how well it
was practised after being preached with eagerness for many years.
Sir Simon Harcourt on Friday stated that matter very justly, though a
precept delivered in Holy Scripture without limitation, as that to
children to obey parents in all things, yet in both instances there might
sometimes be cases in which the contrary was a duty. Yesterday was
taken up by the Doctor's counsel in reading passages out of several
books full of the horridest blasphemy that ever was vented among those
called Christians, others full of base reflections upon the Queen and her
family, one passage that she had no more title to the Crown than my
Lord Mayor's horse, Defoe's wet and dry Martyrdom was not forgot;
none of common understanding but must think the Church and State

too in danger from such christened heathens if suffered to go on without notice taken of them. The Queen heard all this yesterday.

When I writ on Saturday did not know what had passed in the Lords house that day. It seems Judge Powell had bailed one taken up among the mob, for which their Lordships were going to send him to the Tower, Volpone fiery for it, Prince Stira answered him with great warmth, Lord Somers with many of the party for sending him there; upon which the Duke of Argyll defended him briskly, upon which Lord Wharton gave him very ill language which His Grace highly resented and forced him to ask him pardon in the House, told him if he did it not there he would make him do it in another place. I hear my Lord Chief Justice Trevor said if he were sent to the Tower they would all go with him : all the North Britons were against Volpone for the Judge. Chief Justice Holt died Lordsday evening; it is said he will be succeeded by Parker. I am sorry if you have no better a correspondent than myself, and wish I were able to give you a more satisfactory account of affairs than I present to you. You must accept of my poor performances being the best I can do from scraps picked up as I can. There is talk of a plot, letters taken in woolpacks going to France with an account of the commotions here so to hinder peace, and what is most admirable that the persons writ their names to the letters, I suppose that there might be no difficulty in discovering them. I do not know that a word of this is true, only a flying report.

The Doctor's counsel it is said would end to-day their defence, but when the trial will be over is not yet known : I will keep this open till the Governor comes home, if not too late for the post, that you may know what passes.

It is publicly said they will turn Sir Simon Harcourt out of the House : he was not sworn yesterday as was expected. Thank God the Governor is pretty well again, goes constantly to the House.

This is the first day I have been abroad since the mobbing time, am just come home and to my grief the Governor is come and gone again that I cannot give you so good an account as else should. I saw several, both ladies and gentlemen, that came from the trial. What I can collect is this; the Doctor's counsel spoke several times and then he made his own defence which they tell you was done in so fine a manner, in such moving terms, with so harmonious a voice, that the poor ladies wet all their clean handkerchiefs, nay the men could not refrain tears, as they tell you the Duke of Leeds, Lords Rochester and Nottingham shewed their tenderness that way. I question whether ever the Doctor did such a feat in his pulpit. I leave you to believe what you please of this; however, all agree he made an excellent defence for himself with all the courage and decency imaginable, and gave a turn to everything beyond himself. If he made the sermon, be it as it will, Sir Simon Harcourt has the honour of it. The Lords adjourned till Thursday, tomorrow being the Queen's inauguration. I suppose Sir Simon Harcourt was sworn to-day. Good night.

[Henry St. John to Robert Harley.]

[1709-10, March 8]—I went from you to Court where I met Lord R[ochester] and the D. of Ar[gyll] ; they both told me that Hambden had been this day with the D. of Som[erset] to tell him that he was empowered to let his Grace know that, if he was engaged in any measures where their assistance was necessary, he and his friends were ready to follow his directions.   You will please to make your reflections on this tale.

I must add to this two words relating to myself, which I should not have done, had you not mentioned me this morning in giving an account of what passed between the D. of Sh[rewsbury] and yourself.

I am indifferent what employment is reserved for me, but I must own that to succeed Mr. Cardonnel, upon the same foot as Mr. Cardonnel was, is not coming into the service a second time with so good a grace as I came in the first; and keeping one's present situation is a good deal better than sinking whilst one affects to rise.

[HENRY ST. JOHN to ROBERT HARLEY.]

1700-10, March 9—I have heard this morning more than I knew last night of the temper which the Duke of A[rgyll] is in, with relation to the impeachment.   I believe it will be proper for you to endeavour to compound with him, rather than to insist much on convincing him. You will touch the true string, if you insinuate that no one of those embarked in the same interest pretends to drive another, but that where a thing is judged to be right by some, it is natural for those to attempt persuading the rest, without any further consequence if they do not prevail.

I find people strangely alarmed about the two Whig Bishops, which the runners of the Ministry and of the Junto affect to be sure of.

I shall see Lord R[ochester] after he has been with the Duke of somerset ; if anything offers I will trouble you with another billet.

Postscript.—A Chief Justice whom we are jealous of, and two Bishops who will we are sure be against us, must turn all our schemes, and those who go on with them, into a jest.

[ABIGAIL MASHAM to ROBERT HARLEY.]

1709-10, March 10—Last night I had a great deal of discourse with my aunt (the Queen) and much of it about the two men that are named for bishops.   I told her what a wild character Bertan (Barton) had, and that her father never made a worse man one than he is.   She said very little to me, but by what she did say, I suspect from it she has promised he shall be one as well as Bradford, if she has done this I guess it is from Mr. Pickering's recommendation.   Now nobody can serve her if she goes on privately doing these things every day, when she has had so much said to her as I know she has, both from myself and other people ; and because I am still with her people think I am able to persuade her to anything I have a mind to have her do, but they will be convinced to the contrary one time or other.   I desired her to let me see you, she would not consent to that, and charged me not to say anything to you of what passed between us.   She is angry with me and said I was in a passion, perhaps I might speak a little too warm but who can help that when one sees plainly she is giving her best friends up to the rage of their enemies.   I have had no rest this night, my concern is so great, and for my part I should be glad to leave my aunt before I am forced from her, and will see you very soon to talk about that matter whether she will give me leave or no.

The paper I shall let her have as soon as she comes back from the House.

[ABIGAIL HARLEY] to EDWARD HARLEY, at Oxford.

1709-10, March 11. [London]—Yesterday the Commons ended their reply to Sacheverell. Sir Thomas Parker spoke very well at first, but after it was mere Billingsgate, often calling him wretch and miscreant, Sir G. Jeffreys' language. My Lord.Nottingham desired he might have leave to propose a question to the judges; upon this my Lord Steward moved they might adjourn to their own House, which they did and then debated whether it should be proposed there or in the Hall. It was carried for the latter. When they returned thither the question was to this purpose:—whether according to law any man could be condemned for words where the sense was not evidently contained in them? Upon this they adjourned again to their own House, and there the judges unanimously delivered their opinion that no man could. For all this it is uncertain how it will go with him; it is thought there will be no great majority on either side. I was told Lord Wharton said that he would willingly submit to anything, even a fillip upon the nose, so that the Doctor might be found guilty. Before judgment is given it is said many Lords will take occasion to withdraw. This business in all probability will break the Whigs; my foolish fears are it will raise the Tories to their old madness, the extravagance of every party is to be dreaded. If the clergy take up their old way of railing in their pulpits, as some already practise, this will certainly be one consequence, to empty the churches and fill the meetinghouses. I beg your pardon for making any reflections upon such matters, should not to anyone else.

I hear my Lord Carteret is courting Sir Robert Worseley's daughter, a very pretty lady, and 12,000*l.*

[The EARL OF ORRERY to ROBERT HARLEY.]

1709-10, March [14?], Tuesday—I have obeyed your commands to the D[uke] of A[rgyll]; he says he can't bring himself up entirely to vote for an acquittal, because he has very freely and openly given his opinion that the sermon deserves censure, and he does not see how he can with any reputation alter that opinion so suddenly. He thinks too that an absolute acquittal would rather tend to promote a high Tory scheme than to ruin the interest of the Junto, besides he's afraid he should prejudice his interest in Scotland by it; and he thinks at this juncture particularly he ought to run no hazard of lessening that, as well upon account of his friends as upon his own. However he thinks he may fairly oppose any excessive punishment that shall be proposed, and he believes the Duke of So[merset] may be brought to concur with him in that. In all probability too there will be an opportunity to make such a stand as will have the effect you seem to expect from an absolute acquittal, for the punishment designed to be proposed is an incapacity, fine, and imprisonment. Now the Duke of Argyll thinks a man that has made so bad an use of a pulpit ought never to come into it again, but he promises that he will warmly oppose fine and imprisonment, and will endeavour to bring the Duke of Somerset into the same measures. This resolution must be kept very private, for fear the gentlemen on the other side should not propose a punishment that they may think them. selves in danger of losing; in which case we might probably lose that advantage which we now hope for from opposition. I am very glad the Duke of Argyll is brought so great a length, I think his friends cannot in reason desire him to go further.

This morning an order was sent to all the General Officers that serve in Flanders to repair to their posts by the 25th. It comes from the

Queen in Council and is to be complied with upon pain of her highest displeasure, this is so extraordinary that I apprehend 'tis designed to send some people out of the way, as the properest method to defeat the present scheme. I hope you will join with me in opinion that. some step ought immediately to' be taken to .obviate the ill consequence that the strict compliance with this order would undoubtedly have. I think the Queen should be desired to hint that she does not expect the Duke of Argyll and I should go over before we find it absolutely necessary to go, in order to be able to go into the field with the Forces; and in the mean time I think she ought to be pressed to do something without delay that will give such satisfaction to her friends as will leave them no room to doubt of her resolution to pursue those measures they shall advise her to as fast as the circumstances of affairs will permit. For my own part I must confess I much question whether any such ill-consequence is likely to follow from a precipitate declaration of her mind as from a delay.

[The EARL OF ORRERY to ROBERT HARLEY.]

1709-10, March [15?], Wednesday—I have again spoken to the D[uke] of A[rgyll] upon the same subject of the Doctor; he is very sorry that he should differ in opinion with you, for whom he has so much deference, but he cannot yet be brought to think that he should not suffer both in his character and his interest if he should go into an absolute acquittal. He wishes this matter had been sooner thought of, because he believes very proper expedients might have been found to have defeated the impeachment. However he is now come to a resolution to oppose all sorts of punishments that shall be proposed by the Junto, but he cannot do this without coming into some kind of punishment or. other; but he says it shall be as mild as you please. I hope you will consider that the point is not whether Sacheverell ought to be acquitted, but whether the Duke of Argyll ought to give his vote for his acquittal. If you'll please to talk to him freely upon the matter tomorrow night, I daresay you will find him in a reasonable temper. He is a little uneasy about Duke Hamilton who has been with the Queen and asked her for a Garter and a Dukedom of Britain. He thinks that noble Lord has no title to come over him, and therefore if the Queen has any thoughts of making him (Duke Hamilton) a Duke, he hopes that she will make him one first; but at the same time he had rather the matter should rest as it is, which I think 'tis for the Queen's interest it should, for fear she should bring the House of Lords upon her, and encourage a man to be her enemy that has never shown any great inclination to be her friend. You will be pleased to mention this affair tomorrow night in your conversation, 'twill properly be brought in when the Scotch business is upon the tapis. I think it would not be amiss that the Queen should write to order our stay in the manner you propose, but whatever method is taken for it, it must be without delay. I wish the business of the C[hief] J[ustice] be not gone so far as to be past retrieve. I will take upon me to say it might be more properly bestowed at this juncture than upon P[arker]. I wonder the Queen does not give the Duke of Argyll the Garter. I wish that were done, and the scheme finished and agreed to, that we might go out of town with satisfaction.

Postscript.—I forgot to mention that I saw a clergyman today of your acquaintance that said 'twas reported the Whigs had a promise of the vacant bishoprics. I said as much to him as I thought proper to encourage him to believe the contrary, and I hope there will soon be some satisfaction given in that point.

[ABIGAIL HARLEY] to EDWARD HARLEY, at Oxford.

1710, March 25. [London]—I do not hear when the trial will be printed, suppose it will not be long, it is already in parts, but I have read none yet nor design it till the whole may been seen together. Such a one I believe was never seen before, it will make a noble part, with all its circumstances, in our annals. It is said abroad we are all mad, may justly add fools too. Monday the sermon is to be burnt; this might have been done without putting the nation to 60,000l. charge, besides the terrible animosities that are raised throughout the kingdom, of which I pray God avert the fatal consequences. You will see by yesterday's votes what they are doing about the Address; it was moved by Mr. Bromley. The other party opposed it, said it was invading the Queen's prerogative. There were many precedents to clear this, but then the blasphemous books came under debate, and meddling with them stiffly opposed a great deal ; said amongst the rest that it was strange gentlemen should think the Ministry had nothing else to do than to meddle in matters of that nature. Upon this Mr. Annesley told them that it must give the world a strange idea of a Ministry that thought it below them to show any concern for the honour of the great God. They were severely lashed, and after many hours debate carried it in that odd manner as you see. However it is happy that any had courage to appear against that torrent of atheism, that is like a spreading leprosy, and more theatening than anything else to a Christian Church. It is said here great disturbances are with you, the University resolved to defend Sacheverell with their blood.

RICHARD KNIGHT to ROBERT HARLEY.

1710, April 4—I doubt not but you have heard the different treatment that Sir Simon Harcourt and Mr. Lechmere have met with on their circuits at Hereford, Ludlow, and Salop, Sir Simon in all places met by the magistrates and crowds of people and received with all the marks of honour and respect; the other affronted and hissed. At Shrewsbury Sir Simon was met out of town by four hundred horse headed by Mr. Owens and Mr. Cressett, the other hissed. At Ludlow Lechmere was forced to scamper over [to] Witley and steal into Mr. Kettle's by the back way.

Sir Joseph Jekyll had no respect showed him but was affronted rather, and suspected somebody put aqua-fortis on his coach braces, for it fell in Bromfield ; and to gain more respect he ordered Mr. Cornwall to be prosecuted for the sermon he preached before him at Poole, but the Grand Jury refused though Sir Joseph pressed it with some zeal [not] becoming his high station. Mr. Cornwall preached the same sermon before the Judges at Salop with applause, the text, Psalms the 94th and 16th verse, " Who will rise up for me against the evil-doers, or who will stand up for me against the workers of iniquity."

CAPTAIN H. HOWORTH to ROBERT HARLEY.

1710, April 12. Camp before Douay—After ten days march with 10,000 horse and 20,000 foot we joined the grand army at a camp

within an English mile to Tournay on Saturday last. Sunday six
o'clock in the evening we had orders to strike our tents and march.
Accordingly did, and marched all that night and at the break of day
we halted for two hours within a league of the lines; after that,
marched with all the diligence possible in three columns and our horse
and some foot took possession of the lines with little opposition. The
French only detached two hundred men out of fifty battalions of foot
and twenty squadrons of horse, which they had within the lines, and
made two fires and then ran for the fastest. We made two breaches
in the works on the plains of Lens, marched about half a league on the
plains and there encamped that night. The lines were very strong,
they had made a canal one and twenty feet over and two fathoms deep
and a strong breast work the other side, with batteries of cannon.
Tuesday morning ten o'clock, we marched to the river Scarp, where
the French had thrown up a breastwork, and had a great body of men,
but as soon as we appeared they went off, and left some of their tents
and baggage behind them. That night we invested Douay, about
which place we are all encamped, but have not yet laid siege to it,
because the artillery is not yet come up, neither as 'tis thought shall we
break ground this nine days. Sunday night I lost my cart and horses
and all the baggage I had, taken by a partisan party, except what was
about me and the company's tents which were on the Baw horse (*sic*) that
went at the head of the regiment. If it had happened near the end of
the campaign, I should not so much value it, but now it has quite broke
me for this year. Pardon me for troubling you with my misfortunes,
but I wish every branch of yours, and all that belongs to you, success,
it being a thing at present that touches me so near that I cannot forbear
acquainting you with it, though at the same time I acknowledge the
impertinence of it.

Postscript.—Every thing is very scarce yet here, yesterday I saw
half a crown given for a ammunition loaf, but we hope in a short time,
when the convoy comes up, to have everything much more reasonable.
There are but two places we can make an attack to the town because
they overflow the rest with water.

If you have any commands direct for me of Col. Honywood's
Regiment in my Lord Marlborough's army.

[Abigail Masham to Robert Harley.]

1710, April 17—I am very uneasy to see you, but my poor aunt
(the Queen) will not consent to it yet, she puts me off from time to
time which gives me a great deal of trouble. I think it necessary for
her service as well as my own for us to meet, for a great many reasons,
therefore I have a mind to do it without her knowledge and so secret
that it is impossible for any body but ourselves to know it. I would
come to you to-morrow night about eight o'clock to your own house if
you approve of it, but if you have made any appointment with company
any other night will serve me. Send this person to me to-morrow
about ten in the morning to let me know your resolution what I
must do.

[The Same to the Same.]

[1710, April 18 ?] Tuesday—I have been hindered by the person
[Mrs. Danvers] who is to be married to the Bishop of Ossory coming.

to you this night, I could not get rid of her till this moment which is
too late to go out, since I dare not stay out of this house past ten o'clock
without my aunt's leave. Pray let me know what other evening I may
come to you by the bearer, she is very trusty and you may write anything that requires haste for my aunt (the Queen) to know. I go up
to her at ten, so keep her but a little while. You may depend upon it
I will spirit up my friend Mr. Wise to do the business you desire.

[James Cressett to Robert Harley.]

[1710], April 27—I know not how a retired old gentlemen escaped
my memory yesterday when we were talking about The Hague, but
I recovered him this morning. Sir W. Trumbull I am confident
would gladly serve, and I presume may be judged a fitter person to
negociate than such a man whose merit lies in the strong box. These
matters are (as they ought to be) submitted to your thoughts. I discoursed the trusty Doctor last night at large concerning some proper
tools and instruments to be ready upon occasion for the work intended.
The clean and unclean repair to his ark and he will not fail to give you
the best account he can of all he knows; but, to be plain with you, which
I esteem a duty in friendship, I scarce believe any mortal of tolerable
worth and discretion can be found who will undertake mysterious
business during the present situation of affairs. Miserable and desperate
fellows are not wanting who are sure to do more harm than good to those
who employ them, in short the offices must be in sure hands at home
and then without delay effectual service may be done abroad, not before,
everything else will be but trifling to no purpose. Men will move
according to the motion of things and if they suffer a long stand English
virtue is not proof against it. Your Heroes are now gazing at one
another with equal disposition to go forward if encouraged or backward
if it prove convenient. Pray remember the question *quomodo* being
resolved impatience to see the *quando* is very natural. Pardon this long
scrawl and be assured 'tis well meant. I wish you merry with your
select company at dinner.

Mrs. Dela Manley to [Robert Harley].

1710, May 12—My respect only prevents me from waiting upon you
in person (to beg your acceptance of this book), lest I be thought to
have the honour of your acquaintance, which I can only covet, never
hope.
  Your merit, Sir, your great capacity, your zeal for the Church has
made me an unwarrantable intruder. I willingly devote my ease and
interest where my principles are engaged, and, if I have the fortune to
do some small service, my design is answered. I have attempted some
faint representations, some imperfect pieces of painting, of the heads of
that party who have misled thousands. If anything moves your
curiosity, I will explain what you desire, if you send but a note (without
a name) directed to me and under cover, to Mr. Markham at the Bell
and Dragon in Paternoster Row : I give the address to none besides, and
therefore can't fail to know from what part your commands shall come.
  Yet perhaps I am all this time offending where I aim and hope to
please, the uncertainty of that gives me to ask your pardon for my
presumption and to conclude with my profound respect.

The Duke of Somerset to [Robert Harley].

1710, May 24. Kensington—The Duke of Shrewsbury says you desire to talk with me, if so let me know before eight o'clock if you can be at home, or at Northumberland House, this night at nine, accordingly I will come from hence. In case you choose to come to me I will have a servant to conduct you, and if I come to you then have your back door open for me; but if this notice has not the good fortune to fall into your hands by eight o'clock, then any time you shall appoint to-morrow morning I shall obey.

M[artha Lady] M[ansell] to Robert Harley.

1710, May 28—I am almost fright'd to death, with the threats of a great Lady who is now retired from Court, which one that lately came from the Lodge tells of. In a little time she says she shall return with as full power as ever, and that both you and every friend you have shall feel the effects of her utmost revenge. Lady Orkney is often with her, and at the table begins a health to her and all that's for the Duke's interest, and total destruction to those that are not for it.

Duke Hamilton thinks himself neglected by you, and others are caressing him to be of their party, but he is still more inclined to yours and if there was occasion for going into Scotland would convince you of his interest there, and would readily join with whom you approve, and very particularly give the character and inclinations of his countrymen.

The terrible apprehensions I am under have took all rest from me and I was forced to send for my Docter who ordered me something that I had a tolerable night of it; but without some good news, I sha'n't recover mighty soon. I won't mention the writing this to any body living, hope you will pardon the doing it, for the terrors that enraged Lady has put me into is not to be expressed.

Endorsed by Harley:—"Answered immediately."

John Meyricke to ——.

1710, June 2. Pembroke—Your son's friends in this country have prevailed with him to stand for the county at the next election, and we are now taken up wholly in securing our several interests.

According to the best calculation I can make we cannot fail of success, if we can engage Mr. Langhorne, who is now in London, to join with us. Mr. Harley and yourself, or at least one of you, should without loss of time make him a visit and desire his interest which he will be proud to grant to either of you. Mr. Harley visits him, and has a great influence over him. What is done must be done suddenly. Mr. Campbell also has good interest in this country, which I believe may be secured by Mr. Edward Harley, who governs entirely my Lady Campbell and her affairs. The only other persons who have credit enough with Mr. Langhorne to secure him are Mr. Edward Harley and Baron Price.

Earl Poulett to [Robert] Harley.

1710, June 7—I am always obliged to good Mr. Harley for his great goodness towards me and am so sensible of it that I have no respect to myself but in regard to that service. The Duke is our friend and kinsman, and personally I have great esteem for him, but I must be against him, and myself also in respect to that character so useful to the public. Is not the division to be among the Whigs of consequence, must not the Tories be united in order to that, must not the Queen for her own security do something substantial to engage them so as to be depended upon, and must not that appear to be obtained by your credit? Did not you with Earl Rivers at your own house name Anglesey in case I refused? even before I named him, did you or your friends contradict it for·a great while after he was publicly named, did not you desire me to solicit for him and to make Somerset as fond of him as of me, and to give Anglesey all the hints in order to it? Has not Rivers told him Somerset was for him, can it stick any-where but your want of credit with the Queen, is that for your advantage to be known, or for the Queen's to be doubted by men who by her measures she is making necessary to her at this time? Do they not except against me the same as a part of yourself, is not yourself con-vinced so as to refuse what you persuade me to? Has not Anglesey approved himself free to serve from all past friendships and very ready to change his place whenever convenience required it? Has not his party accepted this earnest of your friendship to them, or did they name him at first? Why would you make a useful man disgraced in being dis-appointed, and a real friend who would freely expose life and fortune for you, uneasy to come in against his honour and your credit, will not this make a crack of jealousy in foundation? I once heretofore sank and all this for a Duke of Newcastle, who quietly parted with you in danger and disgrace. Is not he so much above his place as to be beneath it, are not his great riches golden chains to him, has he now for fifty years ever once exerted himself for a friend or the public, can you expect it of him hereafter or is he worth a whole party in time of need? Will not half a score half crown Whigs make up the loss of him, and may not you have as many more of them as you want. For the Queen's, your own, and your friends' sakes consider the want of con-fidence with those most necessary to you, and for my own excuse permit me to say I sacrifice the highest ambition and advantage to myself for the Queen's security and your honour.

Captain H. Howorth to Robert Harley.

1710, June 10, O.S. From the siege before Douay—Thursday night last we stormed the ravelin with one hundred grenadiers and two hundred fusiliers on the right, and the same number on the left. We began our attack at three quarters after nine and it lasted till three quarters after eleven, before we could make a lodgment. Our loss was very considerable, the killed and wounded of the English were two hundred and ninety-five men and twenty-one officers, whereof I had the good fortune to receive but a small flesh wound, which at the present a little disables me, but not so far as to miss my duty that I owe to my country, nor my respect that's due to you. It fell to my lot to be the eldest captain that commanded the fusiliers on the right; and a Dutch Lieutenant Colonel was to head us, but he thought it the securest way not to advance with us, and gave me the honour, (which he should have had), to lead them up the breach of the ravelin, where we were so warmly received that in less than an hour the better half of us were demolished, and not but three officers but what received a hurt. We are now sapping to oblige them to quit the works within the ravelin, as we may be able to raise a battery to make a storming breach in the wall of the town, which we hope we shall get done in four or five days, and when the breach is made, they must either quit the town or venture the being put all to the sword.

Last night a detachment from the Grand Army went under the command of Colonel Newton and surprised two small works of Fort Scarp, and cut off the communication between the town and the fort, which will be of very great advantage to us, because when we oblige the town to surrender, if they have provisions, men or ammunition to spare, they can't supply them. The town expected the Germans would last night have stormed the ravelin on their attack, and that we should have pushed ours on farther, so that they drew what men they could from the fort, with that expectation, which gave us the advantage we have.

Postscript.—Just as I was closing up this the French blew up a mine of theirs on the top of the breach and killed us near one hundred men, but most of them were foreigners. It is expected they have two more there which we are sapping for to find them out. The Germans make their attack to-morrow night.

[The Earl of Orrery to Robert Harley.]

1710, June [10–] 21, New style. Camp near Douay—Mr. Benson will be able to give you a good account of our affairs here, having been in the camp with us about six weeks, where he has been several times entertained by the Vicar-General [Marlborough] and often had discourse with him. I think I already observe an alteration in the behaviour of this great man and his friends upon the prospect of the change in England, they seem to affect a greater air of civility than they once thought they should ever have occasion for, and I am apt to think they will in some little time make overtures of accommodation; for I am persuaded that, though the General should entirely lose his power, he will do all he can to keep his place. The Duke of Argyll and I have yet had but very little correspondence with him, and we have no inclination to have any with him for the future, further than the duty of our posts obliges us to; but it is the custom for all officers when they quit the camp to ask his leave, which is a ceremony we would willingly omit if we could. The only way I think for us to be dispensed with in that respect is for the Queen by letter or any other proper method to signify to us her leave to go out of the camp and return to England when we think fit. I have lately written to H[enry] S[t. John] about my being made a Major General, I hope he will talk about it with you, and I daresay when you know how that matter stands you will not think it unreasonable. I am plainly left out in this last promotion out of pique which has stopped at me though there are not Major Generals enough upon this establish- ment. I shall injure nobody here by it, and I don't design to lay claim to the pay of the post this year, upon which account I hope my friends will do me the justice to believe that I don't desire it for my own par- ticular advantage; but I think it proper for our common cause at this time that this point should be carried, that the Queen may show she will not suffer his Highness to wrong the service or prejudice any person that does not misbehave himself to her or the public.

We have here much discourse and I hope some prospect of peace, for I cannot but flatter myself that the Dutch are more and more inclined to it since they find the French have been able to bring so large and so good an army into the field; and since the siege of this town will cost us so much time and so many men that we cannot probably do anything very considerable after it without venturing a battle at a disadvantage, which I think they will not do from last year's terrible shock, in which we had made a great campaign if we had not gained that victory. The Duke of Argyll gives his humble service to you.

The DUKE OF SOMERSET to [ROBERT HARLEY].

1710, June 18. Kensington—I have spoken to the Queen on the last part of your letter. She was pleased to express her own thoughts on that matter in such a manner that she will not only consider it but will in a few days speak to Mr. Secretary Boyle on it; the further particulars I will at present refer till we meet, which I hope may be to-morrow morning at eleven o'clock at your own house. I desire your porter may be instructed to admit a hackney chair with the curtains drawn round it into your hall without examining the chairmen; or if this time be not convenient let it be at your own hour for it will be the same to me morning, noon, or night.

It is desired Mr. Cressett may not know it before the Queen hath told Mr. Boyle of him.

[ROBERT HARLEY] to ARTHUR MOORE.

1710, June 19—About twelve days since Sir G. Heathcote wrote to a great Lord earnestly desiring that he and some others might speak with the Duke of Devon[shire] and the Lord Privy Seal. In a day or two after a meeting was fixed, at which were present the Duke of Devonshire, Duke of Newcastle, Sir G. Heathcote, Sir William Scawen, Mr. Eyles, and Mr. Nathaniel Gould. Sir G. Heathcote was the spokesman, he in very strong and earnest terms pressed the two Dukes to go to the Queen, and in their name to dissuade her from making any change in the ministry; particularly if Lord Sunderland was put out dismal consequences would follow; that he had nothing to do with, nor any dependence on, the ministers, but that he for the public good could not forbear telling his opinion, and that all credit would be gone, stock fall, and the Bank be ruined, which included the ruin of the nation, with many other tragical expressions.

It was the beginning of last week before this was reported to the Queen, after which the same four gentlemen were introduced to tell their own story themselves to the Queen. The Secretary by that time being removed Sir Gilbert Heathcote thought fit to alter his speech and to speak to her Majesty of the danger of altering her ministers, and dissolving the Parliament.

This is a matter of a very extraordinary nature, that private gentlemen (for it cannot be conceived for their own sakes that the Bank deputed them), that private persons they should have the presumption to take upon them to direct the sovereign. If this be so let us swear allegiance to these four men and give them a right to our passive obedience without reserve.

Draft in Harley's handwriting.

[SIR SIMON HARCOURT to ROBERT HARLEY.]

1710, June 21—I had this morning the honour of a visit from the Duke of Beaufort, after he had been to wait on you. I could wish he had met you at home and since he did not, that you could spare time to see him. He is as well disposed as you can wish him to be, and yet he is not without some apprehensions, which make him as well as many others very uneasy. He tells me he has received a hint of a compliment intended him of a troop of guards, on his buying out my Lord Albemarle. I find he would like it much better if he had a free present made to him, and the Queen would take the payment on herself. However he is determined to be pleased with what her Majesty thinks proper for him. Amongst other things he mentioned Lord Berkeley's dangerous illness, and the vacancy in case of his death of the office of Lord Lieutenant of Gloucestershire; though he did not speak very plain, yet I think he sets his heart on that mark of respect. Lord Wemyss, he says, told him that the Lord Steward was determined to quit, which I do not believe, but on that head he took occasion to mention the Lieutenancy of Derbyshire, which on supposition of his Grace's quitting the Stewardship, he thought the Queen might reasonably resume in this instance. He pressed me to be urgent with you to get the office of Lord Lieutenant of the county of Derby for Lord Scarsdale, who above all things desires it. If I did not mistake his Grace he did not seem uneasy at the Lord Steward quitting, nor would he be so at succeeding him; the usage the Queen has lately received by the insolent admonition and reproof from four citizens has created the utmost dissatisfaction in him, as it has done in all your other friends. The Duke of Newcastle's friends have made such an impression as is not to be wiped off, but by facts, and you must bear my telling you, they become daily more necessary. I had much rather displease you, than not serve you, and therefore take the liberty of telling you, you are in my poor opinion more concerned than any one man living, that something may ere long be done to show the Queen's favour towards the Church of England, if there be a real intention that way. I wish I could go farther than saying, all persons are pleased Lord S[underland] is out. My endeavours have not been wanting that all distrust might be laid aside. But what I say goes but for little anywhere.

The DUKE OF BUCKINGHAMSHIRE to [ROBERT] HARLEY.

1710, July—Since we met I have spoken with some of the best citizens, who besides their good reasoning on this occasion agreeing with yours, will bring Mr. Shepheard at any time, and therefore have promised to be with him whenever I would appoint at your house.

LORD SCUDAMORE to [ROBERT HARLEY].

1710, July 1. Holm Lacy—The early motion of other gentlemen in asking their friends' assistance against a new election for this county [of Hereford] occasions me to acquaint you with my intention of offering my service when there shall be a new parliament, which if you approve of and will favour me with your vote and great interest it will very much add to the obligations already conferred upon me.

[ALEXANDER CUNNINGHAM to ROBERT HARLEY.]

[1710,] July 1—Ever since my coming over I have been seeing the provinces, which has given me abundance of pleasure in this fine season, when everything in nature is most inviting. In our company we had christians of all sorts, but neither aheist nor statesman, nor was it allowed to any man to read a newspper during our progress, so you will easily think we had more laughing than conversation. Perhaps you will not approve this, and to spend English money in jesting and

laughing, but I can assure you even in this there is improvement, and we are not the only gentlemen that do so among you. To what purpose would it be to us to join some old politicians in Guelderland in groaning over the lamentations of their country, which was nothing to us. Loo is well kept, but the hinds and deer are all destroyed, so that there is no more game there, where many men formerly made their fortunes. However this place has been commended yet in my opinion Windsor Forest if well kept is preferable to it. Marsen which is not taken notice of by any of the travel writers that I know, is one of the most delicious places in nature, be it either for art or nature. In two leagues you see a greater variety of pleasure houses and pretty gardens than you can see in all Britain. They have not I own that air of grandeur that some of our houses have, but here you see beauty, cleanness, and symmetry in perfection. Here are the best cherries in the whole country, and I know no landscape where pleasure and profit are mixed with greater judgment. In the middle of this charming place I observed something like a wilderness, which looked like to the contrivance of antiquity and nature. This they told me belonged to a medallist who had lived long in Spain. It minded me of the Hesperian gardens. His being a virtuoso was enough to excite me to see him; he is one of the most accomplished gentlemen that I know of the fraternity; he is married and has children. I was taken up with the fine colony medals, such as the old Hispalis, Gades, Ilerda, Salduba, Calpe, etc., by which I see the Romans did not carry their money out of Italy, but allowed every country to coin for itself, and they had a share of it. The Imperial Court imitates the old Romans in this point, and if our people understood the ancient learning, they would be more saving of their money. Now for example we having taken Douay it would be fit to coin the bullion or plate of the place into English or Dutch coin, and not to fill that place with ours; and if we take more places yet we may do the like, for I see no prospect of peace so very soon, the noise in England helps to keep it off. They make it more here than I know it is at home, and France thinks that we will destroy ourselves, but I hope they are mistaken. You know we have no personal quarrels, all our heats are about a few lucrative places, it matters little who have them provided they that have them will give account what they do in them. No side I know is for this, nor for taking away salaries and pensions, so I am of no side but that of my friends.

Postscript.—If you please to honour me with your commands before I go into Germany direct them for me by Messrs. Drummond and Vanderheyden, merchants in Amsterdam.

They talk that the French plenipotentiaries have offered all but Sicily and Sardinia, and for security offer the bankers in Paris for their paying the Allies a certain sum of money monthly. A money expedient is taking, but bankrupts are no better security than the principal, for by this offer they seem to be playing with us. They did not receive Mr. Pettycum [Petkum]'s last message. Mr. Fletcher is gone to Aix-la-Chapelle for which I am sorry. We have here yet my Lord Lonsdale, my Lord Peters, my Lord Denbigh and his brother. All of them cannot drink so much among them as you made me drink at dinner before I left the town, yet I am not reckoned high church. However you may tell the Duke of Leeds that he may have as great comfort in his grandsons as ever he had trouble with his son.

This day we are told my Lord Dartmouth is Secretary of State.

Endorsed by Harley :—" Mr. Alex. Cunningham the Medallist, from Holland."

The Duke of Somerset to [Robert Harley].

1710, July 3. Kensington—When you sent me back the original
with the copy of the Resolution of the States I acquainted the Queen
with it, who gave me orders to return the copy which is enclosed.

It was tried last night whether Gudgins (*sic*) would bite but in vain,
so we are as we were last week.

Your humble servants do desire you to come here this night to any
other lodging than mine soon after nine o'clock, it being very necessary
to have half an hour's conversation with you before your other
engagement.

The Duke of Somerset to [Robert Harley].

1710, July 5—Your letter came very seasonably by the right use I
have made of it, for it has most effectually procured the resolution
which is to be put in execution to-morrow after an Irish Lord is gone
from the Council on the Irish bills.

If you please to come to Kensington to-morrow night between the
hours of nine and ten I will have a servant at the gate under the clock
who shall conduct you to me.

The Duke of Argyll to [Robert Harley].

1710, July [6-] 17, N.S.—I have been so unfortunate as not to have
had till now an opportunity of writing, otherwise I had sooner acknowledged the honour and favour of your letter. I do assure you your
kind and obliging expressions have entirely the effect on me which they
deserve to have, and you shall always find me most faithfully your
servant. I am extremely obliged to Brigadier Hill that he should
make any mention of me to his friends, I am very sensible I have by no
means merited the favour, though there is no man can love and honour
him more than I do. You may be sure the mortifications he meets
with must needs make him uneasy, but I understand him to have taken
the same resolution which my Lord Orrery and I have done, to serve,
that is to suffer, out this campaign but never to serve another under the
Duke of Marlborough ; his Grace having discharged people on pain of
his displeasure to converse with me, is a step which I am not meek spirited
enough to forgive, and indeed I think it is in some measure an incivility
to the Queen, since she is pleased to approve of what he thinks fit to
find fault with me for. It is a very hard question whether the removal
of my Lord Sunderland gave us most joy, or his Grace and his slaves
confusion ; one might have seen despair in their faces but of late they
have recovered their looks, and do pretend to be well assured that
matters are to go no further, what grounds they may have for it we
know not. The delay indeed gives us some pain, but those gentlemen
have been pleased to have so very little regard to truth in many late
reports they have with great industry spread abroad, that we with very
good reason suspect this to be only an artifice like the rest to keep up
the hearts of their friends.

I will not trouble you with my poor notions of affairs in England,
being at a distance makes it very hard to have a true one of them were I
otherwise capable of judging, which I do not pretend to be, only one
thing I hope you will pardon me if I venture to mention, which is that
I humbly conceive nothing can endanger the Queen's good cause more
than her regulating her affairs at home with regard to what passes on

this side the water, because I take it for granted, that the war and the present Ministry are to end together, and yet that the Plenipotentiaries will not be sent away. I need not say anything in relation to what is practising in the army, I sent my Lord Rivers and my brother some account of it, which no doubt they have communicated to you.

The COUNTESS OF ORKNEY to [ROBERT HARLEY].

1710, July 10—I need not say, 'tis ever very agreeable to me to converse with you, when you have so much leisure; but your being of so great consideration, if 'tis known that you see me, it will be made of more consequence than 'tis possible to be with me who am not of weight enough to give a pretence for our acquaintance. I hope you will soon be at Windsor, and then I flatter myself I may have occasion to invite you to Clieveden; but to show you that fear never governs me, if you choose to come by day-light appoint your own hour and I shall be at home, but if I don't hear again in answer to this I shall expect you to-morrow as soon as it is dark with a great deal of satisfaction.

A[RTHUR] ANNESLEY, M.P. for Cambridge University, to [ROBERT HARLEY].

1710, July 14. Cambridge—Since I came to this place the Vice Chancellor has called the Heads of Houses together three times to consider what should be done to one Mr. Ashenhurst, against whom the enclosed deposition or words to the same effect were sworn by Mr. Craister. Mr. Craister did not keep a copy of his deposition but upon recollection has writ with his own hand, and sent me the enclosed paper. At the third meeting the Vice Chancellor, Dr. Covel, Dr. Balderston, Dr. Ashton, Dr. Fisher and Dr. Laney were of opinion, though the words were spoken out of the Liberties of the University that they might proceed and punish Ashenhurst. Sir John Ellis, Dr. Green, Dr. Bentley, and Dr. Blith (a very old infirm man) were against proceeding in this affair.

Our Statutes requiring a consent of the majority of the Heads (at least nine and there were but ten present) before they can proceed to punish any offence, in a Master of Arts, by expulsion. I hear the Vice Chancellor intends to lay the deposition and the whole proceeding upon it before my Lord Dartmouth. When you see in what manner your name is mentioned in this deposition, I hope you will the more easily pardon my troubling you with this account of what has passed here.

Postscript.—Mr. Ashenhurst is a creature and tool of Dr. Bentley's; Mr. Craister is a man of an unexceptionable character.

I send this by the carrier, not thinking it so safe by the post.

A. LADY PYE to ABIGAIL HARLEY, at Eywood.

1710, July 15. Derby—I heard last post that Lady Hyde's fine daughter was dead of the small pox; Lord Ashburnham and his Lady, a young couple, gone together. The notion with some people is that the Palatines brought in this very ill kind.

The summer hath hitherto passed very dusty, now rain is come, too soon for some whose hay is abroad; 'tis a dear article in this county, and all things else that belong to housekeeping.

I shall be very glad to hear the good news that you have a little nephew or niece in Scotland.

THOMAS FOLEY to his brother-in-law [ROBERT HARLEY].

1710, July 17th. Witley—I received my nephew Harley's letter which brought me the agreeable news of my Lady Dupplin's being delivered of a son, and heartily congratulate you thereon. I have no account of anything here to entertain you with but about Dr. Sacheverell. His sister being at Worcester and he being invited by Mr. Barkley Green came to Cotheridge on Thursday evening by a private way and avoided going through Bewdley. The noise of his coming I am told occasioned our good Diocesan's sending to his clergy not to meet the Doctor, and his great zeal made him go to Worcester and invite the Mayor and Aldermen there to dine with him; but he could not prevail with them not to invite the Doctor, for upon a division they carried it to spend 20l. on a treat at the "Bush" for him on Friday, which it is said was near doubled by private subscriptions. The wise governors of this county, being not sure of all the churchwardens, ordered the clappers to be taken out of the bells of some of the churches. When the Doctor came to Worcester on Friday some men got into St. Nicholas Church and knocked the bells with hammers, upon which the constables were sent for and some of the men committed. It is said that the moderate Doctor of that parish beat a fellow for giving them notice that the constables were coming. Some women made bonfires. The Justices were so careful that they went about themselves to prevent it, and your friend T. W. had an encounter with a woman who would defend her bonfire; it is said that he kicked her and that she threw his periwig into the fire. Other women dressed up King Charles I.'s statue at the Cross with flowers, the zealous men in authority sent the beadles to pull them off; as they were getting up, the women thrust the ladder away; upon which the constables were sent who performed that feat. This no doubt will raise their merit with the party, and certainly the preventing the ringing of the bells and keeping the women from making bonfires with no greater a loss than of a periwig is a piece of service deserves to be taken notice of. Dr. Sacheverell returned Friday evening to Cotheridge, on Saturday dined at Worcester with Lord Folliot and returned at night to Mr. Green's. He is to dine with Mr. Perks at Worcester this day, and I hear in the afternoon goes to Evesham, and to morrow dines with Mr. Savage of Elmley.

[DANIEL] DE FOE to [ROBERT HARLEY].

1710, July 17—I cannot but think that now is the time to find out and improve those blessed mediums of this nation's happiness, which lie between the wild extremes of all parties and which I know you have long wished for.

I know you are blest with principles of peace and concern for your country, and a true taste of its liberty and interest, which are now sadly embarrassed. My lot (in which your favour was my introduction) has been so much abroad that I have had but a small view of things, yet I have room enough to see and lament preposterous conduct on every side. I cannot but hope that Heaven has yet reserved you to be the restorer of your country by yet bringing exasperated parties and the respective mad men to their politic senses, and healing the breaches on both sides, which have thus wounded the nation.

If I can be useful to so good a work without the least view of private advantage I should be very glad, and for this reason I presume to renew the liberty of writing to you, which was once my honour and advantage, and which I hope I have done nothing to forfeit.

My personal obligations to you are very great and cannot be forgotten by me. It would be a double honour to me to have my gratitude mixed with the service of my country.

If you please to admit a short conference on these heads, that honour to me may at least issue in my being rendered more able to guide myself to the public advantage, which is what I sincerely desire to make the end of all my actions, and shall esteem it my singular advantage to take right measures by your direction.

Postscript.—If may have the honour of a line or any order by your servant, the bearer shall attend for it, as you shall please to direct; be pleased to direct it to " A. Goldsmith " as usual.

Charles Cholmondeley to Robert Harley.

1710, July 22. Vale Royal—Since I came here most of our gentlemen have thought fit to fix upon me with Sir George Warburton to oppose our two impeaching members. This puts me upon making use of all our friends, and forces me to beg the favour of your interest with Sir (*sic*) William Penn for the Quakers' votes in this county, where they are numerous, and one Bangs, a very considerable speaker among them, is very warm against us.

Lord Weymouth to [Robert Harley].

1710, July 24. Longleat—I have so entire confidence in your friendship and voluntary promises, that I conclude nothing is yet fixed, proper for the knowledge of an "Outlyer," and yet the common discourse of particular changes makes me think the child is near to the birth, were there strength to bring forth.

The making Mr. Prior the first fruits of a Restoration shows that commission will be continued, and therefore give me leave to remind you of Sir J. Pakington's just pretensions, who twice refused to accept *Onus cum honore.*

I will believe there shall be a new parliament, though I hear the party think with Agag the bitterness of death is past; but we understrappers are as busy as if the writs were sealed, and hope for good success could we see a reformation of the Excise and Custom House officers, whose influence on boroughs is greater than can be imagined.

The Cinque Ports are much guided by the Lord Warden, as well as Kent by a popular Lord Lieutenant, and though Lord Winchilsea's unhappy circumstances forced him with reluctance to make a false step, yet no man is more beloved and pitied there, or capable of doing more service; and greater sinners must be restored, if they did not offend out of malicious wickedness.

I am solicited out of Gloucestershire to join with those gentlemen who propose young Jack Howe for that county. I know the spring that sets it a going, and foresee the consequences hoped from it, which makes me beg your directions how to govern myself, for I would not thwart anything that may be designed, by ignorance or inadvertence.

The DUKE OF SOMERSET to [ROBERT HARLEY].

[1710,] July 26—On this most unfortunate occasion of Mr. Cressett's death it is absolutely necessary you do come to the Queen and to the Duke of Shrewsbury's at or before nine o'clock this night. We have talked it over and do conclude it to be of so very great consequence that somebody ought to go immediately to Hanover and in his way discourse the Pensioner too on the present changes of persons and of the Parliament—of consideration and who hath the honour to be in the Queen's confidence. If it be thought a right thing neither the Duke of Shrewsbury nor myself will decline it, but on the contrary either of us will go very cheerfully, as we don't doubt but my Lord Poulett will say and do the same—to go within less than ten days and to return in less than six weeks. I give you this short hint of our thoughts that you may prepare your own against nine o'clock. The Duke of Shrewsbury hath engaged me this morning to excuse him to the Queen from —— (sic) which I have done.

VISCOUNT DUPPLIN to his father-in-law ROBERT HARLEY.

[1710,] July 26—My father is impatiently waiting to hear that the Parliament is dissolved and wishing that all good designs may be speedily effectuated. He says, if you'll let him know how matters stand, he'll be very ready to use his utmost endeavours to serve you. We have a story here that our two D[uke]s (Queensberry and Hamilton) are divided and quarrelling who shall be preferred. I hope things are upon a better foundation than that either they or any other shall by selfish ends put the least stop to what is so much for the public good. People here really think you slow, but it's hard judging at such a distance. I'm glad to find the generality in this country so much pleased with the expectation of a new Parliament, though your enemies take a great deal of pains to fix their own interests in the elections, both peers and commoners. I hope when a dissolution comes it will be easily managed to get our Scotch elections to your mind.

SIR HARRY PEACHY, M.P. for Sussex, to [E. LEWIS].

1710, July 28. Newgrove—I received yours of the 22nd and desire you to give my service to him [Harley] you mention, and to assure him that I shall be glad to serve him, but that I do not know at present of any other farm then what I have already hinted, which I shall keep my eye upon. If I can hear of any other you shall know it, but wish I had had two or three months more notice, those purchases requiring some management, as well as direct bartering, in a country where there are more buyers than sellers. What lieth in power I shall with pleasure do, for the service of our friend and you, but can think of one only concern more than I have mentioned, which I will enquire after, and if I find any likelihood of dealing will let you know it. I hope that neither you nor our friend will judge of my inclination to you by my forbearing warm and pompous expressions in my letters.

D[ANIEL DE] F[OE] to [ROBERT HARLEY].

1710, July 28—Since I had the honour of seeing you, I can assure you by experience I find, that acquainting some people they are not all to be devoured, and eaten up—will have all the effect upon them could be wished for; assuring them that moderate counsels are at the bottom of all these things; that the old mad party are not coming in; that his Grace the Duke of S[hrewsbur]y and yourself, &c. are at the head of the management; and that neither have been moved, however ill treated, to forsake the principles you always owned; that toleration, succession or union are not struck at, and they may be easy as to the nation's liberties—those things make strong impressions, and well improved may bring all to rights again.

I wish for an occasion to discourse farther on these heads, when your leisure will permit me that favour, when I have also something to offer about ways and means to prevent the ruin of the public credit; and raise things again in spite of some people's endeavour to run them down, in which if I can do any service I shall think myself happy. I should enlarge but rather refer it to discourse, and shall call on your servant myself to receive your commands as to time, promising myself when I have that honour again I shall not break away so rudely as I did last.

The Duke of Somerset to [Robert Harley].

1710, July 30, Sunday night, six o'clock—Some affairs have already happened, but more will before the cabinet council do rise, that the Queen hath commanded me to write to you to come this night to the Duke of Shrewsbury's lodgings and from thence you are to be conveyed to —— (sic) by me.

The Same to [the Same].

Same date, Sunday night, ten o'clock—I am very sorry for the cause of your not coming to us this night, therefore I must desire admittance to-morrow morning between the hours of nine and ten into your own house to discourse on some matters of consequence.

Postscript.—Don't forget to order your porter to open the door to a hackney chair with curtains drawn.

The Earl of Orrery to [Robert Harley].

1710, July 31. Camp before Bethune—I cannot miss the opportunity I have at present of paying my respects to you by an officer that is going for England, though I have not time to be so particular as I should be. I desire to congratulate you upon the success of our affairs in England hitherto, and the fair prospect of carrying it further.

We are told now the Plenipotentiaries are gone, which will destroy the argument against more alterations for fear of hindering the Peace; though I always thought impartial people must be convinced that nothing else could bring it on. The Duke of Argyll and I are much in the dark about the rise and true meaning of several steps that have been made, for want of frequent and distinct accounts from our friends, but we make no doubt but everything is well managed in such able hands. We hope now there will soon be a dissolution and that the kingdom is so well disposed that elections cannot go wrong. In Scotland I dare say with a little care you may have them all as they should be. I find Lord Il[ay] is of that opinion, and I don't question but he has very good grounds for it, for I believe few people know the situation of affairs there better than he; and I am confident you may so absolutely depend upon him without reserve that you cannot possibly find any person more proper than he to consult withal upon all occasions relating to that kingdom. I could heartily wish that he were well settled in some good civil post there. I know he would be well pleased to be Register of Scotland if he could have the place for life, or to be Justice General in the room of Lord Cromartie, to bring about which he has formed a scheme; though I believe the first would be most acceptable to him. I am afraid he is so modest as not to have mentioned anything of this kind to you, but I beg you would take some opportunity of entering upon the subject with him. The merit of the two brothers, especially upon this occasion, entitles them to anything they can ask, and the great respect and value they have for you I'm confident will oblige you to assist them to the utmost in their demands, which I will take upon me to say will be very reasonable considering the service they have already done and their resolution as well as ability to do a great deal more. Some time ago I writ to H. St. [John] pretty earnestly to let him know how necessary I thought it was that some restraint should be put to that exorbitant power Lord Marlborough has in the army. I am every day more convinced of that necessity, for he plainly disposes of preferments here- with no other view but to create a faction sufficient to support him against the Queen and her friends in case every other prop should fail.

I mentioned at the same time my promotion of Major General which I think I have no ill title to, and which I suppose upon the first application to the Queen will be granted. It will be of use to encourage her friends here and will add a little to the present mortification of his Highness.

MRS. L. M. CRESSETT to [ROBERT HARLEY].

1710, August 2—Yesterday Mr. Hill came to town to present my memorial to the Lord Treasurer for the 955*l.* which should have been paid Mr. Cressett for his equipage and advance money. Mr. Boyle has interceded with his lordship, and I am informed that warrants will be drawn for the payment of the money. I entreat your opinion whether it will not be better for me to defer the presentation to the Queen of my petition relating to my poor family until such warrants are passed.

ROBERT HARLEY to LORD CHANCELLOR COWPER.

1710, August 2—By this post I received notice from the clerk of the peace of Herefordshire that I am put out of the commission of the peace for that county. I hear from other hands that a new commission was brought thither July 30; and that care was taken to have a particular remark upon my name by its being rased out. The manner of doing it was sufficiently understood that I was to receive a mortification in the face of my country, therefore I must not doubt but there was particular direction given for the doing it, and the manner it was done in. I do assure your Lordship I receive this with the entire submission that becomes me. I have learnt not to be surprised with affairs of this nature, because my father was turned out by the regulators in King James's time. I thought it my duty to acquaint your Lordship that no one is better pleased with my being turned out than myself. *Draft.*

EDWARD HARLEY to ——.

1710, August 3—I suppose you have heard that my Lord Chancellor has put my father out of the commission of the peace for Herefordshire, and Sir Thomas Mansell for that for Glamorganshire. I think they are very much in the right to show what they are. My father wrote to his Lordship to thank him for his favour, and that he supposed he was turned out for the same reason my grandfather was by the regulators in King James's time.

CHRISTIANE EBERHARDINE, QUEEN OF POLAND, to [ROBERT HARLEY ?].

1710, August 4. Toroau—The letter you have been so good as to write to me gives me as much pleasure as consolation in the state in which I find myself, siuce it is full of hope and honest feeling. You shall have my portrait as soon as possible, to satisfy your ladies and your own curiosity; and in return I accept the offer you make me of the French translation of Archbishop Tillotson's Sermons. They will be the more agreeable as it is known to me that the sermons of your celebrated preachers are very learned and worthy of admiration.

My sole consolation in the present dangerous conjunctures is that your illustrious Queen as well as all the Protestant Powers sympathise in my disgrace, and interest themselves in the safety of my only son the Electoral Prince, whom the opposite party attempt to draw into its meshes by a thousand intrigues, but the good God will never permit that my son shall be the victim of Roman superstition, &c.—*French. Signed.*

LORD CHANCELLOR COWPER to [ROBERT HARLEY].

1710, August 4. Hertingfordbury—I just now received your letter here by the post, and am so surprised as well as vexed with the fact contained in it (to which before I was wholly a stranger), that I cannot rest a moment without sending you my very true answer to it. There lately went a commision of the peace out for Herefordshire, to add a few where I was informed they were wanted; but the Clerk of the Crown had not my fiat to put out any, nor leave out any, except such as I was informed were dead. In short I assure you on my word and honour I never intended the doing it, and 'tis a million to one my secretary Mr. Eugham is so careful as that he has not made the mistake, or laid any fiat before me, which has drawn on such an absurdity ; but if it be as you are informed, it must be the blunder of the Clerk of the Crown, Mr. Wright (my predecessor's son), or his deputy, or his malice to put me in fault whether I will or no. I suggest the latter because I was served such a trick in the case of Sir Simon Harcourt; he was in the Oxford commission with the title of Attorney-General, and when that commission was renewed after Sir Simon laid down, the Clerk of the Crown without my fiat or knowledge left him out as of course, and thereupon Sir Simon and his friends, as they had some ground, looking on it as done by me, I was very much concerned till I let him know the truth. But then the Clerk of the Crown had some excuse, that he thought Sir Simon was put in as Attorney General only, as he was in the other commissions of course, and so left him out of course, as he left that office; but in this your case I can't imagine what should move the brute to commit so unlucky a mistake if it be one. I can only assure you that if you take it patiently I don't, and that if he that has done this was at all in my power, he should not go three hours unpunished by being displaced; as it is I will resent it in the best manner I can. So far am I from doing such a poor, pitiful, spiteful, nay extreme foolish, thing as the putting your name out of that commission, that no force or temptation could have wrought me up, or rather down, to it; and since I have had the honour to be known to you so long, and never, I own, that I know of, received anything from you but favours, I must a little complain, that you would not presume anything rather than believe me guilty of so base an action. I assure you I have learned to be and really am not solicitous about anything in these times of struggle and contest, but to acquit myself as an honest and impartial man. As for my particular disposition towards yourself, since I have this proper occasion of mentioning it, I assure you it is to wish you all imaginable good, and that I think so very well of you as to believe, though you have had great provocation, and have so much in your power, yet you will rather even forego the opportunity of retaliating, than your country should suffer by so doing. I would not say this to flatter you, if I had not these hopes firmly rooted in me. As for the retrieving this vexatious mistake (if it be done) I have sent by this same express, to Engham, to inquire into it, to prepare things against to-morrow, when I will be in town, to seal a new commission for the correcting it; and I hope on inquiry to give you a more particular and satisfactory account of this matter.

Postscript.—Since I wrote this, perusing yours again I find you say your name was rased out: I fear the commission has had some foul play in the country, I beg you to inquire into it.

Robert Harley to the Lord Chancellor [Cowper].

1710, August 4—I received this night the honour of your Lordship's letter and return my hearty thanks for the assurance you are pleased to give me that I have not lost your favour. I am sure I am not conscious to myself of having done anything to forfeit it, and that occasioned my troubling your Lordship with my former letter.

As to my being out of the commission of the peace, that is now over, it has had all its effects and I have had so many letters these two posts upon it that I make it my request to your Lordship no more may be said or done in it. I am now fairly out, and I shall never be willing to be in a possibility of being liable to the same remark another time; therefore I hope I shall be excused if I cannot consent to meddle with that commission any more.—*Draft.*

[The Earl of Ilay to Robert Harley.]

1710, August 5. Edinburgh—I have not troubled you since I came here in hopes that your time has been better employed than to be taken up with any trifles relating to this country. 112 of 19 has I think generally a better appearance than could be expected; as to that of + if 200, 333, and 125 concert measures together the others will not have so much as the show of a 120; nay if 125 acts fairly on the right side nothing 333 can do in my opinion can injure us, but if all enemies are to be excluded one of those two measures is absolutely necessary. 126, 122, and 117's friends meet regularly with 121 and I don't doubt design to declare openly that way, which I wish to God they would, that none of our weak brethren may be drawn into having hopes of them. In my last to 111 I suggested a little blow which may be given to one of 122's creatures if it does not depend too much upon 1000 to be done immediately. I am insensibly troubling you idly with little matters of this kind but hope you will excuse every poor widow valuing her mite. I take all the care I can to say what is proper to every body here ; I could wish you would write the letter you promised to the head of 118 because I know it would do good. I see it necessary every day now that I converse with people here that 200 should be here when 112 approach. 122 came to-day to see me and is the humblest creature in the world, and very inquisitive to know whether he is to be comprehended (as we dissenters speak). I write constantly to 111 who I don't doubt troubles you more upon the subject of 107 than you desire.

The Duke of Somerset to [Robert Harley].

[1710,] August 6—If I was certain to meet you at dinner to-morrow at my Lord Mar's I should have no occasion to write now, but I not knowing how you may stand engaged I send you the Queen's commands to attend her tomorrow night at the usual hour.

Lord Chancellor Cowper to [Robert Harley].

1710, August 6—On my coming to town last night I had the honour of your letter of the 4th, wherein though you are pleased to express yourself desirous to hear no more of a matter which has troubled you so much by letters out of the country about it, I must yet entreat your patience this time, to let you know, (as I promised in my former) the true particulars of which this mistake consisted, since when I was in the country I could only give you my guess concerning it : the rather because you will easily imagine, that one whose weakness must necessarily fall into many errors in the execution of so burdensome a trust, and of such variety of business as mine is, must be very unwilling to bear the least imputation of having done amiss in a matter, where you cannot but be convinced I am wholly blameless, as soon as it is stated : I beg leave to add one reason more for this repeated trouble, which is that I must ever set a very great value on your good opinion and can omit no care in my power to preserve it.

I find there is no mistake in my fiat, but Mr. Sambrook, the Clerk of the Crown's deputy, informs me that whereas that office has ever of course without any warrant inserted the Privy Councillors into all the commissions of peace, and from time to time regulated those commissions according to the alterations in the list of the Privy Councillors ; and he having lately my warrant to insert a few justices and nothing more, set himself to correct the names of the Privy Councillors by a list he had lately received from a Clerk of the Council in which your name being omitted, and standing in the commission prepared in blank among the Privy Councillors he rased it out of the engrossment, not reflecting or not knowing, that as you had always been, so you were entitled in other respects to stand, in that commission. I believe that this account of the Clerk's, as 'tis probable so 'tis true : he was bred under Sir E. Northey, and is one who on inquiry I am told has a very great and particular honour for yourself, so could not intend to affront you. This being the case, I hope now it is submitted to you to judge of, you will not continue any longer such a mark of your resentment, as to say that now you are fairly out and that you desire to be excused from meddling with that commission any more, since 'tis evident your name was not omitted by any sufficient authority, but purely by the mis-apprehension of a subordinate officer, and therefore ought to be restored as soon as can be to the condition it always should have been in. The error till 'I was informed of it was not, I am sure, in the least mine ; but from the time I was so it will become my fault, if I do not see it corrected as soon as possible ; which I have ordered to be done, and the commission sent down, and that the Clerk of the Crown should in his letter to the Clerk of the Peace with the commission acknowledge the nature of his mistake, which, with recording it so soon after, will convince every one, who has not resolved against being convinced, that this was pure chance, and as such not worthy of any consideration.

Endorsed by Harley :—" Answered immediately."

Viscount Dupplin to his father-in-law [Robert Harley].

[1710,] August 8.—I had a letter the other day from Mr. Cunningham, which my father takes to be written by your direction. The substance of it is telling that there is a town where you can get me chosen member of parliament for the House of Commons, if my father and I desire it. My father says you are better judge what is proper for me to do in that matter than either of us, therefore he leaves it to you to do in it as you think fit. But withal his own opinion is that I can spend my time no where so well as in the House of Commons, which I am fully convinced of myself ; so that we both leave it entirely to you.

The Duke of Atholl and several others sent to my father to concert measures with him about the elections, upon the supposition of a new parliament. But he has put them off, not knowing what measures are concerted with you ; for we are made believe here that Duke Hamilton is not entirely Tory as yet, and if it be so, he will create a great deal of trouble in the elections here, both in that of the Peers and Commons ; therefore my father prays you by any means, if possible, to make him of your interest, as being the Scotchman that is by far most capable to do service in the elections. If you can get the four Dukes, Hamilton, Queensberry Argyll and Atholl of your interest you will uncontro-vertedly carry the elections here. The first is most necessary, the second, except in so far as he is supported by the Queen's favour, is of the smallest interest, and for the two last I have no doubt but they will be of your side. We are told here that my Lord Stair, the President of the Sessions, Sir David, and all the Dalrymples with all the interest they can make, are against you, and that my Lord Leven and my Lord Rothes, who were always before in opposition to one another, have now joined their interests in the shire of Fife, to carry the election there against you : but both of them will be disappointed for the Lyon [Sir A. Erskine] will carry it.

Several Peers that were united the last year in one interest against the Squadrony, will now join with them, such as my Lord Seafield, who is very busy caballing at Edinburgh with the Squadrony, who were never so diligent and painful as now. And they will certainly carry off weak brethren, unless the Queen go in to a thorough measure in strengthening the hands of her friends and discouraging her enemies. This I believe will be thought fully as necessary a measure here in Scotland as in England. Wherefore what you do, do it with all your might, and the sooner the better. I am sure you have not the least doubt of my father's inclinations and mine, to be not only good but zealous to serve the interest of the good Queen. Wherefore let us be fully instructed, that we may go on in one joint measure.

My Lord Mar wrote to my father and told him that my Lord Ilay was to call here, and to acquaint my father with what measures they had taken; but he has not yet passed this way. Send down my Lord Mar as soon as you can, and my father and I shall meet him at Edinburgh, and do you all the service we can. It is equal if you write either to my father or me, by yourself, my Lord Mar, or Mr. Cunningham ; but we are resolved not to move one step till we have your instructions. Thus far my father.

My father sends you his most humble service, and had writ this to you with his own hand, if the gout in it had not hindered him. However he is otherwise very well, and able to ride about amongst his workmen. Your daughter I thank God is perfectly well recovered, writ to you herself last post, and now sends you her duty. Little Tommy is as fine a child as ever you saw, sends his duty to his grandpapa in the best manner he can. The Marquis of Annandale is to be here this night or to-morrow, I suppose will stay two or three days, and we shall hear what tune his Lordship sings. I beg your blessing for your daughter, myself, and the child.

J. D[RUMMOND] to ROBERT HARLEY.

1710, August [8–]19, N.S. Amsterdam—I have almost convinced all the men worth applying to of the necessity of what you seem to have gone so heartily about, and there is not now any one who orders their effects to be taken out of your funds that I can discover; some . . . . have indeed sold on the breaking off of the treating for peace in hopes to buy cheaper again, and orders are gone to buy, it stocks should fall upon the dissolution of the Parliament, which your friends once gave the world reason to believe, and we had convinced the reasonable part of mankind here could be of no ill consequence, but on the contrary that your friends would vie with the old party who should go on with most heartiness to carry on the public good, and apply the public's money to most advantage, but by the last post we are made believe you will be all deserted and matters will be managed as formerly. I must say Sir Humphrey (Mackworth) has been very cunning and has secured every thing that could produce money or credit, and got them as much at his devotion as possible. As to the public remittances I know every particular how they have been managed and have been employed less or more by every one concerned in them this war; but unless you can secure the Bank to undertake the remittances into their own hands, or get such a man who has credit abroad as Sir James Bateman, or Sir Theodore Janssen who, next to Furnese, and I may say Sir James preferable to him, has the best interest and credit abroad, I know none can go through with it. Sam. Shepheard is an excellent merchant for shipping, and foreign trade by far the first in England, but no banker, so that unless you could secure these two and Milner with his cabal for the Portugal affair, I know not how you could be well served, for I believe the Bank, Mr. Eylls, and all that party are at Sir Humphrey's devotion. If my private affairs would have permitted me I had certainly come over to your assistance in that particular which I think I have reason to know a good deal of, but I had the misfortune to be under age last war when all the estates were got by that trade, being only yet thirty-four years old, of which I have been above nineteen in this place.

The news from Spain are very seasonable, and the siege of Bethune being calculated to end before the 25th day of this month new style, we are thinking on a new siege, though the people here wish for a battle. I cannot express how barbarously and villainously all your friends are treated in all our printed papers here, and the French refugee scribblers with whom they correspond write them all the scandalous stories which are contrived with you, and they write them as if they were matter of fact. I must see to send you one of our coffeehouse news letters which come from England, and by the French Gazette of this town you may see what pains are taken in your prejudice. ·I wish I knew what we had to depend upon, then one could speak boldly and prepare people for any thing that may be thought useful to be done, and inform them of the reasonableness of doing things after that manner. I am heartily sorry for my old acquaintance Mr. Cresset's death, he would have been an useful [and] valuable man abroad on this occasion. I know nobody would do better there than Mr. Benson, who speaks all languages, fit for that court and knows the world very well, but I believe he may be useful at home. Is my Lord Eyla [Islay] too young? they adore that family at Hanover, for the Duke of Argyll has done more honour to the old Lady's recommendations than any other great man, and has lately given her Highness's page an Ensign's commission in his regiment, which is very kindly taken. I am sorry your premier minister [Shrewsbury] did not come home that way from Italy. I have the honour to be known a little to his Grace, and have lately had a fresh assurance of his favour. I wish the Canon were at London that I could hear some certainty. I am concerned in money matters with a Hereford nobleman's son who lives in Golden Square, has an office at Whitehall; I wish I knew if it were fit for me to retire, he is now down in the country I believe to secure his election for that town. If you could get Mr. Hill to go into the city or meddle again in money matters he could influence some people who were convinced of his integrity and capacity last war, and he has great esteem here; Sir James Bateman will do much for him.

The EARL OF HALIFAX to ROBERT HARLEY.

1710, August 10—I was engaged in company last night when I received the great civilities and compliments you did me the honour to send me. I wish you much joy in the station you have accepted, which, as you foresee, will be attended with so great difficulties, that I tremble at them. Your great abilities and your knowledge of the Revenue, will soon make you master of all the business, but how you will restore credit, and find money for the demands that will be upon you exceeds my capacity.

The duty of my office obliges me to pay your lordships [of the Treasury] all the service I can, and my inclinations dispose me to return the great kindness you show me, in all the friendship and sincerity I can express, and if there is any assistance I can give in healing our divisions, restoring the credit, and carrying on the public business, for the easing and satisfying her Majesty, bringing the war to a happy end, and establishing the Protestant Succession, I shall very cheerfully follow your orders to promote so good a work.

LORD HAVERSHAM to ROBERT HARLEY.

1710, August 10—According to my promise I send you the paper you spoke of; you may, if you like it, dispose of it as you please. There are three or four words added which relate to the House of Hanover at the end, excepting which, those who remember anything of it I believe will find it pretty exact.

Endorsed by Harley:—" With his Speech."

C[HARLWOOD] LAWTON to [ROBERT HAULEY].

1710, August 11. Worcestershire—I go tomorrow from hence and shall be next week at my Lord Shaftesbury's at St. Giles's in Dorsetshire for a few days. A note from a clerk in the Secretary's Office brought word on Thursday that the Queen hath displaced my Lord Godolphin. I have had no reason to grieve at the news, but I had one thought which I believe is pretty natural and that is, that some of his relations and creatures may likewise be displaced; and for that reason I beg leave to give you the character of one of the Commissioners of the Excise who is related to and was put in several years ago by him. I mean Sir Marmaduke Wyvill. Perhaps you may know him yourself, but if you do not, take my word that he is one of the honestest and most friendly men in the world. Perhaps he may rather be called a Tory, but I am sure he would not have any man alive persecuted for his opinion, and he heartily wisheth the good of his country, and in Sir John Fenwick's case he behaved himself extremely well.

When I think of removals I can't but think it possible that there may be some in the Salt Office, and if my brother Ralph Lawton was made Commissioner in it, I am sure nobody could say it was a fault.

If you and my friend in Leicester Fields are entered into any terms of friendship and familiarity, it would be a kind part to tell him accidentally that I have, as you know I always have to you, from time to time, even when he was out of all business, spoken handsomely of him; for such an account of my behaviour from you might make him co-operate with you to do something for my benefit.

COLONEL HORATIO WALPOLE to [ROBERT HARLEY].

1710, August 11. Beckhall—I find by Tuesday's post that her Majesty had removed from her the spring of resistance, Lord Treasurer, and has made choice of you and others to succeed him by commission, whereby I conceive the Parliament will be dissolved, which I would gladly know being very busy in making interest for better members than we had last, I should say have, and at the expense of my own election; for my nephew [Robert] has given me to understand that his brethren the Whigs inform him I am very active, nay the life and spirit of all the opposition they are to expect; so that if I will not compound for one in the county he can't choose me at Castle Rising, which I thought I had an hereditary right in, my nephew and I having the power of the Corporation in our hands but he much the greater share, so I expect to be succeeded by Mr. Comptroller without a staff. And lest you may not have an account of the sense we have of her Majesty's ill-usage and in what manner we are able to show our resentment, I think it no small encouragement to her Majesty for a speedy dissolution when I can with good reason assure her that she may rely upon two for Yarmouth, two for Norwich, two for Thetford, and two for the county, so that the Whigs instead of having ten to two as they have now, if we sit again, we shall have eight to four and they only Castle Rising and Lynn where I am contriving to spirit up an opposition, though I can't as yet promise myself very good success but will set Sir Chas. Turner hard if my nephew stands with him. Therefore I would gladly know your opinion whether there will be a dissolution or no, if not I shall hold my hand a little. But since in my own thoughts the Treasurer being dismissed the rest of the gang will follow and then a new Parliament. Of course I shall not stop till I receive your commands for I would gladly recommend myself to her Majesty's favour,

and that by your kind assistance; and although I be out at Castle
Rising I shall be able to assist in the choice of a Speaker, having good
assurance I shall be chosen, and I have been invited to stand for two
places one of which I am sure of.

The small acquaintance I have with you gave me great discouragement from giving you this trouble, but since it proceeds from the
inclination I have for the cause I have always promoted and you the
chief instrument of retrieving, I hope you will the readier excuse and
accept my weak endeavours and believe I heartily wish you good
success.

Anthony Murray to Robert Harley.

1710, August 11–22. Wolfenbuttel—Having passed more than a
fortnight at Hanover, I came no sooner here than I was surprised with
the melancholy news of Mr. Cresset's death. Knowing his merit I
cannot but with great sorrow lament so great a loss.

It is very necessary to have an honest man at Hanover as soon as
possible; and to send one to King Augustus who is a considerable
prince, and who has been neglected. I earnestly pray you to mind me
with this last, that it may please her Majesty to honour me with being
her envoy at his court, or at any other court that may be thought fit.
I may justly flatter myself with the great Earl of Rochester's protection
in this, and being more known in foreign courts and having been more
abroad perhaps than any of her subjects.

[Daniel] De Foe to [Robert Harley].

1710, August 12—I cannot but heartily congratulate you on the
happy recovery of your honour and trusts in the Government. Her
Majesty is particularly just in placing you in this station, where you
had been so coarsely treated. It is with a satisfaction that I cannot
express that I see you thus established again; and it was always with
regret that when you met with ill treatment I found myself left and
obliged by circumstances to continue in the service of your enemies.
And now, though I am sunk by the change, and know not yet whether
I shall find help in it or no, yet I not only rejoice in the thing, but
shall convince you I do so, by publicly appearing to defend and reconcile
things, if possible, to open the eyes of a wilfully blind and prejudiced
party. In order to this, I shall wait on you in the evening with those
sheets I showed you, finished from the press and to lay before you some
measures I am taking to serve that honest principle which I know you
espouse at a time so nice and when every man thinks 'tis in his power
to wound the government through the sides of the Treasury, and to run
down their masters by running down the public credit. I have two or
three times set pen to paper to move you in my own case, yet cannot
put on assurance enough to do it, believing also your own generosity,
and the former goodness I have had such experience of will move you
in my behalf.

Providence seems to cast me back upon you (I write that with joy)
and lays me at your door; at the very juncture when she blesses you
with the means of doing for me what your bounty shall prompt to.

But in recommending myself to you, I would fain have an eye to
your service. I would not be an *invalid*, and my hope is, that as you
were pleased to reccommend me to another as one that could be made
useful, and who it was worth while to encourage; the same argument

will move you to entertain the man yourself, since your merit, and the voice of the nation places you in the same point, in which you were pleased to present me to another.

I cease to press you on this head; I shall study to make myself useful and leave the rest wholly to your goodness.

Endorsed by Harley "Mr. D. F."

R. Monckton to [Bonert Harley].

1710, August 12. Hodroyd—I perceive our mistress is resolved to be master notwithstanding all the kind advice to the contrary. But what you will believe startles me most is that the Tories tell us positively we are all to be out of her service and that all will not be enough neither. The occasion of giving you this trouble is that the Duke of Leeds's family affirm for certain that he is to be Lord Lieutenant of all our three Ridings. I beg your answer before I tell our friend [the Duke of Newcastle] of what they boast with so much confidence. Though I think it very improbable yet I think also it is a good occasion to try how I stand in your esteem, and if you are pleased to show me any mark of the continuance of your favour. I did presume to congratulate my Lord Dartmouth who I am sure cannot but think I have ever been his servant. Our friend comforted me that though he did not vouchsafe to intimate to me his acceptance yet he hoped he would do it *ore tenus.* When I sued for his patronage in town he used to refer me to a better friend he said I had meaning yourself, and which I believe, and expect if you are not straitened for room; and I am sure you cannot make room, I mean only in your favour, for one that is more cordially and personally addicted to you.

The Earl of Jersey to [Robert Harley].

1710, August 12. Squerries [near Westerham]—I beg leave to express the true satisfaction I have that her Majesty at last has thought fit to declare to the world the great esteem and value she has for you in trusting you with the management of her Treasury. I do not doubt that the public will reap the benefit of it, and you a very great reputation.

[W. Bromley to Robert Harley.]

1710, August 12—I am sensible you must have had great difficulties to struggle with, and can make due allowance for them, but after the grand obstruction is removed I think they must daily lessen.

I congratulate you on the place Dyer had given me which you will much better fill, but am surprised to hear that the first commissions of lieutenancy and custos rotulorum issue to the Lord Chancellor who (besides his other merits), I am told, has lately turned you out of the commission of the peace in Herefordshire and Middlesex. This is as unaccountable as the making Sir R. O[nslow] a privy councillor.

Ralph Freeman to Robert Harley.

1710, August 13. Aspeden Hall—I am mightily surprised to find by the prints that the Lord Chancellor is to be our Lord Lieutenant. Lord Salisbury must of course think himself neglected, and our gentlemen will look upon this as the greatest support of a different interest, that we were now in hopes would be lessened. If this be past recovery

I beg you will take care that the Chancellor of the Duchy may be put
into such hands as will support us, for that post will have some interest
among us.

VISCOUNT WEYMOUTH to [ROBERT HARLEY].

1710, August 13. Longleat—I rejoice much in your good success,
not so much for your sake as that of the public, for the labourer is
worthy of his hire. Having with St. Paul the care of all the churches,
I cannot expect you should throw away any part of your time on me,
and yet upon the score at least of our old friendship I should hope that
you will sometimes remember me.

VISCOUNT DUPPLIN to [ROBERT HARLEY].

1710, August 13—Everybody here in this country is so full of a
new parliament, that both parties are as busy as they can be in laying
themselves out to serve their friends against next elections. One party
go on in such a firm confederacy that they fancy nothing will be able to
break their interest in the elections for several of the shires and
boroughs, and the same folks are in great expectations to get some of
their party chosen amongst the sixteen peers. The other party seem
much supernumerary and large, as good heads and hands as their
enemies; but their antagonists seem to have this advantage over them,
that they have not as yet got a plain measure laid down to them which
they are to prosecute, and they seem to have the best will that can be to
do right things, but do not really know which way to go about it, and
are like a brave, numerous, bold army without a commander to give
them orders. Now some people attribute this to your slowness at
London, and wish you would let your friends know here what way
you would have them unite, and in what measure you would have them
to join, that they might serve their Queen and country to the best
advantage.

My Lord Annandale and my Lord Stormont were here almost all
this week; they are both as right as one could wish. The Marqui s of
Annandale is thoroughly right and very earnest to advance the interest.
They told me one story I was surprised at, that the Duke of Queensberry is setting up a perfect republican in Dumfriesshire to oppose my
Lord Stormont's second son, Mr. James Murray, whom my Lord
Annandale sets up in that shire to stand next election. I wish with
all my heart a way were fallen upon to make that great man let alone
such a thing. For as for Mr. Murray, I can give a character of him
from personal acquaintance, having been his comrade a long time, but
shall let that alone till it be nearer the elections; only his father bid me
tell you, that he has declared to him he will renounce him for ever if he
do not serve his Queen according to your directions, and I am sure he
needed not have done this, his own sense making him as forward in
such a good cause as any could desire. He has entered advocate
at Edinburgh with a great deal of applause, and is a very pretty
gentleman, and I hope he shall carry his election.

We are all in great hopes of a dissolution every day. Pray let me
know your commands by C[unningham?] or any other way. I hear
letters are visited, so I wish I knew if mine come to hand, and if you
desire I should write more frequently. I think it strange Lord Dartmouth does not cause have a care of his friends' letters. Your daughter
and Tommy are well. She sends her duty and we both beg your
blessing and for the child, so adieu.

F[RANCIS] ROBARTES to ROBERT HARLEY.

1710, August 13—I would willingly apply my interest at the next election as may be most acceptable to her Majesty, which I shall be glad to learn from you. At Tintagel all the voices declare for 'me, at Lostwithiel all but the mayor. I also intend to try my fortune at Bodmin and Tregony, for each of which places I have served twice. In a fortnight I may know what probability I have of succeeding there, and my recommendations shall be conformable to your intimation.

WILLIAM ATWOOD to ROBERT HARLEY.

1710, August 14. Inner Temple—You may remember the late Lord Treasurer had an invincible prejudice in relation to what I did as a Chief Justice [of New York] in vindicating the authority of the Crown in a matter which Sir Edw. Northey, then attorney-general, had given to be high treason; and wherein if I had erred in any point, as I am absolutely certain I did not, I should think it no bar to a restitution, much less to the having the salary due between my unconfirmed suspension and the determination of my patent. The sum is but 250*l.*, small in itself but of the utmost consequence to a man loaded with misfortunes as well as misrepresentations. For this I have a petition depending in the Treasury, but put off by an expected representation from the governor of New York.

W. [NICHOLSON] BISHOP OF CARLISLE to K. MUSGRAVE.

1710, August 14—I am not in the least shocked with the account you give me of present and expected changes at Court. Let the contending parties share the lion's skin in their turns; I claim no portion with them. Let her Majesty appoint what Ministry she pleases it will be my standing opinion that it is highly criminal to bespatter them either from the pulpit or the press. I shall always openly pray for God's directing their counsels, and shall keep my fears to myself.

In Westmorland they tell me Col. Graham is much at a loss for an agreeable fellow-knight, though he has taken great pains to magnify the good services (in the main) of his present colleague; but old Mr. Wilson thinks the weather is growing too hot in Parliament for him to venture his only son any more in that region.

Our two present knights of Cumberland seem to threaten one another, but they are two wary gentlemen and will not vainly spend their money.

At Carlisle they talk of four new candidates, Mr. Musgrave, Sir Richard Guy, Capt. Studholme, and the present mayor, Mr. Brougham. Mr. Attorney-General [Sir J. Montague] has done such services for the city that most of the leaders incline to be grateful as yet. I cannot particularly say what is owing to the Brigadier saving the honour done to the place by his being born in it; and others have as high a claim to that obligation. I was this morning assured that J. Reed openly declares his resolution to promote Mr. M.'s interests together with (his master's) the Attorney-General's; he is the likeliest man to divide the rabble, who continue fond of the Spanish officer. I am pretty sure that Mr. Mayor had not a fortnight ago any thoughts of offering his own services, being rather inclined to continue receiver-general of our taxes.

[The Earl of Kinnoull to Robert Harley.]

1710, August 15. Dupplin House—Yours of the 8th instant was most acceptable. The extraordinary thing which you say is fallen out, of the Queen's sending to my Lord Treasurer to break his staff, I confess it is a thing extraordinary but not at all surprising, for after what steps had been made it was very plain that this and a great many more to the same purpose must necessarily follow. I confess, as you say yourself, I do heartily pity you, more by a great deal now than when you went out from being Secretary, though you had then many great and inveterate enemies.

We put it without all doubt that the parliament will now quickly be dissolved. I long to hear what measures are concerted by our friends at London about the election of our peers, that I may endeavour, so far as I can, to bring such as I have any interest with into the same, for nothing can do us so much hurt as differing amongst ourselves. I pray you let me have your directions in those matters, and bring those with you into one concert. I am of opinion we should all agree to make choice of five or six to name the sixteen peers. If you think this a good measure to prevent differences amongst us, you can bring it about better than anybody. I shall heartily go into any measure that shall be thought most proper to advance the Queen's interest.

Your daughter is very well and your grandchild the bravest fellow in Britain.

I just now heard that my Lord Lauderdale is dead. Sir William Calderwood is the fittest man that pleads at bar to succeed him.

[Viscount Dupplin to Robert Harley.]

1710, August 15—In recommendation of Sir William Calderwood to succeed the Earl of Lauderdale as a Lord of Session. Has written to Lord Mar in his favour, and supposes R. Cunningham, who is a mighty well wisher of Sir William's, will be upon them both in his affair.

[Alexander Cunningham to Robert Harley.]

1710, August 16, N.S. Berlin—You know the progress I made through the United Provinces to visit the virtuosi. Soon after that I saw there was nothing to be done at Gertruydenberg, so bent my journey through Westphalia, where we found as little entertainment to our curiosity as there was to our stomachs. Though we went post yet we stopped at Osnabruck to see the Chamber of Peace in which are the pictures of all the plenipotentiaries and Kniperdolian's sword. The mob fancied we were the Duke of Marlborough, but were soon disabused by our drink money. Then they would have us to be the King of Sweden, but by that time our horses were put in, and we got out at the gate with a numerous attendance. All that night we lay on good straw which was the best bedding we had seen for three nights before.

Next day by the Weser we passed the field of battle where Varus lost the Roman legions; I know that doctors differ even on this, but I please myself with my opinion, and will leave my reasons to a greater work. However Varus deserved to be beaten, for entering so wild and desolated a country. As for the manners of the people I shall not trouble you with them, you having read them in Tacitus *De moribus Germanorum*. They are just the same they were then and I fancy will ever be so, there being a great connection between the soil and the manners of the inhabitants. This you doubtless have observed in the countries you have been in, and I think I could give better reasons for the observation than any astrologers have yet given for their hypothesis.

Now having passed the Weser, you will think I may come on politics, which I would certainly do, if I did not think antiquities, architecture, medals, and the beautiful variety of colours that are in butterflies and shells were more agreeable to you than anything I can possibly say in matters of state here. At Hanover, Mr. Leibnitz tells me that his essay on the Origin of Evil, and to reconcile infinite justice and mercy, will be published in a few weeks. Abbé Lockam's collection of medals has more of intrinsic value in it than any thing else. My Lord Rochester's letters were most obliging at court, so were those sent by Ant. Murray; though the reception I met with was more gracious than I could merit, yet I must tell you, that I chose rather to pass my time there incognito than to submit to some ceremonies which I thought were different from our own, by which you see, that I am a good churchman abroad. I heard likewise there that you were made Remembrancer of the Exchequer, if so I wish you much joy, or of something better. I shall be glad to hear both parties are reconciled, though not done by old Ely.

Since I came hither I have not yet seen the King's medals, which you know is one of the best collections in Europe, and I wish other princes might be influenced by his royal example to favour the Muses more than they have done of late. My Lord Baby was pleased to show me his medals the other day. His collection, though yet in its infancy, consists both of modern and ancient; his taste this way you will think makes me partial if I do but justice to his merit, yet I can assure you his Lordship is very much your humble servant, and does you justice and honour on all occasions. Let me as a common friend put you right, if you are wrong in your opinion of his Lordship, because of the miscarriage of the interview when he was last in England. You know the world well enough and that friendship is not restricted to interviews. Perhaps it was your own fault, or your own prudential kind choice, that you both did not meet at that time, and if there be any difference I offer myself as mediator in the peace, which I believe needs not be long a making, and I shall only seek my labour for my pains, it being a particular pleasure to me to serve you both. You know how useful an ally the King of Prussia is, and I can assure you these twenty years past there has not been a minister of any character whatsoever here, that has had so good an interest with his Majesty as his Lordship has at this time. His Lordship is entirely in the Queen's interest, and that of his country, and is your very humble servant, and allows me to do myself the honour to make you the compliment, and for you, I told his Lordship that you were the person in the world farthest from having bad impressions, and the easiest to part with them.

I beg your pardon for going off from the virtuoso, but we may be allowed digressions now and then, especially when they are for good ends and not for our own interest. The urns here are certainly the same that Cæsar mentions in his Commentaries. The plague that is in Prussia has alarmed the Court here. The King takes tobacco, others drink, to drive it away. If these things are preservatives I hope the churchmen will keep it out of England, therefore I hope Convocation may not be called this year.

The Muscovite Ambassadress that was formerly in England raises a plague about precedence wherever she goes; here she embroiled the

the Court to have the *pas* of Madam le Grand Chamberlan. This flame was no sooner quenched than she went to Dresden where she put them all in a confusion and would take the hand of the Princess of Wolfenbuttel, who was to marry the Czar's son.

But before I end, I must tell you a note of a sermon preached by Hanner an old country parson preaching against the evil of our times. He said Duke Anthony of Wolfenbuttel had given one of his daughters to a papist, the other he was to give to a barbarian, and if the devil would ask the third, he believed he would give her to him. However I hear Duke Anthony begins to have some remorses, the Imperial Court being very dilatory in making good some things that they had promised him.

I shall be soon gone from hence, and if you direct your commands for me at Mr. Williams' house in Venice I shall have them.

JOHN RICKARDS to ROBERT HARLEY.

1710, August 17—I waited upon Madam Masham yesterday with Colonel Hill's patent, and she paid me my bill for passing it. As to the other patent concerning which you were pleased to tell me she would give me directions; she desired me to acquaint you that the names to be inserted are Mr. George Gordon, Mr. Edward Webster and my own.

CAPTAIN J. FOLEY to [ROBERT HARLEY].

1710, August 17. Liston—The loss of Major Miranda is so little regarded that one would think the Portuguese insensible of misfortunes, and I myself hear them daily debate what frontier must of course fall to the Castilians the next campaign. The most understanding believe it will be Braganza, unless the Portuguese assume more than a natural vigour to defend a place they pretend to revere as sacred. The government in this reign brings very fresh to remembrance the first years of the last, and the young Prince has such an influence over the people that the Court is not without jealousies and fears.

My Lord Galway has audience next week and then retires and gives himself no more trouble in state or military affairs, which seems very satisfactory to himself and no less to others. I sait here to attend my Colonel the first opportunity to Gibraltar.

EDWARD KNATCHBULL to [ROBERT HARLEY].

1710, August 18. Hatch—I take this occasion of congratulating you on the new honours deservedly conferred upon you which do not only make you surmount your enemies but likewise give you an opportunity of returning them your thanks for their kind usage. I can only tell you that in this corner of the world the joy is universal.

The EARL OF ORRERY to [ROBERT HARLEY].

1710, August [18–]29, N.S. Camp before Bethune—The gentleman who will have the honour to deliver you this is a friend of mine and particularly devoted to the interest of the Duke of Argyll and his family. He is going to Scotland and in his way is ordered to wait upon you and some other of our friends, and to solicit the dispatch of my commission, and the Queen's order for the Duke of Argyll and me to go over to England. I have several times written to H. S[t. John] about them and wish they had been sent some time ago. There is now a gentleman appointed to bring them over to us, and I hope there will be no longer delay in the affair. When the Duke of Argyll is at London he will be advised by you whether it be necessary for him to go to Scotland before the elections, and will be ready to go if it be your opinion that it is for your service ; here I think neither he nor I can be of any further use this campaign, which is or ought to be near an end, for I will be bold to say that after so bloody a campaign as the last, after coming so early as we did this year into the field, after so much sickness as we have had here from the beginning, and two such terrible sieges as that of Douay and Bethune, we cannot undertake another with any other view than to support the General by the destruction of the army. I will not trouble you with a long detail of our circum_ stances here, but refer myself for that account to Capt. Middleton who carries this letter. If you think fit to entrust him with any commands, I will answer for his capacity and fidelity.

The DUKE OF ARGYLL to [ROBERT HARLEY].

1710, August [18-]29, N.S. Camp at Villers Brulin — The joy our last news has given me is infinite, I am too good a Briton not to be transported with my Queen and Country being delivered out of the slavery they have so long been in, and as this blessing is owing to your management I most heartily hope you will receive from both the acknowledgments due to so extraordinary a service.

Count Staremberg's advantage in Spain entertained us a day or two, but your victory in England has put it quite out of our heads, and with very good reason, for I like not only Spain but indeed Britain itself to have depended upon your success.

I have acquainted the gentleman who will have the honour to deliver this letter to you, with everything that I am able to inform you of ; he is by my brother's desire to make the best of his way to Scotland, and will be careful to deliver what commands you are pleased to honour him with to any of your friends there.

The town of Bethune has designed to capitulate, so we shall have it in a day or two. What our mighty Prince of Blenheim will think of doing afterwards, I know not ; but if we pretend to take any more towns, our Infantry will be quite destroyed and our Horse so much out of order that we shall be obliged to stay as long in garrison next spring as the enemy, and I don't know but his Grace may think it his interest to have it so.

JOHN MEYRICKE to [ROBERT HARLEY].

1710, August 19. Carmarthen—No man can wish well to the public and not be infinitely pleased with your return into the administration.

Being told by Mr. Barlow that you desired Mr. Campbell might be chosen next time at Pembroke I have with some difficulty freed myself from an obligation I was under to Brigadier Ferrers of serving him with my interest in that pretention, and am now at liberty to be commanded by you.

I am wholly a stranger to Mr. Campbell and as much unac_ quainted with his principles, but if he be agreeable to you he cannot fail to be so to me. If he resolves to stand he should hasten into the country, and I will meet him here to concert some measures for his service.

THOMAS FOLEY to [HARLEY] the CHANCELLOR OF THE EXCHEQUER.

1710, August 20—Lord Scudamore last Thursday night coming from Hereford was flung with his horse, was so hurt that he has been insensible ever since ; and, if not dead, I find there is no hope of his life. I shall be glad of your direction relating to the county.

JOHN. AISLABIE to [ROBERT HARLEY].

1710, August 20—Give me leave to congratulate you upon the happy turn of affairs, and to praise you the author of so great a revolution. I am not capable of advancing the public service except in respect to such elections as shall serve you.

I am desired by Lord Downe and Sir Arthur Kaye to procure the Duke of Somerset's interest in this county [Yorkshire], for which they have already applied to him, but not having received an answer I beg the favour of you to speak to him in their behalf.

SIR H. BELASYSE to [ROBERT HARLEY].

1710—August 20. Brancepeth Castle nigh Durham—I humbly beg leave to acquaint you with the great joy the county received the news of your being at the head of the new Ministry and that they will pay their taxes very cheerfully, since they now think their Church out of danger.

I hope our four representatives for the next election will be of one mind, Sir Robert Eden and old Mr. Lambton will be for the county, Tom Conyers and I have joined for the city in order to throw out Nicholson, that so we may have four members of one mind. The Duke of Newcastle has proffered Lord Barnard a thousand pounds to defray his son's election if he would set him up again for this county, but Lord Barnard declines it.

I have an humble request to you if you think it proper to move her Majesty, that I may have a commission as Lieutenant General to take rank from the date of my old commission ; this would give me a further credit in my country and do me a further great service at my next election. Her Majesty may employ me or not as she sees occasion. I shall say nothing for my having been laid aside because you are no stranger to that affair, and I must ever own myself obliged to you at that time as well as many others. I shall add no more because I know your minutes are precious.

[WILLIAM BROMLEY to ROBERT HARLEY.]

1710, August 21—My noble friend and neighbour, the Earl of Denbigh, is advised to apply for the Duchy of Lancaster. He is a very honourable, worthy person, and has been a sufferer by the misfortunes of Sir B. Firebrace to a degree that all, who know his circumstances, compassionate. He has just pretensions to be distinguished in the army, having been in that service till the disbanding upon the late peace. He has asked for Essex's Dragoons, but I believe is not likely to succeed.

R. MONCKTON to [ROBERT HARLEY].

1710, August 21—I am returned to the place whither you lately mentioned me. I had never told our friend what I had said to you of

Duke Trinculo's expectations and I understand what you say of me as an answer, and that you thereby infer that it ought not to be supposed that any thing can be done to his prejudice, which therefore deserves no more notice being taken of it; yet because Trinculo has since at his own table publicly said that 33 [the Duke of Newcastle] would soon be out of all, I should think it highly necessary that every thing might be done that is proper to discountenance such rumours that may be prejudicial to 32 [the Queen]'s own interest to which 33 [the Duke of Newcastle] is so affectionately, so faithfully and dutifully, addicted.

For as on the one hand the defeated are in the highest rage and regret against all that carry on the scheme of making 32 [the Queen]'s service safe and easy, so on the other the pride and presumption of the rigids are grown so high that they think of nothing less than deposing and imposing whom they please upon 32 [the Queen], and boast they shall bring it about in a little time and want nothing but the desired dissolution to effect it.

This therefore is wrote with the greatest zeal for 32 [the Queen] and friendship for 48 [yourself] to excite you to make timely provision of engaging such in the scheme as are ready and willing to support it, of which you may exact what proof you please from them, since they must receive the proposition from you of what it is you expect from them and by which you will easily judge of their candour; and thus he concurs with you in your judgment on 41 [Lord Halifax], and that his service with the Bank has been a manifest indication of his sincerity, and as you may exact what test you please from 40 [Lord Cowper] you easily will find whether 33 [the Duke of Newcastle] is mistaken in him, for he is more still confirmed in the opinion he had of his good disposition by the letters he has lately received from him wherein he expresses the most cordial desire of composing matters after the best method for 32 [the Queen]'s service, but as you know his natural reservedness it would not only be more proper for you now but make the greater impression if you yourself made the advance, or at least give such intimation to him as you shall judge fit.

Thus then if the conferences were renewed, which 33 [the Duke of Newcastle] earnestly desires they may be, he verily believes they will be attended with the consequence of gaining the body of that party and all that can be content with the good and quiet of their country into 32 [the Queen]'s interests and that now they having lost their former support they must fall necessarily into a dependence on 48 [yourself]; besides this is a prospect that discovers a scene of fair weather, whereas if the storm be continued and increased no body knows on what rock the ship may be cast, but this is certain, that the crew who at present are caressed think of nothing less then driving the pilots out of the steerage as soon as they get the numbers to support them in it. And I know that at a meeting when things did not proceed so fast as they expected they were not content with ill treating 48 [you] but insolent even upon 32 [the Queen].

Now as men's actions are the surest interpreters of their intentions I will leave you to judge how soon the madness on both sides is like to get together by the facts that happen hereabouts. Had Sir Thomas Willoughby stood to his first disposition every thing in this country would have gone on as you would have it, but he has been persuaded by the rigids to break from his first engagements, and to excuse his treachery has framed a false and artificial tale, and has even gone so far as to set up likewise for Newark in opposition to Mr. Digby whom he himself formerly brought in there. However we hope all will do well when it comes to the trial and as for the county old Turnip will certainly be routed. They have likewise in order to make it easy to Thorold at Grantham found means to bring all their party to acquiesce in my Lord Granby for Leicestershire. On the other side the noble Duke that for such a wise reason retracted his promise to Paget has engaged old Rutland and his son Granby as well as himself to support Curzon and Clarke and they are now making interest against Mr. Cook [Coke] for no other reason but his being in the Queen's service. Now the same thing that will prevent this practice and new associations will also hinder the defection of a whole party, the bulk of whom 'tis thought may be gained by giving them common protection not only to 32 [the Queen]'s service but under 48 [your] direction and this by adding 40 [Lord Cowper] to 33 [the Duke of Newcastle] and 41 [Lord Halifax], whose influence will doubtless bring in the body of them, leaving only those out that must follow their leaders and make room for more reasonable men.

I wish I could have expressed these sentiments as forcibly as they were at first dictated to me, but as you will find it convenient I am commanded to desire you would return your answer to the place you know whence they are sent.

JOHN TOLAND to [ROBERT HARLEY].

1710, [August 22-]September 2, N.S. Leyden — Congratulations on Harley's happy return to the management of affairs and the disgrace of his enemies, confidently predicted and wished for by the writer; and also on the complete victory obtained by King Charles over the Duke of Anjou near Saragossa. Sends extract from a Paris letter.

J. D[RUMMOND] to [ROBERT HARLEY].

1710, [August 22-]September 2, N.S. Amsterdam—My heart is now at ease, and permit me to congratulate you with all the sincerity and gratitude I can express. I am very glad to see you have made a begin with Sir Theodore Janssen, he is truly a fair and just man; I have done good sums with him both on his own and the Bank's account, and I humbly beg that you may be pleased to name me to him. I am overjoyed to hear that the Bank will undertake, nothing can be of so good consequence, even Furnese is a "bable" to the Bank. I know one family here who I have given such an opinion of the Bank to, that they will accept their bills for two hundred thousand pounds, besides several others for forty or fifty thousand. Make much of one Peter Delmé of the Bank, though he be not my friend or correspondent, he deals for the greatest families here, and his accounts are believed as gospel. I wish you could keep Furnese a doing something, that he may not do mischief, till matters go current again; he has been a sad fellow to me, for Lord Godolphin put the tin affair in his hand, and he gave it to a Dutch man here while he was making use of me to facilitate his public payments. He is now sending over the value of fifty thousand pounds sterling worth of tin; if any of your Board would but ask him if Drummond has not the tin commission still, it is very probable he would send me that great parcel, but do in this as may seem good to you, for I would not have you lay under any obligation to him for my account, neither shall I ever desire you to employ me in any thing which another can do better for you. All I entreat is the favour of your recommendation to the undertakers of the public remittances, they all know me and how far I can serve them, and Mr. Brydges the Paymaster General, who I hope keeps his place, knows me, and I must say has been serviceable to me. Mr. James Milner understands the Portugal exchange best, and he has a cabal under him who are concerned in whatever he undertakes, and they are men of substance. Lord Godolphin was terribly imposed upon in that exchange, sometimes ten per cent. for a whole year's business; but in my humble opinion if the Bank will undertake every thing, they ought to have it, and are best able to go through with it, especially between England and Holland, though Sir Theodore Janssen is as good a singleman, and Sir James Bateman, as can be employed, Mr. Brydges knows them very well, and his depute, Mr. Sweet, here has got lately very much the favour of the whole army, especially of the Duke of Argyll, Lord Orkney, Lumley, and Ross, having opposed Cadogan, who is hated as all the Irish favourites are. Mr. Benson can tell you this. I hope you have been pleased to address Earl Rivers to me; there are emissaries gone before him of the other party, a Wortley Montague and an other, they drove past through this. The malicious emissaries at the Hague give out that the Queen has broken her word to the States, having promised as they say to Vrybergen that her Majesty should make no more alterations than Lord Sunderland. All the modest men are sorry for the States undue meddling with such things, but they were put upon it. I tell them that they cannot take it amiss if the Queen name a stadtholder to them, after they pretend to regulate her ministry or confine her Majesty to such as they like. I have made several entertainments to get the best people together to put them right, for your adversaries are industrious and spare neither pains nor money. They all say they will be convinced that all is well and will go well, providing when the parliament comes to sit, the funds be provided before you quarrel. If they see the land tax, malt tax, and a new lottery or annuities for one, two, and three lives granted before Christmas, and generous resolutions at the first sitting down of the parliament taken to carry on the common cause, they will all join and venture as fast as ever. Lotteries and annuities for life are their favourite funds, and will produce ready money viz. for three persons now alive, nine per cent. per annum, for two persons' lives ten per cent., and upon a single life eleven per cent. One million sterling would soon run full, if not one and a half and as much lottery. They seem concerned to have the Duke continued, for they all hate the German Electors or sovereign Princes to command or deal with. I hear it is put through the army that you correspond with Prince Eugene; this is done industriously to see how it would go down with the people.

Sir Robert Davers to [Robert Harley].

1710, August 22. Rushbrooke—Give me leave amongst the rest of your friends to congratulate your glorious success. You have got over the black gentleman. I always thought you a pretty lad and a good raffler. You have often told me you would trip in his heels, and now you have performed nobly. Go on with your blow and restore us. I have often thought of what you have said to me and heartily wish you good success. I am to be opposed by Sir Philip Parker, one not known in our county, set up by two Lords that have little interest in it.

R. Monckton to [Robert Harley].

1710, August 23—I being by the confidence 33 [the Duke of Newcastle] has in my duty to him so far admitted into the present

view as by the letter I addressed to you by his command you will
believe. I cannot be just to the service I have ever had for 48 [you]
if I do not tell you what appears to me so evident when it imports 48
[you] so much for whom yourself are not much more affected. And
that is, that 32 [the Queen] themselves will not be able to protect him
against the malice and subtilty of both sides unless he prevent [the
Duke and Duchess of Marlborough] in what they triumph in going off
with, viz., the interest of the Whig party, and also win that interest for
his own, which if he give way will render itself obvious for him to
effect, for though there is no doubt but they will all readily concur in
their resentment against those whose insolence has brought this fatality
upon them, and may be made most ready to condemn the pride and
ambition of those whose vanity and avarice of usurping so much rendered
them insupportable and their discharge necessary, yet if they that are
innocent, that have constantly contributed their services to 32 [the
Queen], if the whole party are to be branded and disgraced, neither
they themselves nor anybody else will think that they suffer for the sake
of [the Duke and Duchess of Marlborough] but that [the Duke and
Duchess] suffer for the Whigs, and the opinion will prevail both at
home and abroad that it was the merit, the majority, the principles,
the addresses, and the doctrine of the others that have puffed that party
with so much presumption and given the succession, the Allies and the
credit apprehensions that are more like to increase then be removed,
that have produced the change. 48 [You] cannot but have heard
how universally it begins to be declaimed against, and that many
Tories tax the ingratitude of disgracing those that have courted so much
and have been the instruments of gaining greater credit and glory to
the Queen and nation then any of our former Kings or greatest con-
querors ever arrived at. Sure it can be no prudence to let them go off
with a party to blazon their actions and calumniate the advisers. And
suppose it should be thought necessary to retaliate by an accusation?
The cruel people of Rome spared the inveterate enemy of their liberty
Manlius when he shewed them the Capitol he had preserved, and the
nature of this nation is ever to take part with those that are under
persecution and the weakest party will be strong enough to defend the
least claim to merit.

But why should not these extremities be avoided when means and
ways may be taken to keep all still in a dependence, if the violent are
not made already too strong for advice and are become past control and
why should not 48 [you] make himself master of a party that can now
have no other view or protection but by his being supported, when at
the same time it is evident he cannot depend on the others by the hints
they daily give. The old Duke [Rutland] here I mentioned in my last,
who sets up for a pillar of the Church, and who lately had two dozen of
priests with him to give their thanks for the service he had done her,
took occasion at dinner when one that told us was present to open his
heart as well as his bottle and make a representation of the present state
of affairs, and took pains to derogate all he could from 48 [you], and he
thought he made him he meant by it very inconsiderable when he
told them that as for Robin the trickster he had no acquaintance with
him.

I dined yesterday in this neighbourhod with Mr. D'Arcy, Bromley's
brother in law, and I am sure what he said was not his own but the
dictates of the party. As we were mellow and talking of the times, he
immediately fell on 48 [you] whom he represented as a necessary
ladder, but that as soon as the building had got its foundation they
would throw away that part of the scaffolding, that those that had got

up by him could not keep him reared to the frame, but that those that would find other ways of climbing now they were shewn the way would soon kick him down.

I beg your pardon for troubling you with this northern allegory but granting my apprehension of that party's insincerity and falsehood groundless, yet certainly the regret the people express at the fall of [the Duke and Duchess] makes it necessary to take off the load that will be laid on those they presume to be the authors of that advice, and since none but the Whigs will accuse, or can have credit to excuse it, why should you not agree to such an accommodation as may make the nation easy and will be grateful to the greatest and best part of the people, whereas on the contrary 48 [you] will run a risk he may this way avoid. The reputation of 33 [the Duke of Newcastle] will be in danger, and the days and years of 32 [the Queen] uneasy.

THOMAS CONYERS to ROBERT HARLEY.

1710, August 25. Durham—I find all our friends are getting into good posts. I hope I have as just pretensions as others, therefore desire your favour, and where to place me I leave to yourself but shall be unwilling to live constantly in town.

The Church has joined Sir H. Bellasis to me, and I hope I shall bring him in though Nicolson spends very high. Sir H. begins to bleed very freely, if he had begun sooner it would have been much better. We shall have Sir R. Eden and honest William Lambton, I hope without opposition.

Lord Downe and Sir Arthur Kaye are safe; Sir William Hustler will be out at Northallerton, and if any will stand for Hull both will be out.

I hear the Duke of Somerset is now against us. I thought he was for us, therefore went twice to Newcastle to prevent their setting up another to throw out Lord Hertford, so if you would have him out be pleased to let me know, and I dare engage to remove him and with no expense to honest Tom Forster, but this must be known as soon as may be. I'm told that Sir W. Blackett being under age has given his interest to Mr. Wrightson who will join with Alderman Ridley, and will certainly turn out both the old ones. Westmorland and Cumberland will be much better, and I hope it will be so all over England, then my "coyned health" cannot fail to a good Parliament, Mr. Bromley Speaker and Dr. Sacheverell chaplain. Amen!

I will not be further troublesome therefore shall only beg, that you will be pleased to think of me in time that I may not have the trouble of a new election.

Postscript.—My hearty service to all fast friends. I hope you will recommend Mr. Newcomer to Mr. St. John. Sir M. Wharton may turn out Sir C. Hotham.

[HENRY ST. JOHN to ROBERT HARLEY.]

1710, August 25—I have written to our friends in the army as you directed me to do, and have made your compliments to them. Mr. Wade was made Brigadier over the heads of Lord Orrery, Lord Skerrin, Lord Deloraine, Lord Paston, Mr. Breton, Mr. Sutton, Mr. Durel, besides five other colonels, who have since quitted the service. Thus you see it will be no injustice to anybody to make Lord Orrery Major General.

I cannot omit telling you that in the Isle of Wight faction is in its proportion as much encouraged, and as great liberties taken with the Queen's conduct, as in Flanders. I have in few days taken care to have a full account from thence; there cannot be on earth a more peevish, inveterate little creature than Shannon who commands. Five regiments at utmost should only have a Major General and a Brigadier, but the Queen has been at ten pounds a day expense for a Lieutenant General to these troops from Christmas. If you design these troops for no service the whole expense is idle, and if you design them for any, I would appeal to any impartial man in the army, whether they would not be better commanded by Whetham and Breton without Shannon than with him.

In short the Queen pays so much for to encourage a tool against her.

[Sir John Bland to Robert Harley.]

1710, August 25. Kippax Park [co. York]—Lord Downe is now in town so you will hear from him how our elections will go. For Durham county and city I hope you will have four good ones. The gentlemen in Lancashire would have had me stand for the county, but I begged their pardon and told them neither my constitution nor purse was in order to undertake such a fatigue and expense as that must be; but if there be a good Chancellor put in there you may rely upon it that your elections will be good for that county.

R. Monckton to [Robert Harley].

1710, August 26—It is thought very strange you should not return an answer though never so short to what you receive from hence, which is ever intended truly for your service and left to your consideration; for you will best judge of it whether those that can have no other interest in or support with 32 [the Queen] but yourself, and of that you may have an assurance from those I named to you as well as from himself; and others of the most considerable of that party are not likely to prove a surer foundation than the others without them. The example he would always direct you to is that of Cecil who constantly balanced one party by the other, and it is out of the concern for your safety you are advertised of what occurs that may be of any use to you to be told, as the great man I quoted to you before for what he said in relation to yourself. I must tell you now his sense of the great affair of the Parliament, which he says though the dissolution be for some reasons desirable yet, considering the war and posture we are in, is dangerous, and those that are the advisers will be liable to be called to an account for it. Whether this be agreeable to what he said when at London, and at whose door they will be ready to lay the blame, is what your friends cannot be without apprehensions at.

One thing I shall desire and beg of you when I am gone, to tell him if you take any umbrage at the communication he has made to me, and at the same time give me leave to assure you of the respect I owe you and the duty I pay him to which I would as soon forfeit my life as be unjust.

Postscript.—I cannot but again remind you of Burghley, who never suffered one party to be too superior to the other and thereby rendered them both subservient to his mistress, and whether it be not a surer foundation to protect that side who can have no support but from you and by you with 32 [the Queen], than those of whom they that are most in their secrets stick not to say that you are the only obstacle that they have not 32 [the Queen] in their hands entirely, and that they can better maintain themselves and carry on 32 [the Queen]'s business without you than with you. And all the heads of that party say it is of necessity that when you have done their business you must be removed. But you that converse with them can best tell whether there is just ground to suspect them or no.

I am bid tell you, you will likewise receive ▉▉ther letter by this post.

Dr. Charles Davenant to [Robert Harley].

1710, August 27. Sion Hill—I am so full of pleasure to hear of the late glorious success in Spain, that I cannot forbear breaking in upon others with my joy, so many good consequences arising from this battle crowd in upon my imagination, that I know not where to begin. To gain a victory at a time so critical, in the country where it was most needful, least hoped for, and which had been most neglected, is such an auspicious omen to a new ministry, that I must beg leave to felicitate you upon it. All reasonable men must certainly rejoice at a conquest which does not lead us into an endless protraction of the war, nor make us still more and more the prey of, and slaves to, a devouring faction. But this happy news has not been received by all with equal delight, though it gives us the certain prospect of a peace. Sir Thomas Double (for he is now a knight) with whom I still correspond, told me yesterday, with a deep groan, at St. James's coffee house where he often comes, that this advantage in Spain (the term he gave it) would in its effects prove as fatal a blow to the modern Whigs, as to the King of France. But this time must decide.

The Duke of Leeds to Earl Poulett, Albemarle Street.

1710, August 28. Kiveton—Thanks for promise to assist Lord Lempster (Leominster) in his request about the forest of Whittlewood, where for some years one Captain Ryder has been, who has both wasted the deer and made great havoc with the woods.

Sir Rowland Gwynne to [Robert Harley].

1710, [August 29-]September 9, N.S. Hamburgh—Congratulations. I now hope to find more favour with the new ministry and that I may be restored to her Majesty's good opinion of me.

I have passed many days here in retirement with a few books, and though they are the best I can choose, I think that I rust for want of the conversation I was used to in England. But if I cannot be employed there at this time there may be a change of some envoys abroad, and if by your friendship I may be employed in any of these northern countries I shall ever own it as a great obligation, but I would not have any man turned out upon my account.

J. D[rummond] to [Robert Harley].

1710, [August 29-]September 9, N.S. Amsterdam—I am convinced you have no time to write to me, but I must take the freedom to trouble you as often as I think it can be for your service. We have made the rogues alter their style in the Gazettes and the English credit

goes as current as ever again on our exchange. I have ventured all
my small estate, credit, and welfare to serve you as you'll hear by
Sam Shepheard's and Captain Gibbon's offers ; and, as Mr. Brydges
will perhaps do me the justice to tell you, you proceed too slow. Make
all the change you design immediately and let one alarm serve for all,
and not putting of from week to week, and giving new grounds of
diffidence ; make all the noise you can, and do also effectually and
immediately support the service in Spain; and send all the fleet, bound
for the West Indies, I mean the regiments, there if possible, for peace
or war must now be decided there, and our second victory is entire and
glorious as ever anything was. I am let into a piece of a secret to
which I must desire the favour of a speedy answer, or if no answer I
must esteem it a denial, whether you would come to a compromise with
the Duke of Marlborough and on what terms. One that is capable of
doing much in it puts me on this, I run no risk, neither shall they ever
know that I have wrote to you on this subject, so you may answer, or
not as you please ; for I refused to meddle, and told it was out of my
way, I had no interest and would be laughed at.

BARON PRICE to ROBERT HARLEY, Chancellor of the Exchequer.

1710, August 29. Lancaster—Being come to the end of a long
circuit and looking homewards, I could not delay the congratulating
you in your new advancement, may it daily grow and improve with you.
There was a mighty appearance of gentry here, who designed to set up
Mr. Farington in conjunction with Mr. Shuttleworth ; there were many
against Mr. Stanley, which alarmed the Earl his brother who was here
with a very small attendance of the gentlemen. The country in respect
of their harvest did interpose and so the contest is over, my Lord not
concerning himself in other elections.

The two Heyshams are opposed in this town by one Bradley, a
London merchant, but it is thought to little purpose.

Preston will choose Mr. Fleetwood their neighbour and it is thought
will compliment their Chancellor with another, some think Mr. Mainwaring but my Lord is silent as yet. Westmorland does agree to have
Colonel Graham and are at a loss for another, if Mr. Wilson will not
stand ; his father being against it but his uncle Sir William Fleming
for it ; a county depopulated of gentry but the Colonel hopes, if Wilson
stands, his eyes will be opened by next Parliament.

Appleby has new candidates, Mr. Lutwych the lawyer, who is
recommended together with Mr. Duncombe by my Lord Thanet. Mr.
Lutwych has declared he will stand and has visited the borough.
There is one Blackwell, an attorney at Stamford, who has an estate by
his wife in the neighbourhood, does offer his service but will be prevailed
with to acquiesce. The Lord of Ireland drops Lechmere and sets up
one of the Berties of the Lindsey family, I think Albemarle Bertie, and
full orders to spare no money ; but thought to little purpose. My Lord
Thanet is now very hearty ; and if his officers had been so before, there
could not have been an interloper. My Lord Wharton's chief instrument is a tricking attorney, clerk of the peace and an alehouse keeper,
all in one.

Cumberland is in the same case, Lawson is secure, the Bishop and
Lord Carlisle would have compounded with him, to be for him, if he
did not join with any other, which he refused to promise; nor can he
prevail with Sir Richard Musgrave or Sir William Pennington to stand
and so Lowther must come in for the county.

The city of Carlisle wants two candidates, but orders are sent, as the chief manager told me, to let money be spent as free as he will; the price is 400*l.* for each.

Cockermouth, the Duke of Somerset is secure of one, but my Lord Wharton's interest is precarious; as yet they cannot prevail with any to stand. I hear there will be an opposition at Morpeth and Berwick, and one Mr. Wrightson at Newcastle.

I forgot to let you know that Wigan will have the same, Sir Roger Bradshaw's younger brother called Major Bradshaw is mayor of Wigan and has sworn two hundred and fifty burgesses and thereby secure; but he is under Lord Rivers' power. There will be an opposition at Liverpool against Sir Thomas Johnson, but it seems doubtful.

HENRY WATKINS to [ERASMUS] LEWIS.

· 1710, August 30. Villers Brulin—On Thursday as we were making a *feu de joie* for our success in Spain, an *aide-de-camp* brought the Duke word the Governor of Bethune had beat the *chamade*. Next morning the Duke and Prince Eugene went thither and signed the capitulation, by which we had a gate delivered to us last night, and to-morrow the town will be delivered to us, the garrison being to march out with the usual marks of honour and to be conducted to St. Omer.

G. WARBURTON and E. CHOLMONDELEY to [ROBERT HARLEY].

1710, August 30. Vale Royal in Cheshire—Send list of gentlemen to be omitted from the commission of peace, and of others to be added thereto. Among the former, who are charged with poisoning the minds of the people and coercing the voters in the coming election are:—Sir Robert Duckenfield, Sir John Chetwode, Sir Samuel Daniel, John Davenport, Edward Thorneycroft, Roger Mainwaring, Tho. Aldersey, and Peter Warburton. Among the latter are Sir Richard Grosvenor, Leftwyche Oldfeld, George Shakerley, John Waren, and John Egerton of Tatton.

SAMUEL SHEPHEARD to [ROBERT HARLEY].

1710, August 30—According to your commands I send the names of the justices of peace turned out at Cambridge upon my son being chosen for that place viz.: Thos. Ewin, Thos. Fox sen., Char. Chambers sen., and Thos. Fowler, all aldermen of the town and have been mayors several years since. The men put in their stead were Mr. Bendish, Sir Paul Whitchcot, Anthony Thompson and Doctor James Johnson, whereof the last only dwells in the town. My son is very desirous these last three should be all put out, and the former four restored, and if Edward Gatward Esq. the deputy recorder of the town, and William Rumbold, who was mayor two years since and now an alderman, could be added to the number it would conduce to the advancing that interest in the town. All these six are men of estates and the wealthiest in the corporation.

John Hinde Cotton Esq. and my son Samuel are the present members for the town and I hear not of any that will oppose them, and since my son makes it his request that they may both be in the commission for the peace, I must leave it to you whether it is proper, and when your leisure permits, I pray you will send some fit person about it; and when he has executed what you shall have directed him, I entreat he may call on me and give me an account of what he hath done that I may repay him his charges and advise my son who is now at Cambridge.

EARL RIVERS to [ROBERT HARLEY].

1710, September [1-]12, N.S. The Hague—As soon as I came to the Hague Lord Townshend did me the honour to call on me, and I must say has carried himself in all respects very obliging. When he brought me to the Pensioner, he told him he did not present me only as as a man of quality that the Queen had sent to Hanover but by her particular commands, which the Secretary of State communicated to him; and then retired. Mr. Boyle did write very fully to my Lord the Queen's orders to present me to the Pensioner.

I think I did not omit saying any thing I was ordered. He was not much startled at the stocks falling, knowing the tricks of jobbing those matters; and talked as reasonable on that point as could be desired, and was also very well satisfied with the security of our funds, but desired to know how the credit of the nation stood. I told him the present Lords of the Treasury had as great an interest with the moneyed men as any set of people whatsoever, and I did not doubt but they would be able to support it, as well as any Treasurer ever did. What alarmed him most was a new Parliament. I said upon that subject what was commanded me, and he seemed to be better satisfied, but I can't say I left him entirely so. He pressed me very much to tell him if it was resolved to call a new one, to which point I would give no positive answer, but told him 'twas my private opinion the present would be dissolved. He was very earnest to know if the Queen had not promised to make no more changes upon Lord S[underland's] removal, and particularly not 69 (Marlborough). I told him, no, what her Majesty said on that point was, that if she made any more changes, she would take care to choose such ministers as would show their duty to her, their zeal for the common cause in carrying on the war till a good and honourable peace was procured, and that were for the Protestant Succession in the House of Hanover. He pressed me a second time on that subject and desired me to tell him, if I was sure there was no such promise made. I said I was and that 'twas well known by what artifice the Queen's words were turned to the advantage of those concerned, and by whom. I find by the 78 (Pensioner) that the 79, 127 (Dutch envoy) was the chief manager of that matter though I can't say 'twas in words so expressed, but by what fell from him, I have reason to believe it came from thence.

He then asked me if he was to communicate what I said to him to the States, I said I had no public character, that the Queen had ordered me to represent these matters in particular to him, to show the true respect she had for him. He desired me to return her Majesty thanks for the honour she had done him, and ended with a prayer to prosper her and her arms in conjunction with those of the Allies in all their undertakings. Upon this I took my leave, and as I was going to my coach he called me back to ask me if I thought 69 would lay down or be removed. As to the first part of his question I told him, that he had received so many obligations from 66 (the Queen), and was of so grateful a temper that I believed he would serve in any capacity rather than quit 64 (her) service and that I knew nothing of the latter; and so we parted.

I shall set out for Amsterdam to-morrow, when I shall want the letter you promised to give me for 154 (M. Buys). I shall stay there but one night in order to settle my credit and so proceed to Hanover.

As far as I [am] able to judge of the inclination of the people here, they are for the most part prejudiced to the present proceedings in England, so that in my opinion it will be necessary either to gain the person who resides here, which I wish you could, he being very well liked here, or send another who may satisfy them that the late change of our Ministry will not be any way prejudicial to the common cause. I wish you joy of our success in Spain.

[DANIEL] DE FOE to [ROBERT HARLEY].

1710, September 2—What you were pleased to say to me relating to my own particular the last time I had the honour to wait on you has so much goodness in it, and especially so much concern for me, that it extorts my acknowledgements, though I am a man entirely void of ceremony. That you will be pleased to move her Majesty on my behalf, I must look upon as an assurance that it shall be done ; knowing the Queen will deny nothing to your intercession especially when backed with such arguments as I hope my case affords, such as a man entirely given up to, and I had almost said ruined in her Majesty's service. I will say nothing of being capable of serving, willing, faithful, and in the affairs of the Union successful, I leave that to your kindness in recommending. If I would move her Majesty in any part part of it, 'twould be of a wife and six children almost grown up, and perfectly unprovided for, after having been stripped naked in that jail from whence you were once pleased to redeem me.

What I have enjoyed (and that too had its original in your kindness) has constantly gone in expensive travelling, maintaining useful intelligence abroad, family subsistence and a little clearing of encumbering circumstances though far from finishing that unhappy work. This makes the step, which I mentioned to you of almost half a year past, distress me more than I am willing to mention, and really these things too much disable the very capacity of serving usefully, and are a great reason why I move in this matter with more assurance, having no reason to expect from you any thing but as it may render me serviceable to you. 'Tis with too much experience that I express to you that the anxieties and impatience of perplexed circumstances lessen my very capacity of service, sink the spirits, and leave neither the hands free nor the head clear for any valuable performance.

I entreat your pardon for this importunate writing. You may judge of the importuning circumstance by the importunity itself, which you will easily believe is too irksome to me, if the occasion did not urge it.

And yet whatever was the necessity I would not press upon your goodness which has hitherto always prevented me, if I did not persuade myself, that being once made easy I might have some little merit, to render the Queen's bounty to me, and yours also, rational. I would not be an invalid, and hope still I may render you some service, that may save me from the scandal of an unprofitable servant ; yet I forbear to promise for myself, only this, that I shall serve both with principle and inclination, which I cannot say has been so clear to me since I have been out of your service, as it was before, and is now.

I am convinced and thoroughly assured you have in view the true interest of your country, and think it an unaccountable blindness that hides it from some, who ought to see it as well as I. This made me apply myself to you before I saw your present happy restoration in view, or indeed expected it; which clears me of worshipping your fortune rather than your person.

, I persuade myself it shall be in my power to assist the honest but prejudiced people of both kingdoms to know their interest, and their friends, better than hitherto they have done. This I apply myself to with all my might, and begin to meet with unexpected success. But I shall ever be backward in magnifying my own merit, and, therefore, I refrain to say any more of that.

I have since I have served [you] (as you know) established a general correspondence, and at some charge maintained it by which I have a fixed intelligence (I may say) all over Britain. But especially in the north I confess it grieves me to think of letting it fall, because I cannot fail of rendering it very useful to your service on every occasion; and shall, the next time I have the honour to wait on you, show you a proof of it.

I humbly ask your pardon for this long and pressing letter, I will no more be importunate, but resolving to have my entire dependence upon you.

Endorsed by Harley " Mr. Goldsmith."

Capt. T. Foley to [Robert Harley].

1710, September 3. Lisbon—The news of our late victory in Spain has occasioned the Portuguese to make a sort of precipitation to their posts in order to " sortie " it beyond their own frontier, should the enemy draw off any of their troops on this occasion. Lord Galway is quite retired from public business, leaving that of the State to Mr. Le Fevre, and that of the Army to Major-General Newton. His Excellency, on my showing some little discontent at continuing Major Watkins, has complimented me with one of his fashionable favours, a brevet of major to the regiment; but from the apprehensions we have here of the action of King Charles my new feather will be of small use. Therefore I must hope and wish that you may think me capable of serving the government in a civil way.

[John] D[rummond] to [Robert Harley].

1710, September [4–]15. Amsterdam—I gave you the trouble of a confused letter the 9th instant and whatever resolutions you may be pleased to take about what I took the freedom to write to you then, I need not be acquainted with them ; for I shall never meddle with these people, and the honest man who proposed it to me will have as little to do with them, and I believe they think they have gained ground by the Duke of Somerset's going into the country. Though you did not do me the honour to recommend Earl Rivers, my old friend and acquaintance Colonel Worsley came first to me here and brought my Lord with him, who has done the Queen a very singular service at the Hague, where her Majesty was accused of breach of promise and word to the States, her Majesty having according to Monsieur Vrybergen's information promised to make no alteration in the ministry after Lord Sunderland, and my Lord Rivers affirmed to the grand Pensionary that the Queen's answer was, that her Majesty should make no alterations in the ministry but who should be for the carrying on of the war and security of the protestant succession, which I according to my Lord Rivers' order and permission of naming his Lordship for my author have told to our pensionaries and to several of our great men, and I am afraid they have had a pensioner in their service all along of Vrybergen. Monsieurs Buys came to wait on my Lord—who came but late and went away early next day—so that he came too late; but I told him the story, and he said he would write to you himself and I have promised him a long conference with my Lord Rivers at his return. I have got a brave second here, who happens to have his letter of credit on me, one Mr. Archer knight of the shire for Warwick, who is a very hearty and stanch honest gentleman, and knows a great many good and useful things which I was ignorant of, and he shall not want opportunities of imparting his knowledge where he may think it convenient. He is still for the Place Bill, but that is a dispute betwixt him and me and does not concern foreigners. All our officers who are members of parliament are going over with all diligence to secure their elections; some who ventured by the packet boat of Ostend are gone by way of Dunkirk, amongst which Col. Grant, Mr. Speaker Smith's son in law. I am extremely obliged for your kind recommendations; what Captain Gibbon undertakes is by my intelligence and concurrence and we have Sam Shepheard in for a share under us. Be sure to keep Sir Theodore Janssen in your service, and that Dr. (*sic*) Furnese in doing something that he may not do mischief till you can do without him, for all his ready money is laid out on land, and what he undertakes is by credit as well as others do, which is a demonstration that he can do no more than others who have credit, such as Sir T. Janssen, Sir James Bateman and many more. If you could get Sir James Bateman to undertake something for Antwerp where the subsistences of the native British troops are paid he would certainly be the proper person, for he is in great credit there, and I know Mr. Hill has influence on him, and he is disobliged this year by the Whig cabal of the East India Company. The value of eighty thousand pounds sterling of the Queen's tin, if not of a hundred thousand pounds, is just arrived here consigned by Furnese to one Meulenaer a Dutch man, who is just taking the same methods which I showed them when I had the commission, and if the new undertaking of tin at any time burdens you, I shall find money upon any share of it here for you at the rate of four per cent per annum. I send you here inclosed an army letter that you may see what they are doing. This rainy weather will do much harm, the Spanish success is great, and speedy support there will be very necessary. I don't hear that the French yet talk of making any new proposals of peace, I hope the winter may produce some. *Inter nos,* Mr. Stratford of Hamburgh is an entire confident of Sir Humphrey's and Furnese, and both his sense and his estate far inferior to his uncle's whom you knew very well.

WILLIAM PATERSON to [ROBERT HARLEY].

1710, September 4—Mr. Primoli, secretary to Count Gallas, called upon me last night to communicate a letter from a Flemish officer in the service of the Duke of Anjou, dated at Bayonne the 27th of August, to his friend at Brussels, giving a very particular account of what passed in the two armies in Spain from the 26th of July to the 21st of August. It describes a great deal of good conduct on one side, and very indifferent on the other.

I was glad to hear you mention the affair of the Indies, for you may be sure that in all my thoughts for the good of this Island the Indies is always included; and I think that, notwithstanding all the opportunities lost, we have yet a fair occasion, with but common care and a very small expense, to secure our reasonable interest in that matter in not many months to come.

We ought to insist to have the French possessions not only in Newfoundland but also in Canada, and to have two or three cautionary places in South America from Spain, until the repayment of at least some of the vast expenses we have been, and still must be, at for the recovery of that monarchy to the house of Austria.

But what my mind is now most intent upon is sufficiently to apprise myself of the state of the public revenues and debts, in order to the putting an effectual stop to this immense running loss and waste therein, which, according to the gross view I now have of it, will be found not less than 6000*l.* a day, one half of which sum applied towards the extraordinaries of Spain and the Indies will make a happy conclusion of the affairs abroad, as the saving the other will much contribute to the quiet and satisfaction at home. I therefore pray that you will give the requisite assistance towards enabling me effectually to explain myself in this matter, for nothing but time and the necessary tools and materials can do it.

This nation is now brought so far upon the brink of ruin by secrets that it cannot possibly be saved or preserved but by discoveries.

Signed, with the addition thereto in Lord Poulett's handwriting " his secret is to be a C[ommissioner] of Trade."

DR. R. FRIEND to EDWARD (son of Robert) HARLEY.

1710, September 4. [Bath]—Your letters are always welcome to me, but particularly so in this place where we are glad of a line from a good hand. Dyer's letter has made some alteration to-day in people's countenances; they are [not?] so pert as they were all last week when they were positive there would be no dissolution, and that a coalition was very near being concluded. There was a great fondness here too for the report of an invasion, 'twas often attempted to be put upon us but 'twas laughed away and would not go down, though 'twas offered with very serious airs. Lord R[ocheste]r will not be well relished, nor the last paragraph of Dyer, though I think 'tis false as to Hampshire, and I hope as to Cornwall too, though I dare not be positive. I hear Sir Simon has been couched, and shall be glad to know how it has succeeded with him. The noise about credit is quite sunk here now, and they are at a loss for something to supply the place of it since neither the coalition nor invasion will do. Dr. Cheyne was sent for from hence to the Bishop of Salisbury, the messenger that came for the Doctor said his lordship was extremely ill, but we have heard nothing of him since. The Lord Chief Justice [Parker] has found great benefit from pumping; he is very courteous and calm, it seems as if he had a mind to be fair again with his old friends.

[DANIEL] DE FOE to [ROBERT HARLEY].

1710, September 5—I would fain be rendering you some service in return for the favours I daily receive from you and this makes me give you frequent troubles of this nature.

I am not insensible that to bring a certain party of people to a sense of things, viz., to be sensible of their need of friends and to know them, as also to know how to use them is a material work, and a thing which by degrees may be brought to pass, though it must not be attempted abruptly and hastily.

The people are out of humour and alarmed, and to speak to them in the public paper I write would be to do no good at all, yet they should be spoken to; even just as Solomon directs of a certain kind of people, to whom we should *answer* and *answer not*.

I am vain of saying the first step I took has been successful and has done more service than I expected, in which the town does me too much honour, in supposing it well enough done to be your own. I mean the Essay upon Credit.

If you think it proper I would offer another piece of the same kind, which I would call an Essay upon Loans; in which I think it may be of some service to take a certain people a little off of a notion that they can bring the Government to do what they please by refusing to advance their money ; laying no weight upon the advantage the lenders make, and what need they stand in of funds.

This I promise myself shall tend to lessen the vanity of some people who still fancy the Government must be obliged to change hands again, merely to oblige them, if they do but exert themselves by keeping back their money. After this I would offer an Essay upon Banks in which I would attempt to bring those men of paper to know themselves a little, by showing how well the Government can do without the Bank, and how ill the Bank can do without the Government.

These things are the effects of my constant study to render myself useful in the low sphere in which I act, and I humbly offer them for your approbation.

Enclosed I give you the papers I mentioned formerly about Edinburgh, and the proposal as I formerly laid it before the late Lord Treasurer; I lay them before you, that you may be rightly apprized of that matter, when the pickpocket proposal of a dock at Leith shall come to be debated, and doubt not you will be convinced that my scheme is equally of service to Scotland, and only saves her Majesty thirty thousand pounds in her pocket. I shall give you farther hints of this kind, when ever you shall judge it seasonable.

Postscript.—Another paper of insolent queries appears about today, and a most impudent Ballad. Sure there are printers of these things, and I fancy I know them too.

Enclosures.

De Foe's Proposals for Scotland.

Of Improvements in Scotland.

I lay it down as a foundation principle upon which all the following proposals will depend that it is the great interest of England to study and promote the prosperity and increase of Scotland

By the increase of Scotland I mean increase of wealth and people, and that is only to be brought about by increase of trade, which brings home wealth, and increase of employment for the people to keep them at home.

The people of Scotland do not fly abroad, and help to people all Europe, because this country is not equally fruitful and habitable with other places, but because want of employment at home for the people makes it more difficult for them to subsist, and therefore they fly abroad.

If employment for the poor may be found out, and encouragement given by raising the prices of labour and increasing wages the people will stay at home. Nay, people will flock thither from foreign parts and Scotland may be made as populous as other nations. If the number of people increased, the consumption of provisions would increase, and as the value of labour and rate of labour shall rise, the price of provisions would rise, and by consequence land will be improved and the estates of landed men will rise in proportion.

Improvements then being confined to these heads may be farther considered.

Improvements of trade, by navigation and foreign commerce :—

By manufacturing, and employing the poor.

Of land :—

By altering the methods of husbandry in Scotland.

By planting, enclosing, and mending the lands.

By grafting and dairy-keeping, a method which would soon bring Scotland to plenty and quite alter the miserable lives of the poor tenantry.

Of all these I have something to offer, but in my present proposal I confine myself to naval improvements in which I take upon me to say Scotland is as capable of being improved as any nation in the world notwithstanding the present deficiency of materials.

And which is still more to the present purpose, I allege that in this one affair of navigation the Government of Britain have the greatest opportunity imaginable to make a present immediate advance in the improving and encouraging Scotland (viz.)

First for building and repairing ships, and here I cannot but observe that it was a very great mistake in the Commissioners of the Customs in Scotland, when they obtained my Lord Treasurer's order to build three small frigates to cruise upon the coast to preserve the trade, that they should send for an English builder to contract for them, and then give him leave to go back into England and build them at Newcastle, whereas, by a workman I carried down there who has since built them several smaller boats, it has appeared it may even under the present discouragement and scarcity of materials be very well performed in Scotland.

Again the increase of building would encourage the importing materials and in time the producing them in Scotland, particularly hemp for cordage and planting timber for the work, and so make the work cheap.

But all men know that in Holland they have neither timber nor iron, hemp or plank, or pitch or tar, or any materials and yet that they are the greatest builders in the world.

And all men know that whether it be from Archangel, or from the East country, from Sweden or from Norway, Scotland lies nearer and more convenient for the importing naval stores than Holland. Nor do they want the most proper things to export for the purchase of those stores. I mean herrings and which in its course would be a considerable advance to the fishery of Scotland, which otherwise I confess I never promised much from.

But of these things hereafter.

In order to push this advantageous proposal of encouraging Scotland to build, fit out, and repair her own shipping, it seems the Government have an opportunity to give an introduction to it and that with such force as shall (though it may be some charge at first) most infallibly put Scotland in such a posture as for ever after to be able to do it without help, and perhaps not build for herself only but for her neighbours also, and this is the substance of my proposal :—

The Proposal.

The short of my proposal is to erect a yard with docks, store houses, launches, ways and the like for building, laying up, fitting and repairing of ships in Scotland, such as are now at Plymouth, Portsmouth &c. for the use of the Navy and then to appoint a certain squadron of her Majesty's ships to have their winter station and be laid up there.

It seems proper here to examine three things.

1. The occasion of it to England, and its advantages here in order to make it please the English.

2. The practicableness and charge and in that a further explaining the particulars.

3. The advantages to Scotland.

As to England two things prove the occasion or indeed the necessity of this proposal.

1. That since this war with France the naval power of our enemy lying to the west of us it was found so dangerous to our trade to have no port in the west where our ships might winter that the Government was obliged at a prodigious expense to erect a dock and yards at Plymouth though the place was so improper that the dock is cut by force out of a firm solid rock.

But without it our naval affairs were perfectly impotent. And if the French were powerful in the Channel, as sometimes they were, and lay between our ships and their winter ports our squadron could not come home but were obliged to lie in the Roads of Falmouth, Plymouth &c., and not to be repaired or refitted, and so became useless for the next summer, or if they waited till the enemy was retired they came home in the winter and were exposed to storms and tempests by which they were lost and destroyed, all which is now remedied by the yards and stores being placed at Plymouth by which we have always a number of men of war there ready to protect our trade and to join on occasion with the grand fleet who always come that way.

2. There was the like want of a dock &c. to the northward in the late wars with the Dutch and for the very same reason King Charles the 2nd was so sensible of it that having no port capable of receiving the men of war further north than the Humber the King built the citadel of Hull and designed a station there for laying up a squadron, and we found a prodigious disadvantage in the want of it the Dutch getting frequently between us and our northern trade in such a manner that our commerce with the Baltic was almost wholly cut off, and our coal trade so stopped that no ships dared to stir but with very strong squadrons for convoy, whereas had we then had a squadron of men of war in the Firth there had been a retreat for our Eastland fleets and Norway and Russia fleets where they would have been protected and at convenient times brought home with a strong convoy.

These are, I humbly suppose, sufficient precedents to prove the necessity and usefulness of the thing. It is true we all hope there is no probability of a Dutch War. But we are always to provide and be in ready posture for all events.

The explaining the Proposal is next which would require a long discourse, but I shall contract it reserving a further explication to a further occasion.

By a station of men of war in Scotland I mean, that such a certain number of men of war as the Government shall think needful for the security of our northern trade in time of war should be appointed to winter in Scotland in time of peace.

That at some proper place in the Firth of Forth (and I am not to seek for the place) a yard may be erected with dry docks for repairing launches for building, and ways for graving and washing the men of war.

That offices and store houses be built for laying up and securing the sails, rigging, ammunition &c. for the said ships, with victualling offices for provisions that they may be entirely fitted out to sea.

That naval stores be furnished from the proper countries and sufficient quantities laid in for all occasions.

That rope walks and all necessaries be built and provided for making all sorts of cables and cordage with encouragements for planting timber and hemp flax &c. for supplies.

In short, that all things be modelled according to the usage of the Navy for the effectual furnishing and supplying about fourteen men of war of the fourth and fifth rate, or as many as the Government shall appoint, and for building or rebuilding as occasion may require.

And above all that it may be in such a place in the Firth as if possible may be secured from the insults of an enemy and in particular as cannot be bombarded, for which proposals shall be offered when needful.

Of the Advantages of this to Scotland.

It would be very long to enter into all the particular advantages, but without enlarging on the heads, they will be such as these.

1. The expending and circulating a very great sum of money every year in Scotland and especially in the first erecting the yards.

2. The employing a great number of people in the necessary works constantly attending an undertaking of such consequence, such as carpenters, caulkers, labourers &c., about the repairing and building ships, carvers, painters, joiners, blockmakers, anchorsmiths, ropemakers and a multitude of trades which depend upon the fitting out ships.

3. The breeding seamen and encouraging them to stay at home in Scotland, of which a certain number would be always entertained in pay, and the youth of Scotland would have a kind of school to initiate them into the needful arts of building and navigating ships, the said men of war being always manned from Scotland.

4. Increase of shipping and trade for importing the naval stores for these things, and increase of business for goods to export.

5. Consumption of provisions, increase of wages to the poor, increase of labour and by consequence detaining the people at home, and by all these improving the land.

6. Security to the trade of Scotland in time of war. Such a strength being kept at their own doors as will be always able to protect them from pirates and sea robbers, whereas at this time there is not a gun can be fired at an enemy in all the Firth. But all the shipping there lies exposed to every rover, and it seems something wonderful that in all this war the French have not swept the whole Firth and even burnt the very town of Leith, which they might frequently have done but with two men of war, and a bomb ketch.

[*Endorsed.*]—The General Proposal.

The State of the Case of Docks, &c. at Leith.

The first proposal being made for docks, yards, &c. and the town of Edinburgh projecting great advantages to themselves without any view of the public profit, they petition the Queen and Council for docks, yards, &c. in the river or haven of Leith.

Which proposal of theirs being enquired into will be found—

1. Deficient to the main proposal of laying up a squadron of men of war.

2. Impracticable in its nature by the situation and other circumstances of the place.

3. Calculated only for the private advantage of the city of Edinburgh without any view of the public good.

Their proposal consists of a projected wet ▬▬ and enlarging the harbour and pier of Leith, by which they propose to bring in any of the men of war to refit, &c.

Objection—

1. It is humbly suggested that if all this were done the port of Leith cannot be capable of bringing in a squadron, and of all the necessary yards, buildings &c. which are required to that purpose. They do not propose it, nor is there room for the work on the spot they lay out for it.

2. The expense which they propose being at least forty or fifty thousand pounds will seem to be ill laid out, only for bringing in now and then a ship to refit, seeing there is already room enough for all the shipping the place does, or can be expected to employ.

The few ships of war requisite to guard the trade in time of this war cannot be worth while to expend so large sums for refitting them ; in time of peace none are required, and for laying them up their proposal is not calculated for it.

But supposing they would lay up a squadron in Scotland the port of Leith cannot be capable on sundry accounts.

1. The hazard of bringing men of war into a pier or narrow haven, which has always been avoided in the Navy upon any account whatsoever ; and the particular difficulties of the pier of Leith, with respect to a dangerous bar, shoal water, and storms of wind &c. make it on all accounts too great a hazard for the Queen's ships.

2. All the while they are within the harbour and out of the wet dock, they must lie aground at low water which has on all occasions been judged inconvenient and carefully avoided in the Navy.

3. The only piece of ground practicable for a wet dock and where it is proposed has these inconveniences.

 1. That being just on the edge of the shore which is all a sand, it is not probable it can retain the water. But it will drain out with the ebb and leave the ship aground every tide.

 2. That lying just on the edge of the Firth it is exposed to an enemy and may be bombarded at pleasure.

 3. It is believed that it is impracticable to have a depth of water to bring the Queen's ships into it.

But suppose all these things could be answered this seems merely calculated for the advantage of the city of Edinburgh without any view of the public good, since nature has already made a wet dock of the Firth itself, above the Queen's Ferry, and there can be none made like it, so that to make one at Leith can have no pretence but to help the city of Edinburgh, which if her Majesty thinks fit to do so by giving them forty thousand pounds out of her pocket and letting the dock alone it shall be much more to the public advantage.

The Advantages of the Firth for laying up the Ships.

1. For at least eight miles in length from the narrow passage as high as Alloway, the seat of the Earl of Mar, the Channel is safe, the ground good, landlocked from storms, and safe for riding the ships.

2. There is a full depth of water from six fathoms to eighteen fathoms at low water. For the breadth in most places of a mile so that the ships have room to wind upon the flood and ebb and ride clear of one another in case of fire.

3. A small charge will fortify the mouth of the passage at the Queen's ferry, the Island of Inchgarvie lying in the middle, and the main channel not half a mile broad on either side yet deep and safe in some places thirty to forty fathom water, so that no ships can pass but must come under the command of the batteries on both sides.

4. No enemy can come near to bombard them, or to burn the storehouses and yards, unless they bring a land force to go on shore and march round.

Thus the work will be better done and all the charges saved.

Sir Michael Warton to [Robert] Harley.

1710, September 5. Albemarle Street—Not being certain of finding you at home makes me give you this trouble. I find there is mighty intriguing against you new Gentlemen both amongst the English and Scotch. Duke Hamilton is disgusted, pretending a promise made him to make him a Duke here; the other party are at catch for him. Several meetings amongst the English are upon that too, and raising sums to carry on elections. Twice a week great meetings at Putney bowling green and at nights at my Lord Sun[derland's] and Orford's, and elsewhere. I believe you will want people of equal quality to shoulder up and more followers, or else beware of *cul à terre*. If these parties are not broken before the Irish Lieutenant and the General come to reinforce them, you may possibly have slept too much.

Sir Robert Davers to [Robert Harley].

1710, September 6—We have for some time expected a dissolution of this Parliament, but if the Lord Lieutenants of some counties be not turned out, and particularly ours, matters will not go so well as we wish. Our Duke tells us the Pretender is coming, and my Lord Hervey is very much dissatisfied at the present ministry. One of Bury Corporation asked a favour of his Lordship. He answered he would not ask anything of this ministry; and if no other Lord in the House would join with him, he himself would move to have the successor sent for. The man seemeth to be very angry and expressed his anger very much. Many witty things were said against our friends. He says a worse thing could not be done than turning out my Lord Godolphin. Pray let us have my Lord Dysart for our Lord Lieutenant again which will make our country happy.

Another thing the noble Duke said, that our friends are sorry for the victory in Spain, and that we have no religion and are not for a peace. Abundance of fine things they spread about the country.

E[leanor Lady] Oglethorpe to [Robert Harley].

[1710,] September 6. [Godalming]—I take the liberty of giving you this trouble to let you know how affairs go on this side of the world, and hope Lord Guernsey and Mr. Finch will do me justice, having done more for them than I promised; and I begin to believe that the two old knights will lose it, though they exert themselves ten times more than ever, as you may believe, since the Speaker has wrote lately

a most submissive letter to a cobbler at Haslemere to beg the favour of his vote and interest in behalf of himself and his son; that he will stick at no cost to gain his point, which should he miss of, he is undone. By ill luck the cobbler had not learnt to read, not expecting such an honour; I wish I could have prevailed to have kept his letter, but he hugs it as close as his knight does him. If Mr. Oglethorpe can be persuaded to come down, he'll carry in, I am told, above six hundred men for the county; his interest in his borough is very strong. They are already playing tricks with Mr. Mitchell; a nephew of the Speaker has promised to spend a thousand pounds, which I suppose is for Mr. Onslow; but if things are rightly managed, I don't doubt but my son will carry it for himself and a friend, who I hope you'll remember, now that it is so much in your power to assist him, that he may not be the only loyal gentleman that will have cause to complain of this happy change. His father's services and the loss of his brother, I hope, will plead in his behalf who has always flattered himself, that you honoured him with your friendship, and I hope now he will find the effects of it. I dare answer that you can't do for one that will be more zealous in your interest than himself; whatever is intended for him the sooner it is done the greater will be the obligation; besides it will save him the expense of two elections.

A. Lady Pye to Abigail Harley at Auditor Harley's at Eywood.

1710, September 6. Derby—The post hour is come. I now scribble in haste, the hurry I mentioned at first writing is occasioned by the daily expectation of a dissolution. Never was such work in this town. Dick had the best natural interest was ever known here, is opposed by Sir Richard Leving come for that end out of Ireland. Whether it will be worth his while to throw away his money at the rate he does, time must show, though it may go far in this needy age amongst the poor burgesses. God send us peace and quietness, and a recess of lying, of which our young man is well loaded. I fancy you will laugh when I tell you one, that he is much for the Prince of Wales. If he does come in he hopes to meet your nephew there. The vice[chamberlain] Coke is like to be thrown out of the county by his brother in law Clerk. Some think our gentlemen have not used him very civil; Mr. Curzon thought to be at the bottom. Mr. Clerk is our neighbour in Staffordshire, and a very honest gentleman, deserves it well, we think good reason to have his turn. Nottingham are also very busy, at least when I was there, the first time was ever at the horse race which is so famous that many come from London, and all Yorkshire ladies forty miles about, cannot but say it is very pleasant, but less so to me being disappointed of Sir Charles and Dick's company. Now young people are grown up it is fit they should see and be seen. I carried my two eldest girls—but I forget I have scribbled a side since I gave notice to conclude.

Earl Rivers to [Robert Harley].

1710, September [8–]19, N.S. Hanover—I arrived here last night, and that I might not seem dilatory, I was to wait on 86 and 85 (the Elector and Electress) this morning, to deliver them 64 (the Queen's) commands. I cannot say enough of the kind reception I met with, and the particular honours I received, and as I am informed more than was ever known, which I must attribute to the grateful sense they had of 67 (her) letters. I spoke to 86 and 85 upon every head I was ordered to, which 86 answered that

65 (the Queen) had done him a great deal of honour in communicating her affairs so freely to him, and as to whatever regarded his interest, he depended entirely upon 67 (her). 85, who is naturally more open than 86, told me she wondered 64 could bear so long with the ill usage she had met with, and that it was but reasonable she should make choice of such ministers as were most agreeable to her.

If 64 has any farther commands for me, I desire they may be sent me by the first post after the receipt of this, for within three weeks 86 goes to hunt fifty miles from hence, where he is to meet the Prince Royal of Prussia and will stay for some time. 85 is to go at the same time to Wolfenbuttel to the marriage of the hereditary prince of that family.

Sir Robert Cotton to [Robert Harley].

1710, September 8. Hatley St. George—The particular obligation I had to you whilst I served in a public employment, and which all our Cotton family have for that perpetual honour you have done our name in your care and settlement of our Library in that public manner it is done by parliament, makes me from my private country retirement join with your friends in town to congratulate your happy return to the management of the public affairs, always safe in the hands of such ministers as yourself.

Sir Robert Price, Baron of the Exchequer, to Robert Harley.

1710, September 11. Foxley—In my return from the north I lay at Ludlow, where I heard of Sir Thomas Powis who is hard pressed in his election by Baldwin and Walcott, though I believe he is more feared than hurt. Poor Will Gower is set up by some of his old friends, though with little prospect of success. I have persuaded him into Sir Thomas Powis's interest and to act as he shall direct him. There I met with a melancholy scene to find him (Gower), his lady, and ten children under deplorable straits, which has extremely affected my pitying nature. I did promise them to remind you of their circumstances; their whole dependence for bread is upon you. If Gower were made one of the Commissioners of Appeals in the Excise, which is 200*l.* per annum, he might follow his profession besides, which he has neglected being under difficulties; and those places are fitter for men of the law than for Sir James of the Peak and such sort of cattle.

[Erasmus Lewis to Robert Harley.]

1710, September 11—The Duke of Somerset in a conversation last night with Sir Peter King desired him to acquaint all their friends, that he was, is, and ever would be Whig, that he would serve them in all elections, and would oppose a dissolution to the utmost; that he never consented to the removal of the Duke of Bolton, nor the putting in of the Duke of Beaufort, and desired Sir Peter to assure his old friends of his steadiness to them. Sir Edward Lawrence told me this morning that he had all this from Sir Peter last night at Kensington.

H[enry] W[atkins] to ——

1710, September [11-] 22, N.S. Camp at St. André—I am favoured with your billet of the first instant, and have forwarded that you enclosed for "Duke" [Colonel] Disney to Aix la Chapelle, for which place he set out on Thursday last in company of Brigadier Hill, the latter for health, and the former for pleasure.

I believe every man in the army would readily sign an address of thanks for your taking the government of the Isle of Wight out of the hand to which it never belonged and restoring it to the military. If there are any more in England usurped from us, I hope you will think fit to do us the same justice. I will not pretend to tell on whom I would have these bounties conferred, but you know few of our general officers will have any thing else to depend on when the war is ended; and I wonder how it could enter into the thoughts of the two great Dukes of the north and west to ask such posts, and never after think of deserving them.

Our circular will acquaint you with a disgrace we have received, from which I apprehend no other ill consequence than that the Dukes who have been the occasion of it will pay something dearer for this conquest than they expected.

[Daniel] De Foe to [Robert Harley].

1710, September 12—Since I waited on you last I have farther enquired into the Scot's mission I hinted to you, and find it goes forward; the gentleman has signified his going to his congregation, the occasion, as I noted, is purely (so far as appears) the affair of the College.

I am very well assured of the good disposition of the ministers of Scotland to the Queen, and to a quiet peaceable behaviour, and am very sorry to see any attempts to infuse groundless jealousies into their heads, wherefore as the best service I can render her Majesty on this occasion, I shall (if you approve of it) apply myself to weaken the counsels of Achitophel, and prepossess the ministers there, with whom my interest, I believe, is so good that he shall be able to do little mischief. This I did before in the case of Mr. Calamy, and with such success that to this day he has not been able to maintain a correspondence there, and this I do, not to prejudice them on either hand. But I have a double view in it, and both, I hope, very honest and very useful.

First, I would prevent them making the honest poor people in Scotland uneasy to themselves, as I think our dissenters here now are, without any cause.

Secondly, I would prevent their being uneasy to the Government, which now, God be praised, they are not, but if fermented from hence may be.

I am really concerned to see our people diligently spread, and others eagerly receive, the grossest absurdities, by which they would make their disgusts at the late changes appear rational; such as the favouring a French interest, and countenancing the Pretender; terrifying the poor ignorant people with notions of Popery and of persecution, as if our safety was not in her Majesty but in her servants, and the Queen could not govern us, but by such hands as we liked of.

This I apply myself to expose as ridiculous, and in all the correspondence I keep up, which is now all over Britain, I diligently counteract this folly. I relate this not to value myself upon my services, but to have your approbation of it; that I may not ignorantly or officiously take much pains, and do no service.

I know the gentlemen are busy spreading jealousies among all the country people, and I may trace some of their methods too. If to set the people right in their notions, if to prevent the malignity of national jealousy, if to keep up in the minds of her Majesty's subjects their zeal and affection to the person as well as to the government of their Sovereign, be any service to her Majesty, be of any moment, I flatter myself I shall be made useful, especially in Scotland and the north of England.

Matters of credit, and oppressing the public affairs by refusing to lend money, and withdrawing the assistance their duty as well as interest demands, is the great consequence of these discontents and no doubt is the great design in propagating this uneasy temper. To this I shall not fail to apply the best remedy I can, by exposing first the malice and then the folly of it. You see in this a specimen of party fury, and how difficult it is to struggle with the follies of men, but I hope time and a little experience will make our people wiser. I ask your pardon for the length of this.

Endorsed by Harley.—"Mr. Goldsmith."

[JOHN] D[RUMMOND] to [ROBERT HARLEY].

1710, September [12–]23, N.S. Amsterdam—After you have read the inclosed in presence of the person who delivers it to you please seal it up again yourself and give it to him to be returned to me. I am glad with all my heart that you are gaining that great man, for his success. has made him so and covers all faults here. The first of the five mentioned in that letter is Earl Poulett; H. is yourself, it was this person who would have had me meddle to reconcile you and the great man. The Bank having now turned over all their Exchequer notes on the nation by drawing bills for money and buying bills for said notes, by which they have also raised several hundred thousand pounds in money, I hope you will get them to assist you, for they are now full of ready money and have put off all their notes.

Governor Pitt from the East Indies is safe arrived here, and being recommended by Sir Steven Evans and several others to me, I think I have made him yours and have drunk your health heartily with him. He will have a powerful purse in England, and be a thorn in the side of some great men now at the head of the Bank and India Company if they should thwart you. Therefore if you can get him chosen in Cornwall pray do, for he will be more useful to you than ever Dolben was to your predecessor, and I hope you will make a better use of him. He will be here yet ten or fourteen days if not three weeks and then for England. I pray don't show Stratford of Ham(burg?) or any one else my letters for some people through vanity tell all they hear and see.

EARL RIVERS to [ROBERT HARLEY].

1710, September [15–]26, N.S. [Hanover]—I did not write to you by the express I sent with letters to 66, by reason 86 sent me word I should have a copy of his to 64, which I had last night. I think it is very obliging, but I could wish he had been a little more particular in answering what was wrote and said by me to him. It is likely he might believe that I had sent word how he received me, when I delivered him the letters and message, which was in a very obliging manner, approving of 65 conduct in what was done. 85 went farther and wondered at 67 so long patience. I have a very hard task not knowing one of 90 (the Elector's ministers) I can confide in, they being governed by 143 (Robethon), who answers the character you have had of him, but I do not doubt when there is an end of 84 (Parliament), which is not believed here, he and the rest of them will alter their way of talking. 72 (Lord President) has wrote word hither 84 will stand; however, let it be as it will, he is sure to gain his point. If you write to me before you send an express, which I desire you will do if you have anything of consequence, or with your last letters you intend to send me, for I have not had one letter since I left England from you or any of my friends, which I should certainly have had, had they not been somewhere stopped; therefore pray direct your next to Mr. Drummond at Amsterdam. I was in hopes to have received an answer of what I sent you from Holland, in which I gave you an account of what passed between me and 78 (Pensioner). *Signed* " 122."

C[HARLES] CAESAR to ROBERT HARLEY.

1710, September 16—You having asked me yesterday what would be most agreeable to me I let you know that nothing would be so acceptable as having Sir John Holland's staff or a Teller's place in the Exchequer, if either can be obtained for me; but I leave myself wholly to be disposed of as you think most proper.

LORD HALIFAX to [ROBERT HARLEY].

[1710, September 16]—I give you many thanks for representing my endeavours to make this unhappy affair easy to the Queen, in so favourable a manner. I shall always act the same part in everything that may be for her service. I think it would be more proper for me to wait upon her Majesty to thank her for her favour to him, when she has ordered the Patent, than to accompany the surrender. I have heard from Lord Chamberlain and according to his directions my brother will make his surrender to the Queen at six this evening.

SIR JAMES MONTAGUE to [ROBERT HARLEY].

1710, September 17—I did myself the honour to call upon you last night as soon as I returned from the Queen who hath been graciously pleased to accept of the surrender of the Attorney General's office from me, and in testimony of her Majesty's further great grace and favour hath given me assurances of the gratifications you and my Lord Halifax have discoursed of.

As I hitherto have been beholden to you for the kind offices you have done to make this affair the least disagreeable to me, so I must still depend upon your favour and friendship to procure the establishment of what her Majesty hath granted so as it may answer her gracious purposes. I must therefore make it my humble request to you that the warrant for preparing the patent for this pension may be forwarded, now I have done what was expected on my part. Her Majesty may be assured I shall resign this new patent as readily as I have done the former whenever the more valuable part of the proposal shall be made good and her Majesty signifies her pleasure therein. Therefore I do humbly submit it to your consideration whether any mention need be made of the alternative in the Letters patent. If anything more be to be done on my part I shall wait upon you to receive your commands upon the first intimation and shall readily embrace all opportunities to make my acknowledgements for the great favours I have received from you.

[JOHN DRUMMOND to ROBERT HARLEY.]

1710, September [19-]30, N.S. Amsterdam—I delivered the letter into Monsieur Renard's own hand which Mr. Lewis sent me by your order, and I have the honour to forward you this from Earl Rivers, who has sent me a direction how to send any letters safe, which may come to my hands directed for his Lordship. We are all amazed here seeing a new parliament seems necessary that it is not declared, and that the expenses of the war will require money ere it can be granted if the parliament does not consent the usual funds before Christmas. I hope if it is to be at all you will do it, or have done it on Colonel Harrison's arrival with the confirmation of the great success in Spain, which will support the prices of the public funds and stocks as much as the malice of some will be able to lower them at such a juncture.

Some of my friends may have been teasing my Lord Dupplin to write to you about my standing for parliament man; but the Duke of Argyll offered me his interest some time since in his part of the country and I could not accept of it.

LORD HALIFAX to [ROBERT HARLEY].

1710, September 19. Bushey Park—I was at your door to know if you had any further commands for me about the expedition to America, for till I am fuller informed what number of ships and men can be had in a month's time 'tis impossible to form any design, for I believe it will not be advisable, to begin an expedition towards South America later than that. While you are pleased to explain that to me, give me leave to answer one question you asked me more fully than I could remember at that time. In the year 1702-3 there was an intention of sending a great force both English and Dutch into the West Indies to receive those under their protection who would submit to the House of Austria, and to conquer those that were obstinate. To make this expedition more effectual, there were commissaries, and priests sent from Vienna to be sent among the people, and to persuade them to come in to the Emperor, to which they were thought to be disposed. When every thing was almost ready, Count Wratislaw began to start new points and to make difficulties, particularly he insisted upon it, that the garrisons which should be left in any places, as well those that were taken as those who acknowledged the Emperor, should take an oath to the Emperor, and be held in his name, till it was adjusted at the general Peace to whom they should remain. This demand was thought very extraordinary, and contrary to the Grand Alliance, by which we and the Dutch were to keep all we took in America. This occasioned many conferences and disputes between him and the Ministers, and on 7-18 January 1702-3 he presented a memorial to the Queen declaring he must stop the Imperial Commissaries, if this point was not settled to his mind. At the same time the Dutch Ministers gave the Queen a memorial setting forth that their ships had been so long detained by contrary winds, that the season being so far advanced, the States General thought it would be too late to proceed to the West Indies, and were of opinion the forces might be better employed elsewhere. The Queen in the answer which was made agreed to their proposal, and this design was laid aside. This is what I can collect from papers I have, but you may be better informed from those who were then in business. There are many remarks to be made on this passage, one is very obvious that if the Court of Vienna was so stiff in these points at that time, when they were hardly in possession of one foot of ground belonging to the Spanish Monarchy, you may expect pressing instances against it from the Spaniards, if King Charles be at Madrid; and yet without an equivalent in those parts, what Indies have we lavished away.

The tediousness of this will make you cautious of speaking to me of the West Indies which I am always full of.

The DUKE OF ATHOLL to [ROBERT HARLEY].

1710, September 19. Huntingtower—Though I have not the good fortune of your acquaintance it was a great satisfaction to me to hear the Queen had employed you in her service, every unbiassed person being sensible you had the greatest hardships done you; and I must say the bad usage I met with from the same hands made me sympathise very much with you.

My Lord Dupplin who is the bearer can acquaint you particularly of the measures the Earl of Kinnoull and I are taking to support the Queen at this juncture in Scotland. It will be a great satisfaction to me to know they are agreeable to her Majesty. .

[DANIEL DE FOE* to ROBERT HARLEY.]

1710, September 21—The joy I conceived when you were pleased to signify to me that her Majesty has directed the affair in my favour moves me in the humblest manner to apply myself to you in two cases.

First, that the sense I have of her Majesty's goodness may be represented in the best manner possible to her Majesty, so as becomes a subject under the strongest ties of duty and gratitude.

And secondly, that you would be pleased to furnish the occasion how I may render her Majesty such service as may at least testify for me that this bounty is not wrong placed. I do not pretend to be able to merit so much favour, yet the meanest capacity can always do something. There is a difference between not being worthy, and being unworthy, I hope. I need not assure you that I will slip no opportunity of service, but it is wholly in yourself to make me useful, and as the favour comes by your intercession, so the power of serving depends upon your assistance in directing. I remember your discourse about the approaching dissolution, I would humbly offer it to your consideration, whether you think I may not do some service in the country for a mouth or two ; I mean in the North, to argue with, persuade, and bring to their temper and eyesight a certain people who are but too apt to receive impressions from some here who want both.

I do not propose it as a matter of charge ; I shall submit that to you. I shall endeavour rather to be too backward than too forward on that account. But I humbly offer it as my opinion only that at this juncture it may be of more service than perhaps it would be possible at another time. I cannot but remember the journey I once went on such an occasion, I mean at the last election by your order, in which I had such success that I can hardly wish more upon like occasion. I submit it wholly to you, and shall cheerfully obey your orders in it one way or other.

Endorsed by Harley.—" Mr. Goldsmith."

---

* Signature torn off. .   .

THOMAS FORSTER to [ROBERT HARLEY].

1710, September 22. Etherstone, near Belford—Upon intimation from Colonel Dobyns to Mr. Norman that you desired to have as many of your friends in the next Parliament, as you could possibly procure, we made an attempt upon Berwick and Morpeth, but without success. We once thought to propose the joining Sir John Delavall and Colonel Dobyns, but upon inquiry found Sir John's interest would do us no good, so never mentioned it to him; nor did we let any in the Corporation know who was the person intended. I told them it was for one of my friends and got fifty out of the hundred and twenty electors to subscribe for any person I should name. I desired my interest might be kept up and if upon this you think fit to name a person and hazard a petition, we can prove direct bribery upon the other candidates who are named by Lord Carlisle. Whatever direction you give shall be followed.

Postscript.—Lieutenant General Maire would be most acceptable, will be of your interest and I will answer for his obeying your orders. I had forgot one thing which if you please to give the person leave to wait upon you, may be in my humble opinion worth your notice; he will lay a scheme before you which will save ten if not twenty thousand pounds which has by the late Lord Treasurer been universally employed. If you approve of this pray let me know and he shall wait upon you and I with your leave will introduce him.

SIR THOMAS TREVOR, Lord Chief Justice, to [ROBERT HARLEY].

1710, September 22—The matter of your letter is very surprising to me at this time, but having formerly had occasion of considering the subject there mentioned, I am prepared to return an answer without much delay. I hope you have not the least doubt but that I shall upon all occasions be ready to serve the Queen to the utmost of my power, and more especially in the present juncture of affairs, where I am sensible her Majesty meets with great difficulties out of her great zeal for the ease and happiness of her subjects; but I beg I may have the liberty of doing it in my present station. 'Tis not the want of honour or profit which hath hitherto induced me to decline the other you mention, for I think it hath the greatest share of both of any place her Majesty can bestow on one of my profession, but the knowledge of my own weakness and want of strength to discharge the duty of that place. For though I enjoy a tolerable share of health now I have some ease and leisure, the fatigue of that place would utterly destroy it, therefore I beg of you as you are my friend that this thing may rest with you and go no further, as I assure you it shall not be any way divulged by me. I shall always acknowledge and have a grateful sense of your great kindness and friendship for me, and 'tis a great uneasiness to me to be obliged to return an answer that may be unacceptable to so gracious and honourable a proposal, and I earnestly entreat you that this may put a full stop to any further consideration of this matter.

RICHARD HOGARTH to ROBERT HARLEY.

1710, September 23. The Old Bailey within the bounds of the Fleet—Asking for assistance and informing him that though he was not yet forty-six years of age he was perishing in prison under the burden of twenty-two living children; also stating that he was completing a dictionary after the style of Elisha Cole. *Latin.*

[The DUKE OF NEWCASTLE to ROBERT HARLEY.]

1710, September 23—My letters came to me to-day twelve miles from home where I was stag hunting. There were a great many people of quality in the field of those you call Tories and they came from the post house in Mansfield where they had been to see the news. They all seemed to be mightily pleased with one of your great officers but all cried out of the other and wondered what use could be made of him and why he was put in. I will not name him because it might be thought malice in me. This is only writ to divert you.

I cannot add anything to what I writ to you in my last long letter. Your letter I am now answering there seemed to have been an endeavour to open the seal that makes me beg you will put some seal upon your letters that will not be known. I write this because you promised me a particular account in your next to know whether you writ this post because I received none from you, that I may if possible find out the roguery whether in country or town.

The DUKE OF BEAUFORT to ROBERT HARLEY.

1710, September 23—It will take up too much of your time, to give you a whole detail of the proceedings in this country, but I will in as few words as possible let you know that everything has a good face here, and every face full of joy, to see themselves delivered from the management of the Duke of Bolton, whose interest has been carried on more by that and the fear of suppression by the help of his authority, than by any love or personal affection either sex have for him. There is no lie that is possible to be invented that they don't use, they are descended so low as to bully and threaten to stick people by the wall, if they will not vote for them; and tell them that they are confident Robin the Trickster, which is the epithet they give you, will be turned out, and his gang, in a few months and then they will hang and ruin all those that are not of their side especially if they vote for Sir Simeon Stuart or Mr. Pitt. This is the quarter we are to expect from them, so I hope you and the rest of our friends will prevent them from breaking anyone's neck but their own. As it is their business to bully and lie, so I and my friends here make it our business to show all the candour, good humour, and condescension to all people which takes so well amongst them, that I may venture to say, the returns will be better out of this county than we ever expected. So much loyalty I am sure never was seen, than is now in Hampshire, their affection and duty to the Queen are so great, that I am almost deaf with the huzzas for the Queen, Church, prosperity and success to the new faithful Ministry, a good Parliament and a speedy and lasting peace. These healths have almost deafened all the gentlemen of the country and opened the ears and eyes of the honest freeholders and burgesses, that I can see no ill prospect of the loss of any election we have attempted, but that of Portsmouth, which is entirely owing to the Commissioner of the Dock, whose being turned out will be the greatest service to the Queen's friends in this county, and certainly secure the elections of all her friends who stand for any place in it. This makes one press his speedy return to the Board at London, and that you will use your interest to effect it. Long letters I know are troublesome, especially to a person so much and well employed in the retrieving our Queen and Country from such an oppression, that I believe no precedent can be found for, that both the prerogative of the Crown and liberty of the people have been so scandalously struck at by the servants of both.

E[LEANOR, LADY] OGLETHORPE, to [ROBERT HARLEY].

1710, September 24—Since a new parliament is to be called so suddenly I solicit you once more on behalf of my son [Theophilus], to get him into some employment before the election. He would be able to draw many advantages from it. I am this minute going to Hasle-mere where I intend to stay till all is over, and the sooner he comes down the better, for the other gentlemen are there already.

The DUKE OF HAMILTON to [ROBERT HARLEY].

1710, September 24. Sunday night—I return you many thanks for your letter. The Duke of Shrewsbury has acquainted me that it is her Majesty's pleasure I should attend her to-morrow at seven in the evening, when I shall be glad to receive the honour of her commands, for there's nobody covets more to serve her than I.

The EARL OF ORRERY to [ROBERT HARLEY].

1710, September 24--When I waited upon you last you seemed to appoint Monday for settling the Scotch affairs, but fixing no more particular time nor any place either then or since my Lords Ma[r?] and Il[ay] would willingly receive your commands-a little more precisely in that respect. I find these Lords are under some uneasiness that they have not been able all this while to prevail upon you to come to some determination in this matter, and apprehend if they should be strong enough to carry their own elections (which they think is now far from being certain) that they shall not however have it in their power to serve you or the public so effectually as they could have done if proper measures had been taken in time ; but they are particularly afraid lest there should be any design that they should act with the Squadron, with whom they think they can neither safely nor honourably join. I'm confident you will agree with me that the affairs of that kingdom are of too much moment to be any longer neglected, and I know it would be kindly taken if you would settle them immediately with these Lords if they are to have the direction of them, or would open your mind freely to them if they are not. I must own I was in hopes that some steps would have been taken by this in my Lord Il[ay]'s particular affair both in regard to him and his brother, as well as to give him that credit and power which 'tis necessary for him to have in order to serve you ; and I wish still, if it be not too late, that it could be dispatched before he goes to Scotland. I am linked with him and his brother in so particular a manner and so concerned that they should be made easy in all respects, that I must beg whatever is thought fit to be done for them may be done with such a grace as will convince them that the kindness proceeds from a real friendship and not from importunity, and if they are not shocked I dare be answerable you will not find two more faithful servants.

I find by Mr. Aislabie that he would take it well if you would either say something to him yourself or commission me to say something to him before he goes into the country, which I believe he designs to do in a few days. The town has given him a place which I perceive would not be so agreeable to him as another employment in the hands of the same gentleman whom 'tis reported he is to succeed, and as that employment would be more pleasing to him, so in my poor judgment he would be more fit for that than the other. He was to wait upon you according to your own appointment but could not see you.

I cannot but say upon this occasion that I hope there will be such a Secretary at War, and very soon, as will probably give satisfaction in his office to all the officers of the army as well as to his particular friends. I must desire you would excuse the liberty I take in being so plain with you upon all occasions but your multiplicity of business may possibly now and then make you forget some things that are necessary for the public as well as for your own particular service, upon both which accounts I am so zealously and sincerely cone■■■ed that I should hardly forgive myself if I should neglect any opportunity in my power either of preserving your old friends or getting you new ones.

The EARL OF KINNOULL to [ROBERT HARLEY].

1710, September 26. Edinburgh—The Duke of Atholl and some of the Peers in our corner of the country have written to the Queen, assuring her Majesty that when she shall think fit to call a new Parliament, they will make choice of such of the Peers as her Majesty shall think fit. This I thought was the surest measure to unite us and prevent our differing amongst ourselves, and I found it was the only measure that could prevent differences betwixt the Duke of Hamilton and the Duke of Atholl where I am sorry there is too great a breach. We have thought fit to send the letter to the Duke of Shrewsbury to deliver it, which I hope is a measure that you will not dislike, being unwilling to give any ground to think that we were of this or the other party. This is what all of us went cheerfully into, and particularly the Duke of Atholl, who without any terms but merely from the zeal he has to serve the Queen, for he does not so much as desire to be chosen one of the sixteen. I shall write to you more fully with my son who goes from this to-morrow and will be with you in a few days after you receive this. If this be thought a good measure, to be sure the sooner that such of our Scotch Peers, who are with you, write down to their friends to follow the same measure it will be the better, whether they give assurances by separate letters or joint letters, for I find that there are several that would have gone into this measure if they had not been engaged to their friends at London not to move any way till they hear from them. I am perfectly persuaded that a good new Parliament is the only thing can establish the Queen's interest, and I shall to the utmost of my small power do every thing I can for the advancing of it, without any other view than purely to serve so good a Queen.

The EARL OF KINNOULL to [ROBERT HARLEY].

1710, September 27. Edinburgh—Finding that my son had so great a mind to be in the House of Commons and that he was impatient to be with you, your daughter and I have parted with him though not without some reluctance. But I hope it shall not be long before we meet for I am resolved whenever the elections are over to see you at London, whether I be one of the elected or not; for in that matter I shall heartily acquiesce in what shall be thought best for the Queen's service. Though there is none wishes her better and will be readier to serve her to my power, yet there are a great many more capable to whom I shall cheerfully cede.

I know you have an equal concern for my son with myself so that I have not the least doubt but you will be concerned that he makes his first appearance in the world with as great advantage as possible, which you both know better how to direct and can now better assist him in than I. Therefore I leave him entirely to you, do with him what you think fit. I reckon your concern in my family and in little Tommie is now as great as my own so that I promise to myself you will do what you think is proper for my interest; therefore I shall not so much as mention my affair in the Treasury to you but shall patiently wait till you think it convenient.

I confess I have a more than ordinary anxiety to have our elections go right and I have and shall take all the pains in that matter that I can for I always did and still do think that to get a good Parliament is the great business in hand. If the Queen approve of that measure which the Duke of Atholl and some others of us have taken, then make those of our Scotch Peers that are with you write down to their friends here to go into the like measure, to give the Queen assurances either by joint or separate letters that they will go in to her choice of the sixteen peers; and I am fully persuaded there will not one of the Squadron or Whigs be chosen. Whatever may be the measure most proper for advancing the Queen's interest in England I am not capable to judge of, but I am perfectly persuaded that the only measure here in Scotland is to go in entirely to the Tories. I pray you take care that you name none of those to be of the sixteen which you will find necessary afterwards to turn out of their places; there are three or four of such as will pretend to it. My hand is wearied writing and George is just going so I shall say no more.

Charles Caesar to Robert Harley.

1710 September 28—Though I do not in the least doubt being put into some place, I can't help begging that what is intended may be done before my election, which will be on Wednesday, October 4. Mr. Goulston and I are both sure of being chosen [for Hertford] by a great majority.

[Daniel De Foe* to Robert Harley.]

1710, September 29—Though this is sooner than the time I had your orders to attend I could not but give you this trouble to cover the enclosed.

This is another street letter, said to be taken up in the night. I will not presume to anticipate your thoughts of these things; to me they appear very naked and undressed. The design appears villanous, viz., to draw innocent persons into suggested plots, &c. 'Tis the easiest thing in the world to cause traitorous letters to be written to any person and then prompt the intercepting them. The thing, therefore, as it is a vile and most abhorred method, so 'tis withal so foolish, and so ill set out, that the mischief seems taken away, and the mischievous design only left. For surely in vain is the net spread in the sight of any bird.

As to the coming of the Pretender, the vain scarecrow is too visible. I know not whether, if ever we should wish for him, it should not be now, and that an invasion might set us to rights. Then we should see the falsity of the clamours and noise of a party, and many of those who are reproached with being for him would have an opportunity to wipe off that scandal, by discovering the persons who really are so. It is true the experiment might be costly, but a knave discovered is cheap bought almost at any price. If this method be used with success, I

---

* Signature torn off.

expect next counterfeit letters and treasonable papers to be conveyed into houses, and then be searched for ; letters sent and then intercepted, innocent men to be suspected, and then to be falsely accused; and all the wicked things than can be, passed for current law among us. I hope her Majesty will take a right view of these things and will protect her faithful servants from the snares thus laid for their honour and safety.

. There may be other ends in spreading these ▉tters, which without doors a man cannot see. I must confess I see nothing in them to be apprehensive of. They tend indeed to increase jealousies among the people, and make them afraid of one another; but they are so weak, so much malice with so little wit, that I think there is not much to fear from them.

I know you will abate me the ceremony of thanks for the favour done me. The best acknowledgment I can make, either to her Majesty the original, or yourself the means, of my support, is a vigorous application to what is the duty of every honest man, viz., to promote the general peace, and upon all occasions to pursue the best interests both of her Majesty and her people, which is the union of all their hearts in her service. This I take to be the best method to oblige you and the best way to show the sense I have both of my duty and obligation; and in this I shall not be wanting.

This is a day of city hurry. I could have been very glad to have seen a haughty, proud, and (I must own I think) empty man, defeated, and a man of peace, temper and modesty in his room, but I foresee right measures are not taken for it, so if it should happen I must acknowledge myself deceived. This is a day when men of peace and patience are the only useful people either for themselves or the Government. But how few such are to be found ! The zeal of parties has eaten them up, and men seem heated for their country's mischief, as if they were to feel no share of her ruin when it should come to pass.

· I am preparing to receive your commands and persuade myself you will agree in this that the sooner I am there the more service I may do. The gentleman of letters and degrees, who I formerly hinted to you was going northwards, is set out.

Dr. George Smalridge to [Robert Harley].

[1710], September 28—Concerning a misstatement which was being circulated in [Westminster] by Colonel Davenport and Sir H. Colt to the disadvantage of Mr. Crosse's candidature.

The Earl of Orrery to [Robert Harley].

1710, September 29—I find my Lord Ilay by his conversation with you last night thinks you are of opinion that his affair ought to be mentioned to my Lord Roc[hester] and go through the Duke of Queensberry's office, which he is afraid would prove an effectual method to retard if not to defeat it. I told him I was in hopes that he mistook you and that though you might mention that method I could hardly think when you considered it thoroughly that you would insist upon it, for I did not take it to be your interest to fling more power into my Lord Roc[hester]'s hands than was absolutely necessary ; and as for the Duke of Queensberry I thought you were so little inclined to him in the most material points that I could not believe you would make much scruple to disoblige him in a matter of form, especially to serve my

Lord Ilay and in a business which was in some measure your concern to
have dispatched. You will have turned this matter so well in your
thoughts by to-morrow night I hope that you will give my Lord entire
satisfaction in it.

When the agreement is made with Duke Hamilton I hope he will be
made to engage for his brother's behaviour as well as his own, my Lord
Orkney's conduct in the last Parliament is a sufficient pretence to
require security for him in the next, and there is the more reason to
insist upon this because he has expressed more regard this year than he
used to do to my Lord Marlborough.

I wish you would endeavour to speak to Mr. Aislabie as soon as
possible, and make him some civil compliment of your inclinations to
him. He was to wait upon you last night.

The DUKE OF NEWCASTLE to [ROBERT HARLEY].

1710, September 30—I should be sorry if that peevish and stubborn
humour should hinder any of the Commissioners you name from
serving, for though I have been unfortunate not to succeed with some of
the leaders by my being at so great a distance I hope to do it better in
the beginning of the winter with many of the party which will be
chosen. That I have not been more successful to deal plainly with you
I doubt there has been faults on both sides. To show you my poor
endeavours to this end I have enclosed you my Lord Cowper's letter to
me which I beg you will make a great secret to everybody but to 32 if
you think fit to show it them, and when you have perused it be pleased
to return it me back; you may see by the style it was not designed to
be seen by anybody: I assure you this is but one person in a great
many that I have endeavoured with an unfeigned zeal to serve the
Queen and I am not without hopes her Majesty may the next winter
find the effects of it. I have had a long letter from 35 which may
keep cold till I see you. I beg you will make my congratulations to
Mr. St. John and Mr. Granville.

J. D[RUMMOND] to [ROBERT HARLEY].

1710, [September 30—] October 10, N.S. Amsterdam—I hope we
will have a new parliament who will provide plentifully for one campaign
more, which I hope may break the French King's heart as well as his
strength and credit; for though they detain our letters from Madrid
yet, yet it is certain King Charles has been there and was kindly
received, and our siege of Air goes on tolerably well though we very
much want engineers. Our generals resolve to keep their posts in the
army as long as possible to hinder the French making detachments to
Spain, and if the Duke of Savoy's generals do the same we may hope
the French will come to reasonable terms this winter. My Lord Townshend seems earnest for a peace as soon as it can be obtained with reason
and safety; the treaty of barrier which he was so very instrumental in
procuring for the States and his plain honest methods of dealing with
them have got his Excellency an unspeakable interest and reputation
with them, which has sometimes occasioned so great jealousies betwixt
our great Duke and his Lordship, in so far that I am well informed
that he expected to be recalled before you gave this new turn to affairs,
and though my Lord Townshend may be in with some of the Junto, he
has always spoken honourably of the Queen's ministers now employed,

and dealt above board in every respect as much as could be expected, and in all his conversation seems to have more personal respect for the Queen than any of the old set.

The Earl of Orrery to [Robert Harley].

[1710, c. September]. Wednesday—I'm afraid at so short a warning I cannot recollect all my thoughts about the army that I put into the paper which I gave H. St. [John] nor put them into so good a method as I should do; but the most material I think were that the Queen should take the nomination of all Colonels at least to herself, and sign their commissions as well as she does those of all general officers, and that she should for every campaign appoint anew the several general officers for the different establishments and that she should take some public method of declaring these to be stated rules from which she would not depart. In general I believe besides these and other particulars it will be proper that the Queen should take back to herself a good deal of that power which she has given away to the several Commanding Officers in Chief, and that whatever comes before her relating to the army which she does not think fit directly and immediately to determine herself should be referred to whom it shall be judged proper. Perhaps it would not be improper to have those references made to a Committee of the Privy Council consisting of all those officers that are of that Council. I offer this only as an expedient to avoid the inconvenience of referring the business of the army to a Board of general officers that usually sit at the Horse Guards who are most of them, as the army is now, composed in a different interest from that of their real Sovereign. In general I would have the Queen determine every thing and especially grant all favours herself. I am of opinion that the commissions of all commanding Officers in Chief are too large and injurious to the rights of the Crown, but they say my Lord Marlborough's is so particularly extensive that 'tis fit that should have a particular consideration, but I, not having seen it, cannot tell what to say to it. I have given you some of my present thoughts in obedience to your commands but the subject is very copious as well as important and fitter for a conversation than a letter.

Thomas Sclater to [Robert Harley].

1710, October 3. Catley—Last Saturday Lord Anglesey told the University that he could not serve them as a member, which caused a great confusion, for each candidate relying on his late letter to the contrary was absent from the University.

I immediately waited on my Lord to acquaint him, that by the sudden alteration of his Lordship's intention, and by the regulation he designed of obliging each candidate to bring to him a list of their friends of the Honest Party on Tuesday next, in order that all should submit to the candidate that had the majority, it was the advice of my friends that I should not stand, for it was impossible to get such an interest in two days as they had been as many years procuring, especially since his Lordship declared he could not assist me. His Lordship was pleased to tell me that you had obliged him to alter his intentions of standing by inserting in the Gazette his title of Earl of Anglesey. He has taken upon him the sole direction of the election, as an impartial judge, his particular friends solicit for his creature Pask, and his Lordship has so threatened and abused the solicitors for 'Shaw,' that unless a greater spirit of resentment arise than I can yet see,' it is plain who will be chosen, and who has been always designed. I gave your letter to Dr. Gower, who I doubt not but would have done me great service, if my Lord had not pre-engaged him, by telling him I had desisted, before he had any grounds for that assurance.' Your favour in this matter, and in that of the rioters of Ely are additions to those many you have been pleased to do to me.

Postscript.—Mr. Bromley gives you his humble thanks for your favour about the rioters, and begs leave to wait on you when he comes to town to acknowledge it.

DR. WHITE KENNETT to [ROBERT HARLEY].

1710, October 3. Crutched Friars—I humbly beg leave to represent a matter of fact, that I presume is of some consequence to the honour of her Majesty and the regulation of her ministers, as well as to the interest of the church and our Protestant religion.

My brother Mr. Basil Kennett at the desire of the English merchants was sent to Leghorn about four years since to reside and officiate as chaplain to our factory in that port, with a commission from her Majesty and letters of protection. When he had been there a few months the Inquisition began to threaten him, and upon application made by Dr. Newton to the Great Duke, he received an answer to this effect, that the Inquisition was a Court superior to the Civil Power, and his highness could not hinder their proceedings. Upon this report made by Dr. Newton, her Majesty in Council was pleased to command the Secretary of State, the Earl of Sunderland, to write back to this effect, that he should tell the Great Duke and his ministers in her Majesty's name, that if any molestation were given to her chaplain at Leghorn, she should look upon it as an affront done to herself and the nation, a breach of peace, and a violation of the law of nations, and should by her fleets and armies in the Mediterranean not only demand but take satisfaction for any such injury offered. And if they talked any more of the Pope and Court of Rome he must cut that matter short by telling them, that her Majesty has nothing to do with that Court but will treat with the Great Duke as other independent Princes and States.

When this noble resolution was communicated to the Court of Florence, the Inquisition soon desisted, and my brother has continued in the free exercise of his office, to the great benefit of the merchants, and to the honour of her Majesty's Government.

It now so happens that my brother is under a necessity of return, and the factory have desired one to succeed him. Upon this occasion the Lord Archbishop of Canterbury and the Lord Bishop of London recommended one Mr. Taubman (who had been long in her Majesty's service at sea) by letters to the chief merchants in and about London trading to Leghorn, and they were so well satisfied in his good character, as by their letters to the Archbishop and Bishop to approve and accept him, and to desire their Lordships' application to the Queen, that he might be sent over with the like commission and protection that Mr. Kennett had before enjoyed.

But it seems the Envoy of the Great Duke has desired no such mission may be made till he shall put in a memorial in his master's name against the longer allowance of any Protestant chaplain at Leghorn. This is some surprise to the merchants, and puts them in fear that they shall be now deprived of that valuable privilege, which by her Majesty's wisdom and goodness they have quietly enjoyed these four years.

I presume to be a humble petitioner, that there may be no disappointment or long delay in this matter, but that Mr. Taubman may be dispatched to the satisfaction of the merchants, and the continued glory of her Majesty's happy reign.

WILLIAM FYTCHE to [ROBERT HARLEY].

1710, October 4. Danbury Place—Explaining the circumstances under which he had been prevented from being a candidate for Malden instead of Serjeant Comyns.

J. MARLEY to [ROBERT HARLEY].

1710, October 5. Liskeard—The meeting of our gentlemen yesterday was the greatest ever known on such an occasion. Mr. Boscawen and Mr. Edgcomb do join, and having made a very rude opposition against reading a letter my Lord President [Rochester] did the county the honour to write to them, the letter was read and very much applauded, and the gentlemen very much resenting the wrong behaviour of Boscawen and Edgcomb did agree to set up Mr. Granville and Mr. Trevanion in opposition to them. There is a generous spirit in this county. The towns are in a good disposition and I don't question our bringing you a very good return. I am now going to visit the corporations, and hope to meet Mr. Granville on Saturday.

ABIGAIL HARLEY to her nephew EDWARD HARLEY, York Buildings.

1710, October 6. Brampton—A full week this day I've been here, yet till now had not time to tell you so, perhaps you'll wonder what has taken me up, that I can't tell; thus much, I do assure you, Bess and I have not been plotting unless how to spend our time together most agreeably. 'Tis not seldom that we wish your worship with us, I am sure should both be merrier. Among other things a parcel of old letters have been very entertaining, many consumed to their first nothing, as for the rest, if you'll accept them, they are at your service. I fancy you may pick out some will please you. How yours of September 30 came to me last night I know not, only am sure 'tis safe in my hands which it ran a hazard of never touching. I have dispatched the enclosed to the Governor early this morning, hope time enough ere he amble to Leominster where the election will be tomorrow; many apprehend he'll meet with as great a struggle as ever was there, the Quakers and Anabaptists generally against him. I don't hear of one of the other Dissenters but are for him, Mr. Hayley carries himself like an honest prudent man, as he ever has done, neither Lord C[oningsb]y's fawning upon him nor Colt's has any influence to move him or those he has any over. You tell me there is no hopes of the C[hancellor] of the Exchequer coming down, your mother seems to-day to think he will, would I could divine how it will be. I want to be at home yet would be glad to see you all for a day or two and cannot come again this year. I heartily rejoice my Lord Dupplin is safe with you and that your sister will follow the camp, the old stag with other good ladies no doubt will think it their duty to reprove his Lordship for such an irregular action to ride to town. without his wife behind him ; upon my word 'tis a noble subject for the little lady to exert herself in her beloved way of rebuking. I congratulate my own deliverance from the fury of her Ladyship's pen, a scrawl of mine has done me great service that way, yet wish myself in possession of it again ; by some hints guessing according to her prudence, she has exposed it to view, 'twas writ in a heat though had I stayed till next morning instead of mending the matter had made it more stinging, though may be better put together, my comfort is I took a true copy which I never did but twice in my whole life before. You'll think me crazed to say all this to you of a thing you know nothing of, women are ever impertinent and that's sufficient excuse for anything we do.

I trouble you with the enclosed not knowing any other way to have it safely delivered to my sister ; a certificate is in it. My humble service to my Lord Dupplin. When you see Neddy thank him for his letter ; I intend to do it myself very quickly. I'm glad he is more diligent in his learning, your advice to him in that respect will go further than any one else's, and I hope my Lord D. will insinuate the same to him. Idleness is his great fault. You can't now upbraid me with a short letter, may justly for writing a long insignificant one. Adieu.

It evidently appears to all here that the materials for the last " Tatler " were collected in Russell Street, being a lively picture of that lady.

The Duke of Hamilton to [Robert Harley].

1710, October 6. St. Albans—Her Majesty having done me the honour to tell me she was willing to make me Lord Lieutenant of Lancaster, and I having had letters by this last post, giving me an account that they are making great opposition to Mr. Annesley's election at Preston, I think it may be for her Majesty's service that in the next Gazette her Majesty's pleasure be declared, so that as I pass I may have the more authority to promote that election and assist the Heyshams at Lancaster, who meet with opposition there. Pray remember there may be a commission to me for Bow-bearer of the Five (*sic*) Forests, which gives the interest as to the elections, and was last possessed by the Earl of Derby since his being Lord Lieutenant. If this be declared in Wednesday's Gazette I hope it shall come seasonably for my assisting the elections, which is what moves me to desire this expedition and I hope will plead my pardon for giving you this trouble.

Arthur Moore to Robert Harley.

1710, October 6. Grimsby—This day came on the election for this place, the candidates being Mr. Cotesworth, Mr. Vyner, and myself. Mr. Vyner and I are elected by a great majority ; I am well assured he will zealously join with me in such measures as shall be most for the public service.

[Henry] Paget to Robert Harley.

1710, October 7. Stafford—Sir Bryan Broughton has desisted from his candidature but Mr. Bagot having declared yesterday he would stand a poll, I entreat you will excuse my stay here till that is over, it being judged by my friends absolutely necessary. Lord Fer[rer]s that you said was thought of once for a particular thing has acted a very odd part towards me in this election, and I am told here talks wonderful freely of you. This I thought proper to hint that his matters may be respited.

JONATHAN SWIFT.

Paper headed " Dr. Swift's Memorial about the First-fruits of Ireland."

1710, October 7—There are in proportion more impropriations in Ireland than England, which added to the poverty of the country makes the livings of very small and uncertain value, so that five or six united do often hardly amount to 50*l.* per annum ; but these have seldom above one church in repair, the rest being destroyed by the wars, &c.

Hardly one parish in ten hath any glebe, and the rest very small ones and scattered, except very few, and even these have seldom any houses ; for want of which, the clergy are forced to take farms at rack-rents in their own or some neighbouring parish.

The Queen having some years since remitted the first-fruits to the clergy of England, the Bishop of Cloyne, being some time after in London, petitioned her Majesty to grant the same favour for Ireland, and received a gracious answer; but this affair for want of soliciting was not brought to an issue during the government of the Duke of Ormond or Earl of Pembroke.

Upon the Earl of Wharton being nominated Lord Lieutenant, Dr. Swift (having solicited this matter in the preceding government) was desired by the Bishops of Ireland to apply to his Excellency ; who thought fit to receive the motion as wholly new and what he could not consider (as he said) till he were fixed in the government, and till the same application were made to him, as had been to his predecessors, Accordingly, soon after his arrival in Ireland, an address was delivered to his Lordship from both houses of Convocation, with a memorial, and petition to the Queen annexed to it. But a dispute happening in the lower house, wherein his chaplain was concerned, and which was represented by the said chaplain as an affront designed to his Excellency, he was pleased to understand and report it so to the Court; upon which the Convocation was suddenly prorogued, and all further thoughts about the first-fruits let fall as desperate.

The subject of the said petition was to desire, that the twentieth parts might be remitted to the clergy, and the first-fruits made a fund for purchasing glebes and impropriations, and rebuilding churches.

The twentieth parts are twelve pence in the pound paid yearly out of all ecclesiastical benefices, as they were valued at the Reformation, they amount to about 500*l.* per annum, but of little or no value to the Queen, after the officers and other charges are paid, though of much trouble and vexation to the clergy.

The first-fruits paid by incumbents upon their promotion amount to about 450*l.* per annum, so that her Majesty in remitting near 1000*l.* per annum to the clergy, will really lose only 500*l.* per annum.

But there is a greater burden than this, and almost intolerable upon several of the clergy in Ireland ; the easing of which the Convocation for some reasons, of weight at that time, did not make a part of their petition.

In certain dioceses the Queen is impropriator of many parishes, and the incumbent pays her Majesty a yearly rent, generally to the third part of the real value of the living ; and often a full half, nay, some of these parishes are sunk so low by the increase of graziers, that they are seized on by the crown, which out of the whole profits cannot make the reserved rent. The value of all these impropriations is about 2000*l.* per annum to her Majesty.

If the Queen would graciously please to bestow likewise these impropriations to the church; part to be remitted to the incumbent, where the rent is large and the living small, and the rest to be laid out in purchasing glebe &c., it would be a most pious and seasonable bounty.

The utmost value of the twentieth parts, first fruits and impropriations together, is 3000*l.* per annum, of which above 500*l.* is sunk by salaries and other charges of collecting; so that her Majesty by this great benefaction to the church would lose but 2000*l.* (*sic*) per annum.

Upon August 3, 1710, the two Houses of Convocation being met only to be further prorogued, the Archbishops and Bishops conceiving there was now a favourable juncture to resume their applications, did in their private capacities sign a power to the said Dr. Swift, to solicit the remitting the first-fruits and twentieth parts.

(*In Swift's handwriting.*)

T[HEOPHILUS] OGLETHORPE to [ROBERT HARLEY].

1710, October 8. Godalming—Notwithstanding bribery and all other indirect means used I have carried it at Haslemere. My mother tells me you have not been so good as to answer her letters. I am sure you would have done so had not business prevented you.

SIR THOMAS TREVOR to [ROBERT HARLEY].

1710, October 8—I was in hopes my former answer to what you mention in your letter would have been accepted as a final one, without putting me to the great uneasiness of returning the same answer again, for indeed nothing can be more irksome to me than not complying with so gracious an offer from her Majesty accompanied with so many kind circumstances which will make the most lasting impressions of duty and obedience upon me in everything wherein I am capable of serving; and nothing but a perfect knowledge of my inability to discharge the duty of that station could make me persist in this resolution. It is not the consideration of the certainty or profit of the place I now enjoy that weighs with me, for I should be ready to part with that whenever her Majesty commands me, or shall think it for her service. I hope as you are my friend you will represent this matter so to her Majesty that I may not be so unhappy as to incur her displeasure. I should not presume to mention any persons to you, if you had not commanded, and I am sure you can think of persons fitter than any I can suggest; my Lord Guernsey, Sir Ed. Northey, Lord Chief Baron Smythe, Mr. Justice Tracey, are men I think well qualified as to their ability in the law, but whether proper upon any other considerations I cannot pretend to judge. You may rest assured this shall be the greatest secret.

RICHARD STEELE to [ROBERT] HARLEY.

1710, October 9—I presume to write to you lest your servant should omit letting you know I was, according to your commands, a little after four at your house on Saturday.

I think I have an expedient to communicate to you which will effectually prevent further frauds upon stamp-paper.

The Earl of Ilay to [Robert Harley].

1710, October 9—Lord Mar canoot be at Edinburgh till Saturday sevennight, I shall be there on the Sunday. It is now just a month to the day of our elections, and unless Lord Cromartie go in a few days he may happen by reason of his great age and infirmities not to come to Edinburgh in time.

The Duke of Beaufort to [Robert Harley].

1710, October 9. Gloucester—I can't forbear acquainting you that I came this afternoon to this place, where I have met with so handsome an appearance of gentlemen &c. as never yet was seen together in the memory of the old men, so that I believe our success will [be] better than we could express, though we lie under the greatest hardship that ever men did, to have it given out by all the other side, that this Earl of Ber[keley] has kissed the Queen's hand for Lord Lieutenant and that the interest of her Majesty and her officers is to influence all that is possible against us. This we suffer and have no encouragement to contradict them. Let what will happen I am resolved to pursue her Majesty's service to the utmost of my power, but I cannot help regretting that so many honest gentlemen are to be suppressed when they are using the greatest endeavours to support her undoubted hereditary right to that Church she is so zealous in inclination for. If I am troublesome in acquainting you with this I ask pardon, and if no good is to be done in this affair of the Lord Lieutenancy I shall acquiesce.

[Charlwood Lawton to Robert Harley.]

1710, October 9—Though you would not open yourself, I can't but think you have a mind Sir Simon should take the Seals ; I can't deny but that I think him the fittest man you can pitch upon. But I believe you have, as I have, though I have not had great familiarity with him, more than a political friendship for him. I swear I love him as I believe you do heartily, and therefore, unless a good pension is settled upon him for life, I cannot wish he should be put into a post, that is precarious and out of which if he is put, he hath lost the opportunity of increasing his fortune by his profession, at the top of which he now stands as a private man. Thus much for Sir Simon.

Now I come to my own case and must own you sent me home melancholy to death, because I thought you spoke uncertainly when and whether I shall be provided for. I have about ten years served you as faithfully, as carefully, as industriously, whether in or out of place, as if I was to be heir to all you leave. I have loved and do love you from the bottom of my heart, and therefore I conjure you, by all that is sacred in friendship, to let me know before I go out of town, whether anything shall be done for me, whether I must starve, if I will not take oaths I scruple. Let me know the utmost, that I may prepare myself for great poverty, brought upon me by the war, taxes, decay of trade, &c. and not by any one fault of my own. For God's sake be not a statesman towards me ; for, though I may have been an unmannerly monitor, I have been a true friend to you, and though I never did anything inconsistent with my scruples, I have done some things contrary to my inclinations, at your command, particularly soliciting the unmolested increase of wealth for the two insatiably voracious families. When I was used ungratefully, when indeed former promises were not kept, you know you blamed a great man, but now it is in your own power to do any reasonable thing for me. My brother Ralph, whom I have proposed is also a moderate Church Whig, and entirely Anti-Jacobite and is fit for any Commission in the Revenue. He was a rake and spent his fortune upon hunting horses and sports, and then was forced to descend to the lowest step in the Excise. He had first a ride, then a foot walk, and afterwards was an Examiner, and from thence was made Clerk of the Diaries; he is now a Collector, and has been a reclaimed, sober, sedulous man these many years.

[Daniel De Foe* to Robert Harley.]

1710, October 10—Though I am to attend in the evening according to your order yet I could not delay sending you an account, which I received last night after I had the honour of seeing you, of the elections of magistrates for the city of Edinburgh.

Adam Brown, Lord Provost.—Lord Mayor.

William Hutchinson, Archibald Cockburn, John Hay, Thomas Dundas, Bailies.

John Duncan, Lord Dean of Guild. (*La même avec le Provost de marchands à Paris.*)

William Dundas, Treasurer or Chamberlain.

I refer their characters till evening, only hint to you that they are all but two my very particular acquaintances which will, I believe, give me occasion of influencing them very much for her Majesty's service.

T[homas] Coke, Vice-Chamberlain, to [Robert Harley].

1710, October 11. Melbourne—The election for Derby ended so late I could not acquaint you with it by the post that night. Sir Richard Leviug and Mr. Harpur carried it by a very great majority against my Lord James Cavendish and Mr. Pye, who I hear intend to petition and try for that favour upon account of family which they could not obtain by freedom of elections; though my Lord Chief Justice in his session at Derby a little time before the election had gone very great lengths to secure them, of which I hope to bring a true state when I come up to be made use of as you shall see occasion. I have desisted for the county which will be next Monday.

The elections hereabout go very well and what are depending promise very well. I shall set out next week and if you have any commands for me here before I come up they will find me here by Saturday or Tuesday's post. I hope I shall not have the mortification to hear my Lord Scarsdale is our Lord Lieutenant, though he did not decline the compliments upon it before he left the country. My Lord Ferrers sets out for London Monday sevennight.

R. Molesworth to [Robert Harley].

1710, October 11. Edlington, near Doncaster—I have lost my election, the Duke of Newcastle having for some private reasons preferred two sworn junto men to his old friend, so that now I shall have *idleness* but not *Otium:* for this last implies *ease* in one's condition, which my numerous and expensive family deny me. I see many

---

* Signature torn off.

of less merit (if I am not partial to myself) who within this twenty-two years have attained to it *cum dignitate* I am not so presumptuous as to hope for so great good fortune, because as I never could tread in the steps that lead to any degree of it in former times so I am now declining both in years and health.

My principles are the very same they were from the first moment you knew me, and (whatever the appearance may be) I cannot be persuaded that you, the Duke of Shrewsbury, my Lord Poulett, with several others of my acquaintance, after having rescued the nation from the tyranny of one set of men can be for subjecting it to another of priests; and in this confidence I venture to recommend myself to your remembrance.

J. Durden to [Robert Harley].

1710, October 13. Pickering, North Riding [co. York]—As you are one of the principal directors of the revenue, I hope you will not take it amiss that I offer you my opinion as to that small branch of it for which I am concerned. The tax upon houses, &c., by what I can yet find in the course of my survey, will not be much increased by the late Act for additional duties; for though the houses of the nobility and gentry in town or country will be advanced 20s. each, yet these are but few in number in comparison of the houses of people of inferior condition, many of which (though they have hitherto paid 10s.) have by stopping up their lights reduced the charge to 6s.; so that her Majesty instead of getting ten or twenty shillings additional duty will lose four of the old tax unless the Justices or Commissioners contrive the obligation of the new Act to be in force from the day that it passed the Royal Assent. In this case I humbly conceive the design of it can't be eluded by stopping up lights, because that has been done since the Act passed, and no surveyor but what knows, or ought to know, what houses used to pay ten shillings, and may therefore advance them accordingly.

This stoppage as I'm informed is not particular but general throughout England; but the Legislature having engaged to make good any deficiency that shall happen in this case, I shall not presume to say anything more about it.

I understand that twenty seven of my brother officers have been lately discharged, and others put in their places. I am told indeed that I am continued, but am not certain of it, having yet received no new powers from your Lordships of the Treasury. If I am continued I am willing to think that I am solely indebted to your honour for the favour, having not had sufficient notice of the removal of others to take care of my own interest. I therefore thank and esteem myself doubly obliged to your Honour for your care of me; and would gladly flatter myself into a belief that the kindness you have lately done me is an earnest of your future favours.

All the discourse in these as well as in other parts runs only upon elections. I doubt not but you are informed of those that are over already, and the majority by which they were carried. That for this county begins next Wednesday, and 'tis hoped Sir William Strickland will be distanced. The Whigs here (according to their old laudable custom everywhere) are perpetually trumping up some lying story or other to blacken their opponents; but Paul Joddrell's attestation in a late Gazette has so opened the eyes of abundance of misled people, even of the meanest, that truth itself coming from that party would hardly be believed.

I could easily acquaint your Honour with the characters and reputations of the gentlemen in these and the adjacent parts, but fearing to be thought too officious I shall at present decline it : yet I can't but observe to you the satisfaction I had last night to hear unexpectedly one Mr. Robinson, a gentleman in these parts whom I hitherto looked upon as addicted to the Whig interest, begin your health and oblige the company to drink it, which was done heartily.

Postscript.—The aforesaid gentleman stood candidate last Monday with Mr. Worseley for Malton but lost the election by foul play to Palmes and Strickland, but both intend to petition.

MAJOR HENRY FOUBERT to ROBERT HARLEY.

1710, October 13—You encouraged me when I saw you last to find out something in her Majesty's gift to reimburse me for the great loss I have suffered and the great charge I have been in buying and building, what in reason should have been done by the Crown, being for the good of the public. I am advised that Mr. Dyott's place will probably be vacant and not disposed of yet. If you would recommend me for it it would be a means of doing me justice without any charge to her Majesty.

EARL RIVERS to [ROBERT HARLEY].

1710, October [13–]24, N.S.   Hanover—I intended to set out to-morrow for England but resolve to stop till Tuesday as Mr. St. John gives me hope that 107 (Shrewsbury) will write to me in his absence. I am left here alone the Court being all gone to a hunting seat.

W. BROMLEY to [ROBERT HARLEY].

1710, October 14—Mr. Craven and Mr. Gery have an undoubted majority at Coventry, greater than at any time, yet 'tis thought the sheriffs, who are entirely in another interest, will not return them. The Earl of Sunderland, who has been lately among them to take upon him the honourable employment of their Recorder, has certainly given them proper advice on this occasion.

J. BRUCE to ROBERT HARLEY.

1710, October 15. Henley Park, near Guildford—Lord Bruce and my brother are both chosen at Marlborough, as is also Lord Bruce at Bedwin. At the last place there will be a vacancy, both of which and of me you may dispose of as you find most for your service.

My brother stood also at Ludgershall and lost it but by one vote.

SIR THOMAS POWYS to [ROBERT HARLEY].

1710, October 16—If Sir Simon Harcourt should take the Great Seal as justly due to him, I hope you will not wonder at me, if I should desire to be Attorney General, which is a place I could make easy, by wholly applying myself to the execution of that office, and be thereby something freed from the constant attendance of the Bar, which I have so long now laboured under. I should think myself very happy to own it to your favour and friendship, and hope you will place this freedom of request to the claim I make of some relation, neighbourhood of birth, and above all of that (which if it were not too familiar I would also add) of true friendship and service for you.

ABEL BOYER to [ROBERT HARLEY].

1710, October 17—Mr. Steel having resigned his place of Gazetteer, several of my friends would persuade me that few men are better qualified than myself to succeed him. But though I am not so vain as to believe them, yet I will not be so far wanting to myself as to neglect this opportunity of putting your honour in mind of the most humble and most devoted of all your servants.

I presumed some days ago to send to you by Mr. Campbell a paper of my own composing, which has been well received both at home and abroad, where I hear it has been translated. I am now printing something towards the history of the last ministry and Parliament, in which, I hope, I have given such a fair account of the great things you have done for this nation, as may in some measure contribute to the allaying the present ferment.

SIR SIMON HARCOURT to [ROBERT HARLEY].

1710, October 17—Not hearing from you last night I went to bed with the satisfaction you had obtained a reprieve for me. Since I am not to expect it I will labour to overcome the just apprehensions I have hitherto entertained of what may probably be the event of my submission in this case to the Queen's commands. I have with all sincerity represented to you my innumerable defects; which would have been very needless had not your friendship made you overlook them. Let me now conjure you to remember when it shall appear, I have laid the naked truth before you, it was my duty, not ambition placed me in that slippery station, in which I never could have entered, had I not the utmost confidence in her Majesty's goodness. I earnestly beg one half hour with you alone, at your house or where else you please, sometime this afternoon, the sooner you can spare so much time, the favour will be the greater.

Postscript.—Give me leave once more to assure you Sir E. N[orthey] will give infinite more satisfaction that I am able to do.

The DUKE OF HAMILTON to [ROBERT HARLEY].

1710, October 19. Holyrood House—This morning I have received the favour of yours of the 14th and am very much obliged to you for your kind expressions. I hope her Majesty's service shall not suffer by the honour she has been pleased to do me in making me her Lieutenant of the County of Lancaster. I do here humbly entreat you will do me the honour to make my acknowledgments to her Majesty for this mark of her favour. The reason I moved you to desire that if her Majesty did me that honour it might be soon in the Gazette, was that it might strengthen my endeavours in relation to the elections in that county, where I hope ere now you will have some account of what I did as I passed through that county.

It is Chief Ranger of the Four (*sic*) Forests and not Bow-bearer which gives great interest in elections and is not hereditary in the family

of Derby and since her Majesty does me the honour to make me her
Lieutenant I hope she will think it for her service that I be vested with
such powers as may contribute most for her interest, since I am resolved
to lay myself out to serve her Majesty with the utmost zeal.

The Earls of Mar and Loudoun arrived here last night and I hope
you will hasten down the Duke of Argyll and the Earl of Ilay to us.
I am going to the country for a week. At my return I shall take the
liberty of troubling you again to give you an account how our elections
are like to go here, which I hope shall be as successful as those for
London and Middlesex.

DE FOE'S "QUERIES FOR MANAGEMENT," in Scotland.

1710, October 21.

1. Whether the general design be not, to inform and advise the
people of her Majesty's resolutions as well in these changes of things
as any other that shall happen to continue to maintain—

  1. The Union in all its parts.
  2. The Church in all its just rights and established privileges, and
     to discourage and discountenance intrusions and innovations.

That her Majesty will protect and defend their Revolution establishment, and take all occasions to encourage and protect their commerce
and the improvement of their country.

2. Whether I am not to apply myself on all occasions to calm and
make easy the minds of people there, filled with jealousies and fears, and
on every opportunity to detect the false accounts imposed upon them
from hence whether by writing, printing or conversation.

That the poison of a factious spirit may not spread among them, nor
the people be irritated and exasperated against the public administration
of affairs here as if calculated for their destruction.

3. In matters of election whether of the Commons or Peers by all
such methods as shall offer (for 'tis impossible to prescribe them here)
to forward the interest and choice of such men whose tempers are most
moderate and best inclined &c. and as plainly as circumstances will
admit to discourage the contrary.

4. From time to time to give such intelligence of things and persons
as may be for her Majesty's service.

5. To settle and continue such correspondence in every part, whether
the same already settled or such as may be proper for an exact
intelligence in all parts after this journey may be over.

Endorsed by Harley.—" Mr. Goldsmith."

WILLIAM CHURCHILL to [ROBERT HARLEY].

1710, October 24. Dallingoe, near Woodbridge—On behalf of
Mr. Knackston, collector of Customs in Ipswich, who had been drawn
into a combination to defraud the revenue.

P[AUL] METHUEN to ROBERT HARLEY.

1710, October 25. London—I have fully considered the intention of
sending me into Holland to settle with the Dutch their quota of ships
for the next year's service, but I hope I may be excused from that commission. I desire you will consider that I am chosen by my country
as one of its representatives in parliament, but am petitioned against by

Sir Francis Child and Mr. Serjeant Webb. The former has made no scruple of telling me himself to my face that he has interest enough in the House to have me turned out. I cannot therefore leave Great Britain at this time without giving up the just title I have to sit in Parliament and sacrificing the rights of those that have made choice of me to represent them, which I presume her Majesty would not require of me, who whilst in the House have on all occasions made it my business to show that duty and respect to her which become a good subject.

J[OHN] AISLABIE to [ROBERT HARLEY].

1710, October 27. Ripon—I have made use of the liberty you gave me to come down and have carried the County election triumphantly : so there is an end of a Parliament bully ; no more lopping of heads and scandalous minorities. There is a petition against Palmes and Strickland at Malton, a very just one if it is proper to prosecute it ; one of the petitioners is son-in-law to Sir Thomas Frankland, and it will be referred to him whether to prosecute it or no.

I must beg the favour of you to take this county into your protection, and not suffer us to be governed by an old fashioned interest ; it is an easy matter to model it to your service and to make it yours. I hope you will give us an instance of your favour in naming the next High Sheriff, and not suffer it to come from any other hand. There is nothing can show it more than in making the present High Sheriff, Mr. William Turbut, the Sheriff for the ensuing year. Mr. Justice Powell or Baron Price will upon the least order from you make him alight, and I hope I may depend your favour to have him nominated. I am preparing to return to my duty, and desire that Benson may not be suffered to grow fat at Bramham.

[JOHN DRUMMOND] to [ROBERT] HARLEY.

1710, [October 28-]November 7, N.S. Amsterdam—On Sunday last the Earl Rivers returned here, in all appearance, and by the account his Lordship was pleased to give me of his reception, extremely well pleased and satisfied. He showed me your letter in which you ordered me to supply him with what he might want, and gave me his bill on you for the value of what he received of our correspondent at Hanover, and from my partner and me here, amounting to 1000l. sterling payable at twenty days sight, which bill we indorsed to Mr. Mathew Decker and I doubt not it will be punctually paid Mean time I have wrote to Mr. Decker in case you should be scarce of money in the Treasury, to take the value of the bill in tin, out of which the foreign ministers have been paid for some years. Whether that be your method or not I am still ignorant of, but I would much rather have my money if you can spare it, having occasion for all I can scrape together both money and credit to support the public payments, which are made very difficult by the villanous resolution of the Bank of England to discount no foreign bills. So severe a blow to the public credit could not have in any other manner been contained, and unless they alter their resolution you will find nobody can engage farther without ready money. For my share I have one hundred thousand pounds to pay, and nothing but paper to raise it on, and if the Dutch should take the same humour not to discount we would have a hard task. I am glad with all my heart to see elections go so well, all my dependence is on the care you will take of us, for as matters now go a Commission of one-third per cent., or 6s. 6d. (sic) on each 100l. is hardly a premio of the risk that one runs of their credit and establishment, by engaging in such great sums; but its love and not interest that has made me dip so deep. Unless your parliament give very good funds, and encouraging interest, you will get little money from this side, for the States keep an open office to receive money at 10 per cent. upon life rent, and all the best funds of Brabant and Flanders, such as their Post Offices and Custom House revenues, are "paunding" by the States at six per cent. The interest which your Bank gives at present on Exchequer notes comes to $7\frac{1}{2}$ per cent per annum, and the scandalous insinuations of some of your great citizens in their letters that your elections are tumultuous, and people not safe in their houses from the mob, still give apprehensions to the people here who are ignorant of your constitution. All which with humble submission, I hope will make you think of as many ready money funds as you can contrive, such as annuities, lotteries and the like, but annuities for one, two, and three lives at nine, ten and eleven per cent. as I once imagined and went easy five years ago, will not I am persuaded draw money from this, seeing they can have 10 per cent. for one life at home, but I hope you have such a variety of good funds that you will not want what you have ocasion for; only don't starve the cause, it is the latter end of a war and people's ready money for the most part bestowed, and you have many former deficiencies to provide for, which are still remote at least, if not deficient, and I would gladly see as little reason of complaint on this side as has been all this war, though the cause has been half starved at other places to make matters go easy here where the favourite General commands.

I hope you will find some way to make the Bank discount foreign bills for money, as they have done all this war; I mean all bills having but two months to run, which can be of no more hindrance and prejudice to them than it was before the change of the ministry, and it is only pique and revenge of Heathcote's and his party who now govern the Bank absolutely. Such people who value themselves as patriots and on their Revolution principles and are contriving by their resolutions to subvert the credit and constitution, I hope will be distinguished, and I am not surprised that in former violent governments an alderman was tied up, when under so free, mild, easy and just a government they contrive its subversion, discredit and uneasiness. I hope your goodness will pardon all this freedom which proceeds from my concern to have matters go with that ease and reputation which they ought; and I shall return to Earl Rivers who at his arrival was pleased to send for me, and next morning I brought his Lordship to the Pensionary Buys, where he stayed near two hours in close conversation and the Pensionary returned the visit in the afternoon which lasted near an hour. My Lord used all his eloquence to persuade the Pensionary of the reasonableness of the Queen's changing her ministry, and of the unreasonableness of people who had insinuated to the States as if her Majesty had broken her word to them, and took all the reasonable methods to persuade him with what sincerity and heartiness the present ministry would carry on the war, and maintain an entire confidence and friendship with the allies in general and most particularly with the States, all which the Pensionary seemed well satisfied in, and has inclination enough to believe well of your and your friends' sincere intentions for the public good. But the great and earnest question came last, that the States hoped the Duke of Marlborough would be continued at the head of the army, that the whole alliance was easy under his conduct, that the States were used to him, and though they knew his faults as well as his virtues, that there was nobody they would either prefer or equally desire with him. To this my Lord answered it might depend pretty much on his Grace's own behaviour to the Queen and her ministry, that it was entirely in the Queen's own breast to do therein as should seem good to her, that if any, other were sent it would be in a lower station, to be General over the English alone, and to be commanded by Prince Eugene or whoever should be by them esteemed most proper to command in chief, that he would nowise answer for or promise that the Duke would be continued,, and that he wondered to see them so earnest for **that,** he was a mortal man, and had he been taken off in any of the battles must they not have been satisfied. The rest next post.

News Letter.

[1710], October —. Whitehall—The poll for the City of London ended this evening, and a majority has fallen upon Sir William Withers, Sir Richard Hoare, Sir George Newland and John Cass Esquire, the four Churchmen, but the other four Whigs have demanded a scrutiny.

Withers - - - - 3629		Churchmen.
Hoare - - - - 3572		
Newland - - - 3385		
Cass - - - - 3240		
Sir Gilbert Heathcote, Lord Mayor Elect 3185		Whigs.
Ashurst - - - 3048		
Bateman - - - 3104		
Ward - - - - 3222		

[John Drummond] to Robert Harley.

1710, November [1–]11, (new style). Amsterdam—Last post I gave you the trouble of a long letter under Mr. Secretary St. John's cover, and I believe in haste left it without a cover, yet with design that you might read it together, though of very little edification to gentlemen of your penetrating knowledge of all matters at home and abroad. That letter was only gone to the Post Office when I received this in. closed, too late to send it you by the same post, and as soon as you have read it together I earnestly entreat that you may, without letting it go farther, be pleased to seal it up with your little seal and return it to me. I don't press to have you intrust me with your sentiments or resolutions on that head, because by one paragraph you may think that I am very well and intimate with the great man, but as I give no thanks to the writer for ever making mention of me to him, or that I ever courted or coveted friendship there after a very insincere and wrong advice that was given me by him, now three years ago, in a matter too trifling to trouble you with, yet in which you happened to be mentioned about the commission of the tin. Except one dinner at the army with some general company, I have hardly had the honour to speak thrice with him, and never wrote to him, but a long experience of faithful friendship, honesty, and worth in the writer of the enclosed has maintained a very frequent and intimate correspondence betwixt him and me, and it may seem a betraying of that friendship in me to venture to expose so intimate a letter, were I not convinced of your honour, and assured that the person who sent me the inclosed wishes you and your friends as well as I do, and that is no worse than your own brother or child can do, and I know nobody would be more ready to serve you and your interest than this worthy gentleman in every thing not interfering with his fidelity to his master which I think is and ought to be inviolable.

All the weak arguments which I can produce can be but of little influence if matters be otherwise fixed and a scheme laid by which that great man is to lose his command, and I only should reason in the dark if I pretended to give the best reasons I am capable of on that subject, and therefore as to a reconciliation I should think it no wise impracticable if there were a real inclination to it on both sides and that it be the Queen's intention. The true way to begin it is by a mutual complaisance and I could wish there were no dispute who was to begin and make the first advances. I think a faithful honest man who had no by-end, and in whom both had some confidence, might by a mutual consent of both parties break ground, and try by one or two preliminary points, whether there were hopes of succeeding in an entire treaty. I am confident you would strengthen your party more by gaining that one man than by any other thing imaginable, and I believe he is sensible of the intolerable measures which others encouraged him to go into. I know he hates some of their leaders very heartily, and I believe he would abandon his old friend so far as never to desire to have him in play again, but let him lie by the rest of his days. I am also persuaded he would part with any one or all of the damnation club for their ill behaviour, but these may be conjectures and cannot be well known till they are proposed. I know this would be insupportable doctrine to Lord Rivers and the Duke of Argyll, whom I both honour, love, and esteem, but as no private man's interest ought or must come in computation with the present welfare of the public, and to get honourably rid of this bloody, pernicious, expensive, and destructive war, neither any private pique ought to prevail so far as to hinder or any wise encourage the enemy not to renew their proposals for a peace, which the Dutch I am sure and very sure want but to have in a manner on any terms, and if ever proposed if they don't come to a conclusion as well as they can, I shall never pretend to know anything of them or their measures for the future, and we are in no worse circumstances than when the enemy made their last proposals. We have gained two battles in Spain, and four strong towns in Flanders, and the like success another campaign must bring us upon the territories of old France.

What is it are we to imagine that hinders or will hinder their new proposals, but what they write us every day, viz. the hopes they have of the divisions in England and that the Duke of Marlborough will be made so uneasy as to be obliged to retire and abandon the army, who they know has been no less instrumental in keeping the Allies together as in his success in the field. It is not for his person, but for the public good that I argue or presume to meddle in so important an affair, for well do I know all his vices as well as his virtues, and I know as well that though his covetousness has gained him much reproach and ill will on this side of the world, yet his success in the field, his capacity or rather dexterity in council or in the cabinet, and his personal acquaintance with the heads of the Alliance and the faith they have in him make him still the great man with them, and on whom they depend. I can tell you with certainty what I meet in daily conversation, that you will have little money to expect from this if he stay at home, that they wish with all their hearts almost any sort of peace before he be taken from them, that there is no Englishman who they have any opinion of for the command of an army but himself, that his agreeing so well with Prince Eugene is one of their greatest contentments and to make a new acquaintance and intimacy of such a nature with any one is what they fear and abhor the thoughts of.

Pensionary Buys came to me two days after Lord Rivers left this place almost with tears in his eyes, saying "Lord! what shall

become of us, Lord Rivers would give me no satisfaction that the
Duke shall return, for God's sake write to all your friends, let him
but return for one campaign till the French but once make new proposals, let the Queen afterwards do with him what she pleases, but
must the safety of us all be put in the balance with a personal pique
which perhaps may be reconciled if rightly gone about." I hope
the Queen will forbear her farther resentments till a better occasion
though justly deserved by him and all who belong to him. Baron
Gersdorff was last day here he is Envoy at the Hague for the Elector
of Saxony or King of Poland, he assured people in a general assembly
or society that his master would recall his troops if the Duke was not
to command. As to the French flattering themselves of any good befalling them or their interest by the changes, that ought to be no argument,
for I am well assured they never found themselves more disappointed than
they will find themselves three weeks after your new parliament sits
down, as to the provisions that will be made for effectually and vigorously
carrying on the war, yet they will think they gain a great deal if the
commander be removed to whom the successes of this war have been so
generally ascribed both by friends and foes, how justly I shall not pretend
to be a competent judge of; but that they will be more ready to desire a
new conference when they see plentiful provision made for the war, the
Alliance entire, and the same Generals to deal with who have always
baffled them, I think is but reasonable to expect, and as I have already
presumed to say if new Emissarys be sent depend upon it the States
will not let them return without concluding with them what they come
for almost à tout prix.

The chief ground of my troubling you with this long letter is the
alarm which Lord Rivers has given our people, who indeed were very
flatly inquisitive whether the Duke was to return, and whether the
Queen was so far reconciled as to allow him to continue in his command, and his Lordship was pleased to answer almost as plainly that
it was a very dubious matter, and seemed himself of a very contrary
opinion, and that it was entirely in the Queen's breast who had not yet
he believed forgotten the insolences committed by him and his, and that
it was to be feared than when he came to England his Duchess and the
violent men at the head of his party would encourage him to bear as
high and become as insupportable to the Queen as ever, and therefore
thought that he might do as wisely not to come into England this
winter, and I am really of opinion that if he does go his stay will not
be long for he used to say it was easier hearing of heats in England
than being in the heats themselves. Therefore he came over so early
last year, and when a certain minister was exclaiming against Dr.
Sacheverell and the mob he said he would not justify Sacheverell but
that he believed the mob was more owing to Hoadly than to the Doctor.

I hope there is not the least reason to doubt of his returning to command, and therefore all I wish is that anything I have been able to
say may prove an argument of reconciliation which I must again
say I don't think impracticable, and I am sure he is much more
worth gaining than a late Speaker, who was more violent in the time of
your being barbarously prosecuted than ever the Duke was, and who
said to my knowledge harder things. I mind one saying of the Duke's
to Mr. Watkins asking him what pamphlets he had got from England.
Mr. Watkins answered the most considerable one was Greg's trial, the
Duke said did you ever hear of more malice than in that affair, Mr.
Watkins' answer was that you never deserved it either from the Court or
from the Commons. I have troubled you here with a great many long,
simple stories which I hope you will be so good to commit to the fire

when you have had the patience to read them. You will know what is
meant by the damnation club, it is the Lieutenant Generals of our nation
who drink people's damnation sometimes, and there are very few of
the army who care though they were hanged and every one wishes
them out of employ. Mr. H. is yourself and by his master he means
Mr. Cardonnel.

The EARL OF ILAY to [ROBERT HARLEY].

1710, November 1—My Lord Mar will give you an account of what
work we meet with here, everybody sets up not only to be chosen but
to direct; whatever happens your friends here are like to meet with a
good deal of ill will from everybody that is disappointed. The Duke of
Hamilton seems to be in pretty good temper and tells them all that he
is to agree with us. I received the warrant this morning. I hear my
friend the Duke of Queensberry is displeased that he was not consulted
in it, which is very strange since he never advised with me in his affairs,
and in particular, his pension was passed without ever his asking my
consent. My Lord Mar has a letter from my friend my Lord Ruther-
ford wherein he tells him that the other day at my Lord Blantyre's
house, there came a gentleman to him from Sir David Dalrymple, who
told him that in case he would vote for my Lord Stair, he would save
his nephew's life (his nephew is in prison for murder). You may judge
by this piece of history that some people resolve to play all the game. I
have lost several elections in the country by my stay at London, but in
the main you will certainly have a considerable majority of the members
from hence.

Postscript.—My Lord Mar and I when we talk of all that has passed
in Scotch affairs with my Lord Kinnoull are two of the most temperate,
credulous people alive, in comparison of him.

The EARL OF ILAY to [ROBERT HARLEY].

1710, November 2. Liddington, near Haddington—My Lord Mar
and I were astonished this morning at a visit from my Lord Glasgow.
After many professions of friendship &c. he told us the Duke of
Queensberry had sent him the proxies of the Earl of Morton and
Lord Dumblaine (Lord Carmarthen), the first of these I take to be
irretrievable, but I should hope the other of my Lord Carmarthen
might be remedied by his signing another proxy to the Earl of
Wemyss. The aversion the Tories have here to the Squadron is
inexpressible, and not much less to what they call the Duke of
Queensberry's creatures. I am afraid this affair of my Lord Carmarthen
may have fatal consequences as to my Lord Mar and me, if not prevented.
The Tories watch us very narrowly and if they once think they have
good reason to suspect us, we two shall be rejected unanimously.

We wish the Duke of Shrewsbury or some other would write to the
Duke of Atholl to dissuade him from insisting upon the Earl Dumblaine,
which would put us all in confusion and we have some reason to be
apprehensive of his Grace's thoughts that way. In short, forgive me if
I tell you that if Lord Mar and I are not supported we shall grow
perfect scarecrows here, every body imputes his afflictions to us, and
our very friends as yet do but grumble promises of assistance. I have
always told you I would only despair in theory and I assure you I'll
endeavour to show it upon this occasion. I last night received a guinea
from the Earl of Kinnoull for which I am to pay five if the place of

Privy-Seal in Scotland is vacant within a twelvemonth, and I got another upon the place of Commander in-Chief and Governor of the Castle of Edinburgh. He offered the coin and I thought it would not have been civil to have refused it.

G. Granville to [Robert Harley].

1710, November 4. Menabilly—I referred it to Mr. Manley to give you an account of our complete victory for the county [of Cornwall]. We have had a report very industriously spread amongst us that Jack Smith was to be proposed by the Court for Speaker. 'Tis not to be imagined what an alarm it gave for some time. I hope we shall never split twice upon the same rock.

Elizabeth, Lady Pelham, to her cousin Robert Harley.

1710, November 4. Brocklesby—I am desired by Mr. John Anderson to give you some account of him. He is of as considerable a family as any in Lincolnshire, his elder brother is married to one of my daughters and has paid him lately 1,200*l.*, a legacy from his father. He has served an apprenticeship with a linen draper, but likes better to take some place than to set up that trade now we have wars. If he make application to you any favour you are pleased to show him will be gratefully acknowledged by her who begs your pardon for this presumption.

[Robert Harley] to John Drummond, at Amsterdam.

1710, November 7—Sunday night I received the favour of yours of the 11th instant, and though I am at present under the pressure of a great deal of business I cannot suffer the post to go without my hearty acknowledgments of this last mark of your friendship. You have wrote so plain, so prudently and with so much affection that I were very unworthy the name of your friend if I do not ever acknowledge it with the best returns that shall ever be in my power. At this moment I am upon a proposition which will immediately restore all our credit and make all Exchequer Bills equal to money, and this I hope with God's blessing to effect before the Parliament meets, as near as it is now ; and notwithstanding all the villanous and peevish arts of the faction. I mention this as an excuse why I cannot write so largely upon the subject of your letter as I hope in a post or two. The enclosed paper— that which is so great a secret I had seen before—I will seal up as you command and deliver to Mr. Dekker, not being willing to venture them by the post.

As to any reconciliation between me and the [Duke of Marlborough] give me leave to say that I were unworthy the Queen's service, should I not live with any one that her service or the public good requires. I do solemnly assure you I have not the least resentment towards him or any one else. I thank God my mind puts me above that. I never did revenge injuries, and never will sacrifice the public quiet to my own resentment. I believe there is not one here thinks I retain any revenge but have given many instances [of for]giving and forgetting very great injuries. I [have] scarce used the common caution of doing any thing *se defendendo*, for fear it should be thought to be the effect of resentment. In one word I do assure you, I can live and act with the Duke now in the same manner and with the same easiness as the first day that ever I saw him, and that you may be convinced this is my temper and not words only I must tell you some things which have passed since April last and many more I could add. A great Duke a friend of mine, before Lord Sunderland was removed, pressed Lord Treasurer to send over to the Duke and that all matters might be adjusted. Presently after another Duke a near relation of my own pressed it more earnestly. To pass over many other attempts to the same purpose I will add this one more. August 10 last the Commission of the Treasury passed, Lord Poulett wrote to the Duke that very post. I desired an addition to the letter to make my compliments and to desire leave to write. The following week this was repeated again by Lord Poulett at my desire and was absolutely rejected by his letter in answer. Notwithstanding this I have upon many occasions since shewn by actions relating to his particular affairs of Blenheim that I am far from resentment. But this I find by experience those who have done injuries are more difficult to be reconciled than those who have received injuries, and hatred, the more groundless and unreasonable it is, the more durable and violent it most times proves. Now I have opened to you my heart upon this subject and do again assure you that no resentment of mine shall ever obstruct the public service or hinder the co-operating with any one for the good of the common cause.

There is a way which perhaps wou[ld] . . . . friends in Holland aim at, but if it . . . . here it will [ne]ver be accepted; and depend upon it· when he comes over he cannot govern himself, as he will enter into the rage and animosity of those near him, and the party who will apply to him will insensibly draw him into their warmth, and that will naturally draw accusation from the other side which without fresh provocation I do assure you will not be meddled with. I will add but this one thing, your State is a very wise State, but it is inconceivable how they should be so ignorant of the true condition of this country and of its interest, and where the weight and strength of the nation lie, and by what accident the minor part has for some time insulted the majority instead of governing them. Your gentlemen have contented themselves with what they learnt from their minister, or from the general and other officers, or from the scandalous stories and pamphlets which have been written by the mercenary scribblers of the party. I have these three years past mentioned this and foretold the mischiefs which would happen for want of the States having a true account of persons and things here. They might have sent persons without suspicion who could have informed them the truth. I am afraid he who is now to come on that errand will not be able to do them much service unless he get better acquaintance than he had when last in this country, or has improved himself and left off his amours.

It is pretty plain no one in Holland now either has authority enough, or reputation and resolution enough, to give the rule and deliver his country, but will suffer them and us to perish by a lingering consumption. You see, how openly I write to you and I leave it to you to make what use you . . . . and without exposing me. I beg you to . . . . . my sincere compliments to Monsieur the Pensionary Buys. Assure him no one has a greater value than myself for his great virtues, love of his country, just understanding and comprehensive knowledge of all affairs. It was October 9, 1706, about a year and half before I was removed from being Secretary that I wrote last to him. I then saw what was designed and the use which would be made of those surprising victories which happened that year, and would then voluntarily have quitted my place but I could not be suffered. I should willingly renew my correspondence with him, but I cannot tell whether it will be agreeable to his inclinations and the present situation of his affairs.

Monsieur Renaud writ me in a letter that some persons of merit in your city had a mind to join with England in some design on the West Indies. If you have any opportunity of learning from him what it is and how far they would go or anything else of real moment you will do me a favour in communicating it. I will pay Mr. Dekker the 1,000*l.* in money and will discourse him about the quantity of tin. *Copy.*

C. Blackmore and John Butler to Robert Harley, Chancellor of the Exchequer.

1710, November 8. Worcester—We are informed there is or will be a petition brought into Parliament by Mr. Perks against Mr. T. Wild. The ground of which supposed petition is an objection against the Quakers, though if they were cast out Mr. Wild would have a good majority. None of the Quakers refused the affirmation to whom 'twas tendered. In polling them, several of whom polled for Mr. Perks, neither the affirmation nor abjuration was required of several of them by any of the three candidates. Mr. Wild having so much right on his side and being we presume in your own judgment so much the fitter person for estate, sobriety, and on many other accounts to be a member of your honourable House, it is requested you will please to favour his cause with your interest, in doing which we hope you will do a grateful service to the public.

The Earl or Portland to [Robert Harley].

1710, November 8. St. James's Square—The bearer Mr. Philip Pott is the person I took the liberty of recommending to you at Hampton Court. I hope his behaviour in the office he has had has not been such as to make him unworthy of your favour.

The Earl of Ilay to Lord ——

1710, November 9. Thursday—I writ to you by the last post and shall write to-morrow night by the flying packet. Our list is settled thus, as I have enclosed it, I think it is very certain that we shall carry them all. There have been great endeavours used to create differences among us, and nothing but the general rule of excluding all friends to the former Ministry (whom I take to be enemies to the new one) brought us to an agreement. There are several who know this was my opinion when I was last in Scotland, which at last has appeared so necessary that at this very time it would not be safe for us to discover that we had ever any other thoughts. If we had each of us been allowed to make exceptions from the rule and serve his friend there would have been no more to say for one than another and at best we had had the list made up of new converts very ready to serve the Queen so long as their opposition could have done no harm, and impatiently waiting for a proper opportunity of discovering their real inclinations. So long as we did not declare against them the pretentions among the Tories to be chosen were without end, but the moment they saw we acted fairly (as they termed it) they grew very easy. Pray tell Mr. Harley that my Lord Glasgow has threatened us in several places with her Majesty's displeasure, and shows to every body a copy of a letter the Duke of Queensberry has written to the Duke of Hamilton wherein he tells him that he hopes he will support my Lord Glasgow as one the Queen declared to us at London her inclination to have chosen. This is such an affront to us who received the Queen's commands upon promise of secrecy that I think I used no hard words when I said it was either lies or treachery or somewhat of both, I must confess to see such engagements before the Queen's which were strengthened by the ties of duty and honour, such oaths and promises to his fellow servants of mutual confidence and secrecy, I say, all these prostituted to an unaccountable rage of passion for one in whom there has never yet appeared the least shadow of any merit, but on the contrary an universal falseness through the most supine flattery that can be conceived, is what I hope will justify in us all a little warmth upon this subject. I believe my brother will come with the Earl of Mar in his coach, we design to set out on Sunday at farthest.

This will be delivered to you by Sir James Abercromby.

The Earl of Orrery to [Robert Harley].

1710, November 9—I am much concerned to find my friends design me the kindness of bringing me into the House of Commons, where I have resolved never to sit. I desired Mr. St. [John] sometime ago to let you know all my thoughts in relation to myself. I am still of opinion that what I proposed for myself was not unreasonable to be asked by me but if my friends did not think it so I should have nothing more to desire but liberty to retire, which I have thought I should be obliged to do to avoid making a despicable figure in the world, if I had not soon some mark of the Queen's favour.

The Earl of Orrery to [Robert Harley].

1710, November 10—I should think myself very unhappy if I imagined you could think me capable of doubting of your friendship to me. I am sure I should not deserve it if I could have such a thought; but upon the coolest reflection I judged what I chiefly proposed for myself required dispatch upon account of the public service and was as necessary for the Queen's affairs as for my own satisfaction. As to anything of profit I told H. St. [John] I desired only to change what I had, that I thought the place I had in the Treasury was too little and unfit for me to keep, that the post I had my eye upon was the command of the Beefeaters, but that if it was thought proper to give that to anybody else I should acquiesce and take anything else that my friends thought fit for me in lieu of it; that my regiment was a new one, and that I had hopes it would be changed for one of Horse or Dragoons if it could easily be done, and that I should be glad to be of the Privy Council if it could be done without difficulty; but I assured him as I do you, that upon this and every other occasion I would refer myself to the opinion of my friends and if by their determination I thought of anything unreasonable for myself I would readily desist and would endeavour always to show that as I did not want so I would not be over fond of great preferments, and that I did not desire any out of avarice or ambition but to convince the world that I could not have misbehaved myself to those friends that were kind to me, and to put me in a capacity of being as able as I was zealous to be serviceable to them.

The DUKE OF HAMILTON to [ROBERT HARLEY].

1710, November 10. Holyrood House—This comes by Sir James Abercromby who will inform you of the situation of things here. I have taken the liberty to write a few lines to the Duke of Shrewsbury which I make no doubt you'll see and tomorrow I shall give you an account of what passes at our election, which I take to be pretty sure. The other noble lords have shown all the zeal possible in her Majesty's service and I have all the obligation in the world to her Majesty to be conjoined with such honourable persons. There is a thorough good understanding amongst us, the effects of which I hope shall be perceived to-morrow.

G. GRANVILLE to [ROBERT HARLEY].

1710, November .10. Okehampton—If my little services in this part of the world have been acceptable to her Majesty, methinks it might not be difficult for you to obtain a mark of distinction for me which I know you would have readily yielded to my friend Mr. St. John if he would have again accepted his old post, that is to be added to the Privy Council. 'Tis a favour that will cost the Queen nothing, and 'twill give me a great deal of ease in my correspondence with the General when he comes home, by putting me above the servile attendance which he may expect by having been used to it by my predecessors in the same post. It will likewise be a public approbation of my endeavours for her Majesty's service upon the late occasion, which will be very acceptable to my countrymen and add to my credit among them.

The EARL OF ORRERY to [ROBERT HARLEY].

[1710, November]—I am just come from H. St. [John] who promised me to let you know I design to wait upon you to-morrow morning between ten and eleven if that be not an inconvenient hour for you. I would have done myself that honour to-night if I had not been so much tired that I am fit for nothing but to go to bed. I am sorry to find, by the short conversation I have had with some of our friends, that there is so little progress made in the settlement of our affairs, and that there are some considerable difficulties still to be overcome. I hope, however, the prospect mends, and for my own part I shall to the utmost of my poor power contribute to perfect the scheme you have so well begun. This, too, I dare say is the sincere intention of the Duke of Argyll and his brother, who I am confident are faithfully your well wishers.

[JOHN DRUMMOND to ROBERT HARLEY.]

1710, November [10–]21, new style. Amsterdam—You have here inclosed another of our coffee house news letters I made mention of in my former to Mr. Secretary St. J[ohn]. It is from this damned fellow that all our gazetteers print. Some people tell me it is Dyer's Whig letter translated and that he writes another letter for the Jacobites though this may serve for both. I give you the trouble of this (as I am convinced all my letters are but troublesome to you, yet I have my end if at any time they may be useful) to acquaint you that the Earl of Southesk, who is recommended to me, arrived here yesterday coming from Italy, through Berlin and Hanover. At the first place the Prince.

Royal told his Lordship that the army was three months in arrear by the change of ministry in England and that his troops would weary of such service. My Lord who is a very honest young gentleman said the new ministers are those who began and carried on the war the first five or six years, and he was convinced they would maintain it in the same manner to the end. At Hanover the old Electress making several reflections of people being turned out who had made all things go easy, and new people brought in who could not support the credit of the nation, my Lord replied that he had hoped and believed Lord Rivers had satisfied her Royal Highness and the Elector fully on that subject, and that the present ministry were the persons who began the war, &c. Her Royal Highness' answer was that Lord Rivers had told them a great many stories of the Queen's being ill-treated and the like, but to no great purpose. Now as this is intrusted to me in friendly conversation and partly proceeding from my asking how people are satisfied I expect that what I write you must remain sacredly to yourself, and if you incline to have a visit from this young Lord, who is very solid and sober, I shall give him a few lines to you. My Lord Dupplin no doubt knows him very well, and he is much improved in so short a time as he has been travelling.

Sir James Montague to [Robert Harley].

1710, November 11—Last night the dormant warrant for payment of the pension, the Queen has been pleased to settle upon me, was brought to me from the Treasury, and I write in the first place to make known the grateful sense I have of your favours, and in the next place to acquaint you with a particular which perhaps may be no less surprising to you than it was to me when I was first informed of it, which is, that Lieut. Col. Gledhill has been commanded by Mr. Harley and Mr. Secretary St. John to oppose me at the late election for the city of Carlisle, that he has been directed by these great men to spare neither labour nor expense to throw me out of Parliament, and now the election is carried against him, he is ordered to petition upon the assurances that have been given that his cause shall be supported by the new Ministry. My accounts of these particulars come from so many hands that I make no doubt but my opponent hath thought fit to make use not only of Mr. Secretary's name but of yours to support his pretensions, and he has in great measure confirmed the latter part of his account by the petition he has lodged in the hands of Mr. Joddrell which must be founded upon something more than the merits of his cause, since his votes came not within an hundred of mine, and I can defy him to show that I have done anything to invalidate my majority. On the other side he must be sensible that I can't want evidence to prove very many foul practices upon him and his agents. I have all the reason imaginable not to credit his assertions concerning you and in case he thinks fit to proceed in the way he is now in, I shall think it necessary to complain myself of his irregularities and I shall hope for your leave to make use of what he has said and done in your name as part of my charge against him. I persuade myself that as I am a perfect stranger to him, he is not better known to yourself though he boasts so much of his interest in you. If I happen to be mistaken and Mr. Gledhill be one you have a regard for I shall be glad to receive your commands concerning him.

The Earl of Orrery to [Robert Harley].

1710, November 15—I send you all the accounts I had from Scotland last night and this morning and congratulate you upon so good a choice

I must beg leave to put you in mind once more of the Duke of Argyll's affair. I'm confident he expects it should be done by that time he returns and if it be not I know he will be uneasy, for such delays, which are commonly disagreeable to the calmest tempers, are almost insupportable to him. Some time ago I gave a paper to H. St. John that contained some hints about the reformation of the army, 'twas loose and undigested but I can put it into a better form if you desire it, though I hope by this time you have turned that matter so well in your thoughts and laid in such a manner before the Queen that she is come to some determination about it, for certainly 'tis an affair in which not only the dignity but the security too of the Crown is concerned.

[DANIEL DE FOE to ROBERT HARLEY.]

1710, November 16. Edinburgh—The stop I met with at Newcastle prevented my arriving here till the day before the election of Peers. I know I need not give you a list of their names.

Some observations on the conduct of the parties on both sides I shall communicate in my next being not sufficiently furnished for that work at so short notice.

I find the people here alarmed very much, but willing to hope everything shall not issue so bad as the ambassador of a certain party who you know was here before me had suggested. They seem surprised when they hear that moderate thoughts remain among those of whose management they had received such formidable ideas. I flatter myself her Majesty shall be successfully as well as faithfully served in the great work of quieting the minds of her subjects in this part of Britain, and really I find a disposition here, especially amongst the most judicious both of ministers and people, to rest upon the assurances of her Majesty's preserving their liberties, and to leave all other things to her royal justice. The Church here is their great concern, this being untouched they will be the easiest part of the nation in other cases.

This is the foundation I am building upon and indeed I find as many endeavours to embroil them here and disorder the heads of the people as I did in the time of the Treaty, though I hope easier to be defeated. I presume confuting these and informing the people here of their true interest and a little of their duty may be acceptable service to her Majesty and may answer the end of my stay here and in this I shall not fail and shall more constantly now inform you of what occurs. I presume you have an account of what I did at Newcastle in answer to mine. I am very sorry to write that the gentleman I sent my last by from thence is no more to be confided in, of which I shall give a larger account among many things in my next.

Endorsed by Harley.—" Mr. Guilot."

C. GUILOT [*alias* DE FOE]* to [ROBERT HARLEY].

1710, November 18—I wrote you briefly last post but one. I have been in close conference since that with men of all parties; indeed the scenes here have as great a variety as can be imagined, differing not only from themselves but from things of the like nature in England in a most extraordinary manner.

This moves me to be the more particular believing it very much for her Majesty's service to give you a succinct account of the humours of men and parties and of their conduct in the present juncture.

---

* In this and some of the succeeding letters from Edinburgh De Foe makes an attempt to disguise his handwriting.

The Whigs here are balked in their elections of the Peers of whom I need not give you the names though they are in the enclosed list. How unhappily the several parties behave in this case shall be my first remark.

The Tories (as we call them in England) are here a differing kind of people from ours of that denomination, being universally Jacobite and so above board as to own it, in the last of which they certainly show more honesty than discretion. It is so open a thing and so much the mode of the place to own the Pretender, drink his health, and talk most insolently of his being restored, that I think it my duty to represent this to you, for her Majesty's service, and that with the greatest concern.

You will wonder when I shall repeat to you an absurdity of a nature which one would think incapable of deluding anybody, viz. that the 233 (Queen) should have been privately resolved to dissolve the 253 (succession) and to restore 214 (the Pretender) being chagrined, pensive, and in conscience uneasy at his being so long and so much injured—and not only so, but that 233 (the Queen) will resign in favour of the said 214 (Pretender).

I had not mentioned this, for I would not trouble you with trifles, if I did not see a strange use made of it here to encourage the professed Jacobites and to impose upon the poor highlanders and other people in the country who do not look for their Saviour's coming with half the assurance as they do for that of the 214 (Pretender). I doubt not but you will think it proper in its season to represent this to her Majesty, since the encouragement of the Jacobites in the new turn of affairs is the great argument, which the other people make use of to make their quarrel at the late changes become popular. In the late election the conduct of the D[uke] of 60 (Argyll) the E[arl] of 163 (Ilay) and the Earl of 194 (Mar) is very particular; and either their instructions were to use no temper or they discovered most impolitic openness. Many that were willing to come into measures exclaimed openly upon the imprudence of those gentlemen, who treated them with menaces and contempt on the one hand, and declared openly the qualification of those to be chosen, which is now called the test upon which the Peers were closeted by those two above, viz. their agreeing to impeach 140 (Godolphin) and 193 (Marlborough). Nor did the imprudence end there but on all occasions to say in so many words they had her Majesty's orders to choose such and such and it must be done. This was so abandoning all reserves, that it has disgusted the generality, and has put them upon measures of uniting, which may shut the door upon all future measures, whatever the occasion may be. Prudence will never let a wise man play a game so, as he can never play it again, but these gentlemen have not only done so, but exposed their measures so openly that, had a proposal 260 (Stair) made been closed with, all the manage of 60 (Argyll) and 194 (Mar) had been disappointed, and the success of this election is owing to the cowardice not goodwill of 182 (Leven), 138 (Glasgow), with Seafield, Hyndford and (left blank) and not at all to the wisdom and conduct of 60 (Argyll) and 194 (Mar) who certainly lost themselves more in this than any man would have thought possible for men of their character, especially 194 (Mar), to have done, and was within a trifle of spoiling all their work.

Now they have returned their number, it were to be wished they could have avoided a few who are declared professed Jacobites such as 197 (Earl Marischal), Kilsyth, Blantyre, and Hume, who are known to aim in all they do at the Pretender and whose being now chosen has many ill effects here, whatever may be as to overruling them in England.

I mean as to increasing the insolence of Jacobitism in the north, where its strength is far from being contemptible, and the rendering the work of making the other people easy far more difficult than it might otherwise have been. It was very remarkable that when my Lord 163 (Ilay) attempted some of the 100 (clergy) of this city to assure them of the good intentions of the 233 (Queen), and resolutions not to invade their Church, the circumstances of naming Jacobite Peers as the express order from 233 (the Queen) to be chosen was retorted as a bad token for them to rest upon; and the famous tale of the ▮ngman of Edinburgh was told him by one Mr. Miller of Kirkliston, viz., how he used when he had any man to execute to encourage them and bid them not fear till he got them up the ladder and so turned them off.

I hint this to confirm my censure of the conduct aforesaid as imprudent and as what has rendered the quieting these people, which was easy before, very difficult now.

I would not lay down my opinion of things too positively, therefore I cease to enlarge on the affair of this management. How the Whig lords behave, how the Squadron and old Court unite, what measures they took then and are taking now, with some observations on both, shall be the subject of my next. Meantime I should be made easy if I had the honour to know if these accounts come safe to hand, being unexpectedly deprived of the opportunity of conveying by Mr. Bell whom I cannot think of trusting in this affair unless I have again your commands to do so.

Endorsed by Harley :—"Claude Guilot, Edinburgh."

C. GUILOT [*alias* DE FOE] to [ROBERT HARLEY].

1710, November 21. [Edinburgh] — I am unhappily in some perplexity about the conveying my letters as well as my other circumstances in this place, and this causes me giving you this trouble by the ordinary post. I subjoin my humble request that I may receive a line or two signifying that my letters arrive and also that my proceedings are to your satisfaction, if according to my hopes I have the honour to answer your expectation.

I had the honour of your credit to Mr. J. Bell restricting me to twenty pounds, which he readily complied with, but immediately made my having that credit and waiting there for it public all over the town, having himself espoused a contrary interest to what he supposed me acting for, of which I shall add more largely when I am assured my letters arrive safe to your hand. This causes me (however straitened) to offer no further desire of supply that way, choosing rather to struggle with my own circumstances than to hazard the service.

I know if you think fit to continue me here any time, you will not abandon me in your service, and as for methods of supply, if you please to order me any support here, I may draw it in *this hand* and *name* safely and entirely concealed on yourself, or on any person you shall please to appoint. If you do me the honour to leave me to judge whether I am more useful in staying here or not, I must confess I think I can in no spot of ground in Britain render her Majesty like service (though in this I speak against my own interest and affairs), I mean for a month or two yet longer, since these people are infinitely prejudiced and alarmed, and yet not so tenacious and ill-tempered as I expected, and will be soon restored and recovered to their temper.

I humbly lay my own circumstances before you, but submit it entirely to your goodness whose concern for me has always been beyond my merit.

I most humbly and earnestly entreat for a line signifying the receipt of my letters, since I cannot write with equal freedom while I am uncertain whether what I write comes safe to your hands.

Postscript.—I have written at large last post, directed to Mr. Bateman.

Endorsed by Harley :—" C. Guilot."

R[ICHARD] MUSGRAVE to [ROBERT HARLEY].

1710, November 24—The arbitrary proceedings of some noblemen's tools have rendered all my endeavours ineffectual for the borough of Cockermouth. I there carried it by an undoubted majority, but by the base malice of the officers had a return against me. In espousing the interest of Colonel Orfeur my relation, who is zealously devoted to serve you with the last drop of his blood in that revolution which you have judiciously brought about, consequently I cannot despair that you will support his interest at the Committee, and forward as soon as possible his just and legal petition, because the proceedings against him will evidently appear to be extraordinary and surprising and contrary to all rules of Parliament, occasioned partly by such as eat her Majesty's bread ; though in a more particular manner the influences of noblemen, as being foolishly thought to be out of the reach of the law, and able to protect others, though never so great offenders, in the service of them, it would be a hardship if they should happen to go unpunished. Besides their ill-conduct, I am persuaded they are not as you are in the interest of her Majesty, nor have so much at heart the good of her subjects.

I cannot forbear laying before you the conduct and behaviour of Mr. Thomas Brougham, receiver general of the Land Tax for the two counties Cumberland and Westmorland, who exerted his power to an extravagant degree at the election in Carlisle; therefore I flatter myself that you will remove him from his post and indulge me so far as to bestow it upon my brother-in law Mr. John Brisco, who always hath every way showed himself a loyal subject. You'll pardon me if I also mention to you Mr. Brougham's relation, Daniel Brougham, son of a high constable, a man of the same kidney with himself, who behaved at the election in Carlisle in the same manner, with regard to his endeavours, though his interest is nothing. He is Collector of the Customs in Carlisle ; give me leave also to say, and what only is truth, that he is a man of a wicked, debauched, and profligate life and conversation and has lately done things which will ever render him despised and hated even by his former friends, relations, and the very neighbourhood he lives in, not to say his enemies. I am loth and ashamed, nor is it proper to say what I would, therefore let me humbly and earnestly entreat you to displace him, and to give it to my brother; this is the post, though not of the value with the former that I much the rather covet for Mr. Brisco and to ask both would be too presuming, though they might very easily be managed by any one, the Customs in Carlisle being upon the Union very small. I do assure you (and being happy in having been known to you before, I hope you will depend upon it as truth) the disposing of the Collector's place as desired will be looked upon by everybody here as a just return upon the present Collector's scandalous behaviour to my brother's relations, so that I once more beg of you to gratify me in this. As to the Receiver's place, if my brother may be thought by you deserving of it upon the recommendation I make, I will undertake that moneys raised shall more speedily be returned than formerly, yet this I will not press you in, but submit to your judgment wholly in the matter, only pardon me if I again beg the favour of the Collector's post as before. I need not add that upon this and some other alterations in this county a better set of Parliament men may be depended upon when there may be need for it than I doubt at present this county can boast of, though I question not the elections in other places have been so well carried that the Parliament meeting will heartily rejoice with her Majesty upon the choice already made of her Ministry. I had endeavoured, and without any reason to doubt the success, to have been a member myself, but my affairs upon my father's death and other inconveniences attending prevented me in that d■ign, but hope upon future elections to be a sitting member of that honourable House. The bearer my kinsman is the person injured whose cause I hope you'll support.

C. GUILOT [*alias* DE FOE] to [ROBERT HARLEY].

1710, Nov. 25, Edinburgh—I wrote you at large the observations I had made on the conduct of our great men here. I am not the best judge of the reasons of things, but the consequences seem obvious, and any man may determine of them. On this account I presume to assure you, that the unwary openness, which I gave you my thoughts about in my last, has done a great deal of hurt here, in raising the jealousies and uneasinesses of this people, who were very much inclined to acquiesce before in her Majesty's prudence, and rely on the assurances given of the royal protection. The Queen, they say, has always adhered to the law, and never carried it with a high hand. But the D[uke] of 60 (Argyll) destroyed the very appearance of liberty in producing a list, and openly telling the Peers, the Queen would have those men chosen. It is not my business to make comments, her Majesty will judge whether this was her pleasure. The best I can say to them is, that they cannot suppose her Majesty gave his Grace instructions to treat the Peers in that manner, but that the 60 (Duke) might be a little warm; that perhaps her Majesty might have seen such a list, and appear satisfied in the persons, but that her Majesty would command them to choose such, and no other, was not probable. In this, if I do wrong, I shall be very unhappy; since I do it as the only means of quieting the uneasy people, which I take to be very much her Majesty's interest.

I shall go on to acquaint you with this part as the particulars offer. But for the present I cannot avoid representing one thing to you, which as it concerns the public peace here, I believe it my duty to lay before her Majesty.

The uneasiness the people are under here on the affair above said is not little, especially at the returning four of the number professedly 161 (Jacobites). But they are now further alarmed at the confident assurances given them of a change in the great officers here, particularly the military government.

I persuade myself, you will believe me, that I have no interest to make, or persons to serve. I am no bigot to a party much less to persons but when her Majesty shall be informed of the temper of her people here, and of the immediate consequences of a change, I doubt not my notion of that matter will appear to have some weight in it, at least enough to excuse me in the mentioning it.

1. Be it that some (worthless enough) may have the chief hand in the affair, yet to take it from them and leave it to the next in course may

not mend the matter, or to put it into the hands of any of the same party may not be worth the broil such a remove will make among them.

2. To give the military power here which indeed is the supreme, till the country is a little more acquainted with the civil, to the new party, whom the people by the needless and unseasonable conduct aforesaid are so jealous of, is to put them into infinite confusions, and make the uneasiness past any private man's remedy.

3. To let in the Tory party, or indeed those who would be called the Episcopal party, into the military command is to put the Pretender into actual possession of this part of the Island.

I humbly ask your pardon for representing this so positively, yet I am not able to see any medium. I would not reflect on any of her Majesty's episcopal subjects, but certainly if they are in her interest, they act the most impolitic part in the world, for they will not so much as say it themselves; nor in all my knowledge of things and persons in this part of Britain did I ever see, or know, or find any other man that has seen or known, any one man who was purely Episcopal and not also Jacobite avowedly so. Except a very few under the ministry of some of the Episcopal ministers, who are continued in their churches by the Presbyterian government.

I cease to go on with my notes on this till I see how the disposition of the people shall hold, for these things vary as every new notion comes on. But I must offer you one further hint of my own, which I submit to your charity, because I think it acting beyond my sphere. I do not love to be officious, but if you would please to give me leave I could name two or three persons, who while they are in are rendered suspected to the new junto here, and who perhaps may be kept off from them; whereas their being displaced will make them popular and place them at the head of a party which it is very much her Majesty's interest to keep down, and which can never be better kept down than by rendering them suspected to one another. I shall explain myself farther if I may obtain your commands and some hint that my letters come to your hands.

Any letter directed to Mr. William Clift at Mr. Walter Ross's to be left at Mr. David Monroe in Edinburgh will come to my hand. The number of such names is to make it secure.

Endorsed by Harley :—"Mr. Guilot, Edinburgh."

J. D[RUMMOND] to [ROBERT HARLEY].

1710, [November 29-]December 9, new style. Amsterdam—Since I had the honour of writing last to you I have had occasion to make much use of the letter you were pleased to favour me last with, and I dare say with no dishonour or prejudice to you. Mr. Secretary St. John will have acquainted you with what I wrote him of my discourse with ——; the longer he stays at the Hague the more he will be convinced of the necessities he lies under to submit himself to the Queen's pleasure and the measures which her Majesty and her ministers think most for her honour and satisfaction. He has faithfully promised both to the Grand Pensionary and to ours, that he is resolved to live with you if you will make it practicable or possible for him; he will not enter into the heats of party debates, but will go heartily and sincerely into all the measures that may be esteemed proper for carrying on the war, but for other votes he will be at his free liberty. When he said pretty passionately—do they imagine I must make the first advances after all the insults and affronts they have put upon me ? ·1 answered, no, my Lord, they have made once and again offers of correspondence with you, and I did read to him the three instances which you are pleased to mention to me, the last by Earl Poulett. He owned, and said he did not reject your proposal, but desired the Earl as a good friend to you both to make use of his good offices till his arrival in England. As to the two former proposals he believes they may have been made to Lord Godolphin but were not proposed to him. I told him that I had been conversing with Mr. Cardonnel, who believes that his losing his place which his Grace seemed to be so uneasy at proceeded from, and in revenge of, the neglect he had made of your proposals of commencing a correspondence ; even I told him that Mr. Cardonnel and Mr. Watkins had prepared and composed an answer he should make to that period of Earl Poulett's letter, and that he would make no use of it. He seemed concerned that I knew this, I told him he needed be under no concern what I knew, that my design was fair and honest above board, not to widen but to reconcile breaches, not to flatter him into a great opinion of his services and that they could never be rewarded or forgotten, nor to raise his imaginations above his true interest and the safe way he was to take to live easy ; that some people about him had screwed him up to under-value the humble though just advices of honest men who had no design but his own and the public good, while his flatterers were enriching themselves at the expense of his reputation. I read to him another passage in your letter, that though he might now be pretty well resolved to live with the Queen's new ministers and especially with you, that he would be no sooner at home than he would be led into the rage and revenge of some about him, by which instead of abating he would aggravate and inflame the divisions and differences, which if wisely gone about might be removed and converted into affection and friendship. To this he answered, you mean my wife and those I must live with, and that he thanked God he had more temper than some he would have to do with in the new ministry ; and yet he could and would live with Lord Rochester and doubted not he would find friends amongst the old Tories, complaining of some resentments by preferring people under his command who made it their business to lessen him, and be ill with him, meaning Lord Orrery's being made Major General. I told him he was a person of quality and I believed that proceeded from the Queen's own inclination, that I was informed you had been so far from personal resentment that you had shewn as much complaisance in his affair of Blenheim as Lord Godolphin had done. This he consented to, and desired me to write very plainly that he was pretty much desponding, and yet seemed well resolved to carry on the war he had so successfully brought this length, by sticking to her Majesty's service as long as even his greatest enemies should think it possible or practicable for him.

If the wind had been fair you would have had Lieut. Gen. Lumley over with more assurances of this nature, and at the same time Meredith, no doubt with his best respects to his old friends, whom I believe he cannot resolve to abandon till he be sure of new ones.

I told him [Marlborough] at parting that I hoped he was not ignorant how often and how much some of those he thought his friends had endeavoured and still would prostitute him, naming Lord Wharton, which he readily consented to and that he knew all these things very well, and that should make him the less engage in party concerns, but simply satisfy himself in doing his duty. He said Mr. St. John had sent him business enough to keep him here all this month, but that he would be going in ten days at most. I said that in my own opinion I believed he might pass a great part of the winter with as much pleasure here as he would do in England. He answered that he had such advice given him by more, but that he could not think it less for other people's ease than his that such advice was given him; he entreated that I should return to see him before he left the Hague, and he desired the same of Pensionary Buys when he. left the Hague some days before me, and to whom I have made since my return your compliments in the best manner I am capable of, and they were received with no less satisfaction and expressions of sincere friendship by the Pensionary to whom I did read several passages of your letter to convince him that you would not be backward in anything that could be for the public good. I never had more satisfaction than last night in his conversation in which he often expressed also the honour which Mr. Secretary St. John did to the Queen's service, and indeed he is a jewel not enough to be valued, for his expressions are equally lucky and fine in English and French. Monsieur Buys said " If my station allowed me to be the beginner of a correspondence with a foreign minister I had long ago begun it with Mr. H(arley) whom I so much value and esteem, and I am convinced if he knew how much I long to have the honour of seeing him · as well as of hearing from him, we would not stand long upon the ceremony of honouring me with the first letter, which is a necessary preliminary to come to a correspondence with one- in my post, for without the States consent I cannot begin the correspondence, but I will faithfully maintain it and be as punctual in my answers as he can desire." I promised sincerely to acquaint you with his heartiness, friendship and well wishes, and I promised him that I should use my endeavours with you to begin without delay a correspondence which I was sure would be no less useful to the public than pleasant to you both. I made bold to shew him one passage of your letter, which he did read seven times over with much concern, viz.:—

" It is pretty plain no one in Holland now either has authority enough, or spirit and resolution enough, to give the rules, and deliver his country, but will suffer them and us to perish by a lingering consumption."

This sentence struck him, and he said he hoped he should never be wanting to the utmost of his power to approve himself that person you so strongly expresssed, and that had not his *confrater* Vander Dussen and he been threatened out of their senses, yet not so much they as those who sent them, he would have been able to have in some respect personated such a person as you seem to long for, but now that is irrecoverable, and we must have patience till the enemy by our. steady and hearty resolutions be obliged to make new proposals, for I hope in God we shall never be reduced so low as to make them to the enemy. I am truly of opinion that you may with all safety write plainly your opinion to him, and I am convinced you will have much satisfaction in his answers. He said frequently in our conversation, could I but have three hours conversation with Mr. Harley we might do some considerable service, and indeed I wish it could be so contrived that he were sent over to you.

As for Lord Albemarle if he go it will be about his private affairs, he is grown the gentleman of most application in the service, the most affable and obliging in his behaviour, the best husband, and most regular man in his way of living that is in the States dominions; only continues pretty expensive in his equipage and housekeeping. His revenues in the service are great and I don't hear that he is in any one's debt, he complains that the Queen borrowed of him 16,000*l.* sterling which was in the privy purse when the King died, that he has only been paid one thousand pounds of it, and that he had the Queen's promise that it should be paid when he should have occasion for it, which he says he now very much has. I told him that I wondered very much considering the great civilities he had always shewn the Duke of Marlborough by always lodging him ▬ his house, &c. that he did not prevail on Lord Godolphin to pay him at least gradually if he could not all at once, but I find his Lordship has had the fate of others to have fair promises and foul performances. He swears my Lord M. will return from England an excellent Tory, that he would not lose one half of the revenues of his places to become . . . (*sic*) ; and he has the same opinion of Lord Godolphin. He does not make an ill use of the Duke of Shrewsbury's letters to him, I am sure he has read them all to the Grand Pensionary, and to Monsieur Slingerland, Secretary to the Council of State, one of the greatest and best men in the Republic, who with the Grand Pensionary and the Griffier Pagel do the great affairs, and next to them, the Treasurer Hop, and the President of the Council of State, Monsieur de Starenberg of the Wastenaer family, but he grows old and has lived very fast.

When you write to Monsieur Buys be sure to propose the squadron for the West Indies to him, for he has always been a favourer of that project, and had once brought it a great length with Sir David Mitchell, but a man of greater power, rather have the expense than, applied to the land service (*sic*). The properest person you have in England to treat with the Dutch on that subject is Sir James Wishart, who served long in their fleet, speaks their language, and I think commanded once a North Holland man of war ; he is known and beloved by all our Dutch admirals.

I hope you don't go into that villanous proposal of the Bank to make Exchequer notes yield one way and other nine per cent. per annum ; how do you propose to find money on your land and malt tax than at six or even seven per cent.? These eternal rascals have so treated the Queen on this occasion by altering their measures, because the person was out of place from whom they did take their measures, by immediately prohibiting the discount of foreign bills, by drawing immense sums on Holland for Exchequer notes at any exchange, and taking up all the money here which used to circulate and serve the undertakers of your public payments to discount their bills which had two and three months and more to run, and that worthy gentleman Furnese has "paunded" here for one hundred and fifty thousand pounds worth of tin ; I hope you keep no more measures with that instrument of malice. I wish you would be pleased to explain to me or to tell Decker to write me how he came to receive such a prodigious quantity of tin, for it is full five years consumption here unless you enable some one to undersell him a little, which I hope you will ; otherwise all that comes in from the mines in your time will lie so long on your hands. Lord Townshend complains much of want of payments, I told him to get his allowance in tin, that I would sell it off for him and so gradually supply him with the product of the tin for his expenses, and in the same manner any other foreign ministers in Germany or this side of the world. You are very good natured to let one of Molesworth's principles serve the Queen in so fine and easy a station.

Scottish Peers' Pensions.

1710, November—Pensions promised to some people in Scotland—

	Yearly.	Paid as 1st payment.
To The Earl of Glencairne - - -	300*l.*	100*l.*
The Earl of Kincardine what the Queen thinks fit, but he pretends to 500*l.* or his son Mr. Bruce getting the Muster Master's place - - -	500	100
The Earl of Balcarres was promised nothing by me (Lord Dupplin?) but I believe others promised - - -	300	100
Lord Fraser - - - -	200	200
Elphinston - - -	100	100
Banff - - - -	100	100
Rollo - - -	100	100
Mordington - - -	100	100
	1700*l.*	

Lord Sempill had an old promise but is
since provided in a Troop of Dragoons,
he had then - - - - - - 180*l.*

Sum of the money paid then - - 1080*l.*

In Lord Dupplin's handwriting (?)

D[e] F[oe] to [Robert Harley].

1710, December 3. Edinburgh—I have been so anxious about the safe conveying of my letters having not had the honour of the least hint from yourself, that I convey this enclosed by a trusty friend, as well that I may be sure of its coming to your hand, as that I may receive if you please one line for my direction, whether to stay here or return, and whether what I am doing here is for your service and to your satisfaction.

It is a disaster to me that I lost the occasion of writing by Mr. Bell, whose conduct I observed to you renders him suspected to me.

Whatever you please to do me the honour to direct either by word or by writing will be faithfully conveyed to me by Mr. Young the bearer, a faithful and honest man, and on whom I can so far depend, or I would not have entrusted him.

Postscript.—I wrote a long letter this night directed to Mr. Thomas Bateman to which I humbly refer.

J. D[rummond] to Robert Harley.

1710, December [4–]15, new style. Amsterdam—Coming to Lord Albemarle's as he was going to the Pensionary, he was pleased to carry me with him where I was very well received, and I find this great man still under much concern about your affairs, which makes me have the worse opinion of some who I am afraid don't take much pains to put him right. He said very plainly, I am well inclined to believe very well, and every thing that is good of the new ministry by the accounts which Lord Albemarle has given me of them, but they must convince us by their works as well as their words that they are hearty for the public good, and for carrying on the war with vigour till our mutual enemy demands terms of peace, which I am convinced they will do before six months be at an end—if England take cordial resolutions, and the French perceive clearly that they have no good to expect from the changes in England, and they see that England and we are linked together, and that our interest is one, that we go hand in hand to reduce them to such terms, by which we can have a safe and honorable peace. If the Duke of Marlborough has done anything to disoblige the Queen it is none of our business to meddle betwixt her and her subject, but we hope her Majesty will take such a time to shew her resentment as shall not be prejudicial to the service; we hope he will submit to the Queen's pleasure and deserve so well of her as to receive new marks of her favour, [which are] necessary at this juncture, and even more necessary than ever, because we are almost exhausted, and want to have matters carried on without any interruption to bring the enemy to such proposals as in my conscience I believe they will come to very soon if we be but steady. For what can be a greater sign of their hopes to divide us, and that by the changes in England they hope that our interest and that of England will be separate, than in their edicts for prohibiting our trade or calling in their passports. They offer to give passes to English ships, for lately some of our officers wanting to come and go about their private business, the Marshal de Montesque de Artagnan sent word the King had forbid the giving passes to any Dutchman, [but] the English might have as many as they pleased. Therefore I say the new ministry must and I hope will exert themselves to baffle the vain expectations of our enemies, and to remove the fears of their friends who shall heartily stick by them on all occasions, whose safety is placed in their safety and by whose discording together, the French King must become the universal monarch.

To all this and a much finer harangue than I can repeat, I answered, Sir I entreat you will consider on what Lord Albemarle has told you, that the gentlemen now employed by the Queen were as hearty for the Revolution as any in England, that they are firm Protestants, that they are men uninterested, that they have good land estates to lose which they cannot remove, as some new acquired sums of money can be, that before Christmas old style he should be convinced that change of ministers had made no change of measures as to the common cause, unless it were in being more hearty and expeditious, more frugal of the nation's money, and more earnest for a speedy and reasonable peace; that I hoped to be able soon to show him demonstrable proofs of their affection to this State and the carrying on of the common cause with more vigour than ever considering how long the war had lasted, and what a great share England had borne in the expense thereof. Therefore I hope as your new parliament is now sitting you will soon send us over such hearty resolutions as shall rejoice the hearts of the people here, as shall convince them that the Queen has changed for the better, and as shall make ashamed all the disingenuous insinuators of mischief and villany, who will fall into the traps they have prepared for others, and will be ashamed to own the party they have cried up and be glad to shelter under the wings of those they have upbraided and prosecuted.

Some here are afraid you are for weakening the army here to make detachments to Spain, which they are averse to. Lord Albemarle will write the Duke of Shrewsbury next post having sat late with the States.

J. Durden to [Robert Harley].

1710, December 5. Scarborough—Since the last time I did myself
the honour to write to you, some passages happened in public company
here between one Mr. Docker, the minister of this town, and one Mr.
Hannah, the teacher of a dissenting congregation in this corporation,
which because the words spoken immediately concern I think proper
to communicate to you, as I have twice heard them attested from
the parson's own mouth, for I was not in the company myself.

The words were as follows :—

Dissenting Teacher.—Well what think you of Mr. Harley now, is he
of our side or yours?

Church Minister.—If he sides with you he has very little reason for
it, for if one may believe Greg's dying speech (which I have been
told your party endeavoured to smother) you have left no means
unattempted to bring him to the block.

Dissenting Teacher.—But I assure you he has been several times at
our meetings since he came into the new Ministry, and particularly
to hear Mr. Williams, whose prayers he desired : and ordered an
Exchequer bill of 1,000l. to be left for him at his house, but
Mr. Williams refused to accept it and returned it.

The observation that a merry gentleman (to whom the parson told the
story) made upon what was thus confidently affirmed as to the 1,000l.
bill was that granting it true Mr. Harley might design the service of
Government, by so rich a present to a teacher that had the consciences
of perhaps the largest and richest congregation of Separatists in London
under his girdle, and not to promote the dissenting interest: and that if
the design had succeeded, he had played the part of a skilful chemist,
as well as of an able statesman, that can extract something medicinal
and salutary even out of vipers and such like noxious animals.

Please to pardon the freedom with which I relate the whole story;
and likewise the liberty I take to give you some account of two of the
four new members of parliament returned out of this county; viz. :
Mr. Bell of and for Thirsk, and Mr. Raikes of and for Northallerton.
These boroughs are both within my survey, and by that means I have
had opportunities of conversing with their representatives. Mr. Bell
is a mercer in Thirsk, and was, as I am informed, brought up a churchman in his youth; but his father taking some distaste to a former
minister of Thirsk set up a dissenting congregation there, and has ever
since adhered solely to it ; but the son goes to church in the morning,
and, (to humour his father) to the meeting in the afternoon ; but since his
election (or rather since Sir Thomas Frankland and he chose each other,
for these two have much the greatest number of borough houses, and
nobody can come in at Thirsk without their joint consent) he has stuck
wholly to the church, though some of his neighbours say he has been at
the meeting. It would be the highest presumption in me to say anything of his parts and understanding to one that is the best judge in the
world of mankind; his capacity for a legistator will soon discover itself,
if he offers to speech it in the House, but I believe he will yet awhile
be too modest to do that. His present principles as to the disputes on
foot between Whig and Tory, your Honour may be satisfied in by his
recommending to my perusal the four " Letters to a Friend in North
Britain " and other pamphlets of that stamp, which I promised to read,
on condition that he would read over the " Essay upon Public Credit,"
and the "Examiners."

I beg leave here to digress a little to acquaint you that that paper has done excellent service in these, as I doubt not it has in other parts, and proves (as the wise and politic author of the letter to the " Examiner " foresaw it would) a weekly antidote to that weekly poison so industriously scattered through the nation by those two public libellers and incendiaries " The Observator," " The Review," and others. The honest parson before mentioned takes abundance of pains to apply the remedy where it is wanted. Mr. Hungerford sends him the " Examiner " down every Thursday: it comes hither on Sunday and after evening service the parson usually invites a good number of his friends to his house, where he first reads over the paper, and then comments upon the text; and all the week after carries it about with him to read to such of his parishioners as are weak in the faith, and have not yet the eyes of their understanding opened; so that it is not doubted but he will in time make as many converts to the true interest of the State, as ever he did **to the Church.**

I shall now give your Honour some account of the other new member of parliament before mentioned. Mr. Raikes is a barrister of Gray's Inn, but some say more conversant with ladies than law books; an attorney's son of Northallerton. His father left him assets to the value of 5 or 600 pounds, and used often to say that he should go to the D—l to leave young Robin an estate, and some say young Robin will not scruple to go the same way to increase it, and that though he is something extravagant his conscience is not more straitlaced than his father's. He is a famous jockey, talks much in company that are his equals or inferiors, but how well I shall leave others to judge that can do it better. He is a declared Whig but 'tis reasonable to believe from part of his character that he would soon prove a comeover if it should be thought worth while to make him one. I was in company with him about a month since at his borough and he was pleased to say (but gave no reason for it) that he wished her Majesty would dissolve this present Parliament after their first Session; to which nobody replying I answered that I hoped they would give her Majesty no occasion. The discourse ended here, and 'tis high time this letter should after I have begged pardon for the length of it, which I heartily do.

EARL RIVERS to [ROBERT HARLEY].

1710, December 5.—I was surprised to find my name so soon in the Gazette, Mr. St. John told me but yesterday what was designed. I shall think myself very happy if I can do her Majesty service in any capacity. I hope neither the Queen nor yourself do think I have forgot the trade I was brought up in, though I have been discouraged in it of late. As the title I am honoured with is to the full as honourable as Ambassador so I hope the appointments will be the same, considering the present charge I must be at, to send to Hanover to hire and furnish a house; to buy plate, for I have had none since I lost a whole set at sea, for which the late King never allowed me anything, though Blathwayt had 1,500l. for his no loss in the same ship; if my circumstances were as you believe them I should say nothing, but upon my word they are very different.

C. GUILOT [*alias* DE FOE] to [ROBERT HARLEY].

1710, December 6. Edinburgh—I wrote you two letters the last post, one to Mr. Bateman and one in cover to a faithful friend to convey, if possible, to yourself and receive some notice of your having received mine, for which I have been indeed very anxious; and also to receive your further commands.

The notice here that in 212 (Parliament) you have personally spoken against 214 (the Pretender) has fixed the character; I have had the honour to spread here of your steady zeal for the Revolution and confirmed what I hinted in my last that Lieut. General Maitland had avouched publicly in your just defence, viz., that no man in Britain was a greater prop to the constitution than yourself. I was very glad to have so good an assistant in so great a piece of justice to you, who I think have received so much injury from some from whom you have merited much better; and the rather, because it directly contradicted what Dr. Oldfield had been busy here in spreading both of yourself and even of your great mistress the Queen herself.

: Now the joy begins to be visible among the honest people who were and still are firm to her Majesty's person as well as government, but were terrified with the absurd notions of all being to be given up to the 214 (Pretender), even by 233 (the Queen) herself, it is not strange that a thing so ridiculous should prevail if the assurances of those who reported it were considered and that they had obtained to be sent up to 212 (Parliament) where they had peremptorily said it should be done.

: This will satisfy her Majesty that the interest of the Pretender is too great here to be slighted and that nothing but discouragement of it from herself can keep them in bounds, but if her Majesty please on any occasion to express her being pleased with the zeal of her subjects against the Pretender it would strike them here as with a blast from Heaven and weaken his interest more than an army of 10,000 men could do.

As to the people here, I mean the Presbyterians, they come heartily into her Majesty's interest neither do they relish the chagrin of our 288 (Whigs) in 116 (England). The ambassador who has resided here from the 106 (Dissenters) and who has left his Mission here for 249 (secret service) is gone back *re infecta*, and his negotiations have made less impression than indeed I expected; in short nothing but the 214 (Pretender) and encroachments of 100 (clergy) can make them uneasy. I endeavour to assure them and shall hereafter give you some accounts of mediums to preserve her Majesty's interest here and yet make all but the 161 (Jacobites) easy also.

The Duke of Leeds to [Robert Harley].

1710, December 7. London—If my health had permitted me to wait upon you I had acquainted you with something relating to Sir John Bland, who I perceive is not only your acquaintance, but takes you to be his friend. He tells me he was removed from being a Commissioner of the Revenue in Ireland for having voted constantly against that party, and I suppose that is the ground of his writing me the enclosed letter, and I cannot but in justice add that I know he hath been at great charge both in his own elections at the borough of Pontefract, and in the turning out one Lowther there, who is one of the worst of men, and who brought up both a false and counter address to that loyal one which was sent up by the knights of Yorkshire, and I will take this opportunity to say that if the Queen do not lay hold of this time both openly to encourage some of her friends and as openly to discourage some of her enemies the last error will be worse than the first and past any possibility of remedy for the future.

Enclosure.

Sir John Bland to the [Duke of Leeds].

1710, December 7—This very minute Sir William St. Quintin asked me in the House if he might not wish me joy of his place. I answered I knew nothing of his being out or of his successor. His reply was he was out and wished I might succeed him, which was an unexpected compliment. I hope your Grace has had some discourse with Mr. Harley.

Sir John Bland to [Robert Harley].

1710, December 8—The Duke of Leeds has promised to recommend my services to the Queen and would acquaint you that I had spared neither purse nor pains in the elections. I thought I might expect to have some consideration for being displaced five years; perhaps I might have my old place or that of the Green Cloth.

[Mrs. L. M. Cressett to Robert Harley.]

1710, December [8–]19, N.S. Zell—I left Hanover two days ago to return to my mother, after having been there eight days, when their Electoral Highnesses overwhelmed me with a thousand marks of their goodness. It appears to me that I left his Electoral Highness more convinced, if I may say so with presumption, than when I arrived, that the changes which it has pleased her Majesty to make would not be in any way opposed to public affairs, and that all your good intentions, as I understand from the ministers, are better recognised than they were. For we must render this much justice to the Elector that no-one can appear to have better intentions than he has for everything that regards the interests of the Queen; but it is impossible not to let oneself be taken in by certain spirits which are as malicious and as evil intentioned as any that exist upon this weary world. As far as regards financial questions I think I have somewhat improved matters.

He has indeed a very high idea of your capacity and of your devotion to the interests of the Queen and the Protestant succession. He remembers that you were Speaker (orateur) when the first act of the succession was passed. So much had been said of the difficulty and that no one remained who could preserve the credit of the nation, except the man who has just gone out of office, that to tell the truth it was absolutely necessary to reserve this prejudice. He was strongly of opinion that the man who had just gone out had left the finances in very good order, and without contradicting him, what I thought fitting to describe to him has made him change his tone. I did not forget their unworthy attitude towards their sovereign. I know that these are tender places to him and that it was absolutely necessary to open his eyes. I was obliged to have all those conversations with him in the drawing-room and was continually interrupted, but I thought it better not to make myself suspected by those who were examining me closely.

I have rendered the man of whom I spoke to you very assiduous in making his court, for he has never lost an evening whilst I have been here, and I must confess to you that I have never seen any one with such bad intentions. He has in truth spoilt the dispositions of the whole of the ministry here at this court. It is impossible that you should even sufficiently win him over to make an honest man of him. He flattered me extremely seeing that I received so many marks of honour from his master, but he insisted also to make me see that he had

already replied for his master to your letter, for he said to me the
evening before my departure that I could have the reply to the letter
which I had brought when I wanted it; that it was ready. I replied
that I had asked his Electoral Highness, who said nothing to me about
it when I was leaving him. I do not know whether he will send
you the letter or whether he will await my return. Allow me to
represent to you the absolute necessity of having a minister at this
court, devoted, as he ought to be, to her Majesty, in order to inspire
respect in those who are ill-intentioned, for it is really sad that this
prince who is really enlightened, should be so badly informed in regard
to English affairs. I took the liberty of telling him himself that I
should have the honour of communicating with him again when I came
back there, which I expect will be, if you permit me, in about a month,
and I added that I expected to have the honour of receiving your orders
before that time.

I must not forget to ask you to remember the present for the little
Princess Anne. I can tell you in confidence that the Princess Sophia
spoke to me on the subject and seemed much surprised that it had been
neglected to show that the Queen had not disliked the liberty which
their Highnesses had taken in begging the Queen to permit them to
give her name to the young Princess, and that to mark this very
profound respect for her Majesty, they had made her the sole godmother.
That assuredly they had not expected fine presents, but not having
received the smallest token from her Majesty to the child that they were
afraid of having displeased her. On hearing that I thought I ought to
speak and to assure their Electoral Highnesses that the matter had
seemed to give the Queen great pleasure, and I could assure them that
it was like everything else, the fault of the late minister who was
delighted to dishonour the Queen in everything. That trifles like that
ought to open their eyes, but that certainly the first thing of which you
spoke when you became minister was to inform yourself about the
matter and to speak to the Lord Chamberlain whose business partly it
was, and that when I left I knew that you had taken information about
the matter and that if it was not already done it certainly would be.

I hope that you will not take it in bad part that I have represented your care as I ought, on this subject, and that I was quite
sure that the Queen would be very angry when she learned that a thing
like that had been neglected and not honourably performed. It is only
for once, and things of that kind are creditable to her Majesty and those
whom she employs, and I can assure you would have a very good effect.
May I venture to say that I think a diamond necklace costing eight to
ten thousand pieces would be the thing which would make most effect
before the public and would cause confusion to these wretches who only
want to augment the dissensions. Forgive me if I take the liberty
of speaking so openly but I think it is my duty to hide nothing, hoping
that you will believe that in everything I have no other aim than her
Majesty's glory and the welfare of the nation, and the honour of
testifying my zeal for your service.

It seems to me that people here have not properly understood the
mark of distinction which the Queen gave in sending Lord R[ivers].
That is to say, the ill-disposed spirits wished to insinuate everything
which their malice could suggest, but at last I have made his Electoral
Highness understand that it was the greatest mark of distinction which
her Majesty could have given him; that she was not at all obliged to
do it, and that it was only to him that she gave that mark as she considered him more interested than anyone else in regard to the succession
in their family, and wishing to prevent all misrepresentations which

could be made concerning the recent changes. That her Majesty was in a position to make these changes without anyone having a right to say a word, but that if I might say so, his Electoral Highness could never acknowledge too highly the mark of distinction which it had pleased her Majesty to confer on him. After I had said that, he seem to me to understand the matter thoroughly.—*French.*

The Rev. Dr. Lancaster to [Robert Harley].

1710, December 10. Queen's College, Oxford—Refers to some complaint through their representatives in Parliament of the city authorities of Oxford about the pulling down of three old college houses, which had paid seven or eight pounds annually towards the parish tax, to make way for the new building from Queen's College library to High Street. The Vice-Chancellor had made application to the representatives of the University on the subject.

Sir Henry Belasyse to [Robert Harley].

1710, December 12—Desires to succeed Mr. Miseday as governor of Tynemouth Castle, about twelve miles from his house.

Dr. Hugh Chamberlen to [Robert Harley].

1710, December 12–23 [The Hague]—It is a general rumour in these parts that money is very scarce and hard to be procured in England; and that the proposed methods to circulate Exchequer notes will one way or other cost the country twelve per cent. per annum.

He therefore offers his services and makes sundry suggestions with a view to bring about a better state of the country's credit and resources.

Count d'Ursel to [Robert Harley].

1710, December [13–]24, N.S. The Hague—Has begged the Duke of Ormond to deliver this letter not being known to Harley. Desires to explain the unfortunate condition to which his country has been reduced since the battle of Ramillies in hopes that the Queen will give them all the protection which their zeal for the common cause has shown that they deserve. His unhappy country has had to pay for the support of more than thirty battalions and twenty squadrons whose services have for the most part been employed elsewhere and themselves left with little protection; and this with the other contributions towards the support of the levied had brought them to a most impoverished state.—*French.*

The Earl of Ilay to [Robert Harley].

1710, December 14—I cannot avoid putting you in mind of the present state of the affairs of Scotland. My Lords Leven and Glasgow and Seafield are all in town making their court; the two first are supported by the Duke of Queensberry of whom I think it is enough to say he is Secretary of State. All our affairs turn upon that hinge, the eyes of all our friends of that country are on Lord Mar and he above all others of your friends feels the pain of not daring to tell how little he knows. Our elections luckily succeed better than we expected, but you may easily imagine our sixteen Peers &c. will think they have some reason to expect those few places their country affords, especially since they are now in the hands either of declared enemies, or those who would be glad to make use of their places against the interest of the very persons they expect quarter from if their pretended conversion can meet with any credit. I think it is very certain that Lord Mar's interest and my brother's daily decline among our countrymen, and in a little time they will get new habits, and by putting themselves under the protection of the majority be engaged to follow the stream wherever it shall happen to run fastest. For your sake, I hope their interest will never be of great use to you in either House and that you may never have any occasion for their assistance, but if ever that time should come, I cannot help having my own apprehensions of the consequence of their present uneasiness. I assure you I don't think it more my duty to take this liberty in telling you my fears, than to be your fellow sufferer if unfortunately they should come to pass.

[Mrs. L. M. Cressett to Robert Harley.]

1710, December [14-]25, N.S. Zell—I send you the replies to the two letters which I brought. His Electoral Highness has done me the honour to send them to me. I hope that you have received all my letters, of which this is the fourth. I do not hear from England of their having been received, but I can assure you that I have not failed in my duty. I think of returning to my poor little family, but I shall return to Hanover where I shall stay some days. Permit me to put you in mind of sending as soon as possible an envoy here. Chose him so as to do bonour to her Majesty and yourself, and then I am persuaded everything will go well.—*French.*

George Granville to [Robert Harley].

1710, December 17—I am forced to trouble you again about Mr. Austis. Vanbrugh has been with Sir Harry St. George to desire his deputation upon an assurance that the Queen had refused Mr. Anstis's petition. What he contends for is to act at the installation on Friday next, which will give him a pretence of being fixed in the office, which 'tis Mr. Anstis's interest by all means to prevent. Austis petitions therefore to obtain the Queen's pleasure to Lord Suffolk that his patent may be dispatched in such manner that he may be the person to officiate on this occasion.

Postscript.—Mr. Boscawen's friends are triumphing in Cornwall upon notice from him that his interest at the Treasury has carried the collection for Padstow for a friend of his against Mr. Roberts' and my recommendation of Mr. Taylor, which is like to give us a good deal of trouble, we having an election now depending at Tintagel.

C. Guilot [*alias* De Foe] to [Robert Harley].

1710, December 18. Edinburgh—I have wrote frequently since my coming hither, I hope they are all arrived. I had determined to leave this place some days since unless your commands had prevented me, believing it more useful to tender my service nearer your hand. But the unusual tempests, storms and floods have made the country impracticable so that there is no passing the country without imminent danger.

The accounts last post from England seem to make my stay here though otherwise accidental very useful. Some private letters have alarmed the poor people here with a story that an attempt is to be made upon their Church in the case of Greenshields and in the article of patronage, the first tends to a toleration, the other a direct invasion of the constitution of the Church and as they say the Union.

Whether this be fact or no, I can give them no answer as to that, but as I have all along persuaded them that no evil is designed against them in all these alterations, and have satisfied them so well that they began to be very easy; so I assure them now that her Majesty is so tender of the Union that they may be assured nothing will be done of any kind that shall any way encroach upon it. I would value myself upon my having some influence upon things and persons here, if I was pleading my own merit, but when I have an argument so well founded as this of her Majesty's royal promise, I think it very much more to my advantage to say I rather improve that forcible argument than persuade them by my influence. The Queen's promise in her late speech, this I insist upon, and the people depend upon it very much. It is not my business to debate here the reasons for or against a toleration here. I presume from what you were pleased to say to me, that you agree with me in this, that this is not a proper season, and I crave leave to add that whatever some people may pretend it is not the aim of the Dissenters here, nor do they desire it.

However I waive this now, I conceive my proper work here is to calm and quiet the minds of the people here, reconcile them to her Majesty's measures and keep them easy—of this I hope I can give you a good account, and am very thankful for my success.

I fear indeed their uneasiness from these new alarms and wish I knew what answer to give. But it is my misfortune to act wholly by my own judgment. If I am deficient I shall the rather hope for your pardon, but if I had the honour of your instructions I should act with more effect as well as with more courage.

Endorsed by Harley :—" Cl. Guilot."

JOHN DRUMMOND to [ROBERT HARLEY].

1710, December [19–]30. Amsterdam—Introducing the Earl of Southesk who was returning from his travels in Italy and Germany, and would be heartily glad to employ his interest to the Queen's service. He was at some Courts in Germany and will tell you very plainly the conversations he had there. He is yet very young but has very solid sense and very honourable principles. His father had inclined to the *non-jurant* party, which this young gentleman was cured of.

EARL RIVERS to [ROBERT HARLEY].

1710, December 25—I am very much concerned to write to you on this occasion, which is to desire you to acquaint her Majesty that nobody laments the misfortune that has happened in Spain more than myself : and to assure her that if she thinks I can do her any service in any part of the world no one will be more ready to sacrifice his life and all that is dear to him in obedience to her commands.

C. GUILOT [*alias* DE FOE] to [ROBERT HARLEY].

1710, December 26. Edinburgh—I have constantly written to you by the same conveyance as this, and have given you an exact account of everything material in this part. I am particularly unhappy in not having the least hint anyway whether mine come to hand or no, which restrains me very much in my writing, fearing what hands it may fall into and knowing the jealousy and temper of the people I have to do with.

I think I may boast to you of my little management in this place, where the people are brought to be perfectly easy in her Majesty's measures and have a full confidence in her Majesty's concern for the general good. I might assume the words, I have brought them to this, but I leave that to your charity.

I have done myself the honour on all occasions to do justice to her Majesty's measures in the late changes, in answer to the clamour of some certain people, which had reached thus far, and which began to spread here both against yourself and against other of her Majesty's faithful servants, and in this I have the happiness to assure you there is none of that noise heard here; but the dependence of the honest people here is on your zeal for the liberties of your country and her Majesty's justice to the constitution, and when they hear of some let into posts of trust and power, whose former measures they have reason to apprehend, they frequently conclude their safety depends upon her Majesty and the counsels of Mr. H[arley].

This is the plain and true state of the temper here. I hope you will not suspect I flatter myself in it; if it were otherwise I know my duty better than to conceal it.

Here have been two vile illnatured pamphlets prepared, both of which have fallen into my hands in manuscript, and I think I have prevented both their printing. The first was advertised in the Gazette here, and called the "Scots Atalantis." The printer being my 'acquaintance I got a sight of it, but could not get a copy, however I warned him against venturing to print it; upon his refusing which the author sent for it again, and he knows not the messenger. It was full of invectives against the Queen and Government, the Parliament, and especially the members sent from hence to the Peers; it had some banter on the Lord Glennochy and some satire upon families which appeared mere Scottish, but otherwise it seemed to be done in England or at least by some hand that had been lately there. The messenger said, he that sent the advertisement was a lord, and gave the printer 2s. 6d. for putting it in the first time, and paid him for a second; but on my warning the printer he refused to put in the second, and they have never yet sent to know the reason, but I suppose on his returning the copy they care not to be so much known as to receive the money back.

The other pamphlet is called "Atalantis Major" and is a bitter invective against the Duke of Argyll, the Earl of Mar, and the election of the Peers. It is certainly written by some English man and I have some guess at the man, but dare not be positive. I have hitherto kept this also from the press and believe it will be impossible for them to get it printed here after the measures I have taken. The party I got it of pretends the copy came from England, but I am of another opinion. I shall trouble you no farther about it, because if possibly I can get it copied I will transmit the copy by next post, for I have the original in my hand. They expect I shall encourage and assist them in the managing it and till I can take a copy I shall not undeceive them. I beg your favourable construction of my conduct in an age so nice as this.

Endorsed by Harley :—"Mr. Guilot."

EARL RIVERS to [ROBERT HARLEY].

1710, December 26—I was to look for Lord Mohun but find he is gone to Epsom for some days. I met Mr. Methuen whom I find very reasonable, and desires to be employed wherever he can be serviceable.

He says there is a concern of his depending in the Treasury which he desired I would mention to you for dispatch, and give him when that is done six weeks time to settle his affairs in the country, and he'll go wherever it shall be desired. There is not in England nor the world a properer person for foreign affairs. I am very uneasy that Cadogan is not removed from being Viceroy over me, pray prevail with the Queen to dispose of his command as I formerly desired.

Dr. White Kennett to [Robert Harley].

1710, December 27—The merchants trading to Leghorn had a just sense of your good and generous disposition to countenance their earnest desire for the continuance of a chaplain to her Majesty's subjects in that port, and they were put in hopes that there wanted nothing but form in dispatching Mr. Taubman to succeed my brother.

They are under great surprise and trouble to find so much difficulty in that affair, which for four years together created no other trouble than that of a short letter by her Majesty's command to declare her royal resolution to maintain that liberty as founded on the law of nations. They begin to fear that they are not rightly understood; all they desire is that Mr. Taubman may be sent with the like letters of commission and protection that my brother obtained, of which I ordered copies to be presented to my Lord Dartmouth and to be put into your and other hands.

If it be objected that my brother did act as chaplain to the Envoy only, the matter of fact was plainly this:—upon the threats and some attempts of the Pope and Inquisition to disturb my brother, Dr. Newton, her Majesty's Envoy at Florence, did think it a proper expedient at that time to give him another title as his own chaplain, to bring the matter of dispute within a narrower compass, and to dispose the Papal power to a more easy connivance at him. The same prudential method may be taken by her Majesty's present Envoy without raising any new controversy.

But however, if the favour which they think so very reasonable be denied or much longer delayed, I ought to endeavour as much as in me lies to quiet the minds of people who will be apt to look upon the interest of trade and the honour of our religion to suffer too much, if the British factory at Leghorn be now deprived of the exercise of their religion in that free port, where a fuller liberty is still allowed to the Jews and Turks, and is not yet taken away from any other British factory in any other part of the world.

P. Schuyler to the Rev. ——.

1710, December 30. City of Albany—Your primitive zeal for propagating of the Christian Religion, your forwardness in promoting that noble design of the conversion of our Indians, and your kind offers to me when at London, make me presume to trouble you with this letter which after the tender of my humble service comes to acquaint you that our five nations of Indians did not only with great joy receive the glad tidings of the honourable Society's resolutions of sending our missionaries to them, but do heartily long for their coming. I have been in the Indian country and laid out the ground for the fort, the chapel and houses for the missionaries, the officers of the fort, &c. The plan I sent to General Nicolson who will show it to the Society, and the charge will not exceed nine hundred pounds sterling; if it were laid out in goods bought at London and consigned to Robert Livingston, junior, merchant and present Mayor of Albany, that sum would finish the work and something over to the missionaries, for by sending the money in goods'it will give cent. per cent. There is such an earnest desire and longing in these poor nations for the arrival of the missionaries, and they have already discharged the popish emissaries to come among them; if they should meet with a disappointment in this it will be hard to bring them to such a temper again. I doubt not but you will give your assistance and advice in promoting of so pious a work and that the missionaries will be quickly sent over. I heartily wish our American Church were so happy as to have such an overseer as the Reverend Dr. Stubbs, it would be of great advantage of the church. I hope the Society will prosecute their intended designs and not leave our Indians in darkness and so their poor though precious souls be lost for ever. This with my hearty thanks for all your civilities and my sincere wishes for your prosperity.

The Earl of Teviot to [Robert Harley].

1710, December 31. London—I beg your assistance in a case so unprecedented as the usage I have met with from the Duke of Marlborough in relation to my employments, without any shadow of reason disposed of from me, and thereby a strain put upon my reputation for seven years past. Could I take up so much of your time as would explain my case I doubt not you would join in getting me redress.

[Daniel] De F[oe] to [Robert Harley].

1710-11, January 1. Edinburgh—I am humbly to ask your pardon that I have not been able to send you yet the copy of the book which in my last I gave you notice of, yet I have with some difficulty and merely by force prevented its going to the press; I shall yet in a few days compass an opportunity to get it copied. I am very anxious about my letters yet I presume to give you hints of what occurs here.

The concern of the people here has been quieted, as I formerly noted, but a new suggestion rises now of some mischief awaiting them from the case of Greenshields whose petition and appeal lies now before the House of Lords and whose whole case has from its beginning threatened them here with that formidable creature a Toleration. I have with your licence always taken so much freedom in my laying these things before you as to state rather the interest of the government than the merits of the cause; but here, I think, both argue against countenancing this attempt. I am no bigot and farther yet from a friend to coercions of any kind. But the liberty obtained here by connivance is so great, the people that will accept of a Toleration except without oaths to the government so few, the design of seeking it so manifestly a plot upon the public peace, and the consequences apparently so distracting to the people here, who are now so happily easy under all her Majesty's measures, that I cannot but in duty to her Majesty, and in obedience to the orders you were pleased to give me, acquaint you of the case, and humbly offer it to your consideration whether at least this may be a time for it.

There is another affair relating to justices imposing the oaths to the ministers which requires a little [of] your thoughts when at leisure, and which I shall be better qualified to lay before you in a post or two.

I have been so long here without your commands either to stay or to remove that indeed I had presumed to come away, had the roads been passable; my circumstances also unhappily disabling me to subsist longer, without your goodness had been extended as usual for my support. I cannot but presume to hint, however remote to my present sphere, the time for ways and means being at hand, that a contrivance of some people in England to prevent the Government in the article of funds, has gone that length, as they are very sure of success.

I am at a loss how to express myself on this head but I humbly lay it before you, whether it shall be expedient for her Majesty's service, to lay funds and venture there filling *by loans* or rather to think of means to raise the sums within the time, which no doubt, notwithstanding pretences of poverty, bad news abroad and divisions at home, may be effected. My anxiety on this head proceeds from my knowledge of the design above to bank the funds, and my sense of the consequences of such a disappointment.

Endorsed by Harley :—" Cl. Guilot."

J[OHN] D[RUMMOND] to [ROBERT HARLEY].

1711, January [2–]13. Amsterdam—The honour you have procured me of Mr. Secretary St. John's friendship and correspondence hinders me from troubling you with my letters directly to yourself. What I have now to say is properly about matters immediately under your care. I am now paying the last 30,000*l.* of the contract for 350,000*l.* made with you by Messrs. Hoare, Gibbon, &c.

[*Here follows a long financial statement.*]

You have now the Duke with you, and I hope he will be so much his own friend as to approve him yours, at least in what concerns the public; as for his sincerity you are so much used to it that you cannot doubt of it. He takes his measures at this present time very much from the Elector of Hanover which are imparted to him by General Beuls; he had affected to make his court extremely there of late and I am sure with some success, depend upon this, and I need not recommend secrecy to a person of your prudence.

Mr. Cadogan has been pleased to say at the Hague that Lord Albemarle has been playing loose game with the Duke, for that he had promised to go over with his Grace and vote right as he terms it. I think I know Lord A. too well to believe that he would ever have allowed that use to be made of him, but Mr. Cadogan is also something dissatisfied as I am informed with Prince Eugene, for contradicting what he had so industriously spread abroad, that the Prince would not serve if the Duke demitted. By the express which Lord Townshend has sent you over the affairs in Spain you will see are nowise desperate, and people will think the supporting the war here more necessary than they did not long ago, when they were passing their criticism on the Queen's Speech and Commons' Address. We are all sorry that Mr. Hill is not able to come over in room of Mr. Cadogan for he is certainly the properest person in England for that station. There is a great revolution at the Court of Berlin and it will require a good deal of management to keep that king perfectly right, the premier minister Count Wartenberg, through whom both this State and several ministers of the Allies did work, having desired and obtained his demission. It is true the Duke of Marlborough affected to negociate military matters both without him and Lord Raby, and unknown to Monsieur Schmettau the Prussian minister at the Hague, a man of true worth and honesty as ever was born, and made all such bargains with and through Monsieur Gromkau, a travelling military minister, indigent of money and common sense.

Before I conclude I must assure you that the opinion of the leading men of this State in relation to matters in England is in proportion grown as good as our credit in money affairs, and this with daily increase, and I flatter myself that they will tell me when anything happens with you that they dislike, or when they desire that anything should be brought about for the good of the public. I left the Hague last night full of joy that matters in Spain were not so ill as the French made us believe, and at the same time concerned for Mr. Stanhope's misfortune, which Count Staremberg gives the best account of to the Imperial ministers, and you will no doubt have the same with you. I have seen a proposal here for subscribing four millions at six per cent interest, redeemable by Parliament, and that any who subscribe or pay in one hundred pounds in money may bring in two hundred pounds of National Debt. It is very well liked here, and may engage people to send over orders for buying in of Navy bonds and Victualling bonds, especially when they are certain that it will be put in execution.

H. St. John to [Robert Harley,] the Chancellor of the Exchequer.

1710-11, January 8. Whitehall—You must forgive the trouble of one or two letters concerning our West India expedition, and I assure you that you shall have no more about it.

Two frigates, who are to carry to the Colonies of North America the Queen's orders for making the necessary preparations, will be ready to sail in a fortnight. I have got from the Ordnance two thousand muskets and the proportion of ammunition to be sent with them. I have likewise taken care to have thirty old sergeants got ready who must be established at ensign's pay till placed in the country whither they go. The enclosed particulars must likewise be provided against the departure of these ships, and this is all the charge which will require ready money, except some small matter in advance to the sergeants.

I have spoken to Mr. Moore, and he has been with me this morning, to let me know that he has taken effectual care to have in time the things mentioned in the enclosed account; for which I entreat you to let Mr. Brydges issue the money, or to direct some other way of doing it with as little observation as possible.

As to Nicholson I find upon sounding of him, that he will be willing to go immediately back again, which is absolutely necessary. He was established at 20s. per diem, and if his establishment were raised, as indeed it ought to be, I fancy he would be satisfied.

The squadron and troops which are to follow in March we have in our power; morally speaking, if we keep our secret, we shall succeed.

C. Guilot [alias De Foe] to [Robert Harley].

1710-11, January 9. Edinburgh—I have since my last had occasion of doing I hope some little service here, the commission of the Assembly having been sitting for this week past. I have been forward to acquaint you every time I write of the good disposition of the people here, and especially how well the ministers behave, yet at this time the members met being great, they were not without some hot spirits, who had divers projects and made several essays to bring the meeting into some heats. First they were for an address to the Queen, in which they would have been glad to introduce some uneasy things about Greenshields about Toleration and about invasion of Churches in the north. But with some help they have been put off from this.

Then they were for appointing a fast and had that design gone on, it might have been hard to have kept them from bringing in some odd reasons for a fast, for fear of having no good reasons to give; but the news of our loss in Spain falling in some moved for a fast upon that account, which had some real foundation, but then the gentlemen that had a worse design in it dropped their motion, and so the whole fell to the ground for that time.

There fell an unhappy jar in their way of a rabble upon a number of their ministers in a Presbytery meeting in Angus, in which many of the ministers were stoned and beaten. This is put in a way of process in the criminal court and at that they are something pacified. The gentlemen of that country have really acted too imprudently in it and thereby given them advantages against them, which they need not have done.

Last night the Commission rose again and the ministers are most of them dispersed and I am glad to write in this time of uneasiness that they parted so well.

Endorsed by Harley :—" Mr. Guilot."

The EARL OF WEMYSS, Vice-Admiral of North Britain, to [ROBERT HARLEY].

1710-11, January 9. Wemyss—I enclose you an information of an accident that happened ten days ago, of which I have acquainted the Lords of the Admiralty.

There is great complaint made in this country about our convoys and cruisers, and the merchants and gentry who think themselves losers have teased me out of my life to represent it to her Majesty. They say that for want of due orders or due care the Queen's ships lie in Leith Road four, five, and six months at a time. It is as impossible to satisfy all trading people in these concerns as it is to justify these neglects. I shall not decline any trouble if I can be of any use that way. My intelligence upon the coast from my deputies should be better than anybody's else, and the house I live in lying so upon it that by a signal I can hail any of the Queen's ships and inform them what intelligence I have of privateers, or merchantmen kept in port for want of convoy.

[*Encloses* " Information about a Fly-boat now lying in Leith Road " of about 300 tons, suspected to be French.]

The DUKE OF ARGYLL to [ROBERT HARLEY].

1710-11, January 11—I desired Mr. Benson, because I thought he would see you to-day, to tell you that after what passed the other day in your house, I think I should no longer delay putting an end to my affair by sending the warrant to the Attorney. I hope, now that the Queen is no longer in doubt as to the state of our affairs in Spain, you will be so good as to let me know my fate. I was told the other day by Mr. St. John, that you only waited to know how affairs there stood to settle that service, and her Majesty was pleased to tell me that in two or three days she would let me know what service she had for me and that she did think I could not serve in Flanders. Upon which I writ to Holland and gave orders to dispose of my horses and other things there; so that I now know where I cannot serve, and I beg you will not let me be in pain where I am to serve, that is if I am to serve any more.

The Earl of Seafield to [Robert Harley].

1710-11, January 13—I have a great favour to beg of you which I am confident you will not refuse. Lord Godolphin gave me all the volumes of Rymer's *Foedera* except the last. I am informed that others have got the eleventh volume. One word from you to Mr. Lowndes will do it, and I am desirous to have this book complete.

H[enry] St. John to [Robert Harley].

1710-11, January 13 Whitehall— Desires that some part of the money about which he had spoken may be supplied by the following Tuesday, as the stores and goods must then be delivered and sent on board the *Leopard* and *Sapphire*, appointed for this service.

Captain Francis Wyvill to [Robert Harley].

1710-11, January 13. Albemarle Street—Being appointed to command the *Cumberland* at Deptford, yesterday came to me to enter the service, in a fine blue coat, a waterman called Bland, who was concerned in Greg's trial. If I would give him employment he would get me twenty or thirty able seamen. His being in disguise gave me some suspicion of him, which I thought fit to let you know of.

Though I am now Captain of the *Cumberland,* but a third-rate, my pretensions are great in the Navy, and there are two vacant flags. I beg you will intercede with the Queen that I may have no more hardships done me, nor officer preferred over my head.

Sir John Bland to [Robert Harley].

1710-11, January 14—This is only to remind you to remember me in time, for I suppose the rout is begun and will be quickly over. I cannot see what places there are that I can hold except in the Exchequer and Household, and in the last of them you know I had a place promised but was forced to quit my pretensions to it and take another, and was but indifferently used in that.

The Earl of Winchilsea to [Robert Harley].

1710-11, January 15—Being informed this day from hands I cannot but give much credit to, that Lord Jersey is designed the government of the Ports and to be First Lord of the Admiralty, I should be wanting to myself not to urge my own pretensions to one, if not both, of those employments, preferably to any other, not only from my past services and sufferings, but from the late hopes and promises which have been given me, that the Queen designed me some recompense for the large share of my own private fortune I have sacrificed to her service. I shall only add that, as I came to town at a minute's warning on her Majesty's commands, and have continued here some time very much to the prejudice of my own affairs, I cannot doubt but I shall at length have the satisfaction of knowing how her Majesty will be pleased to dispose of me; and I entreat the favour that you will appoint me a speedy time of waiting on you to give me an opportunity of speaking a few words on this subject.

The Duke of Argyll to [Robert Harley].

1710–11, January 16—I hope you will pardon my giving you once more the trouble of begging to know if her Majesty is pleased to have any more service for me in her army. I have all this time had but two reasons given me for the delay, the one by yourself which was that of Lord Peterborough's being here, the other by Mr. St. John, which was your not having heard of Monsieur Staremberg. I think neither of them do now exist, my Lord Peterborough is gone, and you know the state of Monsieur Staremberg's affairs, so that now I hope I shall be no longer in doubt. I neither have nor do I now pretend to say that I deserve anything, but surely I may at this time of day hope at least to be told so, and that is all I pretend to, only that if I am not thought fit to serve any longer, I hope you will not think it unreasonable to give me leave to dispose of the troop of Guards. If this favour is not too much for me, I shall be perfectly pleased with my fate, since I cannot charge myself with having done anything either with regard to my duty to the Queen, my friendship to you, or my service to the public, but what I would be proud to do over again.

J. D[rummond] to [Robert Harley].

1710–11, January [16–]27, new style. Amsterdam—The accounts you are pleased to give me of your credit are very agreeable, and the remittance that is come stops the mouths of your most inveterate enemies of which I must say there are very few now remaining, people's eyes being much opened and will daily grow more clear. If you finish that of the Exchequer notes with the Bank all the rest will easily follow, that is the greatest shock to credit entirely removed.

I wish you may find time to write me such a letter as you are pleased to promise me, I am sure I shall make no ill use of it. Sir Theodore Janssen, I suppose influenced by Furnese or some of that gang, has proposed to Gibbon and some of my friends to employ Furnese's correspondent, one Clifford here, who has been running down your credit with violence. They write to me to apply to you to recommend me to Sir Theodore and that he don't employ the others, but do in this as you please. Gibbon seems much concerned about it and indeed is more than I am.

As for the great man [Marlborough] deal with him as he deserves. I have nothing more to say for him. I believe his wife may advise him sooner to curse God and die than be reconciled to you. If he let such a wife and such a son in law manage him may he fall in the pit they have digged for him. I have a little secret history to trouble you with next post but I am sorry to find one thing public which I wrote, I mean Decker knows that his brother in law had prepared an answer to Lord Poulett's postscript which was rejected; this is wrote over again and does me harm with my friend.

H. St. John to [Robert Harley].

1710–11, January 17—My Lord Marlborough desired me to write you word that he would come to my office whenever you pleased to appoint, that he had something of moment to say to you and to me together.

I find by the Duke of Shrewsbury that he is desirous to have some of the horse guards over with him the next year, in expectation of a battle, and horse being the only article wherein the enemy can pretend to be equal to us. I hope the Queen will let the Scotch, at least a detachment of them, go. Besides these he may have some squadrons of dragoons; and I think after that he cannot grumble if we take five battalions for our attempt upon Quebec. Pray do me the justice to believe that I am not light nor whimsical in this project. It will certainly succeed if the secret is preserved, and if it succeeds you will have done more service to Britain in half a year, than the ministers who went before you did in all their administration. I hope you will support me in it since I have gone so far.

We dine with the Speaker on Friday.

I hope the Queen takes notice by this quarrel between Sutton and Munden that, if she does not exert herself, the army will be none of hers. I am preparing a state of the General Officers, and if she pleases will break Lord Marlborough's faction, by doing what is right in its own nature, and without giving him any just mortification as General.

George Lockhart to [Robert Harley].

1710–11, January 19—On behalf of a kinsman and his neighbour in the country, Major Douglas, who hopes to be appointed governor of the Leeward Islands.

John Drummond to [Robert Harley].

1711, [January 23-]February 2, N.S. Amsterdam—Recommending to Harley's acquaintance and protection his worthy friend Mr. [Henry] Watkins, whose services and good reputation are well known.

Leopold, Duke of Lorraine to [Robert Harley].

1710–11, January 26 [*received*]—Baron de Forstner one of my Chamberlains and Councillors of State is come to England to supplicate her Majesty to remember my interests at the general peace and the assurances she has made of honouring me with her protection. I request your good offices also his in the matter, and beg you to place every confidence in what Baron de Forstner will say to you on my part. *French.*

Ker of Kersland to [Robert Harley].

1710–11, January 29. London—Having since I saw you declined to meet with some who are not in your interest, which I am told this morning is so far resented that enquiry is making if I be owing any debt in town in order to buy it up and affront me. I have been very cautious in that matter for I owe very little in England. So since I am here on the public account and there are designs against my credit, and my estate and effects are at a great distance I shall be much obliged if you procure me some from her Majesty; if not let me know that I may provide another way, for I will not have it in the power of anyone to affront me. I shall attend you at six this evening and shall show you the state of the case which I have drawn up in obedience to your desire, and some other papers.

Charles Rudolph, Duke of Wurtemberg, to the Duke of Marlborough.

1711, [January 31-]February 10, N.S. The Hague—Mr. Sweet has just paid over 157,000 florins for the troops under his command, but this sum is not sufficient to pay off the arrears for 1709, on which account 24,000 florins are still due; and nothing has been received for the year 1710. Desires Marlborough's interest to obtain payment for both years, otherwise the troops will not be in a proper state for another campaign. *Signed. French.*

SIR WILLIAM FLEMING to ROBERT HARLEY.

1710–11, February 1—The importunity of my next brother, Henry Fleming, a doctor of divinity, occasions you this trouble to desire your assistance to get him the deanery of Carlisle, now said to be vacant, who I hope will make all the returns of gratitude in his power. Colonel Graham can give you his character as well as any one.

LORD DARTMOUTH to THE SAME.

1710–11, February 1. Whitehall—Instructions to pay Colonel or Governor Nicholson all arrears due to him on account of his late expedition, a further sum of five hundred guineas as a gratuity, and an allowance of forty shillings a day upon the public establishment from January 1 last—as soon as possible because the service requires that the Colonel should go away on Monday next.

CH. DARTIQUENAVE to Brigadier MASHAM, St. James's.

1710–11, February 3—My very good friend Mr. Clayton, who is one of the agents of the Treasury, has so much business in his other employment in the Exchequer that he finds it impracticable to execute both, and therefore designs to ask leave to resign. I served some years in the same office till Lord Godolphin for reasons unknown to me was pleased to deprive me of almost the only subsistence I then had for myself, father, mother, and sister. I beg you will give my humble service to Mrs. Masham and press her to recommend this matter with some earnestness to Mr. Harley.

I have reason to believe Mr. Lowndes will oppose anything that may be for my advantage.

[EDWARD HARLEY] to his Aunt, ABIGAIL HARLEY, at Eywood.

1710–11, February 6—My Lord Poulett said a thing in the House which has set both W—— and me up in arms against him. In his speech against the Place Bill, which the Commons sent up on Friday, he took occasion to say that the Bill was a phantom that had haunted both Houses for several years and arose from the dregs of the discontented of both parties. Had it been never so true I think it might have been spared at this juncture when there is more occasion for gentle remedies. The Lords threw out the Bill for repealing the Act for a general naturalisation, which makes the common people very angry. I can give you but a very indifferent account of the finery of the day having seen no soul that was at Court but my father, and he was not among the ladies. The Duchess of Bucks and Lady Poulett were scarce able to move under the load of jewels they had on. There has not been so fine nor so full a court since King Charles's time. The common people are very much pleased that so much respect is shewn to the Queen.

E 82470.

T T

CAPTAIN HENRY BAKER.

1710-11, February 8—Affidavit made by George Shuckburgh, clerk, before Thomas Gery, that about August 21, 1710, he fell in company with Captain Baker at Rye, who used language of a seditious and scandalous nature touching the administration of public affairs, the hereditary right of the Queen to the throne; and said that all who were friends to Dr. Sacheverell were rogues and rascals; &c., &c.

EARL RIVERS to [ROBERT HARLEY].

1710-11, February 11—I was this day with the Duke of Shrewsbury and after talking of public matters, I mentioned my own concern; and told him that I had offered my service to Portugal or Spain, but was answered that I could not be spared here. I foresaw long what would be my fate knowing very well the difficulties which would happen with the Duke of Marborough (whom I met there). He was not apprized of my offering my service elsewhere. In the conclusion I told him since matters were so, if I had no mark of the Queen's favour shown me I should make a poor figure in the world; he then asked me what I could propose, I told him since it was so that I could not serve abroad, which I very much desired, it would be some satisfaction to me, that I should be paid as General of the horse, (which I desire may be a New Year's gift) till I am otherwise provided for; by which I mean that if a troop of Guards fall the Duke of Northumberland may be removed to that, and I to his regiment. He was so kind to offer to speak to the Queen immediately, but I desired that you might together propose it to her, I don't doubt of neither of your friendship. I will only add the hardships I suffered in the reign of the last Ministry, compelled to sell my troop for upwards of 5,000l. less than ever troop was sold for, no equipage money when I went for Spain, though Lord Galway and Lord Portman had each of them 3,000l.; and I served the campaign of Liége as Lieutenant-General without pay which comes to 2,000l. I desire you will lay this whole matter before the Queen.

LORD HALIFAX to [ROBERT HARLEY].

1710[-11], February 11—I have considered the scheme of the Lottery, and examined the calculations with all the attention I could, and am extremely pleased with the contrivance; 'tis certainly more advantageous and more inviting than the last, and I have something to tell you, will make you laugh about the comparison. The double chance in this last is finely contrived, for in a lottery where the hopes of good fortune is the chief allurement, the more scope and swing is given to people's expectations and fancies the more certain you are to draw them in. There is one further improvement that I will offer to your better judgment. I believe the smallness of the tickets, and the great number of them, which people are obliged to keep for the several payments that are to be made, are very troublesome; they are apt to be lost or mislaid: for every blank they have 32, and for every benefit 64 little pieces of paper so easily scattered about that they are obliged often to have recourse to Parliament for clauses to renew them that have been lost or destroyed. Now in this new lottery where the course of payment is fixed, might not there be a method established, for giving out orders for their re-payment in the course in which they are drawn; these orders would be more easily kept, assigned, and transferred, and consequently of more value, but this is submitted to you.

[Daniel] De Foe to [Robert Harley].

1710–11, February 13. [London]—Though I confess the honour
you are pleased to do me in frequent and long audience is very great,
yet, considering the weight of public affairs which lie on your hands, and
the several things which after so long absence I have to give you an
account of, some of which, if not all, may be of importance, I thought
it my duty to save as much as possible your time and trouble by
minuting down thus the heads of things. That you may please to call
for such first as you find most proper, and such as you please may be
after laid before you in writing.

Of the temper of the people in Scotland, their temper when I came
there, their temper when I left them, what uneasinesses they have left, and
how they may be kept easy of the affairs of the Church, Greenshields,
toleration, common prayer, intrusion and the rabbles upon their
Presbytery in the North.

Of the mission of Dr. O., the breaking up of all correspondence
between them and the Dissenters in London, and of their new agent, the
Commission's motion for a correspondence, &c.

The state of the civil and military administration there, with
characters of persons, and conduct as they respect the late changes.

Of the state of the debate between Johnston and Hamilton, or between
the merchants and the traders in the election for Edinburgh.

Of the project pushing on by Sir Pat. Johnston at the expense of the
city of Edinburgh for a dock &c. at Leith, of the raising men in the
Highlands and the directing General Maitland to that work.

Of the Assembly, their last division and how cooled, about a medium
for quieting them in the nicety of appointing Fasts &c. about a Commissioner and about her Majesty's letter to their next meeting.

Of all these particulars I may have several things to lay before you,
useful and proper for your observation in your managing that difficult
people in the North.

In matters relating to England I humbly crave leave to offer that if
you think it proper I should turn my thoughts that way, I may have
something to say on the following subjects :—

Credit and of proper means for filling the Lottery, which I hear
already some people please themselves with expectation of seeing
disappointed.

Funds and therein of a clause in the Coal duty, which very much
sinks the Revenue.

Post Office and some circumstances which may enlarge that duty.

Stamp Office and some particulars of increasing that duty.

With some brief hints of other Funds, which if you approve of may
be enlarged upon afterwards.

African Company and how to make them useful to advance a sum
of money on their new proposal which is now preparing.

French trade and how it may be opened most to advantage both of
the nation and of the revenue.

I ask your pardon for the length of this, and hope it is not
impertinent. I shall wait your commands on which of these things to
begin, that I may be as little troublesome, and as much useful as
possible.

Postscript.—Having given you so long a diversion already I should
have forborne saying anything of the unpleasant part; but a long and
expensive journey, family importunities and all the *et ceteras* that make
a dependent always importunate—these force me, in spite of blushes,

T T 2

to remind you of the usual period being passed of that relief, which by whatever hand I received it, was originally owing to your goodness.

I shall venture to say nothing of merit, but this, that as I resolve to have an entire dependence on your hand, so I would gladly be made useful, that I may not be an unprofitable servant.

Endorsed by Harley:—" Mr. Claude Guilot."

[JOHN DRUMMOND to ROBERT HARLEY.]

1710[-11], February [13-]24, new style. [Amsterdam] — Our misfortunes in Spain increase. Gerona is not only surrendered but the Miquilets begin to rebel against King Charles. I hope your fleet will be in time, otherwise matters will have a dismal prospect in Catalonia. If the young Duke [Argyll] can redress these matters in Spain, I hope the old Duke [Marlborough] will not be jealous of his being employed there.

I send you here inclosed a letter to peruse which please return.

I long to know if a certain great man put much money into your funds this year, for 60,000*l.* was put in here in a lump and it is not the first of that nature that has been done; but I entreat, this to yourself.

Mr. Secretary St. John's letters have been of so great use on this side that greater could not be expected.

[*Enclosed is a letter from James Milnes, dated* 30 *January,* 1710-11, *on financial matters.*]

EARL RIVERS to [ROBERT HARLEY].

1710-11, February 14—I hope you have already shown the Queen my last letter or told her the contents of it, so that when I see you, I may know my fate. I ask no great pensions nor force myself into the service, but hope I may be allowed my pay as general of the horse till a troop of guards falls, or the Northumberland regiment. The Duke of Shrewsbury will join with you in recommending me to the favour of her Majesty.

' The DUKE OF ARGYLL to [ROBERT HARLEY].

1710-11, February 17—I have considered the affair I had the honour to hint to you yesterday as well as I am able to do with the little understanding God has given me, and my resolution is settled not to serve any longer unless I may be made serve so as not to be undone every way. The Duke of Shrewsbury and Mr. St. John told me they would lay the matter last night before her Majesty and would let me know her pleasure. To be plain if you have not a mind that I should be forced out of the service something will be done to get things right, but if you think it not fit that I should serve any more I must submit.

[DANIEL] DE FOE to [ROBERT HARLEY].

1710-11, February 19. [London]—In obedience to your commands I have applied myself more particularly to think of a proper person to serve her Majesty, as Commissioner to the General Assembly; and in order to represent things with more clearness, I have with the best of my judgment drawn out short descriptions or characters of the persons that seem proper for that charge, which I beg leave to lay before you for observation, with this exception only, that these characters are more particularly confined to their conduct in the affair before you, their temper, interest, and acceptableness with the people there, and the Government here, since, as I conceive, a person may be fit and acceptable on one side, and not on the other; but that the present case is to find one, if possible, that may be so to both.

From hence I conclude the whole Squadroni utterly unqualified as a set of men though otherwise well enough with the Kirk, yet unfit for the Queen's interest to consist with ; and this is the only objection I have to my Lord Polwarth, who would otherwise be a man without exception, both for sense, moderation and agreeableness to both sides, and perhaps were some method used with him, might be separated from them. This also removes my Lord Yester from my thoughts, though he has also no interest among the ministers, which is an additional exception.

I come next to the persons you were pleased to name and which I humbly objected against :—as first the Marquess of Annandale, and second the Marquess of Lothian. The first is of no reputation on either side, because steady to none, nor would the ministers have any confidence in him or come into anything he should propose. The second has made himself odious by scandalous vices and immoralities, sordid covetousness, and some things so offensive, that it might be some question, whether they would not rather think of delating him for scandal, than receiving him as a Commissioner.

If I did not think it my duty to lay everything nakedly before you, I should not go such a length in characters, especially of men you were pleased to name, but I hope the necessity of giving you a clear view of things will excuse me.

It is really not the easiest thing, in a place where a Church is so generally abandoned of her nobility to find a man who will suit both sides of the present circumstance, yet I shall name a few of such as I think may be depended upon.

The Earl of Polwarth (except as before excepted).

The Earl of Loudoun.—I do not take his character to be so clear with the Church as I take him to have a true view of her Majesty's interest, and yet to be without any visible objection on the side of the Kirk also.

The Earl of Hyndford.—I think a person without exception but doubt if he would serve.

The Earl of Buchan.—I think without exception, also perfectly agreeable to the ministers and yet to be managed ; he parted from the Squadroni in the affair of the Union and was disobliged by the last Ministry in the voting against the Court, for which my Lord Mar quarrelled with him and he lost the government of Blackness Castle. They report him to be hot, but I think I could answer for him on that head ; he is a person of great integrity and understanding, and I believe can do more with the ministers than any nobleman in Scotland.

The Earl of Wemyss.—I cannot say for his steadiness so much, but he stands well enough with the ministers and is generally beloved.

There is another person which for aught I know might be able to manage both sides very well, if other circumstances will admit. This is the old Lord Advocate. But I doubt his being tractable to measures, and is immoderately politic.

The only person I think remaining that both sides would trust is the Earl of Stair, of whom there is only this objection, his late engagement with the Squadroni.

I humbly lay these thoughts before you in' order to be farther discoursed of to-morrow, when I shall attend according to your commands.

I cannot close without some acknowledgement, though small in proportion, of your constant bounty to me; the small return I can make is a steady adhering to your interest and service, and a dependence on your goodness, that her Majesty's bounty to me and your particular favours may not be ill placed.

It is always with regret that I mention my own case to you, and your goodness has been always particular in preventing my blushes on that account. This makes me remember with thankfulness how you were pleased to anticipate my fears by telling me your last bounty, which I am now acknowledging, was not part of her Majesty's appointment. This doubles my thanks and makes me earnest to merit as much as possible so much goodness. I most humbly beg the continuance of your favour and goodness which I shall study never to forfeit.

Endorsed by Harley :—" Cl. Guilot."

CH. DARTIQUENAVE to [Brigadier MASHAM].

1710–11, February 20—This moment I parted with Mr. Clayton, who has lately written to the Treasury resigning his appointment. I beg you will join with Mrs. Masham in recommending my pretensions to the Chancellor of the Exchequer. There is no time to be lost for I know my old friend Mr. Lowndes is never unprovided of some coffeehouse companion to place in that office. If I am not always to be the most unfortunate of mankind, methinks I might promise myself success from the intercession of those persons.

EARL RIVERS to [ROBERT HARLEY].

1710–11, February 22—Matters being now settled with the Duke of Argyll that he goes for Spain, there is no occasion for me as to that service, which I should have readily undertaken (as I told my Lord Keeper) if he had waived it, I must earnestly renew my former request which is that you will intercede with her Majesty to allow me pay as General of the horse, till I am provided for, by a troop of Guards or the Northumberland regiment. I beg you won't think that it is covetousness makes me press you in this matter; but other uneasiness, the chief of which is that if I have no countenance shown me I shall make a sorry figure in the world, considering the part I have acted. There is one reason more, that is, if this is not done, I must as I designed before retire into the country till my circumstances are more easy. I hope you will lay this request before her Majesty to-day or to-morrow that when I wait on you Saturday you will be able to let me know what I may hope for.

[DANIEL] DE FOE to [ROBERT HARLEY].

1710–11, February 26. [London]—Though the other accounts I am preparing seem interrupted by this, yet I thought it my duty to have my eyes about me here also as well as my thoughts intent upon Scotland. I have had but little time since my return to look among our old friends the Whigs, and therefore could say but little when you were pleased to ask me of them. I am sorry to be witness to so much of the weakness of those I thought would have before now have (*sic*) been wiser. When I came among some of my oldest acquaintance they would hardly converse with me, because as they said I had fallen upon them in my "Review" for running down credit, yet I had not discoursed half an hour before they discovered themselves. One said he used to pay six thousand pounds in upon every land tax, but now had not paid in a farthing. Another had constantly discounted Navy bills, but would meddle with no more of them, a third would keep his money by him seven years before he would trust the Government with a farthing, and the like; and yet these gentlemen would not have it said that they run down the public credit.

They now set up to run down and discourage the Lottery and say 'tis a cheat, that the prizes carry a show of smaller odds than the last, but are but trifles except a few, and they inferior to the other; that the Fund is confused and uncertain, and the same suppositious; that the sum appropriated in particular is deficient by a great deal besides the charge of management of which no notice is taken. By this last I perceive the calculator I gave you notice of comes from them and has been among them. I am sorry to see the weakness of these people and indeed not more so, that I am apprehensive of the mischief they can do, as that no men are so inconsiderable but they may do some hurt. If you think it may be of any service, I humbly offer my thoughts that a small tract may be written about the size of the Essay upon Credit, and with the same secrecy, to explain the Lottery itself, and answer a little the coffee house clamour of ill men and make some of them blush. It may be so ordered as to be disposed all over England and into Scotland, principally among those people who are most influenced by these people, and I am verily persuaded will be mighty useful at this time.

I hope your charity will prevent any suspicion that I do this to make a charge. You are too generous to me to have any such thought enter into my heart. My whole design is to render some good service if possible to merit and make rational the bounty I do receive; and if it cost me twenty pound out of my pocket, I shall rejoice to have done anything if possible to restore these wild people to the Government interest; and the rest as well as I may I refer to yourself.

J[OHN] D[RUMMOND] to [ROBERT HARLEY].

1711, [February 28-]March 10, N.S. Amsterdam—I shall go back to the Hague on Saturday morning having promised both the Duke and Lord Orrery. The first seems to have no great hopes of success and seems sorry that there are no proposals of peace from the enemy; and fears the States may hinder him from hazarding a battle. These are all melancholy preliminaries, and before he leaves the Hague I may be able to tell you what power the States give their Deputies.

We will have much difficulty to bring people to have as good an opinion of Lord Raby as they have of Lord Townshend. I hope time and experience will get the better of prejudice and prepossession. I have complaints of you from the Tory side, who I fear want to drive things too suddenly and to extremities. I hope you will agree amongst yourselves and then nothing can hurt you, if otherwise, everything will; and a watchful diligent enemy will make good use of your divisions for their advantage.

DANIEL DE FOE* to [ROBERT HARLEY].

1710-11, March 2. [London]—I am very sorry to write to you on this occasion and indeed never thought the affair could have been

.* Signature torn off.

carried this length—especially considering what assurances were given by her Majesty's express direction at the time of the Union.

I am the more concerned, because of the quiet and good temper things were brought to there, and the difficulty there has been ever since, as well as at the Treaty, to bring it to that pass, which had never been, had not her Majesty been very faithfully served by some who perhaps have not themselves been heard of.

But it is not a time to look back. The business is how to prevent the mischief that will otherwise follow, which according to your order I have been applying myself to.

The first step I have thought of is, to let them know, and make them if possible satisfied in the belief of it :—that this part has not been concerted by the Court, that her Majesty was surprised at it and very much concerned to hear how it was carried; that all the Queen's servants (except &c.) were ordered to oppose it, and that her Majesty will do any reasonable thing to prevent the evil consequences of it.

This I hint, because I have for these three years past given them repeated assurances (and I presume by her Majesty's special direction) that the Queen would upon all such occasions take them into her protection and prevent, as far as possible, the encroachments and invasions which the heat of that party might push them upon, and this was confirmed by letters from the ministers of state at that time and by her Majesty's express command approving of the proceedings of the magistrates against this Greenshiels, whose behaviour was not insolent only to the kirkmen and ecclesiastic judicatories, which he contemned; but even to the magistrates and indeed to magistracy itself; and this is indeed one of the worst things I apprehend as the consequence of this :—that if the magistrates of the capital city may be insulted, as they were then and I fear will be again on this occasion, the little civil government there is in Scotland will be lost, and the matter will be decided in every place by tumults and rabbles;—which though mischievous everywhere will be worse there, and will never end without blood, to the destruction of her Majesty's authority and bringing all things into confusion.

For this reason I most humbly propose that if her Majesty thinks fit, these two steps, or such other as shall appear reasonable, may be taken.

1. As before to quiet them gradually with assurances that the Queen will protect their Church, in all its just rights, and encourage no innovations, &c., and let them have (as before) private hints that the Queen was not pleased with or concerned in the past transaction of the Peers, and this if you please may be my province.

2. To restrain, by management on the other hand, the insolence of those who think themselves let loose by this victory to offer new affronts to the people there, and to invade either their civil or religious rights.

These two things I humbly offer my thoughts in, in obedience to your commands, as what I conceive to be the only method to quiet them under the first surprises, and I doubt not but time and application may reconcile things better ; but if the other side gentlemen go on to renew their insulting of the magistrates, and of the kirk, and set up the common prayer book as it were by authority, I dread the consequences, and am almost assured the rabble will tear them to pieces, the consequence of which I need not insist on to you. And yet I daresay were quiet calm steps taken even that formidable creature the Liturgy would in time come to be a native of Scotland, but by violence the aversions will increase. The proposal I humbly offer here, I make the rather because the ministers there in whom you know much of the people's

, conduct is resolved have been ever since the Union persuaded that their safety depends more upon her Majesty's personal veracity, and pious , adhering to her royal word in the assurances given them of her gracious protection, than in any security by the constitution of the Treaty—and this will not only confirm that opinion, which I have always cultivated , among them, but farther endear her Majesty to them. At the same . time her Majesty may so hold the balance between them, that they may no more oppress the episcopal men, than they may invade the establishment, and I shall lay before her Majesty a scheme of such a temperament whenever you please to command it. I shall omit nothing in this juncture that may contribute to heal this breach, and to restore things , there; and if you think my going may contribute anything to making them easy I am always at your disposal. Though if you please to accept my thoughts upon that, I humbly suggest, it may not be so useful just now as some time hence; lest on my sudden return, they may think they want a correspondent here and return to the notion of settling some other agent, by which I may lose the opportunity (not the office for that is of not a penny advantage) of serving her Majesty's interest with them.

I shall attend in the evening according to your commands in order to receive what instructions you please to give in this affair, and beg if you please that I may receive them this night, because, as you were pleased to say you would not have it delayed longer than next post, I would have time enough to write to all the parts where I correspond, which is seven or eight—that, if possible, the antidote may spread as far as the poison and as fast.

Endorsed by Harley :—" Mr. Guilot, Scotland."

[DANIEL] DE FOE to [ROBERT HARLEY].

1710-11, March 3—I am really perplexing you with letters on the occasion of this new affair of Scotland, but hope my zeal for the service will excuse my impertinence. I have had my thoughts very intent upon the thing itself, and have been up all night writing letters upon the subject, according to my proposal and your commands; but a new thought offering itself I could not but lay it before you for your approbation, and this is, whether if a small pamphlet of two or three sheets at most, were written to allay the fears, and lessen the surprise of the people there, to dispose them to consider calmly of things, and a little encourage them—whether you may not think it useful at such a juncture as this, and follow it with a second at some distance of time to improve and apply the first. This I can send from hence in manuscript and print it at Edinburgh, and privately convey them among the ministers all over Scotland, and I am persuaded, submitting it at the same time to your commands, that it may do a very great service. I am sorry to mention the expense, and should not if my unhappy craving circumstances would bear it. But as I entirely submit that to yourself, so I shall go to the utmost length I can without a demand ; but if I speak my own sense I think if it came to thirty or forty or fifty pounds, it would be well placed, and may do more service just now than modesty will let me name. But I forbear to urge my own opinion. I shall attend in the evening according to your command.

Dr. HUMFREY GOWER to [ROBERT HARLEY].

1710-11, March 3. St. John's College, Cambridge—The gentleman who waits upon you with this letter has not found it an easy matter to engage me thus far in his business. He is a person of prime note and eminence amongst us for his great skill in his faculty, that of music, in which he has commenced Doctor, and is very well known and much esteemed both here and abroad for his abilities in that way. He was bred in and for the Queen's Chapel, and an organist's place there is what he has long hoped for, and he thinks his claim in that particular to be reasonable and just. He was hardly dealt with by some of the late ministry on a very trifling account, for he was by order from above banished the University, in effect, and deprived of his whole subsistence. He was represented as no friend to the government, and yet I know him to have been very zealous in her Majesty's service.

But I have gone further than I gave him reason to expect. He desired a letter from me to help him to gain access to your presence, and I have undertaken to do no more.

[HENRY ST. JOHN to ROBERT HARLEY.]

1710–11, [March 5,] nine at night—I doubt you will think me too great a scribbler but I cannot help it. This moment I came from Lord R[ochester] to whom I opened in the best manner I could the Duke of Shr[ewsbury]'s opinion in relation to the impeachment. I find that I can easily enough prevail with him, provided it were possible to draw the Duke of Somerset into the same measure, but this he thinks impracticable, and urges a promise made by the Duke of Ar[gyll] and himself to vote with Somerset in this affair. The latter it seems told the Queen, when she was commending Harcourt's argument, and in a manner asking him to concur with her, that indeed it was extremely fine, but that it had not convinced him.

However necessary his Grace may be at this time, hereafter I hope good measures will not be neglected, or bad ones pursued, because he cannot be convinced.

I told you Hambden came to the Duke of Somerset, but my information was wrong; it was Morton in the name of Hambden and others.

Parker was with the Dukes of Somerset and Devon[shire] this afternoon. Holt died at three o'clock.

[The DUKE OF SHREWSBURY to ROBERT HARLEY.]

1710–11, March 6—The letters I received from you last night enclosed are of a villanous and dangerous nature, I hope you have or will communicate them soon to the Lord President, and that a time may very soon be appointed to meet and consider what should be done. In my opinion the Duke of Marlborough ought to have advice by this night's post; it may be of consequence for Seissan's correspondence who being discovered should have warning as soon as can be. If a means can be found to have more of Guiscard's letters either on this or the other side the water, it should not be neglected; but my present opinion is that he should be seized without much delay, though perhaps there would be some advantage in its not being done so as that it could be written over to Holland by this post, but that the Duke of Marlborough might know it to give Seissan notice to advertise his correspondence a post before it is made public, as it unavoidably will be as soon as he is seized.

We are to be at the Cockpit this morning, I know not whether you intend to come thither. I am at leisure to wait on you alone, or meet the others any hour you will appoint this whole day, for though her Majesty goes to the House of Lords, I am obliged to no attendance there. I hope you are better but if you are not and keep home let me know what hour it will be convenient for you, and I will be sure to come to you.

[LADY DUPPLIN] to her Aunt, ABIGAIL HARLEY, at Eywood.

1710-11, March 8. London—This family has in a particular manner a great deal of reason to own the providence of God in many signal instances and I hope we shall never forget his goodness to us this day. To-day the Marquis de Guiscard was taken up as he was walking in the Park for high treason, corresponding with France. He was brought before the Cabinet Council to be examined (they met at Mr. Secretary St. John's office in the Cockpit), when they were examining him he pulls out a penknife and strikes at my father with design to stab him but it pleased God the penknife hit upon a bone which broke the knife. The wound is but small and the chirurgeons and doctor say it is not dangerous and that he will be very well. He has been let blood, he lies quiet and is now in a breathing sweat.

The villain reached over the Duke of Ormond and Lord Poulett to get at my father. All immediately drew their swords, they gave him three wounds, but I believe they are not mortal; he is carried to Newgate. Lord Poulett walked home by my father's chair and showed a vast deal of tenderness and care of him.

I forgot to tell you that Guiscard cried to the Duke of Ormond to kill him, but some that were the calmest hindered both the Duke and Mr. St. John, that he might kept for to confess.

—— to her sister ABIGAIL HARLEY at Eywood.

[1711, March 10.] Saturday—I bless God that I can write any comfortable account concerning our dear brother. He has been hitherto kept only with gruel, but to-day the doctor has ordered him chicken-broth with rice and hartshorn boiled in it, and a little sack whey.

Much good may be brought out of this evil. I hope the Dissenters will see whether the Whig lords are their friends; for Lord Scarbrough was one of them and he moved yesterday, when the others moved that Papists might be banished five miles from the Court and the City, that the Dissenters and Non-jurors might be banished also.

Dr. Radcliffe would have another surgeon, not Boushar who dressed him at the Secretary's office. I stayed for Dr. Radcliffe's and Mr. Green's coming till ten o'clock; Lady Dupplin promised she would write you word what they said, so I came away. Mr. Masham came there from the Queen.

RALPH THORESBY to ROBERT HARLEY.

1710-11, March 12. Leeds in Yorkshire—The last post brought a surprising account of a most barbarous assault which fills all good men with horror, but, besides the general concern for one of the greatest of statesmen and best of Privy Councillors, your singular humanity and generosity in permitting me the perusal of some valuable manuscripts in your most noble library have laid so particular an obligation upon me that I am extremely solicitous to hear of the recovery of so great a patron to learned men, and humbly presume to request this additional favour that you would please to order Mr. Wanley or any of your retainers to give notice how it is with you.

The Earl of Orrery to [Robert Harley].

1711, March [15–]26, N.S. Brussels—Nobody can be more heartily concerned than I am upon the occasion of the villanous and unprecedented attempt of M. Guiscard, both for your own sake and that of the public. I hope I shall in a little time congratulate you upon your recovery.

Coroner's Inquisition on Guiscard.

1710-11, March 17—Inquisition taken at the Parish of Christchurch, in the ward of Farringdon within, before George Rivers, Esq., coroner of the City of London on the body of Anthony D'Guiscard commonly known as the Marquis D'Guiscard, and a jury whose names are given, who say that Nathan Williox, of St. James's, Westminster, gent., a messenger in ordinary, had under warrant of Secretary St. John, arrested Guiscard and carried him to the Cockpit in St. Margaret's parish, Westminster, and was called in to the council room just after the attack made by him on Harley in the presence of the other Lords of the Council in order to remove him. Guiscard resisted the attempts to secure him and sustained severe injuries in the struggle, which it was attested were the cause of his death a few days afterwards. *Copy.*

A copy of Williox' or Williock's Information is attached; also that of James Pringle, of St. James's, surgeon, dated March 19, who was sent for to the Cockpit on the 8th inst. after another surgeon Paul Buyssiere had dressed Guiscard's wounds. The two surgeons afterwards visited the prisoner in Newgate, and thought the wounds might be cured, but that the real cause of his death by mortification were certain bruises on his left side which were not at first visible.

Other Informations attached to the same effect are by Edward Coatsworth, doctor in physic, of St. Martin's in the Fields; William Pitt, gent., Keeper of Newgate; Bodenham Rewse, gent., master turnkey; and Paul Buyssiere, surgeon, of St. Martin's in the Fields.

Sir Con[stantine] Phipps, Lord Chancellor of Ireland, to [Robert Harley].

1710-11, March 18. Dublin—The news of the villanous attempt on Harley's life had filled him with so great astonishment, and nothing could equal it but the satisfaction he had received at the same time of Harley being out of danger. It is surprising that any person who had the birth and education of a gentleman could be guilty of such inhumanity, but nothing is too barbarous to be committed by a French subject when nothing is too villanous to be commanded by the French king.

—— Harley to her Sister [Abigail Harley].

1710-11, March 22—Thanks to my dear sister for yours of the 18th. I bless God that I am able still to be a messenger of good tidings for he is still as well as can be expected. It is indeed as you mention a wonderful mercy to me that I was there that day, and was not told it in any surprising manner. My being there that day was wholly accidental I had not been there above a week having been not well, but resolved to go there upon Friday March the 9th, having desired on Thursday to go in the morning to Cousin Bridge's and dine at Mr. Braddle's as they had invited me, and then in the afternoon to Mr. Cotton's lecture; but

Wednesday evening Lord Bellamont (my kind friend) came and begged me to go Thursday morning and speak to my brother on his behalf. I went according to my promise, and when I came he was private in his closet. So soon as his door was open Mr. Secretary St. John came to speak with him; when he was gone he dressed himself and I was called into the dressing room, but several were there, so I could not speak to him, but he said to me be sure you stay till I come home. It being the Queen's inauguration day he had on a new cloth coat and a rich waist-coat, (I believe you remember the waistcoat, it was blue and silver ground flowered with rich gold brocade flowers). Sister had kept it up and that waistcoat served for the birthday and for this occasion (only a silver fringe put round it and looked very well). He went away immedi-ately to the Queen as I think, or else to the Treasury to give some short orders, and then to the Queen. The town says he desired her to forbear going out, but it is certain she did not go to prayers at the Chapel as she used to do. My brother waited on her while she was at dinner. I take it as my brother came to St. James's he saw Guiscard walking in the Mall, and he, with my Lord Chamberlain and others of the Cabinet, filled up the warrant for seizing him. He [Guiscard] had been at the Queen's backstairs that morning, and the day before. Soon after one o'clock Sir Thomas Mansel saw him there, and he came and spoke mighty kind to Sir Thomas Mansel which he wondered at, because he had been angry with the Lords of the Treasury about his pension that he had formerly had, which the Queen had referred to them. He being seized the Lords of the Cabinet Council met at the Cockpit, at Mr. Secretary St. John's office, vizt. The Lord President, The Lord Keeper, the Dukes of Ormond, Newcastle, Buckingham and Queens-berry Secretary for Scotland, and the two English Secretaries St. John and the Earl of Dartmouth, and the Earl Poulett. The Duke of Shrewsbury and the Archbishop were the only members of the Cabinet that were wanting, the former entertained all the foreign ministers that day, and the Archbishop was sick. The Duke of Ormond, the Earl Poulett and our brother sat together. He [Guiscard] stood behind them for the convenience of having his face towards the light, that they might observe his countenance while he was examined, and so he had the opportunity of doing it. They all say they observed he fixed his eyes on my brother so soon as he came in. They all examined him in French; he spoke triflingly in his answers. My brother spoke to him in French to be serious and consider what he said. The Lord President called to have messengers come in and take him out. Some report that he desired to speak with St. John alone but my brother says that is not true. It is said he in French said when the messengers were called for, Now to this villain, meaning my brother (if this be not true that he called him so I will send you word) he reached over my brother's right shoulder, the penknife struck first in the turning up of the right sleeve of his coat, which the surgeon says broke the force of the blow, and turned the knife aside for the back was towards his body, it struck through his coat which was open at the breast, and they now so far as the button holes put a buckram between the cloth and silk lining, through these three it went and into his waistcoat just in one of the gold flowers which also must break the force of the blow. He had on a thin flannel waistcoat and a flannel on his stomach double because his coat was open. It pierced through all and stuck into the breastbone, a little above the gristle that is at the bottom of the breastbone. The penknife broke short off, near half an inch above the handle, and no doubt when the knife broke his hand jobbed down upon the right side of the wound for there was a great bruise. He not finding him fall, and not knowing the knife was broke, repeated his blow (without drawing back his hand) further on the left side, as appears now by a bruise there, though my brother has no notion of the second blow. Had the knife not broke at the first, the second blow had been in all probability fatal being against his heart. The Lords said there was a second blow, but he did not remember it for he was stunned, at first felt only a mighty blow on his breast, but soon recollected himself, felt the smart of the penknife (he told me yesterday for I asked him); he took out the penknife himself, wiped it with his handkerchief, and I think put it up wrapped in his handkerchief into his pocket, then took Lord Poulett's handkerchief held it to the wound and rose up and walked. The seeing him alive they say only could have prevented their killing Guiscard. The Duke of Queensberry ran out, called in the messengers and footmen to seize him; the Dukes of Ormond and Newcastle drew, the one wounded him in the belly, and the other, the shoulder and back, and Secretary St. John in the arm; his sword was broke, but of that I have not yet an exact account, you shall know so soon as I do. He grappled with the Frenchman who stabbed at him (as they think not knowing the knife was broke). St. John then ran out called for a surgeon and I think named Beoushair, and without a sword in the utmost confusion ran away to St. James's, went to Mrs. Masham's lodging in the fright, and haply that day she dined with her sister. He, that is St. John, rested a little and then took the Queen's doctor that is a Scotchman up and told the Queen, who did not believe they had told her truth, but that he was dead, till she had spoke with Beoushair after he had dressed him, when he came to the Secretary's office. My brother before he dressed him obliged him to tell him if the wound was mortal or not. He having dressed him he bid him dress the Frenchman, whom they had knocked down and tied neck and heels. My brother then was brought away in a chair, a sedan I mean, and Lord Poulett came with him for they came upstairs together. And now to let you know how we knew of it: at three o'clock my brother sent word they should go to dinner and not stay. Thus I have given you the best account of all I can. I wish you can make sense of it, I am hardly myself yet.

J[OHN] CHETWYND to [ROBERT HARLEY].

1710-11, March , Sunday Morning—Being ordered by the Queen forthwith to return to Piedmont, has fixed Tuesday to begin his journey. Desires the continuance of Harley's friendship and protection.

ALEXANDER CUNNINGHAM to [ROBERT HARLEY].

1711, [March 25-]April 4, N.S. Rome—Having been entirely taken up with the virtuosi since I came into Italy, I have made several discoveries in the art of printing not yet known in our country, and quite forgot in Italy now. Most of my purchase consists in classics of the first editions, amongst which is Tully, of the Milan edition 1488, and Julius Cæsar by Jenson 1472, which is much finer I am sure than Jacob Tonson can publish now, and I leave it to my Lord Somers and you to judge which is best. I shall not trouble you with more particulars of my purchases, in short most of the classics of the like editions, which I believe will afford you some pleasure to look on. Besides these I have had the good fortune to purchase a very ancient manuscript of Homer, on Egyptian paper and most beautifully writ.

This I humbly offer to the Queen, and can think of none so proper as yourself to make the offer to her Majesty, which I do with the greatest sense of duty. If I did not think it were worthy her Majesty's accepting I would not put it in your hands. Though it want Omega other crowned heads would be glad to have it, but it were a crime in me to deprive her Majesty of a jewel that may give an additional lustre to her reign. Please to let me know how the offer is accepted, and it shall be sent by land to Holland, and her Majesty's ambassador at the Hague will take care to send it to you. If you think you want assistance to make it better received, I presume my Lord Somers will give you his, though I have not writ to him on the head. Please to let me have your answer as soon as is possible. Next week we go to Naples, where we think to stay a month, and will pass the summer here. The functions of this week have taken up my time that I could not be with the learned. Mr. Newton has left a good name here. Mr. Molesworth is arrived at Florence. I heard lately from my Lord Raby who will be proud of your friendship, as I shall also be of having your commands in this place.

Postscript.—Please to direct yours for me under a cover to Mr. Chitty, merchant in Amsterdam, or to Mr. Drummond there.

CHARLES CALDECOT to ROBERT HARLEY.

1711, April 4. Fulnetby, near Lincoln—As one of the grand jury at Lincoln he had drawn up an address of congratulation to Harley on his recovery from the horrid attempt on his life. Only one gentleman of their body, Boucherett by name, had refused to sign it. The Lord Great Chamberlain [Willoughby de Eresby] had promised to concur with them in it, and to desire the same of the rest of the county gentlemen.

BARON ROBERT PRIOR to ROBERT HARLEY.

1711, April 2. Bath—This comes with all my heart and soul to congratulate your recovery and your deliverance from the wicked hands, and designs of unparellelled villainy. I hope you will take more care of yourself for the future.

Here I am on account of my health, having been a cripple from the gout this month, which seized me on circuit, and I carried it round with me, and here I hope to leave it.

Jack Howe is here, a mere walking ghost ; he may with the assistance of the waters linger some weeks, he eats with an appetite and digests it, and yet gains no strength. He has married his daughter to Sir Edmund Thomas, of Glamorganshire, who is 45 years of age, has about 1000*l.* per annum, 5000*l.* to that, and it is said he has given 6000*l.* portion.

We found all the country in very good temper and well satisfied with the conduct of the public (affairs ?) at least seemed so to be.

THOMAS, BISHOP OF ROCHESTER, to [ROBERT] HARLEY, Chancellor of the Exchequer.

1711, April 3. Westminster Abbey—After my most hearty congratulations for the wonderful providence of your escape and recovery, I make bold to acquaint you that we think it absolutely necessary for us to petition Parliament for a continuance of some supply towards the repairing and preserving this royal and ancient church. The Dean and Chapter humbly entreat your direction, encouragement, and patronage in promoting it.

J. MACKY, Master of the pacquet boats, to ROBERT HARLEY.

1711, April 3. Dover—I take the freedom to lay before you an exact calculation which I made some years ago of the monasteries and other seminaries of learning belonging to the English nation in Flanders,* by which you will see the root from whence that great growth of Popery in these nations proceeds, which carries out such vast sums of our money, and yearly returns us shoals of priests and young gentlemen educated in an aversion to our ecclesiastical and civil constitution, and who entering into all our parties of pleasure at home, do more than anything to keep up our unhappy divisions, and a party for the Pretender.

I have an expedient which will moulder all these monasteries insensibly away and root out Popery infallibly, without persecution and with less severity than if the present laws against papists were put in execution.

[ALEXANDER CUNNINGHAM to ROBERT HARLEY.]

1711, April [6-]17 new style. Rome—The advice we had here on the 12th from England gave horror to all good men, especially to those that have the honour to know you. The blackness of the action so damped me that I could not sooner either condole your misfortune nor congratulate your recovery.

I was the first that notified it to the Viceroy of Naples who heard it with the utmost abhorrence, he wondered we should have used so kindly French vagabonds these fifty years past; he added they think nothing black to serve their Prince, which we see by their suffering the greatest hardships from him. Some here say the assassin is dead of his wounds, and that you are not out of danger. I can't but take notice with what air of contentedness they tell these news, but they are such as never speak truth but as it hits with their own inclinations, we can even here despise them, and give a *Viva la Regina di Gr. Britna.* louder than they can on other occasions.

The sudden death of the Emperor is a surprise on us, and the French generals would make us believe that all is in confusion in Germany. We know better what's doing there than they can tell us, we scorn their news, and give them *Quid pro quo,* and are all unanimous for the House of Austria. It is to be wished the Electors will be so too, if not they may do worse. When I'm asked what way I think England will go on this occasion, I would not have them to doubt of our firm adhering to King Charles, and if they will not give it to him no matter though the Czar of Muscovy have it. By this you see we have platonic politicians here as in England you have platonic lovers. For my own part, I can assure you, my time has been wholly taken up since I left Venice, to come to the knowledge of an old town, forty feet underground, which was discovered lately. It lies between Naples and Vesuvius and seems to have been buried when this volcano first broke out of sea. The magnificence of the buildings we see by the entablatures. There are abundance of fine statues digged up already; most of them that I saw are after the Greek manner. There's one of a vestal surprisingly fine, and the painters think it the best model of a Madonna, in being. It is of the *Gusto grande* and thought to be *Maxima Claudia* of the family of *Appius Pulcher;* indeed she is all beautiful and the drapery

---

* Probably the paper assigned to the year 1707, and printed in this volume on pp. 470-472.

curiously wrought, but that which touched me most are the pretty ears that are under the vestal's veil, you cannot imagine how the sculptor could put in the tools to work them so well under the veil. The Hercules you know by the lion's skin, 'tis the least I have seen but well proportioned. The others have not yet got names. I was called to a consultation there about them, my opinion was to do nothing rashly till the congregation of the Virtuosi at Rome were consulted, so that it will come before us soon, then shall let you know the result of this whole matter. I had like to have forgot a statue that was lately found buried at Cuma; though it wants the head yet I own 'tis fine, and take it to be Hygeia by other marks of that deity which I observe on medals.

I will not now trouble you with an account of books old or new, till I have your answer about Homer. It will be a particular pleasure to know that it is accepted and assure yourself 'tis the finest in Europe. If Dr. Bentley had found it he would swear it was the very same Alexander the Great made use of in his *Horæ Subsecivæ*. However as there's a Meseriaque [Meziriac ? *for Dr. Bentley*] in England, so I hope we shall have another ancient manuscript of Phalaris' Epistles in a short time. We have got also Leonard Aretin's History of the Goths, &c. which 'tis said he stole; 'tis printed 1470.

I'll write you no news but for the Gazette. Last night Cardinal Tremoule had two expresses from France, the contents are not known. The Marquis de Prié being much afflicted has dismissed part of his family, the Duke of Aretino is to have a public audience of the Pope next week. Cardinal Ottoboni has not yet accepted the character of protector of France, his civilities to the British are still the same as formerly. The Pope said his prayers this morning in state at the Greeks', the morrow I hope to say mine in another manner, and can have no greater satisfaction, than to hear you are in a condition to say yours at St. James's or where you will.

WILLIAM CLAYTON to [ROBERT HARLEY].

1711, April 13. Liverpool—I rejoice to hear of your perfect recovery from the danger you were in by that villanous attempt on your person.

In 1696 about six of the common council of this corporation and four of the freemen, on their petitioning the late King, obtained a new charter without any due proceeding by law, setting aside the charter of Charles II. under which they had flourished nearly twenty years. The corporate body put in their caveat and desired they might have a fair trial, but this was denied them. The new charter appointed a new mayor, two new bailiffs, and a common council by name, on which the mayor, bailiffs, and all the aldermen under Charles II.s charter except one refused to act, nor was this new charter ever accepted by the corporate body. The latter have now addressed her Majesty on the subject and desire your assistance in obtaining her favourable consideration of their petition.

[The EARL OF ILAY to ROBERT HARLEY.]

1711, April 14—Your cousin Thomas Harley and Lord Dartmouth spoke to me the other day about the envoyship to Spain. The latter added that it had been whispered that my brother (Argyll) and I had supported Mr. Craggs in his pretensions, and that I had carried him to the Duke of Buckingham. All I know of the matter is that Mr. Craggs came to me and told me he was declared and desired me to take him to the Duke. My brother and I had no inclination to meddle in the matter, and had never been asked anything about it. We thought it most reasonable and most dutiful to accept the determination of the Queen and her ministry upon it; and as soon as I was informed that the choice had fallen upon Mr. Craggs I gave him all the little countenance I could. I never had a bad opinion of him, I always thought him a man of honour; but had it been otherwise I should be very unworthy of the Queen's favours if I should decline the company of one she has chosen for her envoy.

[EARL POULETT to ROBERT HARLEY.]

1711, April 18—I did not know you were gone into the country, when I desired leave this morning to wait upon you, and therefore I take the liberty to offer my business in writing till I have the honour to see you return I hope in full strength.

The Emperor's death makes me desire to know whether you would have the Duke of Savoy have half his extraordinaries by next Friday's post, and whether by next Tuesday another month, that is the pay for May, should be sent to Lisbon, and whether we should send 150,000*l.* for Barcelona, only 70,000*l.* of the Portugal stock of money being yet sent there. Lord Raby writes very pressingly for his equipage moneys in Holland and for his pay due to him at Berlin. I therefore take the liberty to send you Powis's state of his account for whatever directions you please to give upon it when you think it proper. Mr. Lowndes is very desirous to reserve a liberty by framing a clause that may apply the money of this year in general to help out upon extraordinary occasion the remainders of last year's service, which with submission I think necessary on several occasions, especially considering the Parliament will not give for this year's service by a great deal what they have voted; and I humbly offer it to your consideration whether it will not be a great help to the credit in the present service, and beg your directions upon this particular.

I likewise beg to know whether you would not have the Post and Leather consolidated into the Annuities with all dispatch, for people's hopes at first sight are I think stronger than their fears, which may balance more into doubt when they see enough to judge more by particulars than they can now in gross. It was mentioned in the Cabinet to acquaint the Parliament with the Emperor's death, as being sure you might get what vote you pleased without the least difficulty in foreign affairs, and that this would be a good occasion to keep up a spirit in Europe with reputation at home, and the ready way to obtain a further power and liberty for the Government to manage a peace which I hope in God will crown all your glories. Lord Halifax, upon common talk which I told him you would not hear of, said he had power to assure you might command him, Somers, and every Whig in England. Anglesey and old Leeds say there will be no government if you do not resolve, only the Cabinet Councillors say nothing to me of it. In short I think you and all with you sink without any chance, if you do not answer the telling call of Heaven upon you, and as it is the Queen's security to discourage the designs of France, to reward the men they intended destruction to, so it will give all a new life in their sufferings beyond any correction, and by their reward will encourage all to follow whatever example you please to lend them.

The Emperor's death makes this a time of perfect changes everywhere in Europe in all likelihood; and as the world is of all hands fully convinced Marlborough and Godolphin shifted only by setting mankind against one another and only throve by wars of all degrees and kinds, so you may now secure your own undertaking by showing your charge is to reconcile all upon a national foot and thereby complete your own power, that all will adore it and none oppose or dare to injure you where all are sensibly interested for your support. I imagine you now take this opportunity of retirement of thinking with yourself what resolution to take and therefore I can't as your servant omit submitting my thoughts to your judgment.

LORD HALIFAX to [ROBERT HARLEY].

1711, April 18—I confess I earnestly wish to have leave to wait upon you and to explain my thoughts to you in this conjuncture which is so extraordinary and so nice, that I think there is no medium between a vigorous asserting the Queen, and her government, or being lost for ever. Men's eyes are turned towards you, expecting their safety from your interest and prudent management under the present difficulties. The danger is great, the trouble infinite, you have courage to undertake and you may have what assistance you please to carry you through so great and glorious a work and may depend upon the good wishes and weak endeavours of myself.

The EARL OF ROCHESTER to [ROBERT HARLEY].

1711, April 18—Your health and strength are to me before all other considerations, but I can't but think the Emperor's death will make your advice highly necessary at this time, whether you can come here or let your friends wait on you where you are gone. I believe the affairs abroad on the part of the Allies must be mightily disjointed and those of the French much the contrary, which perhaps may put thoughts into them they have not hitherto had leisure for. Whether in this very conjuncture the expedition under Walker should not be stopped may be worth consideration, as likewise who may be the fittest man of all the Queen's subjects to be sent into Germany to solicit and attend the election of a new Emperor.

These various and uncomposed thoughts, perhaps fitter to have been kept to myself, may however suggest proper ones to you, so I shall need say no more but that if anything be necessary to be thought on, I shall be ready to wait on you just where it will be most easy to you, with any other you think proper, and shall be glad if I can contribute to the service of the Queen and the public.

The EARL OF ROCHESTER to [ROBERT HARLEY].

1711, April 19—I did not think fit to give you any trouble last night before six, because till the Cabinet had met I had very little to say, and afterwards it was too late, for it was ten. Most of the matters mentioned by you in yours to me were under consideration. The wind at present stops the troops, no other order was given in that affair. All the other particulars I think were agreed to, just as you mentioned them, except that relating to the Duke of Bavaria, which I think was to have a consideration apart. The Queen was desired to acquaint both Houses with the death of the Emperor, and at the same time to call upon them to finish such matters as are necessary to end the Session, which her Majesty agreed to, and that it should be to-morrow; but did not determine whether it should be done by message or by herself.

H. St. John to [Robert] Harley.

1711, April 19—My Lord President surprised me very much last night in Cabinet, when he spoke of stopping Mr. Hill, as what might be expedient upon the alteration in public affairs occasioned by the Emperor's death.

The worse condition we are in, the worse peace we are likely to obtain ; the more reason there is in my humble opinion that the intended expedition should be pushed.

When shall we see you at the House ? You know to be sure how well Aislabie behaves himself towards the Queen. My Lord Mar's Lyon [Erskine ?] and the Duke of Atholl's Murray are not to be forgotten.

Charles Caldecot to [Robert Harley ?].

1711, April 21. Fulnetby, near Lincoln—Thanks for promising to speak to the Lords of the Treasury about his affair, but having no other business at present in town is unwilling to take the journey without some assurance of success.

W. Fytche to [Robert Harley].

1711, April 19—It is with a great deal of pleasure that I congratulate your recovery of the wound received from the villain Guiscard.

The death of Richmond of which I heard on Sunday night occasioned me to go to Maldon and call the corporation together, who unanimously agreed to choose me in his room ; but having applied to you to be Commissioner of the Salt, and being seconded by Secretary St. John in my request, I would not move farther until I had your directions, the post not being consistent with a seat in parliament. The people are in so good a humour that I dare say they would choose any honest gentleman of the country I should name ; and Sir Charles Barrington (who is the most proper person though otherwise averse to the service of the House) has out of pure friendship that I may not be disappointed promised to take my place in case I may be assured of the above employment, which it would be by much the most convenient for me and my affairs to obtain ; but if you would have me come in myself, and you think of any thing I may hold within doors of equal value, I shall most readily submit and go down and be chosen accordingly.

The Duke of Somerset to [Robert Harley].

1711, April 22. Marlborough—Since I am not in town to make you my compliments at your own house, where I sent every day to enquire after your health, I cannot forbear doing it this way, the very next post after I heard you were abroad and had waited on the Queen, to tell you very sincerely that I do most heartily rejoice at the great good fortune you have had to escape the hand of a villain and that I do wish you may be always successful and fortunate, and particularly now at this time in your counsel of a new Emperor and a new King of Spain, for the same person cannot nor must not pretend to both.

I came here last Monday to dispatch some private affairs which I hope to do to-morrow that I may be next Wednesday at Petworth on the same account : the stay I shall make there I cannot at this time determine, but I hope it will not exceed ten days, the next day I return to town, I will either visit you, or your grave porter.

WILLIAM BROMLEY, Speaker of the House of Commons, to
[ROBERT HARLEY].

1711, April 23.—I am very sorry you have suffered so much by going
abroad, and shall be glad to see you are returned to the House, though
it must put me under a difficulty to deliver the commands of the House,
and to express the great satisfaction taken in your recovery.

KER of Kersland to [ROBERT HARLEY].

1711, April 24.—Congratulates Harley on his recovery. Is obliged
to lay before him his inexpressible difficulties for money by the practice
and violence of his enemies, which will hardly promise him freedom
from being affronted one day longer.

REINIER LEERS to DR. STRATFORD, Canon of Christchurch, Oxford.

1711, [April 25–]May 5, N.S. Rotterdam—I shall receive with great
pleasure the set of Rymer's *Foedera*, and entreat you to give my most
humble thanks beforehand to the illustrious Mr. Harley. I am desirous
to know what more power shall be put into his hands because we must
see infallibly the good effects of it. By our former letters it was said
he should be made a Peer of the kingdom and High Treasurer, would
not the last disoblige too much my Lord Poulett and other friends of
Mr. Harley? I send you an abstract of a letter of a friend of St. G.
written to me February 26th last; had acquainted him of my design of
going beyond sea, to discover his mind and satisfaction about the change
of your ministry. He says, *je suis rari que vos affaires particulières
vous engagent à passer la mer, vous y trouverez une confusion extrême,
des inimitiés declarées, des jalousies parmi les associés, et la mauvaise
foi partout*. I do not translate the words, I could not put them in more
significant terms to persuade you of the lamentable idea they have
gotten of the new ministry. It seems all their hopes are quite lost.
Excuse me of not naming him, he is none of the weakest heads of that
court.
  The death of the Dauphin might have produced more inclination to a
peace, if that of the Emperor had not intervened in this fatal time. It
is certain the Duke of Burgundy has declared more than once to his
grandfather and others, that he would not have his future kingdom
ruined upon the account of his brother; his violent temper might have
brought him to great extremities. M. de Torcy and others that were
for continuing the war upon the Dauphin's account, and for no other
reason, were expected to come over in the Duke's sentiments; and we
had reason to believe that his hatred against Vendome should have miscarried the designs of laying a siege in Catalonia. But Providence
having disposed otherwise we must refer to it, till we are a little further,
seeing Charles will be chosen Emperor in all probability. Of nine
Electors, the Duke of Bavaria and his brother will not be admitted to
the election; the Electors of Hanover and Treves have engaged at
their election for the house of Austria; the Electors of Mayence and
Bohemia are surely for the same house; there we have four voices of
the seven. The Elector Palatine and of Saxony would pursue their
own interest if possible; the first may come over to the interest of the
house of Austria, being almost his own, but if the second is chosen
Emperor the kingdom of Poland must fall again in Stanislaus' hands
which may cause sad work to the confederates at the beginning of the

campaign of the King of Sweden with an Ottoman army. For the King of Prussia we do not know as yet what he designs, neither what the King of France may do to assist him, or to recall his troops in case we refuse to be in his interest. All these difficulties may be removed, the greatest in my poor opinion lays in the kingdom of Spain. If King Charles is made Emperor, what have Spain to do with a King that has his residence at Vienna? In which case there is ground to fear Catalonia will submit to Philip.

It is reported the Queen of Spain is with child these four or five months, upon what ground I can not tell. If she was brought to bed of a Prince, Spain will not be for a minority. And if the confederates declare for the Duke of Savoy or for his son, nobody can tell what influence it may have on Spain; in all case we are in a great extremity, perhaps we shall not see an end of it so soon; if we consider maturely the present posture of the affairs of Europe, we have reason to expect more extremities Providence may produce, I hope for the good of the Protestant religion.

Prince Eugene shall not command in Flanders, the wretched condition of the German army and lines destitute of all necessary things, oblige him to stay for a while upon the Rhine to prevent the breaking in of the French army. As soon as the Empire will be secured against the French invasion, and the election of an Emperor regulated or agreed on, it is thought the Prince goes to Catalonia to be Vicar General to King Charles, and to keep that kingdom in obedience, during the absence of the Emperor. What a terrible reversion of affairs!

Pray, dear Sir, do not expect from me any considerable light about the present affairs. We politicians of the last rate on this side do just as our physicians and mountebanks; we reflect and reason upon all the diseases of politic and human bodies, we prescribe drugs and remedies, but we cure none.

As for Guiscard's business you are in the right to say that you are not yet at the bottom of his design. Great suspicions there are that it was on the Queen. If you can send me an abstract of his letter to Toland, and a full account of the Italian gentleman, I could resolve to acquaint M. de Torcy of what is laid to his charge. But he can not clear him [other] than by words, what may not be expected from a minister educated in Popish, tyrannical and arbitrary principles. But let us forbear to declare him guilty till we have a better ground.

About fourteen days ago I had the honour of a visit paid to me by the Admiral Wishart, a man of great judgment and capacity, I could wish to have been acquainted with him at his coming in the country, as well as at his going away. Among other discourses we had together, he seemed to me apprehensive of the King of France, his fitting out of great many men of war and privateers almost in all his sea-ports; and especially of a design of the Pretender of a new invasion in the kingdom. I confess I was not of his opinion neither about the fitting out of a fleet, nor a pretended invasion.

Though I have been already too large, give me leave to tell you something more upon the subject of the Pretender, which perhaps you do not know, and may give you some light, but for God's sake let it not pass beyond Mr. Harley's knowledge.

At the negotiation at Ryswick a separate article was made betwixt the King and the French ambassadors that the annual pension allowed to Queen Mary d'Este by the Parliament at her marriage should be paid. Since that time a sum of fifty thousand pounds sterling has been brought upon the Civil List, ratified by Parliament, but never paid to King James, nor to the Queen. When M. de Torcy came at the Hague and afterwards at Gertrudenberg it was insisted upon by the English that the Prince should abandon France, and retire to another country. The King of France did consent to it, but asked the jointure for the Queen, pretending he could not entertain the Court, if the money was spent without his kingdom. I think the jointure was allowed by the English, but the place not settled.

I confess I could never comprehend the **reason** why the English would force the Prince to retire elsewhere, if they had no mind to restore him upon the throne of his father. I considered always the Roman Catholic religion, and the King of France and his interest, the two chief points of hindrance to keep him from the throne. But if the Prince having succeeded in Scotland had brought Britain in the utmost confusion, as I am apt to think he had, and if the danger is so imminent, especially if the French had a happy campaign, it will be easy for you to get the Prince out of France in paying the jointure, which bears no proportion at all to the danger. The Parliament, you may say, would not have the jointure paid, why is it consented at a time when the family was in France, without any restriction of peace and war? Why is it paid every year upon the Civil List? I reason only *ad hominem* against the Admiral. If the Prince was once out of France, I think all fear of a descent was quite over.

Lord Dartmouth to [Robert Harley].

1711, April 25. Whitehall—It is very unwillingly that I trouble anybody with myself, but especially one that I have more obligation to than all the rest of the world.

The favour I have to beg is what I should take for a very great one at this time as a mark of her Majesty's gracious acceptance of my poor endeavours to serve her, which is that she would be pleased to knight me again. All I can say to induce her to it, is, that I come of a family that has had the honour to be servants to hers above a hundred years, and in as great posts both of honour and trust as any ever were, and I hope without reproach either from Prince or Country, and her Majesty having thought fit to continue the same goodness in putting me in a station much above my desert or expectation, makes me desirous to leave a mark of her favour to my family. But considering I have the substantial part by the bounty of her predecessors, it may be too much vanity, which I hope you will pardon if you are of that opinion, and say nothing to her of it; I know there is no occasion to desire you not to do it to anybody else. All I have to say in alleviation of my im. pertinence is, that since the Revolution half the House of Lords have had brevets granted over my head, and by a late transaction half the world. I depend entirely upon your friendship and goodness to put this into the fire.

John Drummond to [Robert Harley].

1711, [April 25-]May 5. Amsterdam—I have left to more able pens and eloquent orators to make a public condolence on that terrible and barbarous attempt made upon your life, &c.

Lord Raby is like to please very well at the Hague, and the Grand Pensionary is like to find some assistance in his Excellency against the violence of the Imperial ministers who are for sacrificing all to increase the power of the Empire, which it is earnestly wished they would make a better use of. Some think an able Minister at Frankfort against the time of election of a King of the Romans and Emperor will be very necessary; the gentleman you have there is almost esteemed as poor in parts as in money, and he will have difficulty to remove from thence to the new station the Queen has been pleased to bestow on him.

The SAME to the SAME.

[1711, April–May ?]—Lord Peterborough has borrowed about 2300*l.* from my correspondent at Vienna and has drawn bills on Mr. Brydges for that sum. I humbly entreat to know whether, if his Lordship should require any such sums to be further advanced him, we can depend upon the payment of his bills. Three words on this subject without mentioning names will be sufficient.

SIR ROBERT DAVERS to [ROBERT HARLEY].

1711, April 28—I had the pleasure and satisfaction of seeing you in the House though I could not come to speak to you. No friend you have in the world rejoices more for your recovery than myself. God grant you health that you may serve your Queen and country, and complete the great and good work you have begun in delivering —— and all your friends from the slavery we were under.

LORD WANDELL to [ROBERT HARLEY].

1711, April 28—I heartily congratulate your great escape and happy recovery.

Since I depend entirely on your favour, the hope of which, as it has hindered my desiring the assistance of any other, so encourages me to believe you will now be mindful of my affair that I may lose no more time in going to the campaign.

The great confidence which I have in your promise prevailed on me to bargain for horses which are actually now in Flanders, so that if I meet not with very speedy dispatch I shall lose at once my time and credit. I hope I have a title to desire your assistance to preserve both.

—————— to her Aunt ABIGAIL HARLEY, at Aywood.

1711, April 28. London—My dear father is pretty well. His looks are very much mended within these few days.

I hear the Speaker made a very fine speech, my father was received in a very extraordinary manner, there was not one in the House but what took occasion to make their compliments to him and crowded about him. The House was very full. I hear the speech is to be printed.

The COUNTESS OF DORCHESTER to [ROBERT HARLEY].

1711, April 30—Though I have a very high opinion of the Queen's justice and judgment, and even of her kindness towards those that serve her well, yet as I never saw a reign, but had through misrepresentations some odd things done in it, I can't help being a little startled to hear

Earl Orkney say he is promised to be General of the Foot, and others say 'tis resolved, and my Lord not named for the like honour. I beg you'll take the first opportunity to represent to her Majesty that this would be giving away my Lord's rank, who is an older Lieutenant General than Lord Orkney. A thing of that nature is seldom done to the meanest officer, much less to one of my Lord's post actually in the Queen's service. Whatever trouble my application gives you I shall make no excuse, since I can't think it an ill compliment to take you for a man ready to prevent grievances. If there is no occasion for this letter, I humbly beg the Queen's pardon and yours. However I am glad of an opportunity to desire your friendship for my Lord.

Endorsed by Harley:—" Lord Portmore—answered immediately."

JEAN GASSION (*alias* OGILVIE) to [ROBERT HARLEY].

1711, April 30—The last time I waited on you I was going to tell you the story of a negociation betwixt Capt. Griffith and the Duke of Marlborough, but you had not time to hear me, so I have taken the liberty to write it to you. Capt. Griffith being put on by some friends of the Chevalier St. George to pump the Duke to see how he stood affected to him, for they did believe that there was no man so proper as the Captain. He had formerly been a creature of the Duke's in selling places and getting money when his grace was Captain of the guards, and Capt. Griffith was brigadier; so that no man was better acquainted with the Duke's nature. After some discourses with his grace relating to the Chevalier, Capt. Griffith told him that he wanted to write his mind to him, if he were allowed. Griffith therefore sent his letter by old Col. Spicer who is wagon master of the English army. The substance of it was that if the Duke would consider how matters stood with him, there was no way for him to fix his family for ever but to prove himself another Monck, and that would wipe off all "tashes" that might have been cast upon him, and would make him great and glorious to all posterity. It was a very long letter, for I saw a copy of it, but the substance of it ran on that head, that his grace had it now in his power to bring home the Prince and to put his foot on the necks of his enemies.

Capt. Griffith went afterwards with Dr. Taylor to wait on his grace, the doctor being privy to this thing for he told me so himself. The Duke told him he had his letter very safe, called him into his closet and enquired what sort of a Prince the Chevalier was. After the captain had discovered all his advantages he said, but he is a bigot in his religion; the captain told his grace that he was not. Then said his grace, I know it to be true all that you have told me in your letter, but now is not the time; in short we have nothing to say against him but his religion. On this they parted and the Captain got some money from his grace, five guineas, which was a great miracle; this Dr. Taylor told me. After this was all done the Captain sent up a copy of the letter that he wrote to the Duke to my Lord Perth to show it to the Chevalier and to his mother; and prayed my Lord Perth to let him know if his endeavours were approved of and what further instructions the Chevalier would order. Lord Perth was sometime before he sent any answer, so that Griffith wrote to Paris to me to speak to my Lord Perth and to pray him to return an answer to his letters, which I did; whereupon my Lord Perth was frank with me and told me the whole matter and that the Chevalier's answer was he could give the Captain no instructions, for the affair was not ripe enough for that, but he might take his own way. The Captain had his pension of 800 livres a year still continued until his death. The captain's widow knows of this thing, she is Bishop Manningham's sister, she is to be over just now, and I am certain will not refuse to tell her brother this whole story if he but enquire it of her. I have a great deal more to tell you when I wait on you.

LORD DARTMOUTH to [ROBERT HARLEY].

[1711,] April 30. Whitehall—I believe there may be a proper opportunity to send somebody to the Duke of Argyll, Count Maffei having desired the Queen would write to the King of Spain to press him to give some assurance that he will make good the treaties between the late Emperor and Duke of Savoy, as soon as he shall be chosen Emperor, in order to induce him to take the field in person, which he is very well disposed to do at present in respect to the Queen, though he has not received all the satisfaction he had reason to expect from the Court at Vienna. This the Lords at the Committee to night thought very reasonable considering how much the Queen has interposed in that affair already, and have ordered me to acquaint her with it. If you are of the same opinion pray let me know it, and I will propose the gentleman you are so much concerned for to go with it.

EARL RIVERS to [ROBERT HARLEY].

1711, May 1—Desires that three months pay to him as general of the horse may be ordered. Would not be so troublesome had he not made promises of some payments depending on that allowance. Harley and several others are mistaken as to his circumstances. When he has offered to serve her Majesty abroad the answer was that he could not be spared in England. Hopes that some post in the army will fall in soon, that Harley may be eased of this sort of solicitation.

ROBERT HARLEY to [the EARL OF ROCHESTER?].

1711, May 2—Lord Raby finds the Pensionary very well inclined for peace, but that there was a jealousy raised there that England would consult measures with other of the States and leave the Pensionary out; the measures therefore taken by the Queen will obviate that objection.

FRANCIS GWYN to ROBERT HARLEY.

[1711,] May 2—I can only tell you my Lord Rochester is dead. The loss to the public you know, his family may need your protection; but I have that esteem of your regards towards him that I firmly believe they will never want it. My Lady Hyde sent me to the Queen to acquaint her with it; which I did about seven o'clock this evening.

The EARL OF JERSEY to [ROBERT HARLEY].

1711, May 3—I am surprised and do very much lament the sudden death of the Earl of Rochester, I have known him long, and have always esteemed him as a person of great value and consideration; I hope I shall not lessen the respect due to his memory, nor the character of a good natured man, if I so early take the freedom to put you in mind that by this unexpected vacancy her Majesty, free from any engagement, has it now in her power, by making some removes in her family, to dispose of me where I may behave myself with some small capacity.

LADY DUPPLIN to her Aunt ABIGAIL HARLEY, at Eywood.

1711, May 3. London—I believe you will be surprised to hear of my Lord Rochester's death; he dined yesterday at Lady Anne Roberts's, came home about five o'clock, said he was not very well, had a pain cross his stomach. He told Mr. Gwyn he had a mind to see Doctor Radcliffe, he went to fetch him. My Lord writ a letter to the Queen; when he had done he complained his hand shook, sent the letter by Lady Hyde. Before she came back from the Queen he was dead, and also before the Doctor came. They endeavoured to make him bleed, but could not. Nobody about him thought him dying. I think they say he was 72.

Yesterday our friend made the proposal of the fund for paying the nation's debts, which passed, and to-day at the report without any opposition. It has caused great rejoicing, there were bonfires and ringing of bells in the city last night; it is a glorious thing.

The DUKE OF BUCKINGHAMSHIRE to [ROBERT HARLEY,] the Chancellor of Exchequer.

1711, May 3—I most heartily congratulate your success yesterday; though with the just opinion I have of all you undertake I never had the least doubt of that due applause which attended so useful a scheme of affairs. Upon this accident that happened last night I cannot take a better occasion of assuring you of my inclination and interest to see your merit justly rewarded to the highest degree.

The SAME to the SAME.

1711, May ?—Desires to be lord lieutenant of Middlesex in the room of the Duke of Bedford, who has both Cambridgeshire and Bedfordshire, the Duke of Newcastle holding that position in Yorkshire which was formerly his. Is not likely to live much out of the county, and shall go beyond the bishops in residence.

J[ANE, LADY] HYDE, to ROBERT HARLEY.

1711, May 3. Cockpit—I am perfectly persuaded of the sincere concern you have for this surprising and terrible confusion we are all in. My lord is indeed most tenderly concerned for losing the best of parents. Let me see you as soon as you can that your advice and interest may not be wanting to two people that you will never find very unreasonable in their wishes.

EARL POULETT to [ROBERT HARLEY].

1711, May 4—Having read the letter you were pleased to favour me with, I cannot but think with submission that it is the greatest encouragement imaginable for you to go on of yourself, and to hold the scales in your own hand, which at this time is fairly offered to you in every circumstance to balance the fate of Europe and a just settlement at home, by no other distinction but for or against the government. The Crown is reduced so low here, that what in prudence was formerly chosen is now an absolute necessity. If you put Nottingham in and he oversets the balance, you can no more raise the scales again. You know him of no great consequence as he is out, and what service can he do you with the Tories, to make you amends for misleading others to be desperate. Would you give him weight to secure an interest already yours by the greatest obligations imaginable, and after this, may not his being in just now show a shift and make it doubtful by tempting them to hope for their old extravagances with him, which they must despair of as impossible without him. You are the man alone have the turning necessity at will upon others, and though you do wonders if Lord Somers was as dead as Rochester, nobody would respect you a conjuror to raise either of them again to life. The credit of Rochester's confidence and friendship remains alive in you, and every friend he had will be yours to a man. Let the worst come that can, you may at last become a bye interest with Nottingham, who is direct the contrary to your management or interest, for he is party sense in person without respect to the reasons of things, whereas you cannot keep the Tories on their legs as Tories but only as you make them your own followers. Nottingham has undone them once, and you have saved them; and if anything ever disturbs your government, it must be the taint of old courtiers, who I thank God are for the most part worn off the stage, and I cannot but be concerned that you should have no such leaven, except John of Bucks, who can never be dangerous and will many ways be useful, and shows the value of that part of his character in being reckoned a churchman [which] overbalances all his other objections. I cannot but think it for your service not to break with any man you have once engaged, without a very public reason, and therefore think it of the last consequence whom you admit into the Cabinet, and Lord Nottingham may be made as useful with more safety in giving his son Lord Finch a place, rather than in admitting him into the Ministry.

Forgive this freedom which proceeds from my zeal and confidence in your good nature. I beg you burn this letter that it may at no time be ever read by any but yourself.

Endorsed by Harley:—" A prudent letter."

EARL POULETT to [ROBERT HARLEY].

1711, May 5—Though I presumed last night to write you so long a letter, yet I forgot to acquaint you the Duke of Newcastle is positive against being President himself, thinking it a place of less consequence than that he has, and he is not against Buckingham's being so, I having told him how earnestly he desired it. Forgive me if I take the liberty to add, that if your great undertakings should by accident at any time need a man of distinction of either side to be taken into your assistance, this is with respect to your interest a safe place in reserve for any such to be trusted, and which at present John of Bucks will be serviceable in, and may be more so for the time to come, because you may always turn him out without offence to any party, and with great applause of all men either of sense, principle, or interest. But I hope you will never be reduced to necessities of any kind, but that you will be rewarded the remainder of your life to make you amends for your past troubles and dangers, which you have so generously exposed yourself to, for the happiness of us all.

GENERAL HANS HAMILTON to [ROBERT HARLEY].

1711, May 5. London—The difficulties I lie under at present keep me from serving this campaign, the only one I have missed for two and twenty years, which I must own is no small uneasiness to me, but 'twould be a much greater mortification to serve upon the terms I must do.

The government of Berwick being now vacant, 'twould be a favour never to be forgot if you thought me equal to it, and would recommend me to the Queen for it.

THOMAS MADOX to ROBERT HARLEY.

1711, May 5—It would be a great relief if you would let me know by Mr. Wanley the day and hour when I may wait on you at St. James's Palace, because I shall be forced to publish my History [of the Exchequer] in a few days.

COL. HORACE WALPOLE to [ROBERT HARLEY].

1711, May 6—Urging, at the instance of Sir John Wodehouse and eight other members for Norfolk, the claims of Thornhagh Gurdon, Esq., to be general receiver of taxes for that county. Also recommends himself to Harley's favour and protection, having done what in him lay at great expense and industry to carry the Norfolk elections.

The EARL OF ORRERY to [ROBERT HARLEY].

1711, May [7–]18, N.S. Brussels—Our last letters from England give an account of the Parliament congratulating you upon your escape and recovery, which I beg you to believe nobody can take a greater share in than I do, which I think I ought to do not only as a good friend but as a good subject too. I wish I could entertain you with a good account of the situation of affairs in these countries, but I find the management here has been in a great measure of a piece with that in England, and the corrupt and weak administration here with the unavoidable calamities of the war together have so exhausted the country and soured the tempers of the people that I wish the evils here may not be past cure. 'Tis not to be imagined what a jealousy is conceived here upon every step the Dutch make, who to say the truth have given too much reason to suspect that they have very unjustifiable designs upon this country; they have acted I think upon wrong maxims in this matter even for their own interest. The maintenance of the Imperial troops is the great point at present in agitation here, it goes down very heavily with these people, and in my opinion is an unreasonable burden upon them; but the common cause I think is so much concerned to have those troops and Prince Eugene kept here this campaign, if they are not absolutely necessary in Germany, that there must be some method or other found out if possible to maintain them here the rest of the summer. I find the Queen is very averse to enter into any part of the expense for them and therefore I will do all in my power that it shall not light upon her; between the people here on one side and the Dutch on the other 'tis made an affair of inconceivable difficulty, it breaks my rest and perplexes me beyond imagination, but if I can acquit myself to the Queen's satisfaction in it, I shall have no concern at the pains or trouble of it.

I doubt you will not be very well pleased with the beginning of our campaign here, the prospect of the whole is not the best to me; I expect no great matter without some such miracle as we used to have. I will not trouble you with what I have writ lately to my other friends about my money affairs, it will be communicated to you, and whatever you determine I shall acquiesce in, for I desire nothing for my own particular advantage, but now the sessions is so near an end you must give me leave to put you in mind of my peerage. I flatter myself that you wish me so well that you will have a particular regard to my satisfaction in a matter that is so much at my heart, and that has been so long delayed already that I hope my friends will think I have been made sufficiently uneasy about it. I write a private letter to H. St. J[ohn] by this post upon this and some other affairs and I design to write to the Duke of Shrewsbury too, who has made me so handsome an offer of serving me in all my concerns that whatever schemes I may have it in my power to make I shall always think myself his debtor. I have done myself the honour of writing twice to you, once from hence and once from the Hague. I should be glad to know that those letters came to your hands. I correspond with Mr. Drummond, but I don't find you have sent him any cypher for me to write to you by as you promised you would.

Thomas Coutts to Dr. Arbuthnot.

1711, May 10 Loudon.—Concerning a proposal he had made for advancing the revenue upon tobacco which he thinks will bear testing by the Commissioners of the Customs and the merchants trading to Virginia.

Lady Dupplin to her Aunt [Abigail Harley].

1711, May 10. London—A sad accident happened yesterday, Sir Cholmondeley Dering was killed in a duel by one Mr. Thornhill. They fought with pistols; he died in the evening. They were relations and had been great friends. The quarrel was ten days ago at a drinking bout. Mr. Thornhill affronted my Lord Scarsdale, Sir Ch. would have had him beg my Lord's pardon, told him he was very drunk; he said he was not. Sir Ch. knocked him down, set his foot on his mouth, broke his jaw and dashed out several teeth. He lay very ill, but they say Tuesday night sent the knight a challenge, and he called him up, and they went to Tothill Fields. The first shot killed Sir Cholmondeley; he has left two very little boys. Thornhill is in Newgate.

To-day we have been at the Duchess of Shrewsbury's, to return a visit she made here. It is her assembly, but we came away before the crowd came. Cousin Masham, my mother, sister, and I went together.

My Lord Rochester is buried to-night, my father should have been there, but the Queen was so kind to forbid his going for fear he should catch cold.

The Duke of Argyll to [Robert Harley].

[1711, May.—] This waits upon you to beg your interest with her Majesty for the renewal of the pension she was pleased to settle upon me, of which I am informed I am at present dispossessed. I am very far from pretending that my merit got it me, I am sensible it was owing entirely to the Queen's favour, and I am neither ignorant nor forgetful by whose intercession it was obtained; but not being conscious of having done anything to deserve so severe a reproof as the loss of this will be to me, makes me desire to put you in mind of me at a time when I think I have some reason to apprehend my being forgot.

I had the honour before I left England to communicate to you the difficulties I foresaw would attend me in the post I am now in, but have since met with others of such consequence, and which I am so little able to struggle with, that I did from Genoa beg the favour of her Majesty to employ somebody of more merit than I can pretend to be in this difficult post, and have since my arrival here repeated my humble petition for leave to retire.

Some accidents in my private affairs make my presence absolutely necessary in England, which together with my being altogether incapable of managing this confused machine, makes me with the greatest earnestness hope and beg leave to insist to return.

I do not at all doubt but the sketch I have made of the state of our affairs will in some measure surprise you, but however little credit may be due to my informations either from my putting false colours upon things or mistaking them, I have the satisfaction of being pretty sure of having my notions confirmed by the most part of those who have the honour to serve her Majesty in this country.

I am satisfied this melancholy subject can be no ways pleasing to you, I shall therefore only make mention of one particular which comes immediately under your directions, which is the immense debts due upon this establishment. Mr. Mead is to send over the accounts of them, I shall therefore satisfy myself with assuring you, though we are able to keep people quiet for some time, if orders are not given to adjust these debts and at the same time pay them, these few troops that are here will neither be willing nor indeed able to serve. This you will find to be true when it is too late to remedy it, if proper measures are not immediately fallen upon to satisfy these debts.

Lord Halifax to [Robert Harley].

1711, May 11—The points which you spoke to me about were so considerable that they have employed my thoughts ever since; but that which by a fond expression you called your child has a right to be nearest my heart.

In order to nurse that up and make it grow, I have something to offer which I hope you will approve as the most probable way to make it succeed in all its parts. But it cannot be fully digested and prepared before I know your sentiments about some difficulties that are to be removed; this would not detain you long if you could assign me any hour to wait upon you.

Jane, Countess of Rochester, to [Robert Harley].

1711, May 11. Cockpit—I think I have an indispensable reason to write to you, since I find somebody has been applying to the Duke of Ormond that you may succeed my Lord's father [as High Steward] at Oxford; therefore that no person alive may have any jealousy of a misunderstanding between our families, I cannot but think you will believe it the most reasonable (since you have been named) yourself to let the Duke know 'tis what you do not desire.

I have been all this winter so thoroughly acquainted with the intention of ill meaning people to endeavour to have it received in the world that there was not that perfect friendship, that I know is not to be doubted ; sure I am should the Duke of Ormond recommend, considering his alliance and considering my own Lord is personally respected and loved by the University and known by them, it must have this effect with people that would breed ill blood in the world, and between you and my Lord, that they will turn it as if you intended to conquer from us; though I with reason believe you will do nothing towards him but kindness, and serving his interest, that he is of an age that he will preserve. Indeed seeing my Lord at present under so much grief I can never answer to him should I omit anything that I know, when time has made him recollect, he would think of consequence to him.

I know the duty he had to his father will always make him shew himself to the world his son. You may always depend I am sure, of a sincere and honest faithful friend, and he will be glad to give you proofs of being so.

I hope the applications I make to you neither can be difficult or uneasy to you. What you know my mind in I will not repeat, more than that I do not alter, and for any farther trouble I would wish to give you, is only the renewing the lease of this house, and the lives that are fallen. I persuade myself the great goodness of the Queen will be graciously pleased to think this a justice, as much as a grant, since we have never departed from our duty, though oppressed by ambitious people, that, thank God, could not lessen the reputation nor interest of this family.

H[ENRY] WATKINS to ——.

1711, May [14–]25, N.S. The Camp at Warde—If I had now leisure for speculation I should drop the consideration of Lord Orrery, who according to my last information seems to lay down for his fundamental maxim that he is to oppose every thing that comes from the Dutch deputies. There is scarce any good or any bad I have not heard of Vandenberg. I can tell you some of the new magistrates at Ghent are Mr. Cadogan's rogues, and the town has still enough to furnish out another set.

I believe I should now have been in commission and pay as secretary of the Embassy if Lord Raby had not opposed me, and as much as his letter shows him reconciled to me I tell you as a secret I shall infinitely choose rather to continue in the low state I am, than come into subordination to one who can so easily vary his sentiments about me ; though I promise you not to forfeit his favour by any want of respect. I have not the confidence to make any further application either to Mr. Harley or Mr. St. John.

EARL POULETT to [ROBERT HARLEY].

1711, May 14—Knowing how much your quiet is a sacrifice to the public, I do not offer to trouble you with a visit but when a just concern for your interest engages me necessarily to do it.

You having been some time since so kind to propose Townshend's place for me, I readily accepted it as a brevet for the next thing that fell, to keep me in that credit you had placed me in your friendship and the Queen's service, but really now considering what has since happened and has been said, I think it would be setting me aside in that place, and in the sense of the world be throwing that place away upon me, for though it be in itself a very good one, yet it is settling me in as extraordinary a manner in the Cabinet as Queensberry is now, and rather than be like him there, I had much rather be like myself in the country. I thank God the Queen's affairs are now in so good a condition she does not want any one man's assistance immediately besides yourself, and therefore I may be now the easier excused, than sometime past I thought I could, when there were the greatest dangers and difficulties in the service. You have happily overcome them all, and have gained this advantage to the nation in convincing the world nothing is too great for your undertaking. These are obligations you have laid upon every honest man to be your friend, and in that as well as particular obligations, I am very sure I shall always be in earnest your servant, and think I may be so in some degree, being either quit of it, or with so much credit in the Court as to be useful to you.

I beg you would not think this a sally of humour. My respect for you makes me think long and seriously before I offer to acquaint you with my thoughts, and I hope I may take you to witness for me, I have not been ambitious at first, or presumptuous at last, and I assure you it is with a perfect ease and content what I now write for your service and my credit.

Sir William Barker, M.P. for Ipswich, to [Robert Harley].

1711, May 15—Recommends his uncle Mr. Bacon, a gentleman of a very good family, as governor of Landguard Fort, Col. Jones being dead; with the expectation that he will resign the appointment after a time to the writer, who by some management has so disobliged his friends in Ipswich that if he should now vacate his election it would be difficult for him to be re-chosen.

The Earl of Northampton to Robert Harley.

1711, May 17—The assurance you give me that I have the happiness to be in your thoughts makes me presume to acquaint you that all those Lords who had the honour to wait upon her Majesty at the Revolution have received some mark of the Queen's favour, except myself. I do not know that in the late reign or in this I ever neglected any opportunity wherein I could be serviceable to her Majesty, which makes me now hope that distinguishing mark shall not always be upon me.

The Hon. Peregrine Bertie to [Robert Harley].

[1711, May 17, endorsed] Thursday morning, eight o'clock—I think it my duty to inform you, that if you take the title of Oxford you may find yourself under a mistake, for I can assure you from my own knowledge, that I have been present at consultations with my father and brother at several times when they were assured by the best lawyers that could be found that the earldom was certainly in the Heirs General, the heir male being extinct; and therefore you must not be surprised if you find a Caveat entered by my brother Lindsey against her Majesty granting that title.

'Tis what was done by himself and Lord Abingdon when this Duke of Bucks had thoughts of that title.

[Endorsed by Harley:—"Answered immediately."]

The EARL OF STAIR to the EARL OF MAR, at Whitehall.

1711, May [17-]28. Camp at Le Warde—After the battle of Oudenarde her Majesty was pleased to promise me that whenever she made any peers of Great Britain I should be made one; and on several occasions since has renewed her promise and allowed me to kiss her hand upon it.

I think I can never apply myself to a man who can better judge of the service my father and his friends did in the matter of the Union than to yourself. I hope the friendship which was between you and him won't make you averse to the having this mark of honour and distinction put upon his family. In my profession and as far as it lay in my way I have ever been zealous for the Queen's service, without running at any time into the violence of parties.

GEORGE GRANVILLE to [ROBERT HARLEY].

1711, May 18—What I have chiefly to beg of you is so to represent my case to her Majesty that she may not suffer a name and family always so devoted to the service of her ancestors to be buried in the same grave with my Lord Bath.

It is in her Majesty's power by owning me in some distinguishing manner to make every thing easy. Her own service in some measure requires it, for if I am no longer to appear at the head of that interest which I have been collecting with so much pains and expense in the west for the support of her government, it must naturally and inevitably return into the hands of her enemies.

I am very well advised that I cannot fail in my title to the ancient patrimony of my family. If her Majesty might be inclined to revive in me likewise some of its honours, I flatter myself there are sufficient pretensions to induce her, with your assistance and protection. If I am thought unworthy to be continued upon the level with those who have gone before me, I shall think myself unworthy to live, or at least to show my face again in my own country.

The DUKE OF SOMERSET to [ROBERT HARLEY].

1711, May 18. Kensington—Since I cannot obtain leave to wait on you I must try for leave to write on this condition that I do promise to give you as little trouble as any man, but as you are and are to be very soon declared *le premier ministre*, I hope you will allow me to make application to you as occasion shall require; but if I am not to do it tell me so and I will have done.

[JOHN DRUMMOND to the EARL OF OXFORD.]

1711, May [18-]29, N.S. Amsterdam—The Duke of Marlborough I once, I think, wrote you, valued himself on having no hand in the treaty of Barrier with the States. Some letters and expressions of his Grace's on this subject to Prince Eugene and the Imperial ministers being come lately, by what I can hear, to the ears of some of the principal ministers of this State, they in conversation put it on this foot, that this treaty of Lord Townshend's, cutting off all his hopes of being Governor of the Spanish Netherlands and new conquests, makes him against it, and that he will never forgive Lord Townshend for concluding it without his knowledge. Notwithstanding all this, his Grace and Lord Townshend, immediately before my Lord's departure, kept the longest and most frequent conferences with the Grand Pensionary which they had ever been known to do, and I am afraid they agreed in their sentiments on such occasions, to see if they could get that great and honest man to have no faith in the Queen's present ministry but to believe the former and their party the only sincere and faithful friends to Holland.   I am confident notwithstanding the great friendship which Lord Townshend had contracted here, by laying himself entirely out for their service, if that was his doctrine, he has not so entirely succeeded as he may think, for in the last meeting I had with the old gentleman I found him more convinced of the honest and good intentions of the Queen's friends than ever before.

I wrote Mr. Secretary St. John last post a long account of the conference I had, and having read to the Pensionary some passages of Mr. St. John's letters to me, he asked me very earnestly, do you never now get any letters from Mr. Harley? Cannot you prevail on, or encourge him to write plainly to you his own opinion of and thoughts of our present circum-stances?   My answer was, that Mr. Secretary's sentiments were certainly the Queen's and Mr. Harley's; that Mr. Harley had so much other business on his hands, viz. the whole care and management of the finances, the entire direction of the House of Commons to go on in measures and consent to effectual methods for carrying on the common cause, and this long expensive and destructive war, that we may the sooner arrive at a so much longed for peace.   To this he replied, I wish he would resolve to write plain, and I should give you plain answers. I put him in mind that you had once wrote me very plainly which I had shown him, but no effect, in which you wrote those words :—If the Dutch are hearty for us, and mean well with us, whey don't they send over one to whom we could open our hearts freely ?   I told him that at the same time I had acquainted him with the mean opinion Mr. St. John had of Vrybergen and of his trifling behaviour at the late turn of affairs, and yet no pains were taken to supply his place with one more acceptable and in whom the ministry would have the necessary confidence.

He asked me if I had had late complaints or new insinuations to desire some other person to be sent over. I said that there had been so much said on that subject without any new resolution, that it was thought needless to insist farther.   He then began plainly to tell me the many difficulties he was under by cabals and parties, what a confused and turbulent set of men the Zealanders were, out of whom the residing minister from the States to England must be chosen. I told him it was no ordinary residing minister perhaps that was so much wanted, and seeing M. Buys had been sent over before for the Duke of Marlborough's pleasure, why could not he or any other well inclined person be sent over again to please perhaps the Queen as well as her friends. He said he had sounded the tempers of the leading men of the parties as well in confi-dence with him, as of others who some time thwarted some reasonable measures; but he found M. Buys would not be to their liking, having gained himself some enemies by taking much upon him and being very tenacious, and his constant pushing every thing for the private benefit of his town, whether for the universal good or not, had created jealousy against him. Neither could he who was employed as a treating minister with those of the enemy be sent over without giving great hopes to the enemy that it was on account of our inclinations for a sudden peace, and raising the same opinion in the Provinces ; so that he can not be the man. Neither did he know at this time any man who had so good a pretence to go into England about his own affairs as one of the heads of the Nobles, if his employment in the army would allow him, a person of great application, who had improved himself of late years extremely in civil as well as in military affairs, who was beloved and believed by all sorts of men in power in this country; even those who seemed bent to do him prejudice after his master's death are now become his greatest friends and seek opportunities to oblige him. And at last he was, named under faithful promise that I should not name him, till he should see whether it was practicable for him to leave his post during the campaign, and till he sounded the opinions of the leading men of the Provinces whether they would allow him to leave his post on account of private business for a month or two. He then asked me whether I thought he would be acceptable to the present ministry and if they would open their minds freely to him. In answer I desired leave to write about it, but could not obtain it. Then I said I believed in my own opinion he would be very acceptable, the more because he was known to be his favourite. He said he would not have him pass under that term of his favourite, but that I might depend upon his being an honest man, and knew at the same time very well how to behave to those he found otherwise, and that if he came off from the army he must come entirely on pretence of private business, and perhaps even tell another great man or two of the army that he was only coming down to Holland. I believe you can easily guess the person without any farther description, and that you may not be left to guess, it is the person who writes sometimes to the Duke of Shrewsbury and to Van Hues your Dutch friend, who I find writes regularly to the Grand Pensionary.

My Lord Ambassador is very commendably industrious to discover the Jacobite correspondence through this country, particularly through one Taylor, a parson of the Church of England, who it seems was starving at St. Germain and came to Rotterdam some years ago, and has often solicited to get over but has been hindered, refusing to take the oaths. He is also it seems employed in sending them your pamphlets and gazettes, for which it is supposed he has a pension, and I am told he has the charity of some of your nobility called high churchmen because as they term it he has been always a zealous protestant. My Lord Drummond got leave by the Duke of Roxburgh's means contrary to the inclinations and opinions of all his protestant relations to come over to Flanders and to go to the Baths of Aix la Chapelle, having then as they say spit blood and looked to be in a decay. He has lived at Bruges all this winter near a monastery in which his lady's aunt, a sister of the late Duke of Norfolk, is. I refused to supply his Lordship with money that I might have no correspondence with him, yet I am told my name is in one of the intercepted letters, which I cannot help, and I believe it is not my name, for my Lord has two or three Drummonds with him. There is one Mr. Charles Fleming has been pretty much at Bruges with him and was a short while at Utrecht; I am told he wanted leave to go home. My Lord Mar I believe knows him, and it is very like if he were applied rightly to, or let home, he might be able to inform you more certainly about the Pretender's progress than any other; but you cannot be better informed of this person than by Lord Mar, and I entreat you may not name me, for I know not how my Lord might take it.

We meddle much in conversation here with supplying vacancies in your ministry as soon as any happen. Vrybergen wrote over that Lord Somers, Lord Townshend, &c. were to come in immediately as the Lord

President died, but he contradicted it by the very next post. We now talk of Lord Pembroke, the Duke of Somerset, and the Duke of Bucks; the first is our favourite. I have been much afraid that the Emperor's death would entail another campaign on us. I hope through some remarks I have lately made that this may be the last, though it even requires some lucky turns and events to bring it about.

I have made your compliments to Monsieur Buys who received them with much respect and affection, and promises to write to you himself. I find him still hearty for a peace but always saying how shall we get Philip out of Spain; this is a subject he would gladly have me say something on, but I dare not meddle with it. He is afraid when the Imperialists have got their Emperor chosen they will make the best terms they can for the Empire and leave us to conquer Spain or to hire their troops to carry on the war as long as we please. I hope you will find some effectual way to hinder the export of your coin, it is brought over here in great parcels and melted down immediately by the Jews and sold to the mint masters and converted into the current coin of this country.

George Granville to [Robert Harley].

1711, May 19. [London]—You may depend upon it that nothing can be more prejudicial to you than the appointment of Lord Radnor as lord lieutenant of Cornwall, for however that family may be under your direction here, there is that general aversion to it there that they will give everything for lost if such a step be taken; it could end in nothing but an entire loss of that interest which is only able to serve you. I am likewise informed that Lord Carteret puts in for it; I have as much tenderness for him as anybody can have, but to grant this would be making the Queen take part in a private cause and give a decision which I am sure can otherwise never be in his favour. I will say nothing about myself, I have left you to judge and determine the fate of an old friend and faithful servant. But where is the difficulty in the person of Lord Rochester? Is any man more loved or more esteemed by all the gentlemen of the county? You can do nothing more to put them in good humour, and they already expect his appointment.

Sir Simon Harcourt, Lord Keeper, to [Robert Harley].

1711, May 20—I have this morning spoken with Mr. Lutwich who declines taking the Judge's place as I thought he would. I really know no person fitter than Mr. Jeffryes, there is much less choice than you may think there is; I mentioned it to him some months since, and I found him no way fond of it, so that you may think and determine on any other as you think now fit. If you will accept of him, I must immediately give him notice, that he may secure his election, and that the patent may pass as soon as I can hear from him.

I sent for Mr. Dee, I find he will take a Judge's place in Wales, but he told me if he might choose for himself he had rather be a Commissioner of the Appeals from the Excise Office. If that cannot be, I would name him for the Pembroke Circuit. He is an honest man and a good lawyer, I know no objection against his having both. The two together would be a handsome provision, though either will satisfy him. I can't find another to my mind for Pembrokeshire.

As for Lord Bulkeley's circuit I know not what to do. They are fond of two, Serjeant Lloyd and Peisly, and I find the Queen has a disposition for Mr. Peisly, but if you can provide for him as well otherwise, it will I think be better than making him a Judge. I have no opinion of Serjeant Lloyd's ability or usefulness, but since these countries desire him and I am at a loss to find one much better, I think you may let him pass. Baron Price extremely desires it, but your countryman Mr. Bridges is fitter much than either of them. Let me beg you to believe whatever is most acceptable to you will be agreeable to me, all I beg is your speedy resolution, for these removes must be before term, otherwise the Judges who are to be displaced will have the next term's salary, which ought not to be.

You desired me to let you know before 'twas too late what small matters I desired for any of my friends. I have very little trouble to give you on that head. I mentioned Sir James Chamberlain to you last night, a Commissionership in the Salt Office would please him, I think he should not be offered less.

I have a neighbour in the country who has lived reputably there all his time, but having a numerous and expensive family is almost run out of his estate; I should be pleased with your preserving him from ruin, I hope you may have room in the Stamp Office; I mean Mr. Jordan of Witney. If my Lord President had been living he would have been very pressing for him for the Stamp Office or some such Commission. You remember the petition the Chief Justice and I made you for old Courteney for a Commissionership of Appeals.

'Tis expected from me I should get something for Godfrey Harcourt or his son; I believe a reasonable matter in Wales would satisfy. I have no one else to ask for. The Lord Lieutenants and *Custodes Rotulorum* should be I think appointed at the first entrance into your Ministry. The Queen once spoke to me to bring a bill for Lord Scarsdale to be *Custos* for Derbyshire and that I should speak to the Secretary to prepare a bill to make him also Lord Lieutenant of the same county.

I had also the like orders for Lord Denbigh for Leicestershire both for *Custos* and Lord Lieutenant, but on further consideration her Majesty was pleased to tell me it should not be done till towards the rising of Parliament, when she would make all the changes she wished of this kind.

If you make G. G[ranville] a Peer, will you not of course have him succeed upon Lord Rochester's death in Cornwall. The following Lords are not yet displaced :—

Bucks—Lord Bridgwater, Lord Lieutenant and *Custos*. Why not Lord Cheney?

Cambridge—Lord Orford, *Custos*.

Dorset.—Duke of Bolton, Lord Lieutenant and *Custos*.

Hereford—Lord Coningsby, *Custos*. Duke of Kent, Lord Lieutenant. Why not the Earl of Oxford?

Salop—Lord Bradford. Duke of Shrewsbury or Lord Weymouth.

Westmorland—Lord Wharton. *Qu.* Lord Thanet.

Wiltshire—Lord Dorchester, *Custos*. Lord Weymouth.

I desire you to speak to the Queen upon such of these changes as you think proper, and let me know when I may properly desire to receive her commands thereupon.

I forgot to tell you, Sir John Stonhouse sometime since mentioned to me an office in Ireland which is now held by one life, 'tis the Remembrancer of the Exchequer in Ireland; he said it produced in England five or six hundred per annum as he was informed. If there be such an office and it be not disposed of, he would be pleased with a grant in reversion after the present life.

The Dean of Carlisle [Atterbury] desired he might have the making my preamble; if you do really intend to order one for me, I think you must send to him.

THOMAS BLACKWELL to [ROBERT HARLEY].

1711, May 22. Edinburgh—Having seen a most friendly and obliging letter of yours to the Rev. Mr. Carstares, which hath very much called and comforted the spirits of several ministers in this church, I have presumed to lay the following case before you.

Mr. Andrew Burnet, who was before the late happy Revolution one of the Episcopal ministers in the city of Aberdeen, was deprived of his benefice by the Parliament of Scotland and his church appointed to be declared vacant, upon the account of his not taking the oaths to King William and for his protesting against the authority of a Committee of the General Assembly sent up to " cognosce " church affairs in that city. And this was done by the Parliament upon the first day of July 1695.

Notwithstanding of all which, and of his banishment by Parliament from the said city, yet the same Mr. Burnet hath not only for many years intruded into that place and set up a meeting house therein, withdrawing the people from the congregations of the Established ministry, but also within these few weeks upon occasion of the death of one of the Presbyterian ministers in the place, did send three of his congregation to the magistrates of the city, requiring to be " reponed " to the church affirming he was now qualified by taking the oaths to her Majesty Queen Anne; which obliged me to procure letters from her Majesty's Advocate and other persons of influence showing our magistrates and Mr. Burnet that his desire was most illegal and of dangerous consequence to the present Established Church.

Upon what grounds of late Mr. Burnet and others of his party have conceived fondly a great deal of hope, and are thereupon become very bold, I need not inform the judicious Mr. Harley; only if some prudent way be not fallen upon, by some letter to our magistrates who are perfectly friendly, in which Mr. Burnet may be made to know his mistake, it is uncertain what irregular methods may be taken by him, and his party; and what people in this National church are the most sincere faithful and loyal subjects to her Majesty, and cordial well-wishers of the present Government I would gladly hope remains by this time no mystery nor matter of doubt to Mr. Harley.

SIR DAVID DALRYMPLE to DR. ARBUTHNOT.

1711, May 22. Edinburgh—I have been advised from many hands that there is a design to lay me aside and to bring in either him that went before me [Sir W. J. Stewart] or some one who has not until now fallen under consideration for such a post. I would fain know if there is anything in it, and for what cause. Now I do sincerely protest that I did not willingly embrace that office, that it has done good neither to my private business nor to my health, and that it will be neither so reputable nor so easy to return to the bar as it was very honourable to have continued. I shall be the more easy if I do not suffer as one guilty in her Majesty's eyes of something unworthy of her favour. If the change come from any other cause I will bear it as I can, glad to have contributed nothing to it.

Our assembly is not by much so temperate as the last, but has gone on and I think will end peaceably.

GEORGE GRANVILLE to [ROBERT HARLEY].

1711, May 22—I find by my countrymen that there is a general
desire and expectation that the Queen will revive the honours of my
family in myself, and that they may be the same which were borne
by my uncle, two of them being in memory of the place where my
grandfather was slain [Lansdowne]. 'Tis likewise their opinion that a
declaration of her Majesty's pleasure in this case without any delay
would be of public service in the county, as well as fix my own private
affairs. I am by this time in possession of the estate of my family, and
this favour declared at the same time will settle me in the quiet enjoyment of it. I therefore most earnestly entreat you to obtain this request
for me.

[SIR SIMON HARCOURT to the EARL OF OXFORD.]

1711, May 24—Give me leave from the bottom of my heart to wish
you perpetual continuance and increase of honour.

Lord Abingdon tells me 'tis necessary your Lordship should send
notice to the Earl Marshal (my Lord Sussex) of your intention and
desire to be introduced to-morrow that he may order the Heralds to be
at the House of Lords to attend you.

ROBERT HARLEY to [the EARL OF SUSSEX].

1711, May 24—I leave this letter at your house to acquaint your
Lordship that the Queen has had the goodness to create your humble
servant an Earl. The patent will be passed so that I may be introduced
tomorrow into the House of Lords. I make it my humble request that
you will give the directions which are proper on this occasion to the
Heralds.

W. BROMLEY, Speaker, to [the EARL OF OXFORD].

1711, May 28—You are pleased to command my thoughts what the
Queen should say at this conclusion of the session. Some things are so
very obvious I shall presume to trouble you with them :—to begin from
the first paragraph in the speech at the opening of the Session, and to
express an entire satisfaction in what has been done ; to take notice
of the large and effectual supplies granted, and the debts provided after
such a long and expensive war, and to make ample declarations of her
intentions to countenance and encourage those, who by principle have
the greatest zeal and affection for the establishment in church and state.
These cannot be fuller and better declarations to this purpose, than what
are in some of the first speeches after her Majesty's accession to the
throne. After taking notice of the debts it may be proper to add that
care shall be taken by a prudent and frugal management not to run into
the same condition again.

This is in obedience to your Lordship and I hope will be accordingly,
received ; it is not to suggest anything, but what I am sure must occur
to you. Our business in the House of Commons is pressed so fast, that
those who press it propose the Parliament rising on Saturday ; if that
is intended I only offer it to your Lordship whether any time is to be
lost as to the changes in which the members will be concerned. Besides,
the declarations of them, I suppose Commissions and Patents must pass
to make the vacancies.

KER of Kersland, to [the EARL OF OXFORD].

1711, May 29—If I had not assured confidence in your honour and justice no earthly thing is capable of reviving my **drooping spirits under** the present pressure of enemies and straits to which my zealous service to her Majesty, and faithful adherence to your interest, notwithstanding temptations and threats, have exposed me. My innocence and peace of mind would support me in all my trials if an old family which is of significance in Scotland did not perish with me. Do with me as you please, only let me have dispatch and I promise to omit no opportunity of satisfying you.

JOHN CHAMBERLAYNE to [the EARL OF OXFORD].

1711, Restoration day. Petty France, Westminster—When the great men and all my betters have done their duty at your door I shall presume to take my turn too, and in the meantime I make bold to tell your Lordship how much I applaud her Majesty's wise choice of a First Minister; but I should be no less foolish than bold if I should offer this as my own private thoughts; no, my Lord, 'tis the opinion of all the philosophers and unprejudiced men (who are a sort of *squadron volante* without doors, and who *nullius jurant in verba magistri*) which I am now going to lay before your Lordship : and their opinion — which may make the twelfth, when Dr. Swift, or whoever is the author of the *Eleven Opinions about Mr. H———y*, shall reprint that ingenious pamphlet—is that whilst the Earl of Oxford, and our new Lord Treasurer, holds the scales of the contending parties he will produce harmony out of discord, and so long our Church and Nation will be in a safe and flourishing condition : and as this is their opinion, so is their prayer, that the said Earl of Oxford may long hold the balance, and always have weight enough to make an equilibrium; and then he may be able to stop that party tide even with his thumb, which has hitherto borne down all the Ministers before it.

That your Ministry may be more lasting and more glorious than all your predecessors are my sincerest wishes.

The EARL OF SHAFTESBURY to [the EARL OF OXFORD].

1711, May 30. Reigate—The honour you have done me in many kind enquiries after my health, and the favour you have shown me lately in forwarding the only means I have left for my recovery by trying the air of a warmer climate, oblige me 'ere I leave England to return your Lordship my most humble thanks and acknowledgments in this manner, since I am unable to do it in a better.

I might perhaps do injustice to myself, having had no opportunity of late years to pay my particular respects to you, if I should attempt any otherwise to compliment your Lordship on the late honours you have received, than by appealing to the early acquaintance and strict corre. spondence I had once the honour to maintain with you and your family, for which I had been bred almost from my infancy to have the highest regard. Your Lordship well knows my principles and behaviour from the first hour I engaged in any public concern, and with what zeal I spent some years of my life in supporting your interest, which I thought of greater moment to the public than my own or family's could ever be. What the natural effects are of private friendships so founded, and what the consequences of different opinions intervening, your Lordship who is so good a judge of men and things can better resolve with yourself than I can possibly suggest. And being so knowing in friends (of whom you have acquired so many) you can recollect how those ties or obligations have been hitherto preserved towards you; and whose friendships, affections and principles you may for the future best depend on in all circumstances and variations, public and private.

For my own part I shall say only that I very sincerely wish you all happiness and can with no man living congratulate more heartily (*sic*) on what I account a real honour and prosperity. Your conduct of the public will be the just earnest and insurance of your greatness and power. And I shall then chiefly congratulate with your Lordship on your merited honours and advancement, when by the happy effects it appears evidently in the service of what cause, and for the advantage of what interest, they were acquired and employed. Had I been to wish by what hands the public should have been served, the honour of the first part (your Lordship well knows) had fallen to you long since. If others from whom I least hoped have done greatly and as became them, I hope it possible you will still exceed all they have performed, and accomplish the great work so gloriously begun and carried on for the rescue of liberty and the deliverance of Europe and mankind.

CIRCULAR OF THE COMMISSION.

Public Record Office, Chancery Lane,
London, W.C.

HER MAJESTY has been pleased to appoint under Her Sign Manual certain Commissioners to ascertain what unpublished MSS. are extant in the collections of private persons and in institutions which are calculated to throw light upon subjects connected with the civil, ecclesiastical, literary, or scientific history of this country. The present Commissioners are :—

Lord Esher, Master of the Rolls, the Marquess of Salisbury, K.G., the Marquess of Lothian, K.T., the Earl of Rosebery, K.G., Lord Edmond Fitzmaurice, the Bishop of Oxford, the Bishop of Limerick, Lord Acton, Lord Carlingford, K.P., and Mr. H. C. Maxwell Lyte, C.B.

The Commissioners think it probable that you may feel an interest in this object and be willing to assist in the attainment of it; and with that view they desire to lay before you an outline of the course which they usually follow.

If any nobleman or gentleman express his willingness to submit any unprinted book, or collection of documents in his possession or custody to the examination of the Commissioners, they will cause an inspection to be made by some competent person, and should the MSS. appear to come within the scope of their enquiry, a report containing copies or abstracts of them will be drawn up, printed, and submitted to the owner, with a view to obtaining his consent to the publication of the whole, or of such part of it as he may think fit, among the proceedings of the Commission, which are presented to Parliament every Session.

To avoid any possible apprehension that the examination of papers by the Commissioners may extend to title-deeds or documents of present legal value, positive instructions are given to every person who inspects MSS. on their behalf that nothing relating to the titles of existing owners is to be divulged, and that if in the course of his work any modern title-deeds or papers of a private character chance to come before him, they are to be instantly put aside, and are not to be examined or calendared under any pretence whatever.

The object of the Commission is solely the discovery of unknown historical and literary materials, and in all their proceedings the Commissioners will direct their attention to that object exclusively.

In practice it has been found more satisfactory, when the collection of manuscripts is a large one, for the inspector to make a selection therefrom at the place of deposit and to obtain the owner's consent to remove the selected papers to the Public Record Office in London, where they can be more fully dealt with, and where they are preserved with the same care as if they formed part of the muniments of the realm, during the term of their examination. Among the numerous owners of MSS. who have allowed their family paperis of historical interest to be temporarily removed from their muniment rooms and lent to the Commissioners to facilitate the preparation of a report may be named: The Duke of Rutland, the Duke of Portland, the Marquess of Salisbury, the Marquess Townshend, the Earl of Dartmouth, the Earl of Ancaster, Lord Braye, Lord Hothfield, Mrs. Stopford Sackville, Mr. le Fleming, of Rydal, and Mr. Fortescue, of Dropmore.

The costs of inspections, reports and calendars, and the conveyance of documents, will be defrayed at the public expense, without any charge to owners.

The Commissioners will also, if so requested, give their advice as to the best means of repairing and preserving any papers or MSS. which may be in a state of decay, and are of historical or literary value.

The Commissioners will feel much obliged if you will communicate to them the names of any gentlemen who may be able and willing to assist iu obtaining the objects for which this Commission has been issued.

J. J. CARTWRIGHT,
Secretary.

HISTORICAL MANUSCRIPTS COMMISSION.

Date.	—	Size.	Sessional Paper.	Price.
				s. *d.*
1870 (Re-printed 1874.)	FIRST REPORT, WITH APPENDIX - - Contents :— ENGLAND. House of Lords; Cambridge Colleges ·Abingdon, and other Corporations, &c. SCOTLAND. Advocates' Library, Glasgow Corporation, &c. IRELAND. Dublin, Cork, and other Corporations, &c.	f'cap.	[C. 55]	1 6
1871	SECOND REPORT, WITH APPENDIX, AND INDEX TO THE FIRST AND SECOND REPORTS - - - - - Contents :— ENGLAND. House of Lords; Cambridge Colleges; Oxford Colleges; Monastery of Dominican Friars at Woodchester, Duke of Bedford, Earl Spencer, &c. SCOTLAND. Aberdeen and St. Andrew's Universities, &c. IRELAND. Marquis of Ormonde; Dr. Lyons, &c.	„	[C. 441]	3 10
1872 (Re-printed 1895.)	THIRD REPORT, WITH APPENDIX AND INDEX - - - - - Contents :— ENGLAND. House of Lords; Cambridge Colleges; Stonyhurst College; Bridgewater and other Corporations; Duke of Northumberland, Marquis of Lansdowne, Marquis of Bath, &c. SCOTLAND. University of Glasgow; Duke of Montrose, &c. IRELAND. Marquis of Ormonde; Black Book of Limerick, &c.	„	[C. 673]	6 0
1873	FOURTH REPORT, WITH APPENDIX. PART I. - - - - - Contents :— ENGLAND. House of Lords; Westminster Abbey; Cambridge and Oxford Colleges; Cinque Ports, Hythe, and other Corporations, Marquis of Bath, Earl of Denbigh, &c. SCOTLAND. Duke of Argyll, &c. IRELAND. Trinity College, Dublin; Marquis of Ormonde.	„	[C. 857]	6 8
1873	DITTO. PART II. INDEX - - -	„	[C.857i.]	2 6

Date.	—	Size.	Sessional Paper.	Price.
				s. d.
1876	FIFTH REPORT, WITH APPENDIX. PART I. - Contents:— ENGLAND. House of Lords; Oxford and Cambridge Colleges; Dean and Chapter of Canterbury; Rye, Lydd, and other Corporations, Duke of Sutherland, Marquis of Lansdowne, Reginald Cholmondeley, Esq., &c. SCOTLAND. Earl of Aberdeen, &c.	f'cap.	[C.1432]	7 0
,,	DITTO. PART II. INDEX - - -	,,	[C.1432 i.]	3 6
1877	SIXTH REPORT, WITH APPENDIX. PART I. - Contents:— ENGLAND. House of Lords; Oxford and Cambridge Colleges; Lambeth Palace; Black Book of the Archdeacon of Canterbury; Bridport, Wallingford, and other Corporations; Lord Leconfield, Sir Reginald Graham, Sir Henry Ingilby, &c. SCOTLAND. Duke of Argyll, Earl of Moray, &c. IRELAND. Marquis of Ormonde.	,,	[C.1745]	8 6
(Reprinted 1893.)	DITTO. PART II. INDEX - - -	,,	[C.2102]	1 10
1879 (Reprinted 1895.)	SEVENTH REPORT, WITH APPENDIX. PART I. - - - - - Contents:— House of Lords; County of Somerset; Earl of Egmont, Sir Frederick Graham, Sir Harry Verney, &c.	,,	[C.2340]	7 6
(Reprinted 1895.)	DITTO. PART II. APPENDIX AND INDEX - Contents:— Duke of Athole, Marquis of Ormonde, S. F. Livingstone, Esq., &c.	,,	[C.2340 i.]	3 6
1881	EIGHTH REPORT, WITH APPENDIX AND INDEX. PART I. - - - Contents:— List of collections examined, 1869–1880. ENGLAND. House of Lords; Duke of Marlborough; Magdalen College, Oxford; Royal College of Physicians; Queen Anne's Bounty Office; Corporations of Chester, Leicester, &c. IRELAND. Marquis of Ormonde, Lord Emly, The O'Conor Don, Trinity College, Dublin, &c.	,,	[C.3040]	8 6
1881	DITTO. PART II. APPENDIX AND INDEX - Contents:— Duke of Manchester.	,,	[C.3040 i.]	1 9

Date.	—	Size.	Sessional Paper.	Price.
				s. d.
1881	DITTO. PART III. APPENDIX AND INDEX Contents :— Earl of Ashburnham.	f'cap.	[C. 3040 ii.]	1 4
1883 (Re-printed 1895.)	NINTH REPORT, WITH APPENDIX AND INDEX. PART I. - - - - Contents :— St. Paul's and Canterbury Cathedrals; Eton College ; Carlisle, Yarmouth, Canterbury, and Barnstaple Corporations, &c.	„	[C.3773]	5 2
1884 (Re-printed 1895.)	DITTO. PART II. APPENDIX AND INDEX - Contents :— ENGLAND. House of Lords, Earl of Leicester ; C. Pole Gell, Alfred Morrison, Esqs., &c. SCOTLAND. Lord Elphinstone, H. C. Maxwell Stuart, Esq., &c. IRELAND. Duke of Leinster, Marquis of Drogheda, &c.	„	[C.3773 i.]	6 3
1884	NINTH REPORT. PART III. APPENDIX AND INDEX - - - - - Contents :— Mrs. Stopford Sackville.	„	[C.3773 ii.]	1 7
1883 (Re-printed 1895.)	CALENDAR OF THE MANUSCRIPTS OF THE MARQUIS OF SALISBURY, K.G. (or CECIL MSS.). PART I. - - - -	8vo.	[C.3777]	3 5
1888	DITTO. PART II. - - -	„	[C.5463]	3 5
1889	DITTO. PART III. - - -	„	[C. 5889 v.]	2 1
1892	DITTO. PART IV. - - -	„	[C.6823]	2 11
1894	DITTO. PART V. - - -	„	[C.7574]	2 6
1895	DITTO. PART VI. - - -	„	[C.7884]	2 8
1885	TENTH REPORT - - - - This is introductory to the following :—	„	[C.4548]	0 3½
1885 (Re-printed 1895.)	(1.) APPENDIX AND INDEX - - - Earl of Eglinton, Sir J. S. Maxwell, Bart., and C. S. H. Drummond Moray, C. F. Weston Underwood, G. W. Digby, Esqs.	„	[C.4575]	3 7
1885	(2.) APPENDIX AND INDEX - - The Family of Gawdy.	„	[C.4576 iii.]	1 4
1885	(3.) APPENDIX AND INDEX - - Wells Cathedral.	„	[C.4576 ii.]	2 0

Date.	—	Size.	Sessional Paper.	Price.
				_s._ _d._
1885	(4.) APPENDIX AND INDEX - - Earl of Westmorland ; Capt. Stewart ; Lord Stafford ; Sir N. W. Throckmorton, Sir P. T. Mainwaring, Lord Muncaster, Capt. J. F. Bagot, Earl of Kilmorey, Earl of Powis, and others, the Corporations of Kendal, Wenlock, Bridgnorth, Eye, Plymouth, and the County of Essex ; and Stonyhurst College.	8vo.	[C.4576]	3 6
1885 (Reprinted 1895.)	(5.) APPENDIX AND INDEX - - - The Marquis of Ormonde, Earl of Fingall, Corporations of Galway, Waterford, the Sees of Dublin and Ossory, the Jesuits in Ireland.	,,	[C. 4576 i.]	2 10
1887	(6.) APPENDIX AND INDEX - - - Marquis of Abergavenny, Lord Braye, G. F. Luttrell, P. P. Bouverie, W. Bromley Davenport, R. T. Balfour, Esquires.	,,	[C.5242]	1 7
1887	ELEVENTH REPORT - - - - This is introductory to the following :—	,,	[C. 5060 vi.]	0 3
1887	(1.) APPENDIX AND INDEX - - - H. D. Skrine, Esq., Salvetti Correspondence.	,,	[C.5060]	1 1
1887	(2.) APPENDIX AND INDEX - - House of Lords. 1678-1688.	,,	[C. 5060 i.]	2 0
1887	(3.) APPENDIX AND INDEX - - Corporations of Southampton and Lynn.	,,	[C. 5060 ii.]	1 8
1887	(4.) APPENDIX AND INDEX - - Marquis Townshend.	,,	[C. 5060 iii.]	2 6
1887	(5.) APPENDIX AND INDEX - - Earl of Dartmouth.	,,	[C. 5060 iv.]	2 8
1887	(6.) APPENDIX AND INDEX - - Duke of Hamilton.	,,	[C. 5060 v.]	1 6
1888	(7.) APPENDIX AND INDEX - - - Duke of Leeds, Marchioness of Waterford, Lord Hothfield, &c.; Bridgwater Trust Office, Reading Corporation, Inner Temple Library.	,,	[C.5612]	2 0
1890	TWELFTH REPORT - - - - This is introductory to the following :—	,,	[C.5889]	0 3
1888	(1.) APPENDIX - - - Earl Cowper, K.G. (Coke MSS., at Melbourne Hall, Derby). Vol. I.	,,	[C.5472]	2 7
1888	(2.) APPENDIX - - - Ditto. Vol. II.	,,	[C.5613]	2 5

Date.	—	Size.	Sessional Paper.	Price.
				s. d.
1889	(3.) APPENDIX AND INDEX - - - Ditto. Vol. III.	8vo.	[C. 5889 i.]	1 4
1888	(4.) APPENDIX - - - - The Duke of Rutland, G.C.B. Vol. I.	„	[C.5614]	3 2
1891	(5.) APPENDIX AND INDEX - - - Ditto. Vol. II.	„	[C. 5889 ii.]	2 0
1889	(6.) APPENDIX AND INDEX - - - House of Lords, 1689-1690.	„	[C. 5889 iii.]	2 1
1890	(7.) APPENDIX AND INDEX - - - S. H. le Fleming, Esq., of Rydal.	„	[C. 5889 iv.]	1 11
1891	(8.) APPENDIX AND INDEX - - - The Duke of Athole, K.T., and the Earl of Home.	„	[C.6338]	1 0
1891	(9.) APPENDIX AND INDEX - - - The Duke of Beaufort, K.G., the Earl of Donoughmore, J. H. Gurney, W. W. B. Hulton, R. W. Ketton, G. A. Aitken, P. V. Smith, Esqs.; Bishop of Ely; Cathedrals of Ely, Gloucester, Lincoln, and Peterborough; Corporations of Gloucester, Higham Ferrers, and Newark; Southwell Minster; Lincoln District Registry.	„	[C. 6338 i.]	2 6
1891	(10.) APPENDIX - - - The First Earl of Charlemont. Vol. I. 1745-1783.	„	[C. 6338 ii.]	1 11
1892	THIRTEENTH REPORT - - - This is introductory to the following :—	„	[C.6827]	0 3
1891	(1.) APPENDIX - - - - The Duke of Portland. Vol. I.	„	[C.6474]	3 0
	(2.) APPENDIX AND INDEX - - - Ditto. Vol. II.	„	[C. 6827 i.]	2 0
1892	(3.) APPENDIX - - - - J. B. Fortescue, Esq., of Dropmore, Vol. I.	„	[C.6660]	2 7
1892	(4.) APPENDIX AND INDEX - - - Corporations of Rye, Hastings, and Hereford. Capt. F. C. Loder-Symonds, E. R. Wodehouse, M.P., J. Dovaston, Esqs., Sir T. B. Lennard, Bart., Rev. W. D. Macray, and Earl of Dartmouth (Supplementary Report).	„	[C.6810]	2 4
1892	(5.) APPENDIX AND INDEX - - - House of Lords, 1690-1691.	„	[C.6822]	2 4
1893	(6.) APPENDIX AND INDEX - - - Sir W. FitzHerbert, Bart. The Delaval Family, of Seaton Delaval; The Earl of Ancaster and General Lyttelton-Annesley.	„	[C.7166]	1 4

Date.	——	Size.	Sessional Paper.	Price.
				s. d.
1893	(7.) APPENDIX AND INDEX - - - The Earl of Lonsdale.	8vo.	[C.7241]	1 3
1893	(8.) APPENDIX AND INDEX - - The First Earl of Charlemont. Vol. II. 1784–1799.	,,	[C.7424]	1 11
1896	FOURTEENTH REPORT - - - This is introductory to the following :—	,,	[C.7983]	0 3
1894	(1.) APPENDIX AND INDEX - - The Duke of Rutland, G.C.B. Vol. III.	,,	[C.7476]	1 11
1894	(2.) APPENDIX - - - - The Duke of Portland. Vol. III.	,,	[C.7569]	2 8
1894	(3.) APPENDIX AND INDEX - The Duke of Roxburghe; Sir H. H. Campbell, Bart.; the Earl of Strathmore; and the Countess Dowager of Seafield.	,,	[C.7570]	1 2
1894	(4.) APPENDIX AND INDEX - - Lord Kenyon.	,,	[C.7571]	2 10
1896	(5.) APPENDIX - - - J. B. Fortescue, Esq., of Dropmore. Vol. II.	,,	[C.7572]	2 8
1895	(6.) APPENDIX AND INDEX - House of Lords, 1692–1693.	,,	[C.7573]	1 11
1895	(7.) APPENDIX - - - - The Marquess of Ormonde.	,,	[C.7678]	1 10
1895	(8.) APPENDIX AND INDEX - - Lincoln, Bury St. Edmunds, Hertford, and Great Grimsby Corporations; The Dean and Chapter of Worcester, and of Lichfield; The Bishop's Registry of Worcester.	,,	[C.7881]	1 5
1895	(9.) APPENDIX AND INDEX - - The Earl of Buckinghamshire, the Earl of Lindsey, the Earl of Onslow, Lord Emly, Theodore J. Hare, Esq., and James Round, Esq., M.P.	,,	[C.7882]	2 6
1895	(10.) APPENDIX AND INDEX - - The Earl of Dartmouth. Vol. II. American Papers.	,,	[C.7883]	2 9
	FIFTEENTH REPORT. This is introductory to the following :—			
1896	(1.) APPENDIX AND INDEX - - The Earl of Dartmouth. Vol. III.	,,	[C.8156]	1 5
1897	(2.) APPENDIX AND INDEX - - J. Eliot Hodgkin, Esq., of Richmond, Surrey.	,,	[C.8327]	1 8
1897	(3.) APPENDIX AND INDEX - - Charles Haliday, Esq., of Dublin	,,